MANAGING HUMAN RESOURCES

EIGHTH EDITION

GLOBAL EDITION

MANAGING HUMAN RESOURCES

Luis R. Gómez-Mejía
University of Notre Dame

David B. Balkin
University of Colorado, Boulder

Robert L. Cardy
University of Texas at San Antonio

PEARSON

Boston Columbus Indianapolis New York San Francisco Amsterdam
Cape Town Dubai London Madrid Milan Munich Paris Montréal Toronto
Delhi Mexico City São Paulo Sydney Hong Kong Seoul Singapore Taipei

Editor-in-Chief: Stephanie Wall
Acquisitions Editor: Kris Ellis-Levy
Managing Editor, Global Editions: Steven Jackson
Program Manager Team Lead: Ashley Santora
Program Manager: Denise Vaughn
Editorial Assistant: Bernard Ollila
Associate Editor, Global Editions: Paromita Banerjee
Project Manager, Global Editions: Sudipto Roy
Vice President, Product Marketing: Maggie Moylan
Director of Marketing, Digital Services and Products: Jeanette Koskinas
Executive Product Marketing Manager: Anne Fahlgren
Field Marketing Manager: Lenny Ann Raper
Senior Strategic Marketing Manager: Erin Gardner
Project Manager Team Lead: Judy Leale
Project Manager: Karalyn Holland
Senior Manufacturing Controller, Global Editions: Trudy Kimber
Operations Specialist: Diane Peirano
Creative Director: Blair Brown
Senior Art Director: Janet Slowik
Interior and Cover Designer: S4Carlisle Publishing Services
Cover Image: © artqu /Shutterstock
Vice President, Director of Digital Strategy & Assessment: Paul Gentile
Manager of Learning Applications: Paul Deluca
Digital Editor: Brian Surette
Digital Studio Manager: Diane Lombardo
Digital Studio Project Manager: Robin Lazrus
Digital Studio Project Manager: Alana Coles
Digital Studio Project Manager: Monique Lawrence
Digital Studio Project Manager: Regina DaSilva
Media Production Manager, Global Editions: Vikram Kumar
Full-Service Project Management and Composition: S4Carlisle Publishing Services
Full-Service Project Management, Global Editions: SPi Global

Pearson Education Limited
Edinburgh Gate
Harlow
Essex CM20 2JE
England

and Associated Companies throughout the world

Visit us on the World Wide Web at: www.pearsonglobaleditions.com

Authorized adaptation from the United States edition, entitled Managing Human Resources, 8th Edition, ISBN 978-0-13-302969-7 by Luis R. Gómez-Mejía, David B. Balkin, *and* Robert L. Cardy, *published by Pearson Education © 2016.*

ISBN 10: 1-292-09715-9
ISBN 13: 978-1-292-09715-2

British Library Cataloguing-in-Publication Data
A catalogue record for this book is available from the British Library

10 9 8 7 6 5 4 3 2 1

Typeset in Times LT Std, 10/12 by SPi Global Publishing Services
Printed in Malaysia (CTP-VVP)

To my wife Ana, my two sons Vince and Alex,
and my daughter Dulce
—L.G.M.

To my parents, Daniel and Jeanne
—D.B.B.

To my family for their endless support and to Todd Snider
for the endless inspiration
—R.L.C.

Brief Contents

Contents

Preface

Managing Human Resources, Eighth Edition, Global Edition, prepares *all future* managers with a business understanding of the need for human resource management skills. Since the first edition of *Managing Human Resources* was published, the general management perspective has become much more prevalent among practicing managers. Recent environmental and organizational forces have contributed greatly to this trend. Organizations are becoming flatter. Globalized operations have become the norm for most organizations once they reach a certain size, and now one often finds that even firms with fewer than 50 employees may be engaged in cross-border activities. Organizations face great pressure to demonstrate social responsibility and to engage in sustainable practices. In addition to greater diversity at home, this trend requires that managers be prepared to work effectively with people with backgrounds very different from their own. Technology such as the Internet fosters communication among all levels of personnel, and managers are expected to be generalists, with a broad set of skills, including human resource management (HRM) skills. Relatedly, social media is having a significant impact on HR practices, in particular recruitment and selection. At the same time, fewer firms have a highly centralized, powerful human resource (HR) department that acts as monitor, decision maker, and controller of HR practices throughout the organization. The emergence of small businesses as the main employer of the majority of the workforce in the United States and other countries has reinforced this trend. Thus, this eighth edition explicitly covers special challenges in the management of human resources dealing with ethics/social responsibility, technology/social media, globalization, customer satisfaction for the users of HR services, and coping with new emerging trends.

The unprecedented economic upheavals on a global basis in the recent past have made it even more clear that all managers should be able to deal effectively with HR issues such as preparing labor reduction plans; identifying key employees that the firm must keep despite declining profits; managing rising employee stress, anxiety, and depression; rewarding individuals for achieving important milestones; inducing employees to take prudent risks within their purview of responsibilities; cross-training employees so that they are capable of fulfilling different roles; enabling employees to become culturally savvy so that they can relate to diverse audiences both domestically and internationally; and treating employees in an ethical manner.

Most employees are now being asked to make difficult choices regarding benefit plans, and the new federal health insurance mandate has made these choices more complicated, at least in the next few years. Employees are increasingly asked to participate in HR decisions concerning recruitment and selection of new applicants, performance appraisals of peers and team members, enforcement of ethics policies, and the like. We believe that the "nonfunctional" HR approach used in this book makes HR relevant to anyone who has to deal with HR issues, including those who do not hold the title of manager. All materials have been thoroughly updated since the seventh edition (see Chapter-Specific Changes to the Eighth Edition), and we have incorporated new topical areas, in particular those concerning technology/social media and ethics/social responsibility.

New to Eighth Edition

Specific details regarding updates to the eighth edition, Global Edition, can be found later in the preface. However, highlights of changes include the following:

- 700 new references cited within text.
- Most introductory vignettes are either new, substantially revised, or updated.
- Approximately 75 percent of the end-of-chapter cases are new or have been extensively revised and updated.

- More than 80 percent of the boxed features within the text have been replaced with new ones or have been substantially revised and updated.
- New coverage of the special human resource issues concerning social responsibility and ethics as well as technology and social media. This is included in new topical sections of most chapters as well as in new Manager's Notebook features, discussion questions, and cases.
- Updated coverage of how firms respond to dynamic changes in their strategy as a result of environmental jolts, and the important role that human resource management plays in this process.
- Updated coverage of the legal environment of HR such as the changing legal requirements for companies to provide health insurance to employees and emerging regulations that attempt to balance employee and employer rights to engage in religious practices in the workplace.

Manager's Notebooks

The Manager's Notebooks provide exposure to a variety of issues that managers confront daily, from providing feedback during an appraisal session to preparing employees for a layoff. Approximately half of the Manager's Notebooks are new for this eighth edition, Global Edition, and many of the remaining features have been updated with the most current information. Manager's Notebooks are divided into five categories:

- *New:* **Technology/Social Media** notebooks discuss specific opportunities and challenges posed by technology and the rapid increase in the use of social media to the practice of human resource management.
- **Customer-Driven HR** notebooks demonstrate how managers and employees can benefit by approaching employees as internal customers.
- *New:* **Ethics/Social Responsibility** notebooks focus on the role of HR practices in promoting social responsibility and ethical issues that challenge managers and employees.
- **Emerging Trends** notebooks present new developments in HRM practice that are likely to require increased attention in the near future.
- **Global** notebooks focus on HR practices in different countries and offer lessons that can be applied to diverse work contexts within the United States and elsewhere.

You Manage It! Cases

In an effort to make the conceptual material discussed in each chapter come to life, we provide "You Manage It!" case studies at the end of each chapter to support each of the major themes of the book. For each case, we have included critical thinking questions, team exercises, and experiential exercises. Many cases also include individual exercises for students who wish to or who can only work individually as a member of a class (for instance, those taking online courses). These cases are organized as follows:

- *New:* **Technology/Social Media** cases deal with concrete situations where technology/social media affect HR practices related to the subject matter discussed in that particular chapter.
- **Customer-Driven HR** cases illustrate how HRM can add value to an organization by taking a customer-oriented perspective.
- *New:* **Ethics/Social Responsibility** cases illustrate how managing people can involve tough, real-life choices regarding the "right" actions that should be taken and how organizations can act in a more socially responsible manner through appropriate HR practices.
- **Emerging Trends** cases illustrate HR-related issues that are likely to require increased attention in the future.
- **Global** cases draw students' attention outside the boundaries of the United States and illustrate that HR issues may be international in scope.

MyManagementLab Suggested Activities

For the eighth edition we the author(s) are excited that Pearson's MyManagementLab has been integrated fully into the text. These new features are outlined below. Making assessment activities available on line for students to complete before coming to class will allow you the professor more discussion time during the class to review areas that students are having difficulty in comprehending.

Watch It

Recommends a video clip that can be assigned to students for outside classroom viewing or that can be watched in the classroom. The video corresponds to the chapter material and is accompanied by multiple choice questions that re-enforce student's comprehension of the chapter content.

Assisted Graded Writing Questions

These are short essay questions which the students can complete as an assignment and submit to you the professor for grading.

Chapter-Specific Changes to the Eighth Edition

Chapter 1, "Meeting Present and Emerging Strategic Human Resource Challenges," provides new coverage of the effects of layoffs on losing talent to competitors, niche certification for training, challenges and opportunities of rising diversity, the rise of the virtual workforce, electronic monitoring, and an expanded section on ethics and social responsibility. Specific changes and updates in this edition include a new vignette entry on giant Alcatel, a new notebook on the offering of massive open online courses (MOOCs) aimed at meeting specific training needs, a new notebook on how Harley-Davidson has taken advantage of diversity to increase sales, a new notebook on the use of personal information, and two new cases exploring electronic monitoring and embedding sustainability into HR strategies.

Chapter 2, "Managing Work Flows and Conducting Job Analysis," has new content that explains the use of professional employer organizations (PEOs) that provide human resource management services on an outsourcing basis to smaller firms. A new Manager's Notebook looks at the emerging trend of "reshoring" manufacturing jobs to the U.S. that were previously outsourced to China. Two new end-of-chapter cases examine the growing problem of companies giving unpaid internships to students that use them to perform unskilled labor for free as well as the implications from the restrictions on telecommuting at Yahoo announced by its CEO as a controversial tactic to increase employee productivity and innovation.

Chapter 3, "Understanding Equal Opportunity and the Legal Environment," has been updated to include new regulations that require mandatory sexual harassment training in California for all supervisors in firms with more than 50 employees. New content has been added that explains how companies avoid age discrimination by redesigning jobs for older employees so they can work part-time while they extend their working lives to reflect longer spans of life. A new Manager's Notebook brings to light the rampant gender inequity in India and its implications for this emerging economy. Another new Manager's Notebook discusses how to avoid legal difficulties if companies need to install an English-only rule for communication at the workplace. A new end-of-chapter case discusses the implications of having a company policy that forbids employees from displaying visible tattoos at the workplace, which has become challenging because in recent years tattoos have become fashionable for younger-generation employees to display to express their individuality.

Chapter 4, "Managing Diversity," provides updated information on demographic changes, based on recent census reports; new coverage of entrepreneurial firms launched by minorities; coverage of the rapidly changing landscape for legal protection of homosexuals; expanded treatment of religious diversity and recent EEOC religious-bias lawsuits; and expanded coverage of special issues concerning the rapidly expanding Hispanic populations in the United States. All notebooks have been updated or replaced and a new case has been added on technology/social media and how it affects the management of diversity.

Chapter 5, "Recruiting and Selecting Employees," includes a new opening vignette that describes a common retail situation that students can identify with, an updated Manager's Notebook focusing on the global supply and shortage of labor, an updated Manager's Notebook on customer-driven HR, a new Manager's Notebook on technology/social media, a new Manager's Notebook focusing on social responsibility in recruitment and hiring, and two new cases exploring employer uses of social media in the hiring process and the role of social responsibility in business and potential impacts of a clear social responsibility initiative.

Chapter 6, "Managing Employee Separations, Downsizing, and Outplacement," includes a new chapter-opening vignette, a new Manager's Notebook on voluntary employee turnover in China, a new Manager's Notebook focusing on termination of employees for using social media, a new Manager's Notebook focusing on the ethical/social responsibility aspects of the effects of layoffs on survivors, a new Manager's Notebook addressing management actions to minimize the negative effects of a layoff, and two new cases that focus on the management of voluntary turnover and policy that addresses terminations as a result of employee use of social media.

Chapter 7, "Appraising and Managing Performance," includes a new chapter opening with a vignette that illustrates a performance review interaction between a manager and a worker, a new Manager's Notebook focusing on competencies needed in a global workplace, a new Manager's Notebook that focuses on the use of technology in measuring and improving performance, a new Manager's Notebook on using a strength-based approach to provide performance feedback, a new case on the strength-based approach to performance appraisal, and two extensively revised cases on addressing global competencies and the use of technology in appraising performance.

Chapter 8, "Training the Workforce," includes a new chapter opener on employee training, a new Manager's Notebook on the use of technology and social media as a means to shift training toward "learning on-the-fly," a new Manager's Notebook focusing on expatriate training needs, a new Manager's Notebook on customer-based training, and two new cases on the use of social media in training and the training of expatriates.

Chapter 9, "Developing Careers," includes a new Manager's Notebook on the steps involved in international assignments and provides management suggestions for each step, a new Managers Notebook that addresses social media as a skill and as a tool in career development, and a new case that explores the use of social media in career development.

Chapter 10, " Managing Compensation," provides an expanded treatment of the disappearance of entitlements, tying rewards to socially responsible behaviors, the use of non-monetary pay, the rise of telecommuting and compensation, job evaluation in small firms, and updates of legislation concerning compensation. The revised chapter includes a new Manager's Notebook on rewarding employees with non-monetary rewards, a new Manager's Notebook on telecommuters, and a new case on pay and social responsibility.

Chapter 11, "Rewarding Performance," offers new coverage of the effect of pay incentives on employee ethical behaviors, the pitfalls of merit pay and pay-for-performance systems, the complementary relationship of extrinsic and intrinsic rewards, and special issues with pay incentives in small firms. The chapter includes a new Manager's Notebook on healthy living incentives, a new Manager's Notebook on the pros and cons of awarding long-term income, and a new case on providing rewards for key contributors.

Chapter 12, "Designing and Administering Benefits," has been thoroughly revised to include the latest information covering health and retirement benefits. New information on the Patient and Affordable Care Act (PACA) has been added that gives a definition of a full-time employee or part-time equivalent employee for whom employers are required to provide health care coverage, as well as guidelines for the minimum percentage of employees' health care costs that must be paid for by the employer. New content introduces the increasingly popular high-deductible health plan that provides employees with low-cost health coverage that covers only high-cost medical procedures. New laws in a few states that provide paid parental leave that go beyond the unpaid parental leave standards of the FMLA at the federal level are explained. A new Manager's Notebook offers some ways that companies are using wellness practices to lower their health care costs. A new end-of-chapter case explains the wildly popular Superannuation retirement program in Australia, which is similar to the 401(k) retirement benefit in the United States but mandates sizeable minimum employee contributions to the retirement account.

Chapter 13, "Developing Employee Relations," offers new content on the use of workplace chaplains, ordained ministers who provide outreach to employees with personal problems, as an alternative to Employee Assistance Programs (EAPs), which require employees to file a complaint before they can receive access to counseling. A new Manager's Notebook explains how social media is being used to build corporate alumni networks that can be a powerful source of competitive information. A new end-of-chapter case brings to light the fact that many employee feedback systems, which are designed to allow employees to have a voice to complain about unfair treatment, remain unused by employees due to their fear of retaliation by managers. The case challenges students to come up with ways to administer feedback systems that actually get used by employees.

Chapter 14, "Respecting Employee Rights and Managing Discipline," provides expanded content on whistle-blowing, including recent controversies over whether individuals who disclose classified government documents to the WikiLeaks Web site should be considered to be whistle-blowers or criminals. A new Manager's Notebook introduces the emerging employment practice of performing credit checks on applicants' credit histories when they are being considered for a job, which some legal experts claim discriminates against minorities. A new end-of-chapter case introduces the growing problem of incivility in the workplace where employees act rude and disrespectful to each other on a regular basis. Blaming this bad conduct on higher stress and increasing performance expectations, the case challenges students to think of ways to restore civility back into the workplace.

Chapter 15, "Working with Organized Labor," contains updated information on the percentage of the workforce that is unionized in the United States and other countries. A new Manager's Notebook examines how Chinese workers have recently asserted their power and demanded to have unions that actually represent their interests to management rather than act as a tool of the government to pacify the workers and keep them docile. In a new end-of-chapter case, the recent setbacks of public sector unions in Wisconsin are examined and students are challenged to think about whether unions are really necessary in the public sector, which tends to have better job security and benefits than many private-sector workplaces.

Chapter 16, "Managing Workplace Safety and Health," has a new chapter opening that provides summaries of recent workplace safety infractions that resulted in major OSHA fines, a new Manager's Notebook on preventing workers' compensation fraud, an updated Manager's Notebook on company actions regarding AIDS in South Africa, and a new Manager's Notebook on the use of social media in wellness programs.

Chapter 17, "International HRM Challenges," provides new treatment of ethical concerns with outsourcing, new legislation around the world on the use of bribes, equal employment opportunity in a global context, ways to keep the expatriate linked to the home country, and new developments in cross-cultural training. The revised chapter also includes a Manager's Notebook on training expatriates on how to cope with political risks, a new Manager's Notebook on the use of toxic factories in China, and a new case on terrorism.

Instructor Resources

Instructor's Resource Center

At the Instructor Resource Center, www.pearsonglobaleditions.com/Gomez, instructors can easily register to gain access to a variety of instructor resources available with this text in downloadable format. If assistance is needed, our dedicated technical support team is ready to help with the media supplements that accompany this text. Visit http://247.pearsoned.com for answers to frequently asked questions and toll-free user support phone numbers.

The following supplements are available with this text:

- **Instructor's Resource Manual**
- **Test Bank**
- **TestGen® Computerized Test Bank**
- **PowerPoint Presentation**

Video Library

Additional videos illustrating the most important subject topics are available in MyManagementLab.

CourseSmart eTextbooks*

CourseSmart eTextbooks were developed for students looking to save the cost on required or recommended textbooks. Students simply select their eText by title or author and purchase immediate access to the content for the duration of the course using any major credit card. With a CourseSmart eText students can search for specific keywords or page numbers, take notes online, print out reading assignments that incorporate lecture notes, and bookmark important passages for later review. For more information or to purchase a CourseSmart eTextbook, visit www.coursesmart.com.

*This product may not be available in all markets. For more details, please visit www.coursesmart.co.uk or contact your local Pearson representative.

Acknowledgments

The contributions of many people made this book possible. The support and contributions of the editorial staff of Kris Ellis-Levy, Sarah Holle, and Bernard Ollila made a tremendous difference.

The production and manufacturing teams at Pearson Education also deserve special mention. Project Managers Meghan DeMaio and Karalyn Holland handled the details, scheduling, and management of this project with grace and aplomb. Many thanks also to Judy Leale. Without their assistance, many visuals and text items would never have made their way into this book.

Our experience in working with everyone at Pearson Education has been superb. Everyone at Pearson approached this book with commitment and enthusiasm. We were partners with the Pearson staff and feel that we are part of a high-performance team. We appreciate the commitment they displayed and would like to thank them for the experience. The authors would like to acknowledge the following contributors, for writing assessment questions for the new MyLab activities: Erikson Daniel Conkling, Ivy Tech Community College - Northeast, Gordon Schmidt, Indiana University-Purdue University Fort Wayne.

We would also like to thank the many colleagues who have reviewed both the past editions as well as the current edition and have offered valuable feedback.

Uzo Anakwe, Pace University

Kamala Arogyaswamy, University of South Dakota

Kristin Backhaus, SUNY New Paltz

Trevor Bain, University of Alabama

Murray Barrick, University of Iowa

Richard Bartlett, Muskingum Tech College

Kevin Bergin, Dutchess Community College

Deborah Bishop, Saginaw Valley State University

Jim Brakefield, Western Illinois University

Larry Brandt, Nova Southeastern University

Diane Bridge, American University

Mark Butler, San Diego State University

Felipe Chia, Harrisburg Area Community College

Steve Childers, East Carolina University

Denise Daniels, Seattle Pacific University

Kermit Davis, Auburn University

Kerry Davis, Auburn University

Michelle Dean, University of North Texas

Rebby Diehl, Salt Lake Community College

Karen McMillen Dielmann, Indiana University of Pennsylvania

Scott Donaldson, Northeastern Oklahoma A&M College

Cathy DuBois, Kent State University

Rebecca Ellis, California Polytechnic State University

Matt Farron, Schenectady County Community College

Anne Fiedler, Barry University

Hugh Findley, Troy State University

David Foote, Middle Tennessee State University

Debbie Goodwin, Lewis-Clark State College

David A. Hofmann, Michigan State University

Harry Hollis, Belmont University

Deb Humphreys, California Polytechnic State University

Feruzan Irani, Georgia Southern University

David Kaplan, James Madison University

Tim Keaveny, Marquette University

Donald Knight, University of Maryland

Anachai Kongchan, Chulalongkor University

Gregory A. Laurence, University of Michigan—Flint

Lewis Lash, Barry University

Gregory A. Laurence, Syracuse University

Helen Lavan, DePaul University

Stan Malos, San Jose State University

Candice Miller, Brigham Young University—Idaho

Joe Mosca, Monmouth University

Paul Muchinsky, University of North Carolina at Greensboro

Frank Mullins, Syracuse University

Smita Oxford, Mary Washington College

Steve Painchaud, Southern New Hampshire University

Elaine Potoker, Maine Maritime Academy

Dr. Jim Sethi, University of Montana—Western

Marcia Simmering, Louisiana Tech University

Janice Smith, North Carolina A&T

Howard Stager, Buffalo State College

Lisa T. Stickney, University of Baltimore

Gary Stroud, Franklin University

Cynthia Sutton, Indiana University

Thomas Tang, Middle Tennessee State University

Tom Taveggia, University of Arizona

David Wade, Northern Illinois University

Edward Ward, St. Cloud State

Sandy Wayne, University of Illinois at Chicago

Les Wiletzky, Hawaii Pacific University

Carol Young, Wittenberg University

Finally, this book would not have been possible without the indulgence of family and friends. We sincerely appreciate the patience and tolerance that were extended to us as we wrote the eighth edition.

Luis R. Gómez-Mejía
David B. Balkin
Robert L. Cardy

Pearson would also like to thank and acknowledge Jon and Diane Sutherland for contributing to this global edition. We would also like to thank Andy Kwan, City University of Hong Kong; Roshidi Hassan, Universiti Teknologi MARA; Timurs Umans, Kristianstad University; and Yong Wooi Keong, Sunway University for offering valuable feedback that helped improve the global content.

About the Authors

Luis R. Gómez-Mejía holds the Ray and Milann Siegfried Professor of Management Chair in Business at the University of Notre Dame. Prior to that, he was the Benton Cocanougher Chair at Texas A & M University as well as Council of 100 Distinguished Scholars at Arizona State University (ASU), and held the Horace Steel Arizona Heritage Chair at ASU. He was a Regent's Professor at ASU and has recently received the Outstanding Alumni Award from the University of Minnesota and was awarded the title of Doctor Honoris Causa at Carlos III University (Spain). He is a Fellow of the Academy of Management and member of the "Hall of Fame" of the Academy of Management (which includes 33 members out of approximately 20,000 members in the Academy of Management). He has published more than 250 articles and 12 books focused on macro human resource issues. His work has appeared in the best management journals including: *Academy of Management Journal, Academy of Management Review, Strategic Management Journal,* and *Administrative Science Quarterly.* He has received numerous awards for his research, including "best paper" in the *Academy of Management Journal* and "most impactful paper" in *Administrative Science Quarterly.* His publications have been cited approximately 16,000 times (Google), making him one of the most highly cited management scholars. He is past president of the Human Resource Division of the Academy of Management and has served as elected member of the Board of Governors of the Academy of Management. He also served three terms as president of the Iberoamerican Academy of Management.

David B. Balkin is Professor of Management at the Leeds School of Business at the University of Colorado at Boulder. He received his PhD in human resource management and industrial relations from the University of Minnesota. Prior to joining the University of Colorado, he served on the faculties of Louisiana State University and Northeastern University. He has published over 70 articles appearing in journals such as the *Academy of Management Journal, Strategic Management Journal, Personnel Psychology, Journal of Organizational Behavior, Journal of Business Venturing,* and *Journal of Management Studies.* One of his publications (coauthored with Luis R. Gómez-Mejía) was selected as the best article published in 1992 in the *Academy of Management Journal.* Professor Balkin has written or edited several books on human resources, the management of innovation, compensation, and other topics. He has served as Chair of the Management Department at the University of Colorado and also served on advisory boards of nonprofit organizations. Professor Balkin serves as the associate editor for *Human Resource Management Review* and has previously served on the editorial boards of the *Academy of Management Journal* and the *Journal of Management.* He has served as an expert witness on cases dealing with employment and pay discrimination. Professor Balkin has extensive international experience as a scholar and teacher and was a visiting professor at the University of Toulouse (France), Copenhagen Business School (Denmark), Helsinki University of Technology (Finland), University of Regensburg (Germany), ESADE Business School (Spain), National University of Singapore, Hong Kong University of Science and Technology, HEC Montreal (Canada), and Indian School of Business (India).

Robert L. Cardy is a Professor in the Department of Management at the University of Texas at San Antonio. He received his PhD in industrial/organizational psychology from Virginia Tech in 1982. He is an ad hoc reviewer for a variety of journals, including the *Academy of Management Journal* and the *Academy of Management Review.* He is editor and cofounder of the *Journal* *of Quality Management.* Professor Cardy has been recognized for his research, teaching, and service. He was ranked in the top 20 in research productivity for the decade 1980–1989 based on the number of publications in the *Journal of Applied Psychology.* He was doctoral coordinator in Arizona State University's management department for five years and received a University Mentor Award in 1993 for his work with doctoral students. He served as department chair for seven years at UTSA. He authored a regular column on current issues in HRM for over ten years and received an Academy of Management certificate for outstanding service as a columnist for the HR division newsletter. Professor Cardy was a 1992 recipient of a certificate for significant contributions to the quality of life for students at ASU. His research focuses on performance appraisal and effective HRM practices.

CHAPTER 1 Meeting Present and Emerging Strategic Human Resource Challenges

MyManagementLab®

When you see this icon, visit **www.mymanagementlab.com** for activities that are applied, personalized, and offer immediate feedback.

CHALLENGES

After reading this chapter, you should be able to deal more effectively with the following challenges:

1 **Understand** the major challenges affecting HR.

2 **Develop** competence in planning and implementing strategic HR policies.

3 **Develop** competence in selecting HR strategies to increase firm performance.

4 **Become** aware of HR best practices.

5 **Understand** the need to establish a close partnership between the HR department and managers.

6 **Recognize** career opportunities in various human resources management subfields.

Whether in a recession or during boom times, companies compete for talent. Those that are capable of attracting, retaining, and motivating good employees are more likely to achieve and sustain a competitive advantage. Let's take three examples:

- Giant Alcatel-Lucent employs about 72,000 employees worldwide, and it plans to cut approximately 10,000 jobs during 2014 through 2016 to stem years of losses. While this move might be beneficial for the bottom line in the short term, many of its employees (even those who might not get the ax) are being syphoned away by competitors such as Ericsson, Huawei, and Nokia. This loss of talent might accelerate Alcatel-Lucent's decline in the future.[1]
- Not long ago, Google Inc. was considered the ideal place to work and it was repeatedly chosen by *Fortune* in its annual pick of the best companies to work for. Google used to receive more than 1,000 applicants for every five jobs available, and very few employees left the company once they were hired. Yet the situation seems to be changing, making it much tougher for Google to attract and retain top talent despite the company's name recognition and prestige. Google Inc. is now fighting off many growing Internet firms that are poaching its staff. During the years 2011–2015, Facebook, Zynga, and Twitter have increased their staffing by approximately 90 percent, and many of those employees are migrating from Google. To help attract new recruits and preempt defections, all of Google's employees (about 23,000) were given a 10 percent raise, at an estimated cost of $400 million.

Source: epa european pressphoto agency/Alamy.

- In recent years, Motorola has lost thousands of engineers, researchers, and designers to competitors such as Apple; Samsung; Research in Motion (RIM, the maker of the Blackberry); Nokia; Dell; and Sony Erickson. A group of software experts recently laid off by Motorola marketed themselves to Yahoo as a team, and all were quickly hired.[2] Ironically, RIM now is also on the brink of disaster because the market for the Blackberry has dwindled and the company has been unable to muster the engineering talent required to diversify its product offering. Nokia also finds itself in a similar situation—its inability to innovate in the cell phone market has made it a victim of Apple's success in introducing a new stream of devices every year.

The Managerial Perspective

This book is about the people who work in an organization and their relationship with that organization. Different terms are used to describe these people: *employees, associates* (at Walmart, for instance), *personnel*, and *human resources*. None of these terms is better than the others, and they often are used interchangeably. The term we have chosen for the title of this text, and which we will use throughout, is **human resources (HR)**.* This term has gained widespread acceptance over the last decade because it expresses the belief that workers are a valuable—and sometimes irreplaceable—resource. Effective human resource management (HRM) is a major component of any manager's job.

human resources (HR)
People who work in an organization. Also called *personnel*.

human resource strategy
A firm's deliberate use of human resources to help it gain or maintain an edge against its competitors in the marketplace. The grand plan or general approach an organization adopts to ensure that it effectively uses its people to accomplish its mission.

human resource tactic
A particular HR policy or program that helps to advance a firm's strategic goal.

A **human resource strategy** refers to a firm's deliberate use of human resources to help it gain or maintain an edge against its competitors in the marketplace.[3] It is the grand plan or general approach that an organization adopts to ensure that it effectively uses its people to accomplish its mission. A **human resource tactic** is a particular policy or program that helps to advance a firm's strategic goal. Strategy precedes and is more important than tactics.

In this chapter, we focus on the general framework within which specific HR activities and programs fit. With the help of the company's human resources department, managers implement the chosen HR strategies.[4] In subsequent chapters, we move from the general to the specific and examine in detail the spectrum of HR strategies (for example, those regarding work design, staffing, performance appraisal, career planning, and compensation).[5]

Learn It!

If your professor has chosen to assign this go to **www.mymanagementlab.com** to see what you should particularly focus on, and take the chapter 1 warmup.

Human Resource Management: The Challenges

manager
A person who is in charge of others and is responsible for the timely and correct execution of actions that promote his or her unit's success.

line employee
An employee involved directly in producing the company's good(s) or delivering the service(s).

staff employee
An employee who supports line employees.

Managers are people who are in charge of others and who are responsible for the timely and correct execution of actions that promote their units' successful performance. In this book, we use the term *unit* broadly; it may refer to a work team, department, business unit, division, or corporation.

All employees (including managers) can be differentiated as line or staff. **Line employees** are directly involved in producing the company's good(s) or delivering the service(s). A *line manager* manages line employees. **Staff employees** are those who support the line function. For example, people who work in the HR department are considered staff employees because their job is to provide supporting services for line employees. Employees may also be differentiated according to how much responsibility they have. *Senior employees* are those who have been with the company longer and have more responsibility than *junior employees. Exempt employees*

*All terms in boldface also appear in the Key Terms list at the end of the chapter.

FIGURE 1.1
Key HR Challenges for Today's Managers

(sometimes called *salaried employees*) are those who do not receive extra pay for overtime work (beyond 40 hours per week). *Nonexempt employees* do receive overtime compensation. This text is written primarily to help students who intend to be managers deal effectively with the challenges of managing people.

Figure 1.1 summarizes the major HR challenges facing today's managers. Firms that deal with these challenges effectively are likely to outperform those that do not. These challenges may be categorized according to their primary focus: the environment, the organization, or the individual.

Environmental Challenges

Environmental challenges are the forces external to the firm. They influence organizational performance but are largely beyond management's control. Managers, therefore, need to monitor the external environment constantly for opportunities and threats. They must also maintain the flexibility to react quickly to challenges. One common and effective method for monitoring the environment is to read the business press, including *BusinessWeek, Fortune*, and the *Wall Street Journal.* (The Appendix at the end of this book provides an annotated listing of both general business publications and more specialized publications on HR management and related topics.)

environmental challenges
Forces external to a firm that affect the firm's performance but are beyond the control of management.

Eight important environmental challenges today are rapid change, the rise of the Internet, workforce diversity, globalization, legislation, evolving work and family roles, skill shortages and the rise of the service sector, and catastrophic events as a result of natural disasters and terrorism.

RAPID CHANGE Many organizations face a volatile environment in which change is nearly constant.[6] For this reason IBM's ex-CEO, Sam Palmisano, tells his managers that he doesn't believe in forecasts longer than one week.[7] If they are to survive and prosper, firms need to adapt to change quickly and effectively. Human resources are almost always at the heart of an effective response system.[8] Here are a few examples of how HR policies can help or hinder a firm grappling with external change:

- *New company town* As firms experience high pressure to become more productive and deal with very short product life cycles (often measured in months), Americans are working longer, harder, and faster.[9] As a result, the line between home and work is blurred for many employees. To deal with this phenomenon, sociologist Helen Mederer of the University of Rhode Island notes that "companies are taking the best aspects of home and incorporating them into work."[10]

A QUESTION OF ETHICS
How much responsibility does an organization have to shield its employees from the effects of rapid change in the environment? What risks does this type of "shock absorber" approach to management entail?

A survey of 975 employers by consulting firm Hewitt Associates found that an increasing number of companies are providing "home at work" benefits. These include dry cleaner/laundry service, company store, take-home meals, concierge service, oil changes/autocare, hair salon, and pet care.[11]

According to a report in the *New York Times*:[12]

> . . . things like nap rooms and massage recliners may sound out of place to some in a working environment. But such perks can boost productivity when there are older workers with sore backs, or young parents with sometimes sleepless nights. Musical performance, too, may seem at first like an unnecessary distraction. But companies trying them say that they can be done simply and inexpensively, and that they produce better morale, increased motivation and less stress.

- ***Dealing with stress*** Rapid change and work overload can put employees under a great deal of stress. The Bureau of Labor Statistics reported that 50 percent of the 19.8 million Americans who say they work at home at least once a week aren't compensated for it. In other words, millions of employees must work at home just in order to catch up.[13]

  Unless the organization develops support mechanisms to keep stress manageable, both the firm and employees may pay a heavy price.[14] In some extreme cases, workplace violence may result. In 2014 the Centers for Disease Control calls workplace violence a "national epidemic"; the most recent figures indicate that U.S. employees at work were the victims of 18,104 injuries from assault and 609 homicides.[15] Typically, however, the observed results of poorly handled stress are more subtle, yet still highly destructive, costing the company substantial money. According to some estimates, stress-related ailments cost companies about $200 billion a year in increased absenteeism, tardiness, and the loss of talented workers.[16] One survey reports that 67 percent of employees categorize their work-related stress as high.[17] The National Institute of Mental Health estimates that approximately 222.7 million days of work are lost annually due to absence and impairments related to depression alone, costing employers (the majority of which are small firms) $51.5 billion a year.[18] Many firms, including Microsoft, Sysco Food Services, Apple, IBM, General Motors, Google, Chrysler, Johnson & Johnson, Coors Brewing Company, Citigroup Inc., Texas Instruments, and Hughes Aircraft (now merged into Raytheon), among others, have introduced stress-control programs in recent years.

Throughout this book we emphasize how HR practices can enable a firm to respond quickly and effectively to external changes. Two chapters (Chapter 13 on employee relations and Chapter 16 on managing workplace safety and health) specifically deal with issues related to employee stress.

THE INTERNET REVOLUTION The dramatic growth of the Internet in recent years probably represents the single most important environmental trend affecting organizations and their human resource practices. In the mid-1990s, the term *Web economy* had not yet been coined.[19] Now, almost all firms use the Internet as part of their normal business practices. The Internet is having a pervasive impact on how organizations manage their human resources, as the following examples show:

- ***Necessitating greater written communication skills*** Companies have discovered that Internet technology creates a high demand for workers who can deal effectively with e-mail messages.[20] This skill is key if companies want to keep fickle Internet customers loyal, making them less likely to go to a competitor by simply tapping a few keystrokes.

  E-mail writing may also involve legal issues. For instance, an employee's e-mail response to a customer complaint may be legally binding on the firm, and there is the "written" record to prove it. Some jokes among employees may be used as evidence of sexual harassment. Unlike regular mail, electronic communication is not considered private and thus the company and employees may be open to scrutiny by government agencies as well anyone with the basic skills required to access the system.

  Although English is the main language of the Internet, almost half of Internet communication takes place in foreign languages, and only 7 percent of users on a global basis are native English speakers.[21] Major multimillion-dollar blunders due to language problems have already been documented, such as the case of Juan Pablo Davila, a commodities trader in Chile. He typed the word "buy" on the computer by mistake, instead of "sell." To rectify his mistake, he started a frenzy of buying and selling, losing 0.5 percent of his country's GNP. His name has become an Internet-related verb—"davilar"—meaning, "to screw up royally."[22]

- ***Dealing with information overflow*** Although executives spend an average of four hours a day receiving, checking, preparing, and sending e-mails, they are still spending 130 minutes a day in formal and informal face-to-face meetings. According to Neil Flett, CEO of a large communication consulting firm, "Because e-mail consumes so much time it may just be that it just adds to communication time rather than reducing it."[23]

  According to some estimates, almost one-third of e-mails received by employees are not directly relevant to their jobs; considering that employees are now receiving an average of 30 e-mails each day, this may translate into as much as one hour a day of lost productivity.[24]
- ***Breaking down labor market barriers*** More than ever before, the Internet is creating an open labor market where information about prospective employees and firms is available on a global basis and may be obtained quickly and inexpensively.[25] Monster.com, for instance, posted 85 million resumes in 2014.[26] Thousands of specialized search engines (such as *Indeed.com, Simplyhired.com, Workzoo.com*, and *Jobsearch.org*) now scan both well-known and obscure employment boards on the job seeker's behalf.[27] While more and more organizations are relying on Web applications to recruit and screen employees, it is unclear to what extent these highly efficient yet "cold" impersonal approaches to staffing allows organizations to learn about candidates' intangible qualities such as leadership skills, work ethic, business acumen, and flexibility. Applicants often complain that sophisticated computer programs tend to have a narrow focus, relying on numerical and/or concrete criteria that may not truly capture what the person could contribute if given an opportunity (see the Manager's Notebook, "A Cold Way to Get a Job").

MANAGER'S NOTEBOOK

A Cold Way to Get a Job

Emerging Trends

The way people look for jobs has changed dramatically. Employers often require people to submit applications via the Internet, and hiring managers sift through queries with special computer programs. Unless you fit the precise algorithm that the computer program is looking for, you may never get a prospective employer's attention. For instance, you may have four years, 351 days of experience, but not the five years the machine uses as a cutoff, and thus you are out of luck. Or, failure to show evidence that you have used a particular skill during the past two months may be grounds for an automatic rejection (even if maybe you did use the skill but forgot to include it).

In a job market thick with candidates, employers have become extremely selective, and a common complaint among applicants is that computer screening programs are totally inflexible, leading to automatic rejections for small details. The computer makes a decision without giving you a chance to make your case. If an application doesn't make the cut, there is usually no rejection letter or feedback. The process may be efficient for the company, but it can be frustrating and demoralizing to the applicant.

Sources: Based on *www.employtest.com*. (2014); *www.articlesbase.com*. (2014). Computer based recruitment software; *Arizona Republic* (2010, Oct. 31). Networking pays off to get old job back; Black, T. (2011). Every tool you need for hiring, *www.inc.com*. A-8.

- ***Using online learning*** Corporate training has always been dominated by traditional in-house "paper-and-pencil" training programs. Over the last few years, however, there has been a tremendous migration from classroom learning to online learning.[28] For example, 99 percent of employees at the Mayo Clinic opted for online training to learn about new rules on health care privacy (even though the clinic gave them the option to attend a traditional classroom seminar on company time covering the same material).[29] One of the most recent developments in HR is the entry of well-known firms into the online training business for the general public, with a focus on "niche certifications" rather than degree programs (see the Manager's Notebook, "The Growth of Online Niche Certifications to Meet Training Needs").

MANAGER'S NOTEBOOK

Technology/Social Media

The Growth of Online Niche Certifications to Meet Training Needs

While the United States reportedly scores lower than most industrialized nations on math, science, and writing, it is probably second to none when it comes to its pragmatic approach to training. This is reflected in the rapid growth of new niche certifications offered by providers of "massive open online courses," or MOOCs, aimed at meeting specific training needs at a fraction of the cost of a four-year degree. One of these providers is Udacity, which already has 1.6 million students. It offers online courses in specific technical areas of computer science, supply-chain management and "gamification" (the use of video-game mechanics to solve problems). Many "Who's Who" organizations are active participants in the creation and dissemination of these online certification programs, making MOOC providers legitimate education providers and not just diploma mills. These include, for example, Stanford University, Massachusetts Institute of Technology, Google, AT&T, United Parcel Service, Procter & Gamble, Walmart, and Yahoo, among others.

Sources: Based on *www.trainingconference.com*. (2014). Training 2014 Conference & Expo; Belkin, D., and Porter, C. (2013, September 27). Job market embraces massive online courses. *Wall Street Journal*, A-3; Porter, E. (2013, October 10). U.S. must acknowledge the skills gap of its workforce and bridge it. *New York Times*, Global Edition, A-2; Van Horn, C. E. (2013). What workers really want and need. *HRMagazine*, *58*(10), 44-B; Leonard, B. (2013). On the latest talent war's front lines. *HRMagazine*, *58*(10), 42–44. ■■

- ***Enabling HR to focus on management*** The Internet enables firms to handle many operational HR details much more quickly and efficiently. According to Philip Fauver, president and CEO of Employease Inc., the Internet is "the enabler."[30] For a flat fee of about $5 to $6 per employee, Employease manages HR information for 700 small-to-midsize companies. One of its clients is Amerisure Insurance Company in Farmington Hills, Michigan. According to Derick Adams, Amerisure's HR vice president, the Internet allows his 14-member HR department to devote more attention to important managerial challenges. For instance, Adams notes that his department was able to "develop a variable pay plan after handing off the department's data entry work to Employease."[31]

WORKFORCE DIVERSITY Managers across the United States are confronted daily with the increasing diversity of the workforce. In 2014, approximately 35 percent of the U.S. workforce was from a minority group, including African Americans (12%), Asian Americans (4.7%), Latinos (16%), and other minorities (2%).[32] In many large urban centers, such as Miami, Los Angeles, and New York, minorities comprise at least half of the area's workforce. The influx of women workers is another major change in the composition of the U.S. workforce. Women with children under age 6 are now the fastest-growing segment of the workforce. Currently, more than 76 percent of employed men have employed wives, versus 54 percent in 1980.[33]

These trends are likely to accelerate in the future. By 2050, the U.S. population is expected to increase by 50 percent, with minority groups comprising nearly half of the population. Nonwhite immigrants, mostly Hispanics, will account for 60 percent of this population growth. Despite fears that immigrants are not assimilating, children of immigrants actually do better than children of natives in the same socioeconomic class.[34]

Furthermore, never before in history has such a large-scale mixing of the races occurred, due to a sharp rise in the rate of intermarriage.[35] "One day race will not be needed because it will be obsolete," notes Candy Mills, a magazine editor in Los Angeles, who is black. Candy is married to a French-Hungarian with whom she has a child.[36] The best example of this trend, of course, is the current president of the United States, Barack Obama, who is of mixed race. The U.S. Census Bureau has acknowledged this reality, incorporating "mixed" categories for future population censuses.

All these trends present both a significant challenge and a real opportunity for managers.[37] Firms that formulate and implement HR strategies that capitalize on employee diversity are more likely to survive and prosper (see example in the Manager's Notebook, "How Harley-Davidson is Taking Advantage of a Diverse Customer Base"). Chapter 4 is devoted exclusively to the topic of managing employee diversity. This issue is also discussed in several other chapters throughout this book.

MANAGER'S NOTEBOOK

How Harley-Davidson Is Taking Advantage of a Diverse Customer Base

Harley-Davidson had been a highly successful American company by marketing its motorcycles to a particular segment of the market, namely middle-age white males. In the last few years, the company has come to the realization that—to be competitive in the long run—it has to expand its demographic customer base and has to use a more diverse workforce in its dealerships to appeal to potential "non-traditional" buyers. Current sales are down by a third from years past, and better diversity management may be a way to reverse this trend. Keith Wadell, Harley-Davidson's chief executive, recently declared that a major priority for the company's strategic plan in the near future is to target young adults, women, African Americans, and Hispanics. He noted that these diversity efforts are already paying off with domestic sales among these "non-core customers" growing at nearly twice the rate as sales to traditional buyers. These domestic diversity efforts are also helping the company to expand sales outside of North America, with sales in the recent past growing by 25.6% in Asia and by 39% in Latin America.

Sources: Based on *www.harley-davidson.com*. (2014). Workforce and dealer diversity at Harley-Davidson; Diversity Inc. (2014). Do white males really need diversity outreach? *bestpractices.diversityinc.com*; Irwin, N. (2013). How Harley-Davidson explains the U.S. economy. *www.washingtonpost.com*. ■■

GLOBALIZATION One of the most dramatic challenges facing U.S. firms as they enter the second decade of the twenty-first century is how to compete against foreign firms, both domestically and abroad. The Internet is fueling globalization, and most large firms are actively involved in manufacturing overseas, international joint ventures, or collaboration with foreign firms on specific projects. Currently the companies that make up the S&P 500 generate 46 percent of their profits outside the United States, and for many of the biggest U.S. companies, the proportion is much higher.

The implications of a global economy for human resource management are many. Here are a few examples:

- ***Worldwide company culture*** Some firms try to develop a global company identity to smooth over cultural differences between domestic employees and those in international operations. Minimizing these differences increases cooperation and can have a strong impact on the bottom line. For instance, the head of human resources at the European division of Colgate Palmolive notes that the goal of the company is to "make all employees Colgaters."[38]
- ***Worldwide recruiting*** Some firms recruit workers globally, particularly in the high-technology area, where specialized knowledge and expertise are not limited by national

boundaries.[39] For instance, Unisys (an e-business solutions company whose 37,000 employees help customers in 100 countries apply information technology) recruits between 5,000 and 7,000 people a year, 50 percent of whom are information technology (IT) professionals. Unisys is always looking across borders to try to find the best persons.[40]

Global recruitment, however, is no panacea, because good employees everywhere are in high demand, and there may not be as much applicant information available to make the appropriate selection decision.[41] Kevin Barnes, technical director for Store Perform, with facilities in Bangalore, India, notes that "top Indian engineers are world-class, but most are taken. Anyone in India who can spell *Java* already has a job." And the labor market attracts legions of unqualified candidates, Barnes says, making it harder to distinguish the good from mediocre performers.[42]

- ***Industrial metamorphosis*** The proportion of the American labor force in the manufacturing sector has dropped to less than 10 percent, down from 25 percent about 30 years ago. Similar drops have been experienced in several European countries, including England, Germany, and France. According to the *Economist*, "It has happened because rich-world companies have replaced workers with new technology to boost productivity and shifted production from labor-intensive products such as textiles to higher-tech, higher value-added, sectors such as pharmaceuticals. Within firms, low-skilled jobs have moved offshore."[43] Labor unions have lost much of their influence.[44] For instance, in the 1950s almost 40 percent of the U.S. workforce was unionized; by the time President Ronald Reagan took office in the early 1980s this percentage had dropped by almost half (22%); and by the time President Barrack Obama took office less than 20 years later (2009), this proportion had dropped by more than two-thirds (to approximately 7% of the private-sector workforce).
- ***Global alliances*** International alliances with foreign firms require a highly trained and devoted staff. For instance, Philips (a Dutch lighting and electronics firm) became the largest lighting manufacturer in the world by establishing a joint venture with AT&T and making several key acquisitions, including Magnavox, parts of GE Sylvania, and the largest lighting company in France.[45]
- ***A virtual workforce*** Because of restrictive U.S. immigration quotas,[46] U.S. firms are tapping skilled foreign labor but not moving those workers to the United States. The Internet is making this possible with little additional expense. For example, Microsoft Corp. and RealNetworks Inc. use Aditi Corp., a Bangalore, India, company, to handle customer e-mails.[47] In addition, many "virtual" expatriates work abroad but live at home.[48]
- ***The global enterprise*** Internationalization is growing at warp speed, creating a powerful new reality. For instance, most people think of Coca-Cola as emblematic of the United States. Yet its CEO, Muhtar Kent, describes Coca Cola in the following terms: "We are a global company that happens to be headquartered in Atlanta. We have a factory in Ramallah that employs 2,000 people. We have a factory in Afghanistan. We have factories everywhere." Nearly 80 percent of Coca-Cola's revenue comes from 206 countries outside the United States.[49]
- ***Wage competition*** Not too long ago, many U.S. blue-collar workers could maintain a solid middle-class standard of living that was the envy of the rest of the world. This was sustained, in part, by higher productivity and superior technological innovation in the United States and because American manufacturers enjoyed a high market share with little foreign competition. Unfortunately, this is no longer the case in many sectors, particularly the automobile industry. As noted in a recent report, "While businesses have a way to navigate this new world of technological change and globalization, the ordinary American worker does not. Capital and technology are mobile; labor isn't. American workers are located in America."[50]

An entire chapter of this book (Chapter 17) is devoted to the HR issues firms face as they expand overseas. We also include international examples throughout the book to illustrate how firms in other countries manage their human resources.

LEGISLATION Much of the growth in the HR function over the past four decades may be attributed to its crucial role in keeping the company out of trouble with the law.[51] Most firms are deeply concerned with potential liability resulting from personnel decisions that may violate laws enacted by the U.S. Congress, state legislatures, or local governments.[52] Discrimination charges

filed by older employees, minorities, and the disabled, for instance, have been on the rise for years. In some cases, such as charges of sex discrimination by Hispanic and Asian women, the increase has exceeded 65 percent in the past 20 years.[53]

One legal area growing in importance is alleged misuse of "proprietary company information" by ex-employees. Pitney Bowes, the world's largest maker of postage meters and other mailing equipment, recently sued eight ex-employees who opened a small competing firm called Nexxpost. According to a Pitney Bowes' spokesperson:

> The company invests a great deal of time and money in areas of developing our intellectual property, in marketing and training our sales force. We must protect our investment, which also includes our customer lists, information about consumer preferences, as well as pricing. All that has a significant competitive value. When a former employee wants to challenge us, we take that breach very seriously and do what we need to do to protect it.[54]

Operating within the legal framework requires keeping track of the external legal environment and developing internal systems (for example, supervisory training and grievance procedures) to ensure compliance and minimize complaints. Many firms are now developing formal policies on sexual harassment and establishing internal administrative channels to deal with alleged incidents before employees feel the need to file a lawsuit. In a country where mass litigation is on the rise,[55] these efforts may well be worth the time and money.

Legislation may differentiate between public- and private-sector organizations. (*Public sector* is another term for governmental agencies; *private sector* refers to all other types of organizations.) For instance, affirmative action requirements (see Chapter 3) are typically limited to public organizations and to organizations that do contract work for them. However, much legislation applies to both public- and private-sector organizations. In fact, it is difficult to think of any HR practices that are *not* influenced by government regulations. For this reason, each chapter of this book addresses pertinent legal issues, and an entire chapter (Chapter 3) provides an overall framework that consolidates the main legal issues and concerns facing employers today.

EVOLVING WORK AND FAMILY ROLES The proportion of *dual-career* families, in which both wife and husband (or both members of a couple) work, is increasing every year.

More companies are introducing "family-friendly" programs that give them a competitive advantage in the labor market.[56] Companies use these HR tactics to hire and retain the best-qualified employees, male or female. Through the Office of Personnel Management, the federal government provides technical assistance to organizations that wish to implement family-friendly policies. On its 2015 Web page (*opm.gov*), for instance, the office makes available numerous publications on issues such as adoption benefits, child care, elder-care resources, parenting support, and telework.

Family-friendly policies are discussed in detail in Chapter 12 under the heading "Employee Services." Special issues that women confront in the workplace are discussed in Chapter 4.

SKILL SHORTAGES AND THE RISE OF THE SERVICE SECTOR As noted earlier, U.S. manufacturing has dropped dramatically in terms of the percentage of employees who work in that sector. Most employment growth has taken place in the service industry. The categories with the fastest growth are expected to be professional specialties (27 percent) and technical occupations (22 percent). The fastest-growing occupations demand at least two years of college training.[57] Expansion of service-sector employment is linked to a number of factors, including changes in consumer tastes and preferences, legal and regulatory changes, advances in science and technology that have eliminated many manufacturing jobs, and changes in the way businesses are organized and managed.

Unfortunately, many available workers will be too unskilled to fill those jobs. Even now, many companies complain that the supply of skilled labor is dwindling and that they must provide their employees with basic training to make up for the shortcomings of the public education system.[58] For example, 84 percent of the 23,000 people applying for entry-level jobs at Bell Atlantic Telephone (formerly NYNEX) failed the qualifying test. Chemical Bank (now merged with Chase) reported that it had to interview 40 applicants to find one proficient teller.[59] David Hearns, former chairman and CEO of Xerox, laments that "the American workforce is running out of qualified people."[60]

A QUESTION OF ETHICS

What is the ethical responsibility of an employer to employees who lack basic literacy and numeracy skills? Should companies be required by law to provide training opportunities for such employees, as some have proposed?

To rectify these shortcomings, companies spend at least $55 billion a year on a wide variety of training programs. This is in addition to the $24 billion spent on training programs by the federal government each year.[61] On the employee-selection side, an increasing number of organizations are relying on job simulations to test for the "soft skills" needed to succeed in a service environment, such as sound judgment in ambiguous situations, the ability to relate to diverse groups of people, and effective handling of angry or dissatisfied customers.

The improving unemployment picture at the time of this writing makes the skill shortage a greater challenge for U.S. firms. New York has become the first state in the nation to issue a "work readiness" credential to high school students who pass a voluntary test measuring their ability to succeed in entry-level jobs. An article in the *New York Times* notes, "Employers have complained for years that too many students leave high school without basic skills, despite the battery of exams—considered among the most stringent in the nation—that New York requires for graduation."[62] The test covers "soft skills," including the ability to communicate, follow directions, negotiate and make basic decisions, in 10 broad areas. Chapter 8 focuses directly on training; Chapter 5 (staffing), Chapter 7 (appraising employee performance), and Chapter 9 (career development) all discuss issues related to the skills and knowledge required to succeed on the job.

NATURAL DISASTERS AND TERRORISM A stream of recent disasters, including the 2011 Japanese earthquake; the early 2005 tsunami that killed over 250,000 people in Asia; the 2010 Haitian earthquake and subsequent cholera epidemics during 2010–2012, which killed more than 200,000 people; the 2010 oil spill environmental disaster of British Petroleum in the Gulf of Mexico; and a string of devastating hurricanes—most notably Katrina, which destroyed most of the city of New Orleans in August 2005—have increased awareness among HR professionals of the importance of having plans to deal with such catastrophes. A survey conducted by Mercer Human Resource Consulting indicated that almost 3 million employees were affected in one way or another by Katrina.[63] Employers had to suddenly deal with HR issues to which they previously had given little thought. These included: deciding whether to keep paying employees who were unreachable and unable to report to work, paying for a variety of living expenses for displaced staffers in temporary living quarters, providing telecommuting equipment for employees working from hotels, awarding hazardous duty pay, hiring temporary employees (many of whom were undocumented workers) to fill the labor void, and preventing the loss of key talent to competitors outside the disaster area.[64] Time Warner Inc. waived medical deductibles and supported out-of-network medical coverage for affected Katrina families. Walmart, with more than 34,000 employees displaced by Katrina, guaranteed them work in any other U.S. Walmart store and created an "Associate Disaster Relief Fund" for employees whose homes were flooded or destroyed.[65] Surprisingly, even after Katrina, almost half of firms don't have HR policies to deal with major disasters.[66] But this is likely to change as new potential threats (such as avian flu, major earthquakes, chemical contamination, and more hurricanes) loom on the horizon.[67] Another issue of concern to many firms, particularly multinationals, is terrorism, which we discuss later. Recent well-publicized terrorist incidents such as the 2013 Boston Marathon bombings, numerous mass shootings on American soil in the past five years, the 2013 attack on a major Nairobi (Kenya) shopping mall, and continued pirating of ships along the Somalian coast are continuous reminders that organizations need to be prepared to respond to potential terrorist threats.

Organizational Challenges

organizational challenges
Concerns or problems internal to a firm; often a by-product of environmental forces.

Organizational Challenges are concerns or problems internal to a firm. Effective managers spot organizational issues and deal with them before they become major problems. One of the themes of this text is *proactivity:* the need for firms to take action before problems get out of hand. This can be done only by managers who are well informed about important HR issues and organizational challenges.

Competitive Position: Cost, Quality, or Distinctive Capabilities

Human resources represent the single most important cost in many organizations. Organizational labor costs range from 36 percent in capital-intensive firms, such as commercial airlines, to 80 percent in labor-intensive firms, such as the U.S. Postal Service. How effectively a company uses its human resources can have a dramatic effect on its ability to compete (or survive) in an increasingly competitive environment.

Effective HR policies can impact an organization's competitive position by controlling costs, improving quality, and creating distinctive capabilities.

- *Controlling costs* A compensation system that uses innovative reward strategies to control labor costs can help the organization grow, as we discuss in Chapters 10 and 11. Other ways to keep labor costs under control include making better employee selection decisions (Chapter 5); training employees to make them more efficient and productive (Chapter 8); attaining harmonious labor relations (Chapter 15); effectively managing health and safety issues in the workplace (Chapter 16); and reducing the time and resources needed to design, produce, and deliver quality products or services (Chapter 2).
- *Improving quality* Many companies have implemented **total quality management (TQM)** initiatives, designed to improve the quality of all the processes that lead to a final product or service. Continuing evidence shows that firms that effectively implement quality programs tend to outperform those that don't.[68]
- *Creating distinctive capabilities* The third way to gain a competitive advantage is to use people with distinctive capabilities to create unsurpassed competence in a particular area (for example, 3M's competence in adhesives, Carlson Corporation's leading presence in the travel business, and Xerox's dominance of the photocopier market). Chapter 5 (which discusses the recruitment and selection of employees), Chapter 8 (training), and Chapter 9 (the long-term grooming of employees within the firm) are particularly relevant.

total quality management (TQM)
An organization-wide approach to improving the quality of all the processes that lead to a final product or service.

DECENTRALIZATION Organizations commonly centralize major functions, such as HR, marketing, and production, in a single location that serves as the firm's command center. Multiple layers of management execute orders issued at the top and employees move up the ranks over time in what some have called the *internal labor market.*[69] However, the traditional top-down form of organization is being replaced by **decentralization**, which transfers responsibility and decision-making authority from a central office to people and locations closer to the situation that demands attention. The Internet helps companies to decentralize even faster by improving the communication flow among the workforce, reducing the need to rely on the traditional organizational pyramid.[70]

decentralization
Transferring responsibility and decision-making authority from a central office to people and locations closer to the situation that demands attention.

The need for maintaining or creating organizational flexibility in HR strategies is addressed in several chapters of this book, including those dealing with work flows (Chapter 2), compensation (Chapters 10 and 11), training (Chapter 8), staffing (Chapter 5), and globalization (Chapter 17).

DOWNSIZING Periodic reductions in a company's workforce to improve its bottom line—often called **downsizing**—are becoming standard business practice, even among firms that were once legendary for their "no layoff" policies, such as IBM, Kodak, and Xerox.[71] Although U.S. firms traditionally were far more willing than companies in other industrialized nations to resort to layoffs as a cost-cutting measure, globalization is quickly closing the gap. Chinese, Korean, and Indian firms have also experienced massive layoffs in the wake of the economic crisis at the end of the last decade.[72] In recent years, German companies—ranging from electronics giant Siemens to chip-maker Infineon Technologies to Commerzbank—have announced thousands of layoffs. Countries such as France, where authorities have repeatedly blocked management efforts to cut costs via layoffs, often find that these well-intentioned efforts are counterproductive, leading to a wave of bankruptcies. This was the fate of appliance maker Moulinex, once considered an icon of French industry, which shut its doors in 2002, with almost 9,000 employees losing their jobs as a result.[73]

downsizing
A reduction in a company's workforce to improve its bottom line.

In 2013, the socialist government in France passed a more restrictive law whereby the state has the right to disapprove restructuring plans depending on a firm's assets and economic health. At the time of this writing, the French government is applying this new law by blocking Alcatel-Lucent from laying off 900 French employees. Following a period of unprecedented growth, Iceland has experienced since the end of the past decade what amounts to an economic catastrophe, with almost a quarter of its workforce being laid off within a short time.[74] More recently, Ireland and Greece had a similar fate, with Italy, Portugal, and Spain not too far behind. In 2014 the unemployment rate in Spain reached an unprecedented 27%, provoking a large exodus of qualified personnel to other countries in Europe and Latin America (even though unemployment figures are decreasing at the time of this writing, mostly due to temporary hires in low-wage sectors).

Chapter 6 is devoted to downsizing and how to manage the process effectively. Other relevant chapters include those on benefits (Chapter 12), the legal environment (Chapter 3), labor relations (Chapter 15), and employee relations and communications (Chapter 13).

ORGANIZATIONAL RESTRUCTURING Over the past two decades there has been a dramatic transformation in how firms are structured. Tall organizations that had many management levels are becoming flatter as companies reduce the number of people between the chief executive officer (CEO) and the lowest-ranking employee in an effort to become more competitive. Mergers and acquisitions have been going on for decades. Often mergers fail because the cultures and HR systems of the firms involved do not coalesce.[75] A newer and rapidly growing form of interorganizational bonding comes in the form of joint ventures, alliances, and collaborations among firms that remain independent, yet work together on specific products to spread costs and risks.

To be successful, organizational restructuring requires effective management of human resources.[76] For instance, flattening the organization requires careful examination of staffing demands, work flows, communication channels, training needs, and so on. Likewise, mergers and other forms of interorganizational relations require the successful blending of dissimilar organizational structures, management practices, technical expertise, and so forth.[77] Chapter 2 deals specifically with these issues. Other chapters that focus on related issues are Chapter 5 (staffing), Chapter 8 (training), Chapter 9 (career development), and Chapter 17 (international management). Chapters 10 and 11 (compensation issues) address some of the growing controversies with regard to pay inequities between top and lower levels as organizations become flatter.[78]

SELF-MANAGED WORK TEAMS The traditional system in which individual employees report to a single boss (who oversees a group of three to seven subordinates) is being replaced in some organizations by the self-managed team system. Employees are assigned to a group of peers and, together, they are responsible for a particular area or task. It has been estimated that 40 percent of U.S. workers are operating in some kind of team environment.[79]

According to two experts on self-managed work teams, "Today's competitive environment demands intense improvement in productivity, quality, and response time. Teams can deliver this improvement. Bosses can't. . . . Just as dinosaurs once ruled the earth and later faded into extinction, the days of bosses may be numbered."[80]

Very few rigorous scientific studies have been done on the effectiveness of self-managed work teams. However, case studies do suggest that many firms that use teams enjoy impressive payoffs. For example, company officials at General Motors' Fitzgerald Battery Plant, which is organized in teams, reported cost savings of 30 to 40 percent over traditionally organized plants. At FedEx, a thousand clerical workers, divided into teams of 5 to 10 people, helped the company reduce service problems by 13 percent.[81]

HR issues concerning self-managed work teams are discussed in detail in Chapter 2 (work flows), Chapter 10 (compensation), and Chapter 11 (rewarding performance).

THE GROWTH OF SMALL BUSINESSES According to the U.S. Small Business Administration (SBA), the precise definition of a small business depends on the industry in which it operates. For instance, to be considered "small" by the SBA, a manufacturing company can have a maximum of 500 to 1,500 employees (depending on the type of manufacturing). In wholesaling, a company is considered small if the number of its employees does not exceed 100.[82]

An increasing percentage of the 14 million businesses in the United States are considered to be small.[83] One study using tax returns as its source of data found that 99.8 percent of U.S. businesses have fewer than 100 employees and approximately 90 percent have fewer than 20 employees.[84] Another study reports that approximately 85 percent of these firms are family owned.[85] One study found that Latinos and immigrants have substantially higher entrepreneurship rates than U.S. natives, and that African Americans increasingly are becoming entrepreneurs.[86]

Unfortunately, small businesses face a high risk of failure. According to some estimates, 40 percent of them fail in the first year, 60 percent fail before the start of the third year, and only 10 percent survive an entire decade.[87] To survive and prosper, a small business must manage its human resources effectively. For instance, a mediocre performance by one person in a 10-employee firm can mean the difference between making a profit and losing money. In the eighth edition of this book, each chapter has at least a section or a feature concerning special HR issues faced by small businesses.

ORGANIZATIONAL CULTURE The term **organizational culture** refers to the basic assumptions and beliefs shared by members of an organization. These beliefs operate unconsciously and define in a basic "taken for granted" fashion an organization's view of itself and its environment.[88] The key elements of organizational culture are:[89]

organizational culture
The basic assumptions and beliefs shared by members of an organization. These beliefs operate unconsciously and define in a basic taken-for-granted fashion an organization's view of itself and its environment.

- *Observed behavioral regularities* when people interact, such as the language used and the rituals surrounding deference and demeanor
- The *norms* that evolve in working groups, such as the norm of a fair day's work for a fair day's pay
- The *dominant values* espoused by an organization, such as product quality or low prices
- The *philosophy* that guides an organization's policy toward employees and customers
- The *rules of the game* for getting along in the organization—"the ropes" that a newcomer must learn to become an accepted member
- The *feeling or climate* that is conveyed in an organization by the physical layout and the way in which members of the organization interact with one another, customers, and outsiders

Firms that make cultural adjustments to keep up with environmental changes are likely to outperform those whose culture is rigid and unresponsive to external jolts. Campbell's Soup Company's problems in the 2000s are often attributed to norms and values that had not kept up with rapidly changing consumer tastes. As Khermouch wrote in *BusinessWeek*, "It's definitely a risk-averse, control-oriented culture. It's all about two things: financial control and how much they can squeeze out of a tomato. Campbell needs to reward risk-taking, remove organizational roadblocks, and summon up the courage to move bold initiatives from proposal to execution quickly and regularly."[90]

Changing an entrenched organizational culture is not easy. For example, Carly Fiorina, an outsider with a nontechnical background, was brought into Hewlett-Packard (HP) in 1999 as CEO in order to overhaul the company.[91] Yet she was fired just six years later because her marketing focus, aggressiveness, autocratic style, flair for public drama, and what many thought was an overblown ego alienated key HP employees, managers, and members of the board of directors.

TECHNOLOGY Although technology is changing rapidly in many areas, such as robotics, one area in particular is revolutionizing human resources: information technology.[92] *Telematics technologies*—a broad array of tools, including computers, networking programs, telecommunications, and fax machines—are now available and affordable to businesses of every size, even one-person companies. These technologies—coupled with the rise of the Internet—have impacted businesses in a number of ways, specifically:

- ***The rise of telecommuting*** Because technology makes information easy to store, retrieve, and analyze, the number of company employees working at least part-time at home (*telecommuters*) has been increasing by 15 percent annually. Because telecommuting arrangements are expected to continue to grow in the future, they raise many important issues, such as performance monitoring and career planning. A recent survey uncovered that almost half of off-site employees believe that people who work onsite get more recognition than those who work off-site. On the same survey, more telecommuters than onsite employees reported that they are unlikely to stay in their current position and firm if they can find a suitable job elsewhere that pays them a similar amount.[93] Instead of being easy work, telecommuting makes it difficult for most telecommuters to draw a line between personal and work life, sometimes making these jobs very stressful.
- ***The ethics of proper data use*** Data control, data accuracy, the right to privacy, and ethics are at the core of a growing controversy brought about by the new information technologies, particularly the Internet.[94] Personal computers now make it possible to access huge databases containing information on an individual's credit files, work history, driving records, health reports, criminal convictions, and family makeup. One Web site, for example, promises that in exchange for a $7 fee, it will scan "over two million records to create a single report on an individual."[95] A critical observer notes: "Because of the large volume of information errors may creep in and those who are negatively affected may not have a chance to defend themselves."[96] The Manager's Notebook, "What to Do with Personal Information," offers several examples of the ethical issues confronting human resource professionals given easy access to personal data via modern technology.

MANAGER'S NOTEBOOK

What to Do with Personal Information

One of the main ethical challenges facing HR professionals is how to interpret and put to use information about current and prospective employees that can be easily uncovered through the Web. And protecting the data of employees is becoming very difficult. Consider the following recent reports:

- Privacy Rights, an organization that keeps track of data breaches, has documented 613,508,411 records that were breached between 2005 and 2014, involving 3,954 data bases.
- Jessica Bennett, a reporter for *Newsweek*, recently noted a simple experiment. She asked an Internet consultant to do a scrub of the Web giving this person her name and e-mail address to go on. Without doing any hacking, within 30 minutes the consultant had her Social Security number; in two hours, the consultant had identified her address, body type, educational background, hometown, and health status.
- "Most people are still under the illusion that when they go online, they're anonymous," says Nicholas Carr, author of *The Shallows: What the Internet Is Doing to Our Brains.* But in reality, as Carr notes, every key you press is being recorded into a database.
- "It is technically impossible for Yahoo! to be aware of all software or files that may be installed on a user's computer when they visit our site," laments Anne Toth, Yahoo's vice president of global policy and head of privacy.
- Even though there is very little evidence that a credit score is a predictor of job performance, a recent Society for Human Resource Management (SHRM) study showed 60 percent of employers used credit checks (obtained in seconds from the Internet) to vet job candidates. Presumably, a lower credit score is interpreted as evidence of poor working habits, irresponsible behaviors, a higher likelihood of committing fraud, and so forth (but once again, these may be presumptions with little evidence to back them up).

Sources: Based on *www.privacyrights.org*. (2014). Online privacy; *www.aclu.org*. (2014); Murray, S. (2010, Oct. 15). Credit checks on job seekers by employers attract scrutiny. *Wall Street Journal*, A-5; Fowler, G. A., and Morrison, S. (2010, Nov. 4). Facebook expands mobile effort. *Wall Street Journal*, B-12; Vascellaro, J. E. (2010, Nov. 9). Websites rein in tracking tools. *Wall Street Journal*, B-1; Bennett, J. (2010, Nov. 1). Privacy is dead. *Newsweek*, 40; Stecklow, S., and Sonne, P. (2010, Nov. 24). Shunned profiling method on the verge of comeback. *Wall Street Journal*, A-14; Angwin, J., and Thurm, S. (2010, Oct. 8). Privacy defense mounted. *Wall Street Journal*, B-6; Fowler, G. A., and Steel, E. (2010). Facebook says user data sold to broker. *Wall Street Journal*, B-3. ■■

- ***Electronic monitoring*** As illustrated in the You Manage It! case "Electronic Monitoring to Make Sure That No One Steps Out of Line" at the end of this chapter, some companies are experimenting with all sorts of sophisticated devices to measure employee productivity. Approximately 40 percent of firms in 2014 were using artificial intelligence software that monitors when, how, and why workers are using the Internet. According to Clares Voice, a Dallas-based messaging security company, "We look at every piece of mail while it is in motion."[97] E-mail messages are now used as evidence for all sorts of legal cases concerning age discrimination, sexual harassment, price fixing, and the like.[98] "Some 70 percent of the evidence that we routinely deal with is in the form of electronic communication," says Garry G. Mathiason, a senior partner at Littler Mendelson, a prestigious legal firm in San Francisco.[99]
- ***Medical testing*** Genetic testing, high-tech imaging, and DNA analysis may soon be available to aid in making employment decisions.[100] Firms' decisions about how to harness the new information (to screen applicants, to establish health insurance premiums, to decide who should be laid off, and the like) are full of ethical implications. IBM seems to be on the forefront, recently announcing that it will not use genetic data for employment decisions. This is one area where the legal system is still far behind technical advances. A related issue concerns punishing employees who are exposed to health risks; with the

new health care law coming into effect, a growing number of firms are trying to "individualize" the price of health insurance (see the Manager's Notebook, "Watching Over Your Shoulder: Paying a Price for Unhealthy Life Styles").

MANAGER'S NOTEBOOK

Watching Over Your Shoulder: Paying a Price for Unhealthy Life Styles

Ethics/Social Responsibility

As health care costs have increased over the years, more and more companies are imposing financial penalties (mostly in health care monthly premium payments) for workers who show evidence of "unhealthy life styles." In 2015, approximately 20% of large firms had this type of program (including such household names as Home Depot, Pepsi-Co, Safeway, Lowe's, and General Mills), a percentage expected to double or triple in the near future. For instance, Walmart charges $2,000 per year for smokers. While penalizing "bad" behaviors (such as smoking and drug and alcohol abuse) may be fair, demanding that employees who are overweight, have high cholesterol, or have high blood pressure pay more is controversial. These physical traits may not represent a personal choice and could be associated with such involuntary factors as genetic predisposition, stress, and poverty. The new "Affordable Care Act" allows companies to charge up to 30 percent more in insurance costs for an unhealthy lifestyle, although presumably firms can charge workers higher fees only if they are provided with wellness programs. The problem is that federal rules are not explicit in defining wellness programs and many companies are likely to interpret this requirement liberally.

Sources: Based on Society for Human Resource Management. (2014). More employers to penalize workers for unhealthy behaviors. *www.shrm.org*; *www.medscape.com*. (2014). Should people with unhealthy lifestyles pay higher health insurance? Abelson, R. (2013). The smokers surcharge. *www.nytimes.com*. ■■

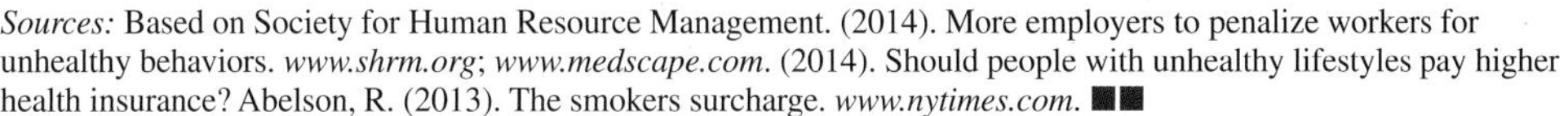

- ***An increase in egalitarianism*** Because information is now available both instantaneously and broadly, organizational structures are becoming more *egalitarian*, meaning that power and authority are spread more evenly among all employees. Groupware networks, which enable hundreds of workers to share information simultaneously, can give office workers corporate and business intelligence previously available only to their bosses.[101] They also enable the rank-and-file to join in online discussions with senior executives. In these kinds of interactions, people are judged more by what they say than by their rank on the corporate ladder.[102]

The challenges and implications of rapidly changing technologies—especially information technologies—for human resources are discussed in every chapter of this book.

INTERNAL SECURITY The 9/11 attacks on the Twin towers and the Pentagon, the Boston Marathon massacre, and several subsequent plots and mass shootings since then have engendered a collective obsession with security in the United States. Many consulting firms are now focusing their attention on how to detect potential security problems, and a wide range of firms and industry groups, from trucking associations to sporting-event organizers, have made security screening a top priority.[103] Apart from conducting background checks, HR departments are increasingly involved in beefing up security details by scanning employees' eyes and fingerprints for positive identification, hiring armed guards to patrol facilities, identifying employees who might pose a violence threat, and even spotting potential spies.[104]

Although few would question that security checks are necessary, one concern from a human resource perspective is to ensure that applicants' and employers' rights are not violated and that due process is followed whenever suspected problems are identified. For example, should a person convicted of a drunken driving violation 15 years ago be denied a job as a flight attendant? What about people whose past reveals some facts that may be warning signals, depending on the bias of the evaluator (for instance, graduation from a Middle Eastern university, frequent job changes, multiple divorces, and the like)? Health sites offer tools used by medical professionals and companies to track data, including test results from HIV and cancer exams.[105] Should firms use this type of information as part of their selection process?

According to a study conducted by Automatic Data Accessing, a computer-based security-service firm, more than 40 percent of résumés misrepresent education or employment history. The same survey shows that many companies are willing to overlook some degree of inaccuracy.[106] In other words, how security-related information is used is a matter of interpretation, except perhaps in the most grievous cases. Chapter 14, "Respecting Employee Rights and Managing Discipline," deals with these and related issues.

DATA SECURITY Numerous cases of unauthorized access to private data have been revealed during the past decade, in some situations leading to widespread identity fraud. (See the Manager's Notebook, "What to Do with Personal Information.") According to a recent *New York Times* report, a well-financed computer underground operates from countries with highly skilled technicians that are subject to very little, if any, government control.[107] "Right now the bad guys are improving more quickly than the good guys," says Patrick Lincoln, director of the computer science laboratory at SRI International, a science and technology research group.[108] The Privacy Rights Clearinghouse, a consumer advocacy group in San Diego, counted over 80 major data breaches involving the personal information of more than 50 million people.[109] In one case, CardSystems (a credit card processor) left the account information of more than 40 million shareholders exposed to fraud.[110] Such well-known organizations as Lexis/Nexis Group, ChoicePoint, Bank of America, the United States Air Force, the Pentagon, and even the FBI experienced serious data breaches during 2005–2012.[111] The recent WikiLeaks dump into the Web of hundreds of thousands of U.S. secrets as well as classified material from the military and the State Department represents the most extreme case so far as to how even one low-level employee can use computer technology to create major damage and embarrassment for an organization. Data security is not just a concern for specialized computer experts; it should also involve HR policies to determine who has access to sensitive information and monitoring systems to prevent abuses by managers and employees.

outsourcing
Subcontracting work to an outside company that specializes in and is more efficient at doing that kind of work.

OUTSOURCING Many large firms now shift work once performed internally to outside suppliers and contractors, a process called **outsourcing**. The motivation is simple: Outsourcing saves money. The *Wall Street Journal* reports that more than 40 percent of Fortune 500 companies have outsourced some department or service—everything from HR administration to computer systems.[112] A survey conducted by the WorldatWork Association (which has more than 10,000

Source: ©Ann Little/Alamy.

members in responsible HR positions) found that the following HR practices are now completely or partially outsourced by a large proportion of participating firms: health and welfare (79%), pension plans (90%), payroll (62%), training (50%), and recruitment and selection (32%).[113]

Outsourcing creates several HR challenges for firms. Although it often helps companies slash costs, employees may face layoffs when their jobs are farmed out to the lowest bidder. For instance, UPS subcontracted 5,000 jobs at its 65 customer service centers.[114] In addition, customer dissatisfaction can result if subcontractors are not carefully watched and evaluated. For instance, a group of former employees at now-liquidated Skillset Software Inc. filed suit against its outside HR provider, TriNet Group Inc., for negligence in handling their claims. Part of the problem is that these HR providers often don't provide enough access and human interaction (many rely extensively on the Web) to handle employee concerns and complaints.[115] Subcontractors may take on more work than they can handle,[116] and small businesses may not receive the best available service and support. When subcontracting HR activities such as training, staffing, and compensation, data security issues become paramount. The organization would have to trust that the subcontractor can effectively protect personal data (such as Social Security numbers, marital status, income level, performance problems, bank accounts) from misuse by insiders or outsiders. Outsourcing that includes a foreign location (which is increasingly common) further complicates the data security issue. Finally, outsourcing poses major difficulties for international firms trying to enforce ethical HR standards among its subcontractors around the world. Nike has been singled out in the press on numerous occasions for issues such as child labor, unsafe working conditions, and slave wages among subcontractors in China, Vietnam, Indonesia, and Thailand that produce 98 percent of its shoes at low cost. Walmart has also been singled out for hiring subcontractors in Bangladesh with very poor working conditions, in one case leading to the death of hundreds of women in a factory fire.

We discuss outsourcing and its challenges for HRM throughout this book. Chapter 2 discusses subcontracting within the context of downsizing, and Chapter 15, on labor relations, discusses how outsourcing affects unions.

PRODUCT INTEGRITY One complex issue that has received much media attention during the last three years is the extent to which firms can effectively monitor the integrity of products or subcomponents that are made in foreign countries. For instance, traces of melamine, which could be deadly for children, have been found in infant formula in the United States and Europe.[117] Similar problems have been reported with bad ingredients imported from China that were used by mainstream drug manufacturers as well as with counterfeit parts used by the U.S. military.[118] The detection and prevention of these problems may require HR policies that involve carefully selecting, training, and providing appropriate incentives for the responsible managers and employees to acquire and monitor inputs from global suppliers (more on this in Chapter 17, which examines international HR issues).

Individual Challenges

Human resource issues at the individual level address the decisions most pertinent to specific employees. These **individual challenges** almost always reflect what is happening in the larger organization. For instance, technology affects individual productivity; it also has ethical ramifications in terms of how information is used to make HR decisions (for example, use of credit or medical history data to decide whom to hire). How the company treats its individual employees is also likely to affect the organizational challenges we discussed earlier. For example, if many key employees leave the firm to join competitors, the organization's competitive position is affected. In other words, there is a two-way relationship between organizational and individual challenges. This is unlike the relationship between environmental and organizational challenges, in which the relationship goes only one way (see Figure 1.1); few organizations can have much impact on the environment. The most important individual challenges today are matching people and organizations, ethics and social responsibility, productivity, empowerment, brain drain, and job security.

individual challenges
Human resource issues that address the decisions most pertinent to individual employees.

MATCHING PEOPLE AND ORGANIZATIONS Research suggests that HR strategies contribute to firm performance most when the firm uses these strategies to attract and retain the type of employee who best fits the firm's culture and overall business objectives. For example, one study showed that fast-growth firms perform better with managers who have a strong marketing and sales background, who are willing to take risks, and who have a high tolerance for ambiguity. However, these managerial traits actually reduce the performance of mature firms that have an established product and are more interested in maintaining (rather than expanding) their market share.[119]

Chapter 5 deals specifically with the attempt to achieve the right fit between employees and the organization to enhance performance.

ETHICS AND SOCIAL RESPONSIBILITY In previous editions of this book, we discussed the well-publicized scandals at Enron, Worldcom, Tyco, and Global Crossings, in which corruption apparently became a way of life at the top. Since then, we can scarcely read any business periodical without being bombarded by multiple cases of egregious unethical behaviors across a wide variety of organizations. These include, for example, American International Group (or AIG, one of the largest insurance companies, which artificially inflated its reserves by $500 million);[120] Time Warner (accused of fraudulent accounting);[121] Bank of America (forced to pay $1 billion in fines for ethical lapses);[122] CitiGroup (several officers are being tried for alleged money laundering);[123] Boeing (where top executives were sentenced in an Air Force procurement scandal involving millions of dollars);[124] ChoicePoint (one of the largest credit reporting agencies, which allegedly kept hidden for a month information about an identity theft ring's access to personal data on about 145,000 people, providing sufficient time for top executives to dump their ChoicePoint stock);[125] Stratton Veterans Affairs Medical Center (at which certain employees posing as doctors conducted unauthorized clinical research on cancer patients, leading to death in some cases);[126] State University of New York at Albany (whose president, Karen R. Hitchcock, was forced to resign after accusations that she hired a contractor who promised to fund an endowed university professorship just for her);[127] the famous Getty Museum in Los Angeles (which is beset by charges of stolen antiquities and profligate executive perks);[128] drug makers accused of systematically hiding the side effects of certain medicines;[129] the ex-governor of Illinois, Rod R. Blagojevich, who brazenly put up for sale his appointment of Barack Obama's successor to the U.S. Senate;[130] and Royal Dutch Shell, found guilty of paying millions of dollars in bribes to secure contracts.[131]

We can safely assume that reported cases of unethical behavior represent only the tip of the iceberg.[132]

In response to these concerns, people's fears that their employers will behave unethically are increasing,[133] so much so that many firms and professional organizations have created codes of ethics outlining principles and standards of personal conduct for their members. Unfortunately, these codes often do not meet employees' expectations of ethical employer behavior. In a poll of *Harvard Business Review* readers, almost half the respondents indicated their belief that managers do not consistently make ethical decisions.[134] To the common person on the street, the economic crisis prompted by dubious financial instruments at the end of the first decade of the twenty-first century and the large bonuses received by top executives during the subsequent deep recession seem to have reinforced that image. President Obama called this situation "immoral."

The widespread perceptions of unethical behavior may also be attributed to the fact that managerial decisions are rarely clear-cut. Except in a few blatant cases (such as willful misrepresentation), what is ethical or unethical is open to debate. Even the most detailed codes of ethics are still general enough to allow much room for managerial discretion. In fact, many of the executives convicted of illegal activities thought they were just buying time to turn the company around or that subordinates were too zealous in implementing "revenue enhancing" directives.[135] Perhaps even more so than in other business areas, many specific decisions related to the management of human resources are subject to judgment calls. Often these judgment calls constitute a catch-22 because none of the alternatives is desirable.[136]

Some companies are using the Web to infuse employees and managers with ethical values. For instance, many of Lockheed Martin's 160,000 employees are required to take a step-by-step online training program on ethics.[137] CitiGroup started an online ethics training program that is mandatory for all of its 300,000 employees.[138] Other companies are using more traditional training methods to implement so called "zero-tolerance policies." For instance, at Goldman Sachs, the chief executive (Henry M. Paulson, Jr., who later became U.S. Treasury Secretary) moderated seminars on various business judgments and ethical issues with all the bank's managing directors.[139] One thing seems certain: Failure to self-regulate leads to constraining legislation. A 2011 federal law, for instance, provides financial incentives for employees to tell regulators directly about securities fraud and other wrongdoings, thus bypassing the company's HR department and management.

A company that exercises *social responsibility* attempts to balance its commitments—not only to its investors, but also to its employees, its customers, other businesses, and the community or communities in which it operates. For example, McDonald's established Ronald McDonald Houses years ago to provide lodging for families of sick children hospitalized away from home. Sears and General Electric support artists and performers, and many local merchants support local children's sports teams. Philip Morris is trying to turn around its "ugly duckling" image by entering the business of treating smoke-related illnesses and supporting research projects on lung-disease prevention.[140]

An entire chapter of this book is devoted to employee rights and responsibilities (Chapter 13); each chapter includes (at selected points) pertinent ethical questions for which there are no absolute answers. Most chapters also include a Manager's Notebook dealing with ethical issues related to the specific topic of that chapter. See the accompanying box for this chapter.

PRODUCTIVITY Most experts agree that productivity gains from technology have altered the economic playing field since the mid-1990s. **Productivity** is a measure of how much value individual employees add to the goods or services that the organization produces. The greater the output per individual, the higher the organization's productivity. For instance, U.S. workers produce a pair of shoes in 24 minutes, whereas Chinese workers take three hours.[141] Intangible human capital comes in many forms, such as designers' creativity at Intel Corp., the tenacity of software architects at Sun Microsystems Inc., marketing knowledge at Procter & Gamble Co., and a friendly culture as in the case of Southwest Airlines.[142] From an HR perspective, employee productivity is affected by ability, motivation, and quality of work life.

productivity
A measure of how much value individual employees add to the goods or services that the organization produces.

ability
Competence in performing a job.

Employee **ability**, competence in performing a job, can be improved through a hiring and placement process that selects the best individuals for the job.[143] Chapter 5 specifically deals with this process. It can also be improved through training and career development programs designed to sharpen employees' skills and prepare them for additional responsibilities. Chapters 8 and 9 discuss these issues.

motivation
A person's desire to do the best possible job or to exert the maximum effort to perform assigned tasks.

Motivation refers to a person's desire to do the best possible job or to exert the maximum effort to perform assigned tasks. Motivation energizes, directs, and sustains human behavior. Several key factors affecting employee motivation are discussed in this book, including work design (Chapter 2), matching of employee and job requirements (Chapter 5), rewards (Chapters 11 and 13), and due process (Chapter 14).

quality of work life
A measure of how safe and satisfied employees feel with their jobs.

A growing number of companies recognize that employees are more likely to choose a firm and stay there if they believe that it offers a high **quality of work life**. A high quality of work life is related to job satisfaction, which, in turn, is a strong predictor of absenteeism and turnover.[144] A firm's investments in improving the quality of work life also pay off in the form of better customer service.[145] We discuss issues related to job design and their effects on employee attitudes and behavior in Chapter 2.

empowerment
Providing workers with the skills and authority to make decisions that would traditionally be made by managers.

EMPOWERMENT Many firms have reduced employee dependence on superiors, placing more emphasis on individual control over (and responsibility for) the work that needs to be done. This process has been labeled **empowerment** because it transfers direction from an external source (normally the immediate supervisor) to an internal source (the individual's own desire to do well). In essence, the process of empowerment entails providing workers with the skills and authority to make decisions that would traditionally be made by managers. The goal of empowerment is an organization consisting of enthusiastic, committed people who perform their work ably because they believe in it and enjoy doing it (*internal control*). This situation is in stark contrast to an organization that gets people to work as an act of compliance to avoid punishment (for example, being fired) or to qualify for a paycheck (*external control*).

Empowerment can encourage employees to be creative and to take risks, which are key components that can give a firm a competitive edge in a fast-changing environment. Empowering employees is "the hardest thing to do because it means giving up control," says Lee Fielder, retired president of Kelly Springfield Tire Co., a unit of Goodyear. "But [according to Fielder], managers who try to tell employees what and how to do every little thing will end up with only mediocre people, because the talented ones won't submit to control."[146] To encourage risk taking, General Electric past-CEO Jack Welch exhorted his managers and employees to "shake it, shake it, break it."[147]

HR issues related to internal and external control of behavior are discussed in Chapter 2 (work flows).

brain drain
The loss of high-talent key personnel to competitors or start-up ventures.

BRAIN DRAIN With organizational success more and more dependent on knowledge held by specific employees, companies are becoming more susceptible to **brain drain**—the loss of intellectual property that results when competitors lure away key employees. Important industries such as semiconductors and electronics also suffer from high employee turnover when key employees leave to start their own businesses. This brain drain can negatively affect innovation and cause major delays in the introduction of new products.[148]

At a national level, brain drain has been a major problem for developing countries because the best educated tend to leave. Universities and R&D labs in the United States are full of faculty and graduate students from China, India, and other emerging economies. In some of the poorest countries, such as Haiti, more than three-fourths of college-educated individuals have emigrated. Even some developed economies like that of Spain have suffered an enormous brain drain in recent years, with approximately 750,000 Spaniards (many with advanced degrees) emigrating to other countries during 2011–2015 as the unemployment rate soared and most new jobs created at the end of the recession were in low-wage, unskilled sectors. According to the National Academy of Engineering, more than half of engineers with advanced degrees in the United States are foreign born, as are over one-third of Nobel-award winners during the past 15 years.[149] At Microsoft, more than 20 percent of employees are from India. This dependence on foreign talent places the United States in a vulnerable position, particularly if giants such as China and India continue their fast growth in the future.[150] In fact, a new term has been coined for this phenomenon: *reverse brain drain.* It refers to foreign-born Americans who decide to return to their homelands, particularly in rapidly growing emergent economies such as China, India, and Brazil.

Brain drain and measures for dealing with it effectively are discussed in several chapters of this book, particularly in Chapter 3 (equal opportunity and the legal environment), Chapter 4 (managing diversity), Chapter 6 (employee separations and outplacement), and Chapter 11 (rewarding performance).

JOB INSECURITY As noted in the introduction, most workers cannot count on a steady job and regular promotions. Companies argue that regardless of how well the firm is doing, layoffs have become essential in an age of cutthroat competition. For employees, however, chronic job insecurity is a major source of stress and can lead to lower performance and productivity. Reed Moskowitz, founder of a stress disorder center at New York University, notes that workers' mental health has taken a turn for the worse because "nobody feels secure anymore."[151]

The corporate crisis at the end of the last decade has produced huge losses in pension plans, meaning that many older employees can no longer afford to retire and will therefore compete for jobs with younger workers.[152] An article in *BusinessWeek* labeled these older adults "the unretired".[153] Except in the public sector, the traditional retirement plans with a guaranteed income for retirees has largely become a thing of the past and a high proportion of older workers in their 70s and beyond are now part of the labor market. *Retirementjobs.com,* a career site for people older than age 50, is currently handling about 600,000 visitors per month, more than double the number just a short time ago.[154]

Paradoxically, voluntary employee turnover is still a problem for many employers (for instance, an annual turnover rate of 50 percent or more in the restaurant and hospitality industry is not unusual), and this can be very costly in terms of recruitment and training costs as well as customer dissatisfaction.[155] Recent crackdowns on illegal immigrants (who work in many of the industries with high turnover, such as meat packing, agriculture, fast-food restaurants, and the like) have made it much more difficult to replace those who quit.[156]

We discuss the challenges of laying off employees and making the remaining employees feel secure and valued in Chapter 6. We discuss employee stress (and ways to relieve it) in Chapter 16. We explore union–management relations in Chapter 15.

Planning and Implementing Strategic HR Policies

To be successful, firms must closely align their HR strategies and programs (tactics) with environmental opportunities, business strategies, and the organization's unique characteristics and distinctive competence.

The Benefits of Strategic HR Planning

The process of formulating HR strategies and establishing programs or tactics to implement them is called **strategic human resource (HR) planning**. When done correctly, strategic HR planning provides many direct and indirect benefits for the company.

strategic human resource (HR) planning
The process of formulating HR strategies and establishing programs or tactics to implement them.

ENCOURAGEMENT OF PROACTIVE RATHER THAN REACTIVE BEHAVIOR Being *proactive* means looking ahead and developing a vision of where the company wants to be and how it can use human resources to get there. In contrast, being *reactive* means responding to problems as they come up. Companies that are reactive may lose sight of the long-term direction of their business; proactive companies are better prepared for the future. For instance, companies on the brink of bankruptcy need to hold on to their key talent, perhaps offering special inducements for star performers to persevere through hard times. Although it might appear counterintuitive to spend money on employee compensation during economic difficulties, it is crucial to retain key employees.[157]

EXPLICIT COMMUNICATION OF COMPANY GOALS Strategic HR planning can help a firm develop a focused set of strategic objectives that capitalizes on its special talents and know-how.

For instance, 3M has had an explicit strategy of competing through innovation, with the goal of having at least 25 percent of revenues generated from products introduced during the past five years. To achieve this goal, 3M's human resource strategy may be summarized as "Hire top-notch scientists in every field, give each an ample endowment, then stand back and let them do their thing. The anything-goes approach has yielded thousands of new products over the decades, from sandpaper and magnetic audio tape to Post-it notes and Thinsulate insulation."[158] One hundred years after its foundation, 3M clearly expresses the philosophy that guides its HR practices: "Every day, 3M people find new ways to make amazing things happen."

STIMULATION OF CRITICAL THINKING AND ONGOING EXAMINATION OF ASSUMPTIONS Managers often depend on their personal views and experiences to solve problems and make business decisions. The assumptions on which they make their decisions can lead to success if they are appropriate to the environment in which the business operates. However, serious problems can arise when these assumptions no longer hold. For instance, in the 1980s IBM deemphasized sales of its personal computers because IBM managers were afraid that PC growth would decrease the profitability of the firm's highly profitable mainframe products. This decision allowed competitors to move aggressively into the PC market, eventually devastating IBM.[159]

Strategic HR planning can stimulate critical thinking and the development of new initiatives only if it is a continuing and flexible process rather than a rigid procedure with a discrete beginning and a specific deadline for completion. This is why many firms have formed an executive committee, which includes an HR professional and the CEO, to discuss strategic issues on an ongoing basis and periodically modify the company's overall HR strategies and programs.

IDENTIFICATION OF GAPS BETWEEN CURRENT SITUATION AND FUTURE VISION Strategic HR planning can help a firm identify the difference between "where we are today" and "where we want to be." Despite a $1 billion budget and a staff of 7,000, 3M's vaunted research laboratory was not able in recent years to deliver fast growth, partly because some of the R&D lacked focus and money wasn't always wisely spent. To speed up growth, 3M announced a series of performance objectives for individual business chiefs who had previously enjoyed much free rein. In addition, 3M introduced specially trained "black belts" to root out inefficiencies in departments ranging from R&D to sales.[160]

ENCOURAGEMENT OF LINE MANAGERS' PARTICIPATION For HR strategy to be effective, line managers at all levels must buy into it. If they do not, it is likely to fail. For example, a large cosmetics manufacturing plant decided to introduce a reward program in which work teams would receive a large bonus for turning out high-quality products. The bonus was part of a strategic plan to foster greater cooperation among employees. But the plan, which had been developed by top executives in consultation with the HR department, backfired when managers and supervisors began hunting for individual employees responsible for errors. The plan was eventually dropped.

IDENTIFICATION OF HR CONSTRAINTS AND OPPORTUNITIES When overall business strategy planning is done in combination with HR strategic planning, firms can identify the potential problems and opportunities with respect to the people expected to implement the business strategy.

A cornerstone of Motorola's business strategy is to identify, encourage, and financially support new-product ventures. To implement this strategy, Motorola relies on in-house venture teams, normally composed of five to six employees, one each from research and development (R&D), marketing, sales, manufacturing, engineering, and finance. Positions are broadly defined to allow all employees to use their creativity and to serve as champions of new ideas.

CREATION OF COMMON BONDS A substantial amount of research shows that, in the long run, organizations that have a strong sense of "who we are" tend to outperform those that do not. A strategic HR plan that reinforces, adjusts, or redirects the organization's present culture can foster values such as a customer focus, innovation, fast growth, and cooperation.

The Challenges of Strategic HR Planning

In developing an effective HR strategy, the organization faces several important challenges.

MAINTAINING A COMPETITIVE ADVANTAGE Any competitive advantage enjoyed by an organization tends to be short-lived because other companies are likely to imitate it. This is as true for HR advantages as for technological and marketing advantages. For example, many high-tech firms have "borrowed" reward programs for key scientists and engineers from other successful high-tech firms.

The challenge from an HR perspective is to develop strategies that offer the firm a sustained competitive advantage. For instance, a company may develop programs that maximize present employees' potential through carefully developed career ladders (see Chapter 9), while at the same time rewarding them generously with company stock with strings attached (for example, a provision that they will forfeit the stock if they quit before a certain date). One company that takes this very seriously is Zappos (whose name is a short form of the Spanish word *zapatos*) because its main business is to sell shoes online. All Zappos' employees, regardless of their positions, are required to undergo a four-week customer loyalty training course that includes at least two weeks of talking on the phone with customers in the call center at full salary. After a week of training, the new employees are offered \$3,000 to leave the company immediately if they wish, no strings attached. This is to ensure that people are there for the love of the job and not the money. Over 97 percent of new employees turn down the buyout. Zappos was recently purchased by Amazon in a deal that was worth \$1.2 billion. Zappos' employees received \$40 million in cash and stocks.

REINFORCING OVERALL BUSINESS STRATEGY Developing HR strategies that support the firm's overall business strategy is a challenge for several reasons. First, top management may not always be able to enunciate clearly the firm's overall business strategy. Second, there may be much

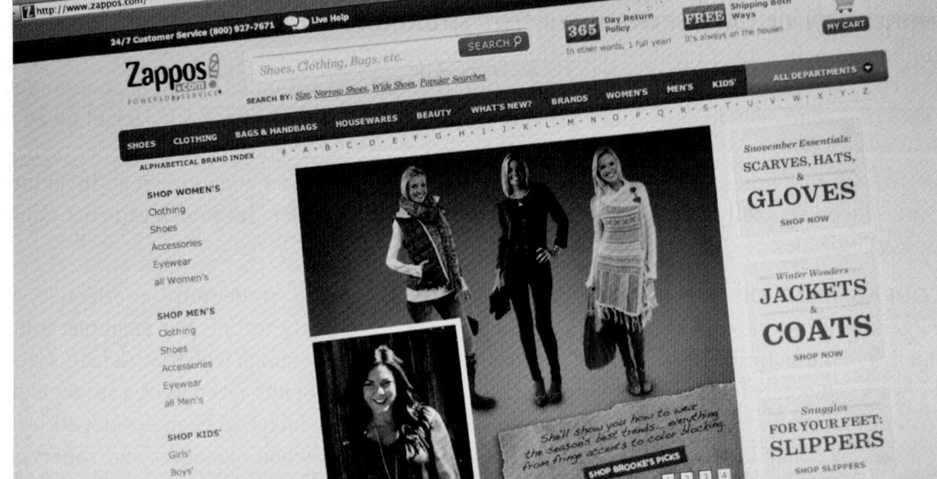

Zappos online shopping Web site.
Source: © NetPhotos/Alamy.

uncertainty or disagreement concerning which HR strategies should be used to support the overall business strategy. In other words, it is seldom obvious how particular HR strategies will contribute to the achievement of organizational strategies. Third, large corporations may have different business units, each with its own business strategies. Ideally, each unit should be able to formulate the HR strategy that fits its own business strategy best. For instance, a division that produces high-tech equipment may decide to pay its engineering staff well above average to attract and retain the best people, whereas the consumer products division may decide to pay its engineers an average wage. Such differentials may cause problems if the engineers from the two divisions have contact with each other. Thus, diverse HR strategies may spur feelings of inequity and resentment.

AVOIDING EXCESSIVE CONCENTRATION ON DAY-TO-DAY PROBLEMS Some managers are so busy putting out fires that they have no time to focus on the long term. Nonetheless, a successful HR strategy demands a vision tied to the long-term direction of the business. Thus, a major challenge of strategic HR planning is prodding people into stepping back and considering the big picture.

In many small companies, staffs are so absorbed in growing the business today that they seldom pause to look at the big picture for tomorrow. Also, strategic HR planning in small companies is often synonymous with the whims of the company owner or founder, who may not take the time to formalize his or her plans.

DEVELOPING HR STRATEGIES SUITED TO UNIQUE ORGANIZATIONAL FEATURES No two firms are exactly alike. Firms differ in history, culture, leadership style, technology, and so on. The chances are high that any ambitious HR strategy or program that is not molded to organizational characteristics will fail.[161] And therein lies one of the central challenges in formulating HR strategies: creating a vision of the organization of the future that does not provoke a destructive clash with the organization of the present.

COPING WITH THE ENVIRONMENT Just as no two firms are exactly alike, no two firms operate in an identical environment. Some must deal with rapid change, as in the computer industry; others operate in a relatively stable market, as in the market for food processors. Some face a virtually guaranteed demand for their products or services (for example, medical providers); others must deal with turbulent demand (for example, fashion designers). Even within a very narrowly defined industry, some firms may be competing in a market where customer service is the key (IBM's traditional competitive advantage), whereas others are competing in a market driven by cost considerations (the competitive advantage offered by the many firms producing cheap computers). A major challenge in developing HR strategies is crafting strategies that will work in the firm's unique environment to give it a sustainable competitive advantage.

SECURING MANAGEMENT COMMITMENT HR strategies that originate in the HR department will have little chance of succeeding unless managers at all levels—including top executives—support them completely. To ensure managers' commitment, HR professionals must work closely with them when formulating policies.

TRANSLATING THE STRATEGIC PLAN INTO ACTION The acid test of any strategic plan is whether it makes a difference in practice. If the plan does not affect practice, employees and managers will regard it as all talk and no action.

Cynicism is practically guaranteed when a firm experiences frequent turnover at the top, with each new wave of high-level managers introducing their own freshly minted strategic plan. Perhaps the greatest challenge in strategic HR planning lies not in the formulation of strategy, but rather in the development of an appropriate set of programs that will make the strategy work.

COMBINING INTENDED AND EMERGENT STRATEGIES Debate continues over whether strategies are *intended* or *emergent*—that is, whether they are proactive, rational, deliberate plans designed to attain predetermined objectives (intended) or general "fuzzy" patterns collectively molded by the interplay of power, politics, improvisation, negotiation, and personalities within the organization (emergent).[162] Most people agree that organizations have intended *and* emergent strategies, that both are necessary, and that the challenge is to combine the best aspects of the two.

Intended strategies can provide a sense of purpose and a guide for the allocation of resources. They are also useful for recognizing environmental opportunities and threats and for mobilizing top management to respond appropriately. On the downside, intended strategies may lead to a top-down strategic approach that squashes creativity and widespread involvement.

Emergent strategies also have their advantages and disadvantages. Among their benefits: (1) They involve everyone in the organization, which fosters grassroots support; (2) they develop gradually out of the organization's experiences and, thus, can be less upsetting than intended strategies; and (3) they are more pragmatic than intended strategies because they evolve to deal with specific problems or issues facing the firm. On the negative side, emergent strategies may lack strong leadership and fail to infuse the organization with a creative vision.[163]

Effectively combining intended and emergent strategies requires that managers blend the benefits of formal planning (to provide strong guidance and direction in setting priorities) with the untidy realities of dispersed employees who, through their unplanned activities, formulate emergent strategies throughout the firm.

ACCOMMODATING CHANGE Strategic HR plans must be flexible enough to accommodate change.[164] A firm with an inflexible strategic plan may find itself unable to respond to changes quickly because it is so committed to a particular course of action. This may lead the organization to continue devoting resources to an activity of questionable value simply because so much has been invested in it already.[165] The challenge is to create a strategic vision and develop the plans to achieve it while staying flexible enough to adapt to change.

Strategic HR Choices

strategic HR choices
The options available to a firm in designing its human resources system.

A firm's **strategic HR choices** are the options it has available in designing its human resources system. Figure 1.2 shows a sampling of strategic HR choices. Keep three things in mind here: First, the list is not exhaustive. Second, many different HR programs or practices may be used separately or together to implement each of these choices. For example, if a firm chooses to base pay on performance, it can use many different programs to implement this decision, including cash awards, lump-sum annual bonuses, raises based on supervisory appraisals, and an employee-of-the-month award. Third, the strategic HR choices listed in Figure 1.2 represent two opposite poles on a continuum. Very few organizations fall at these extremes. Some organizations will be closer to the right, some closer to the left, and others closer to the middle.

A brief description of the strategic HR choices shown in Figure 1.2 follows. We will examine these choices and provide examples of companies' strategic decisions in these areas in later chapters.

WORK FLOWS *Work flows* are the ways tasks are organized to meet production or service goals. Organizations face several choices in what they emphasize as they structure work flows (Chapter 2). They can emphasize:

- Efficiency (getting work done at minimum cost) or innovation (encouraging creativity, exploration, and new ways of doing things, even though this may increase production costs)
- Control (establishing predetermined procedures) or flexibility (allowing room for exceptions and personal judgment)
- Explicit job descriptions (in which each job's duties and requirements are carefully spelled out) or broad job classes (in which employees perform multiple tasks and are expected to fill different jobs as needed)
- Detailed work planning (in which processes, objectives, and schedules are laid out well in advance) or loose work planning (in which activities and schedules may be modified on relatively short notice, depending on changing needs)

STAFFING Staffing encompasses the HR activities designed to secure the right employees at the right place at the right time (Chapter 5). Organizations face several strategic HR choices in recruiting, selecting, and socializing employees—all part of the staffing process. These include:

- Promoting from within (*internal* recruitment) versus hiring from the outside (*external* recruitment)
- Empowering immediate supervisors to make hiring decisions versus centralizing these decisions in the HR department
- Emphasizing a good fit between the applicant and the firm versus hiring the most knowledgeable individual regardless of interpersonal considerations
- Hiring new workers informally or choosing a more formal and systematic approach to hiring

FIGURE 1.2

Strategic HR Choices

EMPLOYEE SEPARATIONS Employee separations occur when employees leave the firm, either voluntarily or involuntarily (Chapter 6). Some strategic HR choices available to the firm for handling employee separations are:

- Use of voluntary inducements (such as early retirement packages) to downsize a workforce versus use of layoffs
- Imposing a hiring freeze to avoid laying off current employees versus recruiting employees as needed, even if doing so means laying off current employees
- Providing continuing support to terminated employees (perhaps by offering them assistance in securing another job) versus leaving laid-off employees to fend for themselves
- Making a commitment to rehire terminated employees if conditions improve versus avoiding any type of preferential hiring treatment for ex-employees

PERFORMANCE APPRAISAL Managers assess how well employees are carrying out their assigned duties by conducting performance appraisals (Chapter 7). Some strategic HR choices concerning employee appraisals are:

- Developing an appraisal system that is customized to the needs of various employee groups (for example, by designing a different appraisal form for each job family) versus using a standardized appraisal system throughout the organization
- Using the appraisal data as a developmental tool to help employees improve their performance versus using appraisals as a control mechanism to weed out low producers
- Designing the appraisal system with multiple objectives in mind (such as training, promotion, and selection decisions) versus designing it for a narrow purpose (such as pay decisions only)
- Developing an appraisal system that encourages the active participation of multiple employee groups (for example, supervisor, peers, and subordinates) versus developing one that asks solely for the input of each employee's supervisor

A QUESTION OF ETHICS

Experts in career development note that in today's increasingly chaotic business and economic environment, individual employees need to prepare themselves for job and career changes. Does an employer have an ethical duty to help employees prepare for the change that is almost certain to come?

TRAINING AND CAREER DEVELOPMENT Training and career development activities are designed to help an organization meet its skill requirements and to help its employees realize their maximum potential (Chapters 8 and 9). Some of the strategic HR choices pertaining to these activities are:

- Choosing whether to provide training to individuals or to teams of employees who may come from diverse areas of the firm
- Deciding whether to teach required skills on the job or rely on external sources for training
- Choosing whether to emphasize job-specific training or generic training
- Deciding whether to hire at a high wage people from outside the firm who already have the required talents ("buy skills") or to invest resources in training the firm's own lower-wage employees in the necessary skills ("make skills")

COMPENSATION Compensation is the payment that employees receive in exchange for their labor. U.S. organizations vary widely in how they choose to compensate their employees (Chapters 10, 11, and 12). Some of the strategic HR choices related to pay are:

- Providing employees with a fixed salary and benefits package that changes little from year to year (and, therefore, involves minimal risk) versus paying employees a variable amount subject to change
- Paying employees on the basis of the job they hold versus paying them for their individual contributions to the firm
- Rewarding employees for the time they have spent with the firm versus rewarding them for performance
- Centralizing pay decisions in a single location (such as the HR department) versus empowering the supervisor or work team to make pay decisions

EMPLOYEE AND LABOR RELATIONS Employee and labor relations (Chapters 13 and 15) refer to the interaction between workers (either as individuals or as represented by a union) and management. Some of the strategic HR choices facing the firm in these areas are:

- Relying on "top-down" communication channels from managers to subordinates versus encouraging "bottom-up" feedback from employees to managers

- Actively trying to avoid or suppress union-organizing activity versus accepting unions as representatives of employees' interests
- Adopting an adversarial approach to dealing with employees versus responding to employees' needs so that the incentive for unionization is removed (enlightened management)

EMPLOYEE RIGHTS Employee rights concern the relationship between the organization and individual employees (Chapter 14). Some of the strategic choices that the firm needs to make in this area are:

- Emphasizing discipline as the mechanism for controlling employee behavior versus proactively encouraging appropriate behavior in the first place
- Developing policies that emphasize protecting the employer's interests versus policies that emphasize protecting the employees' interests
- Relying on informal ethical standards versus developing explicit standards and procedures to enforce those standards

INTERNATIONAL MANAGEMENT Firms that operate outside domestic boundaries face a set of strategic HR options regarding how to manage human resources on a global basis (Chapter 17). Some of the key strategic HR choices involved in international management are:

- Creating a common company culture to reduce intercountry cultural differences versus allowing foreign subsidiaries to adapt to the local culture
- Sending expatriates (domestic employees) abroad to manage foreign subsidiaries versus hiring local people to manage them
- Establishing a repatriation agreement with each employee going abroad (carefully stipulating what the expatriate can expect upon return in terms of career advancement, compensation, and the like) versus avoiding any type of commitment to expatriates
- Establishing company policies that must be followed in all subsidiaries versus decentralizing policy formulation so that each local office can develop its own policies

Selecting HR Strategies to Increase Firm Performance

No HR strategy is "good" or "bad" in and of itself. Rather, an HR strategy's effect on firm performance depends on how well it fits with other factors. Most of the practitioner and scholarly literature in HR suggests that fit leads to better performance, and lack of fit creates inconsistencies that reduce performance.[166] *Fit* refers to the compatibility between HR strategies and other important aspects of the organization.

Figure 1.3 depicts the key factors that firms should consider in determining which HR strategies will have a positive impact on firm performance: organizational strategies, environment, organizational characteristics, and organizational capabilities. As the figure shows, the relative contribution of an HR strategy to firm performance increases:

- The better the match between the HR strategy and the firm's overall organizational strategies
- The more the HR strategy is attuned to the environment in which the firm is operating

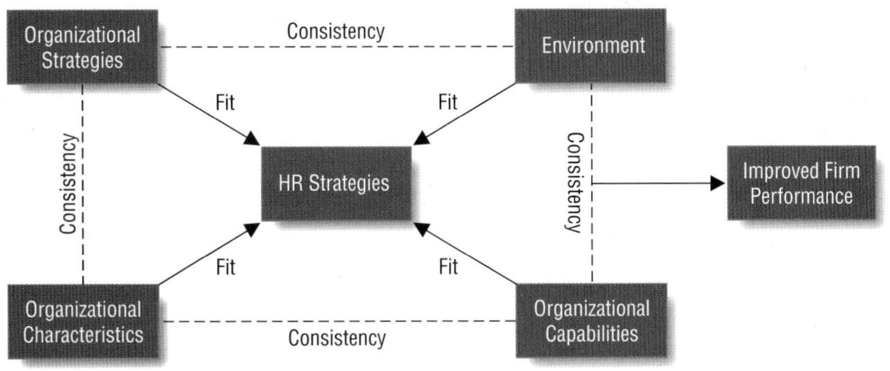

FIGURE 1.3
Effective HR Strategy Formulation and Implementation

- The more closely the HR strategy is molded to unique organizational features
- The better the HR strategy enables the firm to capitalize on its distinctive competencies
- The more the HR strategies are mutually consistent or reinforce one another

Fit with Organizational Strategies

corporate strategy
The mix of businesses a corporation decides to hold and the flow of resources among those businesses.

business unit strategy
The formulation and implementation of strategies by a firm that is relatively autonomous, even if it is part of a larger corporation.

A corporation may have multiple businesses that are very similar to or completely different from one another. **Corporate strategy** refers to the mix of businesses a corporation decides to hold and the flow of resources among those businesses. The main strategic business decisions at the corporate level concern acquisition, divestment, diversification, and growth. **Business unit strategies** refer to the formulation and implementation of strategies by firms that are relatively autonomous, even if they are part of a larger corporation. For instance, AT&T as a corporate entity once owned hundreds of largely independent firms, including perfume makers and Hostess Twinkies, each with its own business strategy.[167] Similarly, diversified giant DuPont combines businesses such as drugs, agriculture, and chemicals under one roof.[168] In firms that produce a single product or highly related products or services, the business and corporate strategies are identical. For companies that have distinct corporate and business unit strategies, it is important to examine each in terms of its fit with HR strategies.

CORPORATE STRATEGIES There are two major types of corporate strategies and matching HR strategies. Corporations adopting an *evolutionary business strategy* engage in aggressive acquisitions of new businesses, even if these are totally unrelated to one another.[169]

In evolutionary firms, the management of change is crucial to survival. Entrepreneurship is encouraged and control is deemphasized because each unit is relatively autonomous. HR strategies that foster flexibility, quick response, entrepreneurship, risk sharing, and decentralization are particularly appropriate. Because the evolutionary corporation is not committed to a particular business or industry, it may hire workers from the external market as needed and lay them off to reduce costs if necessary, with no promise of rehiring them. These HR strategies are appropriate because they "fit" with the organizational reality that change is the only constant.

A QUESTION OF ETHICS
The dark side of strategic planning is that workers are sometimes thought of as numbers on a page or dollars in a budget rather than as flesh-and-blood human beings. When divisions are spun off or merged, individual employees are dramatically affected. What responsibility does the employer have toward its employees in situations like these?

At the other end of the spectrum, corporations adopting a *steady-state strategy* are very choosy about how they grow. They avoid acquiring firms outside their industry or even companies within the industry that are very different from them. Top managers exercise a great deal of direct control over the company, and internal development of new products and technologies and interunit coordination are very important.[170] This is the case at Rubbermaid, a company known for producing such mundane products as trash cans and dustpans. Yet Rubbermaid's record for innovation is anything but mundane. The company brings out new products at the rate of one a day.[171] The HR strategies most appropriate to steady-state firms emphasize efficiency, detailed work planning, internal grooming of employees for promotion and long-term career development, centralization, and a paternalistic attitude.

PORTER'S BUSINESS UNIT STRATEGIES Two well-known business unit strategies were formulated by Porter[172] and Miles and Snow[173] to analyze which HR strategies represent the best fit with a firm's business strategy.

Porter has identified three types of business unit strategies that help a firm cope with competitive forces and outperform other firms in the industry. For each of these strategies, a certain set of HR strategies would fit best.[174]

The *overall cost leadership strategy* is aimed at gaining a competitive advantage through lower costs. Cost leadership requires aggressive construction of efficient plant facilities (which requires sustained capital investment), intense supervision of labor, vigorous pursuit of cost reductions, and tight control of distribution costs and overhead. Firms that have successfully pursued a low-cost leadership strategy include Briggs & Stratton, Emerson Electric, Texas Instruments, Black & Decker, and DuPont.[175]

Low-cost firms tend to emphasize structured tasks and responsibilities, products designed for easy manufacture, and the need to predict costs with minimal margin of error. The HR strategies that fit a low-cost orientation emphasize efficient, low-cost production; reinforce adherence to rational, highly structured procedures to minimize uncertainty; and discourage creativity and innovation (which may lead to costly experimentation and mistakes).

A firm with a *differentiation business strategy* attempts to achieve a competitive advantage by creating a product or service that is perceived as being unique. Some common characteristics of such firms are strong marketing abilities, an emphasis on product engineering and basic research, a corporate reputation for quality products, and amenities that are attractive to highly skilled labor. Approaches to differentiating can take many forms, including design or brand image (Fieldcrest in top-of-the-line towels and linens, Mercedes-Benz in automobiles), technology (Hyster in lift trucks, Coleman in camping equipment), features (Jenn-Air in electric ranges), customer service (IBM in computers), and dealer networks (Caterpillar Tractor in construction equipment).

Differentiation provides a competitive advantage because of the brand loyalty it fosters. This enables the differentiator to enjoy higher profit margins, which, in turn, allow it to invest in extensive research, experiment with new ideas and product designs, cater to the needs of different customers, and support creative initiatives by managers and employees.

HR strategies that fit a differentiation strategy emphasize innovation, flexibility, renewal of the workforce by attracting new talent from other firms, opportunities for mavericks, and reinforcement (rather than discouragement) of creative flair.

The *focus strategy* relies on both a low-cost position and differentiation, with the objective of serving a narrow target market better than other firms. The firm seeks to achieve differentiation either from better meeting the needs of the particular target, or from lowering costs in serving this target, or both.[176] Firms that have used this strategy successfully include Illinois Tool Works (in the specialty market for fasteners), Gymboree (a national franchise providing creative activities and accessories for children under the age of 5), Fort Howard Paper (manufacturer of specialized industrial grade papers), and Porter Paint (producer of paints for professional housepainters).

The HR strategies likely to fit the focus strategy best would be somewhere in the middle of those described for low-cost producers and differentiators. At Illinois Tool Works (ITW), for instance, the chairman stresses working hand-in-hand with customers both to find out what they want and to learn how ITW can help them lower their operating costs. HR strategies reflect this focus by boosting efficiency to hold costs down. ITW's business is decentralized into 200 fairly small operating units, headed by managers whose pay is largely tied to sales and profits at their individual operations. The company's workers are nonunion, which helps to hold costs down. To keep ITW's products geared to customer needs, management puts heavy emphasis on R&D. ITW's R&D spending of almost $40 million a year keeps creativity high; ITW holds over 4,000 active patents.[177]

MILES AND SNOW'S BUSINESS STRATEGIES Miles and Snow created another well-known classification of business unit strategies.[178] They characterize successful businesses as adopting either a defender or a prospector strategy.

Defenders are conservative business units that prefer to maintain a secure position in relatively stable product or service areas instead of looking to expand into uncharted territory. Defenders tend to be highly formalized, emphasize cost control, and operate in a stable environment. Many defenders develop an elaborate internal system for promoting, transferring, and rewarding workers that is relatively isolated from the uncertainties of the external labor market. In exchange for a long-term commitment to the firm, employees are rewarded with job security and the expectation of upward mobility through the ranks.

A proposed set of HR strategies that best fit defenders' needs, categorized according to the six major strategic HR choices we saw in Figure 1.2 earlier, are summarized in Figure 1.4. These strategies include work flows emphasizing managerial control and reliability, staffing and employee separation policies designed to foster long-term employee attachment to the firm, performance appraisals focused on managerial control and hierarchy, structured training programs, and compensation policies that emphasize job security.

Unlike defenders, whose success comes primarily from efficiently serving a stable market, *prospectors* emphasize growth and innovation, development of new products, and an eagerness to be the first in new-product or market areas, even if some of these efforts fail.[179] The prospector's strategy is associated with flexible and decentralized organizational structures, complex products (such as computers and pharmaceuticals), and unstable environments that change rapidly.

The HR strategies that match the strategic orientation of prospectors, also summarized in Figure 1.4, include work flows that foster creativity and adaptability; staffing and employee separation policies that focus on the external labor market; customized, participative employee appraisals used for multiple purposes (including employee development); training strategies targeting broad skills; and a decentralized compensation system that rewards risk taking and performance.

Strategic HR Area	Defender Strategy	Prospector Strategy
Work Flows	• Efficient production • Control emphasis • Explicit job descriptions • Detailed work planning	• Innovation • Flexibility • Broad job classes • Loose work planning
Staffing	• Internal recruitment • HR department makes selection decision • Emphasis on technical qualifications and skills • Formal hiring and socialization process	• External recruitment • Coworkers help make selection decision • Emphasis on fit of applicant with culture • Informal hiring and socialization process of new employees
Employee Separations	• Voluntary inducements to leave • Hiring freeze • Continuing concern for terminated employee • Preferential rehiring policy	• Layoffs • Recruit as needed • Individual on his or her own • No preferential treatment for laid-off workers
Performance Appraisal	• Uniform appraisal procedures • Used as control device • Narrow focus • High dependence on superior	• Customized appraisals • Used as developmental tool • Multipurpose appraisals • Multiple inputs for appraisals
Training	• Individual training • On-the-job training • Job-specific training • "Make" skills	• Team-based or cross-functional training • External training • Generic training emphasizing flexibility • "Buy" skills
Compensation	• Fixed pay • Job-based pay • Seniority-based pay • Centralized pay decisions	• Variable pay • Individual-based pay • Performance-based pay • Decentralized pay decisions

FIGURE 1.4

Selected HR Strategies That Fit Miles and Snow's Two Major Types of Business Strategies

Source: Gómez-Mejía, L. R. (2009). Compensation strategies and Miles and Snow's business strategy taxonomy. Unpublished report. Management Department, Arizona State University. Reprinted with permission.

Fit with the Environment

In addition to reinforcing overall organizational strategies, HR strategies should help the organization better exploit environmental opportunities or cope with the unique environmental forces that affect it. We can examine the environment in terms of four major dimensions: (1) *degree of uncertainty* (how much accurate information is available to make appropriate business decisions), (2) *volatility* (how often the environment changes), (3) *magnitude of change* (how drastic the changes are), and (4) *complexity* (how many different elements in the environment affect the firm, either individually or together). For example, much of the computer and high-tech industry is very high on all four of these dimensions:

- ***Degree of uncertainty*** Compaq thought consumers would continue to pay a premium price for its high-performance computers. The company was proved wrong in the 1990s as low-cost competitors such as Dell, Packard Bell, and AST quickly cut into Compaq's market. More recently thin Macs have taken over much of the PC market, BlackBerries have been largely replaced by iPhones, and Nokia has seen much of its market taken over by Apple.
- ***Volatility*** IBM paid dearly when demand for its mainframe computers declined drastically in the late 1980s and it was caught unprepared.
- ***Magnitude of change*** The advent of each successive new generation of computer microprocessor chips (for example, Intel's 386, 486, Pentium) has almost immediately rendered all previously sold machines obsolete. Polaroid was forced to declare bankruptcy as quick adoption of digital cameras turned its main product (instant photography) obsolete almost overnight.

Environmental Dimension	Low	High
Degree of Uncertainty	• Detailed work planning • Job-specific training • Fixed pay • High dependence on superior	• Loose work planning • Generic training • Variable pay • Multiple inputs for appraisals
Volatility	• Control emphasis • Efficient production • Job-specific training • Fixed pay	• Flexibility • Innovation • Generic training • Variable pay
Magnitude of Change	• Explicit job descriptions • Formal hiring and socialization of new employees • "Make" skills • Uniform appraisal procedures	• Broad job classes • Informal hiring and socialization of new employees • "Buy" skills • Customized appraisals
Complexity	• Control emphasis • Internal recruitment • Centralized pay decisions • High dependence on superior	• Flexibility • External recruitment • Decentralized pay decisions • Multiple inputs for appraisals

FIGURE 1.5

Selected HR Strategies for Firms Low and High on Different Environmental Characteristics

Source: Based on Gomez-Mejia, L. R., and Balkin, D. B. (2012). Management. Englewood Cliffs, NJ: Prentice-Hall; Gomez-Mejia, L. R., Berrone, P., and Franco-Santos, M. (2010). Compensation and organizational Performance. New York, NY: M.E. Sharpe.

- *Complexity* The number and variety of competitors in the computer industry, both domestically and overseas, have grown dramatically in recent years. The life of a product seldom extends more than three years now, as new innovations drive previous equipment and software out of the market.

As Figure 1.5 shows, firms that are high on these four dimensions are more likely to benefit from HR strategies that promote flexibility, adaptivity, quick response, transferability of skills, the ability to secure external talent as needed, and risk sharing with employees through variable pay.

Conversely, firms facing environments that are low on uncertainty, volatility, magnitude of change, and complexity benefit from HR strategies that allow for an orderly, rational, and routine approach to dealing with a relatively predictable and stable environment. The "old" AT&T (before divestment), much of the airline and trucking industry before deregulation, utilities, and government bureaucracies fall at the low end of the scale on these four dimensions. Figure 1.5 shows that the HR strategies that fit firms operating under these conditions tend to be rather mechanistic: detailed work planning, job-specific training, fixed pay, explicit job descriptions, centralized pay decisions, and the like.

Fit with Organizational Characteristics

To be effective, HR strategies must be tailored to the organization's personality. The features of an organization's personality can be broken down into five major categories.

THE PRODUCTION PROCESS FOR CONVERTING INPUTS INTO OUTPUT Firms with a relatively routine production process (such as large-volume steel mills, lumber mills, and automobile plants) tend to benefit from HR strategies that emphasize control, such as explicit job descriptions and job-specific training. The opposite is true for firms with nonroutine production processes (such as advertising firms, custom printers, and biotechnology companies). These firms benefit from flexible HR strategies that support organizational adaptability, quick response to change, and creative decision making. These flexible strategies may include broad job classes, loose work planning, and generic training.

THE FIRM'S MARKET POSTURE Firms that experience a high rate of sales growth and engage in product innovation destined for a wide market segment tend to benefit from HR strategies that support growth and entrepreneurial activities. These HR strategies include external recruitment ("buying" skills), decentralized pay decisions, and customized appraisals. The opposite is true for firms with low rates of growth and limited product innovation destined for a narrow market segment. These firms tend to benefit more from HR strategies that emphasize efficiency, control, and firm-specific knowledge. Such strategies include internal recruitment ("making" skills), on-the-job training, and high dependence on superiors.

THE FIRM'S OVERALL MANAGERIAL PHILOSOPHY Companies whose top executives are averse to risk, operate with an autocratic leadership style, establish a strong internal pecking order, and are inwardly rather than outwardly focused may find that certain HR practices match this outlook best. The HR strategies most often used in these kinds of firms include seniority-based pay, formal hiring and socializing of new employees, selection decisions made by the HR department, and use of top-down communication channels. The HR strategies that fit a managerial philosophy high on risk taking, participation, egalitarianism, and an external, proactive environmental orientation include variable pay, giving supervisors a major role in hiring decisions, up-and-down communication channels, and multiple inputs for performance appraisals.

THE FIRM'S ORGANIZATIONAL STRUCTURE Some HR strategies fit very well with highly formalized organizations that are divided into functional areas (for example, marketing, finance, production, and so on) and that concentrate decision making at the top. The HR strategies appropriate for this type of firm include a control emphasis, centralized pay decisions, explicit job descriptions, and job-based pay. Firms whose organizational structures are less regimented will benefit from a different set of HR strategies, including informal hiring and socializing of new employees, decentralized pay decisions, broad job classes, and individual-based pay.

THE FIRM'S ORGANIZATIONAL CULTURE Companies that foster an *entrepreneurial climate* benefit from supporting HR strategies such as loose work planning, informal hiring and socializing of new employees, and variable pay. Firms that discourage entrepreneurship generally prefer a control emphasis, detailed work planning, formal hiring and socializing of new employees, and fixed pay.

A strong emphasis on *moral commitment*—the extent to which a firm tries to foster a long-term emotional attachment between the firm and its employees—is also associated with certain supporting HR strategies. These include an emphasis on preventive versus remedial disciplinary action to handle employee mistakes, employee protection, and explicit ethical codes to monitor and guide behavior. Firms that are low on moral commitment usually rely on an authoritarian relationship between employee and company. HR strategies consistent with this orientation include an emphasis on discipline or punishment to reduce employee mistakes, employment at will (discussed in Chapters 3 and 14), and informal ethical standards.

Fit with Organizational Capabilities

distinctive competencies
The characteristics that give a firm a competitive edge.

A firm's organizational capabilities include its **distinctive competencies**, those characteristics (such as technical ability, management systems, and reputation) that give the firm a competitive edge. For instance, Mercedes-Benz automobiles are widely regarded as superior because of the quality of their design and engineering. Walmart's phenomenal success has been due, at least in part, to its ability to track products from supplier to customer better than its competitors can.

HR strategies make a greater contribution to firm performance the greater the extent to which (1) they help the company exploit its specific advantages or strengths while avoiding weaknesses and (2) they assist the firm in better utilizing its own unique blend of human resource skills and assets.

The following examples illustrate how one type of HR strategy—compensation strategy—may be aligned with organizational capabilities.[180]

- Firms known for excellence in customer service tend to pay their sales force only partially on commission, thereby reducing their sales employees' potential for abrasive behaviors and overselling.
- Smaller firms can use compensation to their advantage by paying low wages but being generous in offering stock to employees. This strategy allows them to use more of their scarce cash to fuel future growth.
- Organizations may take advantage of their unused capacity in their compensation strategies. For example, most private universities offer free tuition to faculty and their immediate family. With average tuition at private colleges exceeding $30,000 a year in 2014, this benefit represents a huge cash savings to faculty members, thereby allowing private universities to attract and retain good faculty with minimal adverse impact on their cost structure.

Choosing Consistent and Appropriate HR Tactics to Implement HR Strategies

Even the best-laid strategic HR plans may fail when specific HR programs are poorly chosen or implemented.[181] In addition to fitting with each of the four factors just described (organizational strategy, environment, organizational characteristics, and organizational capabilities), a firm's HR strategies are more likely to be effective if they reinforce one another rather than work at cross-purposes. For instance, many organizations are currently trying to improve their performance by structuring work in teams. However, these same organizations often continue to use a traditional performance appraisal system in which each employee is evaluated individually. The appraisal system needs to be overhauled to make it consistent with the emphasis on team performance.

Because it is not always possible to know beforehand whether an HR program will meet its objectives, a periodic evaluation of HR programs is necessary. Figure 1.6 lists a series of important questions that should be raised to examine the appropriateness of HR programs. These questions should be answered as new programs are being chosen and while they are in effect.

HR Best Practices

Several authors have argued that certain HR practices are associated with sustained high firm performance.[182] Figure 1.7 shows the most common HR best practices. Debate continues among academics about whether high firm performance leads to given HR practices, or vice versa (that is, whether introducing particular HR practices causes better firm performance).[183] For instance, can firms that are doing well afford to provide higher wages and more job security, or do firms that pay more and have a more stable workforce derive a performance premium by following these practices? It is extraordinarily difficult to prove the casual relationship one way or the other, yet it seems reasonable that organizations should consider implementation of those practices associated with the highest-performing firms.

HR programs that look good on paper may turn out to be disasters when implemented because they conflict too much with company realities. To avoid this kind of unpleasant surprise, it is important to ask the following questions *before* implementing a new HR program.

1. Are the HR Programs Effective Tools for Implementing HR Strategies?
   - Are the proposed HR programs the most appropriate ones for implementing the firm's HR strategies?
   - Has an analysis been done of how each of the past, current, or planned HR programs contributes to or hinders the successful implementation of the firm's HR strategies?
   - Can the proposed HR programs be easily changed or modified to meet new strategic considerations without violating either a "psychological" or a legal contract with employees?
2. Do the HR Programs Meet Resource Constraints?
   - Does the organization have the capacity to implement the proposed HR programs? In other words, are the HR programs realistic?
   - Are the proposed programs going to be introduced at a rate that can be easily absorbed, or will the timing and extent of changes lead to widespread confusion and strong employee resistance?
3. How Will the HR Programs Be Communicated?
   - Are the proposed HR programs well understood by those who will implement them (for example, line supervisors and employees)?
   - Does top management understand how the proposed programs are intended to affect the firm's strategic objectives?
4. Who Will Put the HR Programs in Motion?
   - Is the HR department playing the role of an internal consultant to assist employees and managers responsible for carrying out the proposed HR programs?
   - Is top management visibly and emphatically committed to the proposed programs?

FIGURE 1.6

But Will It Work? Questions for Testing the Appropriateness of HR Programs Before Implementation

- Offer high employment security because this indicates that the firm is committed to the employee's welfare
- Develop a good selection program that can screen the best applicants
- Offer wages that are highly competitive as this helps reduce employee turnover and helps in the attraction of high-quality employees
- Recognize employees by providing monetary and non-monetary rewards
- Make employees part-owners of the firm by providing them with stock in the firm
- Communicate effectively with employees so that they are kept informed of major issues confronting the organization and any major initiatives
- Encourage employee involvement so that there is strong "buy-in" of human resource practices and important managerial initiatives
- Encourage teamwork so that employees are more willing to collaborate with each other
- Invest in training programs to improve employee skills
- Provide opportunities for learning at work so that employees are "stretched" in the use of their skills
- Give a higher priority to internal candidates for promotion because this enhances employee motivation by providing future career opportunities

FIGURE 1.7
Select HR Best Practices

Sources: Based on www.best-in-classroom.com. (2014). Human resources best practices; www.hrdailyadvisor.blr.com. (2014). Top 10 best practices in HR management; Pfeffer, J. (1995). Producing sustainable competitive advantage through the effective management of people. *Academy of Management Executive,* 10, 55–72; Wright, P. M., Gardner, T. M., Moynihan, L. M., and Allen, M. R. (2005). The relationship between HR practices and firm performance: Examining causal order. *Personnel Psychology, 68*, 409–446; Chuang, C. H., and Liao, H. (2010). Strategic human resource management in service context. *Personnel Psychology, 63*(1), 153–196; Gomez-Mejia, L. R., and Balkin, D. B. (2011). *Management: People, performance and change,* Prentice-Hall.

The HR Department and Managers: An Important Partnership

This book takes a managerial approach to human resources and HR strategy. All managers—regardless of their functional area, their position in the hierarchy, and the size of the firm for which they work—must deal effectively with HR issues because these issues are at the heart of being a good manager. Furthermore, there has been a clear trend in the last decade or so of reducing the size of the Human Resource Department and instead delegating many of the traditional HR duties (such as talent search, selection, and training) to line managers. Part of this trend may be explained by an attempt to reduce "overhead" but perhaps more importantly by a belief that line managers should be empowered and take ownership over major HR decisions in their units.

The role of a company's human resources department is to support, not to supplant, managers' HR responsibilities. For instance, the HR department may develop a form to help managers measure the performance of subordinates, but it is the managers who conduct the actual evaluation. Stated another way, the HR department is primarily responsible for helping the firm meet its business objectives by designing HR programs, but managers must carry out these programs. This means that every manager is a human resource manager.

Companies can take certain steps to foster an effective partnership between managers and the HR department.[184] Specifically, companies should:

- Analyze the people side of productivity rather than depend solely on technical solutions to problems. This requires that managers be trained in certain HR skills and that they value human resources as a key element in organizational performance.
- View HR professionals as internal consultants who can provide valuable advice and support that improve the management of operations.
- Instill a shared sense of common fate in the firm rather than a win/lose perspective among individual departments and units.
- Require some managerial experience as part of the training of HR professionals. This requirement should make HR staff more sensitive to and cognizant of the problems managers face.
- Actively involve top corporate and divisional managers in formulating, implementing, and reviewing all HR plans and strategies in close collaboration with the HR department.

- Require senior HR executives to participate on an equal basis with other key managers from the various functional areas (marketing, finance) in charting the enterprise's strategic direction.

Companies should also periodically conduct an **HR audit** to evaluate how effectively they are using their human resources. The audit, which is typically conducted by the HR department, deals with a broad set of questions, including:

HR audit
A periodic review of the effectiveness with which a company uses its human resources. Frequently includes an evaluation of the HR department itself.

- Is the turnover rate exceptionally low or high?
- Are the people who quit good employees who are frustrated in their present job, or are they marginal performers?
- Is the firm receiving a high return on the money it spends on recruitment, training, and pay-for-performance plans?
- Is the firm complying with government regulations?
- How well is the company managing employee diversity?
- Is the HR department providing the services that line managers need?
- Are HRM policies and procedures helping the firm accomplish its long-term goals?

The HR audit addresses these and other important issues systematically so that effective programs can be maintained and ineffective programs corrected or eliminated.

Specialization in Human Resource Management

While the size of the typical HR department has been shrinking in recent years, the use of external HR consultants has increased considerably. This probably reflects both the growth and complexity of government regulations and a greater awareness that HR issues are important to the achievement of business objectives. It probably reflects as well the need, as noted earlier, to have line managers take ownership of major HR decisions with the assistance of HR advisers (who are often external consultants that might be engaged in program design for personnel selection, incentive systems, training, and the like).

Many colleges and universities now offer specialized degrees in human resources at the associate's, bachelor's, master's, and doctoral levels. The Society for Human Resource Management (SHRM), which at the time of this writing represents 260,000 individual members in over 125 countries, has set up a certification institute to offer HR professionals the opportunity to be certified officially at the PHR (Professional Human Resources) or SPHR (Senior Professional Human Resources) level. SHRM certification requires a certain amount of experience and mastery of a body of knowledge as indicated by successful completion of a comprehensive examination. (For additional information and application materials, write to the Society at 1800 Duke Street, Alexandria, VA 22314 or visit the Web site at *shrm.org*.) Other organizations whose members specialize in a particular area of HRM are WorldatWork (previously the American Compensation Association), the Human Resource Planning Society, and the American Society for Training and Development.[185]

In recent years, the compensation of HR specialists has increased faster than other jobs, and for some HR jobs pay is sharply on the rise, reflecting greater professionalization and increasing awareness by business that a well-managed HR function may help the firm achieve a sustainable competitive advantage. In 2014, experienced HR directors earned approximately $101,000 a year on average; those with the title of vice president for human resources earned approximately $225,000 a year on average, with bonuses as high as $140,000 per year. These are only averages, however. Those at the 90th percentile earn approximately $340,000 per year in base pay. In some of the largest firms, the top job in this field paid more than $900,000. Among the specialized subfields (such as executive trainers, corporate compensation directors, benefit directors, and corporate security managers) average salaries exceeded $135,000.[186]

Summary and Conclusions

Human Resource Management: The Challenges

The major HR challenges facing managers today can be divided into three categories: environmental challenges, organizational challenges, and individual challenges.

The environmental challenges are rapid change, the rise of the Internet, workforce diversity, economic globalization, legislation, evolving work and family roles, skill shortages and the rise of the service sector, and catastrophic events as a result of natural disasters and terrorism.

The organizational challenges are choosing a competitive position, decentralization, downsizing, organizational restructuring, the rise of self-managed work teams, the increased number of small businesses, organizational culture, advances in technology, and the rise of outsourcing.

The individual challenges involve matching people with the organization, treating employees ethically and engaging in socially responsible behavior, increasing individual productivity, deciding whether to empower employees, taking steps to avoid brain drain, and dealing with issues of job insecurity.

Planning and Implementing Strategic HR Policies

When done correctly, strategic HR planning provides many direct and indirect benefits for a company. These include the encouragement of proactive (rather than reactive) behavior, explicit communication of company goals, stimulation of critical thinking and ongoing examination of assumptions, identification of gaps between the company's current situation and its future vision, the encouragement of line managers' participation in the strategic planning process, the identification of HR constraints and opportunities, and the creation of common bonds within the organization.

In developing an effective HR strategy, an organization faces several challenges. These include putting in place a strategy that creates and maintains a competitive advantage for the company and reinforces the overall business strategy, avoiding excessive concentration on day-to-day problems, developing strategies suited to unique organizational features, coping with the environment in which the business operates, securing management commitment, translating the strategic plan into action, combining intended and emergent strategies, and accommodating change.

A firm's strategic HR choices are the options available to it in designing its human resources systems. Firms must make strategic choices in many HR areas, including work flows, staffing, employee separations, performance appraisal, training and career development, compensation, employee rights, employee and labor relations, and international management.

Selecting HR Strategies to Increase Firm Performance

To be effective, HR strategies must fit with overall organizational strategies, the environment in which the firm is operating, unique organizational characteristics, and organizational capabilities. HR strategies should also be mutually consistent and reinforce one another.

The HR Department and Managers: An Important Partnership

Responsibility for the effective use of human resources lies primarily with managers. Hence, all managers are personnel managers. The role of HR professionals is to act as internal consultants or experts, assisting managers to do their jobs better.

Over the past three decades, the number of HR professionals has increased considerably (even though, ironically, HR departments have decreased in size because companies are subcontracting many HR activities to external consultants). This increase reflects both the growth and complexity of government regulations and a greater awareness that HR issues are important to the achievement of business objectives.

Key Terms

ability, 47
brain drain, 48
business unit strategy, 56
corporate strategy, 56
decentralization, 39
distinctive competencies, 60
downsizing, 39
empowerment, 47
environmental challenges, 31
HR audit, 63
human resources (HR), 30
human resource strategy, 30
human resource tactic, 30
individual challenges, 45
line employee, 30
manager, 30
motivation, 47
organizational challenges, 38
organizational culture, 41
outsourcing, 44
productivity, 47
quality of work life, 47
staff employee, 30
strategic HR choices, 52
strategic human resource (HR) planning, 49
total quality management (TQM), 39

Watch It!

Patagonia: Human Resource Management. If your instructor has assigned this, go to **mymanagementlab.com** to watch a video case and answer questions.

Discussion Questions

1-1. Go back to the Manager's Notebook, "A Cold Way to Get a Job." What do you see as the main advantages and disadvantages of Internet-based recruiting? Explain.

1-2. Roughly two generations ago, many HR articles decried problems with performance appraisal. A common complaint was that managers did not devote sufficient time to conducting the appraisals and that biases were rampant. Another common complaint was that most managers gave high ratings to all employees and did not bother to properly differentiate and carefully document the performance evaluation of subordinates. Several old surveys reported that three-quarters or more of employees "hated performance appraisals and found them to be useless, *increasing tension at work*."[187] Today, performance appraisals are standard practice in American businesses and presumably these are used to make key HR decisions, such as distributing merit pay and incentives, screening people for promotions, providing feedback, choosing candidates for layoffs, ensuring equal pay for equal work, and so on (Chapter 7 of this book is devoted to these issues). Many organizations have spent a lot of money in designing and redesigning appraisal systems, and a specialized cadre of HR consultants, industrial psychologists, and other academics have focused most of their efforts and/or research on improving appraisal systems (such as reducing interpersonal biases in the evaluations). Surprisingly, a recent large-scale survey of 750 HR professionals conducted by New York–based consulting firm Sibson Consulting Inc. and WorldatWork, a professional association, found that, if anything, dissatisfaction with performance appraisal systems had gotten worst over the years. Only 3 percent of human resource executives graded their own performance appraisal system as "A," and the majority rated it as "C" or below. In what seems like déjà vu, this new generation of HR executives say they are frustrated that managers don't have the courage to make truthful appraisal decisions and to give constructive feedback to employees.[188] How would you explain this? Do you see this situation as a lack of progress or as an indication that some faulty assumptions continue to be made by the HR professionals who design these programs? Based on what you have learned in this chapter, what implications does this have for HR practices that presumably rely on an accurate assessment of employee performance (such as promotions and merit pay decisions)?[189]

1-3. Go back to Managers' Notebook "How Harley-Davidson Is Taking Advantage of a Diverse Customer Base." If you were an HR manager of a company such as Harley-Davidson, what human resource programs would you put in place to help the company expand its customer base? Explain.

1-4. The Internet is having a pervasive impact on how organizations manage their human resources. How has the Internet impacted HR management? What would you consider the most significant impact? Justify your answer.

1-5. A lot of the growth in the HR practices over the past four decades can be attributed to its crucial role in keeping a company out of trouble with the law. Why has this become such a difficult task?

1-6. Go back to the Managers' Notebook, "Watching Over Your Shoulders: Paying a Price for Unhealthy Life Styles." Do you think it is fair for a company to discipline employees by charging higher fees for those who show evidence of "unhealthy life styles"? According to Dr. Kevin Volpp, Director of the Center for Health Incentives and Behavioral Economics at the University of Pennsylvania, punitive surcharges and tough health targets may hurt those who need assistance the most. Do you agree? Explain.

1-7. 3M's competitive business strategy is based on innovation. 3M requires that at least 25 percent of its annual sales come from products introduced over the previous five years, a goal it often exceeds. Specific HR programs adopted to implement this strategy include the creation of a special fund that allows employees to start new projects or follow up on ideas. 3M's "release time" program, in which workers are given time off during the day to pursue their own interests, is given credit for the creation of new products that management would not have thought of by itself. In addition, 3M's appraisal process encourages risk taking. A senior manager at 3M says, "If you are threatened with dismissal after working on a project that fails, you will never try again." What other types of HR policies might 3M institute to spur product innovation?

1-8. Many believe that top managers care little about human resources compared to such areas as marketing, finance, production, and engineering. What might account for this perception, and what would you do to change it?

MyManagementLab®

If your instructor has assigned this, go to **mymanagementlab.com** for the following Assisted-graded writing questions:

1-9. Outline a set of issues that are most likely to pose a major challenge to the management of human resources during the next few decades. Based on the materials learned in this chapter, explain why you have chosen each of these issues.

1-10. A major complaint one often hears is that the human resource function still remains as one of the weakest and less prestigious functions in many organizations, with the stereotype that it is a "paper shuffling" unit with little impact on the bottom line. Why do you think this is the case? What can the HR manager do to change this real or perceived state of affairs? Explain.

1-11. Some scholars believe that there is a set of "best" human resource practices that advanced companies should follow (see Figure 1.7) while others believe that there is "no one best way" when it comes to HR practices and that these should be adapted depending on organizational strategies, organizational characteristics, environment and organizational capabilities (see Figure 1.3). Are these perspectives contradictory? Which of the two perspectives make the most sense to you? Explain.

You Manage It! 1: Emerging Trends

Electronic Monitoring to Make Sure That No One Steps Out of Line

More and more organizations rely on sophisticated yet inexpensive technologies to keep track of what employees do. A few examples follow:

Use of "Magic Glasses" by Police Officers

Many police departments now use miniaturized video cameras and microphones to record all interactions between police and civilians. The cameras are generally unnoticeable to the untrained eye and are placed on a pair of glasses or on a police cap. A central server automatically uploads all videos, which become part of a reservoir of digital evidence. This allows the department to keep track of any police misconduct and also to avoid any bogus complaints.

Motorola Arm-Mounted Terminals

Motorola is marketing an arm band that allows a company to keep track of how quickly an employee performs his or her job. It looks like something between a Game Boy and a Garmin GPS device. For example, Tesco, a British grocery store chain, uses the arm bands to see how fast employees unload and set goods in a warehouse, assigning a grade to each. It can even maintain a record of when and how often employees take a bathroom break. Employees who do not meet specific productivity score targets (those with a grade of "C" or below) may be terminated. According to Tesco, this has allowed the company to operate stores with 20 percent fewer employees.

Intel Tracking System of Objectives and Key Results

Intel has developed a device to continuously monitor employee productivity. For instance, Zynga (a rapidly growing Internet-startup provider of video games) uses the system to relentlessly aggregate performance data, ranging from the cafeteria staff to the top management team. CEO Mark Pincus purportedly devours all the reports, using multiple spreadsheets and many performance indicators to carefully keep track of the progress of Zynga's roughly 3,000 employees.

Computer Programs at Ann Taylor Stores Corp.

Retailers have a new tool to turn up the heat on their salespeople: computer programs that dictate which employees should work, when, and for how long. Ann Taylor Stores Corp. has installed such a system. When saleswoman Nyla Houser types her code number into a cash register at the store, it displays her "performance metrics": average sales per hour, units sold, and dollars per transaction. The system schedules the most productive sellers to work the busiest hours.

By Building Mathematical Models of Its Own Employees, IBM Aims to Improve Productivity and Automate Management

Samer Takriti, a Syrian-born mathematician, heads up a team that is piecing together mathematical models of 50,000 of IBM's tech consultants. The idea is to inventory all of their skills and then calculate, mathematically, how best to deploy them. Takriti and his colleagues seek to turn IBM's workers into numbers that track what they do.

To put together this system, Takriti requires mountains of facts about each employee. While this sounds Orwellian, he has unleashed some 40 PhDs, from data miners and statisticians to anthropologists, to comb through workers' data. Sifting through resumes and project records, the team can assemble a profile of each worker's skills and experience. Online calendars show how employees use their time and with whom they meet. By tracking the use of cell phones and handheld computers, Takriti's researchers may be able to map workers' movements. Call records and e-mails define the social networks of each consultant. Whom do they copy on their e-mails? Do they send blind copies to certain people?

Creating a Numerical Profile for Recruitment

Amanda Treeline is a manager at an executive recruitment firm that specializes in sales talent, and she gets hundreds of resumes a week. The firm has developed a numerical profile to screen candidates. She claims that their system allows them to screen large databases to identify a small set of candidates on specific criteria that hiring managers are interested in. On average, they are able to decrease the number of candidates from over 1,000 potential hires to just 20 qualified candidates, and then the line managers are sent a detailed profile of each of these candidates including sales stats, resume, LinkedIn profile, picture, and video resume.

Critical Thinking Questions

1-12. Do you think it is feasible to boil down human behavior to a set of numbers? What are the potential advantages and disadvantages of doing so? Explain.

1-13. What do you think are the main reasons for the trend toward "managing by the numbers," as discussed in the case? Do you believe that this is happening in many organizations, or is it an isolated phenomenon? Will this trend grow in the future, or is it another passing fad? Explain.

1-14. Is it possible to use quantitative assessments of the organization's human resources to better link human resource management to firm strategy? Explain.

Team Exercise

1-15. The class is divided into groups of five. Each team is to provide a list of suggestions as to how an organization can implement a numerical human resource system, as discussed in the case. The team should discuss whether such a system could be used to achieve a better fit between HR practices and organizational strategies, the environment, organizational characteristics, and organizational capabilities. Lastly, the team should discuss the extent to which such a numerical system would clash with the "HR best practices" summarized in Figure 1.7. Depending on class size and available class time, each team will be asked to present the results of its deliberation, to be followed by open class discussion moderated by the instructor.

Experiential Exercise: Team

1-16. The class is divided into groups of five. Each team is to choose an organization (which could be a workplace for one or more team members; a hypothetical firm in an industry that is well-known to most people, such as a restaurant; a firm where relatives are employed; and the like). Each team is to provide a list of suggestions as to how the organization can implement a system to "quantify what employees do." Then the team should discuss how this information could be used to improve efficiency. The team may also discuss potential problems that could arise in gathering that information and using it in practice. The instructor may ask each team to make a formal presentation in class, to be followed by open class discussion moderated by the instructor.

Experiential Exercise: Individual

1-17. Each student will interview a manager or an employee (who might be a family member, a friend, or an acquaintance) to determine the extent to which the issues raised in the case are represented in his or her organization and what steps, if any, the firm has taken to make employees more productive. The advantages and disadvantages of such a plan may also be discussed. (Alternatively, if the student has substantial work experience he or she may offer his or her own views based on personal observation.) The instructor will moderate open class discussion based on the findings brought to the class by students.

Sources: Based on Stross, R. (2013). Wearing a badge and a video camera. *www.nytimes.com*; Sudath, C. (2013). Tesco monitors employees with Motorola armbands. *www.businessweek.com*; Rushi, E. M. (2013). Zynga's tough culture risks a brain drain. *http://dealbook.nytimes.com*; Ryan, L. (2013). Because employees can't be trusted. *www.businessweek.com*; Zakaria, F. (2010, Nov. 1). Restoring the American dream. *Time*, 30–35; *www.inc.com*. (2011). Every tool you need for hiring; Shambora, J. (2010, Sept. 27). The algorithm of love. *Fortune*, 28; O'Connell, V. (2008, September 10). Retailers reprogram workers in efficiency push. *Wall Street Journal*, A-12; Baker, S. (2008, September 8). Management by the numbers. *BusinessWeek*, 32–38.

 You Manage It! 2: Ethics/Social Responsibility

Embedding Sustainability into HR Strategy

Many companies are now starting to embed their sustainability efforts into their HR programs so these become part of the employees' everyday life. Companies who adopt this approach believe that this should help employees become engaged in social and environmental causes. A few examples follow:

- Alcatel-Lucent is committed to reducing 50 percent of the company's carbon emissions by 2020. The company has asked the entire workforce to become involved and take steps, no important how small, to accomplish this ambitious goal. Each department (such as facilities operations, logistics, and information technology) is asked to establish specific emissions reduction objectives for the unit, ensuring employee participation in the process.
- Hitachi has announced a program to actively involve employees in corporate social responsibility activities. A cross-functional committee of employees and HR managers has been asked to help in the development of social responsibility e-learning courses, launch global diversity efforts, and introduce work/life balance initiatives. This committee reports directly to the CEO. The company has also set up employee teams to deal with a wide range of social responsibility practices and policies, from labor safety and business ethics to discrimination prevention and protection of the environment.
- Interface (a maker of modular carpets for commercial, institutional, and residential markets) has introduced a system called Quality Using Employee Suggestions and Teamwork (QUEST) to address contamination and unnecessary waste and to reduce carbon footprints. Employees are actively involved in the process and the company offers educational programs to sensitize employees to these issues. The company also provides incentives for employee suggestions that lead to reduced carbon emissions.
- Pfizer (the world's largest biopharmaceutical company) has introduced a "Global Corporate Responsibility Network" that brings together Pfizer employees from different parts of the company to set up initiatives concerning a wide array of social-responsibility issues such as disaster response, employee volunteerism, community health, and ethical business practices.
- Pepsi Cola is one of many firms that encourage employees to engage in organic gardening on company premises. For instance, the company has devoted a track of land in its Purchase, New York, facility for this purpose and provides assistance to employees who wish to participate in this effort. Haberman (a public relations firm in Minneapolis) has rented a plot of land for employee organic gardening and this effort generates sufficient food to satisfy the needs of 30 employee families. HomeStreet Bank in Washington has converted a landscape bed into a vegetable garden that employees are encouraged to cultivate during off-hours. TS Designs (a small T-shirt design business) spends $3,000 to $5,000 a year to maintain an organic garden for employees' use, which includes a beehive as well as a fence to keep out deer and groundhogs.

Critical Thinking Questions

1-18. Would you like to work for a company that offers the sorts of programs that are described in this case? Would this be an important enticement for you to accept a job in such a company and remain employed there? Explain.

1-19. Some skeptics argue that most sustainability programs (such as the ones discussed above) represent an insincere attempt to create a positive company image at low cost. Do you agree or disagree? Do you think these types of programs help or hurt the company's bottom line? Explain.

1-20. What role, if any, should HR professionals play in helping a company become a leader in sustainability efforts? What specific HR challenges is a company likely to face as it tries to become socially responsible? Explain.

Team Exercise

1-21. The class is divided into groups of five. Team members are asked to describe the HR challenges firms are likely to face when trying to implement sustainability programs. Specifically, considering the examples given above, the team should discuss the main HR issues that a company should take into account when implementing these types of programs. For instance, some employees may feel subtle pressures to participate in organic gardening even if this is not something that they enjoy doing.

Experiential Exercise: Team

1-22. The class is divided into groups of five. Each team is asked to role-play a group of employees charged with coming up with a list of HR suggestions to make a hypothetical consumer-products company more environmentally responsible (such as, for instance, providing a bonus for energy savings). Each team will have ten minutes to prepare the list. Depending on class size and available time, the team will present its suggestions to the entire class. The instructor (or another student) will play the role of the HR manager and question the team about the soundness of its recommendations. This will be followed by open class discussion moderated by the instructor.

Experiential Exercise: Individual

1-23. Examine the Web pages of a sample of large firms (such as those listed by *Fortune* in its annual rankings of "best companies to work for") and see if you can identify a particular set of social responsibility programs that involve HR policies. Try to draw some conclusions about the role played by HR, if any, in the implementation of those policies. Also, try to determine the rationale that different companies use for the implementation of these programs.

Sources: Based on Society for Human Resource Management (SHRM). (2013). Advancing sustainability: HR's role: A research report on sustainability by SHRM, BSR and Aurosoorya. *www.shrm.org*; SHRM. (2014). Company gardens reap intangible benefits. *www.shrm.org*; SHRM. (2014). Green jobs—Are they here yet? *www.shrm.org*; SHRM. (2014). Green initiatives during financially challenging times. *www.shrm.org*.

You Manage It! 3: Discussion

Managers and HR Professionals at Sands Corporation: Friends or Foes?

Sands Corporation is a medium-sized company located in the Midwest. It manufactures specialized computer equipment used in cars, serving as a subcontractor to several automobile manufacturers as well as to the military. Federal contracts are an important part of Sands' total sales. In 1985, the firm had 130 employees. At that time, the personnel department had a full-time director (who was a high-school graduate) and a part-time clerk. The department was responsible for maintaining files, placing recruitment ads in the newspaper at management's request, processing employment applications and payroll, answering phones, and handling other routine administrative tasks. Managers and supervisors were responsible for most personnel matters, including whom to hire, whom to promote, whom to fire, and whom to train.

Today Sands employs 700 people. Personnel, now called the human resources department, has a full-time director with a master's degree in industrial relations, three specialists (with appropriate college degrees and certifications: one in compensation, one in staffing, and one in training and development), and four personnel assistants. Sands' top management believes that a strong HR department with a highly qualified staff can do a better job of handling most personnel matters than line supervisors can. It is also convinced that a good HR department can keep line managers from inadvertently creating costly legal problems. One of Sands' competitors recently lost a $5 million sex discrimination suit, which has only strengthened Sands' resolve to maintain a strong HR department.

Some of the key responsibilities the company assigns to its HR department are:

- ***Hiring*** The HR department approves all ads, screens all applicants, tests and interviews candidates, and so forth. Line supervisors are given a limited list of candidates (usually no more than three) per position from which to choose.
- ***Workforce diversity*** The HR department ensures that the composition of Sands' workforce meets the government's diversity guidelines for federal contractors.
- ***Compensation*** The HR department sets the pay range for each job based on its own compensation studies and survey data of salaries at similar companies. The department must approve all pay decisions.
- ***Employee appraisal*** The HR department requires all supervisors to complete annual appraisal forms on their subordinates. The department scrutinizes these appraisals of employees' performance closely; it is not uncommon for supervisors to be called on the carpet to justify performance ratings that are unusually high or low.
- ***Training*** The HR department conducts several training programs for employees, including programs in improving human relations, quality management, and the use of computer packages.
- ***Attitude surveys*** The HR department conducts an in-depth attitude survey of all employees each year, asking them how they feel about various facets of their job, such as satisfaction with supervisor and working conditions.

Over the past few weeks several supervisors have complained to top executives that the HR department has taken away many of their management rights. Some of their gripes are:

- The HR department ranks applicants based on test scores or other formal criteria (for example, years of experience). Often the people they pick do not fit well in the department and/or do not get along with the supervisor and coworkers.
- Excellent performers are leaving because the HR department will not approve pay raises exceeding a fixed limit for the job title held, even when a person is able to perform duties beyond those specified in the job description.
- It takes so long to process the paperwork to hire new employees that the unit loses good candidates to competitors.
- Much of the training required of employees is not focused on the job itself. These "canned" programs waste valuable employee time and provide few benefits to the company.
- Supervisors are afraid to be truthful in their performance ratings for fear of being investigated by the HR department.
- Attitude survey data are broken down by department. The HR department then scrutinizes departments with low scores. Some supervisors feel that the attitude survey has become a popularity contest that penalizes managers who are willing to make necessary (but unpopular) decisions.

The HR department director rejects all of these accusations, arguing that supervisors "just want to do things their way, not taking into account what is best for the company."

Critical Thinking Questions

1-24. What seems to be the main source of conflict between supervisors and the HR department at Sands Corporation? Explain.

1-25. Do you believe that managers should be given more autonomy to make personnel decisions such as hiring, appraising, and compensating subordinates? If so, what are some potential drawbacks to granting them this authority? Explain.

1-26. How should Sands' top executives deal with the complaints expressed by supervisors? How should the director of the HR department deal with the situation? Explain.

Team Exercise

1-27. The CEO of Sands Corporation has called a meeting of four managers, all of whom have lodged some of the complaints noted in the case, and four members of the HR department (the director and three specialists). The instructor or a student acts as the CEO in that meeting. The exercise is carried out as follows: (a) Each side presents its case, with the CEO acting as moderator, and (b) the two groups then try to agree on how Sands' HR department and managers can develop a closer working relationship in the future. The two groups and the CEO may conduct this exercise in separate groups or in front of the classroom.

Experiential Exercise: Team

1-28. One student will role-play the HR department director and three students will fill the roles of disgruntled supervisors. The role-play will take place in front of the entire class for approximately 10 to 15 minutes. At the end, the instructor will moderate class discussion, focusing on key issues that were raised by students during the role-play.

Experiential Exercise: Individual

1-29. Go online and visit the Web sites of the Society of Human Resource Management (*www.shrm.org*) and WorldatWork (*www.worldatwork.com*). Identify a set of resources that may be helpful for the HR director in dealing with this situation. Explain why you think this information might be helpful.

You Manage It! 4: Discussion

Minimum Wage Chaos in Europe

Twenty-two out of twenty-eight governments of the European Union member states have set a minimum wage for their workers. The aim is to guarantee the minimum level of pay they receive. In practice, the minimum levels vary enormously and there are countless caveats, such as training status and age that mean workers rarely receive the minimum pay they are promised on paper. Several key and long-term members of the EU do not even have minimum wage legislation at all, and this group includes Germany, Italy, and Sweden, traditionally collective bargaining has established a higher "natural" minimum wage.

For employers and HR the minimum wage presents a nightmarish situation where a multinational's workforce across the EU can expect to receive a minimum monthly salary of $2593.35 in Luxembourg and a measly $233.55 in Bulgaria. The range of minimum wage levels varies enormously with just three countries guaranteeing over $2,000 and a total of nine with over $1,000 per month. That leaves seventeen countries (including Greece, Portugal, and Poland) where the minimum wage is significantly under $1,000 per month. The EU treaties ensure that minimum wage legislation is a sovereign-state issue. The EU does not have the power to impose minimum wages.

In the run up to the European Parliament elections in 2014, the radical left was calling for a blanket imposition of a new minimum wage based on 60 percent of the average income in each country. Social democratic parties wanted national minimum wages to increase, but fell short of demanding an imposed minimum. Right-leaning parties were completely opposed to any discussion of widening the scope of the minimum wage. Their opinion was that the EU should have nothing to do with what they consider to be the business of a sovereign state.

So where does this leave the employer and their HR departments? The national minimum wage certainly creates some intriguing anomalies for businesses. According to Eurostat, the statistical agency of the EU, it is cheaper to employ British workers (20.9 Euro per hour) than Spanish ones (21.1 Euro per hour). In fact taking wages, bonuses, and non-wage costs (such as employer's social contributions) into account, British workers are significantly cheaper to employ than many other EU countries. Like most things, the equation is much more complex once issues such as productivity are included.

Critical Thinking Questions

1-30. Why do you think there is such a massive difference in the wages paid to employees across the European Union? The EU is a single marketplace, yet the minimum wages are different. Explain.

1-31. What implications are there for businesses that have workers in several different EU countries? What are the ethical issues of offering differential pay?

1-32. What role, if any, should the HR department play in attempting to harmonize pay across a multinational organization? Explain.

Team Exercise

1-33. The class is divided into groups of five and allocated a country in the EU that has either a high or a low minimum wage. Justify the level of wages paid in the country and explain why that makes it an attractive option for employers. If you were pitching to a multinational, what would you say to them to convince them to choose your country to set up in?

Experiential Exercise: Team

1-34. Five students will take the side of the high minimum wage countries and five students will take the opposite side. The two teams will debate the case for a high versus a low minimum wage in front of the entire class for about 15 minutes. The debate may be followed by an open class discussion moderated by the instructor.

Experiential Exercise: Individual

1-35. There are rumors that the European Parliament is broadly in favor of imposing a blanket EU minimum wage. In traditionally high cost countries, wages will be driven down and in most of the rest of the EU wage costs will increase dramatically. If passed by the parliament, this is going to mean significant changes to wage and salary structures across the EU and multinationals will need clear HR guidance. There are fears that some multinationals will abandon traditionally low cost countries. If you were asked for your informed opinion, would you support this change in the law? Carefully justify your answer.

Sources: Based on Fischer, R. (2014). Minimum wages European Union 2014. *www.reinisfischer.com*; FedEE review of minimum wage rates across Europe. (2015). *www.fedee.com*; Should the EU set a European minimum wage? (2014). *www.debatingeurope.eu*; O'Connor, S. (2014). British workers cheaper to employ than Spanish. *www.ft.com*; Eurostat statistics explained. (2015). Minimum wage statistics. http://ec.europa.eu/eurostat/statistics-explained/index.php/Minimum_wage_statistics.

Endnotes

Scan for Endnotes or go to http://www.pearsonglobaleditions.com/Gomez-Mejia.

References

Ahmed, I. (2010). Effects of motivational factors on employees. *International Journal of Business and Management*, *5*(3), 15–29.

Deresky, H. (2011). *International Management*. Upper Saddle River, NJ: Prentice Hall.

Efrati, A., and Tarn, P. P. W. (2010, Nov. 11). Google battles to keep talent. *Wall Street Journal*, 3-1.

Ferraro, G. (2010). *The cultural dimensions of international business*. Englewood Cliffs, NJ: Pearson/Prentice-Hall.

Kim, J., MacDuffie, J. P., and Pil, F. K. (2010). Employee voice and organizational performance: team versus representative influence. *Human Relations*, 10, 1–24.

Luo, L. Cooper, C. L., Kao, S., Chang, T. T., Allen, T. D., Lapierre, L. M., O'Driscoll, M. P., Poelmans, S. A., Sanchez, J. I., and Spector, P. E. (2010). Cross-cultural differences on work-to-family conflict and role satisfaction. *Human Resource Management*, *49*(1), 67–85.

McDonald, D. (2010, Oct. 18). Touched by scandal. *Fortune*, 158.

Salary.com http://swz.salary.com.

CHAPTER 2 Managing Work Flows and Conducting Job Analysis

MyManagementLab®

When you see this icon, visit **www.mymanagementlab.com** for activities that are applied, personalized, and offer immediate feedback.

CHALLENGES

After reading this chapter, you should be able to deal more effectively with the following challenges:

1 **Understand** the organizational perspective of work.

2 **Understand** the group perspective of work.

3 **Understand** the individual perspective of work.

4 **Develop** competence in designing jobs and conducting job analysis.

5 **Have** familiarity with the flexible workforce.

6 **Maintain** human resource information systems.

The powerful forces of technology and global competition are forcing managers to rethink all aspects of business. Work is in a state of flux as companies change basic work processes, job requirements and expectations, and organizational structures to focus more on customers' needs.

One important change is the practice of using work teams instead of individual workers as the basic work unit. Today, many workers spend much of their time on a team established to satisfy customers' needs. For example:

- At Whole Foods Market, a large purveyor of organic foods, teams are the basic unit of organization. Typically, each store has eight teams that run departments such as produce, seafood, and checkout. Teams are given wide latitude with regard to what foods to stock on shelves and how to manage themselves, including the right to hire and fire team members. Information on team performance is transparent, and pay is linked to team, rather than individual, performance.[1]
- General Motors slashed the development time it takes to produce a full mock-up of a car from 12 weeks to only 2 weeks by using collaborative engineering teams that share design information between auto parts suppliers and engineering units within the company. The time saved frees up workers to think more creatively and to develop three or four more alternative designs per car.[2]
- SAP, the German software firm, reduced the time required to produce new, usable application software upgrades from years to 90 days with the use of project teams staffed by some of the company's top software programmers. The increased speed of software development provided by its teams lets SAP compete in more competitive market segments that provide new opportunities for growth, such as database and analytics.[3]

The Managerial Perspective

This chapter is about managing work, which is a highly dynamic process. Managers design structures to organize work into departments, teams, and jobs so that work is performed efficiently and provides a valuable product or service for a customer. Human resource specialists assist managers by keeping track of and documenting the changes for the content of each job through a process called *job analysis*. In this chapter, we explore why job analysis is important to managers and why it is the bedrock of most human resource programs.

Like work teams, organizations are fundamentally groups of people. The relationships among these people can be structured in different ways. In this chapter, we describe how top managers decide on the most appropriate structure for the organization as a whole and for the flow of work within the organization. Although you may never be asked to redesign your organization, it is likely that your company will eventually undergo structural change, because such change is necessary for survival. It is important that you understand structural issues so that you can see the big picture and take an active role in implementing changes.

Work can be viewed from three different perspectives: the entire organization, work groups, and individual employees. We examine each of these perspectives and their implications for human resource management. We also discuss job analysis (a critical HR activity) and the use of contingent workers and alternative work schedules to create a flexible workforce. An understanding of job analysis gives managers a tool to measure how much and what types of work are necessary to achieve organizational objectives. We conclude the chapter with a discussion of human resource information systems.

Learn It!

If your professor has chosen to assign this go to **www.mymanagementlab.com** to see what you should particularly focus on, and take the chapter 2 warmup.

Work: The Organizational Perspective

Organizational structure refers to the formal or informal relationships between people in an organization. **Work flow** is the way work is organized to meet the organization's production or service goals. In this section, we discuss the relationship between strategy and organizational structure, the three basic organizational structures, and the uses of work-flow analysis.

organizational structure
The formal or informal relationships between people in an organization.

work flow
The way work is organized to meet the organization's production or service goals.

Strategy and Organizational Structure

An organization develops a business strategy by establishing a set of long-term goals based on (1) an analysis of environmental opportunities and threats and (2) a realistic appraisal of how the business can deploy its assets to compete most effectively. The business strategy selected by management determines the structure most appropriate to the organization.[4] Whenever management changes its business strategy, it should also reassess its organizational structure.

Recall from Chapter 1 that a company would select a *defender strategy* when it is competing in a stable market and has a well-established product. For example, a regulated electric utility company might adopt such a strategy. Under a defender strategy, work can be efficiently organized into a structure based on an extensive division of labor, with hierarchies of jobs assigned to functional units such as customer service, power generation, and accounting. Management is centralized and top management has the responsibility for making key decisions. Decisions are implemented from the top down via the chain of command. Workers are told what to do by supervisors, who are handed directions from middle managers, who in turn take orders from the company's top executives.

A company would select a *prospector strategy* when operating in uncertain business environments that require flexibility. Companies that are experiencing rapid growth and launching many new products into a dynamic market are likely to select such a strategy. In companies with a prospector strategy, control is decentralized so that each division has some autonomy to make decisions that affect its customers. Workers who are close to the customer are allowed to respond quickly to customers' needs without having to seek approval from supervisors.

A QUESTION OF ETHICS

Implicit in this chapter is the view that organizational change is necessary for survival. However, organizational change often places individual employees under considerable stress, particularly the stress resulting from constantly having to learn new skills and job requirements. Is the organization ethically responsible for protecting employees from these stressful changes?

Management selects HR strategies to fit and support its business strategies and organizational structure. Here are some examples of strategic HR choices regarding structure and work flows that companies have made to achieve cost efficiency and product quality.

- General Electric (GE) signed a 10-year maintenance deal with British Airways to perform engine maintenance and overhaul work. The maintenance agreement helps British Airways save costs by outsourcing this work to GE, which builds, designs, and maintains commercial aircraft engines as a core business.[5]
- Abbey Life Insurance outsourced the claims-adjustment process for its 1.75 million policyholders to Unisys Corp. under a 10-year agreement. Abbey Life saves $80 million over the life of the agreement. Error rates on claims have fallen from 5 percent to 2 percent, and 95 percent of claims are handled within 6 days, down from 10 days.[6]

Designing the Organization

Designing an organization requires choosing an organizational structure that will help the company achieve its goals most effectively. The three basic types of organizational structure are bureaucratic, flat, and boundaryless (see Figure 2.1).

bureaucratic organizational structure
A pyramid-shaped organizational structure that consists of hierarchies with many levels of management.

BUREAUCRATIC ORGANIZATION Companies that adopt a defender business strategy are likely to choose the **bureaucratic organizational structure**. This pyramid-shaped structure consists of hierarchies with many levels of management. It uses a top-down or "command-and-control" approach to management in which managers provide considerable direction to and have considerable control over their subordinates. The classic example of a bureaucratic organization is the military, which has a long chain of command of intermediate officers between the generals (who initiate combat orders) and the troops (who do the fighting on the battlefield).

A bureaucratic organization is based on a *functional division of labor*. Employees are divided into divisions based on their function. Thus, production employees are grouped in one division, marketing employees in another, engineering employees in a third, and so on. Rigid boundaries separate the functional units from one another. At a bureaucratic auto parts company, for instance, automotive engineers would develop plans for a new part and then deliver its specifications to the production workers.

Rigid boundaries also separate workers from one another and from their managers because the bureaucratic structure relies on *work specialization*. Narrowly specified job descriptions clearly mark the boundaries of each employee's work. Employees are encouraged to do only the work specified in their job description—no more and no less. They spend most of their time working individually at specialized tasks and usually advance only within one function. For example, employees who begin their career in sales can advance to higher and higher positions in sales or marketing, but cannot switch into production or finance.

The bureaucratic structure works best in a predictable and stable environment. It is highly centralized and depends on frontline workers performing repetitive tasks according to managers' orders. In a dynamic environment, this structure is less efficient and sometimes disastrous.

flat organizational structure
An organizational structure that has only a few levels of management and emphasizes decentralization.

FLAT ORGANIZATION A company that selects the prospector business strategy is likely to choose the **flat organizational structure**. A flat organization has only a few levels of managers and emphasizes a decentralized approach to management. Flat organizations encourage high employee involvement in business decisions. Nucor (a Charlotte, North Carolina, steel company) has a flat organizational structure. Although Nucor has over 20,000 employees, only a few levels separate the frontline steel workers from the president of the company. Headquarters staff consists of a mere 100 people in a modest cluster of offices.[7]

Flat organizations are likely to be divided into units or teams that represent different products, services, or customers. The purpose of this structure is to create independent small businesses that can respond rapidly to customers' needs or changes in the business environment. For example, Johnson & Johnson, a manufacturer of health care products, is organized into more than 250 operating companies that are located in 60 countries. Each operating company behaves like

Organizational Structure | **Characteristics**

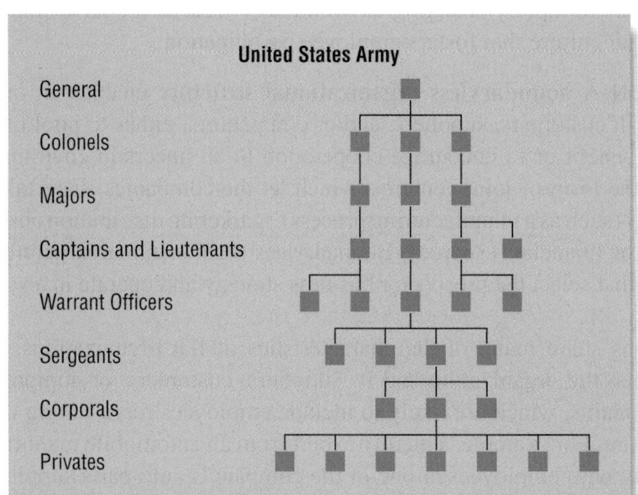

Bureaucratic
- Top-down management approach
- Many levels of management
- Hierarchical career paths within one function
- Highly specialized jobs
- Narrowly specified job descriptions
- Rigid boundaries between jobs and units
- Employees or individuals working independently

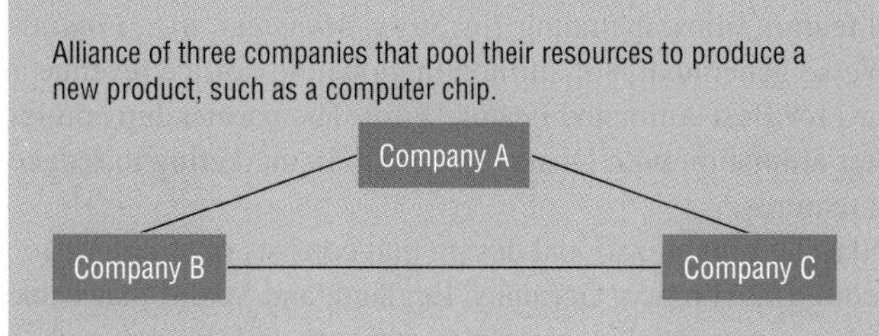

Flat
- Decentralized management approach
- Few levels of management
- Horizontal career paths that cross functions
- Broadly defined jobs
- General job descriptions
- Flexible boundaries between jobs and units
- Emphasis on teams
- Strong focus on the customer

Alliance of three companies that pool their resources to produce a new product, such as a computer chip.

Company A

Company B

Company C

Boundaryless
- Joint ventures with customers, suppliers, and competitors
- Emphasis on teams whose members may cross organizational boundaries
- Shares many characteristics of flat organizational structure

FIGURE 2.1
Organizational Structures

a minibusiness that is responsible for generating profits for the overall company, and employees within each unit feel as if they are working for a small company. The flat organization structure has fostered an entrepreneurial culture that has enabled Johnson & Johnson to innovate.

The flat organizational structure reduces some of the boundaries that isolate employees from one another in bureaucratic organizations. Boundaries between workers at the same level are reduced because employees are likely to be working in teams. In contrast to workers at bureaucratic organizations, employees of a flat organization can cross functional boundaries as they pursue their careers (for instance, starting in sales, moving to finance, and then into production). In addition, job descriptions in flat organizations are more general and encourage employees to develop a broad range of skills (including management skills). Boundaries that separate employees from managers and supervisors also break down in flat organizations because employees are empowered to make more decisions.

Flat organizational structures can be useful for organizations that are implementing a management strategy that emphasizes customer satisfaction. Implementing a customer-focused strategy may require changing work processes so that customers can receive higher-quality products and better service. For example, an auto insurance company may change its claims adjustment process to speed up reimbursement to customers. Rather than using 25 employees who take

14 days to process a claim, the company may create a claims adjustment team that works closely with the customer to take care of all the paperwork within 3 days.

The flat structure works best in rapidly changing environments because it enables management to create an entrepreneurial culture that fosters employee participation.

boundaryless organizational structure
An organizational structure that enables an organization to form relationships with customers, suppliers, and/or competitors, either to pool organizational resources for mutual benefit or to encourage cooperation in an uncertain environment.

BOUNDARYLESS ORGANIZATION A **boundaryless organizational structure** enables an organization to form relationships with customers, suppliers, and/or competitors, either to pool organizational resources for mutual benefit or to encourage cooperation in an uncertain environment. Such relationships often take the form of joint ventures, which let the companies share talented employees, intellectual property (such as a manufacturing process), marketing distribution channels (such as a direct sales force), or financial resources. Boundaryless organizational structures are most often used by companies that select the prospector business strategy and operate in a volatile environment.

Boundaryless organizations share many of the characteristics of flat organizations. They break down boundaries between the organization and its suppliers, customers, or competitors. They also strongly emphasize teams, which are likely to include employees representing different companies in the joint venture. For example, a quality expert from an automobile manufacturing company may work closely with employees at one of the company's auto parts suppliers to train them in specific quality management processes.

Companies often use a boundaryless organizational structure when they (1) collaborate with customers or suppliers to provide better-quality products or services, (2) are entering foreign markets that have entry barriers to foreign competitors, or (3) need to manage the risk of developing an expensive new technology. The boundaryless organization is appropriate in these situations because it is open to change, it facilitates the formation of joint ventures with foreign companies, and it reduces the financial risk to any one organization. Here are some examples of boundaryless organizational structures:

- Pixar, the animation studio, partnered with Walt Disney Pictures to produce a number of highly successful animated feature films, including *Toy Story*, *Monsters, Inc.*, *Finding Nemo*, and *Cars*. *Finding Nemo* generated $865 million in global box office revenue and received the Academy Award for Best Animated Feature Film. The partnership combined Pixar's expertise in computer animation with Disney's strength in marketing to reduce the risk of producing animated features.[8]
- Airbus Industries is a boundaryless organizational design that consists of a partnership of European firms from four countries (France, Germany, England, and Spain) that worked together to market and develop commercial jet aircraft to compete with Boeing and become a leading producer of passenger jets.
- Apple Inc. partners with Foxconn, a Taiwanese electronics firm, to manufacture Apple's iPods, iMacs, and iPhones in China. Apple designs and markets the products, and its Asian partner builds and assembles them according to the design specifications and ships the finished products back to the United States.[9] Apple Inc. also forms partnerships with numerous independent, self-employed software programmers who design new applications to use on Apple's iPhones.

Work-Flow Analysis

We said earlier that work flow is the way work is organized to meet the organization's production or service goals. Managers need to do **work-flow analysis** to examine how work creates or adds value to the ongoing business processes. (*Processes* are value-adding, value-creating activities such as product development, customer service, and order fulfillment.[10]) Work-flow analysis looks at how work moves from the customer (who initiates the need for work) through the organization (where employees add value to the work in a series of value-creating steps) to the point at which the work leaves the organization as a product or service for the customer.

work-flow analysis
The process of examining how work creates or adds value to the ongoing processes in a business.

Each job in the organization should receive work as an input, add value to that work by doing something useful to it, and then move the work on to another worker. Work-flow analysis usually reveals that some steps or jobs can be combined, simplified, or even eliminated. In some cases, it has resulted in the reorganization of work so that teams rather than individual workers are the source of value creation.

Work-flow analysis can be used to tighten the alignment between employees' work and customers' needs. It can also help a company make major performance improvements through a program called *business process reengineering*.

Business Process Reengineering

The term *reengineering* was coined by Michael Hammer and James Champy in their pioneering book *Reengineering the Corporation*. Hammer and Champy emphasize that reengineering should not be confused with restructuring or simply laying off employees in an effort to eliminate layers of management.[11] **Business process reengineering (BPR)** is not a quick fix but rather a fundamental rethinking and radical redesign of business processes to achieve dramatic improvements in cost, quality, service, and speed.[12] Reengineering examines the way a company conducts its business by closely analyzing the core processes involved in producing its product or delivering its service to the customer. By taking advantage of computer technology and different ways of organizing human resources, the company may be able to reinvent itself.[13]

business process reengineering (BPR)
A fundamental rethinking and radical redesign of business processes to achieve dramatic improvements in cost, quality, service, and speed.

BPR uses work-flow analysis to identify jobs that can be eliminated or recombined to improve company performance. Figure 2.2 shows the steps in processing a loan application at IBM Credit Corporation both before and after BPR. Before the BPR effort, work-flow analysis showed that loan applications were processed in a series of five steps by five loan specialists, each of whom did something different to the loan application. The entire process took an average of six days to complete, which gave customers the opportunity to look elsewhere for financing.[14] For much of that time, the application was either in transit between the loan specialists or sitting on someone's desk waiting to be processed.

FIGURE 2.2
Processing a Loan Application at IBM Credit Corporation Before and After BPR

Work Flow Using Specialists

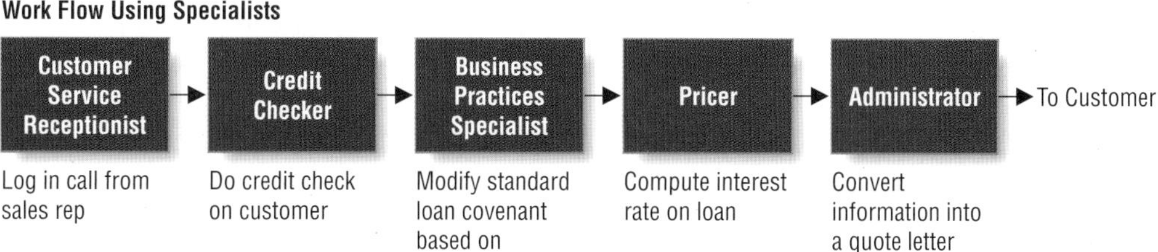

Work Flow After Business Process Reengineering

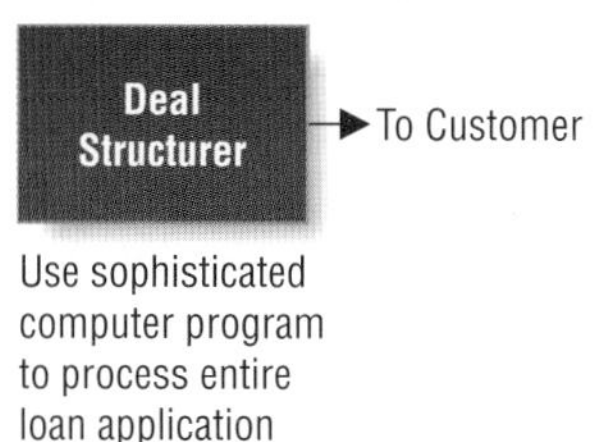

Using BPR, the jobs of the five loan specialists were reorganized into the job of just one generalist called the *deal structurer*. The deal structurer uses a new software program to print out a standardized loan contract, access different credit-checking databases, price the loan, and add boilerplate language to the contract. With the new process, loan applications can be completed in four hours instead of six days.[15]

Work: The Group Perspective

We turn now to an examination of work from the perspective of employee groups. In the flat and boundaryless organizational structures, teamwork is an imperative. Indeed, as we have seen, teams are the basic building blocks of both structures.

team
A small number of people with complementary skills who work toward common goals for which they hold themselves mutually accountable.

What exactly is a team and how does it operate? A **team** is a small number of people with complementary skills who work toward common goals for which they hold themselves mutually accountable.[16] Teams can vary significantly in size, from 2 to 80 members. The upper range may occur with virtual teams where members collaborate on large projects over the Internet. Most teams have fewer than 10 members, with 5 to 6 members considered to be an optimal team size.[17] Unlike *work groups*, which depend on a supervisor for direction, a team depends on its own members to provide leadership and direction.[18] Teams can also be organized as departments. For example, a company may have a product development team, a manufacturing team, and a sales team.

Several types of teams are used in organizations today. The type that is having the most impact on U.S. companies is the self-managed team.

Self-Managed Teams

self-managed team (SMT)
A team responsible for producing an entire product, a component, or an ongoing service.

Organizations are implementing self-managed work teams primarily to improve quality and productivity and to reduce operating costs. **Self-managed teams (SMTs)** are responsible for producing an entire product, a component, or an ongoing service. In most cases, SMT members are cross-trained on the different tasks assigned to the team.[19] Some SMTs have members with a set of complex skills—for example, scientists and engineers with training in different disciplines. Members of the SMT have many managerial duties, including work scheduling, selecting work methods, ordering materials, evaluating performance, and disciplining team members.[20]

One company that has switched over to SMTs is the San Diego Zoo. The zoo's employees traditionally had very narrow and well-defined job responsibilities: Keepers did the keeping and gardeners did the gardening. Then the zoo decided to develop bioclimatic zones, in which plants and animals are grouped together in cageless enclosures that resemble their native habitats. Because the zones themselves are interdependent, the employees who manage them must work together. For instance, the humid 3.5-acre Tiger River exhibit is run by a seven-member team of mammal and bird specialists, horticulturists, and maintenance and construction workers.[21]

HRM practices are likely to change in the following ways when SMTs are established:[22]

- Peers, rather than a supervisor, are likely to evaluate individual employee performance.
- Pay practices are likely to shift from pay based on seniority or individual performance to pay focused on team performance (for example, team bonuses).[23]
- Rather than being based solely on input from managers and HR staff, decisions on new hires may include a decisive amount of input from team members.
- Team leaders are likely to step forward and identify themselves. For example, SEI Investments encourages leaders to emerge on their own initiative in its self-managed teams.[24]
- High-performing SMTs often use a shared leadership style where team members take turns acting as the team leader, depending on the team work context. Shared leadership is common among teams of knowledge workers.[25]

Self-managed teams have made some impressive contributions to the bottom lines of companies that have used them. For instance, after implementing SMTs, Shenandoah Life found it could process 50 percent more applications and customer service requests with 10 percent fewer

EXHIBIT 2.1 TEAMS AT GOOGLE

About half of Google's 34,000 employees (all of those involved in product development) work in small teams, with an average of three engineers per team. Even a large project, such as Gmail, which might occupy 30 people, is broken into teams of three or four, each of which works on a specific service enhancement, such as building spam filters or improving the forwarding feature. Each team has an "über tech leader," a responsibility that rotates among team members depending on shifting project requirements. Most engineers work on more than one team, and no one needs the permission of the HR department to switch teams. Organizations in the technology industry favor small teams because they are agile and can innovate more quickly.

Sources: Based on Hamel, G. (2007, October 1). Break free! *Fortune*, 124; Holstein, W. (2007, December 30). Orders from on high? That's so yesterday. *New York Times*, Sunday Money, 6; Lindberg, O. (2009, October 11). The secrets of Google's design team. *www.techradar.com*; Schrage, M. (2011, December 13). Smart innovators value smaller teams over better processes. *HBR Blog Network. www.blogs.hbr.org/schrage/2011/12/quiet-but-unsubtle-innovation.html.*

employees.[26] Xerox plants using SMTs are 30 percent more productive than Xerox plants organized without them.[27] Boeing used SMTs to reduce the number of engineering problems in the development of the 777 passenger jet by more than half.[28] For a look at how self-managed teams work at Google, the Internet search–services company, see Exhibit 2.1.

Because team members often initially lack the skills necessary for the team to function successfully, it may take several years for an SMT to become fully operational.[29] A company can hasten this evolution by using its HR department to train employees in the skills required of team members. Three areas are important:[30]

1. ***Technical skills*** Team members must be cross-trained in new technical skills so that they can rotate among jobs as necessary. Team members who are cross-trained give the team greater flexibility and allow it to operate efficiently and with fewer workers.
2. ***Administrative skills*** Teams do much of the work done by supervisors in organizations that don't have teams. Therefore, team members need training in such management/administrative skills as budgeting, scheduling, monitoring and evaluating peers, and interviewing job applicants.
3. ***Interpersonal skills*** Team members need good communication skills to form an effective team. They must be able to express themselves effectively in order to share information, deal with conflict, and give feedback to one another.[31]

Other Types of Teams

In addition to the SMT, businesses use other types of teams: the problem-solving team, the special-purpose team, and the virtual team.[32] The **problem-solving team** consists of volunteers from a unit or department who meet one or two hours per week to discuss quality improvement, cost reduction, or improvement in the work environment. The formation of problem-solving teams does not affect an organization's structure because these teams exist for only a limited period; they are usually disbanded after they have achieved their objectives.

problem-solving team
A team consisting of volunteers from a unit or department who meet one or two hours per week to discuss quality improvement, cost reduction, or improvement in the work environment.

The **special-purpose team**, or *task force*, consists of members who span functional or organizational boundaries and whose purpose is to examine complex issues—for example, introducing a new technology, improving the quality of a work process that spans several functional units, or encouraging cooperation between labor and management in a unionized setting. An example of a special-purpose team is the quality of work life (QWL) program, which consists of team members (including union representatives and managers) who collaborate on making improvements in all aspects of work life, including product quality. The QWL programs at Ford and General Motors have focused on improving product quality, whereas the QWL program between the United Steel Workers of America and the major steel companies has concentrated on developing new ways to improve employee morale and working conditions.[33]

special-purpose team
A team or task force consisting of workers who span functional or organizational boundaries and whose purpose is to examine complex issues.

For more on problem-solving teams, refer to the Manager's Notebook titled "Tips on Managing Problem-Solving Teams."

MANAGER'S NOTEBOOK

Customer-Driven HR

Tips on Managing Problem-Solving Teams

Managers should be able to use problem-solving teams consisting of employees with cross-functional skills to solve challenging organizational issues. In designing and managing such teams, the following are some important points to consider:

- If the team is expected to implement new ideas, include members from different levels of the organization. Creating a team with members from different levels (frontline employees and supervisors, for example) can also foster cooperation and reduce barriers between employees and managers.
- Monitor the team to ensure that the free exchange of ideas and creativity is not stifled if managers and employees are on the same team.
- Select members not only for their expertise and diverse perspectives but also for their ability to compromise and solve problems collaboratively.
- Allow the team enough time to complete its task. The more complex the problem, and the more creative the solution needs to be, the more the members will need large blocks of time.
- Coordinate with other managers to free up time for the members.
- Provide clear goals and guidelines on what you expect the team to do. Tell them what they can and cannot address.
- Schedule periodic team meetings to reinforce the process of solving problems collectively. Such meetings can be used to evaluate the effectiveness of the team.

Sources: Based on Gratton, L., and Erickson, T. (2007, November). Eight ways to build collaborative teams. *Harvard Business Review,* 100–109; Kepcher, C. (2005, February). Collegial teams. *Leadership Excellence,* 7–8; Nahavandi, A., and Malekzadeh, A. R. (1999). *Organizational behavior.* Upper Saddle River, NJ: Prentice Hall, 276.

virtual team
A team that relies on interactive technology to work together when separated by physical distance.

The **virtual team** uses interactive computer technologies such as the Internet, groupware (software that permits people at different computer workstations to collaborate on a project simultaneously), and computer-based videoconferencing to work together despite being separated by physical distance.[34] Virtual teams are similar to problem-solving teams because they do not require full-time commitment from team members. The difference is that virtual team members interact with each other electronically, rather than face-to-face.[35]

Because of their part-time nature and flexibility in accommodating distance, virtual teams allow organizations to tap individuals who might not be otherwise available. For example, a management consulting firm working on a project out of its San Francisco office for a local bank includes financial specialists from its New York and Chicago offices on the project team. This type of team also makes it possible for companies to cross organizational boundaries by linking customers, suppliers, and business partners in a collaborative effort that can increase the quality and speed with which the new product or service is brought to market. In writing this textbook, the authors (university professors) formed a virtual team with the publishing company's editors and also with the design specialists who created the graphics and visual images for the text.

One of the best practices that has emerged from research on virtual teams is the use of a virtual work space, which is essentially a Web site that only team members have access to, where the team is reminded of its decisions, rationales, and commitments.[36] The virtual team work space has a home page with links to other "walls," each of which is devoted to a specific aspect of the team project. One wall, for example, contains information about all the people on the virtual team, including contact information and profiles of their expertise and accomplishments. Another wall displays information about teleconference meetings, such as when they are being held, who is supposed to attend, the agendas, and the meeting minutes, which can be shared with team members. Shell Chemicals, for example, has had success with the use of a virtual work space on a company-wide project to develop a new cash-based approach to financial management.[37]

Work: The Individual Perspective

The third and final perspective from which we will examine work flows and structure is that of the individual employee and job. We look first at the various theories of what motivates employees to achieve higher levels of performance and then look at different ways jobs can be designed to maximize employee productivity. In the next section, we look at job analysis, which is the gathering and organization of information concerning the tasks and duties of specific jobs. The section concludes with a discussion of job descriptions, which are one of the primary results of job analysis.

Motivating Employees

Motivation can be defined as that which energizes, directs, and sustains human behavior.[38] In HRM, the term refers to a person's desire to do the best possible job or to exert the maximum effort to perform assigned tasks. An important feature of motivation is that it is behavior directed toward a goal.

motivation
That which energizes, directs, and sustains human behavior. In HRM, a person's desire to do the best possible job or to exert the maximum effort to perform assigned tasks.

Motivation theory seeks to explain why employees are more motivated by and satisfied with one type of work than another. It is essential that managers have a basic understanding of work motivation because highly motivated employees are more likely to produce a superior-quality product or service than employees who lack motivation.

TWO-FACTOR THEORY The *two-factor theory of motivation*, developed by Frederick Herzberg, attempts to identify and explain the factors that employees find satisfying and dissatisfying about their jobs.[39] The first set of factors, called *motivators*, are internal job factors that lead to job satisfaction and higher motivation. In the absence of motivators, employees will probably not be satisfied with their work or motivated to perform up to their potential. Some examples of motivators are the work itself, achievement, recognition, responsibility, and opportunities for advancement.

Notice that salary is not included in the motivator list. Herzberg contends that pay belongs among the second set of factors, which he calls *hygiene* or *maintenance factors*. Hygiene factors are external to the job; they are located in the work environment. The absence of a hygiene factor can lead to active dissatisfaction and demotivation and, in extreme situations, to avoidance of the work altogether. Hygiene factors include the following:

- Company policies
- Working conditions
- Job security
- Salary
- Employee benefits
- Relationships with supervisors and managers
- Relationships with coworkers
- Relationships with subordinates

According to Herzberg, if management provides the appropriate hygiene factors, employees will not be dissatisfied with their jobs, but neither will they be motivated to perform at their full potential. To motivate workers, management must provide some motivators.

Two-factor theory has two implications for job design: (1) Jobs should be designed to provide as many motivators as possible, and (2) making (external) changes in hygiene factors, such as pay or working conditions, is not likely to sustain improvements in employee motivation over the long run unless (internal) changes are also made in the work itself.

WORK ADJUSTMENT THEORY Every worker has unique needs and abilities. *Work adjustment theory* suggests that employees' motivation levels and job satisfaction depend on the fit between their needs and abilities and the characteristics of the job and the organization.[40] A poor fit between individual characteristics and the work environment may lead to reduced levels of motivation. Work adjustment theory proposes that:

- A job design that one employee finds challenging and motivating may not motivate another employee. For example, a mentally disabled employee may find a repetitive job at a fast-food restaurant highly motivating and challenging, but a college graduate may find the same job boring.

- Not all employees want to be involved in decision making. Employees with low needs for involvement may fit poorly on a self-managed team because they may resist managing other team members and taking responsibility for team decisions.

GOAL-SETTING THEORY *Goal-setting theory*, developed by Edwin Locke, suggests that employees' goals help to explain motivation and job performance.[41] The reasoning is as follows: Because motivation is goal-directed behavior, goals that are clear and challenging will result in higher levels of employee motivation than goals that are ambiguous and easy.

Because it suggests that managers can increase employee motivation by managing the goal-setting process, goal-setting theory has some important implications for managers:[42]

- Employees will be more motivated to perform when they have clear and specific goals. A store manager whose specific goal is to "increase store profitability by 20 percent in the next six months" will exert more effort than one who is told to "do the best you can" to increase profits.
- Employees will be more motivated to accomplish difficult goals than easy goals. Of course, the goals must be attainable—otherwise the employee is likely to become frustrated. For example, an inexperienced computer programmer may promise to deliver a program in an unrealistic amount of time. The programmer's manager may work with the programmer to establish a more realistic yet still-challenging deadline for delivering the program.
- In many (but not all) cases, goals that employees participate in creating for themselves are more motivating than goals that are simply assigned by managers. Managers may establish mutually agreed-upon goals with employees through a management by objectives (MBO) approach (discussed in Chapter 7) or by creating self-managed teams that take responsibility for establishing their own goals.
- Employees who receive frequent feedback on their progress toward reaching their goals sustain higher levels of motivation and performance than employees who receive sporadic or no feedback. For example, a restaurant manager can motivate servers to provide better service by soliciting customer feedback on service quality and then communicating this information to employees. The importance of providing feedback to employees for the improvement of their performance is discussed elsewhere in the text in the topic that covers performance appraisal (Chapter 7).

JOB CHARACTERISTICS THEORY Developed by Richard Hackman and Greg Oldham, *job characteristics theory* states that employees will be more motivated to work and more satisfied with their jobs to the extent that jobs contain certain core characteristics.[43] These core job characteristics create the conditions that allow employees to experience critical psychological states that are related to beneficial work outcomes, including high work motivation. The strength of the linkage among job characteristics, psychological states, and work outcomes is determined by the intensity of the individual employee's need for growth (that is, how important the employee considers growth and development on the job).

There are five core job characteristics that activate three critical psychological states. The core job characteristics are:[44]

1. ***Skill variety*** The degree to which the job requires the person to do different things and involves the use of a number of different skills, abilities, and talents.
2. ***Task identity*** The degree to which a person can do the job from beginning to end with a visible outcome.
3. ***Task significance*** The degree to which the job has a significant impact on others—both inside and outside the organization.
4. ***Autonomy*** The amount of freedom, independence, and discretion the employee has in areas such as scheduling the work, making decisions, and determining how to do the job.
5. ***Feedback*** The degree to which the job provides the employee with clear and direct information about job outcomes and performance.

The three critical psychological states affected by the core job characteristics are:[45]

1. ***Experienced meaningfulness*** The extent to which the employee experiences the work as important, valuable, and worthwhile.

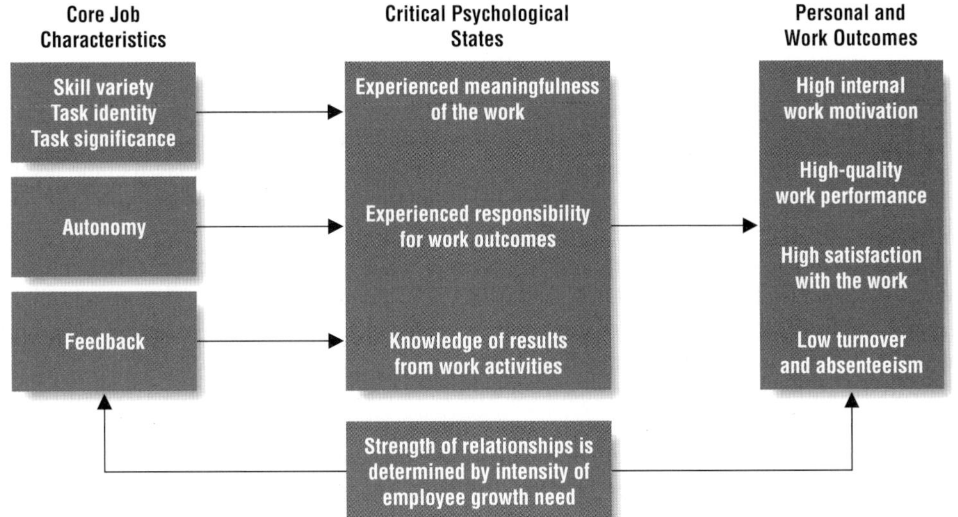

FIGURE 2.3
The Job Characteristics Theory of Work Motivation

2. ***Experienced responsibility*** The degree to which the employee feels personally responsible or accountable for the results of the work.
3. ***Knowledge of results*** The degree to which the employee understands on a regular basis how effectively he or she is performing the job.

As shown in Figure 2.3, skill variety, task identity, and task significance are all linked to experienced meaningfulness of work. Autonomy is related to experienced responsibility and feedback is related to knowledge of results.

A job with characteristics that enable an employee to experience all three critical psychological states provides internal rewards that sustain motivation.[46] These rewards come from having a job where the person can learn (knowledge of results) that he or she has performed well on a task (experienced responsibility) that he or she cares about (experienced meaningfulness).[47] In addition, this situation results in certain outcomes that are beneficial to the employer: high-quality performance, higher employee satisfaction, and lower turnover and absenteeism. Job characteristics theory maintains that jobs can be designed to contain the characteristics that employees find rewarding and motivating.

Designing Jobs and Conducting Job Analysis

All the theories of employee motivation suggest that jobs can be designed to increase motivation and performance. **Job design** is the process of organizing work into the tasks required to perform a specific job.

job design
The process of organizing work into the tasks required to perform a specific job.

Job Design

There are three important influences on job design. One is work-flow analysis, which (you will recall) seeks to ensure that each job in the organization receives work as an input, adds value to that work, and then passes it on to another worker. The other two influences are business strategy and the organizational structure that best fits that strategy. For example, an emphasis on highly specialized jobs could be expected in a bureaucratic organizational structure because work in bureaucratic organizations is built around the division of labor.

We will examine five approaches to job design: work simplification, job enlargement, job rotation, job enrichment, and team-based job design.

WORK SIMPLIFICATION *Work simplification* assumes that work can be broken down into simple, repetitive tasks that maximize efficiency. This approach to job design assigns most of the thinking aspects of work (such as planning and organizing) to managers and supervisors, while giving the employee a narrowly defined task to perform. Work simplification can utilize labor effectively to produce a large amount of a standardized product. The classic twentieth century automobile assembly line, where workers engaged in highly mechanical and repetitive tasks, exemplifies the work simplification approach.

Although work simplification can be efficient in a stable environment, it is less effective in a changing environment where customers demand custom-built products of high quality. Moreover, work simplification often leads to high levels of employee turnover and low levels of employee satisfaction. (In fact, where work simplification is used, employees may feel the need to form unions to gain some control over their work.) Finally, higher-level professionals subjected to work simplification may become so specialized in what they do that they cannot see how their job affects the organization's overall product or service. The result can be employees doing work that has no value to the customer. Over the last decade, many professional employees in highly specialized jobs became casualties of corporate restructurings, because organizations discovered that such work did not provide value to consumers.

Work simplification is not to be confused with *work elimination*. Companies trying to eliminate work challenge every task and every step within a task to see if there is a better way to get the work done. Even if parts of the work cannot be eliminated, some aspect of the job may be simplified or combined with another job. Oryx, a Dallas, Texas–based oil and gas producer, saved $70 million in operating costs in one year after it set up teams to take a fresh look at its operations. The teams discovered many procedures, reviews, reports, and approvals that had little to do with Oryx's business and could easily be eliminated. Work elimination is similar to BPR, though it differs in that work elimination typically focuses on particular jobs and processes rather than on overhauling the entire company.[48]

JOB ENLARGEMENT AND JOB ROTATION Job enlargement and job rotation are used to redesign jobs to reduce fatigue and boredom among workers performing simplified and highly specialized work. **Job enlargement** expands a job's duties. For example, auto workers whose specialized job is to install carpets on the car floor may have their job enlarged to include the extra duties of installing the car's seats and instrument panel.[49]

job enlargement
The process of expanding a job's duties.

job rotation
The process of rotating workers among different narrowly defined tasks without disrupting the flow of work.

Job rotation rotates workers among different narrowly defined tasks without disrupting the flow of work. On an auto assembly line, for example, a worker whose job is installing carpets would be rotated periodically to a second workstation where he or she would install only seats in the car. At a later time period the worker might be rotated to a third workstation, where the job would be to install only the car's instrument panels. During the course of a day on the assembly line, the worker might be shifted at two-hour intervals among all three workstations.

Both job enlargement and job rotation have limitations because these approaches focus mainly on eliminating the demotivating aspects of work and, thus, improve only one of the five core job characteristics that motivate workers (skill variety).

JOB ENRICHMENT Job enrichment is an approach to job design that directly applies job characteristics theory (see Figure 2.3) to make jobs more interesting and to improve employee motivation. **Job enrichment** puts specialized tasks back together so that one person is responsible for producing a whole product or an entire service.[50]

job enrichment
The process of putting specialized tasks back together so that one person is responsible for producing a whole product or an entire service.

Job enrichment expands both the horizontal and the vertical dimensions of a job. Instead of people working on an assembly line at one or more stations, the entire assembly line process is abandoned to enable each worker to assemble an entire product, such as a kitchen appliance or radio.[51] For example, at Motorola's Communications Division, individual employees are now responsible for assembling, testing, and packaging the company's pocket radio-paging devices. Previously, these products were made on an assembly line that broke the work down into 100 different steps and used as many workers.[52]

Job enrichment gives employees more opportunities for autonomy and feedback. It also gives them more responsibilities that require decision making, such as scheduling work, determining work methods, and judging quality.[53] However, the successful implementation of job enrichment is limited by the production technology available and the capabilities of the employees who produce the product or service. Some products are highly complex and require too many steps for one individual to produce them efficiently. Other products require the application of so many different skills that it is not feasible to train employees in all of them. For example, it could take an employee a lifetime to master all the skills necessary to assemble a Boeing 777 aircraft.

Job enrichment can provide opportunities for increased interactions with customers and others who are affected by the results of the work. A job design that has provisions for contact with customers is likely to increase the meaningfulness of an employee's work when he or she learns in the customer's own voice how the customer uses the product and how it affects him or her.[54] For example, putting software engineers in contact with groups of customers on a frequent basis to see how they use the software can motivate the software engineers to create a future version of the software that is easier to use and that has more applications that customers want. Another way to enrich a job is for a company to sponsor an employee in a routine job with the opportunity to do volunteer work in the local community while on the company payroll. The Limited, a women's clothing retailer, has sponsored its employees to provide kindergarten tutoring to local schools.

TEAM-BASED JOB DESIGNS *Team-based job designs* focus on giving a team, rather than an individual, a whole and meaningful piece of work to do.[55] Team members are empowered to decide among themselves how to accomplish the work.[56] They are cross-trained in different skills, then rotated to do different tasks within the team. Team-based job designs match best with flat and boundaryless organizational structures.

McDonald's uses team-based job designs in the operations of a fast-food restaurant. A team of McDonald's employees performs various functions such as food preparation; order taking; operating the cash register; keeping the kitchen and customer areas of the restaurant clean; taking out the trash; and refilling dispensers with napkins, straws, and utensils for the customers to use. Team members are cross-trained on different functions and participate in determining the allocation of work responsibilities for each work shift.

Job Analysis

After a work-flow analysis has been done and jobs have been designed, the employer needs to define and communicate job expectations for individual employees. This is best done through **job analysis**, which is the systematic gathering and organization of information concerning jobs. Job analysis puts a job under the microscope to reveal important details about it. Specifically, it identifies the tasks, duties, and responsibilities of a particular job.

job analysis
The systematic process of collecting information used to make decisions about jobs. Job analysis identifies the tasks, duties, and responsibilities of a particular job.

- A *task* is a basic element of work that is a logical and necessary step in performing a job duty.
- A *duty* consists of one or more tasks that constitute a significant activity performed in a job.
- A *responsibility* is one or several duties that identify and describe the major purpose or reason for the job's existence.

Thus, for the job of administrative assistant, a task might be completing a travel authorization form, which is part of the duty to keep track of the department's travel expenses, which is part of the responsibility to manage the departmental budget.

Job analysis provides information to answer the following questions: Where does the work come from? What machines and special equipment must be used? What knowledge, skills, and abilities (KSAs) does the job holder need to perform the job? How much supervision is necessary? Under what working conditions should this job be performed? What are the performance expectations for this job? On whom must the job holders depend in order to perform this job? With whom must they interact? Job analysis can answer these questions, thereby giving managers valuable information that can help them develop more effective HRM policies and programs, as described in the remaining chapters of this text.

WHO PERFORMS JOB ANALYSIS? Depending on the technique selected, job analysis is performed either by a member of the HR department or by the *job incumbent* (the person who is currently assigned to the job in question). In some businesses a manager may perform the job analysis.

METHODS OF GATHERING JOB INFORMATION Companies use several methods to gather job information: interviews, observation, diaries, and questionnaires. Factors such as cost and job complexity will influence the choice of method.

- ***Interviews*** The interviewer (usually a member of the HR department) interviews a representative sample of job incumbents using a structured interview. The structured interview includes a series of job-related questions that is presented to each interviewee in the same order.

- *Observation* An individual observes the job incumbent actually performing the job and records the core job characteristics from observation. This method is used in cases where the job is fairly routine and the observer can identify the job essentials in a reasonable amount of time. The job analyst may videotape the job incumbent in order to study the job in greater detail.
- *Diaries* Several job incumbents may be asked to keep diaries or logs of their daily job activities and record the amount of time spent on each activity. By analyzing these diaries over a representative period of time (perhaps several weeks), a job analyst is able to capture the job's essential characteristics.
- *Questionnaires* The job incumbent fills out a questionnaire that asks a series of questions about the job's knowledge, skill, and ability requirements; duties; and responsibilities. Each question is associated with a quantitative scale that measures the importance of the job factor or the frequency with which it occurs. A computer can then tally the scores on the questionnaires and create a printout summarizing the job's characteristics.

- *Internet-based data collection* The human resource department puts a job analysis questionnaire on an intranet Web site and instructs employees to complete the questionnaire by a certain date. A software program evaluates the responses and summarizes the job characteristics using standardized descriptors that can be generalized across many different job categories. The Internet-based collection of job data takes less time than many of the other methods, such as face-to-face interviews and direct observation. The U.S. Department of Labor developed the Occupational Information Network (O*NET) as an Internet-based data collection method for collecting job information for over 800 occupations.[57] O*NET provides information on tasks; job-related behaviors; and knowledge, skills, and abilities needed to perform the job.

THE USES OF JOB ANALYSIS Job analysis measures job content and the relative importance of different job duties and responsibilities. Having this information helps companies comply with government regulations and defend their actions from legal challenges that allege unfairness or discrimination. As we will see in Chapter 3, the generic defense against a charge of discrimination is that the contested decision (to hire, to give a raise, to terminate) was made for job-related reasons. Job analysis provides the documentation for such a defense. For instance:

- A company may be able to defend its policy of requiring sales representatives to have a valid driver's license if it can show via job analysis that driving is an essential activity in the sales rep's job. Otherwise, under the Americans with Disabilities Act (see Chapter 3), the employer may be asked to make a reasonable accommodation for a blind job applicant who asserts his rights to be considered for the job.
- The owner of a fast-food restaurant who pays an assistant manager a weekly salary (without any overtime pay) may be able to defend herself from charges of an overtime pay violation with a job analysis proving that the assistant manager job is exempt from the overtime provisions of the Fair Labor Standards Act (see Chapter 10). The owner can prove this by showing that most of the job duties and responsibilities entail supervising and directing others rather than preparing food and providing service to customers.

In addition to establishing job relatedness for legal purposes, job analysis is also useful for the following HR activities:

- *Recruitment* Job analysis can help the HR department generate a higher-quality pool of job applicants by making it easy to describe a job in newspaper ads that can be targeted to qualified job applicants. Job analysis also helps recruiters screen college-student job applicants because it tells them what tasks, duties, and responsibilities the job entails.
- *Selection* Job analysis can be used to determine whether an applicant for a specific job should be required to take a personality test or some other kind of test. For example, a personality test that measures extroversion (the degree to which someone is talkative, sociable, active, aggressive, or excitable) may be justified for selecting a life insurance sales representative. (Such a job is likely to emphasize customer contact, which includes making "cold calls" on potential new accounts.) Job analysis may also reveal that the personality test measuring extroversion has a weak relationship to the job content of other jobs (for example, lab technician) and should not be used as part of the selection process for those jobs.

- ***Performance appraisal*** The performance standards used to judge employee performance for purposes of promotion, rewards, discipline, or layoff should be job related. Under federal law, a company is required to defend its appraisal system against lawsuits and prove the job relatedness of the performance criteria used in the appraisal.
- ***Compensation*** Job analysis information can be used to compare the relative worth of each job's contributions to the company's overall performance. The value of each job's contribution is an important determinant of the job's pay level. In a typical pay structure, jobs that require mastery of more complex skills or jobs that have greater levels of responsibility pay more than jobs that require only basic skills or have low amounts of responsibility.
- ***Training and career development*** Job analysis is an important input for determining training needs. By comparing the knowledge, skills, and abilities that employees bring to the job with those that are identified by job analysis, managers can identify their employees' skill gaps. Training programs can then be put in place to improve job performance.

THE TECHNIQUES OF JOB ANALYSIS Figure 2.4 lists eight major techniques of job analysis. Detailed descriptions of these techniques are beyond the scope of this book. However, we briefly describe four of them—task inventory analysis, the critical incident technique, the position analysis questionnaire, and functional job analysis—to give you a sense of what job analysis entails. For a set of general guidelines on conducting a job analysis effectively, see the Manager's Notebook titled "Guidelines for Conducting a Job Analysis."

Task Inventory Analysis *Task inventory analysis* is actually a collection of methods that are offshoots of the U.S. Air Force task inventory method.[58] The technique is used to determine the **knowledge, skills, and abilities (KSAs)** needed to perform a job successfully. The analysis has three steps: (1) interview, (2) survey, and (3) generation of a task by KSA matrix.

knowledge, skills, and abilities (KSAs)
The knowledge, skills, and abilities needed to perform a job successfully.

The interview step focuses on developing lists of tasks that are part of the job. Interviews are conducted both with workers who currently hold the job and with their managers. The goal of the interviews is to generate specific descriptions of individual tasks that can be used in the task inventory survey.

The survey step involves generating and administering a survey consisting of task statements and rating scales. The survey might ask respondents—the current job holders—to rate each task on importance, frequency, and training time needed. Whether the survey is sent to a sample of the workers or to all of them will depend on the number of workers and the economic constraints on the job analysis.

The final step is the creation of a task by KSA matrix, which is used to rate the extent to which a variety of KSAs are important for the successful completion of each task. An abbreviated example of a KSA rating matrix is presented in Figure 2.5. Ratings in the matrix are usually determined by subject matter experts, who might include supervisors, managers, consultants, and job incumbents.

Task inventory analysis has two major advantages. First, it is a systematic means for analyzing the tasks in a particular situation. Second, it uses a tailor-made questionnaire rather than an already prepared stock questionnaire. Managers can use the technique to develop job descriptions and performance appraisal forms, as well as to develop or identify appropriate selection tests.

Critical Incident Technique The *critical incident technique (CIT)* is used to develop behavioral descriptions of a job.[59] In CIT, supervisors and workers generate behavioral incidents of job performance. The technique uses the following four steps: (1) generate dimensions, (2) generate incidents, (3) retranslate, and (4) assign effectiveness values. In the generating dimensions step, supervisors and workers identify the major dimensions of a job. "Dimensions" are simply aspects of performance. For example, interacting with customers, ordering stock, and balancing the cash drawer are the major dimensions of a retail job. Once they have agreed on the job's major dimensions, supervisors and workers generate "critical incidents" of behavior that represent high, moderate, and low levels of performance on each dimension. An example of a critical incident of high performance on the dimension "interacting with customers" might be:

> When a customer complained to the clerk that she could not find a particular item, seeing no one else was in line, this clerk walked with the customer back to the shelves to find the item.

Technique	Employee Group Focused on	Data Collection Method	Analysis Results	Description
1. Task Inventory Analysis	Any—large number of workers needed	Questionnaire	Rating of tasks	Tasks are rated by job incumbent,* supervisor, or job analyst. Ratings may be on characteristics such as importance of task and time spent doing it.
2. Critical Incident Technique	Any	Interview	Behavioral description	Behavioral incidents representing poor through excellent performance are generated for each dimension of the job.
3. Position Analysis Questionnaire (PAQ)	Any	Questionnaire	Rating of 194 job elements	Elements are rated on six scales (for example, extent of use, importance to job). Ratings are analyzed by computer.
4. Functional Job Analysis (FJA)	Any	Group interview/ questionnaire	Rating of how job incumbent relates to people, data, and things	Originally designed to improve counseling and placement of people registered at local state employment offices. Task statements are generated and then presented to job incumbents to rate on such dimensions as frequency and importance.
5. Methods Analysis (Motion Study)	Manufacturing	Observation	Time per unit of work	Systematic means for determining the standard time for various tasks. Based on observation and timing of work tasks.
6. Guidelines-Oriented Job Analysis	Any	Interview	Skills and knowledge required	Job incumbents identify duties as well as knowledge, skills, physical abilities, and other characteristics needed to perform the job.
7. Management Position Description Questionnaire (MPDQ)	Managerial	Questionnaire	Checklist of 197 items	Managers check items descriptive of their responsibilities.
8. Hay Plan	Managerial	Interview	Impact of job on organization	Managers are interviewed regarding such issues as their responsibilities and accountabilities. Responses are analyzed according to four dimensions: objectives, dimensions, nature and scope, accountability.

*The term job incumbent refers to the person currently filling a particular job.

FIGURE 2.4
The Techniques of Job Analysis

Rating Scale Importance of characteristics for successful performance of task				
1 Very Low	2 Low	3 Medium	4 High	5 Very High

Job Task	Worker Characteristics									
	Mathematical Reasoning	Analytical Ability	Ability to Follow Directions	Memory	Comprehension—Oral	Comprehension—Written	Expression—Oral	Expression—Written	Problem-Solving Ability	Clerical Accuracy
1. Reviews production schedules to determine correct job sequencing										
2. Identifies problem jobs and takes corrective action										
3. Determines need for and provides special work orders										
4. Maintains log book and makes required assignments										
5. Negotiates with foremen to determine critical dates for emergency situations										
6. Analyzes material availability and performs order maintenance										
7. Prepares job packets										
8. Maintains customer order file										
9. Negotiates with Purchasing to ensure material availability										
10. Determines product availability for future customer orders										
11. Determines promise dates and provides to customer										
12. Determines adequacy of materials given document forecast										

FIGURE 2.5
Sample Task by KSA Matrix

An example of low performance on the same dimension might be:

When a customer handed the clerk a large number of coupons, the clerk complained out loud to the bagger that he hated dealing with coupons.

The last two steps, retranslation and assigning effectiveness values, involve making sure that the critical incidents generated in the first two steps are commonly viewed the same way by other employees.

The CIT provides a detailed behavioral description of jobs. It is often used as a basis for performance appraisal systems and training programs, as well as to develop behaviorally based selection interview questions. The appendix to Chapter 7 gives you the opportunity to develop critical incidents.

Position Analysis Questionnaire (PAQ) The PAQ is a job analysis questionnaire that contains 194 different items. Using a five-point scale, the PAQ seeks to determine the degree to which the different items, or job elements, are involved in performing a particular job.[60] The 194 items are organized into six sections:

1. *Information input* Where and how a worker gets information needed to perform the job.
2. *Mental processes* The reasoning, decision-making, planning, and information-processing activities involved in performing the job.
3. *Work output* The physical activities, tools, and devices used by the worker to perform the job.
4. *Relationships with other persons* The relationships with other people required in performing the job.
5. *Job context* The physical and social contexts in which the work is performed.
6. *Other characteristics* The other activities, conditions, and characteristics relevant to the job.

MANAGER'S NOTEBOOK

Customer-Driven HR

Guidelines for Conducting a Job Analysis

Conducting a job analysis requires managers to take five steps:

1. ***Determine the desired applications of the job analysis.*** For example, if used as a basis for performance appraisal, job analysis should collect data that are representative of differing levels of job performance. If used as a basis for determining training needs, then job analysis should collect information on the necessary knowledge, skills, and abilities that lead to effective job performance.
2. ***Select the jobs to be analyzed.*** Factors that make specific jobs appropriate for job analysis include the stability or obsolescence of job content (rapidly changing jobs require more frequent job analysis). Entry-level jobs (which require selection tools that determine who gets hired and who gets rejected) are also analyzed regularly.
3. ***Gather the job information.*** Within budget constraints, collect the desired information using the most appropriate job-analysis technique.
4. ***Verify the accuracy of the job information.*** Both the job incumbents and their immediate supervisors should review the job information to ensure that it is representative of the actual job.
5. ***Document the job analysis by writing a job description.*** Document the job-analysis information in a job description that summarizes the job's essential duties and responsibilities, as well as the knowledge, skills, and abilities necessary for the job. This document allows managers to compare different jobs on various dimensions and is an important part of many HR programs.

Sources: Based on Gatewood, R. D., Field, H. S., and Barrick, M. R. (2011). *Human resource selection* (7th ed.). Mason, OH: South-Western; How to write a job analysis and description. (2010). *www.entrepreneur.com;* Cascio, W. F. and Aguinis, H. (2011). *Applied psychology in human resource management* (7th ed.). Upper Saddle River, NJ: Prentice Hall. ■■

A computer analyzes the completed PAQ and generates a score for the job and a profile of its characteristics.

Functional Job Analysis Functional job analysis, a technique used in the public sector, can be done by either interview or questionnaire.[61] This technique collects information on the following aspects of the job:[62]

1. What the job incumbent does to people, data, and things.
2. The methods and techniques the job incumbent uses to perform the job.
3. The machines, tools, and equipment used by the job incumbent.
4. The materials, projects, or services produced by the job incumbent.

The results of functional job analyses are published by the U.S. Department of Labor in the Occupational Information Network (O*NET), which is a free online database containing hundreds of occupational definitions.[63]

JOB ANALYSIS AND THE LEGAL ENVIRONMENT Because job analysis can be the basis on which a firm wins or loses a lawsuit over how it selects or appraises employees, it is important that organizations carefully document their job-analysis efforts.

There are two important questions regarding job analysis. The first of these questions is: Which job analysis method is best? Although there are many job-analysis techniques, there is no clear choice as to which is best. Some, like task inventory analysis and Guidelines-Oriented Job Analysis, were developed to satisfy legal requirements, but there is no legal basis to prefer one to another. The *Uniform Guidelines* published by the Equal Employment Opportunity Commission state that a job analysis should be done, but do not specify a preferred technique.

As a general rule, the more concrete and observable the job-analysis information, the better. Thus, job-analysis approaches that provide specific task or behavioral statements, such as task inventory analysis or CIT, may be preferable. CIT can be very expensive because of the time commitment required of supervisors and workers.

Given the lack of a single best technique, the choice of job-analysis technique should, within economic constraints, be guided by the purpose of the analysis. For example, if the major purpose for the analysis is the redesign of jobs, then an analysis focusing on tasks would probably be best. But if the major purpose is the development of a training program, a behaviorally focused technique would probably be best.

JOB ANALYSIS AND ORGANIZATIONAL FLEXIBILITY The second question regarding job analysis is: How does detailed job-analysis information fit into today's organizations, which need to be flexible and innovative to remain competitive?

Whatever technique is used, job analysis is a static view of the job as it currently exists, and a static view of jobs is at odds with current organizational trends emphasizing flexibility and innovativeness.[64] For instance, US Airways attempts to keep labor costs down by having employees do a variety of tasks. The same person may be a flight attendant, ticket agent, and baggage handler, all in the same week. And almost all jobs today are affected by the constant advances in information and communication technologies. Such factors can render even the most thorough job analysis virtually useless after a very short time.

In an organizational environment of change and innovation, it is better to focus job analyses on *worker* characteristics than on *job* characteristics. The required tasks in jobs may change, but such employee characteristics as innovativeness, team orientation, interpersonal skills, and communication skills will likely remain critical to organizational success. Unfortunately, most job-analysis techniques are not focused on discovering worker characteristics unless the characteristics are directly related to the immediate tasks. But, because the importance of fit with the organization is being increasingly recognized as a factor that should be considered in selection,[65] job analysis may become more focused on underlying employee factors.[66] Toyota (USA) and AFG Industries are organizations that have expanded job analysis to emphasize fit between prospective employees and the organization.

Job Descriptions

A **job description** is a summary statement of the information collected in the job-analysis process. It is a written document that identifies, defines, and describes a job in terms of its duties, responsibilities, working conditions, and specifications. There are two types of job descriptions: specific job descriptions and general job descriptions.

job description
A written document that identifies, defines, and describes a job in terms of its duties, responsibilities, working conditions, and specifications.

A *specific job description* is a detailed summary of a job's tasks, duties, and responsibilities. This type of job description is associated with work-flow strategies that emphasize efficiency, control, and detailed work planning. It fits best with a bureaucratic organizational structure with well-defined boundaries that separate functions and the different levels of management. Figure 2.6 shows an example of a specific job description for the job of service and safety supervisor. Note that this job description closely specifies the work that is unique to a person who will supervise *safety* employees. The specific job knowledge of safety regulations and Red Cross first-aid procedures included in this job description make it inappropriate for any other type of supervisor (for example, a supervisor at a local supermarket).

Job Title: Service and Safety Supervisor
DIVISION: Plastics
DEPARTMENT: Manufacturing
SOURCE(S): John Doe
JOB ANALYST: John Smith
DATE ANALYZED: 12/26/14
WAGE CATEGORY: Exempt
VERIFIED BY: Bill Johnson
DATE VERIFIED: 1/5/15

Job Summary

The SERVICE AND SAFETY SUPERVISOR works under the direction of the IMPREGNATING & LAMINATING MANAGER: **schedules** labor pool employees; **supervises** the work of gardeners, cleaners, waste disposal, and plant security personnel; **coordinates** plant safety programs; **maintains** daily records on personnel, equipment, and scrap.

Job Duties and Responsibilities

1. **Schedules** labor employees to provide relief personnel for all manufacturing departments; **prepares** assignment schedules and **assigns** individuals to departments based on routine as well as special needs in order to maintain adequate labor levels through the plant; **notifies** Industrial Relations Department weekly about vacation and layoff status of labor pool employees, contractual disputes, and other employment-related developments.
2. **Supervises** the work of gardeners, cleaners, waste disposal, and plant security personnel; **plans** yard, cleanup, and security activities based on weekly determination of needs; **assigns** tasks and responsibilities to employees on a daily basis; **monitors** progress or status of assigned tasks; **disciplines** employees.
3. **Coordinates** plant safety programs; **teaches** basic first-aid procedures to security, supervisory, and lease personnel in order to maintain adequate coverage of medical emergencies; **trains** employees in fire fighting and hazardous materials handling procedures; **verifies** plant compliance with new or changing OSHA regulations; **represents** division during company-wide safety programs and meetings.
4. **Maintains** daily records on personnel, equipment, and scrap; **reports** amount of waste and scrap to cost accounting department; **updates** personnel records as necessary; **reviews** maintenance checklists for towmotors.
5. **Performs** other miscellaneous duties as assigned.

Job Requirements

1. Ability to apply basic principles and techniques of supervision.
   a. Knowledge of principles and techniques of supervision.
   b. Ability to plan and organize the activities of others.
   c. Ability to get ideas accepted and to guide a group or individual to accomplish the task.
   d. Ability to modify leadership style and management approach to reach goal.
2. Ability to express ideas clearly both in written and oral communications.
3. Knowledge of current Red Cross first-aid operations.
4. Knowledge of OSHA regulations as they affect plant operations.
5. Knowledge of labor pool jobs, company policies, and labor contracts.

Minimum Qualifications

Twelve years of general education or equivalent; one year supervisory experience; and first-aid instructor's certification.

OR

Substitute 45 hours classroom supervisory training for supervisory experience.

FIGURE 2.6

Example of a Specific Job Description

Source: Jones, M. A. (1984, May). Job descriptions made easy. *Personnel Journal.* Copyright May 1984. Reprinted with the permission of *Personnel Journal.* ACC Communications, Inc., Costa Mesa, California; all rights reserved.

The *general job description*, which is fairly new on the scene, is associated with work-flow strategies that emphasize innovation, flexibility, and loose work planning. This type of job description fits best with a flat or boundaryless organizational structure in which there are few boundaries between functions and levels of management.[67]

Only the most generic duties, responsibilities, and skills for a position are documented in the general job description.[68] Figure 2.7 shows a general job description for the job of "supervisor." Note that all the job duties and responsibilities in Figure 2.7 apply to the job of *any* supervisor—one who supervises accountants, engineers, or even the safety employees managed by the service and safety supervisor in Figure 2.6.

Job Title: Supervisor
DIVISION: Plastics
DEPARTMENT: Manufacturing
SOURCE(S): John Doe, S. Lee | WAGE CATEGORY: Exempt
JOB ANALYST: John Smith | VERIFIED BY: Bill Johnson
DATE ANALYZED: 12/26/14 | DATE VERIFIED: 1/5/15

Job Summary

The SUPERVISOR works under the direction of the MANAGER: **plans** goals; **supervises** the work of employees; **develops** employees with feedback and coaching; **maintains** accurate records; **coordinates** with others to achieve optimal use of organizational resources.

Job Duties and Responsibilities

1. **Plans** goals and allocates resources to achieve them; **monitors** progress toward objectives and adjusts plans as necessary to reach them; **allocates** and **schedules** resources to assure their availability according to priority.
2. **Supervises** the work of employees; **provides** clear instructions and explanations to employees when giving assignments; **schedules** and assigns work among employees for maximum efficiency; **monitors** employees' performance in order to achieve assigned objectives.
3. **Develops** employees through direct performance feedback and job coaching; **conducts** performance appraisals with each employee on a regular basis; **provides** employees with praise and recognition when performance is excellent; **corrects** employees promptly when their performance fails to meet expected performance levels.
4. **Maintains** accurate records and documents actions; **processes** paper work on a timely basis, and with close attention to details; **documents** important aspects of decisions and actions.
5. **Coordinates** with others to achieve the optimal use of organizational resources; **maintains** good working relationships with colleagues in other organizational units; **represents** others in unit during division or corporate-wide meetings.

Job Requirements

1. Ability to apply basic principles and techniques of supervision.
   a. Knowledge of principles and techniques of supervision.
   b. Ability to plan and organize the activities of others.
   c. Ability to get ideas accepted and to guide a group or individual to accomplish the task.
   d. Ability to modify leadership style and management approach to reach goal.
2. Ability to express ideas clearly in both written and oral communications.

Minimum Qualifications

Twelve years of general education or equivalent; and one year supervisory experience.

OR

Substitute 45 hours classroom supervisory training for supervisory experience.

FIGURE 2.7
Example of a General Job Description

Source: Jones, M. A. (1984, May). Job descriptions made easy. *Personnel Journal.* Reprinted by permission of the author.

The driving force behind a move toward general job descriptions may be a customer-focused management strategy or BPR.[69] For example, the Arizona Public Service (APS), a public utility, moved toward general job descriptions after discovering that it had 1,000 specific job descriptions for its 3,600 workers.[70] This massive number of specific job descriptions erected false barriers among work functions, choked off change, and prevented APS from providing high levels of customer service. By using general job descriptions, APS was able to reduce the number of its job descriptions to 450.

An even more impressive application of general job descriptions is seen at Nissan, the Japanese auto manufacturer. Nissan has only one general job description for all its hourly wage production employees.[71] By comparison, some of the divisions of General Motors have a variety of specific job descriptions for their hourly production workforce. This fact is partially explained by the vigilance of the United Auto Workers' Union (UAW) in defending the rights of its members to work in specific jobs.

ELEMENTS OF A JOB DESCRIPTION Job descriptions have four key elements: identification information, job summary, job duties and responsibilities, and job specifications and minimum qualifications.[72] Figures 2.6 and 2.7 show how this information is organized on the job description.

To comply with federal law, it is important that job descriptions document only the essential aspects of a job. Otherwise, qualified women, minorities, and persons with disabilities may be unintentionally discriminated against for not meeting specified job requirements. For example, a valid driver's license should not be put in the job description if the job can be modified so that it can be performed by a person with physical disabilities without a driver's license.

Identification Information The first part of the job description identifies the job title, location, and source of job-analysis information; who wrote the job description; the dates of the job analysis and the verification of the job description; and whether the job is exempt from the overtime provision of the Fair Labor Standards Act or subject to overtime pay rates. To be certain that the identification information ensures equal employment opportunities, HR staff should:

- Make sure the job titles do not refer to a specific gender. For example, use the job title "sales representative" rather than "salesman."
- Make sure job descriptions are updated regularly so that the date on the job description is current. Job descriptions more than two years old have low credibility and may provide flawed information.
- Avoid inflating a job title to give the job a more impressive-sounding status than it deserves. For example, use the title "sales representative" rather than "sales executive" for a job that does not have executive duties such as supervising a staff of salespeople.[73]
- Ensure that the supervisor of the job incumbent(s) verifies the job description. This is a good way to ensure that the job description does not misrepresent the actual job duties and responsibilities. (A manager who is familiar with the job may also be used to verify the description.)

Job Summary The job summary is a short statement that summarizes the job's duties, responsibilities, and place in the organizational structure.

Job Duties and Responsibilities Job duties and responsibilities explain what is done on the job, how it is done, and why it is done.[74]

Each job description typically lists the job's three to five most important responsibilities. Each responsibility statement begins with an action verb. For example, the job of supervisor in Figure 2.7 has five responsibilities that start with the following action verbs: plans, supervises, develops, maintains, and coordinates. Each responsibility is associated with one or more job duties, which also start with action verbs. For example, the supervisor job in Figure 2.7 has two job duties associated with the responsibility of "plans goals": (1) monitors progress toward objectives and (2) allocates and schedules resources. The job duties and responsibilities statement is probably the most important section of the job description because it influences all the other parts of the job description. Therefore, it must be comprehensive and accurate.

job specifications
The worker characteristics needed to perform a job successfully.

Job Specifications and Minimum Qualifications The **job specifications** section lists the worker characteristics (KSAs) needed to perform a job successfully. The KSAs represent the things that an employee who has mastered the job can do.

When documenting KSAs it is important to list only those that are related to successful job performance. For example, a current computer programmer may have mastered some programming languages that are not necessary for job performance. These should not be included in the job description.

The *minimum qualifications* are the basic standards a job applicant must have achieved to be considered for the job. These can be used to screen job applicants during the recruiting and selection process. Here are some things to watch for when documenting minimum qualifications:

- A college degree should be a minimum qualification only if it is related to the successful performance of the job. For example, a bachelor's degree may be a minimum qualification for an accountant in a major accounting firm, but it is not likely to be necessary for the job of shift supervisor in a fast-food restaurant.
- Work experience qualifications should be carefully specified so that they do not discriminate against minorities or persons with disabilities. For example, the job description in Figure 2.7 provides for a substitution of 45 classroom hours of supervisory training for the one year of supervisory experience minimum qualification. This provision allows people who have been excluded from employment opportunities in the past to be considered for the position. This flexibility allows the company to consider diverse job applicants, who are less likely to meet the supervisory experience qualification.

JOB OR WORK? In this chapter, we saw that in some situations it is more accurate to focus on the *work* that an employee performs rather than the *job*, because some jobs lack clearly defined boundaries due to rapidly changing work responsibilities and duties.[75]

Some companies deal with this dynamic environment by letting teams be responsible for a larger unit of work so that a team member can be deployed on different tasks that the team decides need to be performed, depending on the demands on a given day. Other companies use a general job description—for example, a job with the all-purpose title of "associate"—to provide employees flexibility in interpreting their roles based on the best way to serve a particular customer. For instance, bus drivers serving some of the dangerous neighborhoods of Paris, France, found that their job involved managing hostile customers or ending fights between bus passengers. However, these conflict management skills were not included in the job description of a bus driver. Bus drivers learned to interpret their work role broadly in order to provide a safe environment for their passengers. Thus, although in some cases it may be more accurate to describe what an employee does for an employer as *work* rather than a *job*, we expect that the need to assign employees to perform jobs is going to remain an important feature of the work environment into the foreseeable future. This means that translating the duties and responsibilities of employees' work into job descriptions will continue to be useful and beneficial to both managers and employees.

The Flexible Workforce

We have seen how organizations can be structured and jobs designed to maximize flexibility. In this section, we examine two additional strategies for ensuring flexibility: contingent workers and flexible work schedules.

Contingent Workers

There are two types of workers: core workers and contingent workers. A company's **core workers** have full-time jobs and enjoy privileges not available to contingent workers. Many core workers expect a long-term relationship with the employer that includes a career in the organization, a full array of benefits, and job security. In contrast, the jobs of **contingent workers** are based on the employer's convenience and efficiency needs. Firms hire contingent workers to help them deal with temporary increases in their workload or to do work that is not part of their core set of capabilities. When the business cycle moves into a downturn, the contingent workers are the first employees to be discharged. They thus provide a buffer zone of protection for the core workers. For example, in some large Japanese corporations core workers' jobs are

core workers
An organization's full-time employees.

contingent workers
Workers hired to deal with temporary increases in an organization's workload or to do work that is not part of its core set of capabilities.

protected by a large contingent workforce that can be rapidly downsized when business conditions change.

Contingent workers include temporary employees, part-time employees, outsourced subcontractors, contract workers, and college interns. According to the U.S. Bureau of Labor Statistics in the United States, contingent workers made up 26 percent of the total labor force in 2010. This number includes approximately 27 million part-time employees, 10 million contract workers, and 1.2 million temporary employees. The jobs held by contingent workers are diverse, ranging from secretaries, security guards, sales clerks, and assembly-line workers to doctors, college professors, engineers, managers, and even chief executives.

TEMPORARY EMPLOYEES Temporary employment agencies provide companies with *temporary employees* (or "temps") for short-term work assignments. Temps work for the temporary employment agency and are simply reassigned to another employer when their current job ends. ManpowerGroup, the largest U.S. temporary employment agency, placed 3.5 million people in positions in 2011.[76]

Temporary employees provide employers with two major benefits:

- Temps on average receive less compensation than core workers. They are not likely to receive health insurance, retirement, or vacation benefits from the company that uses their services. A majority of temporary employees do not receive these benefits from the temporary agency because they must meet a minimum service requirement of several months or longer of continuous employment with the agency to qualify for the benefits. For example, as layoffs mounted in the 1990s, the total payroll for professionals and managers employed by temporary firms more than tripled.[77] However, many managers working at temp jobs earn 50 percent less than they earned as core workers.[78]
- Temporary employees may be highly motivated workers, because many employers choose full-time employees from the ranks of the top-performing temps. Because temps can be screened for long-term career potential in an actual work setting and be easily dismissed if the company determines that they have low potential, hiring temps helps employers reduce the risk of selecting employees who prove to be a poor fit.

Employers should understand the legal limits of using a temporary worker on a long-term basis. Several thousand Microsoft temps who held long-term positions but were employed through a temporary agency ("permatemps") filed a class action lawsuit, claiming that Microsoft treated them as full-time workers in every way except in terms of compensation and benefits. A federal court of appeals ruled that workers who were on Microsoft's payroll for more than a few months—even if placed by temporary agencies—should be considered common-law employees who are entitled to the same benefits that permanent employees receive.[79]

Temporary employees are being used with increasing regularity throughout the world. In France, one in five workers is on a temporary or part-time contract, and in Britain more than 25 percent of the workforce is part-time. Almost 33 percent of new jobs created in Spain were for temporary workers. During the height of the recession in 2010, 26 percent of all private-sector jobs in the United States were temporary positions.[80]

PART-TIME EMPLOYEES *Part-time employees* work fewer hours than full-time core employees and receive far fewer employee benefits, thus providing substantial savings to employers. According to the U.S. Bureau of Labor Statistics, a part-time employee is defined as an individual who works less than 35 hours per week due to economic, voluntary, or involuntary reasons.[81] Traditionally, part-timers have been employed by service businesses that have a high variance in demand between peak and off-peak times. For example, restaurants and markets hire many part-time employees to provide service to customers during peak hours (usually evenings and weekends).

Companies are finding many new applications for part-time workers. For example, UPS has created 25-hour-per-week part-time jobs for shipping clerks and supervisors who sort packages at its distribution centers. Companies that downsize their workforces to reduce payroll costs have been known to restructure full-time core jobs into part-time positions.

job sharing
A work arrangement in which two or more employees divide a job's responsibilities, hours, and benefits among themselves.

In a special type of part-time employment called **job sharing**, a full-time job is divided between two or more people to create two part-time jobs. During a downscaling of its workforce,

DuPont used job sharing between employees in its management, research, and secretarial areas to avoid layoffs.[82] Employees who decide to be partners in a job-sharing arrangement must operate as a team and communicate the details of their daily activities to each other so that the quality of service or job output is not affected by the handoffs that occur when the job-sharing partners come and go.[83]

Companies are increasingly using part-time work as a way to reverse the "brain drain" of highly skilled female professionals who need greater work–life balance to provide more time for their family. Johnson & Johnson, the large health care products company, allows professional women with substantial work experience to take a reduced-hour option so the company won't lose them. Pfizer, the pharmaceutical giant, offers part-time work to its pharmaceutical sales professionals who are highly trained in product knowledge and have developed valuable relationships with doctors who are their clients. Sales representatives choosing the part-time option work 60 percent of the hours of full-time employees and can structure their working day around children's school hours. Ninety-three percent of those selecting part-time work at Pfizer are working mothers, and these individuals remain eligible for promotion and may return to full-time status at their discretion.[84]

A QUESTION OF ETHICS

Many employees and union representatives complain bitterly about the practice of outsourcing work, particularly to foreign countries. Part of the complaint is that companies do this to avoid paying fair wages and providing employee benefits that U.S. workers expect. Is this an ethical issue? If so, on what basis should companies make outsourcing decisions?

OUTSOURCING/SUBCONTRACTING As we saw in Chapter 1, outsourcing (sometimes called *subcontracting*) is the process by which employers transfer routine or peripheral work to another organization that specializes in that work and can perform it more efficiently. Employers that outsource some of their nonessential work gain improved quality and cost savings. Outsourcing agreements may result in a long-term relationship between an employer and the subcontractor, though it is the employer who has the flexibility to renew or end the relationship at its convenience.[85]

Outsourcing is the wave of the future as more and more companies look to the "virtual corporation" as an organizational model.[86] A *virtual company* consists of a small core of permanent employees and a constantly shifting workforce of contingent employees.

Consistent with the outsourcing trend, human resource activities are being outsourced by organizations. For example, payroll, benefits, training, and recruiting are often outsourced to external service providers.[87] Previously, these outsourced activities were performed in-house. In fact, human resource outsourcing is a fast-growing $103 billion industry, and total annual industry revenues recently increased 70 percent over a five-year period.[88] Although outsourcing routine human resource activities such as payroll produces efficiencies, the outsourcing of critical HR systems such as training or performance evaluation may lead to a loss of control over important systems or a loss of opportunity to learn from one's best human resource practices that could achieve fundamental improvements in other human resource activities. A firm that provides a wide array of human resource services on an outsourcing basis to small businesses is called a *professional employer organization* (PEO). PEOs provide small businesses with a bundle of human resource management services such as training, benefits administration, and staffing that larger firms have in-house, so that managers in small businesses can focus on achieving strategic business goals.

Establishing the right relationship with service vendors is very important for companies that decide to outsource. Although some companies view their outsourced vendors as strategic partners, others caution that, ultimately, company and vendor do not have identical interests. For example, UOP, an Illinois-based engineering firm that develops technology used to build oil refineries, sued Andersen Consulting, the information-technology firm UOP had hired to streamline and improve some of its work processes. UOP sued for $100 million in damages, alleging breach of contract.[89] The lesson here is that it pays to communicate clearly and specifically with vendors from the beginning.[90]

One company that relies on outsourcing as a source of competitive advantage is Benetton, the Italian multinational corporation that makes clothing sold in 110 countries. Benetton views itself as a "clothing services" company rather than as a retailer or manufacturer.[91] The company outsources a large amount of clothes manufacturing to local suppliers but makes sure to provide its subcontractors with the clothes-making skills that Benetton views as crucial to maintaining quality and cost efficiency.[92]

The Manager's Notebook, "Advantages and Disadvantages of Outsourcing an HR Activity," provides some useful information on factors to consider before outsourcing.

MANAGER'S NOTEBOOK

Advantages and Disadvantages of Outsourcing an HR Activity

Outsourcing an HR activity to a firm that specializes in providing an HR service to customers has both advantages and disadvantages. Here are some important factors to consider:

Outsourcing Advantages

- An outsourcing firm can provide better-quality people and the most current practices and information pertaining to an activity or task. Because the HR activity is the core mission of the outsourcing firm, it can specialize in doing it very well. For example, a firm that specializes in training employees on the use of word processing software is likely to be able to train employees to use the most recent upgrades on the software that contains the newest features and applications. Further, the complexities of meeting the requirements of the Patient Protection and Affordable Care Act—which will require U.S. employers with more than 50 employees to provide health insurance in 2015 (explained in detail in Chapter 12)—can overwhelm employers, who may decide to turn to HR outsourcing firms that specialize in benefits for assistance in complying with the law.
- Outsourcing certain tasks can result in a reduction in administrative costs because the outsourcer can do the task more efficiently and gain economies of scale by virtue of having a large network of customers.
- Outsourcing specific activities and employees that do not fit with company culture may be useful to preserve a strong culture or employee morale. An example is outsourcing the benefits administration activity at a law firm, where the law-firm culture is shared by people who are trained as attorneys.

Outsourcing Disadvantages

- Deploying an HR activity to an outsourcing firm may lead to loss of control over an important activity, which can be a costly problem. For example, by outsourcing employee recruiting to an external recruiting firm, the client company may experience missed deadlines on time-sensitive projects if the recruiting firm has other, more important clients to serve.
- Outsourcing an HR activity may result in losing the opportunity to gain knowledge and information that could benefit other company processes and activities. For example, outsourcing executive training and development to a company that provides a standardized training package can result in a lost opportunity to learn about the unique aspects of a firm's way of shaping leadership with respect to its own culture.

Sources: Based on Korkki, P. (2012, December 2). When the HR office leaves the building. *New York Times,* Sunday Business section, 8; Miller, S. (2007, December). Relationship advice for HR outsourcing buyers. *HRMagazine,* 55–56; Smith, S. (2005, May 9). Look before you leap into HR outsourcing. *Canadian HR Reporter,* 13; Kaplan, J. (2002, January 14). The realities of outsourcing. *Network World,* 33; Baron, J. and Kreps, D. (1999). *Strategic human resources: Frameworks for general managers.* New York: John Wiley & Sons.

Offshore Outsourcing The spectacular economic growth of China and India during the first decade of the twenty-first century has created lucrative opportunities for companies in North America, Europe, and Asia to take advantage of the professional skills and low labor costs provided by outsource firms in those two countries.[93] The labor-cost savings these offshore outsource firms can offer are impressive. For example, an information technology (IT) professional with three-to-five years of work experience would earn an annual salary of around $26,000 in India compared to about $75,000 in the United States. A call-center employee in India would earn around $2,000 a year, compared to $20,000 in Britain.[94] *Offshore outsourcing*, sometimes referred to as *offshoring*, refers to the use of international outsource providers to gain competitive advantage in the market.[95]

Offshore outsource providers in India are particularly competitive in offering services such as call centers, IT consulting, and software development. For example, Indian call-center providers handle customer-service calls and process insurance claims, loans, travel bookings, and credit-card bills.[96]

China has developed a high level of expertise in manufacturing. Chinese outsource firms manufacture a broad range of products for clients. These products range from consumer electronics such as television sets and DVDs to memory chips, to consumer goods such as microwave ovens, dishwashers, and toys for children, as well as autos and trucks. Currently, a large portion of the inventory of the goods sold in Walmart, the world's largest retail store, comes from Chinese suppliers who partner with Walmart. Additional information on offshore outsourcing can be found in Chapter 17 ("International HRM Challenge").

The Manager's Notebook, "Foreign Manufacturing Is Returning to the United States Due to the 'Reshoring' Trend," suggests that companies may have overlooked some of the pitfalls in outsourcing their factories to overseas locations.

MANAGER'S NOTEBOOK

Global

Foreign Manufacturing Is Returning to the United States Due to the "Reshoring" Trend

In a surprising turn of events, some U.S. manufacturers who had outsourced their manufacturing work to China and other low-wage countries have shifted some of their factory production back to the United States—a trend that is called "reshoring." For example, Apple Inc. recently announced it would start manufacturing some of its Mac computers in a newly built American facility. General Electric has opened a U.S. factory in Louisville, Kentucky, to make water heaters that had been made in China and refrigerators that were previously made in Mexico. Here are some of the reasons why factories are being relocated to the United States:

- Wages in China and India have increased at a rate of 10 to 20 percent per year in the last decade while wages in the United States and Europe have remained flat over the same period. Consequently, the wage advantage of doing work offshore has declined.
- Some American firms such as Apple Inc. and General Electric have realized that they went too far in sending their manufacturing overseas and decided they needed to make a correction to achieve a better balance in their supply chain systems.
- Offshoring companies have discovered unexpected costs that result from long lead times to bring products to market from an offshore production facility, as well as quality-control issues resulting from the separation of manufacturing from design and engineering teams. Case in point: The Boeing 787 Dreamliner aircraft has suffered numerous electrical system flaws in addition to the battery problems that led to its grounding in 2013. The engineers at Boeing blame the 787's outsourced supply chain, indicating that poor quality components coming from subcontractors outside Boeing's control are the source of the aircraft's problems.

Sources: Based on *The Economist* (2013, January 19). Special report: Outsourcing and offshoring, 3–5; Smith, A. (2013, March). Foreign factories come back home. *Kiplinger's Personal Finance*, 11; Gates, D. (2013, February 2). Boeing 787's problems blamed on outsourcing, lack of oversight. *Seattle Times*. *www.seattletimes.com*; Denning, S. (2013, January 17). The Boeing debacle: Seven lessons every CEO must learn. *Forbes*. *www.forbes.com*. ■■

CONTRACT WORKERS *Contract workers* are employees who develop work relationships directly with an employer (instead of with a subcontractor through an outsourcing arrangement) for a specific piece of work or time period.[97] They are likely to be self-employed, supply their own tools, and determine their hours of employment. Sometimes contract workers are called *consultants* or *freelancers*.

Many professionals with specialized skills become contract workers.[98] Hospitals use contract workers as emergency room physicians. Universities use them as adjunct professors to teach basic courses. Small businesses also are likely to use contract workers. When things get too busy for its 30 full-time employees, Ippolita, a New York City jewelry manufacturer, brings in a small army of freelancers—fashion experts, sculptors of miniature models, designers, and marketers. The biggest challenge is managing the relationship between freelancers and full-time employees.

Management has found it very beneficial to have written job descriptions for both full-time employees and contract workers so that everyone knows his or her specific assignment.[99]

Contract workers can often be more productive and efficient than in-house employees, because freelancers' time is usually not taken up with the inevitable company bureaucracy and meetings. They can also give companies a fresh outsider's perspective. However, it is not always easy to motivate a freelancer for whom you are one of several clients, each with urgent projects and pressing deadlines.

COLLEGE INTERNS One of the newest developments in the contingency work area is the use of *college interns*, college students who work on full-time or part-time assignments of short duration (usually for one academic semester or summer) to obtain work experience. Some interns are paid, some are not. Employers use interns to provide support to professional staff. Sometimes interns work a trial run for consideration as a potential core employee after graduation from college. Large companies that use college interns include IBM and General Electric (which have internships for electrical engineers), the Big Four accounting firms (which use interns on auditing engagements with clients), and Procter & Gamble (which uses interns in its sales and marketing areas).

College interns are also used extensively by small companies that want to attract employees who will grow with the company. For instance, at Seal Press, a small publishing company in Seattle, Washington, a woman who started as a marketing intern went on to become marketing assistant and is now marketing director. Editorial interns log in and read unsolicited manuscripts, write detailed reader's reports, and sometimes attend staff meetings. Because the work is challenging, there is a long waiting list of applicants.

Flexible Work Schedules

Flexible work schedules alter the scheduling of work while leaving intact the job design and the employment relationship. Employers may get higher levels of productivity and job satisfaction.[100] Employees may feel that they are trusted by management, which can improve the quality of employee relations (see Chapter 13).[101] Employees with flexible work schedules may also experience less stress by avoiding rush hour traffic.

The three most common types of flexible work schedules are flexible work hours, compressed workweeks, and telecommuting.

FLEXIBLE WORK HOURS Flexible work hours give employees control over the starting and ending times of their daily work schedules. Employees are required to put in a full 40-hour workweek at their onsite workstations, but have some control over the hours when they perform the work. **Flexible work hours** divide work schedules into **core time**, when all employees are expected to be at work, and *flexible time* (**flextime**), when employees can choose to organize work routines around personal activities.

flexible work hours
A work arrangement that gives employees control over the starting and ending times of their daily work schedules.

core time
Time when all employees are expected to be at work. Part of a flexible work hours arrangement.

flextime
Time during which employees can choose not to be at work. Part of a flexible work hours arrangement.

Hewlett-Packard's policy gives workers the flexibility to arrive at work between 6:30 A.M. and 8:30 A.M. and leave after they put in eight hours of work. Hewlett-Packard's core hours are between 8:30 A.M. and 2:30 P.M.[102] Meetings and team activities take place in this core time.

COMPRESSED WORKWEEKS *Compressed workweeks* alter the number of workdays per week by increasing the length of the workday to 10 or more hours. One type of compressed workweek schedule consists of four 10-hour workdays. Another consists of four 12-hour workdays in a four-days-on/four-days-off schedule. This schedule gives workers two 4-day blocks of time off every 16 days.[103]

Compressed workweeks create less potential for disruptions to businesses that provide 24-hour-per-day services, such as hospitals and police forces. They also lower absenteeism and tardiness at companies with work sites in remote locations that require long commutes to work (for example, off-shore oil-drilling platforms).

The major advantage of compressed workweeks for employees is that they are given three- or four-day weekends to spend with their families or to engage in personal interests. However, employees who work a compressed workweek may experience increased levels of stress and fatigue.[104]

Figure 2.8 shows the length of the workweek for full-time employment in different countries. Notice that the workweek ranges from 35 hours in France to 48 hours in Hong Kong.

TELECOMMUTING Personal computing devices, smartphones, fax machines, e-mail, and the Internet have created the opportunity for millions of people in the United States to work from a

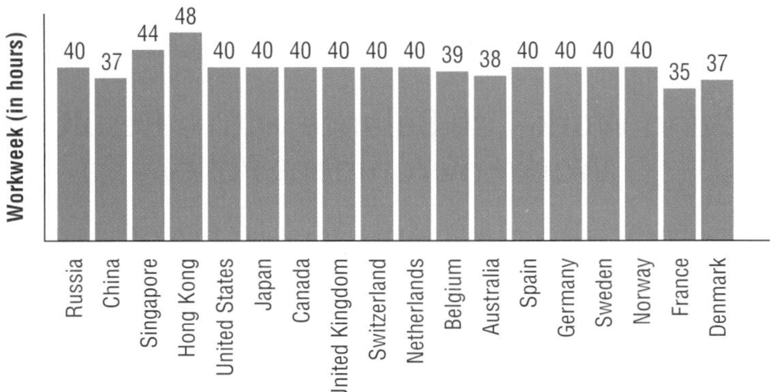

FIGURE 2.8

The Length of the Workweek in Selected Countries

Sources: Based on Briscoe, D., and Schuler, R. 2004. *International human resource management* (2nd ed.). New York: Routledge Press; Counting the hours. *OECD Observer* (2010) *www.oecdobserver.org;* Workweek and weekend. *Wikipedia* (2010) *www.wikipedia.org*.

home office or **telecommute.**[105] Telecommuting allows employees to cultivate tailored lifestyles while working a full-time job.[106]

telecommuting
A work arrangement that allows employees to work in their homes full-time, maintaining their connection to the office through smartphones and personal computing devices.

Telecommuting gives employers the flexibility to hire talented employees who might not otherwise be able to offer their services. Employers also save on office space costs with telecommuting. However, telecommuting does present several challenges to managers. We discuss these in detail in Chapter 13.

The Mobile Workplace

The widespread use of laptops and cell phones and the availability of Wi-Fi hot spots in many public places have given rise to a new work environment, one where employees can work from many different locations. Employees no longer have to be tethered to the office in order to work. Technology has freed employees to work in many different spatial locations, including team spaces, remote work centers, a home office, or the neighborhood coffee shop.[107]

Companies that have embraced the mobile workplace concept include clothing retailer GAP Outlet, Yum Brands, and the retailer Best Buy. The HR staff at Best Buy's corporate headquarters in Minneapolis implemented in 2005 a policy called "results-only work environment," or ROWE, which evaluates employees on output rather than the number of hours spent in the office. The ROWE policy has freed employees to do their work at the location of their choice. One employee was able to spend a few days a week at his vacation home in the woods; another manager was able to leave the office at 2:30 P.M. to pick up her young son from school. Employees viewed the ROWE policy as improving their work–life balance, and Best Buy reported that employee productivity in departments that switched to ROWE increased by an average 41 percent between 2005 and 2007, saving the company $16 million a year.[108] However, in 2013 the new CEO of Best Buy decided to end the ROWE policy as a way to assert more control as the company struggled to meet financial targets. Despite this reversal at Best Buy, ROWE has been implemented in over 40 companies.[109] **Work–life balance** describes the balance between an individual's work and personal life. The flexible workplace provides opportunities for employees to lead lives with better work–life balance so they can spend more time with their families and reduce work-related causes of stress.[110]

work–life balance
The balance between an individual's work and personal life.

The Manager's Notebook, "Improving Work–Life Balance with a Results-Only Work Environment Policy," provides suggestions on how to implement a policy that provides better work–life balance for employees.

Source: Jakub Zak/Shutterstock.

MANAGER'S NOTEBOOK

Emerging Trends

Improving Work–Life Balance with a Results-Only Work Environment Policy

Here are some tips for achieving better work–life balance with a results-only work environment (ROWE) policy so that employees can do whatever they want, whenever they want, as long as the job gets done.

- ***Set measureable goals.*** Create clear, written expectations for every employee, and track progress weekly. However, it is important to let employees decide how and when work will get done.
- ***Eradicate toxic language.*** Snide remarks about the number of hours people are putting in at the office can undermine a results-only effort. Managers should challenge the parties who make these discouraging comments as soon as they occur.
- ***Set an example.*** To get the ball rolling on a results-only effort, a manager should take the afternoon off. Although a manager may have good reasons to spend a lot of time at the office, it is a good idea to set an example of having work–life balance so that employees get the message that it is really OK to leave the office.

Sources: Based on Wescott, S. (2008, August). Beyond flextime: Trashing the workweek, *Inc.*, 1; Cullen, L. (2008, May 30). Finding freedom at work. *Time Online. http://content.time.com/time/business/article/0,8599,1810690,00.html.*

The KPMG accounting firm offers its employees a whole menu of ways to achieve a better work–life balance, including compressed workweeks, flexible hours of work, telecommuting, job sharing, and even reduced workloads. The company also has a policy that provides eight weeks of fully paid maternity leave that includes adoptive parents.[111]

Human Resource Information Systems

Human resource information systems (HRIS) are systems used to collect, record, store, analyze, and retrieve data concerning an organization's human resources.[112] Because most of today's HRIS are computerized, we will briefly explore two relevant issues: the applications of HRIS and the management of security and privacy issues related to HRIS.

human resource information system (HRIS)
A system used to collect, record, store, analyze, and retrieve data concerning an organization's human resources.

HRIS Applications

A computerized HRIS contains computer hardware and software applications that work together to help managers make HR decisions.[113] The software may be a custom-designed program or an off-the-shelf (prepackaged) applications program.

Figure 2.9 shows some HRIS software applications currently available to business. These include:

- An *employee information program* sets up a database that provides basic employee information: name, sex, address, phone number, date of birth, race, marital status, job title, and salary. Other applications programs can access the data in the employee information database for more specialized HR uses.
- An *applicant tracking program* can automate some of the labor-intensive activities associated with recruiting job applicants. These include storing job applicant information so that multiple users can access it and evaluate the applicant, scheduling interviews with different managers, updating the personal status of the job applicant, generating correspondence (for example, a job offer or a rejection letter), and producing the necessary equal employment opportunity (EEO) records required by the government.
- A *skills inventory* keeps track of the supply of job skills in the employer's workforce and searches for matches between skill supply and the organization's demand for job skills.

Applicant tracking	Flexible benefits enrollment system	Payroll
Basic employee information	Goal-setting system	Pension and retirement
Benefits administration	Health and safety	Performance management
Bonus and incentive management	Health insurance utilization	Short- and long-term disabilities
Career development/ planning	Hiring procedures	Skills inventory
Compensation budgeting	HR planning and forecasting	Succession planning
EEO/AA compliance	Job descriptions/analysis	Time and attendance
Employment history	Job evaluation	Travel costs
	Job posting	Turnover analysis
	Labor relations planning	

FIGURE 2.9

Selected Human Resource Information Systems Applications

Sources: Based on Dzamba, A. (2001, January). What are your peers doing to boost HRIS performance? *HR Focus,* 5–6; Kavanagh, M., Gueutal, H., and Tannenbaum, S. (1990). *Human resource information systems: Development and application,* 50. Boston: PWS-Kent; Brown, S. (2010). Human resource information systems–HRIS. *Ezine articles. www.ezinearticles.com.*

- A *payroll applications program* computes gross pay, federal taxes, state taxes, Social Security, other taxes, and net pay. It can also be programmed to make other deductions from the paycheck for such items as employee contributions to health insurance, employee contributions to a tax-deferred retirement plan, and union dues.
- A *benefits application program* can automate benefits record-keeping, administer various benefit programs, or provide advice about benefit choices. Benefits software can also provide an annual benefits statement for each employee.
- An *employee time management program* tracks the way each employee uses time on the job. The program monitors employee attendance, absenteeism, and tardiness.[114]

HRIS Security and Privacy

The HR department must develop policies and guidelines to protect the integrity and security of the HRIS. Unauthorized users of HRIS can create havoc. In one case, an executive who worked for a brokerage house tapped into her company's HRIS to get employee names and addresses for her husband, a life insurance agent who used the information to mail solicitations to his wife's colleagues. The solicited employees brought a million-dollar class-action suit against the company for invasion of privacy.[115] In another case, a computer programmer tapped into a computer company's HRIS, detected the salaries of a number of employees (including top managers and executives), and disclosed this information to other employees. The situation became very disruptive when angry employees demanded to know why large pay discrepancies existed.[116]

To maintain the security and privacy of HRIS records, companies should:

- Limit access to the HRIS by controlling access to the computer and its data files and locking the areas where they are stored and encrypting the data.
- Permit limited access to different portions of the database with the use of passwords and special codes.
- Grant permission to access employee information only on a need-to-know basis.
- Develop policies and guidelines that govern the utilization of employee information and notify employees how this policy works.
- Allow employees to verify and correct their personal records.

Summary and Conclusions

Work: The Organizational Perspective

A firm's business strategy determines how it structures its work. Under a defender strategy, work can be efficiently organized into a functional structure based on division of labor, with hierarchies of jobs assigned to functional units. Under a prospector strategy, decentralization and a low division of labor are more appropriate. The bureaucratic organizational structure is likely to be most effective when an organization is operating in a stable environment. The flat and the boundaryless organizational structures are more likely to be effective when organizations operate in uncertain environments that require flexibility.

Work-flow analysis examines how work creates or adds value to ongoing business processes. It helps managers determine if work is being accomplished as efficiently as possible. Work-flow analysis can be very useful in customer-focused programs and business-process reengineering.

Work: The Group Perspective

Flat and boundaryless organizational structures are likely to emphasize the use of self-managed teams (SMTs), small work units (between 6 and 18 employees) that are responsible for producing an entire product, a component, or an ongoing service. Businesses also use two other types of team designs. Problem-solving teams consist of volunteers from a unit or department who meet one or two hours per week to discuss quality improvement, cost reduction, or improvement in the work environment. Special-purpose teams consist of members who span functional or organizational boundaries and whose purpose is to examine complex issues. Virtual teams allow geographically separated employees to collaborate together on projects or special problems by interacting on the computer or via other technology.

Work: The Individual Perspective

Motivation theory seeks to explain how different job designs can affect employee motivation. Four important work motivation theories are the two-factor, work adjustment, goal-setting, and job characteristics theories.

Designing Jobs and Conducting Job Analysis

Job design is the process of organizing work into the tasks required to perform a specific job. Different approaches to job design are work simplification, job enlargement, job rotation, job enrichment, and team-based job designs.

Job analysis is the systematic process of gathering and organizing information concerning the tasks, duties, and responsibilities of jobs. It is the basic building block of many important HR activities. Job analysis can be used for purposes of legal compliance, recruitment, selection, performance appraisal, compensation, and training and career development. Given the lack of a single best job-analysis technique, the choice of technique should be guided by the purposes of the analysis.

Job descriptions are statements of a job's essential duties, responsibilities, working conditions, and specifications. They are derived from job analysis. Job descriptions, which can be specific or general, have four elements: identification information, job summary, job duties and responsibilities, and job specifications and minimum qualifications.

The Flexible Workforce

Flexible work designs help managers deal with unexpected jolts in the environment and accommodate the needs of a diverse workforce. To maintain flexibility in the workforce, employers can use contingent workers (temporary employees, part-time employees, outsourced subcontractors, contract workers, and college interns). They can also alter work with flexible work schedules (flexible work hours, compressed workweeks, and telecommuting). Employees benefit from flexible work schedules by attaining greater work–life balance.

Human Resource Information Systems

Human resource information systems (HRIS) are systems used to collect, record, store, analyze, and retrieve relevant HR data. HRIS data matched with the appropriate computer software have many applications that support HR activities. These include applicant tracking, skills inventories, payroll management, and benefits administration. It is important that the HR department develop policies to protect the security of the HRIS data and the privacy rights of its employees.

Key Terms

boundaryless organizational structure, 76
bureaucratic organizational structure, 74
business process reengineering (BPR), 77
contingent workers, 95
core time, 100
core workers, 95
flat organizational structure, 74
flexible work hours, 100
flextime, 100

human resource information system (HRIS), 102
job analysis, 85
job description, 91
job design, 83
job enlargement, 84
job enrichment, 84
job rotation, 84
job sharing, 96
job specifications, 94
knowledge, skills, and abilities (KSAs), 87
motivation, 81
organizational structure, 73
problem-solving team, 79
self-managed team (SMT), 78
special-purpose team, 79
team, 78
telecommuting, 101
virtual team, 80
work flow, 73
work-flow analysis, 77
work–life balance, 101

Watch It!

Weather Channel: Talent Management. If your instructor has assigned this, go to **mymanagementlab.com** to watch a video case and answer questions.

Discussion Questions

2-1. Are managers likely to question the work commitment of their contingent workers? What might be the consequences for management when the majority of a company's workforce consists of temporary employees and contract workers?

2-2. What are the drawbacks to using flexible work hours from the organization's perspective? Compressed workweeks? Telecommuting? How should the HR department deal with these challenges?

2-3. For some organizations self-managed teams seem to be the way forward, but why do they need an extended period of time before they are fully effective? It seems to be the case that self-managed teams are more efficient and they can handle the same or greater volume of work with actually less members. If this is the case, why haven't more organizations turned to this solution? What exactly does HRM have to do to provide the necessary training and development? What are the practicalities of dealing with self-managed teams rather than more conventional leader and follower hierarchically orientated structures? Which industries are more likely to favor self-managed teams?

2-4. A recent trend that more and more companies are embracing is to outsource all or most of their human resource management activities. Do you agree or disagree with this trend? What risks is a company taking when it decides to outsource its entire set of human resource management activities? Try to describe a situation in which it is more beneficial to retain most of the human resource management activities within a company so that HR is provided by the human resource management department.

2-5. Temporary employees are being used with increasing regularity throughout the world. In France, one in five workers is on a temporary or part-time contract, and in the UK more than 25 percent of the workforce is part-time. Almost 33 percent of new jobs created in Spain were for temporary workers. During the height of the recession in 2010, 26 percent of all private-sector jobs in the United States were temporary positions. What are the key advantages to employers in hiring temporary workers? Are there any advantages for employees? How common is temporary work in your own country?

MyManagementLab®

If your instructor has assigned this, go to **mymanagementlab.com** for the following Assisted-graded writing questions:

2-6. Are job descriptions really necessary? Provide several of the advantages (at least three) to a company that decides to avoid using job descriptions. Next, briefly describe some situations that would be most favorable for a company that decides to avoid using job descriptions. Include factors such as company size, industry, organization design, work flow, and use of teams in your analysis.

2-7. Companies are currently attempting to develop policies that offer more flexible work arrangements that allow employees to achieve better work–life balance. Briefly describe several popular approaches that could be considered for helping employees achieve work–life balance and indicate the advantages and disadvantages of each work–life balance option.

2-8. Large U.S. companies such as Accenture, AOL, and Dell have outsourced customer-service call centers to India. Customers use these call centers for help when they are having difficulty using the services provided by these companies. Many of the outsourced jobs at the call centers were entry-level jobs that had the potential to lead to higher-skilled jobs at those firms. Provide at least three ethical employment issues that managers who use offshore outsource suppliers in India or other low–labor cost countries should be concerned about.

You Manage It! 1: Ethics/Social Responsibility

Are Companies Exploiting College Students Who Have Unpaid Internships?

More than half of college students who graduate have had one or more internships, according to the National Association of Colleges and Employers. From one-fourth to one-half of the internships for college students are unpaid. Unpaid internships exist in for-profit firms for students to gain entry into careers that receive many job applicants, such as in fashion, book and magazine publishing, art galleries, sports management, and film and television. Internships give college students an opportunity to gain valuable job skills that can lead to job offers after they graduate. According to U.S. Department of Labor regulations, when private-sector companies provide unpaid internships for college students, the internship is expected to benefit the intern and be similar to vocational training so that useful job skills are imparted to the intern. In practice, for-profit firms consider unpaid internships to be legitimate as long as the students receive academic credit for their work. This college-credit loophole has tempted some companies to pile on their interns a large amount of unskilled work.

Many students have reported that they have held internships that involved noneducational and menial work. It is not unusual for unpaid internships to involve some menial work; however, when most of the work consists of unskilled labor, the unpaid internship can be in violation of the law. In one such case, a student at an Ivy League university said she devoted most of her time during an unpaid internship at a magazine publisher packaging and shipping 20 or more apparel samples per day back to fashion houses that had provided them for fashion shoots. In another case, a children's film company provided an unpaid internship to a New York University student who had hoped to work in animation at the film company. Instead, this student was told to work in the facilities department and was ordered to wipe the door handles each day to minimize the spread of swine flu.

It is true that some unpaid internships can provide useful job skills to college students that they can put on their resumes to attract an employer's attention. However, as illustrated by the examples in this case, some unpaid internships end up being little more than a collection of routine tasks and do little to improve a student's professional skill set. With the current high levels of U.S. and European youth unemployment, some companies are tempted to take advantage of unpaid internships as a low-cost source of exploitable labor.

Critical Thinking Questions

2-9. Although it is illegal for profit-based companies to create unpaid internships that require college interns to perform primarily menial tasks, unfortunately this is happening with increasing regularity. What can students do to avoid the experience of having an unpaid internship that consists of mostly menial work with few opportunities to learn new skills?

2-10. Does the university have a responsibility to ensure that a student's unpaid internship will be a legitimate learning experience that earns college credits toward graduation? How can the university ensure that a company provides the unpaid intern a legitimate learning experience while still giving the company the flexibility to deploy the unpaid intern in ways that are useful to the company?

Team Exercise

2-11. Form a small group with several of your class members and take turns sharing your experiences with paid and unpaid internships. Which internships provided better learning experiences—the ones that were paid or the ones that were unpaid by the sponsoring company? After each person in the group has had the opportunity to share their internship experiences, the group will collectively develop a list of three or four practices that students should follow to avoid having a bad experience in an unpaid internship. Be prepared to present your findings to other members of the class.

Experiential Exercise: Team

2-12. What kind of internship would be ideal for you at the end of this program of study? What opportunities do you think there are in your own country or will you have to travel in order to find the right kind of opportunity? In the role of someone looking for imminent internship, investigate the opportunities as a small team. Find at least two others that are looking for similar opportunities. Begin by listing the experiential learning opportunities you would hope to find. Now try and match these against domestic organizations. Do they accept internships? Would you want to have an internship with them? If either question is negative broaden your search to the region and then globally. What hurdles might be in the way of finding internship abroad? Now think about the supporting structures around internship and investigate whether your government, charities, or other organizations help organize and fund internships. What criteria do they use? If no such support exists, how would you "sell" the concept of internship support to them? What have previous cohorts of students done in order to find suitable internships with or without support?

Sources: Based on Greenhouse, S. (2012, May 5). Jobs few, grads flock to unpaid internships. *New York Times. www.nytimes.com*; Chatzky, J. (2011, November 21). The great American internship swindle, *Newsweek,* 22; Guerrero, A. (2013, April 3). Should you take an unpaid internship? *U.S. News & World Report. http://money.usnews.com/money/careers/articles/2013/04/03/should-you-take-an-unpaid-internship*; Greenhouse, S. (2010, April 2). The unpaid intern, legal or not. *New York Times. www.nytimes.com.*

You Manage It! 2: Emerging Trends

Work–Life Balance Is the New Perk Employees Are Seeking

Joe (not his real name) has risen through the corporate ranks to become an executive at a major bank. He thought his workload would become lighter as he moved up, but the opposite has occurred. He now works 6 or 7 days a week, from multiple locations. He keeps an apartment in New York and is on the road another 3 or 4 days per week. Only on weekends does he see his wife and three children, who live in Connecticut.

Does this sound like fun to you? No? Well, you are not alone. Although some ambitious individuals are willing to sacrifice their personal life to satisfy their ambition, a growing number are not. According to a recent survey by the Association of Executive Search Consultants (AESC), 85 percent of recruiters have seen candidates reject a job offer because it lacked work–life balance.

For companies competing for talent, it is becoming increasingly important to provide work–life balance in the positions they are seeking to fill. The AESC survey revealed that two-thirds of companies are developing programs to help top recruits increase their family time without sacrificing their careers.

Job candidates are learning that they can bargain with their employer for more than money. Lisa Patten, a director at the accounting firm PricewaterhouseCoopers (PwC), proved this point when she was being recruited from her previous employer. Because she was not dissatisfied with her former employer, she compiled a list of requests to PwC that included a 4-day workweek so she could spend more time with her children, and the flexibility to work from home if not on a client visit. PwC did not hesitate to approve these flexible work conditions for Patten.

Although Patten's productivity in terms of billable hours and new business brought to the firm increased, PwC has found that flexible work is not a good fit for every employee. It reports that employees most likely to be given flexibility in work hours and location are those who are disciplined and self-motivated and have a clear set of performance measures to ensure accountability.

Critical Thinking Questions

2-13. Which types of jobs are best suited for flexibility with regard to hours and office location? Which types of jobs are less likely to afford this type of flexibility? Explain.

2-14. Earlier in this chapter, you learned that most work in today's workplace is now being done by teams of employees. In your opinion, does the intensive use of self-managed teams make it easier or more difficult for employees to achieve work–life balance? Explain.

Team Exercise

2-15. Form a small group with several class members and discuss the following scenario: The owner-manager of a small, four-person consulting firm works long hours on multiple projects and expects his three associates to spend most of their time in the office to learn consulting skills from him and to attend meetings with clients that take place at the office. What objections would the owner-manager have if the three associates requested policies promoting greater work–life balance? How could the associates present their interest for greater work flexibility in a way that is likely to receive a positive outcome? Be prepared to present your answers to the whole class.

Experiential Exercise: Individual

2-16. The concept of work–life balance is applicable if it is possible to retain and sustain your social and family life at the same time as following a career path. For many, the prospect of having to relocate in order to pursue a career is a very real one and with it there is the danger that the work–life balance will be undermined. Would the need for mobility be a factor in your intended career? How do you think your work–life balance would be impacted if you were to relocate?

Sources: Based on Ridge, S. (2007, March 19). Balance: The new workplace perk. *Forbes.com. www.forbes.com/2007/03/19/work-life-health-lead-careers-worklife07-cz_sr_0319ridge.html*; Hewlett, S., and Luce, C. (2006, December). Extreme jobs: The dangerous allure of the 70-hour workweek. *Harvard Business Review*, 49–59; Shipman, C., and Kay, K. (2009, June 1). A saner workplace. *Businessweek*, 66–69.

 You Manage It! 3: Technology/Social Media

Yahoo CEO Issues a Ban on Telecommuting for Employees

In February 2013 Yahoo CEO Marissa Mayer decided that starting in June, all Yahoo employees would be expected to come to their offices each day to perform their jobs. In effect, this decision resulted in a ban on telecommuting, impacting the work lives of many Yahoo employees who had been working at home. CEO Mayer made this decision after noticing the high number of vacant spaces in the Yahoo corporate parking lot and the scarcity of people occupying cubicles in the building. Yahoo's financial performance had been disappointing for several years prior to announcing the telecommuting ban, and consequently the previous CEO had been dismissed by the board of directors before Ms. Mayer was recruited from Google in 2012 to assume the top job. The justification for the restriction on telecommuting was that by requiring employees to be present at the office, Yahoo would benefit from an anticipated increase in productivity and innovation that should stimulate Yahoo's performance in the competitive technology industry.

The restriction on employee telecommuting runs counter to the conventional wisdom accepted in many companies that giving employees the freedom to work at a location of their choice would have benefits for the company as well as for the employee. Currently, 20 to 30 million Americans work from home at least once a week. For example, IBM is a company in which just under 50 percent of its employees do not have a regular office; instead, they telecommute and occasionally use hoteling offices, which consist of company-owned office space that can be reserved depending on where an employee is situated at a particular time. Under this arrangement IBM—with a global workforce of over 300,000 employees—achieves significant savings on the cost of leasing and maintaining office space. Cisco, a giant technology company based in Silicon Valley, California, claimed in 2009 that it saved $277 million a year by allowing its employees to telecommute.

The decision to tether Yahoo employees to their company offices also generated mixed comments from other executives. Sir Richard Branson, founder of Virgin Atlantic Airways and Virgin Records, wrote a critical blog post that the decision was "a backwards step in an age when remote working is easier and more effective than ever." Taking an opposing position was Donald Trump, chairman and president of The Trump Organization, founder of Trump Entertainment Resorts, and star of the NBC reality show *The Apprentice,* who indicated on Twitter that CEO Mayer was "right to expect Yahoo employees to come to the workplace versus working at home."

Critical Thinking Questions

2-17. Do you agree or disagree with the CEO's decision to ban employees from telecommuting at Yahoo? What is the basis of your position?

2-18. Critics of the decision to restrict telecommuting at Yahoo point to the poor financial and stock market performance of Yahoo in the years prior to this order, and they suggest that the CEO's motive was to impress investors by displaying more control over Yahoo employees. It is likely that the CEO expected—by mandating that employees be present in the office on a regular basis—that they would have more fortuitous conversations in the corridors of Yahoo that would likely lead to increased levels of innovation and new product development. Can you think of alternative ways that the company could engage employee innovation and creativity without restricting their freedom to work at home?

Team Exercise

2-19. Form a small group of four or five students and discuss your preference for the type of learning environment in which you can take a human resource management course for university credit and learn most effectively. Choose between (a) an online learning course, or (b) taking the course in a traditional classroom setting with other students and a professor who teaches the course. What are the advantages and disadvantages of online learning versus learning in a regular classroom environment? What situational factors (type of course, number of students, student learning styles) are most favorable to online learning? Which factors are most favorable to classroom learning? What insights does this comparison between online learning and traditional classroom learning provide regarding the decision at Yahoo to restrict all employees from telecommuting? Be prepared to share your insights with other students in the class.

Experiential Exercise: Individual

2-20. Assume that you are employed at Yahoo as a marketing analyst and you have just been told that you no longer are allowed to telecommute from your home office. Instead, you will now be expected to do all of your work at the headquarters in Sunnyvale, California, in Silicon Valley. The traffic is very heavy during your commute from your home in San Jose to the office in Sunnyvale, and you dislike making the 40-minute commute each way to the office. You enjoyed working at your home office two or three days per week, and now that privilege has been taken away by the new HR policy at Yahoo restricting telecommuting. Which of the following three tactics would you most likely choose if you found yourself in the situation described in this exercise? Would you (a) remain as an employee at Yahoo and voice your feelings to management; (b) remain as an employee at Yahoo and keep silent; or (c) start a job search to find employment at a company that is more supportive of telecommuters? Explain the reasons for your choice of tactics and be prepared to share with other students the thinking behind your decision.

Sources: Based on *The Economist*. (2013, March 2). Corralling the Yahoos, 61; Weise, E. (2013, February 26). Telecommuters to Yahoo: Boo. *USA Today*, 1A; Lawler, E. E. (2011). Creating a new employment deal: Total rewards and the new workforce. *Organizational Dynamics*, 40, 302–309; Suddath, C. (2013, March 4). Work-from-home truths, half-truths, and myths. *Bloomberg Businessweek*, 75; *The Economist*. (2013, March 2). Mayer culpa, 14; Miller, C., and Rampell, C. (2013, February 26). Yahoo orders home workers back to the office. *New York Times*, A1, A3.

You Manage It! 4: Customer-Driven HR

Writing a Job Description

Job descriptions are useful tools that document job content and that can aid decisions for recruitment, staffing, training, compensation, and human resource planning. The purpose of this skill-building activity is to give you some experience writing a job description. In preparation, carefully read the section in this chapter titled "Job Descriptions" and refer to the figures in that section that provide examples of a specific job description and a general job description.

Next, select a job and write a job description. Ideally, your job description should be based on a job you are familiar with—the best candidate for this exercise is one at which you are currently employed or recently experienced. It could be a part-time or full-time job. If you have no work experience to draw from for this exercise, then ask a friend or relative to provide detailed information about his or her job.

Once you have chosen the job for this exercise you are ready to begin.

Critical Thinking Questions

2-21. What do you see as the main differences between a specific job description and a general job description?

2-22. Suppose several people are employed in the same job as the one for which you are writing a job description. Would it be necessary to write a different job description for each person who works in the same job? Explain.

2-23. Carefully follow the format for the "Specific Job Description" provided in Figure 2.6 when writing the job description for the job you selected. Make sure that you include in your job description the following elements: (1) job title and identification information, (2) job summary, (3) job duties and responsibilities, (4) job requirements, and (5) minimum qualifications. Check your work to make sure the style of your job description matches the example in the text as closely as possible.

Team Exercise

2-24. Work with a partner or a small group of three to four people and exchange job descriptions with your partner or a group member. Read each other's job descriptions and make suggestions for improvements based on the example provided in the text. Take turns discussing the suggested revisions with your partner or group so that each person receives some feedback on his or her job description. Make revisions to your job description as needed to improve it. It is normal for a job description to go through several revisions before the document is finished. Now examine the job description you just wrote and revised. Discuss with your partner or group how this job description could be applied to making decisions in the organization that offers the job. Next, discuss what additional steps would be needed to finalize the job description before it could actually be used as a basis for employment decisions in a company.

Experiential Exercise: Individual

2-25. The purpose of this experiential exercise is to learn how managers actually use job descriptions in their organizations. First, you will need to get the names and contact information for three to five managers you know either from your work experience or from personal contact. Or, ask a professor or someone in the career development office at your school for the names of a few managers. You can contact the managers in person, by e-mail, or on the telephone. Ask each manager what uses they have for job descriptions in their organizations. Also, ask the managers how important job descriptions are for making human resource decisions in their organizations—and follow up one more time by asking them to explain why they think that job descriptions are important (or not). Record the responses and summarize your findings. Be prepared to share your findings with other members of the class. Did you find a diversity of opinion from the managers about how they use job descriptions and how important they find them to be? If you did find a diverse set of responses, what do you think accounted for this variety of opinions?

Endnotes

Scan for Endnotes or go to http://www.pearsonglobaleditions.com/Gomez-Mejia.

CHAPTER 3 Understanding Equal Opportunity and the Legal Environment

MyManagementLab®

When you see this icon, visit **www.mymanagementlab.com** for activities that are applied, personalized, and offer immediate feedback.

CHALLENGES

After reading this chapter, you should be able to deal more effectively with the following challenges:

1. **Recognize** why understanding the legal environment is important.
2. **Become** aware of conflicting strategies for fair employment.
3. **Gain** mastery of the equal employment opportunity laws.
4. **Understand** EEO enforcement and compliance.
5. **Have** familiarity with other important laws.
6. **Ensure** avoiding pitfalls in EEO.

Discrimination claims are always difficult for companies, so it is important to stay current with trends in the legal environment. An emerging trend involves claims of employment discrimination based on an employee's appearance. Being aware of the legal standards that are used in such cases can help you prevent a company's employees from taking their discrimination claims to court. The following are some examples of cases related to personal appearance:

Source: © Hero Images Inc./Alamy.

- While many people wear tattoos as a form of personal expression, some companies are not tolerant of visible tattoos in the workplace. Walmart has a standard dress code policy in its stores that requires employees with tattoos to keep them concealed. At Red Robin Gourmet Burgers, an employee was fired for violating a dress code prohibiting visible tattoos on his wrists. However, the tattoos contained religious symbols and the company agreed to pay the discharged employee $150,000 in an out-of-court settlement.[1]
- In California, a female employee refused to wear makeup as required by her employer. The employee alleged that the employer was engaging in gender stereotyping by requiring female beverage servers to wear makeup. Although the employee was unable to provide enough evidence to prevail in this case, in other legal jurisdictions, such as Madison, Wisconsin, city laws forbid discrimination based on physical appearance.
- Debrahlee Lorenzana was fired from her job as a banker at a Citibank branch in New York City because her appearance was too distracting to the men around her, who could not concentrate on their work. Ms. Lorenzana's bosses ordered her to wear modest clothing, and she was forbidden to wear turtleneck sweaters, three-inch heels, or fitted

business suits. Ms. Lorenzana claimed that her female colleagues wore far more revealing clothing than she did, and she refused to let her bosses dictate what clothes she could wear to work. She sued the company based on the discriminatory treatment she is alleged to have received. Ultimately the case never went to court and the plaintiff decided to drop the lawsuit.

Employers can avoid legal entanglements by developing employment policies and practices that avoid the discriminatory treatment of employees. For example, appearance policies should not place an undue burden on one gender and not on the other. In addition, appearance requirements should be applied to employees only when they are necessary to achieve a specific business purpose. If the employers who forced their employees to wear makeup or hide religious symbols had instead considered how to minimize their exposure to employment discrimination, they could have avoided having to defend their employment practices in court.[2]

The Managerial Perspective

Managers must understand the legal issues that affect the practice of HRM because many of their decisions are constrained to some extent by law. They should consider legal issues when making the following decisions:

- Which employees to hire
- How to compensate employees
- What benefits to offer
- How to accommodate employees with dependents
- How and when to fire employees

Legal constraints on HR practices have become increasingly more complex, in large part because of new employment laws and recent court decisions that interpret existing laws. The new employment laws mainly affect people with disabilities and those who seek a medical leave of absence from work. The court decisions relate to numerous issues such as worker safety and sexual harassment. Changes in the law have made HR decisions more difficult and risky—thereby increasing the cost of poor decisions.

HR managers consult and advise managers about the legal aspects of a personnel decision. Legal concerns are not the only priority in employment decisions, but they are heavily considered along with other factors such as timeliness, product quality, and economic efficiency. The dynamism of the legal environment means that managers must seek the advice of HR specialists who, in turn, add value to management decisions with their expertise in employment laws and regulations.

In this chapter, we examine the various aspects of HR law and regulation. First, we look at why managers must understand the HR legal environment. Next we explore several challenges that managers face when they try to comply with the law. Then we discuss *equal employment opportunity (EEO)* law, the enforcement mechanisms in place to ensure compliance, and several other laws that affect HRM. Finally, we describe ways for the effective manager to avoid potential legal pitfalls.

We need to start with a caveat. As with any legal issue you face, you should seek the advice of a qualified attorney to grapple with specific legal questions or problems relating to HRM. Many lawyers specialize in labor and employment law. However, you should not feel that you cannot make *any* decisions without specific legal counsel, and it is a mistake to let legal considerations become so important that you end up making poor business decisions. One goal of this chapter is to give you enough information to know when you need to seek legal counsel.

✪ Learn It!

If your professor has chosen to assign this go to **www.mymanagementlab.com** to see what you should particularly focus on, and take the chapter 3 warmup.

Why Understanding the Legal Environment Is Important

Understanding and complying with HR law is important for three reasons. It helps you to do the right thing, realize the limitations of your firm's HR and legal departments, and minimize your firm's potential liability.

Doing the Right Thing

First and foremost, compliance with the law is important because it is the right thing to do. Although you may disagree with the specific applications of some of the laws we discuss, the primary requirement of all these laws is to mandate good management practice. The earliest of the EEO laws requires that male and female employees who do the same job for the same organization receive the same pay. This is the right thing to do. A more recent EEO law requires that applicants or employees who are able to perform a job should not be discriminated against because of a disability. This, too, is the right thing to do.

Operating within these laws has benefits beyond simple legal compliance. Compensation practices that discriminate against women not only create potential legal liability, but also lead to poor employee morale and low job satisfaction, which can, in turn, lead to poor job performance. Discriminating against qualified employees with disabilities makes no sense; in discriminating, the organization hurts itself by not hiring and retaining the best employees. McDonald's has taken the lead in hiring youth with learning disabilities. This is socially responsible and has created a positive impression among many customers.[3]

Realizing the Limitations of the HR and Legal Departments

A firm's HR department has considerable responsibilities with respect to HR law. These include keeping records, writing and implementing good HR policies, and monitoring the firm's HR decisions. However, if managers make poor decisions, the HR department will not always be able to resolve the situation. For instance, if a manager gives a poor employee an excellent performance rating, the HR department cannot undo the damage and provide the documentation necessary to support a decision to terminate the employee.

Nor can a firm's legal department magically solve problems created by managers. One of the key functions of legal counsel, whether internal or external, is to try to limit damage after it has occurred. Managers should work to prevent the damage from happening in the first place.

Members of the HR department support managers who have to make HR decisions with legal implications. HR staff may monitor managers' decisions or act as consultants. For example:

- A supervisor wants to discharge an employee for unexcused absences and consults the HR department to determine whether there is enough evidence to discharge this person for "just cause." The HR department can help the manager and the company avoid a lawsuit for "wrongful discharge."
- A manager receives a phone call from a company that is inquiring about the qualifications of a former employee. The manager is not sure how of much information in the former employee's work history to reveal, so she seeks the HR department's advice. HR can help the manager and the company avoid a lawsuit for defamation (damage to an employee's reputation as a result of giving out false information to a third party).

Limiting Potential Liability

Considerable financial liabilities can occur when HR laws are broken or perceived to be broken. Typical court awards to victims of age, sex, race, or disability discrimination range from \$50,000 to \$300,000, depending on the size of the employer. Nonetheless, individual awards can actually be much larger.[4] In 2001, the U.S. federal appeals court upheld a jury verdict awarding Troy Swinton \$1.03 million for punitive damages, back wages, and emotional stress for racial discrimination suffered at U.S. Mat in Woodinville, Washington. The only African American of 140 employees, Swinton was subjected to a regular stream of racial "jokes" and slurs during his six months of employment.[5]

Organizations may also face a public relations nightmare when discrimination charges are publicized. In highly publicized cases in the early 1990s, several individual store managers and employees of Denny's restaurant chain were alleged to have discriminated against African

American customers. Not only did the company subsequently have to pay $46 million to African American patrons and $8.7 million in legal fees to settle these complaints, but the company's image with customers was damaged as well.[6] In recent years, though, Denny's has made major strides: As of 2007, minorities owned 43 percent of Denny's 1,030 franchised restaurants. African Americans owned 23, Hispanics owned 60, and Asians owned 359. In 1993, only one franchised restaurant was owned by an African American. Further, *Fortune* has consistently recognized Denny's at the top ranks of its survey of "America's 50 Best Companies for Minorities."[7]

Challenges to Legal Compliance

Several challenges confront managers attempting to comply with HR law. These include a dynamic legal landscape, the complexity of regulations, conflicting strategies for fair employment, and unintended consequences.

A Dynamic Legal Landscape

A quick scan of the Appendix to this chapter clearly demonstrates that many laws affect the practice of HRM. Several have been passed in the last decade.

The opinions handed down in court cases add to this dynamic environment. For example, in 1971 the Supreme Court handed down a landmark civil rights decision in a case titled *Griggs v. Duke Power*.[8] Among other things, this decision placed a heavy burden of proof on the employer in an employment discrimination case. Normally, a Supreme Court decision sets a precedent that the Court is then very reluctant to overturn. However, in a 1989 case the Court revised the standard it had set in *Griggs*, making it more difficult for an employee to win a discrimination case.[9] Then, in 1991, Congress passed a lengthy amendment to the Civil Rights Act of 1964 (discussed later in this chapter) that returned to the burden-of-proof standard established in the *Griggs* decision.

These rapid changes are not limited to issues of courtroom procedure. Sexual harassment regulations were adopted by the Equal Employment Opportunity Commission (EEOC) in the early 1980s and accepted by the Supreme Court in 1986. Since then, companies, lawyers, and judges have been attempting to figure out just what they mean and require. Opinions on these issues vary widely, which means that different courts have made differing decisions about what constitutes sexual harassment. Until the Supreme Court makes several more rulings, or Congress clarifies the underlying law, managers will need to pay close attention to the unfolding developments.

The Complexity of Laws

HR law, like most other types of law, is very complex. Each individual law is accompanied by a set of regulations that can be lengthy. For instance, the Americans with Disabilities Act (1990) is spelled out in a technical manual that is several hundred pages long. To make matters even more complex, one analysis has concluded that there may be as many as 1,000 different disabilities affecting over 43 million Americans.[10] It is very difficult for an expert in HR law, much less a manager, to understand all the possible implications of a particular law.

Nonetheless, the gist of most HR law is fairly straightforward. Managers should be able to understand the basic intention of all such laws without too much difficulty and easily obtain the working knowledge they need to comply with those laws in the vast majority of situations.

Conflicting Strategies for Fair Employment

Society at large, political representatives, government employees, and judges all have different views regarding the best ways to achieve equitable HR laws. One of the major debates in this area centers on the competing strategies used to further the goal of **fair employment**—the situation in which employment decisions are not affected by illegal discrimination. The plain language of most civil rights law prohibits employers from making decisions about employees (hiring, performance appraisal, compensation, and so on) on the basis of race, sex, or age. Thus, one strategy to reach the goal of fair employment is for employment decisions to be made without regard to these characteristics. A second strategy, **affirmative action**, aims to accomplish the goal of fair employment by urging employers to hire certain groups of people who were discriminated against in the past. Thus, affirmative action programs require that employment decisions be made, at least in part, on the basis of characteristics such as race, sex, or age. Obviously, there

fair employment
The goal of EEO legislation and regulation: a situation in which employment decisions are not affected by illegal discrimination.

affirmative action
A strategy intended to achieve fair employment by urging employers to hire certain groups of people who were discriminated against in the past.

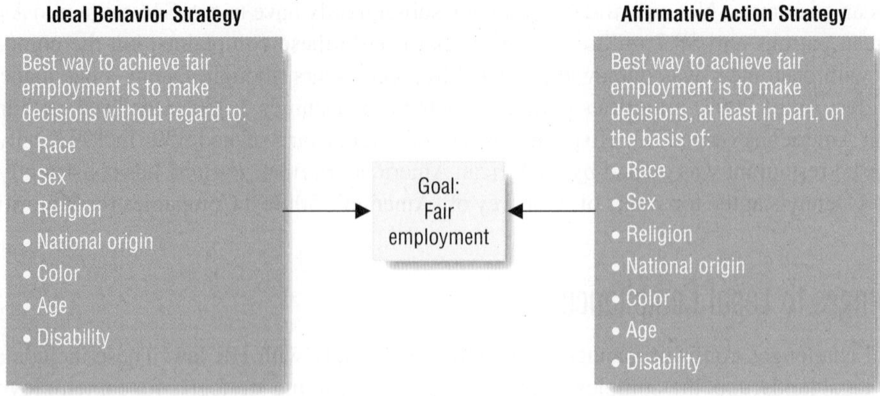

FIGURE 3.1
Competing Strategies for Fair Employment

> A QUESTION OF ETHICS
> Is it ethical to refuse to give preferential treatment to minorities and women, who have been widely discriminated against in the past?

is a conflict between these two strategies—one proposing that only "blind" hiring practices are fair, the other proposing that fairness requires organizations to make an effort to employ certain categories of people (Figure 3.1).

While the battle resulting from these competing strategies is being played out throughout society, the main legal struggle has occurred in the Supreme Court. Based on a series of Supreme Court decisions, the following conclusions seem warranted:

- The affirmative action strategy has been upheld. Specifically, employers are permitted to base employment decisions, in part, on a person's race, sex, age, and certain other characteristics.
- To be permissible, the employment decision cannot be made solely on the basis of these characteristics. Further, the people considered for the position should be "essentially equally qualified" on job-relevant characteristics before these other characteristics are permitted to play a role in the employment decision.
- The one situation in which affirmative action is not permitted is during layoffs. For instance, a white teacher should not be laid off to save the job of a Latino teacher, even if this means that minorities will be underrepresented in the postlayoff workforce.

Unintended Consequences

It is very common for a law, a government program, or an organizational policy to have numerous unanticipated consequences, some of which turn out to be negative. HR law is certainly not immune to this phenomenon. For example, the Americans with Disabilities Act (ADA) was primarily intended to increase the possibility of employment for people with physical and/or mental disabilities. However, since the law has gone into effect, job applicants have filed relatively few ADA complaints. Rather, current employees injured on the job have filed the majority of complaints. Traditionally, state workers' compensation laws (see Chapter 12) regulate the benefits given to employees injured on the job, including income continuation. Nobody intended the ADA to become a national workers' compensation law, but that appears to be just what is happening. The challenge to managers is to anticipate and deal with both the intended and unintended consequences of law.

Equal Employment Opportunity Laws

The laws that affect HR issues can be divided into two broad categories: (1) equal employment opportunity laws and (2) everything else. We will spend the bulk of this chapter on the EEO laws because these are the ones that most affect a manager's day-to-day behavior. In addition, the EEO laws cut across almost every other issue that we discuss in this text. The other laws tend to be more specifically focused, and we discuss them in the context in which they apply. For instance, we discuss the laws governing union activities in Chapter 15 and the Occupational Safety and Health Act (OSHA) in Chapter 16.

The major EEO laws are the Equal Pay Act of 1963, Title VII of the Civil Rights Act of 1964, the Age Discrimination in Employment Act of 1967, and the Americans with Disabilities Act of 1990. The Civil Rights Act of 1964 has been amended through the years, most recently in 1991. The theme that ties these laws together is simple: Employment decisions should not be based on characteristics such as race, sex, age, or disability.

The Equal Pay Act of 1963

The first of the civil rights laws was the **Equal Pay Act**, which became law in 1963. It requires that men and women who do the same job in the same organization should receive the same pay. "Same pay" means that no difference is acceptable.

Equal Pay Act (1963)
The law that requires the same pay for men and women who do the same job in the same organization.

Determining whether two employees are doing the same job can be difficult. The law specifies that jobs are the same if they are equal in terms of skill, effort, responsibility, and working conditions. Thus, it is permissible to pay one employee more than another if the first employee has significant extra job duties, such as supervisory responsibility. Pay can also be different for different work shifts. The law also specifies that equal pay is required only for jobs held in the same geographic region. This allows an organization to make allowances for the local cost of living and the fact that it might be harder to find qualified employees in some areas.

The law contains several explicit exceptions. First, it does not prohibit the use of a merit pay plan. That is, an employer can pay a man more if he is doing a better job than his female coworker. In addition, companies are permitted to pay for differences in quantity and quality of production. Seniority plans also are exempted; a company that ties pay rates to seniority can pay a man more if he has been with the company longer than a female employee. Finally, the law indicates that any factor other than sex may be used to justify different pay rates.[11]

When the Equal Pay Act was passed, the average female employee earned only about 59 cents for each dollar earned by the average male worker. While this gap has narrowed in the intervening years, to about 83 cents in 2010,[12] this average differential remains troubling, and in some jobs it is much higher. For instance, 30-year-old male sales representatives earned an average of $60,000 in 2001, whereas their female counterparts in sales, doing the same amount and same kind of work, earned only an average of $36,000 at the same age.[13] Some states, such as Washington and Illinois, have responded to this issue by requiring that civil service employers pay equally for work of comparable worth.[14] Understanding equal pay and comparable worth requires more knowledge of compensation decisions, so we will return to these issues in Chapter 10.

Title VII of the Civil Rights Act of 1964

Although not the oldest of the civil rights laws, **Title VII of the Civil Rights Act of 1964** is universally seen as the most important passed to date. This law was enacted in the midst of the seething civil rights conflicts of the 1960s, one year after the civil rights march on Washington at which Dr. Martin Luther King, Jr., delivered his "I Have a Dream" speech.

Title VII
Section of the Civil Rights Act of 1964 that applies to employment decisions; mandates that employment decisions not be based on race, color, religion, sex, or national origin.

Before passage of the Civil Rights Act of 1964, open and explicit discrimination based on race, particularly against African Americans, was widespread. *Jim Crow laws* legalized racial segregation in many southern states. The act itself had several sections, or titles, all of which aim to prohibit discrimination in various parts of society. For instance, Title IX applies to educational institutions. Title VII applies to employers that have 15 or more employees, as well as to employment agencies and labor unions.

GENERAL PROVISIONS Title VII prohibits employers from basing employment decisions on a person's race, color, religion, sex, or national origin. The heart of the law, Section 703(a), is reprinted in Figure 3.2. Note that employment decisions include "compensation, terms, conditions, or privileges of employment."

Title VII clearly covers persons of any race, any color, any religion, both sexes, and any national origin. However, as court cases and regulations have grown up around this law, so has the legal theory of a **protected class**. This theory states that groups of people who suffered discrimination in the past require, and should be given, special protection by the judicial system. Under Title VII, the protected classes are African Americans, Asian Americans, Latinos, Native Americans, and women. Although it is not impossible for a nonprotected-class plaintiff to win a Title VII case, it is highly unusual.

protected class
A group of people who suffered discrimination in the past and who are given special protection by the judicial system.

FIGURE 3.2
Title VII of the Civil Rights Act of 1964

Section 703. (a) It shall be an unlawful employment practice for an employer—

1. to fail or refuse to hire or to discharge any individual, or otherwise to discriminate against any individual with respect to his compensation, terms, conditions, or privileges of employment, because of such individual's race, color, religion, sex, or national origin; or
2. to limit, segregate, or classify his employees or applicants for employment in any way which would deprive or tend to deprive any individual of employment opportunities or otherwise adversely affect his status as an employee, because of such individual's race, color, religion, sex, or national origin.

discrimination
The making of distinctions. In HR context, the making of distinctions among people.

disparate treatment
Discrimination that occurs when individuals are treated differently because of their membership in a protected class.

adverse impact
Discrimination that occurs when the equal application of an employment standard has an unequal effect on one or more protected classes. Also called *disparate impact.*

DISCRIMINATION DEFINED Despite the negative connotation the word has acquired, **discrimination** simply means making distinctions—in the HR context, distinctions among people. Therefore, even the most progressive companies are constantly discriminating when they decide who should be promoted, who should receive a merit raise, and who should be laid off. What Title VII prohibits is discriminating among people based on their race, color, religion, sex, or national origin.

Specifically, Title VII makes two types of discrimination illegal. The first type of discrimination, **disparate treatment**, occurs when an employer treats an employee differently because of his or her protected-class status. Disparate treatment is the kind of treatment that you probably first think of when considering discrimination. For instance, Robert Frazier, a bricklayer's assistant and an African American, was fired after quarreling with a white bricklayer. However, Frazier's employer did not discipline the white bricklayer at all, even though he had injured Frazier by throwing a broken brick at him. A federal court judge ruled that Frazier had been treated more harshly because of his race and thus suffered from disparate treatment discrimination.[15]

The second type of discrimination, **adverse impact** (also called *disparate impact*), occurs when the same standard is applied to all applicants or employees, but that standard affects a protected class more negatively (adversely). For example, most police departments around the United States have dropped the requirement that officers be of a minimum height because the equal application of that standard has an adverse impact on women, Latinos, and Asian Americans (that is, any given height standard will rule out more women than men, and more Latinos and Asian Americans than African Americans and nonminority individuals).

The adverse impact definition of discrimination was confirmed in a very important 1971 Supreme Court case that we have already discussed, *Griggs v. Duke Power.*[16] Griggs was an African American employee of the Duke Power Company in North Carolina. He and other African American employees were refused promotions because Duke Power, on the day that Title VII took effect, had implemented promotion standards that included a high school diploma and passing scores on two tests, one of general intellectual ability and one of mechanical ability. The Supreme Court ruled that such standards, even though applied equally to all employees, were discriminatory because (1) they had an adverse impact on a protected class (in this case, African Americans) and (2) Duke Power was unable to show that the standards were related to subsequent job performance.

Griggs v. Duke Power has some important implications. Under the *Griggs* ruling, courts may find that a company is acting in a discriminatory manner even though it works hard to ensure that its HR decision processes are applied equally to all employees. If the outcome is such that a protected class suffers from adverse impact, then the organization may be required to demonstrate that the standards used in the decision process were related to the job. In October 1993, Domino's Pizza lost a case in which it attempted to defend a "no-beard policy." The appellate court ruled that the policy had an adverse effect on African Americans because almost half of male African Americans suffer from a genetic condition that makes shaving very painful or impossible. Almost no white men suffer from this malady. Therefore, African Americans are more adversely affected by this requirement than whites are.[17] Domino's could have won this case if it had shown that not having a beard was necessary for good job performance. It could not, so the court ruled the no-beard policy a violation of Title VII.

In an earlier (1975) case, *Albemarle Paper Company v. Moody*, the Supreme Court established procedures to help employers determine when it is appropriate to use employment tests as a basis for hiring or promoting employees. The Court ruled that employers can use an employment test only when they can demonstrate that the test is a valid predictor of job performance. Thus, *Albemarle* places the burden of proof on the employer to prove that a contested test (for example, a test that has an adverse impact on a protected class) or other selection tool is a valid predictor of job success.[18]

Defense of Discrimination Charges

When a discrimination case makes it to court, it is the responsibility of the plaintiff (the person bringing the complaint) to show reasonable evidence that discrimination has occurred. The legal term for this type of evidence is *prima facie*, which means "on its face." In a disparate treatment lawsuit, to establish a prima facie case the plaintiff only needs to show that the organization did not hire her (or him), that the plaintiff appeared to be qualified for the job, and that the company continued to try to hire someone else for the position after rejecting the plaintiff. This set of requirements, which originated from a court case brought against the McDonnell-Douglas Corporation, is often called the *McDonnell-Douglas test*.[19] In an adverse impact lawsuit, the plaintiff only needs to show that a restricted policy is in effect—that is, that a disproportionate number of protected-class individuals were affected by the employment decisions.

One important EEOC provision for establishing a prima facie case that an HR practice is discriminatory and has an adverse impact is the **four-fifths rule**. The four-fifths rule comes from the EEOC's *Uniform Guidelines on Employee Selection Procedures*, an important document that informs employers how to establish selection procedures that are valid and, therefore, legal.[20]

four-fifths rule
An EEOC provision for establishing a prima facie case that an HR practice is discriminatory and has an adverse impact. A practice has an adverse impact if the hiring rate of a protected class is less than four-fifths the hiring rate of a majority group.

The four-fifths rule compares the hiring rates of protected classes to those of majority groups (such as white men) in the organization. It assumes that an HR practice has an adverse impact if the hiring rate of a protected class is less than four-fifths the hiring rate of a majority group. For example, assume that an accounting firm hires 50 percent of all its white male job applicants for entry-level accounting positions. Also assume that only 25 percent of all African American male job applicants are hired for the same job. Applying the four-fifths rule, prima facie evidence indicates that the accounting firm has discriminatory hiring practices because 50 percent $\times$ 4/5 = 40 percent, and 40 percent exceeds the 25 percent hiring rate for African American men.

Once the plaintiff has established a prima facie case, the burden of proof switches to the organization. In other words, the employer is then placed in a position of proving that illegal discrimination did not occur. This can be very tough to prove. Suppose that a sales manager interviews two applicants for a sales position, a man and a woman. Their qualifications look very much the same on paper. However, in the interview the man seems to be more motivated. He is hired, and the rejected female applicant files a disparate treatment discrimination suit. She can, almost automatically, establish a prima facie case (she was qualified, she was not hired, and the company did hire someone else). Now the sales manager has to prove that the decision was based on a judgment about the applicant's motivation, not on the applicant's sex.

Although these cases can be difficult, employers do win their share of them. There are four basic defenses that an employer can use:

- ***Job relatedness*** The employer has to show that the decision was made for job-related reasons. This is much easier to do if the employer has written documentation to support and explain the decision. In our example, the manager will be asked to give specific job-related reasons for the decision to hire the man for the sales job. As we noted in Chapter 2, job descriptions are particularly useful for documenting the job-related reasons for any particular HR decision.
- ***Bona fide occupational qualification*** A **bona fide occupational qualification (BFOQ)** is a characteristic that must be present in all employees for a particular job. For instance, a film director is permitted to consider only females for parts that call for an actress. An airline company must apply a compulsory age ceiling for pilots, according to Federal Aviation Agency rules, so that age is a BFOQ for airline pilots.
- ***Seniority*** Employment decisions that are made in the context of a formal seniority system are permitted, even if they discriminate against certain protected-class individuals.

bona fide occupational qualification (BFOQ)
A characteristic that must be present in all employees for a particular job.

However, this defense requires the seniority system to be well established and applied universally, not just in some circumstances.

- *Business necessity* The employer can use the business necessity defense when the employment practice is necessary for the safe and efficient operation of the organization and there is an overriding business purpose for the discriminatory practice. For example, an employee drug test may adversely impact a disadvantaged minority group, but the need for safety (to protect other employees and customers) may justify the drug-testing procedure.

Of these four defenses, the job-relatedness defense is the most common because of the strict limitations courts have placed on the BFOQ, seniority, and business-necessity defenses.

When an employer requires employees to speak only English at all times on the job, this *speak-English-only rule* may violate EEOC law, unless the employer can show that the rule is necessary for conducting business.[21] Similarly, an employer may not deny an individual an employment opportunity, such as a job or promotion, if the individual speaks with an accent, unless the employer can show that speaking with an accent has a detrimental effect on job performance.

Title VII and Pregnancy

In 1978, Congress amended Title VII to state explicitly that women are protected from discrimination based either on their ability to become pregnant or on their actual pregnancy. The *Pregnancy Discrimination Act of 1978* requires employers to treat an employee who is pregnant in the same way as any other employee who has a medical condition.[22] For instance, an employer cannot deny sick leave for pregnancy-related illnesses such as morning sickness if the employer allows sick leave for other medical conditions such as other illnesses that cause nausea. The law also states that a company cannot design an employee health benefit plan that provides no coverage for pregnancy. These are strict requirements, as evidenced by the following cases.

In one case that applied the Pregnancy Discrimination Act, a woman who worked at the U.S. Postal Service (USPS) claimed she was subjected to pregnancy discrimination when she was not reappointed after she had served a one-year appointment. The USPS cited her absences from work and that she was considered a high-risk pregnancy and should be doing only light-duty work. However, the EEOC found the complainant was treated less favorably than comparative employees based on her pregnancy. The basis of the EEOC's ruling was that the law requires the employer to treat pregnant employees just as it treats other employees with temporary impairments.[23]

A female police officer in Pinellas Park, Florida, claimed she experienced pregnancy discrimination when she was demoted to dispatcher after becoming pregnant and requesting light duty. She showed evidence that her male supervisor informed her that he was forced to hire women, and he specifically gave women the least desirable shifts and days off to punish them if they became pregnant. The city settled in favor of the complainant and reinstated her as a police officer.[24]

Sexual Harassment

The Title VII prohibition of sex-based discrimination has also been interpreted to prohibit sexual harassment. In contrast to protection for pregnancy, sexual harassment protection was not an amendment to the law but rather a 1980 EEOC interpretation of the law.[25] The EEOC's definition of sexual harassment is given in Figure 3.3. Also shown in the figure is the definition of general harassment that the EEOC issued in 1993. The majority of harassment cases filed to date have dealt with sexual harassment, but this may change in the future.[26] Courts appear to be extending sexual harassment definitions to other protected classes, such as race, age, and disability.

quid pro quo sexual harassment
Harassment that occurs when sexual activity is required in return for getting or keeping a job or job-related benefit.

hostile work environment sexual harassment
Harassment that occurs when the behavior of anyone in the work setting is sexual in nature and is perceived by an employee as offensive and undesirable.

There are two broad categories of sexual harassment. The first, **quid pro quo sexual harassment**, covers the first two parts of the EEOC's definitions. It occurs when sexual activity is demanded in return for getting or keeping a job or job-related benefit.[27] For instance, a buyer for the University of Massachusetts Medical Center was awarded $1 million in 1994 after she testified that her supervisor had forced her to engage in sex once or twice a week over a 20-month period as a condition of keeping her job.[28]

The second category, **hostile work environment sexual harassment**, occurs when the behavior of coworkers, supervisors, customers, or anyone else in the work setting is sexual in nature and the employee perceives the behavior as offensive and undesirable.[29]

1980 Definition of Sexual Harassment

Unwelcome sexual advances, requests for sexual favors, and other verbal or physical conduct of a sexual nature constitute sexual harassment when:

1. submission to such conduct is made either explicitly or implicitly a term or condition of an individual's employment;
2. submission to or rejection of such conduct by an individual is used as a basis for employment decisions affecting such individual; or
3. such conduct has the purpose or effect of unreasonably interfering with an individual's work performance or creating an intimidating, hostile, or offensive working environment.

1993 Definition of Harassment

Unlawful harassment is verbal or physical conduct that denigrates or shows hostility or aversion toward an individual because of his or her race, color, religion, gender, national origin, age or disability, or that of his/her relatives, friends, or associates, and that:

1. has the purpose or effect of creating an intimidating, hostile, or offensive working environment;
2. has the purpose or effect of unreasonably interfering with an individual's work performance; or
3. otherwise adversely affects an individual's employment opportunities.

FIGURE 3.3
EEOC Definitions of Harassment

Consider this example from a Supreme Court case decided in 1993.[30] Teresa Harris was a manager at Forklift Systems, Inc., an equipment rental firm in Nashville, Tennessee. Her boss was Charles Hardy, the company president. Throughout the two and one-half years that Harris worked at Forklift, Hardy made such comments to her as "You're a woman, what do you know?" and "We need a man as the rental manager." He suggested in front of other employees that the two of them "go to the Holiday Inn to negotiate her raise." When Harris asked Hardy to stop, he expressed surprise at her annoyance but did not apologize. Less than one month later, after Harris had negotiated a deal with a customer, Hardy asked her in front of other employees, "What did you do, promise the guy . . . some [sex] Saturday night?" Harris quit her job at the end of that month.

A QUESTION OF ETHICS

Some businesses thrive on a sexual theme. For example, "Hooters" attracts customers by marketing a sexual environment. Many ad campaigns have explicit sexual themes. Are such marketing efforts ethical? What effect might these public images have on the working environment at the company that uses them?

The issue the Court had to decide was whether Hardy violated the sexual harassment regulations based on Title VII. Lower courts had held that Hardy's behavior was certainly objectionable, but that Harris had not suffered serious psychological harm and that Hardy had not created a hostile work environment. The Supreme Court disagreed, holding that the behavior only needed to be such that a "reasonable person" would find it to create a hostile or abusive work environment. Figure 3.4 lists the tests that the Supreme Court said should be considered by judges and juries in deciding whether certain conduct creates a "hostile work environment" and is thus prohibited by Title VII.

Some cases of sexual harassment have involved groups of employees who have lodged hostile work environment claims. In 1998, Mitsubishi Motor Manufacturing of America paid out $34 million to settle a sexual harassment case brought by the EEOC on behalf of more than 300 female employees. Among their complaints were their being groped, gestured to,

The Supreme Court listed these questions to help judges and juries decide whether verbal and other nonphysical behavior of a sexual nature create a hostile work environment:

- How frequent is the discriminatory conduct?
- How severe is the discriminatory conduct?
- Is the conduct physically threatening or humiliating?
- Does the conduct interfere with the employee's work performance?

FIGURE 3.4
Do You Have a Hostile Work Environment?

Anucha Brown Sanders, former senior vice president of the Knicks, settled her sexual harassment lawsuit against the organization and former coach Isiah Thomas for $11.6 million.

Source: Julie Stapen/Newscom.

urged to reveal their sexual preferences, and exposed to sexually explicit pictures.[31] In 1999, Ford Motor Company achieved a settlement with women in two Chicago area factories in regard to their sexual harassment complaints. The female employees claimed a long-term pattern of groping, name-calling, and partying with strippers and prostitutes. The carmaker agreed to set aside $7.5 million to compensate victims of harassment and $10 million more to provide diversity training to managers and male workers.[32] Mitsubishi changed its image from a leader in corporate forgiveness of sexual harassment in 1998 to a model corporate citizen four years later in 2002. Mitsubishi made improvements that included a zero-tolerance policy for sexual harassment and providing training for all employees about the illegality of harassment and how to investigate complaints when they arise.[33]

Sexual harassment cases are not only expensive, but they also can be highly disruptive to business and political organizations. Consider the disruption to the executive branch of the U.S. government when Paula Jones sued President Clinton for sexual harassment. She alleged that the president made an unwanted sexual advance toward her in 1991 while he was the governor of Arkansas and she was a state employee. In 1999, President Clinton paid $850,000 to settle the suit.[34]

More recently, in 2007 a jury found that Madison Square Garden and New York Knicks coach and president for basketball operations Isiah Thomas sexually harassed and discriminated against Anucha Browne Sanders, a former senior vice president of the Knicks, and ordered that the company pay her $11.6 million in punitive damages.[35]

Although most sexual harassment cases involve women as victims, the number of cases in which men are the victims is increasing.[36] In 1995, a federal judge awarded a man $237,257 for being sexually harassed by a female supervisor at a Domino's Pizza restaurant. The female supervisor made unwelcome sexual advances to the male subordinate, creating a hostile work environment. When the man threatened to report the supervisor's inappropriate conduct to top management, he was fired.[37]

Courts also consider same-sex harassment improper work-related behavior. Joseph Oncale, an oil-rig worker who alleged that fellow male workers physically and verbally abused him with sexual taunts and threats, was allowed to bring a sexual harassment lawsuit against his employer. Despite arguments to the contrary, a court reviewing the *Oncale* case ruled in 1998 that same-sex harassment, not just harassment occurring between the sexes, can be the basis for a sexual harassment lawsuit.[38]

As Figure 3.5 indicates, sexual harassment is a major EEO issue for employers. An ABC News/Washington Post poll found that 25 percent of women and 10 percent of men reported that they had been sexually harassed in the workplace.[39] According to the EEOC, plaintiffs filed 11,364 cases of sexual harassment with federal and state agencies in 2011 (Figure 3.5). Men filed approximately 16 percent of those cases.

The Manager's Notebook titled "Reducing Potential Liability for Sexual Harassment" spells out some ways to prevent or correct instances of sexual harassment.

FIGURE 3.5

Number of Sexual Harassment Charges in the United States from 1992 to 2011

Source: The U.S. Equal Employment Opportunity Commission (2012). *www.eeoc.gov/eeoc/statistics/enforcement/sexual_harassment.cfm.*

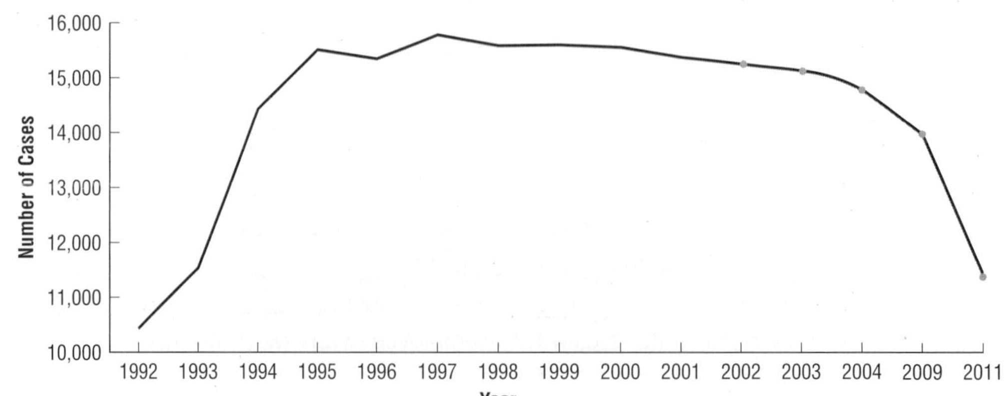

MANAGER'S NOTEBOOK

Customer-Driven HR

Reducing Potential Liability for Sexual Harassment

To reduce the potential liability of a sexual harassment suit, managers should:

- Establish a written policy prohibiting harassment.
- Communicate the policy and train employees in what constitutes harassment.
- Screen potential employees before hiring to make sure they do not have a history of sexually harassing others.
- Establish an effective complaint procedure.
- Quickly investigate all claims.
- Take remedial action to correct past harassment.
- Make sure that the complainant does not end up in a less desirable position if he or she needs to be transferred.
- Follow up to prevent continuation of harassment.

Sources: Based on Kleiner, K. (2012, September/October). What you need to know about sexual harassment. *Nonproprofitworld.org*, 12–13; Commerce Clearing House. (2008). *Sexual harassment prevention training manual* (4th ed.). Chicago: Commerce Clearing House; Equal Employment Opportunity Commission. (2010). Questions and answers for small employers on employer liability for harassment by supervisors. *www.eeoc.gov/policy/docs/harassment-facts.html*. ■■

Recent U.S. Supreme Court sexual harassment rulings directly affect employer liability in sexual harassment cases. First, an employer may be held liable for the actions of supervisors toward their subordinate employees even if the offense is not reported to top management. Second, the Supreme Court has established an employer defense against sexual harassment claims. The employer must prove two items: (1) It exercised reasonable care to prevent and correct sexual harassment problems in a timely manner,[40] and (2) the plaintiff failed to use the internal procedures for reporting sexual harassment.[41]

If the employee reasonably believes that reporting the offensive conduct is not a viable option, then the employer cannot take advantage of the defense. The internal procedures, then, must consist of fair investigations.[42] The Manager's Notebook entitled "How to Handle a Sexual Harassment Investigation " provides some guidelines.

MANAGER'S NOTEBOOK

Customer-Driven HR

How to Handle a Sexual Harassment Investigation

Failure to investigate a sexual harassment complaint can result in an employer liability if the case goes to court. Here are some guidelines for conducting an investigation into sexual harassment:

- ***Timeliness*** Managers should respond quickly, within 24 to 48 hours of a complaint of sexual harassment. Reacting later than that risks a charge of negligence.
- ***Documentation*** Managers should ask open-ended questions to get as much detail as possible about the harassment. Notes taken during the interview should be rewritten or typed after the meeting is concluded. The manager should write the report based on notes from the interview with the complainant.
- ***Employee agreement*** After documenting the facts in the report, the manager should go over the events with the complainant and document the employee's agreement with the report.

- ***Resolution*** Managers should ask what end result the employee is seeking. Those with a genuine complaint usually say they want the harassment to stop. Those with a personal vendetta are often looking to have the alleged perpetrator fired.
- ***Findings of fact*** The manager should interview witnesses who can corroborate or discredit the allegations of sexual harassment. The manager should then interview the alleged harasser. The accused should have the opportunity to defend himself or herself. A "findings of fact" document should be recorded to represent all the facts in the complaint; when this document is completed, the investigation is considered completed.
- ***Remedy*** The employer is obligated only to take steps reasonably likely to stop the harassment and has the right to determine an appropriate course of action. An effective sexual harassment policy gives managers the flexibility to choose from a range of various sanctions, from a written warning to the harasser to stop, to a transfer or demotion, to termination of the harasser.

Sources: Based on Willness, C., Steele, P., and Lee, K. (2007). A meta-analysis of the antecedents and consequences of workplace sexual harassment. *Personnel Psychology*, 127–162; Covey, A. (2001, July). How to handle harassment complaints. *HR Focus*, 5–6; Segal, J. (2001, October). HR as judge, jury, prosecutor and defender. *HRMagazine*, 141–154. ■■

To safeguard against sexual harassment claims, experts recommend that employers develop a zero-tolerance sexual harassment policy, successfully communicate the policy to employees, and ensure that victims can report abuses without fear of retaliation.[43] Furthermore, proactive companies schedule sexual harassment training workshops with mandatory attendance required for all employees. Sexual harassment workshops explain what sexual harassment behaviors look like with role plays or video clips, explain how the company policy works for reporting sexual harassment incidents, and offer opportunities for employees to ask questions. For example, a state law in California requires all employees with supervisory responsibilities in firms with more than 50 employees to take two hours of sexual harassment training at two year intervals.[44]

The Civil Rights Act of 1991

In 1991, believing that the Supreme Court was beginning to water down Title VII, Congress passed a comprehensive set of amendments to it. Together, these amendments are known as the *Civil Rights Act of 1991*. Although the legal aspects of these amendments are fairly technical, their impact on many organizations is very real. Among the most important effects of the 1991 amendment are:

- ***Burden of proof*** As we noted earlier, the employer bears the burden of proof in a discrimination case. Once the applicant or employee files a discrimination case and shows some justification for it, the organization has to defend itself by proving that it had a good job-related reason for the decision it made. This standard was originally established in the *Griggs v. Duke Power* decision in 1971. Then a 1989 Supreme Court case, *Wards Cove Packing Co. v. Antonio*, had the effect of placing more of the burden of proof on the plaintiff.[45] The 1991 law reinstates the *Griggs* standard.
- ***Quotas*** To avoid adverse impact, many organizations (including the Department of Labor) had developed a policy of adjusting scores on employment tests so that a certain percentage of protected-class applicants would be hired. The 1991 law amending Title VII prohibits **quotas**, which are employer adjustments of hiring decisions to ensure that a certain number of people from a certain protected class are hired. Thus, quotas, which had received mixed reviews in Supreme Court decisions before 1991, are now explicitly forbidden. Employers that have an affirmative action program giving preference to protected-class candidates have to walk a very fine line between "giving preference" (which is permissible) and "meeting a quota" (which is forbidden).
- ***Damages and jury trials*** The original Title VII law allowed successful plaintiffs to collect only back pay awards. However, racial minorities were also able to use an 1866 law to collect punitive and/or compensatory damages. **Punitive damages** are fines awarded to a plaintiff to punish the defendant. **Compensatory damages** are fines awarded to a plaintiff to compensate for the financial or psychological harm the plaintiff has suffered as a result

quotas
Employer adjustments of hiring decisions to ensure that a certain number of people from a certain protected class are hired.

punitive damages
Fines awarded to a plaintiff in order to punish the defendant.

compensatory damages
Fines awarded to a plaintiff to compensate for the financial or psychological harm the plaintiff has suffered.

of the discrimination. The 1991 law extended the possibility of collecting punitive and compensatory damages to persons claiming sex, religious, or disability-based discrimination. Such damages are capped at $50,000 to $300,000, depending on the size of the employer.[46] In addition, the law allows plaintiffs to request a trial by jury.

Some believe that by expressly forbidding quotas, the Civil Rights Act of 1991 has prohibited a very useful mechanism for reducing discrimination in employment decisions. Many organizations had found that the best way to prevent adverse impact was to use a combination of quotas and cognitive ability testing. That is, the employer would select a certain percentage of applicants from various groups, and then choose the highest performers on cognitive ability tests from each group. This employment strategy resulted in both the maintenance of a high-quality workforce and greater participation of minorities in that workforce. Yet, by outlawing quotas, the Civil Rights Act of 1991 has prohibited this option.[47]

Executive Order 11246

Executive orders are policies that the president establishes for the federal government and organizations that contract with the federal government. Executive Order 11246 (as amended by Executive Order 11375) was issued by President Johnson in 1965 and is *not* part of Title VII. It does, however, prohibit discrimination against the same categories of people that Title VII protects. In addition, it goes beyond the Title VII requirement of no discrimination by requiring covered organizations (firms with government contracts over $50,000 and 50 or more employees) to develop affirmative action programs to promote the employment of protected-class members. For instance, government contractors such as Boeing and Lockheed Martin are required to have active affirmative action programs.

executive order
A presidential directive that has the force of law. In HR context, a policy with which all federal agencies and organizations doing business with the federal government must comply.

The Age Discrimination in Employment Act of 1967

The **Age Discrimination in Employment Act (ADEA)** prohibits discrimination against people who are 40 or older. When first enacted in 1967, it protected people aged 40 to 65. Subsequently, it was amended to raise the age to 70, and in 1986 the upper age limit was removed entirely.

Age Discrimination in Employment Act (ADEA)
The law prohibiting discrimination against people who are 40 or older.

The majority of ADEA complaints are filed by employees who have been terminated. For instance, a 57-year-old computerized-control salesman for GE Fanuc Automation was the only employee terminated during a "reduction in force"; he was replaced by six younger sales representatives. He brought a lawsuit, claiming that he was fired because of his age, and a Detroit jury awarded him $1.1 million in damages and lost wages and benefits.[48] Employers can also lose lawsuits as a result of ill-informed workplace humor. Employers have lost several age discrimination cases because terminated employees had evidence that supervisors had told jokes about old age.[49] One age-discrimination case involved 1,697 former employees laid off by Sprint Nextel and was settled in 2005 for $57 million for the plaintiffs. In 2012, the EEOC received 22,857 complaints of age discrimination.[50]

An important amendment to the ADEA is the *Older Workers Protection Act (OWPA)* of 1990, which makes it illegal for employers to discriminate in providing benefits to employees based on age. For example, it would be illegal for employers to provide disability benefits only to employees who are age 60 or younger or to require older employees with disabilities to take early retirement. Another OWPA provision makes it more difficult for firms to ask older workers in downsizing and layoff situations to sign waivers in which they give up their right to any future age-discrimination claims in exchange for a payment.[51]

Some companies value older employees and develop policies that help older workers extend their working lives. One such company is Deere & Company, an industrial-equipment manufacturer based in Moline, Illinois. About 35 percent of its 46,000 employees are older than 50 years of age and a number are in their 70s. Deere & Company spends a lot of effort incorporating ergonomics into its factories, making jobs less tiring, which enables older employees to stay on the job longer.[52] With longer life expectancies, there will be greater numbers of employees who will prefer to keep on working beyond their mid-sixties when they qualify for Social Security retirement income and Medicare benefits. Companies will need to rethink how they design careers for older workers who plan to postpone retirement and remain employed. One approach being used to manage older employees is to treat retirement as a process rather than a sudden event and offer older workers "bridge jobs" that provide a transition between full-time employment and retirement. Mercy Health Systems uses such an approach by giving older employees the opportunity to work on jobs during seasonal periods of high demand and then offer long periods of unpaid leave during which these older employees can retain their benefits.[53]

The Americans with Disabilities Act of 1990

Americans with Disabilities Act (ADA)
The law forbidding employment discrimination against people with disabilities who are able to perform the essential functions of the job with or without reasonable accommodation.

The most recent of the major EEO laws is the **Americans with Disabilities Act (ADA)**. Signed into law in 1990 and gradually implemented since then, ADA has three major sections. Title I contains the employment provisions; Titles II and III concern the operation of state and local governments and places of public accommodation such as hotels, restaurants, and grocery stores. The ADA applies to all employers with 15 or more employees.[54]

The central requirement of Title I of the ADA is as follows:

Employment discrimination is prohibited against *individuals with disabilities* who are able to perform the *essential functions* of the job with or without *reasonable accommodation.*

Three parts of this requirement need definition.

individuals with disabilities
Persons who have a physical or mental impairment that substantially affects one or more major life activities.

INDIVIDUALS WITH DISABILITIES For the purposes of ADA, **individuals with disabilities** are people who have a physical or mental impairment that substantially affects one or more major life activities. Some examples of major life activities are:[55]

- Walking
- Speaking
- Breathing
- Performing manual tasks
- Sitting
- Lifting
- Seeing
- Hearing
- Learning
- Caring for oneself
- Working
- Reading

Obviously, persons who are blind, hearing impaired, or wheelchair bound are individuals with disabilities. But the category also includes people who have a controlled impairment. For instance, a person with epilepsy is disabled even if the epilepsy is controlled through medication. The impairment must be physical or mental and not due to environmental, cultural, or economic disadvantages. For example, a person who has difficulty reading due to dyslexia is considered disabled, but a person who cannot read because he or she dropped out of school is not. Persons with communicable diseases, including those who are HIV-positive (infected with the virus that causes AIDS), are included in the definition of individuals with disabilities.

The *ADA Amendments Act* (ADAAA) of 2008 is a law that added amendments to the ADA and broadened the definition of a disability so that it is considered to be less than *substantially limiting* and more than *moderately limiting* to one or more major life activities. The ADAAA adds more life activities for consideration and includes activities such as bending and communicating, and also includes bodily functions such as immune system, bladder, circulatory, endocrine, neurological, and digestive functions.[56] Under the ADAAA, AutoZone was taken to court when it failed to provide a reasonable accommodation for a disabled sales manager who was unable to perform what the court deemed as non-essential job functions (mopping floors and other cleaning tasks) due to back and neck impairments. Even after AutoZone was provided evidence of these impairments, it refused to provide an accommodation and ordered the employee to continue performing cleaning activities that led to additional injury and the need for medical leave. The court awarded the employee a $600,000 settlement and the possibility of obtaining additional back pay.[57]

In addition, the ADA protects persons who are *perceived* to be disabled. For instance, an employee might suffer a heart attack. When he tries to return to work, his boss may be scared that the workload will be "too much" and refuses to let him come back. The employer would be in violation of the ADA because he perceives the employee as disabled and is discriminating against him on the basis of that perception.

Two particular classes of people are explicitly *not* considered disabled: individuals whose current use of alcohol is affecting their job performance and those who use illegal drugs (whether they are addicted or not). However, those who are recovering from their former use of either alcohol or drugs are covered by ADA.

Individuals who are considered morbidly obese, defined as weighing 100 or more pounds above their ideal body weight, may or may not be covered under the ADA. Currently, 9 million U.S. adults are morbidly obese, and many suffer from medical conditions such as hypertension, heart disease, stroke, cancer, depression, rheumatoid arthritis, osteoarthritis, and diabetes. Recent court cases do not consider morbid obesity to be an inherently ADA-eligible condition. To be eligible for ADA coverage, an individual's morbid obesity would require a physiological cause. The individual making a case for ADA coverage would need to provide medical evidence to the employer that he or she was overweight due to physiological causes. For example, if a medical examination revealed that a person was morbidly obese because of overeating and lack of exercise, the employer would be able to deny ADA coverage to the employee seeking it.[58]

INTELLECTUAL DISABILITIES In 2005, the EEOC provided guidelines to address challenges faced by employers in hiring, accommodating, and preventing harassment of employees with intellectual disabilities. The EEOC estimates that within the United States about 2.5 million individuals have *intellectual disabilities* that occur when: (1) the person's intellectual function level (IQ) is below 70–75; (2) the person has significant limitations in adaptive skill areas as expressed in conceptual, social, and practical adaptive skills; and (3) the disability originated before the age of 18. *Adaptive skills* are the basic skills needed for everyday life. They include communication; self-care; home living; social skills; leisure; health and safety; self-direction; functional academics (reading, writing, basic math); and work.[59]

Not everyone with an intellectual impairment is covered by the ADA. An individual's intellectual impairment must substantially limit one or more major life activities, such as walking, seeing, hearing, thinking, speaking, learning, concentrating, performing manual tasks, caring for oneself, and working. The following is an example of someone who has an intellectual impairment that would be covered under the ADA:

> An individual with an intellectual impairment is hired as part of a crew of employees that works at a concession stand at a movie theater. He helps stock the counter with candy and snacks; at closing time, he cleans the counters and equipment and restocks the concession stand with supplies. However, he cannot perform the function of accurately counting money at closing time, nor is he capable of accurately making change for customers from the cash register. This individual is limited in his intellectual ability to perform basic math skills and therefore has a disability that qualifies for ADA coverage.

ESSENTIAL FUNCTIONS The EEOC separates job duties and tasks into two categories: essential and marginal. **Essential functions** are job duties that every employee must do or must be able to do to be an effective employee. *Marginal functions* are job duties that are required of only some employees or that are not critical to job performance. The following examples illustrate the difference between essential and marginal functions:

essential functions
Job duties that each person in a certain position must do or must be able to do to be an effective employee.

- A company advertises a position for a "floating" supervisor to substitute when regular supervisors on the day, night, and graveyard shifts are absent. The ability to work any time of the day or night is an essential job function.
- A company wishes to expand its business with Japan. In addition to sales experience, it requires all new hires to speak fluent Japanese. This language skill is an essential job function.
- In any job requiring computer use, it is essential that the employee have the ability to access, input, or retrieve information from the computer terminal. However, it may not be essential that the employee be capable of manually entering or visually retrieving information because technology exists for voice recognition input and auditory output.
- A group of chemists working together in a lab may occasionally need to answer the telephone. This is considered a marginal job duty because if not every one of the chemists can answer the phone, the other chemists can do so.

ADA requires that employers make decisions about applicants with disabilities solely on the basis of their ability to perform essential job functions. Thus, an employer should not make pre-employment inquiries about a job candidate's disability, although an employer may ask questions about the job candidate's ability to perform essential job functions.

REASONABLE ACCOMMODATION Organizations are required to take some reasonable action to allow employees with disabilities to work for them. The major aspects of this requirement are:

reasonable accommodation An action taken to accommodate the known disabilities of applicants or employees so that disabled persons enjoy equal employment opportunity.

- Employers must make **reasonable accommodation** for the known disabilities of applicants or employees so that people with disabilities enjoy equal employment opportunity.[60] For example, an applicant who uses a wheelchair may need accommodation if the interviewing site is not wheelchair accessible.
- Employers cannot deny a person with disabilities employment to avoid providing the reasonable accommodation, unless providing the accommodation would cause an "undue hardship." Undue hardship is a highly subjective determination, based on the cost of the accommodation and the employer's resources. For instance, an accommodation routinely provided by large employers (such as specialized computer equipment) may not be required of small employers because the small employers do not have the large employer's financial resources.
- No accommodation is required if the individual is not otherwise qualified for the position.
- It is usually the obligation of the disabled individual to request the accommodation.
- If the cost of the accommodation would create an undue hardship for the employer, the disabled individual should be given the option of providing the accommodation. For instance, if a visually impaired person applies for a computer operator position in a small company that cannot afford to accommodate the applicant, then the applicant should be given the option to provide the accommodating technology. (Note, though, that the President's Committee on Employment of People with Disabilities reports that 20 percent of accommodations do not cost anything at all, and less than 4 percent cost more than $5,000.[61])

A wide variety of accommodations is possible, and they can come from some surprising sources. For example, Kreonite, Inc., a small family-owned business of about 250 employees that manufactures specialized photographic film, has been committed to employing persons with disabilities and has several employees who are deaf. Kreonite turned to a local not-for-profit training center for someone to teach sign language to its hearing employees. The training was free, and 30 Kreonite employees volunteered to attend.[62]

Some additional examples of potential reasonable accommodations that the EEOC has suggested are reassigning marginal job duties, modifying work schedules, modifying examinations or training materials, providing qualified readers and interpreters, and permitting use of paid or unpaid leave for treatment.[63] An accommodation the EEOC has suggested for people with intellectual disabilities is to provide a job coach on a temporary basis to assist in training the employee to perform the essential functions of the job.[64]

As we noted earlier in the chapter, the main focus of the ADA and its accompanying regulations is the hiring process. However, the majority of complaints filed so far involve situations in which current employees have become disabled on the job. According to the EEOC, the total number of disability cases filed under the ADA in 2009 was 21,451. The two largest categories of cases were emotional and psychiatric impairments and back injuries, both of which are difficult to diagnose and treat.[65] Managers need to be prepared to deal with a set of issues not anticipated by the lawmakers and regulators who created and passed the ADA.

THE VOCATIONAL REHABILITATION ACT OF 1973 The *Vocational Rehabilitation Act* is the precursor to the ADA. However, this act applies only to the federal government and its contractors. Like Executive Order 11246, the Vocational Rehabilitation Act not only prohibits discrimination (in this case, on the basis of disability), but also requires that the covered organizations have an affirmative action plan to promote the employment of individuals with disabilities. Familiarity with this law is useful to organizations attempting to comply with the ADA because it has led to over 30 years' worth of court and regulatory decisions based on the same central prohibition against disability-based discrimination.

THE VIETNAM ERA VETERANS READJUSTMENT ACT OF 1974 One additional EEO law deserves brief mention. The *Vietnam Era Veterans Readjustment Act of 1974* prohibits discrimination against Vietnam-era veterans (those who served in the military between August 5, 1964, and May 7, 1975) by federal contractors. The law also protects the rights of military veterans who served on active duty during a war, campaign, or expedition for which a campaign badge has been authorized, which includes subsequent military campaigns such as the Gulf War (1991), the war in Iraq (2003–2011), and the war in Afghanistan (2001–2015). It also requires federal contractors to take affirmative action to hire Vietnam-era veterans and those from more recent campaigns.

EEO Enforcement and Compliance

The enforcement of EEO laws is the responsibility of the executive branch of government, which is headed by the president. In this section, we describe the regulatory agencies that enforce the various EEO laws, as well as some of the plans that have been used to comply with affirmative action requirements.

Regulatory Agencies

Two agencies are primarily responsible for the enforcement of EEO law: the Equal Employment Opportunity Commission (EEOC) and the Office of Federal Contract Compliance Programs (OFCCP).

EQUAL EMPLOYMENT OPPORTUNITY COMMISSION (EEOC) The **Equal Employment Opportunity Commission (EEOC)**, which was created by Title VII, has three major functions. The first is processing discrimination complaints. The second is issuing written regulations. The third is information gathering and dissemination.[66]

Equal Employment Opportunity Commission (EEOC)
The federal agency responsible for enforcing EEO laws.

In processing discrimination complaints, the EEOC follows a three-step process:

- *Investigation* An applicant or employee who thinks that he or she has been discriminated against begins the process by filing a complaint with the EEOC. The EEOC then notifies the company that a complaint has been filed, and the company becomes responsible for ensuring that any records relating to the complaint are kept safe. The EEOC usually finds itself with a backlog, so it may take up to two years to begin investigating the complaint. In 2012, 99,412 cases were filed with the EEOC, compared to 62,100 in 1990.

  Of the 99,412 total charges filed with the EEOC in 2012, the common types of discrimination among all filings were:[67]
  - Race: 33,512 (33.7 percent)
  - Sex/Gender: 30,356 (30.5 percent)
  - Age: 22,857 (23.0 percent)
  - Disability: 26,374 (26.5 percent)
  - National Origin: 10,883 (10.9 percent)
  - Religion: 3,811 (3.8 percent)
  - Equal Pay: 1,082 (1.1 percent)

  The average processing time for private-sector charge filings at the EEOC was 180 days.

  After conducting the investigation, the EEOC determines whether it is likely that the company did in fact violate one or more EEO laws. Complainants are always free to file a lawsuit, but the courts are unlikely to rule in their favor without the EEOC's backing.
- *Conciliation* If the EEOC finds that an EEO law was probably violated, it attempts to resolve the case through conciliation. **Conciliation** consists of negotiation among the three parties involved: the complainant, the employer, and the EEOC. The goal of conciliation is to reach a fair settlement while avoiding a trial.
- *Litigation* If conciliation is not possible, the EEOC can choose between two courses of action. The EEOC does not have the power to compel an employer to pay compensation or any other kind of damages; this can be done only as the result of a court's decision. Because pursuing a lawsuit is very expensive, the EEOC takes this course of action only in a relatively small percentage of cases. If the EEOC chooses not to pursue the case, it issues a right-to-sue letter to the complainant, who is then free to pursue court action with the blessing (if not the financial or legal support) of the EEOC.

conciliation
An attempt to reach a negotiated settlement between the employer and an employee or applicant in an EEO case.

In addition to resolving complaints, the EEOC is responsible for issuing regulations and guidelines. These documents put "meat on the bones" of the individual laws. For instance, when the EEOC decided that sexual harassment was prohibited by Title VII, it issued regulations defining what sexual harassment is (see Figure 3.3) and what it expects employers to do in response to employee complaints of harassment. Similarly, when the ADA was signed into law in 1990, the EEOC was given the responsibility of issuing regulations that would inform employers exactly what they would (and would not) be expected to do to comply with the law. The EEOC Web site (*www.eeoc.gov*) also provides a list of its regulations. Figure 3.6 lists some of the most prominent EEOC regulations.

Age: An employment policy or practice that applies to everyone, regardless of age, can be illegal if it has a negative impact on applicants or employees age 40 or older and is not based on a reasonable factor other than age (RFOA).
Disability: The law requires an employer to provide reasonable accommodation to an employee or job applicant with a disability, unless doing so would cause significant difficulty or expense for the employer.
Compensation: The law requires that men and women be given equal pay for equal work in the same establishment. The jobs need not be identical, but they must be substantially equal.
Genetic data: It is illegal to discriminate against employees or applicants because of genetic information.
Bullying: The employer is automatically liable for harassment by a supervisor that results in a negative employment action such as termination, failure to promote or hire, and loss of wages. If the supervisor's harassment results in a hostile work environment, the employer can avoid liability only if it can prove that: (1) it reasonably tried to prevent and promptly correct the harassing behavior; and (2) the employee unreasonably failed to take advantage of any preventive or corrective opportunities provided by the employer.
National origin: The law makes it illegal for an employer or other covered entity to use an employment policy or practice that applies to everyone, regardless of national origin, if it has a negative impact on people of a certain national origin and is not job-related or necessary to the operation of the business.
Pregnancy: The law forbids discrimination based on pregnancy when it comes to any aspect of employment, including hiring, firing, pay, job assignments, promotions, layoff, training, fringe benefits, such as leave and health insurance, and any other term or condition of employment.
Adverse impact: An employment policy or practice that applies to everyone, regardless of race or color, can be illegal if it has a negative impact on the employment of people of a particular race or color and is not job-related and necessary to the operation of the business.
Religion: The law requires an employer or other covered entity to reasonably accommodate an employee's religious beliefs or practices, unless doing so would cause more than a minimal burden on the operations of the employer's business.
Gender discrimination: Sex discrimination involves treating someone (an applicant or employee) unfavorably because of that person's sex.
Sexual harassment: It is unlawful to harass a person (an applicant or employee) because of that person's sex. Harassment can include "sexual harassment" or unwelcome sexual advances, requests for sexual favors, and other verbal or physical harassment of a sexual nature.

FIGURE 3.6
Principal EEOC Regulations

Source: Based on EEOC Regulations (April, 2014). *www.eeoc.gov*.

The EEOC also gathers information to monitor the hiring practices of organizations. It does this by requiring organizations with 100 or more employees to file an annual report (EEO-1) indicating the number of women and minorities who hold jobs in nine different job categories. The EEOC examines this information to identify patterns of discrimination that may exist in organizations.

Finally, the EEOC disseminates posters to employers. These posters explain to workers how to protect themselves from employment discrimination and how to file a complaint. The EEOC requires employers to display the posters in a prominent place (such as the company cafeteria).

Office of Federal Contract Compliance Programs (OFCCP)

Office of Federal Contract Compliance Programs (OFCCP)
The federal agency responsible for monitoring and enforcing the laws and executive orders that apply to the federal government and its contractors.

The **Office of Federal Contract Compliance Programs (OFCCP)** is responsible for enforcing the laws and executive orders that apply to the federal government and its contractors. Specifically, it enforces Executive Order 11246 and the Vocational Rehabilitation Act, which both go beyond prohibiting discrimination to requiring affirmative action programs by covered employers.

Many of the regulations written by the OFCCP are very similar to those issued by the EEOC. However, there are two major differences between the enforcement activities of the two agencies. First, in contrast to the EEOC, the OFCCP actively monitors compliance with its regulations. That is, it does not wait for an employee or applicant to file a complaint. Rather, it requires covered employers to submit annual reports on the state of their affirmative action programs. Second, unlike the EEOC, the OFCCP has considerable enforcement power. Being a government contractor is considered a privilege, not a right. The OFCCP can take away that privilege if it determines that an employer is not complying with the law. It can also levy fines and other forms of punishment.

Affirmative Action Plans

An affirmative action plan is required of all government agencies and businesses that do a significant amount of work for the government. There are three steps to developing an affirmative action plan: conducting a utilization analysis, establishing goals and timetables, and determining action options.

UTILIZATION ANALYSIS The first step in developing an affirmative action plan is conducting a *utilization analysis* to describe the organization's current workforce relative to the pool of qualified workers in the labor force. There are two parts to conducting this analysis. The first involves determining the demographic composition of the current workforce by dividing all the jobs in the organization into classifications. For instance, all management jobs are placed in one classification, all clerical and secretarial jobs in a second, all sales positions in a third, and so on. The percentage of persons from each protected class working in each of these classifications is then determined.

The second part is determining the percentage of those same protected classes in the available labor market. In gathering this information, organizations need to consider the eight different pieces of information listed in Figure 3.7. For instance, what percentage of qualified and available managers are women? What percentage are African Americans? What percentage are Asian Americans? The OFCCP offers guidelines for determining these figures. If the available figures are significantly higher than the currently employed in any category, the protected groups are said to be underutilized in that job category.

GOALS AND TIMETABLES The second step is setting goals and timetables for correcting underutilization. The OFCCP explicitly requires that rigid numerical quotas *not* be set. Rather, the employer should take into consideration the size of the underutilization, how fast the workforce turns over, and whether the workforce is growing or contracting. Another consideration in setting goals and timetables is the types of actions the employer intends to take.

ACTION PLANS The final step in developing an affirmative action plan is deciding exactly what affirmative actions to take. The OFCCP suggests the following guidelines:

- Recruiting protected-class members.
- Redesigning jobs so that the underrepresented workers are more likely to be qualified.
- Providing specialized training sessions for underprepared applicants.
- Removing any unnecessary barriers to employment. For instance, a company located in an area not served by public transportation might consider providing van service from certain areas so that potential applicants who do not have reliable transportation can become employees.

The central concern for organizations is determining how much (if any) preference they should give to applicants who belong to an underutilized protected class. For instance, a few decades ago there was a job opening in the transportation department of Santa Clara County, California. After going through the normal selection process, the candidates for promotion

Determine the percentage of protected-class members for each of the following groups of people:

- Local population
- Local unemployed workers
- Local labor force
- Qualified workers in the local labor market
- Qualified workers in the labor market from which you recruit
- Current employees who might be promoted into the job classification
- Graduates of local education and training programs that prepare people for this job classification
- Participants in training programs sponsored by the employer

FIGURE 3.7
Components of an Eight-Factor Availability Analysis

were ranked according to their performance on tests and in interviews. County rules allowed any of the top seven candidates to be chosen. The supervisors were poised to choose the employee ranked second—Paul Johnson, a white man. Diane Joyce, a white woman who was ranked fourth, called the county's affirmative action officer and ended up with the job.

Johnson filed suit. His argument was straightforward: Title VII prohibits discrimination based on sex, and he did not get the job because he is a man. This is a classic case of alleged **reverse discrimination**, discrimination that occurs as the result of an attempt to recruit and hire more people from the protected classes. In this case, the job classification to which the person was to be promoted had 238 positions, none of which were held by women. Johnson pursued his case all the way to the U.S. Supreme Court. In 1987, the Court ruled that Santa Clara County's decision was permissible.[68]

reverse discrimination
Discrimination against a nonprotected-class member resulting from attempts to recruit and hire members of protected classes.

The Supreme Court has decided over a dozen reverse discrimination cases since the first one in 1977.[69] Although the Court has favored the affirmative action strategy side of the tension outlined in Figure 3.1, almost all these cases were decided by 6–3 or 5–4 margins. Because new justices are added to the Supreme Court fairly regularly, the way these kinds of cases will be decided in the future is very much an open question.

In a landmark 2003 case involving the University of Michigan's affirmative action policies, the U.S. Supreme Court upheld the right of affirmative action in university admissions decisions. First, in upholding the policy of the law school at the University of Michigan, it ruled that race can be one of many factors considered by colleges when selecting their students because it furthers "a compelling interest in obtaining the educational benefits that flow from a diverse student body." Second, it ruled that the University of Michigan's undergraduate admissions policy, which was based on a formula that gave extra points to minorities, needed to be modified because, unlike the law school, it did not take into consideration individual aspects of applicants concerning admission to the university.[70]

The United States is not the only country with affirmative action. Other countries have created similar policies to provide employment or educational opportunities for disadvantaged groups. For example, India has tried to improve the status of the untouchables, the lowest caste in its society, by providing them with preferential treatment in employment and education. This policy has had mixed results because it has enraged some members of the higher castes. Malaysia has favored the Islamic Malays over the Chinese (who on average are wealthier and more highly educated than the Malays) for jobs and higher education opportunities. Significant numbers of Chinese Malaysians have responded to this policy by emigrating to Asia and North America.[71] Other countries have disadvantaged groups in their population but have decided not to create employment policies favorable to these groups. For example, France has a large minority of Muslims from North Africa who have been historically disadvantaged, but it has avoided remedying the high Muslim unemployment rate with a policy similar to affirmative action in the United States. In Great Britain, the government's Commission for Racial Equality concluded that most British firms do little to ensure equal employment opportunity beyond giving verbal support to the idea.[72]

Cultural values can influence how minorities or disadvantaged groups are treated on the basis of equality in countries outside the United States, as described in the Manager's Notebook titled "In India, Gender Inequity in the Workplace Is Widespread."

MANAGER'S NOTEBOOK

Global

In India, Gender Inequity in the Workplace Is Widespread

While India is the world's largest democracy and is rapidly expanding economically, the participation of Indian women has lagged the levels of other rapidly developing countries such as China. The proportion of women in the workforce in India is only 24 percent compared to a 70 percent female participation rate in China. A 2012 Global Gender Gap Report ranked women in 135 countries on economic participation and political empowerment. The report gave India a ranking of 105, which was below countries such as Cambodia, Burkina Faso, and Belize.

India's low female labor participation rate is linked to cultural pressure due to expectations from the family on the role of a married woman. Indian married women are expected to be home taking care of the family, and often that includes taking care of their in-laws as well.

As a result of some well-publicized acts of violence toward women in India, a workplace sexual harassment law was enacted in 2013 that is supposed to prevent acts of sexual harassment of women in the workplace. The law requires that employers with more than 10 employees form an "Internal Complaints Committee" to which a woman who alleges harassment can take her complaint. This committee is supposed to mediate between the complainant and the accused to reach a settlement and will start an investigation only if mediation fails. Critics object to the provision that requires mediation before a formal inquiry takes place because it acts as a deterrent to women coming forward with a complaint.

Sources: Based on Kolhatkar, S. (2013, February 4). Arrested development: India's miserable record on women's rights threatens to stunt its economic growth. *Bloomberg Businessweek*, 6–7; Vasant, K. (2013, April 29). New workplace sexual harassment law 'already out of date.' *India Realtime. www.blogs.wsj.com/indiarealtime/2013/04/29*; Pathak, M. (2012, March 28). India takes steps toward gender equity. *Gazelle Index. www.gazelleindex.com/archives/5410.* ■■

Other Important Laws

We have concentrated on equal employment opportunity laws in this chapter because they have a broad effect on almost all HR issues and are highly likely to influence managers' behavior. The other HR laws, listed in the Appendix to this chapter and discussed elsewhere in the book, are much more narrowly focused. These include laws that affect compensation and benefit plans (state workers' compensation laws, the Social Security Act, the Fair Labor Standards Act, the Employee Retirement and Income Security Act, the Consolidated Omnibus Budget Reconciliation Act, and the Family and Medical Leave Act); union–management relations (the Wagner Act, the Taft-Hartley Act, and the Landrum-Griffin Act); safety and health issues (the Occupational Safety and Health Act); and layoffs (the Worker Adjustment and Retraining Act).

A QUESTION OF ETHICS

Is it ethical for a U.S. employer to require all employees to speak only English at the workplace?

Four laws deserve brief mention. The *Immigration Reform and Control Act of 1986* was intended to reduce the inflow of illegal immigrants to the United States. The law has one provision that affects employers. To discourage the hiring of illegal immigrants, the law mandates that employers hire only people who can document that they are legally permitted to work in the United States.

The Uniformed Services Employment and Reemployment Rights Act of 1994 protects the jobs of employees who take leave to serve in the military reserve. Employers often find the skills that reservists gain through their service are valuable in the workplace.

Source: Shelly Perry/Thinkstock.

The Employment Eligibility Verification (I-9) form specifies which documents employers need to see from new employees. It appears that the major impact of the Immigration Reform and Control Act has been the creation of a market for fake documents.

The *Immigration Act of 1990* was legislated to make it easier for skilled immigrants to enter the United States. This law represents a modification of previous U.S. immigration policy, which favored immigrants who either (1) had family members who are U.S. citizens or (2) were leaving a country that was assigned a large quota of immigrants to the United States based on historical trends.[73]

The *Drug-Free Workplace Act of 1988* requires that government contractors try to ensure that their workplaces are free from drug use. Employers are required to prevent the use of illegal drugs at their work sites and to educate their employees about the hazards of drug use. Although the law does not mandate drug testing, it—along with other more narrowly focused laws and regulations—has led to a general acceptance of drug testing, both of current employees and applicants, across the United States.[74] About 98 percent of Fortune 200 companies now conduct some form of drug testing.[75]

The *Uniformed Services Employment and Reemployment Rights Act of 1994* protects the rights of people who take short leaves from a private-sector employer to perform military service (such as reserve duty). The law protects these employees' seniority rights and benefits. It also protects them from employer discrimination in hiring, promotion, or layoff decisions. Some employers have been giving military reservists returning from combat duty in Iraq perks and benefits that exceed what is legally required, as described in the Manager's Notebook titled "Military Reservists Who Have Returned from Iraq and Afghanistan Are Finding Their Skills in High Demand."

MANAGER'S NOTEBOOK

Emerging Trends

Military Reservists Who Have Returned from Iraq and Afghanistan Are Finding Their Skills in High Demand

Reservists have made up a significant percentage of active duty troops who have served in Iraq and Afghanistan—the largest number of reservists to see combat since World War II. Their average age at the time of their deployment was 32, four years older than the average soldier.

Employers are finding that reservists have returned from duty in Iraq and Afghanistan with seasoned management, people, and communication skills. They also have returned with leadership skills that have been honed in combat. Army Major David Wood, a 41-year-old reservist, commanded a helicopter squadron in Iraq and Afghanistan. Wood says his soldiers always seemed more enthusiastic about a mission when they knew a senior officer was taking part. Back home, as a vice president at Jay Group, a packaging company in Pennsylvania, Wood says he now often goes down to the plant floor to pack and ship products alongside workers. "You can't be what we call a coffee-cup commander," Wood says. "You have to be on the field, leading from the front."

Recognizing the value of skills obtained in the context of military combat, employers are going out of their way to recruit and retain reservists. Although employers are required by law to give returning reservists back their jobs with the same responsibility and pay, some employers go even further than the law requires, offering them such perks as continued pay and benefits while on military duty. Here are a few examples:

- Adolph Coors makes up the difference between a reservist's regular salary and military pay for up to one year of active duty. An internal volunteer organization works with reservists' families, boxing and shipping donated items to the troops.
- American Express provides full pay and benefits for up to five years as well as cash contributions to the employee's retirement plan.
- General Electric pays one month of full salary and makes up the difference in pay for up to three years. GE has a military recruiting division and leadership programs for military members transitioning to the corporate world.

Sources: Based on Palmeri, C. (2004, December 13). Served in Iraq? Come work for us. *BusinessWeek*, 78–80; Dance, S. (2010, February 15). Returning soldiers, employers face post-war challenges. *Baltimore Business Journal. www.bizjournals.com.* ■■

Avoiding Pitfalls in EEO

The great majority of employees and job applicants in the United States fall into one or more protected classes. This means that almost any decision made by a manager that affects a worker's employment status can be challenged in a court of law. In most cases, sound management practices will not only help managers avoid EEO lawsuits, but also contribute to the organization's bottom line. Five specific management practices are recommended: providing training, establishing a complaint resolution process, documenting decisions, being honest, and asking applicants for only needed information.

Provide Training

One of the best ways to avoid EEO problems is to provide training.[76] Two types of training are appropriate. First, the HR department should provide supervisors, managers, and executives with regular updates on EEO and other labor issues, because this area of law is in a constant state of flux.[77] The Supreme Court regularly decides cases that affect HR practice. Although managers can try to read periodicals or search the Web to obtain current information, most find their everyday demands too taxing to allow time for this. Regular, focused training sessions conducted by the HR department are the most efficient method of communicating this information to managers.

Second, employers should focus on communicating to employees their commitment to a discrimination-free work environment. For instance, all employees need to be instructed in what sexual harassment is, how to stop it before it becomes a problem, and what to do if it does become a problem. Honeywell has a council of employees with disabilities, one function of which is to promote awareness of disability issues throughout the company.[78]

Establish a Complaint Resolution Process

Every organization should establish a process for the internal resolution of EEO and other types of employee complaints. It is much less expensive to resolve these concerns if the EEOC, OFCCP, and legal counsel are not involved. More important, employee morale and satisfaction can be improved when employees are able to pass along their concerns to upper-level management. (We describe complaint resolution systems in detail in Chapters 13 and 15.)

Once in place, the complaint resolution process should be followed correctly. AT&T avoided liability in a sexual harassment case because it was able to show that it had acted promptly to remedy the problem once management had been informed of it.[79] Exhibit 3.1, "Alternative Dispute Resolution Methods at Marriott and the EEOC," describes how Marriott and the EEOC have taken the lead in experimenting with new ways to resolve employee EEO complaints.

Document Decisions

Financial transactions and decisions need to be well documented so they can be audited and summarized, problem areas identified, and solutions implemented.[80] The same rationale applies to decisions made about employees. The nature of any HR decision, and the rationale for it, should be clearly documented. Both the EEOC and OFCCP have certain reporting requirements. Employers that have a sound human resource information system in place do not find it difficult to comply with these requirements.

Be Honest

Typically, applicants and employees will not file an EEO complaint unless they think they have been mistreated. Perceptions of mistreatment often result from situations in which employees' or applicants' expectations have not been met. Imagine the following scenario: A 50-year-old employee has consistently received excellent performance evaluations over a 20-year period. He is then abruptly terminated by his manager for poor work performance. This employee is likely to file a lawsuit, because over time he has developed the expectation that he is a valued employee and he now believes that the only possible reason for his termination is his age. Although it may be painful in the short term, providing honest feedback to employees is a good management practice that may reduce legal problems in the long run.

EXHIBIT 3.1 ALTERNATIVE DISPUTE RESOLUTION METHODS AT MARRIOTT AND THE EEOC

Ron Wilensky, vice president for employee relations for Marriott International, was not satisfied with the company's "Guarantee of Fair Treatment" program, which instructed employees with complaints to go first to their immediate supervisor, then to the supervisor's manager, and so on up the ladder, if necessary. Based on his experience with three Fortune 500 companies that had similar policies, he estimated that 75 percent of employees bypass such a policy and consult an attorney. To verify his hunch, he established a committee to examine employee satisfaction with the Guarantee of Fair Treatment. The results indicated that employees did not trust the policy. Instead, they wanted a system that would give those with grievances a chance to air their concerns before impartial listeners and have those concerns addressed promptly—without fear of retribution.

To give employees what they want, Wilensky and his committee have been experimenting with three dispute resolution systems.

1. ***Mutual agreement through mediation*** A neutral person, typically an expert in dispute resolution, meets with both parties to the conflict and tries to arrange a negotiated settlement. Because 80 to 90 percent of litigation is settled out of court anyway, the goal is to reduce attorney fees and other associated costs.
2. ***A helping hotline*** Wilensky found that it was difficult to track employee grievances across so many different geographic locations, so Marriott uses a toll-free 800-number hotline at 300 of its food service locations. Available 24 hours a day, 7 days a week, the hotline is intended to be used only to report cases of perceived wrongful discharge, discrimination, and harassment. Marriott promises to initiate an investigation within three days of receiving the complaint.
3. ***A panel of peers*** In 50 Marriott locations, employees have an opportunity to air their grievance before a panel of their peers. The panel is chosen at random from a group of specially trained volunteers. The panel has the authority to make final, binding decisions on all grievances brought before it.[a]

The EEOC also uses alternative dispute resolution systems. It relies on mediation to achieve faster resolution of its large backlog of cases. The EEOC chairwoman, Ida L. Castro, made a strong commitment to use mediation by increasing the mediation budget by $13 million in 1999 to expand the use of mediation in each EEOC district office. Between 1999 and 2010 about 136,000 mediations at the EEOC took place and almost 70 percent of them were successfully resolved.[b]

Sources: [a]Wilensky, R., and Jones, K. M. (1994, March). Quick response key to resolving complaints. *HRMagazine*, 42–47. Copyright 1999 by Society for Human Resource Management (SHRM). Reproduced with permission of Society for Human Resource Management (SHRM) in the format Textbook & Other book via Copyright Clearance Center. [b]Leonard, B. (1999, February). A new era at the EEOC. *HRMagazine*, 54–62; EEOC Web site. (2014). History of the EEOC mediation program. *www.eeoc.gov/eeoc/mediation/history.cfm.*

Ask Only for Information You Need to Know

Companies should ask only for information that is related to job performance.[81] For instance, you should not ask about an applicant's religious affiliation, although you may ask whether a person can work on specific days of the week. Similarly, you can ask whether the applicant is capable of performing the essential physical aspects of the job (preferably specifically listed), but asking general questions about health would probably be interpreted as a violation of the ADA. Figure 3.8 gives examples of appropriate and inappropriate questions to ask on an application form or during an interview.

A final point to consider in this chapter is that the EEOC rules affect the language that is spoken at the workplace. As described in the Manager's Notebook titled "Employers Should Be Careful When Using English-Only Policies at the Workplace," employers cannot enforce an English-only policy at the workplace unless there is a business necessity to justify that employees speak English on their job.

Subject of Questions	Examples of Acceptable Questions	Examples of Unacceptable Questions	Comments
Name	"What is your name?" "Have you worked for this company under another name?"	"What was your maiden name?"	Questions about an applicant's name that may indicate marital status or national origin should be avoided.
Age	"Are you at least 18 years old?" "Upon employment, all employees must submit legal proof of age. Can you furnish proof of age?"	"What is your date of birth?" "What is your age?" "When did you graduate from high school?"	A request for age-related data may discourage older workers from applying.
Race, Ethnicity, and Physical Characteristics	"After employment, the company must have a photograph of all employees. If employed, can you furnish a photograph?" "Do you read, speak, or write a foreign language?"	"What is your race?" "What are your height and weight?" "Would you please submit a photograph with your application for identification purposes?" "What language do you commonly use?"	Information relative to physical characteristics may be associated with sexual or racial group membership.
Religion	A statement may be made by the employer of the days, hours, and shifts worked.	"What is your religious faith?" "Does your religion keep you from working on weekends?" "What holidays will you need off?"	Questions that determine applicants' availability have an exclusionary effect because of some people's religious practices.
Gender, Marital Status, and Family	"If you are a minor, please list the name and address of a parent or guardian." "Please provide the name, address, and telephone number of someone who should be contacted in case of an emergency."	"What is your sex?" "Describe your current marital status." "List the number and ages of your children." "If you have children, please describe the provisions you have made for child care." "With whom do you reside?"	Direct or indirect questions about marital status, children, pregnancy, and childbearing plans frequently discriminate against women and may be a violation of Title VII.
Physical Conditions	"Are you willing to take a physical exam if the nature of the job for which you are applying requires one?"	"Do you have any physical disabilities, defects, or handicaps?" "How would you describe your general physical health?" "When was your last physical exam?"	A blanket policy excluding the disabled is discriminatory. Where physical condition is a requirement for employment, employers should be able to document the business necessity for questions on the application form relating to physical condition.
Military Service	"Please list any specific educational or job experiences you may have acquired during military service that you believe would be useful in the job for which you are applying."	"Please list the dates and type of discharge you may have received from military service."	Minority service members have a higher percentage of undesirable military discharges. A policy of rejecting those with less than an honorable discharge may be discriminatory.

(continued)

FIGURE 3.8

Examples of Acceptable and Unacceptable Questions Asked on Application Forms or During Interviews

Subject of Questions	Examples of Acceptable Questions	Examples of Unacceptable Questions	Comments
Hobbies, Clubs, and Organizations	"Do you have any hobbies that are related to the job for which you are making application?" "Please list any clubs or organizations in which you are a member that relate to the job for which you are applying."	"Please list any hobbies you may have." "Please list all clubs and other organizations in which you are a member."	If questions on club/organization memberships are asked, a statement should be added that applicants may omit those organizations associated with age, race, sex, or religion.
Credit Rating	None.	"Do you own your own car?" "Do you own or rent your residence?"	Use of credit rating questions tends to have an adverse impact on minority group applicants and has been found unlawful. Unless shown to be job related, questions on car ownership, home ownership, length of residence, garnishments of wages, etc., may violate Title VII.
Arrest Record	"Have you ever been convicted of a crime related to the job you will be expected to perform?" Example: A conviction of embezzlement is related to the job of bank loan officer.	"Have you ever been arrested for a crime?"	Asking if an applicant has ever been arrested violates the applicant's Title VII rights because such questions adversely affect minority applicants.

FIGURE 3.8 (Continued)

Sources: Based on *HR Focus*. (2008, March). Interview with questions that should be on every company's 'don't' list, 9; Gatewood, R. D., and Feild, H. S. (2001). *Human resource selection*, 5th ed. Fort Worth, TX: Harcourt College Publishers. Copyright © 2001 by the Harcourt College Publishers, reproduced by permission of the publisher; and Bland, T., and Stalcup, S. (1999, March). Build a legal employment application. *HRMagazine*, 129–133.

MANAGER'S NOTEBOOK

Ethics/Social Responsibility

Employers Should Be Careful When Using English-Only Policies at the Workplace

Under EEOC rules, it may be unlawful to enforce English-only policies at the workplace. Such policies can be a form of national-origin discrimination against employees who prefer to speak the language of their ethnic background. However, an English-only rule may be justified in the following situations:

- Communications with customers, coworkers, or supervisors who only speak English
- In emergencies or other situations in which workers must speak a common language to promote safety
- For cooperative work assignments in which the English-only rule is needed to promote efficiency
- To enable a supervisor who only speaks English to monitor the performance of an employee whose job duties require communication with coworkers or customers

Even if justified by business necessity in the situations that are listed above, an English-only policy should not be applied to casual conversations between employees who are not performing their job.

Sources: Based on Tuschman, R. (2012, November 15). English-only policies in the workplace: Are they legal? Are they smart? *Forbes. www.forbes.com*; Brook, J. (2012, February 15). Are workplace English-only rules legal? *Continuing Education of the Bar Blog. www.blog.ceb.com*; *Wilson Elser LLP Web Site*. (2010, May). Whether and when English-only rules in the workplace are discriminatory. *www.wilsonelser.com*. ■■

Summary and Conclusions

Why Understanding the Legal Environment Is Important

Understanding and complying with human resource law is important because (1) it is the right thing to do, (2) it helps you realize the limitations of your firm's HR and legal departments, and (3) it helps you minimize your firm's potential liability.

Challenges to Legal Compliance

HR law is challenging for four reasons. Laws, regulations, and court decisions are all part of a dynamic legal landscape. The laws and regulations are complex. The strategies for fair employment required by the laws and regulations sometime compete with, rather than reinforce, one another. And laws often have unanticipated or unintended consequences.

Equal Employment Opportunity Laws

The following are the most important EEO laws: (1) Equal Pay Act of 1963—prohibits discrimination in pay between men and women performing the same job in the same organization. (2) Title VII of the Civil Rights Act of 1964—prohibits employers from basing employment decisions on a person's race, color, religion, sex, or national origin. It has been amended or interpreted to prohibit discrimination based on pregnancy (the Pregnancy Discrimination Act of 1978) and sexual harassment. Most recently, it has been amended by the Civil Rights Act of 1991, which places the burden of proof in a discrimination case squarely on the defendant (employer), prohibits the use of quotas, and allows for punitive and compensatory damages as well as jury trials. Executive Order 11246 prohibits discrimination against the same categories of people that Title VII protects, but also requires that government agencies and contractors take affirmative action to promote the employment of persons in protected classes. (3) Age Discrimination in Employment Act of 1967—prohibits discrimination against employees who are 40 years old or older. (4) Americans with Disabilities Act of 1990—prohibits discrimination against individuals with disabilities who can perform the essential functions of a job with or without reasonable accommodation. The Vocational Rehabilitation Act of 1973, the precursor to ADA, applied only to government agencies and contractors. (5) Vietnam Era Veterans Readjustment Act of 1974—prohibits discrimination against Vietnam-era veterans by federal contractors and requires federal contractors to take affirmative action to hire Vietnam-era veterans.

EEO Enforcement and Compliance

Two main agencies are responsible for enforcing EEO laws. The Equal Employment Opportunity Commission (EEOC) enforces EEO laws. It processes discrimination complaints, issues written regulations, and gathers and disseminates information. The Office of Federal Contract Compliance Programs (OFCCP) enforces the laws and executive orders that apply to the federal government and its contractors. The OFCCP also monitors the quality and effectiveness of affirmative action plans.

Other Important Laws

The Immigration Reform and Control Act of 1986 requires employers to document the legal work status of their employees. The Immigration Act of 1990 makes it easier for skilled immigrants to enter the United States. The Drug-Free Workplace Act of 1988 requires that government contractors try to ensure that their workplaces are free of drug use. The Uniformed Services Employment and Reemployment Act of 1994 protects the rights of private sector employees who take short leaves to perform military service.

Avoiding Pitfalls in EEO

Employers can avoid many pitfalls associated with HR law by engaging in sound management practices. Among the most important of these practices are training, establishing an employee complaint resolution system, documenting decisions, communicating honestly with employees, and asking job applicants only for information the employer needs to know.

Key Terms

Watch It!

UPS: Equal Opportunity Employment. If your instructor has assigned this, go to **mymanagementlab.com** to watch a video and answer questions.

Discussion Questions

3-1. Explain why HR decisions are heavily regulated. Based on your analysis of current social forces, what new laws or regulations do you think will be passed or issued in the next few years?

3-2. Quotas can be seen as means by which resources and opportunities are transferred from an advantaged group to a disadvantaged group. Some justify this approach by stating that it addresses past imbalances and ensures that diversity is recognized. Are imposing quotas to ensure equal opportunity reasonable? Is the very nature of the quota anti-equal opportunity? How would a fair system work?

3-3. What is adverse impact? How does it differ from adverse treatment?

3-4. How can an individual show prima facie evidence for adverse impact discrimination? How would an employer defend itself from this evidence?

3-5. Multi-cultural and multi-religious workforces have complicated the issues surrounding paid holidays for religious festivals and observance. In some countries, where there is a state religion, the basic requirements for employers are fairly clear. In other countries, where there is no statutory requirement to allow leave for religious purposes, the situation is more complex and borders on issues of potential discrimination. In the UK, for example, if an employee wants to take a day off in observance of a religious holiday or festival, employers are urged to accommodate this as long as it does not interfere with their business. How is this matter handled in your country?

MyManagementLab®

If your instructor has assigned this, go to **mymanagementlab.com** for the following Assisted-graded writing questions:

3-6. Kate has severe diabetes that seriously limits her ability to eat. Even when taking insulin to help manage her diabetes, Kate must test her blood sugar several times a day and strictly monitor the availability of food, the time she eats, and the type and quantity of food she eats to avoid serious medical consequences. Does Kate have a disability under the ADA? Explain your answer.

3-7. Under the ADA, is an obese individual considered to have a disability and therefore be eligible for coverage? Explain.

3-8. What are bona fide occupational qualifications (BFOQ)? What is a business necessity? Can race be a BFOQ? Can it be a business necessity? Why or why not?

You Manage It! 1: Emerging Trends

Walgreens Leads the Way in Utilizing Workers with Disabilities

In 2008, Walgreens, one of the nation's largest drugstore retailers, opened a state-of-the-art distribution center in Windsor, Connecticut. It is the company's second facility designed specifically to employ people with disabilities and is patterned after a similar one that opened in 2007 in South Carolina. Managers at both facilities share a goal of having people with disabilities fill at least one-third of the available jobs.

Walgreens has developed a reputation as a company that offers meaningful jobs to people with diverse backgrounds, with equal opportunities for advancement and job mobility. Company leaders intend to open more distribution centers that employ workers with disabilities and plan to use the experience in the facilities in Connecticut and South Carolina to provide managers in other units with information that will result in the hiring of more people with disabilities.

The South Carolina distribution center has a workforce of 400, with 50 percent having a disclosed physical or cognitive disability. Yet the facility's efficiency increased by 20 percent since its opening, after technology and process changes originally intended to accommodate workers with disabilities improved everyone's jobs. According to one of Walgreens' corporate executives of human resources, the experience of creating a disability-friendly environment in its distribution centers has been a transforming event for the company. Walgreens' success in hiring people with disabilities to work at its distribution centers has influenced more than a dozen U.S. companies, including Lowe's, Procter & Gamble, and Best Buy, to follow Walgreens' model.

Many employers do not share or practice Walgreens' level of long-term commitment and investment in hiring people with disabilities, but demographic trends suggest that more companies should—and ultimately will have to—as growth of the traditional labor pool slows, the workforce ages, and disability rates increase. As more business executives recognize and support the hiring and development of workers with disabilities, a chronically underemployed group, the business benefits of tapping this talent pool becomes clear.

Critical Thinking Questions

3-9. What are the tangible and intangible benefits that Walgreens receives by being a leader in hiring employees with disabilities?

3-10. Only about half of the people with disabilities who want to work are employed. What barriers do people with disabilities face in obtaining employment that are not concerns of other groups protected by the EEOC, such as minorities, women, or the aged?

Team Exercise

3-11. A serious barrier to employment of people with disabilities continues to be a perception problem. Managers and co-workers lack knowledge, awareness, and comfort in working with employees with disabilities. Form a team with three or four classmates and develop a strategy to overcome misperceptions surrounding utilizing employees with disabilities. Be ready to present your team's ideas to the rest of the class when called on by the instructor.

Experiential Exercise: Individual

3-12. The purpose of this exercise is to raise your self-awareness of some of the problems faced by employees with disabilities in the workforce. Assume that you have had an accident that will restrict your mobility for a year and that you will need to use a wheelchair while you recover from the accident. Consider how the restrictions on your mobility would affect your life as a student. What accommodations would your teachers need to make for you so you could attend your classes during the academic year? If you are employed on a part-time job, would you be able to continue doing this job as before in a wheelchair? If not, would the employer be able to restructure the job in a way so you could make a significant contribution as an employee? How would the job change? How could you convince your employer that you should be retained in your job? Be prepared to share your answers to these questions with other members of the class.

Sources: Based on Otto, B. (2013, January 14). Walgreens is not always the answer. *Huffington Post. www.huffingtonpost.com*; Wells, S. (2008, April). Counting on workers with disabilities: The nation's largest minority remains an underused resource. *HRMagazine*, 45–49; Medical News Today. (2006, July 8). Walgreens recruits employees with disabilities through new highly accessible web site. *www.medicalnewstoday.com*.

You Manage It! 2: Customer-Driven HR

Can an Employer Refuse to Hire or Retain Employees Who Wear Tattoos?

The wearing of tattoos has become increasingly popular—particularly so with younger people—as a form of personal expression. A survey conducted by the Pew Research Center estimated that 36 percent of people 18 to 25 years of age, and 40 percent of those from 26 to 40, have had at least one tattoo. Despite the growing popularity of tattoos, many companies are not tolerant of the display of visible tattoos on employees in the workplace. For example, according to research from CareerBuilder, 42 percent of corporate managers indicated that their opinion of a job applicant would change for the worse if the individual displayed a tattoo. Tattoos are viewed as unacceptable in some professions or jobs as a consequence of corporate dress codes that forbid the display of visible tattoos. In the medical field, for example, many health care organizations limit the display of tattoos. This policy is in line with the need to demonstrate professionalism to patients in order to gain their trust. The Cleveland Clinic requires that tattoos must be covered during working hours to ensure a professional appearance.

The EEOC laws do not provide protection to persons who are discriminated against by employers in the workplace for wearing visible tattoos. Employers are free to establish dress codes that restrict employees from having visible tattoos if they believe that a tattoo will harm a company's professional image.

If a company decides to limit the display of tattoos in the workplace, it must do so in a fair and consistent manner, or it can be subject to legal actions from tattoo-wearing employees or job applicants. There should be a written personal appearance policy that covers the wearing of tattoos and it should be enforced consistently across different units and locations. If a continuing employee obtains a tattoo while employed, the employer should attempt to make a reasonable accommodation with the employee in order to retain that employee. For example, an employee may be asked to wear long pants to cover a large tattoo on the leg as a reasonable accommodation that makes the tattoo less visible to the public. Employers who act overly harsh in enforcing a policy that restricts wearing tattoos may find themselves in court and will be required to defend their practices.

Critical Thinking Questions

3-13. If a corporation restricts its employees from displaying visible tattoos in the workplace and faces a court challenge of employment discrimination under EEOC regulations, on what basis can the corporation defend its employment practice? Refer to the information in this case as well as in this chapter in the section on "Defense of Discrimination Charges " to answer this question.

3-14. A company's sales representative obtained a highly visible tattoo on her neck after being employed at that company. The company has a dress code policy that restricts the display of visible tattoos for work that has close contact with customers. What would be a reasonable accommodation to present to this employee that would balance the need for enforcement of the dress code policy with a goal of being fair and acting in good faith to company employees?

Team Exercise

3-15. Companies that have dress code policies should balance the company need for regulating the appearance of employees and how it reflects on the company image with the employees' needs to appear in a way that reflects their individual identities. Form a team with several classmates and develop a policy covering the display of tattoos for the Cleveland Clinic, a health care facility, which is referred to in this case. In the policy for tattoos in the workplace, cover the following issues: (1) defining the employees who are covered (and not covered) by the policy; (2) the display of visible tattoos; (3) reasonable accommodations for employees with visible tattoos; (4) sanctions for employees who violate the tattoo policy within the dress code. Be ready to report your team's findings to the rest of the class when called on by the instructor.

Experiential Exercise: Individual

3-16. The purpose of this exercise is to reflect on the implications on a person's career when planning on getting a tattoo. Assume that a friend of yours informed you that she is planning on getting a tattoo. She will be graduating soon from a university with a degree in business and will be looking for a job in marketing, which is the field that she concentrated on for her business degree. What advice would you give to your friend concerning the tattoo she is about to obtain? Your advice will cover the following aspects of getting a tattoo: (1) locations for the tattoo on a person's body that could limit an individual's opportunity to obtain a job offer or promotion into management in the marketing field; (2) images or topics for a tattoo which could be considered controversial or offensive to employers or customers and could limit career advancement; and (3) size and prominence of the tattoo, which can make a strong first impression during interviews. Be prepared to share the advice you gave to the friend with your fellow classmates when called upon by the instructor.

Sources: Based on Green, S. (2013, February 8). Making tattoos and piercings a workplace issue without breaking the law. *Corporate Counsel. www.law.com/corporatecounsel*; Hennessey, R. (2013, February 27). Tattoos no longer a kiss of death in the workplace. *Forbes. www.forbes.com*; Lebros, A. (2010, February 18). Discrimination based on tattoos, a sad reality for those who embrace their permanent inked bodies. *The Famuan. www.thefamuanonline.com*; Fuller, S. (2013). Effects of tattoos on jobs. *eHow. www.ehow.com*.

You Manage It! 3: Discussion

Are Women Breaking Through the Glass Ceiling?

"Glass ceiling" refers to invisible or artificial barriers that prevent women and people of color from advancing above a certain level in an organization. In the United States, women represent 30 percent of all managers but less than 5 percent of executives.

The glass ceiling does not represent a typical form of discrimination that consists of entry barriers to women and minorities within organizations. Rather, it represents a subtle form of discrimination that includes gender stereotypes, lack of opportunities for women to gain job experiences necessary for advancement, and lack of top-management commitment to providing resources to promote initiatives that support an environment for women to advance to the top executive ranks.

As an invisible barrier, the glass ceiling is difficult to crash through legislation. Informal networking and mentoring are often mentioned as ways of increasing opportunities for women to become executives. However, cross-gender relationships between a male mentor and a female employee may be discouraged by the sexual tensions that arise in such relationships, because they can become close, blurring the distinction between their professional and personal lives. In some instances, a mentoring relationship with a younger female may threaten the established male with the potential for a career-wrecking allegation of sexual harassment in which the woman is viewed as the victim, because she ranks lower in the hierarchy. Although same-gender female mentoring relationships are less likely to be as problematic as the cross-gender ones, they depend on the availability of senior female executives willing and able to nurture high-potential women.

Despite the glass ceiling, by 2012 the number of women who achieved the position of chief executive officer (CEO) or chairman of a major Fortune 500 corporation in the United States was much greater than the number of women who were top executives in large corporations in 1997. Here are some women executives who have clearly broken through the glass ceiling, as of 2012:

- Ginni Rometty, CEO and Chairman of IBM
- Indra Nooyi, CEO and Chairperson of PepsiCo
- Irene Rosenfeld, CEO and Chairman of Mondelēz International, Inc.
- Ursula Burns, CEO and Chairman of Xerox
- Meg Whitman, CEO of Hewlett-Packard
- Ellen Kullman, CEO and Chairman of DuPont

Critical Thinking Questions

3-17. Examine the situation of women in senior positions in your own country. Explore the Web sites to learn more about the women who are either the CEO or chairperson at these companies. The Web sites might have profiles so you can learn more about the CEO and other top executives. Another possibility to gather some background on the careers of executive women is to use a search engine such as Yahoo! and search on the company name and name of the CEO or chairperson. Develop a rationale to explain how these women overcame the "glass ceiling" and attained the top executive role in a business in your own country. What country-specific hurdles faced them and how did they overcome them?

3-18. Some male senior executives avoid becoming mentors to younger women because of their fear of possible sexual harassment claims against them (as retribution for a romantic relationship that ends badly) or office gossip suggesting the mentoring pair are having a romance. Do you think it is reasonable for male executives to have fears about what could evolve or be suggested about professional relationships with female managers? How could a woman seeking a mentor go about cultivating a mentoring relationship with a male senior executive, being aware that some men have reservations about establishing close professional relationships with women due to office gossip or the possibility of a romantic relationship that results in the male having to defend himself against charges of sexual harassment?

Team Exercise

3-19. With a team of four or five students, develop an HR plan to break down some of the glass-ceiling barriers in an organization that is male dominated at the upper ranks. Some examples of male-dominated industries include high technology (Intel, Texas Instruments, and Cisco Systems, for example), defense (Boeing, Lockheed Martin, and General Dynamics, for example), and energy (Exxon, BP-Amoco, and Chevron, for example). Think of specific HR activities that could "add value" to the firm by breaking down barriers to women who are seeking to become executives in the organization. Some HR functions that could provide fruitful sources include training, recruitment and selection, compensation, benefits, work systems, HR planning, performance appraisal, employee relations, and discipline. Be prepared to present and defend your plan to other members of your class.

Experiential Exercise: Individual

3-20. Some women avoid the glass ceiling by becoming entrepreneurs. Contact three female entrepreneurs or business owners and ask them some questions that pertain to owning their own business. Start with your own network of family and friends and the entrepreneurship center at the business school at your university or a professor who teaches entrepreneurship. You could also contact the Chamber of Commerce in your city.

Here are some questions to pose in your interviews: Why did you decide to start your own business? What have you learned from the experience of being an entrepreneur? When is the best time in one's career to start a business? Why do you think there is a growing trend among professional women to start their own businesses? Now that more women are becoming CEOs of large corporations, do you think there are fewer obstacles for women to advance to the top of organizations?

After you complete your interviews, summarize the results. What seem to be the key advantages of being a business owner? Do you think that male entrepreneurs would provide the same answers to your questions? Did any of the women you spoke with bring up gender issues related to their former employer as motivations for their career change? Be prepared to share your findings with other members of the class.

Sources: Based on Kowitt, B., Leahey, C., and VanderMey, A. (2012, October 8). The 50 most powerful women. *Fortune*, 128–134; Petrecca, L. (2011, October 27). More women on top to lead top companies. *USA Today*, 3B; Morris, B. (2005, January 10). How corporate America is betraying women. *Fortune*, 64–74; Bell, M., McLaughlin, M., and Sequeira, J. (2002, April). Discrimination, harassment, and the glass ceiling: Women executives as change agents. *Journal of Business Ethics*, 65–76; and Haben, M. (2001, April/May). Shattering the glass ceiling. *Executive Speeches*, 4–10.

You Manage It! 4: Ethics/Social Responsibility

Are Employee Noncompete Agreements Legally Enforceable? It Depends

Once reserved for job-hopping executives and entrepreneurs, noncompete agreements are being used in a range of businesses. From engineering firms in Massachusetts to companies that paint lines on Virginia highways, businesses of all sorts are pushing new hires to sign noncompete agreements that legally restrict them from working for competitors.

When billionaire Ross Perot sold his company Electronic Data Systems to General Motors for $2.4 billion in 1984, he signed a noncompete agreement that restricted him from competing against his former company for four years, after which he started Perot Systems.

Although putting employment restrictions on an executive or entrepreneur, who is likely to know sensitive trade secrets, from competing against a former employer is probably necessary, why should ordinary employees be required to sign noncompete agreements that restrict their employability if they leave their employer? Don't employees have a right to make a living, even after they stop working for their employer?

Noncompete agreements are the most stringent legal barrier that restricts an employee's right to practice his or her profession. Alternatively, some companies ask employees to sign less onerous confidentiality agreements or nonsolicitation agreements, which simply prevent employees from taking company secrets or client relationships when they change jobs.

At Space Care Interiors, a Berkeley, Michigan, office-furniture company, sales employees were asked to sign noncompete agreements to prevent them from taking company clients with them when they changed jobs. The noncompete agreement the employees signed required that employees would not work for a competitor within a 50-mile radius of the company for one to two years after leaving the firm. When a former employee violated the noncompete agreement by working for a nearby competitor shortly after quitting Space Care Interiors, the company threatened legal action and received a negotiated cash settlement from the former employee. The factors that were favorable to the company's interests in this case were that the noncompete agreement was narrowly confined to only 50 miles and one to two years, and that the courts in Michigan are likely to enforce these agreements, as are courts in Florida, Texas, and New Jersey.

Sometimes a judge will decide to throw out an entire noncompete agreement if its terms are too broad. In the recent case of Spivey Pavement Markings, in Chesapeake, Virginia, a Spivey supervisor quit in 2006 and soon started a foreman job at a similar company, Mid-Atlantic Pavement Markings. A year later Spivey sued the supervisor, trying to enforce its noncompete agreement, which was intended to prevent the former employee from taking such a job. Spivey claimed that the supervisor received training in a specific method of painting and road markings and that the firm did not want him sharing his knowledge of the technique with a competitor. However, the judge refused to enforce Spivey's noncompete agreement, calling it "overbroad, ambiguous and vague." The noncompete agreement banned the former employee from doing any kind of work for a competing company, even janitorial work. A legal expert who commented on the decision thought that the noncompete agreement would have been enforceable if it had been written so that it focused on an employee's specific job duties.

Noncompete agreements are less likely to be enforced in a few states that are friendlier to the interests of employees. The states where it is difficult to enforce a noncompete agreement include California, Wisconsin, Georgia, Oregon, and Colorado.

Critical Thinking Questions

3-21. What is the purpose of a noncompete agreement? Do you think it is ethical for a company to require its employees to sign a noncompete agreement as a condition of employment? Under what conditions do you consider it to be acceptable for an employer to ask an employee to sign a noncompete agreement?

3-22. What are alternative ways to manage employee behavior so they do not harm their former employer after they quit? Are there any HR practices that could be used to achieve this outcome?

Team Exercise

3-23. Form a team with several students and develop a generic noncompete agreement that could be used by a company. Describe the company where the noncompete agreement will be used. Which types of jobs will the noncompete agreement cover? How many years will employees who quit the employer be restricted from using their job knowledge at another company? How large a geographic area will the noncompete agreement encompass? What industries will the employees be restricted from working in under the noncompete agreement? Be prepared to share your team's results with other members of the class when called upon by the instructor.

Experiential Exercise: Individual

3-24. In the role of an HR legal specialist, you have been approached by an inventor in your own country who is being threatened by their former employer. The former employee worked for the company for 10 years, after leaving them, the employee invented a gadget that was designed to compete with the devices sold by the former employer. As part of the contract of employment, there was a clause that stated that former employees could neither work for a competitor nor start a business that competed with the employer for a period of 10 years after leaving them. Research whether this non-compete clause is legally binding or not. The employee is of the opinion that when the contract was signed, he was young and in a very junior position with the business.

Sources: Based on Morris, S. (2008, February). Protecting company secrets: More business owners are forcing their new hires to sign noncompetes. Should you? *Inc. Magazine*, 38–39; Workplace Fairness. (2008). Noncompete agreements. *www.workplacefairness.org*.

Endnotes

Scan for Endnotes or go to http://www.pearsonglobaleditions.com/Gomez-Mejia.

APPENDIX TO

CHAPTER 3

Human Resource Legislation Discussed in This Text

The laws are listed in chronological order.

Law	Year	Description	Chapter(s)
Workers' Compensation Laws	Various	State-by-state laws that establish insurance plans to compensate employees injured on the job	12, 15, 16
Social Security Act	1935	Payroll tax to fund retirement benefits, disability and unemployment insurance	12
Wagner Act	1935	Legitimized labor unions and established the National Labor Relations Board	14, 15
Fair Labor Standards Act	1938	Established minimum wage and overtime pay	10, 15
Taft-Hartley Act	1947	Provided some protections for employers and limited union power; permitted states to enact right-to-work laws	15
Landrum-Griffin Act	1959	Protects union members' right to participate in union affairs	15
Equal Pay Act	1963	Prohibits unequal pay for same job	3, 10
Title VII of Civil Rights Act	1964	Prohibits employment decisions based on race, color, religion, sex, and national origin	3, 4, 5, 7, 14, 16, 17
Executive Order 11246	1965	Same as Title VII; also requires affirmative action	3
Age Discrimination in Employment Act	1967	Prohibits employment decisions based on age when person is 40 or older	3, 5
Occupational Safety and Health Act	1970	Establishes safety and health standards for organizations to protect employees	14, 16
Employee Retirement Income Security Act (ERISA)	1974	Regulates the financial stability of employee benefit and pension plans	12
Vietnam-Era Veterans Readjustment Act	1974	Prohibits federal contractors from discriminating against Vietnam-era veterans and encourages affirmative action plans to hire Vietnam veterans	3
Pregnancy Discrimination Act	1978	Prohibits employers from discriminating against pregnant women	3, 16

Law	Year	Description	Chapter(s)
Job Training Partnership Act	1982	Provides block money grants to states, which pass them on to local governments and private entities that provide on-the-job training	8
Consolidated Omnibus Budget Reconciliation Act (COBRA)	1985	Requires continued health insurance coverage (paid by employee) following termination	12
Immigration Reform and Control Act	1986	Prohibits discrimination based on citizenship status; employers required to document employees' legal work status	3, 17
Worker Adjustment and Retraining Act (WARN)	1988	Employers required to notify workers of impending layoffs	6
Drug-Free Workplace Act	1988	Covered employers must implement certain policies to restrict employee drug use	3, 16
Americans with Disabilities Act (ADA)	1990	Prohibits discrimination based on disability	3, 4, 5, 14, 16
Civil Rights Act	1991	Amends Title VII; prohibits quotas, allows for monetary punitive damages	3, 5
Family and Medical Leave Act	1993	Employers must provide unpaid leave for childbirth, adoption, illness	12, 15
Uniformed Services Employment and Reemployment Rights Act	1994	Employers must not discriminate against individuals who take leave from work to fulfill military service obligations	3
Health Insurance Portability and Accountability Act	1996	Employees are allowed to transfer their coverage of existing illnesses to new employer's insurance plan	12
Pension Protection Act	2006	Employees are given greater flexibility to diversify out of company stock in their 401(k) plan	12
ADA Amendments Act	2008	Broadens coverage of ADA to more people	3
Patient Protection and Affordable Care Act	2010	Extends health care coverage to more people and makes it more affordable	12

Laws discussed briefly:

Byrnes Anti-Strikebreaking Act—Chapter 15
Coal Mine Health and Safety Act—Chapter 16
Employee Polygraph Protection Act—Chapter 5
Immigration Act of 1990—Chapter 3
Norris-LaGuardia Act—Chapter 15
Older Workers Protection Act of 1990—Chapter 3
Railway Labor Act—Chapter 15

CHAPTER 4 Managing Diversity

MyManagementLab®

When you see this icon, visit **www.mymanagementlab.com** for activities that are applied, personalized, and offer immediate feedback.

CHALLENGES

After reading this chapter, you should be able to deal more effectively with the following challenges:

1 **Understand** the meaning of diversity.

2 **Develop** familiarity with major challenges in managing employee diversity.

3 **Become** aware of major elements of diversity in organizations.

4 **Learn** how to improve the management of diversity in organizations.

5 **Learn** how to avoid potential pitfalls in diversity management programs.

The second-grade school teacher posed a simple problem to the class: "There are four blackbirds sitting in a tree. You take a slingshot and shoot one of them. How many are left?"

"Three," answered the seven-year-old European with certainty. "One subtracted from four leaves three."

"Zero," answered the seven-year-old African with equal certainty. "If you shoot one bird, the others will fly away."

Which child answered correctly? Clearly, the answer depends on your cultural point of view. For the first child, the birds in the problem represented a hypothetical situation that required a literal answer. For the second child, the birds in the problem had a relationship to known behavior that could be expected to occur.[1]

Source: © Maureen Ruddy Burkhart/Alamy.

The Managerial Perspective

To succeed as a manager in the twenty-first century, you must work effectively with people who are different from you. The labor force is becoming more diverse in terms of ethnicity, race, sex, sexual orientation, disability, and other cultural factors. The managerial challenge is learning how to take advantage of this diversity while fostering cooperation and cohesiveness among dissimilar employees. The HR department can help you meet this challenge by developing training programs, offering assistance and advice, establishing fair selection procedures, and the like. But in the end, the line manager is the person who interacts face-to-face with diverse employees on a daily basis. In this chapter, we explore diversity issues that affect managers and the skills needed to make employee diversity a source of competitive advantage.

The blackbird story clearly illustrates one of the most important truths of HRM: People with different life experiences may interpret reality very differently. By the time people enter an organization, their *cognitive structure*—the way they perceive and respond to the world around them—has been largely determined. This cognitive structure is shaped both by unique personal experiences (with family, peers, school system) and by the socializing influences of the person's culture, and it operates both at home and in the workplace.

Learn It!

If your professor has chosen to assign this go to **www.mymanagementlab.com** to see what you should particularly focus on, and take the chapter 4 warmup.

What Is Diversity?

Although definitions vary, **diversity** simply refers to human characteristics that make people different from one another. The English language has well over 23,000 words to describe personality[2] (such as "outgoing," "intelligent," "friendly," "loyal," "paranoid," and "nerdy"). The sources of individual variation are complex, but they can generally be grouped into two categories: those over which people have little or no control and those over which they have some control.[3]

diversity
Human characteristics that make people different from one another.

Individual characteristics over which a person has little or no control include biologically determined characteristics such as race, sex, age, and certain physical attributes, as well as the family and society into which he or she is born. These factors exert a powerful influence on individual identity and directly affect how a person relates to others.

In the second category are characteristics that people can adopt, drop, or modify during their lives through conscious choice and deliberate efforts. These include work background, income, marital status, military experience, political beliefs, geographic location, and education.

It is important to keep in mind the distinction between the sources of diversity and the diversity itself. Without this distinction, stereotyping tends to occur. Essentially, *stereotyping* is assuming that group averages or tendencies are true for each and every member of that group. For instance, employees who have had significant military experience are generally more accepting of an authoritarian management style than those who have not had such experience. However, if you conclude that *all* veterans favor authoritarian leadership, you will be wrong. Although veterans *on average* are more accepting of authority, there may be, as Figure 4.1 shows, very wide differences among veterans on this score. True, veterans *on the whole* show this characteristic to a greater degree than nonveterans, but the differences *within* each group are far greater than the average difference between groups. In fact, many veterans develop a distaste for authoritarian management *because* of their military experience, and many nonveterans prefer an authoritarian leadership style.

If you take this example and substitute any two groups (male–female, young–old, and so on) and any individual characteristic (aggressiveness, flexibility, amount of education), you will find in the vast majority of cases that the principle illustrated by Figure 4.1 holds true. In fact, it is very difficult to identify individual characteristics that do *not* have a substantial overlap between two groups. The main point of this discussion is to emphasize that, although employees are diverse, a relatively small amount of this diversity is explained by their group membership.

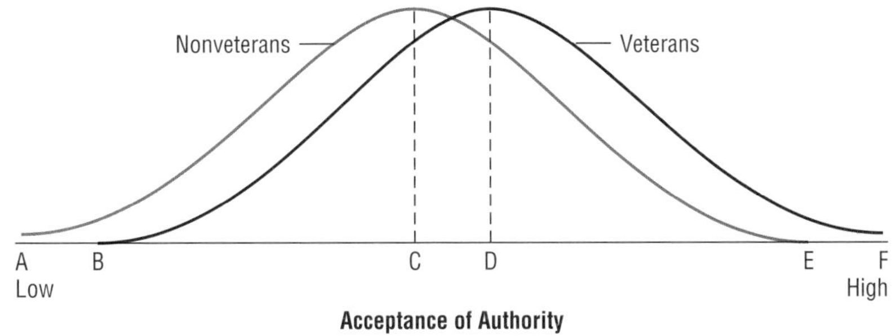

FIGURE 4.1
Group Versus Individual Differences on Acceptance of Authoritarian Leadership

Why Manage Employee Diversity?

To survive and prosper in an increasingly heterogeneous society, organizations must capitalize on employee diversity as a source of competitive advantage. For example, Computer Associates International hires software developers from many nationalities, filling jobs where there is an extreme shortage of personnel.[4] Because many of these employees are non-English speakers, Computer Associates offers free courses in English as a second language.[5] Avon Products provides another example of how firms capitalize on diversity. Avon uses its diversity to create a competitive advantage, using feedback from its workforce to adapt to women's changing needs quickly and effectively. The input of Avon's minority employees—almost one-third of its workforce—helped the firm find a successful niche in an industry that tends to ignore the beauty needs of women of color.[6] AT&T provides formal recognition and support to employee networks formed around a characteristic of diversity (such as the Asian Pacific Islanders' Business Resource Group) if the networks present a business plan to management showing their value to the company.[7] Procter & Gamble has a strong multicultural marketing approach, and it views the diversity of its 38,000-plus employees as a key factor in this regard. According to one top company executive, "Diverse organizations are better connected to their markets."[8] A monthly publication, *DiversityInc.*, offers many examples on the most recent diversity initiatives taken by major employers such as Marriott, IBM, Bank of America, Cox, PriceWaterhouse Coopers, Johnson & Johnson, and Ernst & Young.

Affirmative Action Versus Managing Employee Diversity

management of diversity
The set of activities involved in integrating nontraditional employees (women and minorities) into the workforce and using their diversity to the firm's competitive advantage.

Many people perceive *management of diversity* as a new label for affirmative action. In reality, these are two very distinct concepts.[9] *Affirmative action* first emerged from government pressures on business to provide greater opportunities for women and minorities. **Management of diversity**, in contrast, recognizes that traditional firms, where white men are the majority, are becoming a thing of the past. There is a growing awareness that a key factor in corporate performance is how well women and minorities can be fully integrated and work effectively with one another and with their white male counterparts. Given demographic trends, companies can no longer ignore issues of diversity if they are to be successful. For this reason, many organizations (such as the Society for Human Resource Management, Microsoft, Texas Instruments, and Computer Sciences Corporation) specify diversity as the ability to effectively use the talents of people from various backgrounds, experiences, and perspectives.[10] Another term that is currently used to refer to diversity management is *inclusiveness*, or making all employees feel that they are an integral part of the same organization and that they share a common desire to make the firm succeed regardless of their race, gender, age, and so on.[11]

Demographic Trends

In the next decade or so, we will see a dramatic growth rate in people aged 55 or older (46.6% growth rate). Asian Americans, Hispanic Americans, and other ethnic minorities have shown very rapid growth rates since 1990, and these are projected to continue at a fast pace into the end of the decade. In 2014, approximately 16 percent of the U.S. population was considered Hispanic, surpassing the percentage of African Americans (13.0%), Asian Americans (5.6%), and other minority groups (2.0%). All of these groups have registered increases in workforce participation in recent years, and these are also expected to continue. White Americans still made up a substantial majority of the population in the year 2012 (72%), but less of a majority than in 1990 (79.1%). At current growth rates, in 20-plus years or so white Americans will be a minority (less than 50 percent of the total U.S. population). Women's labor force participation rates (currently 47 percent versus 53 percent for males) are expected to keep rising, and men's participation rates to go on declining.

Source: © Megapress/Alamy.

Note that the data previously described is national. If we focus on the larger metropolitan areas, where most business takes place, the changes have been even more dramatic. Of the top 25 markets, "minorities" now make up a majority of the population in at least 20.[12] In Los Angeles, for example, half of the population is foreign born, mostly Asian and Hispanic. Most corporations are located within or near these metropolitan areas and are highly dependent on the local nonwhite labor supply to meet their needs.[13] In some states—most notably California, where nonwhites account for more than half the population—the future is already here.

The idea that individuals can be pigeonholed into racial categories—which goes back centuries to unscientific racist notions of "pure blood" that were incorporated into law by many states well into the 1960s (in part of the South, for instance, even one-eighth black parentage automatically classified a person as being of African descent rather than white)—is likely to crumble in the coming decades. Many first-, second-, and third-generation Americans are descended from immigrants who were mixed race themselves (usually a combination of European, Native American, and/or black). In addition, the number of interracial marriages has increased, and as a result close to half of the mixed-race population is under age 18.[14] One prime example, of course, is U.S. President Barack Obama, the offspring of a white woman and an African father. Currently 16 percent of blacks, 26 percent of Hispanics, and 31 percent of Asians marry outside their race/ethnicity in the United States.[15] In the western states of the United States, almost one-fourth of all new weddings take place across race and ethnic lines. Eventually this will serve to blur the stereotypical classification of people into racial groupings.

Other statistics provide a glimpse of what the near future will look like in terms of labor force characteristics. In 2014, minority children younger than age five are close to becoming the majority nationally, but this is already the case in the nation's fastest-growing states, such as Florida, Nevada, Georgia, Maryland, New York, Texas, and Arizona. Recent immigration is part of the reason for this trend, but it is not the most important. Although about 15 percent more births than deaths have been recorded among whites since 2000, more than eight times as many Hispanics, four times as many Asians, and twice as many blacks have been born than have died.[16] In the most recent 2010 kindergarten class, one out of four five-year-olds was Hispanic, meaning that approximately 25 percent of high school graduates in 2024 will be Hispanic.[17] Since the last edition of this book was published, the annual inflow of undocumented workers has decreased significantly. However, this may well be a temporary phenomenon as a result of the severe recession experienced by the United States during 2008–2011 and the relatively high unemployment rate since then.[18] One interesting development uncovered by the 2010 census is that the Hispanic population grew far greater than expected in states with smaller and newer immigrant populations. For instance, the Hispanic population increased by more than 10 percent in Alabama, Louisiana, Kansas, Maryland, Delaware, and Minnesota when compared to the 2000 census.[19]

Of the more than 20 million jobs projected to be created over the next decade, 75 percent will be filled by women and minorities. This means that firms must actively compete to attract and retain educated and talented workers from those groups: Most large corporations across different industries are eagerly trying to create receptive environments for nontraditional employees. For instance, Lucent Technologies, Chase Manhattan, Marriott International, FedEx, Xerox, Sun Microsystems, Colgate, Palmolive, Merck, and DuPont, among others, have at least one minority member on their board of directors and close to one-fifth of officials and managers who are minority group members.[20]

At the same time more than one-third of small businesses are started by women and minorities.[21] This is important because small businesses employ more than three-fourths of the U.S. population. Many of these businesses become success stories (see the Manager's Notebook, "Recent Success Stories of Small Businesses Launched by Women and Minorities").

MANAGER'S NOTEBOOK

Emerging Trends

Recent Success Stories of Small Businesses Launched by Women and Minorities

Lexington Consulting, El Cajon, California (35 employees)

This company has revenues exceeding $15 million with a three-year growth rate of 14,017.7 percent. The founder and CEO is Jamie Arundell Latshaw. Latshaw spent eight years in active duty with the U.S. Army. Toward the end of her career as an officer, Latshaw noticed that the military was training soldiers in a new way, setting up mock Afghani and Iraqi villages around the United States so soldiers could experience cultural immersion before they deployed. Based on her observations, Latshaw founded Lexicon Consulting (www.inc.com/inc5000/profile/Lexicon-Consulting), which hires Afghani and Iraqi natives living in the United States to be role players in the mock villages. She attributes Lexicon's growth to the role players' passion. "They're really responsible for our success, because they want the soldiers to be successful."

Pursuit of Excellence (11 employees)

This company has annual revenues of approximately $11 million with a three-year growth rate of 7,054.4 percent. The founder and CEO is Marie Diaz, who is Mexican American. Diaz's father died when she was three years old, so she learned a lot about being a strong female from her single mother. After spending years at a Fortune 500 company, Diaz started her own business, a human resources services company, so that she, too, could have a strong presence in her sons' lives. "I was traveling most of the month and never seeing my children," she says. "You have to keep in mind what your priorities are. Plan your life before your life plans you." At Pursuit of Excellence (www.inc.com/inc5000/profile/Pursuit-of-Excellence), Diaz still works around the clock, but being a business owner affords her flexibility she never had before.

A10 Clinical Solutions, Cary, North Carolina (17 employees)

This company has annual revenues exceeding $1 million with a three-year growth rate of 22,714.29 percent. The founder and CEO is Leah Brown, a black entrepreneur. When one of Brown's close relatives passed away from AIDS, she was inspired to start A10 Clinical Solutions (www.inc.com/inc5000/profile/A10-Clinical-Solutions), which manages and oversees clinical trial processes in humans to get drugs approved by the Food and Drug Administration (FDA). Focusing on ailments prominent within minority communities, Brown's company has also started opening medical checkup centers at businesses, airports, and bus stations.

Zempleo, Lafayette, California (41 employees)

This company has annual revenues exceeding $60 million and has experienced a three-year growth rate of 3,466.1 percent. The founder and CEO is Ramiro Zeron, who immigrated to the United States from Nicaragua when he was 29 years old. Although he didn't speak any English when he arrived, Zeron later earned an MBA and worked his way up from a clerical position at AT&T to an executive director. In 2005, working nights and weekends while he was still at his former employer, he founded Zempleo (www.inc.com/inc5000/profile/Zempleo), a staffing and HR company that also provides consulting for business process outsourcing.

Sources: Based on entrepreneurial success stories listed in *www.inc.com*. (2014); Minority Business Entrepreneurs. (2014). *www.mbemag.com*; Minority and Women in Business. (2014). *www.mwb.com*.

At some firms, including such blue-chip companies as Johnson & Johnson, Xerox, General Mills, and Walt Disney, at least one-fourth of the board of directors are nonwhite.[22] At many Fortune 1000 firms, which not too long ago were almost all white, diversity now permeates every facet of management and technical operations. Recent figures confirm this. At Coca-Cola, approximately 40 percent of managers receiving promotions are African American, Latino, Native American, or Asian, and approximately 60 percent were women. At JPMorgan Chase, more than half of new hires are African American, Asian American, Latino, or Native American. At Ernst & Young, almost half of its most recent management promotions went to women, and one-third went to African American, Latino, Asian American, or Native American employees. At AT&T, half of new hires are nonwhite; 27 percent are African American and 15 percent are Latino. The corporate giant IBM has received hundreds of awards for its diversity initiatives in recent years; it has a worldwide executive council to guide specific corporate-wide diversity initiatives. The examples could go on and on. The basic point is that a growing number of firms realize that a changing labor force requires the active recruitment, retention, and advancement of all talents.

In some respects the changes that have occurred since the first edition of this book in the mid-1990s have been remarkable. For instance, in 1995 not one of the Fortune 500 CEOs was a person of color. Today, 21 Fortune 500 companies are run by people of color, including six blacks, seven Hispanics and eight Asians.[23] And it is now commonplace to have one or more senior executives who is a woman or a minority, something that was rare in the mid-1990s. Currently 21 of the Fortune 500 firms are led by women.[24]

DIVERSITY AS AN ASSET An enormous amount of research on diversity-related issues has been conducted in recent years, with the number of publications doubling every five years.[25] For instance, since 2007 most of the major journals dealing with human resource topics have dedicated at least one full issue to this subject, and in some cases more than one.

Two conclusions may be drawn from this research. The first, and perhaps the most obvious, is that managing employee diversity is not a passing fad or just "politically correct" words. Firms must deal with it on a day-to-day basis, given the demographic trends discussed earlier. If anything, this issue will continue to grow in importance. Second, as recently summarized by two leading researchers, "It is now known that diversity's effects on organizations and groups can be positive, negative or neutral."[26] It all depends on how this diversity is managed. In this section, we discuss the positive aspects of diversity, followed by some of the challenges that organizations face in managing that diversity. Later in the chapter, we discuss approaches that firms can use to improve the management of diversity.

Employee diversity can improve organizational functioning by stimulating greater creativity, better problem solving, and greater system flexibility.[27] Rosabeth Kanter, a well-known business consultant based at Harvard University, notes that "most innovative firms purposely establish heterogeneous work groups to bring a multiplicity of points of views on a particular problem."[28] Employee diversity offers a number of other benefits.

- ***Greater creativity*** Employee diversity can stimulate consideration of less obvious alternatives. Consider the following true story:

  > A Hispanic man and a white woman were members of a task force advising the CEO on a planned organizational downsizing. These two people suggested that the recommendation of the task force majority to lay off 10 percent of the workforce would devastate morale. Upon further consideration, the CEO decided not to lay off employees and opted instead for a plan proposed by these two dissenters. The plan proposed to reduce labor costs by offering early retirement, unpaid vacations, and stock in the firm to employees in exchange for a 5-percent salary cut. Most employees reacted very positively to the plan, with many reporting that it increased their loyalty and commitment to the firm.[29]

- ***Better problem solving*** Homogeneous groups are prone to a phenomenon called *groupthink*, in which all members quickly converge on a mistaken solution because they share the same mind-set and view the problem through the lens of conformity.[30] In a heterogeneous group with a broader and richer reservoir of experiences and cultural perspectives, the potential for groupthink shrinks.
- ***Greater system flexibility*** In today's rapidly changing business environments, flexibility is an important characteristic of successful firms. If properly managed, employee diversity can infuse more flexibility into the firm. The existence of diversity at different levels generates more openness to new ideas in general and greater tolerance for different ways of doing things.
- ***Better information*** A more diverse workforce provides the organization with a broader scope of information and set of skills that may be applied to a variety of situations. For example, see the Manager's Notebook, "Police Comb Their Ranks for Foreign-Language Speakers."

MARKETING CONCERNS Most successful firms realize that effective management of a diverse workforce can lead to better marketing strategies for a multicultural, multiethnic population. For example:

- Colgate acquires the top spot in the oral care market with Total toothpaste, which was designed by a team led by older scientists intent on developing a toothpaste for a maturing population. They discovered Triclosan (an ingredient in Total), a broad-spectrum antibiotic used to fight gingivitis, a bleeding gum disease that people are prone to as they age.[31]
- The appearance of more women online is a boom for e-commerce. Women directly influence more than 80 percent of all retail spending, according to BIGreseach LLC, a market-research firm in Worthington, Ohio. When New York–based Bluefly Inc., a retailer of upscale closeout clothing, was launched in mid-1998, the e-commerce market was still a predominantly male place, and an apparel start-up looked like a sure loser. But the

company looked ahead to the day the Internet would attract more women. "We went after this particular category based on the expected shifts," says Jonathan Morris, executive vice president. "We think that's one of the reasons that we're still here, after the dot.com bust."[32]

Diversity as Part of Corporate Strategy

Many firms now believe that effective management of employee diversity is an integral component of their overall strategy and not just a set of programs run by the human resources function to keep government regulators at bay. It has become standard practice in their annual reports for CEOs of Fortune 1000 firms to explicitly mention diversity management as part of their firm's strategic objectives.[33] In many of the Fortune 1000 firms, the person responsible for diversity issues, often called chief diversity officer, now reports directly to the CEO.

Challenges in Managing Employee Diversity

Although employee diversity offers opportunities that can enhance organizational performance, it also presents managers with a new set of challenges. In other words, greater employee diversity by itself does not ensure positive outcomes. A number of researchers have attempted to quantify the effects of diversity.[34] These challenges include appropriately valuing employee diversity, balancing individual needs with group fairness, dealing with resistance to change, ensuring group cohesiveness and open communication, avoiding employee resentment and backlash, retaining valued performers, and maximizing opportunity for all.

MANAGER'S NOTEBOOK

Customer-Driven HR

Police Comb Their Ranks for Foreign-Language Speakers

At a recent graduation ceremony for the New York City Police Department (NYPD), 24 percent of the newly minted officers were foreign born, representing 48 different countries, including Turkey, Venezuela, Burma, and Albania. That was an increase over the preceding year, which saw a graduating class that was only 20 percent foreign born, yet still represented 65 different countries.

"People are coming here from every corner of the world," says NYPD Commissioner Raymond W. Kelly. "It's incumbent on us to be better positioned to identify them and to service them and be aware of their issues."

The NYPD has a staff of about 40 officers whose full-time job is to actively recruit from the city's immigrant communities. The recruiters work with an ad agency to spread the word that the NYPD is interested in native-level speakers of at least 60 languages, including Kurdish, Pashto, Mandarin, Arabic, and Cambodian. For instance, recruitment ads have appeared in Russian-, Korean-, and Haitian-language papers published in the city. Diversity is "necessary to serve a diverse community," says the head of the Recruitment Section. "It builds trust." Preferred consideration is given to applicants who have skills in languages spoken by small minorities, such as Balochi, Chechen, Laotian, Somali, Swahili, Tamil, Twi, and Wolof. Twenty percent of the workforce in recent years was born overseas, and nearly one out of three of New York police officers is Hispanic.

The "language initiative" seems to be working. NYPD officials say that over the past several years the demographic breakdown of police academy applicants has closely matched that of the city's population: about 35 percent white, 23 percent Hispanic, and 27 percent African American. Hundreds of bilingual officers have been given assignments in community relations, the newly expanded New Immigrant–Special Outreach section, and the antiterrorism unit. According to the New York Police Department's Web page "when the FBI, the Department of Defense, the Secret Service and other Federal agencies need foreign language assistance, they often turn to the NYPD for help."

Sources: Based on NYPD's Foreign Language Outreach. (2014). *www.nyc.gov*; Long, G. (2009, February 9). New book takes readers inside the NYPD's counterterrorism work, *www.theepochtimes.com*; Hays, T. (2007, July 18). "NYPD's diversity reflects demographic shifts." *USA Today, http://usatoday.com*; Buckley, C. (2007, May 31). New York City police seek trust among immigrants. *New York Times*, *www.nytimes.com*; *New York Daily News*. (2006, December 21). Grads make NYPD more melting pot, *www.nydailynews.com*; Porcaro, L. (2005, July 25). Defending the city. *The New Yorker, www.newyorker.com*; *http://nypdrecruit.com*. Accessed March, 2011. ■■

Diversity Versus Inclusiveness

In recent years, there has been some debate about the benefits of emphasizing *diversity* rather than *inclusiveness*, which some see as a way of bringing people together. Although the difference between the two might be one of semantics, it often means that the management of diversity is highly charged and politicized. As recently noted by a leading diversity expert:

> Organizations have expended significant resources in this area in an effort to improve the bottom line, to become an employer of choice, to avoid lawsuits, and to do the right thing. Diversity is also one of the most difficult initiatives to implement in organizations because there are such diverse views on what diversity is and how deeply it should be woven into an organization's culture. Diversity can be difficult also because the dimensions of diversity are closely tied to an individual's personal beliefs, perceptions, and life experiences. These personal beliefs often present barriers to full inclusion and participation in the workforce.[35]

Individual Versus Group Fairness

The extent to which a **universal concept of management**, which leads to standardized management practices, should be replaced by a **cultural relativity concept of management**, which calls for molding management practices to the workforce's different sets of values, beliefs, attitudes, and patterns of behaviors, is an extraordinarily complex question. The proponents of universalism believe that fitting management practices to a diverse workforce sows the seeds for a permanent culture clash in which perceived inequities lead to intense workplace conflict. For instance, when the Lotus software company extended benefits coverage to homosexual couples, unmarried heterosexual employees living with a partner felt that they had been unfairly left out. Conversely, the proponents of relativity argue that failure to adapt HR practices to the needs of a diverse population may alienate much of the workforce and reduce their potential contributions.

universal concept of management
The management concept holding that all management practices should be standardized.

cultural relativity concept of management
The management concept holding that management practices should be molded to the different sets of values, beliefs, attitudes, and behaviors exhibited by a diverse workforce.

Resistance to Change

Although employee diversity is a fact of life, the dominant groups in organizations are still composed of white men. Some argue that a long-established corporate culture is very resistant to change and that this resistance is a major roadblock for women and minorities seeking to survive and prosper in a corporate setting.

Group Cohesiveness and Interpersonal Conflict

Although employee diversity can lead to greater creativity and better problem solving, it can also lead to open conflict and chaos if there is mistrust and lack of respect among groups. This means that as organizations become more diverse, they face greater risks that employees will not work together effectively. Interpersonal friction rather than cooperation may become the norm.

A QUESTION OF ETHICS
Many managers and executives use golfing as an opportunity to combine business and pleasure. How could this practice damage an organization's diversity efforts? Are there any recreational activities that could enhance diversity efforts?

Segmented Communication Networks

Shared experiences are often strongly reinforced by *segmented communication channels* in the workplace. One study found that most communication within organizations occurs between members of the same sex and race. This was found to be true across all professional categories, even at the top, where the number of women and minorities is very small.[36]

The presence of segmented communication poses three major problems to businesses. First, the organization cannot fully capitalize on the perspectives of diverse employees if they remain confined to their own groups. Second, segmented communication makes it more difficult to establish common ground across various groups.[37] Third, women and minorities often miss opportunities or are unintentionally penalized for not being part of the mainstream communication networks. The case at the end of this chapter "Hiring Who You Know as a Threat to Diversity" suggests that heavy reliance on employee referrals and the use of social media to identify prospective employees may inadvertently reinforce segmented communication networks and limit an organization's diversity efforts.

Resentment

Equal employment opportunity (EEO) was imposed by government in the 1960s rather than self-initiated. In the vast majority of U.S. organizations, it was a forced change rather than a voluntary one. One side effect of forced compliance has been the reinforcement of a belief among some managers and mainstream employees that organizations have to compromise their standards to comply with EEO laws. Some have seen EEO laws as legislation of a "forced diversity" that favors political solutions over performance and/or competence.

Given this background, it is perhaps not surprising that twice as many white men as women and minorities feel that promotions received by the latter groups can be attributed to affirmative action.[38] This belief presents two problems. First, women and minorities in positions of authority and responsibility may not be taken as seriously as white men are. Second, the belief that white men are getting the short end of the stick may provoke some of them to vent their frustration against those employees (women and minorities) whom they believe are getting an unfair advantage.

It is important that managers deal with these issues, because affirmative action is here to stay, even though political and legal support for this type of program may be waning as it nears its 50th birthday. Most current polls confirm that big business's commitment to affirmative action continues to be strong, even though most firms now prefer to use the term "diversity" and recently the term "inclusiveness" is generally paired with diversity.[39]

At many large companies, CEOs regularly meet with top managers to ensure that diversity goals are being met. These include firms such as Bank of America (187,000 employees), IBM (387,000 employees), Marriott (151,000 employees), JPMorgan Chase (183,000 employees), Ernst & Young (121,000 employees), AT&T (302,000 employees), and Xerox (54,000 employees).[40]

Retention

The main complaint among female and minority employees is that they lack career growth opportunities. The perception that their upward mobility is thwarted grows stronger at higher levels as women and minorities bump up against the **glass ceiling**, an invisible barrier in the organization that prevents them from rising to any higher position. Lower job satisfaction translates into higher resignation rates, with a resulting loss of valuable talent and greater training costs because of high turnover.

glass ceiling
The intangible barrier in an organization that prevents female and minority employees from rising to positions above a certain level.

Competition for Opportunities

As minorities grow both proportionately and absolutely in the U.S. population, competition for jobs and opportunities is likely to become much stronger. Already there are rising tensions among minorities jockeying for advancement. Employers are being put into the uncomfortable position of having to decide which minority is most deserving.[41] Consider these examples:

A QUESTION OF ETHICS
What ethical problems might arise from giving preferential treatment to certain employees based on their group membership?

- "Blacks have been too successful at the expense of everyone else," grumbles Peter Rogbal, a Mexican American captain in the San Francisco Fire Department. "Other groups have been ignored to placate the black community."
- African Americans fear that newly arrived blacks from places such as Nigeria, Ethiopia, Somalia, Ghana, and Kenya will take away job opportunities from U.S.-born blacks. In the words of Columbia University historian Eric Foner, "Historically, every immigrant group has jumped over American-born blacks. The final irony would be if African immigrants did, too."[42]

There are no fail-proof techniques for effectively handling these challenges. There is, however, one principle that managers should always keep in mind: Treat employees as individuals, not as members of a group. Many of these challenges then become much more manageable.

Diversity in Organizations

The elements of diversity—such as race, ethnicity, and sex—tend to have a profound impact on how people relate to one another. In this section, we discuss (in alphabetical order) the groups that are most likely to be "left out" of the corporate mainstream. Of course, one individual may belong to several of these groups. For this reason, the Census Bureau in 2000 and 2010 allowed Americans to classify themselves into multiple racial categories.

African Americans

African Americans constitute approximately 13 percent of the U.S. workforce. Since the passage of the Civil Rights Act of 1964, the number of African American officials, managers, technicians, and skilled craftspeople has tripled while the number in clerical positions has quadrupled and the number in professional jobs has doubled.[43] However, a significant percentage of African Americans (perhaps as high as 15%) are among the "hardcore" unemployed.

African Americans face two major problems in organizations. First, explicit, intentional racism still exists 50 plus years after the first civil rights victories, even though we now have the first African American president and six of the Fortune 500 CEOs are black, something that not long ago would have almost been considered science fiction.[44] The movie *The Butler*, which came out in 2013, does a great job of illustrating for younger generations how much things have changed in the treatment of African Americans and how difficult the change process has been. African Americans are not the only group to suffer from blatant racism, but it is safe to say that they are the group that suffers the most. The persistence of the Ku Klux Klan and other white supremacy organizations serves as a constant reminder, to both African Americans and U.S. society as a whole, that the struggle for civil rights is not over. This is part of the reason why in 2008 the Florida Legislature formally apologized for the state's "shameful" history of slavery, joining five other states that have expressed public regret for what President Obama calls America's "Original sin."[45] Managers need to be careful to reassure their African American employees, and the entire organization, that racist views will not be tolerated in the workplace. Marriott International, for instance, relies on the film *42*, about Jackie Robinson breaking major league baseball's color line, to make this point. Marriott launched a major campaign in 2013 involving Facebook content, special screenings of the movie, and the showing of "42" (Robinson's number) on hotel rooms and employee lounges.[46]

The second problem African Americans face as a group is less educational preparation than whites.[47] This is not an issue unique to blacks. Both blacks and Hispanics showed approximately half the college graduation rate of whites. Because of the increasing importance of technology and information in the U.S. economy, the discrepancy between the wage rates of college-educated and non–college-educated workers is growing. Therefore, the differential in educational preparation between African Americans (and Hispanic Americans) and whites puts the former at a major disadvantage in the labor market.

There is, however, reason for optimism. An analysis of 291 metropolitan areas indicated that all but 19 were more integrated than in 1990. Whereas in 1972 relatively few whites reported regular interactions with blacks, by 2008 almost two-thirds of whites said they had personal contacts with blacks often or daily.[48] Over the past 50 years, the number of black households at or near the poverty line has fallen by almost one-third, controlling for inflation. Approximately 41 percent of blacks are now solid middle class, making between $42,000 and $108,000 a year, with almost 20 percent considered prosperous (earning more than $108,000 more a year).[49] These positive figures are tamed by a faster dip in median black family income relative to whites following the deepest recession since World War II and the first such significant decline since the 1940s.[50] In 1980, barely one of two blacks over age 25 held a high school diploma. In 2011, nearly four out of five, or just under 80 percent, had a high school diploma; for blacks in the 25–29 age group, it was 86 percent, which was the same as for whites. And in less than 20 years, the number of black college graduates has doubled.[51] African Americans' share of management jobs has increased at least fivefold since 1966.[52] For all of these reasons, a 2008 front-page article in the *Wall Street Journal* concluded that "The growth of the black middle class and integration of the workplace didn't only reshape the black community, it transformed the attitudes of many whites as well."[53]

Asian Americans

Americans of Asian descent constitute approximately 5.6 percent of the U.S. workforce. Their representation in the labor force increased by approximately 63 percent from 1990 to 2014 and is projected to double by 2050.[54] Just as the term "Hispanics" applies to a range of people, "Asian Americans" include a wide variety of races, ethnic groups, and nationalities (for instance, Japanese, Chinese, Koreans, Indians, and Pakistanis).[55] Although Asian Americans have done well in technical fields and are very well represented in institutions of higher education, they are underrepresented in top corporate positions. Employer discrimination probably accounts for this to some extent, because Asian Americans are often stereotyped as being too cautious and reserved to lead.[56] They also suffer from the belief held in some quarters that, because of their educational attainments, they are an advantaged group and, therefore, do not deserve special consideration in hiring and promotion decisions. As a result, they are less likely to benefit from programs intended to improve the employment conditions of women and other minorities. Finally, one survey found that 40 percent of African Americans and Hispanic Americans and 27 percent of whites saw Asian Americans as "unscrupulous, crafty, and devious in business."[57] For all these reasons, some Asian Americans are relegated to technical and support positions that require minimal interpersonal interactions and offer limited opportunities for advancement.

John Yang, a vice president at Hewlett-Packard, notes that although Asians are well represented in the high-technology industry, they seldom make it to the upper echelons. Those Asians who are at the top rung of high-tech companies often started their own companies, like Charles Wang, founder and ex-CEO of New York's Computer Associates.[58]

Most Asian immigrants to the United States today are from the Philippines, Indonesia, Sri Lanka, and Thailand, with a growing number from mainland China. At least half of these immigrants are women, many of whom end up working for very low wages in high-pressure industries such as the garment business.[59] However, we should be cautious of making generalizations. For instance, most Indians who come to the United States are professionals whose average incomes exceed that of native-born Americans.[60] One example is that of Indra Krishnamurthy Nooyi, who grew up in Chennai (formerly Madras) on the southeast coast of India and is now CEO of PepsiCo, a quintessential American company. According to one reporter, "As a vegetarian, she is not who you'd think would be leading the maker of sugary soda and salty snacks."[61] *Inc.* magazine, which focuses on small businesses, has developed a special category listing Indian entrepreneurs who have launched successful companies, many of them in the high-technology sector.

People with Disabilities

There are approximately 43.5 million people with disabilities in the United States, 15 million of whom are actively employed and 6 million of whom subsist on Social Security payments and disability insurance.[62] At least 3.7 million people with severe disabilities are at work.[63] The remainder are either unemployed (presumably supported by their families) or under working age. People who are physically disabled face four main problems at work.

First, social acceptance of disabilities has not advanced much since the Dark Ages.[64] Many people still view people with disabilities with suspicion, even scorn, feeling that those who are physically impaired should stay away from the work world and let "normal" people assume their duties. At a more subtle level, coworkers may not befriend employees with disabilities because they simply do not know how to relate to them. Even extroverts can suddenly become shy in front of a person with a disability.

Second, people with disabilities are often seen as being less capable than others. This misconception persists even though people who are legally blind and deaf can perform many tasks just as well as those with normal sight and hearing, and modern technology allows many paralyzed people to run computers.

Third, many employers are afraid to hire people with disabilities or put them in responsible positions for fear that they may quit when work pressures mount. This myth persists despite the fact that absenteeism and turnover among such employees are only a fraction of those of other employees. For instance, Marriott International reports that turnover among employees with disabilities is only 8 percent annually, compared to 105 percent for workers in general.[65] Pizza Hut has also found a huge difference in turnover rates: 20 percent for employees with disabilities versus more than 200 percent for employees without disabilities.[66]

Fourth, ever since the passage of the Americans with Disabilities Act in 1990, many employers have overestimated the costs of accommodating employees with disabilities. In fact, employers have found that accommodations are usually simple and cheap, costing on average between \$200 and \$500 across different firms.[67] For instance, Griener Engineering, Inc., in Irving, Texas, installed a lighter-weight door on the women's restroom and raised a drafting table by putting bricks under its legs.

The U.S. Supreme Court has established a clear distinction between a physical impairment and a disability under the Americans with Disabilities Act (ADA). For example, Ella Williams, an assembly-line worker at a Toyota plant, was unable to work with power tools after she developed crippling pain in her wrists, neck, and shoulders from repetitive motions. The Sixth Circuit Court of Appeals in Cincinnati said her injury was akin to having "damaged or deformed limbs," and it ruled Toyota should have accommodated her by giving her work as an inspector. Toyota appealed the decision to the U.S. Supreme Court. Citing the so-called "toothbrush test," the Supreme Court ruled that to be disabled a worker must have difficulties in doing everyday tasks. According to

Justice O'Connor, "Even after [Williams's] condition worsened, she could still brush her teeth, wash her face, bathe, tend her flower garden, fix breakfast, do laundry and pick up around the house." This suggests that Williams did not have a true disability but rather a physical impairment. Thus, she was not entitled to the antidiscrimination protection of ADA.[68]

The Americans with Disabilities Act, passed almost 25 years ago, has succeeded in opening access to buildings and providing legal protection, yet significant employment barriers remain. A recent U.S. Bureau of Labor Statistics report covering the recent 2008–2011 recession reveals that, at any one point during the recession, the percentage of disabled people actively looking for work but unable to find employment was almost 70 percent higher than for their nondisabled counterparts.[69]

The Foreign Born

Approximately 14 percent of the U.S. population is foreign born, although in some areas, such as California, southern Texas, southern Florida, and in New York City, the proportion reaches close to one-third of the population.[70] Reliable statistics are hard to find, because of illegal immigration and census undercounts (fearing legal reprisal, many undocumented workers wish to remain incognito), but at least 30 million immigrants have come to the United States over the past 30 years.[71] U.S. Census Bureau data estimates the number of non-naturalized immigrants, both legal and illegal, currently living in the United States at 21.8 million.[72] In addition, half a million foreign students on temporary visas are attending U.S. universities at any one time, spending about $11 billion a year on tuition and living expenses.[73] Many of these people remain in the United States after obtaining their degrees. Although the rate of illegal immigrants seemed to have slowed down considerably during the recent recession, the Pew Research Center estimates that if current trends continue, 19 percent of the U.S. population will be foreign born by 2050.[74]

Regardless of their parents' legal status, all children born in the United States are automatically U.S. citizens under the U.S. Constitution. However, American children of undocumented immigrants face an uncertain future.[75] As noted by one analyst, "As the government steps up its enforcement of immigration laws, the fate of American children is often an afterthought."[76] As of 2014, there are probably about 12 million undocumented immigrants in the United States, compared with 8.4 million in 2000 and 3.5 million in 1990. Mexicans account for about 57 percent of undocumented immigrants, with an additional 24 percent coming from elsewhere in Latin America.[77] A high proportion of these undocumented workers are of childbearing age and they have four children on average (in comparison to two for the rest of the population). This means that a growing percentage of young Americans are raised by parents with few legal rights and who could be subject to immediate deportation. Another major issue that remains unresolved is the legal status of people who came to the United States as children (through no fault of their own) and think of themselves as Americans. President Obama launched a controversial executive order preventing deportation of this group, but nevertheless at the time of this writing they remain in a legal limbo, and some states (such as Arizona) will not issue state-sanctioned IDs to them.

Partly because of security concerns after 9/11 and partly because of a growing belief that our "borders are out of control," public policy has tended toward tightening immigration laws, making it more difficult, for instance, for illegal aliens to obtain a driver's license or even temporary jobs. In one of the largest public-works projects in history, the United States is erecting miles of new fences along much of the Mexican border. Despite these restrictions, it appears that undocumented workers (those who, by definition, cannot achieve legal status) will continue to enter the United States as long as there is demand for their services. In the past, obtaining a "green card" (legal permanent residency) has been an arduous process, and for unskilled workers, a nearly impossible dream.

As of 2014, federal immigration policy is in disarray, and states and local jurisdictions are rushing to fill in the gap. Since the last edition of this book, state legislatures have passed several hundred pieces of immigration legislation. In Arizona, for instance, an employer can lose its license if it knowingly hires an illegal alien.[78] In 2010, Arizona also approved a highly controversial law (being fought in court at the time of this writing) defining all undocumented aliens in the state as "criminals." In Connecticut City (which boasts a population that is 34% foreign born), the Common Council requires local police to work with U.S. Immigration and Customs Enforcement in rounding up workers who are in the country illegally. On the opposite side, a handful of states (such as Illinois, New Jersey, Massachusetts, and Washington) have passed humanitarian legislation that makes integration of immigrants a priority, focusing on language, job, and citizenship training, as well as access to services such as health care and public safety.[79] Likewise California (which hosts at least 3.5 million undocumented people within its borders) recently enacted legislation allowing all residents regardless of immigration status to be jurors and to qualify for state-issued driver licenses. Because many employers find it difficult to do business without access to an immigrant labor force (particularly in agriculture, the hospitality industry, the food and beverage industry, and construction) this confusing situation is creating hardships for firms and foreign workers alike.

Although Americans tend to see immigration as a problem limited to the United States, it has become a major issue in a globalized economy, where approximately 200 million people work outside the country where they were born, with a high percentage living in a legal limbo. In many Western European countries, for instance, which until a few decades ago were largely homogeneous, the proportion of foreign-born residents exceeds 10 percent of the population. Moroccans alone amount to 4,000,000 of those foreign-born residents. A similar situation can be found in Asia (for instance, in Taiwan); in the Middle East (for instance, in Saudi Arabia); in Africa (where, for example, 2 million Indians live); and in Latin America (for instance, in the Dominican Republic where 1 million Haitians live).[80] Recently, the civil war in Syria has provoked the exodus of millions of people into neighboring countries.

Controversial actions by foreign governments in response to immigration pressures are becoming more common. For instance, France has deported hundreds of Romanian Gypsies back to Romania, even though Romania is part of the European Union (EU) and, legally, all citizens of EU member states presumably have the right to settle anywhere they choose within the 27-country EU territory.

The United States has always depended on skilled immigrants to staff science and engineering jobs. In fact, foreigners now account for about 40 percent of all science and engineering PhD holders working in the United States, and more than 50 percent in math and computer fields. In several business fields, 30 percent or more of faculty and doctoral students are foreign born. Fifty-two percent of Silicon Valley startups had immigrant founders. Much of the space program, including the trips to the moon, would not have been possible without teams of German scientists who immigrated to the United States after World War II. For a complex set of reasons, including visa restrictions in the United States, multiyear delays in processing visa applications, and attractive opportunities in other countries (such as Germany, China, India, Korea, and Brazil), a substantial number of highly skilled immigrants are going elsewhere. Unless this trend is reversed, this is likely to create a talent vacuum for the United States in the upcoming decades.

Homosexuals

Although early research dating from the 1940s suggested that about 10 percent of the population is gay, there is considerable debate about the true percentage, with estimates ranging from 1 to 2 percent to 10 percent.[81] In recent years, gay advocacy groups have become very outspoken about their rights, arguing that sexual preference should not be a criterion for personnel-related decisions. But open homosexuality is still taboo in many workplaces.

Federal legislation in the United States offers little legal protection based on sexual orientation at present. Although no federal law prevents overt discrimination against homosexuals, a growing number of states and local jurisdictions have such antidiscrimination laws on their books. An interesting phenomenon is the voluntary decision on the part of a growing number of organizations to embrace employees that do not have a heterosexual orientation (often referred to as lesbian, gay, bisexual and transgender employees, or LGBT). A large number of blue-chip firms and public institutions sponsor gay/lesbian groups in their workforce (including American Express, Deloitte LLP, Prudential, Novartis, General Motors, and Xerox); provide benefits to "domestic partners" (such as Arizona State University, Wachovia Bank, Monsanto, and Microsoft); or do both (such as Microsoft and Monsanto).[82] Even some mainstream religious denominations and organizations, such as the Episcopal Church and the Jewish Theological Seminary, are now accepting openly gay individuals to the ministry and into the seminary.[83] The same is true for the British military. The U.S. military has also abolished the "don't ask, don't tell policy" that was put in place during the Clinton administration. The IRS now allows homosexual couples to file joint tax returns even if their state does not allow gay marriage. Several predominantly Catholic countries (such as Spain, Mexico, and Argentina) now allow weddings for people of the same gender, giving them the identical legal rights, including the same access to fringe benefits, as heterosexual couples. When the first edition of this book was published in the mid-1990s, much of this would have been unthinkable. The Manager's Notebook, "Employee Inclusiveness and Sexual Orientation," addresses this dramatic change.

MANAGER'S NOTEBOOK

Employee Inclusiveness and Sexual Orientation

Although clearly there is no social consensus on this issue, and many people disapprove of the use of sexual orientation to receive legal protection on discrimination grounds, much has changed in the past 10 years or so for the so-called LGBT group. Almost one-third of the states now recognize gay marriage; the "don't ask, don't tell" policy that explicitly barred openly gay people from the military has been repealed; 21 states, the District of Columbia, and more than 160 cities and counties have laws prohibiting employment discrimination based on sexual orientation; and 88 percent of Fortune 500 firms have voluntarily adopted antidiscrimination policies for LGBT employees, including allowance of a "significant other" in lieu of a heterosexual spouse in their benefit program. These firms include such household names as Aetna Inc., Alcatel-Lucent, Apple Inc., Eastman Kodak Co., Nike Inc., JPMorgan Chase & Co., and Xerox Corp. However one still finds large firms that do not share this view. For instance, Exxon Mobil has had an implacable opposition to including sexual orientation in its employment policies and will only do so when mandated by law (such as in Belgium). For many firms, the federal government's refusal to allow anything other than a heterosexual marriage to be recognized for visa purposes continues to pose a major challenge when it comes to global recruitment.

Sources: Based on Stewart, J.B. (2013). Exxon defies calls to add gays to antibias policy, *www.nytimes.com*; Hirsch, E. (2014). Young gay workers predict workplace challenges, *www.shrm.org*; Hastings, R.R. (2014). Companies celebrate gay and transgender equality, *www.shrm.org*. ■■

Latinos (Hispanic Americans)

People from Latin America have traditionally used cultural self-definition to distinguish their cultural identity from that of non-Latino North Americans. The label *Hispanic*, the official name used by the U.S. government, is "essentially a label used by administrative agencies and researchers."[84]

Latinos include people of European descent (there are at least 70 million of them in Latin America) and people of African descent (there are at least 25 million living in the Spanish-speaking Antilles and the Caribbean basin), as well as Latin Indians (who make up a very large proportion of the Mexican and Andean population); Asians (there are probably 10 million Asians of Hispanic descent); and a very large number of people of mixed origin. In fact, over half of Latinos identified themselves as "white" when it came to race in the 2010 Census (which allowed for two separate choices, one on ethnic status and one on race), probably reflecting the fact that in most countries south of the border racial lines are blurred.[85]

There are at least 50 million Latinos in the United States, with some estimates as high as 60 million.[86] The boom in the Hispanic population, 60 percent of which is native born, continues to be the driving force in U.S. demographics.[87] Latino immigrants have birth rates twice as high as those of the rest of the U.S. population. The United States is now the largest Spanish-speaking country in the world except for Mexico.[88] Between now and 2030, Latinos are expected to account for about half of the growth of the U.S. workforce.[89] Many Latinos are professionals and entrepreneurs; others are unskilled laborers and farmers. At the high end of the scale are upper- and middle-class Cubans who came to the United States in the aftermath of the 1959 Cuban Revolution; on the low end are migrant workers.[90]

Latinos face a number of problems in the U.S. workplace. One is language.[91] Second, cultural clashes may occur because of value differences. Some Latinos see non-Latino North Americans as unemotional, insensitive, self-centered, rigid, and ambitious. Meanwhile, non-Latinos often complain that with Latinos "Scheduling, planning, punctuality and attendance might be less rigid than among other employees."[92]

Third, Latinos of African or Latin American Indian descent (many of whom migrate to the United States because of their extreme poverty at home) often face an additional hurdle: racial discrimination because of their skin color. Latinos in the United States have become the target in recent years of anti-immigrant feelings, which are often fueled by politicians who see this as an issue that can win votes for them.

These challenges do not negate the noteworthy progress that Latinos have made in recent years. The largest 500 Latino-owned firms in the United States export more than $1 billion worth of goods each year, generating many U.S. jobs in the process.[93] Almost a quarter of the Fortune 1000 firms have some Latino senior executives, with 70 serving as executive officers and seven who are now CEOs of Fortune 500 firms. Latinos occupy approximately 200 board seats in these companies, double the 1993 number. Hispanic middle-class households (those earning $40,000 to $140,000 annually) have grown 74 percent during the past 23 years, with 15 percent of Latino families reporting incomes of more than $75,000. Total Hispanic purchasing power now exceeds $500 billion. The proportion of college graduates is now over 20 percent, an increase of 45 percent over two decades.[94] There are in excess of 1.5 million Hispanic-owned businesses, and they are forming at a rate three times faster than the U.S. national average.[95]

To quell the fears of those who believe Latinos do not assimilate as well as prior European immigrants assimilated, the evidence shows that the first generation is mostly bilingual and English becomes dominant in the second generation.[96] For this reason, marketers are now starting to focus their attention on the second generation. For instance, Microsoft's MSN Latino, a Spanish-language Web site with about 11 million monthly visitors, now offers marketers an ad service in English that targets second-generation Hispanics.[97] Furthermore, most Latinos do not live in densely packed, highly homogeneous, Spanish-language communities. Rather, most live in neighborhoods with non-Hispanic majorities.[98] Contrary to stereotypes of lack of assimilation, a high proportion of Hispanics marry and establish families with spouses of a different ethnic group, particularly starting in the second generation. As has always been the case throughout history, cultural elements tend to blend, with the dominant culture absorbing what originally was viewed as "foreign." For instance, Mexican restaurants are now common in most neighborhoods and Mexican dishes (with an Americanized twist, sometimes called Tex-Mex) are now part of the American diet. And by the second generation, English rather than Spanish often becomes the main language spoken at home.

Older Workers

The U.S. workforce is getting older. The average U.S. worker is close to age 39 and is expected to reach close to 43 by the year 2020. Forty-seven percent of employees are currently over the age of 40. This is not unique to the United States; in fact, this trend is more pronounced in other developed countries. For instance, in the European Union, close to 40 percent of employees are now over the age of 50.[99] Older workers face several important challenges in the workplace. First, the United States is a youth-oriented culture that has not yet come to terms with its changing demographics.[100] Starting around the age of 40, but particularly after the age of 50, employees encounter a number of stereotypes that may block their career advancement. Partly because of this, the number of age bias claims against private sector employers filed with the Equal Employment Opportunity Commission increased dramatically in recent years.[101] In 2005, the U.S. Supreme Court opened a new door for older workers to sue for age discrimination. The Court ruled that workers over 40 years old could bring charges when the firm's action has a "disparate negative impact" on their age group; they do not have to meet the tougher standard of proving that the employer actually intended to discriminate.[102] Apart from legal considerations, one of the growing ethical issues in human resource management is the extent to which older workers have become easy targets for efforts to reduce salary and health insurance costs.

The economic crisis during 2008–2011, tepid economic growth in subsequent years, and the aging of the baby boom generation (most of whom do not have enough saved for comfortable retirement) have pushed age to the forefront of diversity issues. Most retirement plans are linked to the fortunes of the stock market and few firms now offer a guaranteed monthly payment when an employee reaches retirement age. High rates of divorce and remarriage mean that more and more people start new families in middle age. Because of all of these factors, millions of older workers have changed their minds about quitting their jobs, and some who had already retired decided to reenter the labor market.

To take advantage of this experienced labor pool, a group of employers, including Home Depot, Principal Financial Group, and MetLife, created the National Employer Team, together with the AARP (a national association for people over 50), to endorse "older worker friendly policies." AARP members can access open positions at the companies through the association's Web site.[103] In other words, age is becoming one of the main concerns in human resources when it comes to diversity and inclusiveness (see Manager's Notebook, "The Rise of the Older Worker").

MANAGER'S NOTEBOOK

Emerging Trends

The Rise of the Older Worker

Between 1977 and 2014, the employment of workers 65 and older has more than doubled, a trend that is likely to accelerate as the baby boom generation enters the golden years. The majority of these individuals have less than $200,000 in retirement accounts, not enough to last for more than 10 years living frugally. As a result of this trend, old stereotypes of older workers lacking the speed, technological skills, and stamina of younger workers are quickly fading. Most jobs in the 21st century do not require heavy physical exertion and thus physical impairments are seldom a problem when it comes to age. For this reason, companies such as Google and AT&T publicly proclaim that "we value maturity" and thus will consider older applicants. At Tofulli, a dairy-free product maker, one third of the employees are over 50 and the company advertises itself as an "older worker friendly company." AARP publishes a list every two years of the "Best Employers for Workers Over 50." Despite these changes, in comparison to many other countries the United States remains a youth-oriented culture in which the wisdom of older age is not valued as much. Many managers are still prejudiced when it comes to hiring older applicants because of fears that they might have lower performance, higher absenteeism, and less ability to learn new things and solve problems.

Sources: Based on Sedensky, M. (2013, September 14). Some employers see benefits to hiring older workers, *www.theeagle.com*; AARP. (2014). About the best employers program, *www.aarp.org*; Hennekam, S., and Hersbach, O. (2013). HRM practices and low occupational status of older workers. *Employee Relations*, *35*(3), 339–355.

At the same time, the so-called "generation gap" is creating a challenge for many firms.[104] Citing research at companies such as IBM and Lockheed Martin Corp., one observer notes that "companies worldwide are grappling with generational differences in their workforces. Managers and consultants say they see new workplace problems arising from differing mindsets and communication styles of workers born in different eras. The frictions are aggravated by new technology and work patterns that mix workers of different ages in ever-changing teams."[105] A 2008 survey by the World at Work Association showed that one-third of companies responding now have "generational initiatives" in place to promote better interaction "among the four different generations currently in the workplace."[106]

Among the most common negative assumptions about older workers are that they are less motivated to work hard, that they are "dead wood," that they are resistant to change and cannot learn new methods, and that they are "fire proof."[107] These negative characterizations are not supported by research. Some recent research shows that the absenteeism rate for those 55 and over (4.2 days per year) was almost identical to the absenteeism rate of other age groups (3.9 per year).[108] Recent studies also show that older workers are just as committed to their jobs as younger workers.[109] Many successful companies have implemented programs to use the knowledge and wisdom of older workers to mentor employees. That way they can leverage senior workers as knowledge champions.[110]

Religious Minorities

Although the Jewish population as a percentage of the total population has remained relatively stable in both the United States and Europe, other non-Christian minorities have grown rapidly.

In the United States, approximately 4 million Americans profess Islamic, Hindu, Taoist, or other non-Christian beliefs. In Western Europe, the Muslim population represents the largest minority group, hovering somewhere between 6 and 15 percent of the population in such countries as France, Holland, Spain, Germany, and the United Kingdom.

The tragic events of September 11, 2001, in New York City and Washington, D.C.; the bombings in Boston, Madrid, and London; and multiple other actual or alleged terrorist incidents in the United States and Europe have severely tested tolerance toward people of certain religious backgrounds. The fact that some well-publicized terrorist acts have been carried out by Western-born religious extremists (such as the 2013 attack on a shopping mall in Kenya) adds to this problem. A survey by the Society for Human Resource Management revealed that so-called "ethnic religions" such as Islam now come just after race and gender in U.S. perceptions of "otherness."[111] A 2010 survey conducted by *Time* magazine in the United States revealed that, while only 37 percent of Americans know a Muslim American, 46 percent believe that Islam is more likely than other faiths to encourage violence.[112] In Europe, with a much higher Muslim representation and a short history of immigration, blaming Arab minorities for crime, unemployment, and government budget deficits has become commonplace.[113] In Europe, for example, it is not unusual even for mainstream politicians to use language to refer to religious minorities that in the United States probably would be considered as hateful. Rising intolerance is likely to fuel discrimination in the workplace (see the Manager's Notebook, "Religious Differences Moving to the Forefront of Inclusiveness").

MANAGER'S NOTEBOOK

Emerging Trends

Religious Differences Moving to the Forefront of Inclusiveness

A growing concern in the United States and Western Europe is the extent to which religion has become a source of conflict in the workplace. Firms are now forced to respond to religious tensions as employees (as well as firm owners) openly express their religious sentiments. A few examples follow:

- Employers in France may fire employees for wearing burkas and other full-body robes worn by Muslim women. Similar well-publicized cases have recently occurred in the United States. For instance, Abercrombie & Fitch has been sued for violating federal discrimination laws after it fired an employee for wearing a hijab, or an Islamic religious scarf.
- Some employee groups express open dissatisfaction with certain paid holidays that have religious roots even though they are now part of the secular culture (such as Christmas, Halloween, Good Friday, and St. Valentine's Day).
- A growing number of firms are incorporating an interfaith calendar as part of their HR policies to show that they are aware of holidays that are important to some employees. Employees may then request time off for the holidays (such as Yon Kippur and Ramadan) that are important to their faith.
- Nearly one-third of respondents to a national survey report that they can identify religious biases in their workplace, and one half of those (15% of the total) claim that they find these perceived biases an offense to their personal beliefs.
- Religious beliefs are coming into conflict with work schedules at some companies. Rent-a-Car Center Inc., for example, has been sued by Seventh-Day Adventists who believe they are discriminated against by being forced to work on Saturday (their day of religious observation).
- Some firms are not including contraceptive pills or assisted reproduction as part of their health benefit packages, even though this comes into conflict with federal regulations under so called "Obamacare."

- Hobby Lobby openly sponsors evangelical causes, promoting the owners' faith wherever it operates. For instance, unlike most large retail establishments, it closes on Sundays to give employees a biblical day of rest. Hobby Lobby has recently files a suit against some contraceptive provisions of the Affordable Care Act.

Sources: Based on Leonard, B. (2014). EEOC files two religious bias lawsuits, *www.shrm.org*; Hastings, R. (2014). Religious inclusion requires year-round attention, *www.shrm.org*; Keller, B. (2013). The conscience of a corporation. *New York Times*, *www.nytimes.com*.

Some of this tension has exploded into violence, as in various cities in France and southern Spain. Turkey, which is overwhelmingly Muslim but officially secular, experienced a number of skirmishes during 2010–2014 on the issue of whether women are allowed Islamic head scarves in Turkey's universities.[114] And in 2008, the Vatican publicly condemned physical attacks against religious minorities in Italy, in particular Muslims. On this side of the Atlantic, two issues of Muslim practice—whether the call to prayer should ring out across Harvard Yard and whether the university should grant women separate gym hours—have unleashed small waves of controversy over how Harvard practices tolerance.[115]

Some of this tension may also be found within the Islamic community itself as it tries to adapt to Western society. For instance, there are now more than 200 Muslim student association chapters on U.S. college campuses. One expert notes, "Gender issues, specifically the extent to which men and women should mingle, are the most fraught topic as Muslim students wrestle with the yawning gap between American college traditions and those of Islam."[116]

Unfortunately, as noted by Helen Sanhan, executive director of the Arab-American Institute Foundation, "often the Arab community is negatively displayed in the media."[117] Security fears due to terrorist threats in the United States and Europe have led to many complaints of "racial profiling" and discrimination lodged by people of Arab descent, as well as those who may be mistaken for Muslims, such as some people of East Indian background. Many firms on both sides of the Atlantic are now grappling with policies to cover such issues as permissible garments at work, religious holidays, potential harassment or ridicule based on one's faith, and the display of religious symbols on company premises.[118] The bombing of the Boston Marathon in 2013 by two white Chechen Islamists who had become naturalized American citizens brought the point home that stereotypes based on physical appearances can be misleading.

Women

The projected participation rate for women in the workforce is expected to be about equal that of males.[119] Unfortunately, women's earnings have not mirrored their rising participation trend. After falling to a low of 59 percent of male earnings in 1975, the female-to-male earnings ratio rose slowly and is now approximately 73 percent, just 10 points above its level in 1920, when only 20 percent of women were in the labor force.[120] Over three-quarters of people who earn over $120,000 a year are men.[121]

There may be reason for optimism, however. Women's share of top-management jobs has increased at least threefold during the last three decades.[122] In the past edition of this book, 13 women were CEOs of Fortune 500 firms; at the time of this writing (2014) there are 21. These include some of the most important companies in the world such as Margaret Whitman at Hewlett Packard, Virginia Rometty at IBM, Indra Nooyi at PepsiCo, Marilyn Hewson at Lockheed, Phebe Novakovic at General Dynamics, and Ursula Burns at Xerox.[123] And 55 percent of employed women bring in half or more of their total household income,[124] a trend that has accelerated during the hard economic times of 2008–2012 because many men have lost highly paid jobs in the manufacturing and construction sectors.

Approximately 52 percent of women now hold managerial positions, up from about 12 percent in the early 1970s.[125] Outside the corporate arena, we now have many powerful female role models who were almost totally absent a generation ago. These include, for instance, Oprah Winfrey (one of the richest persons in the world and a very successful entrepreneur), House Speaker Nancy Pelosi, former Secretary of State Hillary Clinton, German Chancellor Angela Merkel, and Janet Yellen, Chair of the Board of Governors of the U.S. Federal Reserve System.[126] In some countries, such as Spain, Norway, and Finland, the cabinet has more women than men,[127] and in the United States it has gone from zero in the 1960s to almost a fourth in recent years. Even in South Korea, which did not ban gender discrimination until 2000, many senior positions in the judiciary, international trade administration, and startups are now held by women.[128]

Still, there is no doubt that most women continue to earn considerably less than their male counterparts, and that 50 years after the women's liberation movement started in the 1960s, males still occupy more than 90 percent of positions on boards of directors, on top management teams, in CEO roles, and other key places in Fortune 1000 firms, even though the gap in educational achievement by gender has largely disappeared. Accordingly, a 2010 large-scale survey of 1,834 business professionals by consulting firm Bain and Co. reveals a huge gap in perceptions as to who has more opportunities in business: men or women. Eighty-one percent of men said that there is no discrimination by gender when it comes to promotions to managerial ranks, compared to 52 percent of women. Similarly, 66 percent of men said that, given equal backgrounds and performance levels, women have an equal chance to be promoted to the top executive levels, versus 30 percent of women.[129] Other than overt sex discrimination (which is, of course, illegal), several factors may account for the earnings differential between women and men and women's lack of upward mobility. These include biological constraints and social roles, a male-dominated corporate culture, exclusionary networks, and sexual harassment.

BIOLOGICAL CONSTRAINTS AND SOCIAL ROLES After five decades of feminism, women continue to encounter a fairly rigid set of expectations regarding their roles and behavior that extend far beyond biological constraints. Women are still primarily responsible for taking care of the children and performing most household duties. A study conducted in the late 1990s estimates that full-time working women still spend three times the amount of time spent by men on household duties.[130] In the words of one woman entrepreneur, who left Dell to start up her own company (the wedding Web site "Weddings Channel") so that she could enjoy more flexibility, "I got pregnant with my first child during my time at Dell. I've always been one of those people who is very driven about work, but I also always wanted to be a mom. All your priorities change when you are shifting your career to accommodate a family."[131]

Perhaps reflecting these societal norms, only a tiny proportion of companies provide day care and other support options (such as job sharing and reduced work hours for employees with young children). For this reason, many talented and highly educated women are forced to curtail their career aspirations and/or quit the organization in their late 20s or early-to-mid 30s—crucial years in one's career—if they wish to have a family. In a recent study that followed the career path of 1,000 women who got Harvard degrees back in the early 1990s, almost one-third of MBA graduates were full-time mothers 15 years later versus 6 percent of doctors. Doctors said they could arrange flexible hours, but most of the women with MBAs agreed that "the infrastructure is not there in the business world."[132]

A MALE-DOMINATED CORPORATE CULTURE Most sex differences are not related to performance, particularly in white-collar occupations, where sheer physical strength is seldom required.

A number of studies have shown that men tend to emerge in leadership positions in U.S. culture because they are more likely than women to exhibit traits believed to "go hand-in-hand" with positions of authority. These include (1) more aggressive behaviors and tendencies; (2) initiation of more verbal interactions; (3) focusing of remarks on "output" (as opposed to "process") issues; (4) less willingness to reveal information and expose vulnerability; (5) a greater task (as opposed to social) orientation; and (6) less sensitivity, which presumably enables them to make tough choices quickly.[133] Thus, cultural expectations may create a self-fulfilling prophecy, with those individuals who exhibit the "female traits" of focusing on process, social orientation, and so on more likely to be relegated to operational and subordinate roles.

old boys' network
An informal social and business network of high-level male executives that typically excludes women and minorities. Access to the old boys' network is often an important factor in career advancement.

Of course, the United States is not alone in this regard. A well-known Japanese author, Marika Bando, notes that "Japanese society hasn't matured enough yet to accept independent and aggressive women. For instance, male managers often address younger workers by adding the diminutive 'chan' or 'kun' to their names instead of 'san.' But female managers should refrain from following that practice because Japanese men are very sensitive about their positions."[134]

EXCLUSIONARY NETWORKS Many women are hindered by lack of access to the **old boys' network**, the informal relationships formed between male managers and executives. Because most high-level positions are filled by men, women are often left out of the conversations that help men get ahead.[135]

SEXUAL HARASSMENT Women have to confront sexual harassment to a much greater extent than men do. Approximately one in five civil suits now concerns harassment or discrimination, compared with one in twenty two decades ago. Sexual harassment litigation is also occurring in Europe.[136] Currently, more than 100 insurance firms in the United States offer employment practice liability insurance, which covers employers' legal costs, damages, and settlements in lawsuits for discrimination and harassment.[137]

Businesses have been getting tougher on this issue by crafting stronger sexual harassment policies and setting up intensive seminars for employees. These educational efforts are particularly important because men and women often have different notions of what kinds of behavior constitute sexual harassment.

Improving the Management of Diversity

Organizations that have made the greatest strides in successfully managing diversity tend to share a number of characteristics. These factors include the creation of a culture that supports inclusiveness, a commitment from top management to valuing diversity, diversity training programs, employee support groups, accommodation of family needs, senior mentoring and apprenticeship programs, communication standards, organized special activities, diversity audits, and a policy of holding management responsible for the effectiveness of diversity efforts.

In recent years, *Fortune* has published a list of the "50 Best Companies for Asians, Blacks, and Hispanics."[138] *DiversityInc.*, a print and online journal dedicated to diversity issues, also publishes an annual list of the best companies for minorities and women. The judges consider many of the factors just mentioned. Here is a sample of some effective diversity practices enacted by the top companies:

- Johnson & Johnson offers a wide variety of family-friendly policies to employees, including retirement transitions for older workers, paid time off for volunteering, a work/life resource and referral program, elder care and adult-management services, child care discounts, resources and referrals and onsite day care, and resources for parenting and grandparenting. The company also encourages the formation and active participation of employees in diversity groups such as the Association of Middle and North African Heritage, South Asian Professional Network, and Veteran's Leading Council. Twenty percent of employees belong to these diversity groups.
- McDonald's makes a concerted effort to purchase from minorities, who now represent half of its vendors.
- Nordstrom weighs minority retention rates as a key factor in manager performance evaluations. The company also has an outreach program to involve minority-owned firms in new store construction.

DiversityInc. also puts together an annual list of the top ten companies for specific groups such as blacks, Latinos, Asian, the disabled, and women. For instance, in 2010, the following widely recognized company names made this list for blacks: Marriott International, AT&T, Sodexo, Northrop Grumman, Altria, McDonald's, Verizon Communications, Southern Company, Intercontinental Hotels Group, and Target.[139] These companies, on average, have:

- 20 percent blacks in their workforce, compared with 14 percent nationally
- 23 percent black women in their workforce, compared with 8 percent nationally
- 17 percent black women among their managers, compared with 3 percent nationally
- 8.2 percent contractor expenditures spent on minority business enterprises, compared with 2 percent nationally

Creating an Inclusive Organizational Culture

As we discussed in Chapter 1, the shared values, beliefs, expectation, and norms prevalent in organizations are likely to have a major influence on the effectiveness of human resource management policies, and the management of employee diversity is particularly sensitive to this culture. In a recent comprehensive review of several hundred diversity studies, two well-known diversity scholars, Susan E. Jackson and Aparna Joshi, concluded that "empirical studies that examined the effects of dissimilarity (employee diversity) in organizations with different cultures seem to support the general argument that organizations with cultures that reflect a belief that diversity is a valuable resource are more likely to realize the potential benefits of team diversity. . . . [O]n the other hand, organizational cultures that endorse a so-called color-blind approach may reinforce majority dominance and result in disengagement by minority employees."[140] As discussed next, several factors go into creating an inclusive culture. Although organizational culture is an elusive concept, it seems clear that some firms are more welcoming and supportive of diversity than others. This also seems to be the case at the industry level. For instance, in the finance industry women have had little luck in breaking through the glass ceiling and it continues to be dominated by entrenched male networks.[141]

Top-Management Commitment to Valuing Diversity

It is unlikely that division managers, middle managers, supervisors, and others in positions of authority will become champions of diversity unless they believe that the chief executive officer and those reporting to the CEO are totally committed to valuing diversity. Xerox, DuPont, Corning, Procter & Gamble, Avon, the *Miami Herald*, Digital Equipment Corporation, U.S. West, and other pacesetters in the successful management of diversity all have CEOs who are fully dedicated to putting this ideal into practice. For example, Avon has established a multicultural participation council (which includes the CEO) that meets regularly. Similarly, in a startling 10-page color brochure, the CEO of Corning announced that management of diversity is one of Corning's three top priorities, alongside total quality management and a higher return to shareholders.[142]

Appraising and Rewarding Managers for Good Diversity Practices

Many companies now explicitly provide or withdraw incentives to managers depending on how well they fare on diversity initiatives. This is based on the idea that what gets measured and rewarded gets done. At Sodexo, for instance, the company links up to 25 percent of managerial compensation to diversity goals. At Wachovia Bank, the CEO personally signs off on senior managers' bonuses tied to meeting diversity goals. Ernst & Young uses a complex system to measure managerial performance in terms of diversity outcomes; these include 20 quantitative and qualitative indicators of retention, promotions, flexible work arrangements, employee satisfaction, and the like. Wells Fargo has mandatory annual reviews that measure team members against four core competencies, one of which is diversity. Time Warner Cable (with a workforce that is approximately 45 percent black, Latino, Asian American, and American Indian) has its CEO personally sign off on annual bonuses and raises tied to the success of diversity initiatives in the managers' responsibility areas. Other companies that use metrics to assess and reward diversity efforts include Novartis, General Mills, Sprint, Abbott, Kaiser Permanente, General Motors, CSX, Hilton Hotels Corporation, and Johnson & Johnson.[143]

Diversity Training Programs

Supervisors need to learn new skills that will enable them to manage and motivate a diverse workforce. Ortho-McNeil Pharmaceutical, Hewlett-Packard, Wells Fargo, Kaiser Permanente, Microsoft, and other companies have developed extensive in-house **diversity training programs** that provide awareness training and workshops to educate managers and employees on specific cultural and sex differences and how to respond to these in the workplace.[144]

diversity training programs
Programs that provide diversity awareness training and educate employees on specific cultural and sex differences and how to respond to these in the workplace.

Much experimentation in this type of training is occurring around the United States.[145] DuPont has sponsored an all-expense-paid conference for African American managers to discuss the problems they encounter and how they can contribute more to the firm. AT&T has offered seminars designed to help straight employees feel comfortable working alongside openly gay employees and to eliminate offensive jokes and insults from the workplace.[146] Corning has introduced a mandatory four-day awareness training program for some 7,000 salaried employees—a day and a half for gender awareness, two and a half days for ethnic awareness.[147]

This provides an excellent opportunity for senior management and staff to learn about diversity. SHRM suggests that effective diversity training programs need to confront complex issues that have more to do with human behavior than with race, gender, age, and the like. For instance, according to SHRM, diversity training needs to consider the fact that human beings find comfort and trust in likeness. However, this report also notes that frequently these programs fall short of expectations. The editors of a special issue of the *Academy of Management Learning and Education* journal came to the same conclusion:

> The most reliable effects [of diversity training] are observed in the impact of knowledge; even the relatively short workshops conducted in organizational settings appear to increase training knowledge. Effects of training on attitudes, which were the most frequently used criteria, are less consistent. Although diversity education appears to affect attitudes toward diversity in general, effects on attitudes toward specific demographic or social groups are less consistent.[148]

Several factors undermine the effectiveness of these programs.[149] First, the training may have come at a time when employees were preoccupied with more urgent priorities (such as downsizing, increased work level, or launching a new product under tight deadlines). Second, if employees perceive that external forces, such as a court order or a politician's decree, have prompted the training, they may resist. Third, if the training poses some as perpetrators and others as victims, those who feel blamed may be defensive. Fourth, if diversity is seen as the domain of a few groups (people of color and women, for example), everyone else may feel left out and view the initiative as being for others, not for them. Lastly, although increasing resources are available for teaching diversity, some experts suggest that the materials provided are less than effective in eradicating stereotypes, sometimes inaccurate, and possibly harmful.[150]

To avoid these problems, SHRM provides recommendations, including holding focus groups with people who may find fault with the training; creating a diversity council that represents a cross section of employees with a wide range of views and attitudes; and exploring ways to deliver the training that do not use a typical classroom format (such as one-on-one coaching to help managers deal with diversity challenges or interventions at team meetings on request).[151]

Support Groups

Some employees perceive corporate life as insensitive to their culture and background, perhaps downright hostile. The perception of an attitude that says "You don't belong here" or "You are here because we need to comply with government regulations" is largely responsible for the high turnover of minorities in many corporations.

To counteract these feelings of alienation, top management at many firms (such as FedEx, Bank of America, Allstate Insurance, DuPont, Marriott, and Ryder) has been setting up **support groups**. These groups are designed to provide a nurturing climate for diverse employees who would otherwise feel shut out. Microsoft, for instance, lists the following employee resource groups on its Web page: Blacks at Microsoft, Arabs at Microsoft, German Speakers at Microsoft, Attention Deficit Disorder at Microsoft, Dads at Microsoft, Working Parents at Microsoft, U.S. Military Veterans at Microsoft, and at least 30 others. As you can see, these groups are truly diverse and are not restricted to traditional categories of gender, race, or age.

support group
A group established by an employer to provide a nurturing climate for employees who would otherwise feel isolated or alienated.

Accommodation of Family Needs

Firms can dramatically cut the turnover rate of their female employees if they are willing to help them handle a family and career simultaneously. Employers can use the following options to assist women in this endeavor. Unfortunately, most organizations do not yet offer these services.[152]

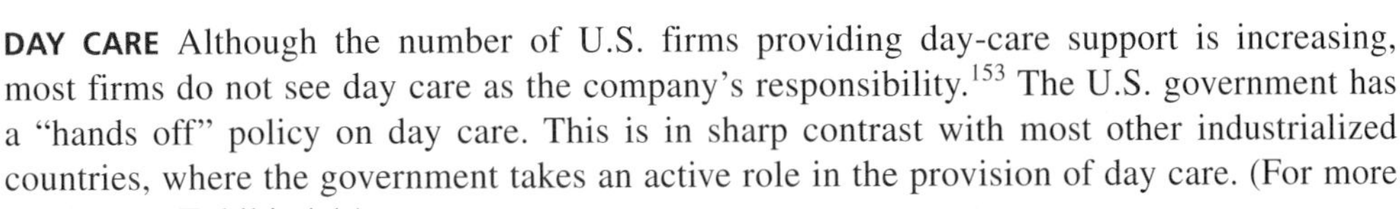

DAY CARE Although the number of U.S. firms providing day-care support is increasing, most firms do not see day care as the company's responsibility.[153] The U.S. government has a "hands off" policy on day care. This is in sharp contrast with most other industrialized countries, where the government takes an active role in the provision of day care. (For more details, see Exhibit 4.1.)

ALTERNATIVE WORK PATTERNS Employers such as Quaker Oats, IBM, Ciba-Geigy, and Pacific Telesis Group have been willing to experiment with new ways to help women balance career goals and mothering, and thereby have retained the services of many of their top performers.[154] As we saw in Chapter 2, these programs come in a variety of forms, including flexible work hours, flextime, and telecommuting. One type of program that is becoming more common is

A QUESTION OF ETHICS
To what extent should employers be responsible for the appropriate care of their employees' children?

EXHIBIT 4.1 WHAT EUROPEAN COUNTRIES DO FOR MUM, MAMAN, MÜTTER, AND MORE . . .

When it comes to creating a family-friendly workplace, more than an ocean separates the United States and European countries. Unlike the United States, many European countries have provisions for maternity leave, child care, and flexible schedules—and they've had them in place for years. For example:

- Germany adopted its maternity leave law back in 1878. German women receive six weeks' prenatal leave at full pay and eight weeks postnatal leave, also at full pay. After mothers return to work, they get time off to breast-feed. In addition, there is a three-year unpaid parental leave for every child for all working parents, both male and female.
- Sweden was the first nation to broaden extended postnatal maternity leave to "parental leave," for either the mother or the father, or for both alternately. Today Swedish parents are guaranteed a one-year leave of absence after childbirth. The first half is reserved for the mother, who receives 90 percent of her salary from social security.
- Denmark, with the highest level of publicly funded services in Europe, offers women 18 weeks' maternity leave, 4 weeks before the birth and 14 weeks afterward. Men can take 10 days' leave after their baby is born, and parental leave policy allows either the mother or the father to take an additional 10 weeks off after the birth.
- France leads the pack in day-care support. In addition to getting at least 16 weeks' maternity leave at 84 percent of their salaries, working mothers can bring their children to state-run day-care centers called *crèches,* which are open 11 hours a day and cost between $3.00 and $17.50 daily.
- Some European companies, such as National Westminster Bank (NWB) in London, have career-break policies that allow employees to take a multiyear leave after the birth of a child. During that period the employee remains in contact with the company, fills in for vacationing employees, and participates in training. At NWB, career breaks of six months to seven years are available to staff at all grades.

"What we tend to find in Europe," says a coordinator of Daycare Trust in London, "is that the more government involvement there is in these issues, the more likely there is to be involvement by employers." In the United States, it is up to individual companies to provide family-friendly programs. This creates some pockets of work–family innovation, but there is no national trend toward providing these kinds of services.

extended leave
A benefit that allows an employee to take a long-term leave from the office, while retaining benefits and the guarantee of a comparable job on return.

job sharing, where two people divvy up what normally is one person's full-time job. A survey of more than 1,000 companies by consulting firm Hewitt Associates found that 28 percent of the organizations offer job sharing, up from 12 percent in 1990.[155] Another option is extended leave. A rare benefit, **extended leave** allows employees to take a sabbatical from the office, sometimes up to three years, with benefits and the guarantee of a comparable job on return. Some companies require leave-takers to be on call for part-time work during their sabbatical.[156]

Many companies now offer day care for employees.
Source: © Jim West/Alamy.

Senior Mentoring Programs

Some companies encourage **senior mentoring programs**, in which senior managers identify promising women and minority employees and play an important role in nurturing their career progress.[157] At Marriott, for instance, newly hired employees with disabilities are paired with Marriott managers who serve as their coaches. Honeywell and 3M team up experienced executives with young women and minorities to give them advice on career strategies and corporate politics, as do Xerox and DQE Corporation, a Pittsburgh utilities firm.[158] At Abbott approximately one-half of managers participate in formal mentoring programs, which Abbot refers to as "cross culturally focused" development.

senior mentoring program
A support program in which senior managers identify promising women and minority employees and play an important role in nurturing their career progress.

Apprenticeships

Apprenticeships are similar to senior mentoring programs, except that promising prospective employees are groomed before they are actually hired on a permanent basis. As with senior mentoring, company managers are encouraged to become actively involved in apprenticeship programs. For example, Sears has established an apprenticeship program that gives students hands-on training in skills such as basic electronics and appliance repair. The best students are hired for 10 hours a week to work at a Sears Service Center. This on-the-job training is integrated into the school curriculum, and the most talented students are hired upon completion of the program.

apprenticeship
A program in which promising prospective employees are groomed before they are actually hired on a permanent basis.

Communication Standards

Certain styles of communication may be offensive to women and minority employees. Examples are the use of "he" when referring to managers and "she" when referring to secretaries; inadequately representing or ignoring minorities in annual reports; failure to capitalize ethnic groups' titles (Asian, Latino, etc.); and using terms, such as *protected classes* and *alien*, that may have a precise legal meaning but are offensive to those being described. To avoid these problems, organizations should set *communication standards* that take into account the sensitivities of a diverse employee population.

Diversity Audits

Often the roots of an employee diversity problem (such as high turnover of minority employees) are not immediately evident. In these instances, research in the form of a **diversity audit** may be necessary to uncover possible sources of bias. Unfortunately, some companies are reluctant to do an official diversity audit for fear that the information uncovered may later be used in a suit against the company. The case of Johnson & Johnson (J&J), the large drug-manufacturing firm, represents one case in point. A voluntary diversity audit by J&J (written in a formal, confidential document) expressed concerns about inadequate tracking of promotions, unequal salaries, and insufficient outreach to recruit women and minorities. The diversity report ended up being used as an unintended legal weapon against J&J when it was uncovered four years later and submitted to a federal court in New Jersey by several African American and Hispanic American employees who argued that "executives knew years ago that they were missing targets for promoting such employees and did little to solve the problem." A company spokesman, Marc Monseau, emphasized that the diversity audit report "should be considered in the larger context of continual self-examination at Johnson & Johnson. We engage in critical self-analysis because we are always looking to improve our process and our performance. That reaches to all aspects of our business, including diversity."[159]

diversity audit
A review of the effectiveness of an organization's diversity management program.

Management Responsibility and Accountability

Management of diversity will not be a high priority and a formal business objective unless managers and supervisors are held accountable for implementing diversity management and rewarded for doing so successfully. At the very minimum, successful diversity management should be one of the factors in the performance appraisal system for those in positions of authority. For instance, at Garrett Company, a manufacturer of jet engines, bonus pay is tied to a supervisor's record on managing diversity. Browsing through the Web pages of companies that are selected as the "best for minorities" by *Fortune* and *DiversityInc.*, one finds that most of them explicitly mention programs to make managers accountable for diversity results. For instance, Xerox keeps track of supplier diversity and uses these figures to hold managers responsible for the success of diversity initiatives.

Some Warnings

Two potential pitfalls must be avoided if diversity management programs are to be successful. These are (1) avoiding the appearance of "white male bashing" and (2) avoiding the promotion of stereotypes.

Avoiding the Appearance of "White Male Bashing"

Disproving the accusation that managing diversity is just another catchphrase for providing opportunities for women and minorities *at the expense of white men* is crucial to the successful management of diversity programs. Otherwise, these programs are likely to engender resentment, heighten anxieties, and inflame the prejudices of those who feel threatened. Management should continually emphasize the positive aspects of capitalizing on employee diversity by framing it as something that (1) must be done to gain a competitive advantage and (2) is in the best interests of all employees. Training programs, if properly designed, may be used as efficient vehicles to convey these messages. Another approach is to use rewards. For instance, Whirlpool distributed an extra $2,700 to each employee in its Benton Harbor, Michigan, plant in a single year in response to productivity and quality improvements. The plant has a significant minority population, and the group incentive induced all employees to work closely together in what they saw as a win-win effort.[160]

Ideally, organizations should adopt an inclusive definition of diversity that addresses all kinds of differences among employees, including (but not limited to) race and gender. A broad definition of diversity will invite participation and decrease resistance.

Avoiding the Promotion of Stereotypes

As we discussed earlier, an inherent danger in diversity programs is inadvertent reinforcement of the notion that one can draw conclusions about a particular person based simply on his or her group characteristics. Remember, differences between individuals *within* any given group are almost always greater than the "average" or typical differences *between* any two groups. **Cultural determinism**—promoting the idea that one can infer an individual's motivations, interests, values, and behavioral traits based on that individual's group memberships—robs employees of their individuality and creates a divisive mind-set of "them versus us."

cultural determinism
The idea that one can successfully infer an individual's motivations, interests, values, and behavioral traits based on that individual's group memberships.

Unfortunately, cultural awareness programs and other diversity training activities tend (unintentionally) to overdramatize diversity. This may lead participants to hold assumptions regarding groups that are totally incorrect (and most likely offensive) when applied to specific employees.[161] Some organizations have begun to use the term *inclusiveness training* to promote the idea that such training is intended to unite people rather than treat them as members of a particular class.

Summary and Conclusions

What Is Diversity?

Diversity refers to human characteristics that make people different from one another. Today's labor force is highly diverse. If effectively managed, this diversity can provide the organization with a powerful competitive edge because it stimulates creativity, enhances problem solving by offering broader perspectives, and infuses flexibility into the firm.

Challenges in Managing Employee Diversity

An organization confronts significant challenges in making employee diversity work to its advantage. These include (1) genuinely valuing employee diversity, (2) balancing individual needs with group fairness, (3) coping with resistance to change, (4) promoting group cohesiveness, (5) ensuring open communication, (6) retaining valued performers, and (7) managing competition for opportunities.

Diversity in Organizations

Some groups are likely to be left out of the corporate mainstream. African Americans still face a certain amount of explicit racism and tend to be less educationally prepared for the workplace. Asian Americans confront two stereotypes—one saying they are too cautious and reserved to lead, and another saying they are unscrupulous in business—as well as the belief that they are too educated to merit special consideration as a minority. Full social acceptance is still denied to people with disabilities, who are often incorrectly perceived as being less capable than others, more prone to quit their jobs under pressure, and costly to accommodate in the workplace.

Foreign-born workers face language and cultural barriers and sometimes ethnic/racial prejudice. They are often resented by Americans of all races, who believe they are taking their jobs.

Homosexuals sometimes face outright discrimination (the refusal to hire or retain them as employees) and ostracism from coworkers or managers. Latinos face language and cultural difficulties and, in some cases, racial discrimination.

Older workers encounter negative stereotypes about their abilities, energy, and adaptability, as well as some physical problems and resentment from younger workers. Women often fare badly in male-dominated corporate cultures that display masculine leadership biases and have old boys' networks that exclude women. They are also subject to sexual harassment to a much greater degree than men.

Improving the Management of Diversity

Organizations that have capitalized the most on their diverse human resources to gain a competitive advantage tend to have top management committed to valuing diversity; solid, ongoing diversity training programs; support groups that nurture nontraditional employees; and policies that accommodate employees' family needs. They also have senior mentoring and apprenticeship programs to encourage employees' career progress, set communication standards that discourage discrimination, use diversity audits to uncover bias, and hold their managers responsible for effectively implementing diversity policies.

Some Warnings

There are two pitfalls in diversity management programs that managers must be careful to avoid: (1) giving the appearance of "white male bashing" and (2) unintentionally promoting stereotypes.

Key Terms

apprenticeship, 169
cultural determinism, 170
cultural relativity concept of management, 153
diversity, 147
diversity audit, 169
diversity training programs, 166
extended leave, 168
glass ceiling, 154
management of diversity, 148
old boys' network, 164
senior mentoring program, 169
support group, 167
universal concept of management, 153

✪ Watch It!

Diversity—Rudi's Bakery. If your instructor has assigned this, go to **mymanagementlab.com** to watch a video case and answer questions.

Discussion Questions

4-1. In the UK, there is an estimate of 270 nationalities and 300 languages. Even this is only part of the story as within these figures are hundreds of sub-groups and identities. With an imperfect knowledge and understanding of diverse groups in our societies, a degree of stereotyping is often inevitable. While membership of a particular group confers a set of characteristics, like behaviors and tastes, to individuals outside that group there is a perceived sameness that is not recognized by members of that group. Individuals can choose to embrace that group identity or they can, to some extent, re-invent themselves by adopting a new set of characteristics and behaviors. How would you describe the diverse nature of the society in which you live? What are the dominant groups and how are they stereotyped? Consider the smaller groups and the factors that distinguish them.

What is the general and stereotypical view of them? How do you think these views actually differ from reality? Are there distinctive reasons for groups to either retain or lose their distinctiveness, what are the reasons for this?

4-2. The European Parliament recently voted 504 to 110 to scold companies for "sexual stereotyping" in marketing their products. One reporter noted that "The lawmakers' ire has many targets, from a print ad for Dolce & Gabbana (which has a woman in spike heels pinned to the ground and surrounded by sweaty men in tight jeans) to Mr. Clean, whose muscular physique might imply that only a strong man is powerful enough." The concern, according to the committee report, is that stereotyping in such ads can "straightjacket women, men, girls, and boys by restricting individuals to predetermined and artificial roles that are often degrading, humiliating, and dumbed-down for both sexes."[163] Do you believe that gender stereotyping in marketing leads to discrimination? Can you think of some examples that illustrate advertising stereotypes? Could this have an effect on how employees perceive the company? Do you think companies should consider how they market their products as part of their diversity efforts? Explain.

4-3. Consider the Manager's Notebook, "Religious Differences Moving to the Forefront of Inclusiveness." Do you think that the owners of a company, major shareholders, or top management have a right to use their religious beliefs as a basis for establishing HR policies for employees? Why or why not? Explain.

✪ 4-4. According to Laura D'Andrea Tyson, Dean of the College of Business at London Business School, in both the United States and Europe women often choose to opt out of high-powered jobs. In her words: "The opt-out hypothesis could explain why, according to a recent U.S. survey, 1 in 3 women with an MBA is not working full-time, versus 1 in 20 men with the same degree. Today, many companies are recruiting female MBA graduates in nearly equal numbers to male MBA grads, but they're finding that a substantial percentage of their female recruits drop out within three to five years. The vexing problem for businesses is not finding female talent but retaining it."[164] In your opinion, how large is the opt-out phenomenon, what are its causes, and what can companies do to retain talented women?

✪ 4-5. Consider the Manager's Notebook "The Rise of the Older Worker." Do you think that young employees now appreciate the wisdom of older workers more than at earlier times? Why do you think the U.S.A has traditionally held older workers at a disadvantage in comparison to other industrialized nations such as Germany, Japan, or Korea? Explain.

4-6. A recent report suggests that pay disparities by gender remain essentially the same whether or not the most senior executive is a man or a woman.[165] Why do you think this is the case? Explain.

✪ 4-7. Many U.S. computer companies fear that if they do not hire foreign talent, then competitors in other countries will. What is your position on this? Explain.

4-8. Are men really fundamentally suited to positions of authority compared to women? Is that truly the case after five decades of feminism, affirmative action, and countless other initiatives across many countries? What is it about men that seem to imply that they have natural leadership traits? What is it in women that make people think they do not?

MyManagementLab®

If your instructor has assigned this, go to **mymanagementlab.com** for the following Assisted-graded writing questions:

4-9. Outline a set of programs that you would put in place to improve the management of diversity in a particular firm. Based on the materials learned in this chapter explain why you have suggested each of the specific programs.

4-10. The Society for Human Resource Management now utilizes the terms "diversity and inclusiveness" together. Why do you think that is the case? What would you do to accomplish both simultaneously? Explain.

4-11. Of all the major demographic trends discussed in this chapter, which one(s) do you think will pose the greatest challenges for firms in the next 50 years or so? Explain.

You Manage It! 1: Technology/Social Media

Hiring Who You Know as a Threat to Diversity

While recommending a friend for a job has always been a natural way of recruiting employees, it might present a major barrier to diversity because employees tend to recommend people like themselves. The social media may compound this problem as more and more companies rely on social media as a source of internal referrals and thus save time and money in their recruitment efforts. For example, both Ernst & Young and Deloitte now hire about half of their employees from these internal referral sources, combing employee networks such as LinkedIn and Facebook to identify potential candidates. These social sites allow companies to trace connections between job candidates and their employees, facilitating the generation of internal referrals and thus avoiding the use of cumbersome job-search sites such as Monster.Com. In fact, prospective candidates using those open-ended job search sites now suffer from negative stereotypes. Some corporate recruiters refer to applicants from Internet job sites as "Homers," referring to the lazy, doughnut-eating character Homer Simpson, and they refer to Monster.Com as "Monster.Ugly." Social sites such as LinkedIn do not carry a stigma for potential applicants because the company can trace the connection between a potential job candidate and current employees, and this removes much of the information uncertainty surrounding other potential candidates who are not part of the network.

Critical Thinking Questions

4-12. Do you really think that social sites may inadvertently reinforce "segmented communication channels" as discussed in this chapter? Explain.

4-13. If you were an HR executive in a company that relies on internal referrals using the social media, what steps would you take to prevent this practice from engendering a more homogeneous workforce and thus blocking the firm from meeting its diversity objectives? Explain.

4-14. Some companies now use incentives for current employees when new hires are socially linked to them and thus their social sites served as a source of internal referrals. What are the pros and cons of this practice? Explain.

Team Exercise

4-15. The director of HR has appointed you to a committee responsible for investigating allegations that reliance on internal referrals through social sites undermines the diversity efforts of the firm. The class is divided into groups of five students, each of which is asked to develop a set of procedures to investigate such allegations.

Experiential Exercise: Team

4-16. In a role-playing exercise, one of the students is asked to take the position in favor of heavy reliance on internal referrals, in particular by combing social sites. Another student is asked to defend the opposite view, arguing that such a practice eliminates equal opportunity for employees outside the network who are more likely to utilize job sites such as Monster.com. Students will debate in small groups for approximately 15 minutes, to be followed by a class discussion of the issues raised to be mediated by the instructor.

Experiential Exercise: Individual

4-17. Research social sites that may be used for internal referrals and those job sites that are open to any potential candidate. Based on this research, do you think that the social sites may promote more segregated employee networks, reducing the firm's access to a more diverse set of candidates? Explain.

Sources: Based on Swartz, N.D. (2013). In hiring, a friend in need is a prospect, indeed, *www.nytimes.com*; Coy, P. (2013) Blacks lose when whites help whites get jobs, *www.businessweek.com*; Society for Human Resource Management (2014). Employers focus on inclusion, *www.shrm.org*.

You Manage It! 2: Emerging Trends

Why Women Lag Behind in MBA Programs

In some professional fields such as medicine and law, women are now exceeding men as a percentage of the entering classes, something that would have been incredible 30 or so years ago when few women entered these fields. Yet colleges of businesses in the United States and abroad seem to be bucking this trend. Although women are now close to matching men in enrollment for undergraduate business programs, the situation is very different at the MBA (graduate) level. Women score higher than men on the GMAT test needed to enter graduate business programs, but in 2014, women still accounted for less than 30 percent of the U.S.-enrolled MBA candidates, a percentage that has not changed much since the early 1990s. Similar findings were recently reported in France, the United Kingdom, Spain, Italy, Germany, Eastern Europe, Russia, and Australia. This data is revealing of future career tracks for men and women because an MBA degree is frequently required to enter mid- to upper-level management.

Critical Thinking Questions

4-18. What do you think is the main reason for the large disparity in the enrollment of women in full-time MBA programs versus enrollment in medical and law school programs? Explain.

4-19. Should business schools actively promote the enrollment of women into their full-time MBA programs? If so, how should they do it? Explain.

Team Exercise

4-20. Assume that you are part of a group of faculty chosen by the dean of the College of Business to help the dean increase the percentage of women in the MBA program. Students divide into groups of six, preferably three males and three females, to role-play this situation and develop some recommendations for the dean. The instructor may play the role of the dean.

Experiential Exercise: Team

4-21. MBA programs are not for everyone, and participation rates not only vary from country to country, but also by gender. In groups of five, one student will role-play an admissions tutor and try to organize a presentation for an MBA program, with the aim of selling the program particularly to women in the group of applicants. The groups should highlight the barriers to participation for women. Students should discuss the percentage of female students enrolled in these programs and have the figures changed over the past decade? At the end of the session, the entire class will discuss the issues raised by the admissions tutor, with the instructor serving as a moderator.

Experiential Exercise: Individual

4-22. Follow up the previous exercise by going online and researching schools offering MBA programs in your country. You may have to broaden your search if there is nothing suitable in your immediate area. Investigate the measures and initiatives that they might take in order to attract more women to their MBA programs. Try to draw some conclusions about how effective their programs are. If applicable, analyze how this type of program may be implemented at your own institution.

Sources: Based on Symonds, M. (2013). Women in business school: Why so few? *www.businessweek.com*; Finn, W. (2011). Flexibility key for women. *The Guardian, www.guardian.com*. Accessed 2011; Gilles, L. (2011). Women and the MBA Forum, Carlson MBA Admissions Blog, *http://blog.lib.umn.edu*; Shellenbarger, S. (2008, August 20). The mommy MBA: Schools try to attract more women. *Wall Street Journal*, C-1.

You Manage It! 3: Ethics/Social Responsibility

Interpreting the Americans with Disabilities Act: The Hot Frontier of Diversity Management

The disabled are making big inroads in the diversity efforts of corporate America, partly because the population is getting older, but also because of a growing awareness of the American with Disabilities Act, which is leading to a rapid increase in disability lawsuits. A few recent examples of legal challenges under the act for the period 2009–2014 are listed as follows:

- Phillis Dewitt says she was fired by Proctor Hospital in Peoria, Illinois, as a result of her disabled husband's extensive medical bills for cancer treatment. Ms. Dewitt, then a clinical nursing manager at Proctor Hospital, says her supervisor pulled her aside and told her the hospital was self-insured and "could not continue to sustain the substantial medical bills incurred" by her husband, Anthony, whose treatment had cost the hospital $177,826 the year before.
- Resources for Human Development (RHD) employed Lisa Harrison as prevention/intervention specialist, working with the young children of mothers being treated for addiction. While she is now deceased, her family claims that RHD perceived Harrison as being disabled because of her obesity and that RHD fired her as a result.
- Chipotle Mexican Grill boasts on its Web site that it offers quality food served quickly in restaurants with a "distinct interior design" more commonly found in the world of fine dining. But a federal appeals court in California has ruled that the chain's "distinct interior design" is also illegal. The 9th U.S. Circuit Court of Appeals in San Francisco ruled that two restaurants in San Diego violated the Americans with Disabilities Act (ADA) because the counters where the staff prepared tacos and burritos were too high and blocked the view for people in wheelchairs.
- A deaf woman, who claims she hasn't been able to sell items on eBay Inc.'s e-commerce Web site, has filed a lawsuit saying the Internet giant violates federal and California state laws that protect disabled people against discrimination. The plaintiff, Melissa Earil of Nevada, Missouri, alleges that she cannot communicate vocally by telephone and hasn't been able to verify her identity with eBay.

Critical Thinking Questions

4-23. Why would employers want to fire employees whose dependents are having serious health problems? Should this practice be illegal? What do you think would be the reaction of employees with healthy dependents who suspect this might be happening? Explain.

4-24. Although the cases discussed above are all very different, what do they have in common? Explain.

4-25. Apart from the potential legal outcomes of the lawsuits discussed, are any larger ethical issues involved? Explain.

Team Exercise

4-26. The class divides into teams of three to five students. Some teams are given the assignment of defending the position of one side (the plantiff). Other teams are asked to argue in favor of the other side (the defendant). All teams should present arguments to support their respective position, with the instructor serving as a moderator. At the end of the discussion, the instructor may take a straw vote as to which side had the more persuasive arguments and then provide his or her own view on the issue.

Experiential Exercise: Team

4-27. One student role-plays Phillis Dewitt and another student role-plays a top manager of Proctor Hospital. (Alternatively, one student may play the role of Lisa Harrison's family and another the HRD staff.) The role play should last approximately 10 minutes and may be repeated with another pair of students playing the same roles. The class will then discuss the issues raised during the role play, with the instructor serving as mediator.

Experiential Exercise: Individual

4-28. As noted in the case, the number of lawsuits under ADA is on the rise. Develop a 5- to 15-page (at instructor's discretion) position paper where you argue in favor of one side or the other for any of the lawsuits listed above.

Sources: Based on *www.ada.gov*. (2014). Information and technical assistance on the American with Disabilities Act; Pokomy, W. R. (2011). EEOC files lawsuit claiming obesity discrimination, *http://mondaq.com*; Conery, B. (2011). Chipotle Mexican Grill in violation of disabilities act, *www.washingtontimes.com*; Morrison, S. (2012). Lawsuit alleges eBay violates disabilities laws, *http://blogs.wsj.com*; Zhang, X. (2008, June 4). Lawsuits test disabilities act. *Wall Street Journal*, D-1.

You Manage It! 4: Discussion

Conflict at Northern Sigma

Northern Sigma, a hypothetical high-technology firm headquartered in New York, develops and manufactures advanced electronic equipment. The company has 20 plants around the United States and 22,000 employees, 3,000 of whom work at a single site in Chicago that is responsible for research and development. About half of the employees at that facility are scientists and engineers. The other half are support personnel, managers, and market research personnel. Corporate executives are strongly committed to hiring women and minorities throughout the entire organization, but particularly at the Chicago site. The company has adopted this policy for two reasons: (1) Women and minorities are severely underrepresented in the Chicago plant (making up only about 13 percent of the workforce), and (2) it is becoming increasingly difficult to find top-notch talent in the dwindling applicant pool of white men.

Phillip Wagner is the general manager of the Chicago plant. In his most recent performance evaluation, he was severely criticized for not doing enough to retain women and minorities. For the past two years, the turnover rate for these groups has been three times higher than that for other employees. Corporate executives estimate that this high turnover rate is costing at least $1 million a year in training costs, lost production time, recruitment expenses, and so forth. In addition, more than 70 charges of discrimination have been filed with the EEOC during the past three years alone—a much higher number of complaints than would be expected given the plant's size and demographic composition.

Under pressure from headquarters, Wagner has targeted the turnover and discrimination problems as among his highest priorities for this year. As a first step, he has hired a consulting team to interview a representative sample of employees to find out (1) why the turnover rate among women and minorities is so high and (2) what is prompting so many complaints from people in these groups. The interviews were conducted in separate groups of 15 people each. Each group consisted either of white men or a mix of women and minorities. A summary of the report prepared by the consultants follows.

Women and Minority Groups

A large proportion of women and minority employees expressed strong dissatisfaction with the company. Many felt they had been misled when they accepted employment at Northern Sigma. Among their most common complaints:

- Being left out of important task forces.
- Personal input not requested very often—and when requested, suggestions and ideas generally ignored.
- Contributions not taken very seriously by peers in team or group projects.
- Need to be 10 times better than white male counterparts to be promoted.
- A threatening, negative environment that discourages open discussion of alternatives.
- Frequent use of demeaning ethnic- or gender-related jokes.

White Male Groups

Most white men, particularly supervisors, strongly insisted that they were interested solely in performance and that neither race nor sex had anything to do with how they treated their staff members or fellow employees. They often used such terms as "equality," "fairness," "competence," and "color-blindness" to describe their criteria for promotions, assignments, selection for team projects, and task force membership. Many of these men felt that, rather than being penalized, women and minorities were given "every conceivable break."

The consulting team asked this group of white men specific questions concerning particular problems they may have encountered at work with women and the three largest minority groups in the plant (African Americans, Asian Americans, and Latinos). The most common comments regarding the white men's encounters with each of these minority groups and with women follow:

African Americans

- Frequently overreact.
- Expect special treatment because of their race.
- Unwilling to blend in with the work group, even when white colleagues try to make them feel comfortable.

Asian Americans

- Very smart with numbers, but have problems verbalizing ideas.
- Stoic and cautious; will not challenge another person even when that person is blatantly wrong.
- Prone to express agreement or commitment to an idea or course of action, yet are uncommitted to it in their hearts.

Latinos

- More concerned with their extended family than with work.
- Often have a difficult time handling structured tasks as employees, yet become dogmatic and authoritarian in supervisory positions.

- Have a difficult time at work dealing with women whom they expect to be submissive and passive.
- Very lax about punctuality and schedules.

Women

- Most are not very committed to work and are inclined to quit when things don't go their way.
- Often more focused on interpersonal relationships than on work performance.
- Respond too emotionally when frustrated by minor problems, thus unsuited for more responsibility.
- Tend to misinterpret chivalry as sexual overtures.
- Cannot keep things confidential and enjoy gossip.

Phillip Wagner was shocked at many of these comments. He had always thought of his plant as a friendly, easygoing, open-minded, liberal, intellectual place because it has a highly educated workforce (most employees have college degrees, and a significant proportion have advanced graduate degrees). He is now trying to figure out what to do next.

Critical Thinking Questions

4-29. What consequences are likely to result from the problems at the Northern Sigma plant? Explain your answer.

4-30. Should Wagner be held responsible for these problems? Explain.

4-31. What specific recommendations would you offer Wagner to improve the management of diversity at the Chicago plant?

Team Exercise

4-32. The class divides into groups of three to five students. Each group should discuss what recommendations it would make to Wagner. After 10 to 15 minutes, each group should present its recommendations to the class. How different are the recommendations from group to group? What principles from the chapter were you able to apply to this problem?

Experiential Exercise: Team

4-33. One to three students will role-play a consultant brought in to interview Phillip Wagner (played by another student) and ask why these diversity problems have emerged at Northern Sigma. Based on the reasons provided by Wagner during the role-play interview, the consultants will offer recommendations to help resolve the problems. The role-play should last approximately 15 minutes, after which the class will discuss the issues raised, mediated by the instructor.

Experiential Exercise: Individual

4-34. Go to *www.diversityinc.com* and examine the 100 companies that have received diversity awards in recent years. What do these companies have in common in terms of effectively dealing with the issues discussed in this case?

Endnotes

Scan for Endnotes or go to http://www.pearsonglobaleditions.com/Gomez-Mejia.

CHAPTER 5

Recruiting and Selecting Employees

MyManagementLab®

When you see this icon, visit **www.mymanagementlab.com** for activities that are applied, personalized, and offer immediate feedback.

CHALLENGES

After reading this chapter, you should be able to deal more effectively with the following challenges:

1 **Understand** human resource supply and demand.

2 **Have** familiarity with the hiring process.

3 **Recognize** challenges in the hiring process.

4 **Learn** practices for meeting the challenge of effective staffing.

5 **Know** the tools of selection.

6 **Develop** awareness of legal issues in staffing.

The Espresso Hut had quickly found success as a coffee shop. The shop catered to coffee lovers and offered fresh-press coffee. The Hut had been able to attract baristas who not only had great knowledge of their coffee products but also provided customers outstanding service. Many customers became regulars, and the Espresso Hut was positioned to expand the business. An assistant store manager was a new position for the Hut, but the additional help was clearly needed.

The store manager, Emily, posted an online ad for an assistant manager. She also put an ad in the classified section of the local newspaper. Emily was contacted by a number of interested candidates. One candidate, Anthony, had never been a barista but had worked in the industry as a repair person for espresso and other equipment commonly found in coffee shops. Anthony clearly had understanding of the industry, and his repair skills could be a useful benefit to have in the store. Anthony had also taken some business courses at a community college. He didn't complete a degree, but the business courses were a plus. Although Anthony didn't have the experience of being a barista, Emily was confident that Anthony could quickly learn the ropes and be an effective store manager. His knowledge of the industry and his exposure to business concepts could be the assets that would lift the performance of the Espresso Hut to a new level.

Source: iofoto/Shutterstock.

Emily's hopes for Anthony as an assistant store manager proved to be overly optimistic. A number of baristas were making complaints to Emily about Anthony's lack of understanding of how the coffee shop worked. Anthony had expressed frustration with how the baristas prepared drinks and processed customers, but the baristas felt that his questioning was annoying and misplaced, particularly because he had never done their jobs. Anthony had also missed ordering needed supplies, and many customers had to be told that they couldn't have their favorite drink for a couple of days. Perhaps the worst for Emily was having a long-term customer share with her that she didn't feel that Anthony treated her well as a customer and just didn't seem to have a customer orientation.

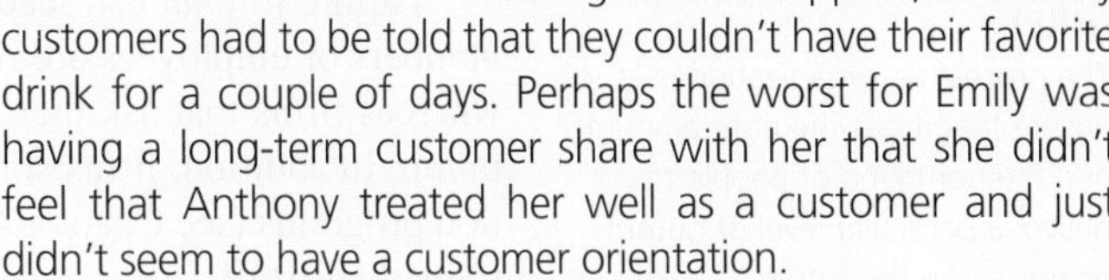

The workers, and apparently even the customers, were wondering why Anthony had been brought in to help manage the shop. Anthony was also unhappy with the situation and was questioning why he had taken on the challenge of managing a group of baristas who would rather manage themselves. For her part, Emily was confronting the reality that her new hire wasn't working out and was wondering how she hadn't seen the misfit before she made the job offer.

The Managerial Perspective

Although HR managers may be responsible for designing employee recruitment and selection systems in many firms, all managers need to understand and use these systems. After all, attracting and hiring the right kind and level of talent are critical elements of business effectiveness. Stocking a company with top talent has been described as the single most important job of management.[1] The ability to attract and hire effective employees is also a key element of a successful management career. As the Espresso Hut example demonstrates, managers may be in charge of recruiting or have a key role in the process. If they do not attract and hire the right people, managers can hurt the organization.

The focus of this chapter is on understanding and conducting effective recruitment and selection. As you think back to the situation at Espresso Hut, consider these important questions:

- Who should make the hiring decision?
- What characteristics should a firm look at when deciding whom to hire, and how should those characteristics be measured?
- Should managers consider how a potential employee "fits" with the firm's culture in addition to that employee's skill level?

In this chapter, we explore how managers plan recruitment efforts effectively by assessing the supply of and demand for human resources. Then we examine the hiring process in detail, the challenges managers face in hiring and promoting, and recommendations for dealing with those challenges. Finally, we evaluate specific methods for making hiring decisions and the legal issues that affect hiring decisions.

Learn It!

If your professor has chosen to assign this go to **www.mymanagementlab.com** to see what you should particularly focus on, and take the chapter 5 warmup.

Human Resource Supply and Demand

labor supply
The availability of workers with the required skills to meet the firm's labor demand.

labor demand
How many workers the organization will need in the future.

human resource planning (HRP)
The process an organization uses to ensure that it has the right amount and the right kind of people to deliver a particular level of output or services in the future.

Labor supply is the availability of workers who possess the required skills that an employer might need. **Labor demand** is the number of workers an organization needs. Estimating future labor supply and demand and taking steps to balance the two require planning.

Human resource planning (HRP) is the process an organization uses to ensure that it has the right amount and the right kinds of people to deliver a particular level of output or services in the future. Firms that do not conduct HRP may not be able to meet their future labor needs (a labor shortage) or may have to resort to layoffs (in the case of a labor surplus).

Failure to plan can lead to significant financial costs. For instance, firms that lay off large numbers of employees are required to pay higher taxes to the unemployment insurance system, whereas firms that ask their employees to work overtime are required to pay them a wage premium. In addition, firms sometimes need to do HRP to satisfy legally mandated affirmative action programs (see Chapter 4). In large organizations, HRP is usually done centrally by specially trained HR staff.

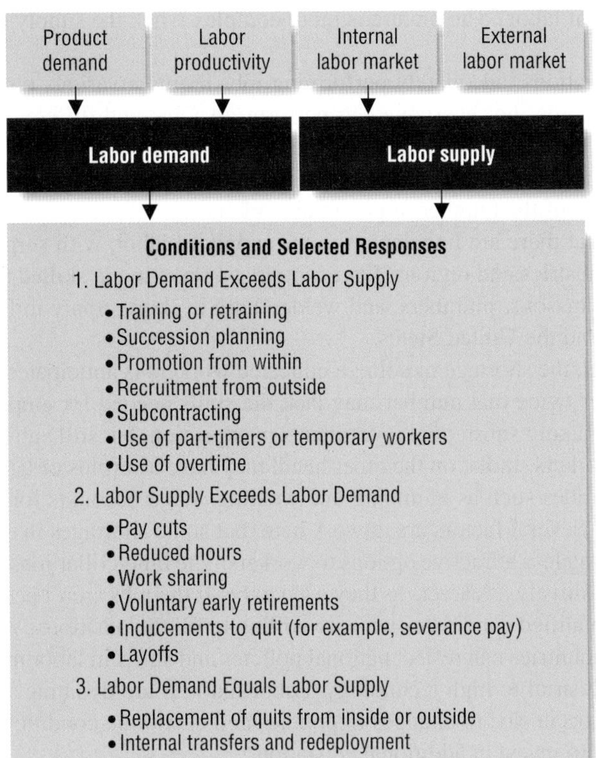

FIGURE 5.1
Human Resources Planning

Figure 5.1 summarizes the HRP process. The first HRP activity entails forecasting labor demand. Labor demand is likely to increase as demand for the firm's product or services increases and is likely to decrease as labor productivity increases (because more output can be produced with fewer workers, usually because of the introduction of new technology).

The second part of the HRP process entails estimating labor supply. The labor supply may come from existing employees (the *internal* labor market) or from outside the organization (the *external* labor market).

After estimating labor demand and supply for a future period, a firm faces one of three conditions, each of which requires a different set of responses. In the first scenario, the firm will need more workers than will be available. A variety of approaches can then be used to increase the labor supply available to a specific firm. These include training or retraining existing workers, grooming current employees to take over vacant positions (*succession planning*), promoting from within, recruiting new employees from outside the firm, subcontracting part of the work to other firms, hiring part-timers or temporary workers, and paying overtime to existing employees.

Whether there is an adequate supply of labor can be a difficult question, as described in the Manager's Notebook, "Global Labor Supply: Surpluses or Shortages? Depends on How You Look at It."

MANAGER'S NOTEBOOK

Global Labor Supply: Surpluses or Shortages? Depends on How You Look at It

Is the supply of labor sufficient? From a macro perspective, the answer must be yes. At the time of this writing, the unemployment rate in the United States is close to 7.50 percent. If you look at the supply of labor as simply the number of bodies willing to work, the unemployment rate indicates that there is a surplus of labor: There are simply more people willing to work than there are jobs. But does viewing labor as simply the number of potential workers adequately depict the status of the supply of labor? The picture is more complex when the supply of labor is looked at more closely.

In most organizations, adequately performing jobs requires various types of skills and experience. In other words, not everyone can perform all jobs, and different types of talent are required to perform different jobs. Thus, recognizing that different skills are needed for different jobs leads to the conclusion that there may be labor shortages, even though there appears to be a labor surplus in terms of the number of potential workers.

The reality is that there are imbalances in the supply of labor, with surpluses and shortages occurring across industries and regions. For example, workers in the skilled trades (such as electricians, carpenters, masons, plumbers, and welders) are in short supply in France, Italy, Brazil, Germany, Canada, and the United States.

At a global level, the shortage of college-educated workers is anticipated to be 40 million by 2020. However, over twice that number may lack the skills needed for employment. China, for example, has been making substantial investments in education, but still anticipates a shortage of college-educated workers. India, on the other hand, may have a surplus of labor but a shortage of workers in skilled trades such as plumbing and welding. What accounts for such imbalances in the supply of labor? Several factors are at work here, but some shortages in the skilled trades are due to these jobs being less attractive options to workers. The blue-collar jobs of the skilled trades are not viewed as positively as careers as they used to be. If the jobs aren't perceived as attractive, it is harder to find qualified candidates who are willing to fill the positions. Variations in the supply of labor across countries can reflect national policies and shifts in labor markets, for instance, from farming to industrial to high technology. Labor markets are dynamic and variations in the supply of labor can occur due to changes in policies and economic conditions as well as people deciding to move or to invest in additional education.

An important message for managers is that the supply of labor isn't just the number of bodies willing to work. Critical issues are the talent that is available in the market and whether a sufficient number of workers are available in an area or industry at a reasonable wage rate.

Sources: Based on Cairns, T. D. (2010). The supply side of labor: HR must be ready to steer organizations to the future, *Employee Relations Today*, *37*, 1–8; Dobbs, R., Lund, S., and Madgakar, A. (2012). Talent tensions ahead: A CEO briefing. *McKinsey Quarterly*, *4*, 92–102; Graham-Leviss, K. (2012). A targeted hiring methodology can hit the bulls-eye in recruiting sales professionals. *Employment Relations Today*, *38*(4), 9–17; *PR Newswire* (2010, August 25). Manpower, Inc. warns global skilled trades shortage could stall future economic growth: Manpower suggests strategic migration, promoting skilled trades key to plugging talent gap. New York. ■■

In the second scenario, labor supply is expected to exceed labor demand. This excess means that the firm will have more employees than it needs. Firms may use a variety of measures to deal with this situation. These include pay cuts, reducing the number of hours worked, and work sharing (all of which may save jobs). In addition, the firm may eliminate positions through a combination of tactics, including early retirement incentives, severance pay, and outright layoffs. (We discuss these issues in detail in Chapter 6.) If the labor surplus is expected to be modest, the firm may be better off reducing the number of hours worked instead of terminating employees. Under federal law, the latter option would force the firm to pay more into the unemployment compensation insurance program. Furthermore, reducing hours worked rather than laying off workers can avoid additional recruiting and training costs when the demand for labor increases.[2]

In the third scenario, labor demand is expected to match labor supply. The organization can deal with this situation by replacing employees who quit with people promoted from inside the business or hired from the outside. The firm may also transfer or redeploy employees internally, with training and career development programs designed to support these moves.

A Simplified Example of Forecasting Labor Demand and Supply

Figure 5.2 shows how a large national hotel chain with 25 units forecasts its labor demand for 16 key jobs two years in advance. Column A indicates the number of employees who currently hold each of these jobs. Column B calculates the present ratio of employees to hotels—that is, the number of current employees divided by the current number of hotels (25). The hotel chain expects to add seven additional hotels by the year 2015 (for a total of 32).

FIGURE 5.2
Example of Predicting Labor Demand for a Hotel Chain with 25 Hotels

	A Number of Employees (2013)	B Ratio of Employees/Hotels (Calculated as Column A ÷ 25)	C Projected 2015 Labor Demand for 32 Hotels (Calculated as Column B × 32)*
Key Positions			
General Manager	25	1.00	32
Resident Manager	9	.36	12
Food/Beverage Director	23	.92	29
Controller	25	1.00	32
Assistant Controller	14	.56	18
Chief Engineer	24	.96	31
Director of Sales	25	1.00	32
Sales Manager	45	1.80	58
Convention Manager	14	.56	18
Catering Director	19	.76	24
Banquet Manager	19	.76	24
Personnel Director	15	.60	19
Restaurant Manager	49	1.96	63
Executive Chef	24	.96	31
Sous Chef	24	.96	31
Executive Housekeeper	25	1.00	32
Total	379		486

*These figures are rounded.

In column C, the expected number of employees for each job in 2015 is calculated by multiplying the current ratio of employees to hotels (column B) by 32. For instance, in 2013 there were 9 resident managers for 25 hotels, or a ratio of 0.36 (9 ÷ 25). When the number of hotels expands to 32 in 2015, it is forecasted that 12 resident managers will be needed (0.36 × 32 = 11.52, or 12.0 after rounding).

The same hotel chain's labor supply prediction is found in columns A to D of Figure 5.3. Column A shows the percentage of employees in each of the 16 key jobs who left the firm during the past two years (2011 to 2013). Multiplying this percentage by the number of present employees in each of these key jobs produces an estimate of how many current employees will have quit by 2015. For example, 38 percent of general managers quit between 2011 and 2013. Because there are now 25 employees holding this job, it is forecasted that by 2015, 10 of them will have left the firm (0.38 × 25 = 9.5, rounded to 10).

The projected turnover for each job is shown in column C. This means that by 2015, 15 of the current general managers (25 minus 10; see column D) will still be working for the company. Because the projected labor demand for general managers in 2015 is 32 (see Figure 5.2), 17 new general managers (32 minus 15) will have to be hired by 2015.

In the past, many firms avoided HRP, simply because their staffs were too swamped with everyday paperwork to manage the planning process effectively. For example, FedEx used to rely on a 20-page employment application. Imagine the labor and paper such a process entailed, especially when thousands of workers were hired. These excesses ended when FedEx moved to a paperless Web-based system that immediately caught errors as a job candidate was completing the employment application form and reduced by more than 50 percent the time needed for applicants to complete the application form and for recruiters to examine it.[3] Furthermore, the

	Supply Analysis				Supply–Demand Comparison	
	A	B	C	D	E	F
	% Quit* (2011–2013)	Number of Present Employees (See Figure 5.2, Column A)	Projected Turnover by 2015 (Column A × Column B)	Employees Left by 2015 (Column B – Column C)	Projected Labor Demand in 2015 (See Figure 5.2, Column C)	Projected New Hires in 2015 (Column E – Column D)
Key Positions						
General Manager	38	25	10	15	32	17
Resident Manager	77	9	7	2	12	10
Food/Beverage Director	47	23	11	12	29	17
Controller	85	25	21	4	32	28
Assistant Controller	66	14	9	5	18	13
Chief Engineer	81	24	16	8	31	23
Director of Sales	34	25	9	16	32	16
Sales Manager	68	45	30	15	58	43
Convention Manager	90	14	13	1	18	17
Catering Director	74	19	14	5	24	19
Banquet Manager	60	19	12	7	24	17
Personnel Director	43	15	6	9	19	10
Restaurant Manager	89	49	44	5	63	58
Executive Chef	70	24	17	7	31	24
Sous Chef	92	24	22	2	31	29
Executive Housekeeper	63	25	16	9	32	23
Total Employees		379	257	122	486	364

*These figures are rounded.

FIGURE 5.3
Example of Predicting Labor Supply and Required New Hires for a Hotel Chain

Web-based job application system was integrated with the human resource information system (HRIS) so that human resource supply and demand data could be updated automatically. Many software companies offer powerful computer-based HRP programs.[4]

Forecasting Techniques

Two basic categories of forecasting techniques are quantitative and qualitative. The example described in Figure 5.2 is a highly simplified version of a *quantitative technique.* A variety of mathematically sophisticated quantitative techniques has been developed to estimate labor demand and supply.[5]

Although used more often, quantitative forecasting models have two main limitations. First, most rely heavily on past data or previous relationships between staffing levels and other variables, such as output or revenues. Relationships that held in the past may not hold in the future, and it may be better to change previous staffing practices than to perpetuate them.

Second, most of these forecasting techniques were created during the 1950s, 1960s, and early 1970s and were appropriate for the large firms of that era, which had stable environments and workforces. They are less appropriate today, when firms are struggling with destabilizing forces such as rapid technological change and intense global competition.

Unlike quantitative techniques, *qualitative techniques* rely on experts' qualitative judgments or subjective estimates of labor demand or supply. The experts may include top managers, whose involvement in and support of the HRP process is a worthwhile objective in itself. One advantage of qualitative techniques is that they are flexible enough to incorporate whatever factors or conditions the expert feels should be considered. However, a potential drawback of these techniques is that subjective judgments may be less accurate or lead to rougher estimates than those obtained through quantitative methods.

As described earlier, forecasting supply and demand is often approached as a separate and fairly specialized function. Further, in some ways it is similar to taking a snapshot of the past to predict the future. A drawback of this approach is the rate of change in many of today's workplaces. Labor supply and demand may shift frequently due to changes in projects, products, technology, competition, and so on.

The Hiring Process

Once the firm has determined its staffing needs, it needs to hire the best employees to fill the available positions. As Figure 5.4 shows, the hiring process has three components: recruitment, selection, and socialization.

Recruitment is the process of generating a pool of qualified candidates for a particular job. The firm must announce the job's availability to the market (inside and outside the organization) and attract qualified candidates to apply.

recruitment
The process of generating a pool of qualified candidates for a particular job; the first step in the hiring process.

Selection is the process of making a "hire" or "no hire" decision regarding each applicant for a job. The process typically involves determining the characteristics required for effective job performance and then measuring applicants on those characteristics, which are typically based on a job analysis (see Chapter 2). Depending on applicants' scores on various tests and/or the impressions they have made in interviews, managers determine who will be offered a job. This selection process often relies on *cut scores;* applicants who score below these levels are considered unacceptable.

selection
The process of making a "hire" or "no hire" decision regarding each applicant for a job; the second step in the hiring process.

The staffing process is not, and should not be, complete once applicants are hired or promoted. To retain and maximize the human resources who were so carefully selected, organizations must pay careful attention to socializing them. **Socialization** orients new employees to the organization and to the units in which they will be working. Socialization can make the difference between a new worker feeling like an outsider or feeling like a member of the team. We discuss the socialization process in more detail in Chapter 8.

socialization
The process of orienting new employees to the organization and the unit in which they will be working; the third step in the hiring process.

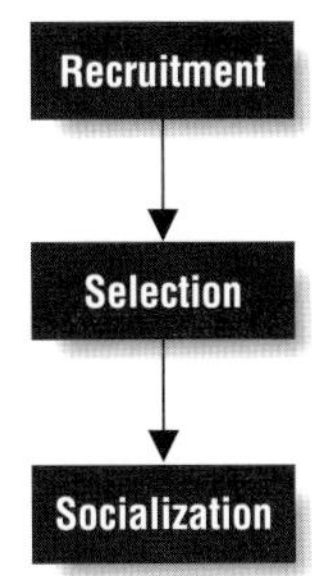

FIGURE 5.4
The Hiring Process

Challenges in the Hiring Process

It has been estimated that above-average employees are worth about 40 percent of their salary more to the organization than average employees.[6] Thus, an above-average new hire in a sales job with a $50,000 salary would be worth $20,000 more to the organization than an average employee hired for the same position. Over 10 years, the above-average employee's added value to the company would total $200,000! If this estimate of added value is multiplied across, for example, 10, 20, or 50 hires, it is easy to see that the monetary value of making above-average hires can total millions of dollars.

Poor hiring decisions are likely to cause problems from day one.[7] Unqualified or unmotivated workers will probably require closer supervision and direction. It has been estimated that managers spend 12 percent of their time managing poor performers,[8] time and energy that could be applied to more productive areas if the poor performers had not been hired. Workers who were hired with inadequate skills or experience may require additional training yet may never reach the required level of performance. They may also give customers inaccurate information or give customers a reason to do business with competitors. Poor hiring decisions can also lead to employee turnover.

Just how costly is employee turnover? A basic estimate is that turnover costs approximately 25 percent of the annual salary and benefits of the employee who is leaving.[9] An examination of turnover costs for park and recreation agencies found that the costs associated with the turnover of a recreation staff member (such as a supervisor or program manager) ranged from $4,208 to $14,464. The turnover costs for operations/support services employees (such as a janitor, an office manager, or a receptionist) ranged from $2,647 to $23,142 per employee. As the level and salary of a worker goes up, so does the turnover cost. The cost to hire another physician for a medical center was found to be $36,743.00, but that cost does not include costs of lost productivity and training costs.[10]

The following list describes the major categories of turnover costs, which can add up to a significant sum.[11] Some may be difficult to estimate, but they are real costs just the same. For example, what is the cost of a disruption to peers and to the work process when someone quits? How much productivity was lost before the worker decided to quit?

Major Turnover Costs[12]

Separation Exit interview, paperwork processing
Recruitment Advertising, recruiter fees
Selection Pre-employment testing, interviewing
Hiring Orientation, training
Productivity Vacancy cost, disruption

Getting and keeping the best not only makes sense in terms of treatment of employees as customers of the management process, but also makes economic sense.

It is essential that line managers, and possibly other line workers, be involved in the hiring process. Although the HR department has an active role to play in recruiting, selecting, and socializing new employees, line personnel will actively be supervising the new hires, and these managers often have job-related insights that members of the HR department may lack.

The hiring process is fraught with challenges. The most important of these are:

- Determining which personal characteristics are most important to performance.
- Measuring those characteristics.
- Evaluating applicants' motivation levels.
- Deciding who should make the selection decision.

We'll look at each of these next.

Determining Characteristics Important to Performance

For several reasons, the characteristics a person needs to perform a job effectively are not necessarily obvious. First, the job itself is very often a moving target. For instance, the knowledge, skills, and abilities (KSAs—see Chapter 2) necessary for a good computer programmer right now are certainly going to change as hardware and software continue to evolve. Second, the organization's culture may need to be taken into account. What kind of place is the organization, and will the worker fit in? The issue of fit can be as important to job performance and employee retention as is the ability to perform the tasks.

Third, different people in the organization often want different characteristics in a new hire. Upper-level managers may want the new manager of an engineering group to be financially astute, whereas the engineers in the group may want a manager with technical expertise.

Measuring Characteristics That Determine Performance

Suppose mathematical ability is considered critical for job performance. You cannot infer from looking at someone what level of mathematical ability he or she possesses. Rather, you must administer some test of mathematical ability. Some tests are better than others at predicting job performance, and they can vary widely in cost.

The Motivation Factor

Most of the measures used in hiring decisions focus on *ability* rather than *motivation*. There are countless tests of mathematical ability, verbal ability, and mechanical ability. But, as the following equation makes clear, motivation is also critical to performance:

$$\text{Performance} = \text{Ability} \times \text{Motivation}$$

This equation shows that a high ability level can yield poor job performance if it is combined with low motivation. Likewise, a high level of motivation cannot offset a lack of ability. (We will discuss another influence on performance, system factors, in Chapter 7.) The performance equation makes conceptual sense, and recent empirical work supports the importance of both ability and motivation in determining performance. For instance, the early career success of M.B.A. graduates has been found to be a function of both ability and motivation levels.[13]

Unfortunately, motivation is very difficult to measure. Many employers try to assess motivation during the employment interview, but (as we will see later in this chapter) there are numerous problems with this method. As a manager, you can look for evidence of motivation in job applicants. For example, have they engaged in extracurricular activities, perhaps sports or in the arts, while attending college? You can try to determine what led to the person being motivated to engage in the activity or to meet the challenge. If similar conditions exist on the job, there will be a chance that the applicant could be inspired and be a motivated worker.[14] However, it is important to recognize that motivation seems to be much more dependent on context than ability is. If you are a typical student, your motivation to work hard in a class depends to a large extent on whether you like the course content, how much you like and respect your instructor, and how grades are determined. Your academic ability is fairly stable from course to course, but your motivation level is much more variable. Work situations are similar to the classroom example: How much you like your job responsibilities, how well you get along with your boss, and how you are compensated all affect your level of effort.

Who Should Make the Decision?

There are two good reasons for letting the HR department run the staffing process. The first (and more important) is that the organization must ensure that its employment practices comply with the legal requirements described in Chapter 3, and making HR staff responsible for all hiring decisions can help avoid problems in this area. The second reason is convenience. Because the HR staff is usually responsible for processing initial contacts with applicants and is often the repository of information about applicants, many organizations find it easier to let the HR department follow through and make hiring decisions.

However, this system leaves the line personnel out of a process that is critical to the operation's effectiveness. If an organization decides to involve line employees in hiring decisions, which ones should it consult? The first, and most obvious, are the managers who will be supervising the new hire. The second group consists of the new hire's coworkers. The third group, where applicable, are the new hire's subordinates. As we saw in the Espresso Hut example that opened this chapter, these groups do not necessarily share the same view of what characteristics are important in the new employee.

Meeting the Challenge of Effective Staffing

Each step of the staffing process—recruitment, selection, and socialization—must be managed carefully. We discuss the first two of these three steps next.

Recruitment

The recruitment process can be viewed as a sales activity. A qualified job candidate is your customer when you are trying to sell the job to him or her. Some keys to approaching recruitment from the perspective of applicants-as-customers are presented in the Manager's Notebook, "Taking an Applicant-Centered Approach to Recruitment."

MANAGER'S NOTEBOOK

Taking an Applicant-Centered Approach to Recruitment

Customer-Driven HR

Finding employees with appropriate qualifications to fill job openings is, of course, a primary purpose for recruitment. However, recruitment can be most effective when it is viewed from the applicant's perspective. Applicants are customers of the organization, and the organization hopes that the applicants make a buy decision about the job openings. Recruitment is your opportunity to sell the job, the organization, and maybe even the community to the job candidates.

- ***Go to where the customers are*** Millions of users are on Facebook, Twitter, and LinkedIn, and many people are now using these and other forms of social media to network and find leads for jobs. Many potential applicants are on the Internet, and using social media can be an effective way to connect with them.
- ***What do they want and what do you have to offer?*** It's about more than the job: People are joining an organization when they take a job. Some of the characteristics that can be important to prospective employees include:
  - working atmosphere (e.g., degree of formality, sense of teams, and fun)
  - career opportunities (opportunity for advancement)
  - work-life value (attractiveness of location, concern for employees)
  - job characteristics (degree to which work is challenging and interesting)
  - pay (level of wages and other benefits)

  These organizational characteristics may not be equally important for all types of potential job applicants. For example, candidates for a managerial-level job might be most interested in work-life value issues and in opportunities for career advancement. Potential applicants for a blue-collar job might focus on, for example, pay and working atmosphere considerations. As a manager, it is important to have a sense of what organizational characteristics are most important to your potential job applicants. Make sure that your recruitment efforts emphasize these characteristics, because it is the potential candidates' perceptions of what your organization can offer on those dimensions that can determine whether they decide to apply.

  Recruitment is your opportunity to attract qualified people to your organization and to provide a picture of the benefits of being a member of your organization that will convince them to be applicants.
- ***Treat applicants like customers*** Do your job applicants feel like they were treated as customers? Applicants who feel they were treated positively are more likely to pursue employment with an organization. If applicants view the hiring process as inconvenient or overly intrusive, it could mean the loss of some great hires. To avoid this problem, try to maintain a customer-oriented approach in the recruitment and selection process. Are interviews and other assessments explained, particularly if some of them might seem to delve into areas that don't seem to be directly related to work? For example, providing applicants with an explanation of why aspects of personality are being measured, or why social media use is an issue, can assure applicants that they are dealing with a transparent and fair employer. Likewise, making sure that interviews and other assessments are scheduled as conveniently as possible can convey the message that this organization cares for its employees and would be a good place to work.

If applicants are treated as customers, even those who are not hired are likely to have a positive impression of the organization. As a result, they may become customers of the organization's products or services and recommend the organization to other potential customers and applicants.

Sources: Based on Baum, M., and Kabst, R. (2013). How to attract applicants in the Atlantic versus the Asia-Pacific region? A cross-national analysis on China, India, Germany, and Hungary. *Journal of World Business*, *48*, 175–185; Bettencourt, L. A., Brown, S. W., and Sirianni, N. J. (2013). The secret to true service innovation. *Business Horizons*, *56*, 13–22; Madera, J. M. (2012). Using social networking websites as a selection tool: The role of selection process fairness and job pursuit intentions. *International Journal of Hospitality Management*, *31*, 1276–1282. ■■

Sources of Recruiting

A great number of recruitment sources are available to organizations.[15] The most prominent are:

- ***Current employees*** Many companies have a policy of informing current employees about job openings before trying to recruit from other sources. Internal job postings give current employees the opportunity to move into the firm's more desirable jobs. However, an internal promotion automatically creates another job opening that has to be filled.
- ***Referrals from current employees*** Studies have shown that employees who were hired through referrals from current employees tended to stay with the organization longer and displayed greater loyalty and job satisfaction than employees who were recruited by other

means.[16] Some organizations offer incentives to their employees for successful referrals. For example, the Container Store pays employees between $200 and $500 for successful referrals, after the new hire has completed a probationary period. REI, the outdoor outfitter, found that employee referrals increased by 850 percent after it doubled its referral bonus to $100 per hire.[17] Employee referrals can be an effective recruitment tool, because employees have a good sense of what it takes to be a successful worker and member of the organization. However, to the extent current employees tend to refer people who are demographically similar to themselves, it can create equal employment opportunity (EEO) problems.

- ***Former employees*** A firm may decide to recruit employees who previously worked for the organization. Typically, these are people who were laid off, although they may also have worked seasonally (during summer vacations or tax season, for example). Forming an online alumni network could be a simple and cost-effective way to maintain a hiring pool of competitive candidates.[18] Furthermore, a network of former employees can be a source of employee referrals because they are familiar with the company, its culture, and its values.
- ***Former military*** Since the war on terror began, employers have had the option to hire discharged soldiers. This is more than patriotism. Some organizations recruit former military in the belief that military experience will result in better and more consistent job performance. In some situations, the link between military experience and the job that needs to be filled is direct. The U.S. Border Patrol, for example, has been hiring thousands of new border patrol agents. The job involves protecting the U.S. border from illegal immigration and illegal contraband, as well as from infiltration by terrorists. The job requirements of a border patrol agent line up well with the basic experience of many military, and it is little wonder that the U.S. Border Patrol is targeting former military as a source of new agents.[19]
- ***Customers*** Customers can be a convenient and cost-effective source of employees. Customers are already familiar with the organization's products or services. Recruiting customers can capitalize on this familiarity, as well as on enthusiasm and alignment with the brand that often goes along with being a committed customer.[20]
- ***Print and radio advertisements*** Advertisements can be used both for local recruitment efforts (newspapers) and for targeted regional, national, or international searches (trade or professional publications).
- ***Internet advertising, career sites, and social media*** Employers are increasingly turning to the Web as a recruitment tool because online ads are relatively cheap, are more dynamic, and can often produce faster results than newspaper help-wanted ads. The Web is not only an economical, efficient means to recruit, but it is also a convenient tool for job seekers. Thousands of career Web sites exist, and almost all are free to people searching for jobs. One of the best known sites is Monster.com. Job seekers can search for jobs by industry, geographic location, and, in some cases, by job description. Social media sites such as Facebook, LinkedIn, and Twitter are also being used by applicants and employers as a way to connect with each other. The Manager's Notebook, "Don't Get Screened Out in a Social Media Screen," points out, however, that employers may also use these sites to evaluate you as a potential employee.

MANAGER'S NOTEBOOK

Don't Get Screened Out in a Social Media Screen

Technology/Social Media

The popularity of social networking sites has made social media an attractive recruitment tool for employers. Having an online presence to promote the business and to recruit new employees makes sense when the increasing number of people using social media is considered. For example, Facebook was founded in 2004[a] and now has over one billion users. If Facebook were a country, it would have a population greater than the United States. It's no wonder that many employers have recognized social media as an important marketing and communication tool. Social media has permeated our culture, and it has become increasingly common for employers to use social media in their recruitment efforts.

An increasing number of employers are going beyond the use of social media as a recruitment tool and are using social media to screen applicants. Some companies, such as Microsoft, openly state that the use of social medial to screen applicants is typical.[b] Surveys indicate that over a third of employers report using social networking sites to screen applicants, and the actual percentage is probably higher. Further, a third of those employers who do social media screening report that they have found content that led them to not hire job candidates.[c]

You might believe that someone's pictures and their postings on social networking sites should not influence an employment decision. You might be right! Nonetheless, the reality is that employers are increasingly using social media not only to recruit but also to screen applicants. Being aware that what is publically accessible could be viewed by potential employers is a basic starting point for making sure that your use of social media doesn't cause you difficulty in being recruited for job openings.

Here are some additional tips for building an online image that will be positive to employers.

- ***No inappropriate or provocative information*** About half of employers who didn't offer a job to a candidate due to information on social networking sites said it was due to pictures or information that were inappropriate. Make sure this type of material is not something you post, or at least that it is not something publically available.
- ***Build strong social networks*** Building a positive online image means more than avoiding or eliminating inappropriate content. Building connections with people who can post or provide positive references can be very helpful. How do you build these connections? It takes being active and stepping in where you can. For example, can you direct someone to a helpful online source or article? Did you follow up when someone in your field asked for input?
- ***Present a professional image*** Make sure that the information you post in a profile is accurate and consistent across social networking sites. Take time to make sure that your profile and postings are well stated and free of typos.

Sources: Based on [a]Brown, V. R., and Vaughn, E. D. (2011). The writing on the (Facebook) wall: The use of social networking sites in hiring decisions. *Journal of Business & Psychology*, *26*, 219–225; [b]Ebnet, N. J. (2012). It can do more than protect your credit score: Regulating social media pre-employment screening with the Fair Credit Reporting Act. *Minnesota Law Review*, *97*, 306–336; [c]Smith, J. (2013). How social media can help (or hurt) you in your job search. *Forbes*, online posting on April 16, 2013, accessed on May 31, 2013 at *www.forbes.com*. ■■

A fun social posting could screen you out of a job.
Source: Daniel Berehulak/Getty.

- ***Employment agencies*** Many organizations use external contractors to recruit and screen applicants for a position. Typically, the employment agency is paid a fee based on the salary offered to the new employee. Agencies can be particularly effective when the firm is looking for an employee with a specialized skill.
- ***Temporary workers*** Temporary workers provide employers the flexibility to quickly meet fluctuating demands. Bringing in temporary workers enables employers to bypass the time-consuming hiring process of job interviews and background checks. Temporary workers also provide a buffer between the changing business environment and the permanent workforce. For example, a decrease in demand for the product or service provided by a business could be balanced with a layoff of temporary workers. The temporary workers may have been hired with the hope they would become permanent, but the presence of temporary workers can mean that permanent workers aren't affected by a business downturn.

The demand for temporary workers can increase in times of economic uncertainty. In difficult and uncertain times, firms may be reluctant to hire permanent staff, preferring instead to bring in temporary workers who can be dismissed more easily than permanent employees.[21] In addition to providing flexibility, the increase in the demand for temporary workers may also be due to employers using temporary workers as a way to avoid paying benefits. However, this practice can lead to abuse, unfair treatment, and, as we saw in Chapter 3, potential legal liability.

- *College recruiting* Your school probably has a job placement office that helps students make contacts with employers. Students whose majors are in accounting, engineering, computer programming, and information systems at the undergraduate level and those with graduate degrees in business and law are often considered the most desirable candidates because of the applied training they have received.

  You might think that college recruiting may change in its nature and shift from face-to-face meetings to Web-based interactions. For example, Hewlett-Packard has a Web site specifically focused on college recruiting at *www.jobs.hp.com*. However, savvy organizations recognize that the Internet cannot do the entire recruiting job.[22] There is value in interacting with college students, developing relationships, and generating interest in the college pool of candidates. Company visits to college campuses, job fairs, and various relationships such as internships are likely to continue for the long term.

Finding qualified and motivated employees is a key concern for small businesses. Bad hires can be catastrophic for small businesses, which do not have the luxury of reassigning workers who are not well suited for their positions.[23]

How do employers evaluate the effectiveness of different recruitment sources? One way is to look at how long employees recruited from different sources stay with the company. Studies show that employees who know more about the organization and have realistic expectations about the job tend to stay longer than other applicants.[24] Current employees, employee referrals, and former employees are likely to turn up applicants with realistic expectations of the job.

Another way of evaluating recruitment sources is by their cost. There are substantial cost differences between advertising and using cash awards to encourage employee referrals, and between hiring locally and hiring beyond the local area (which entails relocating the new employee).

Comparing the effectiveness of various recruiting sources is easier with the use of a simple spreadsheet. As shown in Figure 5.5, the spreadsheet could have recruiting sources in the rows and effectiveness measures (say, on a scale of 1 to 10) in the columns. The columns might track various outcomes from each of the recruitment sources, such as number of employment offers, number of acceptances, turnover at one year, and employee performance ratings at one year.

NONTRADITIONAL RECRUITING Recruiting new workers is a central concern for managers in U.S. organizations when unemployment rates are low. Regardless of current conditions, a long-term perspective leads to the expectation of a labor shortage because the baby boomer generation is nearing retirement and relatively fewer young people are entering the workforce.[25] Furthermore, even in times of high employment and a general labor surplus, there can be shortages of workers with particular skills or in particular areas.

When faced with a labor shortage, companies spend more to advertise job openings via radio, the Web, billboards, television, and print media and at job fairs. Many firms also use employment agencies and employee leasing firms to recruit and select new hires. In addition, many companies recruit from nontraditional labor pools and use innovative methods to attract new employees.

Nontraditional labor pools can include prisoners, welfare recipients, senior citizens, and workers from foreign countries. An innovative and inspiring example of an organization that

Source	Number of Employment Offers	Number of Acceptances	Total Cost	Turnover After 1 Year	Average Performance Rating at 1 Year
Referrals					
Print ads					
Internet ads and career sites					
Agencies					
College recruitment					
Customers					

FIGURE 5.5
Example Criteria for Assessing Effectiveness of Recruitment Sources

embraces a nontraditional labor pool is Greyston Bakery in Yonkers, New York (see *www.greystonbakery.com*). Greyston, a gourmet bakery, has supplied cakes and tarts to the White House and bakes the brownies and blondies used in Ben & Jerry's ice cream and yogurt. Greyston produces all these products with employees who had been chronically unemployed. Greyston Bakery is committed to giving people opportunities—people who may be homeless or drug addicts. Its choice of a nontraditional labor pool helps people get off the streets and into the workforce. Greyston's CEO and president states, "We don't hire people to make brownies, we make brownies to hire people."[26]

EXTERNAL VERSUS INTERNAL CANDIDATES Hiring externally gives the firm the advantage of fresh perspectives and different approaches. Sometimes it also makes economic sense to search for external specialists rather than bear the expense of training current workers in a new process or technology.

On the downside, current employees may see externally recruited workers as "rookies" and, therefore, discount their ideas and perspectives, limiting their impact. Another disadvantage is that it may take weeks before a new recruit has learned the job. Bringing in someone from the outside can also cause difficulties if current workers resent the recruit for filling a job they feel should have gone to a qualified internal worker.

Internal recruiting, usually in the form of promotions and transfers, also has its advantages and disadvantages. On the positive side, it is usually less costly than external recruiting. It provides a clear signal to the current workforce that the organization offers opportunities for advancement. And internal recruits are already familiar with the organization's policies, procedures, and customs.

One drawback of internal recruiting is that it reduces the likelihood of introducing innovation and new perspectives. Another is that workers being promoted into higher-level jobs may be undercut in their authority if, for example, former coworkers expect special treatment from a supervisor or manager who used to be a colleague.

RECRUITING PROTECTED CLASSES An integral part of many organizations' recruitment efforts, both externally and internally, is attracting women, minorities, people with disabilities, and other employees in the protected classes. Although the Equal Employment Opportunity Commission guidelines stipulate only that government employers and government contractors must have written affirmative action policies, many private sector employers believe that such policies make good business sense for them. It stands to reason, for instance, that newspapers with diverse readerships would want to increase the diversity of their editorial and reporting staffs.

A good rule of thumb is to target potential recruits through media or recruitment methods that focus on minorities. For example, recruitment efforts could include black colleges and Hispanic organizations.[27] When a company puts too much emphasis on hiring of minorities in ads, candidates may feel resentful or believe they are being hired simply to fill a quota. Recruitment experts say that minority candidates should be addressed the same way all candidates are.[28]

PLANNING THE RECRUITMENT EFFORT To be effective, recruitment should be tied to HRP.[29] As we saw earlier in this chapter, HRP compares present workforce capabilities with future demands. The analysis might indicate, for example, a need for 10 more staff personnel given the firm's expansion plans and anticipated market conditions. This information should play a key role in determining the level of the recruitment effort.

How many candidates should the recruitment effort attempt to attract for each job opening? The answer depends on *yield ratios*, which relate recruiting input to recruiting output. For example, if the firm finds that it has to make two job offers to get one acceptance, this offer-to-acceptance ratio indicates that approximately 200 offers will have to be extended to have 100 accepted. Perhaps the interview-to-offer ratio has been 3:1. This ratio indicates that the firm will have to conduct at least 600 interviews to make 200 offers. Other ratios to consider are the number of invitations-to-interview ratio and the number of advertisements or contacts-to-applicant ratio. Ratios and other measures of effectiveness can vary across sources of recruitment. Investing in the best ways to recruit employees requires a comparison of the effectiveness of the various recruitment sources used by your company. Figure 5.5 provides a listing of basic recruitment sources and criteria that can be important in assessing effectiveness.

PLANNING YOUR JOB SEARCH The flip side of recruitment is the job search process in which people search for the right employer. Are you looking for your first job or a change in your career? In addition to the sources listed in Figure 5.5 another place to start your job search is the local library. In addition to online sources, libraries offer print resources that can be useful to job seekers.[30] For example, *The Dictionary of Occupational Titles* describes job responsibilities and requirements for a wide array of jobs. However, the Occupational Information Network, or O*NET, is an online database that is replacing the book system used in the *Dictionary of Occupational Titles*. You can access this online resource at *onetonline.org*.

Selection

Selection determines the overall quality of an organization's human resources. Consider what happens when the wrong person is hired or promoted. How do you, as a customer, like being served by someone who is slow and inept? How would you, as a line supervisor, like to deal with the problems caused by a worker who cannot perform necessary tasks on a production line? Hiring the wrong person can also cause friction among staff as other workers become resentful of having to pick up the slack for inept employees. Inappropriate hires may even lead better employees to seek employment elsewhere. We've seen that all these effects have economic ramifications.

In fact, the economic value of good selection procedures is higher than most people realize. For example, an academic study in 1984 estimated that the federal government's use of ability testing for entry-level jobs saved the government over $15 billion per year.[31] This amazing figure, which can only be larger in today's dollars, is derived from the cumulative effects of modest job performance increases by people hired because they scored better than average on the selection test. Continually hiring people who perform, say, 20 percent above average can make a tremendous difference to an organization that hires many workers.

A variety of tools can be used in the selection process. Before we consider these techniques, though, you should be aware of two concepts important for selection tools: reliability and validity.

Reliability and Validity

Reliability refers to consistency of measurement, usually across time but also across judges. If a measure produces perfectly consistent results, that measure is perfectly reliable. For example, if you take a math test every week for five weeks and always obtain the same score, then that measure of your mathematical skill level would be considered to be perfectly reliable. Likewise, if five different interviewers all judged you to have the same level of social skill, the interjudge reliability would be perfect.

reliability
Consistency of measurement, usually across time but also across judges.

However, perfect reliability is rarely if ever achieved. Measurement almost always involves some error and that error is "noise," or unreliability. The greater the amount of noise in a measure, the harder it is to determine the true signal that the measure is trying to detect. Reliability is an index of how much error has influenced the measures.

The error with which something is measured can be broken down into two types: deficiency error and contamination error.[32] *Deficiency error* occurs when a component of the domain being measured is not included in the measure. Not including subtraction questions in a test of basic math skills would yield a deficient measure: one that does not capture the true level of basic math skill.

Contamination error occurs when a measure includes unwanted influences. For example, an interviewer may be under undue time pressure from other job duties and not take the time to accurately assess a job candidate. Or, an interviewer might rate an average job candidate lower than average because of the contrast with an outstanding candidate who preceded him.

Validity is the extent to which the technique measures the intended knowledge, skill, or ability. In the selection context, this means that validity is the extent to which scores on a test or interview correspond to actual job performance. A technique that is not valid is useless and may even present legal problems. When discrimination in hiring practices is charged, the critical evidence will be the job relatedness (validity) of the selection technique.[33] Documentation of validity is critical.

validity
The extent to which the technique measures the intended knowledge, skill, or ability. In the selection context, it is the extent to which scores on a test or interview correspond to actual job performance.

There are typically two basic strategies for demonstrating the validity of selection methods: content and empirical. A *content validity* strategy assesses the degree to which the content of the selection method (say, an interview or a test) is representative of job content. For instance, applicants for the job of commercial airline pilot are required to take a series of exams administered by the Federal Aviation Administration. These exams assess whether the candidates have the necessary knowledge to pilot safely and effectively. However, passing these tests does not guarantee that the applicant has the other abilities necessary to perform well in the cockpit.

An *empirical validity* strategy demonstrates the relationship between the selection method and job performance. Scores on the selection method (say, interview judgments or test scores) are compared to ratings of job performance. If applicants who receive higher scores on the selection method also turn out to be better job performers, then empirical validity has been established.

concurrent validity
Extent of correlation between selection and performance scores, when measured at the same time.

There are two types of empirical (also known as criterion-related) validity: concurrent and predictive.[34] **Concurrent validity** indicates the extent to which scores on a selection measure are related to job performance levels, when both are measured at roughly the same time. To illustrate, say that a company develops a test to use for hiring additional workers. To see how well the test might indicate job performance levels, the company gives the test to its current workforce. The company then correlates the test scores with the performance appraisal scores that supervisors just completed. The correlation between the test scores and job performance scores indicates the concurrent validity of the test because both the test and job performance scores were measured concurrently in time.

predictive validity
Extent to which selection scores correlate with performance scores, when performance is measured later in time.

Predictive validity indicates the extent to which scores on a selection measure correlate with future job performance. For example, the company gives the test to all applicants and then checks new hires' job performance levels 12 months later. The correlation between the test scores and job performance in this case indicates the predictive validity of the test because the selection measure preceded the assessment of job performance.

Even if empirical validity is the goal when developing or choosing a selection measure, all measures should have content validity.[35] That is, what is being measured to assist in making the hiring decision should be job related. The starting point for establishing job-related content is a job analysis (see Chapter 2). However, content validity does not necessarily guarantee empirical validity. For instance, a measure that is content valid but so difficult that no one can earn a passing score will probably not be found to have empirical validity. Further, if empirical validity is assessed, the two forms, concurrent and predictive, each have their advantages and disadvantages.

Concurrent validation can be done relatively quickly and easily. However, the validity found with the concurrent approach may not be a good estimate of how valid a measure may be when used for assessing job applicants. To illustrate, current workers may not be representative of job applicants in that they may be older and tend to be white and male. We see, then, that concurrent validity may not be a good estimate of how valid a selection measure might be in practice.

In contrast, predictive validation most closely matches the hiring problem of trying to predict who will develop into the best performers for the organization. However, determining the predictive validity of a measure requires a fairly large number of people, at least 30, for whom both selection and job performance scores are available. Further predictive validity cannot be determined until job performance is measured, perhaps 6 to 12 months later.

Selection methods can be reliable but not valid; however, selection methods that are not reliable cannot be valid. This fact has a great deal of practical significance. Whether someone has an M.B.A. or not can be measured with perfect reliability. But if having an M.B.A. is not associated with improved job performance, attainment of an M.B.A. is not a valid selection criterion for that job. It seems clear that more highly motivated applicants make better employees, but if the selection method used to measure motivation is full of errors (not reliable), then it cannot be a valid indicator of job performance.

A QUESTION OF ETHICS

Suppose you are asked to write a recommendation letter for a friend whom you like but consider unreliable. Would it be ethical for you to write a positive reference even though you anticipate that your friend will not be a good employee? If not, would it be ethical for you to agree to write the letter knowing that you will not be very positive in your assessment of your friend's abilities?

Selection Tools as Predictors of Job Performance

In this section we look at the most commonly used methods of selection, in no particular order. Each approach has its limitations as well as its advantages.

LETTERS OF RECOMMENDATION In general, letters of recommendation are not highly related to job performance because most are highly positive.[36] This does not mean that *all* letters of recommendation are poor indicators of performance, however. A poor letter of recommendation may be very predictive and should not be ignored.

A content approach to considering letters of recommendation can increase the validity of this selection tool. This approach focuses on the content of the letters rather than on the extent of their positivity.[37] Assessment is done in terms of the traits the letter writer attributes to the job candidate.[38] For example, two candidates may be given equally positive letters, but the first candidate's letter may describe a detail-oriented person, whereas the second candidate's letter describes someone who is outgoing and helpful. The job to be filled may require one type of person rather than the other. For example, a job in customer relations requires an outgoing and helpful person, whereas clerical work requires someone who is good at details.

A more proactive approach to increasing the validity and usefulness of letters as well as verbal references (see "Reference Checks ," p. 170) is to focus the reference on key job competencies. Rather than asking a reference broad questions, such as "Tell me what you think of this job candidate?" ask the reference about the applicant's specific skill in areas relevant to the job opening.[39]

APPLICATION FORMS Organizations often use application forms as screening devices to determine whether a candidate satisfies minimum job specifications, particularly for entry-level jobs. The forms typically ask for information regarding past jobs and present employment status.

A recent variation on the traditional application form is the *biodata form.*[40] This is essentially a more detailed version of the application form in which applicants respond to a series of questions about their background, experiences, and preferences. Responses to these questions are then scored. For instance, candidates might be asked how willing they are to travel on the job, what leisure activities they prefer, and how much experience they have had with computers. As with any selection tool, the biodata most relevant to the job should be identified through job analysis before the application form is created. Biodata have moderate validity in predicting job performance.

Application forms are often the first formal contact a job seeker has with an organization. Typically, most job applicants are eliminated in this initial stage, and it is therefore important that the application form be seen as fair and nondiscriminatory. If an applicant feels that he or she was rejected based on personal information collected in the application form, a charge of discrimination and a lawsuit may result. Based on an analysis of federal court cases involving application forms, items about an applicant's gender, age, race, and national origin were most frequently associated with charges of discrimination involving the application form.[41] To lower this legal risk, organizations need to be sure that information concerning an applicant's gender, age, race, or national origin is not collected on the application forms.

ABILITY TESTS Various tests measure a wide range of abilities, from verbal and qualitative skills to perceptual speed. *Cognitive ability tests* measure a candidate's capability in a certain area, such as math, and are valid predictors of job performance when the abilities tested are based on a job analysis.

A number of studies have examined the validity of *general cognitive ability* (*g*) as a predictor of job performance. General cognitive ability is typically measured by summing the scores on tests of verbal and quantitative ability. Essentially, *g* measures general intelligence. A higher level of *g* indicates a person who can learn more and faster and who can adapt quickly to changing conditions. People with higher levels of *g* have been found to be better job performers, at least in part because few jobs are static today.[42]

Some more specific tests measure physical or mechanical abilities. For example, the *physical ability tests* used by police and fire departments measure strength and endurance. The results of these tests are considered indicators of how productively and safely a person could perform a job's physical tasks. However, companies can often get a more direct measure of applicants' performance ability by observing how well they perform on actual job tasks. These types of direct performance tests, called *work sample tests*, ask applicants to perform the exact same tasks that they will be performing on the job. For example, one of Levi Strauss's work sample tests asks applicants for maintenance and repair positions to disassemble and reassemble a sewing machine component.[43] Work sample tests typically have high reliability and validity, the essential ingredients for an effective and legal selection tool.[44]

Work sample tests are widely viewed as fair and valid measures of job performance, as long as the work samples adequately capture the variety and complexity of tasks in the actual job. Work sample test scores have even been used as criteria for assessing the validity of general mental ability selection measures.[45] However, physical ability measures have been found to screen out more women and minorities than white men. Physical preparation before the testing has been found to reduce this adverse impact significantly.[46]

Another form of ability, emotional intelligence, has become popular to measure. Emotional intelligence has been variously defined by researchers,[47] but can probably be fairly described as the ability to perceive and manage emotions in the self and in others.[48] Although the concept is popular, its validity has yet to be proven convincingly.[49] For instance, one study found no correlation between a measure of emotional intelligence and grade point average. However, a measure of general cognitive ability and personality measures were found to be correlated with grade point average. Similar findings for work performance has led researchers to question whether emotional intelligence really adds to our ability to predict performance beyond measures of general intelligence and ability.[50]

PERSONALITY TESTS Personality tests assess *traits,* individual workers' characteristics that tend to be consistent and enduring. Personality tests were widely used to make employee selection decisions in the 1940s and 1950s,[51] but then fell out of favor as predictors of job-related behaviors.[52] The arguments against using personality tests revolve around questions of reliability and validity. It has been argued that traits are subjective and unreliable,[53] unrelated to job performance,[54] and not legally acceptable.[55] Research on the use of personality measures in selection continues, and the use of personality measures in organizations continues to increase.[56]

Many traits can be measured in a variety of ways, and this lack of consistency produces problems with reliability and validity. However, recent research on personality measurement has demonstrated that personality can be reliably measured[57] and summarized as being composed of five dimensions.[58] The "Big Five" factors, now widely accepted in the field of personality psychology, follow:[59]

- ***Extroversion*** The degree to which someone is talkative, sociable, active, aggressive, and excitable.
- ***Agreeableness*** The degree to which someone is trusting, amiable, generous, tolerant, honest, cooperative, and flexible.
- ***Conscientiousness*** The degree to which someone is dependable and organized and conforms and perseveres on tasks.
- ***Emotional stability*** The degree to which someone is secure, calm, independent, and autonomous.
- ***Openness to experience*** The degree to which someone is intellectual, philosophical, insightful, creative, artistic, and curious.

Of the five factors, conscientiousness appears to be most related to job performance.[60] It is hard to imagine a measure of job performance that would not require dependability or an organization that would not benefit from employing conscientious workers. Conscientiousness is thus the most generally valid personality predictor of job performance. Conscientiousness has also been found to be related to safety at work.[61] For example, people with low levels of conscientiousness tend to ignore safety rules and regulations and, thus, tend to have more accidents and injuries than people with higher levels of conscientiousness.

The validity of the other personality factors seems to be more job specific, which bring us to two warnings about personality tests. First, whether personality characteristics are valid predictors of job performance depends on both the job and the criteria used to measure job performance. A job analysis should be done first to identify the personality factors that enhance job performance. Second, personality may play little or no role in predicting performance on certain measures, such as the number of pieces produced on a factory line (which may depend largely on such factors as speed of the production line). However, personality factors may play a critical role in jobs that are less regimented and demand teamwork and flexibility. Clearly, then, selection procedures should take both personality and the work situation into account.[62] Some types of people may be better suited for some work situations than for others. Overall, although the validity of personality tests can vary across work situations, research supports the conclusion that personality measures are valid for predicting job performance.[63] It remains to be seen, however, whether personality measures are sufficiently valid so as to be useful tools in the hiring process.[64]

HONESTY TESTS Employee theft is a serious problem for organizations, thus it is no surprise that employers want to make sure that they are hiring honest workers. The polygraph test measures an interviewee's pulse, breathing rate, and galvanic skin response (perspiration) while he or she is asked a series of questions. The theory is that these physiological measures will change when the interviewee is not telling the truth. However, the passage of the federal Employee Polygraph Protection Act in 1988 has eliminated the use of polygraph tests by most employers.

Honesty or integrity tests are designed to identify job applicants who are likely to engage in theft and other undesirable behavior. Integrity tests can now be administered in a variety of forms, including paper and pencil, via telephone, and via the Internet, among others. The typical test measures attitudes toward honesty, particularly whether the applicant believes that dishonest behavior is normal and not criminal.[65] For example, the test might measure the applicant's tolerance for theft by other people and the extent to which the applicant believes most people steal regularly.

A study by independent researchers appears to confirm the validity of honesty testing.[66] It found that those who scored more poorly on the honesty test were more likely to steal from their employer. A study reported by one of the major honesty test publishers supports the validity of the measure. Specifically, a retailer began using an integrity test in 600 of its 1,900 locations. Within one year there was a 35 percent drop in the rate of inventory shrinkage in the stores using the test while there was a 10 percent rise in the shrinkage rates in the stores not using the tests.[67]

Nevertheless, honesty tests are controversial. Most of the arguments against integrity testing center on the issue of false-positive results: people who are honest but score poorly on the tests. Typically, at least 40 percent of the test takers receive failing marks.[68]

INTERVIEWS Although the job interview is probably the most common selection tool, it has often been criticized for its poor reliability and low validity.[69] Countless studies have found that interviewers do not agree with one another on candidate assessments. Other criticisms include human judgment limitations and interviewer biases. For example, one early study found that most interviewers make decisions about candidates in the first two or three minutes of the interview.[70] Snap decisions can adversely affect an interview's validity because they are made based on limited information. More recent research, however, indicates that interviewers may not make such hasty decisions.[71]

Another criticism is that traditional interviews are conducted in such a way that the interview experience is very different from interviewee to interviewee. For instance, it is very common for the interviewer to open with the following question: "Tell me about yourself." The interview then proceeds in a haphazard fashion depending on the applicant's answer to that first question. Essentially, each applicant experiences a different selection method.

Dissatisfaction with the traditional unstructured interview has led to an alternative approach called the structured interview.[72] The **structured interview** is based directly on a thorough job analysis. It applies a series of job-related questions with predetermined answers consistently across all interviews for a particular job.[73]

structured interview
Job interview based on a thorough job analysis, applying job-related questions with predetermined answers consistently across all interviews for a job.

Figure 5.6 gives examples of the three types of questions commonly used in structured interviews:[74]

- ***Situational questions*** try to elicit from candidates how they would respond to particular work situations. These questions can be developed from the critical incident technique of

FIGURE 5.6

Examples of Structured Interview Questions

Type	Example
Situational	You are packing things into your car and getting ready for your family vacation when you realize that you promised to meet a client this morning. You did not pencil the meeting into your calendar and it slipped your mind until just now. What do you do?
Job knowledge	What is the correct procedure for determining the appropriate oven temperature when running a new batch of steel?
Worker requirements	Some periods are extremely busy in our business. What are your feelings about working overtime?

job analysis: Supervisors and workers rewrite critical incidents of behavior as situational interview questions, then generate and score possible answers as a benchmark.[75]

- ***Job knowledge questions*** assess whether candidates have the basic knowledge needed to perform the job.
- ***Worker requirements questions*** assess candidates' willingness to perform under prevailing job conditions.

Structured interviews are valid predictors of job performance.[76] First, the content of a structured interview is, by design, limited to job-related factors. Second, the questions asked are consistent across all interviewees. Third, all responses are scored the same way. Finally, because a panel of interviewers is typically involved in conducting the structured interview, the impact of individual interviewers' idiosyncrasies and biases is limited.

Structured interviews have been used very successfully at numerous companies. Interviewing panels range from two to six members and typically include an HR professional, the hiring manager, and the person who will be the candidate's manager. The panels often also include key people from other departments who will have to work very closely with the new hire.

The usual practice is to interview all candidates over a one- or two-day period. This makes it easier to recall interviewee responses and compare them equitably. Immediately after an interview, panel members rate the interviewee using a one- to two-page sheet that lists important job dimensions along with a five-point rating scale. After each interviewer has rated the candidate, one member of the panel—usually either the HR professional or the hiring manager—facilitates a discussion in which the panel arrives at a group rating for the candidate. After all applicants have been interviewed, the panel creates a rank order of acceptable job candidates.[77]

If the structured interview is so effective, why does the traditional interview remain popular? One reason is that many equate the panel format of structured interviews with a stress test. Another is that organizations find the traditional interview quite useful, probably because it serves more functions than just selection.[78] For example, it can be an effective public relations tool in which the interviewer gives a positive impression of the organization. Even a candidate who is not hired may retain this positive impression. In addition, the unstructured interview may be a valid predictor of the degree to which a candidate will fit with the organization. Finally, the open-ended nature of unstructured interviews may provide an opportunity for unsuitable candidates to demonstrate the qualities that make them less desirable as potential employees.

Whatever the interview procedure, employers are assessing interviewees for the role of employee. In addition to responses to interview questions, the assessment of job candidates may include mannerisms and behavior during the interview, as well as dress. If you want to make a good impression during the job interview, you might begin by avoiding some of the real-life interviewing mistakes presented in Figure 5.7.

Whether employers choose to use structured or unstructured interviews, they need to make sure their interview questions are not illegal. Companies that ask job applicants certain questions (for example, their race, creed, sex, national origin, marital status, or number of children) either on application forms or in the interview process run the risk of being sued.

To operate within the limits of the law, interviewers should remember the "nine don'ts" of interviewing:[79]

1. Don't ask applicants if they have children, plan to have children, or what child-care arrangements they have made.
2. Don't ask an applicant's age.
3. Don't ask whether the candidate has a physical or mental disability that would interfere with doing the job. The law allows employers to explore the subject of disabilities only *after* making a job offer that is conditioned on satisfactory completion of a required physical, medical, or job skills test.
4. Don't ask for such identifying characteristics as height or weight on an application.
5. Don't ask a female candidate for her maiden name. Some employers have asked this to ascertain marital status, another topic that is off limits in interviewing both men and women.
6. Don't ask applicants about their citizenship.
7. Don't ask applicants about their arrest records. You are, however, allowed to ask whether the candidate has ever been convicted of a crime.

The impression you make through your behavior at a job interview is critical to your being favorably considered for the job. No matter how stellar your résumé, inappropriate behavior during the interview can ruin your chances for a job offer. The following are some real situations that indicate how unusual (even bizarre) the behavior of some job seekers can be.

- The applicant wore a Walkman and said she could listen to me and the music at the same time.
- A balding candidate abruptly excused himself and returned to the office a few minutes later wearing a hairpiece.
- The applicant asked to see the interviewer's résumé to determine if the interviewer was qualified to judge his capabilities for the job.
- The interviewee announced she hadn't had lunch and proceeded to eat a hamburger and french fries in the interviewer's office—wiping the ketchup on her sleeve.
- When I asked the candidate about his hobbies, he stood up and started tap dancing around my office.
- After arriving for a morning interview, the candidate asked to use the employer's phone. She called her current employer, faked a coughing fit, and called in sick to her boss.
- In response to the interviewer's offer to answer questions, a job seeker replied, "What happens if I wake up in the morning and don't feel like going to work?"
- The applicant brought his mother to the interview.
- The applicant swore throughout the interview.
- A candidate interrupted a discussion of work hours and the office environment to say that he would take the job only if he could move his desk to the courtyard outside.
- Asked what he would like to do in his next position, a candidate replied, "I'll tell you what I don't want to be doing—sitting in boring meetings, doing grunt work, and having to be nice to people all day long."
- Question: "Why do you want this job?" Answer: "I've got a big house, a big car, and a big credit card balance. Pay me and I'll be happy."

FIGURE 5.7
Unusual Job Interview Behaviors

8. Don't ask if a candidate smokes. Because there are numerous state and local ordinances that restrict smoking in certain buildings, a more appropriate question is whether the applicant is aware of these regulations and is willing to comply with them.
9. Don't ask a job candidate if he or she has AIDS or is HIV-positive.

The key point to remember is not to ask questions that are peripheral to the work itself. Rather, interviewers should stay focused on the objective of hiring someone who is qualified to perform the tasks required by the job.

ASSESSMENT CENTERS An **assessment center** is a set of simulated tasks or exercises that candidates (usually for managerial positions) are asked to perform. Observers rate performance on these simulations and make inferences regarding each candidate's managerial skills and abilities. Many organizations use assessment centers for external recruitment and for internal promotion.[80]

assessment center
A set of simulated tasks or exercises that candidates (usually for managerial positions) are asked to perform.

Although expensive, the assessment center appears to be a valid predictor of managerial job performance.[81] Assessment centers also appear to be an effective technique for judging key leadership competencies.[82] Assessment centers may be well worth the price when the costs of poor hiring or promotion decisions are high.[83] However, given a tight budget, the cost of an assessment center can be prohibitive. For example, the State of Maryland used to require the use of assessment centers in hiring public school principals, but that requirement was dropped because the expense of $1,200 to $1,500 per candidate became too onerous.[84] A strategy to reduce the costs associated with using an assessment center is to not conduct an assessment for those candidates with exceptionally poor or good prescreening scores (such as scores on ability tests). Thus, the relatively expensive and more involved assessment-center procedure is used to focus on those candidates in the middle range who are not clearly acceptable or unacceptable for the job.[85]

Assessment centers are usually conducted off-premises, last from one to three days, and may include up to six candidates at a time. Most assessment centers evaluate each candidate's abilities in four areas: organizing, planning, decision making, and leadership. Task-based assessment

A QUESTION OF ETHICS

Some experts contend that urinalysis is an invasion of privacy and, therefore, should be prohibited unless there is reasonable cause to suspect an employee of drug use. Is it ethical for companies to insist that applicants undergo urinalysis? Suppose a company that wants to save on health insurance costs decides to test the cholesterol levels of all job applicants to eliminate those susceptible to heart attacks. Would this practice be ethical? Would it be legal?

centers focus more directly on work-related situations and how well people perform on these specific tasks.[86] There is considerable variability in what exercises an assessment center includes, how these are conducted, and how they are scored.[87] Candidates who can put an activity behind them and focus on the next challenge are likely to perform better in the assessment center.[88] In addition, candidates who are not too dominant or too timid but who can effectively interact with others are likely to perform better.

The *in-basket exercise* is probably the exercise most widely associated with assessment centers. It includes the kinds of problems, messages, reports, and so on that might be found in a manager's in-basket. The candidates are asked to deal with these issues as they see fit, and then are assessed on how well they prioritized the issues, how creative and responsive they were in dealing with each one, the quality of their decisions, and other factors. Performance on an in-basket exercise can be highly revealing. Often it points up the skills of a candidate who might otherwise have appeared average.[89]

DRUG TESTS Preemployment drug testing typically requires job applicants to undergo urinalysis as part of routine selection procedures. Applicants whose test results are positive are usually eliminated from further consideration. Alternatively, they may be given the option of taking another test at their own expense if they challenge the test's outcome.[90]

The purpose of preemployment drug testing is to avoid hiring people who may become problem workers. Given this purpose, the critical question is: Do drug test results correlate to an applicant's later job performance? The answer is yes. In one study done by the U.S. Postal Service, urine samples were taken from more than 5,000 job applicants, but the results were not used in hiring. Six months to one year later, it was found that the applicants who had positive tests were absent 41 percent more often and fired 38 percent more often than those who did not. It appears that drug testing is a valid predictor of job performance.[91]

REFERENCE CHECKS One of the best methods of predicting the future success of prospective employees is to look at their past employment record. Fear of defamation suits has often caused companies to not provide job-related information about former employees. However, checking employees' references is an employer's best tactic for avoiding negligent hiring suits, in which the employer is held liable for injuries inflicted by an employee while on the job. What should companies do?

Courts in almost every state have held that employers—both former and prospective—have a "qualified privilege" to discuss an employee's past performance. But to enjoy that privilege, a company must follow three rules. First, it must determine that the inquirer has a job-related need to know. Second, the former employer must release only truthful information. Third, EEO-related information (such as an employee's race or age) should not be released.[92]

BACKGROUND CHECKS Background checks can be distinguished from reference checks and can include, depending on the job opening, criminal background checks, verifications of academic achievements, driving histories, immigration status checks, and Social Security checks. A primary motivation for organizations to conduct background checks is to avoid a lawsuit charging negligent hiring. However, after the terrorist attack of September 11, 2001, some organizations broadened their screening efforts out of a concern for security. The Patriot Act, passed in November 2001, requires background checks on people who work with certain toxins and bans felons and illegal aliens, among others, from working with these materials.[93] Surveys have found that some employers very infrequently uncover potential problems through the background-check process.[94] However, it is well worth having performed a background check if a problem and consequent lawsuit alleging negligent hiring were to occur. In fact, conducting a background check has largely become an expected practice, and not conducting one can be considered evidence of negligence in hiring.[95]

HANDWRITING ANALYSIS Graphology, the study of handwriting for the purpose of measuring personality or other individual traits, is routinely used to screen job applicants in Europe, the birthplace of the technique. Analysis looks at over 300 aspects of handwriting, including the slope of the letters, the height at which the letter *t* is crossed, and the pressure of the writing. Although graphology is not as widely used in the United States as it is in Europe, it has been estimated that over 3,000 U.S. organizations use the procedure as part of their screening process. Furthermore, the covert and occasional use of graphology may be even more widespread and may be growing.[96] The important question, of course, is whether handwriting is a valid predictor of job performance. Research on this issue indicates that the answer is no.

One study collected handwriting samples from 115 real estate associates and gave them to 20 graphologists, who scored each sample on a variety of traits, such as confidence, sales drive, and decision making.[97] Later, these results were compared with the subject's actual performance ratings as well as with objective performance measures such as total sales volume. There was a fair amount of consistency across graphologists' judgments of the handwriting samples (reliability). However, none of the judgments made by the graphologists correlated with any of the performance measures, so graphology cannot be considered a valid measure. This conclusion is echoed by other research on graphology.[98] Thus, it should not be used as an employment screening device, and you should be wary when you see graphology touted as a valuable selection tool in magazines and other popular press outlets.[99]

Combining Predictors

Organizations often use multiple methods to collect information about applicants. For instance, managers may be selected on the basis of past performance ratings, an assessment center evaluation, and an interview with the manager to whom they will be reporting.

How should these pieces of information be combined to make an effective selection decision? There are three basic strategies. The first requires making a preliminary selection decision after completion of each method. This approach is called *multiple-hurdle strategy*, because an applicant has to clear each hurdle before moving on to the next one. Those who do not clear the hurdle are eliminated from further consideration.

Both the remaining approaches require collecting all the information before making any decision; the difference is in how that information is combined. In a *clinical strategy,* the decision maker subjectively evaluates all the information and comes to an overall judgment. In a *statistical strategy,* the various pieces of information are combined according to a mathematical formula, and the job goes to the candidate with the highest score.

The multiple-hurdle strategy is often the choice when a large number of applicants must be considered. Usually, the procedure is to use the less-expensive methods first to screen out clearly unqualified applicants. Research studies indicate that a statistical strategy is generally more reliable and valid than a clinical strategy,[100] but many people—and probably most organizations—prefer a clinical strategy.

Selection and Person/Organization Fit

Many companies have successfully used various selection tools to hire above-average employees who have made a significant contribution to the firm's bottom line.[101] However, the traditional approach to selection may not be sufficient for a growing number of organizations. For a growing number of organizations, the business involves more than material gain and the bottom line. There may also be values and responsibilities that are considered core to the business. Various social responsibilities, for example, can be core obligations for organizations. These responsibilities can become part of the culture and employment brand of the organization. These characteristics can make a potential employer more attractive to job applicants and, for those who are hired, they are more likely to be committed and loyal employees the better their values fit with the organization.[102]

In addition, a problem with fit can be difficult to solve. In general, it may be possible to reduce a deficit in knowledge or expertise with training, but changing a person's values is typically very difficult or impossible. Thus, hiring people who share the organization's desired priorities and characteristics might be much better than trying to remedy problems later. The Manager's Notebook, "A Larger Purpose: Social Responsibility in the Recruitment and Hiring Process," considers social responsibility as an important component in person/organization fit.

Providing opportunities to contribute to the community can be an important part of an employer's brand.
Source: © aberCPC/Alamy.

MANAGER'S NOTEBOOK

Ethics/Social Responsibility

A Larger Purpose: Social Responsibility in the Recruitment and Hiring Process

You want a job to make money, right? But is that all you are looking for? Companies are finding that many workers, and especially younger workers who are part of Generation Y, want more from work. They have ambitions to also make a positive difference in society and, thereby, find meaning and value in their jobs. For these workers, the job is more than just about a paycheck. As a manager, how can you meet that ambition and have your business benefit from the motivation and loyalty that can result from workers finding a fit with their desire to make a positive contribution? Some basic, but important suggestions regarding social responsibility and maximizing person/organization fit in recruitment and selection are presented below.

- ***How is your business socially responsible?*** Does your business support particular causes or contribute to the local community? Is your company particularly focused on being environmentally responsible? If your organization emphasizes various aspects of social responsibility, these commitments need to be clarified. For example, if there are core values that reflect social responsibility commitments, they need to be identified. Likewise, if there are actions such as community projects, charity drives, or environmental programs that your organization engages in, these actions need to be highlighted in a description of the organization's social responsibility efforts.
- ***Include your social responsibility message in your recruitment efforts*** Social responsibility efforts can attract applicants and increase the likelihood they will accept a job offer. If social responsibility is to have an effect, people need to know about it. Including social responsibility in your recruitment efforts can get out the message that your organization is a place where workers can, indeed, find a larger purpose.
- ***Job performance remains a priority*** Although you hope that social responsibility efforts of the organization resonate with job candidates, the ability to perform the job is the primary concern. In other words, the fit between the person and the job should be satisfied before the degree of fit between the person and the organization is a focus.
- ***A larger purpose isn't for everyone*** Finding meaning through work by contributing to social responsibility efforts is important for some people, but not for everyone. For some people, a job is primarily a job and a way to make money, not a way to make a positive social difference. For these people, the social responsibility message may not make much difference in terms of the attractiveness of the organization and the likelihood of applying for a job.

Sources: Based on Chuang, P. M. (2013). Gen Y staff want meaning in work, employers told. *The Business Times*, April 22; Gully, S. M., Phillips, J. M., Castellano, W. G., Han, K., and Kim, A. (2013). A mediated moderation model of recruiting socially and environmentally responsible job applicants. *Personnel Psychology*, *66*, 1–39; Roberts, B. (2012, March). Values-driven HR. *HRMagazine*, 44–48; Zhang, L., and Gowan, M. A. (2012). Corporate social responsibility, applicants' individual traits, and organizational attraction: A person-organization fit perspective. *Journal of Business and Psychology*, *27*, 345–362. ■■

Reactions to Selection Devices

Over the last several pages, we have discussed how well the various selection tools predict job performance. Next, we consider reactions to selection tools. How do applicants and managers respond to the selection methods we have discussed? The answer is clearly important, because these responses may be the determining factor in a decision to file a lawsuit.

1. *Applicant reactions to selection devices* Applicants are a major customer of selection systems; they want and may demand fair selection devices. Moreover, applicants' reactions to selection methods can influence their attraction to and opinions of an organization and their decision to accept or reject an offer of employment.[103] Applicants' reactions to selection tools also influence their willingness to purchase the company's products.[104]

To which selection tests do applicants respond most favorably and least favorably? Some interesting findings have emerged. For example, despite the increasing use of personality assessment devices as predictors, many job applicants believe that personality traits are not job relevant. A more negative reaction to personality tests tends to be characteristic of U.S. applicants, whereas job applicants in Europe and other areas don't seem to have as much of a problem with personality assessment being a part of the hiring process.[105]

2. ***Manager reactions to selection systems*** Managers need selection systems that are quick and easy to administer and that deliver results that are easy to understand. However, very little research has considered manager reactions to selection systems. One study surveyed 635 managers from 38 agencies in state government.[106] The study assessed the managers' perceptions of various factors related to the selection process, including selection methods. These findings were used to revise selection systems and other HR practices in those agencies.

Although validity must remain a central concern in selection, applicant and manager reactions to selection methods also need to be considered in the design of a selection system. Managers who are not happy with a selection method may ignore the data collected using that method or find a way to eliminate the use of the method. Applicants who perceive a method to be unfair may be more likely to file a discrimination charge over its use. In short, validity is critical, but applicant and manager perceptions can determine whether a method is going to be useful in practice.

Legal Issues in Staffing

Legal concerns can play an exceptionally important role in staffing, particularly in selection. A number of legal constraints, most notably federal legislation and its definition of illegal discrimination, affect selection.

Discrimination Laws

The Civil Rights Act of 1964 and its extension, the Civil Rights Act of 1991, provide broad prohibition against discrimination based on race, color, sex, religion, and national origin. These laws, which state that such discrimination in *all terms and conditions* of employment is illegal, affect selection as well as many other organizational programs, including performance appraisal and training.

To decrease the chances of lawsuits claiming discrimination, firms should ensure that selection techniques are job related. In other words, the best defense is evidence of the validity of the selection process. For example, if a minority group member who was turned down for a job claims discrimination, the organization should have ample evidence to document the job relatedness of its selection process. This evidence should include job analysis information and evidence that test scores are valid predictors of performance.

The Age Discrimination in Employment Act of 1967 and the 1978 amendments to the act prohibit discrimination against people aged 40 and older. Again, the organization needs evidence of the validity of the selection process if older applicants are turned away—particularly if comparable but younger applicants are hired.

The Americans with Disabilities Act (ADA) of 1991 extends the Vocational Rehabilitation Act of 1973 and provides legal protection for people with physical or mental disabilities. ADA requires employers to provide reasonable accommodations for people whose disabilities may prevent them from adequately performing essential job functions, unless doing so will create an undue hardship for the organization. Thus, employers need to determine what constitutes a job's essential functions. Although the law does not clearly define "reasonable accommodation," the courts may deem reasonable such actions as modifications in schedules, equipment, and facilities. In terms of selection, ADA prevents employers from asking applicants whether they have a disability and prohibits the requirement of medical examinations before making job offers. However, an employer can ask applicants whether they can perform a job's essential functions. Also, job offers can be made contingent on the results of a medical examination.

Affirmative Action

Affirmative action must also be considered. Federal Executive Order 11246 requires organizations that are government contractors or subcontractors to have affirmative action programs in place. These programs are designed to eliminate any underutilization of protected group members that might occur in an organization's employment practices (see Chapter 3). Affirmative action is not the same as the equal employment opportunity required by Title VII of the Civil Rights Act and related legislation. Making job-related selection decisions while not discriminating against subgroups is not the same as setting utilization goals. However, organizations that are not government contractors or subcontractors can lose the privilege of selecting employees solely on the basis of expected job performance if they are found guilty of discrimination. In that case, they can be ordered to put an affirmative action program in place.

Negligent Hiring

The final legal issue in staffing concerns claims of *negligent hiring.* Negligent hiring refers to a situation in which an employer fails to use reasonable care in hiring an employee, who then commits a crime while in his or her position in the organization. Because claims of negligent hiring have increased over the years,[107] managers need to be particularly sensitive to this issue. For example, Avis Rent A Car hired a man without thoroughly checking his background; the man later raped a female coworker. Avis was found guilty of negligent hiring and had to pay damages of $800,000. Had the company carefully checked the information provided in the man's job application, it would have discovered that he was in prison when he claimed he was attending high school and college. Employers are responsible for conducting a sound investigation into applicants' backgrounds. Factors such as gaps in employment or admission of prior criminal convictions should prompt closer investigation. To avoid liability for negligent hiring, employers should:[108]

- Develop clear policies on hiring as well as on disciplining and dismissing employees. The hiring policy should include a thorough background check of applicants, including verification of educational, employment, and residential information.
- Check state laws regarding hiring applicants with criminal records. What is legal in this area varies widely among states.
- Learn as much as possible about applicants' past work-related behavior, including violence, threats, lying, drug or alcohol abuse, carrying of weapons, and other problems. Keep in mind that privacy and discrimination laws prohibit inquiries into an applicant's personal, non–work related activities. Behavioral problems may be investigated only in the context of their possible effect on job performance.

Summary and Conclusions

Human Resource Supply and Demand

HRP is the process an organization uses to ensure that it has the right amount and right kinds of people to deliver a particular level of output or services at some point in the future. HRP entails using a variety of qualitative or quantitative methods to forecast labor demand and labor supply and then taking actions based on those estimates.

The Hiring Process

The hiring process consists of three activities: recruitment, selection, and orientation.

Challenges in the Hiring Process

The hiring process is filled with challenges. These include (1) determining which characteristics are most important to performance, (2) measuring these characteristics, (3) evaluating applicants' motivation, and (4) deciding who should make hiring decisions.

Meeting the Challenge of Effective Staffing

Because choosing the right person for a job can have a tremendous positive effect on productivity and customer satisfaction, it is important that each step of the hiring process be managed carefully.

Recruitment

Recruiting should focus on attracting qualified candidates, internally and/or externally. Recruiting efforts should be tied to the firm's HRP efforts. To ensure proper fit between hires and their jobs and to avoid legal problems, firms should conduct job analyses.

Selection

Many selection tools are available. These include letters of recommendation, application forms, ability tests, personality tests, psychological tests, interviews, assessment centers, drug tests, honesty tests, reference checks, and handwriting analysis. The best (and most legally defensible) selection tools are both reliable and valid.

Legal Issues in Staffing

Several federal legal issues govern staffing practices. The Civil Rights Act, the Age Discrimination Act, and the Americans with Disabilities Act all prohibit various forms of discrimination. Executive Order 11246 spells out affirmative action policies. Employers must also take steps to protect themselves from negligent hiring litigation.

Key Terms

Watch It!

Gawker Media: Personnel Planning and Recruiting. If your instructor has assigned this, go to **mymanagementlab.com** to watch a video case and answer questions.

Discussion Questions

5-1. Recent economic difficulties, restructurings, and plant closing have left many people without jobs and looking for new career paths. A hiring employer can now enjoy being able to select from among far more applicants than typical. Unfortunately, many of these applicants lack qualifications for the jobs. How can a hiring employer avoid or deal with a potentially large number of unqualified applicants? How can the problem be approached in recruitment? In selection, what tools would you recommend when an employer is facing a large number of applicants?

5-2. Should applicants be selected primarily on the basis of ability or on personality/fit? How can fit be assessed?

5-3. A company uses a series of selection measures to try and predict future job performance. The company gives the test to all applicants and then checks new hires' job performance levels 12 months later. Theoretically, there should be a correlation between the test scores and job performance. The problem is that the first cohort of employees show a marked over-estimation of job performance in selection compared to the results a year later. There is little correlation between the two sets of scores and this leads the company to assume that the selection process test is somehow flawed. What could be the problem? How could this problem be sorted out? What can the company do about the seemingly under-performing employees after one year of employment with the company?

 5-4. You have been asked by your company to hire a new worker for your unit. You have been given responsibility for conducting the recruitment and selection. How would you recruit a new worker for your unit? Explain why you would use those particular methods and sources.

How will you select the applicant who will actually get the job? Would you use some sort of tests and an interview? If so, what kind and in what order?

5-5. Interviewing unqualified applicants can be a frustrating experience and a waste of time for managers, peers, or whoever is responsible for interviewing. How can the HR department minimize or eliminate this problem?

5-6. You work for a medium-sized organization that has very distinct core values and social responsibilities. It is the only major employer in the locality and takes its community responsibilities very seriously. This does mean that there is a tension between recruiting those local to the organization and those who hold a similar set of values and feel similar responsibilities. How can this tension be handled as an integral part of the recruitment process?

 5-7. Your boss has stated that he wants the hiring program to hire the best workers and to be legally defensible. Are those two goals compatible? What would be your basic recommendations to your boss to achieve those two goals?

MyManagementLab®

If your instructor has assigned this, go to **mymanagementlab.com** for the following Assisted-graded writing questions:

5-8. A job applicant complained that his job interview was positively evaluated by one member of the interview panel and negatively evaluated by another panel member. Is the applicant describing a problem of reliability or validity? Explain. Why is this type of disagreement a problem?

5-9. A manager explained that he denied a promotion to a worker due to the results of his personal test. His personal test consisted of examining a workers' car in the parking lot to determine if it was clean and well kept. A car in disrepair and with material strewn around the interior indicated the worker was disorganized and could not be counted on to take care of details. Should the manager's personal test be used to make promotion assessments? Why or why not? What alternatives to the personal test would you suggest?

5-10. One of your managers thinks that ability to do the job is the most important issue in assessing job applicants. Another manager thinks that personality and fit issues are most important. Assuming that both characteristics are important, how would you recommend that abilities needed to do the job be identified and measured? How would you recommend that personality be measured?

You Manage It! 1: Customer-Driven HR

Women: Keeping the Supply Lines Open

Women leave the workforce at higher rates than men. In part, this may help explain why only about 2 percent of top CEO positions are held by females. But why do women quit? Further, do they later rejoin the labor force? Can they, after leaving? Let's take a look at these issues.

First, there is little doubt that women are more likely than men to leave the labor force. For example, a recent survey focused on a nationally representative group of women who had a graduate, professional, or high-honors undergraduate degree. The survey included over 2,400 women. A major finding of the survey was that 24 percent of men had voluntarily left their job whereas nearly 40 percent of women had voluntarily left. These women invested in education that positioned them for successful careers, yet many of them chose to leave the workforce.

Why do women choose to leave the workforce? There is, of course, no single answer. Family and child-care issues certainly can "pull" women away from work. However, a surprising number of women report leaving their jobs due to boredom and frustration. That is, in order to feel challenged and to increase their chances for growth and opportunity, women feel that they have to leave their current employer.

The factors that "push" women to leave jobs would seem to be most directly manageable by organizations. Some organizations offer programs such as coaching and mentoring programs for women, family-friendly policies, and training targeted at women returning to the workforce in an attempt to retain and attract high-quality female workers.

Critical Thinking Questions

5-11. Why is the departure of women an issue for organizations?

5-12. When trying to reenter the workforce, women often find that they have to take a lower pay rate to "get back in the game." Do you think this is fair? Why or why not?

5-13. If push factors can be controlled by employers, what could stop them from doing so?

Team Exercise

5-14. "Pull" factors are issues or characteristics that draw a woman away from her job responsibilities. "Push" factors are characteristics that repel a woman from her current job responsibilities. Join team members in your class and identify reasons why women leave their jobs. Classify each as a pull or push factor and judge the extent to which each tends to affect women rather than men. (You can use the following rating scale to make these judgments.)

1	2	3	4	5	6	7
Mainly affects men			Affects men and women equally			Mainly affects women

Experiential Exercise: Team

5-15. Join team members and research what companies are doing to retain women employees. Classify these management initiatives as addressing either "push" or "pull" factors. Are there approaches that you think would be effective for retaining women but that you did not find being used by organizations? List and describe what you consider to be the best approaches. Be prepared to discuss expected costs and benefits and to justify your recommendations.

Experiential Exercise: Individual

5-16. Design a job that you think would maximize the retention of women. What characteristics would the job have in terms of policies, benefits, and so on? Would any costs associated with these job characteristics be worth it for men as the job holders? Why or why not? Share the job characteristics with the rest of the class.

Sources: Based on Deutsch, C. H. (2005, May 3). Boredom is the culprit: Exodus of women executives has a cure. *Arizona Republic,* D-4; Hewlett, S. A., and Luce, C. B. (2005). Off-ramps and on-ramps: Keeping talented women on the road to success. *Harvard Business Review, 83,* 43–54; Booth, N. (2007, November 13). Scheme aims to attract women back into IT. *Computer Weekly,* 41.

You Manage It! 2: Ethics/Social Responsibility

What a Fraud!

The economy is tight, and there is competition among applicants to land jobs. This setting is expected to lead to an increase in the number of applicants who will misrepresent their background and credentials. The hope, of course, is that this bit of fudging will help them get the job. The misrepresentations might involve a change in the date of birth, shifting a college major, or maybe even the fabrication of a degree. There may also be lies about criminal records. The fact of the matter is that these misrepresentations, whether "little white lies" or major fabrications, are fraud. It is expected that fraud will be engaged in by approximately 30 percent of job applicants.

Critical Thinking Questions

5-17. Do you think fraud on resumes and job applications is an important issue for organizations? Why or why not?

5-18. In some countries, fake qualifications and forged certificates are as common as the real thing. To what extent do you think that this devalues the real thing? If it is so easy to obtain convincing forged documents, is there any incentive for people to study at all?

5-19. If a fraudulent imposter can perform the job, what's the harm?

Team Exercise

5-20. With your team members, identify how companies try to detect fraud. Do you think it is worth the cost? What could be the cost if it wasn't done?

Experiential Team Exercise

5-21. With your teammates, consider various jobs and the potential liability for each. For example, a cable installer would have access to private property, and teachers would work with children. Some jobs may have high stress, and some jobs involve driving vehicles. With your team, identify as many of the potential liability areas as you can, and list each as a row in a matrix or spreadsheet.

For the columns in your matrix, identify the types of characteristics or backgrounds that should be checked. For example, propensity for violence, driving record, and criminal record could be some of your major columns.

Mark the cells in the matrix to indicate where a check should occur. Are there some checks that appear more important than others? Describe. How can an organization use the type of matrix you developed?

Sources: Based on Guthrie, J. (2009, March 5). Beware the risky business of resume fraud. *Financial Times,* London, 15; Levashina, J., and Campion, M. A. (2009). Expected practices in background checking: Review of the human resource management literature. *Employee Responsibilities and Rights Journal, 21,* 231–249; Patel, P. (2009). Experts expect resume fraud to rise. *IEEE Spectrum, 46,* 24.

 You Manage It! 3: Technology/Social Media

Social Media in the Hiring Process

As discussed in the Manager's Notebook, "Don't Get Screened Out in a Social Media Screen ," as a job applicant, it is best to recognize that many employers are using social media screening and accordingly to put your best foot forward. In this case, we take another look at the use of social media in the hiring process and ask you to consider issues from the perspectives of an applicant and a manager.

Many employers are using social media, such as Facebook and LinkedIn, in their recruitment and hiring process. As illustrated in Figure 5.8, the use of social media ranges from promotion, to public screening, and to private screening. Employers use social media as a promotion tool when they place ads and recruit for job applicants on social networking sites. Public screening refers to employer use of publically available digital information, such as postings, profiles, and blogs, in the evaluation of job applicants. Private screening, on the other hand, involves employers' asking applicants to provide access to their private social networking accounts.

There has been surprisingly little research on the effectiveness of social media as a recruitment tool or as a screening tool. However, there have been an increasing number of legal protections offered to job applicants regarding private screening. Employers may be overstepping a line of expected privacy by asking applicants for passwords to their social networking sites or by asking applicants to log in so that the employer can review the account. Given privacy concerns, legislation prohibiting this practice has been proposed or passed in various states and at the federal level.

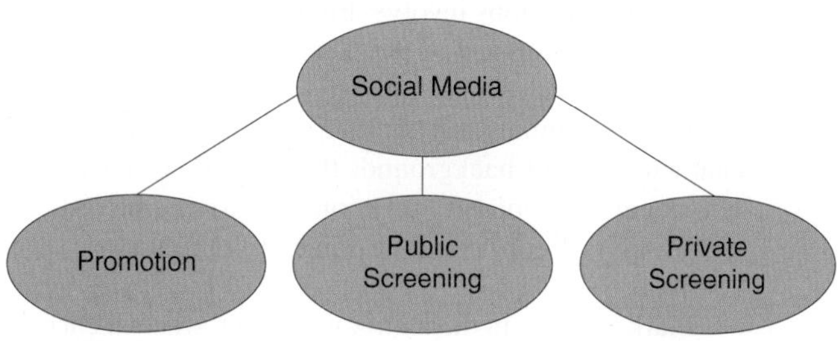

FIGURE 5.8
Categories of Employer Use of Social Media

Critical Thinking Questions

5-22. Do you think that the use of social media for recruitment is an effective approach to recruit workers?

5-23. As a manager looking to hire additional workers, what steps would you take to maximize the effectiveness of your recruitment efforts using social media?

5-24. Using social media to recruit for job openings may disproportionately tap into younger applicants. Older workers could be unintentionally precluded from the applicant pool to the extent they are less present and active on social networking sites. Why would this be a problem? What would you recommend to eliminate or reduce this problem?

5-25. What advice would you give someone who is actively seeking work in relation to their activities on social media? What should they avoid saying or doing? Should they consider "tidying up" their profiles, comments, and content? How likely is it that a potential employer will look at their social media activities? How should they react if a potential employer asks for access to their accounts?

Team Exercise

5-26. The use of social media for public screening of job applicants can offer benefits to an employer such as a relatively low cost recruitment alternative and a means for finding information about applicants that may be more honest than what is found in cover letters and resumes. However, costs may also be involved with this use of social media. For example, a charge of discrimination may occur (see Critical Thinking Question 5-25); postings that appear to have been by a candidate may have been made by someone else; or information about a candidate's activities may be old and no longer valid.

As a team, identify potential benefits of the use of social media for public screening. Also, identify potential costs of this approach. How could the potential costs be reduced?

Experiential Exercise: Team

5-27. Validity of measures is a critical concept in hiring: it is needed to identify those who will be better workers, and it is needed to legally defend the selection process. In the case of using social media to screen applicants, there is little evidence of validity of the various types of information that might be collected. How could the content validity of social media be developed?

a. As a team, pick a job and identify aspects of the job, such as task or competencies needed. Are there types of social media information that would reflect these aspects? Why would this job-driven approach be useful?

b. As a team, identify how you could assess the criterion-related validity of the types of social media information you identified in in Question 5-27a. How would this validity information be useful?

Share the assessments of your team with the rest of the class.

Experiential Exercise: Individual

5-28. Companies have recently been created, such as Social Intelligence, that offer pre-employment social media screening. Using an Internet search, identify some of the companies offering this service. What do the companies offer? Would you recommend the use of such a third-party approach to performing social media screening of job applicants? Why or why not?

Sources: Based on Brown, V. R., and Vaughn, E. D. (2011). The writing on the (Facebook) wall: The use of social networking sites in hiring decisions. *Journal of Business and Psychology*, *26*, 219–225; Ebnet, N. (2012). It can do more than protect your credit score: Regulating social media pre-employment screening with the Fair Credit Reporting Act. *Minnesota Law Review*, *97*, 306–336; Davison, H. K., Maraist, C., and Bing, M. N. (2011). Friend or foe? The promise and pitfalls of using social networking sites for HR decisions. *Journal of Business and Psychology*, *26*, 153–159; Martucci, W. C., and Shankland, R. J. (2012). New laws prohibiting employers from requiring employees to provide access to social-networking sites. *Employee Relations Today*, *39*, 79–85.

You Manage It! 4: Ethics/Social Responsibility

Fitting in Social Responsibility

As discussed in the Manager's Notebook, "A Larger Purpose: Social Responsibility in the Recruitment and Hiring Process ," social responsibility commitments can make an organization a more attractive employer. Furthermore, fit between an individual's values and interests and the organization's social responsibility commitments is associated with other positive outcomes, such as higher job performance and worker commitment. These positive outcomes can't be expected to materialize just from a policy statement regarding social responsibility. If managed well, however, social responsibility efforts can be a source of competitive advantage for an organization by attracting applicants and improving the chances that they will join as motivated workers.

Critical Thinking Questions

5-29. Traditionally, hiring decisions were primarily based on the extent to which an applicant's qualifications fit the job. In other words, the focus has been on hiring the person who, based on information collected through the selection process, was expected to best perform the job. To what extent do you think an applicant's fit with the social responsibility commitments of the organization should be considered? If, for example, person/organization fit is to be considered in the selection process, should this fit assessment be given weight equal to expected job performance? Or, should fit be given less weight or somehow taken into account in another way in the selection process?

5-30. What steps would you take to make sure that potential applicants are aware of the social responsibility commitments of your organization? That is, what would you recommend be done to make social responsibility part of the employer brand for the organization?

5-31. In the roles of an employer, how would you handle a situation where employees have taken on a greater sense of social responsibility than that is immediately apparent in your organization? How would you handle the potential tensions? Do you think it is important to adjust the organization's social responsibilities, or demand that the employees fall in line with the organization's stance? To what extent do you think that the absence of shared commitment might damage the organization?

Team Exercise

5-32. You may have management colleagues who think that social responsibility isn't an important issue for organizations and, therefore, it shouldn't play a role in employee recruitment and selection. The issue, as they see it, might be summarized as, "It's all about doing the job and making money." As a team, what arguments could you offer that might convince these colleagues of the usefulness of social responsibility? Share your arguments with the rest of the class.

Experiential Exercise: Team

5-33. With your teammates, look at some of the online job-opening announcements. Consider at least a dozen ads and summarize those that include a description of social responsibility commitments or activities. What social responsibility aspects are highlighted? Do you think the ads that include social responsibility information are more effective?

Experiential Exercise: Individual

5-34. Consider your own interests and values. What is important to you and in what do you find meaning or purpose? Given this reflection, what type of social responsibility activities would most appeal to you?
   a. How important is it to you to have a positive social impact through your work?
   b. Given the above considerations, can you identify employers that look like they would be a good person/organization fit for you?

Sources: Based on Aguinis, H., and Glavas, A. (2012). What we know and don't know about corporate social responsibility: A review and research agenda. *Journal of Management*, *38*, 932–968; Gully, S. M., Phillips, J. M., Castellano, W. G., Han, K., and Kim, A. (2013). A mediated moderation model of recruiting socially and environmentally responsible job applicants. *Personnel Psychology*, *66*, 1–39; Zhang, L., and Gowan, M. (2012). Corporate social responsibility, applicants' individual traits, and organizational attraction: A person-organization fit perspective. *Journal of Business and Psychology*, *27*, 345–362.

You Manage It! 5: Emerging Trends

One Job, Many Roles

Teamwork is how many organizations operate today. Rather than being independent contributors, team members have some degree of interdependence and share in getting the work done. The informal reality in many teams is that tasks or responsibilities are allocated depending on the relative strengths and weaknesses of the team members. For example, a technical problem faced by a team might be allocated to the team member who has the best technical skills, whereas a potential conflict is given to the person with the best interpersonal skills. The informal reality is that team members often end up playing different roles, depending on their natural strengths. Research has found that allowing people to play to their strengths can yield maximum performance and employee satisfaction. It makes sense that if people can do what they do best, performance should also be maximized.

If team members take on different roles, there really isn't one job for all of the workers, but different roles. Some people might do well in some of these roles and in others they might do poorly. Recognizing that people might take on different roles in a team environment can have important implications for the hiring process.

Critical Thinking Questions

5-35. If there are distinct roles to be played on a team, how would you go about recruiting and hiring for them?

5-36. The characteristics needed by individual team members depend on the team and the strengths and weaknesses of others who are on the team. In other words, the situation is much more dynamic than assuming that there is one static job with a single set of qualifications. How could you model or include this dynamic and interactive nature in the recruitment and hiring process?

Team Exercise

5-37. As a team, identify the roles that you think are important for teams in the small business workplace. To help you get started, here are some possible basic team roles that have been identified in research: contributor, collaborator, communicator, and challenger. A number of other roles have been identified in research or could be useful in practice. Don't limit yourself to this set of roles.

a. Identify the skills needed to perform each role.
b. In addition to skills, a natural tendency or motivation to perform in a particular type of role can be critical. How could you measure the motivation needed for each role?
c. How could you measure the skills needed for each role?
d. How could you effectively recruit for the various positions or roles?
e. Present your recruitment and selection plan to the rest of the class.

Individual Exercise

5-38. Suppose that you worked for an organization that promoted the establishment and running of self-managed teams. As head of HR, you have traditionally taken the lead role in the recruitment and selection process. You have developed sophisticated and effective selection methods over the course of the past few years and have made very few recruitment mistakes as a result. The suggestion is to now devolve some of those recruitment and selection duties to the self-managed teams. They will take the lead in the selection process and HR will provide the necessary logistical support and guidance. In effect, you will provide the guidelines and safety for them. In a short document, outline how you think this might work. What are the practicalities of the situation? You should assume that the organization is at least committed to employing these guidelines for a trial period. You should, therefore, make sure that checks and balances will be put in place to ensure that the process has a chance of working.

Sources: Based on Black, B. (2002). The road to recovery. *Gallup Management Journal, 1,* 10–12; Mumford, T. V., Van Iddekinge, C. H., Morgeson, F. P., and Campion, M. A. (2008). The team role test: Development and validation of a team role knowledge situational judgment test. *Journal of Applied Psychology, 93,* 250; Lupuleac, S., Lupuleac, Z., and Rusu, C. (2012). Problems of assessing team roles balance–team design. *Procedia Economics and Finance, 3,* 935–940.

Endnotes

Scan for Endnotes or go to http://www.pearsonglobaleditions.com/Gomez-Mejia.

CHAPTER 6 Managing Employee Separations, Downsizing, and Outplacement

MyManagementLab®

When you see this icon, visit **www.mymanagementlab.com** for activities that are applied, personalized, and offer immediate feedback.

CHALLENGES

After reading this chapter, you should be able to deal more effectively with the following challenges:

1. **Understand** employee separations.
2. **Gain** mastery in identifying types of employee separations.
3. **Have** familiarity with managing early retirements.
4. **Learn** practices for managing layoffs.
5. **Recognize** the role of outplacement.

Maintaining the fiscal health of an organization, particularly in difficult economic times, often means cutting costs. In most organizations, a significant portion of the cost of doing business is the cost of labor. Layoffs are one tool organizations use to reduce labor costs.

The reduced employment level due to a downsizing is typically meant to improve productivity and the financial situation of the firm. However, there can be difficulties in using layoffs as a means to improve organizational performance. Below are some points to consider regarding layoffs.

- Downsizing became a common practice and familiar term by the mid-1980s. The number of layoffs peaked in the 1990s and again in the recent recession during 2007 through 2009. The layoff numbers declined in 2010, but the practice continues.[1]

Employee separations need to be handled fairly.
Source: David De Lossy/Thinkstock.

- In the 1960s and 1970s, job cuts tended to affect blue-collar workers. Although the initial focus of layoffs was elimination of lower-skilled and hourly workers, that is no longer true. For example, Zynga, an online gaming pioneer, has eliminated hundreds of employees from its workforce.[2]
- Until the early 2000s, layoffs were largely seen as a means to get a boost in stock price. Large, publicly traded firms would get noticed for their layoff announcements, and there was a belief that investors rewarded the cost-cutting measures with an increase in the stock prices. Recent research, however, indicates that layoff announcements are generally associated with a negative stock price response.[3]
- Layoffs have been associated with a number of negative outcomes. Internal to the organization, morale can

decline and concerns over job security can become a focus for surviving workers.[4] External to the organization, the reputation of the organization may suffer. For example, a former employee may post negative comments about their former employer, particularly if he or she feels that the layoff was unfair.[5] More broadly, a major layoff can have a negative effect on an entire community. If a company is a major employer in town, a layoff could affect the livelihood of many people and the economic health of families in the community.

Overall, layoffs, as with any kind of employee separation, can have negative or positive consequences. An important factor is how well the employee separation process is managed.

The Managerial Perspective

Global competition and technological advances have changed the rules of competition, forcing many firms to become increasingly productive with smaller workforces. In addition, voluntary turnover—people choosing to leave their jobs—can be an issue for companies. People can choose to leave their jobs for a variety of reasons, including job opportunities that can arise, even in tight economic times.

Managers must not only develop skills to help an employee who leaves the company voluntarily, but they must also aid employees who have been fired for cause or are being let go for economic reasons. A badly managed ending to the employment relationship can damage a firm's reputation in its industry or community and limit its ability to attract the scarce, talented employees that it may need in the future.

This chapter deals with the sometimes unpleasant task of managing an organization's outflow of human resources. We explore the process leading up to an employee's exit from the firm and how to manage that process effectively.

Learn It!

If your professor has chosen to assign this go to **www.mymanagementlab.com** to see what you should particularly focus on, and take the chapter 6 warmup.

What Are Employee Separations?

employee separation
The termination of an employee's membership in an organization.

turnover rate
The rate of employee separations in an organization.

An **employee separation** occurs when an employee ceases to be a member of an organization.[6] The **turnover rate** is a measure of the rate at which employees leave the firm. Well-managed companies try to monitor their turnover rate and identify and manage causes for turnover. The goal is to minimize turnover and the costs of replacing employees. Replacement costs, particularly for highly skilled positions, can be surprisingly high. For example, replacing a U.S. Navy fighter pilot may cost more than $1,000,000.[7] However, multiple turnover rates can be calculated, and it is important to focus on the correct numbers. Exhibit 6.1 presents the basics about calculating turnover rates. An excessively high turnover rate compared to the industry standard is often a symptom of problems within the organization.

Employee separations can and should be managed. Before we discuss the management of separations, however, we examine both the costs and the benefits of separations.

The Costs of Employee Separations

The cost of turnover can differ across organizations, and some costs associated with turnover can be difficult to estimate. For example, an organization's geographic location may necessitate a particularly high cost of recruiting new employees, which causes the cost of turnover in that organization to be unusually high. The effect of lost talent on sales, on productivity, or on research and development all may be tremendous, but difficult to estimate.

EXHIBIT 6.1 A QUICK LOOK AT THE NUMBERS: A TURNOVER RATE PRIMER

Turnover happens in all organizations. The rate of turnover can vary over time and across companies and industries. Before determining whether your turnover rate is high compared to other time periods or to other organizations, be sure you calculate it accurately.

You need the number of employees exiting each month and the average number of employees on staff during each of those months. The following formula calculates this rate:

$$\text{Turnover} = \frac{\text{Number of employees leaving the job}}{\text{Average number of employees during the period}} \times \frac{12}{\text{Number of months in the period}}$$

Let's consider the following situation. Over the course of 6 months, you have had 12 employees leave a department. The average number of employees in the department is 50. Given these numbers, your annualized turnover rate is:

$$12/50 \times 12/6 = .48$$

Over the 6 months your turnover rate has been 24 percent; however, the formula indicates that this rate is 48 percent on an annual basis.

Knowing the overall turnover rate can provide a rough comparison point. However, breaking the overall rate down into various components can help you to understand the sources for turnover and help to determine whether you have a problem. A helpful way of breaking out the overall rate is to use the categories in Figure 6.1.

"Source of turnover" refers to whether the employee decided to leave the organization (voluntary) or management made the decision to end the employment relationship (involuntary). "Type of turnover" can be divided into people who left the organization (external) and employees who left the job but took another position in the organization (internal).

You can calculate turnover rates for each of the four cells in the source-by-type matrix. A high rate of turnover that is voluntary and external, a high quit rate, could be of particular concern and be symptomatic of organizational problems.

Type of Turnover \ Source of Turnover	Voluntary	Involuntary
External	Quits	Terminations
Internal	Voluntary Transfers	Mandatory Transfers

FIGURE 6.1
Source and Type of Turnover

Source: Cleveland, B. (2005, June 1). Tackling turnover. *Call Center*, 16. Reprinted with permission.

Employee turnover affects the bottom line. A recent survey of over 200 insurance brokerages demonstrates the relationship between employee turnover and firm profitability.[8] The brokerages were arbitrarily divided into two groups: those with profitability that exceeded 20 percent of sales and those with profitability under 20 percent of sales. Employee turnover in the lower-profit group was approximately twice as high as turnover in the higher-profit group. The profit level in the high-profit group was 30.3 percent of sales, and the profit level in the lower profit group was 11.4 percent of sales. Although turnover might not be the only cause of these profit levels, these findings indicate that employee turnover is an important factor in bottom-line performance.

Unfortunately, organizations can find it difficult to reduce employee separations when turnover is part of the system. The Manager's Notebook, "Voluntary Turnover in China," is part of the business reality in China.

It is common to estimate the cost of turnover from a conservative 25 percent[9] to 300 percent of the lost employee's annual compensation.[10] Looking at the most conservative end of that range, at an average salary of $30,000, the cost of a turnover would be $6,000.

Recruitment Costs	Selection Costs	Training Costs	Separation Costs
• Advertising	• Interviewing	• Orientation	• Separation pay
• Campus visits	• Testing	• Direct training costs	• Benefits
• Recruiter time	• Reference checks	• Trainer's time	• Unemployment insurance cost
• Search firm fees	• Relocation	• Lost productivity during training	• Exit interview
			• Outplacement
			• Vacant position

FIGURE 6.2
Human Resource Replacement Costs

For a company with 1,000 employees and a 20 percent turnover rate, the annual cost of turnover would be at least $1,200,000—not a trivial cost, and it could be much higher depending on the situation. Figure 6.2 presents only some of the costs associated with replacing an employee. The costs can be categorized as *recruitment costs, selection costs, training costs,* and *separation costs.*

RECRUITMENT COSTS The costs associated with recruiting a replacement may include advertising the job vacancy and using a professional recruiter to travel to various locations (including college campuses). To fill executive positions or technologically complex openings, it may be necessary to employ a search firm to locate qualified individuals, who most likely are already employed. A search firm typically charges the company a fee of about 30 percent of the employee's annual salary.

MANAGER'S NOTEBOOK

Global

Voluntary Turnover in China

Employee turnover in the United States and Europe average around 5 percent annually, while voluntary turnover in China is approximately 19 percent. Turnover rates in China have been found to vary across companies and range from 11 to 40 percent. Multinational companies doing business in China face an employee turnover rate that is approximately 25 percent above the global average.

What accounts for the high quit rate in China? Simply stated, demand for labor exceeds supply. Companies in China are dealing with labor shortages and fighting for the talent they need to effectively operate their businesses. A shortage of talent in China is identified as a barrier by multinational and Chinese companies. A slowdown in the Chinese economy is expected to somewhat lessen the overall shortage of labor, but a need for talented managers is expected to grow.

The need for experienced workers, particularly those with management experience and training, means that there are a number of job openings that can hire employees away from their current jobs. The highly competitive job market makes for a more mobile workforce and a higher employee turnover rate.

Wage rates in China have increased as a means to retain and attract labor. However, it is not just about wages. Companies in China are also finding that they need to provide employees a good value proposition in order to retain their talent. For example, offering leadership and management skills training can be a valuable benefit to employees and increase their commitment to stay with the employer. Providing paths for people to move forward in the organization and being transparent about what it takes to move forward on those paths can also contribute to employees deciding to stay with the organization. Although there are steps that organizations can take to reduce employee turnover, it is part of the business reality in China that job opportunities are plentiful. Having those opportunities certainly makes voluntary turnover a more difficult problem to manage.

Sources: Based on Huang, J. (2013). Developing local talent for future leadership. *The China Business Review*, *40*, 28–30; John, I. S. (2013). Average salary increases of 9.1%, turnover rate of 18.9%. *China Benefits and Compensation International*, *42*, 51; Silva, J. D. (2012). The war for talent in China. *Ivey Business Journal Online*, retrieved on June 9, 2013 from Proquest. ■■

SELECTION COSTS Selection costs are associated with selecting, hiring, and placing a new employee in a job. Interviewing the job applicant includes the costs associated with travel to the interview site and the productivity lost in organizing the interviews and arranging meetings to make selection decisions. For example, a law firm's decision to hire a new associate may require the participation of many junior associates as well as senior partners who may charge clients hundreds of dollars per hour for their time.

Other selection costs include testing the applicant and conducting reference checks to make sure the applicant's qualifications are legitimate. Finally, the company may have to pay relocation costs, which include the costs of moving the employee's personal property, travel costs, and sometimes even housing costs. Housing costs may include the costs of selling one's previous house and the transaction costs of buying a house in a more expensive market.

TRAINING COSTS Most new employees need some specific training to do their job. Training costs also include the costs associated with an orientation to the company's values and culture. Also important are direct training costs—specifically, the cost of instruction, books, and materials for training courses. Finally, while new employees are being trained they are not performing at the level of fully trained employees, so some productivity is lost.

SEPARATION COSTS A company incurs separation costs for all employees who leave, whether or not they will be replaced. The largest separation cost is compensation in terms of pay and benefits. Most companies provide *severance pay* (also called *separation pay*) for laid-off employees. Severance pay may add up to several months' salary for an experienced employee. Although length of service is the main factor in determining the amount of severance pay, many companies also use formulas that take into account factors such as salary, grade level, and title.

Less frequently, employees may continue to receive health benefits until they find a new job. In addition, employers who lay off employees may also see their unemployment insurance rates go up. Companies are penalized with a higher tax if more of their former employees draw benefits from the unemployment insurance funds in the states in which they do business.

Other separation costs are associated with the administration of the separation itself. Administration often includes an **exit interview** to find out the reasons why the employee is leaving (if he or she is leaving voluntarily) or to provide counseling and/or assistance in finding a new job. It is now common practice in larger firms to provide departing employees with **outplacement assistance**, which helps them find a job more rapidly by providing them with training in job-search skills. Finally, employers incur a cost if a position remains vacant and the work does not get done. The result may be a reduction in output or quality of service to the firm's clients or customers.

exit interview
An employee's final interview following separation. The purpose of the interview is to find out the reasons why the employee is leaving (if the separation is voluntary) or to provide counseling and/or assistance in finding a new job.

outplacement assistance
A program in which companies help their departing employees find jobs more rapidly by providing them with training in job-search skills.

Who conducts the exit interview? The exiting worker's manager is usually a bad choice, because he or she is often the reason for voluntary separations. The interviewer should have very good communication skills and be in a neutral position regarding the employee's departure. Some organizations are moving to Web-based exit interviews, assuming that people may be more open about their reasons for leaving without a face-to-face interaction.[11] However, some workers may find that the human interaction and concern of a skilled interviewer allows them to open up more than would a Web-based interaction.

An overriding issue is how turnover and the various costs associated with it can be reduced. One important factor to recognize in managing employee turnover is that turnover often occurs early in the employment relationship. For example, an organization may experience most employee turnover within the first 30 to 60 days of employing a worker. However, many organizations calculate only annual turnover rates, and this gross measure can mask the reality that most of the turnover occurs in the first two months of employment. A reduction in turnover in the first months of employment can pay dividends for the rest of the year. Reducing the voluntary quit rate in the first month of employment can mean that fewer workers need to be hired as replacements for the rest of the year.[12]

The Benefits of Employee Separations

Although many people see separations negatively, they have several benefits. When turnover rates are too low, few new employees will be hired and opportunities for promotion are sharply curtailed. A persistently low turnover rate may have a negative effect on performance if the workforce becomes complacent and fails to generate innovative ideas.

Employees may receive some potential benefits from a separation, too. An individual may escape from an unpleasant work situation and eventually find one that is less stressful or more personally and professionally satisfying.

REDUCED LABOR COSTS An organization can reduce its total labor costs by reducing the size of its workforce. Although separation costs in a layoff can be considerable, the salary savings resulting from the elimination of some jobs can easily outweigh the separation pay and other expenditures associated with the layoff.

REPLACEMENT OF POOR PERFORMERS An integral part of management is identifying poor performers and helping them to improve their performance. If an employee does not respond to coaching or feedback, it may be best to terminate him or her so that a new (and presumably more skilled) employee can be brought in.

INCREASED INNOVATION Separations create advancement opportunities for high-performing individuals. They also open up entry-level positions as employees are promoted from within. An important source of innovation in companies is new people hired from the outside who can offer a fresh perspective.

THE OPPORTUNITY FOR GREATER DIVERSITY Separations create opportunities to hire employees from diverse backgrounds and to redistribute the cultural and gender composition of the workforce while maintaining control over hiring practices and complying with the government's Equal Employment Opportunity Commission policies.

Types of Employee Separations

Employee separations can be divided into two categories. Voluntary separations are initiated by the employee. Involuntary separations are initiated by the employer. To protect themselves against legal challenges by former employees, employers must manage involuntary separations very carefully with a well-documented paper trail.

Voluntary Separations

voluntary separation
A separation that occurs when an employee decides, for personal or professional reasons, to end the relationship with the employer.

Voluntary separations occur when an employee decides, for personal or professional reasons, to end the relationship with the employer. The decision could be based on the employee obtaining a better job, changing careers, or wanting more time for family or leisure activities. Alternatively, the decision could be based on the employee finding the present job unattractive because of poor working conditions, low pay or benefits, a bad relationship with a supervisor, and so on. In most cases, the decision to leave is a combination of having attractive alternatives and being unhappy with aspects of the current job.

Voluntary separations can be either *avoidable* or *unavoidable.* Unavoidable voluntary separations result from an employee's life decisions that extend beyond an employer's control, such as a spouse's decision to move to a new area that requires the employee to relocate. However, recent studies show that approximately 80 percent of voluntary separations are avoidable, and many of those are due to staffing mistakes. By investing in quality HRM recruiting, selection, training, and development programs (see Chapters 5 and 8), companies can avoid a poor match between the employee and the job.[13]

The two types of voluntary separations are quits and retirements.

QUITS The decision to *quit* depends on (1) the employee's level of dissatisfaction with the job and (2) the number of attractive alternatives the employee has outside the organization.[14] The employee can be dissatisfied with the job itself, the job environment, or both.

In recent years, some employers have been using pay incentives to encourage employees to quit voluntarily. Employers use these *voluntary severance plans*, or *buyouts*, to reduce the size of their workforce while avoiding the negative factors associated with a layoff. The pay incentive may amount to a lump-sum cash payment of six months to two years of salary, depending on the employee's tenure with the company and the plan's design.

RETIREMENTS A *retirement* differs from a quit in a number of respects. First, a retirement usually occurs at the end of an employee's career. A quit can occur at any time. (In fact, it is in the early stages of one's career that a person is more likely to change jobs.) Second, retirements usually result in the individual receiving retirement benefits from the organization. These may include a retirement income supplemented with personal savings and Social Security benefits. People who quit do not receive these benefits. Finally, the organization normally plans retirements in advance. HR staff can help employees plan their retirement, and managers can plan in advance to replace retirees by grooming current employees or recruiting new ones. Quits are much more difficult to plan for.

Most employees postpone retirement until they are close to 65 because that is the age at which they are entitled to Medicare benefits from the government (see Chapter 12).[15] Without these benefits, many workers would find it difficult to retire. It is illegal for an employer to force an employee to retire on the basis of age.

Many Fortune 500 companies have found *early retirement incentives* to be an effective way to reduce their workforces. These incentives make it financially attractive for senior employees to retire early. Along with buyouts, they are used as alternatives to layoffs because they are seen as a gentler way of downsizing. We discuss the management of early retirements in detail later in this chapter.

involuntary separation
A separation that occurs when an employer decides to terminate its relationship with an employee due to (1) economic necessity or (2) a poor fit between the employee and the organization.

Involuntary Separations

An **involuntary separation** occurs when management decides to terminate its relationship with an employee due to (1) economic necessity or (2) a poor fit between the employee and the organization. Involuntary separations are the result of very serious and painful decisions that can have a profound effect on the entire organization and especially on the employee who loses his or her job.

Although managers implement the decision to dismiss an employee, the HR staff makes sure that the dismissed employee receives "due process" and that the dismissal is performed within the letter and the spirit of the company's employment policy. Cooperation and teamwork between managers and HR staff are essential to effective management of the dismissal process. HR staff can act as valuable advisers to managers in this arena by helping them avoid mistakes that can lead to claims of wrongful discharge. They can also help protect employees whose rights are violated by managers. There are two types of involuntary separations: discharges and layoffs.

Can using social media at work be a problem?
Source: © RTimages/Alamy.

DISCHARGES A *discharge* takes place when management decides that there is a poor fit between an employee and the organization. The discharge is a result of either poor performance or the employee's failure to change some unacceptable behavior that management has tried repeatedly to correct. Sometimes employees engage in serious misconduct, such as theft or dishonesty, which may result in immediate termination. Recently, employee use of social media has become the basis for employee discharges. The Manager's Notebook, "Social Media and Work Can Be a Terminal Mix," explores this practice.

MANAGER'S NOTEBOOK

Technology/Social Media

Social Media and Work Can Be a Terminal Mix

Social media, such as Facebook and Twitter, have become integrated into our personal lives and have been adopted as routine tools by many people. For both individuals and organizations, social media offers many benefits, such as being able to immediately reach out and connect with friends or customers. However, casual use of social media by employees has probably caused heartburn for a number of managers and has definitely resulted in some employees being discharged. Consider the following examples of actual employee terminations.

- A flight attendant lost her job after posting suggestive pictures of herself in her company uniform.
- Two employees of a pizza chain franchise were terminated after posting a video on YouTube in which one put mucus on the food and the other put cheese up his nose.
- Thirteen Virgin Atlantic cabin crew members were terminated after the airline learned that the employees had posted inappropriate comments on Facebook about their employer and about their customers.
- An employee of a car dealership was fired after posting criticism on Facebook of the dealership's promotional event for including only water and hot dogs.

As the preceding examples illustrate, people have been fired due to their activity on social media. If you are like many college-age (18–24 years old) students, you might feel that employer monitoring of social media is inappropriate. However, employers have a right to protect themselves from defamation and from actions that might negatively impact the reputation of the business. Just where the legal line is regarding employee expectations of privacy and free expression in social media is something that will remain somewhat blurry until the legal framework evolves in this area. It is clear, though, that employers can't use social media information to discriminate, and there would probably be a lack of legal support to use such information for any purpose that is not strictly business related. Other than these broad prohibitions, it appears that use of social media can be a basis for employee termination.

From a management perspective, it is important to note that, at present, most employers do not have a policy regarding the use of social media. Developing a policy could clarify expectations and prevent problems. A couple of key issues that could be addressed in such a policy include:

- whether social media can be used during work hours.
- what is acceptable for an employee to post.

Clarity regarding these issues could provide guidance to employees and lower the chances of the employer having to discipline, or even terminate, someone for misuse of social media.

Sources: Based on Abril, P. S., Levin, A., and Del Riego, A. (2012). Blurred boundaries: Social media privacy and the twenty-first century employee. *American Business Law Journal*, *49*, 63–111; Cavico, F. J., Mujtaba, B. M., Muffler, S. C., and Samuel, M. (2013). Social media and employment-at-will: Tort law and practical considerations for employees, managers, and organizations. *New Media and Mass Communication*, *11*, 25–41; Field, J., and Chelliah, J. (2012). Social media misuse a ticking time-bomb for employers. *Human Resource Management International Digest*, *20*, 36–38; Jacobson, W. S., and Tufts, S. H. (2013). To post or not to post: Employee rights and social media. *Review of Public Personnel Administration*, *33*, 84–107. ■■

Managers who decide to discharge an employee must make sure they follow the company's established discipline procedures. Most nonunion companies and all unionized firms have a *progressive discipline procedure* that allows employees the opportunity to correct their behavior before receiving a more serious punishment. For example, an employee who violates a safety rule may be given a verbal warning, followed by a written warning within a specified period of time. If the employee does not stop breaking the safety rule, the employer may choose to discharge the employee. Managers must document the occurrences of the violation and provide evidence that the employee knew about the rule and was warned that its violation could lead to discharge. In this way, managers can prove that the employee was discharged for just cause. Chapter 14 details the criteria that managers can use to determine whether a discharge meets the standard of just cause.*

An example illustrates how costly discharging an employee can be if handled poorly or without due process. Sandra McHugh won $1.1 million in damages in an age discrimination lawsuit against her employer.[16] McHugh was forced out of her job because of her age—which was 42 at the time.

It is usually more involved than simply saying "You're fired!"
Source: Thinglass/Shutterstock.

LAYOFFS *Layoffs* are a means for an organization to cut costs. For example, the recent layoff announcement by Zynga, mentioned in the opening of this chapter, was based on financial considerations. Changes in online gaming and a reduction in revenues led Zynga to make the decision to let go hundreds of its employees.

A layoff differs from a discharge in several ways. With a layoff, employees lose their jobs because a change in the company's environment or strategy forces it to reduce its workforce. Global competition, reductions in product demand, changing technologies that reduce the need for workers, and mergers and acquisitions are the primary factors behind most layoffs.[17] In contrast, the actions of most discharged employees have usually been a direct cause of their separation. Although we can make these conceptual distinctions between a layoff and a discharge, the Zynga workers who endured being cut simply know that they lost their jobs, whatever the process is called.

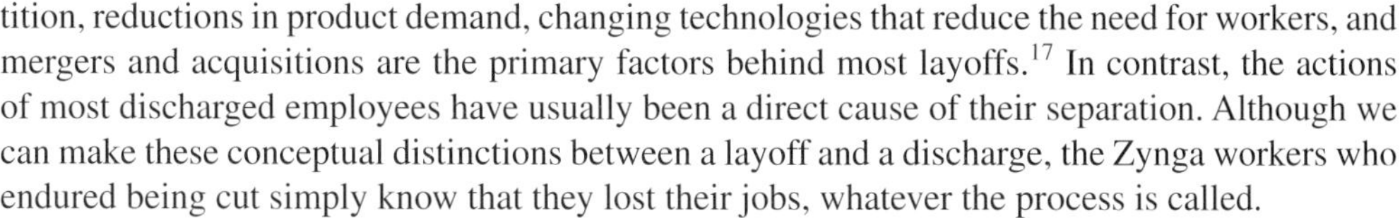

Layoffs have a powerful impact on the organization. They can affect the morale of the organization's remaining employees, who may fear losing their own jobs in the future. In addition, layoffs can affect a region's economic vitality, hurting the merchants who depend on the workers' patronage to support their businesses. Layoffs can also affect the perceptions of the safety and security of an area.

Investors may be affected by layoffs as well. The investment community may interpret a layoff as a signal that the company is having serious problems. This, in turn, may lower the price of the company's stock on the stock market. Finally, layoffs can hurt a company's standing as a good place to work and make it difficult to recruit highly skilled employees who can choose among numerous employers.

LAYOFFS, DOWNSIZING, AND RIGHTSIZING Let's clarify the differences between a layoff, downsizing, and rightsizing. A company that adopts a **downsizing** strategy reduces the scale (size) and scope of its business to improve its financial performance.[18] When a company decides to downsize, it may choose layoffs as one of several ways of reducing costs or improving profitability.[19] In recent years many firms have done exactly this, but we want to emphasize that companies can take many other measures to increase profitability without resorting to layoffs.[20] We discuss these measures later in this chapter.

downsizing
A company strategy to reduce the scale (size) and scope of its business in order to improve the company's financial performance.

Rightsizing means reorganizing a company's employees to improve their efficiency.[21] An organization needs to rightsize when it becomes bloated with too many management layers or bureaucratic work processes that add no value to its product or service. For example, companies that reconfigure their frontline employees into self-managed work teams may find that they are overstaffed and need to reduce their headcount to take advantage of the efficiencies provided by the team structure. The result may be layoffs, but layoffs are not always necessary. As with downsizing, management may have several alternatives to layoffs available when it rightsizes its workforce. Whatever the label, the result of downsizing or rightsizing is that people are losing their jobs.

rightsizing
The process of reorganizing a company's employees to improve their efficiency.

Managing a layoff is an extremely complex process. Before we examine the specifics, however, we'll examine an important alternative: early retirements.

*In some jurisdictions, it is possible for management to discharge an employee based on evidence that does not meet the standard of just cause. However, the authors recommend meeting this standard as a good business practice.

Managing Early Retirements

When a company decides to downsize its operation, its first task is to examine alternatives to layoffs. As we mentioned earlier, one of the most popular of these methods is early retirement.[22]

The Features of Early Retirement Policies

Early retirement policies consist of two features: (1) a package of financial incentives that makes it attractive for senior employees to retire earlier than they had planned and (2) an *open window* that restricts eligibility to a fairly short period of time. After the window is closed, the incentives are no longer available.[23]

The financial incentives are usually based on a formula that accelerates senior employees' retirement eligibility and increases their retirement income. It is not unusual for companies to provide a lump-sum payment as an incentive to leave. Many companies also offer the continuation of health benefits so that early retirees enjoy coverage until they are eligible for Medicare at age 65.

Early retirement policies can reduce the size of a company's workforce substantially. For example, Progress Energy, a public utility company headquartered in Raleigh, North Carolina, had a stronger response to an early retirement program than was expected.[24] As a result, the company had to hire additional people to make up for the shortfall.

Avoiding Problems with Early Retirements

When not properly managed, early retirement policies can cause a host of problems. Too many employees may take early retirement, the wrong employees may leave, and employees may perceive that they are being forced to leave, which may result in age discrimination complaints.

One way to avoid excess resignations is to restrict eligibility to divisions that have redundant employees with high levels of seniority (instead of making the policy available to all employees throughout the corporation). Another way is to ask senior employees how they would respond to a specific early retirement plan. If too many would leave, the incentives could be fine-tuned so that a controlled number of employees take early retirement.

Sometimes the most marketable employees with the best skills can easily find another job and decide to "take the money and run." To avoid this situation and keep its most valuable people, the company can develop provisions to hire back retired employees as temporary consultants until suitable replacements can be promoted, hired, or trained.

Early retirement programs must be managed so that eligible employees do not perceive that they are being forced to retire and consequently file age discrimination charges. Situations that could be interpreted as coercive include the following:

- A longtime employee who has performed satisfactorily over many years suddenly receives an unsatisfactory performance evaluation.
- A manager indicates that senior employees who do not take early retirement may lose their jobs anyway because a layoff is likely in the near future.
- Senior employees notice that their most recent pay raises are quite a bit lower than those of other, younger workers who are not eligible for early retirement.

A former employee who sued IBM for age discrimination was awarded $315,000 in compensatory damages because he convinced the jury that he was forced to take early retirement.[25] The employee introduced evidence showing that his job had been reclassified after he voiced some reservations about taking early retirement. Shortly after that, he claimed, he received a warning that his next performance evaluation would be unsatisfactory.

Managers can avoid lawsuits by following one simple guideline: All managers with senior employees should make certain that they do not treat senior employees any differently than other employees. HR staff members play an important role here by keeping managers aware of the letter and the spirit of the early retirement policy so that they do not (consciously or unconsciously) coerce senior employees during the open window period.

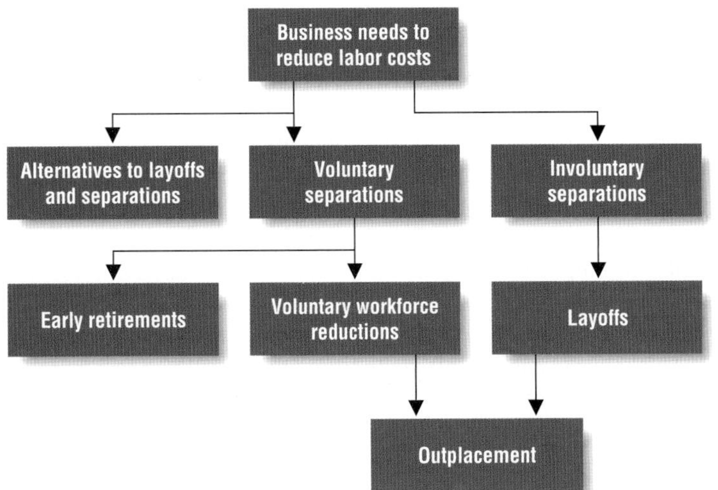

FIGURE 6.3
The Layoff Decision and Its Alternatives

Managing Layoffs

Typically, an organization will institute a layoff when it cannot reduce its labor costs by any other means. Figure 6.3, which presents a model of the layoff decision and its alternatives, shows that there are alternatives to layoffs, such as early retirements and other voluntary workforce reductions, that managers can consider as means to reduce labor costs. After managers make the decision to implement a layoff, they must concern themselves with the outplacement of the former employees.

Alternatives to Layoffs

Most organizations search for alternative cost-reduction methods before turning to layoffs. Attrition is a common strategy. Other approaches include freezing employment, not renewing contract workers, and encouraging employees to take time off voluntarily. Figure 6.4 shows the major alternatives to layoffs. These include employment policies, changes in job design, pay and benefits policies, and training. Managers can use these alternatives both to reduce labor costs and to protect the jobs of full-time employees.

EMPLOYMENT POLICIES The first alternatives to layoffs that managers are likely to consider are those that intrude the least on the day-to-day management of the business. These alternatives usually focus on adjustments to employment policies.

Employment Policies	Changes in Job Design	Pay and Benefits Policies	Training
• Reduction through attrition	• Transfers	• Pay freeze	• Retraining
• Hiring freeze	• Relocation	• Cut overtime pay	
• Cut part-time employees	• Job sharing	• Use vacation and leave days	
• Cut internships or co-ops	• Demotions	• Pay cuts	
• Give subcontracted work to in-house employees		• Profit sharing or variable pay	
• Voluntary time off			
• Leaves of absence			
• Reduced work hours			

FIGURE 6.4
Alternatives to Layoffs

attrition
An employment policy designed to reduce the company's workforce by not refilling job vacancies that are created by turnover.

hiring freeze
An employment policy designed to reduce the company's workforce by not hiring any new employees into the company.

The least disruptive way to cut labor costs is through **attrition**. By not filling job vacancies that are created by turnover, firms can improve the bottom line. When greater cost reductions are needed, a **hiring freeze** may be implemented. Other employment policies aim to decrease the number of hours worked and, therefore, the number of hours for which the company must pay its employees. Workers may be encouraged to take voluntary (unpaid) time off or leaves of absence, or they may be asked to put in a shorter workweek (for example, 35 hours rather than 40).

The strategic application of employment policies to provide job security for a firm's full-time, core employees is called a *rings of defense* approach to job security. Under this approach, headcounts of full-time employees are purposely kept low. An increase in the demand for labor will be satisfied by hiring part-time and temporary employees or subcontracting work to freelancers. The advantage of this approach is that it provides some stability and security, at least for the core employees. This security can pay off in the form of workers who feel more comfortable and can, therefore, be more innovative—an important competitive characteristic in many industries. However, the increasing use of temporary, or contingent, workers as a strategy to smooth out variations in demand for labor means that more workers are vulnerable and treated as expendable by employers.

CHANGES IN JOB DESIGN Managers can use their human resources more cost-effectively by changing job designs and transferring people to different units of the company. Alternatively, they may relocate people to jobs in different parts of the country where the cost of living and salaries are lower. The cost of relocating an employee plus the fact that some employees do not want to move sometimes make this alternative problematic. Another practice, common in unionized companies, allows a senior employee whose job is eliminated to take a job in a different unit of the company from an employee with less seniority. This practice is called *bumping*.

A QUESTION OF ETHICS
Is it ethical for top managers to receive cash bonuses while at the same time asking lower-level employees to accept a pay freeze?

Companies can also use *job sharing* (which we discussed in Chapter 2) when it is possible to reconfigure one job into two part-time jobs. The challenge here is to find two people willing to share the job's hours and pay. Finally, as a last resort, highly paid workers may be demoted to lower-paying jobs.

PAY AND BENEFITS POLICIES As one way of reducing costs, managers can enforce a *pay freeze* during which no wages or salaries are increased. Pay freezes should be done on an across-the-board basis to avoid accusations of discrimination. These policies can be augmented by reductions in overtime pay and policies that ask employees to use up their vacation and leave days. Many state governments have enforced annual pay freezes on their employees. Unfortunately, pay freezes often cause some top-performing, highly marketable employees to leave the company.

A more radical and intrusive pay policy geared toward reducing labor costs is a *pay cut*. This action can be even more demoralizing to the workforce than a pay freeze and should be used only if employees are willing to accept it voluntarily as an alternative to layoffs. Unions in several U.S. industries have accepted wage reductions in return for job security.

A long-term pay policy that may protect workers from layoffs structures compensation so that profit sharing (the sharing of company profits with employees) or variable pay (pay contingent on meeting performance goals) makes up a significant portion of employees' total compensation (around 15 to 20 percent). When the business cycle hits a low point, the company can save up to about 20 percent of the payroll by not paying out profit sharing or variable pay, but still retain its employees by paying them the salary portion of their total compensation. Few companies in the United States use this approach, but it is very common in Japan.

TRAINING By retraining employees whose skills have become obsolete, a company may be able to match newly skilled workers with available job vacancies. Without this retraining, the workers might have been laid off. For example, IBM has retrained some of its production workers in computer programming and placed them in jobs requiring this skill.

Implementing a Layoff

Once the layoff decision has been made, managers must implement it carefully. A layoff can be a traumatic event that affects the lives of thousands of people. The key issues that managers must settle are notifying employees, developing layoff criteria, communicating to laid-off employees, coordinating media relations, maintaining security, and reassuring survivors of the layoff.

NOTIFYING EMPLOYEES The **Worker Adjustment and Retraining Notification Act (WARN)** requires U.S. employers with 100 or more employees to give 60 days' advance notice to employees who will be laid off as a result of a plant closing or a mass separation of 50 or more workers.[26] This law, passed in 1988, was designed to give workers more time to look for a new job. Employers who do not notify their employees must give them the equivalent of 60 working days of income. Employers who lay off fewer than 50 employees have greater flexibility as to when they can notify the affected employees.

Worker Adjustment and Retraining Notification Act (WARN)
A federal law requiring U.S. employers with 100 or more employees to give 60 days' advance notice to employees who will be laid off as a result of a plant closing or a mass separation of 50 or more workers.

There are several arguments in favor of giving at least several weeks' notice before a layoff. It is socially and professionally correct to extend employees this courtesy. Also, this treatment is reassuring to the employees who will remain with the company. But there are also arguments in favor of giving no notification. If the labor relations climate is poor, there is the potential for theft of or sabotage to company equipment. In addition, the productivity of employees who are losing their jobs may decline during the notice period.[27]

A QUESTION OF ETHICS
How much notice of a layoff should a company be obligated to give?

DEVELOPING LAYOFF CRITERIA The criteria for dismissal must be clear. When the criteria are clearly laid out, the managers responsible for determining who will be laid off can make consistent, fair decisions. The two most important criteria used as the basis for layoff decisions are seniority and employee performance.

Seniority, the amount of time an employee has been with the firm, is by far the most commonly used layoff criterion. It has two main advantages. First, seniority criteria are easily applied; managers simply examine all employees' dates of hire to determine the seniority of each (in years and days). Second, many employees see the seniority system as fair because (1) managers cannot play "favorites" under a seniority-based decision and (2) the most senior employees have the greatest investment in the company in terms of job rights and privileges (they have accrued more vacation and leave days and have more attractive work schedules, for example).

There are disadvantages to using the "last in, first out" method, however. The firm may lose some top performers, as well as a disproportionate number of women and minorities—who are more likely to be recent hires in certain jobs. Nonetheless, the courts have upheld seniority as the basis for layoff as long as all employees have equal opportunities to obtain seniority.

When the workforce is unionized, layoff decisions are usually based on seniority. This provision is written into the labor contract. However, when the workforce is nonunion, and especially when cuts must be made in professional and managerial employees, it is not unusual for companies to base layoff decisions on performance criteria or on a combination of performance and seniority. Using performance as the basis for layoffs allows the company to retain its top performers in every work unit and eliminate its weakest performers. Unfortunately, performance levels are not always clearly documented, and the company may be exposed to wrongful discharge litigation if the employee can prove that management discriminated or acted arbitrarily in judging performance. Because of these legal risks, many companies avoid using performance as a basis for layoff.

If a company has taken the time to develop a valid performance appraisal system that accurately measures performance and meets government guidelines, then there is no reason why appraisal data cannot be used as the basis for layoff. When using this criterion, managers should take the employee's total performance over a long period of time into account. Managers who focus on one low performance appraisal period and ignore other satisfactory or exceptional performance appraisals could be viewed as acting arbitrarily and unfairly. We discuss this topic in detail in the next chapter.

COMMUNICATING TO LAID-OFF EMPLOYEES It is crucial to communicate with the employees who will be laid off as humanely and sensitively as possible. No employee likes being told he or she will be discharged, and the way a manager handles this unpleasant task can affect how the employee and others in the organization accept the decision.

Laid-off employees should first learn of their fate from their supervisor in a face-to-face private discussion. Employees who learn about their dismissal through a less personal form of communication (for example, a peer or a memo) are likely to be hurt and angry. The information session between supervisor and employee should be brief and to the point. The manager should express appreciation for what the employee has contributed, if appropriate, and explain how much severance pay and what benefits will be provided and for how long. This information can be repeated in greater detail at a group meeting of laid-off employees and should be documented in a written pamphlet handed out at the meeting.

An argument can be made that the best time to hold the termination session is in the middle of the workweek. It is best to avoid telling workers they are being laid off during their vacation or right before a weekend, when they have large blocks of time on their hands.[28]

One example of how *not* to communicate a layoff is provided by the following example: A petroleum company brought employees together for a rather unsettling meeting. Each employee was given an envelope with the letter *A* or *B* on it. The A's were told to stay put while the B's were ushered into an adjacent room. Then, en masse, the B's were told that they were being laid off.

COORDINATING MEDIA RELATIONS Rumors of an impending layoff can be very dangerous to the workforce's morale as well as to the organization's relationships with customers, suppliers, and the surrounding community. Top managers, working with HR staff members, should develop a plan to provide accurate information about the layoff to external clients (via the media) as well as the workforce (via internal communications).[29] In this way, managers can control and put to rest rumors that may exaggerate the extent of the firm's downsizing efforts. It is also important that direct communication take place with the employees directly affected by the layoff *and* the surviving employees and that all communication be coordinated with press releases to the media. In addition, HR staff must prepare to answer any questions that employees or the media may have regarding outplacement, severance pay, or the continuation of benefits.

MAINTAINING SECURITY In some situations, a layoff may threaten company property. Laid-off employees may find themselves rushed out of the building, escorted by armed guards, and their personal belongings delivered to them later in boxes. Although such treatment may seem harsh, it may be necessary in certain industries (such as banking and computer software), where sabotage could result in substantial damage.

For instance, Timothy Lloyd worked for Omega Engineering, Inc., a company that designs and manufactures instruments and process control devices. After he was dismissed but before his last day at the company, Lloyd allegedly set a "program bomb" in the company's computer system. About two weeks after his last day, the bomb deleted key files from Omega's database, resulting in $10 million in damage. Al DiFrancesco, Omega's director of human relations, noted that the company could have avoided the problem with better security, but "hindsight is 20/20 . . ." As a result of the damage, Omega tightened its security policies and procedures to safeguard against disgruntled employees.[30]

In most cases, security precautions are probably not necessary when implementing a layoff, and using armed guards and other heavy-handed tactics will only lead to hard feelings and resentment. Treating laid-off employees with dignity and respect generally reduces the potential for sabotage.

REASSURING SURVIVORS OF THE LAYOFF On paper, a layoff may have the positive effect of reducing labor costs and restoring financial balance to an organization. As a practical reality, layoffs can have some negative effects on the organization. The Manager's Notebook, "Effects of Layoffs on Survivors" considers the possible negative impacts of a layoff. It is important to be aware of the negative fallout that can happen following a layoff. As a manager, if you are aware of these downsides, you can take steps to lower or eliminate their occurrence. The Manager's Notebook, "Survivor Management 101," addresses some of the basic steps you can take as a manager to lessen the negative effects of a layoff on the surviving workers.

MANAGER'S NOTEBOOK

Ethics/Social Responsibility

Effects of Layoffs on Survivors

Those workers who survived a layoff might be considered the lucky ones. However, research has found that layoffs can have a number of negative effects on those who got to keep their jobs. Some of the negative effects on survivors can include:

- Increased absenteeism and turnover.
- Lower productivity and poorer job satisfaction.
- Increased sabotage.

Why such negative effects from people who should feel lucky that they didn't lose their jobs? When you consider the situation, the negative impacts may make more sense. Consider, for example, that when labor is reduced through a layoff, the amount of work that is expected to be done often stays the same. The layoff survivors have more to do. A layoff can also make clear to remaining workers that they are dispensable and their jobs could be on the chopping block next. It's little wonder that the "lucky" layoff survivors can experience negative effects.

Sources: Based on Cotter, E. W., and Fouad, N. A. (2012, November 27). Examining burnout and engagement in layoff survivors: The role of personal strengths. *Journal of Career Development*, published online; Long, B. S. (2012). The irresponsible enterprise: The ethics of corporate downsizing. *Critical studies on Corporate Responsibility, Governance, and Sustainability, 4*, 295–315; Sobieralski, J., and Nordstrom, C. R. (2012). An examination of employee layoffs and organizational justice perceptions. *Journal of Organizational Psychology, 12*, 11–20. ■■

MANAGER'S NOTEBOOK

Survivor Management 101

Customer-Driven HR

What can you do as a manager to minimize the negative effects of a layoff on the surviving workers? Jobs, of course, still need to be done and products or services need to be provided to customers. In the wake of a layoff, what steps can you take to help assure that morale stays as positive as possible and that work continues to be done as well as possible? The following are some suggestions to help you keep up the morale of your surviving employees.

- *Provide clear communication about the layoff* Surviving workers are more likely to remain positive about their organization and job if they understand why people were laid off and how. If people understand why the layoff was needed and they think the process of how people were let go was fair, they can move forward with a positive attitude. As a manager, you need to make sure, as best as possible, that your surviving employees have an understanding of the layoff process.
- *Mark the occasion* Ignoring a layoff will not make it go away. Having an event or gathering regarding a negative outcome, such as a layoff, can give people a transition point. Whether you hold a formal meeting to discuss the layoff or have an informal get-together, you can be providing people some closure that will help them to put that chapter behind them. Without some transition or closure point, people can continue to look back rather than adapt and move forward.
- *Listen to your workers* A layoff is something that the surviving workers didn't have control over. They may feel that other arbitrary treatment may also be in store for them. It is important to assure your workers that their input is heard and that they will have input into the work processes in the new work environment.

Sources: Based on Bies, R. J. (2013). The delivery of bad news in organizations: A framework for analysis. *Journal of Management, 39*, 136–162; Dierendonck, D. V., and Jacobs, G. (2012). Survivors and victims, a meta-analytical review of fairness and organizational commitment after downsizing. *British Journal of Management, 23*, 96–109. ■■

Outplacement

As we mentioned at the beginning of this chapter, outplacement is an HR program created to help separated employees deal with the emotional stress of job loss and to provide assistance in finding a new job.[31] Outplacement activities are often handled by consulting firms retained by the organization, which pays a fee based on the number of outplaced employees. Companies are often willing to pay for outplacement because it can reduce some of the risks associated with layoffs, such as negative publicity or an increased likelihood that unions will attempt to organize the workforce.[32] Employers who provide outplacement services tend to give the goal of social responsibility a high priority as part of their HR strategy.

The Goals of Outplacement

The goals of an outplacement program reflect the organization's need to control the disruption caused by layoffs and other employee separations. The most important of these goals are (1) reducing the morale problems of employees who are about to be laid off so that they remain productive until they leave the firm, (2) minimizing the amount of litigation initiated by separated employees, and (3) assisting separated employees in finding comparable jobs as quickly as possible.[33] In addition, providing an outplacement service can help keep the remaining employees focused on their work. Without outplacement, a natural tendency for remaining workers would be to concentrate on how their former coworkers were treated badly and didn't find jobs, rather than concentrate on moving the organization forward.[34] Overall, providing outplacement can protect an employer's reputation and help the organization be known as an employer of choice.

Outplacement Services

The most common outplacement services are emotional support and job-search assistance. These services are closely tied to the goals of outplacement.

EMOTIONAL SUPPORT Outplacement programs usually provide counseling to help employees deal with the emotions associated with job loss—shock, anger, denial, and lowered self-esteem. Because the family may suffer if the breadwinner becomes unemployed, sometimes family members are also included in the counseling as well.[35] Counseling also benefits the employer because it helps to defuse some of the hostility that laid-off employees feel toward the company.

JOB-SEARCH ASSISTANCE Employees who are outplaced often do not know how to begin the search for a new job. In many cases, these people have not had to look for a job in many years.

An important aspect of this assistance is teaching separated employees the skills they need to find a new job. These skills include résumé writing, interviewing and job-search techniques, career planning, and negotiation skills.[36] Outplaced employees receive instruction in these skills from either a member of the outplacement firm or the HR department. In addition, the former employer sometimes provides administrative support in the form of clerical help, phone answering, access to e-mail, and fax services.[37] These services allow laid-off employees to use computers to prepare résumés, post résumés on the Web or send them via fax and e-mail, and to use copiers to copy résumés.

Summary and Conclusions

What Are Employee Separations?

Employee separations occur when employees cease to be members of an organization. Separations and outplacement can be managed effectively. Managers should plan for the outflow of their human resources with thoughtful policies. Employee separations have both costs and benefits. The costs include (1) recruitment costs, (2) selection costs, (3) training costs, and (4) separation costs. The benefits are (1) reduced labor costs, (2) replacement of poor performers, (3) increased innovation, and (4) the opportunity for greater diversity.

Types of Employee Separations

Employees may leave either voluntarily or involuntarily. Voluntary separations include quits and retirements. Involuntary separations include discharges and layoffs. When an employee is forced to leave involuntarily, a much greater level of documentation is necessary to show that a manager's decision to terminate the employee was fair.

Managing Early Retirements

When downsizing an organization, managers may elect to use voluntary early retirements as an alternative to layoffs. Early retirement programs must be managed so that eligible employees do not perceive that they are being forced to retire.

Managing Layoffs

Layoffs should be used as a last resort after all other cost-cutting alternatives have been exhausted. Important considerations in developing a layoff policy include (1) notifying employees, (2) developing layoff criteria, (3) communicating to laid-off employees, (4) coordinating media relations, (5) maintaining security, and (6) reassuring survivors of the layoff.

Outplacement

No matter what policy is used to reduce the workforce, it is a good idea for the organization to use outplacement services to help separated employees cope with their emotions and minimize the amount of time they are unemployed.

Key Terms

attrition, 220
downsizing, 217
employee separation, 210
exit interview, 213
hiring freeze, 220
involuntary separation, 215
outplacement assistance, 213
rightsizing, 217
turnover rate, 210
voluntary separation, 214
Worker Adjustment and Retraining Notification Act (WARN), 221

Gordon Law Group: Employee Separation. If your instructor has assigned this, go to **mymanagementlab.com** to watch a video case and answer questions.

Discussion Questions

6-1. Following a series of acquisitions, a company has looked at its pool of employees and geographical locations. In order to cut costs and streamline operations, largely by merging finance and administration, HR and other support services, three remote locations are to be closed over the course of the next six months. The company recognizes that there will be unavoidable separation costs, but also wants to be seen to be doing the right thing. What is the value of additional efforts to support employees who will have little option other than to leave the company? The company has a tried and tested severance pay package in place, so why is it necessary to offer something more than this?

6-2. The Manager's Notebook, "Voluntary Turnover in China," addresses the high rate at which workers in China have been choosing to quit their jobs. Do you think voluntary turnover is becoming more of an issue in the United States? If you are a manager, do you think that voluntary turnover is an issue? How would you deal with it?

6-3. Would an employer ever want to increase the rate of employee turnover in a company? Why or why not?

6-4. In an age when more and more companies are downsizing, an increasingly important concept is the "virtual corporation." The idea is that a company should have a core of owners and managers, but that, to the greatest degree possible, workers should be contingent—temporary, part-time, or on short-term contracts. This gives the corporation maximum flexibility to shift vendors, cut costs, and avoid long-term labor commitments. What are the advantages and disadvantages of the virtual corporation from the points of view of both employers and the workers?

6-5. Under what circumstances might a company's managers prefer to use layoffs instead of early retirements or voluntary severance plans as a way to downsize the workforce?

6-6. Under what set of conditions should a company lay off employees without giving them advance notice?

6-7. Carrying out terminations usually is the responsibility of the manager. However, the manager may not always be involved in determining who should be let go. Do you think direct managers should have input into which of their workers should be laid off? Why or why not? If a manager and HR staff disagrees on who should be laid off, how do you think the disagreement should be resolved?

6-8. Managing survivors in a layoff is important. As a manager, what concerns would you have about the surviving workforce after a layoff? How can the HR management staff be of assistance in providing support for the survivors to a layoff?

6-9. Why should management be concerned with helping employees retire from their organization successfully?

6-10. The departure of senior workers through retirement can mean that years of experience and knowledge are walking out an organization's doors. This "brain drain" can cripple an organization's ability to remain competitive, particularly if it is difficult to regularly hire younger talent. What approaches would you recommend to reduce this problem?

6-11. You have noticed that the overall turnover rate for your company is about average for your industry. Does this average rate mean their turnover isn't a problem? Considering the source and type of turnover discussed in Exhibit 6.1, describe how this average rate might or might not indicate a problem.

MyManagementLab®

If your instructor has assigned this, go to **mymanagementlab.com** for the following Assisted-graded writing questions:

6-12. Employees have been terminated due to their postings on social media. Do you think that social media postings should be a cause for termination? Are there circumstances that might make termination a more justifiable management action? For example, what if the postings are critical of the company? Describe.

6-13. Can employee turnover be a good thing? Explain. When is employee turnover a bad thing?

6-14. Survivors of layoffs might be considered the lucky ones who still have a job. However, layoff survivors can present a number of problems. What kind of problems might you expect layoff survivors to exhibit? Assuming a layoff of workers is a necessity, what would you recommend be done to lessen problems associated with layoff survivors?

You Manage It! 1: Global

Turnover: A Global Management Issue

As discussed in the Manager's Notebook, "Voluntary Turnover in China," voluntary turnover is a problem faced by organizations in China. This turnover is particularly a problem in management-level positions and in areas such as sales, marketing, and human resources. The issue is expected to continue, even though the growth in the Chinese economy may be slowing.

Facing voluntary turnover is a problem in more areas than China. For example, companies in India face high levels of voluntary turnover. The common element to the level of voluntary turnover is a demand for labor that exceeds the supply. The demand creates job opportunities for the too-few employees who have the desired competencies.

Critical Thinking Questions

6-15. What steps do most companies take to reduce voluntary turnover? Are they effective?

6-16. Do you think the voluntary turnover rate in an area should be considered before opening a business operation there? Why?

6-17. A company discovers that a poorly performing factory has a significant level of voluntary turnover compared to other locations. The company is not sure if it is a symptom of poor management or something else. Is there an optimal voluntary turnover rate and what are the costs and benefits of it?

Team Exercise

6-18. As a team, identify the steps you could take as managers to reduce the problem of high voluntary turnover you face in an overseas operation. For example, you could use domestic workers for the operation or you could increase the wage rate offered in your foreign operation. What are the advantages and disadvantages of these and other actions you could take?

Experiential Exercise: Team

6-19. As a team, consider the following situation and then outline an action plan as to how you would propose to deal with it. Your company has traditionally had a young employee profile. As a retailer catering for the late teen market, your sales force has always reflected this fact. However, it has meant, over the past ten years, an average voluntary turnover rate of 43 percent. Last year that rocketed to 58 percent. Sales are falling, customer satisfaction has dropped, and supervisors and managers (mainly in their 30s) report having to spend 60 percent of their time recruiting and training. This leaves little time for marketing initiatives.

Experiential Exercise: Individual

6-20. Where there is high voluntary turnover, managers often face difficulty in finding replacement workers. If you are a manager in a high–voluntary turnover situation and one of your workers decides to leave, you will likely find yourself on the market, fighting to replace the talent that just left. A high–voluntary turnover problem also usually means difficulty in finding and hiring replacements.

a. An alternative to trying to hire scarce talent is to grow your own. That is, an organization may decide to provide training and development opportunities to current workers in order to development needed talent. What are the advantages and disadvantages of this approach?
b. Do you think internal development of talent would also have an effect on voluntary turnover? Why? What would be the downside?
c. Do you know of or can you locate any companies that focus on internal development? Does it seem to be effective? Share your conclusions and findings with the rest of the class.

Source: Based on Huang, J. (2013). Developing local talent for future leadership. *The China Business Review*, *40*, 28–30; Sanchez-Arias, F., Calmeyn, H., Driesen, G., and Pruis, E. (2013). Human capital realities pose challenges across the globe. *T & D*, *67*, 32–35; Silva, J. D. (2012). The war for talent in China. *Ivey Business Journal Online*, retrieved on June 9, 2013 from Proquest.

 You Manage It! 2: Ethics/Social Responsibility

Employment-at-Will: Fair Policy?

As an employee, you have the right to quit your job, right? The policy of employment-at-will (see Chapter 14) gives a similar right to employers to end the employment relationship. The rationale behind employment-at-will is that if an employee can quit at any time and for any reason, so, too, should an employer be free to end the employment relationship at any time and for any reason. A practical implication of this common-law doctrine is that employees can't be sued by employers for leaving, even if their departure disrupts the workplace. Likewise, the employer cannot be held responsible for terminating the employee.

However, there are exceptions to the employment-at-will policy. For example, an employer cannot terminate an employee for refusing to engage in an illegal act or because of the employee's race or gender. Another limitation is that employment-at-will applies only when there is not some sort of agreement, understanding, or contract between the employer and employee about the duration or permanence of employment. For example, an employee who has an employment contract can sue the employer for breach of contract if termination violates the terms of the contract. Likewise, a terminated employee may be able to convince the court that he or she wasn't an at-will employee because of an implied contract formed by statements in the employee handbook. For example, a handbook might offer the positive and supportive statement that as long as you perform, you have a job with the organization. This sort of statement could be viewed as implying permanence of the employment relationship, at least as long as performance is satisfactory.

Critical Thinking Questions

6-21. Do you agree with the concept of employment-at-will? Why or why not?

6-22. If you had a choice, would you rather be employed as an at-will employee or have some employment protection? Why?

6-23. Most workers are not covered by explicit or implicit contracts and are at-will employees. Thus, an employer should be able to terminate these workers at any time and for any reason. A practical reality, however, is that a charge of discrimination as a basis for a termination needs to be defended against. How can an employer defend against a charge that a termination decision was based on discrimination? Does this limit an employer's right to fire-at-will? Explain.

Team Exercise

6-24. Exceptions to employment-at-will vary by state. As a team, choose a state and use the Internet to research the exceptions to employment-at-will there. Report your findings to the class.

a. As a class, identify which states seem most and least employer-friendly with regard to these exceptions.

Experiential Exercise: Team

6-25. Two small groups will be formed to represent pro and con employment-at-will positions. The two groups should debate the merits of the employment-at-will policy. Each team has five minutes to make its major statement in support of or against the policy. Issues that might be considered include ethical treatment, balance of power between employer and employee, and cost of litigation. Each team has an opportunity to rebut and rejoin. The instructor mediates the debate. The major issues and positions will be summarized in the class following the debate.

Sources: Based on Grossenbacher, K. (2005, April 11). What happened to "at will"? *Podium, 26*, 26; Knight, D. (2005, April 8). Understanding employment-at-will. *Kansas City Daily Record.*

You Manage It! 3: Customer-Driven HR

From Turnover to Retention: Managing to Keep Your Workers

Turnover is costly for organizations. In addition to the direct costs of recruiting, hiring, and training new talent, turnover can have negative effects that can be difficult to quantify. The loss of front-line employees, for example, can have a negative effect on customer service and can reduce the morale of remaining employees. In addition, employee turnover can result in a loss of expertise and knowledge that is critical to the operation.

One way to reduce turnover is to approach the issue from the perspective of what can be done to get employees to stay. The employee-equity model provides a framework for addressing strategies for increasing employee retention.

As shown in the "Employee Equity Model" graphic, the employee-equity model indicates that employee retention is a function of three equity levels: value, brand, and retention. Value equity is the employees' perception of the employment exchange. It is the fairly objective assessment of the costs and benefits of the job. For example, how does the pay measure up against the effort and difficulty of performing the job? Although working conditions are a central value-equity concern, convenience can also be a factor. For example, the worker's value-equity assessment might be affected negatively if the job is located in an area that is difficult to reach or the hours of the job are difficult to accommodate. Brand equity is a more subjective emotional assessment of an organization's desirability. In making a brand-equity assessment, a worker might consider how the employer treats workers, the organization's culture, and how it approaches ethics. Brand equity reflects the extent to which a worker is happy, or even proud, to be working for the organization. Retention equity is the worker's perceived benefit of staying with the organization. Key factors in retention-equity assessments are seniority and pension plans. Other factors that can influence retention equity are the opportunities in the organization for development and for career advancement. In addition, the extent to which organizational members have a sense of community can influence retention equity levels.

Critical Thinking Questions

6-26. The employee-equity model provides value, brand, and retention equity perceptions as important determinants of whether an employee stays with an organization. Do you think that the three components are independent, or do they influence each other? Is this a problem for managing retention with the employee equity model? Why or why not?

6-27. How would you measure value, brand, and retention equity in an organization? How often do you think the three characteristics should be measured?

6-28. Given your response to item 2, how would these measures be useful? What could they be used for?

6-29. Value, brand, and retention characteristics could be used as criteria, or standards, for assessing management programs and actions. For example, consider recruitment and/or performance appraisal. If you were trying to maximize employee retention, how might you go about recruitment or performance appraisal so that value, brand, or retention equity is influenced positively?

Employee Equity Model

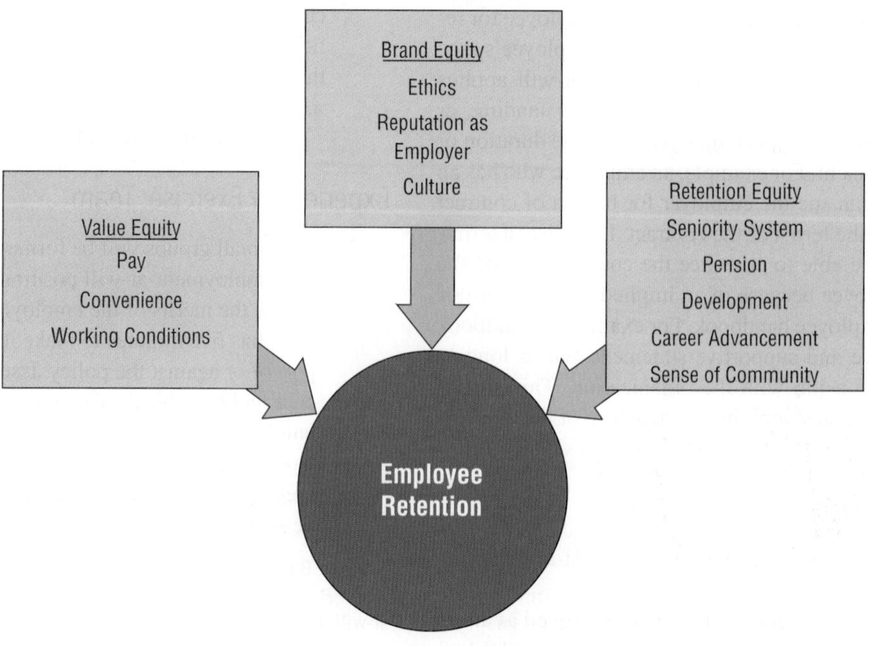

Team Exercise

6-30. The things that might lead a person to quit might not be the same things that lead a person to stay with an organization. For example, another job offer or the tendency to always be looking for new opportunities elsewhere can lead a person to quit.

a. Using the employee equity framework, identify the types of things that the organization could do to improve retention. Organize these actions or programs according to whether the primary focus is on improving value, brand, or retention equity.

b. What is the management advantage of focusing on these retention efforts? That is, instead of focusing on why someone quits, why focus on retention?

Experiential Exercise: Team

6-31. Divide the team into three groups. Each group will choose value, brand, or retention equity. Or, if team sizes are smaller, each team will select an equity component. For each equity component, generate survey items or interview questions that would measure that form of equity. For each item or question, identify organizational characteristics or management actions that would maximize the measure. Share your measures and proposed management actions with the rest of the class.

Experiential Exercise: Individual

6-32. Generate survey or interview items that would capture value-, brand-, or retention-equity levels in workers. If possible, ask a sample of your friends and neighbors to take a survey based on your items. Are value, brand, and retention equities high or low? For low levels, ask your survey respondents what they think their employers could do to improve these levels.

a. Are there differences among groups of employees in terms of the importance placed on value, brand, or retention equity? For example, might production, sales, and staff workers weigh the three equity components differently? If so, identify the component that you think would be most important for each group. How might differentiating among groups of employees in terms of the importance placed on the three equity components be useful to management? Share your findings and conclusions with the rest of the class.

Sources: Cardy, R. L., and Lengnick-Hall, M. (2011). Will they stay or will they go? Exploring a customer-oriented approach to employee retention. *Journal of Business and Psychology*, *26*, 213–217; Cardy, R. L., (2012, December). Performance management: Managing for retention. Featured article in *Personnel Testing Council of Metropolitan Washington Newsletter, VIII*(4), 4–7; Rust, R. T., Ziethaml, V. A., and Lemon, K. N. (2000). *Driving customer equity: How customer lifetime value is reshaping corporate strategy*. New York: Free Press.

You Manage It! 4: Technology/Social Media

You're Fired!

On *The Apprentice* television show, Donald Trump has made the statement "You're fired!" part of the entertainment. The reality in the workplace, however, is that having to let someone go is not easy and far from entertaining. Nonetheless, it is sometimes necessary. The use of social media has dramatically increased, and it has increasingly become a basis for employee terminations.

The use of social media isn't, of course, illegal. People have, nevertheless, gotten themselves into trouble at work with the use of social media. Common issues that can lead to termination include the sharing of inappropriate material and the inappropriate use of company equipment. Consider the following scenarios:

- George has been a valuable employee and Lori has been working hard to make sure he stays with the company. One of her fellow managers just informed Lori that he entered George's office and found him watching a revealing video. George apologized to the manager, quickly shut it off, and explained that it was a personal video sent to him by a friend. The manager described the video to Lori as being pornographic. The manager told Lori that something had to be done, and that type of behavior didn't fit with the company culture and couldn't be tolerated.
- Don is a supervisor and had two of his workers in his office. He had called them into his office to ask if the story he had heard was true. What Don had heard was that one of the workers had taken a picture of a female colleague when she was bent over a piece of equipment. The photo revealed the female worker's underwear. The two workers had apparently distributed the photo by posting it on their Facebook pages and sending links to other workers.
- A manager was at a company party and left his phone on a table while he left to use the restroom. Some of his workers at the party thought it would be funny to use his phone to post some critical comments about the company. Unfortunately, the manager had not exited from a social media page. At the time, the workers thought it was a hilarious prank, but upper management didn't see the humor in it.

The preceding types of incidents have led to people losing their jobs.

Critical Thinking Questions

6-33. Do you think terminations for the types of incidents presented here are fair? Why or why not?

6-34. Assume that the employees or managers in each of the scenarios perform at an above-average level. Should that matter in the decision to terminate or not terminate? Why or why not?

6-35. How could these social media–driven issues be prevented? Are there steps that you, as a manager, could take that would prevent these issues from happening in the first place?

Team Exercise

6-36. Many private companies do not have a policy regarding the use of social media. As a team, identify why a social media policy would be useful.

a. Draft an ideal social media policy. What are its key characteristics? For example, would your policy ban any use of social media during working hours? How would inappropriate postings be treated? Share your policy and why it would be useful with the rest of the class.

Experiential Exercise: Team

6-37. Telling someone that they are being terminated can be a difficult and emotionally draining task. Using any of the scenarios presented in this case, or other relevant scenarios of your choosing, role-play terminating someone for inappropriate use of social media. One member of your team should take on the role of manager and another member takes on the role of the employee being terminated. Other team members should observe the interaction and provide feedback to the person playing manager about how the interaction went and how it might be improved.

Experiential Exercise: Individual

6-38. Many companies do not have a policy regarding the use of social media. Identify why such a policy would be useful if an employee disputed a social media–based termination. Conducting an Internet search, can you locate social media policies used by companies? Are there common features of these policies? As a manager, which parts of such policies would you find most useful?

Endnotes

Scan for Endnotes or go to http://www.pearsonglobaleditions.com/Gomez-Mejia.

CHAPTER 7 Appraising and Managing Performance

MyManagementLab®

When you see this icon, visit **www.mymanagementlab.com** for activities that are applied, personalized, and offer immediate feedback.

CHALLENGES

After reading this chapter, you should be able to deal more effectively with the following challenges:

1 **How** to effectively carry out each of the steps in performance appraisal.

2 **Have** familiarity with challenges to effective performance measurement.

3 **Develop** competence in managing performance.

George was prepared for the upcoming performance reviews. He had carefully gone through the performance data. The new performance-review software had made the task much easier, with written feedback automatically inserted depending on the performance ratings George entered for each worker. As a manager of a small group of customer service employees, George was grateful for how much easier and quicker the software had made his task of evaluating the performance of his workers.

Estelle was the first worker scheduled for the annual face-to-face performance reviews. Overall, Estelle was the best worker in terms of customer service, but she didn't do well at some of the record-keeping aspects of the job. George had given Estelle high ratings on customer service, but rated her as "needing improvement" on technical aspects. As Estelle sat down across from George, he handed her the performance evaluation and started to talk through the points with her.

Source: Monkey Business Images/Shutterstock.

George started with the summary of the performance of the unit, a nice broad picture of the group provided by the software. Estelle quickly flipped to the sections addressing the aspects of her performance. At a glance, she saw the poor ratings George had given her on technical aspects, such as filing paperwork, placing orders, and keeping account information up-to-date. Estelle was deflated and angry at the same time. George could tell that Estelle was already upset and wondered whether he had been too harsh in his ratings of her. He quickly moved to the section of the performance review that Estelle was focused on. The following exchange rapidly played out:

George: Look, Estelle, I know you are the best at customer service. All of our customers think you are wonderful. But, you have to admit that paperwork isn't your strong suit.

Estelle: Yes, I know what I'm doing with customer service. I know my job and my customers. I have been doing his awhile, and I can't believe you're nailing me on this Mickey Mouse paperwork stuff. We operate as a team, and I let other people take care of some of the technical details, since they can do that. Frankly, for some of them, it's better they not do much interacting with customers, since they just don't do that very well.

George: Everyone is supposed to be responsible for customer service and for technical areas. That's the job and everyone has the same job.

Estelle: Well, that might be what's on paper in the official job description, but the reality is that people do what they do best and that means everything works better and customers get better service and are happier.

George: That may be, but I can't very well give you high performance ratings on an area that even you admit isn't your strength.

Estelle: I'm sure you didn't rate other people this low on customer service, even though they are terrible at it. Besides, the "Needs Improvement" rating is embarrassing, and I think it might mean that I am not eligible for merit pay. I don't think it's fair.

George: I forgot about that merit pay rule and didn't mean for you to not get a bonus. Again, you are outstanding at customer service, and you are a stand-out worker in that respect and deserve to be in the running for merit pay. However, you have to admit that your poor follow-through on record keeping has caused some problems. There was that one incident last month where we had to scramble to get supplies because the order wasn't done correctly and was late.

Estelle: Yeah, right. While you're at it, why don't you beat me up for that snafu? My name may have been on the paperwork, but the problems with the order weren't my fault.

George: What do you mean?

Estelle: What I mean is that Don was doing that order for me. He didn't want to make the visit to a new customer, and I took that on for him, and he did the order. I don't know what he was doing, why it took him so long, or how he got it messed up. Of course, you could have asked me about this before you jumped to conclusions and your performance evaluations, but it's a little late for that, isn't it?

George: Well, Estelle, I had no idea that is what was going on. Based on the paperwork, it looked pretty clear.

Estelle: You could have checked. Also, are you really questioning whether I have a complete understanding of the operational details of the job and that I should consider revisiting the technical training modules offered by the company?

George: Does the review say that?

Estelle: Yes, of course—right here! You didn't even write this, did you? What's the point of having these performance reviews, anyway? I'm evaluated unfairly and things I didn't do are held against me. And, the feedback is machine generated! Well, if the point of this process is to push me out of here, mission accomplished. If my contribution isn't valued, I will be on my way out as soon as I line up an alternative. In the meantime, I'll be sure to allocate more of my time and effort to record keeping, and others will have to step up on service. I'm sure that will work out well.

George: Really, Estelle, don't take this so negatively. I tried to provide the best ratings I could with the information I had.

George had the feeling that he had been the one who was just evaluated, and it hadn't gone too well. It sounded like there were things he missed and didn't take into account. The reality was that Estelle was a star player on the team, someone who knew what she was doing and was a kind of glue holding things together. She certainly didn't need retraining so that she knew how to do the job. He was now kicking himself for not catching that recommendation that the performance review software had automatically entered. The software made the job of evaluation easier, but now he was paying a price for it. If Estelle left her job over this, her experience and customer service skills would be difficult to replace.

George realized he had a number of performance review meetings scheduled for the afternoon. Many of those meetings were with workers with poorer performance than Estelle, and he wasn't looking forward to how these might go. He couldn't help but wonder if holding those performance reviews was worth it.

The Managerial Perspective

The situation involving George and Estelle (a fictitious scenario, but based on real-life incidents) illustrates common problems with performance appraisal—the process of assessing employee performance and diagnosing and improving performance problems. Maintaining and improving your performance and the performance of other people in the organization will be an important part of your role as a manager. To conduct this process, you may rely on appraisal forms and systems that are often designed by HR personnel or provided by third-party vendors. Although these forms and systems are key elements of the appraisal process, they are only a starting point.

Effective performance appraisal requires managers to measure and improve performance. If performance is to be improved, the manager needs to have a good understanding of the cause for a performance problem. Not getting your facts straight and, for example, blaming the wrong person for a problem, can mean that the problem isn't solved and can result in negative outcomes. As George learned, if the cause of a performance problem is not correctly diagnosed, the mistake can lead to a worker with reduced motivation and commitment.

The performance appraisal process includes providing feedback to workers so that they can improve their performance. We all need, want, and deserve feedback regarding how we are doing in the workplace. Feedback from a direct supervisor, rather than from an automated system, will typically be the most meaningful and useful. As the situation with George and Estelle illustrates, feedback is important, but it needs to be relevant and accepted by the worker. Like most of us, Estelle assumed that feedback would be feedback that comes directly from the supervisor, who can take into account various work situations and has knowledge of the worker. Like Estelle, in the end, most of us want to know more what our boss thinks of our work performance than what an automated system or software has to say. Our first goal in this chapter is to acquaint you with the foundation, design, and implementation of performance measurement systems. Our second is to describe the principles of effective performance management.

✪ Learn It!

If your professor has chosen to assign this go to **www.mymanagementlab.com** to see what you should particularly focus on, and take the chapter 7 warmup.

What Is Performance Appraisal?

Performance appraisal, as shown in Figure 7.1, includes the *identification, measurement*, and *management* of human performance in organizations.[1]

performance appraisal
The identification, measurement, and management of human performance in organizations.

- *Identification* means determining what areas of work the manager should be examining when measuring performance. Rational and legally defensible identification requires a measurement system based on job analysis, which we explored in Chapter 2. The appraisal system, then, should focus on performance that affects organizational success rather than performance-irrelevant characteristics such as race, age, or sex.
- *Measurement,* the centerpiece of the appraisal system, entails making managerial judgments of how "good" or "bad" employee performance was. Performance measurement must be consistent throughout the organization. That is, all managers in the organization must maintain comparable rating standards.[2]
- *Management* is the overriding goal of any appraisal system. Appraisal should be more than a past-oriented activity that criticizes or praises workers for their performance in the preceding year. Rather, appraisal must take a future-oriented view of what workers can do to achieve their potential in the organization. This means that managers must provide workers with feedback and coach them to higher levels of performance.

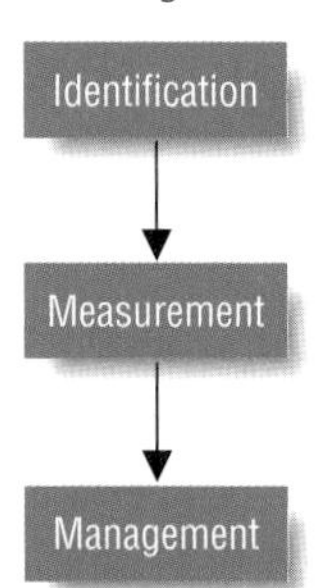

FIGURE 7.1
A Model of Performance Appraisal

The Uses of Performance Appraisal

Organizations usually conduct appraisals for *administrative* and/or *developmental* purposes.[3] Performance appraisals are used administratively whenever they are the basis for a decision about the employee's work conditions, including promotions, termination, and rewards. Developmental uses of appraisal, which are geared toward improving employees' performance and strengthening their job skills, include providing feedback, counseling employees on effective work behaviors, and offering them training and other learning opportunities.

Performance appraisal offers great potential for a variety of uses, ranging from operational to strategic purposes.[4] If done effectively, performance appraisal can be the key to developing employees and improving their performance. In addition, it provides the criteria against which selection systems are validated and is the typical basis on which personnel decisions, such as terminations, are legally justified. Further, performance appraisal makes the strategy of an organization real. For example, performance measures that assess courtesy and care can make a stated competitive strategy based on customer service very tangible to employees.

Despite the many uses of performance appraisals, companies struggle to realize the potential in their performance appraisal systems.[5] If managers aren't behind the system and can't see its value, it is little wonder that workers also don't see the value in it. To be effective, the performance appraisal system may require considerable time and effort of managers and may require employees to gather information and receive feedback. Unfortunately, some managers do not take the task seriously or do not have the skills needed to do a good job of evaluating performance and providing feedback. Some employees do not calmly accept the feedback. Others may become frustrated with an ineffective performance appraisal system and end up believing that the system is unfair and doesn't matter.

Although performance appraisal systems can have problems and are the target of many criticisms, employees still want performance feedback, and they would like to have it more frequently than the typical once-a-year performance evaluation.[6] Although more frequent formal appraisal can be positive, the practical reality is that informal appraisal, including feedback and discussion with workers, should occur on a continuous basis.

If appraisal is not done well—if, for instance, performance is not measured accurately and feedback is poorly given—the costs of conducting the appraisal may exceed its potential benefits.[7] It makes good business sense to engage in a practice only if the benefits exceed the cost. Some people take the position that performance appraisal should not be done at all.[8] From this perspective, the practice of performance appraisal is staunchly opposed as a hopelessly flawed and demeaning method of trying to improve performance.[9] Thus, performance appraisal should be eliminated as a practice in organizations because of the problems and errors in evaluating performance.[10] One basis for the position against doing performance appraisal is the quality philosophy[11] that performance is mainly due to the system and that any performance differences among workers are random.

Although there is selected opposition, the vast majority of organizations conduct performance appraisal. Figure 7.2 lists several reasons, from both the employer's and employee's perspectives, why appraisal is valuable despite the criticisms that have been leveled against it.

In the next two sections, we explain the issues and challenges involved in the first two steps of performance appraisal: identification and measurement. We conclude the chapter by discussing some of the key issues involved in managing employee performance.

Identifying Performance Dimensions

The first step in the performance appraisal process (see Figure 7.1) is identifying what is to be measured. Consider the following example:

dimension
An aspect of performance that determines effective job performance.

As part of her job as team manager, Nancy has to allocate raises based on performance. She decides to take a participative approach to deciding which aspects, or **dimensions**, determine effective job performance. In a meeting, she and her team start generating dimensions of performance. One of the first suggestions is the *quality of work* done. However, Nancy realized that some of the workers she supervises took three times longer than others to complete assignments, so she offered *quantity of work performed* as another dimension. One worker volunteered that how well someone interacted with peers and "customers" inside the organization was pretty important. The team added *interpersonal effectiveness* as another performance dimension.

Employer Perspective

1. Despite imperfect measurement techniques, individual differences in performance can make a difference to company performance.
2. Documentation of performance appraisal and feedback may be needed for legal defense.
3. Appraisal provides a rational basis for constructing a bonus or merit system.
4. Appraisal dimensions and standards can help to implement strategic goals and clarify performance expectations.
5. Providing individual feedback is part of the performance management process.
6. Despite the traditional focus on the individual, appraisal criteria can include teamwork and the teams can be the focus of the appraisal.

Employee Perspective

1. Performance feedback is needed and desired.
2. Improvement in performance requires assessment.
3. Fairness requires that differences in performance levels across workers be measured and have an effect on outcomes.
4. Assessment and recognition of performance levels can motivate workers to improve their performance.

FIGURE 7.2
The Benefits of Performance Appraisal

Sources: Based on Cardy, R. L., and Carson, K. P. (1996). Total quality and the abandonment of performance appraisal: Taking a good thing too far? *Journal of Quality Management, 1,* 193–206; Heinze, C. (2009). Fair appraisals. *Systems Contractor News, 16,* 36–37; Tobey, D. H., and Benson, P. G. (2009). Aligning performance: The end of personnel and the beginning of guided skilled performance. *Management Revue, 20,* 70–89.

Raising and considering additional work dimensions might continue until Nancy and her team have identified perhaps six or eight dimensions they think adequately capture performance. The team might also decide to make the dimensions more specific by adding definitions of each and behavioral descriptions of performance levels.

As you have probably realized, the process of identifying performance dimensions is very much like the job-analysis process described in Chapter 2. In fact, job analysis is the mechanism by which performance dimensions should be identified.

What is measured should be directly tied to what the business is trying to achieve,[12] because the performance appraisal process needs to add value to the business and not be done simply as a measurement exercise. Many organizations identify performance dimensions based on their strategic objectives. This approach makes sure that everyone is working together toward common goals.[13]

competencies
Characteristics associated with successful performance.

competency model
Set of competencies associated with a job.

An increasingly popular approach to identifying performance dimensions focuses on **competencies**, the observable characteristics people bring with them in order to perform the job successfully.[14] In order to make adequate evaluations, it is important to define competencies as observable characteristics, rather than as underlying and unseen characteristics (see the discussion and difficulties associated with personality traits as performance measures in the following section). The set of competencies associated with a job is often referred to as a **competency model**. An example of a competency model is presented in the Manager's Notebook, "Competencies in a Global Workplace."

Source: Ambrophoto/Shutterstock.

Measuring Performance

To measure employee performance, managers can assign numbers or a label such as "excellent," "good," "average," or "poor."[15] Whatever system is used, it is often difficult to quantify performance dimensions. For example, "creativity" may be an important part of the advertising copywriter's job. But how exactly can we measure it—by the number of ads written per year, by the number of ads that win industry awards, or by some other criterion? These are some of the issues that managers face when trying to evaluate an employee's performance.

Measurement Tools

Managers today have a wide array of appraisal formats from which to choose. Here we discuss the formats that are most common and consider their legal defensibility. Appraisal formats can be classified in two ways: (1) by the type of judgment that is required (relative or absolute) and (2) by the focus of the measure (trait, behavior, or outcome).

relative judgment
An appraisal format that asks supervisors to compare an employee's performance to the performance of other employees doing the same job.

RELATIVE AND ABSOLUTE JUDGMENTS Appraisal systems based on **relative judgment** ask supervisors to compare an employee's performance to the performance of other employees doing the same job. Providing a *rank order* of workers from best to worst is an example of a relative approach. Another type of relative judgment format classifies employees into groups, such as top third, middle third, and lowest third.

Relative rating systems have the advantage of forcing supervisors to differentiate among their workers. Without such a system, many supervisors are inclined to rate everyone the same, which destroys the appraisal system's value. For example, one study that examined the distribution of performance ratings for more than 7,000 managerial and professional employees in two large manufacturing firms found that 95 percent of employees were crowded into just two rating categories.

Most HR specialists believe the disadvantages of relative rating systems outweigh their advantages.[16] First, relative judgments (such as ranks) do not make clear how great or small the differences between employees are. Second, such systems do not provide any absolute information, so managers cannot determine how good or poor employees at the extreme rankings are. For example, relative ratings do not reveal whether the top-rated worker in one work team is better or worse than an average worker in another work team. This problem is illustrated in Figure 7.3. Marcos, Jill, and Frank are the highest-ranked performers in their respective work teams. However, Jill, Frank, and Julien are actually the best overall performers.

Third, relative ranking systems force managers to identify differences among workers where none may truly exist.[17] This can cause conflict among workers if and when ratings are disclosed. Finally, relative systems typically require assessment of overall performance. The "big picture" nature of relative ratings makes performance feedback ambiguous and of questionable value to workers who would benefit from specific information about the various dimensions of their performance. For all these reasons, companies tend to find relative rating systems most useful only when there is an administrative need (for example, to make decisions regarding promotions, pay raises, or terminations).[18]

absolute judgment
An appraisal format that asks supervisors to make judgments about an employee's performance based solely on performance standards.

Unlike relative judgment appraisal formats, **absolute judgment** formats ask supervisors to make judgments about an employee's performance based solely on performance standards. Comparisons to the performance of coworkers are not made. Typically, the dimensions of performance deemed relevant for the job are listed on the rating form, and the manager is asked to rate the employee on each dimension. An example of an absolute judgment rating scale is shown in Figure 7.4.

FIGURE 7.3
Rankings and Performance Levels Across Work Teams

Actual	Team 1 Ranked Work	Team 2 Ranked Work	Team 3 Ranked Work
10 (High)		Jill (1)	Frank (1)
9			Julien (2)
8		Tom (2)	Lisa (3)
7	Marcos (1)	Sue (3)	
6	Uma (2)		
5			
4	Joyce (3)	Greg (4)	
3	Bill (4)	Ken (5)	Jolie (4)
2	Richard (5)		Steve (5)
1 (Low)			

FIGURE 7.4
Sample of Absolute Judgment Rating Scale

PERFORMANCE REVIEW

Three-month (H&S)☐ Annual (H-Only)☐
Six-month (H&S) ☐ Special (H&S) ☐
H = Hourly S = Salaried

Employee Name

Social Security # Hourly ☐ Salaried ☐

For probationary employee review: Do you recommend that this employee be retained? Yes ☐ No ☐

Classification/Classification Hire Date

Review period: From ________ To ________

Department/Division

For each applicable performance area, mark the box that most closely reflects the employee's performance.
1 = unacceptable 2 = needs improvement 3 = satisfactory 4 = above average 5 = outstanding

PERFORMANCE AREA	1	2	3	4	5	PERFORMANCE AREA	1	2	3	4	5
Ability to make job-related decisions						Effective under stress					
Accepts change						Initiative					
Accepts direction						Knowledge of work					
Accepts responsibility						Leadership					
Attendance						Operation and care of equipment					
Attitude						Planning and organizing					
Compliance with rules						Quality of work					
Cooperation						Quantity of acceptable work					
Cost consciousness						Safety practices					
Dependability						**SUPERVISOR'S OVERALL APPRAISAL**					

For overall appraisals at the 1 or 2 level: Is the employee to remain or be placed on probationary status? Yes ☐ No ☐
If yes, what is the approximate date of next performance review? ________

JOB STRENGTHS AND SUPERIOR PERFORMANCE INCIDENTS:

AREAS FOR IMPROVEMENT:

PROGRESS ACHIEVED IN ATTAINING PREVIOUSLY SET GOALS:

SPECIFIC OBJECTIVES TO BE UNDERTAKEN PRIOR TO NEXT REVIEW FOR IMPROVED WORK PERFORMANCE:

SUPERVISOR COMMENTS:

EMPLOYEE COMMENTS:

Use separate sheet, if necessary, for additional comments by supervisor or employee. Please note on form if separate sheet is used.
Signing a review does not indicate agreement, only acknowledgment of being reviewed.

Employee's Signature | Date | Rating Supervisor's Signature | Social Security # | Date

Second Level Supervisor's Signature | Date | Department Head's Signature | Date

Theoretically, absolute formats allow employees from different work groups, rated by different managers, to be compared to one another. If all employees are excellent workers, they all can receive excellent ratings. In addition, because ratings are made on separate dimensions of performance, the feedback to the employee can be more specific and helpful. Absolute formats are also viewed as more fair than relative formats.[19]

Although often preferable to relative systems, absolute rating systems have their drawbacks. One is that all workers in a group can receive the same evaluation if the supervisor is reluctant to differentiate among workers. Another is that different supervisors can have markedly different evaluation standards. For example, a rating of 6 from an "easy" supervisor may actually be lower in value than a rating of 4 from a "tough" supervisor. But when the organization is handing out promotions or pay increases, the worker who received the 6 rating would be rewarded.

Nonetheless, absolute systems do have one distinct advantage: They avoid creating conflict among workers. This, plus the fact that relative systems are generally harder to defend when legal issues arise, may account for the prevalence of absolute systems in U.S. organizations.

It is interesting to note, though, that most people *do* make comparative judgments among both people and things. A political candidate is better or worse than opponents, not good or bad in an absolute sense. If comparative judgments are the common and natural way of making judgments, it may be difficult for managers to ignore relative comparisons among workers.

FIGURE 7.5
Sample Trait Scales

Rate each worker using the scales below.						
Decisiveness						
1	2	3	4	5	6	7
Very low			Moderate			Very high
Reliability						
1	2	3	4	5	6	7
Very low			Moderate			Very high
Energy						
1	2	3	4	5	6	7
Very low			Moderate			Very high
Loyalty						
1	2	3	4	5	6	7
Very low			Moderate			Very high

TRAIT, BEHAVIORAL, AND OUTCOME DATA In addition to relative and absolute judgments, performance measurement systems can be classified by the type of performance data on which they focus: trait data, behavioral data, or outcome data.

trait appraisal instrument
An appraisal tool that asks a supervisor to make judgments about worker characteristics that tend to be consistent and enduring.

Trait appraisal instruments ask the supervisor to make judgments about *traits*, worker characteristics that tend to be consistent and enduring. Figure 7.5 presents four traits that are typically found on trait-based rating scales: decisiveness, reliability, energy, and loyalty. Although some organizations use trait ratings, trait ratings have been criticized for being too ambiguous[20] and for leaving the door open for conscious or unconscious bias. In addition, because of their ambiguous nature trait ratings are less defensible in court than other types of ratings.[21] Definitions of reliability can differ dramatically across supervisors, for example, and the courts seem to be sensitive to the "slippery" nature of traits as criteria.

Assessment of traits also focuses on the *person* rather than on the *performance*, which can make employees defensive. This type of person-focused approach is not conducive to performance development. Measurement approaches that focus more directly on performance, either by evaluating behaviors or results, are generally more acceptable to workers and more effective as development tools. It is not that personality traits are not important to performance; the problem is with using a broad person characteristic, such as *reliability*, as a performance measure. To categorize an employee as "unreliable" will likely make the worker defensive, and the basis for the assessment and how to improve may not be clear. It would be preferable to assess and provide feedback on more observable and performance-relevant measures, such as number of times the employee has been late, the number of missed deadlines, and so on.

behavioral appraisal instrument
An appraisal tool that asks managers to assess a worker's behaviors.

Behavioral appraisal instruments focus on assessing a worker's behaviors. That is, instead of ranking leadership ability (a trait), the rater is asked to assess whether an employee exhibits certain behaviors (for example, works well with coworkers, comes to meetings on time). Probably the best-known behavioral scale is the Behaviorally Anchored Rating Scale (BARS). Figure 7.6 is an example of a BARS scale used to rate the effectiveness with which a department manager supervises his or her sales personnel. Behaviorally based rating scales are developed with the *critical-incident technique.* We describe the critical-incident technique in the Appendix to this chapter.

The main advantage of a behavioral approach is that the performance standards are unambiguous and observable. Unlike traits, which can have many meanings, behaviors across the range of a dimension are included directly on the behavioral scale. Because behaviors are unambiguous and based on observation, BARS and other behavioral instruments are more legally defensible than trait scales, which often use such hard-to-define adjectives as "poor" and "excellent." Behavioral scales also provide employees with specific examples of the types of behaviors to engage in (and to avoid) if they want to do well in the organization, and they encourage supervisors to be specific in their performance feedback. Having behavioral examples can make clear to employees how to enact organizationally prescribed values that may otherwise be unclear to them. For example, acting with integrity or being ethical may sound like great concepts, but workers

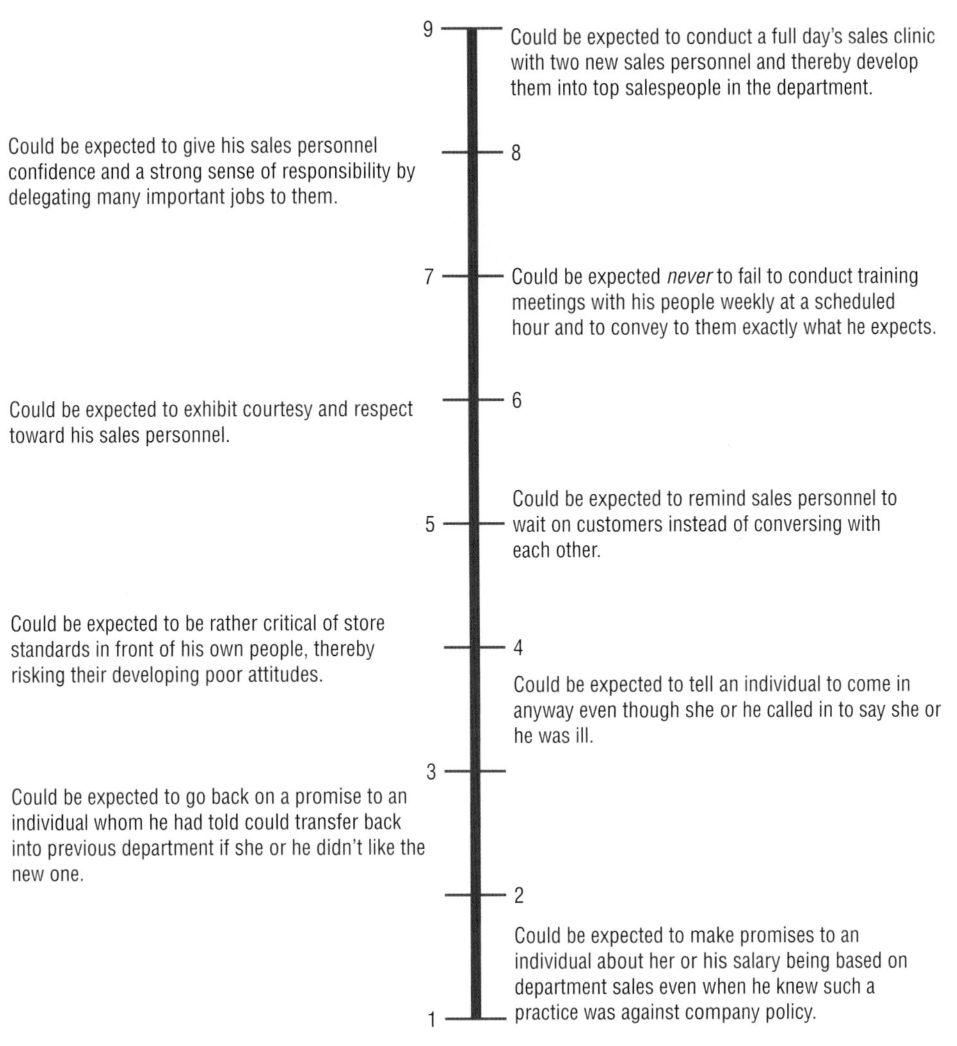

FIGURE 7.6

Sample BARS Used to Rate a Sales Manager

Source: Campbell, J. P., Dunnette, M. D., Arvey, R. D., and Hellervik, L. V. (1973). The development and evaluation of behaviorally based rating scales. *Journal of Applied Psychology*, 15–22. © 1973 by the American Psychological Association. Reprinted with permission.

may be unclear about what these concepts should mean for their day-to-day work performance. The Manager's Notebook, "Make Ethics Part of Appraisal," suggests how you can operationalize these concepts. Finally, both workers and supervisors can be involved in the process of generating behavioral scales.[22] This is likely to increase understanding and acceptance of the appraisal system.

MANAGER'S NOTEBOOK

Make Ethics Part of Appraisal

Performance appraisal is typically focused on tasks and business accomplishments. However, how duties are carried out and how goals are achieved can be critically important in organizations. Specifically, the ethical conduct of employees can be an important issue, but it is often not directly measured. Ethical conduct is often identified as a guiding value at the organizational level. But how does this value translate into everyday performance on the job? Many organizations have codes of ethics, but it may not be clear to employees how it should translate into how they perform their jobs. For example, a code emphasizing integrity and fairness may sound great, but what the code should mean for how the worker carries out his or her tasks may be ambiguous.

Including ethics in the appraisal of performance sends a clear signal about the importance of ethics in the organization. Taking a behavioral approach to the assessment of ethical performance can make clear the types of actions workers should and shouldn't do.

Source: Image Source/Getty Images.

The dimensions described here are examples of ethical characteristics that have been found to occur in organizations. A positive and negative behavioral example is provided for each of these dimensions of ethical performance. These behavioral examples are general and provide only a broad behavioral description of each dimension. The behavioral descriptions would probably be most useful if they were customized for each organization's setting.

Dimensions	General Behavioral Examples
Misrepresentation	+ This worker accurately states work situations. − This worker misconstrues work situations.
Information Sharing	+ This worker openly shares information with coworkers. − This worker withholds information from coworkers.
Collegiality	+ This worker supports colleagues and provides a positive influence. − This worker attacks colleagues and is a negative influence.
Adherence to Work Rules	+ This worker follows standards for work processes. − This worker does not follow standards for work processes.

Sources: Based on Cardy, R. L., and Selvarajan, T. T. (2004, March). Assessing ethical behavior: Development of a behaviorally anchored rating scale. Paper presented at the Southern Management Association meeting, Orlando, FL; Selvarajan, T. T., and Cloninger, P. A. (2007). The influence of job performance outcomes on ethical assessments. *Personnel Review, 38,* 398–412; Selvarajan, T. T., and Sardessai, R. (2010). Appraisal of ethical performance: A theoretical model. *Journal of Applied Business Research, 26,* 1–8; Whyatt, G., Wood, G., and Callaghan, M. (2012). Commitment to business ethics in UK organizations. *European Business Review*, *24*, 331–350. ■■

Behavioral systems are not without disadvantages, however. Developing them can be very time consuming, easily taking several months. Another disadvantage is their specificity. The points, or *anchors*, on behavioral scales are clear and concrete, but they are only examples of behaviors a worker *may* exhibit. Employees may never exhibit some of these anchor behaviors, which can cause difficulty for supervisors at appraisal time. Also, significant organizational changes can invalidate behavioral scales. For example, computerization of operations can dramatically alter the behaviors that workers must exhibit to be successful. Thus, the behaviors painstakingly developed for the appraisal system could become useless or, worse, operate as a drag on organizational change and worker adaptation. To avoid this problem of obsolescence, behavioral examples could be developed that reflect general performance capabilities rather than very job-specific task performance. **Outcome appraisal instruments** ask managers to assess the results achieved by workers, such as total sales or number of products produced. The most prevalent outcome approaches are **management by objectives (MBO)**[23] and naturally occurring outcome measures. MBO is a goal-directed approach in which workers and their supervisors set goals together for the upcoming evaluation period. The rating then consists of deciding to what extent the goals have been met. With *naturally occurring outcomes*, the performance measure is not so much discussed and agreed to as it is handed to supervisors

outcome appraisal instrument
An appraisal tool that asks managers to assess the results achieved by workers.

management by objectives (MBO)
A goal-directed approach to performance appraisal in which workers and their supervisors set goals together for the upcoming evaluation period.

and workers. For example, a computerized production system used to manufacture cardboard boxes may automatically generate data regarding the number of pieces produced, the amount of waste, and the defect rate.

MANAGER'S NOTEBOOK

Competencies in a Global Workplace

Competencies needed to adequately perform in an organization can go beyond being able to complete tasks. Global aspects of today's organizations can mean that additional competencies are needed. For example, working with customers from various parts of the world or working with fellow employees on virtual teams from around the globe can require additional skills.

Competencies are often identified based on either an analysis of what is done on a job or based on the core mission and strategy of an organization. In the case of basing competencies on job requirements, the focus begins with what needs to be done. Based on what the employee needs to do on the job, competencies are identified. For example, for a job that requires assembly of parts, a manager or human resources representative might identify mechanical skill as a core competency area.

Competencies can also be based on the strategy of the firm. An organization might, for example, set its sights on becoming known for its customer service, even though its current emphasis has been on manufacturing. Basing competencies on the current jobs would not capture this customer-service focus. However, basing competencies on the strategy of the organization will help move it closer to reaching that customer service target. Identifying customer service behaviors as a competency that will be measured and developed as part of the performance appraisal system can make the strategic goal of competing on customer service a reality for the business.

Globalization in the business world is also a source for competencies in many organizations. Certainly, having the competencies to perform the required tasks or the competencies that have strategic value is necessary if employees are to add value to the business. Simply being able to operationally perform tasks is not the whole story—it's also how the tasks are carried out and knowing when a situation calls for different approaches. Differences in culture can be one of those key situational factors that need to be taken into account. People from different countries or backgrounds can differ in their beliefs, experiences, and values. These differences can affect a wide variety of work-related issues. In the extreme, differences in language can make communication difficult and negatively impact areas such as sales and decision making in the organization. Less dramatic, but also important, cultural differences can also impact styles of communication, priorities, and preferred styles of working. For example, people from more individualistic cultures, such as the United States, Australia, and United Kingdom, would generally be more responsive to performance feedback that focuses on their individual contributions. In contrast, people from more collectivist cultures, such as China and Singapore, would look for feedback that focuses on how their work team is doing as a whole.

In situations where jobs include working with customers or fellow employees from diverse backgrounds, cultural competency may be as important as job- or strategy-based competencies. The sources of competencies are summarized in the following illustration.

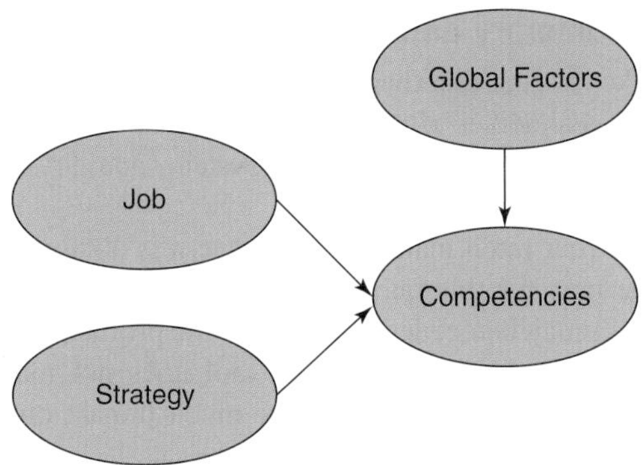

The ability to do the tasks that are part of the job and the ability to contribute to the strategic mission of the organization are core competencies. In today's global environment, awareness of cultural differences and the ability to take those differences into account can also be critical competencies.

Sources: Based on Aguines, H., Roo, H., and Gottfredson, R. K. (2012). Performance management universals: Think globally and act locally. *Business Horizons*, *55*, 385–392; Hall, M. G., and Gurdry, J. J. (2013). Literature review of cultural competence curriculum within the United States: An ethical implication in academic preparational programs. *Education in Medicine Journal*, *5*, 6–13; Hill, J. (2012, January 30). Competency model helps HR add value. *Canadian HR Reporter*, January 20–21. ■■

The outcome approach provides clear and unambiguous criteria by which worker performance can be judged. It also eliminates subjectivity and the potential for error and bias that goes along with it. In addition, outcome approaches provide increased flexibility. For example, a change in the production system may lead to a new set of outcome measures and, perhaps, a new set of performance standards. With an MBO approach, a worker's objectives can easily be adjusted at the beginning of a new evaluation period if organizational changes call for new emphases. Perhaps the most important thing is that outcomes can easily be tied to strategic objectives.[24]

Are outcome-based systems, then, the answer to the numerous problems with the subjective rating systems discussed earlier? Unfortunately, no. Although they are objective, outcome measures may give a seriously deficient and distorted view of worker performance levels. Consider an outcome measure defined as follows: "the number of units produced that are within acceptable quality limits." This performance measure may seem fair and acceptable. However, when the machine is not running properly, it can take several hours—sometimes an entire shift—to locate the problem and resolve it. If you were a manager, you would put your best workers on the problem. But consider what would happen to their performance. Your best workers could actually end up looking like the worst workers in terms of the amount of product produced.

This situation actually occurred at a manufacturer of automobile components.[25] Management concluded that supervisors' subjective performance judgments were superior to objective outcome measures. The objective numbers were deficient measures of performance and didn't accurately portray who were the better and poorer workers. Some of the best workers were assigned to difficult situations and were given responsibility to resolve problems with machinery, giving these workers poor productivity numbers. The objective data couldn't take these factors into account, but the supervisors could consider difficulty of assignments when assessing employee performance. Another potential difficulty with outcome-based performance measures is the development of a "results at any cost" mentality.[26] Using objective measures has the advantage of focusing workers' attention on certain outcomes, but this focus can have negative effects on other facets of performance. For example, an organization may use the number of units produced as a performance measure because it is fairly easy to quantify. Workers concentrating on quantity may neglect quality and follow-up service to the long-term detriment of the organization. Likewise, a "results at any price" mentality can lead workers to disregard ethics in the conduct of their job so that goals are achieved.[27] Although objective goals and other outcome measures are effective for increasing performance levels, these measures may not reflect the entire spectrum of performance.[28]

A QUESTION OF ETHICS

Is it appropriate for organizations to evaluate and compensate employees according to objective measures of performance, even though performance is at least partially determined by factors beyond their control? Should a salesperson, for instance, be paid completely on commission even in the midst of a recession that makes it practically impossible to sell enough to make a decent living?

Measurement Tools: Summary and Conclusions

Our discussion so far makes it clear that there is no single best appraisal format. Figure 7.7 summarizes the strengths and weaknesses of each approach in the areas of administration, development, and legal defensibility. The choice of appraisal system should rest largely on the appraisal's primary purpose.

For example, say that your main management concern is obtaining desired results. An outcome approach would be best for this purpose. However, when outcomes are not adequately achieved, further evaluation may be needed to diagnose the problem.

Empirical evidence suggests that the type of tool does not make that much difference in the accuracy of ratings.[29] If formats do not have much impact on ratings, what does? Not

Appraisal Format	Administrative Use	Developmental Use	Legal Defensibility
		CRITERIA	
Absolute	0	+	0
Relative	+ +	+	−
Trait	+	−	− −
Behavior	0	+	+ +
Outcome	0	0	+

− − Very poor − Poor 0 Unclear or mixed + Good + + Very good

FIGURE 7.7
Evaluation of Major Appraisal Formats

surprisingly, it's the person doing the rating. Characteristics such as the rater's intelligence, familiarity with the job,[30] and ability to separate important from unimportant information[31] influence rating quality. Thus, the person doing the rating is an important determinant of the quality of ratings.

Who does the rating is commonly referred to as the *source* of the appraisal. The most common source is the worker's direct supervisor. However, other sources can provide unique and valuable perspectives to the performance appraisal process. Self, peers, subordinates, and even customers are increasingly common sources of appraisal.

Self-review, in which workers rate themselves, allows employees input into the appraisal process and can help them gain insight into the causes of performance problems. For example, there may be a substantial difference in opinion between a supervisor and an employee regarding one area of the employee's evaluation. Communication and possibly investigation are warranted in such a case. In some situations, people can find themselves having to rely on self-appraisal as a guide to managing performance.

self-review
A performance appraisal system in which workers rate themselves.

In a **peer review**, workers at the same level of the organization rate one another. In a **subordinate review**, workers review their supervisors.

peer review
A performance appraisal system in which workers at the same level in the organization rate one another.

subordinate review
A performance appraisal system in which workers review their supervisors.

In addition to feedback from within the organization, some companies look to customers as a valuable source of appraisal. Traditional top-down appraisal systems may encourage employees to perform only those behaviors that supervisors see or pay attention to. Thus, behaviors that are critical to customer satisfaction may be ignored.[32]

Indeed, customers are often in a better position to evaluate the quality of a company's products or services than supervisors are. Supervisors may have limited information or a limited perspective, whereas internal and external customers often have a wider focus or greater experience with more parts of the business.

The combination of peer, subordinate, and self-review and sometimes customer appraisal is termed **360° feedback**. A 360° system can offer a well-rounded picture of an employee's performance, one that is difficult to ignore or discount, because it comes from multiple perspectives. Many organizations are now employing technology to make 360° appraisal an efficient and cost-effective system.

360° feedback
The combination of peer, subordinate, and self-review.

Challenges to Effective Performance Measurement

How can managers ensure accurate measurement of worker performance? The primary means is to understand the barriers that stand in the way. Managers confront at least five challenges:

- Rater errors and bias
- The influence of liking
- Organizational politics
- Whether to focus on the individual or the group
- Legal issues

Rater Errors and Bias

rater error
An error in performance appraisals that reflects consistent biases on the part of the rater.

A **rater error** is an error in performance appraisal that reflects consistent biases on the part of the rater. One of the most prominent rater errors is *halo error*, the tendency to rate similarly across dimensions.[33]

There are at least two causes of halo error:[34] (1) A supervisor may make an overall judgment about a worker and then conform all dimensional ratings to that judgment and/or (2) a supervisor may make all ratings consistent with the worker's performance level on a dimension that is important to the supervisor. If Nancy rates Luis low on all three performance dimensions (quality of programs written, quantity of programs written, and interpersonal effectiveness) even though his performance on quality and quantity is high, then she has committed a halo error.

Another type of rater error is *restriction of range error*, which occurs when a manager restricts all of his or her ratings to a small portion of the rating scale. Three different forms of range restriction are common: *leniency errors*, or restricting ratings to the high portion of the scale; *central tendency errors*, or using only the middle points of the scale; and *severity errors*, or using only the low portion of the rating scale.

Suppose that you are an HR manager reviewing the performance ratings given by the company's supervisors to their subordinates. The question is: How can you tell how accurate these ratings are? In other words, how can you tell what types of rating error, if any, have colored the ratings? It is very difficult to tell. Let us say that a supervisor has given one of her subordinates the highest possible rating on each of five performance dimensions. There are at least three possible explanations. The employee may actually be very good on one of the dimensions and has been rated very high on all because of this (halo error). Or the rater may only use the top part of the scale (leniency error). Or the employee may be a very good all-around worker (accurate). Although sophisticated statistical techniques have been developed to investigate these possibilities, none is practical for most organizations or managers. Further, current research indicates that "errors" in ratings can sufficiently represent "true" ratee performance levels (the "accurate" possibility presented previously), such that rater errors are *not* good indicators of inaccuracy in rating.[35]

Personal bias may also cause errors in evaluation. Consciously or unconsciously, a supervisor may systematically rate certain workers lower or higher than others on the basis of race, national origin, sex, age, or other factors. Conscious bias is extremely difficult, if not impossible, to eliminate. Unconscious bias can be overcome once it is brought to the rater's attention. For example, a supervisor might be unconsciously giving higher evaluations to employees who went to his alma mater. When made aware of this leaning, however, he may correct it.

Blatant, systematic negative biases should be recognized and corrected within the organization. Negative bias became an issue at the U.S. Drug Enforcement Agency (DEA) in the early 1980s when a lawsuit, *Segar v. Civiletti*, established that African American agents were systematically rated lower than white agents and, thus, were less likely to receive promotions and choice job assignments. The DEA failed to provide supervisors with any written instructions on how to evaluate agents' performance, and virtually all the supervisors conducting the evaluations were white.[36]

comparability
In performance ratings, the degree to which the performance ratings given by various supervisors in an organization are based on similar standards.

A major difficulty in performance measurement is ensuring comparability in ratings across raters.[37] **Comparability** refers to the degree to which the performance ratings given by various supervisors in an organization are based on similar standards. In essence, the comparability issue is concerned with whether supervisors use the same measurement yardsticks. What one supervisor considers excellent performance, another may view as only average.

frame-of-reference (FOR) training
A type of training that presents supervisors with fictitious examples of worker performance (either in writing or on video), asks the supervisors to evaluate the workers in the examples, and then tells them what their ratings should have been.

One of the most effective ways to deal with errors and bias is to develop and communicate evaluation standards via **frame-of-reference (FOR) training**,[38] which uses prepared behavioral examples of performance that a worker might exhibit. After rating the performance presented on video or paper, the trainees in a typical FOR session are told what their ratings should have been. Discussion of which worker behaviors represent each dimension (and why) follows. This process of rating, feedback, and discussion is followed by the presentation of another example. Again, rating, feedback, and discussion follow. The process continues until the appraisers develop a common frame of reference for performance evaluation. In other words, FOR training is all about calibrating everyone to the same performance standards.[39]

FOR training has consistently been found to increase the accuracy of performance ratings.[40] Perhaps even more important, it develops common evaluation standards among supervisors.

The FOR training procedure does have a number of drawbacks, though. One glaring problem is the expense, which can be prohibitive owing to the amount of time and number of people involved. Another drawback is that it can be used only with behaviorally based appraisal systems.

The Influence of Liking

Liking can cause errors in performance appraisals when raters allow their like or dislike of an individual to influence their assessment of that person's performance. Field studies have found rater liking and performance ratings to be substantially correlated.[41] Findings of a correlation might indicate that performance ratings are biased by rater liking. However, good raters may tend to like good performers and dislike poor performers.

The fundamental question, of course, is whether the relationship between liking and performance ratings is appropriate or biased.[42] It is appropriate if supervisors like good performers better than poor performers. It is biased if supervisors like or dislike employees for reasons other than their performance and then allow these feelings to contaminate their ratings. It can be difficult to determine if an influence of liking on performance ratings is appropriate or due to bias. Managers may be able to separate their liking from employee performance and, thus, eliminate the possibility that liking biases the performance ratings.[43] Nonetheless, most workers appear to believe that their supervisor's liking for them influences the performance ratings they receive.[44] The perception of bias can cause communication problems between workers and supervisors and lower supervisors' effectiveness in managing performance.

Given the potentially biasing impact of liking, it is critical that supervisors manage their emotional reactions to workers. One approach that may be helpful is to keep a performance diary of observed behavior for each worker[45] to serve as the basis for evaluation and other managerial actions. An external record of worker behaviors can dramatically reduce error and bias in ratings.

Recordkeeping should be done routinely—for example, daily or weekly. Keeping records of employee performance is a professional habit worth developing, particularly to safeguard against litigation that challenges the fairness of appraisals.[46] To prevent error and bias, the record should reflect what each worker has been doing, not opinions or inferences about the behavior. Further, the record should present a balanced and complete picture by including all performance incidents—positive, negative, or average. A good question to ask yourself is whether someone else reading the record would reach the same conclusion about the level of performance as you have.

In one field study of such recordkeeping, supervisors reported that the task took five minutes or fewer per week.[47] More important, the majority of supervisors reported that they would prefer to continue, rather than discontinue, the recording of behavioral incidents. By compiling a weekly record, they did not have to rely much on general impressions and possibly biased memories when conducting appraisals. In addition, the practice signaled workers that appraisal was not a personality contest. Finally, the diaries provided a legal justification for the appraisal process: The supervisor could cite concrete behavioral examples that justified the rating.

Two warnings are in order here. First, performance diaries are not guarantees against bias due to liking, because supervisors can be biased in the type of incidents they choose to record. However, short of intentional misrepresentation, the keeping of such records should help reduce both actual bias and the perception of bias.

Second, it is unfair to keep a secret running list of "offenses" and then suddenly unveil it to the employee when he or she commits an infraction that can't be overlooked. The message for managers is simple: If an employee's behavior warrants discussion, the discussion should take place immediately.[48]

Organizational Politics

Thus far, we have taken a *rational perspective* on appraisal.[49] In other words, we have assumed that the value of each worker's performance can be estimated. Unlike the rational approach, the *political perspective* assumes that the value of a worker's performance depends on the agenda, or goals, of the supervisor.[50] Consider the following quote from an executive with extensive experience in evaluating his subordinates:

> As a manager, I will use the review process to do what is best for my people and the division. . . . I've got a lot of leeway—call it discretion—to use this process in that manner. . . .

> I've used it to get my people better raises in lean years, to kick a guy in the pants if he really needed it, to pick up a guy when he was down or even to tell him that he was no longer welcome here. . . . I believe that most of us here at ______________ operate this way regarding appraisals.[51]

Let's examine how the rational and the political process differ on various facets of the performance appraisal process.

- The *goal* of appraisal from a rational perspective is accuracy. The goal of appraisal from a political perspective is *utility*, the maximization of benefits over costs given the context and agenda. The value of performance is relative to the political context and the supervisor's goals. For example, a supervisor may give a very poor rating to a worker who seems uncommitted in the hopes of shocking that worker into an acceptable level of performance.
- The rational approach sees supervisors and workers largely as passive agents in the rating process: Supervisors simply notice and evaluate workers' performance. Thus, their accuracy is critical. In contrast, the political approach views both supervisors and workers as motivated participants in the measurement process. Workers actively try to influence their evaluations, either directly or indirectly.

The various persuasion techniques that workers use to alter the supervisor's evaluation are direct forms of influence. For example, just as a student tells a professor that he needs a higher grade to keep his scholarship; a worker might tell her boss that she needs an above-average rating to get a promotion. Indirect influences are behaviors by which workers influence how supervisors notice, interpret, and recall events,[52] ranging from flattery to excuses to apologies. The following quote from a consulting group manager demonstrates how employees in the organization used impression-management tactics:[53]

> Phone calls from customers praising a consultant's performance were rarely received except during the month before appraisals. These phone calls were often instigated by the consultants to highlight their importance.

- From a rational perspective, the *focus* of appraisal is measurement. Supervisors are flesh-and-blood instruments[54] who must be carefully trained to measure performance meaningfully. The evaluations are used in decisions about pay raises, promotions, training, and termination. The political perspective sees the focus of appraisal as management, not accurate measurement. Appraisal is not so much a test that should be fair and accurate as it is a management tool with which to reward or discipline workers.
- *Assessment criteria*, the standards used to judge worker performance, also differ between the rational and political approaches. The rational approach holds that a worker's performance should be defined as clearly as possible. In the political approach, the definition of what is being assessed is left ambiguous so that it can be bent to the current agenda. Thus, ambiguity ensures the necessary flexibility in the appraisal system.
- Finally, the *decision process* differs between the rational and political approaches. In the rational approach, supervisors make dimensional and overall assessments based on specific behaviors they have observed. For instance, Nancy would rate each programmer on each dimension and then combine all the dimensional ratings into an overall evaluation. In the political approach, appropriate assessment of specifics follows the overall assessment. Thus, Nancy would first decide who in her group should get the highest rating (for whatever reason) and then justify that overall assessment by making appropriate dimensional ratings.

Appraisal in most organizations seems to be a political rather than a rational exercise.[55] It appears to be used as a tool for serving various and changing agendas; accurate assessment is seldom the real goal. But should the rational approach be abandoned because appraisal is typically political? No! Politically driven assessment may be common, but that does not make it the best approach to assessment.

Accuracy may not be the main goal in organizations, but it is the theoretical ideal behind appraisal.[56] Accurate assessment is necessary if feedback, development, and HR decisions are to be based on employees' actual performance levels. Basing feedback and development on managerial agendas is an unjust treatment of human resources. Careers have been ruined, self-esteem lost, and productivity degraded because of the political use of appraisal. In addition to these negative effects, politically driven appraisal is also associated with increased intention of workers to quit their jobs.[57] Such costs are difficult to assess and to ascribe clearly to politics. Nonetheless, they are very real and important for workers.

A QUESTION OF ETHICS

Performance appraisal is a management tool. As such, managers often use the tool to benefit themselves or the company. For example, a manager may use overly positive performance ratings as a reward for someone who spearheaded a project for the manager. Likewise, a manager may use overly harsh ratings as punishment for someone who objected to a project the manager promoted. Do you think such use of the appraisal system is acceptable? Why?

Individual or Group Focus

If the organization has a team structure, managers need to consider team performance appraisal at two levels: (1) individual contribution to team performance and (2) the performance of the team as a unit.[58] To properly assess individual contributions to team performance, managers and employees must have clear performance criteria relating to traits, behaviors, or outcomes. Behavioral measures are typically most appropriate for assessing individual contributions to team performance because they are more easily observed and understood by team members and others who interact with the team.

The individual contribution measures could be developed with the input of team members. However, a good starting point is the set of competencies for individual contribution to team performance identified in recent research.[59] The following example describes the use of these competencies at Pfizer, a large pharmaceutical company. Peers assess team members online in the finance area of Pfizer.[60]

> The assessment is based on a four-dimensional model of collaboration, communication, self-management, and decision making. Feedback reports are used as a discussion point to improve the functioning of teams. Over time, there has been significant improvement in the average level of ratings given to team members.

Whatever measures are already in existence or are developed for measuring team performance, here are some points to keep in mind.

First, the measurement system needs to be balanced. For example, although financial objectives may be apparent and easy to develop as criteria, these kinds of objectives may not reflect the concerns of customers.

Another point to keep in mind is that outcome measures may need to be complemented with measures of process. For example, achieving a result may be important but so, too, are interpersonal relations. With a balance of measures, it should be clear to team members that achieving outcomes by running roughshod over peers and customers is not acceptable performance.

Assessing the performance of a team as a unit means that managers must measure performance at the team, not individual, level. Dimensions for measuring team performance may be set at higher levels in the organization; if this is not the case, then team members can be great sources for identifying and developing team-level criteria. Going to team members to help develop criteria encourages their participation in selecting measures that they feel they can directly influence.

Overall, given the individual focus in the United States, it is recommended that individual performance still be assessed, even with a team environment.[61] As with individual assessment, there is no consensus as to what type of appraisal instrument should be used for team evaluations. The best approach may include internal and external customers making judgments across both behavioral and outcome criteria.[62]

Legal Issues

The major legal requirements for performance appraisal systems are set forth in Title VII of the Civil Rights Act of 1964, which prohibits discrimination in all terms and conditions of employment (see Chapter 3). This means that performance appraisal must be free of discrimination at both the individual and group levels. Some courts have also held that performance appraisal systems should meet the same *validity* standards as selection tests (see Chapter 5). As with selection tests, *adverse impact* may occur in performance evaluation when members of one group are promoted at a higher rate than members of another group based on their appraisals.

Probably the most significant court test of discrimination in performance appraisal is *Brito v. Zia Company*, a 1973 U.S. Supreme Court case. In essence, the Court determined that appraisal is legally a test and must, therefore, meet all the legal requirements regarding tests in organizations.

In practice, however, court decisions since *Brito v. Zia* have employed less stringent criteria when assessing charges of discrimination in appraisal.

Appraisal-related court cases since *Brito v. Zia* suggest that the courts do not wish to rule on whether appraisal systems conform to all accepted professional standards (such as whether employees were allowed to participate in developing the system).[63] Rather, they simply want to determine whether discrimination occurred. The essential question is whether individuals who have similar employment situations are treated differently.

The courts look favorably on a system in which a supervisor's manager reviews appraisals to safeguard against the occurrence of individual bias. In addition, the courts take a positive view of feedback and employee counseling to help improve performance problems. An analysis of 295 court cases involving performance appraisal found judges' decisions to be favorably influenced by the following additional factors:[64]

- Use of job analysis
- Providing written instructions
- Allowing employees to review appraisal results
- Agreement among multiple raters (if more than one rater was used)
- The presence of rater training

In the extreme, a negative performance appraisal may lead to the dismissal of an employee. Management's right to fire an employee is rooted in a legal doctrine called *employment-at-will.* Employment-at-will is a very complex legal issue that depends on laws and rulings varying from state to state. We discuss employment-at-will more fully in Chapter 14. Here, the major point is that managers can protect themselves from lawsuits by following good professional practice. If they provide subordinates with honest, accurate, and fair feedback about their performance, and then make decisions consistent with that feedback, they will have nothing to fear from ongoing questions about employment-at-will.

Managing Performance

The effective management of human performance in organizations requires more than formal reporting and annual ratings. To be useful to the organization, performance appraisal has to be more than measurement. As illustrated in the Manager's Notebook, "From Performance Appraisal to Performance Management," technology can be used to integrate performance measures and feedback into an everyday system that can improve performance. However, even with the best technology, performance management requires the involvement of managers. People want and expect to hear how they are doing and discuss plans to move forward in a face-to-face meeting with their manager. Managers may also need to be proactive and deal with performance problems and be involved in finding solutions. In this section, we discuss the third and final component of performance appraisal, performance management.

MANAGER'S NOTEBOOK

Technology/Social Media

From Performance Appraisal to Performance Management

A primary purpose for performance appraisal is to improve performance. Increasingly, companies are using technology to help make sure that the appraisal process leads to performance improvement. Nearly 75 percent of companies utilize web-based performance management systems. Although technology won't necessarily solve all problems with performance appraisal, it can simplify the task of evaluating performance and facilitate getting feedback and improvement suggestions to workers.

Performance appraisal software, such as Halogen Software, allows employees and managers to electronically access performance information. For example, competencies and goals might be identified by employees. Managers can then check to assure that the employee has selected targets that are linked to the strategic goal of the organization and then give electronic approval.

The electronic platform can then be used by the employees as a place to log their activities and accomplishments, and managers or other sources, such as peers and subordinates, can enter their performance evaluations.

Technology can be used to provide suggestions to the employee for performance improvement, such as online training. Some companies, such as Klick Health Systems in Toronto, Canada, have developed this internal communication and workflow management system to the point that it provides real-time performance support. The system, for example, can give coaching tips and suggest short instruction videos when someone is going to do a task they haven't done before.

Social media is also being used to allow peer-based feedback and recognition of performance. For example, Kudos is a company that provides software to businesses that is similar to Facebook and allows peers to write on each other's walls and give feedback on performance. The software also allows people to award points for particularly positive contributions made by a fellow employee. The points can later be turned in by the recipient for prizes such as gift cards and paid time off. This system provides a means for people to quickly provide feedback and recognize contributions that managers may not always be aware of.

Web-based technology can be an important tool to help improve employee performance. It may not replace human judgment and face-to-face performance meetings, but technology can be a supplement that shifts annual appraisal into performance management that is an everyday part of work.

Sources: Based on Dobson, S. (2013). Upgrading talent management processes leads to fully integrated approach, efficiencies. *Canadian HR Reporter*, *26*, 20; Lawler, E. E., Benson, G. S., and McDermott, M. (2012). What makes performance appraisal effective? *Compensation & Benefits Review*, *44*, 191–200; Lewis, T. (2012). The talent score. *Medical Marketing and Media*, *47*, 58–60, 62; Zielinski, D. (2012). Giving praise. *HR Magazine*, *57*, 77–78, 80. ■■

The Appraisal Interview

Upon completing the performance rating, the supervisor usually conducts an interview with the worker to provide feedback—one of the most important parts of the appraisal process. Many managers dread the performance interview, particularly if they do not have good news to deliver. The HR department or an external group, such as a management association or consulting group, can help managers by offering training in conducting interviews, providing role-play practice, and offering advice on thorny issues. Figure 7.8 summarizes several communication "microskills" that managers need to effectively conduct an appraisal interview.

Performance reviews are sometimes separated into two sessions: one to discuss performance, the other to discuss salary.[65] The logic behind this system was based on two assumptions. First, managers cannot simultaneously be both a coach and a judge. Thus, the manager was expected to play the coach role during the performance development meeting and the judge role during the salary meeting. Second, if performance and salary discussions were combined, employees probably would not listen to their performance feedback because their interest would be focused on salary decisions.

However, research has found that discussion of salary in an appraisal session has a *positive* impact on how employees perceive the appraisal's usefulness.[66] Managers who have to justify a low salary increase will probably take time to carefully support their performance assessments, and this more detailed feedback should make the appraisal session more valuable to the employee. Second, feedback, goal setting, and making action plans can become a hollow and meaningless exercise when salary implications are divorced from the session.

Overall, it appears that the best management practice is to combine development and salary discussion into one performance review. Informal performance management throughout the appraisal period requires a combination of judgment and coaching.

It makes sense that the appraisal interviews focus on gaps in performance and provide suggestions to workers for improvement. However, feedback that focuses only on shortcomings can be demoralizing rather than motivating. It can be useful to focus feedback on what workers do well so that they hear positives as well as any necessary negatives. The Manager's Notebook, "Accentuate the Positive," explores a strength-based approach to providing performance feedback.

Face-to-face communication during the performance appraisal interview can be more effective if managers use "microskills"—communication factors that must be present for effective interpersonal communication. Several examples follow:

Skills	Benefit	Description	Example
Nonverbal Attending	Suggests interest and active listening.	Rater sits with a slight forward, comfortable lean of the upper body, maintains eye contact, and speaks in a steady and soothing voice.	While the ratee is speaking, the rater looks at the person and gently nods head to signal interest.
Open and Closed Questions	Appropriate use of open and closed questions can ensure an effective flow of communication during an interview.	Open questions encourage information sharing and are most appropriate early in an interview or in complex, ambiguous situations.	Open questions start with words like "Could," "Would," "How," "What," or "Why."
		Closed questions evoke short responses and are useful for focusing and clarifying.	Closed questions start with words like "Did," "Is," or "Are."
Paraphrasing	Paraphrasing can clarify and convey to the ratee that you are listening actively.	A paraphrase is a concise statement in your own words of what someone just said. It should be factual and nonjudgmental.	You might begin by saying "If I have this right . . ." or "What you're saying is . . ." and end with "Is that correct?" or "That's what you are saying?"
Reflection of Feeling	Shows that you are sensitive to and trying to understand the emotional dimension of the workplace. The empathy and sensitivity of reflection can open up communication and allow task-related issues to be addressed more meaningfully.	Similar to paraphrase, a reflection of feeling is a factual statement of the emotions you sense the other person is feeling. Be cautious about using this technique insincerely or with those who need professional help.	Start by saying something like "It sounds like you're feeling . . ." End as you would a paraphrase ("Is that right?").
Cultural Sensitivity	Communication is more effective when you are sensitive to the possible influence of cultural differences.	Pay attention to cultural differences that may influence how another person communicates and how you might communicate with others.	When dealing with employees from a culture that is highly formal, avoid addressing them in the workplace by their first names. Doing so may signal disrespect.

FIGURE 7.8

Communication Skills for the Appraisal Interview

Sources: Based on Kikoski, J. F. (1998). Effective communication in the performance appraisal interview: Face-to-face communication for public managers in the culturally diverse workplace. *Public Personnel Management, 27*, 491–513; Ivey, A. B., Ivey, M. B., and Simek-Downing, L. (1987). *Counseling and psychotherapy: Integrating skills, theory, and practice* (2nd ed). Upper Saddle River, NJ: Prentice Hall; Cardy, R. L., and Leonard, B. (2011). *Performance management: Concepts, skills, and exercises* (2nd ed.). Armonk, NY: M. E. Sharpe, Inc.

MANAGER'S NOTEBOOK

Customer-Driven HR

Accentuate the Positive

The traditional approach to providing performance feedback focuses on gaps in performance, those areas where an employee's performance is below expected levels. Those gaps are deficiencies that need to be resolved in order for performance to improve. Taking this traditional approach in a performance review session seems rational: identify the employee's weaknesses and discuss how to improve. From the employee's perspective, however, such a review will likely be a negative experience that consists of criticism and lowers motivation. Given this potential response from workers, it may be no surprise to learn that performance feedback, although sometimes effective, can also lead to decreased performance.

A promising approach meant to improve the positive impact of performance feedback is to focus on the strengths that an employee brings to his or her job. Rather than focusing on deficiencies to eliminate weaknesses, the idea is to recognize strengths and to build on how the worker contributes to the organization. The focus on strengths is, of course, better received by workers than negative feedback. Strengths-based feedback has been found to be motivating to workers and to improve productivity.

To the extent that people have natural strengths and weaknesses, the strengths-based approach focuses on building on natural talents rather than on trying to change someone's weak areas. Trying to change a naturally weak area can be difficult and frustrating for you, as a manager, as well as for the employee. Recognizing someone's strengths can make performance feedback a more positive and motivating experience.

Sources: Based on Aguinas, H., Gottfredson, R. K., and Joo, H. (2012). Delivering effective performance feedback: The strengths-based approach. *Business Horizons, 55*, 105–11; Cardy, R. L., and Leonard, B. (2011). *Performance management: Concepts, skills, and exercises* (2nd ed.). Armonk, NY: M. E. Sharpe, Inc.; De Nisi, A. S., and Kluger, A. N. (2000). Feedback effectiveness: Can 360-degree appraisals be improved? *Academy of Management Executive, 14*, 129–139. ■■

Performance Improvement

Because formal appraisal interviews typically are conducted only once a year,[67] they may not always have substantial and lasting impact on worker performance.[68] Much more important than the annual interview is informal day-to-day performance management. Supervisors who manage performance effectively generally share three characteristics:

- Explore the causes of performance problems.
- Develop an action plan and empower workers to reach a solution.
- Direct communication at performance and provide effective feedback.[69]

Each of these characteristics is critical to achieving improved and sustained performance levels.

Identifying the Causes of Performance Problems

Identifying the causes of performance problems may sound like an easy task, but it is often quite challenging. Performance can be the result of many factors, some of which are beyond the worker's control. In most work situations, though, supervisors tend to blame the worker when they observe poor performance, whereas workers tend to blame external factors.[70] This tendency is called *actor/observer bias.*[71] The experience of baseball teams provides an analogy. When a team is losing, the players (workers/actors) point to external causes such as injuries, a tough road schedule, or bad weather. The manager (supervisor/observer) blames the players for sloppy execution in the field. And the team's owner and the sportswriters (top management/higher observers) hold the manager responsible for the team's poor performance.

It is important that managers determine the causes of performance deficiencies accurately for three reasons. First, determination of causes can influence how performance is evaluated. For example, a manager is likely to evaluate an episode of poor performance very differently if he thinks it was due to low effort than if he thinks it was due to poor materials. Second, causal determination can be an unspoken and underlying source of conflict between supervisors and their workers. Supervisors often act on what they believe are the causes of performance problems. This is only rational. But when the supervisor's perception significantly differs from the worker's, the difference can cause tension. Third, the cause affects the type of remedy selected; what is thought to be the cause of a performance problem determines what is done about it.

How can the process of determining the causes of performance problems be improved? A starting point is to consider the possible causes consciously and systematically. Traditionally, researchers believed that two primary factors, ability and motivation, determined performance.[72] A major problem with this view is that situational factors external to the worker, such as clarity of the task, quality of materials, and degree of management support, also affect worker performance.[73]

A more inclusive version of the causes of performance embraces three factors: ability, motivation, and situational factors. The *ability* factor reflects the worker's talents and skills, including characteristics such as intelligence, interpersonal skills, and job knowledge. *Motivation* can be affected by a number of external factors (such as rewards and punishments), but is ultimately an internal decision: It is up to the worker to determine how much effort to exert on any given task. **Situational factors** (or **system factors**) include a wide array of organizational characteristics that can positively or negatively influence performance. System constraints include poor quality of materials, poor supervision, and other factors listed in Figure 7.9.[74]

situational factors or system factors
A wide array of organizational characteristics that can positively or negatively influence performance.

Performance depends on all three factors. The presence of just one cause is not sufficient for high performance to occur; however, the absence or low value of one factor can result in poor performance. For example, making a strong effort will not result in high performance if the worker has neither the necessary job skills nor adequate support in the workplace. But if the worker doesn't put forth any effort, low performance is inevitable, no matter how good that worker's skills and how much support is provided.

In determining the causes of performance problems, managers should carefully consider situational factors. The factors in Figure 7.9 are only a starting point; they are too generic for use in some situations. Involving workers in generating examples of situational constraints can send a signal that managers are serious about considering workers' input. The supervisor and worker (or work team) can go over the list together to isolate the causes of any performance difficulties.

After the supervisor and the worker have discussed and agreed on the causes of performance problems, the next step is to take action to control them. Depending on whether the cause of performance problems is related to ability, effort, or situational characteristics, very different tactics are called for, as Figure 7.10 makes clear. Leaping to a remedy like training (a common reaction) will not fix a problem that is caused by poor effort and will be a waste of the organization's resources.[75]

FIGURE 7.9
Situational (System) Factors to Consider in Determining the Causes of Performance Problems

Situational factors

- Poor coordination of work activities among workers
- Inadequate information or instructions needed to perform a job
- Low-quality materials
- Lack of necessary equipment
- Inability to obtain raw materials, parts, or supplies
- Inadequate financial resources
- Poor supervision
- Uncooperative coworkers and/or poor relations among people
- Inadequate training
- Insufficient time to produce the quantity or quality of work required
- A poor work environment (for example, cold, hot, noisy, frequent interruptions)
- Equipment breakdown

Cause	Questions to Ask	Possible Remedies
Ability	Has the worker ever been able to perform adequately? Can others perform the job adequately, but not this worker?	Train Transfer Redesign job Terminate
Effort	Is the worker's performance level declining? Is performance lower on all tasks?	Clarify linkage between performance and rewards Recognize good performance
Situation	Is performance erratic? Are performance problems showing up in all workers, even those who have adequate supplies and equipment?	Streamline work process Clarify needs to suppliers Change suppliers Eliminate conflicting signals or demands Provide adequate tools

FIGURE 7.10

How to Determine and Remedy Performance Shortfalls

Sources: Based on Schermerhorn, J. R., Gardner, W. I., and Martin, T. N. (1990). Management dialogues: Turning on the marginal performer. *Organizational Dynamics, 18*, 47–59; Rummler, G. A. (1972). Human performance problems and their solutions. *Human Resource Management, 19*, 2–10; Cardy, R. L., and Leonard, B. (2011). *Performance management: Concepts, skills, and exercises* (2nd ed.). Armonk, NY: M. E. Sharpe, Inc.

Developing an Action Plan and Empowering Workers to Reach a Solution

Effective performance management requires empowering workers to improve their performance. As in a sports team, the supervisor-as-coach assists workers in interpreting and reacting to the work situation. The role is not necessarily one of mentor, friend, or counselor. Rather, it is that of enabler. The supervisor-as-coach works to ensure that the necessary resources are available to workers and helps employees identify an action plan to solve performance problems. For example, the supervisor may suggest ways for the worker to eliminate, avoid, or get around situational obstacles to performance. In addition to creating a supportive, empowered work environment, coach/supervisors clarify performance expectations; provide immediate feedback; and strive to eliminate unnecessary rules, procedures, and other constraints.[76]

Directing Communication at Performance

Communication between supervisor and worker is critical to effective performance management. Exactly what is communicated and how it is communicated can determine whether performance improves or declines. Although there is merit to providing positive feedback regarding a worker's strengths (see the Manager's Notebook, "Accentuate the Positive"), performance problems can't be ignored.

Performance discussions can be difficult for managers, and a worker may disagree that there is a performance issue and become emotional. For example, say that a manager tells an employee that her late arrivals and long lunches are affecting the performance of the office. Instead of understanding and promising to improve, the employee denies that there is a problem, claims that the manager is unfairly focusing on her small errors, and begins yelling at the manager. Handling this type of situation professionally is a key competency to being an effective manager. Unfortunately, these types of situations will occur during your management career.

A key question is how you will handle these situations. Following some simple steps can help keep the communication effective and focused on performance.[77] First, define the performance problem. If performance is to improve, understanding the performance issue is a necessary starting point. Second, make it a discussion. Performance improvement will be more likely to occur if there is a dialogue, rather than a one-sided lecture. Third, be plain and direct in communicating the performance issue. Although it might make you more comfortable to be vague and dance around the issue, focusing on the performance issue will move the discussion toward a clear plan of action. Last, and most important, maintain your composure. If you become emotional and say things out of anger or frustration, you will likely regret them later.

It is important that communication regarding performance be directed at the performance itself and not at the person. While it might be tempting to summarize a worker's behavior and tell the employee that she or he is, for example, unreliable or adversarial, these conclusions about person characteristics are not likely to be helpful. Even if these conclusions about a worker are correct, they have to do with personal characteristics and are not likely to be helpful in improving performance. The conclusions can be seen as personal attacks and can cause an employee to become defensive. Further, conclusions about personal characteristics may address aspects of someone's nature that can be difficult to change. For instance, it may be difficult for someone to become a more reliable person. However, it may be more doable for that person to hear feedback about the importance of arriving on time and meeting delivery targets and to control these work-related behaviors. Communication focused on performance, rather than the person, can be the more effective route to improving performance.

Summary and Conclusions

What Is Performance Appraisal?

Performance appraisal is the identification, measurement, and management of human performance in organizations. Appraisal should be a future-oriented activity that provides workers with useful feedback and coaches them to higher levels of performance. Appraisal can be used administratively or developmentally.

Identifying Performance Dimensions

Performance appraisal begins by identifying the dimensions of performance that determine effective job performance. Job analysis is the mechanism by which performance dimensions should be identified.

Measuring Performance

The methods used to measure employee performance can be classified in two ways: (1) whether the type of judgment called for is relative or absolute, and (2) whether the measure focuses on traits, behavior, or outcomes. Each measure has its advantages and disadvantages. But it is clear that the overall quality of ratings is much more a function of the rater's motivation and ability than of the type of instrument chosen.

Managers face five challenges in measuring performance: rater errors and bias, the influence of liking, organizational politics, whether to focus on the individual or the group, and legal issues (including discrimination and employment at will).

Managing Performance

The primary goal of any appraisal system is performance management. To manage and improve their employees' performance, managers must explore the causes of performance problems, develop action plans, empower workers to find solutions, and use performance-focused communication.

Key Terms

absolute judgment, 236
behavioral appraisal instrument, 238
comparability, 244
competencies, 235
competency model, 235
dimension, 234
frame-of-reference (FOR) training, 244
management by objectives (MBO), 240
outcome appraisal instrument, 240
peer review, 243
performance appraisal, 233
rater error, 244
relative judgment, 236
self-review, 243
situational factors or system factors, 252
subordinate review, 243
360° feedback, 243
trait appraisal instrument, 238

Watch It!

Hautelook: Appraising. If your instructor has assigned this, go to **mymanagementlab.com** to watch a video case and answer questions.

Discussion Questions

7-1. Organizations usually conduct appraisals for administrative and developmental purposes. Performance appraisals are used administratively whenever they are the basis for a decision about the employee's work conditions, including promotions, termination, and rewards. How would you go about framing a compelling argument for a company to introduce a formal version of performance appraisal? What is it about the process that could be beneficial to the organization?

7-2. It seems preferable to use objective performance data (such as productivity figures), when available, rather than subjective supervisory ratings to assess employees. Why might objective data be less effective performance measures than subjective ratings?

7-3. How important are rating formats to the quality of performance ratings? What is the most important influence on rating quality?

7-4. What is comparability? How can it be maximized in performance appraisal?

7-5. "Occasionally an employee comes along who needs to be reminded who the boss is, and the appraisal is an appropriate place for such a reminder." Would the manager quoted here be likely to use a rational or a political approach to appraisal? Contrast the rational and political approaches. To what extent is it possible to separate the two?

7-6. Do you think performance appraisal should be done? Is it worth the cost?

7-7. What criteria do you think should be used to measure team performance? What sources should be used for the appraisal? Should individual performance still be measured? Why or why not?

7-8. You own a small company and your income relies on four key sales personnel who have, for the fifth year in succession, increased sales by over 12 percent. Margins are the same as last year, but profit has fallen by 5 percent so you need to look elsewhere for the reasons behind the profit fall. Normally, you would reward all employees with a blanket increase in salaries on a percentage basis of 50 percent of the increase in profit. Following the profit results, this would mean a salary reduction of 2.5 percent. What situational factors do you need to look at in this year's appraisals before considering this?

7-9. Would you design a performance appraisal system based on behaviors, outcomes, or both? Why would you design it in this way?

7-10. Your company is considering using relative ratings for its performance appraisal system. Are there potential problems with a relative system? What type of rating system, relative or absolute, would you recommend and why?

MyManagementLab®

If your instructor has assigned this, go to **mymanagementlab.com** for the following Assisted-graded writing questions:

7-11. Your workers complain that they don't like the performance appraisal system since it seems like all they get is negative evaluations and feedback. What approach to performance feedback could reduce this problem? Describe how this approach would differ from the traditional approach of focusing on weaknesses.

7-12. Some people have argued that performance appraisal should not be done. Take the position that performance appraisal is useful and should be done. Describe three benefits of conducting performance appraisal.

7-13. A goal of performance management is to improve performance. Describe the factors that should be considered when diagnosing and improving performance.

 You Manage It! 1: Ethics/Social Responsibility

Rank and Yank: Legitimate Performance Improvement Tool or Ruthless and Unethical Management?

Forced ranking is a performance appraisal system popularized by Jack Welch when he was CEO of General Electric. It is a system that has been given the derogatory label of "rank and yank" by its critics. The intent of the forced-ranking system is to improve the performance level of an operation by getting rid of the bottom 10 percent of performers and hiring replacements who will perform at a high level. Ranking judgments can be made in a variety of ways. For example, a forced distribution can pre-assign a set percentage of employees that must be placed into categories such as "most effective," "average," and "needs improvement." Alternatively, a simple ranking of workers from best to worst can be used. Top performers may be rewarded and offered promotion or training. Low performers may be given a warning or terminated.

Forced ranking has been employed by a number of companies, but some legal challenges have been made. For example, Microsoft successfully defended several discrimination suits challenging its use of a forced-ranking system. Conoco used a forced-ranking system and reached an out-of-court settlement in a discrimination lawsuit. Ford Motor Company, Goodyear, and Sprint have all faced lawsuits relating to forced ranking systems.

The advantage of using the forced ranking approach is to regularly trim the lowest performers and thereby regularly raise the bar for performance and create a team of top performers. Unfortunately, the practice of forced ranking can have important disadvantages. The use of forced ranking can be detrimental to a collaborative culture, creating instead competitiveness among workers. If the bottom 10 percent of workers are terminated each year, the forced ranking system can also produce a lack of continuity in work teams. You could, for example, just be learning to work well as a team when some of them are replaced due to forced ranking. The pressure of forced ranking may also influence workers to focus on performance to the extent that ethical corners might be cut.

Critical Thinking Questions

7-14. Do you think forced ranking is a good performance management system? Why or why not?

7-15. Part of the forced-ranking label reflects the intent to force distinctions among worker performance levels. In an absolute-rating system, everyone could be rated "above average." Does this difference between the absolute- and relative-rating approaches mean that the absolute performance judgments are wrong? Explain.

7-16. As a manager, would you prefer to rely on an absolute performance rating system or a relative system, such as forced ranking? Why?

7-17. Can you devise an absolute-rating system that would guarantee differentiation among workers? Why or why not?

Team Exercise

7-18. As a team, address the effectiveness of the forced-ranking approach for improving the level of performance in an organization.

Address the following issues:

a. What is the logic of forced ranking? That is, on paper, why might you expect forced ranking to improve the performance level of your group?

b. The logic behind the forced-ranking approach is that performance in a workplace is normally distributed. Do you think this is an accurate assumption? Why or why not?

c. If performance in a workplace is not normally distributed (for example, maybe your organization has outstanding hiring and training programs that positively impact performance), do you think a forced-ranking approach would still improve the average level of performance in the organization? Explain.

Share your judgments on these issues with the rest of the class.

Experiential Exercise: Team

7-19. Proponents of forced ranking see the system as a means for a quick exchange of personnel in a way that lifts the average performance level of the organization. Critics see the approach as possibly damaging the culture and camaraderie in an organization and would prefer to keep people and develop their skills.

Select representatives as members of a pro or con forced-ranking team. Each team identifies its assumptions about how performance is distributed in the workplace. They will then offer reasons why they are for or against forced ranking. Some of the issues to be addressed include:

a. What is the expected impact of forced ranking on performance in an organization?

b. Turnover has costs associated with it (see Chapters 5 and 6). How would these costs affect your position?

c. What would be the impact of forced ranking on the organization's culture? What about the culture without the system?

d. Is it better to replace a poor performer or to try to develop and improve that worker?

In a debate-style format, each team makes its presentation of position and rationale and has the opportunity to question and rebut and rejoin the other team. The instructor moderates this process. At the end of the debate, the instructor leads the class in identifying the key reasons for and against the use of forced ranking. Is there a clear consensus in the class for or against this system?

Sources: Based on Amalfe, C. A., and Steiner, E. G. (2005). Forced ranking systems: Yesterday's legal target. *New Jersey Law Journal*; Hill, A. (2012, July 16). Forced ranking is a relic of an HR tool. *Financial Times*; Marchetti, M. (2005). Letting go of low performers. *Sales and Marketing Management, 157*, 6; Rajeev, P. N. (2012). Impact of forced ranking evaluation of performance on ethical choices: A study of proximal and distal mediators. *International Journal of Business Governance and Ethics*, *7*, 37–62; Scullen, S. E., Bergey, P. K., and Aiman-Smith, L. (2005). Forced distribution rating systems and the improvement of workforce potential: A baseline simulation. *Personnel Psychology*, *58*, 1–32.

You Manage It! 2: Global

Competencies in a Global Environment

As discussed in the Manager's Notebook, "Competencies in a Global Workplace," competencies can come from a variety of sources, including the job, the strategic direction of the organization, and the global nature of the business. Whatever the source, once competencies are identified, they typically become the key aspects measured in a performance appraisal system. For example, a competency for a salesperson's job would likely include customer service. The formal performance appraisal for this job might then include a customer service dimension and include, for example, behavioral standards, such as "salesperson greets customer" and "salesperson helps resolve customer complaints," on which salespeople are evaluated. In short, competencies become the criteria by which performance is measured.

Competencies should reflect what workers do on the job. For example, a job might include dealing with customers, putting together customer products, and expediting orders. Competencies associated with this type of job might include interpersonal skills, negotiation ability, problem solving, and organization skills. These competencies could then be illustrated and measured with observable reflections of these competencies, such as behaviors.

Competencies can reflect more than the core tasks that make up a job. As presented in the Manager's Notebook, "Competencies in a Global Workplace," competencies can be based on the strategic direction of an organization. For example, a manufacturing organization might commit to a strategy of customer service in order to have a competitive advantage in its industry. Engaging in customer service isn't how the company currently operates, and it isn't reflected in its current manufacturing jobs. However, customer service is a strategic target for the company. If it is going to reach this strategic target, customer service needs to be included as a competency and become part of how jobs are performed in the company.

Competencies can also reflect the global nature of business. The ability to recognize and deal with diverse values and cultures can be critical in today's global environment. Global businesses routinely confront diversity in culture and language. However, increases in minority and immigrant populations are forcing local organizations to adapt to culturally and linguistically diverse groups. Cultural competency is increasingly being recognized as an important capacity. Cultural competency means that you not only have knowledge of a culture, but that you also have the skills needed to work with that particular ethnic group and the attitude to do so effectively.

Many organizations would benefit from improvements in their cultural competency. Teamwork and productivity suffer if a diverse workforce lacks cultural competency. Further, a lack of cultural competency could negatively affect service and sales to customers.

Critical Thinking Questions

7-20. Is there a distinction between diversity and cultural competency, or are they the same thing? Explain.

7-21. Of the three sources of competencies discussed—job, strategy, and global factors—what is their relative importance? That is, how would you weigh each of the three categories of competencies? For example, should they all be weighted the same, or should the ability to perform the current tasks take precedence over strategically important competencies or cultural competency?

7-22. Do you think that cultural competency should be included as a core competency in most businesses? Why or why not?

Team Exercise

7-23. Join your team members to work on operationalizing cultural-competency criteria.

a. Specifically, start by identifying the dimensions of cultural competency. For example, if you think of cultural competency as a general duty or area of responsibility, what aspects make up that area? Perhaps communication is one dimension. In other words, part of cultural competency may be the capability to understand someone's language and to be able to effectively express yourself in that language. Understanding of a culture could be another aspect. Identify as many dimensions as you think are needed to capture the general concept of cultural competency.

b. Refer to this chapter's Appendix detailing the critical-incident technique. Using the Appendix as a guide, generate behavioral examples for each of the cultural-competency dimensions your team identified (see step 2 in the Appendix). These "critical incidents" should describe both good and poor levels of each cultural competency dimension.

Share your team's dimensions and behavioral examples with the rest of the class.

c. Can a common or core set of dimensions be identified? As a class, address the issue of the utility of these dimensions and the behavioral incidents. Specifically, what could they be used for?

Experiential Exercise: Team

7-24. Select representatives as members of a pro or con cultural-competency team. Each team identifies a rationale for their position. This rationale can include, but should not be limited by, the following aspects:

a. What is the impetus behind the push for cultural competency?

b. What role does cultural competency have in business?

c. If it is a competency, should it be measured? How?

d. What about the bottom line? Can a positive return on an investment be expected?

In a debate-style format, each team makes its presentation of position and rationale and has the opportunity to question and rebut and rejoin the other team. The instructor moderates this process. At the end of the debate, the instructor leads the class in identifying the key reasons for and against the use of cultural-competency in performance appraisal. Is there a clear consensus in the class for or against this performance measure?

You Manage It! 3: Technology/Social Media

Going Digital with Appraisal

Many managers avoid performance appraisals because the task makes them uncomfortable. Some managers may not do a very good job of appraising the performance levels of their workers. A growing number of companies are now offering technology that promises to solve these difficulties.

A number of software programs can make the rating task a paperless process. Further, some performance review software even automates improvement suggestions. As presented in the chapter-opening illustration involving George using technology to appraise the performance of Estelle, clicking a score on a performance dimension could automatically generate the text of a performance review. A below-average score could generate text that identifies the performance as deficient and recommends steps that the employee should take to improve performance.

Depending on the vendor, electronic performance review systems can use generic goals and competencies as evaluation criteria or they can be customized so that organizationally specific goals and competencies are used. The software can report the extent to which an employee has contributed to the goals of the organization.

Critical Thinking Questions

7-25. Place yourself in the position of an employee receiving a performance review. Would it matter to you whether your performance review, the narrative description of your performance levels, and suggestions for improvement were generated by computer or by your manager? Why?

7-26. From the perspective of a manager, what advantages might be associated with taking an electronic approach to reviewing the workers' performance levels? List these advantages into two categories: rational and political. The rational category is for advantages such as the speed with which the appraisal task could be completed. The political category is for advantages such as being able to blame the computer software for a poor performance review that a worker is not happy with.

7-27. What rational and political disadvantages are associated with the use of electronic performance review?

7-28. Given your answers to the previous questions, would you recommend the use of electronic performance reviews? Justify your position.

Team Exercise

7-29. A number of companies offer software for reviewing worker performance. Some offer technology that can be installed on computers within an organization. Others offer Web-based services.

As a team, identify a couple of companies that offer electronic performance review technology. (Some company names you will likely run across in a computer search include Halogen, Workscape, and PerformanceReview.com.) For each company selected by your team, describe the performance review service that is provided.

a. What claims do the vendors make with regard to the benefits their services provide?
b. If possible, determine the typical cost associated with the use of the technology for a small or medium-sized firm. Estimate the per-employee cost of the electronic approach. Given your cost figures, do you think purchasing electronic review technology is something you would recommend to a small or medium-sized firm? Share your findings and conclusions with the rest of the class.

Experiential Exercise: Team

7-30. As discussed in the Manager's Notebook, "From Performance Appraisal to Performance Management," social media is being used in some organizations as a tool to support performance. As a team, consider the possible roles for performance appraisal software, social media, and face-to-face performance reviews. Does each serve a purpose?

a. An organization has asked for a recommendation from your team regarding how they should measure and manage employee performance. Consider yourselves a team of consultants and make recommendations regarding how they should measure and manage employee performance.
b. Also make recommendations regarding the use of appraisal software, social media, and face-to-face review. Should all three be used, or should only one or two be relied on? Why? For what purposes should each be used? Share your recommendations with the rest of the class.

Experiential Exercise: Individual

7-31. Develop a set of criteria for judging the effectiveness of performance appraisal. For example, are the evaluation and feedback likely to be accepted? Will performance appraisal be useful? Will it improve performance? Does it support an organizational goal of coaching and developing employees? Given your criteria, evaluate the use of appraisal software, social media, and face-to-face performance review meetings.

Present a summary of your criteria and evaluations to your class. Share your recommendations regarding the use of the three approaches.

 You Manage It! 4: Ethics/Social Responsibility

Let's Do It Right

In any business, an employee's unethical behavior can set a bad example for other workers and be a negative influence on the culture in the business. For example, a worker taking extended breaks or recording hours that weren't worked can cause inequity and friction with other workers. If unchecked, the unethical behavior can become the norm and prompt others to behave in the same way. Without clear and concrete norms and accountability, employees may be unclear about ethical expectations and may be swayed by the unethical behaviors of some employees. Actions such as inaccurate reporting of time worked and taking of supplies can become crippling costs in organizations.

Of course, you want to hire workers who aren't likely to engage in these unethical behaviors. Once workers are hired, however, it may not be enough to simply tell them that you expect them to be ethical. The employees may view this expectation as a great concept but may be unclear as to how to operationalize it in their jobs. Just what, for example, does being ethical mean for my job of janitor, secretary, clerk, and so on? Including ethical performance in the appraisal system is a way to make clear to employees that how they reach business goals is equally as important as reaching them in the first place.

Critical Thinking Questions

7-32. Place yourself in the position of a manager. Describe situations when ethical performance appraisal for your employees would be useful.

7-33. Are there disadvantages to a focus on ethics in performance appraisal? Describe.

7-34. How should a manager develop an appraisal system that measures ethical performance? Identify the steps.

Team Exercises

7-35. Reread the Manager's Notebook, "Make Ethics Part of Appraisal." As a team, use the dimensions and behavioral examples in the notebook as starting points.

a. Select a business and generate dimensions and behavioral examples for the setting. In addition to developing a measure of ethical performance, what else can be done with the dimensions and behavioral examples generated by your team?

b. Generate an example of the ethical appraisal instrument that your team would recommend for use in the business. Share your example with the rest of the class.

Experiential Exercise: Team

7-36. As a team, consider the ethical issues and the practical problems for an organization that runs peer assessment and appraisal as the main form of employee appraisal. They do incorporate a degree of management observation in the appraisal decision making process, but that is very much an add-on and an overview of the situation. In many cases, the departments are sufficiently large, and managers only have some knowledge about employees they have direct day-to-day contact with, hence the development of the peer system. The peers assess team members online using an assessment based on a four-dimensional model of collaboration, communication, self-management, and decision making. Feedback reports are used as a discussion point to improve the functioning of teams. Over time, there has been significant improvement in the average level of ratings given to team members. Choose a team member to present your team's assessment to the class. Following the presentation of other teams' assessment, engage in a class discussion and debate. Identify a comprehensive assessment of the ethical and practical issues and a conclusion as to whether this form of performance appraisal is workable as an alternative to more traditional options.

Experiential Exercise: Individual

7-37. After completing the team experiential exercise, individually reflect on the class resolution or vote. If business outcomes were considered the priority among your fellow future managers, how does this bode for the importance of ethics in organizations in the future? If ethics was the priority, how realistic do you think this position is in today's business environment? Summarize your assessment in a reflection paper to hand into your instructor or to share with the class.

 You Manage It! 5: Customer-Driven HR

Build on Their Strengths

People bring different strengths and weaknesses to the workplace. Some of these strengths and weaknesses are the result of fairly fixed characteristics. For example, one person may be very methodical and follow steps in a project in a prescribed manner. However, another person might approach issues in a more free-form manner. The first person might excel at following detailed procedures, but not do well at finding novel and innovative approaches to work issues. Of course, the second person would be much stronger in terms of innovating, but struggle with detailed steps that need to be closely followed. To the extent that the weak areas for each person are due to weaknesses that the person might not be able to change, what good would it do to focus on these weak areas?

The strength-based approach to performance appraisal, discussed in the Manager's Notebook, "Accentuate the Positive," recognizes the above issue and encourages managers to focus on positive feedback. The core ideas of focusing on strengths are that people want to contribute and that receiving evaluations and feedback that recognize their positive contributions can motivate workers. On the other hand, providing negative assessments can lead a worker to become defensive and less motivated.

Critical Thinking Questions

7-38. Not everyone can be good at everything about a job. Providing only positive performance feedback can give workers inaccurate pictures off their performance. What are the disadvantages of this inaccuracy?

7-39. Motivating workers is an important goal for managers. Do you think that providing feedback on strengths helps accomplish this goal? Identify other purposes for performance appraisal. How well does a strength-based approach meet with those purposes?

7-40. If a worker has some weak areas that affect how well they perform aspects of a job, the traditional approach would be to provide evaluation and feedback to the worker to try to improve those deficiencies. How else could those deficiencies be improved?

Team Exercise

7-41. Workers often share the same formal job title and set of tasks that need to be done. The practical reality in many organizations is that workers gravitate to particular tasks that they perform well. What is one formal job that can informally be made up of people playing different roles?

With your teammates, assess the practice of people taking on different roles. From the strengths-based performance appraisal approach, would people engaging in various roles—rather than one consistent job performed by all workers—be a positive or negative way of structuring work? Why or why not? Share your assessment and rationale with the rest of the class.

Experiential Exercise: Team

7-42. As a team, you want to reconfigure an appraisal system and incorporate aspects of ability, effort, and situational factors. Frame a series of questions that would focus on:

a. Has the worker ever been able to perform adequately? Can others perform the job adequately, but not this worker?

b. Is the worker's performance level declining? Is performance lower on all tasks?

c. Is performance erratic? Are performance problems showing up in all workers, even those who have adequate supplies and equipment?

How would you assess the questions that you propose to pose? What remedies would you propose? Each team should take on the role of consultants and provide a draft version of the performance appraisal questions and how to interpret them to your instructor.

Endnotes

Scan for Endnotes or go to http://www.pearsonglobaleditions.com/Gomez-Mejia.

The Critical-Incident Technique: A Method for Developing a Behaviorally Based Appraisal Instrument

The critical-incident technique (CIT) is one of many types of job-analysis procedures. The CIT is often used because it produces behavioral statements that make explicit to an employee what is required and to a rater what the basis for an evaluation should be.

CIT Steps

The following steps are involved in a complete CIT procedure:

1. *Identify the major dimensions of job performance* This can be done by asking a group of raters and ratees to brainstorm and generate dimensions relevant to job performance. Each person lists, say, three dimensions. The group members then combine their lists and eliminate redundancies.
2. *Generate "critical incidents" of performance* For each dimension, the group members should list as many incidents as they can think of that represent effective, average, and ineffective performance levels. Each person should think back over the past 6 to 12 months for examples of performance-related behaviors that they have witnessed. Each incident should include the surrounding circumstances or situation.

   If you are having trouble generating incidents, you might want to think of the following situation: Suppose someone said that person A, who you feel is the most effective person in the job, is a poor performer. What incidents of person A's behavior would you cite to change the critic's opinion?

   Try to make sure that the incidents you list are observable *behaviors* and not *personality characteristics* (traits).
3. *Double-check that the incidents represent one dimension* This step is called *retranslation.* Here you are trying to make sure there is clear agreement on which incidents represent which performance dimension. If there is substantial disagreement among group members, this incident may need to be clarified. Alternatively, another dimension may need to be added or some dimensions may need to be merged.

   In the retranslation process, each person in the group is asked to indicate what dimension each incident represents. If everyone agrees, the group moves on to the next incident. Any incidents on which there is disagreement are put to the side for further examination at the end of the process. At that time they may be discarded or rewritten.
4. *Assign effectiveness to each incident* Effectiveness values are assigned to all the incidents that survived retranslation. How much is incident "A" worth in our organization, on, say, an effectiveness scale of 1 (unacceptable) to 7 (excellent)? All group members should rate each incident. If there is substantial disagreement regarding the value of a certain behavior, that behavior should be discarded.

Note: Disagreement on incident values indicates differences in evaluative standards or lack of clarity in organizational policy. Disagreement regarding evaluative standards can be a fundamental problem in appraisal. The CIT procedure can help to reduce these differences.

The chart on the following page shows some CIT worksheets for you to try your hand at. The dimensions included are a subset of those generated in a research project conducted for a hospital that wanted a common evaluation tool for all non-nursing employees.*

The jobs covered ranged from floor sweeper and clerical worker to laboratory technician and social worker. Of course, the behavioral standards for each dimension differed across jobs—an excellent floor sweeper behavior would not be the same as an excellent lab technician behavior. The dimensions included in the worksheets appear fairly generic, though, and are probably applicable to jobs in most organizations. You may want to develop more specific dimensions or other dimensions altogether.

Remember, after generating incidents, your group should determine agreement levels for the dimension and value for each incident. An easy way to do this is for one person to recite an incident and have everyone respond with dimension and value. This process could be informal and verbal or formal and written.

*Goodale, J. G., and Burke, R. J. (1975). Behaviorally based rating scales need not be job specific. *Journal of Applied Psychology, 60,* 389–391.

Critical Incidents Worksheet
Job Title:
Job Dimension: Knowledge of Job—Understanding of the position held and the job's policies, techniques, rules, materials, and manual skills.

Instructions: Provide at least one behavioral statement for each performance level.

1. Needs improvement:
2. Satisfactory:
3. Excellent:
4. Outstanding:

Critical Incidents Worksheet
Job Title:
Job Dimension: Initiative—The enthusiasm to get things done, energy exerted, willingness to accept and perform responsibilities and assignments; seeks better ways to achieve results.

Instructions: Provide at least one behavioral statement for each performance level.

1. Needs improvement:
2. Satisfactory:
3. Excellent:
4. Outstanding:

Critical Incidents Worksheet
Job Title:
Job Dimension: Personal Relations—Attitude and response to supervision, relationships with coworkers, flexibility in working as part of the organization.

Instructions: Provide at least one behavioral statement for each performance level.

1. Needs improvement:
2. Satisfactory:
3. Excellent:
4. Outstanding:

Critical Incidents Worksheet
Job Title:
Job Dimension: Dependability—Attention to responsibility without supervision, meeting of deadlines.

Instructions: Provide at least one behavioral statement for each performance level.

1. Needs improvement:
2. Satisfactory:
3. Excellent:
4. Outstanding:

CHAPTER

8

Training the Workforce

MyManagementLab®

✪ When you see this icon, visit **www.mymanagementlab.com** for activities that are applied, personalized, and offer immediate feedback.

CHALLENGES

After reading this chapter, you should be able to deal more effectively with the following challenges:

1 **Have** familiarity with key training issues.

2 **Become** aware of training versus development.

3 **Recognize** challenges in training.

4 **Learn** practices for managing the training process.

5 **Become** aware of a special case: orientation and socialization.

Jim was hired as a unit manager, and he was happy to be in his first management position. He also felt very fortunate to have a new administrative assistant, Suzy, who was very good at her job and a great asset to Jim. Suzy had been hired shortly after Jim arrived because the previous staff person had retired.

Jim was discussing some work issues with Suzy when she asked him a question he didn't anticipate. Suzy wanted to know why Jim hadn't recommended her for any of the recent training sessions being offered to staff. Jim didn't see any problems with Suzy's job performance and couldn't understand why she thought she needed training. Nonetheless, he asked her what training session she might be interested in. Her response was vague, but she mentioned that maybe one of the sessions on teamwork or on interpersonal skills could be interesting. He told her he didn't think she had issues in those areas. Suzy thanked him for the compliment but said that there was always room for improvement.

Source: © aleksandar kamasi/Fotolia.

Jim was confused over this exchange and informally checked with some other unit managers who had been in their management positions awhile. Jim learned that the staff was accustomed to being recommended for training as a reward for good performance. Going to a training session was a way for staff to spend a few hours, or maybe a half day, away from the office. The training was usually kept pretty fun and upbeat and included coffee and snacks. The staff had a chance to network at these training sessions, and Jim had noticed that staff members getting together to walk to the training locations was also part of the social function. Jim also learned from a long-time manager that the staff members kept informal track of who regularly attended training and made judgments about who was performing their jobs well according to who got to go to the most training.

Overall, what Jim found out was that training had become a reward and was an indicator of social status for the staff. By not sending Suzy to training, Jim had been inadvertently sending the message that he wasn't too happy with Suzy's performance. Of course, Suzy knew that wasn't the case, but it looked like that to her fellow staff members. Suzy was getting uncomfortable with not being in attendance at any training sessions and with having her peers conclude that her boss didn't think enough of her to let her be included in these sessions.

Jim made the commitment to himself to recommend Suzy for training at the next opportunity. He knew Suzy would be happy with his decision.

After Jim had recommended Suzy for a couple of training sessions, he opened up a message from the corporate office. The note indicated that HR would be conducting a survey on employee training that would include an assessment of staff training needs and would look at the return on investment in the current training program. Jim hoped that this assessment didn't reflect badly on him as a manager; but the truth was that his staff person didn't really need training, and he wondered how a positive return on investment could be found if training, by and large, wasn't really addressing a performance problem.

The Managerial Perspective

The preceding illustration involving Jim recommending Suzy for training is based on the training program in a real organization. Rationally, training should be focused on improving performance by making sure everyone knows the correct way of doing their jobs. The reality, however, is that sometimes training serves other purposes. Training is not, however, cost-free. Training costs include, for example, the cost of developing the training; the cost of materials and delivery of the training; and, sometimes most important, the cost of employees being away from their jobs to attend training. If the training is done well and addresses a performance need in the organization, then these employee training costs won't be an expense but rather an investment that should return improved performance. As a manager, you will want your staff to have the best skills and the broadest understanding of the organization and its customers. This chapter examines key training issues and the training process, identifies the major types of training available, and explores how to evaluate the effectiveness of training.

✪ Learn It!

If your professor has chosen to assign this go to **www.mymanagementlab.com** to see what you should particularly focus on, and take the chapter 8 warmup.

Key Training Issues

Some of the important training issues facing today's organizations are presented as follows:

- *How can training keep pace with a changing organizational environment?* Many training topics are provided online. As products, sales procedures, and equipment change, online content can be easily created or changed and disseminated to employees. However, does this flexibility come with a cost of poorer learning or application on the job?
- *Should training take place in a classroom setting or on the job?* Classroom training may lack realism and not be as effective as training that occurs while on the job. However, on-the-job training can cause slowdowns that decrease production or irritate customers.
- *How can training be effectively delivered worldwide?* Many of today's organizations conduct operations around the world. Consistent quality of products or service is critical to organizational survival in today's competitive markets. Providing training content online is an efficient way to distribute information. However, learning advanced skills or interpersonal skills may

require an approach that incorporates both classroom time and face-to-face interaction. The cost of bringing employees to one central training location could become a costly proposition as a firm expands geographically. An option for a widely dispersed firm could be to offer hands-on training on a regional basis, such that face-to-face training takes place at various regional centers.

- ***How can training be delivered so that trainees are motivated to learn?*** Lectures and workbooks may have outstanding content but will be ineffective if they do not engage the trainees or motivate them to learn. A key to motivating trainees is to make sure that what they are learning is for them and their jobs. When employees are sent to training, they should be able to see how the content of the training is related to performance of their jobs. If this relevance link isn't there, employees can't be expected to be motivated to learn the content. Similarly, consider how motivated you are to learn course material when you don't see how the content is relevant to you. In addition to relevance, making training a fun and active experience can be positive for the motivation levels of trainees. Incorporating activities that get people involved, such as team exercises, and including humor can improve trainees' motivation to learn the material.

In this chapter, we distinguish between training and development. Then we discuss the major challenges managers face in trying to improve workers' performance through training. Next we offer some suggestions on managing the three phases of the training process, explore selected types of training, and consider ways to maximize and evaluate training effectiveness. We close with a section on what is arguably the most important training opportunity: the orientation of new employees.

Training Versus Development

Although training is often used in conjunction with development, the terms are not synonymous. **Training** typically focuses on providing employees with specific skills or helping them correct deficiencies in their performance.[1] For example, new equipment may require workers to learn new ways of doing the job or a worker may have a deficient understanding of a work process. In both cases, training can be used to correct the skill deficit. In contrast, **development** (the subject of Chapter 9) is an effort to provide employees with the abilities the organization will need in the future.

training
The process of providing employees with specific skills or helping them correct deficiencies in their performance.

development
An effort to provide employees with the abilities the organization will need in the future.

Figure 8.1 summarizes the differences between training and development. In training, the focus is solely on the current job; in development, the focus is on both the current job and jobs that employees will hold in the future. The scope of training is on individual employees, whereas the scope of development is on the entire work group or organization. That is, training is job specific and addresses particular performance deficits or problems. In contrast, development is concerned with the workforce's skills and versatility.[2] Training tends to focus on immediate organizational needs and development tends to focus on long-term requirements. The goal of training is a fairly quick improvement in workers' performance, whereas the goal of development is the overall enrichment of the organization's human resources. Training strongly influences present performance levels, whereas development pays off in terms of more capable and flexible human resources in the long run.

FIGURE 8.1
Training Versus Development

	Training	Development
Focus	Current job	Current and future jobs
Scope	Individual employees	Work group or organization
Time Frame	Immediate	Long term
Goal	Fix current skill deficit	Prepare for future work demands

Source: Orada Jusatayanond/Alamy.

Keep in mind one other distinction between training and development: Training can have a negative connotation. Although being sent to training can be a reward, as in the training program described in the opening of this chapter, when training is focused on removing performance deficiencies, being selected for training can be a negative. Who, after all, wants to be considered deficient? People might appreciate an opportunity for development but resent being scheduled for training.[3] Employees may view their selection for training as a negative and embarrassing message rather than an improvement opportunity.

Changing negative perceptions of training can be difficult. To help engender more positive attitudes toward training, a company can focus on the improvement potential offered through training rather than on correction of skill deficits. In other words, the "training" is portrayed as development. Although this tactic muddies the distinction between training and development, the two terms are often used interchangeably in practice. Given the rapid rate of change in many workplaces, training is becoming a necessity. Some organizations are turning to technology as a means to deliver needed training and are changing the nature of training from removing deficiencies to providing support. This approach can provide training in a timely fashion and holds promise for improving any negative attitudes toward training. This evolving approach to training is discussed in the Manager's Notebook, "From Removing Deficiencies to Improving Capability: The Changing Nature of Training."

MANAGER'S NOTEBOOK

Technology/Social Media

From Removing Deficiencies to Improving Capability: The Changing Nature of Training

Many of today's organizations face unprecedented change. Changes in competition, customer preferences, machinery, and software can translate into workers having to confront new processes in their jobs. Learning new ways to perform a job requires training, and the dynamic nature of many of today's workplaces means that there is a great need for training.

The traditional approach to a change in a work process would be to deliver training on the new procedure. The company could avoid performance problems by making sure that the steps for the new way of performing the task were clearly covered in the training. Performance deficiencies could be avoided by delivering training to everyone who would be affected by the change in the work process. This traditional approach would typically consist of structured sessions, either offered in face-to-face classes or electronically delivered. The traditional approach assumes that workers repeatedly perform certain tasks and that the best way of carrying out these tasks can be specified. If that is the case, then it makes sense to take the traditional approach and roll out the necessary training so that people have the knowledge they need to perform the new or changed task. But what if changes are coming so fast that you can't reasonably keep up using the typical structured training approach? Or what if it is difficult to anticipate just what situations workers might encounter in the future? These practical realities are leading some companies to explore the use of technology as means to deliver training in a different way.

Social media provides a means for people to learn "on-the-fly" what they need to use in order to solve issues and perform adequately. Instructional videos that can be found on YouTube can provide a means for employees to learn a process or to refresh their memory for how a task should be performed. Social media, such as Facebook or Twitter, or internally developed software, can be used by employees to improve performance. For example, Sabre

Holdings, the company that owns Travelocity, created a system called SabreTown[a] that is a virtual community for its thousands of employees. Sabre employees create a profile that reflects their skills and job experience. Questions that an employee might ask about a problem or job situation are directed by the software to fellow employees who have relevant knowledge and experience.

The use of social media connects people so that they can solve work-related issues. This use of technology can also change the focus of training from removing deficits to assisting employees in their jobs. The social media approach means that this help can happen any time it is needed by an employee. In dynamic work situations where training needs may be difficult to specify, social media can be an effective training tool.

[a]Galagan, P. (2009). Letting dgo. *T & D, 63*, 26–28.

Sources: Based on Dachner, A. M., Saxton, B.M., Noe, R. A., and Keeton, K. E. (2013). To infinity and beyond: Using a narrative approach to identify training needs for unknown and dynamic situations. *Human Resource Development Quarterly*, *24*, 239–267; Lassk, F. G., Ingram, T. N., Kraus, F., and Mascio, R. D. (2012). *Journal of Personal Selling and Sales Management*, *32*, 141–154; Thomas, K. J., and Akdere, M. (2013, January 31). Social media as collaborative media in workplace learning. *Human Resources Development Review*, available at *http://hrd.sagepub.com/content/early/2013/01/29/1534484312472233l.* ■■

Challenges in Training

The training process brings with it a number of questions that managers must answer. These are:

- Is training the solution to the problem?
- Are the goals of training clear and realistic?
- Is training a good investment?
- Will the training work?

Is Training the Solution?

A fundamental objective of training is the elimination or improvement of performance problems. However, not all performance problems call for training. Performance deficits can have several causes, many of which are beyond the worker's control and would, therefore, not be affected by training.[4] For example, the effects of unclear or conflicting requests, morale problems, and poor-quality materials cannot be improved through training.

Are the Goals Clear and Realistic?

To be successful, a training program must have clearly stated and realistic goals. These goals will guide the program's content and determine the criteria by which its effectiveness will be judged. For example, management cannot realistically expect that one training session will make everyone a computer expert. Such an expectation guarantees failure because the goal is unattainable.

Unless the goals are clearly articulated before training programs are set up, the organization is likely to find itself training employees for the wrong reasons and toward the wrong ends. For example, if the goal is to improve specific skills, the training needs to be targeted to those skill areas. In contrast, the company's training goal may be to provide employees with a broader understanding of the organization.

A QUESTION OF ETHICS

Some companies reimburse the educational expenses of employees who take classes on their own. In an era when people can count less and less on a single employer to provide them with work over the course of their careers, do you think employers have a responsibility to encourage their employees to pursue educational opportunities?

Is Training a Good Investment?

The economic climate has been challenging and organizational budgets can be strained. Nonetheless, many organizations fervently believe in the importance of training. Although training can be expensive, it can also pay off in more capable and loyal workers. An international survey of more than 5,000 organizations in 26 countries examined the relationship between firms' investments in training and their profitability.[5] A key finding of the survey was that the greater the investment in employee training, the more profitable the firm. Interestingly, the study statistically controlled for past profitability. Thus, the relationship between training and profitability does not appear to be due to firms with more profitable histories having more dollars to put into training. Rather, the findings indicate that training is a good investment that can have a bottom-line payoff. We can't conclude from the survey findings that training caused the higher profitability, but an emphasis on training certainly differentiates more profitable firms from less profitable ones. Training also appears to be positively related to the stock price of an organization.[6] Organizations that expend more on training their employees have been found subsequently to have a higher stock value. A direct interpretation of this finding is that training results in better performance that is recognized by the market. It is also possible that organizations that put more resources into training employees take a longer-term view of building value, and this approach is valued in the stock market. Whatever the causal paths, it appears that investments in training can pay off in bottom-line results.

It isn't really the cost, per se, that should be the important issue as much as the effectiveness of the investment. In some cases, training may be appropriate but not cost-effective. Before beginning a training program, managers must weigh the cost of the current problem against the cost of training needed to eliminate it.

Not conducting training can be a costly choice. A federal appeals court upheld a judgment against an employer because it failed to train its managers in the basic requirements of discrimination law. Phillips Chevrolet Inc. was found guilty of age discrimination. A general manager who had ultimate hiring authority admitted that he often considered the age of applicants when making hiring decisions and that he wasn't aware that it was an illegal practice. The courts stated that the failure of the organization to train its managers in the basics of discrimination law was an "extraordinary mistake" and justified the conclusion that the company was recklessly indifferent to antidiscrimination law.[7] The court awarded $50,000 in punitive damages. The cost of training these managers in discrimination law was little relative to the cost levied against the company for not providing that training. Sometimes a company may be legally obligated by the state to invest in training. For example, a California law requires all supervisors in companies with more than 50 employees to receive two hours of interactive preventive sexual harassment training every two years.[8]

Determining whether training is a good investment requires measuring the training's potential benefits in dollars. Training that focuses on "hard" areas (such as the running and adjustment of machines) that have a fairly direct impact on outcomes (such as productivity) can often be easily translated into a dollar value. Estimating the economic benefits of training in "softer" areas—such as teamwork and diversity training—is much more challenging. However, demonstrating the value of a training investment is important, particularly when budgets are tight. It is estimated that only approximately 7 percent of organizations calculate the dollar return on the costs of their training programs.[9] Although it cannot provide a financial estimate, assessing whether trainees apply the new skills and knowledge covered in training when back on the job can be an important indicator of the effectiveness of that training. However, it is estimated that only 9 percent of organizations assess the extent to which training impacts job performance.[10] Although evaluation may be lacking, the best companies try to maximize return on their training investment by aligning their training with their mission, strategy, and goals.[11] However, only an analysis of costs and benefits will indicate whether a training investment, no matter how well planned and positioned, was worth it or is worth continuing.

Will Training Work?

Designing effective training remains as much an art as a science, because no single type of training has proved most effective overall. For example, an organizational culture that supports change, learning, and improvement can be as much a determinant of a training program's effectiveness as any aspect of the program itself. Participants who view training solely as a day away from work, as in the chapter-opening example, are unlikely to benefit much from the experience. In addition to the role of participants in determining the effectiveness of training, managers of trainees need to endorse the content and purpose of training in order for the training program to have a positive influence on work processes.

Finally, training will not work unless it is related to organizational goals. A well-designed training program flows from the company's strategic goals; a poorly designed one has no relationship to—or even worse, is at cross-purposes with—those goals. It is the manager's responsibility to ensure that training is linked with organizational goals.

Managing the Training Process

Poor, inappropriate, or inadequate training can be a source of frustration for everyone involved. To maximize the benefits of training, managers must closely monitor the training process.

As Figure 8.2 shows, the formal training process consists of three phases: (1) needs assessment, (2) development and conduct of training, and (3) evaluation. The *needs assessment phase* involves identifying the problems or needs that the training must address. In the *development and conduct phase*, the most appropriate type of training is designed and offered to the workforce. In the *evaluation phase*, the training program's effectiveness is assessed. In the pages that follow, we provide recommendations for maximizing the effectiveness of each of these phases.

In large organizations, surveys of workers and input of managers can be important for determining what training is needed (phase 1), but the actual training (phase 2) is usually provided by either the organization's own training department or an external resource (such as a consulting firm or a local university). After the training program is complete, managers may become involved to determine whether it has been useful (phase 3). In small businesses, the manager may be responsible for the entire process, although external sources of training may still be used.

The Needs Assessment Phase

The overall purpose of the needs assessment phase is to determine whether training is needed, and if so, to provide the information required to design the training program. Needs assessment consists of three levels of analysis: organizational, task, and person.

THE LEVELS OF NEEDS ASSESSMENT *Organizational analysis* examines broad factors such as the organization's culture, mission, business climate, long- and short-term goals, and structure. Its purpose is to identify both overall organizational needs and the level of support for training. Some of the key issues to be addressed at the organizational level of analysis are the external environment and the organization's goals and values.[12] An analysis of the external environment may indicate a shortage of skilled workers and changes in technology. Training can help the organization to meet these challenges. The goals of an organization are the targets it is trying to achieve—perhaps increased market share or expansion into a new market. Training may be needed to give employees the skills to achieve the organizational goals. Similarly, values can be the core of how an organization operates. Employees should understand these values and have the skills to work within them. In sum, the organizational level of needs assessment looks at external influences and the direction and principles of the organization to determine whether training is needed.

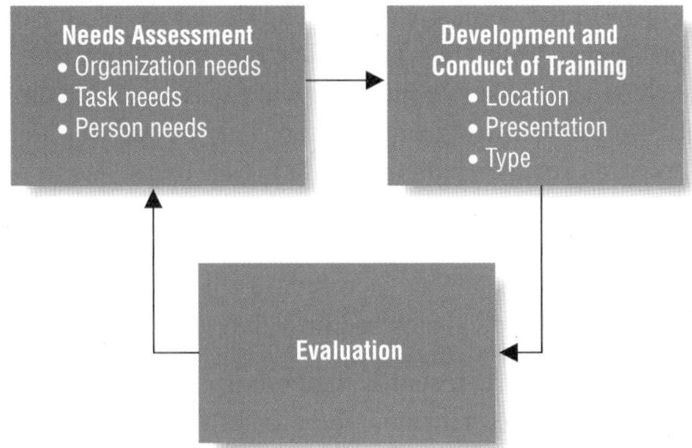

FIGURE 8.2
The Training Process

Source: bikeriderlondon/Shutterstock.

Task analysis is an examination of the job to be performed. A recent and carefully conducted job analysis should provide all the information needed to understand job requirements. These duties and tasks are used to identify the knowledge, skills, and abilities (KSAs) required to perform the job adequately (see Chapter 2). The KSAs are then used to determine the kinds of training needed for the job.

Person analysis determines which employees need training by examining how well employees are carrying out the tasks that make up their jobs.[13] Training is often necessary when there is a discrepancy between a worker's performance and the organization's expectations or standards. Often a person analysis entails examining worker performance ratings and then identifying individual workers or groups of workers who are weak in certain skills. The source of most performance ratings is the supervisor, but (as we saw in Chapter 7) a more complete picture of workers' strengths and weaknesses may be obtained by including other sources of appraisal.

As we noted in Chapter 7, performance problems can come from numerous sources, many of which would not be affected by training. The only performance problem that training can address is a deficiency that is under the trainee's control.[14] For example, sales training will improve sales only if poor sales techniques are the source of the problem. If declining sales are due to a poor product, high prices, or a faltering economy, sales training is not going to help.

Training is not the only option available for responding to a worker deficiency. For example, if decision makers determine that the training needed would be too costly, transferring or terminating the deficient workers may be the more cost-effective course. Strict KSA requirements can then be used to select new employees and eliminate the performance gap. The obvious drawbacks of terminating or replacing employees deemed deficient are that these options are likely to harm commitment and morale in the workforce.

Training needs are an important consideration whenever employees are assigned new tasks. The importance of assessing training needs is heightened when the new tasks involve international assignments that can be expensive and strategically important to the organization. The Manager's Notebook, "Expatriate Assignments and Training Needs," identifies some important factors that should be taken into account when determining the training needs for workers given international assignments.

MANAGER'S NOTEBOOK

Global

Expatriate Assignments and Training Needs

Expatriates, employees assigned to work in other countries, can determine whether a firm's international efforts succeed or fail. Expatriates who might control operations in the foreign location transfer knowledge and play other important roles. Obviously, it is important that employees given international assignments have the needed competencies, and training may be needed. What has been less recognized is that training may also be needed to help the transition when the employee returns to the domestic operation. The return of an expatriate to their home country is called repatriation. Difficulties in making this transition back to the home country have resulted in employees with valuable international experience deciding to leave their organizations. As illustrated in the following figure, there may be training needs that an employee faces in order to be prepared for the transition to being an expatriate as well as to prepare for repatriation.

As a manager, there are three basic categories to consider when looking at possible training needs for expatriates and repatriates: (1) the country, (2) the job, and (3) the worker. In the following, we consider each of these categories and how they may prompt training needs.

- *Country characteristics* How different is the country from the one where the employee currently resides? In terms of expatriates, the greater the difference between their home country and the country to which they are being assigned, the more there can be a

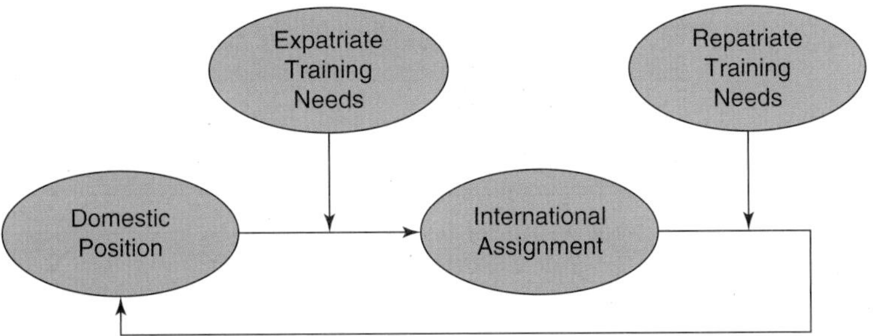

training need. For example, is a different language spoken in the foreign location and is the employee conversant in that language? Is there a large difference between the countries in terms of values, customs, and practices? Is the employee aware of and comfortable with these differences? The answers to these and similar questions can indicate whether cross-cultural training might be needed for expatriates. However, these types of issues can also apply to repatriation. If, for example, a foreign assignment has been long term and the person was immersed in a very different culture, training that sensitizes the employee to the cultural differences when she or he returns home can make for a smoother transition.

- ***Job characteristics*** Characteristics of the international assignment can have training implications. The international assignment may pose challenges such as difficulty in obtaining supplies, the quality of the materials, and how smoothly the work process operates. At repatriation time, the nature of the job that the employee will be taking on could also call for training. Repatriates sometimes return to jobs that are different from the one they left. Providing job training to repatriates can help refresh their competencies and provide information on any changes.
- ***Worker characteristics*** The worker's competencies can have obvious implications for training needs. If the expatriate doesn't have a competency needed to adequately perform the foreign assignment, there is an obvious training need. Similarly, lack of a competency to perform the job at repatriation time is a training need. In addition to having the competency to perform the jobs, another important worker characteristic is adaptability.

Overall, training may be needed for both expatriates and repatriates. In addition to addressing potential deficits, offering training to expatriates and repatriates provides support to workers when they may need it to successful make these transitions. In addition to the content of the training, it can be important to these employees to know that there is support from their organization to make the needed adjustments.

Sources: Based on Cox, P. L., Khan, R. H., and Armani K. A. (2012). Repatriate adjustment and turnover: The role of expectations and perceptions. *Global Conference on Business and Finance Proceedings*, *7*, 431–443; Lee, L. Y., and Croker, R. (2008). A contingency model to promote the effectiveness of expatriate training. *Industrial Management & Data Systems*, *106*, 1187–1205; Nery-Kjerfve, T., and McLean, G. N. (2012). Repatriation of expatriate employees, knowledge transfer, and organizational learning. *European Journal of Training and Development*, *36*, 614–629. ■■

Clarifying the Objectives of Training

The objectives for a training program should be based on the assessment phase. Each objective should relate to one or more of the KSAs identified in the task analysis and should be challenging, precise, achievable, and understood by all.[15] It only makes good business sense for organizations to focus training on the competencies that have been identified as being important to the job.

Whenever possible, objectives should be stated in behavioral terms and the criteria for judging the training program's effectiveness should flow directly from the behavioral objectives. Suppose the cause of a performance deficiency is poor customer service. The overall objective of the training program designed to solve this problem, then, would be to improve customer service.

FIGURE 8.3
Example of Development of Behavioral Training Objectives

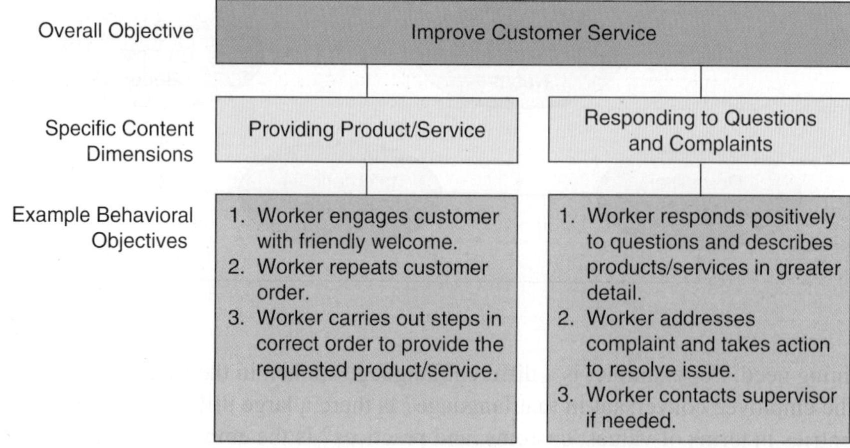

Although "improving customer service" is a noble training goal, the term is ambiguous and does not lead to specific content for a training program or to specific criteria by which the training's effectiveness can be judged. Stating this objective in behavioral terms requires determining what an employee will know, do, and not do after training.

Figure 8.3 shows how the overall objective of improving customer service provides a starting point that can be broken down into dimensions (specific aspects of job performance) for which managers can develop specific behavioral goals. The overall objective reflected in the figure is to improve customer service. This overall objective then is divided into the job tasks that are relevant to customer service. In the case of our example, there are two relevant job areas: providing the product/service and responding to questions and complaints. Then specific behaviors that are part of these dimensions are identified, both to guide the training effort and to help evaluate whether the training has been successful.

The Training and Conduct Phase

The training program that results from assessment should be a direct response to an organizational problem or need. Training approaches vary by location, presentation, and type.

LOCATION OPTIONS Training can be carried out either on the job or off the job. In the very common *on-the-job training (OJT)* approach, the trainee works in the actual work setting, usually under the guidance of an experienced worker, supervisor, or trainer. OJT provides hands-on experience that is based on the actual job. If more experienced employees provide guidance, the OJT can also help the new worker to be part of the social network in the workplace. For example, on-the-job training is a focus at Brady Ware, a CPA firm in the Midwest.[16] The firm has determined that its young accountants must quickly and thoroughly learn through hands-on experience that is guided by an experienced accountant. In addition to improved learning and performance, the guided on-the-job training approach helps build relationships between the experienced and newer accountants, which can help develop loyalty in the new employees.

Job rotation, apprenticeships, and internships are all forms of OJT.

- *Job rotation*, as we saw in Chapter 2, allows employees to gain experience in different kinds of narrowly defined jobs in the organization. It is often used to give future managers a broad background.
- *Apprenticeships*, OJT programs typically associated with the skilled trades, derive from the medieval practice of having the young apprentice learn a trade from an experienced worker. In Europe, apprenticeships are still one of the major ways for young men and women to gain entry to skilled jobs. In the United States, apprenticeships are largely confined to adults wanting to work in certain occupations, such as carpentry and plumbing. These apprenticeships generally last four years, and the apprentice's pay starts at about half that of the more experienced "journeymen" workers.

- Just as apprenticeships are a route to certain skilled blue-collar jobs, *internships* are a route to white-collar or managerial jobs in a variety of fields. Internships are opportunities for students to gain real-world job experience, often during summer vacations from school (see Chapter 2 for further discussion of internships). Although many internships offer low pay, student interns can often gain college credits and, possibly, the offer of a full-time job after graduation.

OJT has both benefits and drawbacks. This type of training is obviously relevant to the job because the tasks confronted and learned are generated by the job itself. Very little that is learned in the context of OJT would not transfer directly to the job. OJT also spares the organization the expense of taking employees out of the work environment for training. On the negative side, OJT can prove quite costly to the organization in lost business when on-the-job trainees cause customer frustration. (Have you ever been caught in a checkout line that moves like molasses because a trainee is operating the cash register?) Even if only a handful of customers switch to a competitor because of dissatisfaction with trainee service, the cost to the organization can be substantial. Errors and damage to equipment that occur when a trainee is on the job may also prove costly. Another potential drawback is that trainers might be top-notch in terms of their skills but inadequate at transferring their knowledge to others. In other words, those who can, cannot always teach.

Finally, the quality and content of OJT can vary substantially across organizations. This variability makes it difficult for employers to judge the skill level of a potential worker from another organization. A new worker may claim that he or she received OJT for operating a piece of machinery or conducting a task, but the employer can be left wondering what the worker really learned and what skill level she or he brings to the operation.

Consider how the woodworking industry is trying to relieve the problem of variability of OJT. The woodworking industry is developing national standards for worker skills. The intent of the development of these skills standards is to have the ability to train, test, and score employees using a common set of standards for woodworking skills. The effort began with wood manufacturers in the state of Washington performing a task analysis (see "The Needs Assessment Phase" in this chapter) to identify the skills needed by woodworkers. The goal of the national woodworking standards project is a credentialing process for workers who demonstrate that they meet the skills criteria. The existence of a common set of skills standards will assure both employers and employees that they have the skills needed to effectively and safely operate woodworking machinery. Without a common set of standards, assessment of skills can differ across employers and can be assumed based on past experience. Thus, without common standards, a worker who has developed efficient, but unsafe, work habits at a previous employer could be assumed to be a skilled and desirable woodworker by another employer. The project has resulted in the development of standards and a set of evaluators that are now in place to evaluate the skills levels of woodworkers in the use of common tools and machines.[17]

Off-the-job training is an effective alternative to OJT. Common examples of off-the-job training are formal courses, simulations, and role-playing exercises in a classroom setting. One advantage of off-the-job training is that it gives employees extended periods of uninterrupted study. Another is that a classroom setting may be more conducive to learning and retention because it avoids the distractions and interruptions that commonly occur in an OJT environment. The big disadvantage of off-the-job training is that what is learned may not transfer back to the job. After all, a classroom is not the workplace, and the situations simulated in the training may not closely match those encountered on the job. Also, if employees view off-the-job training as an opportunity to enjoy some time away from work, as was illustrated in the opening of this chapter, not much learning is likely to take place.

PRESENTATION OPTIONS Trainers use a variety of presentation techniques in training sessions. The most common presentation techniques are slides and videotapes, teletraining, computers, simulations, virtual reality, classroom instruction, and role-plays.

Slides and Videotapes Slides and videotapes can be used either off-the-job or in special media rooms in an organization's facility. Slides and videotapes provide consistent information and, if done well, can be interesting and thought provoking. However, these presentation media do not allow trainees to ask questions or receive further explanation. Many companies prefer to use slides, film, or tapes to supplement a program led by a trainer, who can answer individuals' questions and flesh out explanations when necessary.

Teletraining A training option that can be useful when trainees are dispersed across various physical locations is teletraining.[18] Satellites are used to beam live training broadcasts to employees at different locations. In addition to the video reception, the satellite link can allow trainees to ask questions of the instructor during the broadcast.

Two disadvantages of teletraining are the need for an expensive satellite connection and the difficulty of scheduling the broadcast so that everyone will be able to attend. A company can solve the scheduling problem by videotaping the presentation and then offering the videotape to people in locations where schedules conflicted with the live broadcast. The training instructor can be available via phone or computer to respond to questions. This method makes the trainer's expertise available to trainees without requiring him or her to redeliver the entire training program. The reality is that Web-based technology, such as web conferencing, can be a more attractive choice for delivering training when people are geographically dispersed.

Computers Computer-based training can range from the use of a CD-ROM to training over the Internet. A number of companies are still exploring what type of computer-based training works best for them. However, Web-based training is fast becoming the training method of choice.

Both small and large businesses are finding computer-based training to be a cost-effective medium. In particular, if a job requires extensive use of computers, then computer-based training is highly job related and provides for a high degree of transfer of training back to the job. Computers also have the advantage of allowing trainees to learn at a comfortable pace. As a trainer, the computer never becomes tired, bored, or short-tempered. Further, computers can be a multimedia training option in which text can be combined with film, graphics, and audio components.

Using the Internet or company intranet for training, e-learning has been increasing in popularity for obvious reasons. This approach not only offers the content but also administers the training. E-learning also offers a way to standardize training across far-flung employees and centers of operation.[19] Perhaps the most apparent reason is the elimination of travel and lodging costs. A general estimate is that companies can reduce their training costs by 50 to 70 percent by using electronic courses rather than traditional classroom-style training.[20] Because individuals can access training at any time and from any place where an Internet connection is available, it is not surprising that e-learning is a success story at many organizations.

Although e-learning offers cost savings and convenience over traditional face-to-face training, most organizations have found that e-learning is most effective when it is combined with other forms of training.[21] Simply having online training content available doesn't mean that it will be learned and influence performance in the organization. Likewise, having sophisticated technology to deliver training can't be expected to be effective if the content being delivered is poor.

simulation
A device or situation that replicates job demands at an off-the-job site.

Simulations Particularly effective in training are **simulations**, devices or situations that replicate job demands at an off-the-job site. Organizations often use simulations when the information to be mastered is complex, the equipment used on the job is expensive, and/or the cost of a wrong decision is high. The performance of jobs in the military, law enforcement, and security can sometimes mean life or death. Simulations can be particularly effective at safely training people to handle these situations. Firearms Training Systems Inc. (FATS) provides simulation training for military organizations around the world.[22] The training includes simulated weapons that realistically portray the real things, including recoil. A FATS simulation for training police officers uses a computer and a 10-foot video screen to confront police officers-in-training with the sights and sounds of a number of situations commonly encountered in police work. For example, a dangerous suspect is fleeing on a crowded street. Should the officer shoot at the suspect and risk injuring or killing innocent bystanders? The FATS system offers a variety of scenarios for police-officer training, ranging from domestic violence situations to dealing with agitated people with weapons.[23] Simulation systems, such as FATS, give police trainees the opportunity to practice making such snap decisions in a safe but realistic setting.

The airline industry has long used simulators to train pilots. Flight simulations often include motion in addition to visual and auditory realism. This aspect substantially increases the cost of the simulation but makes the training even more realistic. The NASA Ames Research Center has, for example, developed a virtual control tower simulator with a price tag of approximately $10 million. Viewers can see any airport in the world outside the control tower's 12 glass windows in a 360-degree view. The tower can simulate any time of day or night, any weather pattern, and the movement of up to 200 aircraft and ground vehicles.

Traditionally, simulators have been considered separate from computer-based training. With advances in multimedia technology, however, the distinctions between these two methods have blurred considerably.

A product called CathSim is an example of the melding of computerized and simulator types of training. The CathSim AccuTouch System gives medical personnel the chance to practice giving shots before giving them to a real patient. The training system combines computer software with tactile-feel robotics so that students, nurses, and doctors can get a realistic experience without practicing on animals or humans.[24] In addition, the CathSim provides trainees with report cards on their effectiveness and allows supervisors to track trainees' progress.

The CathSim works with a PC and includes a small robotic box, called the AccuTouch, which is about the size of a paperback book. A computer program allows users to select from a variety of options, such as whether the patient is an elderly woman or a drug user. The program then presents on screen a number of materials and needle sizes to choose from. After that, the trainee inserts a real needle into the AccuTouch box. The box has a rubber-like substance and mimics resistance and other factors of a real patient's arm. If the needle is inserted improperly, the computer program may yell "ow" in response. Immersion Medical, the company responsible for CathSim, provides a similar simulation with touch feedback so that surgeons can improve their suturing and knot-tying skills.[25]

Research supports the effectiveness of simulation training. For example, one study found that pilots who trained on simulators become proficient at flight maneuvers nearly twice as fast as pilots who trained only in the air.[26] The importance of this difference is underscored by the fact that the cost of simulator training is only about 10 percent of the cost of using the real equipment to train pilots. In a very different domain, simulation training for call-center operators was found to have the greatest impact on performance.[27]

Virtual Reality **Virtual reality (VR)** uses a number of technologies to replicate the entire real-life working environment rather than just several aspects of it, as do simulations. VR immerses a participant in a computer-generated virtual environment that changes according to head and body movements.[28] Within these three-dimensional environments, a user can interact with and manipulate objects in real time.

virtual reality (VR)
The use of a number of technologies to replicate the entire real-life working environment in real time.

The military uses VR training and continues to invest in the technology. Immersing soldiers in the types of situations they may face on the battlefield can provide valuable experience and can help them to be better prepared for combat. Additionally, VR may provide a stress inoculation for military personnel and lower their chances of developing psychological problems when placed in actual combat.[29]

Virtual reality technology is also being used to help maintain military equipment. The 3D software developer NGRAIN helped to develop a virtual reality system used by the Canadian military to maintain its C130 Hercules aircraft.[30] With the virtual system, a technician can generate a 3D view of the engine of the aircraft and focus on subsystems. A technician can also view a quick demonstration of a maintenance task and rehearse the procedure before actually performing it. The virtual system eliminates the time and difficulty of going through lengthy manuals, because everything is presented through the computer system. The Canadian military has also found that students complete maintenance training more quickly with the virtual-training approach than with the traditional book-based method.

Tasks that are good candidates for VR training are those that require rehearsal and practice, working from a remote location, or visualizing objects and processes that are not usually accessible. VR training is also excellent for tasks in which there is a high potential for damage to equipment or danger to individuals.

For example, VR training is becoming the method of choice for training physicians in how to implant carotid stents—devices that hold open the carotid arteries.[31] In the VR training, physicians thread a catheter through an artificial circulatory system and view angiograms of the human mannequin. The improved skills were obtained without putting individuals at risk.

Classroom Instruction and Role-Plays Although widely viewed as "boring," classroom instruction can be exciting if other presentation techniques are integrated with the lecture. For example, a video could complement the discussion by providing realistic examples of the lecture material. In-class case exercises and role-plays (both of which are found throughout this book) provide an opportunity for trainees to apply what is being taught in the class and transfer that knowledge back to the job. Solving and discussing case problems helps trainees learn technical material and content, and role-plays are an excellent way of applying the interpersonal skills being emphasized in the training. If done well, role-plays give trainees the opportunity to practice the skills they've been studying via books, video, computer, or some other medium.[32]

TYPES OF TRAINING We focus here on the types of training that are commonly used in today's organizations: skills, retraining, cross-functional, team, creativity, literacy, diversity, crisis, and customer service.

Skills Training Skills training is probably the most common in organizations. The process is fairly simple: The need or deficit is identified via a thorough assessment. Specific training objectives are generated, and training content is developed to achieve those objectives. The criteria for assessing the training's effectiveness are also based on the objectives identified in the assessment phase.

Skills training is often approached as a separate task that provides the needed knowledge to employees. The reality is that specifics and steps are sometimes forgotten. What can be helpful for employees trying to apply the training back on their jobs is a means of reminding them of key information or steps. A performance support system[33] is an electronic means for employees to quickly access information that can help them quickly determine the correct step or process to follow. A performance support system can supplement the skills learned in a training program and provide employees with a way to remind themselves of specifics that they may have forgotten since the training was delivered. At a more simple and low-tech level, trainees can be provided with materials such as pamphlets and reference guides to ensure that the training results in improved performance. These sorts of materials, **job aids**, are external sources of information that workers can access quickly when they need help in making a decision or performing a specific task.[34]

job aids
External sources of information, such as pamphlets and reference guides, that workers can access quickly when they need help in making a decision or performing a specific task.

A performance support system or job aids offer the advantage of reducing errors and increasing efficiency by allowing workers to quickly access key information instead of memorizing details. Although performance support systems and job aids can't replace training, they can be an effective supplement to help ensure that the training transfers back to the job. Job aids, in particular, offer a relatively inexpensive approach that can be developed and delivered quickly.

Retraining A subset of skills training, *retraining* gives employees the skills they need to keep pace with their job's changing requirements. For instance, however proficient garment workers may be at a traditional skill such as sewing, they will need retraining when the company invests in computerized sewing equipment. Unfortunately, even though retraining is much cited in the media as an item at the top of the corporate agenda, many companies rush to upgrade their equipment without taking comparable steps to upgrade their employees' skills. They erroneously believe that automation means a lower-skilled workforce when, in fact, it often requires a more highly skilled one.

Unfortunately, retraining efforts are not always as effective as hoped. Over 4,000 workers in North Carolina lost their jobs when Pillotex, a textile manufacturer, closed its doors.[35] However, after five years less than half of those workers had sought retraining. The Pillowtex example makes clear that retraining can only be effective if people take advantage of it. In addition, even if pursued, retraining doesn't work for everyone. Despite the retraining, some people will not be able to find jobs. Of course, not being able to find a job may not be the fault of the retraining; it could be due to general economic conditions or a worker's unwillingness to move to take a new job, among other factors.

Cross-Functional Training Traditionally, organizations have developed specialized work functions and detailed job descriptions. However, today's organizations are emphasizing versatility rather than specialization.

Cross-functional training teaches employees to perform operations in areas other than their assigned job. Cross-training offers value to employers because it makes current workers more versatile, and this flexibility can be more efficient than hiring new workers. For employees, cross-training can add variety to their work and can be a welcome break from doing the same thing over and over again.

cross-functional training
Training employees to perform operations in areas other than their assigned job.

A job rotation program can be a useful way to expose workers to other areas of an operation and allow them to learn new responsibilities in another area. **Peer trainers** can also be useful in developing needed skills. A peer trainer can provide instruction and model tasks for workers who are being cross-trained into the peer's area. If the cross-trained positions require unique or additional knowledge, then a formal training program, such as a blended approach of e-learning with hands-on experience, may be the most efficient means to provide the cross-functional training.

peer trainers
High-performing workers who double as internal on-the-job trainers.

For cross-training to work effectively, managers need to know what skills each area of an operation requires and which employees have those skills. In large operations, software can be used to assess workers and to store skill data. However, it is instructive to see how a smaller operation has handled cross-training. Auto-Valve, Inc. is an aviation valve manufacturer in Ohio with about 40 employees.[36] The operations manager realized that it was difficult to complete daily tasks when a worker was absent. The manager then developed a spreadsheet of the necessary job functions (150 of them) and rated each one according to how critical it was to the organization. The manager then offered cross-training (a mixture of electronically available information and hands-on experience), starting with the most critical functions. Auto-Valve now has at least three people who can perform each job function, and an electronic list identifies those employees who can perform the functions of a missing worker. Skills assessment and the development of a training plan are now annual events for each employee. Daily operations are now carried out more smoothly due to the flexibility provided by the cross-training. Further, the operations manager reports that employee turnover has decreased, perhaps due to the variety and challenge offered by the cross-training.

Team Training Teams have become a common fixture in organizations, with many operations involving empowered teams of workers. Team structure can be effective, but team-level issues, such as communication and trust, can be stumbling blocks and stop teams from reaching their full potential. Thus, just as with individuals, teams can be in need of training.

Team training can be divided into two areas based on the two basic team operations: content tasks and group processes.[37] *Content tasks* directly relate to a team's goals—for example, cost control and problem solving. *Group processes* pertain to the way members function as a team—for example, how team members behave toward one another, how they resolve conflicts, and how extensively they participate. Unlike traditional individual training, team training goes beyond the content skills and includes group processes.[38]

One innovative approach involves moving work teams into the kitchen as a means to improve team processes.[39] Culinary team-building programs can be competitive and involve recipe competitions between teams. Or, they can be designed as collaborative efforts, such as when teams need to work together to prepare a multicourse meal. One culinary team-building company assigns teams various dishes to prepare and culinary coaches provide basic instructions. The teams are given 30 minutes to prepare their dish, but after 25 minutes everyone is told to stop and move to the next station on the left! At the new station, no one knows what to do. The team-building company has seen a wide array of responses to this problem, ranging from teams just walking away from their stations to teams leaving one person behind to help the new group through the recipe. The exercise focuses on how teams can better communicate to support each other and improve overall performance. This lesson is certainly pertinent to the workplace, where dynamic changes and unanticipated problems may be encountered at any time.

The reality in many organizations is that teams often involve members who do not regularly interact in a face-to-face fashion. These "virtual teams" involve members from around the country or the globe who are collaborating on common tasks or goals. Virtual teams allow organizations to capitalize on the diverse skills and backgrounds of workers, no matter where they are physically located. Virtual team members can communicate using technologies such as e-mail, teleconferencing, and videoconferencing, among other options. These means of communication can eliminate the cost of travel involved in bringing people together for face-to-face meetings. Although reduced expenses can be an important benefit, the virtual nature of these teams can present difficulties. For example, the teams might experience difficulties in communication, cultural differences, technological problems, and lack of trust when team members do not know each other.

Some organizations have been proactive in trying to reduce these barriers to the effective operation of virtual teams.[40] For example, Sabre Inc. holds team-building sessions with new virtual teams that are focused on setting team objectives, clarifying roles, and building team identity.

A survey of virtual team practices in organizations identified a common set of recommended virtual team training topics:[41]

- Initial face-to-face team-building session
- Use of technology
- Communication
- Team management

An initial face-to-face physical meeting can help to build trust among team members and help establish team norms and the team's mission. In terms of use of technology, training may be needed to ensure that all virtual team members can use any relevant software and teleconference or videoconference technology. Training in communication could address cultural sensitivity, electronic etiquette, and decision-making processes when people are geographically dispersed. Team management training can help virtual team members to define team members' roles, determine how to resolve conflicts, and create a method to track the team's progress.

Creativity Training Creativity training is based on the assumption that creativity can be learned. There are several approaches to teaching creativity, all of which attempt to help people solve problems in new ways.[42] One common approach is the use of **brainstorming**, in which participants are given the opportunity to generate ideas as wild as they can come up with, without fear of judgment. Only after a good number of ideas have been generated are they individually submitted to rational judgment in terms of their cost and feasibility. Creativity is generally viewed as having two phases: imaginative and practical.[43] Brainstorming followed by rational consideration of the options it produces satisfies both phases. Figure 8.4 presents some other approaches to increasing creativity.

brainstorming
A creativity training technique in which participants are given the opportunity to generate ideas openly, without fear of judgment.

Critics of creativity training argue that its effectiveness is hard to measure and that any effects are short-lived. Although the effectiveness of creativity training continues to be debated,[44] there can be little doubt that poor management support can negate any impact of creativity training.

Literacy Training The abilities to write, speak, and work well with others are critical in today's business environment. Unfortunately, many workers do not meet employer requirements in these areas. U.S. companies spend more the $3 billion annually for remedial training for employees.[45]

Creativity can be learned and developed. The following techniques can be used to improve a trainee's skill in generating innovative ideas and solutions to problems.

1. **Analogies and Metaphors** Drawing comparisons or finding similarities can improve insight into a situation or problem.
2. **Free Association** Freely associating words to describe a problem can lead to unexpected solutions.
3. **Personal Analogy** Trying to see oneself as the problem can lead to fresh perspectives and, possibly, effective solutions.
4. **Mind Mapping** Generating topics and drawing lines to represent the relationships among them can help to identify all the issues and their linkages.

FIGURE 8.4
Techniques to Increase Creativity

Source: Based on Higgins, J. M. (1994). *101 creative problem solving techniques: The handbook of new ideas for business.* Winter Park, FL: New Management Publishing Company.

The term **literacy** is generally used to mean the mastery of *basic skills*—that is, the subjects normally taught in public schools (reading, writing, arithmetic, and their uses in problem solving). It is important to distinguish between general literacy and functional literacy. *General literacy* is a person's general skill level, whereas *functional literacy* is a person's skill level in a particular content area. An employee is functionally literate if he or she can read and write well enough to perform important job duties (reading instruction manuals, understanding safety messages, filling out order slips). The most pressing issue for employers is not the general deficiencies in the workforce, but rather their workers' ability to function effectively in their jobs. For example, a generally low level of reading ability may be cause for societal concern, but it is workers' inability to understand safety messages or fill out order slips that is the immediate concern for business. Functional illiteracy can be a serious impediment to an organization's productivity and competitiveness. For instance, the Occupational Safety and Health Administration (see Chapter 16) believes that there is a direct correlation between illiteracy and some workplace accidents.

literacy
The mastery of basic skills (reading, writing, arithmetic, and their uses in problem solving).

Functional literacy training programs focus on the basic skills required to perform a job adequately and capitalize on most workers' motivation to get help or advance in a particular job. These programs use materials drawn directly from the job. For example, unlike a reading comprehension course (which teaches general reading skills), functional training teaches employees to comprehend manuals and other reading materials they must use on the job.

Different approaches can be taken to literacy training. A company can, for example, offer its own in-house literacy training program. McDonald's, for example, offers a variety of e-learning opportunities for its employees, including a literacy module.[46] Another option for conducting literacy training is for a firm to partner with a local school to provide the needed literacy training. Whatever the approach, providing training to bring employees up to acceptable functional literacy levels is a concern of and a cost to employers. A survey of over 700 organizations in England found that the majority reported concerns about the literacy levels of new employees. However, the majority of the employers also felt that it should be up to the government to address literacy problems.[47]

A QUESTION OF ETHICS
Are companies ethically responsible for providing literacy training for workers who lack basic skills? Why or why not?

Diversity Training Ensuring that the diverse groups of people working in a company get along and cooperate is vital to organizational success. As we saw in Chapter 4, *diversity training programs* are designed to teach employees about specific cultural and sex differences and how to respond to these in the workplace. Diversity training is particularly important when team structures are used. To be successful, it must include and be sensitive to all groups, including white males who may perceive that the training is directed at or against them.[48] Diversity training that focuses on individual strengths and weaknesses rather than on differences between groups can be a positive experience for all employees. Making the link between diversity and the business is also important. For example, effective organizations are moving their diversity training beyond debunking stereotypes to the need to engage employees from diverse backgrounds.[49] Kodak includes training for all its employees that addresses the importance of diversity for its business.[50] (See Chapter 4 for additional information about diversity training.)

Crisis Training Unfortunately, accidents, disasters, and violence are part of life. Events such as plane crashes, chemical spills, and workplace violence can wreak havoc on organizations. Yet many organizations are ill prepared to deal with these tragedies and their aftermath. Consider the criticism leveled against the Federal Emergency Management Agency (FEMA) for its response to the devastation of the New Orleans area due to Hurricane Katrina. The agency was accused of delay and inadequacy and the agency director resigned amid criticisms of how the catastrophe was managed.

In addition to after-the-fact crisis management, *crisis training* can focus on prevention. For example, organizations are becoming increasingly aware of the possibility of workplace violence, such as attacks by disgruntled former employees or violence against spouses. Prevention training often includes seminars on stress management, conflict resolution, and team building.[51]

Ethics Training Due to widely publicized ethical breaches at organizations such as Enron, WorldCom, and Tyco, ethics in business has taken on increased importance. Although ethical guidelines can be helpful, ethics training can clarify the policies and help employees apply them to their everyday work. According to a survey of HR professionals, approximately one-third of organizations offer ethics training.[52] If there is to be a meaningful effect, it is important that ethics training make the translation from company's guidelines or principles to actual on-the-job behavior. Creating an ethical and productive workplace environment means that people need to be equipped to deal with unethical behavior when they encounter it. The Manager's Notebook, "That's Not Right: Training to Help Workers Confront Unethical Actions," looks at how training can help give workers the skills they need to challenge unethical situations.

MANAGER'S NOTEBOOK

Ethics/Social Responsibility

That's Not Right: Training to Help Workers Confront Unethical Actions

Despite the best efforts of an organization, unethical practices will occur. The unethical behavior could take many forms, such as cutting corners by engaging in unsafe work practices, bullying and intimidating others, or stealing from the employer. For example, bullying behaviors at work (e.g., name calling, false allegations, and taking undue credit) are all too common, with one survey finding 62 percent of respondents reporting that they had experienced bullying at work. Bullying and other unethical behaviors can have a negative impact on workers. If the offensive behavior continues, employee satisfaction and productivity can suffer. Sometimes incidents of unethical behavior are not reported because workers are concerned about possible negative repercussions, particularly if the offender is in a superior position to them in the organization. Helping to provide workers with skills to challenge unethical actions can help eliminate offending behaviors and can send a clear signal to workers that the organization is taking a strong, proactive stance on ethics.

Training that focuses on recognizing unethical behavior and, most import, addresses how to challenge such behaviors can be helpful for workers. For example, covering communication techniques and exploring how to challenge inappropriate behavior effectively can improve skills and raise awareness. However, understanding and improved communication skills can still leave workers lacking the confidence to actually challenge someone who is engaged in unethical behavior, such as bullying others. Providing opportunities to practice challenging unacceptable behavior can be effective. For example, using role plays that incorporate how to challenge an offender and feedback on performance can improve both skill and confidence levels.

Sources: Based on Sexton, T. L. (2009). Beating the bullies. *Intheblack, 79,* 58; Wells, A., Swain, D., and Fieldhouse, L. (2010). How support staff can be helped to challenge unacceptable practice. *Nursing Management, 16*, 24–27; Kurtz, L., and Kucsan, R. (2009). Using scenario training to handle difficult employees *T&D, 63,* 28–30. ■■

Customer Service Training Organizations are increasingly recognizing the importance of meeting customers' expectations. In addition to establishing philosophies, standards, and systems that support customer service, many companies are turning to customer service training to give employees the skills they need to meet and exceed customer expectations. Customer-service skills, particularly for frontline workers, can determine the very survival of a business. Better customer-service skills can impact the business by influencing sales and customer loyalty. In addition to improving customer service, customer service training for frontline workers also appears to improve employee job satisfaction and retention.[53] Helping frontline workers to develop the skills to do their jobs may not only improve how well they perform their jobs, but may make for happier and potentially more loyal workers. The goal of customer service training is, of course, to improve customer service. In order to achieve that goal, it can be important to look at how a product or service is provided to a customer from the perspective of the customer. An organization might, for example, emphasize the speed at which it can deliver a product or service and train employees to maximize efficiency and speed. However, if its customers are more interested in the quality of the product or service and how it is presented, the company, despite trying very hard, could miss the mark. The Manager's Notebook, "Customer-Based Training," considers employee training from the customer perspective.

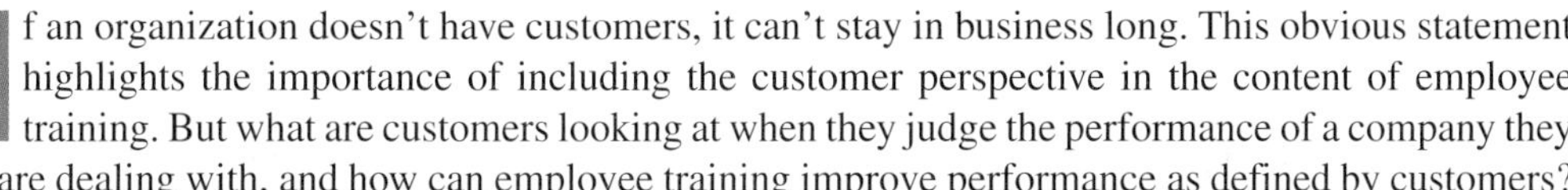

Customer-Driven HR

Customer-Based Training

If an organization doesn't have customers, it can't stay in business long. This obvious statement highlights the importance of including the customer perspective in the content of employee training. But what are customers looking at when they judge the performance of a company they are dealing with, and how can employee training improve performance as defined by customers?

Research with customers has found that how a service interaction is carried out is an important determinant of how the customer evaluates the performance. For example, how friendly and helpful a worker was could be a critical factor in how a customer assesses the experience of interacting with the company. The tasks could have been performed adequately, but customers are likely also considering how the process of providing the product or service was carried out. When looking at performance from the customer's perspective, interpersonal aspects could be just as important as more technical aspects of a product or service.

To be effective, employee training needs to go beyond simply telling workers that how they interact with customers is important. Concrete examples of successes and failures from customers can be very helpful for directing employees toward improved customer service. Customer-provided incidents of good and poor performance can be the basis for training that meaningfully improves customer service. For example, the incidents could be used to develop role-plays so that employees can practice dealing with the various issues and concerns brought by customers. Because customers are the source of the content of the training, the efforts at improvement would result in improvements from the customer perspective.

Sources: Based on Groth, M., and Grandey, A. (2012). From bad to worse: Negative exchange spirals in employee-customer service interactions. *Organizational Psychology Review*, *2*, 208–233; Johnson, L. (2012). Using the critical incident technique to assess gaming customer satisfaction. *UNLV Gaming Research & Review Journal*, *6*, 1–12; Turel, O., Connelly, C. E., and Fisk, G. M. (2013). Service with an e-smile: Employee authenticity and customer use of web-based support services. *Information & Management*, *50*, 98–104; Verhoef, P. C., and Lemon K. N. (2013). Successful customer value management: Key lessons and emerging trends. *European Management Journal*, *31*, 1–15; Victorino, L. and Bollinger, A. R. (2012). Scripting employees: An exploratory analysis of customer perceptions. *Cornell Hospitality Quarterly*, *53*, 196–206. ■■

The Evaluation Phase

In the evaluation phase of the training process, the effectiveness of the training program is assessed. Companies might measure effectiveness in monetary or nonmonetary terms. Whatever the terms, the training should be judged on how well it addressed the needs it was designed to meet. For example, it would make sense for a business to evaluate a training program designed to increase workers' efficiency by assessing its effects on productivity or costs, but not in terms of employee satisfaction.

All too often the evaluation phase of the training process is neglected. This is tantamount to making an investment without ever determining whether you're receiving an adequate (or any) return on it. Calculating a return on investment can require a study of the costs and benefits of training, and funding such a study can be difficult if funding for the training was barely adequate to begin with. Granted, collecting the necessary data and finding the time to analyze training results may be difficult. But at the very least companies should estimate the costs and benefits of a training program, even if these cannot be directly measured. Without such information, training's financial value cannot be demonstrated, and upper management may feel there is no compelling reason to continue the training effort.

Assessing the effectiveness of training is more than simply estimating financial costs and benefits. A four-level framework for evaluation[54] has been widely accepted in the training area. Level 1 refers to the *reaction* of the trainees, and it may consist of ratings on a satisfaction scale that assesses how happy trainees are with the training. Level 2 refers to how much the trainees *learn*, and it may be assessed with a skill exercise. Level 3 refers to the trainees' *behavior*, and it may be measured by observers of the work operation. Level 4 refers to the *results*, which are generally assessed through the financial measure of return on investment (ROI). Evaluating the results, the highest level of measurement, seems to be the most desirable way of assessing the

FIGURE 8.5
Training Effectiveness: Four Measurement Levels

Level	Type of Measurement
1	Subjective reactions to training, such as perceived usefulness.
2	Objective measure of learning, such as a test of concepts covered in training.
3	Application of training back on the job, such as behaviors and decisions made on the job.
4	Financial impact of the training, such as an ROI estimate.

success of a training program. However, other levels of measurement, particularly level 3, behavior, can also be important.

Applications of the four levels of evaluation to measure training effectiveness are illustrated in the following example. Employees attend a training program offered by their company that is focused on improving skills to operate as a team. Following the team training, the employees complete a questionnaire asking for evaluations of how useful they felt the program was and how knowledgeable the trainers were. After returning to work, the employees are asked to complete an online assessment regarding the team training. The assessment is a set of items that test knowledge about concepts and procedures covered in the training. A week after the training, observers are in the workplace and take notes about work processes and how employees are interacting with each other. A month later the training numbers are pulled together into a spreadsheet that reflect aspects such as the number of jobs completed and the number of errors.

As summarized in Figure 8.5, each of the above measures relates to one of the four levels of evaluation. The first level of evaluation focuses on the reaction of trainees to the program. Although a positive reaction can be important, the second level of evaluation assesses the extent to which trainees learned material covered in the program. And although learning key concepts and procedures can be important, the third level of evaluation addresses the question of whether the training had an impact on how people perform their jobs. Finally, the fourth level of measurement looks at whether there was a financial return on the investment made in offering the training.

Although the financial return on training expenditures is important, it is not always the most appropriate measure of effectiveness. A better measurement might be whether the training resulted in attaining the business goal.[55] In a competitive fight for survival, achieving business goals may be more important than a cost/benefit analysis.

Also, the purpose of evaluation may be more than assessment.[56] For example, measures of training effectiveness might serve as a source of learning and motivation if they are provided as feedback to trainees. A business could use data on behavioral change, for instance, to give workers feedback about their work-related improvements.

Legal Issues and Training

Like all other HRM functions, training is affected by legal regulations. The major requirement here is that employees must have access to training and development programs in a nondiscriminatory fashion. Equal opportunity regulations and antidiscrimination laws apply to the training process, just as they do to all other HR functions.

As we discussed in Chapter 3, determining whether a training program has adverse impact is a primary means of deciding whether a process is discriminatory. If relatively few women and minorities are given training opportunities, it would appear that there is discrimination in terms of development offered to different groups of employees. This situation could trigger an investigation and the company may have to demonstrate that development opportunities are offered on a job-relevant and nondiscriminatory basis.

A Special Case: Orientation and Socialization

orientation
The process of informing new employees about what is expected of them in the job and helping them cope with the stresses of transition.

It is possible, though difficult to prove, that the most important training opportunity occurs when employees start with the firm. At this time managers have the chance to set the tone for new employees through **orientation**, the process of informing new employees about what is expected of them in the job and helping them cope with the stresses of transition. Orientation is an important aspect of the socialization stage of the staffing process as briefly discussed in Chapter 5.

Although many people use the terms *orientation* and *socialization* synonymously, we define socialization as a long-term process with several phases that helps employees acclimate themselves to the new organization, understand its culture and the company's expectations, and settle into the job. We view orientation as a short-term program that informs employees about their new position and the company. Many companies refer to this orientation process as onboarding.

The socialization process is often informal and, unfortunately, informal can mean poorly planned and haphazard. A thorough and systematic approach to socializing new employees is necessary if they are to become effective workers. The first step should be an orientation program that helps new employees understand the company's mission and reporting relationships and how things work and why.

Socialization can be divided into three phases: (1) anticipatory, (2) encounter, and (3) settling in.[57] At the *anticipatory stage*, applicants generally have a variety of expectations about the organization and job based on accounts provided by newspapers and other media, word of mouth, public relations, and so on. A number of these expectations may be unrealistic and, if unmet, can lead to dissatisfaction, poor performance, and high turnover.

A **realistic job preview (RJP)** is probably the best method of creating appropriate expectations about the job.[58] As its name indicates, an RJP presents realistic information about the demands of the job, the organization's expectations of the job holder, and the work environment. This presentation may be made either to applicants or to newly selected employees before they start work. For example, a person applying for a job selling life insurance should be told up front about the potentially negative parts of the job, such as the uncertain commission-based income and the need to try to sell insurance to personal acquaintances. Of course, the positive parts of the job, such as personal autonomy and high income potential, should also be mentioned. Studies have found RJPs to have beneficial effects on important organizational outcomes such as performance and turnover.[59]

realistic job preview (RJP)
Realistic information about the demands of the job, the organization's expectations of the job holder, and the work environment.

In the *encounter phase*, the new hire has started work and is facing the reality of the job. Even if an RJP was provided, new hires need information about policies and procedures, reporting relationships, rules, and so on. This type of information is helpful even for new employees who have had substantial experience elsewhere because the organization or work unit often does things somewhat differently than what these employees are used to. In addition, providing systematic information about the organization and job can be a very positive signal to new workers that they are valued members of the organization.

During the *settling-in phase*, new workers begin to feel like part of the organization. If the settling in is successful, the worker will feel comfortable with the job and his or her role in the work unit. An *employee mentoring program*, in which an established worker serves as an adviser to the new employee, may help ensure that settling in is a success.[60] (We talk about mentoring programs at length in Chapter 9.)

Summary and Conclusions

Training Versus Development

Although training and development often go hand in hand and the terms are often used interchangeably, the terms are not synonymous. Training typically focuses on providing employees with specific skills and helping them correct deficiencies in their performance. Development is an effort to provide employees with the abilities that the organization will need in the future.

Challenges in Training

Before embarking on a training program, managers must answer several important questions: (1) Is training the solution to the problem? (2) Are the goals of training clear and realistic? (3) Is training a good investment? (4) Will the training work?

Managing the Training Process

The training process consists of three phases: assessment, development and conduct of training, and evaluation. In the assessment phase, organizational, task, and person needs are identified and the goals of training are clarified. Several options are available during the training phase. Training can take place either on the job or off the job and can be delivered through a variety of techniques (slides and videotapes, teletraining, computers, simulations, virtual reality, classroom instruction, and role-plays). The most appropriate type of training (for example, skills, retraining, cross-functional, team, creativity, literacy, diversity, crisis, or customer service) should be chosen to achieve the stated objectives. In the evaluation phase, the costs and benefits of the training program should be assessed to determine its effectiveness.

A Special Case: Orientation and Socialization

Organizations should pay particular attention to socializing employees. The first step in socializing them is orientation, or informing new employees about what is expected of them in the job and helping them cope with the inevitable stresses of transition. Companies and managers who recognize that socialization is a long-term process and should be carefully planned will benefit from lower turnover.

Key Terms

brainstorming, 278
cross-functional training, 277
development, 265
job aids, 276
literacy, 279
orientation, 282
peer trainers, 277
realistic job preview (RJP), 283
simulation, 274
training, 265
virtual reality (VR), 275

✪ Watch It!

Wilson Learning: Training. If your instructor has assigned this, go to **mymanagementlab.com** to watch a video case and answer questions.

Discussion Questions

8-1. Your company wants to introduce a series of new policies and procedures covering all interactions with external stakeholders. There is a need to ensure that all employees are trained in the same and consistent way so that there is a standardized approach to interactions in the future. Outline your views as to whether this training should be classroom based or on-the-job.

8-2. How effective do you think training can be in raising employee motivation?

8-3. Illiterate workers can suffer from embarrassment and fear that keeps them from admitting their problem. Instead, they may cope by asking questions, observing others, and relying on informal assistance from others. If illiterate workers can effectively cope with a work environment, do you think there is still a problem? Explain. How would you go about identifying workers who should receive literacy training?

✪ 8-4. How important is it that the effectiveness of a training program be measured in dollar terms? Why is it important to measure training effectiveness in the first place?

✪ 8-5. Training provides workers with skills needed in the workplace. However, many organizations have dynamic environments in which change is the norm. How can training requirements be identified when job duties are a moving target?

8-6. Your distribution company operates in several remote locations around the world. Annually, there is an opportunity for regional managers to meet with their counterparts for a week's training and updating. The results of this are supposed to be passed on to other employees by the regional managers. This is not working, so alternatives have been sought. A training option, which can be useful when employees are dispersed across various physical locations, is teletraining. Satellites are used to beam live training broadcasts to employees at different locations. In addition to the video reception, the satellite link can allow trainees to ask questions of the instructor during the broadcast. This could be a way forward, but some people in the company are reticent about it. How would you summarize the potential drawbacks?

a. What does Simuflite's experience suggest about the limitations of interactive media and CBT?

b. In what situations is CBT most likely to be beneficial to trainees?

8-7. Organizations recognize that crisis training is a necessary step. The problem is predicting the likelihood of a crisis and its nature. It begs the question as whether it should be preventive or post-crisis. What are the arguments for and against these radically different approaches?

8-8. In 2013, Ryanair were named the United Kingdom's worst brand for customer service by *Which?*, a Consumer's Association that had evaluated 100 companies on factors such as staff attitude and their ability to deal with problems. Ryanair was at least consistent with 2 stars out of 5. As a result of their poor customer service standards, Ryanair reported a significant financial loss compared to a profit in the previous financial year and there was a 13 percent fall in the value of their shares. It does prove that poor customer service can hit the bottom line. The problems can be identified and rectified with good training; usually this is carried out by a dedicated in-house team, but some organizations take the approach of bringing in an objective external training company. The unbiased opinion of an outside team can help to identify where the training is really needed, whether it is a focus on dealing with complaints or simply building a rapport with customers. Explain why customer service training is so important to all organizations.

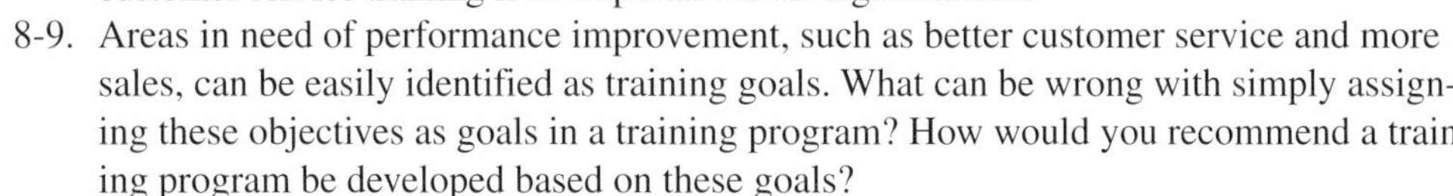

8-9. Areas in need of performance improvement, such as better customer service and more sales, can be easily identified as training goals. What can be wrong with simply assigning these objectives as goals in a training program? How would you recommend a training program be developed based on these goals?

MyManagementLab®

If your instructor has assigned this, go to **mymanagementlab.com** for the following Assisted-graded writing questions:

8-10. Traditionally, employee training has primarily been used to remove deficiencies. As described in this chapter, how can technology be used to shift training toward a tool that can improve capability?

8-11. Training is often used to improve performance problems. Describe when training would and would not be expected to improve performance.

8-12. Your boss has asked for an evaluation of the effectiveness of a training program. Describe the various levels of evaluation you could include in a report to your boss.

You Manage It! 1: Technology/Social Media

Social Media and Workplace Training

As discussed in the Manager's Notebook, "From Removing Deficiencies to Improving Capability: The Changing Nature of Training," the use of social media has the potential to significantly change the delivery of training in organizations. Traditionally, training has been focused on delivering a structured experience to employees so that all know how to properly perform tasks. The traditional approach grew out of the typical workplace in which jobs were defined and repetitious, and there was an identifiable right way of doing the tasks. A job on a production line provides an example of such a job.

Today, jobs can be more dynamic and involve less repetition. In a customer service setting, for example, it can be difficult to anticipate what complaint or problem a customer may confront an employee with. It may not be possible to identify every possible scenario and then train employees on the exact steps to follow in each situation. Additional examples of more dynamic workplaces include jobs that are project-based and workplaces that experience fast-paced change due to factors such as changing technology or changes in the marketplace.

As discussed in the Manager's Notebook, the more dynamic the workplace, the more it may make sense to deliver training when it is needed by employees. In a dynamic environment, rather than providing structured training aimed at removing present or anticipated deficiencies, the use of technology such as social media can provide helpful direction to employees precisely when they need it.

Critical Thinking Questions

8-13. The traditional training approach is meant to remove a deficit. The use of social media in training can shift the impact of training to supporting performance. Which approach do you think is better? Explain.

8-14. The use of social media allows training to be on demand and available when needed. Can you still apply the four levels of training evaluation (reaction, learning, application, and financial return) to this type of training? Describe.

8-15. Can both the traditional deficit-reduction approach to training and the social media style of training be useful in the same organization? Describe.

Team Exercise

8-16. Join your teammates and develop your approach to using social media to deliver training. What features would your approach have? For example, would you use a collaborative Facebook-like approach? Why or why not?

Experiential Exercise: Team

8-17. The vast majority of organizations have some kind of presence on Facebook or Twitter. Others have LinkedIn, Pinterest, and Instagram accounts, which are an integral part of their overall social media marketing strategy. Increasingly, organizations are coming around to the realization that their employees have their own personal social media profiles and that these could be used as branding and marketing tools. As a team, consider the following:

a. Consumers don't tend to buy brands as such; they buy from people that they know and they trust.

b. When consumers search the Internet for products and services, social profiles should appear and these should support the brand and the marketing strategies.

As a team, come up with a strategy that recognizes these statements and how you could encourage employees to post content that presents an organization in a positive light. The purpose is to drive traffic to a Web site or to generate sales. Entitle your strategy "Leveraging your employees' social networks" and suggest how you would train employees to do this.

Experiential Exercise: Individual

8-18. A workplace situation may be dynamic, but deficiencies in performance can still occur. For example, a selection error might occur and a worker may not have a needed skill. Or, equipment or procedures may be substantially changed.

a. Identify basic causes for deficiencies in performance. Which of these deficiencies can be improved or eliminated through training?

b. Finally, given a dynamic environment, how would you approach the deficiencies that can be reduced through training?

You Manage It! 2: Customer-Driven HR

Costs and Benefits: Assessing the Business Case for Training

No matter what your business, to stay in business you have to attract and retain customers. How do you do that? One way is to deliver a quality product or service in a high-quality manner. In other words, it is a combination of what is offered and how it is offered that determines whether a buyer will become a loyal customer. Training is one way to make sure that employees' technical skills and customer-service skills meet customer expectations.

When making a business decision, two basic elements are typically considered: costs and benefits. In the case of training, the issues are: (1) how much does the training reduce costs? and (2) how much does the training increase revenues? If the training sufficiently reduces costs and/or increases revenues, then there is a strong business case to conduct the training. Your ability to identify the potential sources of revenue and costs and to estimate their levels can be an important business skill. It can be the basis by which you can successfully make the case for needed training for your employees.

Critical Thinking Questions

8-19. Given your answers to the previous questions, estimate the combined impact on the bottom line of direct and indirect savings generated by training. Extrapolate this number over a one- or two-year time period.

8-20. As you have read, training can increase revenue. The revenue could come from increased quality of the customer experience due to the impact of training. Consider, as an example, the following table of customer survey responses before and after training.

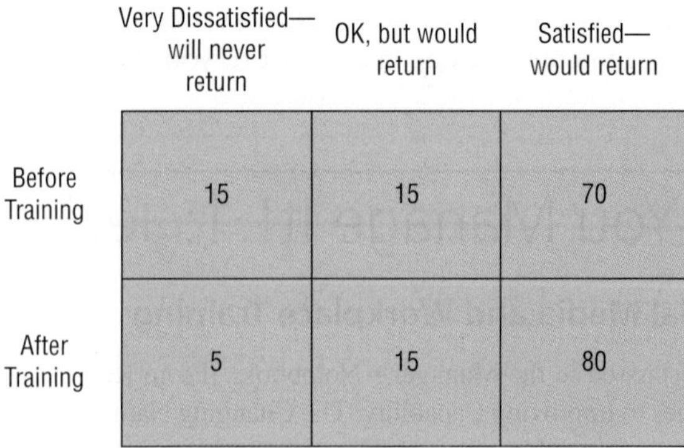

Customer Satisfaction

	Very Dissatisfied—will never return	OK, but would return	Satisfied—would return
Before Training	15	15	70
After Training	5	15	80

The numbers are percentages of customers in each satisfaction category six months before and six months after employees received their training. A key change is a reduction in the "Very dissatisfied—will never return" category of customers, which fell from 15 to 5 percent.

a. What will this 10-percent change mean to the bottom line? Assume that the average revenue generated per month by a customer is $500.00. Also assume that you have 500 customers.

b. What is the increased revenue due to the training for the past six months?
c. What would be the revenue generated if you had 1,000 customers?

Training can also impact the bottom line by reducing a number of direct costs. For example, employee costs may be reduced because fewer overtime hours will be needed due to improved performance. Another cost reduction can be seen in reduced returns, because training may reduce errors or damage that can occur when the product or service is provided.

8-21. Make assumptions about the costs in each of these direct cost categories and any other direct costs you can think of. Also assume that you can expect a 10-percent reduction in each of these categories. Generate the direct cost savings estimate due to the training.

Training can also impact the bottom line by reducing indirect costs. These are costs that may not be obvious, but that are still important. For example, the safety of work processes or equipment can be improved due to training if workers handle materials or equipment more safely. Employee turnover can also be reduced, because of improved job satisfaction due to the training.

8-22. Assume that training results in a 10-percent reduction in your turnover rate. Also, assume that the cost of a turnover is 1.5 times the departing employee's salary. For a given average employee salary of your choosing, estimate the reduced costs due to the reduction in turnover.

Team Exercise

8-23. When employees leave an organization, they will have to be replaced and the replacement will need to be hired and trained. Estimates vary, but in order to recruit and get an employee up to speed in terms of training, the average cost is around $5,500. To recruit and train a new nurse sees the training costs rocket to an average of $40,000 and a hi-tech employee can see the costs exceed $100,000. It does go to prove that hiring and training is not only a time consuming task, but an expensive one too. On average it costs 38 percent of someone's salary to replace them. How could training opportunities avoid the need to replace employees?.

Experiential Exercise: Team

8-24. Join your teammates and consider the impact of training in technical and soft skills. For example, consider training in a production-related process and training in interpersonal skills.
a. Using the revenue and cost criteria discussed in this case, how do the two types of training stack up?
b. Does one training approach appear better in terms of increasing revenue?
c. Is another approach better at reducing costs? Share your team's findings and conclusions with the rest of the class.

Experiential Exercise: Individual

8-25. Create a spreadsheet, either electronically or on paper, that includes the revenue and cost criteria discussed in this case. Include in the matrix a comparison of training a technical skill (such as a production technique) and training a soft skill (such as interpersonal communication). Use the spreadsheet to assess the two approaches. How do the two approaches compare? Share your spreadsheet estimates and conclusions with the rest of the class.

Sources: Based on Howe, S. (2008). Training ROI revisited. *Fleet Maintenance, 12*, 32–33. Carman, M. (2013). Hitting the mark: Using training needs analysis to improve customer satisfaction. *Training and Development, 40*, 10–11; Mattox, J. (2011). ROI: The report of my death is an exaggeration. *Training and Development, 65*, 30–31, 33; Rogers, S. S. (2013). Great expectations: Making ROI successfully work for you. *Training and Development, 40*, 8–9.

 You Manage It! 3: Ethics/Social Responsibility

The Ethics Challenge

Training to help workers confront unethical behavior was discussed in the Manager's Notebook, "That's Not Right: Training to Help Workers Confront Unethical Actions." Offering this training to workers assumes that they may run into unethical behaviors and need the skills to deal with these situations.

Critical Thinking Questions

8-26. If you have a clear code of ethics, do you think training to challenge unethical behavior would still be needed? Why or why not?

8-27. Might challenging someone who is engaging in unethical behavior have some risk? How can this risk be minimized?

8-28. Using the evaluation framework presented in Figure 8.5, which level would the ethics training attempt to improve?

Team Exercise

8-29. Join your teammates and consider the training to help employees challenge unethical behavior.
a. How can the effectiveness of this training be maximized?
b. Do your team members agree that this ethics training is a good idea? Why or why not?
c. Share you assessments with the rest of the class.

Experiential Exercise: Team

8-30. As a team, identify some examples of unethical behavior that college students might engage in. For each of these examples, determine whether challenges from other students would be effective or too risky and give some reasons why this is so.

8-31. Do you think students can benefit from training focused on challenging unethical behavior? Why or why not? Share your team's assessment with the rest of the class.

Experiential Exercise: Individual

8-32. Generate examples of unethical behavior (either in a university or workplace setting).
a. What behaviors reflect intimidation or bullying?
b. How can these behavioral examples be used in training to help challenge those examples of unethical behavior?

You Manage It! 4: Global

Training for Expatriates

A global foreign assignment can be an exciting opportunity and challenge for the employee. However excited or cautious someone might be about the opportunity, it is in everyone's interest to prepare the worker for a successful experience. As discussed in the Manager's Notebook, "Expatriate Assignments and Training Needs," a variety of training needs should be considered for expatriates. Specifically, the three categories of country, job, and worker characteristics are sources of potential training needs.

Inadequate preparation for a foreign assignment can result in a job not being done well and could result in longer term costs, such as derailed international opportunities for the organization. Inadequate preparation for repatriation could also have negative effects on job performance and could result in dissatisfied workers who decide to take their international experience elsewhere. Whether training is needed by expatriates is an important consideration to make as a manager.

Critical Thinking Questions

8-33. How could you measure the training needs for each of the three areas of country, job, and worker characteristics?

8-34. Do you think that the three categories of potential training needs (country characteristics, job characteristics, worker characteristics) should receive the same or different weights? That is, should a deficit in a job competency be viewed as more critical than a deficit in a cultural competency?

8-35. If time or budget were limited, what areas of training would be the top priority?

8-36. How do you think the effectiveness of training for expatriate positions should be measured?

8-37. Training for repatriation is also an important consideration. How do you think the effectiveness of training for repatriates should be measured?

Team Exercise

8-38. As a team, consider training for repatriation.
- a. Do your team members agree that training for repatriates should be offered?
- b. How could you know whether the training is effective?
- c. Share your team's judgment of repatriation training and how its effectiveness could be assessed.

Experiential Exercise: Team

8-39. Decide for yourself or have your instructor assign your team to focus on either expatriates or repatriates.

As a team, consider the three sources of possible training needs: country, job, and worker characteristics.
- a. How would you assess training needs in each of these areas, for either expatriation or repatriation? For example, would you conduct a survey, interview, or something else?
- b. What would you measure? That is, what items or question might you include? Provide examples.
- c. Share your approach with the rest of the class.

Experiential Exercise: Individual

8-40. The effectiveness of training is an important consideration, and the effectiveness of training for expatriates is no exception. Consider the four levels of measuring training effectiveness (Level 1: reaction; Level 2: learning; Level 3: behaviors; Level 4: financial return on the investment).
- a. How could each of these levels be measured to assess the effectiveness of expatriate training and of repatriate training?
- b. Generate examples of how you could measure effectiveness at each of these levels.
- c. Which level of measurement seems best to assess the effectiveness of expatriate training? Why?
- d. Which level of measurement seems best to assess the effectiveness of repatriate training? Why?

Endnotes

Scan for Endnotes or go to http://www.pearsonglobaleditions.com/Gomez-Mejia.

CHAPTER 9 Developing Careers

MyManagementLab®

When you see this icon, visit **www.mymanagementlab.com** for activities that are applied, personalized, and offer immediate feedback.

CHALLENGES

After reading this chapter, you should be able to deal more effectively with the following challenges:

1. **Understand** what is needed for career development programs to be successful.
2. **Have** familiarity with challenges in career development.
3. **Learn** practices for meeting the challenges of effective development.
4. **Gain** competence in self-development.

Tom had been happy to get the job at the men's clothing company. He started the job almost two years ago as he was graduating from college with a marketing degree. At the time, Tom had thought that there were a lot of opportunities at the company and that it was a good fit with his education. However, he has just heard from a friend that another company is looking for more talent in the marketing area. The friend suggested that Tom should consider making a move.

Tom can't help but think about what working for the other company might be like and whether the other job might be a better opportunity. The issues he finds himself reflecting on have to do with how satisfied he really has been with his current employer. Have there been as many opportunities with his current employer as he thought there would be? Has he had a chance to apply his skills and to develop them further? Has he had a chance to develop new skills? Has he been challenged with meaningful assignments? Has he increased his marketability? Is he happy with how his career has been progressing?

Source: Golden Pixels LLC/Shutterstock.

The prospect of a new job has also forced Tom to think about whether he has progressed in the company. Has his pay level increased at the rate he thinks it should? What about his job title? Could he get ahead if he tried? Is it clear how he could move ahead in the company, and is there even room to move up?

Tom isn't comfortable with all of the questions that have been raised by the prospect of another career path. He is also a little troubled that the answers to the questions aren't always clear or positive. He isn't sure what he is going to do, but he now realizes that careers don't simply happen—they must be planned for and managed. It is also painfully clear to him that he has to take responsibility for his career—no one else is going to do it for him.

The Managerial Perspective

Tom's reflection on his career is not uncommon. A job opening, an anniversary, a certain goal that was or wasn't reached—among many other possible triggers—can cause people to consider where they are at in a job and where they are going.

As a manager, emphasizing career development for your workers can provide some insurance that they won't pursue other opportunities when these "triggers" occur. Giving employees opportunities to grow and develop can ensure that your workforce keeps pace with the demands of the changing business environment. In addition, if you make this kind of investment in your employees, you are more likely to keep workers instead of seeing them lured away by competitors.

The employer and employee often share the responsibility for career development. In your job as a manager, then, you will likely be partially responsible for your own career development as well as that of your workers. As part of that responsibility, you may become involved in a formal or informal mentor relationship.

In this chapter, we investigate how you can help manage others' career development as well as your own. First, we define *career development*. Second, we explore some of the major challenges connected with career development and offer some approaches to help managers avoid problems in this area. We conclude by discussing self-development.

Learn It!

If your professor has chosen to assign this go to **www.mymanagementlab.com** to see what you should particularly focus on, and take the chapter 9 warmup.

What Is Career Development?

career development
An ongoing and formalized effort that focuses on developing enriched and more capable workers.

As we noted in Chapter 8, career development is different from training. Career development has a wider focus, longer time frame, and broader scope. The goal of training is improvement in performance; the goal of development is enriched and more capable workers. **Career development** is not a one-shot training program or career-planning workshop. Rather, it is an ongoing organized and formalized effort that recognizes people as a vital organizational resource.[1]

The career development field, though relatively young, has seen tremendous change, largely because career opportunities and paths are less structured and predictable than they were a few decades ago.[2] Instead of job security and career-long tenure with one organization, downsizing and technological change now characterize the business world.

Greater uncertainty in the workplace has made clear to most employers and employees that job security and loyalty are being replaced by marketability of skills. Traditionally, a worker's career consisted of a series of positions of increasing levels of authority at the same organization. Although a formal path within one organization can still define a person's career, the reality for many workers is that careers are not so linear nor are they limited to one organization. For many of today's workers, a career may go in a number of directions and encompass a number of employers.

Despite the uncertain business environment, career development remains an important activity. It can play a key role in helping managers recruit and retain the skilled, committed workforce an organization needs to succeed.[3] But it can only do so if it meets the dynamic needs of employers and employees.

In the 1970s, most organizations instituted career development programs to help meet organizational needs (such as preparing employees for anticipated management openings) rather than to meet employees' needs.[4] Today, career development usually tries to meet employee and employer needs. Figure 9.1 shows how organizational and individual career needs can be linked to create a successful career development program. Many organizations view career development as a way of preventing job burnout (see Chapter 16) and improving the quality of employees' work lives.[5]

This changed emphasis has largely resulted from a combination of competitive pressures (such as downsizing and technological changes) and workers' demands for more opportunities for growth and skill development.[6] These factors have made career development a more difficult endeavor than it used to be. There may no longer be a strict hierarchy of jobs from which a career path can easily be constructed. Career development today requires workers' active participation in thinking through the possible directions their careers can take.

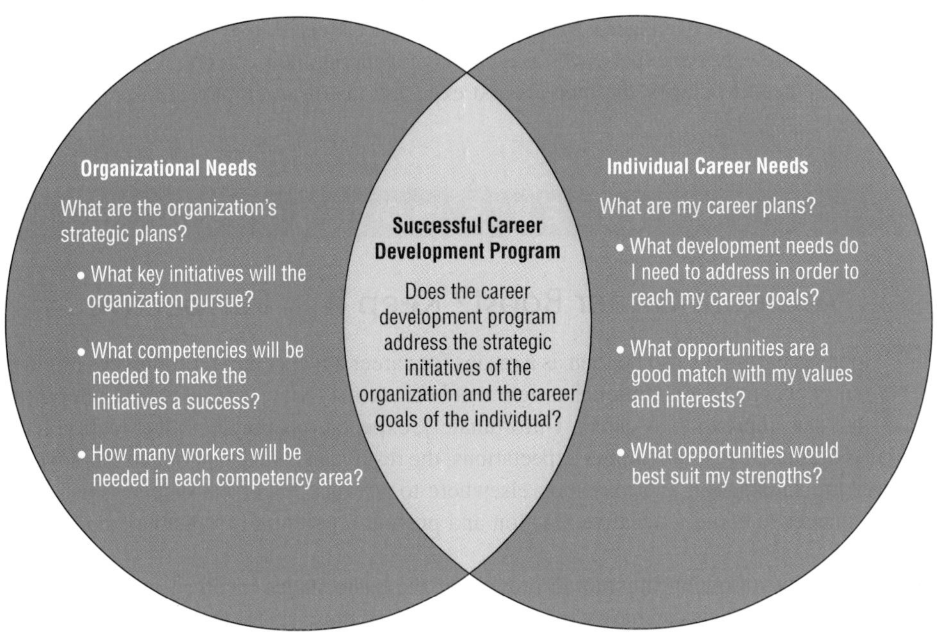

FIGURE 9.1

Successful Career Development Programs Address Organizational and Individual Needs

Source: Based on Gutteridge, T. G., Leibowitz, Z. B., and Shore, J. E. (1993). Organizational career development: Benchmarks for building a world-class workforce.

An organization must make career development a key business strategy if it intends to survive in an increasingly competitive and global business environment.[7] In the Information Age, companies will compete more on their workers' knowledge, skill, and innovation levels than on the basis of labor costs or manufacturing capacity.[8] Because career development plays a central role in ensuring a competitive workforce, it cannot be a low-priority program offered only during good economic times.

Challenges in Career Development

Although most businesspeople today agree that their organizations should invest in career development, it is not always clear exactly what form this investment should take. Before putting a career development program in place, management needs to consider three major challenges.

A QUESTION OF ETHICS

How much responsibility does a company have for managing its employees' careers? Can a company take too much responsibility for employee career development? In what ways might this be harmful to employees?

Who Will Be Responsible?

The first challenge is deciding who will be ultimately responsible for career development activities. In traditional, bureaucratic organizations development was something done "for" individual employees. For instance, the organization might have an assessment center to identify employees who have the characteristics necessary to hold middle- and upper-management positions. Once identified, these individuals would be groomed through a variety of programs: special project assignments, positions in international divisions, executive training programs, and so on. The individual employee, although certainly not kept in the dark about the company's plans, would not actively participate in the development decisions.

In contrast, many of today's organizations have concluded that employees must take an active role in planning and implementing their own personal development plans. Continuing mergers, acquisitions, and downsizings have led to layoffs and employees' realization that they cannot depend on their employers to plan their careers for them. Added to this economic turmoil is the emergence of the empowerment movement, which shifts decision-making responsibility down through the organizational hierarchy. Both these trends have led companies to encourage their employees to take responsibility for their own development. We will look at strategies for personal development at the end of this chapter.

Career development can occur in many ways in today's organizations. In an increasing number of organizations, career development responsibility is being shifted to the employee. Although an employee-empowerment approach to development can be positive, it can be negative if taken too far. Giving employees total responsibility for managing their own careers can create problems in today's flatter organizations, where opportunities to move up through the hierarchy are far fewer than in traditional bureaucratic organizations. Employees need at least general guidance regarding the steps they can take to develop their careers.

As discussed in the Manager's Notebook,"A Global Career Boost? Keep It in Perspective," employees can view global experiences as a path to advancing their careers. As a manager, however, you may need to clarify the motives and expectations of an employee taking on a global assignment.

MANAGER'S NOTEBOOK

Global

A Global Career Boost? Keep It in Perspective

Global assignments can be seen as a means for career advancement. Employees might seek out or accept an international assignment because they view it as an exciting opportunity that can improve their career. Unfortunately, expectations may not meet reality. If international assignments result in unmet expectations, the result can be a disappointed employee who has lower job satisfaction and may look elsewhere to advance his or her career. What can you do as a manager to avoid a negative reaction and prevent a potentially valuable employee from leaving?

Consider the following illustration presenting the basic stages involved in an international assignment. An expatriate can have expectations at each of these stages that might be unmet. As a manager, you can take steps to make sure that employee expectations are realistic and avoid later having to deal with a dissatisfied employee.

Motive	Assignment Characteristics	Repatriation
• To escape or a development opportunity?	• Unreasonably positive expectation or recognize challenges?	• Expect significant advancement or have a realistic assessment?

In the first stage, employees will have expectations about the international assignment as a way to get away. An employee may be wrestling with family or money issues and an international assignment may be a ticket to get away from those troubles. Alternatively, an employee may view the international assignment as a challenge and opportunity to develop knowledge and skills.

In the second stage, employees will have expectations regarding the international assignment and what it will be like. The employee may anticipate an exotic international setting that offers outstanding support. Or, the employee might anticipate that the location of the assignment will mean lack of conveniences and technology and will anticipate a difficult experience.

Finally, in the third stage expatriates will have expectations regarding their return to their home operation. An employee might, for example, expect that the international assignment will be followed by being placed in a higher-level and better-paying position.

An international assignment can be an important growth opportunity and offer unique career development opportunities. However, unrealistic expectations can mean that a potentially positive outcome turns negative. To limit this downside, as a manager, you can follow the goals summarized below for each of the above three stages.

Stage	Management Action
1. Motivation	Have employee view the assignment as a development opportunity.
2. Assignment Characteristics	Employee should have an accurate appraisal of the international experience.
3. Repatriation	Employee needs to have a realistic assessment of their job when returning home.

In terms of the first stage, employees need to understand that taking on an international assignment will not, in and of itself, resolve personal issues. If there are relationship or money problems, they will likely not go away and could get worse over the course of an international assignment. As a manager, you can work with employees to recognize the international assignment as a development opportunity and not as a means to escape. You can emphasize the new experiences, skills, and network that can result from an international experience.

Employees also need a realistic assessment of the international assignment. An employee needs to have as accurate a picture as possible of the international environment and the challenges that will be faced in the job. You can make sure that your employees have the best information possible.

You also can help employees have realistic expectations about their repatriation. Employees might expect that their international experience will be utilized in a new job or that the experience will lead to a higher-level position in the company. Those aspirations could be wrong, and it is probably best to help your employees avoid being disappointed. There may be no room for promotion and the employee might be asked to return to the employee's original job. If that is the situation, the employee should at least understand what is reasonable to expect at repatriation.

Sources: Based on Harvey, M., Buckley, M. R., Richey, G., Moeller, M, and Novicevic, M. (2012). Aligning expatriate managers' expectations with complex global assignments. *Journal of Applied Social Psychology*, *42*, 3026–3050; Selmer, J., and Lauring, J. (2012). Reasons to expatriate and works outcomes of self-initiated expatriates. *Personnel Review*, *41*, 665–684; Shaffer, M. A., Kraimer, M. L., Chen, Y. P., and Bolino, M. C. (2012). Choices, challenges, and career consequences of global work experiences: A review and future work agenda. *Journal of Management*, *38*, 1282–1327. ■■

How Much Emphasis Is Appropriate?

Career development is generally seen as a positive way for companies to invest in their human resources. However, too great an emphasis on career enhancement can be detrimental to organizational effectiveness.[9] Employees with an extreme careerist orientation can become more concerned about their image than their performance and be poorer organizational citizens.[10]

It is difficult to pinpoint where an employee's healthy concern for his or her career becomes excessive. However, there are warning signs managers should watch for:

- Is the employee more interested in capitalizing on opportunities for advancement than in maintaining adequate performance?
- Does the employee devote more attention to managing the impressions the employee makes on others than to the reality of his or her job responsibilities and skill levels?
- Does the employee emphasize networking, flattery, and being seen at social functions over job performance? In the short run, people who engage in these tactics often enjoy advancement. However, sooner or later they run into workplace duties or issues they are not equipped to deal with.

For better or for worse, studies have found that such strategies are effective in helping employees advance through the organization.[11]

Managers should also be aware that a career development program can have negative side effects—including employee dissatisfaction, poor performance, and turnover—if it fosters unrealistic expectations for advancement.

How Will the Needs of a Diverse Workforce Be Met?

To meet the career development needs of today's diverse workforce, companies need to break down the barriers to advancement that some employees may face. In 1991, the first major government study of the glass ceiling revealed that women and minorities are held back not only from top executive positions, but also from lower-level management positions and directorships. The study revealed that women and minorities are frequently excluded from informal career development activities such as networking, mentoring, and participation in policy-making committees. In addition to outright discrimination, some of the practices that contribute to their exclusion are informal word-of-mouth recruitment, companies' failure to sensitize and instruct managers about equal employment opportunity requirements, lack of mentoring, and the too-swift identification of high-potential employees.[12] Barriers to the advancement of minorities and women continue to exist after more than two decades since the initial government study of the glass ceiling. For example, recent statistics indicate that females make up approximately 47 percent of the U.S. workforce, but less than 3 percent are CEOs of Fortune 500 companies.[13]

dual-career couple
A couple whose members both have occupational responsibilities and career issues at stake.

Another group of employees who may need special consideration are **dual-career couples.** Nearly 80 percent of all couples are working couples. The two-income family has replaced the

Source: Brendan Delany/Thinkstock/Getty Images.

single-income family as the norm.[14] When both members of a couple have career issues at stake, personal lives can complicate and become intertwined with occupational lives. A career opportunity for one member that demands a geographic move can produce a crisis for both the couple and their companies.

Both couples and organizations can take steps to help deal with dual-career issues. Rather than waiting until a crisis point, it is better if the couple resolves competing career issues by planning their careers and discussing how they will proceed if certain options become available. This approach also reduces the possibility of abrupt personnel losses for organizations. Some of the organizational approaches used to deal with the needs of dual-career couples include flexible work schedules, telecommuting (both discussed in Chapter 4), and child-care services (see Chapter 12). These kinds of practices have become more common.

Meeting the Challenges of Effective Development

Assessment Phase → Direction Phase → Development Phase → Assessment Phase

FIGURE 9.2
The Career Development Process

Creating a development program almost always consists of three phases: the assessment phase, the direction phase, and the development phase (Figure 9.2). Although presented separately in Figure 9.2, in an actual program the phases of development often blend together.

The Assessment Phase

The *assessment phase* of career development includes activities ranging from self-assessment to organizationally provided assessment. The goal of assessment, whether performed by employees themselves or by the organization, is to identify employees' strengths and weaknesses. This kind of clarification helps employees (1) to choose a career that is realistically obtainable and a good fit and (2) to determine the weaknesses they need to overcome to achieve their career goals. Figure 9.3 lists some tools that are commonly used for self-assessment and for organizational assessment.

SELF-ASSESSMENT Self-assessment is increasingly important for companies that want to empower their employees to take control of their careers. Traditionally, the major tools used for self-assessment are workbooks and workshops. There are now a growing number of online sites that provide self-assessment and assistance with setting realistic career goals. For example, CareerOneStop is sponsored by the U.S. Department of Labor Employment and Training Administration and offers a variety of self-assessment tools, available in its "Explore Careers" portal at *www.careeronestop.org*.

In addition to the exercises included in a generic career workbook or website, tailored workbooks and company-specific career sites might contain a statement of the organization's policies and procedures regarding career issues as well as descriptions of the career paths and options available in the organization.

Career-planning workshops, which may be led either by the company's HR department or by an external provider such as a consulting firm or local university, give employees information about career options in the organization. They may also be used to give participants feedback on their career aspirations and strategies. Participation in most workshops is voluntary, and some organizations hold these workshops on company time to demonstrate their commitment to their workforce.

FIGURE 9.3
Common Assessment Tools

Self-Assessment	Organizational Assessment
Career workbooks	Assessment centers
Career-planning workshops	Psychological testing
Career websites	Performance appraisal
	Promotability forecasts
	Succession planning

FIGURE 9.4
Sample Skills Assessment Exercise

Use the scales below to rate yourself on each of the following skills. Rate each skill area both for your level of proficiency and for your preference.

Proficiency:

1	2	3
Still learning	OK — competent	Proficient

Preference:

1	2	3
Don't like to use this skill	OK — Don't particularly like or dislike using this skill	Really enjoy using this skill

Skill Area	Proficiency	×	Preference	=	Score
1. Problem solving	______		______		______
2. Team presentation	______		______		______
3. Leadership	______		______		______
4. Inventory	______		______		______
5. Negotiation	______		______		______
6. Conflict management	______		______		______
7. Scheduling	______		______		______
8. Delegation	______		______		______
9. Participative management	______		______		______
10. Feedback	______		______		______
11. Planning	______		______		______
12. Computer	______		______		______
13. Social media	______		______		______

Whether done through workbooks, face-to-face workshops, or with online exercises, self-assessment usually means performing skills assessment exercises, completing an interest inventory, and clarifying values.[15]

- As their name implies, *skills assessment exercises* are designed to identify an employee's skills. For example, a workbook exercise might ask the employee to compile a brief list of his or her accomplishments. Once the employee has generated a set of, say, five accomplishments, he or she then identifies the skills involved in making each accomplishment a reality. In a workshop situation, people might share their accomplishments in a group discussion, and then the entire group might help identify the skills underlying the accomplishments.

  Another skills assessment exercise presents employees with a list of skills they must rate on two dimensions: their level of proficiency at that skill and the degree to which they enjoy using it. A total score is then generated for each skill area—for example, by multiplying the proficiency by the preference rating. Figure 9.4 shows an example of this approach to skills assessment. Scores below 6 indicate areas of weakness or dislike, whereas scores of 6 or above indicate areas of strength. The pattern of scores can guide employees regarding the type of career for which they are best suited.
- An *interest inventory* is a measure of a person's occupational interests. Numerous off-the-shelf inventories can give employees insight into what type of career will best fit their interests. One of the best-known inventories is the Strong Vocational Interest Inventory.[16] The interest inventory asks people to indicate how strong or weak an interest they have in activities such as dealing with very old people, making a speech, and raising money for charity. Responses to items on the inventory are then scored to identify the occupations in which the individual has the same interests as the professionals employed in those fields.
- *Values clarification* involves prioritizing personal values. The typical values-clarification exercise presents employees with a list of values and asks them to rate how important each value is to them. For example, employees may be asked to prioritize security, power, money, and family in their lives. Knowing their priority values can help employees make

satisfying career choices. The Manager's Notebook, "Anchor Yourself," provides an example of a values-based approach to career development. It presents eight items that describe career "anchors" and identifies implications for effective management for each anchor.

MANAGER'S NOTEBOOK

Ethics/Social Responsibility

Anchor Yourself

When your career's direction matches what you are really about, the result can be finding meaning and fulfillment in your work. Isn't it only ethical to try to provide the kind of work experience that matches the core values of a worker?

These core values might be considered to be career "anchors" according to Dr. Edgar Schein, an MIT professor who has developed this concept to identify what a worker wants from a career. There is some discussion among researchers that the concept of anchors might be better thought of as orientations that can change over time. Overall, the career anchors framework has largely been supported by research and career counselors often use the career anchors framework when working with clients. To determine someone's career anchor, have the person select one of the following eight statements that best describes him or her. Go through the exercise yourself to identify your career anchor:

Career Anchor Assessment

1. I identify with my profession and like to use my skills.
2. I like having a broad overview and enjoy responsibility.
3. I like to work independently.
4. I like it when things are stable and predictable.
5. I like the challenge of starting something new.
6. I want to make the world a better place.
7. I like competition and enjoy solving problems.
8. I want balance in my life.

Even if you determine your workers' career anchors, what can you do about it? The nature of a job should enable a worker to express his or her career anchor. You will probably find that there is enough flexibility in how a job can be structured that you can help a worker to express his or her career anchor. The following list of management implications presents actions that you as a manager could take for each of the eight career anchors.

Basic Management Implications for Each Career Anchor

1. Give the worker opportunity to develop work standards and to mentor others.
2. Give the worker opportunities to lead projects or teams.
3. Ask the worker to take on the role of an internal consultant and tackle a workplace problem.
4. Let the worker know that staying in his or her current position is an option.
5. Give this worker new projects and let him or her develop ideas as an internal entrepreneur.
6. Offer this worker some responsibility for a company program, such as diversity, or the opportunity to partner with a local charity.
7. Set stretch goals with the worker and empower him or her to make the decisions needed to get there.
8. Offer this worker flexibility in his or her work schedule and the opportunity to work from home.

Sources: Based on Barclay, W. B., Chapman, J. R., and Brown, B. L. (2013). Underlying factor structure of Scheen's career anchor model. *Journal of Career Assessment*, in press, online version downloaded from *jca.sagepub.com* on June 23, 2013; Danziger, N., Rachman-Moore, D., and Valkency, R. (2008). The construct validity of Schein's career anchors orientation inventory. *Career Development International, 13*, 7–19; Kanchier, C. (2006, May 6). What anchors your career? Workplace unhappiness may simply be a matter of a poor personality fit. *Calgary Sun* (Alberta, Canada), News section, 62; Rodrigues, R., Guest, D., and Budjanovcanin, A. (2013). From anchors to orientations: Towards a contemporary theory of career preferences. *Journal of Vocational Behavior, 83*, 142–152. Wils, L., Wils, T., and Trembley, M. (2010). Toward a career anchor structure: An empirical investigation of engineers. *Relations Industrielles, 65*, 236–254; Wong, A. L. Y. (2007). Making career choice: A study of Chinese managers. *Human Relations, 60*, 1211–1233. ■■

ORGANIZATIONAL ASSESSMENT Some of the tools traditionally used by organizations in selection (see Chapter 5) are also valuable for career development. Among these are assessment centers, psychological testing, performance appraisal, promotability forecasts, and succession planning.

- *Assessment centers* are situational exercises, such as interviews, in-basket exercises, and business games, that are often used to select managerial talent. A developmentally oriented assessment center stresses giving feedback and direction to the worker.[17] The assessment center measures competencies needed for a particular job and provides participants with feedback about their strengths and weaknesses in the competency areas as uncovered in the exercises.

  Like many other tools, assessment centers are being developed in computerized versions.[18] For example, one computerized assessment tool evaluates management skills such as coaching, problem solving, and team building. A variety of scenarios simulate workplace situations in which judgments have to be made about performance, problems need to be solved, and confrontations need to be dealt with. Based on the person's performance in these scenarios, the program provides a development plan for career growth.

  A limited number of studies indicate that assessment centers have significant and positive effects on participants, even months after the assessment center exercise.
- Some organizations also use *psychological testing* to help employees better understand their skills and interests. Tests that measure personality and attitudes, as well as interest inventories, fall into this category.[19]
- *Performance appraisal* is another source of valuable career development information. Unfortunately, appraisals are frequently limited to assessment of past performance rather than oriented toward future performance improvements and directions. Future-oriented performance appraisal can give employees important insights into their strengths, their weaknesses, and the career paths available to them. Performance appraisal should be more than simply evaluation; it needs to include learning and lead to improvement in performance and direction for development.[20]
- **Promotability forecasts** are decisions made by managers regarding the advancement potential of their subordinates. These forecasts allow the organization to identify people who appear to have high advancement potential.[21] The high-potential employees are then given developmental experiences (such as attending an executive training seminar) to help them achieve their advancement potential.
- **Succession planning** focuses on preparing people to fill executive positions. Formally, succession planning means examining development needs given a firm's strategic plans. That is, the formal approach identifies the organization's future direction and challenges and then derives the competencies new leaders need.[22] Then the organization identifies internal and external target candidates. Once a short list of potential executives is created, the candidates are researched and tracked using the required competencies as evaluation areas. This tracking and monitoring process continues indefinitely so that an up-to-date list is available when inevitable turnover in leadership occurs. Succession planning is necessary when the organization needs key positions filled without interruption. Without it, the business may sacrifice profitability and stability as the price for not being prepared.

  Although the formal approach is advisable, most succession planning is done informally. Informal succession planning means that high-level managers identify and develop their own replacements. The employees identified as having upper-management potential may then be given developmental experiences that help prepare them for the executive ranks, such as workshops on the organization's values and mission.

  Succession planning can pose difficulties. For example, organizations have been accused of discriminating against women and minorities when filling high-level positions. Rather than outright discrimination, it can be the informality of much succession planning that makes companies unwittingly exclude these groups as candidates. Formal succession planning programs can make the identification of high-potential employees and replacement candidates a more egalitarian procedure.

promotability forecast
A career development activity in which managers make decisions regarding the advancement potential of subordinates.

succession planning
A career development activity that focuses on preparing people to fill executive positions.

In small companies, succession planning is crucial because the sudden departure or illness of a key player can cause the business to flounder. Yet just as some people shy away from drafting a will for fear of recognizing their own mortality, some small-business owners shy away from succession planning for fear of recognizing that they will not always be in control of their business. Other small-business owners are too caught up in the daily pressures of running a business to plan for the future.

The majority of employers recognize the importance of having a succession plan. However, a survey of over 1,000 organizations found only approximately 20 percent to be effective at succession planning.[23] Organizations recognize the importance of having a leadership pipeline, but many don't appear to put effective succession plans into operation.

The Direction Phase

The *direction phase* of career development involves determining the type of career that employees want and the steps they must take to realize their career goals. Appropriate direction requires an accurate understanding of one's current position. Unless the direction phase is based on a thorough assessment of the current situation, the goals and steps identified may be inappropriate. For example, a task force assembled by the Healthcare Financial Management Association reviewed credentials, experience, and other data for more than 5,000 senior finance executives. They also reviewed certification standards and graduate school curricula and worked with two panels of experts. Through this review, the task force developed the competency model shown in Figure 9.5.

FIGURE 9.5

A Competency Growth Model for Healthcare Financial Managers: Basis for Career Development Direction

Source: Based on *Healthcare Financial Management.* (1999). Dynamic healthcare environment demands new career planning tools, *52*, 70–74. Reprinted with permission.

A Healthcare Financial Management Association task force identified behavioral characteristics having to do with the skill, knowledge, social, trait, or motive qualities needed to excel in the profession. These competencies were grouped into the following three components:

Component 1: Understanding the Business Environment

Competencies:

1. Strategic thinking—the ability to integrate knowledge of the industry with an understanding of the long-range vision of an organization.
2. Systems thinking—an awareness of how one's role fits within an organization and knowing when and how to take actions that support its effectiveness.

Component 2: Making It Happen

Competencies:

1. Results orientation—the drive to achieve and the ability to diagnose inefficiencies and judge when to take entrepreneurial risks.
2. Collaborative decision making—actions that involve key stakeholders in the decision-making processes.
3. Action orientation—going beyond the minimum role requirements to boldly drive projects and lead the way to improved services, processes, and products.

Component 3: Leading Others

Competencies:

1. Championing business thinking—the ability to energize others to understand and achieve business-focused outcomes. Fostering an understanding of issues and challenges through clear articulation and agenda setting.
2. Coaching and mentoring—the ability to release the potential of others by actively promoting responsibility, trust, and recognition.
3. Influence—the ability to communicate a position in a persuasive manner, thus generating support, agreement, or commitment.

The competency model can be most useful for career development by focusing on the type of role the person desires. For example, someone who aspires to be the leader of an enterprise may need to develop the highest competency levels in the area of leading others. Someone aspiring to the role of business advisor might be best served by developing a balanced portfolio of competencies.

The direction phase, represented by the competencies, should be based on a careful assessment of what is needed in the profession. Further, career development direction should not be a stand-alone effort. To be effective, career development must be integrated with other HRM efforts, such as staffing, performance appraisal, and training.

One manager who participated in a study by PricewaterhouseCoopers quoted Mark Twain: "Never try to teach a pig to sing. It wastes your time and annoys the pig."[24] In other words, for your organization's development efforts to be successful, you need to first make sure that you are hiring people who generally match your skill requirements and culture. Two major approaches to career direction are individual counseling and various information services.

INDIVIDUAL CAREER COUNSELING *Individual career counseling* refers to one-on-one sessions with the goal of helping employees to examine their career aspirations.[25] Topics of discussion might include the employee's current job responsibilities, interests, and career objectives. Although career counseling is frequently conducted by managers or HR staff members, some organizations use professional counselors.[26]

Career counseling resources and other career planning resources can also be found online. The National Career Development Association, for example, develops standards for the career development field and provides resources and tools at *www.ncda.org*. Their website includes a search function that can be used to locate career counselors.

When line managers conduct career counseling sessions, the HR department generally monitors the sessions' effectiveness and provides assistance to the managers in the form of training, suggested counseling formats, and the like. Having managers conduct career counseling sessions with their employees has several advantages. First, managers are probably more aware of their employees' strengths and weaknesses than anyone else. Second, knowing that managers understand their employees' career development concerns can foster an environment of trust and commitment.

Unfortunately, assigning career counseling responsibility to managers does not guarantee that the task will be carried out carefully. As with performance appraisal and many other important HR activities, managers may treat employee career development simply as a paper-shuffling exercise unless top management signals its strong support for development activities. If managers only go through the motions, there is likely to be a negative impact on employee attitudes, productivity, and profits.

INFORMATION SERVICES As their name suggests, information services provide career development information to employees. Determining what to do with this information is largely the employee's responsibility. This approach makes sense, given the diversity of the interests and aspiration of employees in today's organizations.

The most commonly provided information services are job-posting systems, skills inventories, career paths, and career resource centers.

- **Job-posting systems** are a fairly easy and direct way of providing employees with information on job openings. The jobs available in an organization are announced ("posted") on a bulletin board, in a company newsletter, through a phone recording or computer system, or over a company's intranet. Whatever the medium, all employees have access to the list. All postings should include clear descriptions of both the job's specifications and the criteria that will be used to select among the applicants.

  Job-posting systems have the advantage of reinforcing the notion that the organization promotes from within.[27] This belief not only motivates employees to maintain and improve their performance, but also tends to reduce turnover.

job-posting system
A system in which an organization announces job openings to all employees on a bulletin board, in a company newsletter, or through a phone recording or computer system.

Alternative Career Paths for a Hotel Employee

Busperson → Waiter/Waitress → Pantry Worker → Pastry Cook → Sauce Cook → Short-Order Cook → Sous-Chef

Busperson → Host/Hostess → Storeroom Clerk → Assistant Steward → Liquor Storeroom Steward → Beverage Manager → Assistant Banquet Manager → Banquet Manager

FIGURE 9.6
Alternative Career Paths for a Hotel Employee

This is a generic example of alternative career paths. Actual career paths should specify a time frame for each job.

Not everyone who applies for a posted job will get the promotion. It is important for managers to turn this potentially negative feedback into a positive development opportunity.[28] For example, a worker who applied for a posted opening but wasn't selected for the promotion should be told why he or she did not get the promotion. Most important, the manager needs to discuss with the worker what he or she can work on so that the next time a similar promotion opportunity comes along, the worker will be better positioned for it.

skills inventory
A company-maintained record of employees' abilities, skills, knowledge, and education.

- **Skills inventories** are company-maintained records with information such as employees' abilities, skills, knowledge, and education.[29] The company can use this comprehensive, centralized HR information system to get an overall picture of its workforce's training and development needs, as well as to identify existing talent in one department that may be more productively employed in another.

  Skills inventories can prove valuable for employees as well. Feedback regarding how they stack up against other employees can encourage them to improve their skills or seek out other positions that better match their current skill levels.

career path
A chart showing the possible directions and career opportunities available in an organization; it presents the steps in a possible career and a plausible timetable for accomplishing them.

- **Career paths** provide valuable information regarding the possible directions and career opportunities available in an organization. A career path presents the steps in a possible career and a plausible timetable for accomplishing them. Just as a variety of paths may lead to the same job, starting from the same job may lead to very different outcomes. Figure 9.6 provides an example of alternative career paths that a bus person in the hotel business might follow.

  To be realistic, career paths must specify the qualifications necessary to proceed to the next step and the minimum length of time employees must spend at each step to obtain the necessary experience. This information could be generated by computer.

  Figure 9.7 presents examples of two survey forms based on jobs in the hotel industry that might be used to collect career path information. Form A asks employees to indicate how important certain skills are for the performance of their job. The skills included on the form can be determined by examining job-analysis information and by interviewing individual employees. Employee responses can then be used to develop lists of critical and desirable skills for each job.

  Form B asks employees to judge the extent to which experience in other jobs in the organization is needed to perform their current job adequately. The lowest-level jobs, which still involve the skill requirements uncovered with the use of Form A, would not require previous job experience within the organization. Higher-level or more complex jobs would likely require more job experience.

  Career paths point out development needs and options for workers. Whereas traditional career paths usually become very narrow at the top, broader options are available if lateral career moves, such as across departments or functions, are allowed. The types of options offered through broad career paths can be particularly appealing for younger workers who are looking to keep their jobs varied and interesting.[30]

Form A: Skill Requirements

Instructions: A list of various skills that apply to various jobs is presented below. Use the scale provided to indicate the extent to which each skill is applicable to your current position.

	Circle the Most Appropriate Number			
	Not applicable	**Somewhat desirable, useful at times**	**Very desirable, but not essential**	**Critical—could not perform job without it**
Skills				
1. Determine daily/forecasted production and service equipment requirements.	1	2	3	4
2. Clean guest rooms.	1	2	3	4
3. Set up, break down, and change over function rooms.	1	2	3	4
4. Handle security problems.	1	2	3	4
5. Clean public areas/restrooms.	1	2	3	4
6. Assist in menu development.	1	2	3	4
7. Register/preregister guests into hotel.	1	2	3	4
8. Participate in the preparation of sauces, soups, stews, and special dishes.	1	2	3	4
9. Prepare and serve salads, fruit cocktails, fruits, juices, and so on.	1	2	3	4
10. Participate in the rating of meats and other dishes.	1	2	3	4
11. Care for, clean, and distribute laundry items.	1	2	3	4

Form B: Experience Requirements

Instructions: A list of work experience by job titles is presented below. Use the scale provided to indicate for each item: (a) how important previous experience in this work is for the successful performance of your current job duties; and (b) the amount of experience that constitutes adequate training or exposure so that you are able to function efficiently in your current position.

	Circle the Most Appropriate Number							
	Importance of Requirement			**Minimum Experience**				
	Not very important	**Very desirable, but not essential**	**Critical—could not perform job without it**	**0–6 mos**	**7–11 mos**	**1–2 yrs**	**3–5 yrs**	**6 yrs**
Work Experience								
1. *Storeroom Clerk:* Accurately compute daily food costs by assembling food invoices, totaling food requisitions, taking monthly inventory of food storeroom, and so on.	1	2	3	1	2	3	4	5

(continued)

FIGURE 9.7

Two Career Path Information Forms

	Circle the Most Appropriate Number							
	Importance of Requirement			Minimum Experience				
	Not very important	Very desirable, but not essential	Critical—could not perform job without it	0–6 mos	7–11 mos	1–2 yrs	3–5 yrs	6 yrs
2. *Liquor Storeroom Steward:* Maintain adequate levels of alcoholic beverages and related supplies; properly receive, store, and issue them to user departments.	1	2	3	1	2	3	4	5
3. *Pantry Worker:* Prepare and supply to waiters salads, fruit cocktails, fruit juices, and so on.	1	2	3	1	2	3	4	5
4. *Pastry Cook:* Prepare mixes for baking cakes, pies, soufflés, and so on.	1	2	3	1	2	3	4	5
5. *Short-Order Cook:* Prepare short-order foods in assigned restaurant areas.	1	2	3	1	2	3	4	5
6. *Sous Chef:* Assist executive chef in all areas of kitchen production; directly supervise the operations of the kitchen in his or her absence.	1	2	3	1	2	3	4	5
7. *Waiter or Waitress:* Take food and beverage orders from customers and serve them in a restaurant or lounge.	1	2	3	1	2	3	4	5
8. *Beverage Manager:* Supervise and schedule personnel as required and maintain budgeted liquor cost and supplies for the lounge and/or banquet functions.	1	2	3	1	2	3	4	5
9. *Assistant Banquet Manager:* Assist in the coordination and successful completion of all banquet functions, such as coordinating staffing requirements, ensuring that function room is properly set and tidied, and keeping banquet manager fully informed of all problems or unusual matters.	1	2	3	1	2	3	4	5

FIGURE 9.7 (Continued)

- A **career resource center** is a collection of career development materials such as workbooks, tapes, and texts. These resources might be maintained by the HR department either in its offices or in an area that is readily accessible to employees. Companies with many locations might publicize the availability of these materials and lend them to employees who express interest. Some colleges and universities maintain career resource centers, and many consulting firms (particularly those specializing in employee outplacement) provide career development materials as well. Career resource centers can help people identify for themselves their strengths and weaknesses, career options, and educational and training opportunities.

career resource center
A collection of career development materials such as workbooks, tapes, and texts.

In addition to the traditional career information sources, social media is emerging as a means to share career information. Competence with social media is also increasingly becoming a skill that is needed to perform many jobs. The Manager's Notebook, "Reaching Out to Develop Careers: Social Media as a Skill and a Tool," explores these issues.

MANAGER'S NOTEBOOK

Technology/Social Media

Reaching Out to Develop Careers: Social Media as a Skill and a Tool

Social media may be more of a factor in your career than you might recognize. Having facility with social media is a factor that employers are seeing as relevant to many jobs. In addition to core job skills, social media can be important because it is increasingly being used as a means to connect with customers. Some employers are finding that expertise with social media can differentiate them in the marketplace. Certificate programs and continuing education classes in social media are being offered by universities and community colleges. Because social media is becoming integrated into how many businesses connect with customers, having competency in this area could facilitate your career opportunities.

Social media is also being used to reach out and help people to develop their careers. In addition to building a customer base, social media is being used to develop a talent base of potential employees. For example, The Limited, a fashion retailer that you might be familiar with, is using social media to ask customers for their success stories. These stories can reflect how someone got ahead in their personal or professional life. The stories are being collected as a means for people to share life experiences and what they have learned about moving forward. You can find some of these stories at *http://50.thelimited.com*. For each story submission, The Limited is donating $1.00 to Dress for Success, a nonprofit organization devoted to career advancement for disadvantaged women. Through these efforts, The Limited is positively contributing to the community while helping to build a talent pool by helping people recognize the company as a career opportunity.

Some organizations are bringing technology to people who often don't have access to the Internet and may not have an understanding of career options. Fifth Third Bank has retrofitted city buses with satellite technology and is taking these "eBuses" into areas of low-to-moderate income. The facilities on the eBuses can be used by community members to access financial information and to receive credit counseling. In addition to providing banking-related services to traditionally underserved neighborhoods, the eBuses offer a multimedia program that includes topics such as resume and cover letter preparation, assessment of career direction, and interviewing skills. The eBuses provide the bank a means to penetrate a relatively untapped market but also provide people with awareness of career options. Some of the community members might choose a career with the bank. Whatever the nature of the careers, if the eBus project has a positive effect, it will end up providing the bank with better customers and improved business.

Sources: Based on Donston-Miller, D. (2013, July 15). Social business skills in high demand. InformationWeek-Online, retrieved from *http://search.proquest.com*; Fifth Third Bank highlights job seeker's toolkit. (2013, August 9). Entertainment Close-Up, retrieved from *http://search.proquest.com*; The Limited celebrates 50 year anniversary. (2013, July 11). Entertainment Close-Up, retrieved from *http://search.proquest.com*. ■■

The Development Phase

Meeting the requirements necessary to move up in an organization can require a great deal of growth and self-improvement. The *development phase*, which involves taking actions to create and increase skills to prepare for future job opportunities, is meant to foster this growth and self-improvement. The most common development programs offered by organizations are mentoring, coaching, job rotation, and tuition assistance.

mentoring
A developmentally oriented relationship between senior and junior colleagues or peers that involves advising, role modeling, sharing contacts, and giving general support.

MENTORING **Mentoring** is a developmentally oriented relationship between senior and junior colleagues or peers. Mentoring relationships, which can occur at all levels and in all areas of an organization, generally involve advising, role modeling, sharing contacts, and giving general support. Mentoring can be either voluntary and informal or involuntary and formal. Informal mentoring is generally more effective than mentoring done solely as a formal responsibility,[31] although there are situations in which a formal mentoring program may be the better choice.

Mentoring has been found to make a real difference in careers, with executives who were mentored early in their careers tending to make more money at a younger age and more likely to follow a career plan than those who were not mentored. Research findings support the conclusion that effective mentoring can improve outcomes such as performance levels, promotion rates, upward mobility, income, and job satisfaction.[32] For mentors, particularly those nearing retirement, the mentoring role can offer new challenges and reignite enthusiasm and motivation. A survey of mentees found that the supervisors are often considered the most effective mentors.[33] However, survey respondents also viewed the roles of supervisor and mentor quite differently, with the supervisor focused on results and the mentor focused on the person. Mentees report that mentors build confidence, stimulate learning, and serve as a role model and sounding board.

The mentoring program at Intel provides an innovative example of matching mentors and mentees.[34] The Intel program matches people by skills and needs, not by position in the organization. The company utilizes interest and e-mail to make global mentor and mentee matches.

Mentoring relationships can be particularly important for minority employees.[35] For example, African American managers who have had mentors have been found to achieve greater levels of career advancement. The promotion rate for African American women was found in one study to be 70 percent for those with mentors and 50 percent for those without. An effective mentor can help sensitize and educate a mentee about political and cultural issues that might arise to which a minority employee may not have had previous exposure.

Like women and minorities in large firms, people who work for a small business or are self-employed may find it difficult to find a mentor. These people can benefit from membership in professional and trade associations. This form of "group mentoring" may complement individual mentoring or serve as a substitute for it.

COACHING Employee *coaching* consists of ongoing, sometimes spontaneous, meetings between managers and their employees to discuss the employee's career goals and development. Working with employees to chart and implement their career goals enhances productivity and can spur a manager's own advancement. Then why do so many managers give short shrift to employee coaching? For one thing, in today's flatter organizations managers have more people under their supervision and less time to spend on developing each employee. For another, some managers may view "employee development" as a buzz phrase unless top management clearly and strongly supports it. Finally, managers may be more comfortable working on job-related tasks and may believe they lack the skills needed to be an effective coach.[36] Many managers view their role as one of providing answers, pointing out weaknesses, and diagnosing and solving problems. This role is effective if the purpose is judgment or assessment, but it is not conducive to effective coaching.

JOB ROTATION *Job rotation* assigns employees to various jobs so that they acquire a wider base of skills. Broadened job experience can give workers more flexibility to choose a career path. And, as we discussed in Chapter 8, employees can gain an even wider and more flexible experience base through cross-functional training.

In addition to offering more career options for the employee, job rotation results in a more broadly trained and skilled workforce for the employer. The job rotation process can also keep things fresh for employees and keep them energized.[37]

Although job rotation programs do have advantages, note that they can also have some disadvantages. Such programs do not suit employees who want to maintain a narrow and specialized focus. From the organization's perspective, job rotation programs can slow operations as workers learn new skills. Although the development benefits of job rotation may be high in the long run, firms should be aware of the short-run and intermediate costs. From an employee's perspective, the opportunity of job rotation may be a survival mechanism. Specifically, downsizing in an organization may focus on eliminating an obsolete area. When employees broaden their skills through job rotation, they help to ensure their longevity and usefulness to the organization.

Source: © Marmaduke St. John/Alamy.

TUITION ASSISTANCE PROGRAMS Organizations offer *tuition assistance programs* to support their employees' education and development. Tuition and other costs of educational programs (ranging from seminars, workshops, and continuing education programs to degree programs) may be entirely covered, partially covered, or covered contingent upon adequate performance in the program.

Verizon Wireless is recognized as a company that invests in its employees. The company has partnerships with numerous universities and colleges and offers on-site degree programs with prepaid tuition at some of its locations. Bases on its assessments, Verizon has concluded that the tuition reimbursement program has increased job performance and reduced turnover.[38]

Self-Development

We conclude this chapter by examining how to manage your personal career. The reality of today's workplace is that things are uncertain—workers must contend with layoffs, international competition, and rapid changes in technology. In the face of this dynamic reality, most people want to find meaning in their work and do something that somehow "fits" them and provides some satisfaction. In order to find satisfaction with what you do and to successfully navigate the ever-changing business environment, you need to be responsible for your own career. The tradition of remaining loyal to and retiring after working 30 years for the same employer is rapidly fading. The new reality is that workers will have to take responsibility for their own careers, or risk obsolescence and stagnation.

An initial step in career self-management is determining how you define personal success. You might be very serious about managing your career, but what are you striving toward? You want to avoid being disappointed at the end and regretting choices you made along the way. In order to be in the position of saying it was all worth it, you first need to have a firm grasp of what success means to you. The Manager's Notebook, "The Three Domains: Where's Your Balance Point?" offers an overall framework that can be helpful in determining your big picture approach to success.

At the beginning of this chapter, we considered a worker, Tom, who was faced with a possible job change. Tom's concerns reflect two basic issues in careers: development and advancement. Development has to do with enhancing your skills and potential. Advancement has to do with positioning yourself to move ahead in the organization.

MANAGER'S NOTEBOOK

The Three Domains: Where's Your Balance Point?

What makes for a successful career and life? The balance between work and personal life has remained an important focus, even in the recent tough economic times. Many workers aren't happy just to have a job. They want more balance. A recent survey found that 89 percent of Americans indicated that work/life balance is a problem, and 54 percent indicated that it is a serious problem. Although some employers are sensitive to concerns about work/life balance and can offer flexibility, most workers, as these survey results indicate, remain frustrated about this imbalance.

A basic starting point for you is to recognize your own preferences in regard to work/life balance and a successful career. Success means different things to different people with, for example, some people placing greater emphasis on money than others. When it comes to your career, you need to be attuned to what success means to you, not how it is defined by others. One way to begin to focus on your own definition of career success is to recognize that success is not one-dimensional. There are at least three domains in which people often think about and define their degree of success: money, work, and life. Overall career success can be thought of as the balance struck among these three domains. There are trade-offs of costs and benefits for emphasizing one domain over another, and people differ in their balance points.

Consider the following figure. Each circle represents one of the three domains to consider in defining career success. We'll consider each of them in turn.

The Three Domains

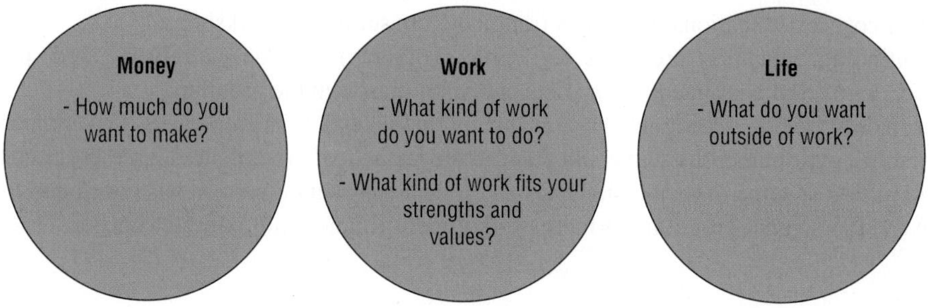

Money

Compensation is a key issue and measure of success for many people. How much do you want to make? How important is money to you? Is it the most important thing you think of when considering your own success, or are there other things that you place a higher priority on? If you want a much higher level of compensation than you are making now, consider what sacrifices and investments need to be made in order to achieve that income level. Are you willing to make these investments and sacrifices?

Work

Now turn to the work domain and consider the kind of work you would like to do. Make a list of the kinds of tasks that energize you and that you are good at. It might be helpful to first identify the things you don't like to do. What level of responsibility do you want? What are your strengths and values? Given those, what kind of job best fits your skills and interests?

Life

What do you want from life outside of work? Consider the weight you place on this domain. How important is family to you? Do you want to have dinner with your family every day, or does that not matter to you?

Your personal definition of success lies in the balance among the domains of money, work, and life. You need to evaluate whether the aspirations you have for compensation are realistic given the kind of job you want. Both the job and money expectations need to be evaluated based on what you want from life outside of work. Recognizing the three domains is a starting point in developing a personal definition of success. There isn't a simple formula for balancing the various costs and benefits when you are considering how much weight to put on each of the domains. How you make the trade-offs is up to you. The important thing is to explicitly consider the trade-offs up front so that you know where you are trying to go in your career.

Consideration of the three domains and where the balance point is for you is something that needs to be revisited periodically, perhaps every three to five years. Things change in the world of work and in our personal lives.

Sources: Based on Hopke, T. (2010). Go ahead, take a few months off. *HRMagazine, 55,* 71–73; North, M. (2008). The three circles of career advancement. *Healthcare Financial Management, 62,* 110–112; Pan, J., and Zhou, W. (2013). Can success lead to happiness? The moderators between career success and happiness. *Asia Pacific Journal of Human Resources, 51,* 63–80; Smith, S. (2010, Sept. 1). Despite economic woes, Americans still seriously concerned about work/life balance. *EHS Today, http://ehstoday.com/health/wellness/economic-woes-concerned-work-life-balance-9438.* ■■

Development	Advancement
1. Identify your mission.	**1.** Market yourself.
2. Keep learning.	**2.** Understand business trends.
3. Develop competencies.	**3.** Resolve problems.
4. Find a mentor.	**4.** Improve your communication skills.

FIGURE 9.8

Suggestions for Self-Development

Sources: Based on Brown, M. (2008). Take charge of your career. *T&D, 62,* 84–85; Lanigan, K. (2008). Moving on up: Making success the return on investment in your career. *Accountancy Ireland, 40,* 56–57; *Agri Advance* (2010). Tips to marketing your career. *48,* 16.

Figure 9.8 identifies suggestions for development and for advancement. Each of these dimensions can be important in your career. However, it is important to keep in mind that it is difficult to advance if you don't have the necessary skills. In other words, development makes sure that you can bring the skills that are needed to the table. Advancement activities can help you get noticed so that you get invited to the table.

Development Suggestions

The development suggestions in Figure 9.8 reflect the reality that the responsibility for career development is increasingly being shifted to individual workers. These development suggestions can help you and your workers make sure that you are ready for future workplace challenges.

1. ***Identify your mission*** Like an organizational mission statement, a *personal mission statement* should indicate the business you would like to be in and the role you would like to play.[39] You should see the statement as changeable over time, not a commandment to which you must blindly adhere regardless of situational or personal factors. Once completed, the mission statement should help you set your strategic direction, clarify your priorities, and avoid investing time and energy in pursuits that are not instrumental to achieving your mission. Overall, you should think of yourself as a business that has a core mission statement and a set of core values.
2. ***Keep learning*** Look beyond your current skills and immediate tasks at work. What can you do to improve your potential? What skills would complement your current set of skills? Continual learning could occur through formal workshops and classes. You can also increase your skill set through informal means by taking on challenging projects or by volunteering to be involved in activities that stretch your current skills.
3. ***Develop competencies*** Look beyond preparing yourself for a particular job. Jobs can change and can be limiting. To develop your potential, think about developing areas of competencies. Focus on developing competencies in areas that are likely to be required in your industry in the future. These packages of skills can help to positively position you in your industry.
4. ***Find a mentor*** To maximize your development, you need to find someone who can provide you with honest feedback and support. A mentor can help you identify your strengths and weaknesses and give you a picture of your development needs. Your career progression can be enhanced with the support of and input from a mentor.

Advancement Suggestions

The advancement suggestions in Figure 9.8 focus on the steps you can take to improve your chances of being considered for advancement. The development suggestions are fundamental and provide the necessary base, but the advancement suggestions provide the necessary attitudes and organizational presence.

1. ***Market yourself*** Make yourself known in your organization and industry. For example, increase your standing in the market by attending seminars and conferences. Attendance at these functions provides networking opportunities because you can meet colleagues and other employers. You also need to let people know that you are interested in advancement.

Not everyone wants the increased responsibility that comes with progression, and you don't want people to wrongly assume that you aren't interested in getting ahead.

2. ***Understand business trends*** Keep up with what is going on in your area of business. Be familiar with the issues and difficulties. You also want to know who your business competitors are. If you can bring this understanding to bear in conversations with higher-level managers, you can become recognized as someone who has a grasp of the bigger picture—someone who is informed beyond their immediate tasks in the organization. Demonstrating your understanding of the business environment can help to differentiate you from your competition for advancement.
3. ***Resolve problems*** Don't let conflict fester and become a problem. It can be difficult to confront conflict, but conflicts will occur and you do need to get along with others. Rather than personalize a disagreement and place blame, try to learn from the interaction and ask questions. If your intent is positive and you want to move forward, dealing with the conflict can have a positive impact on your advancement.
4. ***Improve your communication skills*** Improved written and verbal communication skills are consistently on the wish list of management for their workforces. Communication may not be a critical component of your current job. However, improving your communication skills can get you noticed. Many successful businesspeople point to interpersonal communication skills as an important factor in their career advancement.[40] You might improve your skills by taking a speech class or by attending workshops on communication. If you can deliver a standout presentation to management or demonstrate good business writing in your communication, it can be another facet that differentiates you from the competition and helps you to move ahead.

Summary and Conclusions

What Is Career Development?

Career development is an ongoing organized and formalized effort that focuses on developing enriched and more capable workers. It has a wider focus, longer time frame, and broader scope than training. Development must be a key business strategy if an organization is to survive in today's increasingly competitive and global business environment.

Challenges in Career Development

Before putting a career development program in place, management needs to determine (1) who will be responsible for development, (2) how much emphasis on development is appropriate, and (3) how the development needs of a diverse workforce (including dual-career couples) will be met.

Meeting the Challenges of Effective Development

Career development is a continuing cycle of three phases: an assessment phase, a direction phase, and a development phase. Each phase is an important part of developing the workforce.

In the assessment phase, employees' skills, interests, and values are identified. These assessments may be carried out by the workers themselves, by the organization, or by both. Self-assessment is often done through career workbooks and career-planning workshops. Organizational assessment is done through assessment centers, psychological testing, performance appraisal, promotability forecasts, and succession planning.

The direction phase involves determining the type of career that employees want and the steps they must take to make their career goals a reality. In this phase, workers may receive individual career counseling or information from a variety of sources, including a job-posting system, skills inventories, career paths, and career resource centers.

The development phase involves taking actions to create and increase employees' skills and promotability. The most common development programs are mentoring, coaching, job rotation, and tuition assistance programs.

Self-Development

Employees must increasingly take an active role in their own development. To do otherwise is to risk stagnation and obsolescence.

Key Terms

career development, 290
career path, 300
career resource center, 303
dual-career couple, 293
job-posting system, 299
mentoring, 304
promotability forecast, 297
skills inventory, 300
succession planning, 297

Watch It!

Verizon: Career Planning. If your instructor has assigned this, go to **mymanagementlab.com** to watch a video case and answer questions.

Discussion Questions

9-1. It has been argued that training can lead to turnover, but career development can reduce it. Differentiate between training and career development. Why might training lead to turnover whereas career development might improve retention? Explain.

9-2. How would you go about retaining and developing older employees who are part of a dual-career couple?

9-3. Today's organizations are flatter and offer fewer opportunities for advancement. How do you think careers should be developed in this type of organizational environment?

9-4. What challenges do nontraditional family units pose to company career development plans? How can companies meet these challenges?

9-5. Skills assessment exercises are designed to identify an employee's skills. One such skills assessment exercise presents employees with a list of skills they must rate on two dimensions: their level of proficiency at that skill and the degree to which they enjoy using it. A total score is then generated for each skill area. Figure 9.4 shows an example of this approach to skills assessment. Scores below 6 indicate areas of weakness or dislike, whereas scores of 6 or above indicate areas of strength. The pattern of scores can guide employees regarding the type of career for which they are best suited. Carry out the process for your group and share the results. What does the exercise tell you about others?

9-6. Companies use various tactics to encourage managers to make employee development a top priority. What do you think of the policy of tying financial rewards to people development? What are some other ways companies can hold managers accountable for developing those they supervise?

9-7. As a manager, what could you do to offer career development for your workers? Do you think it would be worth it? Why or why not?

9-8. What would you suggest about the use of social media as a career development tool? Is it a good option? How could it be better used in career development?

9-9. People have different comfort zones and aspirations that can affect their careers. How does the career anchor system (see Manager's Notebook, "Anchor Yourself," take these individual differences into account? Do you think if people are guided by their "anchors" that they will be happier in their careers? Why or why not?

MyManagementLab®

If your instructor has assigned this, go to **mymanagementlab.com** for the following Assisted-graded writing questions:

9-10. Describe the concept of career anchors. Why are they important in career development?

9-11. Distinguish between career development and advancement. Describe at least two steps that can be taken to improve development and two that can be taken to improve advancement.

9-12. Can being too focused on career enhancement have negative effects? Describe. Can a careerist orientation also have positive effects? Describe.

You Manage It! 1: Customer-Driven HR

Be Strategic About Your Career

As discussed in this chapter, workers are increasingly becoming responsible for their careers. Further, it is useful to think of yourself as a business in order to effectively manage your career. If you take this advice seriously, then it could be helpful to apply a strategic business tool to your own career. A SWOT (strengths–weaknesses–opportunities–threats) analysis is a common technique used by businesses to analyze their internal and external environments. The technique can be applied to individual careers as well.

Consider each area of a SWOT analysis. Recognize that the analysis can provide input for strategic decisions, but it doesn't directly provide strategic solutions.

- *Strengths* What are you good at? What skills and experience do you have that employers might want? What tasks do you find rewarding?
- *Weaknesses* This may not be the most enjoyable step in the SWOT analysis process, but you need to make an honest assessment of your shortcomings. You might ask for feedback from a mentor or from a previous manager. The point here is to identify areas where you need improvement.
- *Opportunities* What options do you see in terms of work? What do you want to be doing five years from now? Are there broader roles you might want to consider or new trends that might translate into new job opportunities?
- *Threats* What could stop you from reaching your career goals? Is there strong competition in your area of business? Are there financial problems and layoffs that might occur in your industry?

After identifying the strengths, weaknesses, opportunities, and threats, the next step is to develop an action plan. Again, the SWOT analysis only provides information, not the answer. Just as with strategic planning in a business, you need to go through a process of thinking through what the pattern of strengths, weaknesses, opportunities, and threats should mean for your actions. Perhaps you need to obtain additional training or move to a different region or industry. A variety of actions can be taken, and there is no one right or wrong action plan. The SWOT analysis can provide the information you need to develop an action plan that is right for you.

Critical Thinking Questions

9-13. Do you think that SWOT analysis is a useful tool for career development? Why or why not?

9-14. Opportunities and threats have to do with external factors. What sources could be useful for obtaining this information?

9-15. Which should drive action planning more, strengths or weaknesses? That is, is it more important to build on your strengths or to reduce your weaknesses? Explain.

Team Exercise

9-16. As a team, consider how the SWOT analysis might be streamlined for use by individuals. For example, develop a list of strengths that people could use to rate themselves. What key skills would your team list? Could this same list be used to assess weaknesses? Similarly, generate a list of possible opportunities. Could this list be used to assess threats? How could the lists and rating scales be used by people planning their careers? Are there advantages/disadvantages of using the lists and rating scales? Share your lists and assessments with the rest of the class.

Experiential Exercise: Team

9-17. As a team, apply the SWOT framework to an individual's career. Identify strengths, weaknesses, opportunities, and threats for a fictitious colleague (thus avoiding the possible discomfort of asking a volunteer to discuss his or her weaknesses). Given the analysis, generate an action plan. Share the analysis and action plan with the rest of the class. Do other people in the class have alternative action plan suggestions?

Experiential Exercise: Individual

9-18. Ask peers and acquaintances about their career plans. Do most people have a career plan that they can state succinctly? Also ask how they arrived at their career plans. Consider the responses. Do you think people came up with their action plans based on a careful SWOT analysis? If not, might there be benefits to conducting a SWOT analysis? Describe.

Sources: Based on *Occupational Health.* (2008). How to find your strengths and weaknesses, *60*, 24; Lindberg, H. J. (2010). Curbing career fears. *Quality Progress, 43,* 52–53; Barrett, M., and Simmonds, M. (2008, November). Brand planning your career. *Training Journal,* 37–41.

 You Manage It! 2: Technology/Social Media

Career Building with Social Media

Career development is a process that can be viewed as consisting of three phases: assessment, direction, and development. The process of career development used to be mainly the responsibility of the organization, but career development today has largely become the responsibility of individuals. However, individuals can still use help in developing their careers, and many organizations find that assisting with career development is an investment in employees that offers a positive return. As described in the Manager's Notebook, "Reaching Out to Develop Careers: Social Media as a Skill and a Tool," some organizations are utilizing social media as a means to develop careers. Although the use of this technology in career development is still emerging, there may be much potential in using this technology to efficiently provide career development.

Critical Thinking Questions

9-19. Do you think social media can be effectively used as a career development tool? Why or why not?

9-20. As discussed in the Manager's Notebook, "Reaching Out to Develop Careers: Social Media as a Skill and a Tool," what is the difference between social media being a skill and social media being a tool in career development? Describe. How important do you think social media is becoming as a skill?

9-21. Social media is a collaborative tool. Do you think there could be downsides to a collaborative approach to developing your career? For example, might there be repercussions from your boss for you being part of a social media network and being aware of your efforts to shift your career? Could this type of potential downside be eliminated or reduced? How?

Team Exercise

9-22. As a team, revisit the topic of self-development at the end of his chapter. Specifically, self-development efforts can be directed toward the categories of development and advancement. Do you think that the use of social media as a career development tool would be more useful in efforts to develop, to advance, or both? Are there different ways you might use social media to aid development versus advancement? As a team, describe your conclusions and suggestions with the rest of the class.

Experiential Exercise: Team

9-23. As a team, consider the career development phases of assessment, direction, and development.

a. How could technology, such as social media, be used at each phase? Assume that your team is responsible for making a proposal regarding the use of social media in each of these phases. How could this tool be used in each phase? Is there a phase in which social media would seem to fit best and be most effective?

b. Where do the company examples presented in the Manager's Notebook, "Reaching Out to Develop Careers: Social Media as a Skill and a Tool," fit into the phases of career development? That is, are the featured companies using social media in only the assessment phase, or development phase, and so on? Also look for information on how other organizations are using social media in the career development process. Given your analysis, are there phases where social media isn't being used? Could this be an area in which your company could differentiate itself and offer something of value to employees that is unique?

Share the basics of your proposal with the rest of the class. What are your major conclusions and recommendations?

Experiential Exercise: Individual

9-24. Consider your use of social media and your career development. How separate are these two activities? Identify ways you could utilize social media for your development and for your enhancement.

 You Manage It! 3: Ethics/Social Responsibility

Anchors II

As described in the Manager's Notebook, "Anchor Yourself," employees' career anchors may be motivated by different sets of values. The anchors have important implications for the type of career an individual will find most motivating and satisfying. Review the eight anchors and their implication as presented in the Manager's Notebook on page 268.

Critical Thinking Questions

9-25. The concept of career anchors indicates that there is more to career development than having and matching skills to competency requirements. Some managers view development as a moral imperative. That is, business is about making money, but it also should be about helping people to grow and realize their career aspirations. Do you agree? Explain why or why not.

9-26. Competencies are important to career success, but so, too, are career anchors. These two factors are analogous to ability and motivation being predictors of performance (see Chapter 5). Construct a parallel equation using competencies and anchors as predictors of career success. How is this simple equation useful?

9-27. In some work environments, career aspirations are ignored and immediate performance is the focus. Do you think this lack of attention to career anchors is an ethical issue? Explain why or why not.

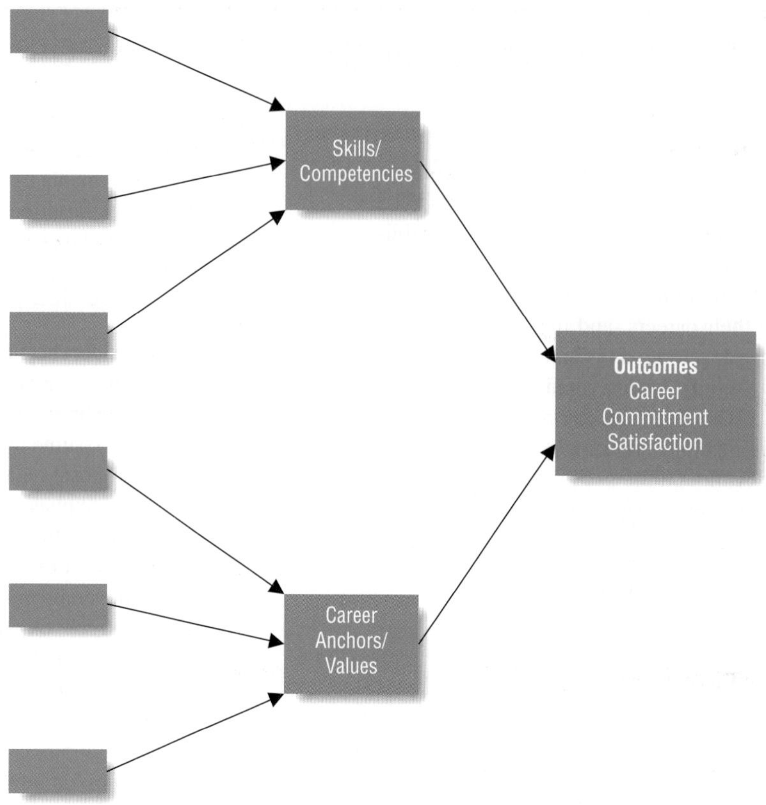

Team Exercise

9-28. A key issue in career development has to do with the competencies associated with different career paths. Strengths and weaknesses on various competencies can be assessed and then a plan for development can be put into place. Another key issue is the career anchor that employees bring with them. A misfit between an employee's anchor and the company and/or career chosen would likely result in employee dissatisfaction and other difficulties.

a. As a team, develop a framework or model for how these two sides of career development should be managed. You might label one concern as skills competencies and the other as career anchors/values. Your team could develop a model that uses boxes and arrows to indicate the causes or predictors for both the skills side and the anchors side. Your model might take a form similar to the one above.

b. Given the predictors identified in your model, what are the implications for management? Specifically, if skills are low or don't match what is needed, what could you, as a manager, do? Likewise, if career anchors don't match, what, if anything, can be done?

c. Alternatively, your team could develop a 2 × 2 framework using the skill and anchor variables. You can use two levels of each variable: low and high levels of match or fit. Your resulting framework would look something like the following:

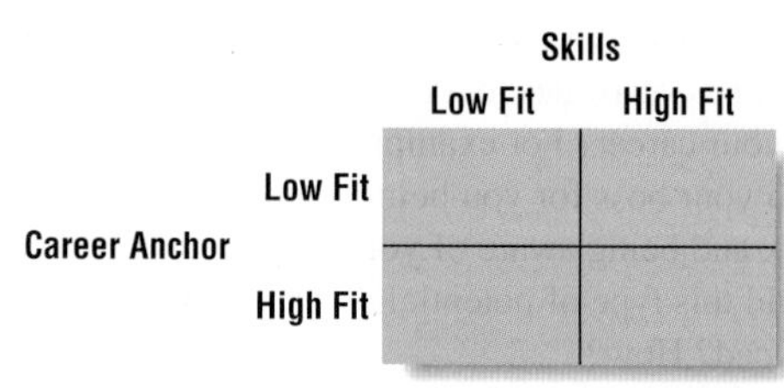

For each cell in the matrix, describe the particular combination of skills and career values. Identify management implications for each of the four cells. For example, what should be done, from a management perspective, in regard to employees whose skills have a high fit but whose career anchors are a misfit?

Experiential Exercise: Team

9-29. As a team, select a member to share career anchors and plans. As a class, assess whether there is a high degree of fit with career anchors. What is the consensus of the class regarding the importance of this fit?

Experiential Exercise: Individual

9-30. Use the Manager's Notebook, "Anchor Yourself," to assess your top career anchor(s). What type of career do you think you want to pursue? Does it match with your anchor? Do you think the degree of match is an important consideration? Why or why not?

You Manage It! 4: Global

Mentoring as Global Development

Organizations face enormous challenges in bringing people together and having them understand and trust the organization and its systems. Some groups of people may have experienced discrimination and/or disrespect, or come from a cultural background that is not the norm in the organization. It may be difficult for these workers to trust and embrace an organization's system. As employees, these workers may need support and opportunities if they are to get ahead. A mentoring program can provide the support and guidance they need. Employees can run into roadblocks to their advancement and feel ill equipped to deal with the problem. Organizations may also want employees in far-flung places across the globe to understand their organization's values, processes, and culture. Mentoring can also be an effective means for dealing with these issues.

Critical Thinking Questions

9-31. Do you think that people should be required to serve as mentors? What characteristics should these mentors possess?

9-32. Workers can learn about policies, procedures, and so on by reading electronic or hard-copy documents. What else does mentoring bring to the situation that apparently makes this form of employee development so effective?

9-33. How do you think mentors and mentees should be matched? Should they be assigned, or should they be allowed to choose each other?

Team Exercise

9-34. As a team, consider the mentoring activity from the mentee perspective. Place yourselves in the position of someone who does not feel like part of the organization, has hit a plateau, or may be in another country and not have a deep understanding of the organization. What would you be looking for from this person's mentor? Are there potential difficulties that the mentor should be aware of? How should mentors be identified and assigned (from your mentee position)? Share your team's judgments with the rest of the class.

Experiential Exercise: Team

9-35. With your team, identify mentor selection criteria for mentors whose primary purpose would be to share organizational knowledge with international employees who need to develop this knowledge base. What characteristics should employees have in order to serve in this mentor role? Identify selection criteria for mentors who will focus on disadvantaged workers or workers who seem to have hit barriers in their careers. Should two sets of selection criteria be developed for these two roles? With your team members, identify the needed mentor characteristics. Share your selection criteria with the rest of the class.

Experiential Exercise: Individual

9-36. Do you think mentoring is effective for developing a more unified organization? Ask peers, family members, and friends whether they have had a mentor in their career. Was the relationship helpful? Why or why not?

Sources: Based on *Development and Learning in Organizations*. Mentors and minorities: How to create a united workplace. *24*, 28; Dimorski, V., Skerlavaj, M., and Man, M. M. K. (2010). Comparative analysis of mid-level women manager's perception of the existence of 'glass ceiling' in Singaporean and Malaysian organizations. *The International Business and Economics Research Journal, 9*, 61–77; Francis, L. M. (2009). Shifting the shape of mentoring. *T & D, 63*, 36–40.

Endnotes

Scan for Endnotes or go to http://www.pearsonglobaleditions.com/Gomez-Mejia.

CHAPTER 10 Managing Compensation

MyManagementLab®

When you see this icon, visit **www.mymanagementlab.com** for activities that are applied, personalized, and offer immediate feedback.

CHALLENGES

After reading this chapter, you should be able to deal more effectively with the following challenges:

1. **Learn** about the components of total compensation.
2. **Learn** how to design a compensation system.
3. **Understand** the difference between job and individual pay options.
4. **Develop** familiarity with compensation tools.
5. **Become** familiar with the legal environment affecting compensation and pay system governance.

Sigma, Inc., is a medium-sized biotechnology firm specializing in genetic engineering. The firm was founded in 2004 by Dr. Roger Smith, who is still Sigma's chief executive officer and continues to be actively involved in all hiring and pay decisions. He repeatedly tells his line managers that Sigma "will pay whatever it takes to hire the best talent in the market."

During the past year Smith has noticed an erosion in Sigma's "family atmosphere" and an increase in the number of dissatisfied employees. There have been three pay-related complaints during the past week alone, and Smith suspects that this is only the tip of the iceberg. The first complaint came from a software developer who has been with Sigma for five years. He is upset that another developer was hired last year at a salary 15 percent higher than his. Smith explained that such starting salaries are necessary to attract top experienced programmers from other firms despite the severe recession at the end of the last decade. The second complaint came from a software engineer who feels that Sigma's best technical people—the lifeblood of a biotechnology firm—are discriminated against in pay because supervisors (who, in his words, are often "failed engineers") receive 30 percent more pay. The third complaint was filed by a head secretary who has been with Sigma from the start. She is angry that janitors are getting more money than she is, and she is not satisfied with Smith's explanation that it is difficult to hire and retain reliable people who are willing to clean up and dispose of dangerous chemicals.

Source: © ZUMA Press, Inc./Alamy.

In addition, a 49-year-old engineer who was purportedly terminated for poor performance has just filed an age discrimination suit against the company, arguing that the firm is replacing older, higher-earning employees with Indian employees on temporary visas who are willing to work at much lower wages.

The Managerial Perspective

Sigma's experience raises several important questions that managers and HR personnel must face in designing and administering compensation programs, such as the following:

- Who should be responsible for making salary decisions?
- Should pay be dictated by what other employers are paying?
- What types of activities should be rewarded with higher salaries?
- What criteria should be used to determine salaries?
- Which employee groups should receive special treatment when scarce pay resources are allocated?
- How does an employer balance ethical concerns for employees' welfare versus the need to save on labor costs?

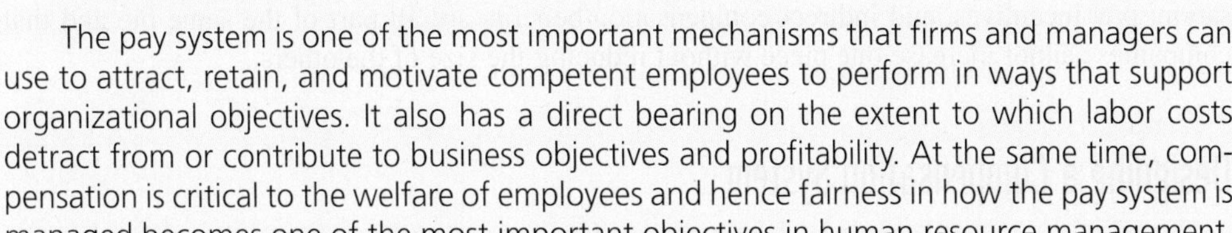

The pay system is one of the most important mechanisms that firms and managers can use to attract, retain, and motivate competent employees to perform in ways that support organizational objectives. It also has a direct bearing on the extent to which labor costs detract from or contribute to business objectives and profitability. At the same time, compensation is critical to the welfare of employees and hence fairness in how the pay system is managed becomes one of the most important objectives in human resource management.

In the first part of this chapter, we define the components of compensation and examine the nine criteria used to develop a compensation plan. Then we explore the process of designing a compensation plan and the legal and regulatory influences on compensation.

✪ Learn It!

If your professor has chosen to assign this go to **www.mymanagementlab.com** to see what you should particularly focus on, and take the chapter 10 warmup.

What Is Compensation?

As Figure 10.1 shows, an employee's **total compensation** has three components. The relative proportion of each (known as the *pay mix*) varies extensively by firm.[1] In most firms the first and largest element of total compensation is **base compensation**, the fixed pay an employee receives on a regular basis, either in the form of a salary (for example, a weekly or monthly paycheck) or as an hourly wage. The second component of total compensation is **pay incentives**, programs designed to reward employees for good performance. These incentives come in many forms (including bonuses and profit sharing) and are the focus of Chapter 11. The last component of total compensation is *benefits*, sometimes called *indirect compensation*. Benefits encompass a wide variety of programs (for example, health insurance, vacations, and unemployment compensation), the costs of which approach 42 percent of workers' compensation packages.[2] A special category of benefits called *perquisites*, or perks, is available only to employees with some special status in the organization, usually upper-level managers. Chapter 12 discusses benefit programs in detail.

total compensation
The package of quantifiable rewards an employee receives for his or her labors. Includes three components: base compensation, pay incentives, and indirect compensation/benefits.

base compensation
The fixed pay an employee receives on a regular basis, either in the form of a salary or as an hourly wage.

pay incentive
A program designed to reward employees for good performance.

Compensation is the single most important cost in most firms. In 2014, private-industry employers spent an average of $29.67 per hour in employee compensation. For the same period, total compensation for state and local government workers averaged $41.73 per hour.[3] Personnel

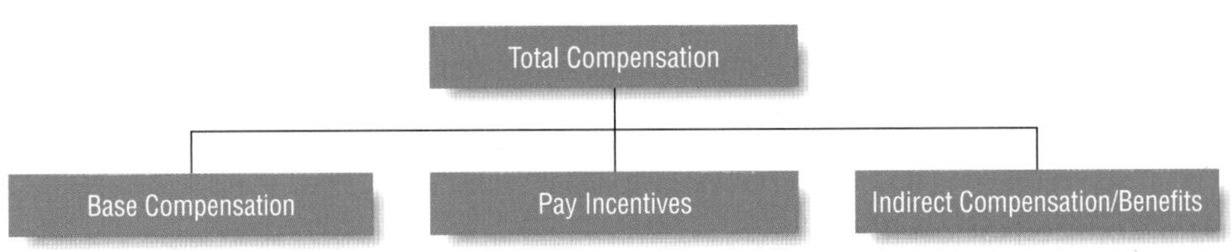

FIGURE 10.1
The Elements of Total Compensation

costs are as high as 60 percent of total costs in certain types of manufacturing environments and even higher in some service organizations. This means that the effectiveness with which compensation is allocated can make a significant difference in gaining or losing a competitive edge. Thus, *how much is paid* and *who gets paid what* are crucial strategic issues for the firm.[4]

Research shows that employees severely undervalue their employer's contributions to indirect compensation or benefits (which is estimated at close to $21,500 per employee, on average, in 2014),[5] and as a result they often take their employer-funded benefits for granted.[6] This situation may be changing as a growing number of companies—including General Motors, IBM, Boeing, Lucent Technologies, and others—are transferring a significant portion of these costs to employees.[7] Firms are also becoming savvier in explaining to employees how much these benefits cost, and that this leaves them with less money for raises.[8] According to a recent survey of 350 large firms, 85 percent are increasing employee communication about the real cost of benefits.[9] This means that employees are more likely to become acutely aware that base compensation, pay incentives, and indirect compensation/benefits are all part of the same pie and that companies cannot increase one piece without reducing the size of the others.

Designing a Compensation System

An employee's paycheck is certainly important for its purchasing power. In most societies, however, a person's earnings also serve as an indicator of power and prestige and are tied to feelings of self-worth. In other words, compensation affects a person economically, sociologically, and psychologically.[10] For this reason, mishandling compensation issues is likely to have a strong negative impact on employees and, ultimately, on the firm's performance.[11]

The wide variety of pay policies and procedures presents managers with a two-pronged challenge: to design a compensation system that (1) enables the firm to achieve its strategic objectives and (2) is molded to the firm's unique characteristics and environment.[12] We discuss the criteria for developing a compensation plan in the sections that follow and summarize these options in Figure 10.2. Although we present each of these as an either/or choice for the sake of simplicity, most firms institute policies that fall somewhere between the two poles.

1. **Internal Versus External Equity** Will the compensation plan be perceived as fair within the company, or will it be perceived as fair relative to what other employers are paying for the same type of labor?
2. **Fixed Versus Variable Pay** Will compensation be paid monthly on a fixed basis—through base salaries—or will it fluctuate depending on such preestablished criteria as performance and company profits?
3. **Performance Versus Membership** Will compensation emphasize performance and tie pay to individual or group contributions, or will it emphasize membership in the organization—logging in a prescribed number of hours each week and progressing up the organizational ladder?
4. **Job Versus Individual Pay** Will compensation be based on how the company values a particular job, or will it be based on how much skill and knowledge an employee brings to that job?
5. **Egalitarianism Versus Elitism** Will the compensation plan place most employees under the same compensation system (egalitarianism), or will it establish different plans by organizational level and/or employee group (elitism)?
6. **Below-Market Versus Above-Market Compensation** Will employees be compensated at below-market levels, at market levels, or at above-market levels?
7. **Monetary Versus Nonmonetary Awards** Will the compensation plan emphasize motivating employees through monetary rewards such as pay and stock options, or will it stress nonmonetary rewards such as interesting work and job security?
8. **Open Versus Secret Pay** Will employees have access to information about other workers' compensation levels and how compensation decisions are made (open pay), or will this knowledge be withheld from employees (secret pay)?
9. **Centralization Versus Decentralization of Pay Decisions** Will compensation decisions be made in a tightly controlled central location, or will they be delegated to managers of the firm's units?

FIGURE 10.2
The Nine Criteria for Developing a Compensation Plan

Internal Versus External Equity

Fair pay is pay that employees generally view as equitable. There are two forms of pay equity. **Internal equity** refers to the perceived fairness of the pay structure within a firm. **External equity** refers to the perceived fairness of pay relative to what other employers are paying for the same type of labor.

internal equity
The perceived fairness of the pay structure within a firm.

external equity
The perceived fairness in pay relative to what other employers are paying for the same type of labor.

In considering internal versus external equity, managers can use two basic models: the distributive justice model and the labor market model.

THE DISTRIBUTIVE JUSTICE MODEL The *distributive justice model* of pay equity holds that employees exchange their contributions or input to the firm (skills, effort, time, and so forth) for a set of outcomes. Pay is one of the most important of these outcomes, but nonmonetary rewards, such as a company car, may also be significant. This social–psychological perspective suggests that employees are constantly (1) comparing what they bring to the firm to what they receive in return and (2) comparing this input/outcome ratio with that of other employees within the firm. Employees will think they are fairly paid when the ratio of their inputs and outputs is equivalent to that of other employees whose job demands are similar to their own.

THE LABOR MARKET MODEL According to the *labor market* model of pay equity, the wage rate for any given occupation is set at the point where the supply of labor equals the demand for labor in the marketplace (W_1 in Figure 10.3). In general, the less employers are willing to pay (low demand for labor) and the lower the pay workers are willing to accept for a given job (high supply of labor), the lower the wage rate for that job.[13]

The actual situation is a great deal more complicated than this basic model suggests. People base their decisions about what jobs they are willing to hold on many more factors than just pay. Moreover, the pay that an employer offers is based on many factors besides the number of available people with the skills and abilities to do the job. A complete exploration of this topic is beyond the scope of this book. However, the basic point of the labor market model is that external equity is achieved when the firm pays its employees the "going rate" for the type of work they do.[14] For a growing number of managerial, professional, and technical occupations, the "going rate" is determined not only by local and domestic factors, but also by global forces.[15]

In general, salary dispersion increases for higher occupational levels and for broader geographic areas. For instance, according to Salary.com, in 2013 the salary range for a chief financial officer at a U.S. firm was between $179,820 (lowest 10%) and $466,341 (highest 10%). In contrast, the salary range for an administrative assistant was from $33,217 (lowest 10%) to $56,607 (highest 10%).[16]

BALANCING EQUITY Ideally, a firm should try to establish both internal and external pay equity, but these objectives are often at odds. For instance, universities sometimes pay new assistant professors more than senior faculty who have been with the institution for a decade or more,[17] and firms sometimes pay recent engineering graduates more than engineers who have been on board for many years.[18]

Many firms also have to determine which employee groups' pay will be adjusted upward to meet (or perhaps exceed) market rates. This decision is generally based on each group's relative

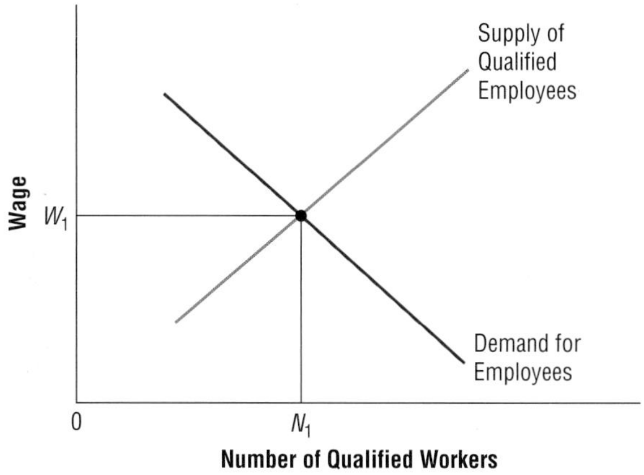

FIGURE 10.3
The Labor Market Model

importance to the firm. For example, marketing employees tend to be paid more in firms that are trying to expand their market share and less in older firms that have a well-established product with high brand recognition.

Once a decision has been made as to which groups will be adjusted upward, one difficult challenge remains: What to do with "superstars." In some cases, these individuals command a much higher salary than the average of those holding the same title. For instance, U.S. universities are expanding their business faculty. This has driven up business faculty salaries, which averaged more than $155,150 a year in 2014, making it one of the highest-paid occupational groups that the government tracks.[19] Yet even at an elite school, a top business faculty member can earn more than double the average earnings of his or her peers of the same rank in the same department. Some compensation professionals refer to this type of pay as having **individual equity**, because it is based on the value to the institution of specific people rather than of the job group, position title, or class to which they belong. Individual equity decisions are becoming more important in professions where some key people can make a big difference and where there is high performance variance. These typically include such occupations as top executives, sales, scientists and engineers, software development, and the like. Individual equity decisions may be controversial because these generally require subjective judgments as to how much each employee is worth to the firm; if not justified carefully, real or perceived favoritism would tarnish the whole process.

individual equity
The perceived fairness of individual pay decisions.

In general, emphasizing external equity is more appropriate for newer, smaller firms in a rapidly changing market. These firms often have a high need for innovation to remain competitive and are dependent on key individuals to achieve their business objectives.[20]

When faced with choosing between internal and external equity, an increasing number of firms have opted to offer large "sign-on bonuses" to new employees in order to entice good candidates without disrupting the existing salary schedules. A survey of 348 large and small firms that use sign-on bonuses indicated 80 percent of them use sign-on bonuses for professional staff and executives; 70 percent for midlevel managers and information technology personnel; 60 percent for sales, lower-level managers, and technical staff; and 20 percent for clerical workers. In a sense, the new employee receives a big pay raise "up front"—in many cases 25 percent or more of annual salary—and the company avoids the need to reduce posted salary differentials between junior and senior employees.[21]

In recent years, another interesting twist to the balancing equity dilemma is the practice in which companies facing uncertain financial futures shower "retention bonuses" on key employees. The objective is to retain needed expertise without having to raise the entire salary schedule—which might hasten the firm's demise. For instance, a few years back Kmart spent upward of $92 million in retention bonuses for 9,700 key employees as it filed for bankruptcy protection. Other well-publicized cases of companies that did the same include Enron, Polaroid, Bradlees Inc., and Aerovox, Inc.[22] Some financial institutions bailed out by the federal government during 2008–2011 paid retention bonuses to key employees, a move that some people thought was akin to rewarding those who were responsible for the crisis in the first place. A 2013 survey indicates that 59.1 percent of companies are very concerned with losing good employees and the majority of these utilize incentives to reduce turnover.[23]

Firms can also provide "adds ons" or "caps," which are renegotiable on an individual basis. Going back to the example of business faculty, one way many universities handle the individual-equity challenge is to base all professors' salaries on a nine-month academic year schedule (usually mid-August to mid-May). Those who are exceptional contributors receive a summer stipend that often adds up to a third of the nine-month salary. They may also receive other perks, such as large travel budgets, research support, secretarial assistance, and the like. These "chairs" or "fellowships," as they are usually called, are often renegotiated at certain fixed intervals.

Lastly, a growing number of firms have developed explicit "counteroffer" policies. This means that the organization will match or closely match the compensation offer an employee receives from a competitor, but only if certain criteria are met (for example, the offer comes from a leading-edge company). According to a recent survey, 55 percent of firms make counteroffers, but only for employees who are in key positions and those who are outstanding performers.[24]

Fixed Versus Variable Pay

Firms can choose to pay a high proportion of total compensation in the form of base pay (for example, a predictable monthly paycheck) or in the form of variable pay that fluctuates according to some preestablished criterion. On average, approximately 75 percent of firms offer some form of variable pay and this proportion continues to increase over the years.[25]

There is a great deal of variation in the way firms answer the fixed versus variable pay question. On average, 10 percent of an employee's pay in the United States is variable. This compares to 20 percent in Japan. However, the range is huge in both countries—from 0 percent up to 70 percent. For select employee groups (such as sales), variable pay can be as high as 100 percent.[26] In general, the proportion of variable pay increases as an employee's base pay increases, indicating that those in higher-level positions earn more but their overall compensation is more subject to risk. According to most recent estimates, for employees earning more than $950,000 a year in base pay, variable compensation is close to 90 percent of base pay. For those earning less than $35,000 a year in base pay, this percentage drops to less than 5 percent.[27]

Fixed pay is the rule in the majority of U.S. organizations largely because it reduces the risk to employees and it is easier to administer. However, variable pay can be used advantageously in smaller companies, firms with a product that is not well established, companies with a young professional workforce that is willing to delay immediate gratification in hopes of greater future returns, firms supported by venture capital, organizations going through a prolonged period of cash shortages, and companies that would otherwise have to institute layoffs because their revenues are volatile. The Manager's Notebook, "Compensation Entitlements Are Going Out the Window," gives examples of the many risks employees now bear with regard to their pay.

MANAGER'S NOTEBOOK

Compensation Entitlements Are Going Out the Window

Not too long ago employers divided pay into fixed (salaries), variable (incentives), and benefits components. Except for incentive pay, which for most employees was a small percentage of their total compensation, workers could count on a promised salary and future benefits as a condition for employment. But this is changing rapidly, as the following examples demonstrate.

Shift to Variable Pay Plans Continues

In a recent survey, Perrin Watson Consulting found that 82 percent of companies have a variable pay program for nonexecutive employees and 49 percent have a variable pay plan for all employees. Furthermore, 46 percent are increasing the goals that employees are required to meet in order to earn an award.

Race to the Bottom: Mexico Lowers Wages to Snare International Auto Production

Wage concessions were apparently key to persuading Ford Motor Co. to direct many of the 4,500 new jobs involved in building its Fiestas to the Ford plant in Cuautitlan, which is on the outskirts of Mexico City. Wages for new hires were cut to about half of the standard wage of $4.50 per hour. With labor costs like these, Mexico is staying competitive with China, where an average worker at a foreign-owned factory or joint venture can make $2 to $6 per hour. In the United States, General Motors, Chrysler, and Ford have reduced salaries of nonunion staff by as much as 28 percent in an effort to boost profits.

Making Wage Concessions at Airlines

Frontier Airlines, which employs 6,000 aviation professionals, made cuts of up to 20 percent in wages and benefits for the executive management team during 2009–2011 and has asked all of its employees to make wage and benefit concessions in the upcoming years. Similarly, United Airlines has cut pilots' pay by 12 percent and flight attendants' pay by 9.5 percent, in addition to reducing benefits. United has joined the ranks of American Airlines, Continental (which later merged with United), Delta, and US Airways (which later merged with American), which have all made salary and benefit cuts. The wave of mergers in the industry has compounded this problem for employees as there are fewer and fewer options in alternative airlines to find another job.

Pensions Going Up in Smoke

It used to be that pensions were a sacred cow, particularly in the public sector where employees often accepted lower salaries in exchange for generous pension plans. But employees are increasingly faced with big surprises in what they thought was a sure deal. The city of Detroit is just the latest example of a municipality using bankruptcy to negotiate reduced pension payments to employees. As another recent example, The City of Stockton, California, owes $900 million to CalPERS, the state-run pension plan, and is reneging on its pension promises to employees.

Medical Doctors Being Squeezed

Not long ago medical doctors were at the top of all professions in terms of earned income. However, their enviable position has eroded over the years due to shrinking payments by private insurance companies, lower government reimbursement for patients covered under Medicaid and Medicare, and higher malpractice insurance. As a result, an increasing number of doctors are filing for bankruptcy. A recent example is that of oncologist Dr. Dennis Morgan from Enfield, Connecticut: "Revenues began to fall when reimbursements for treatment and drugs to oncologists started shrinking. I made cutbacks but began having trouble meeting expenses and my debt grew. Critical chemotherapy drug and medical supply providers eventually cut me off."

Documenting Pay Cuts Around the World

A quick search through Google at the time of this writing (2015) shows numerous Web sites documenting hundreds of organizations in the United States and abroad that have implemented pay cuts.

Sources: Based on Fisher, D. (2013). Municipal bankruptcies set up war between pensioners and bondholders. *www.forbes.com*; Kavilaz, P. (2013). Doctors driven to bankruptcies. *www.money.cnn.com*; Hellerman, M., and Kochanski, J. (2011). Society for Human Resource Management. Reducing the sense of entitlement, *www.shrm.org;* Vlasic, B., and Bunkley, N. (2009, January 6). Automakers fear a new normal of low sales. *New York Times,* B-1; Evans, K., and Mathews, R. G. (2009, January 3). Manufacturing tumbles globally. *Wall Street Journal*, A-1; Laise, E. (2009, January 3). Mutual fund fought off bears but now is clawed. *Wall Street Journal*, B-1; Sorkin, A. R. (2009, January 6). Eating crow at a dinner for Wall Street. *New York Times*, B-1. ■■

Apple Inc. provides an excellent example of a firm that used variable pay to its own and its employees' advantage. In its early years, employees were willing to work for low salaries for several years in exchange for company stock; many who persevered became millionaires after the value of Apple's stock went sky high in the mid-1980s. Software maker Symantec saw its stock increase 150 percent during 2003–2005, and a high percentage of employees received huge gains during that period because they were all eligible for stock options.[28]

As we will discuss in Chapter 11, tax regulations in effect since fiscal year 2006 are putting a damper on the use of stock options. But this has not stopped firms from experimenting with other types of variable pay. For example, Nordstrom recently gave each employee who worked at least 1,000 hours a year a profit-sharing bonus that was triple what it had been in prior years.[29] Pella, a maker of windows and doors with more than 8,000 employees, has an official policy of giving employees 25 percent of its pretax profits in addition to their normal salaries. Network Appliance, a hardware and software provider, gives employees $5,000 to $10,000 for each patent they file.

Not all variable-pay plans work out well for employees, however. Employees at Enron and Global Crossing saw their stock holdings drop from $90 per share to about 50 cents per share within months, partly due to company mismanagement and partly due to corruption at the top.[30] In less than a year, in response to the housing crisis, employees saw their stock options drop dramatically in value during 2008–2009 at now-bankrupt Lehman Brothers (95%), Merrill Lynch (69%), and AIG (90%). In fact, from 2009 to 2011, approximately 10 percent of salaried employees across a wide variety of firms were unpleasantly surprised to find that the wealth they thought they accumulated during years of hard work had evaporated, and in some cases had left them with a big tax bill as well.[31] On the other hand, most employees have seen significant increases in their shareholdings' value during 2012–2014, showing that the risk is real but so are the potential high returns. What is clear, however, is that fixed pay as a percentage of total compensation continues to decline, and firms are asking employees to share more risks with them.[32] Those firms that treat employees fairly and that clearly communicate to them the downside and upside of the compensation risk they face are more likely to prevent a deterioration of morale in spite of the added stress. For example, Emmis Communications, a chain of magazines and radio and TV stations, recently cut pay 10 percent when faced with a profit crunch. Surprisingly, few people left, and employees accepted the bad news as well as could be expected.[33]

Performance Versus Membership

A special case of fixed versus variable compensation requires a choice between performance and membership.[34] A company emphasizes performance when a substantial portion of its employees' pay is tied to individual or group contributions and the amount received can vary significantly from one person or group to another. The most extreme forms of *performance-contingent compensation* are traditional piece-rate plans (pay based on units produced) and sales commissions. Other performance-contingent plans use awards for cost-saving suggestions, bonuses for perfect attendance, or merit pay based on supervisory appraisals. All these options are provided on top of an individual's base pay (see Chapter 11).

Firms that emphasize *membership-contingent compensation* provide the same or a similar wage to every employee in a given job, as long as the employee achieves at least satisfactory performance. Employees receive a paycheck for logging in a prescribed number of hours of work per week (normally 40). Typically, salary progression occurs by moving up in the organization, not by doing the present job better.

The relative emphasis placed on performance and membership depends largely on the organization's culture and the beliefs of top managers or the company's founder. Most companies that emphasize performance tend to be characterized by fewer management levels, rapid growth, internal competition among people and groups, readily available performance indicators (see Chapter 7), and strong competitive pressures.[35] Regardless of company size, there seems to be a trend not only in the United States, but also in many other countries, away from membership-contingent compensation.[36] Global competition is likely to accelerate this trend as we progress through the second decade of the twenty-first century.[37] This raises another question: should a multinational measure performance at the plant level, at the national level, or across the entire globe? IBM has decided to measure profitability for the entire corporation with the objective of focusing employees' attention, no matter where they work, on worldwide performance. Other companies, however, believe that the "line of sight" between employee behavior and performance is more direct if rewards are based on the profitability of local units.

Most organizations struggle with the choice of criteria to reward performance. For example, some companies such as Intel consider community service as a performance criterion. As another example, teachers in many jurisdictions are being held accountable for how much students learn as well as for enhancing students' welfare. One challenge in the choice of performance criteria is determining how much control the employee actually has over the criteria in question. The Manager's Notebook, "Paying Teachers for Student Welfare," discusses how well-meaning attempts to measure important performance aspects may lead to charges of unfairness.

MANAGER'S NOTEBOOK

Ethics/Social Responsibility

Paying Teachers for Students' Welfare

There has been a major push in recent years to reward teachers for promoting the welfare of students. In one midwestern state, for instance, teachers are given bonuses for ensuring that students meet state-defined targets for physical education "such as consistently demonstrating correct skipping techniques with a smooth and effortless rhythm and strike consistently a ball with a paddle to a target area with accuracy and good technique." In many jurisdictions around the country, pay-for-performance in K–12 now translates into rewards for teachers pegged to improvements in test scores. Common complaints with these well-intentioned programs are that teachers are induced to teach students how to do well on the tests (perhaps while sacrificing critical thinking and general learning) and that the system is unfair because teachers are made accountable for variables they can't control (such as the socioeconomic status of students, school funding, and family life).

Sources: Based on Will, G. F. (2013). In Chicago, a battle over schools' future. *www.washingtonpost.com*; Gates, B. (2013). A fairer way to evaluate teachers. *www.washingtonpost.com*; Munnell, A. H., and Fraenkel, R. C. (2013). Compensation matters: The case of teachers. *Center for Retirement Research of Boston College, 28*, 1–10. ■■

Job Versus Individual Pay

Most traditional compensation systems assume that in setting base compensation, a firm should evaluate the value or contributions of each job, not how well the employee performs it.[38] This means that the minimum and maximum values of each job are set independently of individual workers, who must be paid somewhere in the range established for that job.

knowledge-based pay or skill-based pay
A pay system in which employees are paid on the basis of the jobs they can do or talents they have that can be successfully applied to a variety of tasks and situations.

In a **knowledge-based pay or skill-based pay** system, employees are paid on the basis of the jobs they *can* do or the talents they have that can be successfully applied to a variety of tasks and situations.[39] Thus, the more hats an individual can wear, the more pay he or she will receive. Employees' base compensation increases as they become able to perform more duties successfully.

Although the traditional job-centered pay system is still predominant, more and more firms are opting for a knowledge-based approach. Proponents argue that knowledge-based pay provides greater motivation for employees, makes it easier to reassign workers to where they are most needed, reduces the costs of turnover and absenteeism because other employees can assume missing employees' duties, and provides managers with much more staffing flexibility. However, critics maintain that a skill-based system may lead to higher labor costs, loss of labor specialization, greater difficulty in selecting applicants because the qualifications are less specific, and a chaotic workplace where "the left hand does not keep track of what the right hand is doing."[40]

How, then, should managers approach the job versus individual pay question? A job-based pay policy tends to work best in situations where:

- Technology is stable.
- Jobs do not change often.
- Employees do not need to cover for one another frequently.
- Much training is required to learn a given job.
- Turnover is relatively low.
- Employees are expected to move up through the ranks over time.
- Jobs are fairly standardized within the industry.

The automobile industry fits most of these criteria. Individual-based compensation programs are more suitable when:

- The firm has a relatively educated workforce with both the ability and the willingness to learn different jobs.

- The company's technology and organizational structure change frequently.
- Employee participation and teamwork are encouraged throughout the organization.
- Opportunities for upward mobility are limited.
- Opportunities to learn new skills are present.
- The costs of employee turnover and absenteeism in terms of lost production are high.[41]
- Individual-based pay plans are common in manufacturing environments that rely on continuous-process technologies.[42]

Another related issue in this category is the extent to which the firm and employee share some of the financial benefits derived from the employee's ideas or inventions. In the United States, this practice is uncommon because the employee is already being compensated for performing a particular job. Any extra payments to this individual are optional and discretionary. However, this is not the case in other countries, which presents a challenge to multinational organizations (particularly high-technology firms) that employ skilled personnel around the world (see the Manager's Notebook "Who Is Entitled to the Profits: The Employee Who Came up with the Idea That Made the Company Money or the Company That Paid His or Her Salary?").

MANAGER'S NOTEBOOK

Global

Who Is Entitled to the Profits: The Employee Who Came Up with the Idea That Made the Company Money or the Company That Paid His or Her Salary?

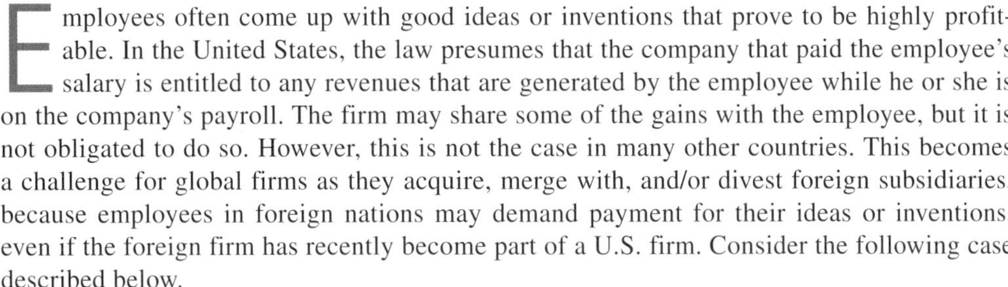

Employees often come up with good ideas or inventions that prove to be highly profitable. In the United States, the law presumes that the company that paid the employee's salary is entitled to any revenues that are generated by the employee while he or she is on the company's payroll. The firm may share some of the gains with the employee, but it is not obligated to do so. However, this is not the case in many other countries. This becomes a challenge for global firms as they acquire, merge with, and/or divest foreign subsidiaries, because employees in foreign nations may demand payment for their ideas or inventions, even if the foreign firm has recently become part of a U.S. firm. Consider the following case described below.

Dr. Andreas Paul Schueppen is a former employee of Atmel Germany GmbH. He is claiming he is owed 42 million euros (about $60 million) as an "inventor's bonus." Schueppen joined the Daimler-Benz research center in Ulm, Germany, in 1993, where he worked on SiGe (silicon-germanium) technology and improved it in 1994 (he brought it up to the then–world record for silicon-based transistors: to a 160 GHz maximum frequency of oscillation). During 1995 and 1996, he transferred the SiGe technology from Daimler in Ulm to production at TEMIC Telefunken Microelectronics in Heilbronn, Germany. Silicon germanium was also being researched by many leading semiconductor companies, and the technology is now widely used in mobile applications, such as mobile phones, wireless large-area networks (LANs), global positioning satellite (GPS) receivers, park distance control, and anti-collision radars. Schueppen filed his case in Germany and claims that it is only with his patents and his inventions that TEMIC was able produce the technology in its facility in Heilbronn, Germany. Daimler sold part of TEMIC to Atmel Corp, which is now based in the United States and is the target of the suit.

Sources: Based on *www.faqs.org/patents*. (2013). System and method for distributing mobile compensation and incentives for inventors; *www.electronics-eetimes.com*. (2011). Engineer seeks $60 million bonus from Atmel; *www.Atmel.com*. (2011); *www.patentstorm.us*; *www.spoke.com*. (2011), Atmel Germany GmbH. ■■

Elitism Versus Egalitarianism

egalitarian pay system
A pay plan in which most employees are part of the same compensation system.

elitist pay system
A pay plan in which different compensation systems are established for employees or groups at different organizational levels.

Firms must decide whether to place most of their employees under the same compensation plan—an **egalitarian pay system**—or to establish different compensation plans by organizational level and/or employee group—an **elitist pay system**. For example, in some firms only the CEO is eligible for stock options.[43] In other companies, even the lowest-paid worker is offered stock options. Some companies offer a wide menu of pay incentives only to specific employee groups[44] (such as salespeople), whereas others make these available to most employees. At the Vermont-based ice cream company Ben & Jerry's Homemade Holdings, Inc., the compensation system is linked to company prosperity. When the company does well, everyone does well. The profit-sharing plan awards the same percentage to all employees, from the top to the bottom.[45]

Some top executives have recently tried to reinforce an egalitarian perspective by pegging their fortunes to those of employees. For instance, at Synovus, a large financial firm with almost 12,000 employees, executives have forfeited their bonuses in order to provide employees higher pay.[46] At SEI Investments, with close to 2,000 employees, workers own nearly half of SEI stock. Whole Foods Market limits the maximum compensation anyone can receive (including top executives) to 14 times the average pay of its full-time workers (this ratio often exceeds 300 to 1 across different organizations in the United States). As we will discuss in Chapter 11, these egalitarian policies are probably the exception rather than the norm; pay differentials between upper echelons and lower ranks have steadily increased during the past 25 years. As another sign of how globalization is creating diffusion in compensation practices, internal pay differentials are becoming increasingly similar when comparing the United States to other Western nations.

Most compensation experts would agree that both systems have their advantages and disadvantages. Egalitarianism gives firms more flexibility to deploy employees in different areas without having to change their pay levels. It can also reduce barriers between people who need to work closely together. Elitist pay structures tend to result in a more stable workforce because employees make more money only by moving up through the company.

Elitist compensation systems are more prevalent among older, well-established firms with mature products, a relatively unchanging market share, and limited competition. Egalitarian compensation systems are more common in highly competitive environments, where firms frequently take business risks and try to expand their market share by continually investing in new technologies, ventures, and products.

Below-Market Versus Above-Market Compensation

A QUESTION OF ETHICS
Some people argue that it is wrong for CEOs to earn multimillion-dollar salaries while some of their employees are earning the minimum wage or being laid off. Some suggest that a firm's top earner should earn no more than 20 times what the lowest-ranked employee earns. What do you think?

Employees' pay relative to alternative employment opportunities directly affects the firm's ability to attract workers from other companies. Pay satisfaction is very highly correlated with pay level, and dissatisfaction with pay is one of the most common causes of employee turnover. The decision to pay above market for all employee groups also allows the firm to hire the "cream of the crop," minimize voluntary turnover, and create a climate that makes all employees feel they are part of an elite organization.[47] This has traditionally been the choice for "blue-chip" firms such as IBM, Microsoft, and Procter & Gamble. However, few companies can afford such a policy. Instead, most firms recognize the importance of certain groups explicitly by paying them above market and cover these costs by paying other groups below market. For example, many high-tech firms compensate their R&D workers quite well while paying their manufacturing employees below-market wages.

Companies that are trying to grow rapidly in a tight labor market must consider paying above-market wages. For instance, Goldman Sachs increased its workforce by 42 percent within a two-year period in the late 1990s. Its pay is at the top of the scale, with executive secretaries, for example, earning $50,000 a year.[48] Unions, which we discuss in detail in Chapter 15, also contribute to above-market pay. Unionized workers receive approximately 9 to 14 percent higher wages than similar nonunionized workers do.[49]

A recent trend, even among firms that traditionally have paid high wages, is to provide a base salary pegged to the market median, combined with more aggressive incentives. According to one expert, "While it is difficult to cut base salary levels, the salary can be frozen for several years until the competitive market catches up."[50] In the meantime, more incentives are given so that total direct compensation (salary plus incentives) may position the firm at a higher percentile in the relevant labor market.

One thing that should be made clear is that firms enjoy a great deal of latitude as to how much they will pay a specific employee relative to the market, even when compensation surveys for most jobs are readily available at the local, national, and international levels. As noted earlier, pay dispersion gets larger for professional and managerial jobs, giving the company more discretion as to how much it will pay "John Doe" to perform a particular job. For instance, say a firm is trying to set a salary for an HR manager. In 2015, the firm may choose a range of base pay from $50,000 to over $500,000 after consulting salary survey data. How much the firm decides to pay the HR manager within that huge market range depends on the importance of the position to the organization as well as individual characteristics (past experience, education, performance appraisal ratings, and the like).

Monetary Versus Nonmonetary Rewards

One of the oldest debates about compensation concerns monetary versus nonmonetary rewards. Unlike cash or payments that can be converted into cash in the future (such as stocks or a retirement plan), nonmonetary rewards are intangible. Such rewards include interesting work, challenging assignments, and public recognition.[51]

Many surveys have shown that employees rank pay low in importance. For example, a large-scale survey found that only 2 percent of Americans declared that pay is a very important aspect of a job.[52] This finding should be viewed with skepticism, however. Most people may find it culturally desirable to downplay the importance of money. Two well-known commentators say, "pay may rank higher than people care to admit to others—or to themselves. In practice, it appears that good old-fashioned cash is as effective as any reward that has yet been invented."[53]

The relative importance of monetary and nonmonetary rewards is illustrated by an annual study of more than 1,000 large-to-midsized firms conducted by *Fortune* magazine to identify the 100 best places to work and how they got that way. For instance, winners during the past three years include:

- ***eBay*** The company offers perks such as golf lessons, bike repair, dental services, and prayer and meditation rooms. Four-week paid sabbaticals every five years are also offered.
- ***Google*** The firm allows engineers to devote 20 percent of their time to projects of their choosing. In addition, it offers on-site child care, an on-site fitness center, subsidized gym membership, and telecommuting.
- ***General Mills*** The company allows women to phase back into work after maternity leave on a part-time basis. It also offers paid sabbaticals, on-site child care, and an on-site fitness center.

As we already noted in some of the company examples drawn from the *Fortune* best-company-to-work-for list, one type of nonmonetary reward that is becoming more common falls under the umbrella of "family-friendly policies" or "work–life balance programs." It includes flexible work hours, personal time (not to be confused with sick time), fitness centers, day care, backup care when children are sick, and the like. Other examples of smaller firms offering these nonmonetary awards include A.G. Edwards, a brokerage firm that provides its employees an indoor walking track, yoga classes, running clubs, and more, and First Horizon National (formerly known as First Tennessee), which offers its employees time off during the school year for parents to visit their children's classrooms.[54]

In general, companies that emphasize monetary rewards want to reinforce individual achievement and responsibility. Those that emphasize nonmonetary rewards prefer to reinforce commitment to the organization. Thus, a greater emphasis on monetary rewards is generally found among firms facing a volatile market with low job security, firms emphasizing sales rather than customer service, and firms trying to foster a competitive internal climate rather than long-term employee commitment. A greater reliance on nonmonetary rewards is usually found in companies with a relatively stable workforce, those that

Source: © David Buffington / Blend Images / Alamy.

emphasize customer service and loyalty rather than fast sales growth, and those that want to create a more cooperative atmosphere within the firm.[55] Several other recent examples of organizations that emphasize nonmonetary rewards and that tend to fit this profile are described in the Manager's Notebook, "Rewarding Employees with Nonmonetary Compensation." One important issue here is that organizations should be realistic about how employees feel about nonmonetary rewards. In a recent survey of 1,400 firms, the investigators concluded that "when budgets are tight, nonmonetary perks such as time off or a departmental celebration can be valuable tools to acknowledge employee accomplishments. But employees also expect financial compensation for their efforts."[56]

A related trend is to offer high performers tangible incentives rather than cash. For instance, each Four Seasons Hotel location provides its "employee of the year" with an all-expense-paid trip for two and an extra week's vacation. Recreational Equipment (REI) provides top performers with up to $300 per year to tackle an outdoor goal.[57]

One important nonmonetary reward for many employees—particularly those with families—is being allowed to work from home. In recent years technology has made this possible by enabling employees to be fully functional from a distant location. Perhaps for this reason (as discussed in the Manager's Notebook "Telecommuters No Longer at a Pay Disadvantage") telecommuters are no longer underpaid relative to their counterparts at the office.

MANAGER'S NOTEBOOK

Emerging Trends

Rewarding Employees with Nonmonetary Compensation

Money isn't everything, and in difficult times it might be hard for cost-cutting firms to shower employees with regular raises, bonuses, and other forms of monetary compensation. However, many companies are finding that employees value more than money on the job and often respond well to other forms of rewards. Public recognition, for instance, goes a long way toward building loyalty and multiplying the positive effects of one employee's stellar performance.

A recent poll asked Canadian executives what they are doing to recognize staff without spending extra funds, and 9 in 10 reported using morale-boosting strategies. "People just want to feel valued," said a management science professor at the University of Waterloo. Other managers suggest strategies such as negotiating employee discounts at local merchants. Cut rates at hotels and restaurants can make it easier for workers to afford family vacations, for instance. Small incentives such as gift cards also make employees feel appreciated. Offering membership in a credit union is another plus; these organizations encourage savings and offer lower loan rates than most banks. Flex time, telecommuting, job sharing, and other family-friendly benefits are widely popular. Time—whether extra time off (with pay) or more face time with managers—is highly valued and seldom costs the company real money. Epcor Utilities Inc., which builds power plants in Canada and the United States, gives its 3,000 employees an extra Friday off every month to use as they wish. Some firms give paid time off for volunteering and community work.

But not even the most generous nonmonetary rewards can make up for inequitable or noncompetitive salaries or for expectations that employees will "pay" for such benefits with long hours and unreasonable workloads. As one company's compensation director put it, "Everybody needs to feel they're being paid fairly. You really have to be within 5 percent of the market—otherwise, these things will niggle at them."

Sources: Based on Aguinis, H., Joo, H., Gottfredson, R. K. (2013). What monetary rewards can and cannot do: How to show employees the money. *Business Horizons, 56*(2), 241–249; Sowanane, P. (2013). Non-monetary rewards: employee choices and organizational practices. *Indian Journal of Industrial Relations, 44*(2), 256–272; *www.writeforhr.com*. (2011). Can't afford to boost your employees' salaries? Think creatively; *www.glenture.com*. (2011). Compensation solutions. Compensation solutions; Grant, T. (2009, March 21). "Thanking staff without a fistful of dollars," Globe and Mail, http://business.theglobeandmail.com; Bergfeld, C., and Calabrese, P. (2009, February 1). Recession-friendly employee perks. Portfolio.com, www.portfolio.com, February 1, 2009; Paul B. Brown, "Making Hard Times Work for Your Business," New York Times, www.nytimes.com

Open Versus Secret Pay

Firms vary widely in the extent to which they communicate openly about worker's compensation levels and company compensation practices. At one extreme, some firms require employees to sign an oath that they will not divulge their pay to coworkers; the penalty for breaking the oath is termination. At the other extreme, every employee's pay is a matter of public record (for instance, Whole Foods Market); in public universities, this information may even be published in the student newspaper. Many organizations are somewhere in between: they do not publish individual data, but they do provide information about pay and salary ranges.

Open pay has two advantages over secret pay.[58] First, limiting employees' access to compensation information often leads to greater pay dissatisfaction because employees tend to overestimate the pay of coworkers and superiors. Second, open pay forces managers to be more fair and effective in administering compensation because bad decisions cannot be hidden and good decisions can serve as motivators to the best workers.

But open pay forces managers and supervisors to defend their compensation decisions publicly. Regardless of good-faith attempts to explain these judgments, it may be impossible to satisfy everyone (even those who are doing very well may feel that they should be doing better). To avoid time-consuming and nerve-wracking arguments with employees, managers may eliminate pay differences among subordinates despite differences in performance levels. The result may be turnover of the better performers, who feel underpaid.

Recent research suggests that greater pay openness is more likely to be successful in organizations with extensive employee involvement and an egalitarian culture that engenders trust and commitment.[59] This is so because open pay can foster perceptions of fairness and greater motivation only in a climate that nurtures employee relations. In more competitive climates, it may unleash a destructive cycle of conflict and hostility that is difficult to stop.

MANAGER'S NOTEBOOK

Telecommuters No Longer at a Pay Disadvantage

Technology/Social Media

It used to be that employees working from home were at a major disadvantage relative to those who work at the office. However, technology has created a level playing field as companies realize that by allowing employees to "telework," they can save on real estate costs and at the same time offer a reward that most employees value. A recent survey shows that 9 out of 10 parents place a higher value on workplace flexibility than higher pay. And fortunately telecommuters are now receiving salaries comparable to in-office employees, so that employees "do not necessarily have to choose between the convenience of working from home and the size of their paycheck." On top of that, telecommuters enjoy substantial cost savings in transportation, wardrobe, cleaning bills, eating out, and day care.

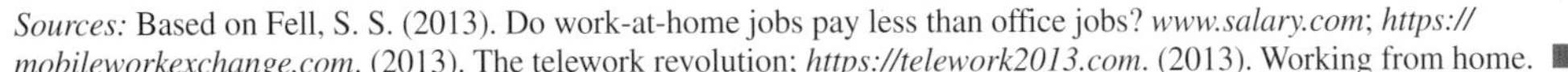

Sources: Based on Fell, S. S. (2013). Do work-at-home jobs pay less than office jobs? *www.salary.com*; *https://mobileworkexchange.com*. (2013). The telework revolution; *https://telework2013.com*. (2013). Working from home.

Centralization Versus Decentralization of Pay Decisions

In a centralized system, pay decisions are tightly controlled in a central location, normally the HR department at corporate headquarters. In a decentralized system, pay decisions are delegated deep down into the firm, normally to managers of each unit.

Centralized pay is more appropriate when it is cost-effective and efficient to hire compensation specialists who can be located in a single place, and made responsible for salary surveys, benefits administration, and recordkeeping.[60] If the organization faces frequent legal challenges, it may also be prudent to centralize major compensation decisions in the hands of professionals.

A centralized system maximizes internal equity, but it does not handle external equity (market) concerns very well. Thus, large and diverse organizations are better served by a decentralized pay system. For example, Mars, Inc., a worldwide leader in the candy market with estimated annual revenues of $11 billion and 30,000 employees, has only two HR people at corporate headquarters. Each Mars unit is responsible for its own pay decisions.[61]

Summary

Compensation is a complex topic that has a significant impact on organizational success. The good news is that there are not as many separate compensation systems as the nine criteria options might suggest. The bad news is that none of these options is a simple either/or decision. Rather, each pair of criteria defines two end points on a continuum, with many possibilities between them.

One final point: compensation policies that apply to a unionized workforce are subject to negotiation and bargaining. Thus, managers in union shops are often severely restricted in what they can and cannot do with regard to compensation issues.

Compensation Tools

Compensation tools can be grouped into two broad categories depending on the unit of analysis used to make pay decisions: job-based approaches and skill-based approaches.

Job-based approaches include the most traditional and widely used types of compensation programs.[62] These plans assume that work gets done by people who are paid to perform well-defined jobs (for example, secretary, bookkeeper). Each job is designed to accomplish specific tasks (for example, coding, recordkeeping) and is normally performed by several people. Because all jobs are not equally important to the firm and the labor market puts a greater value on some jobs than on others, the compensation system's primary objective is to allocate pay so that the most important jobs pay the most.

A simplified example of a typical job-based pay structure appears in Figure 10.4. It shows the pay structure of a hypothetical large restaurant with 87 employees performing 18 different jobs. These 18 jobs are grouped into six **pay grades**, with pay levels ranging from $8.50 an hour for jobs in the lowest grades to a maximum of $34.00 an hour for the job in the highest grade (chef). Employees are paid within the range established for the grade at which their job is classified. Thus, a dishwasher or a busser would be paid between $8.50 and $9.25 an hour (Grade 1).

pay grades
Groups of jobs that are paid within the same pay range.

The *skill-based approach* is far less common. It assumes that workers should be paid not according to the job they hold, but rather by how flexible or capable they are at performing multiple tasks. Under this type of plan, the greater the variety of job-related skills workers possess, the more they are paid. Figure 10.5 shows a simple example of a skill-based approach that could be used as an alternative to the job-based approach depicted in Figure 10.4. Workers who master the first set of skills (Block 1) receive $9 an hour; those who learn the skills in Block 2 (in addition to those in Block 1) receive $10.50 an hour; those who acquire the skills in Block 3 (in addition to those in Blocks 1 and 2) are paid $13.50 an hour; and so on.

In the sections that follow, we discuss these two major types of compensation programs in greater depth. Because compensation tools and pay plans can be very complex, we avoid many of the operational details, focusing instead on these programs' intended uses and their relative strengths and weaknesses. Excellent sources that provide step-by-step procedures to implement such programs are available elsewhere.[63]

Job-Based Compensation Plans

There are three key components of developing job-based compensation plans: achieving internal equity, achieving external equity, and achieving individual equity. Figure 10.6 summarizes how

	Jobs	Number of Positions	Pay
GRADE 6	Chef	2	$23.50–$34.00/hr.
GRADE 5	Manager	1	$14.50–$24.00/hr.
	Sous-Chef	1	
GRADE 4	Assistant Manager	2	$10.50–$15.00/hr.
	Lead Cook	2	
	Office Manager	1	
GRADE 3	General Cook	5	$9.50–$11.00/hr.
	Short-Order Cook	2	
	Assistant to Lead Cook	2	
	Clerk	1	
GRADE 2	Server	45	$9.00–$10.00/hr.
	Hostess	4	
	Cashier	4	
GRADE 1	Kitchen Helper	2	$8.50–$9.25/hr.
	Dishwasher	3	
	Janitor	2	
	Busser	6	
	Security Guard	2	

FIGURE 10.4

Pay Structure of a Large Restaurant Developed Using a Job-Based Approach

Skill Block	Skills	Pay
5	• Create new items for menu • Find different uses for leftovers (e.g., hot dishes, buffets) • Coordinate and control work of all employees upon manager's absence	$26.00/hr.
4	• Cook existing menu items following recipe • Supervise kitchen help • Prepare payroll • Ensure quality of food and adherence to standards	$20.00/hr.
3	• Schedule servers and assign workstations • Conduct inventory • Organize work flow on restaurant floor	$13.50/hr.
2	• Greet customers and organize tables • Take orders from customers • Bring food to tables • Assist in kitchen with food preparations • Perform security checks • Help with delivery	$10.50/hr.
1	• Use dishwashing equipment • Use chemicals/disinfectants to clean premises • Use vacuum cleaner, mop, waxer, and other cleaning equipment • Clean and set up tables • Perform routine kitchen chores (e.g., making coffee)	$9.00/hr.

FIGURE 10.5

Pay Schedule of a Large Restaurant Designed Using a Skill-Based Approach

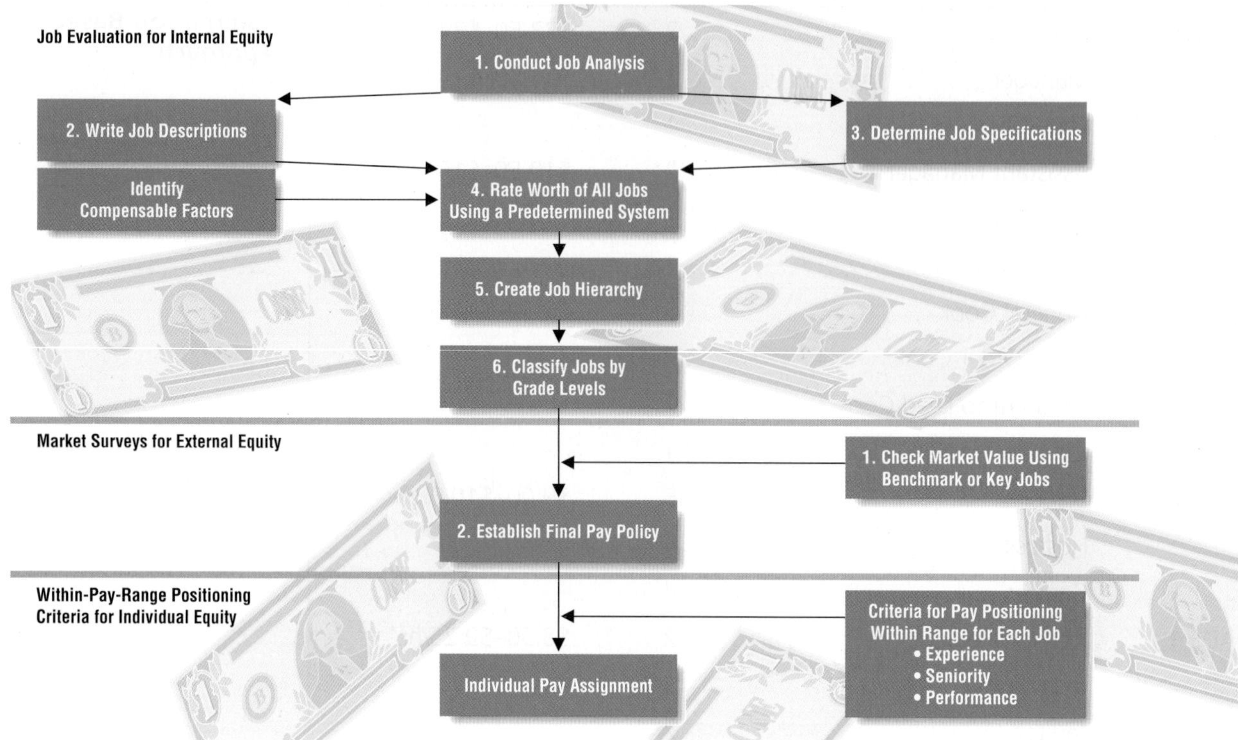

FIGURE 10.6
The Key Steps in Creating Job-Based Compensation Plans

these are interrelated and the steps involved in each component. The large majority of U.S. firms rely on this or a similar scheme to compensate their workforce.[64]

job evaluation
The process of evaluating the relative value or contribution of different jobs to an organization.

ACHIEVING INTERNAL EQUITY: JOB EVALUATION Job-based compensation assesses the relative value or contribution of different jobs (*not* individual employees) to an organization. The first part of this process, referred to as **job evaluation**, is composed of six steps intended to provide a rational, orderly, and systematic judgment of how important each job is to the firm. The ultimate goal of job evaluation is to achieve internal equity in the pay structure.

Step 1: Conduct Job Analysis As we discussed in Chapter 2, job analysis is the gathering and organization of information concerning the tasks, duties, and responsibilities of specific jobs. In this first step in the job-evaluation process, information is gathered about the duties, tasks, and responsibilities of all jobs being evaluated. Job analysts can use personal interviews with workers, questionnaires completed by employees and/or supervisors, and business records (for example, cost of equipment operated and annual budgets) to study the what, how, and why of various tasks that make up the job. Sample items from a commonly used job analysis questionnaire, the Position Analysis Questionnaire, appear in Figure 10.7. For each question, the job analyst considers what is known about the job and decides which of the five descriptions is most appropriate.

Step 2: Write Job Descriptions In the second step in the job-evaluation process, the job-analysis data are boiled down into a written document that identifies, defines, and describes each job in terms of its duties, responsibilities, working conditions, and specifications. This document is called a *job description.* (You will recall this term from Chapter 2.)

Step 3: Determine Job Specifications Job specifications consist of the worker characteristics that an employee must have to perform the job successfully. These prerequisites are drawn from the

Mental Processes

Decision Making, Reasoning, and Planning/Scheduling

36. Decision making

Using the response scale below, indicate the level of decision making typically involved in the job, considering the number and complexity of the factors that must be taken into account, the variety of alternatives available, the consequences and importance of the decisions, the background experience, education, and training required, the precedents available for guidance, and other relevant considerations.

Level of Decision

1. *Very limited* (e.g., decisions such as those in selecting parts in routine assembly, shelving items in a warehouse, cleaning furniture, or handling automatic machines)
2. *Limited* (e.g., decisions such as those in operating a wood planer, dispatching a taxi, or lubricating an automobile)
3. *Intermediate* (e.g., decisions such as those in setting up machines for operation, diagnosing mechanical disorders of aircraft, reporting news, or supervising auto service workers)
4. *Substantial* (e.g., decisions such as those in determining production quotas or making promoting and hiring decisions)
5. *Very substantial* (e.g., decisions such as those in approving an annual corporate budget, recommending major surgery, or selecting the location for a new plant)

37. Reasoning in problem solving

Using the response scale below, indicate the level of reasoning required in applying knowledge, experience, and judgment to problems.

Level of Reasoning in Problem Solving

1. *Very limited* (use of common sense to carry out simple or relatively uninvolved instructions, e.g., hand assembler or mixing machine operator)
2. *Limited* (use of some training and/or experience to select from a limited number of solutions the most appropriate action or procedure in performing the job, e.g., sales clerk, electrician apprentice, or library assistant)
3. *Intermediate* (use of relevant principles to solve practical problems and to deal with a variety of concrete variables in situations where only limited standardization exists, such as that used by supervisors or technicians)
4. *Substantial* (use of logic or scientific thinking to define problems, collect information, establish facts, and draw valid conclusions, such as that used by petroleum engineers, personnel directors, or chain store managers)
5. *Very substantial* (use of logical or scientific thinking to solve a wide range of intellectual and practical problems, such as that used by research chemists, nuclear physicists, corporate presidents, or managers of a large branch or plant)

FIGURE 10.7

Sample Items from Position Analysis Questionnaire

Source: Purdue Research Foundation, West Lafayette, IN 47907-1650. Used with permission.

job analysis, although in some cases they are legally mandated (for example, plumbers must have a plumbing license). Job specifications are typically very concrete in terms of necessary years and type of prior work experience, level and type of education, certificates, vocational training, and so forth. They are usually included on job descriptions.

Step 4: Rate Worth of All Jobs Using a Predetermined System After job descriptions and job specifications have been finalized, they help determine the relative value or contributions of different jobs to the organization. This job evaluation is normally done by a three- to seven-person committee that may include supervisors, managers, HR department staff, and outside consultants. Several well-known evaluation procedures have evolved over the years, but the *point factor system* is used by the vast majority of firms.[65]

compensable factors
Work-related criteria that an organization considers most important in assessing the relative value of different jobs.

The point factor system uses **compensable factors** to evaluate jobs. Compensable factors are work-related criteria that the organization considers most important in assessing the relative value of different jobs. One commonly used compensable factor is knowledge. Jobs that require more knowledge (acquired either through formal education or through informal experience) receive a higher rating and, thus, more compensation. Although each firm can determine its own compensable factors, or even create compensable factors suitable to various occupational groups or job families (clerical, technical, managerial, and so on), most firms adopt compensable factors from well-established job-evaluation systems. Two point-factor systems that are almost universally accepted are the *Hay Guide Chart Profile Method* and the Management Association of America (MAA) *National Position Evaluation Plan* (formerly known as the NMTA point factor system). The Hay Method, which is summarized in Figure 10.8, uses three compensable factors to evaluate jobs: know-how, problem solving, and accountability. The MAA (NMTA) plan has three separate units: Unit I for hourly blue-collar jobs; Unit II for nonexempt clerical, technical, and service positions; and Unit III for exempt supervisory, professional, and management-level positions. The MAA (NMTA) plan includes 11 factors divided into four broad categories (skill, effort, responsibility, and working conditions).[66]

In both systems, each compensable factor is assigned a scale of numbers and degrees. The more important factors are given higher point values and the less important factors lower values.

Know-How

Know-how is the sum total of every kind of skill, however acquired, necessary for acceptable job performance. This sum total, which comprises the necessary overall "fund of knowledge" an employee needs, has three dimensions:

1. Knowledge of practical procedures, specialized techniques, and learned disciplines.
2. The ability to integrate and harmonize the diversified functions involved in managerial situations (operating, supporting, and administrative). This know-how may be exercised consultatively as well as executively and involves in some combination the areas of organizing, planning, executing, controlling, and evaluating.
3. Active, practicing skills in the area of human relationships.

Problem Solving

Problem solving is the original "self-starting" thinking required by the job for analyzing, evaluating, creating, reasoning, and arriving at conclusions. To the extent that thinking is circumscribed by standards, covered by precedents, or referred to others, problem solving is diminished and the emphasis correspondingly is on know-how. Problem solving has two dimensions:

1. The environment in which the thinking takes place.
2. The challenge presented by the thinking to be done.

Accountability

Accountability is the answerability for an action and for the consequences thereof. It is the measured effect of the job on end results. It has three dimensions:

1. Freedom to act—the degree of personal or procedural control and guidance.
2. Job impact on end results.
3. Magnitude—indicated by the general dollar size of the areas(s) most clearly or primarily affected by the job (on an annual basis).

FIGURE 10.8
Hay Compensable Factors

Source: Courtesy of Hay Group

For instance, the highest possible points under the MAA (NMTA) system are earned for experience, with each degree of experience being worth 22 points. The value of the other two MAA (NMTA) skill factors is 14 points per degree. All other factors are worth either 5 or 10 points per degree.

This scale allows the evaluation and compensation committee to assign a number of points to each job on the basis of each factor degree. For example, let us assume that job X is rated at the fifth degree for physical demand (50 points), equipment or process (25 points), material or product (25 points), safety of others (25 points), and work of others (25 points); at the fourth degree for mental or visual demand (20 points), working conditions (40 points), and hazards (20 points); at the second degree for experience (44 points); and at the first degree for knowledge (14 points) and initiative and ingenuity (14 points). The total points for this job across all 11 MAA (NMTA) compensable factors is, thus, 302.

Step 5: Create a Job Hierarchy The four steps described thus far produce a **job hierarchy**, a listing of jobs in terms of their relative assessed value (from highest to lowest). Figure 10.9 illustrates a job hierarchy for office jobs in a typical large organization. Column 1 of the figure shows the total points assigned to each job in descending order. These range from a high of 300 for customer-service representative to a low of 60 for receptionist.

job hierarchy
A listing of jobs in order of their importance to the organization, from highest to lowest.

Step 6: Classify Jobs by Grade Levels For the sake of simplicity, most large organizations classify jobs into grades as the last step in the job-evaluation process. Typically, the job hierarchy is reduced to a manageable number of grade levels, with the assigned points used to determine where to set up dividing lines between grades. For example, column 2 in Figure 10.9 shows how the hierarchy of 18 clerical jobs is divided into five grade levels. All jobs in a given grade are judged to be essentially the same in terms of importance because the points assigned to each are very close in number.

FIGURE 10.9
Hierarchy of Clerical Jobs, Pay Grades, and Weekly Pay Range for a Hypothetical Office

	1 Points	2 Grade	3 Weekly Pay Range
Customer Service Representative	300	5	$600–$750
Executive Secretary/ Administrative Assistant	298		
Senior Secretary	290		
Secretary	230	4	$550–$650
Senior General Clerk	225		
Credit and Collection Clerk	220		
Accounting Clerk	175	3	$525–$575
General Clerk	170		
Legal Secretary/Assistant	165		
Senior Word Processing Operator	160		
Word Processing Operator	125	2	$490–$530
Purchasing Clerk	120		
Payroll Clerk	120		
Clerk-Typist	115		
File Clerk	95	1	$450–$500
Mail Clerk	80		
Personnel Clerk	80		
Receptionist	60		

Other job-evaluation systems are the *ranking system* (in which the evaluation committee puts together a hierarchy of job descriptions from highest to lowest based on an overall judgment of value); the *classification system* (in which the committee sorts job descriptions into grades without using a point system, as in the federal civil service job classification system); *factor comparison* (a complex and seldom-used variation of the point and ranking systems); and *policy capturing* (in which mathematical analysis is used to estimate the relative value of each job based on the firm's existing practices).

You should keep two key aspects of our discussion so far in mind. First, job evaluation is performed internally and does not take into account the wage rates in the marketplace or what other firms are doing. Second, job evaluation focuses only on the value of the tasks that make up each job, not the people performing them. The MAA (NMTA) booklet distributed to all employees whose jobs are evaluated under that system makes this very explicit: "The plan rates each job based on compensable factors used to assess the contributions of each job to the organization and does not judge the performance of any given individual employee."[67]

ACHIEVING EXTERNAL EQUITY: MARKET SURVEYS To achieve external equity, firms often conduct *market surveys*. The purpose of these surveys is to determine the pay ranges for each grade level. An organization may conduct its own salary surveys, but most purchase commercially available surveys. Consulting firms conduct literally hundreds of such surveys each year for almost every type of job and geographic area. Users can create customized reports based on position, job family, geographic area, industry classification, organization size, and the like by using simple pull-down menus and point-and-click technology. For additional salary survey sources that are user friendly and instantly available to HR professionals and line managers via the Web, see the Manager's Notebook, "How Much Is a Position Worth in the Marketplace?" You might want to try some of these online sources and check the salary range of a job of interest to you by state, metropolitan area, and even zip code.

MANAGER'S NOTEBOOK

Customer-Driven HR

How Much Is a Position Worth in the Marketplace?

Salary survey data were commonly obtained by the HR department. But technology is making this process almost obsolete. Line managers can now instantly access salary data analyzed by location, by industry, and by work experience for hundreds of positions. This is possible through online compensation surveys; three of them are Comp Quest Online, Global Directory of Salary Surveys, and Survey Finder.

Comp Quest Online (*www.towerswatson.com*)

Towers Watson Comp Quest Online is a powerful Web-based service that helps managers and HR professionals conduct competitive pay assessments (both domestically and internationally) over the Internet. It allows users to generate custom reports. For example, users can:

- Create their own peer groups of companies by selecting specific companies by name, industry, size, or performance measure.
- Access new data as it is submitted to the database throughout the year.
- Customize report formats and content (for example, select preferred percentiles and currencies, show incumbent's data, and tailor report titles and labels).

Global Directory of Salary Surveys (*http://jobmob.co.il*)

This site will connect you to more than 100 salary surveys around the world. You can click on the home Web page (for instance, India, the Philippines, the United Kingdom, or South Africa) and it will take you to the appropriate site.

Survey Finder (*hrcom.salary.com*)

The Survey Finder enables HR professionals and line managers to search a database of hundreds of up-to-date compensation surveys offered from more than 100 independent vendors, including major human resource consulting firms, compensation consulting firms, survey companies, and industry associations. To make searches easier, the Survey Finder catalogs every survey according to industrial, geographic, and employee population.

Sources: Based on Comp Quest Online™ (*www.towerswatson.com*), Global Directory of Salary Surveys (*http://jobmob.co.il*), and Survey Finder (*hrcom.salary.com/surveyfinder*).

Similarly, the federal government regularly conducts salary surveys on a regional and national basis for close to 800 occupations. The results are currently available for free on the Internet (Bureau of Labor Statistics, 2014, National Employment and Wage Estimates by Occupation and Industry, *www.bls.gov/bls/blswage.htm*).

Why spend time and money on internal job evaluations when market data can be used to determine the value of jobs? First, most companies have jobs that are unique to the firm and therefore cannot be easily matched to market data.[68] For instance, the job of "administrative assistant" in Company Y may involve supporting top management in important tasks (such as making public appearances for an executive when he or she is not available), whereas in Company Z it may involve only routine clerical duties. Second, the importance of a job can vary from firm to firm. For example, the job of "scientist" in a high-tech firm (where new-product creation is a key to competitive advantage) is usually far more important than in a mature manufacturing company (where scientists are often expected to perform only routine tests).

Using market surveys to link job-evaluation results to external wage/salary data generally requires two steps: benchmarking and establishing a pay policy.

Step 1: Identify Benchmark or Key Jobs To link the internal job-evaluation hierarchy or grade-level classification to market salaries, most firms identify **benchmark or key jobs**—that is, jobs that are similar or comparable in content across firms—and check salary surveys to determine how much these key jobs are worth to other employers. The company then sets pay rates for nonkey jobs (for which market data are *not* available) by assigning them the same pay range as key jobs that fall into the same grade level.

benchmark or key job
A job that is similar or comparable in content across firms.

An example will help here. Let's say five of the jobs in our office example in Figure 10.9 are identified as key. (These are briefly described in Figure 10.10.) The company purchases a salary survey for office workers in the area showing both average weekly pay and the 25th, 50th, and 75th percentiles in weekly pay for these key jobs. For example, Figure 10.11 shows that 25 percent of the customer-service representatives in organizations included in the survey earn $500 per week or less, 50 percent earn $600 or less, and 75 percent earn $750 or less. The average weekly salary in the area for this job is $595. The company uses these market data to assign a pay range for all jobs that were evaluated as being at the same grade level as the key job of customer-service representative—in this case, executive secretary and senior secretary. But first it needs to establish a pay policy.

Customer Service Representative Establishes and maintains good customer relations and provides advice and assistance on customer problems.

Credit and Collection Clerk Performs clerical tasks related to credit and collection activities; performs routine credit checks, obtains supplementary information, investigates overdue accounts, follows up by mail and/or telephone to customers on delinquent payments.

Accounting Clerk Performs a variety of routine accounting clerical work such as maintaining journals, subsidiary ledgers, and related reports according to well-defined procedures or detailed instructions.

Word Processing Operator Operates word processing equipment to enter or search, select, and merge text from a storage device or internal memory for continuous or repetitive production of copy.

Clerk-Typist Performs routine clerical and typing work; follows established procedures and detailed written or oral instructions; may operate simple types of office machines and equipment.

FIGURE 10.10
Sample Benchmark Jobs for Office Personnel

Sources: AMS Foundation. *Office, Secretarial, Professional, Data Processing and Management Salary Report,* AMS Foundation, 550 W. Jackson Blvd., Suite 360, Chicago, IL 60661; see also Salary Wizard. (2012). Salary report for administrative support, and clerical job categories. *www.sw2.salary.com.*

FIGURE 10.11
Market Salary Data for Selected Benchmark Office Jobs

Benchmark Jobs	Weekly Pay Percentile 25th	50th	75th	Weekly Pay Average
1. Customer Service Representative	$500	$600	$750	$595
2. Credit and Collection Clerk	$500	$550	$650	$555
3. Accounting Clerk	$470	$525	$575	$523
4. Word Processing Operator	$480	$490	$530	$494
5. Clerk-Typist	$430	$450	$500	$443

pay policy
A firm's decision to pay above, below, or at the market rate for its jobs.

Step 2: Establish a Pay Policy Because market wages and salaries vary widely (look again at Figure 10.11), the organization needs to decide whether to lead, lag, or pay the going rate (which is normally defined as the midpoint of the wage/salary distribution in the survey). A firm's **pay policy** is determined by how it chooses to position itself in the pay market. The hypothetical firm shown in Figure 10.11, for example, decided to set a pay policy pegging the minimum pay for each grade to the 50th percentile and the maximum pay to the 75th percentile in the market (see column 3 of Figure 10.11). Some firms use more complex methods to achieve the same objective.

ACHIEVING INDIVIDUAL EQUITY: WITHIN-PAY-RANGE POSITIONING CRITERIA After the firm has finalized its pay structure by determining pay ranges for each job, it must perform one last task: Assign each employee a pay rate within the range established for his of her job. Companies frequently use previous experience, seniority, and performance appraisal ratings to determine how much an employee is to be paid within the stipulated range for his or her job. The objective of this last step is to achieve individual equity. Individual equity refers to fairness in pay decisions for employees holding the same job.

EVALUATING JOB-BASED COMPENSATION PLANS Job-based compensation programs are rational, objective, and systematic, all features that minimize employee complaints. They are also relatively easy to set up and administer. However, they have several significant drawbacks:

- Job-based compensation plans do not take into account the nature of the business and its unique problems. For example, jobs are harder to define and change more rapidly in small, growing companies than in larger, more stable companies (such as those in the insurance industry).
- The process of establishing job-based compensation plans is much more subjective and arbitrary than its proponents suggest.
- Job-based systems are less appropriate at higher levels of an organization, where it is more difficult to separate individual contributions from the job itself. To force people to conform to a narrowly defined job description robs the organization of much-needed creativity.
- As the economy has become more service oriented and the manufacturing sector has continued to shrink, jobs have become more broadly defined. As a result, job descriptions are often awash in generalities. This makes it more difficult to evaluate the relative importance of jobs.
- Job-based compensation plans tend to be bureaucratic, mechanistic, and inflexible. Thus, firms cannot easily adapt their pay structure to a rapidly changing economic environment. In addition, because they rely on fixed salary and benefits associated with each level in the hierarchy, these plans tend to result in layoffs to save on costs during economic downturns. Japanese firms often provide 20 to 30 percent of their employees' pay in variable form and have greater flexibility to absorb the economy's ups and downs.
- The job-evaluation process is biased against those occupations traditionally filled by women (clerical, elementary school teaching, nursing, and the like). Although empirical studies are inconclusive on this issue, critics often use vivid examples to make their point, such as sanitation jobs (garbage collection) in New York City being evaluated higher than teaching jobs.

- Wage and salary data obtained from market surveys are not definitive. After adjusting for job content, company size, firm performance, and geographic location, differences ranging from 35 to 300 percent in the pay of identical jobs within the same industry are not uncommon.[69]
- In determining internal and external equity, it is the employees' perceptions of equity that count, not the assessments of job-evaluation committees and paid consultants. Job-based compensation plans assume that the employer can decide what is equitable for the employee. Because equity is in the eye of the beholder, this approach may simply rationalize an employer's pay practices rather than compensate employees according to their contributions.
- In a knowledge-based economy, workers—particularly those who work in scientific and technical fields—may compete for work in an open market; hence, they are not tied to a particular organization. They may not want to be constrained by salaries that are set by a job-evaluation procedure. They are more loyal to the profession than to the firm. As a result, they may see themselves as "freelancers" and may resent organizational controls on their earnings.

Despite all these criticisms, job-based compensation plans continue to be widely used, probably because no alternative systems are both cost-efficient and generally applicable.

SUGGESTIONS FOR PRACTICE Rather than dismissing job-based compensation plans completely, it is more realistic to take steps to reduce the potential problems associated with them:

- ***Think strategically in making policy decisions concerning pay*** For example, it may be in the firm's best interests to design a certain number of jobs very broadly and flexibly. The firm may also find it advantageous to pay at the top of the market for critical jobs that are central to its mission and at the low end of the market for jobs it considers less important. In short, the firm's business and HR strategy should drive the use of compensation tools rather than the other way around.
- ***Secure employee input*** Employee dissatisfaction will be reduced to the extent that employees have a voice in the design and management of the compensation plan. Computer-assisted job-evaluation systems allow employees to describe their jobs in a way that can be synthesized, displayed, rearranged, and easily compared. This tends to improve the acceptability of job-evaluation results and offers an inexpensive way to update job descriptions regularly.
- ***Increase each job's range of pay while expanding its scope of responsibility*** This approach, commonly called **job banding**, entails replacing narrowly defined job descriptions with broader categories (bands) of related jobs.[70] For instance, Fine Products, Inc., a consumer products company, collapsed 13 separate plant, regional, and production manager job titles down to four jobs with increased responsibility. The maximum salary in a range is set at 90 percent greater than the minimum within each band (from $28,500 to $54,500 for "Band C," for instance).[71]

job banding
The practice of replacing narrowly defined job descriptions with broader categories (bands) of related jobs.

Job banding permits employees to receive a substantial pay raise without having to change jobs or get promoted. It has three potential benefits. First, it gives the firm more flexibility because jobs are not narrowly defined. Second, during periods of slow growth, the firm can reward top performers without having to promote them. Third, the firm may save on administrative costs because with banding there are fewer layers of staff and management. However, banding needs to be monitored, because managers enjoy substantial discretion in "slotting" an employee within a large allowable salary range. Over time, this flexibility may create unjustifiable salary inequities from one unit to another and from one employee to another.

- ***Examine statistical evidence periodically to ensure that the job-evaluation system is doing what it is supposed to*** For instance, high turnover or difficulty in hiring employees in certain job classifications may be a good indicator that job evaluation is not working properly.
- ***Expand the proportion of employees' pay that is variable (bonuses, stock plans, and so forth)*** Variable-pay programs provide the firm with the flexibility to reduce costs without resorting to layoffs.

FIGURE 10.12
Example of a Dual-Career Ladder

Band	Managerial	Individual Contributor
13	President	
12	Executive Vice President	Vice President for Research
11	Vice President	Executive Consultant
10	Assistant Vice President	Senior Consultant
9	Director	Consultant
8	Senior Manager	Senior Adviser
7	Manager	Adviser
6		Senior Specialist
5		Specialist
4		Senior Technician
3		Senior Administrative Support, Technician
2		Administrative Support Senior Manufacturing Associate
1		Clerical Support, Manufacturing Associate

Source: LeBlanc, P. Banding the new pay structure for the transformed organization. *Perspectives in Total Compensation, 2014, 3*(8). WorldatWork. Scottsdale, AZ. Used with permission of WorldatWork.

- ***Develop policies for so-called knowledge workers that specify the types of paid external opportunities they may pursue while still remaining employed by the firm*** For example, many universities stipulate that faculty can devote an average of eight hours per week to consulting activities, although they need to file a report listing the external organizations for which they provide services.
- ***Establish dual-career ladders for different types of employees so that moving into management ranks or up the organizational hierarchy is not the only way to receive a substantial increase in pay*** In some situations, such as in a large organization with multiple business units and several layers of management, a tall job hierarchy is appropriate; in others, a relatively flat hierarchy with much room for salary growth (based, for instance, on performance and seniority) makes more sense. Figure 10.12 is an example of a dual-career ladder. The Manager's Notebook, "Go Your Own Way," discusses how more companies are adopting this practice.

MANAGER'S NOTEBOOK

Go Your Own Way

Despite the job title and pay, not everyone wants to be a manager. But for many years, companies offered few other paths to advancement for highly skilled and technical workers, even their star performers.

Now, however, valued employees who love their work rather than the idea of managing other people have more options than ever before. Firms are creating new paths, both formal and informal, to help these employees continue to achieve, improve, and win recognition without having to assume a management role they don't want and in which they might not do well. And companies are finding that these programs help them retain critical employees, too.

At Abbott Laboratories, for example, Dale Kempf advanced through the ranks for several years thanks to his work as a research chemist in the pharmaceutical discovery division. Then his manager nominated him for membership in a prestigious honorary society of Abbott's 200 top scientists, where he continues to win recognition and rewards.

At PricewaterhouseCoopers, Tania Chebli fills the highly regarded and well-paid role of managing director, where her expertise in matters of risk and credit quality is well respected. She mentors other employees, but has no direct reports to manage. Earning the spot required the support of her boss and other colleagues and a formal presentation to a committee. "It was a huge process," Ms. Chebli says now, but "I feel rewarded, I feel recognized."

Johnson Controls offers nonmanagerial technical career tracks, but it also offers technical workers a chance to try a management role without the risk of derailing their careers. "They might say, 'I'm not 100 percent sure, but I want to try it,'" said the company's CIO. "Afterward, they can at least say we tried. We allow for that freedom." To give these technical workers every opportunity to succeed, the company reviews their performance as managers every 30 days. If the job isn't a good match, they return to the technical track, where each position has a three-level salary range and room for advancement.

Other firms that offer nonmanagement tracks for skilled individuals include organizations as diverse as Microsoft, Chevron, Nordstrom, and the Mayo Clinic.

Sources: Based on *www.careerladdersproject.org*. (2014); Different science careers. (2011). *www.nature.com*; Bersin & Associates. (2009, March 9). Succession management for non-management roles. *www.bersin.com/blog*; White, E. (2008, April 14). Go your own way. *Wall Street Journal, http://online.wsj.com*; Plus, J. V. (2008, January 7). Non-management career tracks need not derail tech careers. *WTN News, http://wistechnology.com*.

Skill-Based Compensation Plans

Unlike job-based compensation plans, skill-based compensation plans use skills as the basis of pay.[72] All employees start at the same pay rate and advance one pay level for each new skill they master.[73]

Three types of skills may be rewarded. Employees acquire *depth skills* when they learn more about a specialized area or become expert in a given field. They acquire *horizontal* or *breadth skills* when they learn more and more jobs or tasks within the firm and *vertical skills* when they acquire "self-management" abilities, such as scheduling, coordinating, training, and leadership. Skill-based pay has been adopted by a wide range of industries, such as telecommunications (AT&T and Northern Telecom), insurance (Shenandoah Life Insurance), hotels (Embassy Suites), and retailing (Target).[74]

Skill-based pay offers several potential advantages to the firm.[75] First, it creates a more flexible workforce that is not straitjacketed by job descriptions specifying work assignments for a given job title. Second, it promotes cross-training, thus preventing absenteeism and turnover from disrupting the work unit's ability to meet deadlines. Third, it calls for fewer supervisors, so management layers can be cut to produce a leaner organization. Fourth, it increases employees' control over their compensation because they know in advance what it takes to receive a pay raise (learning new skills).

Skill-based pay does pose some risks to the organization, and this may help explain why only a relatively small proportion (5% to 7%) of all firms use it.[76] First, it may lead to higher compensation and training costs that are not offset by greater productivity or cost savings. This can happen when many employees master many or all the skills and thus receive a higher wage than they would under a job-based pay rate. Second, unless employees have the opportunity to use all the skills they have acquired, they may become "rusty." Third, when employees hit the top of the pay structure, they may become frustrated and leave the firm because they have no further opportunity to receive a pay raise. Fourth, attaching monetary values to skills can become a guessing game unless external comparable pay data are available. Finally, skill-based pay may become part of the problem it is intended to solve (extensive bureaucracy and inflexibility) if an elaborate and time-consuming process is required to monitor and certify employee skills.

One final observation about skill-based pay: This is the pay system that many new and small businesses use by default. Because flexibility is crucial for continued growth, flexible employees are more highly valued and paid accordingly. When a business is fairly new, of course, there is no formalized system relating specific skills to specific compensation values. However, at some point the company must systematize its compensation structure. It is then that the design issues described earlier become critical.

Special Compensation Issues in Small Firms

Smaller firms can seldom implement the more elaborate compensation plans discussed in this chapter. First, they may not have enough positions to justify a pay structure such as the one in our hypothetical restaurant (see Figure 10.4). Second, they may not have the time or

Source: © ZUMA Press, Inc./Alamy.

the employees in place to create and administer a complex compensation program. Third, in many small firms, jobs are broadly defined so that employees are expected to perform multiple tasks and hence, job descriptions are not very meaningful. That is, the value of contributions tends to reside more in the person than in a job title or job content. With these caveats in mind, small firms still face most of the issues discussed in this chapter and need to find effective ways to deal with them. An employee who feels that he or she is treated inequitably with pay is more likely to leave. A good candidate who receives a job offer that is far below the compensation offered by other alternative employers is unlikely to take the lowest bid. Employees who believe that salary and salary raises are given arbitrarily without taking into account responsibility and performance are likely to become demoralized. In short, small firms must provide sufficient inducements to have a qualified and motivated workforce. Even if done more informally, the pay system should be administered so that employees believe pay decisions have adequate distributive and procedural justice.

Small firms can appoint committees that give employees some voice; thus, managers and/or owners can take corrective action if needed based on employee feedback. It is also critical for smaller firms to have a good sense of what other similar firms in the community pay for similar jobs. Hiring underqualified applicants "on the cheap side" or losing key contributors may be devastating to these firms. Online salary surveys can be helpful, although (as discussed earlier) most surveys show a big salary range for various positions, so the firm still needs to choose the most appropriate compensation level. Depending on the strategic needs of the company, this might involve paying above market for some positions (to attract the "cream of the crop") and below market for other positions. For instance, some startup high-technology firms pay above market to engineers and scientists in key positions. Smaller firms often rely on nonmonetary rewards as a substitute for high compensation that the company can't afford (see the You Manage It! feature titled "Helping Employees Take Care of Home Tasks" near the end of this chapter). In some growing sectors, it is common to offer stock to employees in lieu of higher salaries. Most frequently, smaller firms offer substantial bonuses to employees depending on how well the company has performed during the year. Employees may feel that it is fair to receive lower assured compensation (in the form of a fixed salary) in return for the potential to earn additional income in the form of bonuses and stock appreciation.

Many small firms are owned and managed by families. Nonfamily employees who work alongside family employees can sometimes feel an inequity in their positions as nonfamily members. Favoritism toward family employees could prove disastrous to the morale of the workforce. To prevent this problem, family-owned firms should seek the advice of an impartial, external compensation consultant. If the company can afford it, hiring some professional managers and nonfamily supervisors can also be helpful in creating more objectivity in the system. Establishing clear expectations (in terms of scheduling, workloads, tasks, and so on) that are applied equally to all employees—family and nonfamily alike—may also help establish a climate of fairness.

The Legal Environment and Pay System Governance

The legal framework exerts substantial influence on the design and administration of compensation systems. The key federal laws that govern compensation criteria and procedures are the Fair Labor Standards Act, the Equal Pay Act, and the Internal Revenue Code. In addition to these, each state has its own sets of regulations that complement federal law. Labor laws may also limit managerial discretion in setting pay levels.

Fair Labor Standards Act (FLSA)
The fundamental compensation law in the United States. Requires employers to record earnings and hours worked by all covered employees and to report this information to the U.S. Department of Labor. Defines two categories of employees: exempt and nonexempt.

The Fair Labor Standards Act

The **Fair Labor Standards Act (FLSA)** of 1938 is the compensation law that affects most pay structures in the United States. To comply with the FLSA, employers must keep accurate records of earnings and hours worked by all covered employees and must report this information to the Wage and Hour Division of the U.S. Department of Labor. Most businesses are covered by the FLSA, except those with only one employee or annual gross sales under $500,000.

The FLSA defines two categories of employees: exempt and nonexempt. **Exempt employees** are not covered by the provisions of the act; **nonexempt employees** are. Exempt categories include professional, administrative, executive, computer-related jobs, motor carriers, and outside sales jobs. The Department of Labor provides guidelines to determine whether a job is exempt or nonexempt. Although these regulations are subject to change, currently there are specific minimum weekly dollar figures below which a job may not be classified as exempt, namely $455/week for executive, administrative, professional, and computer positions. Managers are often tempted to classify as many jobs as possible as exempt to avoid some of the costs associated with nonexempt status, principally the minimum wage and overtime payments. However, there are heavy penalties for employers who unfairly classify nonexempt jobs as exempt.

exempt employee
An employee who is not covered by the provisions of the Fair Labor Standards Act. Most professional, administrative, executive, and outside sales jobs fall into this category.

nonexempt employee
An employee who is covered by the provisions of the Fair Labor Standards Act.

This means that employers must be alert to new interpretations of the FLSA because they do occur from time to time. For instance, the deputy administrator of the FLSA recently announced that mortgage loan officers are no longer considered exempt under the FLSA and therefore are entitled to overtime pay. This announcement was a reversal from the department's long-time policy on the status of mortgage loan officers and requires banks and other financial institutions to alter their pay practices accordingly to bring themselves into compliance.

MINIMUM WAGES The federal minimum wage set by the FLSA is currently $7.25 per hour, although in some states and cities it is considerably higher. For instance, in Connecticut and Illinois the minimum wage ($8.25 per hour) is almost 14 percent higher than the federal minimum wage, while in the state of Washington the minimum wage ($9.00 per hour) is 24 percent higher. Minimum wage legislation is controversial. Those in favor believe that it raises the standard of living for the poorest members of society. Those who oppose it argue that it results in higher levels of unemployment and poverty among low-skilled workers because it discourages firms from hiring and/or retaining workers. Opponents also claim that minimum wages encourage U.S. firms to open overseas plants in low-wage countries (such as Mexico and the Philippines), thereby creating more unemployment at home. This debate has not yet been resolved, probably because the minimum wage is set at a much lower level than most U.S. firms are willing to pay. However, the debate is being rekindled by a growing number of local governments passing "living wage" (wage needed to secure a decent standard of living) legislation that sets the minimum wage at a much higher level than the federal minimum of $7.25 per hour. For instance, the city of Santa Cruz, California, passed a requirement for public sector employers who contract or subcontract with the county to pay a "living wage" of $13.08 per hour, or $14.27 per hour if they do not provide benefits. At the time of this writing there is legislation pending in Congress to raise the minimum wage to $10.10 per hour minimum.

OVERTIME The FLSA requires that nonexempt employees be paid one and a half times the standard wage for each hour they work over 40 hours a week. This provision was intended to stimulate hiring by making it more costly to expand production using existing employees. In fact, however, many firms would rather pay overtime than incur the costs associated with hiring additional employees (recruitment, training, benefits, and so on).

The U.S. Department of Labor requires that employers guarantee overtime for workers who earn up to $23,600 a year, up from the ceiling of $8,660 established in 1975. The change covers manual laborers, other blue-collar workers, and managers who earn $23,660 per year or less, whether they are paid a salary or an hourly wage. Employers can exempt white-collar workers from overtime pay who make more than $23,660 per year if they do some "professional, administrative, or executive" duties or are "team leaders," whether or not they supervise workers.[77]

Overtime can make a big difference in an employee's paycheck, and it can also derail an organization's cost-cutting efforts. Consider, for instance, the following story. Like many other state employees in California, prison nurse Nellie Larot was hit with furloughs that cut her annual salary: It dropped $10,000, to $92,000. But she more than made up for it by working extra shifts, raking in $177,512 in overtime, according to state records. Her total $270,000 in earnings the same year eclipsed the $225,000 paid to Matthew Cate, then-head of the entire California state prison system. Ex-Governor Arnold Schwarzenegger's decision to furlough workers three days a month was made to save money. Ironically, to make up for these lost hours and maintain minimum service levels, many employees who are filling the gap are taking home paychecks fattened by overtime—more than $1 billion in a single year.[78]

The Equal Pay Act

The Equal Pay Act (EPA) was passed in 1963 as an amendment to the FLSA. As we discussed in Chapter 3, it requires that men and women be paid the same amount of money if they hold similar jobs that are "substantially equal" in terms of skill, effort, responsibility, and working conditions. The EPA includes four exceptions that allow employers to pay one sex more than the other: (1) more seniority; (2) better job performance; (3) greater quantity or quality of production; and (4) certain other factors, such as paying extra compensation to employees for working the night shift. If there is a discrepancy in the average pay of men and women holding similar jobs, managers should ensure that at least one of the four exceptions to the EPA applies to avoid legal costs and back pay to affected employees.

COMPARABLE WORTH Equal pay should not be confused with comparable worth, a much more stringent form of legislation enacted in some countries and used in a few public jurisdictions in the United States. **Comparable worth** calls for comparable pay for jobs that require comparable skills, effort, and responsibility and have comparable working conditions, even if the job content is different. For instance, if a company using the point-factor job-evaluation system we described earlier finds that the administrative assistant position (held mostly by women) receives the same number of points as the shift supervisor position (held mostly by men), comparable worth legislation would require paying employees in these jobs equally, even though they might be exercising very different skills and responsibilities.

comparable worth
A pay concept or doctrine that calls for comparable pay for jobs that require comparable skills, effort, and responsibility and have comparable working conditions, even if the job content is different.

The considerable controversy surrounding comparable worth legislation centers mainly on how it should be implemented rather than on its main goal of pay equity between the sexes. Supporters of comparable worth legislation favor using job-evaluation tools to advance pay equity, pointing out that many private firms already use this method to set wages. Opponents argue that job evaluations are inherently arbitrary and that they do not take sufficient account of jobs' market value. For example, comparable worth proponents have often said that markets treat nurses unfairly because society links the profession to women's unpaid nurturing role in the family. Despite all the problems with implementation, comparable worth is already being used in many countries, including Britain, Canada, and Australia.[79]

ROLE OF THE OFFICE OF FEDERAL CONTRACT COMPLIANCE PROGRAMS (OFCCP) The OFCCP may evaluate compensation in an effort to monitor compliance with EEO. This agency has extensive powers because it may revoke federal government contracts from employers—a costly loss in revenue for many firms.

During the past 40 years, OFCCP has focused most of its efforts on the implementation of affirmative action plans (see Chapter 3). Recently, however, that emphasis seems to have shifted to more focused investigations of discrimination claims, sometimes involving groups who are not considered protected classes (see Chapter 3). For instance, recently more than 530 African American and Caucasian workers who were turned down for jobs with Tyson Refrigerated Processed Meats, Inc. in Vernon, Texas, recovered $560,000 in back pay and interest under a conciliation agreement the company signed with the OFCCP. Fifty-nine of the workers will receive job offers as laborer positions become available at the bacon-processing plant. "The Labor Department is committed to leveling the playing field for all workers," said OFCCP director Patricia A. Shiu. "A company that profits from taxpayer dollars must not discriminate, period!" The settlement, known as a conciliation agreement, resolves an investigation by OFCCP into the facility's hiring practices, which showed that African American and Caucasian job applicants were much less likely to be hired than similarly situated Hispanics applicants. As a federal contractor, Tyson is prohibited from discriminating against workers on the basis of gender, race, sex, religion, nationality, disability, or status as a protected veteran.[80] Other recent cases where the OFCCP negotiated major settlements for past wage discrimination include Goodwill Industries, Bertucci Contracting Co. LLC, and shipping giant Federal Express.[81]

The Internal Revenue Code

The **Internal Revenue Code (IRC)** affects how much of their earnings employees can keep. It also affects how benefits are treated for tax purposes, as we discuss in Chapter 12. The IRC requires the company to withhold a portion of each employee's income to meet federal tax obligations (and, indirectly, state tax obligations, which in most states are set as a percentage of the federal tax withholding).

Internal Revenue Code (IRC) The code of tax laws that affects how much of their earnings employees can keep and how benefits are treated for tax purposes.

Tax laws change from time to time, and these changes affect an employee's take-home pay as well as what forms of compensation can be sheltered from taxes. An employer's failure to take advantage of IRC legislation may result in wasted payroll dollars. For instance, the tax laws currently treat short-term capital gains (profits) on the sale of stock as ordinary income. This reduces the motivational value of stock as a long-term pay incentive because employees bear more risk with stock than with a cash-based form of pay. However, setting the capital gains tax below the tax on ordinary income could make stock more attractive to employees as a pay incentive.

Summary and Conclusions

What Is Compensation?

Total compensation has three components: (1) base compensation, the fixed pay received on a regular basis; (2) pay incentives, programs designed to reward good performance; and (3) benefits or indirect compensation, including health insurance, vacations, and perquisites.

Designing a Compensation System

An effective compensation plan enables the firm to achieve its strategic objectives and is suited to the firm's unique characteristics as well as to its environment. The pay options managers need to consider in designing a compensation system are (1) internal versus external equity, (2) fixed versus variable pay, (3) performance versus membership, (4) job versus individual pay, (5) egalitarianism versus elitism, (6) below-market versus above-market compensation, (7) monetary versus nonmonetary rewards, (8) open versus secret pay, and (9) centralization versus decentralization of pay decisions. In all situations, the best choices depend on how well they "fit" with business objectives and the individual organization.

Compensation Tools

There are two broad categories of compensation tools: job-based approaches and skill-based approaches. The typical job-based compensation plan has three components: (1) To achieve internal equity, firms use job evaluation to assess the relative value of jobs throughout the firm. (2) To achieve external equity, they use salary data on benchmark or key jobs obtained from market surveys to set a pay policy. (3) To achieve individual equity, they use a combination of experience, seniority, and performance to establish an individual's position within the pay range for his or her job.

Skill-based compensation systems are more costly and more limited in use. Skill-based pay rewards employees for acquiring depth skills (learning more about a specialized area), horizontal or breadth skills (learning about more areas), and vertical skills (self-management).

The Legal Environment and Pay System Governance

The major federal laws governing compensation practices are the Fair Labor Standards Act (which governs minimum wage and overtime payments and provides guidelines for classifying employees as exempt or nonexempt), the Equal Pay Act (which prohibits pay discrimination based on gender), and the Internal Revenue Code (which specifies how various forms of employee pay are subject to taxation). Some countries and municipalities have comparable worth legislation, which calls for comparable pay for jobs that require comparable skills, effort, and responsibility and have comparable working conditions, even if the job content is different.

Key Terms

Watch It!

Joie de Vivre Hospitality: Pay for performance and financial incentives. If your instructor has assigned this, go to **mymanagementlab.com** to watch a video case and answer questions.

Discussion Questions

10-1. According to a 2010 study by economists Angus Deaton and Nobel Prize winner and psychologist Daniel Kahnerman, "High incomes don't bring you happiness. . . . [T]he further a person's household income falls below $75,000, the unhappier he or she is. But no matter how much more than $75,000 people make, it doesn't bring them any more joy."[82] How do you explain these results? Do you agree with their conclusion or with the conclusion in the You Manage It! feature titled "Money Doesn't Buy Happiness. Well, on Second Thought . . . "? Explain.

10-2. Walgreens Alliance Boots (previously known as Alliance Boots), a major pharmaceutical retailer, employs some 70,000 workers in the UK, many of whom earn less than $9 an hour. The company is headed by Stefano Pessina, who spearheaded Alliance Boots' merger with Walgreens—a deal that increased his personal fortune by $6.6 billion. The company was criticized for locating its headquarters in Switzerland to reduce its tax liabilities in the UK.[83] What are the implications of a CEO channeling corporate revenues overseas to avoid tax while paying employees less than the "living wage"?

10-3. Go to any of the salary survey sources listed in the Manager's Notebook, "How Much Is a Position Worth in the Marketplace?" and research the salary ranges of four to five positions of your choice. Assume that you are planning to recruit five individuals into each of those positions. How would you use the salary survey data to arrive at a specific offer? Explain.

10-4. In a recent article by professors Hannah Riley Bowless from Harvard and Linda Babcock from Carnegie Mellon, the authors argue that "policy makers, academics, and media reports suggest that women could shrink the gender pay gap by negotiating more effectively for higher compensation. Yet women entering compensation negotiations face a dilemma: They have to weigh the benefits of negotiating against the social consequences of having negotiated. Research shows that women are penalized socially more than men for negotiating higher pay." Do you agree or disagree? Explain.

10-5. As noted in the Manager's Notebook, "Compensation Entitlements Are Going out the Window," fixed or secure pay is becoming rare. What impact do you think this has on employees' outlook? What, if any, are the negative and positive aspects of this trend? Explain.

10-6. According to a recent report by the Society for Human Resource Management "many job evaluation methods are subjective. Evaluators' decisions about which jobs are worth more can be personal and emotional. If the evaluation team knows the job incumbents, they may consider employees' personal qualities as job factors." (*http://www.shrm.org.* [2013] Performing job evaluations.) Based on what you have learned in this chapter, how can job evaluation be made more objective? Explain.

10-7. Some people believe that the recent trend towards giving employees non-monetary rewards is simply a way to save money by using a cheaper way to retain, attract, and motivate employees. Do you agree? Do you think this is fair? Explain.

10-8. Some people argue that it is wrong for CEOs to earn multimillion-dollar salaries while some of their employees are earning the minimum wage or being laid off. Some suggest that a firm's top earner should earn no more than 20 times what the lowest-ranked employee earns. What do you think? Explain your answer.

MyManagementLab®

If your instructor has assigned this, go to **mymanagementlab.com** for the following Assisted-graded writing questions:

10-9. Several companies are moving in the direction of compensating employees with nonmonetary rewards in lieu of higher wages (see the Manager's Notebook, "Rewarding Employees with Nonmonetary Compensation"). Why do you think this is happening? Do you think this is a good thing for companies and employees? Explain.

10-10. One observer argues that external equity should always be the primary concern in compensation, noting that it attracts the best employees and prevents the top performers from leaving. Do you agree? Explain.

10-11. Do you think a company should keep pay secret and demand that all employees not disclose their pay to coworkers? Why or why not?

You Manage It! 1: Global

Money Doesn't Buy Happiness. Well, on Second Thought . . .

If money can't buy you love, can it still buy you happiness? A now-famous 1974 study seemed to indicate that the answer was *no.* U.S. economist Richard Easterlin, then at the University of Pennsylvania, studied comparative data on moderately wealthy and very wealthy countries and concluded that although rich people are happier than poorer people, rich countries are *not* happier than poorer ones, and they do *not* grow happier as they grow increasingly rich. The explanation for this apparent paradox, said Easterlin, was that only relative income—your income compared to that of your peers and neighbors—matters to happiness, not absolute income.

Now, however, two Wharton professors, Betsey Stevenson and Justin Wolfers, say that the Easterlin paradox, as it has come to be called, does not exist. Based on new research, they say that the truth isn't paradoxical at all, but is in fact very simple: "1. Rich people are happier than poor people. 2. Richer countries are happier than poorer countries. 3. As countries get richer, they tend to get happier."

Pointing out that Easterlin had little data to work with 35 years ago, Stevenson and Wolfers draw their conclusions from data about more countries, including poor ones, over longer periods of time. Public opinion surveys and other studies show that life satisfaction is highest in richer countries. In the United States, for instance, 9 in 10 Gallup Survey respondents in households making more than \$250,000 a year called themselves "very happy," compared to only 4 in 10 with incomes below \$30,000. "On balance," Stevenson and Wolfers conclude, "GDP and happiness have tended to move together." The bottom line, they say, is that absolute income matters.

What do these new findings mean in practice? A pair of British economists suggest that government's policy goals should focus less on growing GDP and more on improving measures that directly affect happiness.

Easterlin would probably agree. He now concedes that people in wealthy countries do report more happiness than those in poorer countries. But he still doubts that money alone is the reason. Comparing Denmark and Zimbabwe, for instance, he says, "The Danes have social welfare policies directed toward some of the most salient concerns of families—their health, care for the aged, child care. If you ask why the Danes are happier, an alternative hypothesis is they have a set of public policies that deal more immediately with people's fundamental concerns."

And the tiny Himalayan kingdom of Bhutan has, in fact, replaced GDP with a measure it calls "gross national happiness."

Critical Thinking Questions

10-12. What do you think is the role of money as a determinant of a person's satisfaction at work and with life in general? Should organizations worry about this issue? Explain.

10-13. As discussed in this chapter, firms vary widely on the extent to which they emphasize money as an incentive. Do you think an emphasis on financial incentives is good or bad? Explain.

Source: Betsey Stevenson and Justin Wolfers, Wharton School at the University of Pennsylvania. Reprinted with permission by the authors.

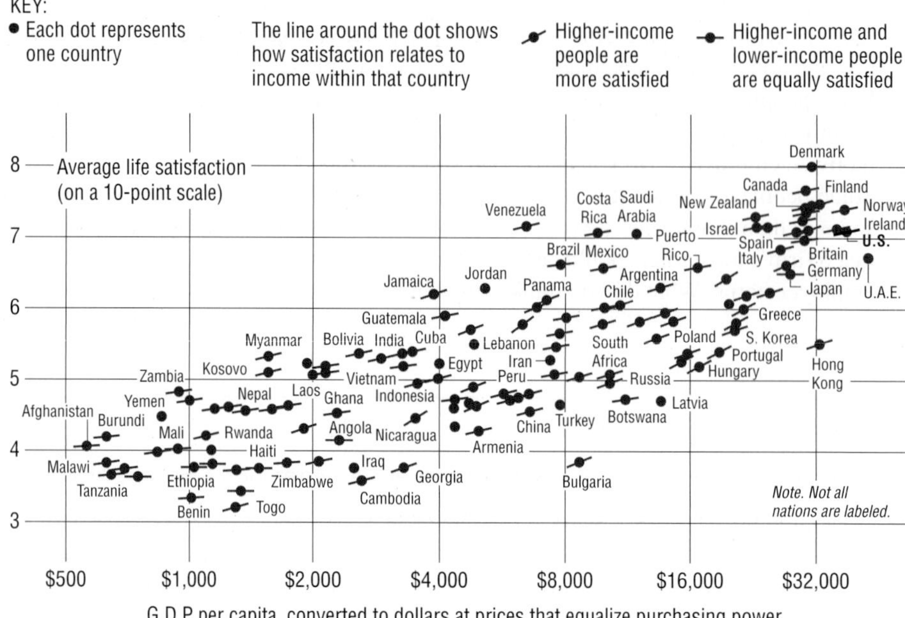

10-14. For the past 90 years or so, job evaluation as a compensation tool has been designed to assess the value of each job rather than to evaluate the person doing the job, prompting a relatively flat pay schedule for all incumbents in a particular position. Some HR experts believe that the emerging trend is for pay inequality to become "normal." Employers are using variable pay to lavish financial resources on their most prized employees, creating a kind of corporate star system. "How do you communicate to a workforce that isn't created equally? How do you treat a workforce in which everyone has a different deal?" asks Jay Schuster of Los Angeles–based compensation consultants Schuster-Zingheim & Associates, Inc. If you were asked these questions, how would you answer them? Given the issues just discussed in this case study, what effect do you think this trend toward greater pay inequality will have on employees' satisfaction with their pay, their job, and life in general? Explain.

Team Exercise

10-15. The HR director of an investment bank has called a meeting of senior employees to discuss the year's bonuses. While rival banks are giving out bonuses of over $3 million to each senior employee, the HR director is arguing that the bonuses in this organization should be more evenly spread among the entire workforce. The HR director has worked out a complex formula that takes into account the pay scale and years of service of each employee. Senior employees argue that there is no personal performance element to the bonus. They consider themselves to be the profit-makers and reject the proposals. Students divide into groups of five to role-play this situation. First, they should discuss the implication this is likely to have on employee satisfaction with their pay, jobs, and life in general. Second, they should discuss what repercussions, if any, this inequity is likely to have for the firm. Finally, the team should develop a plan for explaining to employees why the changes are happening.

Experiential Exercise: Team

10-16. One student will role-play a retail store manager who has traditionally been paid a flat basic salary and a percentage of sales generated by their store. The chain has merged with another company and the new owners want to replace the payment system with a fixed salary plus a yearly bonus. Managers are not happy with the decision. Another student will role-play the human resources manager of the merged company defending its decision. Both sides will role-play in front of the class for approximately 15 minutes. The instructor will then moderate an open class discussion.

Experiential Exercise: Individual

10-17. Would you conclude that an organization that offers greater pay improves employee satisfaction with their pay, their job, and life in general? Review the papers by Easterlin and Stevenson and Wolfers and discuss which of the two positions seems most reasonable to you and the implications this has for compensation.

Sources: Based on Rowley, L. (2011). Money & Happiness, *www.moneyandhappiness.com*; Investing Strategy. (2009, March 4). Does Money Make You Happier? *www.fool.co.uk*; Vendantam, S. (2008, June 23). Financial hardship and the happiness paradox. *The Washington Post, www.washingtonpost.com*; Wolfers, J. (2008, April 16). The Economics of happiness, part 1: Reassessing the Easterlin paradox. *New York Times, http://freakonomics.blogs.nytimes.com*; Leonhardt, D. (2008, April 16). Maybe money does buy happiness after all. *New York Times, www.nytimes.com*; Caulkin, S. (2008, March 9). Cutting the payroll means unhappy dividends, *The Guardian, www.guardian.com.uk*; Casey, E. (2008). *Empowering Women, 3*(1), 26–29.

 You Manage It! 2: Ethics/Social Responsibility

Helping Employees Take Care of Home Tasks

A recent trend is for companies to actively try to help employees improve life at home, with many of these companies claiming that this is a form of social responsibility toward their employees, sometimes referred to as "internal stakeholders." According to management professor David Lewis at UCLA, this represents "a growing effort by American business to reward people with time and peace of mind instead of more traditional financial tools like stock options and bonuses." Consider the following:

- Evernote, a software company, pays each of its 250 employees—from receptionists to top executives—to have their homes cleaned twice a month.
- Facebook provides each employee who becomes a new parent with $4,000 to help with expenses.
- Stanford School of Medicine offers doctors not only housecleaning but also in-home dinner delivery.
- Genentech helps parents with take-home dinners, housecleaning, and last-minute babysitting for a sick child.
- Deloitte, the consulting firm, offers employees a wide array of family support services including backup care for workers with sick family members, personal trainers, nutritionists, and 24-hour counseling services "on demand" for family-related problems such as marital strife and infertility.
- Patagonia, a clothing company based in Ventura, California, is legendary for its environmental focus. It is beloved by its employees, who enjoy an almost unparalleled degree of autonomy and flexibility. According to its CEO Yvon Chouinard, for every opening at Patagonia, the company has an average of 900 applicants. With a high percentage of women employees, the company tries to offer perks that are particularly attractive to working women. In the words of Chouinard, "One gets pregnant, I can't afford to lose her. The average cost to replace an employee is $50,000, including headhunter fees, lost productivity, training. So I say, put in child care. Give people flextime. Let my people go breastfeeding, for God's sake. Before we had a child care center, employees came to work with their babies and kept them on their desks in cardboard boxes."

Critical Thinking Questions

10-18. Do you think companies provide these types of family-oriented rewards for altruistic reasons? Do you see this as a trend? Explain.

10-19. Do you think employees who take advantage of these forms of family-assistance support truly value these services more than they would an equivalent amount in take-home pay? Explain.

10-20. If you had a choice of working for a firm that offers you a higher wage but little in the way of family support services versus a firm that offers you a lower wage but better family support services, which one would you pick and why? Explain.

Team Exercise

10-21. Form teams of five. Each team is to develop a proposal for a medium-size company in the retail, hospitality, transportation, or manufacturing sectors to provide family-support rewards to employees. Team members should consider some of the rewards discussed in the case opening and decide in favor of or against this idea. Each team will make recommendations in class. The instructor will serve as a mediator for the discussion.

Experiential Exercise: Team

10-22. Role-play a human resources manager trying to convince the company CEO and two of his executives (role-played by three students) that introducing some of the rewards discussed in the case opening is good for the firm. The CEO and the two executives should ask probing questions of the HR manager about the wisdom of introducing such a program. Alternatively, the instructor may play the role of CEO.

Experiential Exercise: Individual

10-23. Research firms that have introduced some of the family-support rewards programs discussed in the case opening. What, if anything, do these firms have in common? Is there sufficient evidence to recommend offering this type of reward for employees in other organizations? Justify your conclusions.

Sources: Based on *www.dss.gov.au*; *www.man4soft.com/evernote*. (2013); *www.gene.com*. (2013); *www.deloitte.com*. (2013); Rithtel, M., 2012. Housecleaning, then dinner? Silicon Valley perks come home. *www.nytimes.com*; Best small-business workplaces. (2013). *www.entrepreneur.com*; Giving back as a company. (2011). *www.inc.com*; A little enlightened self-interest. (2011). *www.inc.com*; Special financial report: Employee compensation. (2011). *www.inc.com*.

You Manage It! 3: Discussion

An Academic Question

Mountain States University is a medium-sized public university with 21,000 students and 1,200 faculty members. The College of Business Administration is the largest one on campus, with 8,000 students and 180 faculty members. For the past few years, the dean has had to deal with a large number of dissatisfied faculty members who complain that they are underpaid relative to newly hired faculty. Many of the complainants are senior tenured professors who refuse to engage in committee activities beyond the minimum service requirements and who are seldom in their offices because they

	1997		2004	
Rank	New Hires	Current	New Hires	Current
Full professors	$68,000	$56,000	$79,000	$62,000
Associate professors	$62,000	$51,000	$73,000	$61,000
Assistant professors	$52,000	$48,000	$61,000	$59,000
	2011		Now	
Rank	New Hires	Current	New Hires	Current
Full professors	$99,935	$76,217	$120,000	$85,000
Associate professors	$92,345	$70,797	$ 98,000	$77,000
Assistant professors	$80,644	$69,443	$108,000	$71,000

feel aggrieved. They teach six hours a week, spend two hours in the office, and then disappear from campus. Recently, the head of the college's faculty council compiled some statistics and sent these to the dean, demanding "prompt action to create more equity in the faculty pay structure." The average salary statistics are shown in the table on the following page.

The dean replied that he has little choice but to make offers to new faculty that are competitive with the market and that the university will not give him enough funds to maintain equitable pay differences between new and current faculty or between higher and lower ranks.

Critical Thinking Questions

10-24. Based on the data collected by the faculty council, name three compensation problems that exist at Mountain States University.

10-25. Is the dean's explanation for decreased pay differences by rank and/or seniority justifiable?

10-26. How would you suggest the dean deal with senior faculty who feel underpaid?

Team Exercise

10-27. A group of six faculty members has come to see the dean to express dissatisfaction with pay compression (reduced pay differentials between lower and higher ranks) at the college. All six represent current faculty; two are assistant professors, two are associate professors, and two are full professors. Students divide into groups of seven and role-play this situation as the dean attempts to deal with the pay complaints raised by the faculty. The dean doesn't have the money to correct the pay-compression problem, yet he can't afford to alienate the faculty.

Experiential Exercise: Team

10-28. One student will role-play a department chair who has just hired a full professor from another institution at a much higher salary than a full professor who has spent 20 years at the university. Another student will role-play the 20-year veteran who will go to the department chair for explanations. Overall, both professors have approximately the same number of publications in journals of similar quality and their teaching ratings are comparable, but over the past two years the professor who was hired from the outside has published a couple of pieces in a top journal whereas the 20-year veteran has not. Role-play will last for approximately 10 minutes. Open class discussion will follow moderated by the instructor.

Experiential Exercise: Individual

10-29. Interview a number of professors or instructors of your choice and ask them if pay compression is a problem. If so, ask them to give you reasons as to why this happens, the consequences, and suggestions for resolving the problem. Analyze their answers and provide your own recommendations based on the information in this chapter.

You Manage It! 4: Emerging Trends

More Suits for Overtime Pay

Alleged violations of the Fair Labor Standards Act (FLSA) are on the increase. For instance, in a recent year:

- More than 31,000 complaints were registered against employers.
- More than 342,000 employees received back wages.
- Back wages (not including penalties) totaled more than $200 million.
- More than 70 percent of the violations were initiated by an employee complaint.

Another report notes the following recent cases and settlements where the company allegedly misclassified some employees as exempt so it would not have to pay them overtime:

- Caribou Coffee agreed to pay $2.7 million in a suit initiated by three former employees who alleged the company misclassified retail coffeehouse managers as exempt.
- Starbucks paid an $18 million settlement to coffeehouse managers. Another suit is ongoing.
- Farmers Insurance paid a $200 million settlement for failing to pay claims agents for overtime.
- Eckerd paid a settlement of $8 million for improperly docking the pay of employees misclassified as exempt.
- Cingular Wireless paid $5.1 million to call-center customer-service representatives entitled to overtime.

This same report indicates that FLSA cases are outnumbering employment discrimination class-action cases.

Let's Take a Look at a Specific Case

Pacific Software Publishing Inc., a Bellevue, Washington, company that translates English software into Japanese, hired Hidetomo Morimoto to serve as translator. Morimoto says he was soon working 60-hour weeks without getting any overtime pay, even though he sometimes worked until 1 a.m. in the morning. When he lost his job after complaining online about Japanese firms taking advantage of their employees' strong work ethic, he sued Pacific Software for the overtime pay he believes he is owed. The company contends that Morimoto's extra hours were spent on personal matters and has filed a countersuit for defamation.

Pacific Software Publishing Inc. is not alone. In one suit, several former salesmen accused Oracle Corp. of failing to keep accurate time records of their work in order to avoid paying them overtime. A former IBM technician has sued IBM, alleging that managers asked him to manipulate his time cards to reduce overtime pay. The technician, Ray Wheeler, says he was laid off when he complained.

Labor suits for overtime pay such as these are hitting technology outfits—from startups to mature companies—in waves. "Wage-and-hour class-action lawsuits have now invaded high-tech in the valley," says Lynne Hermle, an attorney representing several companies.

One result is the kind of wage-and-hour suits previously seen in such old-line industries as retailing and hotels. "Reality has set in," says Harvey Sohnen, a labor attorney in Orinda, California. He says that "many tech workers are net slaves, putting in unconscionable hours and getting nothing but ashes in their mouth . . . Now they just want to get paid."

Critical Thinking Questions

10-30. Why do you think there is an increase in the number of cases alleging violations of the FLSA, one of the oldest pieces of legislation governing compensation passed back in the 1930s? Explain.

10-31. If you were a manager at one of the affected companies, how would you make sure that the company is in compliance with FLSA regulations when dealing with employees such as Mr. Morimoto? Explain.

10-32. Do you think that workers who complain against employers for FLSA violations may hurt themselves in the marketplace because other firms may refuse to hire them? If you were in Mr. Morimoto's shoes, what would you have done? Explain.

Team Exercise

10-33. According to one observer, not too long ago professional employees "bragged about their long hours and disdained overtime pay as the mark of a clock-watcher." The class is divided into teams of five. Each team is asked to analyze the reasons for what seems to be recent changes in employee attitudes toward overtime pay and their willingness to sue employers for alleged FLSA violations, which until now has been unprecedented among professional employees.

Experiential Exercise: Team

10-34. You have been asked by a company to write a section in its employee handbook that specifically outlines the criteria that must be met before employees are eligible for overtime as required by law. The instructor will select some of the best examples produced by class members and distribute them to the class. These will then serve as a rallying point for class discussion.

Experiential Exercise: Individual

10-35. According to a labor attorney, the Fair Labor Standards Act (FLSA) "does not define 'work' . . . what is compensable 'worktime' continues to be one of the most hotly debated issues in FLSA." For instance, does it include off-the-clock work and preparatory work at home? If you were the owner of a small business, how would you define "worktime" for purposes of FLSA compliance?

Sources: Based on McKay, D. R. (2014). Exempt employee. *http://careerplanning.about.com*; Woodman, C. (2014). Exempt versus non-exempt salaried employees. *www.ehow.com*; Unpaid overtime lawsuits (2011). *www.overtime.com*; Fair Labor Standards Act (FLSA) compliance. (2011). *www.workforcesofficial.com*; Alper, D. E., and Gerard, D. (2005, March). FLSA update. *Workspan*, 38–41; Andrews, J. M. (2008, May 7). FLSA update. Presented at the Annual meeting of the Labor and Employment Section of the Utah State Bar. Salt Lake City, UT; Pui-Wing, T., and Wingfield, N. (2005, February 24). As tech matures, workers file a spate of salary complaints. *Wall Street Journal*, A-1.

 You Manage It! 5: Customer-Driven HR

A Challenge at Antle Corporation

Antle Corporation (a fictitious name for a company known to one of this book's authors) is a large electronics and computer firm headquartered on the East Coast. It has more than 100,000 employees. Founded in 1912, Antle was generally regarded as the world's number-one designer and manufacturer of large computer equipment from the late 1940s until the early 1990s. At its peak, its share of the market was estimated at 80 percent.

The compensation system at Antle has evolved through the decades, and top managers as well as employees report high levels of satisfaction with it. The following are the essential elements of the compensation system:

- All jobs are evaluated using a point factor approach once every 10 years, with minor adjustments made in between evaluations to correct inequities.
- The company hires a consulting firm once a year to conduct a salary survey for benchmark jobs. The company's pay policy is to peg salaries at the 75th percentile of the market.
- There are 25 grade levels in the company. Employees increase their pay level mainly by moving up the corporate hierarchy over time. The typical employee remains three years in one job before being promoted to a job at the next grade level. All employees are hired at the entry level and are groomed within the company. Although promotions are ostensibly based exclusively on performance, in practice "time on grade" plays an important role in deciding who is ready to move up.
- Perquisites and special benefits are closely tied to grade level. Stock options, for instance, are available only to employees in grades 17 through 25.
- Pay and promotion decisions are highly centralized.
- The only variable compensation comes from a profit-sharing plan under which the company funds a retirement plan for each employee based on the firm's profitability over the preceding year.
- Although "pay for performance" is the company's official policy, most employees view job security and upward mobility over time as the main rewards offered by the firm.
- A strict pay-secrecy policy is in force.

For the past 10 years, Antle's market share has been declining at an average rate of 2 percent annually. The board of directors decided to offer early retirement to Antle's chief executive officer, Alan Steven, who had been at the helm for almost 20 years, and replaced him with Peter Merton, who was hired from a smaller but fast-growing competitor. Merton's mandate is to reverse the company's declining market share by fostering growth and enhancing flexibility.

Because labor costs are almost 70 percent of Antle's total costs, one of Merton's first actions was to appoint a committee to examine the firm's compensation practices. The committee included the vice president for human resources, the comptroller, and two external human resource consultants. Four months later, the committee produced a report identifying several key problems with Antle's compensation system and related HRM practices. These problems, according to the report, add to Antle's production costs and reduce the company's flexibility and capacity to respond to market changes. The committee's report presented the following conclusions:

- The firm has too many management layers. This is expensive and slows communication.
- Most employees have developed a sense of entitlement; that is, they feel they "deserve" regular raises and promotions. This perception has had a negative effect on motivation.
- The promotion-from-within policy has meant that once hired, very few employees are terminated, even if they are not performing up to standard. As a result, many employees are trapped at Antle because they cannot earn an equivalent salary at any other company.
- Jobs are too narrowly defined, increasing labor costs and preventing people from working to their full potential.
- The company is top heavy with highly paid employees whose best days are over but who are still many years from retirement.
- The firm's tradition of providing job security is now putting it at a disadvantage because it cannot reduce its labor force to remain competitive.
- The firm has not been taking advantage of outsourcing to foreign locations in order to preserve employee loyalty. But this means that competitors who are going to places such as China and India enjoy a substantial compensation edge, which improves their bottom line.

After reading the report, Merton is trying to decide what to do about the problems that have been identified.

Critical Thinking Questions

10-36. Based on what you've read about Antle, do you agree with the problems identified by the committee? If not, what alternative set of problems or issues do you see?

10-37. What are the pros and cons of Antle's compensation policies? Are they attuned to its new business strategies of fostering growth, increasing market share, and enhancing flexibility to respond to competitors?

10-38. What recommendations would you offer Peter Merton for redesigning Antle's compensation system?

Team Exercise

10-39. Peter Merton has set up a committee composed of the HR director, two general managers, two senior employees, and one external HR consultant. The committee, composed of six students each, will provide recommendations to Merton (played by the instructor) as to what the company should do next to deal with the problems outlined in the report. Depending on the size of the class, several teams (each representing a committee of six) will make a 15-minute presentation. The instructor will then discuss issues raised with the entire class.

Experiential Exercise: Team

10-40. Students will assume various roles (HR director, general manager, senior employee, and external HR consultant) and each will represent his or her perspective depending on the assigned role. Role-play should last approximately 15 minutes, to be followed by an open class discussion. Roles include Peter Merton (CEO), the HR director, one senior employee with more than 20 years with the company, one union member representing factory workers, and an independent external consultant.

Experiential Exercise: Individual

10-41. If you were hired by a company such as Antle, would you feel comfortable working under the compensation system it has in place? Why or why not? Depending on your response, outline what features of the compensation system would make you the happiest.

Endnotes

Scan for Endnotes or go to http://www.pearsonglobaleditions.com/Gomez-Mejia.

CHAPTER 11

Rewarding Performance

MyManagementLab®

When you see this icon, visit **www.mymanagementlab.com** for activities that are applied, personalized, and offer immediate feedback.

CHALLENGES

After reading this chapter, you should be able to deal more effectively with the following challenges:

1. **Grasp** the major challenges in pay for performance systems.
2. **Develop** competence in dealing with potential problems with pay for performance systems.
3. **Have** familiarity with various types of pay for performance plans and their advantages/disadvantages.
4. **Develop** competence in designing pay for performance plans for executives and sales people.
5. **Learn** about how to reward excellence in customer service.
6. **Become** aware of special concerns with pay for performance programs in small firms.

Century Telephone Company bases its employees' annual pay raises on how well employees perform their job duties. For the past 10 years, these "merit raises" have averaged 3.5 percent of base pay. About two years ago the HR department conducted an employee attitude survey. One of its most striking findings: More than 75 percent of employees felt that pay raises and performance were unrelated. In response, top managers asked the HR staff to determine whether pay raises were indeed based on performance (as required by policy) or on some other unrelated factors. Surprisingly, the data showed that employees were right: Supervisors rated more than 80 percent of their workers as "excellent," and there was only minimal differentiation in the percentage raises received by individual employees.

Source: Pressmaster/Shutterstock.

Top management concluded that supervisors were equalizing performance ratings and raises, sidestepping their responsibility to reward employees on the basis of performance.

To remedy the situation, Century instituted a new procedure a year ago. Under this new system, supervisors must distribute employee performance ratings as follows: excellent (top 15%), very good (next 20%), good (next 20%), satisfactory (next 35%), marginal or unsatisfactory (lowest 10%). Pay raises are pegged to these performance classifications, with employees at the top receiving a 10 percent raise and those at the bottom receiving nothing.

Shortly after the system was put in place, it became obvious that something had gone wrong. A large number of employees could not understand how or why their performance had "dropped" compared to the previous year. Many believed that favoritism played a big role in who received pay increases. Irate employees hounded their supervisors, who in turn complained that increased tension was poisoning interpersonal relationships and interfering with performance.

The Managerial Perspective

Attempting to motivate employees with pay incentives can backfire, as the experience at Century Telephone (a real company given a fictitious name) shows. Nonetheless, the use of pay incentives is increasing. In 1988, the number of U.S. companies offering pay for performance (chiefly in the form of bonuses) to all salaried employees was 47 percent. By 2014, experts estimated that close to 95 percent of U.S. companies do so, and this practice is spreading rapidly around the world. A more dramatic change is observed at the top executive ranks, where stock-related pay increased from approximately 1 percent of total compensation in the 1970s to over 70 percent at the present time.[1]

What these numbers do not tell us about is the flourishing of creative incentive plans that are being implemented. For instance, almost all of the publicly traded "Best Companies" in *Fortune*'s list are experimenting with all kinds of monetary and nonmonetary incentives for employees. JM Family Enterprises in Florida offers top performers free haircuts, manicures, and day trips to the Bahamas on the company yacht. When Jim Moran, the company's founder, died in 2007, he left his stock in a trust to continue funding these "employee-friendly" policies. Kingston Technology Co., Inc., besides buying free monthly lunches, offers quarterly performance-based bonuses that sometimes exceed the typical employee's full year's salary.[2]

At Men's Wearhouse, a clothing company with almost 10,000 employees, executives gave away 113 trips to Hawaii for top performers. After five years, outstanding employees are also eligible for a three-week paid sabbatical.[3]

In this chapter, we discuss the design and implementation of pay-for-performance (incentive) systems. First, we address the major challenges facing managers in their attempts to link pay and performance. Second, we offer a set of general recommendations to deal with these challenges. Third, we describe specific types of pay-for-performance programs and the advantages and disadvantages of each. We conclude with a discussion of unique pay-for-performance plans for two important employee groups, executives and sales personnel.

✪ Learn It!

If your professor has chosen to assign this go to **www.mymanagementlab.com** to see what you should particularly focus on, and take the chapter 11 warmup.

Pay for Performance: The Challenges

Most workers believe that those who work harder and produce more should be rewarded accordingly. If employees see that pay is not distributed on the basis of merit, they are more likely to lack commitment to the organization, decrease their level of effort, and look for employment opportunities elsewhere.[4]

Pay-for-performance systems, also called **incentive systems**, reward employee performance on the basis of three assumptions:[5]

1. Individual employees and work teams differ in how much they contribute to the firm—not only in what they do, but also in how well they do it.
2. The firm's overall performance depends to a large degree on the performance of individuals and groups within the firm.
3. To attract, retain, and motivate high performers and to be fair to all employees, a company needs to reward employees on the basis of their relative performance.

Before talking about specific types of pay-for-performance plans, we will discuss nine challenges facing organizations that want to adopt an incentive system.

pay-for-performance system or incentive system
A system that rewards employees on the assumptions that (1) individual employees and work teams differ in how much they contribute to the firm; (2) the firm's overall performance depends to a large degree on the performance of individuals and groups within the firm; and (3) to attract, retain, and motivate high performers and to be fair to all employees, the firm needs to reward employees on the basis of their relative performance.

The "Do Only What You Get Paid For" Syndrome

To avoid the charge that pay is distributed on the basis of subjective judgments or favoritism, pay-for-performance systems tend to rely on objective indicators of performance.[6] This may lead some managers to use whatever "objective" data are available to justify pay decisions. Unfortunately, the more closely pay is tied to particular performance indicators, the more employees tend to focus on those indicators and neglect other important job components that are more difficult to measure. Consider the following examples:

- In some school systems where teachers' pay has been linked to students' scores on standardized tests, teachers spend more time helping students do well on the tests than helping them understand the subject matter. Teachers report that they fear negative evaluations for themselves and their schools unless they teach to the test.[7]
- Many blame the meltdown of the financial system in the United States at the end of the prior decade to executive bonus systems at companies such as Lehman Brothers, Merrill Lynch, and Bear Stearns. These bonus systems pegged executives' and analysts' incentives to the achievement of challenging financial targets, inducing these individuals to make risky, speculative investments and to engage in creative financial maneuvers (so called "derivatives") that resulted in "paper wealth," but not much real value in terms of goods and services. This generated a situation where executives of some of these firms garnered large bonuses while their company's debt was socialized, with the federal government becoming the "investor of last resort." Despite these well-documented cases of imprudent risk taking in response to badly designed incentives, one still finds that the practice of taking poor risks in order to secure higher rewards is alive and well. In 2013, for instance, the British bank Barclays, one of the largest in the world, agreed to pay a $450 million settlement after its executives were found to have taken bad risks on behalf of their clients "because of a bonus system that encouraged risk taking over serving clients."[8]
- Part of the reason for the scandals associated with Arthur Andersen (once one of the five largest accounting firms, with 85,000 employees) and its subsequent legal problems may have been the way its managers were rewarded for the volume of revenues generated through consulting and accounting fees. This may have led managers to poorly monitor their clients (and in some cases approve of outright fraud) for fear of losing lucrative contracts.[9] Because auditing firms depend on a good reputation for their business, the legendary Arthur Andersen never recovered from the scandals and ended up closing its doors almost a century after its founding.

Unethical Behaviors

By creating pressure to produce and to "keep score," incentives may induce employees to engage in undesirable behaviors, to cut corners, deceive, misinform, hide negative information, take more credit than they deserve, and the like. Managers may look the other way, because it could be to their advantage to preside over a unit that "meets or exceeds" targets. What starts as a matter of interpretation, or perhaps "white lies," may eventually cross over into unethical or even illegal terrain. Several examples have recently come to light across a variety of industries, as discussed in the Manager's Notebook, "Incentives Come to Medicine: Do They Promote Unethical Behaviors Among Doctors?" These examples are only the tip of the iceberg. The majority of cases are never reported; hence, it is difficult to know the extent of the problem.

Unfortunately, employee cynicism about company ethics and senior leadership are also on the rise. A survey showed that only 50 percent of employees believed their top executives had high integrity, and approximately the same percentage shared similar feelings about the entire organization.[10] As a result, employees may unconsciously blame their employer for their own questionable behaviors or ethical lapses in order to meet incentive criteria ("they made me do it," or "that is the way things get done around here") rather than take full responsibility for their actions.

Negative Effects on the Spirit of Cooperation

The experiences of Century Telephone Company clearly show that pay-for-performance systems may provoke conflict and competition while discouraging cooperation.[11] For instance, employees may withhold information from a colleague if they believe that it will help the other person get ahead. Those who are receiving less than they feel they deserve may try to "get back" at those who are receiving more, perhaps by sabotaging a project or spreading rumors. Internal competition may set off rivalries that lead to quality problems or even cheating.

Lack of Control

Factors beyond an employee's control include the supervisor, performance of other work group members, the quality of the materials the employee is working with, working conditions, the amount of support from management, and environmental factors.[12]

For instance, many medical doctors in group practices now receive a substantial portion of their pay in the form of a bonus. As can be seen in the Manager's Notebook, "Incentives Come to Medicine: Do They Promote Unethical Behaviors Among Doctors? " these programs are generating a great deal of controversy. Doctors commonly complain that managed-care bureaucrats try to slash revenues as doctors' overhead costs rise. As a result, the managed-care system pressures physicians to see more patients in less time. This means that nurses and pharmacists can take over some of the duties previously reserved for doctors.[13] Union membership is soaring among doctors as many see such a situation as demoralizing and inequitable.[14]

MANAGER'S NOTEBOOK

Ethics/Social Responsibility

Incentives Come to Medicine: Do They Promote Unethical Behaviors Among Doctors?

Unknown to their patients, doctors often receive incentives from pharmaceutical firms, private insurance companies, and even the federal and state governments. Some estimate that more than half of all health maintenance organizations (HMOs), accounting for 80 percent of HMO enrollees in the United States, make such payments. Incentives are cropping up in the federal Medicare program; they already exist in more than half of state-run Medicaid programs (which provide health care for low-income individuals). The United Kingdom's state-run primary care system includes a broad-based pay for performance program for doctors.

Could incentives cloud a doctor's judgment, tempting someone to put financial gain ahead of patient welfare? Here is a sample of controversial situations that have arisen in the wake of physician incentives.

Rewarding Hospitals for Quality Care

The U.S. federal government as well as the British Health Service are trying to set reimbursements for hospitals based on how well they do on quality measures. These reimbursements in turn will affect the income of doctors affiliated with the hospitals. Although this sounds good in theory, most physicians believe that the difficulties of accurately measuring hospital quality are insurmountable. As noted by one doctor "[quality of health care] outcomes studies require controlling for so many patient factors from genetics to diet and premorbid exercise levels that they are almost impossible to do across large populations, so that it becomes like deciding the quality of an artist's work by the staying ability or vibrance of his paintings' colors over time."

Gainsharing for Doctors

Because doctors might be tempted to use more expensive procedures than are necessary, some insurance companies are providing incentives to minimize this problem. They are doing this through gainsharing plans. The idea is simple: The doctor's practice or clinic receives a lump sum payment per year from the insurance company based on number of patients. If the doctors do not use the full amount allocated by the insurance company, at the end of the year the savings revert to the doctors in the form of a bonus. The downside? Although gainsharing may discourage unnecessary procedures and treatments, it is difficult to know the extent to which patients may receive suboptimal care, because doctors may cut corners to keep expenses to a minimum.

Source: Rob Byron/Shutterstock.

Doctors Paid to Prescribe Generic Pills

Some health insurance plans pay doctors $100 for prescribing a generic drug instead of a name-brand one. The rationale is that generics save money for patients, employers, and insurers. Some practitioners say it takes time to decide which drug is better for a specific patient's health, and they feel they should be reimbursed for that effort.

Report Cards for Surgeons

Some states try to improve the quality of coronary bypass surgery by issuing report cards for surgeons who perform the procedure. Hospitals and surgeons who failed to meet standards were required to improve. An unintended result of this effort is that many cardiologists now report that it is difficult to find surgeons who are willing to operate on their sickest patients. In New York State, for instance, a survey found that almost two-thirds of cardiac surgeons responded to the report card process by accepting only relatively healthy patients for heart-bypass surgery.

What the Doctor's Aren't Disclosing

Researchers at Duke University were recently surprised to discover that four of five published studies on heart stents lacked an important detail required by many medical journals—whether the studies' authors were paid consultants. When the companies funding the research *were* identified, stent manufacturers Johnson & Johnson, Boston Scientific, and Medtronic were named most often. Only one-quarter of the articles describing clinical trials identified who paid for the testing; top research supporters included Bristol-Meyers Squibb and Sanofi-Aventis, which comarket a drug for stent patients. Some journal editors say there's a limit to their power to police their contributors. "I'm not a cop. I'm not the FBI," says the editor-in-chief of the *Journal of the American Medical Association*.

Use of Orthopedic Devices

When orthopedic devices such as replacement hip and knee joints are brought to market, their manufacturers often hire doctors to train other doctors and medical sales reps on how to use them. These are often the same doctors who have already served as consultants to help develop the devices. Some companies spend more than $1 million a year compensating surgeons who use their device instead of another manufacturer's, even though the devices are all very similar in performance.

Sources: Based on Andorno, N. B., and Lee, T. H. (2013, March). Ethical physician incentives—from carrots and sticks to shared purpose. *New England Journal of Medicine*, 980–982; Schmidt, H., Asch, D., and Halpern, S. D. (2013). Fairness and wellness incentives: What is the relevance of the process-outcome distinction? *Preventive Medicine*, *55*(1), 118–123; *www.pbs.org*. (2011). As Medicare moves toward pay-for-performance, study highlights need for better data; *www.sciencedaily.com*. (2011). Pay for performance programs may worsen medical disparities; Rangel, D. (2011). When pay for performance does not work and may impair patient care. *www.kevinmed.com*; Gemmil, M. (2008). Pay-for-performance in the US: What lessons for Europe? *Eurohealth, 13*(4), 21–23; Fuhrmans, V. (2008, January 24). Doctors paid to prescribe generic pills. *Wall Street Journal,* B-4; Jauhar, S. (2008, September 9). The pitfalls of linking doctor's pay to performance. *New York Times*, D-5–D-6; Weintraub, A. (2008, May 26). What the doctor's aren't disclosing. *BusinessWeek*, 56; Feder, B. (2008, March 22). New focus of inquiry into bribes: Doctors. *New York Times*, B-1. ■■

Difficulties in Measuring Performance

As we saw in Chapter 7, assessing employee performance is one of the thorniest tasks a manager faces, particularly when the assessments are used to dispense rewards.[15] At the employee level, the appraiser must try to untangle individual contributions from those of the work group while avoiding judgments based on a personality bias (being a strict or a lenient rater), likes and dislikes, and political agendas. At the group or team level, the rater must try to isolate the specific contributions of any given team when all teams are interdependent.[16] Appraisers experience the same difficulties in attempting to determine the performance of plants or units that are interrelated among themselves and with corporate headquarters. In short, accurate measures of performance are not easy to achieve, and tying pay to inaccurate measures is likely to create problems. For instance, pay-for-performance programs for teachers are criticized for focusing on narrow criteria of student achievement (such as test scores) while ignoring more general problems that limit student learning such as crowded classrooms, lack of up-to-date equipment, and dysfunctional families.

Psychological Contracts

Once implemented, a pay-for-performance system creates a psychological contract between the employee and the firm.[17] A *psychological contract* is a set of expectations based on prior experience, and it is very resistant to change.

Breaking a psychological contract can have damaging results. For instance, when a computer-products manufacturer changed the terms of its pay-for-performance program three times in a two-year period, the result was massive employee protests, the resignation of several key managers, and a general lowering of employee morale.

Two other problems may arise with respect to the psychological contract. First, because employees feel entitled to the reward spelled out in the pay-for-performance plan, it is difficult to change the plan even when conditions call for a change. Second, it is sometimes hard to come up with a formula that is fair to diverse employee groups.

The Credibility Gap

Employees often do not believe that pay-for-performance programs are fair or that they truly reward performance, a phenomenon called the *credibility gap.*[18] Some studies indicate that as many as 75 percent of a typical firm's employees question the integrity of pay-for-performance plans.[19] If employees do not consider the system legitimate and acceptable, it may have negative rather than positive effects on their behavior. A big part of the problem is that, to defend their egos, employees who receive lower performance-related payments than others tend to blame management rather than themselves. Unless an effective performance appraisal and feedback system is in place (see Chapter 7), incentive programs are unlikely to produce the expected results.

Going back to the case of teachers noted earlier, in a well-intended attempt by the British government to reward good teaching, "superhead" teachers can earn up to $140,000 a year, a big change from a system where teachers were stuck at the $46,000-per-year level. The "bumper" pay raises are linked to exam results, lower truancy rates, and improved mathematical and literacy rates. Even though no teacher would receive a pay cut (that is, there is only upside potential to earn more money), teachers' unions have vigorously opposed the program. They argue that teachers cannot always be blamed if pupils do badly and that the bonus received may depend more on luck than performance.[20]

Job Dissatisfaction and Stress

Pay-for-performance systems may lead to greater productivity but lower job satisfaction.[21] Some research suggests that the more pay is tied to performance, the more the work unit begins to unravel and the more unhappy employees become.[22] For instance, Lantech (a small manufacturer of machinery in Kentucky) experimented with various incentive programs, yet the company dropped them altogether after the CEO and founder Pat Lancaster concluded that the competition for bonuses means that managers may have to spend much of their time in conflict resolution.[23]

A QUESTION OF ETHICS

How much consideration should the organization give to the psychological health of its employees when designing a pay-for-performance system?

Potential Reduction of Intrinsic Drives

Pay-for-performance programs may push employees to the point of doing whatever it takes to get the promised monetary reward, and in the process may stifle their talents and creativity. Thus, an organization that puts too much emphasis on pay in attempting to influence behaviors may

EXHIBIT 11.1 INCENTIVES THAT BACKFIRED: CROWDING OUT INTRINSIC MOTIVATION

The story goes that "A man was upset that his neighbor's children would always play on his lawn and damage it. So he decided to pay each child to play on his lawn. The surprised children gladly accepted. After a few days, the man told them that he could afford to pay them only half of the initial rate. The children accepted this reduced rate but were less than enthusiastic. After a few more days, the man cut the children's pay to almost nothing, and the children were so upset that they left, vowing never to play on his lawn again unless he increased their pay. Problem solved." The moral of the story is that by paying the kids the man crowded out the intrinsic drives that led the kids to play on his lawn (enjoying the autonomy and having fun as the only reason for the activity).

A recent study published in *The British Medicine Journal* confirmed a similar crowded-out effect. The study was based on 2,523,659 adults who are members of Kaiser Permanente Northern California health care system. Doctors were given incentives to screen patients for diabetic retinopathy and cervical cancer. During the five years when the incentives were given, the rate of screening went up considerably. But when the incentives were withdrawn the rate of screening fell substantially below the rate prior to the start of the incentive program. The authors of the study concluded that once extrinsic rewards are given to the doctors for conducting desired procedures, it becomes a double-edged sword: removing financial incentives means that use of the procedures declines to a level lower than it was before the bonuses were started.

This is yet another example of how the results of relying on economic incentives can be counterintuitive and counterproductive. One would assume that performance would increase linearly with increased rewards, but in many contexts, researchers have found the opposite effect. The mechanism is thought to work this way: an external reward or punishment (apart from base compensation) has the effect of decreasing internal motivators (based on autonomy, mastery, and purpose) so much so that this diminishes or even reverses the positive effects of a person's external motivators (the drive to earn more) such that the individual's total motivational drive and hence her or his work performance are decreased. On the other hand, recent research suggests that this dilemma is not as black and white as it appears. There is the possibility that extrinsic and intrinsic rewards might work together to the extent that employees believe that doing the right things will be noticed by management and that, to be fair, management may recognize those who are intrinsically motivated.

Sources: Based on Baumann, O., and Stieglitz, N. (2014). Rewarding value-creating ideas in organizations: The power of low-powered incentives. *Strategic Management Journal,* available online as doi:1002/SMJ.02093; Speckbacher, G. (2013). The use of incentives in non-profit organizations. *Nonprofit and Voluntary Sector Quarterly*, available online in *http://nvs.sagepub.com*; Rangel, C. (2011). Why pay for performance does not work and may impair patient care, *www.kevinmed.com*; Feder-Ostroy, B. (2011). At Kaiser Permanente, seeing how financial incentives affect healthcare. *www.reportingonhealth.org*; Lester, H., Schmittdiel, J., Selby, J., Fireman, B., Campbell, S., Lee, J., Whippy, A., and Madvig, P. (2010). *British Medical Journal* (open access). *www.bmj.com.*

reduce employees' *intrinsic drives,* or internally driven motivation. One expert argues that the more a firm stresses pay as an incentive for high performance, the less likely it is that employees will engage in activities that benefit the organization (such as overtime and extra-special service) unless they are promised an explicit reward.[24] Exhibit 11.1 illustrates how extrinsic motivation may crowd out intrinsic motivation when incentives are introduced.

Meeting the Challenges of Pay-for-Performance Systems

Properly designed pay-for-performance systems present managers with an excellent opportunity to align employees' interests with those of the organization. The following recommendations can help to enhance the success of performance programs and avoid the pitfalls we just discussed.

Develop a Complementary Relationship Between Extrinsic and Intrinsic Rewards

Recent psychological research suggest that hybrid intrinsic-extrinsic rewards may be effective motivators and that one type of reward may not necessarily compete with the other but rather they serve as complements to each other.[25] For instance, "3M offers rewards that nourish both self-esteem and personal bank accounts while Google has a policy of giving outsized rewards to people who come up with outsized ideas . . . Google set up its Founders' Awards program with restricted stock options that were awarded quarterly to those teams that came up with the best ideas to increase profitability."[26]

Link Pay and Performance Appropriately

In a few instances, managers can justify paying workers according to a preestablished formula or measure. Traditional **piece-rate systems**, in which workers are paid per unit produced, represent the tightest link between pay and performance. Many piece-rate systems have been abandoned because they tend to create the kinds of problems discussed earlier, but there are situations in which piece-rate plans are appropriate. The primary requirement is that the employee has complete control over the speed and quality of the work. Interestingly enough, the Internet is creating a new type of piece-rate system in which employees have control over the speed and quality of work (because it is available 24 hours a day and it can easily trace what the person has done). It has allowed many firms, particularly high-tech companies, to have employees work elsewhere (including at home), thereby saving office space, overhead, and supervisory time. Many of the employees work on a contract basis, so the company saves on benefits.

piece-rate system
A compensation system in which employees are paid per unit produced.

Use Pay for Performance as Part of a Broader HRM System

Pay-for-performance programs are not likely to achieve the desired results unless they are accompanied by complementary HRM programs. For instance, performance appraisals and supervisory training usually play a major role in the eventual success or failure of a pay-for-performance plan. As we saw in Chapter 7, performance ratings are often influenced by factors other than performance. Because a defective appraisal process can undermine even the most carefully conceived pay plan, supervisors should be rigorously trained in correct rating practice.

Poor staffing practices can also damage the credibility of a pay-for-performance program. For instance, if employees are hired because of their political connections rather than for their skills and abilities, other employees will get the message that good performance is not that important to the organization.

Employees should also receive training to make them more productive so they are able to earn more. For instance, the U.S. division of Swiss giant Roche, based in Indianapolis, puts all its employees with high leadership potential through a 10-month development program.[27]

Build Employee Trust

Even the best-conceived pay-for-performance program can fail if managers have a poor history of labor relations or if the organization has a cutthroat culture. Under these conditions, employees are likely to attribute rewards not to good performance, but rather to chance or good impression management. If a pay-for-performance program is to have a chance of succeeding, managers need to build employee trust, which may require making major changes in the organization's climate.[28]

Managers should start by answering these questions from their employees' perspective: Does it pay for me to work longer, harder, or smarter? Does anyone notice my extra efforts?

If the answers are "no," managers need to go all out to show that they care about employees and are aware of the work they do. Even more important, they need to keep employees informed and involved when making any changes in management or the compensation plan.[29]

Promote the Belief That Performance Makes a Difference

Because of the problems noted earlier, managers may shy away from using pay to reward performance.[30] However, unless an organization creates an atmosphere in which performance makes a difference, it may end up with a low-achievement organizational culture. In a sense, then, pay-for-performance systems are the lesser of two evils, because without them performance may drop even lower.[31] The Manager's Notebook, "Using Incentives to Motivate Employees and Customers," shows how some organizations try to accomplish this.

MANAGER'S NOTEBOOK

Customer-Driven HR

Using Incentives to Motivate Employees and Customers

Companies spend approximately $46 billion a year on incentives, and some experts say they should retain that focus regardless of general economic conditions. "In good times or bad, organizations are well served by creating a culture of recognition for their employees as well as their customers," says the executive director of the Incentive Marketing Association (IMA). "Incentive programs allow a company to focus people's activities and tasks on what produces financial outcomes," agrees IMA's president. "They align what the individual does to what the company would like them to do, and they allow companies to keep the investment they place in people and the intellectual property they develop in those employees."

Some firms are using incentives as simple as $5 Subway gift cards, which in one recent year helped U.S. Air Conditioning Corp. increase sales more than 7 percent. At the other extreme was the owner of a five-person business who rewarded one long-term employee with a fur coat, only to be disappointed by her less than enthusiastic reaction. "I've been an employee with you for 25 years and you've never noticed that I'm a vegetarian," the employee explained. "I would never wear a fur coat."

Safer incentives than fur coats, and less costly, are brand-name consumer electronics such as digital cameras, which rank among the most popular, according to Canon USA's manager of special markets. "They're desired by everyone," she says, "young and old, male and female. They make the selection process much easier for the decision makers who are trying to get the right mix of items to incentivize."

Another option is to give employees as much choice as possible. At T-Mobile USA, all employees are eligible to earn points or credits to purchase merchandise in the company's top-rated incentive program. Top-scoring employees are honored by senior executives at banquets, and exotic trips reward the very best of the group.

Sources: Based on *Fortune*. (2014). The best companies to work for. *www.fortune.com*; McLoone, S. (2008, December 10). How do I offer employee incentives? *Washington Post,* B-1; Gallo, C. (2008, April 11). A simple employee incentive. *BusinessWeek*, 21–26. ■■

Use Multiple Layers of Rewards

Because all pay-for-performance systems have positive and negative features, providing different types of pay incentives for different work situations is likely to produce better results than relying on a single type of pay incentive. With a system based on multiple layers of rewards, the organization can realize the benefits of each incentive plan while minimizing its negative side effects. For instance, at AT&T Credit, variable pay (in the form of bonuses) was based on 12 measures reflecting the performance of both regional teams and the entire business unit. Team members had to meet their individual performance goals to qualify for variable pay.[32]

Increase Employee Involvement

An old saying among compensation practitioners is: "Acceptability is the ultimate determinant of success in any compensation plan." When employees do not view a compensation program as legitimate, they will usually do whatever they can to subvert the system—from setting maximum production quotas for themselves to shunning coworkers who receive the highest rewards. The best way to increase acceptance is to have employees participate in the design of the pay plan.[33] Employee involvement will result in a greater understanding of the rationale behind the plan, greater commitment to the pay plan, and a better match between individual needs and pay-plan design.[34]

Employee participation in designing the plan is not the same as employee dispensation of the rewards. Managers should still control and allocate rewards because employees may not be able to separate self-interest from effective pay administration. Managers can, however, solicit employee input by instituting an appeal mechanism that allows workers to voice their complaints about how rewards have been distributed. Such a mechanism is likely to enhance the perceived fairness of the system, particularly if a disinterested third party acts as an arbitrator and is empowered to take corrective actions.[35]

Stress the Importance of Acting Ethically

Once a pay-for-performance system is in place, employees may be tempted to manipulate whatever criteria are being used to trigger incentives. Even the tightest monitoring systems may not be able to catch all transgressions. Hence, the organization is better off if employees can monitor themselves. To this end, ethics as a corporate value cannot be emphasized enough, and training programs providing examples of "gray" or unethical behaviors may help employees better decide when it is appropriate or inappropriate to act in a particular way in order to meet performance expectations.

Use Motivation and Nonfinancial Incentives

One of the most basic facts of motivation is that people are driven to obtain the things they need or want. Although pay is certainly a strong motivator, it is not an equally strong motivator for everyone. Some people are more interested in the nonfinancial aspects of their work. A growing trend, as shown in the Manager's Notebook, "Healthy Living Incentives," is for companies to offer financial rewards to attain worthwhile goals that are not directly related to performance objectives. In that sense, the company is using a mix of monetary (bonus) and nonmonetary (opportunities to improve health) rewards for employees. The company may also derive some indirect financial benefits as well (for instance, lower health insurance premiums and fewer sick leaves), making this a "win–win" situation.

MANAGER'S NOTEBOOK

Healthy Living Incentives

Ethics/Social Responsibility

Half the companies in a recent survey of more than 450 firms use incentives to get employees to improve their health by quitting smoking or losing weight. The survey indicates that nearly three-quarters of firms will soon have such programs in place. Although privacy experts warn that they must be carefully designed to avoid discrimination, incentives are increasingly popular, and they seem to be working.

"Small changes in daily habits can lead to big improvements in health," says the medical officer for Humana Inc. "We need to invest in prevention programs to keep people healthy and motivate them to do the right thing." At Humana, that means setting up a rewards program that offers points redeemable for gift cards and merchandise for employees who undergo health assessments and coaching and follow up with preventive care. Those who meet established goals receive discounts on their company medical and dental insurance plans.

Obesity is estimated to cost U.S. companies $13 billion a year. At CFI Westgate Resorts in Florida, a company-wide employee weight-loss contest, inspired by the president's shedding of more than 20 pounds, rewards winners with cash prices or luxury vacations. Some employees have lost as much as 60 pounds.

Pepsi Bottling Company employees earn $75 gift cards for taking a health-risk assessment and $100 if they join a lifestyle-management program. Nicotine replacement therapy is free, as are annual physicals and other basic health care services.

Aetna, the health care insurance company, has enrolled almost 60 percent of its employees in its incentive-based health program. The program was recently expanded to include spouses and family members; spouses are eligible for the same $600 cash per year that employees get for proving they exercise regularly.

Employees of the state of Alabama pay zero health insurance premiums as long as they are working on reducing their risk of high blood pressure, cholesterol, obesity, and diabetes. And diabetic employees at Affinia Group who stay on their regimen of medication, doctor visits, and blood-sugar monitoring can reduce their health care costs by up to $600 a year and qualify for free prescriptions. In Nova Scotia, Canada, the Healthy Living Tax Incentive was passed in 2013. It offers a tax credit per child of up to $500 for registering in an approved organized sport or a physical recreation program

Sources: Based on DTE Energy. (2013). Healthy living program. *www.dteenergy.com*; Government of Nova Scotia. (2013). Healthy living tax incentives. *http://www.novascotia.ca/finance/en/home/taxation/tax101/personalincometax/healthyliving.aspx*; Ganster, K. (2011). Incentives for healthy habits. *http://chamberpost.com*; Kavilanz, P. B. (2009, March 26). Unhealthy habits cost you more at work. CNN Money.com, *www.cnnmoney.com*; Business Wire. (2009, February 27). Healthy rewards: New health incentive program rewards employees and employers for healthy decision making; Appleby, J. (2009, January 19). Firms offer bigger incentives for healthy living. *USA Today*, A-1; Knowledge@Wharton. (2008, January 9). From incentives to penalties: How far should employers go to reduce workplace obesity? *http://knowledge.wharton.upenn.edu*. ■■

Nonfinancial rewards include public and nonpublic praise, honorary titles, expanded job responsibilities, paid and unpaid sabbatical leaves, mentoring programs, and 100-percent tuition reimbursements.[36] Even if it is impossible to provide a financial reward for a job well done, many employees appreciate overt recognition of excellent performance. However, as discussed in Chapter 10, organizations need to be careful that employees do not come to see nonfinancial rewards as a ruse to justify compensation savings at their expense.

Types of Pay-for-Performance Plans

As Figure 11.1 shows, pay-for-performance plans can be designed to reward the performance of the individual, team, business unit or plant, entire organization, or any combination of these. All these plans have advantages and disadvantages, and each is more effective in some situations than in others. Most organizations are best served by using a variety of plans.

Individual-Based Plans

At the micro level, firms attempt to identify and reward the contributions of individual employees. *Individual-based pay plans* are the most widely used pay-for-performance plans in industry.[37]

merit pay
An increase in base pay, normally given once a year.

Of the individual-based plans commonly used, merit pay is by far the most popular; its use is almost universal.[38] **Merit pay** consists of an increase in base pay, normally given once a year. Supervisors' ratings of employees' performance are typically used to determine the amount of merit pay granted. For instance, subordinates whose performance is rated "below expectations," "achieved expectations," "exceeded expectations," and "far exceeded expectations" may receive 0, 3, 6, and 9 percent pay raises, respectively. Once a merit pay increase is given to an employee, it remains a part of that employee's base salary for the rest of his or her tenure with the firm (except under extreme conditions, such as a general wage cut or a demotion).

bonus program or **lump-sum payment**
A financial incentive that is given on a one-time basis and does not raise the employee's base pay permanently.

Individual **bonus programs** (sometimes called **lump-sum payments**) are similar to merit pay programs but differ in one important respect. Bonuses are given on a one-time basis and do not raise the employee's base pay permanently. Bonuses tend to be larger than merit pay increases because they involve lower risk to the employer (the employer is not making a permanent financial commitment). For instance, Devon Energy, an independent oil and natural gas producer, recently awarded a bonus averaging $21,332 per employee.[39] Bonuses can also be given outside

FIGURE 11.1
Pay-for-Performance Programs

Unit of Analysis			
Micro Level		Macro Level	
Individual	**Team**	**Business Unit/Plant**	**Organization**
Merit pay	Bonuses	Gainsharing	Profit sharing
Bonuses	Awards	Bonuses	Stock plans
Awards		Awards	
Piece rate			

the annual review cycle when employees achieve certain milestones (for example, every month that Continental, now merged with United, ranked among the top five airlines in on-time arrivals, employees received a check for at least $65); offer a valuable cost-saving suggestion; or simply "go the extra mile" (for instance, Los Alamos National Laboratory allows supervisors to offer an up-to-$75 award certificate when an employee displays "exceptionally high quality work under tight deadlines").[40] One survey shows that 92 percent of firms offer special one-time spot awards, and 28 percent provide lump-sum payments to their employees. These types of bonuses often exceed 5 percent of annual salary.[41]

Awards, like bonuses, are one-time rewards but tend to be given in the form of a tangible prize, such as a paid vacation, a television set, or a dinner for two at a fancy restaurant. For instance, once a year Nike invites top, long-time performers to a luxurious "Decathlete's dinner" at the company's expense.[42]

award
A one-time reward usually given in the form of a tangible prize.

ADVANTAGES OF INDIVIDUAL-BASED PAY-FOR-PERFORMANCE PLANS Individual-based plans have four major advantages:

- ***Performance that is rewarded is likely to be repeated*** A widely accepted theory of motivation, known as **expectancy theory**, explains why higher pay leads to higher performance. People tend to do those things that are rewarded. Money is an important reward to most people, so individuals tend to improve their work performance when a strong performance–pay linkage exists.[43]
- ***Individuals are goal oriented and financial incentives can shape an individual's goals over time*** A pay incentive plan can help make employees' behavior consistent with the organization's goals.[44] For instance, if an automobile dealer has a sales employee who sells a lot of cars, but whose customers rarely return to the dealership, the dealer might implement a pay incentive plan that gives a higher sales commission for cars sold to repeat buyers. This plan would encourage the sales staff to please the customer rather than just sell the car.
- ***Assessing the performance of each employee individually helps the firm achieve individual equity*** An organization must provide rewards in proportion to individual efforts. Individual-based plans do exactly this. If individuals are not rewarded, high performers may leave the firm or reduce their performance level to make it consistent with the payment they are receiving.
- ***Individual-based plans fit in with an individualistic culture*** National cultures vary in the emphasis they place on individual achievement versus group achievement (see Chapter 17). The United States is at the top of the list in valuing individualism, and U.S. workers expect to be rewarded for their personal accomplishments and contributions.

expectancy theory
A theory of behavior holding that people tend to do those things that are rewarded.

In contrast to U.S. firms, the Japanese do not tend to reward individual performance but economic pressures seem to be moving the Japanese toward a more "American" model. In a recent survey, 70 percent of Japanese leaders said they plan to cut wages and that only top performers may be able to keep (or exceed) their prior earnings.[45]

DISADVANTAGES OF INDIVIDUAL-BASED PAY-FOR-PERFORMANCE PLANS Many of the pitfalls of pay-for-performance programs are most evident at the individual level. Two particular dangers are that individual plans may (1) create competition and destroy cooperation among peers and (2) sour working relationships between subordinates and supervisors. And because many managers believe that below-average raises are demoralizing to employees and discourage better performance, they tend to equalize the percentage increases among employees, regardless of individual performance. This, of course, defeats the very purpose of an incentive plan.

Other disadvantages of individual-based plans include the following:

- ***Tying pay to goals may promote single-mindedness*** Linking financial incentives to the achievement of goals may lead to a narrow focus and the avoidance of important tasks, either because goals are difficult to set for these tasks or because their accomplishment is difficult to measure at the individual level. For instance, if a grocery store sets a goal of happy and satisfied customers, it would be extremely difficult to link achievement of this goal to individual employees.
- ***Many employees do not believe that pay and performance are linked*** Although practically all organizations claim to reward individual performance, it is difficult for employees to determine to what extent their companies really do so. So it should come as no surprise

- Performance appraisal is inherently subjective, with supervisors evaluating subordinates according to their own preconceived biases.
- Regardless of the appraisal form used, supervisors tend to manipulate the ratings.
- Merit systems emphasize individual rather than group goals, and this may lead to dysfunctional conflict in the organization.
- To maintain an effective working relationship with all subordinates and prevent interpersonal conflict within the team, the supervisor may be reluctant to single out individuals for special recognition with pay.
- The use of a specified time period (normally one year) for the performance evaluation encourages a short-term orientation at the expense of long-term goals.
- Employees try to defend their ego by ignoring negative performance feedback, blaming the organization for their problems.
- Supervisors and employees seldom agree on the evaluation, leading to interpersonal confrontations.
- Supervisors often do not know how to justify a particular pay raise recommendation to an employee.
- Increments in financial rewards are spaced in such a way that their reinforcement value for work behaviors is questionable. For example, becoming twice as productive now has little perceived effect on pay when the employee must wait a whole year for a performance review.
- Individual merit pay systems are less appropriate for the service sector, where many people in the United States work. In knowledge-based jobs (such as "administrative assistant"), it is even difficult to specify what the desired product is.
- Supervisors typically control a rather limited amount of compensation, so merit pay differentials are normally quite small and, therefore, of questionable value.
- A number of bureaucratic factors that influence the size and frequency of merit pay (for example, position in salary range, pay relationships within the unit and between units, and budgetary limitations) have little to do with employee performance.
- Performance appraisals are designed for multiple purposes (training and development, selection, work planning, compensation, and so forth). When a system is used to accomplish so many objectives, it is questionable whether it can accomplish any of them well. It is difficult for the supervisor to play the role of counselor or adviser and evaluator at the same time.

FIGURE 11.2
Factors Commonly Blamed for the Failure of Individual-Based Pay-for-Performance Systems

that many surveys over the past three decades have found that up to 80 percent of employees do not see a connection between personal contributions and pay raises.[46] The beliefs underlying this perception, many of which have proved to be very resistant to change, are summarized in Figure 11.2.

- ***Individual pay plans may work against achieving quality goals*** Individuals rewarded for meeting production goals often sacrifice product quality. Individual-based plans also work against quality programs that emphasize teamwork because they generally do not reward employees for helping other workers or coordinating work with other departments.
- ***Individual-based programs promote inflexibility in some organizations*** Because supervisors generally control the rewards, individual-based pay-for-performance plans promote dependence on supervisors. Thus, they prop up traditional organizational structures, which make them particularly ineffective for firms trying to take a team approach to work.

WHEN ARE INDIVIDUAL-BASED PLANS MOST LIKELY TO SUCCEED? Despite the challenges they present to managers, rewards based on individual performance can be highly motivating, usually under the following conditions:

- ***When the contributions of individual employees can be accurately isolated*** Identifying any one person's contributions is easier for some jobs than for others. For instance, a strong individual incentive system can work well with salespeople because it is relatively easy to measure their accomplishments. In contrast, research scientists in industry are generally not offered individual-based performance incentives because they typically work so closely together that individual contributions are hard to identify.
- ***When the job demands autonomy*** The more independently employees work, the more it makes sense to assess and reward the performance of each individual. The performance

of managers of individual stores in a large retail chain like Gap can be rated fairly easily, whereas the performance of the HR director in a large company is much more difficult to assess.

- ***When cooperation is less critical to successful performance or when competition is to be encouraged*** Practically all jobs require some cooperation, but the less cooperation needed, the more successful an individual-based pay program will be. For example, less employee cooperation is expected of a stockbroker than of a pilot in an Air Force squadron.

Team-Based Plans

A growing number of firms are redesigning work to allow employees with unique skills and backgrounds to tackle projects or problems together. For instance, at Compaq Computer Corp. (now part of Hewlett-Packard) as many as 25 percent of the company's 16,000 employees are on teams that develop new products and bring them to market.[47] Employees in this new system are expected to cross job boundaries within their team and to contribute in areas in which they have not previously worked. Other companies that have implemented a team approach to job and work design are Clairol (now part of Procter and Gamble), Bristol-Myers Squibb, Hershey Chocolate (North America), Newsday/Times Mirror, Pratt & Whitney/United Technologies, General Motors, TRW, Digital Equipment, Shell Oil, and Honeywell.[48] A team-based compensation system can provide integral support for effective team arrangements.

Team-based pay plans normally reward all team members equally, based on group outcomes. These outcomes may be measured objectively (for example, completing a given number of team projects on time or meeting all deadlines for a group report) or subjectively (for example, using the collective assessment of a panel of managers). The criteria for defining a desirable outcome may be broad (for example, being able to work effectively with other teams) or narrow (for example, developing a patent with commercial applications). As with individual-based programs, payments to team members may be made in the form of a cash bonus or in the form of noncash awards such as trips, time off, or luxury items.

Some firms allow the team to decide how its bonus will be distributed within the group. Other companies couple team-based incentives with team-building exercises. Monsanto, for instance, made it onto *Fortune*'s 100 Best Companies a few years back largely because of activities, such as snowshoe softball, intended to improve team cohesiveness. At several Monsanto sites, "people teams" of staffers are charged with designing employee bonding activities.[49]

ADVANTAGES OF TEAM-BASED PAY-FOR-PERFORMANCE PLANS When properly designed, team-based incentives have two major advantages:

- ***They foster group cohesiveness*** To the extent that team members have the same goals and objectives, work closely with one another, and depend on one another for the group's overall performance, team-based incentives can motivate group members to behave and think as a unit rather than as competing individuals. In this situation, each worker is more likely to act in a way that benefits the entire group.[50]
- ***They aid performance measurement*** A number of studies have shown that performance can be measured more accurately and reliably for an entire team than for individuals.[51] This is true because less precise measurement is required when an individual's performance does not need to be identified and evaluated in relation to others in a group.

DISADVANTAGES OF TEAM-BASED PAY-FOR-PERFORMANCE PLANS Managers need to be aware of potential pitfalls with team-based plans. This may account for the limited adoption of these types of incentives, which are used by firms about a third as often as individual-based incentives.[52] The disadvantages are as follows:

- ***Possible lack of fit with individualistic cultural values*** Because most U.S. workers expect to be recognized for their personal contributions, they may not react well to an incentive system in which individual efforts take a back seat to the group effort, with all team members rewarded equally. On the other side of the coin, individual incentives are likely to fail in societies with a collective orientation. In a striking display of cultural insensitivity, many U.S. companies have introduced high-risk individual incentives to their Japanese subsidiaries. These plans have generally failed.[53]

- *The free-riding effect* In any group, some individuals put in more effort than others. In addition, ability levels differ from one person to the next. Those who contribute little to the team—either because of low effort or limited ability—are *free riders.*[54]

  When all team members (including free riders) are rewarded equally for a group outcome, there are likely to be complaints of unfairness. The result may be conflict rather than the cooperation the plan was intended to foster, with supervisors having to step in to judge who is contributing what.[55]

  To minimize the free-riding effect, some companies have been adjusting pay incentives to encourage individual performance within teams. W. L. Gore, the maker of Gore-Tex fabric, has its 4,000-plus employees evaluate fellow team members each year to individualize team-based incentives (each team member receives a payment according to his or her personal contributions as assessed by peers).[56]
- *Social pressures to limit performance* Although group cohesiveness may motivate all team members to increase their effort and work to their full potential, it can also dampen team productivity. When commercial airline pilots want to express a grievance, for instance, they sometimes agree among themselves to fly "by the book." This means that they follow every rule without exception, leading to an overall work slowdown. Group dynamics may also encourage team members to try to beat the game—cheating to get the reward, for instance—as a way to get back at management.[57]
- *Difficulties in identifying meaningful groups* Before they decide how to distribute rewards based on team performance, managers must define a *team.* Coming up with a definition can be tricky, because various groups may be highly interdependent, making it difficult to identify which ones did what. Also, a person may be a member of more than one team, and teams may change members frequently.
- *Intergroup competition leading to a decline in overall performance* A team may become so focused on maximizing its own performance that it ends up competing with other teams. The results can be quite undesirable. For instance, the manufacturing group may produce more units than the marketing group can possibly sell, or the marketing group may make sales commitments that manufacturing is hard pressed to meet on schedule.[58]

UNDER WHICH CONDITIONS ARE TEAM-BASED PLANS MOST LIKELY TO SUCCEED? Although managers need to be aware of the potential disadvantages of team-based plans, they should also be on the lookout for situations conducive to their successful use. Such plans are likely to be successful under the following circumstances:

- *When work tasks are so intertwined that it is difficult to single out who did what* This is often the case in research and development labs, where scientists and engineers work in teams. It is also the case with firefighter crews and police units, which often think of themselves as one indivisible entity.
- *When the firm's organization facilitates the implementation of team-based incentives* Team-based incentives are appropriate when:
  1. *There are few levels in the hierarchy, and teams of individuals at the same level are expected to complete most of their work with little dependence on supervisors or upper management* Both public- and private-sector organizations that have had to lay off workers to maintain efficiency and profitability have found that teamwork becomes a necessity. For instance, when the city of Hampton, Virginia, underwent a massive downsizing and restructuring that resulted in the loss of several layers of supervision, it had to redesign its work processes. The city created self-managed teams and incorporated team-based pay into a multilayered pay-for-performance plan.[59] At W. L. Gore, which, as noted earlier, uses a lot of team-based incentives, the firm's culture is highly supportive of the practice. American scientist Bill Gore, who founded the company with his wife Vievi in 1958, believed that a nonhierarchical environment allows creative individuals to flourish and work collaboratively. Hence, almost 55 years later (in addition to team incentives), W. L. Gore does not have job descriptions, titles, or managers, just leaders.[60]
  2. *Technology allows for the separation of work into relatively self-contained or independent groups* This can be done more easily in a service unit (such as a telephone

repair crew) than in a large manufacturing operation (such as a traditional automobile assembly line).

3. ***Employees are committed to their work and are intrinsically motivated*** Such workers are less likely to shirk responsibility at the expense of the group, so free riding is not a serious concern. Intrinsic motivation is often found in not-for-profit organizations, whose employees are emotionally committed to the organization's cause.
4. ***The organization needs to insist on group goals*** In some organizations, this is a paramount need. For example, high-tech firms often find that their research scientists have their own research agendas and professional objectives—which are frequently incompatible with those of the firm or even their peers. Team-based incentives can focus such independent-minded employees' efforts on a common goal.[61]
5. ***Team-based incentives can help blend employees with diverse backgrounds and perspectives and focus their efforts on goals important to the organization*** At Intel, for instance, "customer-focused teamwork" is now the firm's mantra. Long-dominant hardware engineers are learning to work more closely with marketers and software engineers, and their incentives are tied directly to how well they cooperate with each other.[62]

- ***When the objective is to foster entrepreneurship in self-managed work groups*** Sometimes, to encourage innovation and risk taking within employee groups, a firm will give certain groups extensive autonomy to perform their task or achieve certain objectives. This practice is often referred to as *intrapreneuring* (a term coined by Gifford Pinchot, who published a book with that title in 1985).[63] In an intrapreneuring environment, management often uses team-based incentives as a hands-off control mechanism that allows each group to assume the risk of success or failure, as entrepreneurs do.

Figure 11.3 summarizes the advantages and disadvantages of individual- and team-based pay-for-performance plans.

Plantwide Plans

Plantwide pay-for-performance plans reward all workers in a plant or business unit based on the performance of the entire plant or unit. Profits and stock prices are generally not meaningful performance measures for a plant or unit because they are the result of the entire corporation's performance. Most corporations have multiple plants or units, which make it difficult to attribute financial gains or losses to any single segment of the business. Therefore, the key performance indicator used to distribute rewards at the plant level is plant or business unit efficiency, which is normally measured in terms of labor or material cost savings compared to an earlier period.

FIGURE 11.3
Advantages and Disadvantages of Individual- and Team-Based Pay-for-Performance Plans

	Individual-Based Plans	Team-Based Plans
Advantages	• Rewarded performance is likely to be repeated • Financial incentives can shape a person's goals • Can help the firm attain individual equity • Fit an individualistic culture	• Fosters group cohesiveness • Aids performance measurement
Disadvantages	• Can promote single-mindedness • Disbelief that pay and performance are linked • May work against achieving quality goals • May promote inflexibility	• Possible lack of fit with individualistic culture • May lead to free-riding effect • Group may pressure members to limit performance • Hard to define a team • Intergroup competition

gainsharing
A plantwide pay-for-performance plan in which a portion of the company's cost savings is returned to workers, usually in the form of a lump-sum bonus.

Plantwide pay-for-performance programs are generally referred to as **gainsharing** programs because they return a portion of the company's cost savings to the workers, usually in the form of a lump-sum bonus. Three major types of gainsharing programs are used. The oldest is the *Scanlon Plan,* which dates back to the 1930s. It relies on committees of employees, union leaders, and top managers to generate and evaluate cost-saving ideas. If actual labor costs are lower than expected labor costs over an agreed-on period (normally one year), the difference is shared between the workers (who, as a group, usually receive 75% of the savings) and the firm (which usually receives 25% of the savings). A portion of the savings may also be set aside in a rainy day fund.

The second gainsharing program, the *Rucker Plan,* uses worker–management committees to solicit and screen ideas. These committees are less involved and simpler in structure than those used by the Scanlon Plan. But the cost-saving calculation in the Rucker Plan tends to be more complex because the formula encompasses not only labor costs but also other expenses involved in the production process.

The last type of gainsharing program, *Improshare* ("*Im*proved *pro*ductivity through *shar*ing"), is a relatively new plan that has proved easy to administer and communicate. First, a standard is developed—based on research by an industrial engineering group or some set of base-period experience data—that identifies the expected number of hours required to produce an acceptable level of output. Any savings arising from production of this agreed-on output in fewer than the expected hours are shared between the firm and the workers.

ADVANTAGES OF PLANTWIDE PAY-FOR-PERFORMANCE PLANS The primary rationale for gainsharing programs can be traced to the early work of Douglas McGregor,[64] a colleague and collaborator of Joseph Scanlon, founder of the Scanlon Plan. According to McGregor, a firm can be more productive if it follows a participative approach to management—that is, if it assumes that workers are intrinsically motivated, can show the company better ways of doing things if given the chance, and enjoy being team players.

In contrast to individual-based incentive plans, gainsharing does not embrace the idea that pay incentives motivate people to produce more. Rather, gainsharing suggests that cost savings result from treating employees better and involving them intimately in the firm's management. The underlying philosophy is that competition between individuals and teams should be avoided, that all workers should be encouraged to use their talents for the plant's common good, that employees are willing and able to contribute good ideas, and that the financial gains generated when those ideas are implemented should be shared with employees.

Gainsharing plans can provide a vehicle to elicit active employee input and improve the production process. They can also increase the level of cooperation across workers and teams by giving everyone a common goal. In addition, gainsharing plans are subject to fewer measurement difficulties than individual- or team-based incentives. Because gainsharing plans do not require managers to sort out the specific contributions of individuals or interdependent teams, it is easier both to formulate bonus calculations and to achieve worker acceptance of these plans.[65]

DISADVANTAGES OF PLANTWIDE PAY-FOR-PERFORMANCE PLANS Like all other pay-for-performance plans, plantwide gainsharing programs may suffer from a number of difficulties, among them:

- ***Protection of low performers*** The free-rider problem can be very serious in plants where rewards are spread across a large number of employees. Because so many people work together in a plant, it is less likely that peer pressure will be used to bring low performers into the fold.
- ***Problems with the criteria used to trigger rewards*** Although the formulas used to calculate bonuses in gainsharing plans are generally straightforward, four problems may arise. First, once the formula is determined, employees may expect it to remain the same forever. A too-rigid formula can become a management straitjacket, but managers may not want to risk employee unrest by changing it. Second, improving cost savings will not necessarily improve profitability, because the latter depends on many uncontrollable factors (such as consumer demand). For example, an automobile production facility can operate at high efficiency, but if it is producing a car that is in low demand, that plant's financial performance will not look good. Third, when gainsharing is first instituted, it is easier for inefficient than for efficient plants or business units to post a gain. This occurs because opportunities for

dramatic labor-cost savings are much higher in the less-efficient units.[66] Thus, gainsharing programs may seem to penalize already efficient units, which can be demoralizing to those who work in them. Fourth, there may be only a few labor-saving opportunities in a plant. If these are quickly exhausted, further gains will be difficult to achieve.

- *Management–labor conflict* Many managers feel threatened by the concept of employee participation. When the gainsharing program is installed, they may be reluctant to give up their authority to committees, thus creating conflict and jeopardizing the program's credibility. In addition, only hourly workers are included in many gainsharing plans. The exclusion of salaried employees may foster hard feelings among them.

CONDITIONS FAVORING PLANTWIDE PLANS A number of factors affect the successful implementation of gainsharing programs.[67] These are:

- *Firm size* Gainsharing is more likely to work well in small-to-midsize plants, where employees can see a connection between their efforts and the unit's performance.
- *Technology* When technology limits improvements in efficiency, gainsharing is less likely to be successful.
- *Historical performance* If the firm has multiple plants with varying levels of efficiency, the plan must take this variance into account so that efficient plants are not penalized and inefficient plants rewarded. It is difficult to do this where there are scanty historical records. In these cases, past data are insufficient for establishing reliable future performance standards, making it difficult to implement a gainsharing program.
- *Corporate culture* Gainsharing is less likely to be successful in firms with a traditional hierarchy of authority, heavy dependence on supervisors, and a value system that is antagonistic to employee participation. Gainsharing can be used effectively in a firm that is making the transition from a more autocratic to a more participative management style, but it probably cannot lead the charge as a stand-alone program.
- *Stability of the product market* Gainsharing is most appropriate in situations where the demand for the firm's product or service is relatively stable. Under these circumstances, historical data may be used to forecast future sales reliably. When demand is unstable, the formulas used to calculate bonuses may prove unreliable and force management to change the formula, which is likely to lead to employee dissatisfaction.

Corporatewide Plans

The most macro type of incentive programs, *corporatewide pay-for-performance plans,* reward employees based on the entire corporation's performance. The most widely used program of this kind is **profit sharing**, which differs from gainsharing in several important ways:[68]

profit sharing
A corporatewide pay-for-performance plan that uses a formula to allocate a portion of declared profits to employees. Typically, profit distributions under a profit-sharing plan are used to fund employees' retirement plans.

- In a profit-sharing program, no attempt is made to reward workers for productivity improvements. Many factors that affect profits (such as luck, regulatory changes, and economic conditions) have little to do with productivity, and the amount of money employees receive depends on all of these factors.
- Profit-sharing plans are very mechanistic. They make use of a formula that allocates a portion of declared profits to employees, normally on a quarterly or annual basis, and do not attempt to elicit worker participation.
- In the typical profit-sharing plan, profit distributions are used to fund employees' retirement plans. As a result, employees seldom receive profit distributions in cash. (This deferral of profit-sharing payments is commonly done for tax reasons.) Profit sharing that is distributed via a retirement plan is generally viewed as a benefit rather than an incentive. Some companies do have profit-sharing programs that are true incentives, however. A notable case is Andersen Corporation, the Minnesota-based manufacturer of windows and patio doors. Employees have received up to 84 percent of their annual salary in a lump-sum check at the end of the year from Andersen's profit-sharing pool.[69]

employee stock ownership plan (ESOP)
A corporatewide pay-for-performance plan that rewards employees with company stock either as an outright grant or at a favorable price that may be below market value.

Like profit sharing, **employee stock ownership plans (ESOPs)** are based on the entire corporation's performance—in this case, as measured by the firm's stock price. ESOPs reward employees with company stock, either as an outright grant or at a favorable price that may be below market value.[70] Employers often use ESOPs as a low-cost retirement benefit for employees because stock contributions made by the company are nontaxable until the employee redeems the stock.[71] Under the right conditions, ESOPs may result in a bonanza for employees. For example, stocks of *Fortune*'s 100 Best Companies beat the market by a wide margin during the past 20 years or so.[72] Employees whose retirement plans are based on ESOPs are exposed to risk, however, because the price of the company's stock may fluctuate as a result of general stock market activity or mismanagement of the firm.

Risk was not in the mind of most stock-owning employees as the stock market skyrocketed during the 1990s and part of the following decade. Examples of firms that offered ESOPs to all employees who saw at least a tripling of their original value during this period include Amgen, Arrow Electronics, Autodesk, Hewlett-Packard, Intel, Lucent Technologies, Marriot International, Merck, Sun Microsystems, and Whole Foods Market.[73] However, many employees were shocked to find that during 2008–2011 the value of their stockholdings declined by a third or more within a year and, in some cases, in a matter of months, or even days. Yet again stockholdings took a big turn for the best starting in 2013. Given their cyclical nature, it is important for employers offering ESOPs to warn employees not to take for granted the value of their stockholdings or to assume that the value of these stockholdings will rise rapidly in the next few years.

Firms in the United States have led the world in ESOPs, particularly in industries such as high technology. Now, multinational firms and foreign firms are extending stock ownership opportunities to their employees at home and abroad. Companies offering stock options to employees include Siemens and SAP in Germany, Marconi and British Telecom in the United Kingdom, and Suez-Lyonnaise des Eaux and Alcatel in France.[74] Many foreign governments are establishing the legal framework to permit such plans, which until recently were unknown outside the United States. Depending on the specific country, many U.S. companies are surprised to find that, contrary to U.S. practice:[75]

- Option gains may be included in mandatory severance payments.
- Suspending vesting during a maternity leave may not be legal.
- Excluding part-time employees from participating in the plan based solely on the criterion that they are part time may be impermissible.
- An employee's consent and/or notification to a government agency may be required before information necessary to determine an option grant is collected and transferred to a U.S. database.
- The company may have to provide stock options to all employees, regardless of their rank as employees or managers, and seniority may determine who gets how much.

The Internal Revenue Service now requires all firms to "expense" the cost of stock-based programs, which means that the firm must estimate the value of the stocks handed out to employees and executives even though the price of the stock (and hence its value) lies in the future (assuming stockholders have yet to convert their shares into cash).

ADVANTAGES OF CORPORATEWIDE PAY-FOR-PERFORMANCE PLANS Corporatewide pay-for-performance plans have distinct advantages, several of which are economic rather than motivational. These are:

- ***Financial flexibility for the firm*** Both profit sharing and ESOPs are variable compensation plans: Their cost to the firm is automatically adjusted downward during economic downturns. This feature allows the firm to retain a larger workforce during a recession. In addition, these plans allow employers to offer lower base compensation in exchange for company stock or a profit-sharing arrangement. This feature gives the firm "float," the flexibility to direct scarce cash where it is most needed. ESOPs may also be used to save a foundering company—one whose cash is running out or is facing a hostile takeover bid. Weirton Steel, Hyatt Clark, Polaroid, and Chevron have effectively used ESOPs for this purpose.[76]
- ***Increased employee commitment*** Employees who are entitled to profit sharing and ESOPs are more likely to identify themselves with the business and increase their commitment to it. Many consider the sharing of profits between the firm's owners and workers as a just distribution of income in a capitalistic society.
- ***Tax advantages*** Both profit sharing plans and ESOPs enjoy special tax privileges. In essence, they allow the firm to provide benefits (discussed in detail in Chapter 12) that are subsidized in part by the federal government. Although these types of plans are sometimes

blamed for the loss of enormous amounts in tax revenues, it can be argued that they let firms that cannot afford to pay employees high salaries grow and prosper, thereby creating more jobs and tax revenues in the long run. Apple Inc., Sun Microsystems (now part of Oracle Corporation), Quantum Corporation, and Microsoft might not be around today were it not for tax-subsidized ESOPs and profit-sharing plans.

DISADVANTAGES OF CORPORATEWIDE PAY-FOR-PERFORMANCE PLANS Like all other pay-for-performance programs, corporatewide plans have their drawbacks:

- *Employees may be at considerable risk* Under profit-sharing or ESOP plans, workers' financial well-being may be threatened by factors beyond their control. Often workers are not fully aware of how much risk they face because the factors affecting profits or stock prices can be very complex. The more that long-term employees become reliant on these programs for savings (for their children's college tuition, their own retirement, or some other purpose), the more vulnerable they are to the firm's fate.

  Many employees of Fortune 500 firms saw their life savings take a huge fall after the bull market turned into a bear market late in 2008, with the Dow dropping more than 30 percent. Others have seen a windfall in 2013 as the market picked up steam. As the Enron case and its aftermath traveled through the legal and legislative process, it became evident that employers can subject employees to great financial risk when (1) they impose restrictions that prohibit employees from selling or diversifying their company stock until a certain age, or (2) when they allow employees to bet 100 percent of their long-term savings on their company stock. Among entrepreneurial firms, the risk can be huge: Many of these firms do not survive past five years, so the stock employees own may not be worth the paper it is printed on.[77] Unfortunately many employees are not fully aware of the risks, or perhaps they don't want to recognize the risk in these programs and focus instead on the possibility of high returns. The ethical thing for employers to do is to keep insisting on the fact that losses are a distinct possibility when it comes to employees holding company stocks (although this might be difficult to do given that most firms that institute stock-based programs believe that they are good for both employees and the company).
- *High exposure to macroeconomic forces* Related to the prior point, most companies have switched over the years from fixed pensions to 401(k) accounts, which are largely funded through profit sharing (see Chapter 12). Because these are unsecured investments, retirees and those approaching retirement age risk losing big chunks of their savings in a single day's trading, as many experienced in recent years.[78]
- *Limited effect on productivity* Because the connection between individual goal achievement and firm performance is small and difficult to measure, corporatewide programs are not likely to improve productivity. However, they should reduce turnover if seniority strongly affects how much an employee is entitled to under the plan.
- *Long-run financial difficulties* Both profit sharing and ESOPs often appear painless to the company in the short run, either because funds are not paid out to employees until retirement or because employees are paid in "paper" (company stock). As noted earlier, firms are now required to expense this "paper money," but they may still trim the option expenses in a number of ways. This illusion may induce managers to be more generous with these types of compensation than they should be, leaving future management generations with less cash available, lower profits to distribute to investors, and a firm that has decreased in value.

CONDITIONS FAVORING CORPORATEWIDE PLANS A number of factors influence the successful implementation of corporatewide pay-for-performance plans:

- *Firm size* Although they may be used at firms of any size, profit sharing and ESOPs are the plans of choice for larger organizations, in which gainsharing is less appropriate.[79]
- *Interdependence of different parts of the business* Corporations with multiple interdependent plants or business units often find corporatewide plans most suitable because it is difficult to isolate the financial performance of any given segment of the corporation.
- *Market conditions* Unlike gainsharing, which requires relatively stable sales levels, profit-sharing and ESOP programs are attractive to firms facing highly cyclical ups and downs in

FIGURE 11.4
Conditions That Favor Various Pay-for-Performance Plans

Type of Plan	Favorable Conditions
Individual-Based Plans	• The contributions of individual employees can be accurately isolated • The job demands autonomy • Successful performance does not depend on cooperation, or competition should be encouraged
Team-Based Plans	• Work tasks are so intertwined that it is difficult to single out who did what • The firm's organization supports the implementation of team-based incentives • The firm's objective is to foster entrepreneurship in self-managed work groups
Plantwide Plans	• Firm size is small to midsize • Technology does not limit efficiency improvements • Clear records of historical performance are available • Corporate culture supports participative management • A stable product market is present
Corporatewide Plans	• Firm size is large • Different parts of the business are interdependent • A relatively unstable (cyclical) product market is present • Other incentives are present

the demand for their product. The structuring of these incentives helps the firm cut costs during downturns. (This is why these programs are often called "shock absorbers.") Employees (except those who are closer to retirement) are not immediately affected by these fluctuations in short-term earnings because most profit-sharing benefits are deferred until retirement.

- ***The presence of other incentives*** Because corporatewide pay-for-performance plans are unlikely to have much motivational impact on individuals and teams within the firm, they should not be used on their own. When used in conjunction with other incentives (for example, individual and team bonuses), corporatewide programs can promote greater commitment to the organization by creating common goals and a sense of partnership among managers and workers.

Figure 11.4 summarizes the conditions that favor individual, team, plantwide, and corporatewide pay-for-performance plans.

Designing Pay-for-Performance Plans for Executives and Salespeople

Executives and salespeople are normally treated very differently than most other types of workers in pay-for-performance plans. Because pay incentives are an important component of these employees' total compensation, it is useful to examine their special compensation programs in some detail. It is also useful to examine how companies are rewarding excellence in customer service—a key source of competitive advantage today.

Executives

According to most recent figures, the median chief executive of a United States company with more than five billion dollars in revenues earns about $14 million per year; however, some can pocket more than $100 million.[80] CEO pay creates a lot of controversy in the media each year as these figures are released (see the Manager's Notebook "High-Priced CEOs: Are They Worth It?"). Approximately 38 percent of this amount is cash compensation (salary, bonus); the rest is stock-based compensation (which normally accounts for the largest pay packages reported in the media).

MANAGER'S NOTEBOOK

High-Priced CEOs: Are They Worth It?

Every year all U.S. publicly traded companies are required to release CEO pay data. And shortly after their release, one is likely to see a flurry of articles claiming that CEO pay is out of control, while some commentators (usually in the minority) argue that these executives deserve high pay because of their ability to create value for the corporation. Some examples of highly paid CEOs in recent 2013 filings include Disney's Bob Iger ($40.2 million), Direct T.V.'s Michael White ($18 million), Hewlett Packard's Meg Whittman ($15.4 million), and 37-years-old Marissa Mayer (who obtained a $117 million ironclad five-year contract from Yahoo! Inc.). As seen in this chapter, most of that pay is in the form of stock options. According to Harvard professor Mihir Desai, "Unfortunately the idea of market-based compensation [through stock options] is both remarkably alluring and deeply flawed. Financial markets cannot be relied upon in simple ways to evaluate and compensate individuals because they can't easily disentangle skill from luck . . . [as a result] these incentives provided huge windfalls for individuals who now consider themselves entitled to such rewards." In contrast, writing for *BusinessWeek*, consultant Larry Popelka rebukes this perspective, arguing that "CEO compensation packages are rising because more companies are realizing the value of good CEOs, and their pay—much like contracts for top tier professional athletes—is getting bid up . . . of course, everyone in a corporation is important and should be compensated fairly. But good companies with poor CEOs are rudderless and fail."

Source: Monkey Business Images/Shutterstock.

Sources: Based on *http://money.cnn-com*. (2013). 20 top-paid CEOs; *www.nytimes.com*. (2013). The infinity pool of executive pay; Bruce, S. (2013). Where is the public's breaking point on exec pay? *http://hrdailyadvisor.blr.com*; Joshi, P. (2013). Out of spotlight, a lucrative payday. *www.nytimes.com*; Murphy, T. (2013). CVS Caremark CEO compensation climbs 51 percent. *www.boston.com*; *www.washingtonpost.com*. (2013). Departing Wellpoint CEO's compensation ballooned to 20.6 M last year, as insurer's shares fell; Kerber, R., and Rothacker, R. (2013). Exclusive: BofA's Moynihan to hold stock longer in new pay policy. *www.reuters.com*; *www.bloomberg.com*. (2013). Verizon retirees win 2013 executive compensation change; Desai, M. (2012, March). The incentive bubble. *Harvard Business Review,* 2–11; Popelka, L. (2013). More companies need high-priced CEOs. *http://businessweek.com*.

According to some estimates, each of the Fortune 500 CEOs could live to age 95 among the top 2 percent of Americans if he or she saved just one year's pay. At the higher end, some could have $1.2 million a year for life by saving one year's pay.[81] U.S. CEOs earn approximately 500 times what the average employee makes, up from 42 times in 1980, and far more than in any other industrialized nation, both on absolute and relative grounds. That is, U.S. CEOs make more money than CEOs in other countries and they earn more compared to what the average worker does than CEOs from other nations earn. For instance, in Japan the CEO is paid 33 times what the average Japanese worker is paid.[82] However, some recent evidence suggests that international differences in CEO pay (both in absolute numbers and relative to lower-level employees) are diminishing, probably a reflection of globalization (good CEOs are in high demand, no matter their national background, so that the CEO labor market is slowly becoming more integrated around the world).[83]

The trend during the past 20 years or so has been for CEO pay to be less in the form of salary and more in the form of stocks. This trend was the result of several forces, including (1) favorable tax treatment for long-term income (for the CEO, stock gains are tax deferred, and when stocks are cashed in they are taxed at the capital gains rate, which is lower than the rate on salary and bonuses); (2) stock grants not counted as an expense in the balance sheet (although this changed starting in 2006); (3) a rising stock market over most of this period, with some short-term exceptions (such as during 2008–2012); and (4) investor calls for greater CEO accountability (unlike salary, long-term income is not assured and reflects growth in shareholder value).

Ironically, the trend toward greater emphasis on long-term income to reward executives has had several unintended consequences. First, a bull market can make CEO pay soar, fueling the belief that CEO pay is out of control. During the 1991–2001 decade, the nation's corporate elite saw their average pay increase by more than 550 percent, almost 20 times faster than raises to the typical worker.[84] Except for a short hiatus during 2008–2012, most executives have seen an expansion in their equity-based wealth year after year, and critics see this as unfair given that they receive the benefits of the market rise on top of high salaries.

Second, because executives may decide at any time to cash the stock options they received years earlier, it is difficult to see the link between CEO pay and firm performance. For example, Lawrence J. Ellison, CEO of Oracle Corporation, received a "windfall" of $706 million in 2001, even though that year had been a disaster for Oracle (the total return to Oracle's shareholders declined 57% during 2001). The huge amount received by Ellison (which exceeds the gross domestic product of many countries) came from exercising long-held stock options, and his decision to cash them in 2001 probably had nothing to do with Oracle's poor showing in 2001. Moving forward to 2013, Ellison again saw his pay jump 24 percent in a single year to $96.2 million (with $90.7 million of that amount attributed to cashing in stock options at Oracle during a bull market). In other words, it is difficult to see the chronological tie between stock-based pay and firm performance because of the elapsed time between receiving and cashing in a stock option. Many complex methods have been devised by academics to estimate the true linkage of long-term income to firm performance, yet these are arcane, often controversial, and the results tend to be inconsistent.[85]

And, third, when the stock market changes from a bull market to a bear market, firms face the problem of what to do for executives whose stocks are "under water" (that is, when the current market price is below the market price when they were provided to the executive, so the options have become worthless). Many firms believe that "underwater" options are demotivating to executives and could make those executives an attractive recruitment target by competitors. This happened, for instance, after the Wall Street financial meltdown of the late 2000s. To deal with this possibility, firms might make new additional grants to compensate the executive for the loss of value of previously granted stocks, cancel and reissue stock options to ensure they are not under water, or buy underwater stock with cash.[86] This strategy may reinforce the notion that top executives incur little risk with their pay while employees are often asked to bear the brunt of employment and compensation risk because they are more likely to be laid off and see their bonus cut during a downturn.[87]

A QUESTION OF ETHICS

Do you think it is ethical for a company to give its CEO and its other top executives multimillion-dollar pay packages that are not closely tied to the company's performance?

A large number of plans are used to link executives' pay to firm performance, but there is little agreement on which is best. The disagreement is only heightened by the huge sums of money involved and the weak or inconsistent correlation between executive earnings and firm performance.[88] Given the widespread belief that reckless risk taking, fueled by CEO incentive systems, was partly responsible for the recent financial meltdown, there is some consensus at the time of this writing (2014) that salary should play a more prominent role than incentives when designing compensation packages for executives.

SALARY AND SHORT-TERM INCENTIVES The amount of executives' base pay increases as firms get larger[89]—practically all CEOs of Fortune 500 firms earn a base of at least half a million dollars a year, with an average of $3.1 million in cash compensation annually based on 2011 estimates.[90] Executives' bonuses are usually short-term incentives linked to the firm's specific annual goals; in 2014 the average annual executive bonus among large firms was about $2 million. More than 90 percent of U.S. firms reward executives with year-end bonuses, but the criteria used to determine these bonuses vary widely.

Two major concerns are often expressed regarding executives' annual bonuses. First, because executives are likely to maximize whatever criteria are used to determine their bonuses, they may make decisions that have short-term payoffs at the expense of long-term performance. For instance, long-term investments in research and development may be crucial to the firm's success in introducing new products over time. Yet if bonus calculations treat such investments as costs that reduce net income, executives may be tempted to scale back R&D. Second, many bonus programs represent salary supplements that the CEO can expect to receive regardless of the firm's performance. For instance, an examination of the *Wall Street Journal*'s executive pay survey in published every year shows that approximately three-fourths of the CEOs in the survey receive a substantial bonus. An earlier study found that if we focus on companies with a drop in total shareholder return of 40 percent or more, we find that a surprising number of those CEOs received a bonus in excess of half a million dollars during the same period (including, for instance, Aplera, Crown Cork & Seal, Continental Airlines, and Boeing).[91]

The almost automatic payment of lavish bonuses to top executives has led to much resentment among middle managers. One vice president at a major bank expressed a common middle-management frustration: "It disturbs me when someone on high dictates that no matter how hard you work or what you do, you're only going to get a 6 percent increase, and if you don't like it, you can take a hike. Yet whatever they've negotiated for themselves—10 percent, 20 percent, or 30 percent—is a different issue from the rest of the staff." Although this is pure speculation at the moment, it is conceivable that political pressures in response to the economic meltdown at the end of the 2000s, the negative public image of many CEOs, and the necessity for vast federal "bailouts" may force boards of directors to place greater limits on CEO pay in the foreseeable future.

LONG-TERM INCENTIVES Most executives also receive long-term incentives, either in the form of equity in the firm (stock-based programs) or a combination of cash awards and stock. In 2014, these incentives amounted to approximately $6 million on average per executive of the largest U.S. firms. A brief description of the most commonly used executive long-term incentive plans appears in Figure 11.5.

The primary criticism of long-term incentive plans is that they are not very closely linked with executive performance. There are three reasons for this: First, even executives themselves rarely know how much their equity in the firm is worth because its value depends on stock prices at redemption. Second, the executive is likely to have very little control over the value of a company's stock (and thus the worth of his or her own long-term income) because stock prices tend to be highly volatile. (As noted earlier, depending on the time period, this can benefit the executive, as during 1995–2007; hurt the executive, as during 2008–2012; or make the executive wealthy again, as in the bull market that started in 2013). This is one reason that many critics see this as unfair given that the market has a logic of its own, and they claim that CEOs have very little influence over share prices, not even for their own firm.[92] Third, designing long-term incentive plans involves many judgment calls, and these are not always addressed in a manner consistent with achieving the firm's long-term strategic objectives. The major questions that firms should address in designing executive long-term incentive programs are listed in Figure 11.6.

GOLDEN PARACHUTES Following the demise of major financial investment and mortgage companies in recent years, one aspect of CEO pay that has received much negative publicity is the so called "golden parachute," which provides a CEO with a large lump-sum payment if he or she is terminated by the firm. These "parachutes" represent a contractual obligation on the part of the company to the CEO, even if the CEO is fired for poor performance. A 2013 study of large U.S. firms found that 92 percent of CEOs have golden parachutes and 87 percent have an additional severance payment agreement if they lose their jobs.[93] In 2014, the average payment that would be owed to the CEOs at 200 large companies if those CEOs were terminated would be close to $45 million.

REWARDS FOR SOCIAL RESPONSIBILITY Recently, some firms began to reward and penalize executives depending on the firm's record of social responsibility. For instance, apart from profitability, executive bonuses and long-term income in polluting industries may be pegged to reducing the level of dangerous emissions. For example, in 2013, Chevron Corporation reduced the bonus of its CEO John S. Watson by 13 percent, or $520,000, due to accidents the preceding year. These included underwater oil leaks in Brazil, a deadly rig fire in Nigeria, and a blaze at a refinery in Richmond, California.[94]

Stock-Based Programs

Stock Options Allow the executive to acquire a predetermined amount of company stock within a stipulated time period (which may be as long as 10 years) at a favorable price.

Stock Purchase Plans Provide a very narrow time window (usually a month or two) during which the executive can elect to purchase the stocks at a cost that is either less than or equal to fair market value. (Stock purchase plans are commonly available to all employees of the firm.)

Restricted Stock Plans Provide the executive with a stock grant requiring little, if any, personal investment in return for remaining with the firm for a certain length of time (for example, four years). If the executive leaves before completing the specified minimum length of service, all rights to the stock are forfeited.

Stock Awards Provide the executive with "free" company stock, normally with no strings attached. Often used as a one-time-only "sign-on" bonus for recruitment purposes.

Formula-Based Stock Stock provided to the executive either as a grant or at a stipulated price. Unlike other stock-based programs, the value of the stock to the executive when he or she wishes to redeem it is not its market price but one calculated according to a predetermined formula (normally book value, which is assets minus liabilities divided by the number of outstanding shares). Used when the board believes that the market price of an organization's stock is affected by many variables outside the control of the top-management team.

Junior Stock Stock whose value is set at a lower price than common stock, so that the executive is required to spend less cash up front to acquire it. Unlike the owners of common stock, the owners of junior stock have limited voting and dividend rights. However, junior stock can be converted to common stock upon achievement of specific performance goals.

Discounted Stock Options Stock with a strike price lower than the market value of the stock at the date of the grant. Introduced during the bear market of 2001–2003, when there was a reasonable probability that the market value of the stock would rise slowly or may drop.

Tracking Stock Options A class of shares linked to the performance of a specific business or unit of the parent company rather than linked to the performance of the corporation as a whole.

Programs That Combine Cash Awards and Stocks

Stock Appreciation Rights (SARs) Provide the executive with the right to cash or stocks equal to the difference between the value of the stock at the time of the grant and the value of that same stock when the right is exercised. Thus, the executive is rewarded for any increase in the value of the stock, although no stock was actually granted by the firm. No investment on the executive's part is required. May be offered alone or mixed with stock options.

Performance Plan Units Under this plan, the value of each share is tied to a measure of financial performance such as earnings per share (EPS). For example, for every 5 percent increase in EPS, the firm may provide the executive with $1,000 for every share he or she owns. Therefore, if EPS increases by 15 percent, the executive will receive $3,000 for each share owned. The payment may be made in cash or common stocks.

Performance Share Plans Offer the executive a number of shares of stock based on profitability figures using a predetermined formula. The actual compensation per share depends on the market price per share at the end of the performance or award period.

Phantom Stock Pays executives a bonus proportional to the change in prices of company stocks, rather than changes in profitability measures. A phantom stock is only a bookkeeping entry because the executive does not receive any stock per se. The executive is awarded a number of shares of phantom stock to track the cash reward that will be received upon attaining the performance objectives. The award may be equal to the appreciation or the value of the share of phantom stock.

FIGURE 11.5
Commonly Used Long-Term Executive Incentive Plans

perquisites ("perks")
Noncash incentives given to a firm's executives.

PERKS In addition to cash incentives, many executives receive a large number of **perquisites**, or "**perks**." A 2013 report shows a wide array of "special deals" for most top executives, including physical exams, financial counseling, club memberships, company plane, airline VIP clubs, chauffer service, and concierge service, among other similar perquisites.[95] These may keep the executive happy, but they are seldom linked to business objectives.[96] They are also an easy target of criticism for those who feel that executive compensation is already excessive and who believe that perks are a form of "stealth wealth," representing "a hidden way [for executives] to increase their compensation."[97] To make CEO pay more transparent, the Internal Revenue Service and the

1. How long should the time horizon be for dispensing rewards?
2. Should length of service be considered in determining the amount of the award?
3. Should the executive be asked to share part of the costs and, therefore, increase his or her personal risk?
4. What criteria should be used to trigger the award?
5. Should there be a limit on how much executives can earn or a formula to prevent large unexpected gains?
6. How often should the awards be provided?
7. How easy should it be for the executive to convert the award into cash?

FIGURE 11.6

Key Strategic Pay Policy Questions in the Design of Executive Long-Term Incentive Programs

Sources: Gomez-Mejia, L. R., Berrone, P., and Franco-Santos, M. (2010). *Compensation and organizational performance*. New York: M. E. Sharpe Inc; Makri, M. (2008). Incentives to stimulate innovation in global context. In Gómez-Mejía, L. R., and Werner, S. (Eds.), *Global compensation: Foundations and perspectives.* London: Routledge, 72–85; Berrone, P., and Gómez-Mejía, L. R. (2008). Beyond financial performance: Is there something missing in executive compensation schemes? In Gómez-Mejía, L. R., and Werner, S. (Eds.), *Global compensation: Foundations and perspectives.* London: Routledge, 205–218; Makri, M., and Gómez-Mejía, L. R. (2007). Executive compensation: Something old, something new. In Wemer, S. (Ed.), *Current Issues in Human Resource Management.* London: Routledge.

SEC passed new rulings to provide for better disclosure of CEO pay, including perks, starting in 2007. It is very difficult to understand what the whole compensation package consists of.[98]

There are no easy answers to these criticisms. Executive compensation will probably always be more an art than a science because of all the factors that must be considered and each firm's unique conditions. Nonetheless, it is safe to say that an executive compensation plan is more likely to be effective if (1) it adequately balances rewarding short-term accomplishments with motivating the executive to consider the firm's long-term performance, (2) the incentives provided are linked to the firm's overall strategy (for example, fast growth and risky investments versus moderate growth and low business risks), (3) the board of directors can make informed judgments about how well the executive is fulfilling his or her role, and (4) the executive has some control over the factors used to calculate the incentive amount.[99]

DIRECTORS AND SHAREHOLDERS AS EQUITY PARTNERS The board of directors is responsible for setting executive pay. Traditionally, the board members have been paid in cash. In recent years, however, the relative elements of director compensation have changed fundamentally, as we see a shift toward payment in stock and stock options to tie the financial interests of directors to those of the firm and thus increase their incentive to monitor the executives more closely. Currently, the vast majority of firms include at least some stock as part of the annual compensation of directors, with an estimated $60,000 in stock on average per director.[100]

Although in theory this change in director compensation is a good idea, two well-known researchers warn us that it could be tantamount to the fox watching the chickens. In other words, boards may be tempted to act in a self-serving manner because in most cases the board sets its own compensation.[101] For instance, directors may set lower performance targets for the granting of stock options. And even if the board acts in good faith with the best interest of shareholders in mind, the appearance of a conflict of interest would always loom in the background.[102]

Historically, boards of directors have played mostly a ceremonial role, meeting a few hours a year and seldom challenging the CEO. However, the large number of corporate scandals in recent years as well as the financial troubles of Wall Street giants in 2008–2009; the appearance of unjustifiably high CEO compensation; and passage of the Sarbanes-Oxley Act (which outlines a set of accountability standards for public companies in the areas of financial reporting, disclosure, audits, conflicts of interest, and governance) are forcing boards of directors to become active watchdogs.[103] In a cover story, *BusinessWeek* summarized this dramatic change: "Boards used to be hired as much for their golf handicaps as for any other expertise. They read reports from management, offered occasional bits of advice, and generally greenlit decisions the CEO had already made. These days, they are apt to become involved in key corporate functions, from strategies to succession to auditing. And if there is a difference with the CEO, they will lawyer up in a heartbeat."[104] In a recent report on executive compensation, the *Wall Street Journal* notes, "Boards flex their pay muscles: directors, facing unprecedented pressure from investors, lawmakers and regulators . . . are retaining their own lawyers, holding frequent executive sessions, and evaluating management rigorously."[105] Following the "Great Recession" of 2008–2012, boards are creating specialized risk-management committees to "anticipate corporate crises, intensify efforts to review risks and dodge disasters."[106] Apparently, the United States is not alone in this respect. In Japan, for instance, after a decade of disappointing corporate results, "oversight of top decisions, from staffing to compensation is now handled by committees governed by a majority of outside directors."[107] One danger with board overzealousness is that executives may try to please boards composed of people with diverse backgrounds, perspectives, and interests rather than use their own best judgment. Boards are probably better at advising than decision making, which is the primary role of the CEO.[108]

SALESPEOPLE Sales professionals, working with the marketing staff, are responsible for bringing revenues into the company. There are several reasons why setting up a compensation program for salespeople is so much different from setting up compensation programs for other types of employees.[109]

- The spread in earnings between the lowest-paid and highest-paid salespeople is usually several times greater than the earnings spread within any other employee group in the company.
- The reward system for salespeople plays a supervisory role because these employees generally operate away from the office and may not report to the boss for weeks at a time.
- Perceptions of pay inequity are a lesser concern with this group than with others because few employees outside the company's marketing organization have knowledge of either sales achievement or rewards.
- Sales compensation is intimately tied to business objectives and strategies.
- The performance variation among salespeople tends to be quite large. Most organizations rely on relatively few stars to generate most of the sales.
- The salesperson generally works alone and is personally accountable for results.
- Accurate market data on pay practices and levels are extremely difficult to find for salespeople, and commercial salary surveys are usually unreliable.
- The positive motivational impact of compensation plan designs is based largely on the accuracy of sales goals and forecasts.[110]

Sales professionals may be paid in the form of *straight salary* (with no incentives), *straight commission* (in which all earnings are in the form of incentives), or a *combination plan* that mixes the two. Straight salary is most appropriate when maintaining good customer relations and servicing existing accounts are the key objectives, with increased sales a secondary goal. Straight commission is most appropriate when the key objective is to generate greater sales volume through new accounts. Only one-fourth of all firms use either a straight-salary or straight-commission method. Three-quarters use a combination of the two, though the relative proportion of salary versus incentives varies widely across firms. The trend has been to put more emphasis on commissions in a mixed plan.[111]

As Figure 11.7 shows, all three sales compensation methods have their pros and cons. The main criterion that should determine the type of plan chosen is overall marketing philosophy, which is derived from the firm's business strategies.[112] If increased sales is the major goal and these sales involve a one-time transaction with the customer and little expectation of a continuing relationship, then a greater proportion of incentives in the pay mix is appropriate. If customer service is crucial and the sales representative is expected to respond to clients' needs on a long-term basis, then greater reliance on straight salary is appropriate. For example, used car salespeople are often paid in the form of straight commission, whereas sales representatives for highly technical product lines (which often require extensive customer service) tend to be paid on straight salary.

Rewarding Excellence in Customer Service

More and more companies are using incentive systems to reward and encourage better customer service. A survey of 1,400 employers revealed that 35 percent of the respondents factor customer satisfaction into their formula for determining incentive payments. Another third are considering

Straight-Commission Sales Compensation Plan

Goods	*Bads*
• May generate more accounts • May motivate sales force to sell more • May foster entrepreneurial orientation • May reduce supervisory expenses • May reduce fixed costs • May attract employees who are willing to take risks	• Quality of service may suffer • Sales representative may overstate the positive features of the product • Sales representative may become overly aggressive with customers and they might not come back

Straight-Salary Sales Compensation Plan

Goods	*Bads*
• Sales force may be willing to spend more time with customer • May reduce stress levels among sales force, reducing turnover • May engender greater cooperation and less competition among the sales workforce	• May reduce the motivation to sell • Increases fixed compensation costs • Best sales performers may go to a firm that provides incentives • Greater need to appoint sales managers to supervise sales workforce

Combining Salary with Straight Commission Sales

Goods	*Bads*
• Reinforces good citizenship behavior and at the same time provides an incentive to sell more • May offer a good middle solution to the conflicting demands of spending time with customers versus selling to a broader customer base • Support a greater variety of marketing goals	• Plan could be complex to design and administer • Sales force may not be clear as to which objectives or targets are most important • Top sales people may find it more advantageous to get a job with another employer in order to make more money

FIGURE 11.7

How Should Employees in Sales Be Compensated? The Goods and the Bads of Paying with Salary and Commission

doing so. Common measures of customer satisfaction used to determine incentive payments are customer surveys, records of on-time delivery of products and services, and number of complaints received.[113]

Customer service rewards may be individual-, team-, or plant-based. For example, Storage Technology in Louisville, Colorado, uses customer service as part of its formula to distribute gainsharing monies to all employees covered by the plan. To ensure that sales representatives and managers do not shortchange the customer for the sake of increasing sales and short-term profits, IBM introduced a plan in which 40 percent of incentive earnings are tied to customer satisfaction. IBM uses a survey to determine whether buyers are happy with the local sales team.[114] AT&T Universal Card provides a $200 on-the-spot bonus for employees who deal effectively with customers' complaints on the phone; phone calls are randomly monitored for this purpose.[115]

Pay-For-Performance Programs in Small Firms

As noted in the preceding chapter, smaller firms face some of the same compensation issues that larger firms face when it comes to the attraction, retention, and motivation of employees through the use of pay (for instance, ensuring the perception of fairness and accurately assessing salary rates in the labor market for various positions). When the objective is to reward employees based on their performance, small firms face some unique challenges, including the following:

- Smaller firms seldom have trained personnel capable of designing and administering complex pay-for-performance systems and/or may be unable to afford this kind of professional help.
- Smaller firms seldom have in place a grievance procedure to deal with situations that particular employees feel are unfair. In a small-group setting, it is almost impossible to treat a

grievance confidentially, much less anonymously. This often means that perceived unfairness may be more difficult to detect and resolve through an impartial process that gives employees a voice.

- Because information travels quickly in small groups and most employees are interconnected, one or more disgruntled employees can have a major impact on the morale of the entire organization.
- In a larger organization, the negative effect of a few unhappy employees is more likely to be diluted and thus the consequences are not as bad. Smaller firms typically do not have enough leeway to handle disruptive conflict that interferes with the work that needs to get done. As noted by one observer, "Each of us has our own unique version of events. Owners and managers tend to see things one way and employees another, particularly when it comes to shortfalls in individual performance that is used to justify lower incentive pay for one person than another . . . [E]ach of us builds up a self-image, and a positive one is critical to our well being." In other words, differential pay allocations based on performance (as judged by owners and/or managers) within a small group can hurt the egos of those who get less, provoking interpersonal conflict that may be damaging to the firm. Small firms seldom have sufficient buffer among employees, units, or departments to prevent the conflict from spreading quickly.
- Unlike larger firms, the dividing line between work and personal relations tends to be thin in small firms. In these small organizations, emotional distance tends to be shorter because owners, managers, and employees know each other well and may socialize outside normal working hours. Pay-for-performance plans that allocate incentives differentially may generate deep resentments among those who get less (and perhaps embarrassment among those who get more) that are felt at a very personal level. Another way of looking at this is that feelings of betrayal and disillusionment are most likely to arise in smaller firms when some employees receive more incentives than others. This is compounded by the fact that management may not have good options for handling these emotional reactions (for instance, through a grievance procedure or by transferring the employee to another department).
- It is very difficult in small firms to link pay incentives to team performance because the work is seldom divided among teams. Employees often perform multiple tasks, and teams may come together in a fluid come-and-go fashion, with people expected to help each other as needed.
- In most small firms, opportunities for promotion are rather limited. Hence, a major challenge is to find ways for good employees to earn extra income in a way that does not involve a formal change in job title or moving up the organizational pyramid.

The issues noted here may be difficult to resolve if the small firm desires to implement a pay-for-performance system at the individual or team level. As discussed in Exhibit 11.1, the downside of such a system may overcome any potential benefits. The following suggestions seem particularly appropriate for smaller organizations:

- Active employee participation in the development of the pay-for-performance system can generate greater commitment to the firm and increase perceptions of fairness. Small size can be a great advantage to the organization in this regard because it is easy to get more people involved.
- Because of the firm's smaller size, it is easier for each employee to discern his or her personal contributions to the achievement of organizational goals. Given a "shorter line of sight" between individual contributions and organizational results, pay-for-performance plans linked to overall organizational performance can have two important advantages. First, they encourage the employee to work harder to improve overall firm performance. Second, they may bring employees closer together so that they cooperate with each other to achieve organizational goals.
- Given the close personal nature of relationships in most small firms and frequent interactions among employees, managers, and owners, informal feedback should be used more often, with the goal of helping employees improve performance rather than justifying differentials in incentive allocations.
- Smaller firms should be generous in sharing profits with employees. In addition to any motivational impact, this offers the firm an opportunity to attract and retain good employees while reducing fixed costs, because the firm may be able to get away with paying lower salaries. Employees may accept this in exchange for the potential to earn more money in the future.

- Smaller firms should be generous in offering stock options to employees. Stock options should increase employee identification with the firm because it makes them part owners. Just like profit sharing, employees may be willing to accept lower salaries in exchange for equity participation in the firm.

Summary and Conclusions

Pay-for-Performance: The Challenges

Pay-for-performance (incentive) programs can improve productivity, but managers need to consider several challenges in their design and implementation. Employees may be tempted to do only what they get paid for, ignoring those intangible aspects of the job that are not explicitly rewarded. Cooperation and teamwork may be damaged if individual merit pay is too strongly emphasized. Individual merit systems assume that the employee is in control of the primary factors affecting his or her work output, an assumption that may not be true. Individual performance is difficult to measure, and tying pay to inaccurate performance measures is likely to create problems. Pay incentive systems can be perceived as an employee right and can be difficult to adapt to the organization's changing needs. Many employees do not believe that good performance is rewarded (the credibility gap). Emphasizing merit pay can place employees under a great deal of stress and lead to job dissatisfaction. Finally, merit pay may decrease employees' intrinsic motivation.

Meeting the Challenges of Pay-for-Performance Systems

To avoid the problems sometimes associated with pay-for-performance systems, managers should (1) link pay and performance appropriately, (2) use pay for performance as part of a broader HRM system, (3) build employee trust, (4) promote the belief that performance makes a difference, (5) use multiple layers of rewards, (6) increase employee involvement, and (7) consider using nonfinancial incentives. Employee participation in the design of the plan can enhance its credibility and long-term success.

Types of Pay-for-Performance Plans

There are four types of incentive programs. At the level of individual employees, merit pay (which becomes part of base salary) and bonuses and awards (given on a one-time basis) determined via supervisory appraisals are most common. At the next level, team-based plans reward the performance of groups of employees who work together on joint projects or tasks, usually with bonuses and noncash awards. At the level of the plant or business unit, gainsharing is the program of choice. Gainsharing rewards workers based on cost savings, usually in the form of a lump-sum bonus. At the fourth and highest level of the organization—the entire corporation—profit sharing and employee stock option plans (ESOPs) are used to link the firm's performance with employees' financial rewards. Both plans are commonly used to fund retirement programs.

Designing Pay-for-Performance Plans for Executives and Salespeople

Two employee groups, top executives and sales personnel, are normally treated very differently than most other workers in pay-for-performance plans. Short-term annual bonuses, long-term incentives, and perks may be used to motivate executives to make decisions that help the firm meet its long-term strategic goals. Sales employees are revenue generators, and their compensation system is normally used to reinforce productive behavior. A reliance on straight salary for salespeople is most appropriate where maintaining customer relations and servicing existing accounts are the key objectives. A heavy reliance on straight commission is most appropriate if the firm is trying to increase sales. Most firms use a combination of the two plans. In today's globally competitive marketplace, many firms are also using incentive programs to reward customer service.

Designing Pay-for-Performance Plans in Small Firms

Small firms face some special challenges when designing pay-for-performance systems because they are less likely to have the necessary professional support to develop and administer these plans. Real or perceived mistakes in allocating incentives can have a large impact on these firms.

Because information travels quickly, because there is often a fine line between personal and work life, and because people are supposed to cooperate closely with each other, pay-for-performance plans in these firms are more likely to be successful if there is active employee participation in the development of the plan, incentives are linked to the achievement of organizational goals, and frequent informal feedback is provided to employees. In designing these plans, most small firms find it beneficial to offer generous profit sharing and equity-based pay for employees.

Key Terms

award, 335
bonus program or lump-sum payment, 334
employee stock ownership plan (ESOP), 341
expectancy theory, 335
gainsharing, 340
merit pay, 334
pay-for-performance system or incentive system, 325
perquisites ("perks"), 348
piece-rate system, 331
profit sharing, 341

Discussion Questions

11-1. This chapter identifies three assumptions underlying pay-for-performance plans. Do you believe these assumptions are valid?

11-2. One observer notes that "the problem with using pay as an incentive is that it is such a powerful motivational weapon that management can easily lose control of the situation." Do you agree? Why or why not?

11-3. Reread the Manager's Notebook, "Incentives Come to Medicine: Do They Promote Unethical Behaviors Among Doctors? " Do you agree that it is a good idea to offer incentives to doctors for better patient care? What are the drawbacks? Can these problems be avoided? Explain.

✪ 11-4. Some critics of pay-for performance programs warn that incentive pay may promote unethical behaviors among employees. Do you agree? Why or why not? What system would you put in place, if any, to prevent this from happening? Explain.

11-5. Based on your experiences working in a group task (for instance, completing a course project), what major problems have you observed when the team is rewarded as a group (for instance, a grade for entire team based on the quality of a completed class project)? What can be done to mitigate the problems you have identified? What could possibly go wrong if your recommendations are implemented? Explain.

11-6. Reread the Manager's Notebook, "Healthy Living Incentives." Do you believe that most employees value these incentives over cash? Do you think these incentives are capable of changing employees' unhealthy habits? Explain.

✪ 11-7. Reread the Manager's Notebook, "High-Priced CEOs: Are They Worth It? " Develop a list of arguments in favor of the position of Prof. Desai (that CEO pay is irrational) and a list of arguments in favor of consultant Popelka (that CEO pay is rational). Which of the two sets of arguments seem to make most sense to you? Explain.

11-8. In early 2014, video game company Nintendo released its nine-month financial results. In the period ending December 31, 2013, its earnings and profits were down by 8.1 percent and 30 percent respectively. Nintendo's president and CEO, Satoru Iwata, announced that he would implement a personal 50 percent pay cut for 5 months in recognition of the poor results. Other board members would take a pay cut of between 20 and 30 percent.[116] Do you think more CEOs and board members should follow this example? Explain.

11-9. More companies are using a compensation system that incorporates customer satisfaction as a more reasonable formula to give incentives to employees. Discuss how you would use such a system. What are the potential pitfalls of using incentive payments based only on sales?

MyManagementLab®

If your instructor has assigned this, go to **mymanagementlab.com** for the following Assisted-graded writing questions:

11-10. Outline a set of features that you would put in place if you were asked to design a pay for performance system. Based on the materials learned in this chapter explain why you have suggested each of the specific features.

11-11. In recent years most companies have relied heavily on the use of stock based compensation programs to reward senior executives. What are the advantages and disadvantages of using these incentive programs for executives? A smaller proportion of firms have also introduced employee stock ownership plans for the entire workforce. What are the advantages and disadvantages of using these incentive programs for employees?

11-12. A group of scholars have argued that use of extrinsic rewards tend to reduce intrinsic motivation. Why do they reach that conclusion? Do you agree? Explain.

You Manage It! 1: Global

Is There a Downside to Meritocracy?

Pay-for-performance systems are predicated on the simple idea that rewarding employees based on their contribution is not only fair but also important in order to attract, retain, and motivate the best performers. This view is widely shared in the United States, and most U.S. companies devote a substantial amount of their compensation dollars to achieve this (what is referred to as "individual equity" in this chapter). However, critics in other countries often note that too much meritocracy may create a blind spot for management because the organization may allocate insufficient resources to other important aspects of the employment relationship. A few examples follow:

- *Sick Leave* The United States, unlike most Western countries, does not have a mandatory sick-leave policy for employees. The Healthy Family bill, which would require such a policy, has been introduced in Congress during the past 10 years but has always failed to pass due to opposition by powerful business groups. According to U.S. Department of Labor statistics, more than a third of civilian workers in the United States do not get sick leave. Supporters of the Healthy Family bill argue that this represents a health hazard to both employees and the public because low-wage workers can't afford to stay away from work when sick.
- *Child Care* Unlike most European nations, American firms seldom provide day care for their employees' children and there is no government policy that supports it. The U.S. National Institute of Child Health Development rates only 10 percent of day care centers as high quality, with the median annual salary of a day care worker below that of a parking lot attendant. At the same time, day care consumes over 40 percent of the median income of many low-wage workers. Compare this to France, for instance, which devotes more than twice the amount of its GDP to day care than does the United States. As a result, day care is available in France to all parents, with the fee tied to the parents' personal income.
- *The Myth of the "Lone Star"* Most American firms believe in snapping up and retaining top talent through targeted incentives for so called "key contributors." In collectivist countries, such as in China and South Korea, it is the team that matters rather than the lone star. A group of Harvard business professors warns against the obsession of U.S. firms with identifying and rewarding lone stars: "The idea that you can catapult your firm into the big leagues with one or two top performers is a myth . . . the truth is, in the absence of equally talented colleagues, stars probably won't excel at their jobs or stick around for very long."

Critical Thinking Questions

11-13. Do you think offering incentives to key contributors motivates them as well as other employees to do a better job? Why or why not? If not, what alternative ways do you propose? Explain.

11-14. Are there any potential problems with devoting most compensation dollars to rewarding top performers, even if this means neglecting investments to improve the welfare of all employees (such as day care or paid sick leave)? If you were asked the hypothetical question of what percentage of compensation dollars should be directed toward individual contributors versus directed to investments in programs to improve the welfare of all employees, what percentage would you choose? Justify your answer.

11-15. In examples of profit-sharing with employees, once the total pool is established, the business needs to develop a methodology for providing individual rewards that are clear, logical, and fair. If the business fails to do this, they may end up creating animosity, undermining team cohesion, and eroding trust. How do you think profit-sharing schemes should really work? How should they be structured?

Team Exercise

11-16. Class is divided into teams of five. Some teams are asked to defend the view that most financial incentives should be targeted for key contributors. The other teams are asked to defend the contrarian view; that is, that devoting most compensation resources to the welfare of all employees is a better policy. Each pair of teams (pro and con) will debate for about 15 minutes, moderated by the instructor. Debate is then opened to discussion for the entire class.

Experiential Exercise: Team

11-17. Class is divided into two groups. One group must defend and support the awarding of bonuses on the basis of annual financial targets. The second group needs to support a more complex range of goals, including revenue targets, cash collection, and a break-even target on profit; they can also include a personal target for each employee based on job specifications. The groups should be given 20 minutes to prepare a workable scheme and suggest a series of advantages. The instructor will mediate, asking each team probing questions as to why they think their version of an incentive is better, more workable, and fairer.

Experiential Exercise: Individual

11-18. Research the success (or failure) of pay-for-performance systems for individual employees. Based on your research, would you recommend that these systems be expanded, limited, or eliminated altogether? Justify your recommendations.

Sources: Based on Plumer, B. (2013). Five shocking facts about child care in the United States. *www.washingtonpost.com*; McGregor, J. (2013). Should paid sick leave be mandated for all employees? *www.washingtonpost.com*; Groysberg, B., Lee, L., and Abrahams, R. (2013). The myth of the lone star: Why one top performer may not shine as brightly as you hope. *http://online.wsj.com*; Bruce, S. (2013). News flash—30% do pay for performance well! Do you? *http://hrdailyadvisor.blr.com* (note: interview with Jim Kochanski at Sibson reported in this article).

You Manage It! 2: Discussion

Loafers at Lakeside Utility Company

Lakeside Utility Company provides electrical power to a county with 50,000 households. Pamela Johnson is the manager in charge of all repair and installation crews. Each crew consists of approximately seven employees who work closely together to respond to calls concerning power outages, fires caused by electrical malfunctions, and installation of new equipment or electric lines. Fourteen months ago Johnson decided to implement a team-based incentive system that will award an annual bonus to each crew that meets certain performance criteria. Performance measures include indicators such as average length of time needed to restore power, results of a customer satisfaction survey, and number of hours required to complete routine installation assignments successfully. At the end of the first year, five crews received an average cash bonus of $12,000 each, with the amount divided equally among all crew members.

Soon after Johnson announced the recipients of the cash bonus, she began to receive a large number of complaints. Some teams not chosen for the award voiced their unhappiness through their crew leader. The two most common complaints were that the teams working on the most difficult assignments were penalized (because it was harder to score higher on the evaluation) and that crews unwilling to help out other crews were being rewarded.

Ironically, members of the crews that received the awards also expressed dissatisfaction. A surprisingly large number of confidential employee letters from the winning teams reported that the system was unfair because the bonus money was split evenly among all crew members. Several letters named loafers who received "more than their share" because they were frequently late for work, took long lunches and frequent smoking breaks, and lacked initiative. Johnson is at a loss about what to do next.

Critical Thinking Questions

11-19. What major issues and problems concerning the design and implementation of pay-for-performance systems does this case illustrate? Explain.

11-20. Are team-based incentives appropriate for the type of work done by Johnson's crews?

11-21. Might it be desirable to use a combination of team-based and individual incentives at Lakeside Utility Company? How might such a plan be structured?

Team Exercises

11-22. Students form pairs. One student takes the role of Pamela Johnson; the other, the role of an HRM consultant Johnson has hired to help her decide what to do next. Role-play the meeting between the two. Johnson explains what has happened and the consultant reacts.

The class divides into groups of five students each. One of the students takes the role of a consultant hired by Pamela Johnson to help her decide what to do. The remaining four students take the roles of line workers, each from a different crew. The consultant is gathering information from the crews about how they feel about the bonus system and what changes they would like to see.

Experiential Exercise: Team

11-23. This experiential exercise involves a group of six students. One will be a manager and five will be part of a team that has worked closely together during the past year. A bonus of $12,000 is to be divided among the five team members. A peer evaluation based on a scale of 1 (low) to 5 (high) shows that Ana, Robert, Steve, Peter, and Tom received scores of 4.4, 4.1, 3.7, 3.2, and 3.0, respectively. The manager is responsible for allocating the bonus. The manager must explain to each team member the rationale for the pay amount decided upon.

Experiential Exercise: Individual

11-24. Go online and find recent publications and case studies on the use of team-based incentives in industry. Based on this information, would you recommend the use of team-based incentives? Why or why not? Do you think team-based incentives are more appropriate in certain situations? Are there any policies that make team-based incentives more effective? Explain.

You Manage It! 3: Discussion

How Should Incentive Money Be Distributed?

Aetna Communications Inc. is a small firm with 90 employees installing telecommunication equipment. A team of consultants has advised the company owners to introduce the following incentive program. Any increase in profits from one year to the next would be divided as follows: 20 percent would be divided among employees and 80 percent would go to the firm's owners, savings, and future capital investments. The total pool of money for employees would then be allocated as follows. One half, or 50 percent, would be allocated among those employees who receive the top appraisal rating (which is a 5 in the company's rating scale). The next one third, or thirty-three percent, of the money would be allocated among those employees who received the next highest appraisal rating (which is a 4 in the company's ratings scale). The remaining 17 percent of the money would be allocated among those employees who were rated in the middle of the scale (or those who were rated as 3). Those who were rated in the two lowest categories (1 or 2) would receive zero from the pool of money.

Let's assume, for instance, that profits increased $900,000 from one year to the next. According to the formula described here, the total incentive pool of money to be distributed among employees would be $180,000, or 20 percent of the profit increase. Ninety thousand dollars of that incentive amount (50 percent) will go to those employees who were rated at the top or as a 5, $60,000 of the incentive amount will go to those employees who were rated as 4, and the remaining $30,000 would be distributed among those who were rated as 3.

Critical Thinking Questions

11-25. Do you agree with the proposal put forward by the consulting firm? Why or why not? Explain.

11-26. What do you see as the main advantages and disadvantages of this proposal? Explain.

11-27. As a small-firm owner, do you think it is a good idea to distribute profit gains across the board among all employees or would you rather distribute the profit gains based on individual contributions? Explain.

Team Exercise

11-28. Divide the class into teams of five. Some teams are asked to defend the position that the proposed plan is fair and reasonable; other teams are asked to argue that this is a dangerous proposal that may create widespread conflicts among employees, leading to future declines in overall performance. After each team meets for approximately 15 minutes, both sides will then discuss their respective position in class, with the instructor acting as a moderator.

Experiential Exercise: Team

11-29. Divide the class into teams of five. Each team is asked to evaluate the proposed plan and develop a set of conclusions about whether the plan should be accepted as is or should be modified, and, if so, how. Teams will present their conclusions to the entire class. The instructor will moderate discussion among various teams and provide his or her own views on the issue.

Experiential Exercise: Individual

11-30. There is much in the literature on gainsharing and profit sharing, and one of the key issues is the extent to which any money generated by that incentive plan should be divided equally among employees or differentially based on criteria such as individual performance, seniority, job title, level in the organizational hierarchy, and so on. Based on your review, what do you think is the best criterion that should be used to allocate the pool of incentive money? Justify your answer.

You Manage It! 4: Ethics/Social Responsibility

The Pitfalls of Merit Pay and Pay for Performance

Merit Pay? For Whom?

Three recent studies suggest that the link between pay and performance may not always show in the pay checks of women and minorities. A joint study of nearly 200 British executives by the University of Exeter in Britain and Tilburg University in the Netherlands found when men and women with similar experience achieved improved results, the women were rewarded far less. Bonuses for men rose over 250 percent at poorly performing companies that began to improve, whereas bonuses for women rose an average of merely 4 percent. An MIT study of nearly 9,000 nonmanagement information technology workers at a U.S. firm found that minorities received lower raises, even after controlling for variables such as job titles, starting pay, and education levels. Another study by the National Security Personnel System (NSPS) evaluated the Pentagon's pay-for-performance system and concluded that "Employees in higher-level, higher-paid positions got higher performance ratings and payouts than lower-level, lower-paid employees. The report further found that, in general, being a racial minority had a negative effect on one's rating and payout, and being black had a more negative effect than membership in other racial groups."

Pay for Performance

The following situations emerged in very different organizational settings after incentives were introduced to reward good employees:

- Prior to the financial crisis of 2008–2012, banks and security firms have been accused of fostering imprudent risk taking by showering employees with bonuses linked to revenues and volume of transactions. After 2008, large financial firms tried to defuse public anger and political retaliation by limiting these practices. But according to a recent *Wall Street Journal* report, "Bank of America Corp. and Citigroup Inc. are doling out shares that employees can sell within months—much sooner than normally allowed. Other giant banks, including Goldman Sachs Group Inc., Morgan Stanley and Royal Bank of Scotland Group PLC, let certain employees borrow money to relieve personal cash crunches. And some U.K. banks have considered raising base, or cash salaries—funds that won't be subject to the country's new 50% tax on bonuses."
- Several large banks were recently sued for housing foreclosure fraud. The lawsuits allege "common law fraud and misrepresentation as well as violations of consumer fraud statutes." Part of the problem may be traced to the incentive system that rewarded bank employees for expediting the foreclosure paperwork. The banks have admitted problems in the paperwork, uncovering evidence of "employees not verifying documents their signature suggested they verified."
- Green Giant had to abandon a bonus plan intended to reward employees for thoroughly cleaning the peas harvested for its vegetable packages. Employees had begun bringing their own insect parts to the factory, dropping them in the peas, and removing them to qualify for the incentive pay.
- Insects of a different sort were the undoing of another incentive pay plan, when a software developer found its programmers actually creating coding "bugs" in order to be rewarded for removing the glitches from their own work.
- By late 1996, ailing Sunbeam's well-paid new CEO Al Dunlap had fulfilled his mission to turn the company around and help its stock value soar. Then in 1998 the value of Sunbeam stock fell precipitously, from $53 a share to less than $4, and the SEC began an investigation of the company's accounting practices. Dunlap had improved Sunbeam's short-run performance, but he had not been able find a company willing to purchase it, leading Sunbeam's board of directors to fire him.

Critical Thinking Questions

11-31. What is the common thread across the widely different examples of "merit pay" and "pay for performance" given in this case?

11-32. What are some of the pros and cons of linking pay to objective criteria that are important to the organization such as quality control measures, profitability, and low turnover?

11-33. What can an organization do to ensure that merit pay and other incentives are administered fairly? What kind of data would you gather to ensure that the pay-for-performance system is not biased in favor of any particular group? Explain.

11-34. How would you prevent the problems that arose at Green Giant, the software developer, and Sunbeam and still reward good performance? Explain.

11-35. Assuming you are a top executive at Green Giant or the software developer, would you punish the employees who engaged in those unethical acts, the managers who devised the incentive system, or both?

11-36. Some people believe that most employees will act ethically even though they have a chance to take advantage of an incentive system through inappropriate behaviors. Do you agree?

Team Exercise

11-37. Divide the class into groups of three to five students. One set of teams will defend the proposition that incentives can be beneficial to a firm by reinforcing desired behaviors. Another set of teams will defend the position that in most cases incentives promote a "let's beat the game" attitude among employees that leads to poor performance.

Experiential Exercise: Team

11-38. A large retailer wants to link two key issues into one neat solution. Employee purchases are problematic as they are irregular and unpredictable. At the same time, there is a need to overhaul the rewards and incentive programs. The proposal is to issue each employee with a prepaid card. The card will be credited with their bonuses and rewards, which the employees can then use to buy products from the ranges sold by the store, at a predetermined discount level. One half of the class should prepare a strong case for the proposal and the other half should come up with a list of potential problems it might present. They should then present their thoughts, after which the instructor will moderate an open class discussion on the issue.

Experiential Exercise: Individual

11-39. Many have blamed the Wall Street debacle of 2008–2012, which the *Wall Street Journal* has referred to as the "worst crisis since 1930s," to the inappropriate use of pay incentives for top executives of large financial giants. According to this view, these executives earned huge bonuses if profit increased, inducing them to take imprudent risks "with other people's money" and to actively engage in speculation (particularly in the housing market). Despite tough talk about clamping down on pay abuses, many people feel that banks and security firms are finding ways to ease the toll on employees who were responsible for the crisis in the first place, except that now these institutions have access to a large infusion of money from the federal government (what some people refer to as bailout money). Research this issue and come up with a set of recommendation to reward top executives in a way that does not reinforce bad behaviors.

Sources: Based on Davidson, J. (2011). Lessons learned from pay-for-performance. *www.washingtonpost.com;* Enrich, D., Munoz, S. S., and Lucchetti, A. (2010, January 28). Banks see past pay limits. *Wall Street Journal*, A-1; Ng, S. (2010, Jan. 19). AIG tries to defuse bonus pay showdown. *Wall Street Journal*, C-3; Benoit, D. (2010, Nov. 10). Investors sue J. P. Morgan. *Wall Street Journal*, C-2; McGregor, J. (2008, September 22). Merit pay? Not exactly. *BusinessWeek*, 17; Bloom, M. (1999). The art and context of the deal: A balanced view of executive incentives. *Compensation and Benefits Review, 31*(1), 25–31; Hilsenrath, J., Serena, N. G., and Paleita, D. (2008, September 18). Worst crisis since '30s, with no end yet in sight. *Wall Street Journal*, A-1.

Endnotes

Scan for Endnotes or go to http://www.pearsonglobaleditions.com/Gomez-Mejia.

References

Buchanan, L. (2014). Opening the books and motivating workers. www.inc.com.

Cooper, J. (2010). Best Small-Business Places 2010. www.entrepreneur.com.

CNNMoney.com. (2014). 100 best companies to work for. http://money.cnn.com/magazines/fortune.

CNNMoney.com. (2014). Top things to know about stock options. http://money.cnn.com.

Festing, M., and Sahakiants, I. (2010). Compensation practices in Central and Eastern European EU member states. *Thunderbird International Business Review, 52*(3), 201–216.

Fowler, D., and Edquist, P. M. (2011). Tips for managing compensation in the family firm. www.bizjournals.com.

Ganster, K. (2011). Incentives for healthy habits. http://chamberpost.com.

Martochio, J. J. (2014). *Strategic compensation*. Upper Saddle River, NJ: Prentice-Hall

Robbins, S. (2011). How to set salaries. www.entrepreneur.com.

www.sciencedaily.com. (Accessed 2014). Pay for performance programs may worsen medical disparities, study finds.

CHAPTER 12 Designing and Administering Benefits

MyManagementLab®

When you see this icon, visit **www.mymanagementlab.com** for activities that are applied, personalized, and offer immediate feedback.

CHALLENGES

After reading this chapter, you should be able to deal more effectively with the following challenges:

1 **Grasp** an overview of benefits.

2 **Develop** the benefits strategy.

3 **Know** the legally required benefits.

4 **Have** familiarity with the voluntary benefits.

5 **Learn** practices for administering benefits.

Employee benefits in the twenty-first century have increased in complexity from the standard benefits of health insurance, retirement plans, and vacation time that all companies offer to employees. Google, the world's largest search-engine company, uses a vast array of benefits to differentiate itself from competitors that want to hire people with the same talents, according to Steven E. Gross, a consultant practice leader at Mercer Human Resource Consulting.[1]

One of the benefits that is noticed right away at Google is the food. Google provides 11 free gourmet cafeterias at its campus in Mountain View, California, that provide a variety of international foods, including a Spanish-style tapas bar and Indian, Chinese, Italian, Thai, and Mexican restaurants.[2] It also offers a 24-hour on-site fitness center, as well as personal trainers. There is an in-house doctor, nutritionist, a dry cleaner, and a massage service. A biodiesel bus equipped with Wi-Fi shuttles commuters to the office. For employees who wish to drive their cars to work, Google supplies onsite car washes and oil changes.

Source: © ZUMA Press, Inc./Alamy.

In addition, Google offers employees a $5,000 subsidy to buy a hybrid car.[3]

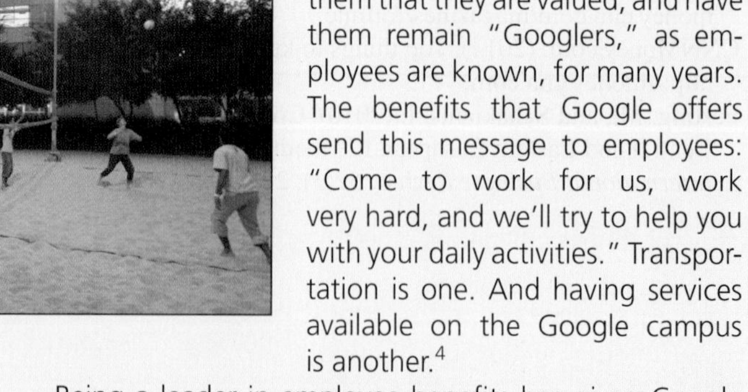

Is Google's generosity purely altruistic? Of course not! Google uses the benefits to achieve several goals: Attract the best knowledge-workers it can in the intensely competitive environment for high achievers; help them work long hours by feeding them gourmet meals onsite and handling other time-consuming personal chores; show them that they are valued; and have them remain "Googlers," as employees are known, for many years. The benefits that Google offers send this message to employees: "Come to work for us, work very hard, and we'll try to help you with your daily activities." Transportation is one. And having services available on the Google campus is another.[4]

Being a leader in employee benefits has given Google recognition as an outstanding place to work. Google was ranked number one in *Fortune's* "100 Best Companies to Work For" list in 2012 and 2013.[5]

Of course, not all companies have the resources to offer the benefits that Google does for its employees. The challenge is for managers and HR professionals to work together to (1) give employees meaningful benefit choices that match their needs, (2) keep the costs of these benefits under control, and (3) ensure that employees are fully informed of their benefit options.

The Managerial Perspective

In the United States, unlike most other developed countries, the employer provides most of an employee's benefits. The benefits, which are part of a group benefit plan, are designed to safeguard employees and their families against problems due to sickness, accidents, or retirement. More than almost any other issue addressed in this text, an organization's HR staff controls benefits programs. Still, managers must be familiar with benefits for several reasons:

- ***Benefits issues are important to employees*** Managers must help employees understand and make the best use of their benefits. For instance, if an employee has a child who needs urgent medical attention, the employee's manager should be able to explain the company's medical benefits to ensure that the employee obtains all available coverage.
- ***Benefits are a powerful recruiting tool*** Managers at firms that offer enticing benefits can use this advantage to recruit high-quality applicants.
- ***Benefits help retain talented employees*** Firms that offer an attractive benefits package to employees give managers an advantage because the package often helps reduce turnover.
- ***Certain benefits play a part in managerial decisions*** Some benefits—such as vacations, family and medical leave, and sick days—give employees scheduling flexibility. Managers need to be aware of these benefits to effectively manage work schedules.
- ***Benefits are important to managers*** Managers need to be aware of their own benefit options. Some decisions, particularly those concerning retirement plans, have long-term consequences. Good decisions in this area made early in a career can affect quality of life at the end of and after a career.

However, understanding benefit plan designs is not an easy task. As we see in the chapter, cost-control measures, the need to offer benefits that attract and retain employees, and new laws and regulations have led to many changes in the design of benefit programs.

In this chapter, we explain benefits in detail. We begin with an overview of employee benefits and the relationship of benefits to the rest of the compensation package. We then examine strategies for designing benefits programs. Next, we describe the scope and significance of two categories of employee benefits programs: legally required benefits and voluntary benefits. Finally, we discuss some important issues in benefits administration.

✪ Learn It!

If your professor has chosen to assign this go to **www.mymanagementlab.com** to see what you should particularly focus on, and take the chapter 12 warmup.

An Overview of Benefits

Employee benefits are group membership rewards that provide security for employees and their family members. They are sometimes called **indirect compensation** because they are given to employees in the form of a plan (such as health insurance) rather than cash. A benefits package complements the base-compensation and pay-incentives components of total compensation. According to the U.S. Bureau of Labor Statistics, benefits cost U.S. companies about $19,947 per year for the average employee.[6] Figure 12.1 shows how the benefit dollar is divided in the average firm.

employee benefits or indirect compensation
Group membership rewards that provide security for employees and their family members.

FIGURE 12.1
How the Benefit Dollar Is Spent

Source: U.S. Bureau of Labor Statistics (2013). Employer costs for employee compensation.

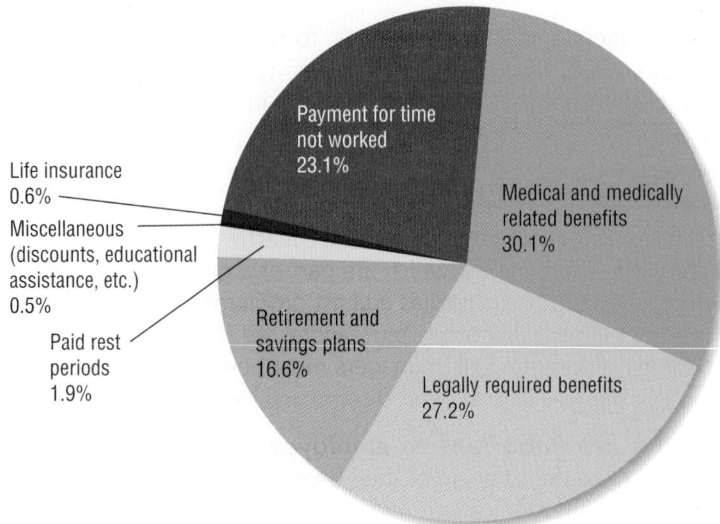

Employee benefits protect employees from risks that could jeopardize their health and financial security. They provide coverage for sickness, injury, unemployment, and old age and death. They may also provide services or facilities that many employees find valuable, such as child-care services or an exercise center.

In the United States, the employer is the primary source of benefits coverage. The situation is quite different in other countries, where many benefits are sponsored by the government and funded with taxes. For example, in the United States employers provide their employees with health insurance, whereas in Canada health insurance is a right bestowed on all citizens by the country's national health system. For a brief summary of Canada's health care policy, see Exhibit 12.1, "Benefits Across the Border: A Look at Canada's Health Care System."

EXHIBIT 12.1 BENEFITS ACROSS THE BORDER: A LOOK AT CANADA'S HEALTH CARE SYSTEM

When Tommy Bettis from Arkansas broke his arm and cut his head while helping to repair the garage of his Ontario friend, Kristopher Goering, Bettis received emergency care at a Canadian hospital by presenting Goering's health card. Although this case involved an emergency occurring in Canada, thousands of Americans are routinely borrowing Canadian health cards to get medical care.

Why are ailing Americans going to another country and using illegal means to get health care there? Because in Canada health care is free. In the debate on U.S. health care reform, the U.S. media have alternately portrayed Canada's national health care system as a medical miracle or as a bureaucratic nightmare. The truth seems to be somewhere in between.

Canada's national system covers all residents' medical and hospital bills and is funded through income taxes (top bracket: 48% on income over $50,000) and through a payroll tax on employers. Doctors and hospitals are reimbursed directly by provincial governments according to a negotiated schedule of fees, while patients pay nothing—except higher taxes than U.S. citizens. Health care expenditures are 40 percent lower per capita than in the United States, however, and the burden is lighter for employers, too. But does Canada get more out of its health system for less? Statistics seem to say so: Canada boasts the eighth-highest life expectancy in the world, 77.03 years as opposed to 75.22 for the United States, which ranks thirty-third. Canada's infant mortality rate of 7.9 per 1,000 live births is the tenth lowest in the world, whereas the U.S. rate of 10 per 1,000 is twenty-first. Canadians view health care as a right that must be distributed equitably to every citizen and not as a commodity to be sold to the highest bidder.

Is there a catch in the Canadian system? Canadians sometimes have to wait for nonemergency procedures, but rarely for run-of-the-mill services.

Sources: Based on Reid, T. (2009, September 21). No country for sick men. *Newsweek,* 42–45; Krauss, C. (2005, June 10). In blow to Canada's health system, Quebec law is voided. *New York Times,* A-3; Krauss, C. (2003, February 13). Long lines mar Canada's low-cost health care. *New York Times,* A-3; Farnsworth, C. H. (1993, December 20). Americans filching free health care in Canada. *New York Times,* A-1; Crossette, B. (2001, October 11). Canada's health care shows strains. *New York Times,* A-12.

The benefits package offered by a firm can support management's efforts to attract employees. When a potential employee is choosing among multiple job offers with similar salaries, a firm offering an attractive benefits package will be ahead of the pack. For example, Swedish Medical Center, a hospital in Denver, Colorado, uses its on-site child-care center as a recruiting tool to attract high-quality staff.[7] It is one of only a few organizations in its region that offer this benefit.

Benefits can also help management retain employees. Benefits that are designed to increase in value over time encourage employees to remain with their employer. For instance, many companies make contributions to employees' retirement funds, but these funds are available only to employees who stay with the company for a certain number of years. For this reason, benefits are sometimes called "golden handcuffs." An excellent example of the power of benefits to retain employees is the U.S. military, which provides early retirement benefits to personnel who put in 20 years of service. This "20 years and out" retirement provision allows retired military people to start a second career at a fairly young age with the security of a lifelong retirement income to supplement their earnings. These generous benefits help the armed forces retain valuable officers and professionals who would otherwise be attracted to higher-paying civilian jobs.[8]

Basic Terminology

Before we proceed, let us define some basic terms that we will use throughout this chapter:

- *Contributions* All benefits are funded by contributions from the employer, the employee, or both. For example, vacations are an employer-provided benefit: The salary or wages paid to the employee during the vacation period come entirely from the employer. Premiums for health care insurance are often paid partly by the employer and partly by the employee.
- *Coinsurance* Payments made to cover health care expenses that are split between the employer's insurance company and the employee. For instance, under an 80/20 insurance plan, the employer's insurance company would pay 80 percent of the employee's health care costs and the employee would pay the remaining 20 percent.
- *Copayment* A small payment that the employee pays, usually $15 to $30 dollars, for each office visit to a physician under the health plan. The health plan pays for additional medical expenses that exceed the copayment at no cost to the employee.
- *Deductible* An annual out-of-pocket expenditure that an insurance policyholder must make before the insurance plan makes any reimbursements. For instance, the 80/20 plan described previously may also have a $500 deductible, in which case the employee would be responsible for the first $500 of medical expenses before the insurance company makes its 80 percent coinsurance payment.
- *Flexible benefit programs* A **flexible benefits program**, also called a **cafeteria benefits program**, allows employees to select the benefits they need most from a menu of choices. Unlike employers that try to design a one-size-fits-all benefits package, employers with a flexible benefits program recognize that their employees have diverse needs that require different benefits packages. A 30-year-old married female employee with a working spouse and small children is likely to need child-care benefits and may be willing to forgo extra paid vacation days in exchange for this benefit. A 50-year-old married male employee with grown children may prefer a larger employer contribution to his retirement plan.

contributions
Payments made for benefits coverage. Contributions for a specific benefit may come from the employer, employee, or both.

coinsurance
Payments made to cover health care expenses that are split between the employer's insurance company and the insured employee.

copayment
A small payment made by the employee for each office visit to a physician under a health plan. The health plan pays for additional medical expenses that exceed the copayment at no cost to the employee.

deductible
An annual out-of-pocket expenditure that an insurance policyholder must make before the insurance plan makes any reimbursements.

flexible or cafeteria benefits program
A benefits program that allows employees to select the benefits they need most from a menu of choices.

The Cost of Benefits in the United States

The cost of employee benefits in the United States has increased dramatically over the decades as businesses have offered more and more benefits. The cost of employee benefits as a percentage of an employer's payroll increased from 3 percent in 1929 to about 30.9 percent in 2013.[9] This growth can be explained by a combination of factors, including federal tax policy, federal legislation, the influence of unions, and the cost savings of group plans.

FEDERAL TAX POLICY Since the 1920s, the federal government has provided favorable tax treatment for group benefit plans that meet certain standards (discussed later in this chapter).[10] Employers who meet the tax policy guidelines receive tax deductions for their benefits expenditures.

Employees also receive favorable treatment under the tax policy because they receive many of their benefits on a *tax-free* basis. For example, employees receive their employer's contribution to a health insurance plan tax-free. In contrast, self-employed individuals have to pay for health insurance out of their taxable income. Other benefits are received on a *tax-deferred* basis. For example, employee contributions to a qualified retirement plan (up to a maximum amount) may be tax-deferred until the employee retires, at which time the person may be taxed at a lower rate. Federal tax policy on benefits has encouraged employees to demand additional benefits, because each additional dollar a company allocates for benefits has more value than a dollar allocated as cash compensation, which is taxed as ordinary income.

FEDERAL LEGISLATION In 1935, federal legislation decreed that all employers must provide Social Security and unemployment insurance benefits to their employees. We take a closer look at these benefits later in this chapter. At this point, we only wish to make the point that federal law requires some benefits and that federal legislation will probably continue to cause significant growth in the cost of benefits.

UNION INFLUENCE Unions have been in the forefront of the movement to expand employee benefits for the last half century. In the 1940s, powerful unions such as the United Auto Workers and the United Mine Workers obtained pensions and health insurance plans from employers. In recent years, unions have been asking for dental-care coverage, extended vacation periods, and unemployment benefits beyond those required by federal law.

Once benefit patterns are established in unionized firms, these same benefits tend to spread to nonunionized companies, which often wish to avoid union organization drives.

COST SAVINGS OF GROUP PLANS Employers can provide benefits for much less money than employees would pay to obtain them on their own. When insurance companies can spread risk over a large group of individuals, they can reduce the cost of benefits per person. This fact causes employees to put considerable pressure on their employers to provide certain benefits.

Types of Benefits

Benefits can be organized into six categories. These categories, which we examine in detail later in this chapter, are:

1. ***Legally required benefits*** U.S. law requires employers to give four benefits to all employees, with only a few exceptions: (1) Social Security, (2) workers' compensation, (3) unemployment insurance, and (4) family and medical leave. In addition, it is a legal requirement that employers with 50 or more employees provide health insurance to employees starting in 2015. All other benefits (including health insurance at small companies with less than 50 employees) are provided by employers voluntarily.
2. ***Health insurance*** Health insurance covers hospital costs, physician charges, and the costs of other medical services. Because of its importance, health insurance is usually considered separately from other types of insurance.
3. ***Retirement*** Retirement benefits provide income to employees after they retire.
4. ***Insurance*** Insurance plans protect employees or their dependents from financial difficulties that can arise as a result of disability or death.
5. ***Paid time off*** Time-off plans give employees time off with or without pay, depending on the plan.
6. ***Employee services*** Employee services are tax-free or tax-preferred services that enhance the quality of employees' work or personal life.

Figure 12.2 shows the percentage of full-time U.S. employers providing selected benefits plans. As the figure makes clear, large- and medium-sized private firms (those that employ more than 100 individuals) and state and local governments offer a wider variety of benefits than small businesses do.

The growth of benefits over the years, coupled with increased benefits costs, has encouraged employers to hire more part-time or temporary employees when their business grows. Companies often do not provide benefits to part-time employees and temporary employees. However, both Starbucks and UPS discovered that it pays to offer good benefits even to part-time employees, as explained in the Manager's Notebook, "Starbucks and UPS Offer Generous Benefits to Part-Time Employees."

	Medium and Large Private Firms*	Small Private Firms**	State and Local Governments
Health Insurance	85	57	89
Retirement Plan	82	49	79
Insurance Plans			
Life Insurance	78	39	82
Long-Term Disability Insurance	45	25	35
Time-Off Plans			
Paid Vacations	86	69	100
Paid Holidays	87	68	100
Paid Sick Leave	72	51	90
Flexible Benefits Plans	12	4	34

*Firms employing 100 workers or more.
**Firms employing fewer than 100 workers.

FIGURE 12.2

Percentage of Employers Providing Selected Benefit Plans

Source: U.S. Department of Labor, Bureau of Labor Statistics (2013).

MANAGER'S NOTEBOOK

Ethics/Social Responsibility

Starbucks and UPS Offer Generous Benefits to Part-Time Employees

Starbucks and UPS depend heavily on part-time employees to provide services to their customers. Each company offers a generous and broad array of employee benefits to its part-time employees. This runs counter to the practices of most companies, which treat part-timers as second-class citizens. Both Starbucks and UPS recognize that it is a good business practice to treat part-time employees well when it comes to benefits. Here we discuss some highlights of the benefits provided by these two companies.

Starbucks employs many part-time employees, called "baristas," at its ubiquitous coffee shops to serve customers during peak demand times. Part-time employees (those who work between 20 and 40 hours) receive the following benefits:

- Health care benefits (medical, prescription drugs, dental, and vision care)
- Retirement savings plan
- Life insurance and disability insurance
- Adoption assistance
- Domestic partner benefits
- Referral programs and support resources for childcare and eldercare
- Discounted Starbucks merchandise
- Participation in stock program

UPS employs many part-time employees (and a large percentage of these part-timers are college students) to sort packages at its package-distribution centers. The shipping business alternates between bursts of activity and slack time throughout the day, which requires a high utilization of part-time employees. UPS part-time employees who work 15 or more hours per week have access to the following benefits:

- Comprehensive medical and life insurance for the employee and dependents
- 401(k) retirement plan
- Funds for tuition assistance
- Funds available on UPS Earn & Learn Student Loans
- Paid vacations and holidays
- Discounted stock-purchase plan

Although most companies only offer benefits to their full-time employees, Starbucks offers benefits to all part-time employees who work 20 hours or more. Offering benefits such as health insurance and retirement plans helps Starbucks attract and retain part-time help.

Source: CandyBox Images/Shutterstock.

Sources: Based on Starbucks Web site. (2014). Working at Starbucks. *www.starbucks.com/careers/working-at-starbucks*; UPS Web site. (2014). Working at UPS—Benefits. *https://ups.managehr.com/benefits.htm*; Clark, J. (2004, August). Steppingstone jobs for recent grads: These employers offer health insurance and more, even for part-timers. *Kiplinger's*, 107–108. ■■

The Benefits Strategy

To design an effective benefits package, a company needs to align its benefits strategy with its overall compensation strategy. The benefits strategy requires making choices in three areas: (1) benefits mix, (2) benefits amount, and (3) flexibility of benefits. These choices provide a blueprint for the design of the benefits package.

A QUESTION OF ETHICS

Most larger employers provide some sort of retirement fund for their employees. Do you think that companies are ethically bound to offer this benefit? Does the financial condition (good or poor) or size of the firm make any difference to your analysis?

The Benefits Mix

The **benefits mix** is the complete package of benefits that a company offers its employees. At least three issues should be considered when making decisions about the benefits mix: the total compensation strategy, organizational objectives, and the characteristics of the workforce.[11]

benefits mix
The complete package of benefits that a company offers its employees.

The total compensation strategy issue corresponds to the "below-market versus above-market compensation" decision we discussed in Chapter 10. The company must choose the market in which it wants to compete for employees and then provide a benefits package attractive to the people in that market. In other words, management tries to answer the questions: Who are my competitors for employees, and what kinds of benefits do they provide?

For example, a high-tech firm may want to attract people who are risk takers and innovators. The firm's management may decide not to offer retirement benefits because high-tech companies are usually considered desirable places to work by people in their 20s, and people this young are generally not concerned about retirement. As an upstart challenger to IBM, Apple Inc. at first chose not to offer retirement benefits because management did not think this benefit would attract the entrepreneurial employees it wanted.[12] Later, when Apple's workforce became older, its employees expressed a need for retirement benefits, and Apple redesigned its benefits mix and offered retirement benefits in response to employees' needs.

The organization's objectives also influence the benefits mix. For instance, if the company philosophy is to minimize differences between low-level employees and top management, the benefits mix should be the same for all employees. If the organization is growing and needs to retain all its current personnel, it needs to ensure that it offers the benefits its workforce desires.

Finally, the characteristics of the workforce must be considered when choosing the benefits mix. If the firm's workforce consists largely of parents with young children, it is likely that child-care and other family-friendly benefits will be important. A professional workforce will probably want more say in decisions about its retirement funds. A unionized workforce is likely to demand a guaranteed retirement plan.

Benefits Amount

The choice of benefits amount governs the percentage of the total compensation package that will be allocated to benefits as opposed to the other components of the package (base salary and pay incentives). This choice corresponds to the "fixed versus variable pay" decision covered in Chapter 10. Once management determines the amount of money available for all benefits, it can establish a benefits budget and decide on the level of funding for each part of the benefits program. Management will then know how much it can contribute for each benefit and how much it will need to ask employees to pay toward that benefit. In larger companies, these calculations are usually performed by the benefits administrator; smaller companies often hire a benefits consultant to do the math.

A company that focuses on providing job security and long-term employment opportunities is likely to devote a large portion of its compensation dollars to benefits. One company that prides itself on its excellent employee benefits is Procter & Gamble (P&G). Its profit-sharing plan—the oldest such plan in continuous operation in the United States—was started in 1887. P&G was also one of the first companies to offer all its employees comprehensive sickness, disability, and life insurance programs.[13]

Flexibility of Benefits

The *flexibility of benefits choice* concerns the degree of freedom employees have to tailor the benefits package to their personal needs. This choice corresponds to the "centralization versus decentralization of pay" decision described in Chapter 10. Some organizations have a relatively standardized benefits package that gives employees few options. This system makes sense in organizations that have a fairly homogeneous workforce. In these firms, a standardized benefits package can be designed for a "typical" employee. However, because of the changing demographics of the U.S. workforce—more women working full-time, dual-career marriages, and single-parent families—there is now a greater variety of employee needs. In organizations that cannot develop a "typical" employee profile, a decentralized benefits package that emphasizes choice will probably be more effective. We discuss flexible benefits packages in detail at the end of this chapter.

Legally Required Benefits

With only a few exceptions, all U.S. employers are legally required to provide Social Security, workers' compensation, and unemployment insurance coverage for their employees—benefits that are designed to give the workforce a basic level of security. The employer pays a tax on an employee's earnings for each of these three required benefits. In the case of Social Security, the employee also pays a tax to fund the benefit. A fourth legally required benefit has been added in recent years: Employers must offer unpaid leave to employees in certain family and medical circumstances.

Social Security

Social Security provides (1) income for retirees, the disabled, and survivors of deceased workers and (2) health care for the aged through the Medicare program. Established by the Social Security Act in 1935, Social Security is funded through a payroll tax paid in equal amounts by the employer and the employee. The Social Security tax in 2014 was 7.65 percent of an employee's annual earnings on the first $117,000 of income. This means that both the employer and employee pay a tax of 7.65 percent on the employee's earnings. The Social Security tax actually has two components: a tax of 6.2 percent to fund the retirement, disability, and survivor benefits,

Social Security
A government program that provides income for retirees, the disabled, and survivors of deceased workers, and health care for the aged through the Medicare program.

Benefit	Eligibility	Provisions
Retirement income	• Age 65–67 (full benefits) *or* • Age 62–64 (benefits reduced up to 20%)	Monthly payments for life beginning at retirement. Average benefit provides between 28 and 54 percent of earnings prior to retirement depending on level of earnings.
Disability income	• Totally and continuously disabled for 5 months. • Disability should be expected to last at least 12 months or result in death.	Monthly payments comparable to retirement benefits as long as totally disabled. Provisions payments to dependents.
Medicare	• Age 65 *or* • Receiving Social Security disability payments for 24 months.	Covers hospital expenses, nursing home and home health agency expenses, subject to a deductible payment. Medical expenses are covered, subject to monthly premium.
Survivor benefits	• Family members of the deceased person, including widow or widower age 60 or over, child or grandchild under age 18, or dependent parent age 62 or over.	Monthly payments related to the deceased worker's primary Social Security retirement benefit.

FIGURE 12.3
Social Security Benefits

Source: Adapted from the 2010 Social Security online Web site, *www.ssa.gov*.

and a tax of 1.45 percent to fund Medicare. Employees who earn more than $117,000 are taxed for Medicare at 1.45 percent of all their additional earnings. This 1.45 percent tax for Medicare is also matched by the employer.

To be eligible for full Social Security benefits, a person must have worked 40 quarter-year periods (which equals 10 years of total employment) and have earned a minimum of $1,200 per quarter. Figure 12.3 spells out the provisions of the four Social Security benefits—retirement income, disability income, Medicare, and survivor benefits—and who is eligible to receive them.

RETIREMENT INCOME Social Security provides retirement income to people who retire between age 65 to 67 depending on the year that they were born. Workers can retire as early as 62 and receive benefits reduced by as much as 20 percent.

The retirement income provided by Social Security averages about 54 percent of one's earnings in the final year before retirement at age 65 for those with low incomes and 28 percent of earnings for those with high incomes. This means that people need to develop other sources of postretirement income if they want to maintain a lifestyle similar to the one they enjoyed before retirement. These sources might include a company-provided pension plan, personal savings, or another job. According to the Social Security Administration, people who retired at age 66 in 2010 could expect a monthly Social Security check ranging from $744 to $2,346, depending on their preretirement earnings. In the future, the minimum age for receiving Social Security benefits will increase. For people born between 1943 and 1959, the minimum retirement age for full benefits will be 66, and for individuals born in 1960 or later, it will be age 67. The average monthly retirement income provided by Social Security in 2013 was $1,221 for an individual and $1,978 for a retired married couple. The amount of Social Security retirement income for recipients is adjusted each year based on an automatic *cost of living adjustment* (COLA), computed by economists at the Social Security Administration in order to protect the standard of living of retirees (for additional information on COLAs, see Chapter 15).

DISABILITY INCOME For people who become disabled and cannot work for at least 12 months, Social Security provides a monthly income comparable to retirement benefits. Because the level of disability income averages only about 30 percent of one's earnings from the job, workers need to derive disability income from other sources. These sources include short- and long-term disability insurance and personal savings and investments. The average amount of Social Security disability income provided to beneficiaries in 2014 was $1,148 per month.

MEDICARE **Medicare** provides health insurance coverage for people 65 and older. Medicare has two parts. Part A covers hospital costs. People who pay an annual deductible ($1,216 in 2014) receive up to 60 days of hospital expenses covered under Medicare. Part B, for which individuals pay a monthly fee ($104.90 in 2014), covers medical expenses such as doctors' fees and the cost of medical supplies. The deductibles and monthly fees for Medicare are adjusted periodically as the cost of medical care increases. Part C, called Medicare+Choice, is an alternative to the original program (Parts A and B) and provides health care from different options, such as managed care or private fee-for-service plans. Part D provides coverage for prescription drugs. The retiree in 2013 pays a $325 deductible, after which Medicare pays 75 percent of drug costs, up to $2,970. After that, the beneficiary pays 100 percent of drug costs from $2,970 to $6,733. Finally, Medicare pays 95 percent of prescription drug costs above $6,733.[14]

Medicare
A part of the Social Security program that provides health insurance coverage for people aged 65 and over.

SURVIVOR BENEFITS A deceased employee's surviving family members may receive a monthly income if they qualify. Survivor benefits are related to the deceased worker's primary retirement benefit. Those eligible to receive survivor benefits are (1) widows and widowers age 60 and over, and (2) widows and widowers of any age who care for a child age 16 or younger, an unmarried child or grandchild younger than age 18, or a dependent parent age 62 or over.

Workers' Compensation

Workers' compensation provides medical care, income continuation, and rehabilitation expenses for people who sustain job-related injuries or sickness. "Workers' comp" also provides income to the survivors of an employee whose death is job related.

workers' compensation
A legally required benefit that provides medical care, income continuation, and rehabilitation expenses for people who sustain job-related injuries or sickness. Also provides income to the survivors of an employee whose death is job related.

Workers' compensation is designed to provide a *no-fault remedy* to workers who are injured on the job. This means that even workers who were wholly at fault for their accidents can still receive a benefit. Employers who provide workers' compensation coverage cannot be sued by injured employees.

Workers' compensation is administered by state governments and is required by 48 of 50 states for all employees, including part-time workers. In Texas and New Jersey, workers' comp is elective. It is funded by a payroll tax, the proceeds of which go to a state workers' compensation fund or to a private insurance company. Only the employer pays for workers' compensation. Although the average workers' compensation cost is only about 1 percent of total payroll expense, companies in accident-prone industries may pay more than 25 percent of their payroll in workers' compensation taxes.[15]

The rates that employers pay for workers' compensation are based on three factors: (1) the risk of injury for an occupation, (2) the frequency and severity of the injuries sustained by a company's workforce (called the company's injury *experience rating*), and (3) the level of benefits provided for specific injuries within the state where the company is located. Because the company's experience rating is based on its own safety record, managers have an incentive to design and promote a safe work environment: A better safety record leads directly to a lower payroll tax rate. Some states offer greater benefits to injured workers, which leads to higher workers' comp taxes assessed on employers in those states. States with the highest workers' compensation costs are California, Oklahoma, Louisiana, Rhode Island, Texas, and Florida.[16]

Small businesses in industries such as construction and food service have had great difficulty dealing with cost increases in workers' compensation taxes resulting from increasing claims. Consider the following examples:

- Workers' compensation costs for William Solburg, the owner of a small construction company near Tallahassee, Florida, have skyrocketed. More than 25 percent of Solburg's total payroll costs go to cover workers' compensation insurance, and he foresees a significant increase in the near future. Solburg is uncertain whether his business can survive much longer with workers' compensation costs rising so quickly.[17]

A QUESTION OF ETHICS
One way for companies to lower their workers' compensation costs is to move from a state with a high workers' compensation tax rate to one with a lower rate. Is this a legitimate reason for moving a business? What other ethical issues should employers think about when trying to decrease workers' comp costs?

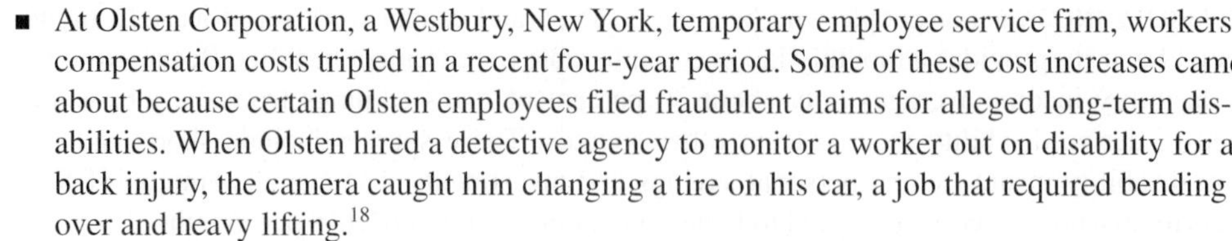

- At Olsten Corporation, a Westbury, New York, temporary employee service firm, workers' compensation costs tripled in a recent four-year period. Some of these cost increases came about because certain Olsten employees filed fraudulent claims for alleged long-term disabilities. When Olsten hired a detective agency to monitor a worker out on disability for a back injury, the camera caught him changing a tire on his car, a job that required bending over and heavy lifting.[18]

Some small companies are fighting back by banding together to form *self-insurance* pools. L.E. Mason Company, a Boston maker of lighting fixtures and other construction materials, joined a self-insurance group because its rates were 40 percent below Mason's other alternatives. Here's how a self-insurance fund works: A fund's member companies, often in the same industry, band together and hire an administrator. The administrator contracts with actuaries, investment managers, health care providers, and anyone else necessary to perform the functions of an insurance company. Fund members share one another's risk, paying losses out of premiums and investment returns. A typical fund member has between 60 and 100 employees and pays between $50,000 and $100,000 a year for coverage. By 2005, 49 states allowed self-insurance funds, with North Dakota the exception.

Self-insurance funds are not the answer for all companies. In firms that go it alone, HR staff can help managers control workers' compensation costs in several important ways:

- The HR department should stress safe work procedures by impressing upon employees the importance of safety (see Chapter 16). Many accidents are caused by carelessness, ignorance of safe work practices, personal problems, or the use of alcohol or drugs. HR staff should train managers and supervisors to communicate and enforce the company's safety program. Employees who disregard safe work practices should be disciplined.[19]

- The HR department should audit workers' compensation claims. The National Insurance Crime Bureau estimates that workers' compensation fraud in the United States costs insurance companies $5 billion each year. These costs are then passed on to employers, who must pay higher premiums to insure their employees with workers' compensation. Managers should challenge any claim they suspect is fraudulent or not job related. For example, a manager can ask an injured worker to submit to a drug test. A positive result from the drug test can be a reason for denying a claim. Or after a serious accident a safety specialist could conduct an investigation at the scene of the accident. Information gathered from the investigation may reveal inconsistencies in the story that may indicate the employee's claim is fraudulent.[20]
- HR should manage how workers' comp benefits work with employers' health insurance benefits when workers sustain job-related injuries. HR should establish controls so that duplicate medical benefits are not paid out to employees.

- HR staff should design jobs and work assignments so that there are fewer risks of injuries such as back strain and repetitive motion injuries. For example, employees can have their video display terminals adjusted daily to avoid strain on the arms and wrists.[21]
- HR can encourage workers who are partially disabled to return to work under a *modified duty plan.* Under such a plan, a manager or HR staff member works with injured employees to develop modified tasks that they can perform until they are ready to handle their regular job. For instance, a maintenance worker with a back injury might be assigned to help schedule the work orders. Modified duty plans can save the company money on benefits that provide income continuation for employees who may be needlessly postponing their return to employment.

Unemployment Insurance

unemployment insurance
A program established by the Social Security Act of 1935 to provide temporary income for people during periods of involuntary unemployment.

The Social Security Act of 1935 established **unemployment insurance** to provide temporary income for people during periods of involuntary unemployment. The program is part of a national wage stabilization policy designed to stabilize the economy during recessionary periods. The logic underlying this policy is fairly simple: If unemployed workers have enough income to maintain their consumption of basic goods and services, the demand for these products will be sustained, which ultimately will preserve the jobs of many people who might otherwise be added to the ranks of the unemployed.

Unemployment insurance is funded by a tax paid by employers on all employees' earnings. The tax averages 6.2 percent on a set amount of annual earnings by each employee subject to the tax. Employee earnings subject to the tax range from $7,000 in Arizona to $39,800 in Washington.[22] The proceeds of the tax are split between the state government and the federal government, which provide different services for the unemployed. The federal government levies a tax of 0.8 percent, a rate that does not change from employer to employer. In contrast, the states' assessments range from at or near zero to more than 10 percent (the average is about 5.4%). All the states give employers an experience rating comparing the employer's contributions to the unemployment insurance fund against the benefits drawn by the employer's workers from the fund over a period of time. This system allows the state to lower the unemployment tax rate for employers that discharge only a small number of employees, and raise it for those that discharge large numbers of employees for any reason (including layoffs).

To be eligible for unemployment insurance, employees must meet several qualifications: First, they must be available for and actively seeking employment. Second, they must have worked a minimum of four quarter-year periods out of the last five quarter-year periods and have earned at least $1,000 during those four quarter-year periods combined. Finally, they must have left their job involuntarily.

Employees may be disqualified for unemployment insurance benefits for several reasons. The following people are not eligible for unemployment insurance:

- An employee who quits voluntarily.
- An employee who is discharged for gross misconduct (for example, for failing a drug test).
- An employee who refuses an offer of suitable work (that is, a job and pay level comparable to the employee's previous position).
- An employee who participates in a strike (48 of 50 states deny benefits to strike participants).
- A person who is self-employed.[23]

Unemployment benefits were designed to cover an employee's basic living expenses but not to be a disincentive against actively seeking employment. For this reason, unemployment benefits seldom cover more than 50 percent of lost earnings, and people discharged from high-paying jobs generally receive only a small fraction of their lost earnings. States have developed their own schedules for unemployment benefits and cap them at a maximum level that ranges from $230 per week in Mississippi to $942 per week in Massachusetts.[24] Unemployment benefits last for 26 weeks, although in states with persistently high unemployment rates, extensions of benefits in 13-week periods may be given. In addition, some companies provide **supplemental unemployment benefits (SUB)** to their laid-off employees. These benefits are most often written into the union contract.

supplemental unemployment benefits (SUB)
Benefits given by a company to laid-off employees over and above state unemployment benefits.

It is interesting to compare the level of replacement income and duration of benefits provided by unemployment insurance in the United States to the benefits provided to unemployed workers in other countries.[25]

- United States: 50 percent of salary for 6 months
- Italy: 80 percent of salary for 6 months
- Japan: 80 percent of salary for 10 months
- France: 75 percent of salary for 60 months
- Germany: 60 percent of salary for 12 months
- Sweden: 80 percent of salary for 15 months

The amount and duration of unemployment benefits in the United States are modest compared to benefits in other countries. In the United States, government policy is designed to encourage unemployed workers to actively seek employment, and it views generous benefits as suppressing an employee's motivation to search for a new job.

Containing the costs of unemployment insurance is an important priority for management. The HR department can make significant contributions here by establishing practices that lower the firm's experience rating. Here are some useful HR practices in this area:

- HR planning can tell management whether an increase in the company's workload is due to short or long-term causes. Short-term increases in the workload should be handled by hiring temporary employees or consultants rather than by creating full-time positions. Because neither temporary employees nor consultants can claim unemployment benefits, it costs the company nothing to let them go when the workload decreases. If the increased workload appears to be long-term, however, the company may decide to hire more full-time employees.

- The employee benefits administrator should audit all unemployment claims filed by former employees. Employers have the right to appeal these claims, and in about half the cases they win.[26]
- Managers or members of the HR department should conduct exit interviews with all discharged employees to (1) come to a mutual understanding on the reason for termination and (2) advise them that the company will fight unemployment claims not made for good reason. For example, if an employee discharged for theft makes a claim for unemployment benefits, the company will contest the claim.

Unpaid Leave

Family and Medical Leave Act (FMLA) of 1993
A federal law that requires employers to provide up to 12 weeks' unpaid leave to eligible employees for the birth or adoption of a child; to care for a sick parent, child, or spouse; or to take care of health problems that interfere with job performance.

Employees occasionally need long periods of time off to take care of their families or their own health problems. Until recently, most employers refused to give workers unpaid leave for any reason other than the birth of a child. The **Family and Medical Leave Act (FMLA) of 1993**, enacted under the Clinton administration, now requires most employers to provide up to 12 weeks' unpaid leave to eligible employees for the following reasons:[27]

- The birth of a child
- The adoption of a child
- To care for a sick spouse, child, or parent
- To take care of the employee's own serious health problems that interfere with effective job performance

The FMLA applies only to businesses with 50 or more employees and to employers with multiple facilities that have 50 workers within a 75-mile radius. The law requires employers to give employees returning from FMLA leave the same job they held before taking the leave or an equivalent job. Employers must maintain coverage of health insurance and other employee benefits while the employee is on FMLA leave.[28] Employees are eligible to take FMLA leave after accumulating one year of service with their employer. "Highly compensated" employees—those at the top 10 percent of the pay scale and who tend to be the company's top managers—are not eligible for FMLA leave because it may be a hardship for the employer to replace them for a 12-week period.

A 2008 amendment to the FMLA permits a spouse, son, daughter, parent, or next of kin to take up to 26 work weeks of leave to care for a member of the Armed Forces, including a member of the National Guard or Reserves, who is undergoing medical treatment, recuperation, or therapy, is otherwise in outpatient status, or is otherwise on the temporary disability retired list for a serious injury or illness.[29]

The FMLA forces companies to develop contingency plans to keep their operations running with a minimum of disruption and added cost when employees are on leave. Managers may want to consider (1) cross-training some workers to cover for employees on leave or (2) hiring temporary workers.[30]

Mandatory unpaid leave also forces companies to confront some troublesome issues, such as:

- Can employees substitute accrued sick days for unpaid leave?
- What sort of illnesses are serious enough to justify a leave?[31]
- How can FMLA leave be coordinated with other laws, such as the Americans with Disabilities Act?
- Just what constitutes an "equivalent" job when a leave-taker returns and finds his or her job filled?

The last question was the subject of a Wisconsin lawsuit filed well before the FMLA was passed. Elizabeth Marquardt returned from maternity leave to find that her Milwaukee-based employer, Kelley Company, had eliminated her job as credit manager during a restructuring. Kelley gave Marquardt a new job with the same pay and benefits. However, the new job involved supervising one employee instead of four, and unlike the old position, it included about 25 percent clerical work. Marquardt resigned the next day. Kelley claimed that the reassignment was intended to sidestep Marquardt's longstanding problems with customers. But a Wisconsin appeals court ruled that the jobs were not equivalent because Marquardt's "authority and responsibility were greatly reduced in the new position." HR professionals and line managers will have to work together to avoid such court challenges.[32] The Manager's Notebook, "What to Do When an Employee Returns from FMLA Leave ," specifies an employer's duties and obligations.

Surveys that have examined how employees have used FMLA show that over 80 percent of the time, it was used by workers recovering from an illness or caring for a sick family member. More than 14 percent of eligible workers use FMLA every year, and 35 percent of leave-takers were off more than once, according to a survey by the Employment Policy Foundation. The method employers were most likely to use to cover for an employee taking FMLA leave was to assign the work temporarily to other employees; the second-most prevalent method was to hire an outside temporary replacement to do the work.[33]

MANAGER'S NOTEBOOK

Ethics/Social Responsibility

What to Do When an Employee Returns from FMLA Leave

Employers have both duties and rights when an employee returns from FMLA leave. Here are some key points to consider:

1. Although an employer is not required to hold an employee's specific position open for an indefinite period of time, the employee is entitled to an "equivalent" job when he or she returns. Under FMLA, an equivalent position is one that is virtually identical to the former position in terms of pay, benefits, and working conditions. The job must also have the same or substantially similar duties and responsibilities. An employee who returns from FMLA leave is entitled to an equivalent job even if the employee has been replaced or the position has been restructured while the employee was on leave.
2. On returning from FMLA, the employee must receive any unconditional pay raises, such as cost-of-living increases, given to other employees during the leave period. The employee must also be given all benefits accrued at the time his or her leave began, such as paid vacation, sick leave, or personal leave, unless this has been substituted for FMLA leave.
3. An employer is not required to apply the time taken for FMLA to seniority or length of service schedules that are used to determine pay increases, promotions, or other rewards unless the employer's policy is to recognize all unpaid leave taken by employees as an input to seniority.
4. Employers are not required to provide an equivalent position to a returning employee who took FMLA leave if the employee is laid off during the leave period, or his or her work shift is eliminated. Similarly, if an employee would have been terminated because of misconduct or incompetence that occurred before the leave, the employer isn't required to reinstate the employee after the leave.

Sources: Based on United States Department of Labor. (2013). *Family and medical leave act advisor.* www.webapps.dol.gov; Flynn, G. (1999, April). What to do after an FMLA leave. *Workforce,* 104–107; Kuhn, B. (2008). Rights and responsibilities under the FMLA. *www.employment.findlaw.com.* ■■

Voluntary Benefits

The benefits provided voluntarily by employers include health insurance, retirement benefits, other types of insurance plans, time off, and employee services. Health insurance is a benefit that is required by law starting in 2015 companies with 50 or more employees. However for companies with fewer than 50 employees, the law allows health insurance to be provided on a voluntary basis, which is the reason why health insurance is categorized as a voluntary benefit. Future legislation may move some of these benefits from the voluntary category to the legally required category.

Health Insurance

Health insurance provides health care coverage for both employees and their dependents, protecting them from financial disaster in the wake of a serious illness. Because the cost of individually obtained health insurance is much higher than that of an employer-sponsored group health plan,

FIGURE 12.4
Health Spending in Various Countries 2011

Source: OECD health data (2013), *www.oecd.org*.

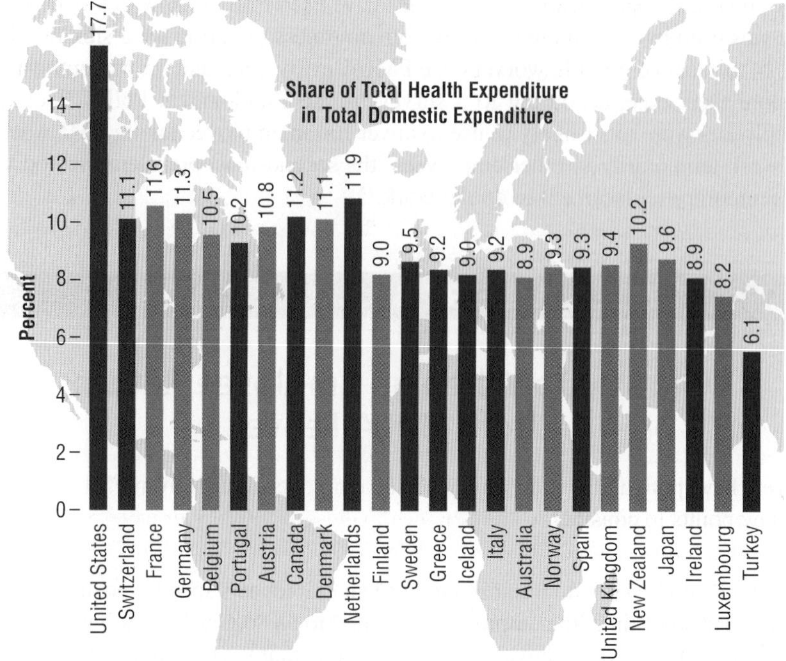

many people could not afford health insurance if it were not provided by their employer. As Figure 12.2 shows, 85 percent of large- and medium-sized private businesses in the United States offer health insurance to their employees. However, only 57 percent of small firms (those with fewer than 100 employees) do so. It has been estimated that about 45 million people in the United States do not have any health insurance coverage.[34]

During the early 1990s, U.S. health care costs increased at an astonishing 10 to 20 percent per year. By 2014, spending on health care accounted for about 18 percent of the U.S. gross domestic product (GDP). This is the highest percentage found in any country in the world. For example, per capita health spending in the United States exceeds that of Canada by 58 percent, of Germany by 57 percent, and of the United Kingdom by 88 percent. And unlike the United States, these countries provide health care coverage for all their citizens. Figure 12.4 compares health care expenditures across the 24 countries that were members of the Organization for Economic Cooperation and Development (OECD) in 2011.

Obviously, containment of health spending costs will be an important issue for companies and the nation for many years. The benefits specialist in the HR department can make an important contribution to the bottom line by keeping spending on health insurance under control. For example, many companies are now requiring employees to make larger contributions toward the cost of their health insurance.

Consolidated Omnibus Budget Reconciliation Act (COBRA) of 1985
Legislation that gives employees the right to continue their health insurance coverage for 18 to 36 months after their employment has terminated.

Health Insurance Portability and Accountability Act (HIPAA)
A federal law that protects an employee's ability to transfer between health insurance plans without a gap in coverage due to a preexisting condition.

preexisting condition
A medical condition treated while an employee was covered under a former employer's health plan and requires treatment under a new employer's different health plan.

The health insurance benefits that a company offers are significantly affected by the **Consolidated Omnibus Budget Reconciliation Act (COBRA) of 1985**, which gives employees the right to continue their health insurance coverage after their employment has terminated. COBRA applies to all employers with 20 or more employees. Employees and their dependents are entitled to 18 to 36 months' additional coverage from the group health insurance plan after separation from the organization. Employees who quit or are discharged from an organization are entitled to 18 months of continued group health coverage under COBRA, whereas a divorced spouse of an employee or a survivor of a deceased employee can receive up to 36 months of continued coverage. The former employee (or relative of the employee) must pay the full cost of coverage at the group rate, plus a 2-percent administrative fee, which is still considerably less than the individual rate that could be purchased from a health insurance company on the open market. All employees who are covered by an organization's health care plan are also covered by COBRA provisions.

The ability of an employee to transfer between health insurance plans without a gap in coverage due to a preexisting condition is protected by a federal law enacted in 1996 called the **Health Insurance Portability and Accountability Act (HIPAA)**. A **preexisting condition** is a medical condition that was treated while the employee was covered under a former employer's health plan and requires further treatment under a new employer's different health plan. Under HIPAA, an employee earns a credit of coverage for every month he or she is covered by the former employer's health insurance plan. When an employee earns 12 months of credit with the former employer, he or she is immediately covered by the new employer's health plan and cannot be denied coverage due to a preexisting condition.[35] In 2004, new provisions were added to HIPAA that require employers to ensure protection of employees' privacy concerning health information so that it is not used in any employment-related decisions without an employee's consent. Employers are expected to erect a privacy shield around employees' personal health information, so that if an employee has been diagnosed with cancer, for example, this information is not disclosed to a manager without the employee's permission.[36]

Patient and Affordable Care Act (PACA)
A federal law passed in 2010 that guarantees that affordable health care is available to people in the United States.

The **Patient and Affordable Care Act (PACA)** is a federal law passed in 2010 that guarantees that affordable health care is available to people in the United States. It also regulates the health insurance industry so that it provides more consistent health care coverage. Individuals cannot be dropped from their insurer when they are sick or because they have a preexisting medical condition, nor can they be denied a necessary medical procedure that exceeds a lifetime cost cap on coverage on a health insurance policy. The law requires that, starting in 2015 all employers with more than 50 full-time employees (or 50 full-time equivalent part-time employees who work at least 30 hours per week) must provide health insurance to these employees or pay a $2,000 tax penalty for each employee. Individuals not covered by an employer-provided plan in 2014 will be required to purchase a health insurance policy or pay a penalty of $95 or 1 percent of income (whichever is greater), which will rise to $695 or 2.5 percent of income in 2016. Individuals and small businesses with fewer than 100 employees in 2014 will be able to purchase health insurance policies from state-based health insurance exchanges. The law also requires employers with 50 or more full-time equivalent employees to cover at least 60 percent of an employee's total health care costs.[37] The law is expected to extend health insurance coverage by 2019 to 32 million uninsured people.[38]

There are three common types of employer-provided health insurance plans: (1) traditional health insurance, (2) health maintenance organizations (HMOs), and (3) preferred provider organizations (PPOs). Figure 12.5 summarizes the differences among these plans.

TRADITIONAL HEALTH INSURANCE Provided by an insurance company that acts as an intermediary between the patient and health care provider, *traditional health insurance plans* (also

Issue	Traditional Coverage	Health Maintenance Organization (HMO)	Preferred Provider Organization (PPO)
Where must the covered parties live?	May live anywhere.	May be required to live in an HMO-designated service area.	May live anywhere.
Who provides health care?	Doctor and health care facility of patient's choice.	Must use doctors and facilities designated by HMO.	May use doctors and facilities associated with PPO. If not, may pay additional copayment/deductible.
How much coverage of routine/preventive medicine?	Does not cover regular checkups and other preventive services. Diagnostic tests may be covered in part or full.	Covers regular checkups, diagnostic tests, and other preventive services with low or no fee per visit.	Same as HMO if doctor and facility are on approved list. Copayment and deductibles are much higher for doctors and facilities not on list.
What hospital care costs are covered?	Covers doctors' and hospitals' bills.	Covers doctors' bills; covers bills of HMO-approved hospitals.	Covers bills of PPO-approved doctors and hospitals.

FIGURE 12.5
Employer-Provided Health Insurance Plans

Source: Milkovich, G., and Newman, J. (2009). *Compensation* (9th ed.). New York: McGraw-Hill, 473. Reprinted with permission by The McGraw-Hill Companies, Inc.

called *fee-for-service plans*) develop a fee schedule based on the cost of medical services in a specific community. They then incorporate these fees into the costs of insurance coverage. The best-known examples of traditional health insurance plans are the Blue Cross and Blue Shield organizations. Traditional health insurance covers hospital and surgical expenses, physicians' care, and a substantial portion of expenses for serious illnesses. In 2012, traditional health plans were selected by 17 percent of employees in large companies who had health insurance coverage.[39]

premium
The money paid to an insurance company for coverage.

Traditional health insurance plans have several important features: First, they include a deductible that a policyholder must meet before the plan makes any reimbursements. Second, they require a monthly group rate (also called a **premium**) paid to the insurance company. The premium is usually paid partially by the employer and partially by the employee. Third, they provide for coinsurance. The typical coinsurance allocation is 80/20 (80% of the cost is covered by the insurance plan and 20% is picked up by the employee). The deductible, premium, and coinsurance can be adjusted, so the employer's and employee's costs of health care insurance vary depending on how the parties agree to allocate the costs. A type of traditional health plan that is gaining in popularity is the high-deductible health plan (HDHP) which is designed to help employers keep the costs of employee health care plans under control. The HDHP has a high deductible of several thousand dollars that employees are required to pay each year before the plan provides any coverage for health care costs. The plan provides health care coverage only for expensive medical procedures and protects employees from going into debt from unexpected medical costs. Employees are expected to pay the full cost of regular recurring health care expenses under the HDHP.

Traditional plans give employees the greatest amount of choice in selecting a physician and a hospital. However, these plans have several disadvantages: First, they often do not cover regular checkups and other preventive services. Second, calculating the deductible and coinsurance allocation requires a significant amount of paperwork. Each time they visit a physician, employees must fill out claims forms and obtain bills with long, itemized lists of services. This can be frustrating for patients and costly to physicians, who often need to hire clerical workers solely to process forms.

health maintenance organization (HMO)
A health care plan that provides comprehensive medical services for employees and their families at a flat annual fee.

HEALTH MAINTENANCE ORGANIZATIONS (HMOS) A **health maintenance organization (HMO)** is a health care plan that provides comprehensive medical services for employees and their families at a flat annual fee. People covered by an HMO have unlimited access to medical services, because the HMO is designed to encourage preventive health care to reduce ultimate costs. (The "stitch in time saves nine" analogy applies here.) HMO members pay a monthly premium, plus a small copayment or deductible. Some HMOs have no copayment or deductible. The HMOs' annual flat fee per member acts as a monetary disincentive to the HMOs' participatory doctors, who might otherwise be tempted to give patients unnecessary medical tests or casually refer them to expensive medical specialists. In 2012, HMOs were selected by 17 percent of employees in large companies who have health insurance coverage.[40]

HMOs have two major advantages: First, for a fixed fee, people covered by the HMO receive most of their medical services (including preventive care) without incurring coinsurance or deductibles or having to fill out claims forms. Second, HMOs encourage preventive health care and healthier lifestyles.

The major disadvantage of HMOs is that they restrict people's ability to select their physicians and the hospitals at which they receive medical services. The HMO may service a limited geographic area, which may restrict who can join the plan. People may be forced to leave their existing doctor and choose one from a list of those who belong to the HMO. In the case of serious illnesses, the specialists consulted must also belong to the HMO, even if there are doctors in the area with better reputations and stronger qualifications. In addition, some consumer groups have criticized HMOs for skimping on patient care to save money on medical costs.

To deal with the problem of patients being denied health care services by administrators under an HMO, federal lawmakers have proposed a "Patient's Bill of Rights," which is intended to protect patients from abuses of cost-control policies. Although federal lawmakers continue to debate this issue, 38 states now have laws allowing patients to appeal medical decisions to external review boards that have independent experts. In addition, 10 states, led by Texas, have passed laws giving patients the right to sue HMOs, and 23 more are considering such legislation.[41]

PREFERRED PROVIDER ORGANIZATIONS (PPOS) A **preferred provider organization (PPO)** is a health care plan in which an employer or insurance company establishes a network of doctors and hospitals to provide a broad set of medical services for an annual flat fee per participant. The fee is lower than that which doctors and hospitals normally charge their customers for the bundle of services, and the monthly premium is lower than that charged by a traditional plan for the same services. In return for charging a lower fee, the doctors and hospitals who join the PPO network expect to receive a larger volume of patients. Members of the PPO can use it for preventive health care (such as checkups) without paying a doctor's usual fee for the service. PPOs collect information on the utilization of their health services so that employers can periodically improve the plan's design and reduce costs. In 2012, PPOs were selected by 63 percent of employees in large companies who have health insurance coverage.[42]

preferred provider organization (PPO)
A health care plan in which an employer or insurance company establishes a network of doctors and hospitals to provide a broad set of medical services for a flat fee per participant. In return for the lower fee, the doctors and hospitals who join the PPO network expect to receive a larger volume of patients.

PPOs combine some of the best features of HMOs (managed health care and a wide array of medical services for a fixed fee) with the flexibility of the traditional health insurance plan. They include provisions that allow their members to go outside the PPO network and use non-PPO doctors and medical facilities. People who select non-PPO doctors and hospitals pay additional fees in the form of deductibles and copayments determined by the PPO. Because PPOs have few of the disadvantages of traditional health insurance plans or HMOs, they are expected to continue growing rapidly.

Some employers go beyond just giving their employees several different choices of health insurance benefit plans, such as between an HMO or a PPO, and provide on-site medical clinics that make it convenient for employees to receive health care right where they work. The Manager's Notebook, "On-Site Medical Clinics at Companies Reduce Health Care Costs," explains why Toyota decided to offer on-site health care to its employees at its truck plant in San Antonio, Texas.

MANAGER'S NOTEBOOK

On-Site Medical Clinics at Companies Reduce Health Care Costs

Employees are enthusiastic about the on-site medical center Toyota built at its truck factory in San Antonio, Texas. Louis Aguillon, a line worker, went to the clinic with a nagging back pain and paid just $5 for the visit and saw the doctor for 20 minutes. Aguillon says, "You're not just a number there."

Toyota views the medical center as a business investment. It spent $9 million in 2007 to build the facility, but it expects to save many additional millions over the next decade. Managed by Take Care Health Systems, whose business is running clinics, the clinic has helped Toyota slash big-ticket medical items, including referrals to highly paid specialists, emergency room visits, and the use of costly brand-name drugs. In addition, Toyota has seen productivity gains, because workers don't have to leave the plant for routine medical care.

Toyota's on-site medical clinic is part of a new trend being driven by the spiraling cost of health insurance benefits. Other companies offering on-site medical care for employees include Nissan Motors, Harrah's Entertainment, Google, and the Walt Disney Parks and Resorts group. A recent study by benefits-consulting firm Watson Wyatt Worldwide found that 32 percent of all employers with more than 1,000 workers either have an on-site medical center or plan to build one.

At Toyota, the copayment for an employee for a visit to a doctor is $5, versus $15 if the worker visits an outside doctor. At the San Antonio Toyota plant, workers who have signed up to use the on-site clinic often see little reason to seek outside care. The on-site team of three doctors, plus dentists, physical therapists, and others, can take x-rays, treat broken bones, and handle various emergencies. The doctors perform many of these procedures for as little as half of the physician fees that a specialist or local hospital charges. At the San Antonio Toyota plant, 60 percent of the employees signed up to use the on-site medical facility.

Sources: Based on Welch, D. (2008, August 11). The company doctor is back. *BusinessWeek*, 48–49; LaPenna, A. (2009, March–April). Workplace medical clinics: The employer-redesigned "company doctor." *Journal of Healthcare Management*. *www.entrepreneur.com*. ■■

HEALTH INSURANCE COVERAGE OF EMPLOYEES' PARTNERS Traditionally, health insurance benefits have been offered only to employees and their spouses or dependents. Today, however, employers are being asked to offer the same health insurance benefits to employees' domestic partners—that is, unmarried heterosexual or homosexual partners.

More than half of Fortune 500 companies offer health benefits for domestic partners, according to the Human Rights Campaign, the nation's largest gay-advocacy group.[43] Among the firms that offer such benefits are some of the most prestigious names in U.S. business: Silicon Graphics, Microsoft, Viacom, Apple Inc., and Warner Bros. Companies that also cover unmarried heterosexual couples include Ben & Jerry's Homemade, Levi Strauss, and the Federal National Mortgage Association (Fannie Mae).

Research shows that health care costs for gay partners and unmarried heterosexual couples are often lower than those for married couples. Moreover, many homosexual employees do not sign up for the benefits because they want to keep their sexual orientation private. Employers can protect themselves against abuse by asking eligible employees to file affidavits of "spousal equivalency" showing a history of living together and sharing assets. The question of pitting heterosexual employees against gay and lesbian employees may become moot because the growing threat of discrimination lawsuits may force employers to offer coverage to all domestic partners in the near future.[44]

health savings account (HSA) A qualified health plan with a high deductible that lets individuals save money for health care expenses with pretax dollars and lets unspent money accumulate as a tax-free stash of money.

HEALTH SAVINGS ACCOUNTS In 2004, a new type of medical plan, called a **health savings account (HSA)**, became available to employees. An HSA lets individuals save money for health care expenses with pretax dollars. Employers offer the accounts in conjunction with a qualified health plan that has a high deductible—at least $1,250 for single coverage and $2,500 for a family, to a maximum in 2014 of $3,300 for singles and $6,550 for families.[45] The account's earnings are not taxed, nor are withdrawals taxed that are used to pay for qualified medical expenses. HSAs allow unspent money to be rolled over from one year to the next, potentially building up a tax-free stash of money. In exchange for higher deductibles, premiums on HSAs are lower than on other health insurance policies, making them attractive for relatively healthy families that do not need a lot of routine care and preventive services.

The theory behind the HSA concept is that the more of one's own money a customer of medical services spends, the more likely that person will make financially responsible decisions, such as skipping a visit to an emergency room for a minor problem or choosing a generic rather than a brand-name drug.[46]

HEALTH CARE COST CONTAINMENT The annual cost of premiums for employee health insurance coverage in 2012 was $5,615 for single coverage and $15,745 for family coverage, according to a survey by the Kaiser Family Foundation.[47] Employee contributions cover on average about 18 percent of the cost of a premium for single coverage and 24 percent of a premium for family coverage. The employer covers the rest of the health insurance premium costs. A company's HR benefits manager can control health care costs by designing (and modifying) health insurance plans carefully and by developing programs that encourage employees to adopt healthier lifestyles. Specifically, HR staff can:

- ***Develop a self-funding arrangement for health insurance*** A company is self-funding when it puts the money it would otherwise pay in insurance premiums into a fund to pay employee health care expenses. Under this type of plan, the employer has an incentive to assume some responsibility for employees' health. Self-funding plans can be designed to capture administrative efficiencies that translate into lower costs for the same services provided by a traditional health insurance plan.[48]
- ***Coordinate health insurance plans for families with two working spouses*** HR staff can encourage spouses who have duplicate coverage under two different insurance plans to establish a cost-sharing arrangement. Many companies, such as General Electric, require employees whose working spouses decline their own employers' health insurance to pay a significantly higher premium than nonworking spouses or those who cannot get insurance elsewhere.[49]

- ***Develop a wellness program for employees*** A *wellness program* assesses employees' risk of serious illness (for example, heart disease or cancer) and then teaches them how to reduce that risk by changing some of their habits (such as diet, exercise, and avoidance of harmful substances such as alcohol, tobacco, and caffeine).[50] Adolph Coors Company, the Colorado-based beer producer, has a wellness program composed of six areas: health hazard appraisal, exercise, smoking cessation, nutrition and weight loss, physical and cardiovascular rehabilitation, and stress and anger management. It has been estimated that Coors' wellness program returns $3.37 to the company for each dollar spent on it.[51]

- ***Offer high-deductible health plans for employees*** A **high-deductible health plan (HDHP)** is a way that employers can manage the costs of employee health care plans. An HDHP has a high deductible, which requires that each employee pay for the first few thousand dollars of medical costs each year (the plan pays only when an employee has a major medical problem). An HDHP is sometimes referred to as a *catastrophic health plan* because it can be used only when there is a serious medical event. An HDHP can be linked to a health savings account, which also has high deductibles in the plan design. The idea behind the HDHP is that people make smarter, less wasteful health care decisions when they have a larger financial stake in their own health care. Due to the high deductibles, these health care plans are less costly for employers, and employees' premiums cost less, too.[52] The Affordable Health Care Act places some limits on the use of HDHP plans because it specifies that health plans must pay on an annual basis at least 60 percent of allowed medical expenses and limit out-of-pocket spending at $6,350 for individuals and $12,700 for families.

high-deductible health plan (HDHP)
A way that employers can manage the costs of employee health care plans. The high deductible requires that employees pay for the first few thousand dollars of medical costs each year, which means that the plan pays only when employees have major medical problems.

The Manager's Notebook, "Wellness Practices Improve Employee Health and Lower Company Health Care Costs," gives some idea of the diversity of wellness practices that companies are using to improve their employees' health and reduce health care costs.

MANAGER'S NOTEBOOK

Ethics/Social Responsibility

Wellness Practices Improve Employee Health and Lower Company Health Care Costs

Here are some examples of practices used by companies to support employee wellness in the workplace:

- ***Give employees more flexible work schedules so they can exercise regularly*** At Bandwidth, a communications technology company, employees are given longer lunch periods so they can exercise at the gym. The company also encourages physical activity by sponsoring sports teams.
- ***Provide healthy food for employees to eat*** Scripps Hospitals installed self-service kiosks stocked with healthy food, including complete meals. The company also partially subsidizes the cost of the healthy food, making it a more attractive option for employees.
- ***Offer financial incentives to employees who participate in wellness activities*** Nationwide Financial pays its employees close to $300 for completing health-risk assessments and following through on requirements for improvement. Nationwide's focus on wellness has contributed to reductions in health care benefit costs at the company.
- ***Appeal to employees' sense of competition*** Manufacturing company Ashcroft set up a fitness program that focuses on friendly competition. Employees form teams or compete individually in programs developed by GlobalFit. After one year, 68 percent of the company's employees voluntarily participated in the competitions.

Sources: Based on Lucas, S. (2013, May 6). Wellness programs that work for small businesses. *Inc.*, *www.inc.com*; Mannino, B. (2012, June 14). Wellness programs finally catching on with companies. *Fox Business. www.foxbusiness.com*; Lorenz, M. (2010, July 8). 7 habits of highly successful corporate wellness programs. *The Hiring Site. www.thehiringsite.careerbuilder.com.* ■■

Retirement Benefits

After retiring, people have three main sources of income: Social Security, personal savings, and retirement benefits. Because Social Security can be expected to provide only between 25 and 50 percent of preretirement earnings, retirees must rely on additional employer-provided retirement benefits and personal savings to maintain their standard of living. Retirement benefits support an employee's long-term financial goal of achieving a planned level of retirement income.

An important service that the HR department can provide to employees nearing retirement is preretirement counseling. *Preretirement counseling* sessions give employees information about their retirement benefits so that they can plan their retirement years accordingly.[53] A benefits specialist can answer questions such as:

- What will my total retirement income be when Social Security is added to it?
- Would I be better off taking my retirement benefits in the form of a lump sum or as an annuity (a fixed amount of income each year)?
- What would be the tax effects on my retirement benefits if I earn additional income from a part-time job?

Retirement benefit plans that are "qualified" by the Internal Revenue Service receive favorable tax treatment under the Internal Revenue Code. To qualify, the retirement plan must be available to broad classes of employees and must not favor highly compensated workers over lower-paid workers. Under a qualified retirement plan, employees pay no taxes on the contributions made to the plan until these funds are distributed at retirement. Also, the earnings on the fund's investments accumulate without being taxed each year. Employers may also take a tax deduction for the annual contributions they make to a qualified retirement plan.

ERISA The major law governing the administration of retirement benefits in the United States is the **Employee Retirement Income Security Act (ERISA).** Passed in 1974, ERISA protects employees' retirement benefits from mismanagement.[54] The key provisions of ERISA cover who is eligible for retirement benefits, vesting, and funding requirements.

Employee Retirement Income Security Act (ERISA)
A federal law established in 1974 to protect employees' retirement benefits from mismanagement.

- ***Eligibility for retirement benefits*** ERISA requires that the minimum age for participation in a retirement plan cannot be greater than 21. However, employers may restrict participation in the retirement plan to employees who have completed one year of service with the company.
- ***Vesting*** A guarantee that accrued retirement benefits will be given to retirement plan participants when they retire or leave the employer is called **vesting**. Under current ERISA rules, employee vesting rules must conform to one of two schedules: (1) full vesting after three years of service; or (2) 20 percent vesting after two years of service and a further 20 percent vesting each year thereafter, until the employee is fully vested at six years of service. Employers are allowed to vest employees faster than this if they wish. Vesting pertains only to employer contributions to the retirement plan. Any contributions the employee has made to the plan are always the employee's property, along with any earnings that have accumulated on those contributions. These employee-provided funds, and any employer contributions that are vested, are said to be **portable**—that is, they stay with the employee as he or she moves from one company to another.
- ***Funding requirements and obligations*** In addition to establishing guidelines for a retirement plan's minimum funding requirements, ERISA requires that retirement plan administrators act prudently in making investments with participants' funds. Plans that do not meet ERISA funding standards are subject to financial penalties from the Internal Revenue Service.

vesting
A guarantee that accrued retirement benefits will be given to retirement plan participants when they retire or leave the employer.

portable benefits
Employee benefits, usually retirement funds, that stay with the employee as he or she moves from one company to another.

To protect employees from an employer's possible failure to meet its retirement obligations, ERISA requires employers to pay for plan termination insurance, which guarantees the payment of retirement benefits to employees even if the plan terminates (either because of poor investment decisions or because the company has gone out of business) before they retire. Termination insurance for defined benefit plans (discussed next) is provided by the **Pension Benefit Guaranty Corporation (PBGC)**, a government agency.

Pension Benefit Guaranty Corporation (PBGC)
The government agency that provides plan termination insurance to employers with defined benefit retirement programs.

DEFINED BENEFIT PLANS A **defined benefit plan**, also called a **pension**, is a retirement plan that promises to pay a fixed dollar amount of retirement income based on a formula that takes into account the average of the employee's last three to five years' earnings before retirement. The amount of annual income provided by defined benefit plans increases with the years of service to the employer. For example, based on a final five-year preretirement average salary of $50,000, Eastman Kodak's pension plan pays a retired employee with 30 years of service $20,523 per year at age 65. Merck, the pharmaceutical giant, pays an employee with the same salary and 30 years of service $24,000 per year at age 65.[55]

defined benefit plan or pension
A retirement plan that promises to pay a fixed dollar amount of retirement income based on a formula that takes into account the average of the employee's last three to five years' earnings prior to retirement.

Under a defined benefit plan, the employer assumes all the risk of providing the promised income to the retiree and is likely to make all of the financial contributions to the plan. Defined benefit plans are most appropriate for firms that want to provide a secure and predictable retirement income for employees. Michigan-based Dow Chemical is one such company.[56] Such plans are less appropriate for firms that stress risk taking and want employees to share in the risk and responsibility of managing their retirement assets.

Most companies that use defined benefit plans for retirement provide the maximum retirement income only after an employee has spent an entire career of 30 to 35 years with the company. Those who change jobs by moving to different companies are penalized with much lower retirement incomes. Employees currently entering the labor market expect to change jobs and employers several times. Defined benefit plans are less attractive to these employees, because few will spend an entire career at one company. Consequently, there has been a decline in the number of companies offering defined benefit plans for their employees' retirement.[57]

DEFINED CONTRIBUTION PLANS A **defined contribution plan** is a retirement plan in which the employer promises to contribute a specific amount of funds into the plan for each participant. For example, a defined contribution plan may require the employer to contribute 6 percent of the employee's salary into the plan each pay period. Some defined contribution plans also allow or require employees to make additional contributions to the plan. The retirement income that the participants receive depends on the success of the plan's investments and therefore cannot be known in advance.[58] Companies that value employee risk taking and participation are likely to offer defined contribution plans. Under these plans, employees and employers share both risk and responsibility for retirement benefits. Employees may need to decide how to allocate their retirement funds from different investment choices that represent various levels of risk. Because they require fewer obligations from employers than defined benefit plans, most of the new retirement plans established in recent years have been defined contribution plans.

defined contribution plan
A retirement plan in which the employer promises to contribute a specific amount of funds into the plan for each participant. The final value of each participant's retirement income depends on the success of the plan's investments.

There is a dark side to this trend toward defined contribution plans. Whereas highly educated and highly paid employees may benefit from such risk-taking arrangements, defined contribution plans are likely to be devastating for low-wage workers, according to a report by the Senate Labor and Human Resources Committee. By the year 2020, more than 50 million U.S. men and women will be of retirement age, but many will not be able to retire because, as low-wage earners, they could not afford to invest in the defined contribution plans established by their employers. Many of these low-wage workers are women.[59]

Figure 12.6 summarizes the most common defined contribution retirement plans: the 401(k) plan, the individual retirement account (IRA), the simplified employee pension (SEP), and the profit-sharing Keogh. These plans all have tax benefits that can prove very valuable in the long run.

401(k) Plan To understand the features and benefits of a *401(k) plan* (as well as other tax-deferred retirement plans), consider the following situation. Suppose you want to save $100 per month for your retirement, you are in the 28 percent federal income tax bracket, and the money you invest will earn 8 percent per year. If you save the money out of your salary and put it into a personal savings account, the $1,200 that you set aside each year would, in effect, be reduced to $864 because of taxes (Figure 12.7). With one year's interest, that $864 would grow to $891. Each year the investment earnings would also be taxed at the 28 percent rate. If you continue to set aside $1,200 each year in a personal account, your retirement fund would grow to $67,514 in 30 years.

With tax-deferred retirement plans like the 401(k), the money you save each month is not taxed. Therefore, each year you are saving the full $1,200 you put into your retirement account. In addition, the earnings on your investment are not taxed. After the first year, the value of your account would be $1,251 (compared to $864 under the personal account scenario).

Plan	Available to	Appropriate for	Maximum Contributions	Tax Break on Contributions/ Earnings
401(k)	Employees of for-profit businesses	Everyone who qualifies	15 percent of salary up to $17,500 in 2014	Yes/Yes
IRA	Anyone with earned income	Those without company pension plans or who have put the maximum into their company plan	100 percent of salary up to $5,500, $11,000 if joint with spouse	Sometimes/Yes
SEP	The self-employed and employees of small businesses	Self-employed person who is a sole proprietor	25 percent of gross self-employment income or $52,000, whichever is less	Yes/Yes
Profit-Sharing Keogh	The self-employed and employees of unincorporated small businesses	Small-business owner who is funding a plan for self and employees	Same as SEP	Yes/Yes

FIGURE 12.6

A Comparison of Defined Contribution Retirement Plans

Source: Internal Revenue Service Web site (2014), *www.irs.gov*.

FIGURE 12.7

Personal Account Versus Deferred Compensation Plan

Source: State of Tennessee. *Introduction to the deferred compensation programs.*

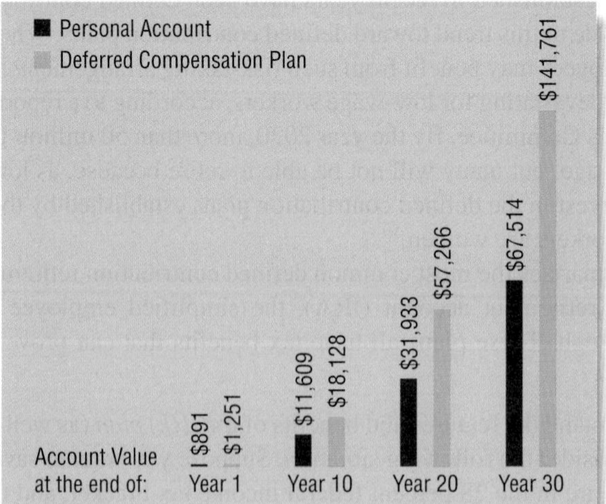

After 30 years, the value would grow to $141,761, more than twice the size of the personal account. When you retire and draw the funds, your withdrawals will be taxed at your retirement tax rate.

Anyone who works for a for-profit business is eligible to participate in a 401(k) plan.[60] Most companies that establish 401(k) plans will match 25 to 100 percent of employee contributions up to 6 percent of the employee's salary.[61] In 2014, the maximum employee annual contribution that could be made to a 401(k) plan was 15 percent of salary up to a limit of $17,500. Employees in not-for-profit companies can also save for retirement with a 403(b) retirement plan, which has the same features as the 401(k) plan. The 403(b) plan lets employees in not-for-profit organizations take advantage of the same retirement savings opportunities as those offered to employees in the for-profit sector who are eligible to participate with a 401(k) plan.

The 401(k) plan's matching feature makes it attractive to both employers and employees. Employees benefit by accumulating tax-deferred retirement funds; employers benefit by reducing their risk, because there is no payment required when the employee leaves or retires. Usually, employees are free to decide individually how they wish to invest their funds. The basic choice is between an investment strategy with a high potential return, but the risk of a low or even a negative return, and a strategy with low risk and a low-to-moderate return. Investing in the stock market is an example of the first investment strategy; investing in a savings account is an example of the second.

One controversial aspect of 401(k) plans is a practice that permits many large companies to provide their matching contribution to an employee's 401(k) contribution in the form of company stock. For example, Procter & Gamble, Pfizer, General Electric, and McDonald's use company stock for matching an employee's 401(k) contribution.[62] An employee who has a large portion of her retirement savings in the stock of one company puts her retirement investment at considerable risk. This risk became apparent in 2001 with the bankruptcy of Enron, a large energy company, and the subsequent collapse of its stock price that wiped out the retirement savings of thousands of Enron employees.[63] Even worse, Enron restricted employees from selling their stock until they were close to retirement age.

In 2006, the Pension Protection Act was enacted, which gives employees greater flexibility to diversify out of the company stock in their 401(k) plan and into less risky investments, such as mutual funds. Employers must now allow workers to cash out their company stock within three years to diversify their 401(k) investments, and many firms now allow their employees to transfer out at any time.[64]

A recent development in the use of 401(k) plans is an automatic enrollment feature that has been adopted by 59 percent of companies that use the plans, according to Hewitt Associates, a benefits consulting firm. This feature is designed to increase enrollment among the 25 percent of employees who do not sign up for their company 401(k) plan because they may be overwhelmed with benefits decisions when they start their jobs. With automatic enrollment, employees are enrolled in a 401(k) plan at the time they are hired, and they are given an opt-out choice that they can use if they do not want to participate. When Alon USA, a Texas oil refiner, instituted automatic enrollment into its 401(k) plan, the employee participation level increased from 40 to 80 percent of the workforce.[65]

IRA An *individual retirement account (IRA)* allows people in 2014 to contribute up to $5,500 per year tax free (or $11,000 per year into a joint account with a spouse). Unlike the other defined contribution plans, IRAs are personal savings plans—that is, employers do not contribute to them. As with the 401(k) plan, the interest on an IRA account is tax deferred until the employee cashes it in at retirement. This tax-free benefit is eliminated for employees who participate in a qualified retirement plan with their employer and/or employees who have an adjusted gross income of at least $70,000 (single people) or $116,000 (married people filing a joint return).[66] However, there are no such restrictions on the IRA's tax-deferred earnings. IRAs are available to both those without company pension plans and those who have contributed the maximum to their company plan.

In 1998, a new version of the IRA called the *Roth IRA* became available. The Roth IRA allows people to contribute up to $5,500 per year of after-tax income into a savings plan in which the accumulation of interest on the contributions is not taxed and the distributions of income are not taxed after retirement. The Roth IRA (similar to the regular IRA) requires a person to attain a minimum age of 59½ before income can be taken out of the savings without a penalty. Roth IRAs are restricted to people with adjusted gross incomes of less than $129,000 as a single person or $191,000 for married people filing joint returns. The Roth IRA is advantageous for people who anticipate being in higher tax brackets in the future, because the tax savings possible under the traditional IRA would be more than offset by the tax-free distributions of retirement income taken when the person moves to a higher tax bracket.[67]

SEP A *simplified employee pension (SEP)* is similar to an IRA, but although IRAs are available to people who also participate in a retirement fund through their employer (subject to the limits described earlier), SEPs are available only to people who are self-employed or who work for small businesses that do not have a retirement plan. Those who are eligible for an SEP can invest up to 25 percent of their annual income or $52,000 (whichever is less) on a tax-deferred basis.

Profit-Sharing Keogh Plan A *profit-sharing Keogh plan* provides for the same maximum contribution as an SEP but allows the employer to contribute to an employee's retirement account on the basis of company performance as measured by profits. Profit-sharing Keogh plans allow employers to make smaller contributions when profits are modest and larger contributions when profits are high. Keogh plans have three main advantages: First, because they allow employees to share in the company's success, they foster a sense of teamwork. Second, they let employers make contributions to the retirement plan that reflect their ability to pay. Third, their tax benefits are similar to those of SEPs.

Hybrid Pension Plans Several hybrid pension plans have sprung up to address the limitations of both defined benefit plans and defined contribution plans. Defined benefit plans reward long-term service in a world in which employees are more and more mobile. And although defined contribution plans offer greater portability than defined benefit plans, defined contribution plans are tied more to investment returns than to job performance. Thus, fast-trackers who move from job to job may end up with less retirement income than those who work in a company with a traditional pension plan. One of the most popular hybrid plans developed to bridge these two types of pensions is the *cash balance plan,* which works like this: Employees are credited with a certain amount of money for their tax-deferred retirement account each year, based on their annual pay. These contributions are compounded using an agreed-upon interest rate (such as the interest rate on five-year Treasury bills). The employees take the cash balances with them when they change jobs. One drawback of cash balance plans is the time-consuming and expensive recordkeeping required for individual accounts. Another problematic issue is the effect on employees when a company decides to convert from a traditional pension plan to a cash balance pension plan. In some cases the cash balance plan provides lower retirement income than traditional pensions for more senior employees. IBM employees legally challenged the company's decision to switch from a traditional pension plan to a cash balance plan based on alleged age discrimination. However, a federal appeals court ruled in favor of IBM's right to convert its traditional pension plan into a cash balance plan. This 2006 court ruling on cash balance plans has given the green light for other companies to make the conversion.[68]

Despite these potential drawbacks, cash balance plans are becoming popular because they are effective for retaining younger employees. Duracell International and Bank of America are two companies that have cash balance plans.[69]

Insurance Plans

A wide variety of insurance plans can provide financial security for employees and their families. Two of the most valued company-provided insurance benefits are life insurance and long-term disability insurance.

LIFE INSURANCE Basic *term life insurance* pays a benefit to the survivors of a deceased employee. The typical benefit is one or two times the employee's annual income. For example, both Citicorp and AT&T offer their employees life insurance that will pay one year's salary to their survivors. In most cases, company-provided term life insurance policies cover workers only while they are employed by the organization. Companies with a flexible benefits policy may allow employees to purchase insurance beyond the basic level. An employee with a nonworking spouse, for example, may need a benefit of three to five years' salary to provide for his or her survivors. Approximately 78 percent of medium and large businesses provide a life insurance benefit to full-time employees.

LONG-TERM DISABILITY INSURANCE About one-third of 20-year-old workers today will become disabled before they hit retirement age at 67, according to the Social Security Administration. The primary cause of disability is chronic disease—cardiovascular problems, musculoskeletal issues, and cancer are the leading diagnoses—rather than work-related accidents, according to a study for the Life and Health Insurance Foundation for Education.[70] These employees need replacement income to cover the earnings lost while they are recovering from an illness or accident or, if they are permanently disabled, for the rest of their lives. Workers' compensation does not provide disability income for people who have had off-duty accidents, and Social Security provides only a modest level of disability income to cover the most basic needs.

An extended period of disability can exhaust a person's financial resources fairly quickly. Besides regular living expenses, many people who are disabled face medical bills and other expenses, such as the cost of rehabilitation to recover from a disability. Many rehabilitation services are not covered by health insurance.[71]

Long-term disability insurance provides replacement income to disabled employees who cannot perform their essential job duties. An employee is eligible to receive disability benefits after being disabled for six months or more. These benefits range from 50 to 67 percent of the employee's salary.[72] For example, Xerox provides 60 percent replacement income under its long-term disability insurance plan, whereas IBM provides 67 percent.[73] Employees who are disabled for less than six months are likely to receive replacement income under a sick leave policy (discussed later in this chapter). Employees can also purchase short-term disability insurance, which provides coverage until the long-term coverage takes over.

With Social Security benefits added to long-term disability insurance benefits, an employee's total replacement income is likely to be 70 to 80 percent of his or her salary. Long-term disability insurance plans usually take Social Security into account and are designed so that disabled employees do not receive more than 80 percent of their salary from these combined sources—the theory being that a higher percentage might be a disincentive to return to work. Approximately 45 percent of medium and large companies offer long-term disability insurance benefits to their workers (see Figure 12.2).

Paid Time Off

Paid time off provides breaks from regularly scheduled work hours so that employees can pursue leisure activities or take care of personal or civic duties. Paid time off includes sick leave, vacations, severance pay, and holidays. Paid time off is one of the most expensive benefits for the employer. Paid time off costs U.S. employers 7.0 percent of total payroll.[74]

SICK LEAVE *Sick leave* provides full pay for each day that an employee experiences a short-term illness or disability that interferes with his or her ability to perform the job. Employees are often rewarded with greater amounts of sick leave in return for long-term service to the company. According to the U.S. Bureau of Labor Statistics, employers with sick leave benefits provide an average of 15 days of sick leave for employees with one year of full-time service to the company. Many employers allow employees to accumulate unused sick leave over time. For example, an employee with 10 years on the job may accumulate 150 sick days if he or she has not used any sick time (10 years × 15 days per year of sick leave = 150 days). This accumulated coverage would be more than enough to give the employee full replacement income for the first six months of a serious illness, after which long-term disability coverage takes over.

Some companies allow retiring employees to collect pay for accumulated unused sick leave and vacation time. For example, when John Young retired as the CEO of Hewlett-Packard, he collected $937,225 in lieu of unused sick pay and vacation leave accumulated during his 34 years with the company.[75]

An HR benefits specialist must monitor and control sick leave benefits to prevent employees from using sick leave to take care of personal business or to reward themselves with a "mental health day" off from work. A survey from Kronos, a workplace productivity consulting firm, reported that 57 percent of U.S. salaried employees take sick days when they are not really sick.[76] The HR department should consider instituting the following policies:

- Set up a "wellness pay" incentive program that monetarily rewards employees who do not use any sick days. Wellness programs may also encourage employees to adopt healthier lifestyles and file for fewer health benefits. For example, Quaker Oats provides bonuses of as much as $500 for employees who exercise, shun smoking, and wear seat belts.[77]
- Establish flexible work hours so that employees can take care of some personal business during the week, thereby decreasing their need to use sick days for this reason.
- Reward employees with a lump sum that represents their unused sick days when they leave or retire from the organization. Alternatively, give employees the chance to accrue vacation days as a percentage of unused sick leave.

- Allow employees to take one or two personal days each year. This helps to discourage employees from regarding sick days as time off to which they are entitled even if they do not get sick. A poll conducted by job Web site CareerBuilder indicated that 29 percent of employees took a sick day in the most recent year, even though they were not actually sick.[78]
- Establish a paid time off (PTO) bank, which is a policy that pools time off in a bank of days that employees use for vacation, sick leave, personal days, and floating holidays. PTO programs allow employees to choose how they will use their time off without feeling the pressure to justify their absence to the boss. With PTOs, employees can take time off for any reason as long as it is scheduled with supervisors. Time off can also be used for unplanned reasons such as sickness and emergencies.[79]

VACATIONS Employers provide paid vacations to give their employees time away from the stresses and strains of the daily work routine. Vacation time allows employees to recharge themselves physically and emotionally and can lead to improved job performance.[80] Many companies reward long-term service to the company with more vacation time. For example, Hewlett-Packard employees with one year of service are eligible for 15 days' vacation; after 30 years of service, they are entitled to 30 days. A new development in paid time-off benefits is an *unlimited paid vacation policy* that some companies are using in the hopes of lowering employee stress and reducing disruptive turnover. Unlimited paid vacation policies trust employees to take paid vacation days when they need to take time off from work. The company benefits by reducing the need to keep records of paid vacation time allocations. Companies in Silicon Valley, California, such as Netflix and Zynga, as well as software startup Evernote, have adopted unlimited vacation policies to help in the recruiting of engineering talent.[81]

Figure 12.8 is an international comparison of the average annual number of paid vacation days that employees receive from their companies. U.S. employees average about 10 days (two weeks) of paid vacation. This is the same as in Japan, but far less than in most European Union nations. For example, French workers receive 35 days (seven weeks) and British workers receive 25 days (five weeks) of paid vacation. Many European countries have laws stipulating the number of paid vacation days that workers must receive, but the United States has no such laws.

Some U.S. businesses are starting to offer employees *sabbatical leave,* which is an extended vacation with pay. Sabbaticals, which can be considered a vacation with a purpose, help employees improve their skills or provide a service to the community. Sabbaticals are very common for college and university faculty, for whom they are a tradition. In the business world, where they are much newer, they are most likely to be found in the high-tech industries, where employee skills become obsolete rapidly and need to be renewed. At Intel, for example, engineers and technical employees who have worked for the company for seven years are entitled to an eight-week paid sabbatical in addition to their annual paid vacation. Employees have used these sabbaticals to continue their education, teach in public schools or colleges, or do volunteer work for nonprofit organizations.[82] At Intel, some 4,350 workers, or about one in every 20 full-time employees, take sabbaticals in a given year. According to the Society for Human Resource Management,

FIGURE 12.8

Average Annual Number of Vacation Days in Various Countries for Employees

Sources: Galvan, S. (2004, July 6). Wake up and smell the beach, Americans. *Denver Post,* B-6; Minimum vacation time around the world. (2010). *www.nationmaster.com.*

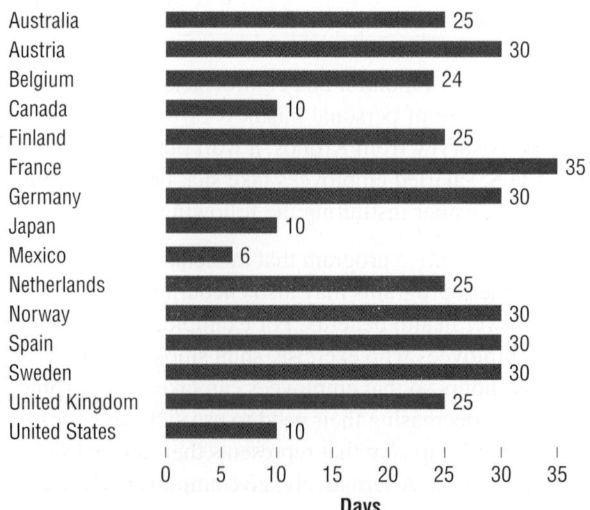

23 percent of businesses in the United States offer either paid or unpaid sabbaticals to employees. Another company that has adopted a sabbatical program for employees is McDonald's. At McDonald's, full-time employees receive eight weeks of paid time off every 10 years, in addition to vacation.[83]

SEVERANCE PAY Although not typically thought of as a benefit, the severance pay given to laid-off employees is also a form of paid time off. The type of severance pay offered varies widely. Some organizations offer one month's pay for each year the employee has worked for them, often capped at one year's salary. Severance pay is provided to cushion the shock of termination and to finance the employee's search for a new position.

PAID PARENTAL LEAVE In the United States, the Family and Medical Leave Act (FMLA) provides up to 12 weeks of unpaid leave for employees who become parents of a newborn child, but only two states, California and New Jersey, have enacted laws that provide up to six weeks of paid parental leave for employees. The paid parental leave law in California covers 55 percent of weekly pay, and in New Jersey it covers 67 percent of weekly pay.[84] Outside the United States, many countries have enacted laws that require paid parental leave for employees. Sweden provides working parents up to 16 months of paid leave per child at 80 percent of pay, the cost being shared between the employer and the state. Germany provides up to 14 months of paid parental leave at 65 percent of pay, and Japan provides 14 weeks of paid parental leave at 60 percent of pay.[85]

HOLIDAYS AND OTHER PAID TIME OFF Many employers give their employees paid holidays or pay extra to employees who are required or volunteer to work on holidays. In the United States, employers provide an average of 10 paid holidays per year to employees. Other countries provide similar or more paid holidays, with an average of 10 paid holidays in the United Kingdom, 13 in Brazil, 14 in Japan, and 11 in France.[86] Although they are not required to, many employers also provide paid leave for jury duty. In manufacturing environments where employees work on tight time schedules, many employers provide (either voluntarily or through a union contract) time for employees to eat, clean up, and get dressed. Some union contracts (particularly those in railroad and other transportation firms) also stipulate that employees will be paid if they are scheduled for work even though no work is available.

Employee Services

The last category of employee benefits is *employee services,* which employers provide on a tax-free or tax-preferred basis to enhance the quality of employees' work or personal life. Figure 12.9 lists some well-known employee services. These include child care, health club memberships, subsidized company cafeterias, parking privileges, and discounts on company products.

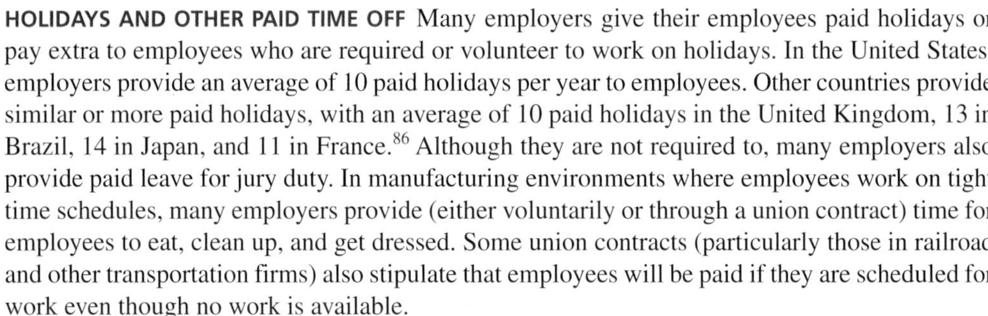

1. Charitable contributions
2. Counseling
   - Financial
   - Legal
   - Psychiatric/psychological
3. Tax preparation
4. Education subsidies
5. Child adoption
6. Child care
7. Elder care
8. Subsidized food service
9. Discounts on merchandise
10. Physical awareness and fitness programs
11. Social and recreational opportunities
12. Parking
13. Transportation to and from work
14. Travel expenses
    - Car reimbursement
    - Tolls and parking
    - Food and entertainment reimbursement
15. Clothing reimbursement/allowance
16. Tool reimbursement/allowance
17. Relocation expenses
18. Emergency loans
19. Credit union
20. Housing
21. Employee assistance programs
22. On-site health services
23. Laptop computers
24. Concierge services

FIGURE 12.9

Selected Tax-Free or Tax-Preferred Employee Benefits or Services

Sources: HR Focus. (2000, June). What benefits are companies offering now? 5–7; 100 best companies to work for (2010). *www.cnnmoney.com.*

Companies are taking a fresh look at employee services and their value to employees. For years, employers offered services tentatively and experimentally, often as kind of a side dish to the main course of medical and health insurance and pension plans. But today companies are using a wide array of services to attract and retain employees, particularly if they cannot offer competitive salaries or raises. John Hancock Mutual Life Insurance of Boston recruits prospective employees with a heavy emphasis on its variety of benefits, including flexible scheduling, dependent-care services, fitness center, and take-home food from the company cafeteria.[87] Accenture, an IT consulting firm, provides concierge services as a benefit for its busy consultants who spend a lot of time away from home traveling on consulting projects. Concierge services take care of personal errands for employees such as car care, taking clothes to the cleaners, event planning, gift buying, and ticket purchasing. This support helps decrease employee stress by reducing the time busy employees spend on personal tasks.[88]

One of the most valued employee services today is child care.[89] Currently, about 7 percent of U.S. employers provide some child-care benefits, and this percentage is likely to increase because of the growing number of single parents and dual-career households with children.[90]

Companies that decide to offer child-care services have several options. The most expensive is an on-site child-care center. Other child-care options include subsidizing employee child-care costs at off-site child-care centers and establishing a child-care referral service for working parents.[91] Because child care is expensive, employers usually subsidize 50 to 75 percent of the costs and require employees to pay the rest.[92]

In addition to child-care benefits, many employees are finding a need for elder care benefits to provide care for their aging parents. A recent trend in employee benefits is offering a combined child and elder care benefit, called "backup care," that serves as a safety net for employees' children and elder family members by providing trusted and affordable temporary care so they can remain at work when their regular care-giving arrangements are unavailable due to unexpected illness, recovery from surgery, or school closures.[93]

Multinational firms that do business on a global basis have discovered that employees' preferences for benefits are highly diverse, as explained in the Manager's Notebook, "A Global Perspective on Employee Benefits."

MANAGER'S NOTEBOOK

Global

A Global Perspective on Employee Benefits

Employees' benefit needs are even more diverse when doing business on a global basis, as many multinational companies are discovering. For example, in some Latin American countries employees are not interested in 401(k) retirement plans, which are so popular in the United States. Many Latin American countries have experienced financial crises, and employees in those countries do not want their money tied up in stocks and bonds that could rapidly lose their value.

Here are some popular benefits offered in different countries that are not likely to be offered in the United States:

- ***India*** A popular benefit in India is health care benefits for aging parents of employees. Indian employees are more likely to have their parents living with them in a multigenerational household.
- ***Hong Kong*** Hong Kong workers often have coverage for traditional Chinese medicine as a supplement to their regular health insurance.
- ***Philippines*** Filipinos traditionally received bags of rice as a benefit from their employer. Employers later converted the sacks to "rice allowances," which were paid in cash, and now offer "flex" packages, whereby less tradition-minded workers can exchange the cash for items such as free mobile phones.
- ***Brazil*** It is more of an essential safety precaution than a benefit, but to foil kidnappers top executives in Brazil are chauffeured in bulletproof cars and followed by bodyguards.
- ***Russia*** Company-sponsored mortgages are viewed as an attractive benefit in Russia, where consumers have traditionally had less access to credit and the cost of living is high.

- *France* Some French employers offer the use of company-owned ski chalets and beach houses to employees for a nominal fee. This benefit is offered by some German companies, too. European employees have longer vacation periods to spend time at the mountains or the beach.
- *Sweden* In Sweden, each pair of parents of new born infants is entitled to 16 months of paid leave at 80 percent of salary starting from the birth of their infant. The parents are free to decide how to allocate the paid leave beyond the 60 days reserved for each parent.

Sources: Based on McGregor, J. (2008, January 28). The right perks: Global hiring means how different cultures view salaries, taxes, and benefits. *BusinessWeek*, 42–43. Working in Sweden—employee guide. (2010). *www.investsweden.se.*

Administering Benefits

We conclude this chapter by examining two critical issues in the administration of employee benefits: (1) the use of flexible benefits and (2) the importance of communicating benefits to employees. The HR department usually takes the lead in administering benefits, but managers need to help communicate options to employees, provide advice occasionally, keep records (vacation time, sick days), and be prepared to call on the HR department if disputes arise.

Flexible Benefits

Employees have different benefits needs, depending on a number of factors: age, marital status, whether the employee's spouse works and has duplicate benefits coverage, and the presence and ages of children in the household. A flexible benefits program allows employees to choose from a selection of employer-provided benefits such as vision care, dental care, health insurance coverage for dependents, additional life insurance coverage, long-term disability insurance, child care, elder care, more paid vacation days, legal services, and contributions to a 401(k) retirement plan.[94]

As Figure 12.2 shows, 12 percent of large- and medium-sized U.S. employers have a flexible benefits plan in place, among them TRW Systems, Educational Testing Services, Chrysler, and Verizon.[95] In the future, as the workforce becomes even more diverse, it is likely that more companies will implement flexible benefits plans.

TYPES OF FLEXIBLE BENEFITS PLANS The three most popular flexible benefits plans are modular plans, core-plus options plans, and flexible spending accounts.[96]

Modular plans consist of a series of different bundles of benefits or different levels of benefits coverage designed for different employee groups. For example, Module A might be the basic package paid for entirely by employer contributions. It would include only the most essential benefits and would be designed for single employees. Module B might include everything in Module A plus additional benefits such as family coverage under the health insurance plan, dental care, and child care. This module might be designed for married employees with young children and could require both employer and employee contributions.

Core-plus options plans consist of a core of essential benefits and a wide array of other benefits options that employees can add to the core. The core is designed to provide minimum economic security for employees, and usually includes basic health insurance, life insurance, long-term disability insurance, retirement benefits, and vacation days. Core-plus options plans give employees "benefits credits" that entitle them to "purchase" the additional benefits that they want. In most cases, all employees receive the same number of credits and may use them either to purchase higher levels of coverage in the core benefits package or to purchase additional benefits such as dental care or child care.

Flexible spending accounts are individual employee accounts funded by the employer, the employee (with pretax dollars), or both. Employees "pay" for the combination of benefits from their accounts. The result can be added take-home pay because employees do not pay taxes on the dollars that they have spent on benefits from their flexible spending accounts. Employee benefits administrators must design flexible spending accounts that conform to the rules specified in Section 125 of the Internal Revenue Code, which governs which benefits are exempt from taxes and which are not. For example, educational benefits and van pooling cannot be included in a flexible spending account because they are taxable benefits.

CHALLENGES WITH FLEXIBLE BENEFITS Flexible benefits offer employees the opportunity to tailor a benefits package that is meaningful to them at a reasonable cost to the company. However, they do pose some challenges to benefits administrators. These are:

- ***Adverse selection*** The *adverse selection* problem occurs when enough employees use a specific benefit more than the average employee does. Intensive use of a benefit can drive up the benefit's cost and force the employer either to increase spending on benefits or reduce the amount of coverage it provides. For example, employees who know they will need expensive dental work may select a dental-care option instead of some other benefit. Or employees who know they have a high probability of an early death (due to a health condition such as high blood pressure or even a terminal condition such as cancer) may choose extra life insurance coverage. In both cases, the cost of the insurance coverage will eventually be driven up.

  Benefits administrators can deal with the adverse selection problem by placing restrictions on benefits that are likely to result in adverse selection problems. For instance, the company might require those applying for higher life insurance coverage to successfully pass a physical examination. They can also bundle a broad package of benefits together into modules to ensure a more balanced use of each benefit.[97]
- ***Employees who make poor choices*** Sometimes employees make a poor choice of benefits and later regret it. For example, an employee who selects additional vacation days instead of long-term disability insurance is likely to regret his choice if he experiences a long-term illness that exceeds his accumulated amount of sick leave. Benefits administrators can manage this problem by (1) establishing core benefits that minimize an employee's risks and (2) communicating benefits choices effectively so that employees make appropriate choices.

- ***Administrative complexity*** A flexible benefits program is difficult to administer and control. Employees must be kept informed of changes in the cost of benefits, the coverage of benefits, and their utilization of benefits. They must also be given the opportunity to change their benefits selection periodically. In addition, the potential for errors in recordkeeping is high. Fortunately, computer software packages can help the HR department manage the recordkeeping aspect of benefits administration. Benefits consultants can assist HR staff in selecting and installing these software programs.

Benefits Communication

Benefits communication is a critical part of administering an employee benefits program. Many employees in companies with excellent benefits packages have never been informed of the value of these benefits and are therefore likely to underestimate their worth.[98] The two major obstacles to effective benefits communication are (1) the increasing complexity of benefits packages and (2) employers' reluctance to devote enough resources to explain these complex packages to employees.

Traditionally, benefits have been communicated via a group meeting during new-employee orientation or a benefits handbook that describes each benefit and its level of coverage. In today's dynamic world of employee benefits, however, more sophisticated communication media (such as video presentations on a company intranet and computer software that generates personalized benefits status reports for each employee) are needed. Here are a few of the approaches employers are taking to inform employees about additions to or changes in their benefits:

- General Electric (GE) uses its benefits Web site to give its employees access to benefits information 24 hours a day. GE's benefits Web site has reduced the number of calls to its benefits department by 25,000 calls per month, resulting in substantial cost savings of $175,000 per month. GE reported that a telephone inquiry to the benefits department cost $8.00, whereas a Web site inquiry cost only $1.00.[99]
- In its innovative 15½ minute video, the Los Angeles County Employees Retirement Association (LACERA) uses a Sam Spade–type detective character to "crack the case" of confusing retirement plans. During the course of the video the animated detective discovers what confusing terms like *noncontributory* and *defined benefits* mean—and so do LACERA's 500 new members each month.[100]

Figure 12.10 lists some of the ways a company can keep its employees informed about their benefits or answer questions about coverage.

Benefits Web Sites
Let employees access information about their benefits from home, a hotel, or anywhere with an Internet connection. Employees can also enroll in a different HMO health insurance plan, for example, on the Web site without having to go to the company benefits office and wait for an appointment with a benefits specialist.

Colorful Fliers or Newsletters
Can be mailed to employees' homes so they can read them at their leisure.

Posters
Eye-catching posters can be an effective way to announce enrollment dates for benefits or notify employees of upcoming changes to their benefits. They must be brief and designed to be noticed.

Audio-Visual Presentations
Slides and videos that present concepts in an upbeat fashion can ensure that employees at different locations receive the same information.

Toll-Free Number
Lets employees call to enroll in a benefits program or hear automated information about these programs 24 hours a day.

Computer Software Package
Allows employees to play "what-if" scenarios with their benefits. For example, they can determine the amount that will be deducted from their paychecks if they enroll in medical plan A as opposed to plan B, or how much money they would save by age 60 if they contribute 6 percent a year to the 401(k) plan.

FIGURE 12.10
Selected Methods of Employee Benefits Communication

Sources: Based on Hope Health. (2012). *Employee benefits communications: New approaches for a new environment.* Florence, SC: Hope Health; Wojcik, J. (2004, December 6). As workers' benefit needs change, so do methods of communication. *Business Insurance,* 10–11; and Cohen, A., and Cohen, S. (1998, November/December). Benefits Web sites: Controlling costs while enhancing communication. *Journal of Compensation and Benefits,* 11–18.

Summary and Conclusions

An Overview of Benefits

Benefits are group membership rewards that provide security for employees and their families. Benefits cost companies about $19,947 per year for the average employee. The cost of employee benefits has increased dramatically in recent years. Although benefits programs are usually centrally controlled in organizations, managers need to be familiar with them so they can counsel employees, recruit job applicants, and make effective managerial decisions.

The Benefits Strategy

The design of a benefits package should be aligned with the business's overall compensation strategy. The benefits strategy requires making choices in three areas: (1) benefits mix, (2) benefits amount, and (3) flexibility of benefits.

Legally Required Benefits

The four benefits that almost all employers must provide are Social Security, workers' compensation, unemployment insurance, and unpaid family and medical leave. These benefits form the core of an employee's benefits package. All other employer-provided benefits are designed to either complement or augment the legally required benefits.

Voluntary Benefits

Businesses often provide five types of voluntary benefits to their employees: (1) Health insurance provides health care for workers and their families. The major types of health insurance plans are traditional health insurance, health maintenance organizations (HMOs), and preferred provider organizations (PPOs). (2) Retirement benefits consist of deferred compensation set aside for an employee's retirement. Funds for retirement benefits can come from employer contributions, employee contributions, or a combination of the two. The Employee Retirement Income Security

Act (ERISA) is the major law governing the management of retirement benefits. There are two main types of retirement benefit plans: defined benefit plans and defined contribution plans. In a defined benefit plan, the employer promises to provide a specified amount of retirement income to an employee. A defined contribution plan requires employees to share with their employer some of the risk of and responsibility for managing their retirement assets. The most popular defined contribution plans are 401(k) plans, individual retirement accounts (IRAs), simplified employee pension plans (SEPs), and profit-sharing Keogh plans. (3) Insurance plans protect employees or their survivors from financial disaster in the case of untimely death, accidents that result in disabilities, and serious illnesses. Two kinds of insurance likely to be included in a benefits package are life insurance and long-term disability insurance. (4) Paid time off, which gives employees a break to pursue leisure activities or take care of personal and civic duties, includes sick leave, vacations, severance pay, holidays, and other paid time off. (5) Employee services consist of a cluster of tax-free or tax-preferred services that employers provide to improve the quality of their employees' work or personal life. One of the most valued employee services is child-care benefits.

Administering Benefits

Two important issues involving benefits administration are the use of flexible benefits and communicating benefits to employees. Although the benefits administration is likely to be performed by an HR benefits specialist, managers need to understand their companies' benefits package well enough to help communicate benefits to their employees and keep records.

Key Terms

benefits mix, 394
coinsurance, 391
Consolidated Omnibus Budget Reconciliation Act (COBRA) of 1985, 402
contributions, 391
copayment, 391
deductible, 391
defined benefit plan or pension, 409
defined contribution plan, 409
employee benefits or indirect compensation, 389
Employee Retirement Income Security Act (ERISA), 408
Family and Medical Leave Act (FMLA) of 1993, 400
flexible or cafeteria benefits program, 391
Health Insurance Portability and Accountability Act (HIPAA), 402
health maintenance organization (HMO), 404
health savings account (HSA), 406
high-deductible health plan (HDHP), 407
Medicare, 397
Patient and Affordable Care Act (PACA), 403
Pension Benefit Guaranty Corporation (PBGC), 408
portable benefits, 408
preexisting condition, 402
preferred provider organization (PPO), 405
premium, 404
Social Security, 395
supplemental unemployment benefits (SUB), 399
unemployment insurance, 398
vesting, 408
workers' compensation, 397

Watch It!

Elm City Market: Designing and Administering Benefits. If your instructor has assigned this, go to **mymanagementlab.com** to watch a video case and answer questions.

Discussion Questions

12-1. How might the increasing diversity of the workforce affect the design of employee benefits packages in large companies?

12-2. Paid time off (PTO) policies pool vacation, sick leave, personal days, and floating holidays into a bank of days that employees can have for personal use. Normally, the use of one of these days requires notification of the supervisor in advance. However,

PTO can also be used for unplanned reasons, such as sickness and emergencies. Suppose an employee feels he or she needs a "mental health" day and calls in sick to the supervisor in order to use a PTO day to avoid the routine of going to work that day. What are the ethics and consequences of using a PTO day this way? What would you do if you were the manager?

12-3. Why should younger employees (those in their 20s and 30s) care about retirement benefits?

12-4. What is the average number of paid holidays per year that most employees receive from their employers? What are the usual arrangements in terms of remuneration if employees work on designated national holidays? What other paid leave entitlements do most employees receive? Do these entitlements differ according to industries or length of service?

 12-5. Some benefits experts claim that unemployment insurance and workers' compensation benefits create a disincentive to work. Why do you think they say this? Do you agree or disagree with this position?

MyManagementLab®

If your instructor has assigned this, go to **mymanagementlab.com** for the following Assisted-graded writing questions:

12-6. How do managed-care health insurance plans (HMOs and PPOs) differ from traditional fee-for-service health insurance plans? What are the advantages and disadvantages of each to the employer? To the employee?

12-7. The United States mandates only four required benefits, yet U.S. employers provide many other benefits—such as health insurance, retirement benefits, and paid vacations—voluntarily. What are the reasons (at least three) that so many employers provide these benefits even though they are not legally required to do so?

12-8. Cost containment is an important issue in employee benefits programs. Provide at least three employee benefits where cost containment is a high priority and explain how it works for each benefit.

You Manage It! 1: Global

Australia's 'Super' Retirement Program Is a Source of National Pride

Australia currently has one of the most highly regarded retirement systems in the world. It is based on compulsory employee contributions that are put into a retirement fund. The retirement system is called Superannuation and it functions similarly to a 401(k) retirement plan in the United States. Currently employers in Australia are required to send 9 percent of an employee's salary into the Superannuation program, which provides a menu of different investment funds that allows employees to make choices regarding how to allocate their retirement funds into investments that differ according to risk. Employees' contributions and investment earnings are taxed at 15 percent, substantially below the ordinary income tax rate. Around 20 percent of employees put additional earnings into the retirement fund and some employers match the contributions that employees put in the fund. More than 90 percent of employed Australians contribute to Superannuation, compared to 40 percent of American employees who participate in their employer's retirement plan.

The Superannuation retirement program augments a national pension system in Australia that is funded by taxes and is similar to the Social Security retirement program in the United States. At present, the Superannuation program has grown to an amount equal to the equivalent of $1.5 trillion, which represents over half the amount that Americans have put into their 401(k) accounts, despite the fact that the United States has a population that is 14 times larger than that of Australia. Consequently, experts estimate that an Australian employee who contributes to the Superannuation program over a 30-year period can expect to have a retirement income equivalent to 70 percent of his or her preretirement income. This is the percentage of retirement income that financial experts recommend.

The Superannuation program began in 1992 and initially it required a compulsory contribution of 3 percent of an employee's salary. Over the years, Australians have voted for increases in the size of the mandatory contributions to Superannuation, so that the employee contribution now currently stands at 9 percent of salary. However, in a recent election Australians approved a gradual year-by-year increase in the contribution amount, which will end up at 12 percent by 2019 because people in future generations will be likely to require a greater amount of retirement funds to cover longer life expectancies. By comparison, U.S. employees save an average of about 6 percent of their salaries into a 401(k) retirement fund, and consequently many Americans are concerned that they will not have enough retirement income saved when they decide to retire. Due to the success of the Superannuation program, when Australians think about their retirement they have a good reason to smile.

Critical Thinking Questions

12-9. What can retirement benefits specialists in the United States learn from the successful experience of the Australian Superannuation retirement program? Do you think that American citizens would support a law that requires that 9 percent of employee salaries must be contributed into a 401(k) retirement fund? Explain your reasoning.

12-10. Although Australia's Superannuation program has been successful, experts have pointed out a flaw in the design—it does not provide for an annuity option for most of the retirees. An annuity provides a consistent retirement income that continues for the life of a retiree and it is created when individuals voluntarily roll over their retirement fund accumulations into the annuity. Why do you think experts consider that the lack of an annuity option in the Superannuation program could be a problem for Australian retirees?

Team Exercise

12-11. Although the Superannuation retirement program in Australia uses a defined contribution retirement plan design, retirement benefits in many countries base their retirement system on a defined benefit design. For example, the retirement system in France consists of a pension plan (i.e., defined benefit) that has the following features: (a) retiree must reach age 65 to receive full retirement benefits and have worked for a total of 40 years; (b) the retirement salary is based on providing 70 percent of the average salary over the 20 best salary years during an individual's employment history; (c) the system is funded on taxes taken from the incomes of the working population in France and these funds are transferred directly to the population of retirees. With a group of four or five students compare the advantages and disadvantages of the French retirement system based on a defined benefit plan, and the Australian retirement system which is explained in the case presentation. Which system does your team prefer? Be prepared to share your team findings with the class.

Experiential Exercise: Individual

12-12. The Melbourne Mercer Global Pension Index, compiled by Mercer and the Australian Centre for Financial Studies, is a comparison of 18 pension schemes that together account for around 50 percent of the world's population. The pension schemes are compared using over 40 different indicators. Top of the class with an A grade for its pension scheme was Denmark, the United Kingdom scored a C+, and the United States, Germany, and France were given straight Cs. Countries at the bottom of this list, receiving the lowest grade D, were India, China, Japan, and South Korea. As the best pension provider, Denmark has a public basic pension scheme with a means-tested supplementary pension benefit. In addition, it has fully funded mandatory private schemes. These are organized by large funds as opposed to spate company. Investigate your country's pension provisions and compare them to that of its near neighbors. Do you prefer any scheme in particular? Explain.

Sources: Based on Summers, N. (2013, June 3). Retirement saving done right. *Bloomberg Businessweek,* 44–45; Greenhouse, S. (2013, May 15). Retirement: How they do it elsewhere. *New York Times,* F1, F7; Australian Securities & Investments Commission. (2013). How super works. *MoneySmart. www.moneysmart.gov.au*; White, J. (2013, March 21). 11 things about 401(k) plans we need to fix now. *CNBC Personal Finance. www.cnbc.com*; Francoz, K. (2010, September 23). Retirement reform in France 2010. Peter G. Peterson Foundation. *www.pgpf.org*. Evans, R. (2013, March 3). The best pensions in the world. *The Telegraph. www.telegraph.co.uk.*

You Manage It! 2: Ethics/Social Responsibility

Should Employers Penalize Employees Who Do Not Adopt Healthy Habits?

In an effort to motivate workers to kick unhealthy habits, U.S. companies are hitting them where it hurts—their wallets. Employers who provide health insurance often use financial incentives such as contributions toward health insurance premiums to encourage workers to participate in wellness programs, such as smoking cessation or nutrition improvement courses. Now some companies are penalizing employees who are overweight, smoke, or have high cholesterol, for example, and do not participate in supplementary wellness programs. The penalty for not participating in a wellness programs is a higher health insurance premium for the employee, so that in extreme cases the employee's insurance deductible could rise by $2,000 per year.

Although the motive behind company policies that pressure employees to adopt healthier lifestyles is to reduce health insurance costs, the use of financial penalties could put a firm at risk of lawsuits. The U.S. Equal Employment Opportunity Commission indicates it is looking into wellness program policies to see if some of them violate the Americans with Disabilities Act (ADA).

The Tribune Company, which owns newspapers in Chicago and other cities, applies a monthly surcharge of $100 to family health insurance premiums of workers or dependents who use tobacco. Wal-Mart applies an annual surcharge of $2,000 to employees who smoke. Clarion Health, an Indianapolis-based hospital chain, will charge employees who are smokers $5 each paycheck. Employment law experts recommend that a company should not discriminate against smokers by asking them to pay higher insurance premiums unless the higher fee is derived from a broader effort to help smokers quit smoking.

Another way employers are making intrusive interventions into employees' health habits is by eliminating unhealthy foods that employees enjoy for snacks or meals within the company premises. Recently the HR director at Littler Mendelson, a San Francisco law firm, eliminated high carbohydrate and sugary breakfast foods that employees enjoyed, such as Krispy Kreme donuts, gooey sweet rolls, and huge muffins. These were replaced with yogurt, hard-boiled eggs, cottage cheese, and fresh fruit. Other companies, such as Yamaha Corp. of America and Caterpillar, are putting more healthful foods in corporate break rooms, cafeterias, and vending machines, while dumping donuts and other unhealthy foods. Florida Power & Light, Dow Corning, and Sprint all charge more money for unhealthy food and less for healthier fare. For example, Caterpillar offered garden burgers in its cafeteria for one dollar, and sales soared fivefold.

One company, Crown Laboratories in Johnson City, Tennessee, has gone so far as to require each employee to take an annual health assessment to force employees to live healthier lives. Based on a number of indicators, including blood pressure, weight, physical activity, and cholesterol levels, the employees are given a "wellness

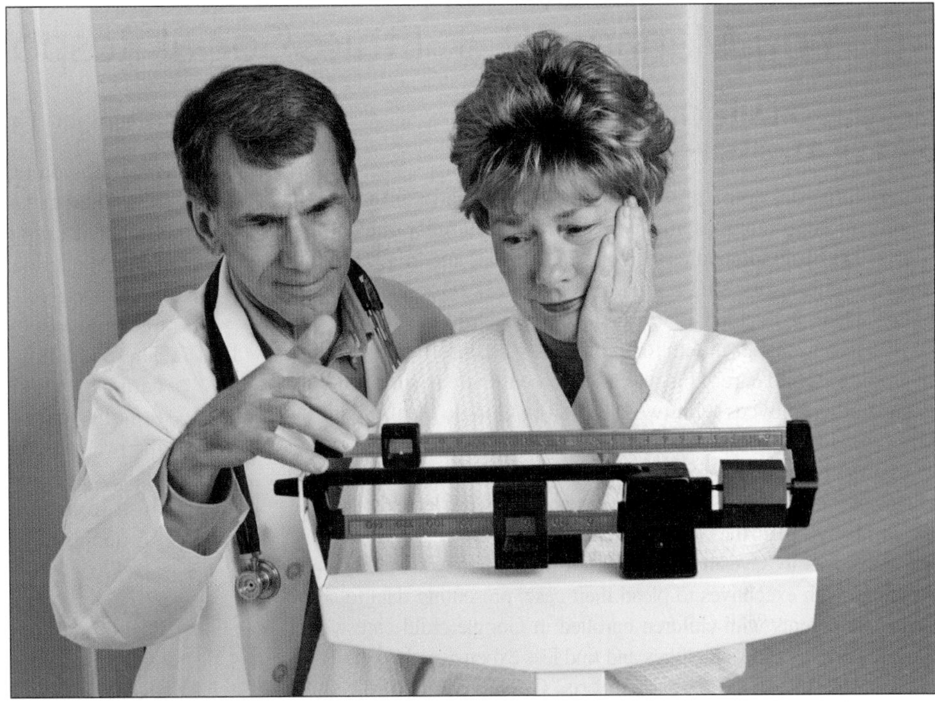

It has become common for companies to offer insurance discounts to employees who maintain a healthy weight. Some companies, however, are now offering standard health insurance plans only to those employees who are considered healthy. In these firms, overweight employees and employees who smoke are eligible for plans that have higher out-of-pocket expenses.

Source: forestpath/Shutterstock.

number" of up to 24 points. Those who improve their scores by at least 3 points a year, or maintain a score of 20 or more, will get a $500 bonus and extra days off. More than two-thirds of workers at Crown Laboratories are clinically obese, so the bonus compensates slender employees more than overweight ones. Smoking is officially against company policy, even during off-hours, and nicotine levels are measured in the health assessment. Employees who smoke are given approximately six months to quit, and if they don't they are required to pay for their own health insurance premiums.

Critical Thinking Questions

12-13. Why are employers implementing policies that require employees to adopt healthier lifestyles? Do you think it is ethical when an employer decides to penalize employees who eat their favorite junk foods and gain weight or smoke cigarettes, which are a legal product?

12-14. The enforcement of the wellness policies described in this case often falls into the domain of the HR staff, and they may be viewed by employees as the "wellness police." How might this enforcer role undermine the credibility of HR staff in their work in other areas—such as EEOC compliance, training, and compensation—that require managers and employees to cooperate?

Team Exercise

12-15. With a group of four or five students, discuss the legal implications of penalizing employees for not adopting healthy habits within wellness programs, as explained in the case. For example, can overweight employees seek protection under the ADA for being discriminated against by an employer that requires them to pay higher health insurance premiums than nonoverweight employees? What about when employers deny workers bonuses because they are overweight? Can an employee who smokes only away from the job and is penalized with higher health insurance rates claim under the law that he or she is a victim of discrimination? In fact, a number of states have passed smoker rights laws that protect the rights of smokers to use tobacco products within a state. Would these laws protect workers who smoke from being assessed higher health insurance rates by employers for violating an employee wellness policy when they smoke? Be prepared to present your findings to the other students in the class when called upon by your instructor.

Experiential Exercise: Individual

12-16. Suppose you worked at a company that implemented a new wellness policy that required that you take health screenings each year for weight, cholesterol, tobacco use, and other health indicators. According to the wellness policy, if you do not achieve a high enough wellness score you will be required to make changes in your diet, exercise habits, or eliminate tobacco. Those who do not comply with the wellness policy face financial penalties. How would this wellness policy make you feel about working for this employer? Would you feel better (the employer cares about my health), worse (the employer is being unfair by trying to regulate my lifestyle), or indifferent to your employer for having this wellness policy? How would the policy affect your job behavior? Would you increase your effort, maintain it, decrease it, or start looking for another job? What explains your positive or negative reactions to this wellness policy? When called upon by your instructor, be prepared to offer your reactions to the wellness policy to other members of the class and see how they compare.

Sources: Based on Tozi, J. (2013, May 20). The doctor will see you now. And now. And now. *Bloomberg Businessweek*, 27–28; *The Economist*. (2011, July 30). Keeping employees healthy: Trim staff, fat profits, 58–59; Abelson, R. (2011, November 17). The smokers'surcharge. *New York Times*, B1, B4; Conlin, M. (2008, April 28). Hide the Doritos! Here comes HR: With an eye on soaring health care costs, companies are getting pushy about employees' eating habits. *BusinessWeek*, 94–96; Knight, V. (2007, December 4). Employers tell workers to get healthy or pay up. *Wall Street Journal*, D4; Gill, D. (2006, April). Get healthy . . . or else. *Inc.*, 35–37.

 You Manage It! 3: Ethics/Social Responsibility

Google's On-Site Child-Care Policy Stirs up a Controversy

Google provides some of the best employee benefits offered anywhere, an important reason why it was ranked number one on *Fortune*'s 100 Best Companies to Work For in 2012 and 2013. Despite this recognition of being a great place to work, Google stumbled badly when it decided to raise its on-site child-care cost from $1,425 to $2,500 per month to employees who enroll their children in Google's child care. This was a 75 percent increase in child-care costs, and employees with two children in Google's child-care facility would pay $57,000 per year, up from $33,000.

At the first of three focus groups set up to discuss the changes in child-care benefit costs, parents wept openly. As word leaked out about the company's plan, the Google parents began to fight back. They came up with ideas to save money and used the company's weekly open meetings with executives to plead their case, presenting data to show that most parents with children enrolled in Google child care would have to leave Google's facilities and find less expensive child care.

As a result of the parent's efforts, Google decided to reduce its price increase only slightly and phase in the higher price over five quarters, but the original decision to raise the price remains basically unchanged. At one of the weekly meetings, according to several people who attended the meeting, one of the Google founders, Sergey Brin, said that he had no sympathy for the parents and that he was tired of Google employees who felt entitled to perks such as bottled water and M&M's.

Google's on-site child-care facility is one of the finest child-care facilities in the country. It is designed for highly creative children who are encouraged to chart their own paths of learning. The unique facility has the best teachers with the most advanced teaching philosophies and offers the children highly creative toys to play with. To run this facility, Google had been subsidizing each child to the tune of $37,000 per year, compared to the average of $12,000 per year that other comparable Silicon Valley, California, companies contribute to the child-care benefit. In addition, Google had a waiting list of 700 employees who were waiting up to two years to enroll their children into Google's on-site child care. Google managers gathered data that predicted that by raising the price of the child care to the new price, the waiting list would disappear, because price would be used as a mechanism to ration child care to those who really wanted it for their child. This is an economically efficient solution, but is it a fair and just solution?

Google may be providing the greatest child care available, but so what? Does it matter how good the child care is, when only the wealthiest employees can use it? Wouldn't it have been better to redesign the child-care plan, which is targeted at wealthy parents and children with a potential for genius, and instead offer child care to all employees who have children? Shouldn't Google rethink its attitude about child care and view it as a benefit that should be available to every parent, rather than a luxury available to those who are willing to pay for it?

Critical Thinking Questions

12-17. What do you think about Google's policy to increase parents' financial contribution for child-care benefits? Why is Google asking parents to pay more for the child care benefits? What does this tell you about what happens when a company gives a benefit and then threatens its availability to employees by raising its price?

12-18. There is a long waiting list for Google's on-site child-care benefit. Google's solution is to let the market ration the spaces to enroll children in child care by raising the price. Is this a good idea? What principle is Google using to decide who gets child care? Do you agree with this? If not, what principle of allocation would you use for deciding whose child gets to enroll in on-site child care?

12-19. What do you think of the fact that Google's child care is designed for children who are intellectually gifted and uses expensive learning techniques and highly paid teachers?

Team Exercise

12-20. With a group of four or five students, assume that you are consultants that Google has invited to study the controversy surrounding the change in cost of the child-care benefits policy due to the emotional reactions of the parents who are affected by it. First, group members need to gather some background information on Google's other benefits it offers to employees by rereading the opening vignette of this chapter and visiting a site that explains Google's child care and other benefits (see *http://computer.howstuffworks.com/googleplex4.htm*). Then discuss whether the child-care policy should remain unchanged or be revised so that it is consistent with the other Google employee benefits. What changes (if any) to the child-care benefit plan does your group recommend? What is the basis of your recommendation? Be prepared to share your group's findings with other members of the class when asked by your instructor.

Experiential Exercise: Individual

12-21. Assume you have a child enrolled at an on-site child care facility at the company where you work. This policy lets you have lunch with your child every day, and you can drop in and see your child playing with other children whenever you feel like it. How would you react when the company decides to increase your cost by 75 percent over what you have been paying (similar to what happened at Google) and this unexpected cost increase strains your budget? What would you do? How would you feel toward the company? What actions would you take to persuade management that this is an unfair decision that discriminates against less affluent employees and favors the wealthier ones? Be prepared to discuss your answers to these questions with other members of the class when called upon by your instructor.

Sources: Nocera, J. (2008, July 5). On day care, Google makes a rare fumble. *New York Times*, A1, A12; Thomas, O. (2008, June 13). Google daycare now a luxury for Larry and Sergey's inner circle. *www.valleywag.com; The HR Capitalist.* (2008, July 16). Comparing the cost of Google daycare with the rest of the free world. *www.hrcapitalist.com*.

You Manage It! 4: Customer-Driven HR

IBM's 401(k) Plan Sets the Standard

IBM currently uses its 401(k) defined contribution plan as the primary retirement benefit for all of its 100,000 U.S. employees. The company has devoted a lot of resources to designing its 401(k) plan with many of the latest features. These efforts have reduced some of the uncertainty that employees face about their financial security because most companies, including IBM, have dropped paternalistic defined benefit pension plans in favor of the riskier defined contribution plans. Defined contribution plans require that employees take responsibility for managing the allocation of their financial assets for retirement and bear the risk if their investments do not perform up to their expectations.

When designing its 401(k) retirement plan, IBM adopted many of the best features from plans at other companies and negotiated low fees from investment companies that manage employees' retirement assets. The IBM 401(k) plan boasts a 94 percent participation rate among U.S. employees and an average balance of $127,000, which is more than double the national average. The following are some of the key features of the IBM 401(k) plan:

- IBM matches 100 percent of employee contributions to the 401(k) plan, up to 6 percent of base salary. The typical company match in industries in which IBM competes is only 50 percent of employee contributions, up to 6 percent of base salary.
- IBM provides financial coaches to assist employees and their families with decisions about allocating their retirement funds into different types of investments in financial securities. The financial coaches are paid by IBM to give one-on-one advice to employees about any aspect of their financial lives. Most companies do not offer this service to employees and expect them to figure out how to invest their retirement funds on their own.
- The IBM 401(k) plan uses an opt-out feature that automatically enrolls employees into the retirement plan unless they decide to opt out. Another feature is auto-escalation, which automatically increases employees' contributions each year to coincide with annual raises in pay, unless employees opt out.

Critical Thinking Questions

12-22. The opt-out feature of the 401(k) plan is designed to increase the enrollment of employees in the plan because, without this feature, 25 percent of employees on average are not likely to enroll in it. What do you think would happen if the IBM 401(k) plan had an opt-in feature instead? [An opt-in feature would mean that all IBM employees must take positive steps to enroll in the 401(k) plan, because the default position is that an employee is not enrolled in the 401(k) plan.] In the majority of companies, employees must opt in to a 401(k) plan. Are there any advantages to a company that uses an opt-in requirement for enrolling employees in the plan?

12-23. By offering its employees one of the best 401(k) plans available, how does IBM benefit from this investment in its employees? How might employee behavior and performance be affected by the IBM 401(k) plan in its current form? What changes in employee behavior and performance would you expect if IBM decided to modify its 401(k) plan to be just average in the market (for example, a 50-percent company match to employee contributions, up to 6 percent of base salary) compared to what other competing firms offer for employee retirement?

Team Exercise

12-24. According to Fidelity, one of the largest financial services firms, the average 401(k) fund lost 31 percent of its value between 2007 and 2009 in the aftermath of the financial crisis. People who were close to retirement realized that they would need to work for several additional years to have enough savings to be able to retire. Exacerbating this situation was the fact that many companies needed to economize their labor costs during the recession and decided to eliminate the employer matching funds for employees' 401(k) accounts until their economic prospects improved. In light of these events, does it make sense for employees to continue to contribute to their company 401(k) plan? With a group of three or four classmates, decide whether it still makes sense for employees to contribute to their company 401(k) plan or not. In your presentation, compare the 401(k) to other alternatives that employees have for saving for their retirement.

Experiential Exercise: Individual

12-25. This exercise is designed to raise your awareness about 401(k) retirement plans. Assume that the company you work for has a 401(k) retirement benefit—most companies do have these plans. Answer the following questions concerning 401(k) retirement benefits:

a. Will you enroll in the 401(k) plan as soon as you join the company? If yes, why did you decide to join right away? If no, when will you decide to enroll in the 401(k) plan?

b. What percentage of your base salary (between 1 and 15 percent) will you set aside to contribute to your 401(k) plan? What factors affect how much you will save in your 401(k) plan?

c. What percentage of your retirement contributions will you put into mutual funds that invest in stocks? What percentage of your retirement contributions will you put into mutual funds that invest in bonds?

d. What would you do if there is another financial crisis, similar to the one during 2007 to 2009, and your retirement investments in your 401(k) fund drop in value by 40 percent?

Be prepared to share the answers to these questions with other members of the class if called upon by the instructor.

Sources: Based on Feldman, A. (2009, July 13). Why IBM's 401(k) is the leader of the pack. *BusinessWeek*, 58–62; Kansas, D. (2009, June 22). Has the 401(k) failed? *Fortune*, 94–98; Franklin, M. (2010, October). Fix your 401(k). *Kiplinger's Personal Finance*, 45–51.

Endnotes

Scan for Endnotes or go to http://www.pearsonglobaleditions.com/Gomez-Mejia.

CHAPTER 13 Developing Employee Relations

MyManagementLab®

When you see this icon, visit **www.mymanagementlab.com** for activities that are applied, personalized, and offer immediate feedback.

CHALLENGES

After reading this chapter, you should be able to deal more effectively with the following challenges:

1. **Know** the roles of the manager and the employee relations specialist.
2. **Become** aware of developing employee communications.
3. **Learn** practices for encouraging effective communications.
4. **Describe** employee recognition programs.

One approach companies are using to sustain positive employee relations and morale is by valuing fun in the workplace. This trend was displayed in the popular TV series *The Office*, which featured a manager, a character named Michael Scott, who likes to play light-hearted pranks on his employees and encourages them to play pranks on him and each other. In one episode, Scott invites the entire office to a local restaurant where he presents a recognition award to each employee based on their having done something humorous during the year, modeling the event after an Academy Awards show. After receiving the award from Scott, each employee attempts to make a humorous speech to thank their coworkers for their support, or lack of it. For example, one of the female characters receives an award for having the cleanest tennis shoes, after which she thanks a long list of people for making her achievement possible.

Source: Monkey Business Images/Shutterstock.

One real-life company that institutionalizes fun in the workplace is Blazer Industries, a $35 million maker of modular buildings located in Aumsville, Oregon. Marv Shetler, founder and CEO of Blazer Industries, appointed Kendra Cox, a project manager with an outgoing personality, to be a "chief fun director," a role like a cruise director on a ship. Kendra organizes fun activities, such as holiday parties and pizza nights, and is responsible for taking candid photos of colleagues having fun. She is also responsible for personally inviting each of the 220 employees to events.

Paul Spiegelman, CEO of Beryl Companies, a call-center company in Bedford, Texas, plans fun events for his employees to reduce the stress and tedium of their jobs (the call-center industry is known for low morale and high attrition). One time he arranged for the staging of a murder mystery on the call-center floor, and teams spent the next eight weeks solving it. Every August there is a talent show where employees sing, play an instrument, or perform a stand-up comedy routine to try to get a laugh. The point of these events is to have fun on a consistent basis. Often the CEO allows himself to be on the receiving end of a joke so that employees can see that he does not take himself too seriously. On one occasion, he roller-skated in a matador outfit and another time he played a short-order cook at a company party.[1]

The Managerial Perspective

By instigating fun in the workplace, the managers in the examples given strive to provide an environment with positive employee relations, the subject of this chapter. Companies with strong employee relations benefit because their employees are highly motivated to expend their best efforts. In exchange, the employees expect to be treated fairly and recognized for their achievements. To develop and sustain relations, employers must keep employees informed of company policies and strategies. That way, employees can learn new behaviors or skills as needed and understand the workings of the firm more fully. In addition, employers must have policies that allow employees to discuss problems with or communicate important information to company representatives who can respond effectively.

As a manager, you will play a key role in employee relations. You must listen to your employees' concerns and feelings, observe their experiences, and help keep employees informed about changes in the business and the effects of such changes.

HR specialists also play a crucial role in employee relations. If they develop communication policies and procedures that apply appropriate communication tools in a timely manner, employees can access more abundant, higher-quality information and can communicate more effectively with management. Managers and HR specialists must work in partnership to ensure that the communication policies and procedures bolster employee relations.

In this chapter, we explore how managers and employee relations specialists can work together to coordinate an employee relations program. Next, we present a model of communication and explore specific policies that give employees access to important information. Finally, we examine some programs for recognizing employees' individual and team contributions to company goals.

✪ Learn It!

If your professor has chosen to assign this go to **www.mymanagementlab.com** to see what you should particularly focus on, and take the chapter 13 warmup.

The Roles of the Manager and the Employee Relations Specialist

Having good *employee relations* means providing fair and consistent treatment to all employees so that they will be committed to the organization.[2] Companies with good employee relations are likely to have an HR strategy that places a high value on employees as stakeholders in the business. Employees who are treated as *stakeholders* have certain rights within the organization and can expect to be treated with dignity and respect. For example, Johnson & Johnson, a company known for its excellent employee relations, is committed to a philosophy of respect for the individual. To foster good employee relations, managers must listen to and understand what employees are saying and experiencing, keep them informed about what management plans to do with the business, and tell them how those plans may affect their jobs. They should also give employees the freedom to air grievances about management decisions. There may be good reasons for not changing the decision, but management should at least listen to the grievances.

employee relations representative
A member of the HR department who ensures that company policies are followed and consults with both supervisors and employees on specific employee relations problems.

employee relations policy
A policy designed to communicate management's thinking and practices concerning employee-related matters and prevent problems in the workplace from becoming serious.

Effective employee relations require cooperation between managers and **employee relations representatives**. These specialists are members of the HR department who act as internal consultants to the business. They try to ensure that company policies and procedures are followed and they advise both supervisors and employees on specific employee relations problems. **Employee relations policies** provide channels to resolve such problems before they become serious.

For example, an employee whose supervisor has denied her request for two weeks' vacation (to which she is entitled according to the employee handbook) may ask the employee relations representative to speak to her supervisor and clarify why she is being denied her preferred vacation time. Or, a supervisor may request assistance because he suspects that one of his subordinates has an alcohol abuse problem that is affecting job performance. In both these cases, the employee relations representative will try to resolve the problem within the letter and spirit of the appropriate employment policy, while carefully balancing the interests of the supervisor, the employee, and the company.

Employee relations representatives may also develop new policies that help maintain fairness and efficiency in the workplace. The client in this situation may be a top manager who needs assistance in drafting a new policy on smoking in the workplace or the hiring of employees' spouses and other relatives.

Developing Employee Communications

Many companies have found that the key to a good employee relations program is a *communication channel* that gives employees access to important information and an opportunity to express their ideas and feelings. When supervisors are familiar with employment policies and employees are aware of their rights, there is less opportunity for misunderstandings to arise and productivity to drop.

Because corporations are very complex, they must develop numerous communication channels to move information up, down, and across the organizational structure. For instance, Intel provides many communication channels that allow employees and managers to speak with one another and share information. Managers communicate with their employees by walking around and talking to them informally, sponsoring newsletters, and providing a Web site with key employment policies. Employees give feedback to managers through e-mail, memos, meetings, and other forms of face-to-face communication. As today's organizations have delegated more responsibilities and decision-making authority to employees, the importance of making more information available to employees has increased substantially.[3]

Types of Information

Two forms of information are sent and received in communications: facts and feelings. *Facts* are pieces of information that can be objectively measured or described. Examples are the cost of a computer, the daily defect rate in a manufacturing plant, and the size of the deductible payment in the company-sponsored health insurance policy. Recent technological advances have made factual information more accessible to more employees than ever before. Facts can be stored in databases and widely distributed to employees by networks of personal computers.

Feelings are employees' emotional responses to the decisions made or actions taken by managers or other employees. Managers who implement decisions must be able to anticipate or respond to the feelings of the employees who are affected by those decisions. If they cannot or do not, the plan may fail. For example, a public university changed its health insurance coverage without consulting the employees affected by the change. When these employees learned of their diminished coverage, they responded so negatively that the manager of employee benefits resigned. (The health insurance policy was subsequently changed to be more favorable to the employees.)

A company must be especially careful of employees' feelings when it is restructuring or downsizing and laying off a considerable portion of its workforce. A production employee at a large East Coast manufacturing firm remembers how top management kept issuing memos that said, in effect, "we're doing fine, we're doing fine," and then suddenly announced layoffs. Survivors of the layoff were shocked and hurt and became highly distrustful of management.[4]

Organizations need to design communication channels that allow employees to communicate facts and feelings. In many cases, these channels must provide for face-to-face communication because many feelings are conveyed nonverbally.[5] Employees cannot write on a piece of paper or record on a computer database their complex emotional reactions to a decision that they fear will cost them their jobs.

How Communication Works

Figure 13.1 is a simple representation of the communications process within an organization. Communication starts with a *sender*, who has a message to send to the *receiver*. The sender must *encode* the message and select a *communication channel* that will deliver it to the receiver. In

FIGURE 13.1
The Communications Process Within an Organization

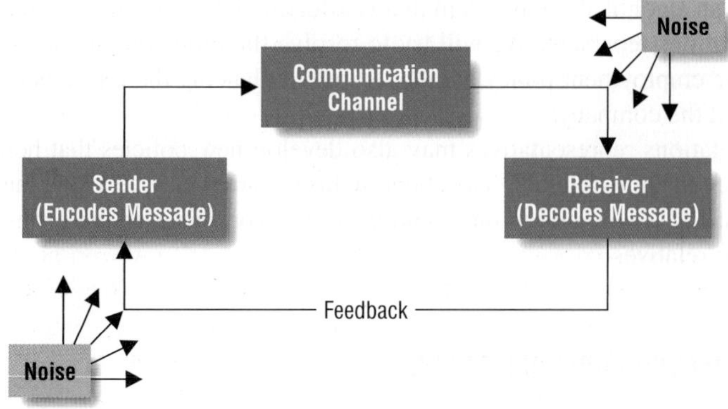

communicating facts, the message may be encoded with words, numbers, or digital symbols; in communicating feelings, it may be encoded as body language or tone of voice.

Some communication channels are more appropriate than others for sending certain messages. For example, memos are usually not very effective for sending information that has a lot of feeling in it. A more effective channel for conveying strong emotions is a meeting or other form of face-to-face communication.

Communication is not effective unless the receiver is able to *decode* the message and understand its true meaning. The receiver may misinterpret a message for many reasons. For example, the message may be filled with technical jargon that makes it difficult to decode, the receiver may misinterpret the sender's motives for sending the message, or the sender may send a message that lends itself to multiple interpretations.

Because of the strong possibility of miscommunication, important communications should include opportunities for *feedback* from the receiver. This way the sender can clarify the message if its true meaning is not received. In addition, noise in the sender's or receiver's environment may block or distort the message. *Noise* is anything that disrupts the message: inaccurate communication by the sender, fatigue or distraction on the part of the receiver, or actual noise that distorts the message (other people talking, traffic, telephone ringing). Very often noise takes the form of information overload. For example, if the receiver gets 100 e-mail messages in one day, she may not read the most important one carefully enough because she is overwhelmed by the barrage of information.

Communications that provide for feedback are called *two-way communications* because they allow the sender and receiver to interact with each other. Communications that provide no opportunity for feedback are one-way communications. Although ideally all communications should be interactive, this is not always possible in large organizations, where large amounts of information must be distributed to many employees. For example, top executives at large companies do not usually have the time to speak to all the employees they need to inform about a new product about to be released. Instead, they may communicate with the employees via a memo, report, or e-mail. In contrast, top executives at small businesses have much less difficulty communicating with their employees. The Manager's Notebook, "How to Communicate Useful Feedback to Employees," offers tips for managers who want to improve the communication process of giving and receiving feedback. (Note additional information in Chapter 7 on giving feedback during performance appraisals.)

MANAGER'S NOTEBOOK

Customer-Driven HR

How to Communicate Useful Feedback to Employees

Here are some ways to communicate useful feedback to subordinates and other employees.

- *Focus on specific behaviors* Provide feedback that lets employees know what specific behaviors are effective or need improvement. That way, they are able to sustain and intensify the desired behaviors and are motivated to change those that may be inappropriate.

Avoid vague statements such as "you have a bad attitude." It is better to give more specific feedback such as "you ignored the customer when she tried to get your attention."

- ***Keep the feedback impersonal*** Try to keep the feedback descriptive rather than judgmental or evaluative. To do this, focus on job-related behaviors rather than make value judgments about the employee's motivations. Rather than telling an employee "you are incompetent," it would be preferable to say, "I noticed some gaps in your product knowledge when you gave a presentation to the marketing group."
- ***Give the feedback at the appropriate time and place*** The best time to give feedback is right after the person who should receive the feedback engages in the behavior at issue. A manager who waits months until the formal performance appraisal to give the feedback has lost an opportunity to coach and motivate an employee to improve at the time the behavior was observed. Similarly, the appropriate place to provide critical feedback is in private. Giving negative feedback publicly can humiliate the person being critiqued and is likely to provoke anger rather than the intended result of the message. Conversely, giving positive feedback in front of others can be motivational not only to the person who is being praised, but also to others who may learn from the good example set by the employee whose behaviors are positively recognized.
- ***Focus negative feedback on behaviors that can be controlled by the employee*** When giving negative feedback to another employee, focus on behaviors that the employee can control. For example, it may be appropriate for a manager to criticize an employee who is late arriving at a team meeting. However, if the manager asked the employee to handle a customer service problem that took longer to solve than originally anticipated, the criticism about tardiness may be unfair.

Sources: Based on Gomez-Mejia, L., and Balkin, D. (2012). *Management.* Upper Saddle River, NJ: Prentice-Hall; Robbins, S. P., and Hunsaker P. L. (2009). *Training in interpersonal skills* (5th ed.). Upper Saddle River, NJ: Prentice Hall. ■■

DOWNWARD AND UPWARD COMMUNICATION Employee relations specialists help to maintain both downward communication and upward communication in an organization. **Downward communication** allows managers to implement their decisions and to influence employees lower in the organizational hierarchy. It can also be used to disperse information controlled by top managers. **Upward communication** allows employees at lower levels to communicate their ideas or feelings to higher-level decision makers. Unfortunately, many organizations erect serious barriers in their upward communication channels. For example, in many companies it is considered disloyal for an employee to go "over the head" of an immediate supervisor and communicate with a higher-level executive about a problem.

downward communication
Communication that allows managers to implement their decisions and to influence employees lower in the organizational hierarchy.

upward communication
Communication that allows employees at lower levels to communicate their ideas and feelings to higher-level decision makers.

One final but very important note concerning communication in general: The U.S. economy is shifting from an industrial base to an information base. This revolution is as significant as the move from an agrarian to an industrial economy over a century ago. In an industrial economy, production processes are the focus of concern. In an information economy, communication (the production and transmission of information) is the focus. How information is communicated, both internally and externally, is becoming more and more important to organizational success.

Encouraging Effective Communications

Working with supervisors and managers, employee relations representatives can aid effective communications by developing and maintaining three types of programs: information dissemination, employee feedback, and employee assistance.

Information Dissemination Programs

Information is a source of power in organizations. In traditional top-down hierarchies, top managers zealously guard information as their special preserve. But the information age has forced many businesses to forge a new set of rules. Today, organizations depend more and more on knowledge workers to produce their product or service. **Knowledge workers** (for example,

knowledge worker
A worker who transforms information into a product or service.

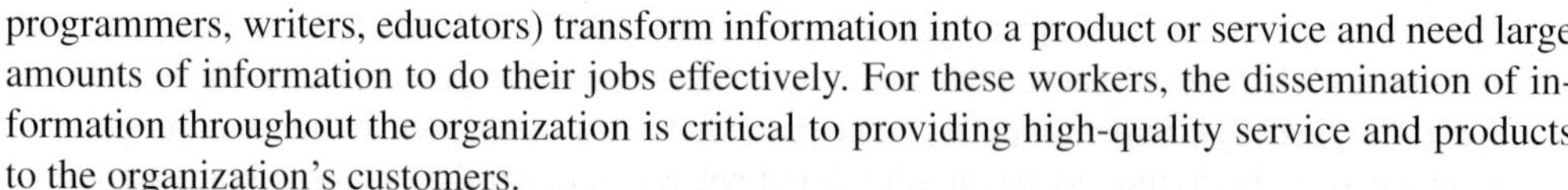

programmers, writers, educators) transform information into a product or service and need large amounts of information to do their jobs effectively. For these workers, the dissemination of information throughout the organization is critical to providing high-quality service and products to the organization's customers.

information dissemination
The process of making information available to decision makers, wherever they are located.

Information dissemination involves making information available to decision makers, wherever they are located. Employees who have access to abundant information are more likely to feel empowered and are better able to participate in decision making. Information dissemination also helps managers adopt more participative leadership styles and work configurations, leading to greater employee involvement and, ultimately, to better employee relations.

A QUESTION OF ETHICS
Some companies attempt to restrict the behavior of employees while they are off the job. The most common restriction is a prohibition against smoking. Less common is a prohibition against public drinking. Is it ethical for a company to try to control its employees' behavior while they are not on the job?

The most important methods of disseminating information to employees are employee handbooks, written communications, audiovisual communications, electronic communications, meetings, retreats, and informal communications.

The Employee Handbook

The *employee handbook* is probably the most important source of information that the HR department can provide. It sets the tone for the company's overall employee relations philosophy,[6] informing both employees and supervisors about company employment policies and procedures and communicating employees' rights and responsibilities. The handbook lets employees know that they can expect consistent and uniform treatment on issues that affect their job or status in the company. It also tells supervisors how to evaluate, reward, and discipline their employees. It can protect supervisors and the company from making uninformed and arbitrary decisions that may hurt the workforce's morale or lead to litigation from angry employees.

A QUESTION OF ETHICS
Should companies have the right to read and monitor their employees' e-mail?

Employee handbooks cover issues such as employee benefits, performance evaluation, dress codes, employment of family members, smoking, probationary employment periods, drug-testing procedures, family leave policies, sexual harassment, discipline procedures, and safety rules.[7] Handbooks need to be updated annually to reflect the current legal environment and to remain consistent with the company's overall employee relations philosophy. Although employee handbooks are usually printed and distributed to employees, it is becoming more common for companies to put them online as electronic documents that can be updated easily. Online handbooks reduce printing costs, because employees can print only the pages they need.[8]

Although they are sometimes considered a tool for only large corporations, small businesses can also benefit from the use of employee handbooks. For example, a restaurant owner recently discharged an employee who did not pay for a meal, even though there was no written policy on meals and the owner had previously allowed some other employees to eat meals at the restaurant. The ex-employee took the owner to court over this misunderstanding. The owner spent over $7,000 in legal fees defending the decision to discharge the ex-employee. This dispute could have been avoided if an "employee meals" policy had been distributed in an employee handbook.[9]

Court decisions in some states have suggested that employee handbooks may constitute an implied contract between employer and employee that restricts the employer's freedom to discharge employees without just cause. To avoid such restrictive interpretations by the courts, employers should include at the end of their handbook a disclaimer stating that employees can be discharged for any reason or no reason and that the handbook does not constitute an employment contract, but rather it is a set of guidelines.[10] Some firms go even further to protect themselves: They ask all new employees to sign an employee handbook acknowledgment form stating they have received the handbook; will refer to it for company rules, regulations, and policies; and understand that it is in no way a contract. Not surprisingly, such forms have been controversial because the legal protection they provide the employer also tends to undermine the goodwill the handbook was designed to foster.[11]

Still, employee handbooks can help prevent or solve problems in the workforce. Figure 13.2 shows how a firm might communicate an enlightened nepotism policy through its employee handbook. (**Nepotism** is the practice of favoring relatives over others in the workplace.) The policy communicated in Figure 13.2 protects the rights of family members but balances those rights with the company's need to avoid conflicts of interest that could affect the efficiency of its business.

nepotism
The practice of favoring relatives over others in the workplace.

In family-owned businesses in which owners often groom sons, daughters, or other family members to take over the company, nepotism is taken for granted. How much nepotism is okay? It is not uncommon for company owners to put their children in positions of power and grant

Nepotism Policy

Section 1. **Family Member Employment.** The company considers it an unlawful employment practice regarding a member of an individual's family working or who has worked for the Company to:

a. Refuse to hire or employ that individual;
b. Bar or terminate from employment that individual; or
c. Discriminate against that individual in compensation or in terms, conditions, or privileges of employment.

Section 2. **Conflict of Interest.** The Company is not required to hire or continue in employment an individual if it:

a. Would place the individual in a position of exercising supervisory, appointment, or grievance adjustment authority over a member of the individual's family, or in a position of being subject to the authority that a member of the individual's family exercises; or
b. Would cause the Company to disregard a bona fide occupational requirement reasonably necessary to the normal operation of the Company's business.

Section 3. **Member of an Individual's Family.** Member of an individual's family includes wife, husband, son, daughter, mother, father, brother, brother-in-law, sister, sister-in-law, son-in-law, daughter-in-law, father-in-law, mother-in-law, aunt, uncle, niece, nephew, stepparent, or stepchild of the individual.

FIGURE 13.2

Sample Nepotism Policy Statement from an Employee Handbook

Sources: Based on Decker, K. H. (1989). *A manager's guide to employee privacy: Policies and procedures*, 231–232. New York: Wiley; Thiname, H. (2010). How to establish a workers nepotism policy. *www.ehow.com*; Sample nepotism policies. (2010). *www.mrsc.org*.

them pay, titles, and privileges denied to more experienced or qualified company employees. Naturally, this antagonizes nonfamily employees. Family business consultants Craig E. Aronoff and John L. Ward recommend that family members meet the following three qualifications before making the family business a permanent career:

- Get an education appropriate for the job sought.
- Work three to five years outside the family business.
- Start in an existing, necessary job within the family business and honor precedents for pay and performance.[12]

WRITTEN COMMUNICATIONS: MEMOS, FINANCIAL STATEMENTS, NEWSLETTERS, AND BULLETIN BOARDS There are many other forms of written communication besides the employee handbook. *Memos* are useful for conveying changes in policies or procedures. For example, when there is a change in coverage of a specific type of medical procedure, the affected group of employees can be notified by written memo. In addition, the company should disseminate *financial reports* to make employees knowledgeable about the company's performance. Shareholders are routinely given this information, but employees should receive it, too, because it is an important source of feedback on their aggregate performance.[13] Many companies choose to distribute a *triple bottom-line report* that informs both shareholders and stakeholders how a company has performed on meeting its social, environmental, and financial performance goals. Social performance goals listed in a triple bottom-line report are likely to include how effective a company was at improving employee satisfaction over the previous year or a report on the state of employee wellness based on preestablished employee health goals encompassing smoking cessation, weight loss, cholesterol maintenance, and the like.[14]

One activity for which the HR department is likely to have direct responsibility is the production and distribution of an employee newsletter. The *newsletter* is usually a short monthly or quarterly publication designed to keep employees informed of important events, meetings, and transitions and to provide inspirational stories about employee and team contributions to the business.[15] Newsletters help foster community spirit in a company or unit. The advent of desktop publishing packages for personal computers has made newsletter production and distribution feasible for even the smallest of companies. Some managers use a simple *bulletin board* to post current team performance data and comparisons with outside competitors or other teams with the company. Moreover, a common feature of a company Web site is to have an *electronic bulletin board* that contains announcements of interest to employees that can be posted quickly and can be viewed by all the employees regardless of their location. For example, an employee who anticipates the start of a one-year international assignment may want to post an announcement on the electronic bulletin board that he is willing to sublease his home for a year.

teleconferencing
The use of audio and video equipment to allow people to participate in meetings even when they are a great distance away from the conference location or one another.

AUDIOVISUAL COMMUNICATIONS New technologies have made it possible to disseminate information that goes beyond the printed word. **Teleconferencing** allows people with busy schedules to participate in meetings even when they are a great distance away from the conference location (or one another). Through video cameras and other sophisticated equipment, teleconferencing makes it possible for employees at remote locations to interact with one another as if they were all seated in the same conference room. One four-hour video conference that keeps five people off an airplane and out of hotels and restaurants could save a company at least $5,000.

With teleconferencing systems ranging in price from $10,000 to $40,000, however, the costs are still prohibitive for many companies. One way companies can teleconference affordably is to rent the equipment as needed. For instance, FedEx Office rents rooms equipped with teleconferencing equipment in many of its locations.

Electronic Communications

voice mail
A form of electronic communication that allows the sender to leave a detailed voice message for a receiver.

Advances in electronic communications have made interactive communications possible even when the sender and receiver are separated by physical distance and busy schedules. With **voice mail**, an employee can avoid playing "telephone tag" with busy managers and instead leave a detailed voice message for them. The sender can also transmit a prerecorded voice mail message to some or all of the people within the company's telephone network. For example, an executive can send a personalized greeting to a large group of employees. In addition, the receiver can leave different voice mail messages for different types of callers by creating a menu of messages.

Like any technology, voice mail has some drawbacks. Many people still dislike speaking to a machine. And this machine has plenty of potential for misuse. People often use it to screen calls, avoiding callers they do not want to talk to by pretending they are not there. This is fine in private life, but screening too many calls at the office can create problems. The following guidelines can help managers improve the efficiency of the voice mail system:[16]

- ***Leave a brief message*** Limit the length of the voice mail message to 30 seconds or less.
- ***Provide a timeframe for returning the call*** When leaving a voice mail message give the person a timeframe when you can be reached for a return call.
- ***Give people other options*** Sometimes a voice mail system gets filled with calls and it is not possible to leave a message. Give the return caller other options to reach you such as a cell phone number or an e-mail address.
- ***Provide a context for the voice mail message*** Give the listener a reason for the purpose of your call and provide a context for how the listener may know you such as the name of a mutual friend you both have in common.

electronic mail (e-mail)
A form of electronic communication that allows employees to communicate with each other via electronic messages sent through personal computer terminals linked by a network.

Electronic mail, or **e-mail**, allows employees to communicate with each other via written electronic messages sent through personal computer terminals linked by a network. In addition, e-mail allows employees to offer feedback to anyone in the organization, no matter what that person's rank. E-mail is a very fast way to convey important business results or critical events to a large number of employees.[17] It also permits the sharing of large information databases among employees and even members of different organizations. E-mail has made it possible for professors at different universities worldwide to collaborate on research studies, write manuscripts, and share data as quickly as if they were working next door to each other at the same university. Interorganizational electronic communication is likely to increase significantly in the coming years, thanks to the rise of the Internet.

Another advantage of e-mail is that it allows lower-echelon employees to communicate with managers and executives when urgent information needs to be given to those who need it. For example, a functional team located on a different continent can advocate for a change in suppliers or warn of a competitive maneuver that no one in charge seems to see coming. An entire factory floor can call for the ouster of a manager who has been treating subordinates abusively and withholding performance information from key decision makers.[18]

Despite its many advantages, e-mail has created some problems for managers. One problem is that because e-mail is so easy to use it contributes to information overload. Some senders create large mailing lists for a document that needs to be read by only a few targeted people.

Another problem with e-mail is that mobile devices such as the smart phone and tablet PCs make it easy for managers to communicate job related e-mail messages to employees outside the office during off-hours, which can infringe upon employees' personal time. This ease of accessibility with mobile devices can add extra hours to the workweek. A 2012 survey of 2,600 workers in the United States, United Kingdom, and South Africa sponsored by the *Harvard Business Review* on employee e-mail use found that 40 percent of respondents respond to work e-mail messages during non-work hours.[19] The survey also found that employees spend an average of 111 workdays per year responding to e-mail.

Firms that set up e-mail systems with the idea of boosting productivity are sometimes dismayed to find that they are actually *decreasing* productivity. Here are some guidelines for using e-mail productively:

- Establish an e-mail improvement team to develop protocols and procedures for getting the most out of the system.
- Create electronic files for messages that need to be saved and organize them in subject folders for quick retrieval.
- Set up a common folder or electronic bulletin board to which senders can route reports and memos intended for general distribution. An electronic bulletin board can save considerable system space and time.[20]
- Shut off the computer beep that alerts the receiver to incoming messages to prevent constant interruptions of work.
- Assume that your e-mail from a company computer will be read by management. Use other communication channels for private or controversial messages.
- Protect sensitive documents with encryption software so that private information is not accessible to hackers or other unintended receivers.
- If you are unable to respond to an e-mail for several days, acknowledge that you have received the message and tell the sender when you are likely to answer it.[21]
- HR and management can develop a policy that limits off-hours e-mail work messages to specific times (for example between 8:00 a.m. and 6:00 p.m.) so that employees' personal time is protected from intrusive requests from the office.

The thorniest problem managers confront with e-mail requires consultation with HR professionals. This is the tendency of employees to view their e-mail messages as private property, immune to employer inspection. This assumption can lead them to use e-mail to communicate about off-hours activities or to spread rumors, misinformation, and complaints throughout the organization. Some managers have been shocked to find that disgruntled employees have developed grievance Web sites that encourage workers to use e-mail to sabotage managers' plans.[22] For these reasons, employers sometimes decide to monitor their employees' e-mail. Employees usually resent this, regarding it as an invasion of their privacy.[23] A survey of 435 employers sponsored by the American Management Association found that about 62 percent of the employers exercise their legal right to monitor employees' e-mail.[24]

For example, when setting up Epson America's e-mail system, e-mail administrator Alana Shoars reassured 700 nervous Epson employees that their e-mail would be private. When Shoars found out that her supervisor was copying and reading employees' e-mail messages, she complained—and lost her job. She filed suit, but the judge agreed with the company. Because state privacy statutes did not make specific reference to e-mail or the workplace, the judge said, the law did not protect electronic messages in the office. Epson has since notified employees that it cannot guarantee e-mail privacy, citing in part its need to protect itself from computer crime. Unless HR staff members develop e-mail policies that are explicit and reasonable, employee relations may suffer.[25] A company may violate employee privacy if it captures its employees' electronic profiles when they visit the company Web or intranet site and then sells those profiles to marketers. The marketers may in turn send unwanted marketing messages by e-mail, telephone, and junk mail to employees who match the target market profile.[26]

In many workplaces, e-mail reigns as the primary form of communication with colleagues, clients, and suppliers. Overdependence on e-mail can lead to misunderstandings that increase conflict and cause strained work relationships, due to the limits on e-mail's ability to transmit emotional content between the sender and receiver. By choosing e-mail communication over face-to-face communication, the sender is deprived of the opportunity to display nonverbal information such as tone of voice, facial expressions, body posture, and eye gaze, which receivers often depend on to figure out what someone really means.[27] Whenever a message has a high potential for emotional content from either the sender's or receiver's perspectives, it is advisable to deliver it face-to-face during a meeting or through management by walking around, both of which are discussed later in this chapter.[28]

An unusual approach to wean employees away from e-mail is to make rules that restrict its use. The CEO of PBD Worldwide Fulfillment Services in Alpharetta, Georgia, suspected that his 275 employees were so dependent on e-mail that it was hurting sales and productivity. So he instituted a "no e-mail on Fridays" rule that required employees to either pick up the phone or meet in person each Friday and to reduce e-mail use the rest of the time. Although this rule did not go down well with some employees, within four months the CEO noticed quick problem solving, better teamwork, and more satisfied customers following the limits placed on the use of e-mail.[29]

social networking
Interacting over the Internet and sharing text messages, photos, and video clips.

Social networking Web sites such as LinkedIn or Facebook are online services that facilitate the building of social networks among people. These Web sites allow people to interact over the Internet with each other and share text messages, photos, and video clips. Social networking sites allow employees to stay connected with current and former colleagues. Employees who join a social networking service create a public profile that identifies their current occupation, work history, interests, and activities. They also display a list of people who are in their network on their profile for others in the network to view. A person who shares a common friend with another network member can ask the friend for an introduction, which can make it easier to do business with the person of interest.

Social networking has many uses in human resource management. For example, it can be used to learn about job vacancies by sending a message to all people in a person's network inquiring about a specific job. The social network can also be useful to an employer who is considering a person for a job. The employer can ask former colleagues who are familiar with the person about his or her work habits and what the person is like to work with as a coworker. This information is unlikely to be available in letters of recommendation. The head of global recruiting at Accenture, a multinational consulting firm, expects to identify about 40 percent of the people it will hire in the coming years with social networking tools such as LinkedIn.[30]

Social media, by reducing the power distance, can enable managers to form closer emotional bonds with large groups of employees. For example, Tupperware developed an internal social media community of part-time sales consultants that gave sales managers a better understanding of the reasons for costly turnover in these positions. The turnover rate was ultimately improved with the introduction of new practices based on ideas extracted from the conversations on the social media.[31] The Manager's Notebook, "Using Social Media to Build Corporate Alumni Networks," explains how, when corporate alumni networks are in place, relationships between employees and organizations can continue and be mutually beneficial, even after an employee leaves.

MANAGER'S NOTEBOOK

Using Social Media to Build Corporate Alumni Networks

When an employee leaves an organization for a new job, the relationship between the employee and the organization does not have to end. Corporate alumni networks are social networks that companies create whose purpose is to maintain long-term relationships with valued former employees. Companies benefit from alumni networks in different ways. Former employees can recommend colleagues to fill job vacancies in highly skilled positions. They can share competitive information, effective business practices, or new industry-wide trends. Alumni employees can also provide hard-to-obtain information, for example, on the work habits of a coworker who is seeking a job at the former employer but may be a poor fit with the organization's culture.

The application of social media technology has been an enabler to forming corporate alumni networks that allow former employees to stay in touch and learn from each other's professional experiences. Online corporate alumni networks are likely to be password-protected, and can include message boards, blogs from executives, profiles of prominent alumni, and both internal and external job postings. LinkedIn, the social networking Web site, currently sponsors thousands of corporate alumni groups including those of 98 percent of the Fortune 500 companies. Many companies use intranets to create more personalized and secure alumni network sites. There are even informal alumni associations for companies that no longer exist such as Lehman Brothers and Arthur Andersen.

The use of corporate alumni networks is pervasive in the management consulting industry. McKinsey & Company, the renowned strategy consulting firm, has a corporate alumni network of 24,000 members including over 200 CEOs of large companies. It is not unusual for McKinsey to obtain new consulting projects from former employees who stayed in close contact with their colleagues at McKinsey. Professional services firms are also heavy users of corporate alumni networks and include Deloitte, PricewaterhouseCoopers, and Ernst & Young.

Sources: Based on Hoffman, R., Casnocha, B., and Yeh, C. (2013, June). Tours of duty: The new employer-employee compact. *Harvard Business Review*, 48–58; Lambert, L. (2012, September). After the breakup: The business case for corporate alumni networks. *Gibbs & Soell Newsletter*. *www.gibbs-soell.com*; Korn, M. (2011, October 24). Boomerang employees: More companies tap into alumni networks to re-recruit best of former workers. *Wall Street Journal*. *www.online.wsj.com*; *The Economist*. (2001, November 29). Corporate alumni networks. *www.economist.com*. ■■

---

multimedia technology
A form of electronic communication that integrates voice, video, and text, all of which can be encoded digitally and transported on fiber optic networks.

Multimedia technology—integrating voice, video, and text, all of which are encoded digitally and can be transported on fiber optic networks—make it possible to interact with video images of employees located across the country or around the world as if they were in the same room.

Multimedia technology has potential applications in many areas. One is in employee training programs (see Chapter 8). For example, pilots can develop aviation skills on a multimedia flight simulator without risking an accident to the plane. Many textbooks now offer multimedia disks that help students learn skills and apply the information they've learned from the text.[32] These multimedia programs include voice and video clips and ask the student to make a decision from a menu of possible choices. After making a decision, the student can see the outcome on video.

Another application of multimedia technology is in telecommuting, a trend that is already changing the face of companies across the nation.[33] More and more employees are working with company-equipped computer systems and faxes in their homes.[34] According to a study by the Telework Research Network, the typical person who is a teleworker is 47 years old; has worked with the company for 12 years; and is likely to work in service occupations such as management consultant, salesperson, or insurance claims adjuster.[35]

The Manager's Notebook, "Keys to Managing Telecommuters," addresses the managerial implications of this new workplace development.

MANAGER'S NOTEBOOK

Keys to Managing Telecommuters

Telecommuting must be planned carefully. The following suggestions can make managing telecommuters a little easier:

- Select telecommuters with care, considering the work habits of the employee and the type of work involved. People who are not very self-motivated may not be able to manage their time well at home.
- Maintain schedules and make sure telecommuters stick to deadlines. Although it is okay for telecommuters to work off-hours, they should be available for consultation when the company needs them.
- It is recommended that a telecommuter should make regular phone or e-mail status reports so that colleagues can observe the progress being made by the telecommuter.
- Make sure the technology works. Without the right compatibility between employers' and telecommuters' computer systems, there will be delays in communication and traffic tie-ups on the electronic highway.

- Have home-based workers come in to the office on a regular basis so they can attend meetings and interact with managers. Doing so not only keeps these employees in the flow but also helps combat their feelings of isolation.
- Develop a carefully crafted telecommuters plan that includes performance expectations with measurable results. Managers of telecommuters must develop new skills and learn to transition from managing with a focus on employees' behaviors and time to one with an emphasis on managing by results.
- Don't make telecommuting a term of employment. State in the plan that the company can require changes to telecommuting based on business needs.

Sources: Based on Elsbach, K., and Cable, D. (2012, Summer). Why showing your face at work matters, *MIT Sloan Management Review*, 10–12; *HR Focus*. (2008, April). Planning enhances the potential of telecommuting success, 51–54; Fisher, A. (2005, May 30). How telecommuters can stay connected. *Fortune*, 142; *HR Focus*. (2002, May). Time to take another look at telecommuting, 6–7. ■■

MEETINGS Formal meetings are opportunities for face-to-face communication between two or more employees and are guided by a specific agenda. Formal meetings facilitate dialogue and promote the nurturing of personal relationships, particularly among employees who may not interact frequently because they are separated by organizational or geographic barriers. Meetings are particularly useful in the formation of teams; team members can work out their interpersonal differences and build mutual trust in order to develop collaborative working relationships necessary for effective performance.

Meetings take place at different organizational levels. For example, staff meetings allow managers to coordinate activities with subordinates in their units.[36] Division or corporate meetings involve issues that have a larger impact and may include managers or employees from all divisions across the corporation. For instance, when a company such as Microsoft decides to unveil a new product, organization-wide meetings are sometimes used to make sure that everyone in the organization is communicating the same message. Task force meetings may be called to discuss specific goals such as a change in marketing strategy or compensation policies.

It has been estimated that managers and executives spend as much as 75 percent of their time in meetings.[37] Poorly managed meetings can be a colossal waste of time that lower a company's productivity. Think about what it might cost for several highly paid executives to spend three hours at a meeting without accomplishing their objectives—and then multiply that amount by 260 workdays a year. However, meetings do not have to be a necessary evil. Here are some guidelines for making meetings more productive:

1. Decide whether it is even necessary to hold a meeting. If a matter can be handled by a phone call or memo, do not schedule a meeting.
2. Make meeting participation match the meeting's purpose. For instance, if a meeting is being held for the purpose of sharing information, a large group might be appropriate. For a problem-solving session, a smaller group is usually more productive.
3. Distribute a carefully planned agenda before the meeting. This will provide participants with purpose and direction and give them a chance to plan their own contributions.
4. Choose an appropriate meeting space and time. It is difficult for people to accomplish much when they are crowded into a small room with notepads balanced on their laps. Holding a meeting in a room that is too large may encourage participants to spread out and not develop the necessary cohesion. Timing is crucial, too. At meetings scheduled in the hour before lunch, attendees may be listening to their stomachs growl rather than to their colleagues. Some managers like to schedule meetings in the morning, when people are more alert. To encourage promptness, they set a time that is not exactly on the hour—such as 10:10 a.m. instead of 10:00 a.m.
5. In the case of a problem-solving or policy-setting meeting, close with an action plan and follow up with a memo outlining what happened at the meeting and what steps need to be taken.[38]

Skillful management of the dynamics among meeting participants is even more important than logistics. It is inevitable that some participants will attempt to dominate the proceedings with either helpful or negative contributions. Meeting leaders must strive to establish an atmosphere in which everyone feels at ease—one in which differences of opinion are encouraged and treated with respect.

Further clouding the air in the conference room are gender differences. Women often complain that they find it difficult to get—and hold—the floor in meetings with male colleagues. Sociolinguist Deborah Tannen has found that women and men have different communication styles that lead to misunderstandings both at work and at home.[39] Cultural differences also crop up in the meeting room. In a U.S. business meeting, the focus tends to be on action. In contrast, the objective of Japanese business meetings is to gather information or to analyze data before planning action. In Italy, meetings are often a way for managers to demonstrate their authority and power.[40]

In addition to scheduled formal meetings with specific work-related goals, managers can use informal meetings to build personal relationships among employees. Friday social hours have become a regular part of business at high-technology companies, including Cisco Systems and Google. At these social hours, technical employees talk among themselves and with managers and marketing staff about projects and share information that may not be communicated through formal channels. This practice has spread to many other types of businesses.

RETREATS A *retreat* is an extended meeting in which the company takes employees to a relaxing location, such as a mountain lodge or a seaside resort, where they mix business with recreational activities, such as golf, tennis, or sailing. Some retreats are designed to develop creative ideas for long-term planning or for implementing changes in business practices. Others, such as the outdoor adventures organized by Outward Bound, encourage employees to develop interpersonal skills by involving them in such activities as mountain climbing or whitewater rafting, where they are forced to be interdependent. These intense shared experiences can foster mutual appreciation among coworkers.[41] A retreat can also be an excellent way of improving employee relations. For example, one medium-sized law firm in the Denver area used a retreat to improve relations between partners and associates. All the firm's members spent two days at a mountain lodge talking in small groups about ways to improve their relationships with one another. These discussions brought into the open many touchy issues that had been simmering. In the retreat setting, the firm's members could deal with them constructively.

Many family businesses are discovering the value of retreats. Two brothers, Steve and Elliott Dean, bought all the stock in their father's company, Dean Lumber Company in Gilmer, Texas. Three years later Steve realized that he had been so busy with day-to-day affairs that he had not spoken with family members about his plans for the company's future. The solution: a family retreat at which all 15 members of the Dean clan gathered for two days to discuss Steve's vision for Dean Lumber, helped by a facilitator from the Family Business Institute at Baylor University in Waco, Texas. The retreat, which included facilities with meals, the facilitator, and guest speakers, cost the Deans $5,000.

informal communications
Also called "the grapevine." Information exchanges without a planned agenda that occur informally among employees.

Most family business consultants recommend using a nonfamily facilitator at the first retreat, to get the process going and keep emotions from running too high. Later on the role of facilitator can be rotated among family members. To help the Dean family get a grip on the issue of succession, for example, the facilitator asked the group to pretend that Steve and Elliott had been killed in a plane crash and asked what they would do. This proved a shocking exercise for the brothers because it made them realize how very little short- or long-term planning they had done.[42] In addition to using retreats to air important issues, many family businesses use them to set up a *family council,* an organizational and strategic planning group whose members regularly meet to decide values, policy, and direction.[43]

Source: Tim Robbins/Getty Images.

INFORMAL COMMUNICATIONS Sometimes called the "grapevine," **informal communications** consist of information exchanges without a planned agenda that occur informally among employees. Many informal communications take place among employees who form friendships or networks of mutual assistance at the water fountain or in the hallway, company cafeteria, offices, or parking lot. Informal communications pass along information that is usually not available through more formal communication channels—for example, the size of upcoming merit pay increases, who is in line for a big promotion, who has received an outside job offer, and who has gotten a low performance evaluation and is upset about it.

Informal communications can be the source of creative ideas. Qwest, a regional telecommunications company that is now part of CenturyLink, designed a new research facility to take advantage of the benefits of informal communication. The architect designed "breakout rooms" and hallways to optimize spontaneous interactions between technicians and scientists so that informal groups could brainstorm together to solve technical problems and generate ideas.

Managers and HR staff need to be aware of informal social groups among employees called *cliques*, which may disrupt the flow of information among employees by excluding those who are not part of the clique. Cliques often form among employees who are similar to each other, which results in the exclusion of those who are different on factors such as age, race, gender, or ethnicity. In one case, a top executive at Adams-Blake, a California software firm, noticed that within one of the company's software development teams, a clique had formed that prevented two team members from obtaining information from those on the team who were part of the clique. Team performance was negatively affected by the social tension between the clique and the excluded employees. The executive was able to improve team performance in the short run by threatening to discharge anyone in the clique who withheld information.[44] Better ways to deal with some of the harmful effects of cliques over the long term include rotating team members between different projects, allowing employees to form working relationships with diverse members of the organization. Company-sponsored social events also open new channels of communication so that more information is shared, thus reducing some of the harmful effects of cliques.

When organizations allow too much information to be communicated informally, there is a good chance that it will be distorted by rumor, gossip, and innuendo. The result may be poor employee morale and poor employee relations. To guard against this, the HR department and managers need to monitor informal communications and, when necessary, clarify them through more formal channels. One effective way to monitor informal communications is through **management by walking around (MBWA)**. MBWA, championed by Tom Peters and Robert Waterman in their wildly successful book *In Search of Excellence*, is a management technique in which the manager walks around the company so that employees at all levels have an opportunity to offer suggestions or voice grievances. This management style is used to build rapport with employees and monitor morale at IBM and many other companies.[45] Management behavior in the workplace can communicate trustworthiness to other employees. The Manager's Notebook, "Managerial Behaviors That Promote Interpersonal Trust," offers tips on behavior that communicates and builds trust with others.

management by walking around (MBWA)
A technique in which managers walk around and talk to employees informally to monitor informal communications, listen to employee grievances and suggestions, and build rapport and morale.

MANAGER'S NOTEBOOK

Ethics/Social Responsibility

Managerial Behaviors That Promote Interpersonal Trust

The way managers behave in the workplace communicates their trustworthiness to other employees. Here are some examples of trustworthy behaviors that managers can engage in to build trust with others:

- ***Act with discretion and keep secrets*** Keeping a secret means not exposing another employee's vulnerability. Divulging a confidence makes a person seem malevolent and unprofessional.
- ***Be consistent between word and deed*** People who don't say one thing and do another are perceived as being caring about others (i.e., they do not mislead) and being competent enough to follow through. Managers should set realistic expectations when committing to do something, and then deliver.
- ***Engage in collaborative communication*** People are more willing to trust someone who shows a willingness to listen and share, to get involved, and talk things through. In contrast, people are wary of someone who seems closed and will only answer clear-cut questions or discuss complete solutions. Thus, it is important for managers to be willing to work with people to improve on their partially formed ideas.

- ***Ensure that decisions are fair and transparent*** People take their cues from the larger environment. As a result, the way management treats other people influences the way employees treat each other. Therefore, fair and transparent decisions, in which the decision process and outcomes are revealed to all, can translate into a more trusting environment for all employees.
- ***Demonstrate loyalty to other employees*** A good way a manager can show loyalty to employees is by acknowledging their contributions and giving them credit for successful results. By sharing credit with employees, a manager supports a more trusting environment where people feel free to share ideas with each other, which can lead to an increase in workplace innovations.

Sources: Based on Abrams, L., Cross, R., Lesser, E., and Levin, D. (2003, November). Nurturing interpersonal trust in knowledge-sharing networks. *Academy of Management Executive*, 67; Covey, S. M. R. (2006). *The speed of trust*. New York: Free Press; Sutton, R. (2010). *Good boss, bad boss*. New York: Business Plus. ■■

Gossip may sometimes be helpful to people in organizations, which means that managers should use discretion when attempting to discourage employees from exchanging gossip. Research shows that employees derive some benefits from gossip. They can learn which employees are likely to be free riders, which bosses are bullies, and which employees are difficult to work with. This is valuable information that people need to know when taking on new work assignments or bringing new members into a high-performing team, and it may not be available through other, more formal channels of communication.[46]

Employee Feedback Programs

To provide upward communications channels between employees and management, many organizations offer **employee feedback programs**. These programs are designed to improve management–employee relations by (1) giving employees a voice in decision making and policy formulation and (2) making sure that employees receive due process on any complaints they lodge against managers. The HR department not only designs and maintains employee feedback programs, but is also expected to protect employee confidentiality in dealing with sensitive personal issues. HR personnel are also charged with ensuring that subordinates are not subject to retaliation from angry managers.

employee feedback program
A program designed to improve employee communications by giving employees a voice in policy formulation and making sure that they receive due process on any complaints they lodge against managers.

The most common employee feedback programs are employee attitude surveys, appeals procedures, and employee assistance programs. Here we discuss the first two kinds of programs, which are intended to resolve work-related problems. We discuss employee assistance programs (EAPs), which are designed to help employees resolve personal problems that are interfering with their job performance, later in this chapter.

EMPLOYEE ATTITUDE SURVEYS Designed to measure workers' likes and dislikes of various aspects of their jobs, **employee attitude surveys** are typically formal and anonymous. They ask employees how they feel about the work they do, their supervisor, their work environment, their opportunities for advancement, the quality of the training they received, the company's treatment of women and minorities, and the fairness of the company's pay policies. The survey responses of various subgroups can be compared to those of the total employee population to help managers identify units or departments that are experiencing poor employee relations.

employee attitude survey
A formal anonymous survey designed to measure employee likes and dislikes of various aspects of their jobs.

Making specific improvements in employee relations can avert acts of sabotage or labor unrest (such as strikes, absenteeism, and turnover) that are directly attributable to strains between subordinates and managers. For example, in analyzing attitude survey data, a chain of retail stores in the Midwest found that employees at one store had much lower levels of satisfaction than the employees at any other store in the chain. The chain's top managers immediately realized this was the same store that had experienced several serious acts of sabotage. Instead of retaliating against employees, corporate management set out to solve the store's supervision problems with training and mediation.

To manage an employee attitude survey effectively, managers should follow three rules: First, they should tell employees what they plan to do with the information they collect and then inform them about the results of the survey. There is no point in surveying opinions unless the firm intends to act on them. Second, managers should use survey data ethically to monitor the

state of employee relations, both throughout the company and within employee subgroups (such as women, accountants, or newly hired workers), and to make positive changes in the workplace. They should not use the information they collect to fire someone (for example, a supervisor whose workers are unhappy) or to take away privileges. Finally, to protect employee confidentiality and maintain the integrity of the data, the survey should be done by a third party, such as a consulting firm.

The application of the Internet with custom-designed software provides employee attitude survey feedback on a just-in-time basis. For example, eePulse, an Ann Arbor, Michigan, company, produces weekly reports of employee job satisfaction and other work attitude measures for its clients based on taking the pulse of various employee subgroups with an e-mail survey. The Web-based attitude survey lets managers identify the factors that cause declines in employee satisfaction more rapidly than is possible with traditional paper-and-pencil surveys.[47]

Best Buy, a retail chain, allows employees to share and discuss their ideas and experiences on an employee-run intranet called Blue Shirt Nation. Employees can offer advice for tackling job-related problems or candid feedback on what they think about specific company programs. The benefit to management from unfiltered information from employees is that they learn what employees really think about company programs and they can identify best practices that employees truly value. For example, Blue Shirt Nation ran a contest in which employees submitted videos they had conceived and produced to improve employee adoption of 401(k) retirement plans. The result was a 30-percent increase in plan enrollment.[48]

In which countries are workers the most satisfied with their jobs and their employers? According to a survey, Swiss workers are the happiest, whereas Japanese workers are the least happy. The United States falls in the middle range—at about the same level as Germany and Sweden, two countries known for their enlightened approaches to management.[49] Experts in employee relations recommend several practices that can enhance employee satisfaction and happiness in the workplace: (1) provide fair treatment, security, and recognition of employees; (2) select employees for fit in the organization as well as the job; and (3) ensure that competent leadership is provided at all levels of an organization.[50]

appeals procedure
A procedure that allows employees to voice their reactions to management practices and to challenge management decisions.

APPEALS PROCEDURES Providing a mechanism, an **appeals procedure**, for employees to voice their reactions to management practices and challenge management decisions enhances employees' perception that the organization has fair employment policies. Organizations without an effective set of appeals procedures increase their risk of litigation, costly legal fees, and back-pay penalties to employees who use the courts to obtain justice.[51] Effective appeals procedures give individual employees some control over the decisions that affect them and help to identify managers who are ineffective or unfair.

Some of the most common management actions appealed by employees are:

- The allocation of overtime work
- Warnings for safety rule violations
- The size of merit pay increases
- The specification of job duties
- The employer's reimbursement for medical expense claims filed by employees
- Performance evaluations

Managers may choose from several different types of appeals procedures that vary in formality.[52] The most informal is an *open-door program.* Although the specifics of open-door programs vary from company to company, the common theme is that all employees have direct access to any manager or executive in the organization. IBM's open-door policy has been much admired. An IBM employee can walk into the office of any manager, up to and including the CEO, and ask for an opinion on a complaint or any other problem worrying the employee. The manager consulted must conduct a fair investigation into both sides of the issue and provide an answer within a specified period of time. For example, an employee who is dissatisfied with his or her performance evaluation may seek a second opinion from another manager. The open-door policy has two major benefits: It makes employees feel more secure and committed to IBM, and it makes managers less likely to act arbitrarily.

Like the open-door policy, a *speak-up program* is informal and flexible. It differs in that it prescribes specific steps for the employee to take in bringing a work problem to management's attention. CIGNA, a financial services and insurance company, has a speak-up program called Speak Easy that guarantees employees access to higher levels of management, but only after they bring their problems to the attention of their immediate supervisor.

Companies use hotlines as a way to enable employees to report complaints anonymously and confidentially through a neutral third party. Workers can call a toll-free number, available around the clock, and talk to a trained interviewer, who routes a written summary of the complaint to the employer. Callers get a case number so they can check on the status of a complaint later. The number of employers providing telephone hotlines has increased since the passage of the Sarbanes-Oxley Act of 2002, which requires publicly traded companies to have a confidential, anonymous mechanism for employees to report suspect accounting matters. Some companies use hotlines for a wider set of issues than as a compliance tool to report fraud or ethics violations. Cabela's, an outdoor-outfitter chain based in Sidney, Nebraska, uses hotlines to measure the satisfaction of its workforce. Cabela's hotline vendor responds to calls within 48 hours of notification.[53]

An *ombudsman* is a neutral person whose role is to handle employee complaints by mediating between the parties who are in a dispute. Employees may lodge concerns anonymously to an ombudsman without fear of retaliation. General Electric uses an ombudsman system as a communication channel to give its employees a voice so they can anonymously report activities that can compromise the company's integrity or ethics. Depending on the nature of the problem, the ombudsman may attempt to mediate it or refer concerns to financial, legal, or HR staffs for investigation.[54]

The grievance panel and the union grievance procedure are the most formal mechanisms used by organizations to handle employee complaints. *Grievance panels* are used in nonunion firms. They are composed of the complaining employee's peers and managers other than the employee's direct manager. The grievance panel conducts an investigation into the grievance brought before it. Grievance panels are typically the last step in the appeal process. For example, Honeywell's grievance panel, called the Management Appeals Committee, is asked to resolve a grievance only if solutions have not been found at earlier steps involving, first, the employee's supervisor and, second, an employee relations representative.

The *union grievance procedure* is the appeals procedure used by all employees working under a union contract. Like the grievance panel procedure, it entails multiple steps leading to a final and binding decision made by a neutral decision maker called an arbitrator. The union grievance procedure is an important feature of labor contracts, and we explain it in greater detail in Chapter 15.

Organizations should use a mix of appeals procedures. For instance, a company might implement an open-door policy to deal with fairly simple problems that can be resolved quickly (such as determining whether an employee violated a safety rule). Next, it might institute an employee assistance program to deal with sensitive problems that involve an employee's privacy (such as a terminal illness). Finally, it might set up a grievance panel to examine complex problems affecting employee relations within a group or organizational unit (such as the definition of a fair production quality standard).

Employee Assistance Programs

Employee assistance programs (EAPs) help employees cope with personal problems that are interfering with their job performance. These problems may include alcohol or drug abuse, domestic violence, elder care, AIDS and other diseases, eating disorders, and compulsive gambling.[55] Organizations with EAPs publicize the programs to employees and assure them that their problems will be handled confidentially. When an employee's personal problem interferes with job performance, the individual is considered a *troubled employee.*[56] In a typical company, about 10 percent of the total employee population at any given time is troubled.

employee assistance program (EAP)
A company-sponsored program that helps employees cope with personal problems that are interfering with their job performance.

Figure 13.3 shows some of the symptoms of a troubled employee. A troubled employee generally behaves inconsistently in terms of attendance, quality of work, attention to detail, and concern for personal appearance.[57] A great deal of the person's energy is devoted to coping with a personal crisis that he or she may want to keep secret from the company. Until this personal problem is resolved, the employee will be in emotional and/or physical pain and the company will be deprived of the full benefit of his or her skills. It is, therefore, in the interests of both the troubled employee and the employer to resolve the problem.

FIGURE 13.3
Symptoms of a Troubled Employee

Sources: Based on Filipowicz, C. A. (1979, June). The troubled employee: Whose responsibility? *Personnel Administrator*, 8; Identifying the troubled employee. (2010). Employee Assistance Network. *www.eannc.com*; Posey, B. (2010, September 22). Five tips for working with a troubled employee. *www.blogs.techrepublic.com*.

1. Excessive absenteeism patterns: Mondays, Fridays, days before and after holidays
2. Unexcused absences
3. Frequent absences
4. Tardiness and early departures
5. Altercations with coworkers
6. Causing injuries to other employees through negligence
7. Poor judgment and bad decisions
8. Unusual on-the-job accidents
9. Increased spoilage and breaking of equipment through negligence
10. Involvements with the law—for example, a DWI (driving while intoxicated) conviction
11. Deteriorating personal appearance
12. Obsessive behavior such as inappropriate discussion of personal problems with customers
13. High accident rate

An EAP involves four steps (Figure 13.4):

1. The first step is identifying troubled employees and referring them for counseling. About half of all referrals are self-referrals by employees who realize they are in a crisis and need help, but want to keep their problem confidential. The other half are made by supervisors who observe some of the symptoms of a troubled employee. When job performance is deficient, the EAP referral is usually linked to the company's discipline procedure—it may be the last step taken before the employee is dismissed. Employees have the right to refuse to participate in the EAP, but refusal may mean termination if the problem has a significant negative impact on their work. In fact, though, many employees appreciate the company's willingness to help them through EAP counseling.
2. The second step after referral is a visit with an EAP counselor, who interviews the employee to help identify the problem. In the case of a complex personal problem such as alcohol abuse, employees may strongly deny having a problem. The counselor, however, is trained to identify the problem and arrange for treatment. The location of an EAP can be at an on-site facility, with counselors available on the company premises, or an off-site facility. Offsite EAP facilities can provide counseling services to employees by the use of an 800 telephone line with counselors on call on a 24-hour per day basis. However, because EAPs are driven by relationships between counselors and employees, a recent survey

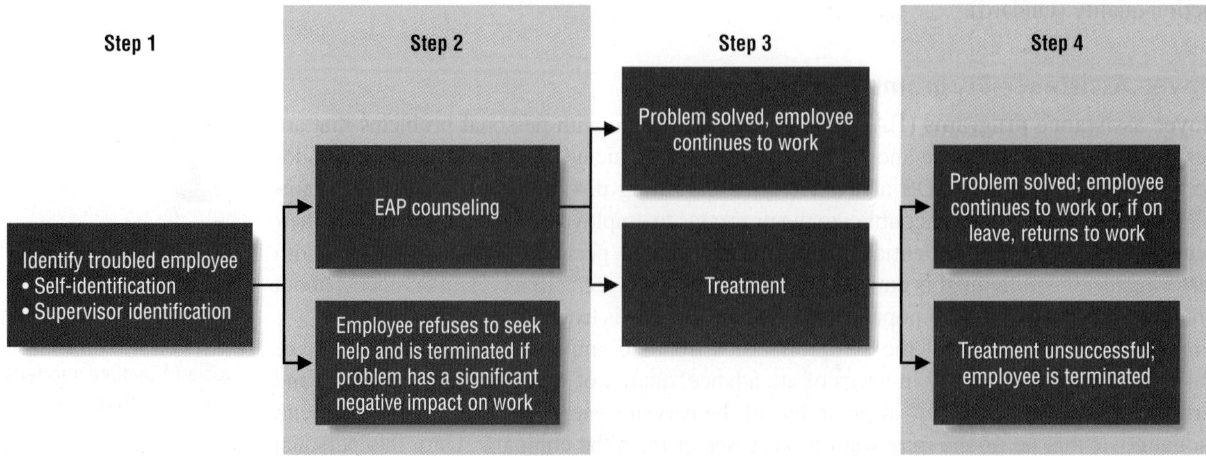

FIGURE 13.4
An Employee Assistance Program

by consulting firm EAP Support Systems found that overall use of off-site EAP programs was one-third less than that of on-site EAP programs.[58]

3. The third step is to solve the problem. Sometimes the EAP counselor is able to help the employee do this in a short time (three sessions or fewer). For example, an employee in financial difficulty may need only short-term counseling in how to manage personal finances. Some problems, however, take longer to resolve. For these, the EAP counselor will send the troubled employee to an outside agency equipped to provide the necessary treatment. The counselor will try to find a service that best fits the employee's needs and is also cost-effective. For example, an EAP counselor who determines that an employee needs treatment for alcoholism must decide whether the employee should receive inpatient residential treatment, receive outpatient treatment, or attend Alcoholics Anonymous (AA) meetings.[59] Inpatient residential treatment may require a 30-day hospitalization period that costs between $8,000 and $12,000. The other two alternatives cost much less.
4. The fourth and final step depends on the outcome of the treatment. If the employee has been placed on leave and the treatment is successful, the employee is allowed to return to work. In some cases, treatment does not require the employee to take a leave of absence; the employee remains on the job while being treated and continues after treatment has been successfully concluded. If the treatment is unsuccessful and the difficulty continues to disrupt the employee's work performance, the employer usually terminates the employee.

EAPs can help employees suffering from anxiety and stress due to restructurings or downsizings. The EAP at Rohm & Haas, a specialty chemical company headquartered in Philadelphia, played an important role in easing the effects of downsizing the company's production facility. When employment was cut from 800 to about 550, the company negotiated with its EAP vendor for an on-site psychologist who, in addition to maintaining office hours at the plant, sat in on management meetings and walked around the plant talking to employees. At GTE, EAPs are used to identify and provide support for managers who are dealing with people who are being let go or transferred.[60]

In the United States, there are more than 12,000 EAPs; 74 percent of large companies use them[61] to deal with a wide variety of problems. Gambling casinos in the Atlantic City, New Jersey, area have used EAPs to deal with the high incidence of alcohol- and drug-related performance problems that employees in the gambling industry experience. The EAP for the Association of Flight Attendants, which represents flight attendants from 19 airlines, has an unusually large number of individuals seeking help with weight loss.[62] At Harmon International Industries, a California manufacturing firm, the EAP for the company developed some special programs to help Harmon's employees deal with domestic violence, a problem that costs U.S. industry $700 million in lost productivity a year, according to the Family Violence Prevention Fund. The EAP provided awareness training to managers to show them how to detect warning signs of domestic violence and how to make referrals to the EAP counselor. The EAP helped one of Harmon's employees who reported domestic violence, Martha Rodriguez, to obtain a restraining order and obtain psychiatric care for her husband, herself, and her children.[63]

EAPs contribute to effective employee relations because they represent a good-faith attempt by management to support and retain employees who might otherwise be dismissed because of poor performance. The annual cost per employee of an EAP runs about $20 to $30.[64] However, employers gain financial benefits that outweigh their out-of-pocket EAP expenses in terms of savings on employee turnover, absenteeism, medical costs, unemployment insurance rates, workers' compensation rates, accident costs, and disability insurance costs. One study showed that the rate of problem resolution for EAPs is about 78 percent.[65] PricewaterhouseCoopers consultants estimate that each dollar invested in an EAP could return four to seven times that amount in cost reductions.[66]

Through over 12,000 EAPs in the United States, workers have access to therapy for issues such as divorce, death, and addictions.
Source: Rob Marmion/Shutterstock.

An alternative to EAPs for the purpose of helping employees cope with personal problems is the growing use of

workplace chaplains, who are usually ordained ministers that provide counselling services to employees. Workplace chaplains are proactive and do outreach with employees rather than waiting for complaints to be reported to the EAP, which are likely to occur on a telephone hotline. Employers receive written reports from a workplace chaplain on a regular basis that will reveal the patterns of problems that are troubling to employees. Companies that use workplace chaplains include R. J. Reynolds Tobacco, McDonald's, and Tyson Foods. Marketplace Chaplains is a company that supplies workplace chaplains to businesses, and currently employs 2,700 of them.[67]

Employee Recognition Programs

employee recognition program
A program that rewards employees for their ideas and contributions.

Companies operating in global markets need employees who continuously improve the way they do their jobs to keep the company competitive. Employees are more likely to share their ideas for work improvements when managers give them credit for their contributions. **Employee recognition programs** can enhance employee relations by communicating that the organization cares about its employees' ideas and is willing to reward them for their efforts.[68] The HR department can help here by developing and maintaining formal employee recognition programs, such as suggestion systems and recognition awards.

Suggestion Systems

A *suggestion system* is designed to solicit, evaluate, and implement suggestions from employees and then reward the employees for worthwhile ideas.[69] Although the reward is often monetary, it does not have to be. It might instead be public recognition, extra vacation time, a special parking spot, or some other benefit. Suggestion systems have been successfully implemented in such diverse organizations as hospitals, universities, the U.S. Postal Service and other branches of government, and private-sector companies such as BP, Eastman Kodak, Black & Decker, Simon & Schuster, and Lincoln Electric Company.[70] Firms that use suggestion systems in the United States average approximately 10 suggestions per 100 employees. Although this yield of suggestions appears modest, management experts indicate that many incremental workplace improvements are normally made outside of a formal suggestion system.[71]

Managers should adhere to certain guidelines when designing a suggestion system. They should:

- Provide a simple, easy process for submitting suggestions.[72]
- Use a suggestion evaluation committee to evaluate each suggestion fairly and provide an explanation to employees why their suggestions have not been used.
- Implement accepted suggestions immediately and give credit to the suggestion's originator. The company newsletter can be used to publicly recognize employees whose suggestions have resulted in improvements.
- Make the value of the reward proportional to the suggestion's benefit to the company. For example, a loan manager at Bank of America who made a suggestion that saved the bank $363,520 per year received a cash award of $36,520 for her idea.[73] The average award that companies paid per employee suggestion was $235, according to a survey by the Employee Involvement Association. The survey also reported that the value received by employers from these suggestions was about 10 times greater.[74]
- Let the HR department track and manage the suggestion program by taking a coordinating role to ensure that employees buy into the program.[75]

Suggestion systems, long a part of U.S. business, have become more popular globally in recent years. For example, Japanese companies such as Toyota, Honda, and Mitsubishi have successfully gathered numerous suggestions from their employees resulting in significant improvements in their products (including automobiles). At Honda, employees who provide suggestions that result in quality improvements earn points that can be applied to prizes such as a new Honda Accord or two international airline tickets.[76] Companies that depend on innovation should reward employee suggestions liberally, as explained in the Manager's Notebook, "Good Employee Suggestions Should Be Rewarded Substantially."

MANAGER'S NOTEBOOK

Good Employee Suggestions Should Be Rewarded Substantially

Companies that offer substantial rewards for innovative suggestions can expect to see a substantial increase in the number of workable innovations. All too often, rewards for suggestions do not inspire employees to share their ideas with the company because of the modest size of the reward.

At Interminds, a consulting firm founded by Bill Townsend in the San Francisco area, employee suggestions can be well rewarded. An employee who comes up with an idea to save money while promoting the company's vision gets half of the first year's savings. The suggestion policy was instrumental in obtaining a great idea from an executive assistant who earned a salary of $38,000 a year. Her process improvement was to automate the manual system of tracking 900 field representatives. She was able to prove her concept's validity to an individual in the finance department, who then implemented her suggestion. The company saved $304,000 in the first year from this suggestion, which earned the employee a $152,000 bonus. By publicizing this success story within the company, Interminds saw the number of workable suggestions increase by 20 to 40 percent.

Sources: Based on Carini, G., and Townsend, B. (2007, April). $152,000 for your thoughts. *Harvard Business Review*, 23; Conlin, M. (2009, March 23). The case for unequal perks. *BusinessWeek*, 54–55; *The Economist*. (2009, September 19). A market for ideas, 75–76. ■■

Recognition Awards

Recognition awards give public credit to people or teams who make outstanding contributions to the organization. These people or teams may become role models for others by communicating what behaviors and accomplishments the company values. McDonald's Employee of the Month award consists of a notice posted in each restaurant for all employees and customers to see. IBM employees who make major contributions are recognized in a host of different ways, ranging from a simple thank-you letter from a division manager to a cash award of $150,000 (given to two company scientists who won the Nobel Prize in science).

The recognition of teams and people who make important quality contributions can be either monetary or nonmonetary. For example, FedEx allows supervisors to confer instant cash awards to employees for quality efforts.[77] FedEx has earned the Malcolm Baldrige National Quality Award, the highest recognition of quality that a U.S. company can receive.

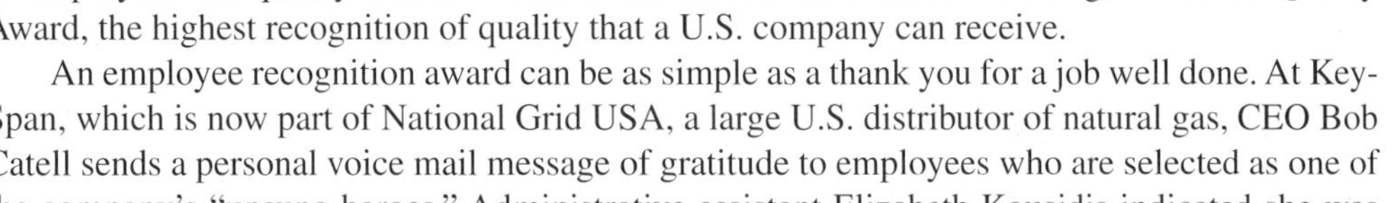

An employee recognition award can be as simple as a thank you for a job well done. At KeySpan, which is now part of National Grid USA, a large U.S. distributor of natural gas, CEO Bob Catell sends a personal voice mail message of gratitude to employees who are selected as one of the company's "unsung heroes." Administrative assistant Elizabeth Kousidis indicated she was "surprised and happy" when CEO Catell recognized her as an unsung company hero.[78]

A recognition award can be initiated by a manager or by an internal customer of an individual or a team, with nominees evaluated by a recognition and awards committee. To emphasize that quality improvement should be continuous, there should be no limit on the number of times that a person or team can receive a recognition award. At Yum! Brands, a global corporation of fast food restaurants, recognition is given to the employee or team right away and it is always personalized. For example, at Pizza Hut (one of Yum! Brands' restaurant chains) an employee can be recognized for doing good work on a particular day with a cheesehead (a funny hat shaped like a slice of cheese) and have a personal note written on it.[79]

A recognition award should be a celebration of the team or individual's success that encourages all organization members to work toward the organization's goals.[80] Recognition awards that focus attention on team or individual accomplishments include:

- A company-paid picnic to which all team members and their families are invited.
- T-shirts, coffee mugs, or baseball caps with a team insignia encouraging team commitment.

- A company-paid night on the town (such as dinner at a nice restaurant or tickets to a concert or sports event) for an employee and his or her spouse.[81]
- A plaque engraved with the names of individuals or teams that have made outstanding contributions.
- A donation in the name of an employee to the charity of his or her choice.

Recognition programs can serve purposes other than providing positive feedback to employees.[82] A Phoenix-area hotel rewarded employees who made outstanding contributions with a free night's stay at the hotel. Not only was this a valued prize, but it also gave employees the chance to view their organization from the customer's perspective. Management hoped that this experience would prompt new suggestions for improving customer service.

Although public recognition can be a powerful tool to sustain employee and team motivation, the Manager's Notebook, "Guidelines for Public Recognition Rewards," shows managers how to avoid pitfalls with public recognition awards. For example, when a reward appears to be motivated by favoritism or becomes a popularity contest rather than clear recognition of excellent performance, it can depress rather than improve company morale.[83]

MANAGER'S NOTEBOOK

Customer-Driven HR

Guidelines for Public Recognition Rewards

Public recognition rewards can have a high upside impact on employee and team levels of motivation if they are administered well. Most employees find it very rewarding to be recognized and honored in front of their peers. However, a public reward that is poorly administered due to favoritism or being perceived as a popularity contest can demotivate employees and embarrass the recipient of the reward. Here are some key points to keep in mind when administering public recognition rewards to employees:

- ***Have clear reward criteria*** Reward criteria that are clear, unambiguous, and well communicated to employees beforehand are likely to result in an employee perception of fairness and deservedness of the reward on the part of its recipient.
- ***Ensure that judges of the recognition reward are not personally related to the recipient*** The individuals on the committee who determine the winner of the public recognition reward should have an arm's-length relationship to the reward recipient. For example, if an employee's supervisor or coworker is on the rewards committee, this person may need to excuse himself or herself from the voting to avoid a perception of favoritism.
- ***The presentation of the reward should be given on a sincere basis*** The speaker who presents the reward to the recipient in front of peers should focus on giving a sincere message of appreciation to the employee being honored. The presenter should avoid engaging in theatrics and exaggerated gestures that make the recipient feel undeserving and embarrassed.
- ***Try to personalize the reward if possible*** Rewards that are personalized to the needs of the recipient have the greatest impact on motivation. An employee who loves sports will probably appreciate tickets to a baseball game more than tickets to hear an orchestra play classical music. A personalized plaque given in a public ceremony will have longer-lasting memory value than cash because the cash is soon spent whereas the plaque remains in an employee's office or in his or her home.
- ***Recognize multiple top performers*** Avoid limiting the recognition reward to only one person if several employees have made contributions that deserve to be recognized.

Sources: Based on Buchanan, L. (2011, July). And the award goes to . . . Rethinking annual honors. *Inc.*, 108–110; Wiscombe, J. (2002, April). Rewards get results. *Workforce*, 42–48; Ginther, C. (2000, August). Incentive programs that really work. *HRMagazine*, 117–120; Demos, T. (2010, April 12). Motivate without spending millions. *Fortune*, 37–38. ■■

Summary and Conclusions

The Roles of the Manager and the Employee Relations Specialist

Good employee relations involve providing fair and consistent treatment to all employees so that they will be committed to the organization. The backbone of an effective employee relations program is the manager, who is expected to evaluate, reward, and discipline employees in line with the company's employee relations philosophy. Employee relations representatives from the HR department ensure that employment policies are being fairly and consistently administered within the company. They often consult with both supervisors and employees on specific employee relations problems.

Developing Employee Communications

To develop effective employee relations, a company needs communication channels to move information up, down, and across the organization. Effective communications in an organization involve (1) a sender who encodes the message, (2) a communication channel that transmits the message, (3) a receiver who decodes the message, and (4) provisions for feedback because noise in the environment may distort the message's true meaning.

Encouraging Effective Communications

Working with supervisors and managers, employee relations representatives can facilitate effective communications by developing provisions for (1) information dissemination, (2) employee feedback, and (3) employee assistance programs.

Information dissemination involves making information available to decision makers, wherever they are located. Employee handbooks, written communications (memos, financial statements, newsletters, and bulletin boards), audiovisual communications, electronic communications (voice mail, e-mail, and multimedia applications), meetings, retreats, and informal communications are some of the choices available for disseminating information to employees.

Employee feedback programs are designed to improve communications by giving employees a voice in decision making and policy formulation and making sure they receive due process on any complaints they lodge against managers. Two programs that the HR department can establish to solicit employee feedback are (1) employee attitude surveys and (2) appeals procedures.

Employee assistance programs are designed to help employees whose emotional or psychological troubles are affecting their work performance. The employee is given the opportunity and resources to resolve the problem. Successful resolution of personal problems benefits both the employer and the employee.

Employee Recognition Programs

Employee recognition programs can enhance communications and employee relations by recognizing and rewarding employees who make important contributions to the organization's success. Recognition programs often use suggestion systems and recognition awards. The rewards given to individuals or teams may be monetary or nonmonetary.

Key Terms

appeals procedure, 442
downward communication, 431
electronic mail, 434
e-mail, 434
employee assistance programs (EAPs), 443
employee attitude surveys, 441
employee feedback programs, 441
employee recognition programs, 446
employee relations policies, 428
employee relations representatives, 428
informal communications, 439
information dissemination, 432
knowledge workers, 431
management by walking around (MBWA), 440
multimedia technology, 437
nepotism, 432
social networking, 436
teleconferencing, 434
upward communication, 431
voice mail, 434

✪ Watch It!

Gawker Media: Managers and Communication. If your instructor has assigned this, go to **mymanagementlab.com** to watch a video case and answer questions.

Discussion Questions

13-1. Employee privacy has been called "today's most important workplace issue." What kinds of dilemmas have the new technologies created regarding employee privacy? What other kinds of problems have the new technologies created in employee relations and communications, and how might managers deal with them?

13-2. Shelly Wexler tells her supervisor, Rob Levine, that having to care for her aging mother is forcing her to leave work early and is making her feel increasingly "stressed out." Rob refers her to the company's EAP, but he also tries to convince her to put her mother in a home for the aged and even gives her some information about nursing homes in the area. Do you think Rob is just showing ordinary concern for his employee, or do you think he is overstepping managerial boundaries? Discuss the supervisor's role in implementing an EAP. Should a supervisor try to diagnose an employee's personal problem? Why or why not?

✪ 13-3. Do you think most employees have reservations about using an appeals procedure such as an open-door policy? What can managers do to convince employees that the available procedures are fair and effective?

✪ 13-4. Some communication experts claim that men and women have different styles of communication that create barriers to decoding messages from a sender of the opposite sex.

What do you think are the important differences between the way men and women communicate with each other in a work environment? What are the implications of these sex differences in communication from the perspective of effective employee relations?

13-5. A minority of employees are actually demotivated by being given public recognition in front of their coworkers. Why might some employees feel uncomfortable being recognized in a public ceremony? Do you think that this could be an issue related to diversity in the workplace? Assuming that you are a manager and you are aware that one of your employees does not respond well to public recognition, what can you do to recognize this employee's good performance as an individual or part of a team?

MyManagementLab®

If your instructor has assigned this, go to **mymanagementlab.com** for the following Assisted-graded writing questions:

13-6. List three ways the HR department can contribute to positive employee relations in a company.

13-7. Do you think it is a good idea for a company and its managers to keep in touch with employees who have quit and taken jobs elsewhere? Provide two of the advantages and two disadvantages with staying in touch with former employees who have moved on with their careers.

13-8. Millions of people use social networking Web sites, such as Facebook and MySpace, to share personal information, including photos and videos with their friends. Should companies use social networking Web sites as a communications tool to build employee networks? What are two of the advantages and two of the disadvantages of using social networking Web sites as informal communication channels for employees?

You Manage It! 1: Ethics/Social Responsibility

Employees Don't Always Speak Up When There Is Bad News to Communicate

As discussed in this chapter, companies establish feedback systems such as speak-up programs, open-door policies, grievance panels, or corporate ombudsmen in order to give employees an opportunity to lodge a complaint or voice their reactions to what they perceive as unfair treatment. These systems are designed to improve situations that are sources of employee dissatisfaction and to avoid costly turnover as well as keep upper management informed on what employees are feeling about their relationship with management and company policies. Despite the presence of feedback systems, employees do not always use these channels of upward communication because they fear for their job security as well as fear possible retribution from powerful managers who may want to discipline an employee who provides critical feedback. A manager may view an employee who uses the feedback program as a whistle blower or someone lacking in team spirit. For example an employee who feels rightly or wrongly that her supervisor is being unfair in allocating work assignments or pay raises may not use her company's speak-up program because it requires that she first try to resolve the dispute with her supervisor, and she may fear making the relationship even more stressful and being forced to quit before she is ready to leave for another job.

The fears that some employees have for their safety and job security when using a feedback program to voice a concern may indeed have a basis in reality. When an employee goes to an HR representative or a corporate ombudsman—who is supposed to be an impartial party that helps to resolve an employee's problem—the employee knows that the designated person that listens to his or her problem in the workplace is still being paid by the company. The employee may hesitate to use the feedback program because the problem resolver is likely to have interests that are more closely aligned with those of management.

Critical Thinking Questions

13-9. Assume that you are working in a company and you believe that your supervisor gave you a pay raise that is unfair and less than you deserve based on your performance. This is not the first time this has happened with the current supervisor and you believe your performance has also been evaluated unfairly by him. You are considering using one of the company feedback programs to complain that your pay raise is not fair and that you deserve more pay. The company has an open-door policy, a corporate ombudsman, and a speak-up program. Which one will you use and which one will you avoid using? Explain the basis for your choice.

13-10. A company has a speak-up feedback program but unfortunately few employees use it. Managers learn about employee problems only during the exit interview when the employees are leaving to work for a different employer. Provide some ways that a feedback program can be improved to increase the likelihood that employees will use it.

Team Exercise

13-11. Academic cheating on exams occurs at a high frequency at many universities and yet most students are not willing to inform on cheating students and use university feedback channels designed to let the university administration be aware of the parties who are cheating. With a group of four or five other students, develop a list of reasons why university students avoid using university feedback channels to let the administration know that cheating is going on in a class. How would you design a feedback channel that has the potential to be used by more students to inform the administration about cheating when it occurs? Be prepared to share your ideas with other members of the class when called on by your instructor.

Experiential Exercise: Individual

13-12. In this experiential exercise, think about how you would react to the following situation. During the first few months of your first professional job since graduating from the university, you discover that your supervisor is a difficult person and treats you badly. Here are some examples: (1) At team meetings the supervisor humiliates you in front of other employees by calling you a nickname "Booby" rather than your given name of Bob; (2) the supervisor has described several of your mistakes that you have made learning your new job on his Facebook page and coworkers have teased you about these mistakes, which makes the workplace seem hostile to you; and (3) the supervisor likes to play practical jokes on employees and you believe you are often the target of these pranks. You want the supervisor to stop treating you disrespectfully and are not sure how to get him to treat you in a better fashion. You are considering using one of the following company feedback programs: the open-door policy, the speak-up program, or the corporate ombudsman. Which one will you use and what is the basis of your choice? Should you just quit the job? Quitting after only a few months of employment may look bad on your resume and make it difficult to secure a new job. Be prepared to explain what you decide to do when the instructor calls on you.

Sources: Based on Klaas, B. S., Olson-Buchanan, J. B., and Ward A. (2012). The determinants of alternative forms of workplace voice: An integrative perspective. *Journal of Management*, 38, 314–345; Bies, R. J. (2013). The delivery of bad news in organizations: A framework for analysis. *Journal of Management*, 39, 136–162; Burris, E. R. (2012). The risks and rewards of speaking up: Managerial responses to employee voice. *Academy of Management Journal*, 55, 851–875.

 You Manage It! 2: Customer-Driven HR

Should Having Fun Be a Job Requirement?

The trend of having fun in the workplace influences employee relations at many companies. Several software firms in Silicon Valley, California, have installed rock-climbing walls in their reception areas and put inflatable animals in their offices. TD Bank, a U.S. subsidiary of Canada's Toronto Dominion Bank, has a "Wow!" department that sends festive, costume-wearing teams to "surprise and delight" successful employees. Red Bull, a beverage company, has set up a slide in its London office. Google has embraced workplace fun in a big way. Its office park has volleyball courts, bicycle paths, a yellow brick road, a model dinosaur, regular games of roller hockey, and several professional masseuses.

A company that has turned "fun and a little weirdness" in the workplace into one of its core values is Zappos, an online shoe retailer. Zappos has made having fun at work into a job requirement. At Zappos, some people are assigned the job of making workers happy because many employees work in the call center taking orders for shoes, which can be routine work. Call-center work traditionally has high turnover rates, but the fun culture at Zappos has helped the company retain employees at rates exceeding industry norms. Some of the fun activities at Zappos include parades, pajama parties, and happy hours, where employees go bar hopping after work in Las Vegas, where the company is located. One of the unique policies at Zappos is that managers are required to spend 10 to 20 percent of their time socializing with people they manage, which includes time spent outside the office. These social activities can go late into the night because Las Vegas is a city where bars and clubs stay open all night.

The rationale behind the trend to install fun in the workplace is that workers who are having fun will be more fully engaged with their jobs and be more creative. However, when having fun at work becomes formalized into a policy and turns into a job requirement, the "fun" may cease. Employees may feel resentment toward a company that stages fun as a business strategy to increase productivity.

Most of the youthful employees at Zappos are in their twenties, and the CEO, Tony Hsieh, is in his forties. As the Zappos workforce ages, the game-playing and bar-hopping activities that were once viewed as fun may seem more like an unnecessary chore. Managers may prefer to have a greater work-life balance so they can focus on the needs of their families and friends outside Zappos. Is the culture of fun at Zappos sustainable?

Critical Thinking Questions

13-13. When managers at Zappos get older, they are likely to prefer to spend more time with their families and less time after hours partying with their subordinates. What HR policies can enable Zappos to maintain its fun-loving culture that is based on socializing between employees and their bosses?

13-14. Why do companies such as Google let employees play volleyball, roller hockey, and other games at work? Is there a business reason why employees are permitted to play games at the workplace? Wouldn't it be more fun to play these games away from the workplace with friends who are not coworkers?

Team Exercise

13-15. Laura Brounstein is the special projects direction for Cosmopolitan magazine. She believes that work and fun should be synonymous. In 2014, she designed the "Fun Fearless Life Weekend". Brounstein is firmly of the opinion that employees do a much better job if they are enjoying themselves doing it. Work should be something that employees look forward to and not dread. It does appear that the most successful people derive a great deal of happiness and satisfaction from their day to day work. The fun and enjoyment gets them through the more difficult times. What do you think about the notion that having fun at work and being really effective in your job role are not mutually exclusive? With a group of three or four classmates, if you were creating a Fun Fearless Life Weekend to kick start this approach in an organization, what would you include in the program? What key points would you want participants to take away with them? Be prepared to share your ideas for events and motivational messages with your instructor and other members of the class.

Experiential Exercise: Individual

13-16. In this exercise, think how you would react to some specific situations where you may be required to have fun as a job requirement. Can you see yourself having fun in the situations listed here? If not, would you still be willing to perform these activities in a company that has a fun-loving culture? Do you see yourself fitting into a company culture that encourages participation in several of these activities?

a. Sing a karaoke song solo in front of your coworkers during after-hours socializing at a bar, which is a ritual expected of each employee.
b. Dress up as a well-known celebrity such as Elvis or Dolly Parton and perform your work in costume during a company dress-up day activity.
c. Go out for drinks after work with coworkers on your team on a regular basis, which includes socializing with a coworker you do not particularly like.
d. As a manager, order a birthday cake with candles and sing happy birthday to each of your subordinates on her or his birthday.
e. Participate in a weekly poker game with coworkers after work.

Which activities, if any, would you prefer not to participate in? There could be social pressure from coworkers to participate in some of these activities. How would you explain to your boss and fellow employees that you would prefer not to participate in a certain activity and avoid any hurt feelings that may strain your relationships with them?

Sources: Based on *The Economist*. (2010, September 18). Down with fun: The depressing vogue for having fun at work, 82; O'Brien, J. (2009, February 9). Zappos knows how to kick it. *Fortune*, 55–60; Chafkin, M. (2009, May). Get happy: How Tony Hsieh uses relentless innovation, stellar service, and a staff of believers to make Zappos.com an e-commerce juggernaut—and one of the most blissed-out businesses in America. *Inc.*, 67–73.

 You Manage It! 3: Ethics/Social Responsibility

Going Green Keeps New Belgium Brewing Company in the Black

Kim Jordan and Jeff Lebesch, the husband and wife founders of New Belgium Brewing Company, envisioned building a world-class beer brand while minimizing the company's footprint on the planet. Nearly two decades later, they have built a workplace where employees are engaged and enthusiastic about supporting the company's environmental cause. New Belgium currently has 320 employees and generates $96 million in annual revenues.

One of the secrets of the company's success is finding fun and communal ways for employees to be involved. Another is not preaching from the top. "I think it is very important not to be heavy handed and instead set an example that employees can follow if they want to," says Jordan, New Belgium's chief executive officer.

The company gives employees ample ways to be environmentally conscious at work and in their free time. It also ties those efforts into its signature beer, Fat Tire, by encouraging bicycling. Each New Belgium employee is given a cruiser bike after one year of employment, and roughly half of the employees based in Fort Collins, Colorado, commute by bike in the summer months. What is more, every summer the company hosts an 11-city event called Tour de Fat, where New Belgium employees dress in costumes and lead local residents on a bike tour. Not all of the company's initiatives are centered on bikes. New Belgium leases Toyota Prius hybrids for its sales force to drive to meetings.

The company also tries to make environmental sustainability a big influence at the workplace. An on-site recycling center allows employees to recycle goods such as old car batteries and motor oil. The company also donates 1 percent of its profits to "1% For The Planet," a global philanthropic network. New Belgium also has been using wind-power electricity—a clean energy source—for its brewing process since 1999 when employees voted to use wind power instead of electricity from the local coal-based utility company. Employees voted to subsidize the higher cost of wind-powered electricity over cheaper coal-based alternatives from their profit-sharing bonuses.

One challenge has been to keep the feel of a close-knit community, even as the company grows quickly and adds employees in cities outside of the Fort Collins headquarters. Each month, New Belgium holds a videoconference meeting for all employees to discuss new developments, and every employee gets invited to an annual retreat. After five years of employment, each worker gets a one-week complimentary trip to Belgium to learn about Belgian beer culture.

Jordan says that employee ownership has also helped boost engagement. Employees own about 32 percent of New Belgium through a stock ownership plan, and the company practices open-book management, hosting monthly meetings where it walks employees through the company's financial statements.

Chris Winn, the self-titled "event evangelist" for New Belgium, says the company has made the work environment fun and collaborative by letting employees be themselves and by not setting strict rules for employees to follow.

Critical Thinking Questions

13-17. How do New Belgium's green business practices contribute to positive employee relations?

13-18. What communication and HR practices does New Belgium use to keep employees in the loop so they feel involved with the company and part of a community?

13-19. How does New Belgium introduce fun into the workplace? How does having fun keep employees engaged and enthusiastic about their work and the company?

Team Exercise

13-20. As described in the case on New Belgium Brewing Company as well as in this chapter's opening vignette, companies are coming up with creative ways to introduce fun into the workplace in order to encourage employees to feel more involved with their work and experience positive emotions (happiness, joy, passion, etc.) at the workplace. With a group of four or five students, discuss your most recent work experiences in light of whether the employer tried to consciously introduce some fun workplace activities. What were the fun activities? Did they work? That is, did they draw employees in and increase their level of work engagement, or did they simply distract employees from doing the real work that was expected from them? Be prepared to share your ideas with other members of the class when asked by the instructor.

Experiential Exercise: Individual

13-21. Visit the New Belgium Brewing Web site (*www.newbelgium.com*) to learn more about the company. The company has a strong culture that values environmental sustainability. Here are its core beliefs:

We believe, to be environmental stewards, we need to:

a. Lovingly care for the planet that sustains us.
b. Steward natural resources by closing the loops between waste and input.
c. Minimize the environmental impact of shipping our beer.
d. Reduce our dependence on coal-fired electricity.
e. Protect our precious Rocky Mountain water resources.
f. Focus our efforts on conservation and efficiency.
g. Support innovative technology.
h. Model joyful environmentalism through our commitment to relationships, continuous improvement, and the camaraderie and cheer of beer.

How do the stated core values fit with the employee-relations activities described in the case? How do these company values compare to those of other companies where you have worked? How do the values of New Belgium compare to your own personal values? Do you think you could fit into the employee community at New Belgium? For example, would you be willing to sacrifice part of your bonus to support the higher cost of wind power, as did all the employees at New Belgium? Be prepared to explain your answers to these questions when called upon by the instructor.

Sources: Based on New Belgium Brewing Company Web site. (2008). *www.newbelgium.com*; Spors, K. (2008, October 13). Top small workplaces, 2008. *Wall Street Journal*, R8; New Belgium Brewery: Four principles of sustainable business. (2008, June 7). *www.triplepundit.com*.

 You Manage It! 4: Global

In Praise of Nepotism?

Nepotism is a global HR practice that gives preference in the workplace to relatives and friends of organization members in decisions such as hiring, promotions, and pay. In places such as China and Africa, nepotism has been used to favor members of one's kinship group or tribe over others. In Western Europe and the United States, nepotism has been used to favor members of one's family or social class.

Nepotism challenges some of the core values in the U.S. workplace, such as the principles of merit and equal opportunity. Yet nepotism is still applied in the United States in business, public life, and the creative arts. Bill Ford, great-grandson of founder Henry Ford, was the CEO of Ford Motor Company, and his ascendency to the top job at Ford is related to the fact that there is a special class of voting shares owned by the Ford family that allows them to have a strong voice in the company's affairs. U.S. President John Kennedy chose his 34-year-old brother, Robert Kennedy, for attorney general, and U.S. President George W. Bush is son of former President George H. W. Bush. It is unlikely if either of these political leaders would have held their respective office without the assistance of their relative who was a U.S. president. Former Mayor Richard Daley of Chicago had the same job as his father with the same name, who was mayor from 1955 to 1976. In the movie industry, children or relatives of actors and actresses such as Goldie Hawn (daughter Kate Hudson), Kirk Douglas (son Michael Douglas), and Rosemary Clooney (nephew George Clooney) are presented opportunities to work in the entertainment business that are difficult to obtain for those without family connections.

Nepotism can be good or bad, according to Adam Bellow, author of *In Praise of Nepotism: A Natural History*. Bellow indicates that factors that affect the good or bad use of nepotism include merit and the distinction between private and public. Consider the following:

- In his bestselling book *Good to Great*, Jim Collins found that companies that markedly outperform their peers in terms of total shareholder return over extended periods of time are disproportionately led by CEOs who are the descendants of founders.
- In recent years, some highly publicized CEO failures occurred with descendants of company founders in firms such as Motorola (Chris Galvin) and Seagrams (Edgar Bronfman, Jr.).
- President Suharto of Indonesia excelled at nepotism and "crony capitalism" when he lavished business monopolies on his six children, whose wealth was estimated to exceed $40 billion. This blatant favoritism of family members had a major effect on influencing Indonesians to overthrow his government in 1998.
- In some of America's top universities, children of university alumni (called "legacies") are given preference in filling 10 to 15 percent of spots in the entering freshman class. For example, William Fitzsimmons, dean of admissions of Harvard College, admits that 40 percent of legacy student applications are accepted compared to only 11 percent of ordinary applicants. Even at good public universities such as the University of Virginia, legacy applicants are two to four times more likely to be admitted than nonlegacy applicants.

Adam Bellow argues that nepotism can create family dynasties such as the Rothschilds (banking), Rockefellers (finance and philanthropy), and Hiltons (hotels) that become brands offering perceived value to customers when the family remains involved in the business. He argues that the family member who is hired in a dynastic organization is more likely to perform better and make greater sacrifices for the company than others in order to protect the reputation of the family name and the business, which are closely related.

Critical Thinking Questions

13-22. Why do you think people are more accepting of the application of nepotism in the workplace in a privately owned business than in one that is publicly owned by many shareholders? Why is there little tolerance for nepotism in the government, such as when the mayor of a city puts friends and family members on the government payroll?

13-23. Under what conditions could it be considered acceptable to hire a relative of an employee or executive in a public organization, such as in federal government, or a publicly owned business, such as General Motors?

13-24. Do you agree or disagree with Bellow's argument that relatives of company owners have a greater motivation to perform well and make sacrifices for the business to protect the family reputation than do nonrelatives? Explain.

Team Exercise

13-25. Form a team with four or five of your classmates to learn why some organizations have implemented *antinepotism policies*, which are employment rules that restrict the hiring of relatives of employees in an organization. The team should find one or two examples of an antinepotism policy to share with the class. (For example, these policies are quite common in city government units such as police or firefighting departments.) For each antinepotism policy, indicate which relatives are not permitted to seek employment and which ones are (possibilities may include in-laws, step relations, or grandchildren). Develop a theory or explanation why you think each organization implemented its antinepotism policy. Do you agree or disagree that the organizations should use antinepotism policies?

Experiential Exercise: Team

13-26. Find a partner in the class for this exercise and take turns sharing your opinions about the long-entrenched practice used by elite universities such as Harvard, Yale, and Princeton to reserve 10 to 15 percent of the spaces in the incoming freshman class for legacy students who are related to former alumni. Some critics of this practice call it "affirmative action for the wealthy." Is this a fair comment? Why do highly selective schools continue this form of nepotism? Would it make a difference if you learned that many selective schools that help children of alumni gain admission also give full financial scholarships to economically disadvantaged students who meet their admission standards? After both partners have shared their opinions, summarize the key points and be prepared to share your ideas with other members of the class.

Sources: Based on Jaskiewicz, P., Uhlenbruck, K., Balkin, D., and Reay, T. (2013). Is nepotism good or bad? Types of nepotism and implications for knowledge management. *Family Business Review,* 26, 121–139; Ciulla, J. (2005, January). In praise of nepotism? *Business Ethics Quarterly*, 153–160; *The Economist.* (2004, January 10). The curse of nepotism, 27; Bellow, A. (2003, August 5). When in doubt, hire your kin. *Wall Street Journal*, B-2.

Endnotes

Scan for Endnotes or go to http://www.pearsonglobaleditions.com/Gomez-Mejia.

CHAPTER 14

Respecting Employee Rights and Managing Discipline

MyManagementLab®

When you see this icon, visit **www.mymanagementlab.com** for activities that are applied, personalized, and offer immediate feedback.

CHALLENGES

After reading this chapter, you should be able to deal more effectively with the following challenges:

1. **Understand** employee rights.
2. **Understand** management rights.
3. **Become** aware of employee rights challenges: a balancing act.
4. **Learn** practices for administering and managing discipline.
5. **Develop** competence for managing difficult employees.
6. **Become** aware of preventing the need for discipline with human resource management.

All employees have rights that are based on laws, company employment policies, and traditions. Employers also have rights that support their authority and what they can expect from their employees. Sometimes these two sets of rights conflict. Consider the following situations:

- Aligo, a Mountain View, California, producer of "mobile services," sells a product called Worktrack that enables employers to monitor employees electronically to see where they are and what they are doing at any time. Among the principal customers of Worktrack are employers in the heating and air conditioning business. Workers have cell phones equipped with a GPS (global positioning satellite) chip that transmits their locations to computers in the back office. The location coordinates can be compared to the location of the work site where the employee is expected to be. If an employee is not in the right area, he or she is considered to be not working, and a notification will be sent to the employee's office. The system also tracks how fast the workers drive, so the employer can verify to insurance companies that no one is speeding. This monitoring is legal, because employers have the right to monitor their workers. However, when employees are constantly monitored by an employer, does this practice infringe on employees' rights to ethical treatment in the workplace?[1]

Employers can use electronic devices to monitor the location of employees while they are on the job.
Source: Monty Rakusen/Getty Images.

- Verified Person performs background checks of new hires for employers and then continues to provide automated biweekly updates on an employee's activities, alerting the company of any new misdemeanor or felony convictions. Automated ongoing screening can be useful for employers in certain industries, such as financial services, that have statutes prohibiting employees convicted of certain crimes from being on the payroll. However, such monitoring could be troubling for white-collar employees who would rather not have their employers discover a marijuana infraction or drunk-driving charge.[2]

- Hearsay Social is a company that lets large companies control how their employees interact with customers on Facebook and other social media. Hearsay Social provides customers such as 24 Hour Fitness with a dashboard to monitor employees on Facebook, LinkedIn, and Twitter. The software provided by Hearsay Social looks for compliance violations between employees and customers, such as when bankers discuss an unauthorized deal.[3]

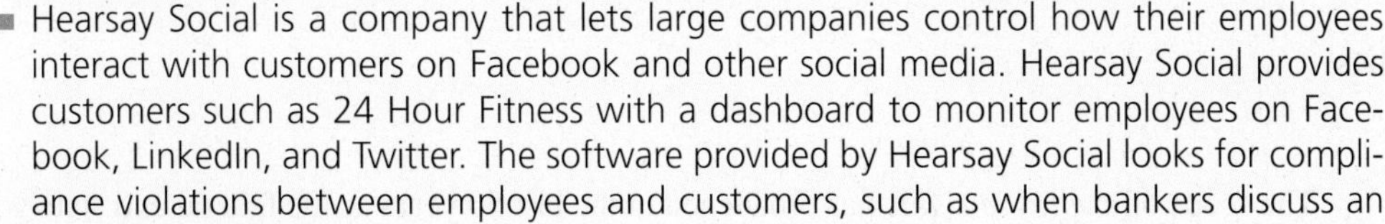

The Managerial Perspective

The three examples in the chapter opener suggest that the rights of both employees and employers should be clearly spelled out in every employment relationship. The HR department can help in several ways, such as:

- Developing and enforcing policies that inform employees of their rights and responsibilities.
- Making managers aware of employees' rights and managers' obligations to employees.
- Acting as an employee advocate, especially in cases where a supervisor misunderstands or disregards discipline policy.

But it is the manager who can make a tremendous difference here. Managers who respect employees' rights are more likely to have employees with higher levels of morale and job satisfaction than managers who ignore these rights. Respecting employees' rights also lessens the likelihood of a costly grievance procedure or lawsuit. As a result, managers need to learn what their employees' rights are, conduct thorough investigations on behalf of employees with a complaint, and learn to administer discipline as a way to correct a behavior or habit that is nonproductive—rather than as a form of punishment.

In this chapter, we examine employee rights and employee discipline. These two issues are closely related to the quality of employee relations (discussed in Chapter 13). Organizations with effective employee relations ensure that their managers respect employees' rights and use fair and consistent discipline procedures.

First, we examine the concepts of employee rights, management rights, and the employment-at-will doctrine that governs many nonunion employers. Second, we explore some challenges that managers encounter in balancing employee rights with the rights of management. Next, we discuss employee discipline and offer some suggestions for managing difficult employees. We conclude by examining how the HR department can support managers with proactive policies that minimize the need for disciplinary procedures.

✪ Learn It!

If your professor has chosen to assign this go to **www.mymanagementlab.com** to see what you should particularly focus on, and take the chapter 14 warmup.

Employee Rights

A **right** is the ability to engage in conduct that is protected by law or social sanction, free from interference by another party (such as an employer). For example, employees have the legal right to form a union. It is illegal for an employer to discourage employees from exercising their right to form a union by withholding pay increases from those who support the union.

right
The ability to engage in conduct that is protected by law or social sanction, free from interference by another party.

Statutory Rights	Contractual Rights	Other Rights
• Protection from discrimination	• Employment contract	• Ethical treatment
• Safe working conditions	• Union contract	• Privacy (limited)
• Right to form unions	• Implied contracts/employment policies	• Free speech (limited)

FIGURE 14.1
Categories of Employee Rights

The scope of *employee rights* has broadened in the last 50 years as the federal and state governments have enacted laws giving employees specific protections. Additionally, in the last few decades courts have been more willing to protect employees from wrongful discharge than they were in the past. Many believe that the courts have been more proactive in protecting employees' rights because of the shrinking proportion of the labor force that is protected by union contracts.

Figure 14.1 shows the three different categories of employee rights that managers must consider: (1) statutory rights, (2) contractual rights, and (3) other rights.

Statutory Rights

statutory right
A right protected by specific laws.

Employees' **statutory rights** are protected by specific laws enacted by government. A key statutory right of employees is protection from discrimination based on race, sex, religion, national origin, age, handicap, or other protected status under Title VII of the Civil Rights Act of 1964 and other equal employment opportunity laws (see Chapter 3). The *Equal Employment Opportunity Commission (EEOC)* regulates employer conduct to ensure that employees are not discriminated against.

Another important employee statutory right is protection from unsafe or unhealthy working conditions. The Occupational Safety and Health Act (OSHA) requires employers to provide safe working conditions for workers and has established the *Occupational Safety and Health Administration* to regulate health and safety practices at companies (see Chapter 16).

Employees also have the legal right to form unions and participate in union activities (see Chapter 15). The *National Labor Relations Board (NLRB)* regulates employer and employee conduct to ensure fair labor practices.

Contractual Rights

contractual right
A right based on the law of contracts.

contract
A legally binding promise between two or more competent parties.

employment contract
A contract that spells out explicitly the terms of the employment relationship for both employee and employer.

Contractual rights are based on the law of contracts. A **contract** is a legally binding promise between two or more competent parties.[4] A breach of contract, in which one of the parties does not perform his or her promised duty to the other party, is subject to legal remedy.

Both employers and employees have rights and obligations to each other when they enter into a contract. An **employment contract** spells out explicitly the terms of the employment relationship for both employee and employer. In general, such contracts state that the employee is expected to work competently over a stipulated period of time and that the employer is expected to provide a mutually agreed upon amount of pay, as well as specific working conditions, over this time period.[5] Employees covered by employment contracts include nonunionized public school teachers, college football coaches, actors in film and television, top-level executives, and middle management.[6] Only a very small percentage of the labor force works under employment contracts.

The provisions of the employment contract give the employee job security and are, at least theoretically, negotiated individually. We say "theoretically" because there are cases in which contracts are so similar as to be standard. For instance, many public school teachers not covered by union contracts are hired on a year-to-year basis by the school district. In theory, each teacher negotiates his or her own contract. In practice, however, because of the volume of contracts that must be written, the vast majority of these contracts follow a standard pattern.

Some industries have standard contract provisions to protect their interests more fully. For instance, employers in competitive technology and service industries often have several employment contract provisions that forbid employees to (1) disclose trade secret information during or after their employment, (2) solicit business from former customers, or (3) attempt to hire former coworkers after leaving the company.[7] For some high-profile jobs, such as top-level executives, the contract will not follow the standard pattern and will, in fact, be negotiated individually.[8] An employee under contract may be fired for reasons other than nonperformance, but he or she is then entitled to compensation for the life of the contract.

A significant percentage of employees in the U.S. labor force (around 11%) are covered by *union contracts,* which protect groups of unionized workers. Union contracts do not provide as much job security as individually negotiated employment contracts do, but they do provide some job security through seniority and union grievance procedures. Seniority provisions protect the jobs of the most senior workers through the "last in, first out" layoff criterion that is commonly written into the union contract (see Chapter 6). Union grievance procedures subject all disciplinary actions (including discharge) to **due process**, which requires a fair investigation and a showing of just cause to discipline employees who have not performed according to expectations. An arbitrator who is empowered to decide discipline and rights cases can restore the job rights and back pay of an employee who has been wrongfully discharged. (**Wrongful discharge** is discharge for reasons that are either illegal or inappropriate, such as age or the refusal to engage in illegal activities.)

due process
Equal and fair application of a policy or law.

wrongful discharge
Termination of an employee for reasons that are either illegal or inappropriate.

Sometimes employers and employees enter into a contract even though no formal contract exists. In this case, the employer and the employee are said to have entered into an *implied contract.* Certain employment policies and practices may unintentionally create an implied contract. The courts have interpreted statements made by an interviewer or manager such as "You will always have a job as long as you do your work" as a promise of job security.[9] Employees who lost their jobs because of layoffs have successfully obtained legal remedies when such promises were made.

Employee handbooks can be another source of implied employment contracts if they offer job security. Some courts have interpreted statements like "Employees will be dismissed only for just cause" as placing the burden of proof on the company for a termination decision.[10] In addition, when an employee handbook or employment policy makes a distinction between "probationary" and "permanent" employees, the courts have held that employers are promising continued employment to workers who successfully complete the probationary period and become permanent employees. To date, at least 38 states have recognized that employee handbooks can be interpreted as enforceable contracts.[11]

Other Rights

Employees often expect certain other rights in addition to statutory and contract rights. These include a right to ethical treatment and limited rights to free speech and privacy. These rights differ from the first two categories of rights in an important way: Although employees may expect these rights, they may have no legal recourse if they feel that these rights have been violated. Even though the law does not require employers to extend these other rights to employees, doing so is likely to result in more satisfied workers who are willing to go the extra mile for the organization.

RIGHT TO ETHICAL TREATMENT Employees expect to be treated fairly and ethically in return for providing their employer with a fair and reasonable amount of work. This expectation is called the *psychological contract.*[12] Employers who uphold the psychological contract generally have more productive employees. In contrast, those who violate the psychological contract may cause employees to quit or to form a union. Because employee turnover is costly and unionization results in some loss of control over the business, managers should be aware of the importance of the psychological contract to employees.[13] One way of sealing the psychological contract is to develop and publicize a code of ethics.[14] HR can contribute to maintaining an ethical environment by integrating the code of ethics into employment policies, orientations for new employees, and formal training programs.[15]

Managers and supervisors can influence their companies' climate of fairness and ethical behavior by the tone they set for employees in their work units.[16] Specifically, managers and supervisors should:

- Take actions that develop trust, such as sharing useful information and making good on commitments.
- Act consistently so that employees are not surprised by unexpected management actions or decisions.

- Be truthful and avoid white lies and actions designed to manipulate others by giving a certain (false) impression.
- Demonstrate integrity by keeping confidences and showing concern for others.
- Meet with employees to discuss and define what is expected of them.
- Ensure that employees are treated equitably, giving equivalent rewards for similar performance and avoiding actual or apparent special treatment of favorites.
- Adhere to clear standards that are seen as just and reasonable—for example, neither praising accomplishments nor imposing penalties disproportionately.
- Demonstrate respect toward employees, showing openly that they care about employees and recognize their strengths and contributions.[17]

LIMITED RIGHT TO PRIVACY The right to privacy protects people from unreasonable or unwarranted intrusions into their personal affairs. Although this right is not explicitly stated in the U.S. Constitution, the Supreme Court found in a 1965 ruling that it is implicit in the Constitution. For instance, the Constitution does explicitly prohibit unreasonable searches and seizures, and this prohibition is consistent with a more general right to privacy.

There are two additional legal bases for privacy rights. First, several state constitutions (including those of Arizona and California) contain an explicitly stated right to privacy. Second, several federal laws protect specific aspects of an employee's privacy. For instance, the Crime Control and Safe Streets Act of 1968 has a provision that prevents employers from viewing or listening to an employee's private communications without obtaining prior consent.

Because the U.S. and state constitutions limit the powers of the government, federal and state employees' privacy rights are protected, although not absolutely. For instance, under a program mandated by Congress, employees whose jobs in U.S. aviation are directly related to safety must undergo periodic blood alcohol testing.[18] However, the same constitutional protections do not apply to private employee arrangements. For instance, government employers are typically prohibited from searching their employees' personal work space (desks, lockers, etc.) unless they have reasonable cause, but private employers typically are not prohibited from this kind of activity. Still, because employees expect certain privacy rights, it is almost always good policy for an employer to respect employee privacy.

personnel file
A file maintained for each employee, containing the documentation of critical HR-related information, such as performance appraisals, salary history, disciplinary actions, and career milestones.

A sensitive issue involving employee privacy rights is the maintenance of personnel files. Each worker's **personnel file** contains the documentation of critical information, such as performance appraisals, salary history, disciplinary actions, and career milestones. Access to the personnel file should be denied to all people except managers who have a job-related "need to know" certain information. Employees should be able to review the information in their personnel file periodically to ensure its accuracy. If personnel files are stored in a human resource information system (HRIS), access to this sensitive information should be controlled by the use of passwords or special codes to protect employees' privacy rights.

Privacy Act of 1974
Guarantees the privacy of personnel files for employees of the U.S. federal government.

Employees of the U.S. federal government have the privacy of their personnel files protected under the **Privacy Act of 1974**. The act requires federal agencies to permit employees to examine, copy, correct, or amend employee information in their personnel file. The act also includes provisions for an appeal procedure if there is a dispute over the accuracy of the information or what is to be included in the file.[19]

Employers may be able to discover personal information about employees through social networking sites, such as Twitter and Facebook, where people describe their nonwork activities to friends and post photos. Individuals should use discretion when posting indiscreet photos or stories on social networking sites that could potentially damage their reputation for conforming to conventional morality and ethics or having sound judgment. An increasing number of employers are scanning social networking sites as an informal recruitment practice to narrow the applicant pool and eliminate individuals prior to the interview phase.[20] An example of a young woman who lost her job as a teacher when her employer saw a photo of her at a party that had been posted online is provided in the Manager's Notebook, "Think Twice Before Posting Photos on the Internet."

MANAGER'S NOTEBOOK

Technology/Social Media

Think Twice Before Posting Photos on the Internet

Employee privacy is not protected in regard to photos or descriptions of employees' off-the-job activities that are posted on the Internet. Poorly chosen words or photos posted online regarding one's leisure-time experiences can have career-altering consequences. Stacy Snyder, who was a senior at Millersville University in Millersville, Pennsylvania, provides an instructive example. Snyder was dismissed from the student teaching program at a nearby high school and denied her teaching credential after the school staff came across her photograph on her MySpace profile. In response, Snyder filed a lawsuit in a federal court contending that her right to free expression under the First Amendment had been violated, but so far no trial date has been set.

Snyder's photo, preserved at the *Chronicle of Higher Education*'s "Wired Campus" blog, turns out to be surprisingly innocent. In a head shot snapped at a costume party, Snyder, with a pirate's hat perched atop her head, sips from a large plastic cup whose contents cannot be seen. When posting the photo, she fatefully captioned her self-portrait "drunken pirate," although whether she was serious cannot be determined by looking at the photo.

Millersville University, in a motion asking the court to dismiss the case, contends that Snyder's student teaching had been unsatisfactory for many reasons. However, it affirms that she was dismissed and barred from re-entering the school shortly after the high school staff discovered her MySpace photograph. The university backed the school authorities' contentions that her posting was "unprofessional" and might "promote underage drinking." It also cited a passage in the teacher's handbook that said staff members are "to be well-groomed and appropriately dressed."

Although social networking sites such as MySpace have privacy settings that can be adjusted to restrict public access, Snyder had not adjusted the privacy settings. She anticipated that her profile page would be seen by school authorities but felt that because she was an adult over 21 years of age she had nothing to hide.

Sources: Based on Stross, R. (2007, December 30). How to lose your job on your own time. *New York Times,* Business, 3; Grasz, J. (2009, August 24). 45% employers use Facebook-Twitter to screen job candidates. *The Oregon Biz Report—Business News from Oregon. www.oregonbusinessreport.com*; Finder, A. (2006, June 11). For some, online persona undermines a résumé. *New York Times. www.nytimes.com.* ■■

LIMITED RIGHT TO FREE SPEECH The First Amendment to the U.S. Constitution guarantees all U.S. citizens the right to free speech. This right is therefore more explicit than the right to privacy. However, it too is limited.[21] Again, government employees are more fully protected than those who work for private employers. For instance, an IRS agent who disagrees with the current president's tax policies is perfectly free to say so publicly without fear of official retribution. However, if a Sears' store manager publicly disagrees with corporate pricing strategy, Sears is free to discipline or terminate that manager. Thus, managers in the private sector can legally discipline employees who say something damaging to the company or its reputation. Similarly, a company can and should discipline an employee for using demeaning language that insults a person based on his or her race or gender. Texaco did not discipline the managers who insulted African American employees on the basis of race, which resulted in an expensive discrimination lawsuit.[22] There are important exceptions to this situation, however. When employees reveal management misconduct to outsiders, they are engaging in whistle-blowing, which is a legal right under federal and some state laws. We discuss whistle-blowing in detail later in this chapter.

As with the right to privacy, managers should interfere as little as possible with employees' free speech because this right is so deeply ingrained in U.S. culture. Managers need to balance the costs and benefits of extending versus not extending privacy and speech rights. For instance, we saw in Chapter 13 that e-mail has become a very popular method of communication. Should companies establish a policy allowing managers to read all their employees' electronic communications? For example, an employer could have employees sign a consent form acknowledging the

A QUESTION OF ETHICS

A computer programming manager suspects that one of her programmers is sharing programming information with a competitor through electronic mail. Is it appropriate for the manager to examine her employee's e-mail files without the suspected programmer's permission?

company's right to access e-mail messages.[23] Employees who know that managers are looking at their communications are likely to "censor" them to some degree, and the loss of candor may lead to less-than-optimal decisions. In addition, such a policy would injure the trust relationship between employees and their employer. Thus, any theoretical benefit a company might gain from such a policy—such as guarding against criminal activity—would almost certainly be offset by work-related and psychological costs.

Management Rights

management rights
Management's rights to run the business and retain any profits that result.

The rights of the employer, usually called **management rights**, can be summed up as the rights to run the business and to retain any profits that result. In the United States, management rights are supported by property laws; common law (a body of traditional legal principles, most of which originated in England); and the values of a capitalistic society that accepts the concepts of private enterprise and the profit motive.[24] The stockholders and owners who control a firm through their property rights delegate the authority to run the business to managers.

Management rights include the right to manage the workforce and the rights to hire, promote, assign, discipline, and discharge employees. Management's right to direct the workforce is moderated by the right of employees (at least those who have not signed an employment contract) to quit their jobs at any time. Thus, it is in management's interest to treat employees fairly.

Management rights are influenced by the rights of groups who have an interest in decisions made in the workplace. For example, managers have the right to hire the employees they wish to hire, but this right is affected by EEOC laws that prevent the employer from discriminating on the basis of certain applicant characteristics (age, race, sex, and so on). Furthermore, managers have the right to set pay levels for their employees, but the presence of a union labor contract with a pay provision requires managers to pay employees according to the contract's terms.

Management rights are often termed *residual rights* because they pertain to the remaining rights that are not affected by contracts or laws that represent the interests of employees or other parties (such as a union).[25] According to the residual rights perspective, managers have the right to make decisions that affect the business and the workforce except where limited by laws or contract provisions.

One of the most important employer rights is employment at will.

Employment at Will

employment at will
A common-law rule used by employers to assert their right to end an employment relationship with an employee at any time for any cause.

Employers have long used **employment at will**, a common-law rule, to assert their right to end their employment relationship with an employee at any time for any cause. U.S. courts adopted the rule in the nineteenth century to promote flexibility in the labor market by acknowledging the existence of a symmetrical relationship between employer and employee. Because workers were free to terminate their relationship with their employer for any reason, the courts deemed it fair for employers to be able to end their relationship with employees whenever they see fit to do so. Employment at will can be a particularly important management right in small business, where a low-performing employee can make the difference between a healthy profit and an unhealthy loss.

Although the courts originally assumed that employment at will would give both parties equal footing in the employment relationship, it is apparent that employment at will has stacked the deck in favor of employers. Because of the employment-at-will doctrine, many employees who are wrongfully discharged each year have no legal remedies.[26] One labor relations expert has estimated that approximately 150,000 employees are wrongfully discharged by their employers each year.[27] Virtually all these wrongful discharges occur in the 70 percent of the U.S. labor force that is not protected by either a union contract or *civil service rules,* which guarantee government employees the right of due process in termination procedures. Employment at will is not accepted in other parts of the world, including Japan and the nations of the European Union. These countries have enacted laws that make it difficult for employers to discharge a worker without good cause. In France, Belgium, and the United Kingdom, the only grounds for immediate dismissal are criminal behavior.[28] In many other countries, employers who discharge employees for noncriminal reasons face costly mandatory severance pay requirements that provide many weeks of pay. For example, employment laws provide discharged workers 32 weeks of pay in France,

34 weeks of pay in the United Kingdom, 75 weeks of pay in Mexico, 78 weeks of pay in India, 90 weeks of pay in China, and 165 weeks of pay in Brazil. By comparison, in the United States employers are not legally required to provide severance pay to discharged employees, although some U.S. companies voluntarily offer modest amounts of severance pay.[29]

LEGAL LIMITATIONS TO EMPLOYMENT AT WILL For the past 35 years or so, state courts have been ruling that employment at will is limited in certain situations.[30] Because these are state rather than federal cases, they have varied widely. In general, however, employment-at-will limitations can be grouped into three categories: public policy exceptions, implied contracts, and lack of good faith and fair dealing. In some states, plaintiffs have received sizable settlements for punitive damages as well as back pay. Although juries have given an average award of $500,000 to plaintiffs in wrongful discharge cases, in one case at a Wall Street investment bank a manager was awarded $1.9 million by his former employer to settle his claim.[31]

Public Policy Exceptions The courts have ruled that an employee may not be discharged for engaging in activities that are protected by law. Examples are filing a legitimate workers' compensation claim; exercising a legal duty, such as jury duty; refusing to violate a professional code of ethics; and refusing to lobby for a political candidate favored by the employer.[32]

Implied Contracts As we saw earlier, the courts have determined that an implied contract may exist when an employer makes oral or written promises of job security. For instance, an implied contract may exist when an employee handbook promises job security for good performance, or when a manager who is unaware of this doctrine makes promises during the selection interview, such as "good performers will always have opportunities at our company." To prevent implied contract lawsuits, employers should carefully rewrite employee handbooks to eliminate any language that could be interpreted as an implied contract. In addition, employers must train managers to refrain from implying promises of job security in conversations with new and current workers.

LACK OF GOOD FAITH AND FAIR DEALING Courts in some jurisdictions expect each party in the employment relationship to treat the other in good faith. If one party acts with malice or bad faith, the courts may be willing to provide a remedy to the injured party. For example, the courts may reason that firing a worker shortly before he or she becomes eligible for a retirement plan indicates bad faith. In this situation, the burden of proof may be on the employer to show that the discharge was for just cause.

The following case makes it plain how costly it can be for an employer to act in bad faith in discharging employees:

> In 1987 two employees of a New Jersey real estate management firm took maternity leave. One was dismissed after she returned to work; the other was fired seven weeks before her planned return. Both women sued, and in 1992 a jury awarded them $210,000 and $225,000, respectively, in compensatory damages. They were awarded another $250,000 each in punitive damages, and on top of that the judge added another $374,000 in interest and legal fees. Total cost to the employer: $1.3 million.[33]

To minimize the risk of wrongful discharge lawsuits based on an implied contract, many employers have drawn up employment-at-will statements that all new employees must sign, acknowledging their understanding that the employer can terminate their employment at any time for any reason.[34]

A QUESTION OF ETHICS

Is it ethical to require all employees to sign an employment-at-will statement acknowledging that they understand that the employer can terminate their employment at any time for any reason?

Employee Rights Challenges: A Balancing Act

Four workplace issues are particularly challenging to HR professionals and managers because they require walking a thin line between the rights of employees and those of management: (1) random drug testing, (2) electronic monitoring, (3) whistle-blowing, (4) moonlighting, and (5) office romance.

Random Drug Testing

The practice of random drug testing pits management's duty to protect the safety of its employees and customers against an employee's right to privacy. *Random drug testing* screens employees for the use of drugs randomly, without suspicion or cause. The test usually includes the analysis of a urine specimen provided by the employee.

Many employees consider random drug testing an unreasonable and illegal invasion of their privacy.[35] Although random drug testing is required by law for specific occupations where safety is critical, such as airline pilots and military personnel, it has been challenged in cases where the employer has other methods available to ensure a drug-free work environment. For example, the International Association of Fire Fighters will permit clauses in its labor contracts that allow drug testing based on "probable cause" but will not agree to random drug testing. Numerous employers also use preemployment drug testing as a condition of employment.[36]

Because no employee groups have succeeded in stopping drug testing under the U.S. Constitution, the legal battle between employee privacy and employer-mandated drug testing is being played out at the state level.[37] Not only do state constitutions vary widely in their protections of employee privacy—for example, New Jersey and California have added employee privacy provisions to their state constitutions, whereas Utah and Texas have not[38]—but the courts' interpretation of these protections has veered from one side to the other as well. For instance, the California Supreme Court dealt what was considered a death blow to random drug testing in that state when it ruled in 1990 that an employer must have a "compelling interest" to require employees not in safety-sensitive positions to submit to random drug tests.[39] Pro-employee groups cheered the ruling, but four years later the California Supreme Court allowed the National Collegiate Athletic Association to conduct random drug testing of student athletes. The court said that the private sector, like the government, must abide by the state constitution's right of privacy, but that the private sector can invade privacy for "legitimate" interests.[40]

Every professional sports league tests its athletes for drugs, including performance-enhancing drugs such as steroids and stimulants. Most of the professional sports leagues require random drug testing to deter the use of drugs by their athletes, as shown in the following examples:[41]

- Major League Baseball (MLB) requires each player to be tested twice a season, once during the first five days of reporting to spring training and again on a randomly selected date. In addition, 600 players chosen at random are tested a third time each year. A player who tests positive for a performance-enhancing drug is subject to three additional tests in a year, with incremental penalties of a 50-game suspension, a 100-game suspension, and then a permanent suspension. In August, 2013, 12 professional baseball players admitted to using performance-enhancing drugs and each player was suspended for 50 games during the baseball season that year.
- The National Football League (NFL) tests all players at least once a year as part of their training-camp physicals and randomly selects 10 players per team per week during the regular season for additional drug testing. Players can also be randomly selected for testing up to six times during the off-season.
- The National Basketball Association (NBA) allows players to be randomly tested no more than four times each season. Players testing positive receive incremental penalties of a 10-game suspension, a 25-game suspension, a one-year suspension, and then a permanent ban.
- The National Association for Stock Car Auto Racing (NASCAR) requires random drug testing as part of its substance abuse policy. Drug testing is conducted with all drivers beginning at the Daytona 500 race in February. Random testing includes all drivers, crew members, and NASCAR officials. Failure of a drug test results in an immediate, indefinite suspension; a third violation results in a lifetime ban.

Designing a random drug-testing policy poses numerous challenges. The HR staff can be helpful in counseling management on how to deal with some of the following issues:

- How should employees who have positive drug test results be treated? Should the manager discharge them or attempt to rehabilitate them?
- If an employee has a positive test for a legitimate reason, such as using a prescription drug or eating a poppy seed bagel (poppy seeds are the source of opium), how can the employer ensure that the employee is not charged with using illegal drugs? How can an employer protect employees from false-positive results in general?
- What can managers do to maintain security over urine specimens provided for the drug test so that they are free from adulteration designed to alter the results? Should managers

require that employees be monitored while providing the urine sample to ensure its authenticity? Or does such monitoring violate the employee's privacy rights?

Motorola's random drug-testing policy was designed specifically to deal with these issues. Motorola decided to implement random drug testing after it estimated the cost of employees' drug use in terms of lost time, reduced productivity, and health care and workers' compensation claims at $190 million annually. This amounted to 40 percent of the company's net profits.[42]

The jury is still out on whether the benefits of random drug testing outweigh the resentment and mistrust this policy often generates. A survey of workers at one of the nation's largest railroads found that only 57 out of 174 respondents expressed support for periodic drug testing—and all stipulated that it was justifiable only for safety reasons. Many commented that drug testing undermined their loyalty to the company. One worker wrote:

> I am a faithful and loyal employee. I felt like a common criminal, and I didn't even do anything wrong. . . . I happen to have bashful kidneys. The first time I took a drug test it took me almost three hours of drinking water and coffee before I could give a sample. Needless to say I was upset, angry, humiliated, defensive, etc. . . .[43]

Employees' anger and humiliation about random drug testing is compounded by the evidence that it does not help deter accidents: In 1991, a Federal Railroad Administration report found that only 3.2 percent of workers involved in railroad accidents tested positive for drugs.[44]

In order to avoid some of the disadvantages related to having employees submit to random drug-testing procedures, management in firms that are not involved with transportation or safety-sensitive jobs may decide to use either a preemployment drug test or a probable cause drug test.[45] A *preemployment drug test* is given to each job applicant as part of the hiring process. For example, the preemployment drug test may be taken as part of a physical examination that a job candidate must take before being given a job offer. Those who fail the test are not hired.[46] A *probable cause drug test* is given to employees who have accidents, engage in unsafe job behavior, or show behavioral signs of drug use, which may include having impaired judgment or slurred speech. Notice that neither the preemployment drug test nor the probable cause drug test is given on a random basis but instead is given either at a predetermined time (such as the time an employee is hired) or for a predetermined reason, such as having an accident or being reprimanded for unsafe conduct in the workplace. In a survey taken in 2004 by the American Management Association, 62 percent of U.S. firms reported using some form of drug testing.[47]

Moreover, there is an alternative to drug testing that does not invade employee privacy and that is much more reliable for determining an employee's fitness for work: the performance test. For example, computer-based performance tests are available that test workers' hand–eye coordination to measure their ability to do their jobs. Every morning at Silicon Valley's Ion Implant Services, Inc., delivery drivers line up in front of a computer console to "play" a short video game. Unless the machine spits out a receipt confirming they have passed the test, they cannot climb behind the wheel of their trucks. What happens to workers who fail their performance tests? Some companies refer them to a supervisor, others to an employee assistance program. Besides being both more reliable and less invasive of employees' privacy, performance testing has another advantage over random drug testing: It is cheaper. Performance tests cost from $0.60 to $1 per employee compared with the $10 per employee that the cheapest drug test costs.[48]

Many employers justify random drug testing on the grounds that drug use is illegal. In recent years, however, some companies have also begun testing employees who engage in *legal* activities, such as smoking. Exhibit 14.1 examines the controversy surrounding employer policies that reject all applicants who smoke on or off the job.

Electronic Monitoring

Experts estimate that employee theft costs U.S. business over $400 billion a year.[49] "Theft" includes theft of merchandise, embezzlement, industrial espionage, computer crime, acts of sabotage, and misuse of time on the job. While the average annual loss a bank suffers from embezzlement is $42,000, the average computer crime costs around $400,000.[50] A retail store loses an average of $213 in a shoplifting incident (when a store customer steals merchandise) but loses an average of $10,587 for an employee theft incident.[51] The country with the highest level of shrinkage (losses from shoplifting and employee theft) is India; the countries with the lowest levels of shrinkage

EXHIBIT 14.1 CAN AN EMPLOYER DENY JOBS TO PEOPLE WHO SMOKE?

In one of the first court cases dealing with off-the-job smoking as part of the screening and selection process, the U.S. Supreme Court refused to hear the appeals of job applicants who were rejected from consideration for employment with the City of North Miami, Florida, because they are smokers. The denied appeal leaves in place an earlier Florida Supreme Court decision in favor of a city regulation requiring that all job applicants sign an affidavit stating that they have not used any tobacco products for one year before seeking a job with the city.[a]

Arlene Kurtz, a cigarette smoker who applied for a job as a clerk-typist, filed suit, claiming that the city's action interfered with her privacy rights to smoke during her time away from the job. Kurtz offered to comply with any reasonable on-the-job smoking restrictions but indicated that she had smoked for 30 years and had tried to quit smoking without success. The city argued that it established the policy because employees who use tobacco cost as much as $4,611 per year more than nonsmokers. The court noted that the regulation was the least intrusive way to accomplish the city's interest because it does not affect current employees, only job applicants.[b]

An even more restrictive employee smoking policy went into effect at Weyco, an insurance benefits administrator in central Michigan, which alerted all incumbent employees that they will be randomly tested annually for smoking on or off the job. Employees who fail the test are fired.[c] Some companies penalize employees who smoke with sizeable financial surcharges to their health insurance. Direct General, an insurance company, penalizes its employees who smoke with a $480 annual surcharge to their health insurance premiums.[d]

Other companies have taken a more moderate approach to controlling smoking behavior. They have enacted nonsmoking policies that restrict on-the-job smoking due to safety concerns and to protect nonsmoking employees from secondary smoke exposure. For example, FedEx has a nonsmoking policy that prohibits the use of tobacco products in all company buildings, facilities, vehicles, and aircraft, but does not try to regulate employee's off-duty smoking behavior.[e]

Outside Florida, a number of other states have recently enacted laws that protect employees' legal off-duty activities such as smoking or skiing (a high-risk leisure activity that an employer might also object to because of higher insurance costs). These state laws prohibit employers from using an applicant's off-the-job smoking as a basis for hiring or continuing the employment relationship.[f]

Sources: [a]Barlow, W., Hatch, D., and Murphy, B. (1996, April). Employer denies jobs to smoker applicants. *Personnel Journal,* 142; [b]*Ibid.*; [c]Peters, J. (2005, February 8). Company's smoking ban means off-hours, too. *New York Times,* C5; [d]Wieczner, J. (2013, March 5). Companies make smokers pay. *MarketWatch. www.marketwatch.com*; [e]Grensing-Pophal, L. (1999, May). Smokin' in the workplace. *Workforce,* 58–66; [f]Barlow et al., 1996.

are Germany and Taiwan.[52] Industrial spies who steal competitive trade secrets, such as software codes or plans for a microprocessor chip, may take property so valuable that its theft threatens the very existence of the business. Employees' theft of time from employers can also be costly. Employees steal time when they take long lunches, use the telephone for private conversations, misuse sick leave for extra vacation time, or surf the Internet for personal reasons.

Companies are attempting to fight these various forms of theft by using electronic surveillance devices to monitor employees.[53] In industries such as telecommunications, banking, and insurance, as many as 80 percent of employees are subject to some form of electronic monitoring.[54] To eavesdrop on employees, companies use hidden microphones and transmitters attached to telephones and tiny fish-eye video lenses installed behind pinholes in walls and ceilings. In a survey published by *Macworld* magazine, more than 21 percent of respondents said they have "engaged in searches of employee computer files, voice mail, electronic mail or other networking communications." Most said they were monitoring work flow or investigating thefts or espionage.[55]

The increased sophistication of computer and telephone technology now makes it possible for employers to track employees' job performance electronically—for example, to count the number of keystrokes an employee makes on a computer terminal or determine how many reservations a travel agent books in a given time period.[56] As noted in the chapter opener, air conditioning service employees who drive to serve clients can be monitored by special cell phones containing chips that are tracked by global positioning satellites so that the employer knows the employees' location at any time and can compare it to where they are expected to be.[57] This use of electronic monitoring has raised concerns not only about employee privacy, but also about the dehumanizing effect such relentless monitoring can have on employees.[58] Many employees whose work is tracked electronically feel that monitoring takes the human element out of their work and causes too much stress. One study comparing monitored and nonmonitored clerical workers showed that 50 percent of monitored workers felt stressed, compared with 33 percent of nonmonitored workers; and that 34 percent of monitored workers lost work time because of stress-induced illness, compared with 20 percent of nonmonitored workers.[59] Some research suggests that there is a higher incidence of headaches, backaches, and wrist pains among monitored employees.[60]

Employees are most likely to see electronic monitoring as legitimate when management uses it to control theft. But even in this area some managers have exceeded reasonable standards. For example, experts estimated that in 2000 thirty million U.S. workers were subjected to secret electronic monitoring.[61] In one case, the nurses at Holy Cross Hospital in Silver Spring, Maryland, became quite upset after discovering that a silver box hanging on the locker room wall was a video camera monitored by the hospital security chief—who was a man.[62]

Some employers use electronic monitoring devices to control employee theft of time when they are on the company payroll. This wasted time is sometimes spent playing video games or visiting pornographic Web sites. Employers monitor to eliminate such wastage. In the retail industry, employee theft is monitored through the use of data-mining programs that are synchronized with video monitors to permit a more comprehensive look at activity at the cash register. With the press of a button, managers can highlight irregular register transactions on their computers and pull up corresponding video. This could enable companies to catch cashiers who cut deals for their friends or pocket cash refunds for themselves.[63]

To use electronic monitoring devices to control theft while not intimidating or invading the privacy of honest employees (who make up the majority of the workforce), managers should:

- Avoid secret monitoring, except with specific individuals whom managers have reason to believe are stealing from the company. In those cases, management should obtain a court order to perform the secret surveillance.
- If the company decides to monitor employees' e-mail and Internet use, then management should provide guidelines to employees for exchanging e-mail messages and accessing Web sites. The guidelines may also state that employees should not access Web sites that are related to gambling, chat rooms, or online game playing, or sites with violent or sexually explicit images.[64]
- Find positive uses for electronic monitoring devices that are beneficial to employees as well as to the employer. Avis Rent A Car System, for example, has used monitoring devices to provide feedback on employee performance. This practice has been accepted as a valuable training tool.
- Develop a systematic antitheft policy and other practices to discourage theft, such as reference checks; pencil-and-paper honesty or integrity tests that screen out applicants who are likely to behave dishonestly; and internal controls that control the use of cash (accounting controls), merchandise (inventory controls), computers and databases (computer security controls), and company trade secrets (security badges and clearance procedures).

A controversial employment practice that affects individual privacy rights occurs when employers monitor the credit histories of job applicants during the hiring process and eliminate those with poor credit reports. The Manager's Notebook, "Employers Are Using Credit Checks in Hiring Decisions," explains how credit histories are being used in the employment process and why some parties believe that this employment practice is unfair.

MANAGER'S NOTEBOOK

Technology/Social Media

Employers Are Using Credit Checks in Hiring Decisions

According to a 2012 survey by the Society for Human Resource Management, 47 percent of employers use credit checks when making a hiring decision. Using a credit check as part of an employment screening can be a simple data-driven way for a company to gather evidence on a potential employee's reliability. Although most companies are selective in terms of using credit checks only for specific jobs, the survey found that 17 percent of the companies use credit checks for every hire. Privacy and civil rights advocates argue that employers are using credit histories unfairly to eliminate the people at the bottom of the income scale who are likely to be unemployed or belong to a minority. When a person loses a job they have difficulty paying their bills, and consequently their credit history collects some bad marks that make it even more difficult to find a job and improve their credit history. In addition, credit checks contain errors. In a Federal Trade Commission study, 25 percent of consumers identified errors on their credit reports that could affect their credit history.

Some lawmakers have been convinced that the use of credit checks in making employment decisions is discriminatory and infringes on privacy rights. A total of 25 states have proposed bills that are being debated that aim to restrict the use of credit histories in the hiring process. Currently nine states have adopted laws that limit the use of credit reports to evaluate people being considered for jobs.

Sources: Based on Rivlin, G. (2013, May 12). *New York Times, Sunday Business*, 1, 4; Emple, H. (2013, May 14). Putting the kibosh on using credit checks in hiring decisions. *New America Foundation. www.assets.newamerica.net*; Acohido, B. (2011, April 8). Limits sought to employers' use of credit reports. *USA Today. www.usatoday30.usatoday.com.* ■■

Whistle-Blowing

whistle-blowing
Employee disclosure of an employer's illegal, immoral, or illegitimate practices to persons or organizations that may be able to take corrective action.

Whistle-blowing occurs when an employee discloses an employer's illegal, immoral, or illegitimate practices to persons or organizations that may be able to take corrective action.[65] Whistle-blowing is risky because managers and other employees sometimes deal harshly with the whistle-blower.[66] Although whistle-blowers often have altruistic motives, they may be shunned, harassed, and even fired for their efforts.[67] For example:

- Jared Bowen, a Wal-Mart executive, gave the company information to investigate expense-account abuses and false invoices for as much as $500,000 made by vice chairman Thomas Coughlin that resulted in the board's asking for Coughlin's resignation from the company in 2005. Shortly afterwards, Wal-Mart also discharged Bowen, claiming that he had tampered with his college transcripts by reporting an inflated grade point average and number of college credits. Bowen filed a complaint with the U.S. Department of Labor claiming that Wal-Mart violated federal whistle-blower rules by firing him. In 2006 Bowen decided to drop the claims that he had made against Wal-Mart.[68]
- Two Federal Aviation Administration (FAA) inspectors became targets of intimidation after repeatedly alerting higher-ups to lapses in enforcement of safety rules at Southwest Airlines. Southwest Airlines knowingly flew 46 jet aircraft that had not received required inspections for cracks in the fuselage. One of the inspectors, Douglas Peters, testified how a supervisor issued a veiled threat—while holding a family photo Peters kept in his office—that Peters and his wife, also an FAA employee, would jeopardize their careers if Peters continued to press for safety issues. The Transportation Department investigated this incident and fined Southwest Airlines $10.2 million for safety violations, yet the supervisor who intimidated the whistle-blowers was only reassigned to another work site, and no disciplinary action was taken against him.[69]
- Bradley Manning, a U.S. Army private, disclosed thousands of pages of sensitive classified documents from the Department of Defense and State Department to the WikiLeaks Web site. The documents disclosed information on how the United States conducted its wars in Iraq and Afghanistan that included violations of international law and rules of the U.S. Army. Manning believed he was a whistle-blower and that his disclosure of the secret documents was a patriotic act that informed citizens of the missteps of Defense Department and State Department officials. However, Manning violated Army regulations and the Espionage Act when he leaked secret documents to the Internet, and the Army and the government treated him as a traitor rather than a heroic whistle-blower. After spending three years in a military prison, in 2013 Manning received a court martial and dishonorable discharge from the Army and a 35-year prison sentence for disclosing secret information to the public.[70]

A QUESTION OF ETHICS
You discover that your supervisor has been billing the company for business trips that he never took. When you ask him about it, he says this is common practice throughout the company, the other department heads do the same thing, and corporate headquarters has set reimbursement rates so low that employees have to pad their expense accounts to be fairly reimbursed. What should you do?

Dealing with whistle-blowing requires balancing employees' right to free speech with the employer's right to prevent employees from disregarding managers' authority or disclosing sensitive information to outsiders. Although whistle-blowers who work for the federal government and some state and local governments have certain legal protections, there is far less protection for private-sector employees, except in states that have enacted whistle-blower laws. Many times the whistle-blower is subject to the employment-at-will rule and may be discharged in retaliation for going public about an illegal or unethical company activity. A potential whistle-blower should have good documentation of the evidence of wrongdoing before disclosing it to others. The whistle-blower should also be prepared to deal with employer retaliation and have a contingency plan, which may include lining up another job in case the worst happens.

Despite all these risks, many employees have used whistle-blowing to call their employers to account. For example, Enron executive Sherron Watkins wrote a blunt memo in 2001 to Enron CEO Kenneth Lay warning him that the company might "implode in a wave of accounting scandals." Instead of thanking her, management factions tried to squelch the bad news and intimidate her for not being a team player. After the financial scandal broke and became a media event, Watkins was praised for her courage and became a positive role model for whistle-blowers.[71] For this reason, many companies have realized that it is in their best interests to establish a whistle-blowing policy that encourages people to reveal misconduct internally instead of exposing it externally. This way the company can avoid negative publicity and all the investigative, administrative, and legal actions associated with it.[72] Figure 14.2 lists some of the most important elements of an effective whistle-blowing policy. Probably the most important is support by top management, including the CEO. Other important elements of a whistle-blowing policy are provisions for the whistle-blower to remain anonymous initially and to be protected from retribution. Some companies that have effective whistle-blowing policies are Bank of America, Pacific Gas & Electric, McDonald's, and General Electric.[73]

The financial scandals at Enron and WorldCom prompted the passage of the Sarbanes-Oxley Act in 2002. The whistle-blower provision in Sarbanes-Oxley protects whistle-blowers from retaliation from the company or its employees and holds those who violate the law liable for both civil and criminal penalties. Enacted in 2010, the Dodd-Frank Wall Street Reform and Consumer Protection Act strengthened the rights of whistle-blowers with provisions that both extend the time to file for an investigation that focuses on management financial misconduct and offer a

1. Get input from top management as you develop the policy and obtain approval of the final version.
2. Develop a written policy that is communicated to employees through multiple media, such as the employee handbook, e-mail, and the company intranet site, and at department meetings and training sessions. Communicating the written policy signals the company's commitment to exposing misconduct.
3. Make it possible for employees to submit their initial complaint anonymously.
4. Develop a streamlined process that makes it easy for employees to report misconduct. Designate a special representative to hear initial employee complaints so that employees do not have to report to their supervisor first.
5. Safeguard against reprisals employees who report suspected misconduct in good faith.
6. Develop a formal investigative process and communicate to employees exactly how their reports will be handled. Use this process consistently in all cases.
7. If the investigation reveals that the employee's allegations are accurate, take prompt action to correct the wrongdoing. Whatever the outcome of the investigation, communicate it quickly to the whistle-blower.
8. Establish an appeals process for employees dissatisfied with the outcome of the initial investigation. Provide an advocate (probably from the HR department) to assist the employee who wishes to appeal an unfavorable outcome.
9. To ensure the success of the whistle-blowing policy, the organization—from top management on down—must be committed to creating an ethical work environment.

FIGURE 14.2

Developing an Effective Whistle-Blowing Policy

Sources: Based on Dworkin, T., and Baucus, M. (1998). Internal vs. external whistleblowers: A comparison of whistleblowing processes. *Journal of Business Ethics, 17,* 1281–1298; Barrett, T., and Cochran, D. (1991). Making room for the whistleblower. *HRMagazine, 36*(1), 59; Eaton, T., and Akers, M. (2007, June). Whistleblowing and good governance: Policies for universities, government entities, and nonprofit organizations. *The CPA Journal. www.nysscpa.org*.

pro-employee legal burden of proof for what it takes to win a case. Whistle-blowers who win can receive back pay, compensatory damages, and attorney fees along with reinstatement to their former jobs. The Internal Revenue Service (IRS) pays a reward to whistle-blowers who provide the agency with information on wealthy Americans who hide their assets or cheat on disclosing income when they pay their taxes. Whistle-blowers receive 30 percent of the sums of money recovered from tax cheats. In the 2012 fiscal year the IRS issued 128 whistle-blower rewards, and 12 of those were for sums greater than $2 million in unpaid taxes.[74]

Restrictions on Moonlighting

moonlighting
Holding a second job outside normal working hours.

Moonlighting is holding a second job outside normal working hours.[75] Employees moonlight for different reasons. Some moonlight to earn extra income. When the economy is in a recession and employees are affected by pay freezes, work-hour reductions, or pay reductions, they may take second jobs to maintain their standard of living. Other employees work second jobs for the enjoyment of the work, such as an accountant who teaches an evening accounting class at the local university. In the United States, about 5 percent of employees with full-time jobs hold a second job. When an employer becomes aware of an employee who is moonlighting, it may be tempting for the manager of that employee to prevent the employee from working the other job. Restrictions on employees who moonlight may be appropriate in some situations to protect the employer's interests; in other situations, such restrictions may be a violation of an employee's rights. Consider the following situations:

- A sales executive manages his blossoming second job as a motivational speaker by cell phone and laptop during work hours on his day job.
- A police officer works a few evenings a week as a bouncer at a local nightclub.
- A truck driver has a job moonlighting during off hours as a local delivery person for a pizza restaurant.

Moonlighting brings with it the need to balance the rights of the employer, who expects employees to come to the workplace and be fully engaged in performing their jobs, with the rights of employees, who expect to be free to use their off-duty time any way they want, which includes working a second job.

The best way for managers to handle moonlighting is to treat it on a case-by-case basis rather than attempt to have a policy that restricts moonlighting for all employees. Management should rely on job performance and conflict-of-interest policies to manage moonlighting.[76] The sales executive from the moonlighting situation already listed can be required by the employer to curtail his cell phone calls and laptop use for his motivational speaker business at the workplace and limit it to nonwork hours. Speaking with clients on the phone and scheduling business engagements on the laptop for the second job can detract from job performance as a sales executive and can be addressed as a performance issue. A full-time truck driver has the number of driving hours per day regulated by federal Department of Transportation (DOT) law. A second job that requires additional driving time can increase the legal liability of the trucking company for its driver to have an accident. The trucker who drives in excess of the driving time that is permitted will be in violation of DOT rules. In this situation, the trucking company can restrict its drivers from driving on a second job to remain in compliance with the law. In the situation where the police officer is moonlighting as a nightclub bouncer, this second job can be permitted as along as the officer is able to perform the job duties of a police officer at expected levels of performance, which includes coming to work alert and well rested.

An employer may need to restrict a specific employee from moonlighting when the second employer is a direct competitor and a conflict of interests exists. One video-game firm handles this situation by having its engineers and artists receive approval from managers in advance, and approval is likely as long as the work is not done for a competitor.[77]

Restrictions on Office Romance

The office is an inviting place for romance. People fall in love at work because that is where they spend much of their time and meet people with similar interests. Some controversial high-profile office romances, such as the affair between President Clinton and Monica Lewinsky, a young White House intern, have influenced many companies to view office romance with a critical eye. The challenge of dealing with an office romance forces management to balance the need to protect the company from its liability for preventing sexual harassment with the need to protect the privacy of employees during their off-duty hours so they feel free to develop romantic relationships with people of their choosing. The biggest danger occurs when a person in authority dates a subordinate. If the romance goes sour, the subordinate may claim that the boss forced the relationship, which opens the door for a sexual harassment case.[78] A survey conducted by the Society for Human Resource Management (SHRM) found that 24 percent of employer respondents reported having had a sexual harassment claim filed against them as a result of a workplace romance.[79]

How organizations deal with office romance depends on the goals and culture of the organization. The U.S. military restricts personal relationships between officers and enlisted personnel when the relationship compromises the chain of command. In the military, the need for a highly disciplined, strongly bonded group of individuals is critical to a combat unit's success. A minority of companies have enacted *no-dating policies* that attempt to eliminate the presence of romantic relationships at the workplace between employees. Enforcing no-dating policies can be difficult. A senior executive at Staples, an office supply company that instituted a no-dating policy, was forced to resign when it was revealed he was having a consensual affair with his secretary. Staples lost a valued officer, and the manager forfeited his lucrative job for violating company rules, even though he committed no illegal act.[80]

Other companies view office romance more positively by recognizing the beneficial effect it may have on employee morale due to the fact that many office romances lead to marriage. For example, Microsoft's former CEO Bill Gates met his wife, Melinda French, at the company when she was a marketing executive. Representative of companies that do not interfere with office romance is Delta Airlines, which does not have any rule against dating between employees. Delta expects its employees to maintain a professional and business-like approach to work, which includes all work-related relationships. The only exception it makes is that the company does not allow a spouse or romantic partner to supervise the other. If that were to happen, one of the partners would be transferred to another work unit.[81] Some companies go beyond tolerating office romance and condone it. At Princeton Review, a well-known New York test-preparation company, 6 of the 10 top executives, including the CEO and president, are married to people on the payroll. More than 40 couples who met at the company have married. So far there have been no divorces and no lawsuits—though more than 20 children have been born from these marriages. The CEO of Zappos, an online shoe retailer, encourages dating among employees as a form of work–life integration.[82] The employment trend of longer work hours in U.S. firms suggests that more employees will be tempted to develop a romantic relationship with a colleague at the workplace. A recent survey on employee attitudes about office romance by the American Management Association revealed that 67 percent of respondents said they approved of dating at the office, and 30 percent said they had done it themselves.[83] Management can be expected to look for guidance on how to deal with office romance from HR representatives as they struggle with balancing the privacy rights of employees with the company's liability to prevent sexual harassment.

The following are some basic guidelines that employees should consider if they are involved in an office romance, according to Andrea Kay, a career consultant and author:[84]

- Think before you disclose your relationship to the office. Discuss with your partner how you will inform the office that you are in a relationship with a colleague. It is also important to plan who will be the recipient of this personal information, which may include someone in human resources, your supervisor, or coworkers.
- Know the rules regarding office romance in your company. According to a recent survey by the Society for Human Resource Management (SHRM), only 28 percent of companies have a formal written policy that covers dating in the workplace. Those companies that have a policy indicate who needs to be informed if there is a consensual relationship between two employees.
- It is recommended that the parties involved in an office romance behave in a subtle fashion in how they conduct their relationship at the office. Don't flaunt the relationship. Public displays of affection should be kept to a minimum. Also, avoid sending love notes to each other on the company's e-mail account.

Jim and Pam (far right) from the television show *The Office* exemplify the virtues of a workplace romance.

Source: Splash News/Newscom.

Disciplining Employees

Employee discipline is a tool that managers rely on to communicate to employees that they need to change a behavior. For example, some employees are habitually late to work, ignore safety procedures, neglect the details required for their job, act rudely to customers, or engage in unprofessional conduct with coworkers. Employee discipline entails communicating the unacceptability of such behavior along with a warning that specific actions will follow if the employee does not change the behavior.[85]

Employee discipline is usually performed by supervisors, but in self-managed work teams employee discipline may be a team responsibility. For instance, at Hannaford Bros., a food distribution center outside Albany, New York, the 120 warehouse employees are divided into five teams, each of which has a serious conduct committee. The committee handles employee discipline and makes recommendations to management, including counseling and even termination. Management usually adopts these recommendations. The committees generally come up with creative solutions for handling discipline problems. In fact, it has rarely proved necessary to terminate an employee.[86]

Employee and employer rights may come into conflict over the issue of employee discipline. Sometimes employees believe they are being disciplined unfairly. In such situations, a company's HR staff may help sort out disputed rights. This HR contribution is particularly valuable because it can enable the employee and the supervisor to maintain an effective working relationship.

Two different approaches to employee discipline are widely used: (1) progressive discipline and (2) positive discipline. In both these approaches, supervisors must discuss the behavior in question with their employees. Managers almost invariably find it difficult to confront an employee for disciplinary purposes. Reasons for their discomfort range from not wanting to be the bearer of bad news, to not knowing how to start the discussion, to a fear that the discussion will get out of control. The Manager's Notebook, "Five Steps for Effective Disciplinary Sessions," offers some guidelines that should make it easier for managers to handle an admittedly distasteful task.

MANAGER'S NOTEBOOK

Ethics/Social Responsibility

Five Steps for Effective Disciplinary Sessions

1. Determine whether discipline is called for. Is the problem an isolated infraction or part of a pattern? Consult with HR experts and get some feedback before making a disciplinary decision.[a]

2. Outline clear goals for the discussion in your opening remarks. Do not rely on indirect communication or beat around the bush. The employee should gain a clear idea of your expectations for improvement.[b]
3. Ensure two-way communication. The most helpful disciplinary meeting is a discussion, not a lecture. The objective of the meeting, after all, is to devise a workable solution, not to berate the employee.[c]
4. Establish a follow-up plan. The agreement to a follow-up plan is crucial in both the progressive and positive disciplinary procedures. It is particularly important to establish the time frame in which the employee's behavior is to improve.[d]
5. End on a positive note. You may want to emphasize the employee's strengths so that he or she can leave the meeting believing that you—and the company—want the employee to succeed.[e]

Sources: [a]Cottringer, W. (2003, April). The ABC's of employee discipline. *Supervision,* 5–7; [b]*Ibid.*; [c]Day, D. (1993, May). Training 101. Help for discipline dodgers. *Training & Development,* 19–22; [d]*Ibid.*; [e]*Ibid.* ■■

Progressive Discipline

The most commonly used form of discipline, **progressive discipline**, consists of a series of management interventions that gives employees opportunities to correct their behavior before being discharged. Progressive discipline procedures are warning steps, each of which involves a punishment that increases in severity the longer the undesirable behaviors persist.[87] If the employee fails to respond to these progressive warnings, the employer is justified in discharging the individual.[88]

progressive discipline
A series of management interventions that gives employees opportunities to correct undesirable behaviors before being discharged.

Progressive discipline systems usually have three to five steps, although a four-step system is the most common, as shown in Figure 14.3. Minor violations of company policy involve using all the steps in the progressive discipline procedure. Serious violations, sometimes referred to as *gross misconduct,* can result in the elimination of several steps and sometimes even begin at the last step, which is discharge. Examples of gross misconduct are assaulting a supervisor and falsifying employment records. However, most applications of discipline involve minor rule infractions like violating a dress code, smoking at an inappropriate time or place, or being habitually late. Figure 14.4 shows more examples of minor and serious violations.

A four-step progressive discipline procedure includes the following steps:[89]

1. ***Verbal warning*** An employee who commits a minor violation receives a verbal warning from the supervisor and is told that if this problem continues within a specific time period, harsher punishment will follow. The supervisor provides clear expectations for improvement.

1. Verbal Warning
The employee has an unexcused absence from work. He or she receives a verbal warning from the supervisor and is told that if he or she takes another unexcused absence within the next month, harsher punishment will follow.

2. Written Warning
Two weeks after the verbal warning from his or her supervisor, the employee takes another unexcused absence. He or she now receives a written warning that if he or she fails to correct the absenteeism problem within the next two months, more severe treatment will follow. This warning goes into the employee's personnel file.

3. Suspension
Six weeks later the employee fails to show up for work for two consecutive days. This time he or she is suspended from work without pay for one week. He or she also receives a final warning from his or her supervisor that if there is another unexcused absence within three months after returning from suspension, he or she will be terminated.

4. Discharge
Two weeks after his or her return from suspension, the employee does not show up for work. Upon his or her return to work the following day, he or she is discharged.

FIGURE 14.3
Four Steps in a Progressive Discipline Procedure

FIGURE 14.4
Categories of Employee Misconduct

Minor Violations	Serious Violations
• Absenteeism	• Drug use at work
• Dress code violation	• Theft
• Smoking rule violation	• Dishonesty
• Incompetence	• Physical assault upon a supervisor
• Safety rule violation	• Sabotage of company operations
• Sleeping on the job	
• Horseplay	
• Tardiness	

2. ***Written warning*** The employee violates the same rule within the specified time period and now receives a written warning from the supervisor. This warning goes into the employee's records. The employee is told that failure to correct the violation within a certain time period will result in more severe treatment.
3. ***Suspension*** The employee still fails to respond to warnings and again violates the work rule. The employee is now suspended from employment without pay for a specific amount of time. He or she receives a final warning from the supervisor, indicating that discharge will follow upon violating the rule within a specified time period.
4. ***Discharge*** The employee violates the rule one more time within the specified time period and is discharged.

Figure 14.3 illustrates how an employer would use progressive discipline with an employee who has a pattern of unexcused absences from work.

For infractions that fall between the categories of minor violation and serious violation, one or two steps in the procedure are skipped. These infractions are usually handled by supervisors, who give the employees an opportunity to correct the behavior before discharging them. For example, two employees get into a fistfight at work, but there are mitigating circumstances (one employee verbally attacked the other). In this situation, both employees may be suspended without pay and warned that another such violation will result in discharge.

Positive Discipline

The emphasis on punishment in progressive discipline may encourage employees to deceive their supervisor rather than correct their actions. To avoid this outcome, some companies have replaced progressive discipline with **positive discipline**, which encourages employees to monitor their own behaviors and assume responsibility for their actions.

positive discipline
A discipline procedure that encourages employees to monitor their own behaviors and assume responsibility for their actions.

Positive discipline is similar to progressive discipline in that it too uses a series of steps that increase in urgency and severity until the last step, which is discharge. However, positive discipline replaces the punishment used in progressive discipline with counseling sessions between employee and supervisor. These sessions focus on getting the employee to learn from past mistakes and initiate a plan to make a positive change in behavior.[90] Rather than depending on threats and punishments, the supervisor uses counseling skills to motivate the employee to change. Rather than placing blame on the employee, the supervisor emphasizes collaborative problem solving. In short, positive discipline alters the supervisor's role from adversary to counselor.

To ensure that supervisors are adequately prepared to counsel employees, companies that use positive discipline must see that they receive appropriate training either from the company's own HR department or from outside professional trainers. At Union Carbide, which began using positive discipline in the late 1970s, managers attend a two-day training program to gain familiarity with positive discipline policies and practices. Because Union Carbide had long used a progressive discipline approach, a key element of the training is helping managers abandon their tendency to respond to performance problems in a punitive way. Managers also receive training in documenting their discussions specifically, factually, and defensibly.[91]

A four-step positive discipline procedure starts with a first counseling session between employee and supervisor that ends with a verbal solution that is acceptable to both parties. If this solution does not work, the supervisor and employee meet again to discuss why it failed and to develop a new plan and timetable to solve the problem. At this second step, the new agreed-upon solution to the problem is written down.

If there is still no improvement in performance, the third step is a final warning that the employee is at risk of being discharged. Rather than suspend the employee without pay (as would happen under progressive discipline), this third step gives the employee some time to evaluate his or her situation and come up with a new solution. In doing so, the employee is encouraged to examine why earlier attempts to improve performance did not work. Some companies even give the employee a "decision-making day off" with pay to develop a plan for improved performance.[92]

Managers often resist this aspect of positive discipline because they feel that it rewards employees for poor performance. Some suspect that employees intentionally misbehave to get a free day off. According to the employee relations director of Union Carbide, which uses a paid decision-making day off as part of its disciplinary procedure, this is not so. The company believes a paid day off is more effective than the unpaid suspension used in progressive discipline procedures because (1) workers returning from an unpaid suspension often feel anger or apathy, which may lead to either reduced effectiveness on the job or subtle sabotage; (2) paying the employee for the decision-making day off avoids making the employee a martyr in the eyes of coworkers; and (3) paying for the decision-making day off underscores management's "good faith" toward the employee and probably reduces the chances that the employee will win a wrongful discharge suit if he or she is eventually terminated.[93]

Failure to improve performance after the final warning results in discharge, the fourth step of the positive discipline procedure. Incidents of gross misconduct (such as theft) are treated no differently under a positive discipline procedure than under a progressive discipline procedure. In both systems, theft will most likely result in immediate discharge.

In addition to the costs of training managers and supervisors in appropriate counseling skills and approaches, positive discipline has another drawback. Counseling sessions require a lot of time to be effective, and this is time during which both the supervisor and employee are not working on other tasks. Nonetheless, positive discipline offers considerable benefits to both employees and managers. Employees prefer it because they like being treated with respect by their supervisors. Counseling generally results in a greater willingness to change undesirable behaviors than discipline does. Supervisors prefer it because it does not demand that they assume the role of disciplinarian. Counseling makes for better-quality working relationships with subordinates than discipline does. In addition, under a system of positive discipline, managers are much more likely to intervene early to correct a problem.

Finally, positive discipline can have positive effects on a company's bottom line, as evidenced at Union Carbide. Studies in five of the company's facilities have shown an average decline in absenteeism of 5.5 percent since the company switched from punitive to positive discipline procedures. Moreover, in one unionized facility at the company, disciplinary grievances went down from 36 in one year to 8 in the next. Union Carbide executives estimate that taking an employee complaint through all steps of the grievance procedure (short of arbitration) costs approximately $400 at this facility, thus the switch in discipline procedures saved the company over $11,000 per year.[94] Pennzoil, General Electric, and Procter & Gamble also have adopted the positive discipline procedure and have reported successful outcomes with it.[95] In addition, many city police forces and some universities use positive discipline. For example, one university used positive discipline with a professor who would yell at, criticize, and belittle students when they volunteered the wrong answers to his questions or avoided class participation. The department chair and the professor worked together to develop a plan to control his temper in the classroom. The department chair saw a positive change in the professor's classroom behavior that would not have occurred had the chair used a more confrontational form of discipline, such as the progressive discipline procedure.

Administering and Managing Discipline

Managers must ensure that employees who are disciplined receive due process. In the context of discipline, *due process* means fair and consistent treatment. If an employee challenges a disciplinary action under the EEO laws or a union grievance procedure, the employer must prove that the employee engaged in misconduct and was disciplined appropriately for it. Thus, supervisors should be properly trained in how to administer discipline.[96] Two important elements of due process that managers need to consider in this area are (1) the standards of discipline used to determine whether the employee was treated fairly and (2) whether the employee has a right to appeal a disciplinary action.

BASIC STANDARDS OF DISCIPLINE Some basic standards of discipline should apply to all rule violations, whether major or minor. All disciplinary actions should include the following procedures at a minimum:

- ***Communication of rules and performance criteria*** Employees should be aware of the company's rules and standards and the consequences of violating them. Every employee and supervisor should understand the company's disciplinary policies and procedures fully. Employees who violate a rule or do not meet performance criteria should be given the opportunity to correct their behavior.
- ***Documentation of the facts*** Managers should gather a convincing amount of evidence to justify the discipline. This evidence should be carefully documented so that it is difficult to dispute. For example, time cards could be used to document tardiness; videotapes could document a case of employee theft; the written testimony of a witness could substantiate a charge of insubordination. Employees should have the opportunity to refute this evidence and provide documentation in self-defense.
- ***Consistent response to rule violations*** It is important for employees to believe that discipline is administered consistently, predictably, and without discrimination or favoritism. If they perceive otherwise, they will be more likely to challenge discipline decisions. This does not mean that every violation should be treated exactly the same. For example, an employee with many years of seniority and an excellent work record who breaks a rule may be punished less harshly than a recently hired employee who breaks the same rule. However, two recently hired employees who break the same rule should receive the same punishment.

hot-stove rule
A model of disciplinary action: Discipline should be immediate, provide ample warning, and be consistently applied to all.

The **hot-stove rule** provides a model of how a disciplinary action should be administered. The rule suggests that the disciplinary process is similar to touching a hot stove: (1) Touching a hot stove results in an immediate consequence, which is a burn. Discipline should also be an immediate consequence that follows a rule infraction. (2) The hot stove provides a warning that one will get burned if one touches it. Disciplinary rules should inform employees of the consequences of breaking the rules as well. (3) A hot stove is consistent in administering pain to anyone who touches it. Disciplinary rules should be consistently applied to all.[97]

The Just Cause Standard of Discipline

In cases of wrongful discharge that involve statutory rights or exceptions to employment at will, U.S. courts require the employer to prove that an employee was discharged for *just cause.* This exacting standard, which is written into union contracts and into some nonunion companies' employment policies and employee handbooks, consists of seven questions that must be answered in the affirmative for just cause to exist.[98] Failure to answer "yes" to one or more of these questions suggests that the discipline may have been arbitrary or unwarranted.

1. ***Notification*** Was the employee forewarned of the disciplinary consequences of his or her conduct? Unless the misconduct is very obvious (for example, theft or assault), the employer should make the employee aware, either verbally or in writing, that he or she has violated a rule.
2. ***Reasonable rule*** Was the rule the employee violated reasonably related to safe and efficient operations? The rule should not jeopardize an employee's safety or integrity in any way.
3. ***Investigation before the discipline*** Did managers conduct an investigation into the misconduct before administering discipline? If immediate action is required, the employee may be suspended pending the outcome of the investigation. If the investigation reveals no misconduct, all of the employee's rights should be restored.
4. ***Fair investigation*** Was the investigation fair and impartial? Fair investigations allow the employee to defend himself or herself. An employee who is being interviewed as part of a disciplinary investigation has a right based on federal law to have another employee present to be his or her advocate, or to have someone to consult with, or simply to be a witness.[99]

5. ***Proof of guilt*** Did the investigation provide substantial evidence or proof of guilt? Management may need a "preponderance of evidence" to prove serious charges of gross misconduct, and a less stringent (but still substantial) amount of evidence to prove minor violations.
6. ***Absence of discrimination*** Were the rules, orders, and penalties of the disciplinary action applied evenhandedly and without discrimination? It is not acceptable for managers to go from lax enforcement of a rule to sudden rigorous enforcement of that rule without notifying employees that they intend to do so.
7. ***Reasonable penalty*** Was the disciplinary penalty reasonably related to the seriousness of the rule violation? The employer should consider related facts, such as the employee's work record, when determining the severity of punishment. There might be a range of penalties for a given rule infraction that depend on the length and quality of the employee's service record.

Because the just cause standard is fairly stringent and can prove unwieldy in cases of minor infractions that require immediate supervisory attention, nonunion employers who believe that their employees work under employment at will may choose a less demanding discipline standard.[100]

The Right to Appeal Discipline

Sometimes employees believe they have been disciplined unfairly, either because their supervisors have abused their power or because their supervisors are biased in dealing with individuals whom they like or dislike. For a disciplinary system to be effective, employees must have access to an appeals procedure in which others (who are perceived to be free from bias) can examine the facts. As we discussed in Chapter 13, good employee relations requires establishing appeals procedures that employees can use to voice their disagreement with managers' actions. For challenging disciplinary actions, two of the most useful appeals procedures are the open-door policy and the use of employee relations representatives. These two methods are attractive because of their flexibility and their ability to reach quick resolutions. The Manager's Notebook, "Mistakes to Avoid When Administering Discipline," lists some common pitfalls that can occur when disciplining employees and ways to avoid them.

MANAGER'S NOTEBOOK

Mistakes to Avoid When Administering Discipline

Customer-Driven HR

1. ***Losing your temper*** When you lose control of your temper, you may say things that damage your relationship with the employee and that you may later regret. Your loss of self-control may also encourage the employee to lose control and yell right back at you. It is preferable to step back and take a deep breath before you begin to speak to the employee who is misbehaving, no matter how angry you are feeling. Once you are calm you can have a more constructive conversation with the employee.
2. ***Avoiding disciplinary action entirely*** Many supervisors avoid disciplinary action entirely because they associate it with punishment and fear harming the relationship with an employee. A supervisor needs to understand that the purpose of discipline is to correct behavior, not necessarily to punish an individual. Avoiding disciplinary action may actually harm an employee who is deprived of the chance to learn how to correct his or her behavior.
3. ***Playing therapist*** Trying to get to the root causes and motives for a behavior may send the wrong message to an employee. Unless a supervisor is trained as a therapist, the employee may misinterpret the supervisor's personal questions as being nosy or overly analytical, which is unlikely to achieve the desired change in behavior. Employees respond more positively to a supervisor who is more decisive and points out the inappropriate behavior and communicates clearly what kind of performance is expected in its place.
4. ***Making excuses for an employee*** It is common for employees to make excuses that explain their mistakes. Some employees become adept at creating sympathy for themselves

by telling tales of woe involving their family or personal hardships. By falling for these excuses, supervisors deprive employees the chance to accept responsibility for their mistakes and instead enable them to continue rationalizing their performance deficiencies. If an employee truly has a serious personal problem that is affecting work performance, he or she should seek help with the EAP.

5. ***Using a nonprogressive approach to discipline*** Managers sometimes postpone disciplinary action until the employee's behavior is so intolerable that it must be addressed immediately. At this point, the manager feels the need to apply harsh sanctions because the inappropriate behavior has become intolerable. Nonprogressive measures (harsh initial action) that are administered to a long-standing but untreated problem often seem unfair and overly harsh by the target employee and sometimes by his or her coworkers, too. The solution is to curtail inappropriate employee behavior at the beginning with a more moderate sanction before the offense becomes severe and requires more forceful action.

Sources: Based on Bielous, G. A. (1998, August). Five worst disciplinary mistakes (and how to avoid them). *Supervision,* 11–13; Lisoski, E. (1998, October). Nine common mistakes made when disciplining employees. *Supervision,* 12–14; Bacal, R. (2010). Five sins of discipline. *www.conflict911.com.* ■■

Managing Difficult Employees

So far we've focused on the challenges of administering discipline. We now turn to some common problems that managers are likely to encounter. All of the problems we discuss here—poor attendance, poor performance, insubordination, workplace bullying, and substance abuse—often lead to disciplinary actions. Managing the discipline of difficult employees requires good judgment and common sense.

Poor Attendance

The problem of poor attendance includes absenteeism and/or tardiness. Poor attendance can become a serious problem that leads to discharge for just cause. If poor attendance is not managed properly, employee productivity can decline and group morale can suffer as those with good attendance are forced to increase their efforts to compensate for people who shirk their responsibilities.

Sometimes employees are absent or tardy for legitimate reasons—for example, sickness, child-care problems, inclement weather, or religious beliefs. Managers should identify those employees who have legitimate reasons and treat them differently than they treat those who are chronically absent or tardy.

When disciplining an employee for poor attendance, managers need to consider several factors:

- ***Is the attendance rule reasonable?*** Attendance rules should be flexible enough to allow for the emergencies or unforeseen circumstances that most employees experience from time to time, including religious or cultural holidays celebrated by a diverse workforce. Most companies deal with this issue by showing leniency when an employee gives notice that he or she is sick or experiencing an emergency.
- ***Has the employee been warned of the consequences of poor attendance?*** This could be particularly important when an employee is unaware of how much time flexibility is possible in reporting to the job.
- ***Are there any mitigating circumstances that should be taken into consideration?*** Sometimes special circumstances need to be considered. These circumstances include work history, length of service, reason for absence, and likelihood of improved attendance.[101]

Managers should be aware of patterns of poor attendance within a work unit. Employees may dread coming to work because coworkers are unpleasant, the job has become unchallenging, they are experiencing conflicting demands from job and family, or supervision is poor. A disciplinary approach is not the best way to deal with this type of absenteeism. Possible solutions to such job avoidance are redesigning jobs or, when the problem is widespread, restructuring the organization.

For employees whose absences are due to overwhelming family demands, flexible work schedules or permission to work at home (telecommuting) may be desirable. Flexible work schedules are gaining popularity at companies both large and small. Ten months into Xerox Corporation's experiment with flexible work schedules, absences had fallen by one-third, teamwork had improved, and worker surveys showed that morale had risen.[102]

Poor Performance

Every manager must deal with employees who perform poorly and who do not respond to coaching or feedback. In most cases, the performance appraisal (see Chapter 7) can be used to turn around poor performers by helping them develop an action plan for improvement. Sometimes, however, the poor performance is so serious that it requires immediate intervention. Consider the following situations:

- A restaurant manager receives daily complaints from angry customers about the quality of one waitress's service.
- A partner's poor interpersonal skills affect his working relationships with the other two partners in his firm. The firm is now failing to meet its goals because of the severe conflicts and disruptions instigated by this one person.

These examples suggest a glaring need for progressive or positive discipline procedures. If these employees failed to improve their performance after receiving some warnings or counseling, dismissal would be justified.

Companies and managers should follow three guidelines when applying discipline for poor performance:

1. The company's performance standards should be reasonable and communicated to all employees. Job descriptions can be used for this purpose.
2. Poor performance should be documented, and poor performers should be told how they are not meeting the expected standards. One source of documented evidence can be the pattern of the employee's performance appraisals over a period of time.
3. Managers should make a good-faith attempt to give employees an opportunity to improve their performance before disciplining them.

Sometimes poor performance is the result of factors beyond the employee's control. In these cases, managers should avoid using discipline except as a last resort. For example, an employee may be unable to perform at expected standards because of incompetence. An *incompetent employee* (one who is lacking in ability, not effort) may be given remedial training (see Chapter 8) or be transferred to a less demanding job rather than be dismissed. An incompetent employee's poor performance may be the result of a flaw in the organization's selection system that caused a poor match between the employee's skills and the job requirements.

Some organizations use a *probationary employment period* (a period of time that allows the employer to discharge any employee at will) to weed out incompetent employees early. Probationary employment periods typically last one to three months. In Europe, where permanent employment is the norm, many companies insist on a six-month trial period as part of the employment contract. However, this policy can present a problem when recruiting executives, who understandably want to be guaranteed a permanent position before leaving their current job.

It is not only inappropriate but also illegal to use discipline to correct poor performance when an employee has a physical or mental disability.[103] The Americans with Disabilities Act (ADA, see Chapter 3) requires employers to make reasonable accommodation for disabled employees who cannot perform the job as it is structured. Accommodation may include redesigning the job or modifying policies and procedures. For example, an employee who is diagnosed with a terminal illness may request a change from a full-time job to a part-time job or one with a more flexible work schedule. The EEOC, which regulates how employers respond to the needs of employees with disabilities, would probably consider this a reasonable request, so failure to make such an accommodation could lead to government sanctions.

Unfortunately, many myths hinder firms' compliance with the ADA. One myth is that reasonable accommodation always involves prohibitive expense. Actually, accommodation is not necessarily costly, and more often than not, the money spent to accommodate a disabled individual is minor compared with the cost of litigation. Samsonite Corporation, a luggage company located in Denver, has employed deaf production workers for years. The only accommodation necessary—beyond an accommodating attitude and the willingness of many employees to learn some sign language—has been the use of lights in the production area in addition to the standard beepers alerting employees to the presence of forklifts.[104]

Insubordination

The willingness of employees to carry out managers' directives is essential to a business's effective operations. For example, consider the case of a sales representative who refuses to submit the weekly activity reports requested by his manager.[105] How should the sales manager react to the sales representative's behavior?

insubordination
Either refusal to obey a direct order from a supervisor or verbal abuse of a supervisor.

Insubordination, an employee's refusal to obey a direct order from a supervisor, is a direct challenge of management's right to run the company. Insubordination also occurs when an employee is verbally abusive to a supervisor. The discipline for insubordination usually varies according to the seriousness of the insubordination and the presence or absence of mitigating factors. Mitigating factors include the employee's work history and length of service and whether or not the employee was provoked by a supervisor's verbal abuse.

To justify disciplining an employee for insubordination, managers should document the following: (1) The supervisor gave a direct order to a subordinate, either in writing or orally; and (2) the employee refused to obey the order, either by indicating so verbally or by not doing what was asked. The discipline for a first insubordination offense ranges from applying the first step of the progressive discipline procedure to immediate suspension or discharge.

Two exceptions allow an employee to disobey a direct order: illegal activities and safety considerations. For instance, a California court found that an employer had violated public policy when it fired an employee who refused to commit perjury. Other illegal orders that employees can refuse with legal protection are participation in price-fixing and improper bookkeeping.[106] The whistle-blowing laws passed in some states provide further protection to employees who can prove they were discharged for refusing to break the law. The Occupational Safety and Health Administration protects the rights of employees who refuse to expose themselves to serious jeopardy. For insubordination to be acceptable, the employee should have "reasonable cause" to fear for his or her safety—for example, knowing that a truck the worker is ordered to drive has defective brakes.

Because the penalties for insubordination are severe, companies should create internal systems and cultures (open-door policies, appeal systems) that allow employees to appeal charges of insubordinate behavior. The legal and monetary penalties to companies for refusing to hear an employee's reasons for insubordination can be severe. Managers should be sure that insubordination charges are not being used to protect their own illegal or unethical behavior. For instance, a supervisor who charges an employee with insubordination may be attempting to force out someone who objects to the supervisor's illegal behavior. Companies that ignore such signs of trouble may find that a small problem has escalated into a very difficult and/or expensive situation.

Workplace Bullying

workplace bullying
A form of harassment that consists of a persistent pattern of offensive, abusive, intimidating, malicious, or insulting behavior focused at a target employee.

Employees have a right to be treated with dignity and respect in the workplace. Unfortunately, many are not. They wake up in the morning and go to work dreading that they will face another day of abuse.[107] Employees who feel this way likely experience **workplace bullying**, a form of harassment that results in employees experiencing mental distress, physical illness, loss of productivity, and a higher propensity to quit to avoid being in a toxic workplace.[108] Workplace bullying consists of ". . . persistent, offensive, abusive, intimidating, malicious or insulting behavior, abuses of power or unfair penal sanctions, which makes the recipient feel upset, threatened, humiliated, or vulnerable, which undermines their self-confidence and which may cause them to suffer stress."[109] The bully could be a boss chewing out a subordinate in front of colleagues, a peer who spreads a damaging rumor that harms an employee's reputation, or a subordinate who withholds support to the boss during a crisis.

Although legal remedies are available for sexual harassment, other forms of antisocial behavior, such as workplace bullying, are not considered to be illegal, yet can be equally harmful to the employees who are being targeted. Therefore, it is up to the organization, with the assistance of the HR staff, to provide remedies to employees being bullied by abusive colleagues.

Swearing at an employee in a hostile manner	Threatening an employee to reveal private or embarrassing information to others
Treating an employee in a rude and/or disrespectful manner	Subjecting an employee to temper tantrums when disagreeing
Subjecting an employee to obscene or hostile gestures	Criticizing an employee for his or her personal life and activities
Subjecting an employee to mean pranks	Subjecting an employee to unwanted terms of endearment
Subjecting an employee to derogatory name calling	Treating an employee in a condescending and insulting manner
Targeting an employee with rumors or gossip with intentions to harm	

FIGURE 14.5

Examples of Bullying Behaviors in the Workplace

Sources: Based on Neuman, J., and Keashly, L. (2005, August 9). Reducing aggression and bullying: A long-term intervention project in the U.S. Department of Veterans Affairs. In J. Raver (chair), *Workplace bullying: International perspectives on moving from research to practice.* Symposium conducted at the meeting of the Academy of Management, Honolulu, Hawaii; Roscigno, V., Lopez, S., and Hodson, R. (2009). Supervisory bullying, status inequalities and organizational context. *Social Forces, 87*(3), 1561–1589; *Workplace Bullying: What everyone needs to know.* (2008, April). Safety & Health Assessment & Research for Prevention Report #87-2-2008.

The media have focused attention on some high-profile situations in which individuals assumed it was permitted to treat employees harshly, and then found out the hard way that it is not:

> Staff sergeant Michael G. Rhoades, a drill sergeant at Fort Knox, Kentucky, used abusive methods to train soldiers, including calling them humiliating names such as "fat nasty," and punching a recruit in the stomach. Rhoades was court-martialed and found guilty of cruelty and dishonorably discharged for mistreating recruits.[110]
>
> In 2005, CEO Philip J. Purcell was asked by the board of directors to resign his job as CEO of Morgan Stanley, a financial services giant, after a stream of top-performing executives quit in recent years, adversely affecting company performance. Former employees indicated that CEO Purcell treated employees ruthlessly, and was intolerant of dissent or argument with his ideas. He pushed away and demeaned strong executives and preferred to surround himself with yes men and women.[111]

Some examples of bullying behaviors are listed in Figure 14.5. Although a single occurrence of one of the specified behaviors in Figure 14.5 is not likely to be perceived as a form of bullying, a persistent pattern of displaying one or more of these behaviors to a targeted employee has the cumulative effect of undermining an employee's self-confidence and morale to the point where the workplace becomes a stressful and toxic environment.

Unless an organization has a communication channel such as an open-door policy that encourages the reporting of workplace bullying behavior and provides remedies for it, employees will tolerate it, and targets of bullying will suffer in silence until they are able to quit. Two social scientists, Christine Pearson and Christine Porath, conducted a survey of employees who have been targeted by bullies to discover practices that reduce these incidents of uncivil conduct between employees. One of the recommendations from this study was for organizations to develop policies that promote zero tolerance for bullying and other forms of employee-to-employee incivility (rude conduct). Supporting this idea, organizations need value statements similar to that of AT&T, which states "we treat each other with respect and dignity."[112] Such statements set the tone for conduct that is acceptable and indicate that bullying behavior is not tolerated. Once there is a general consensus that employees need to be treated with dignity and respect, incidents of bullying can be treated as any other discipline problem.

Another approach to dealing with workplace bullying is provided by Robert Sutton, a business professor at Stanford University, who offers advice to companies who seek to implement and enforce a no-jerk rule when hiring and firing employees. Sutton defines a "jerk" as one who oppresses, humiliates, de-energizes, or belittles a subordinate or colleague. Sutton differentiates between "temporary jerks," who have a lapse in good judgment and may act rudely on an infrequent basis, and "certified jerks," who are routinely nasty to people. He says that certified jerks are the employees who pose the greatest threat to an organization's culture and are the targets of the no-jerk rule. One way of applying the no-jerk rule is to carefully screen job candidates during the recruiting process by getting groups of employees involved in the interview process. In addition, he recommends seeking out former coworkers of a recruit who are not listed as a reference and gathering information about a recruit's interpersonal conduct at the former employer. When evidence confirms that a job candidate is a certified jerk, the no-jerk rule is used to eliminate that individual from the applicant pool.[113]

Alcohol-Related Misconduct

Employees' use of alcohol presents two separate challenges to managers. First, there is the challenge of managing an employee who is an alcoholic. Second, there is the challenge of managing an employee who uses alcohol or is intoxicated on the job. Each of these employees should be disciplined differently.

Alcoholic employees are generally viewed sympathetically because alcoholism is an illness and medical treatment is the generally accepted remedy for it. However, as we mentioned in Chapter 13, some alcoholic employees have a strong denial mechanism that prevents them from admitting that they are alcoholics: Others may not view them as alcoholics either because alcoholism is often masked by behavioral symptoms such as poor attendance. Thus, a supervisor may perceive an alcoholic employee as someone who has an attendance or performance problem rather than an alcohol problem and discipline the employee accordingly. Organizations with EAPs give employees with performance problems the opportunity to visit a counselor as the last step in progressive discipline before discharge. This is where the alcoholism may finally be discovered and the employee referred to an alcohol rehabilitation facility.

Sometimes employees claim to be alcoholic to cover up their misconduct. If the EAP counselor determines that the individual is not an alcoholic, the discipline procedure is the appropriate managerial response to the problem.

Using alcohol on the job and coming to work intoxicated are both considered serious misconduct and can lead to harsh discipline. Organizations that have job-related reasons to restrict alcohol use at work or working "under the influence" should have clearly stated and reasonable policies. For example, it is reasonable to restrict the alcohol use, on or off the job, of heavy equipment operators at a construction site. It is more difficult to forbid a sales representative to drink alcohol when entertaining a prospective client at a lunch.

The best way to prove that an employee has come to work intoxicated is to administer a blood alcohol content test. A supervisor can ask an employee to submit to this test if there is a reasonable suspicion that the worker is intoxicated. Supervisors may suspect an individual is intoxicated if he or she engages in unusual behavior (talking particularly loud or using profanity), has slurred speech, or has alcohol on the breath.

A first intoxication offense may result in suspension or discharge because of the potential for damage that an alcohol-impaired employee can create. An extreme example of an alcohol-impaired employee's cost to an organization is the accident in which the oil tanker *Exxon Valdez* spilled oil off the coast of Alaska in March 1989. A blood alcohol test revealed that the ship's captain was intoxicated at the time of the oil spill, which cost Exxon over $1 billion to clean up.

Illegal Drug Use and Abuse

Drug use and abuse by employees also presents a serious challenge to managers. *Illegal drug use* refers to any use of prohibited substances such as marijuana, heroin, and cocaine as well as the illegal use of prescription drugs such as Valium. The problems associated with drug use are very similar to those associated with the use of alcohol. The key difference is that the use of illegal drugs is socially unacceptable, whereas the use of alcohol in moderation is socially acceptable.

We examined the specifics of drug-use detection systems earlier in this chapter, and we will address the health aspects of drug use in Chapter 16. Here we note only that illegal drug use is often masked by symptoms such as inattention and unexplained absences. Managers who suspect that drug use or addiction is the source of a performance problem should refer the employee to EAP counseling if the organization has such a program. Simultaneously, they should document performance problems and begin disciplinary procedures. These will prove valuable should it be necessary to terminate the employee because of failure to overcome the substance abuse problem after counseling and treatment. Managers who refer employees to an EAP program for problems that are not strictly related to performance may create some risk for the company, as we see in Chapter 16.

Preventing the Need for Discipline with Human Resource Management

By taking a strategic and proactive approach to the design of HRM systems, managers can eliminate the need for a substantial amount of employee discipline. HR programs designed to use employees' talents and skills effectively reduce the need to resort to discipline to shape employee behavior. In this section we briefly revisit some of the functional areas of HR we discussed in earlier chapters to show how each can be designed to prevent problem employees.[114]

Recruitment and Selection

By spending more time and resources on recruiting and selection, managers can make better matches between individuals and the organization.

- Workers can be selected for fit in the organization as well as the job. Choosing applicants who have career potential in the company decreases the likelihood that employees will exhibit performance problems later.
- Checking references and gathering background information on applicants' work habits and character are useful preliminaries to making a job offer.
- Multiple interviews that involve diverse groups in the company can reduce biases that lead to poor hiring decisions. When women, minorities, peers, and subordinates, as well as senior people, are involved in the interviewing process, companies stand a better chance of obtaining an accurate portrait of the applicant.
- Personality tests or honesty tests can be administered to job candidates. Candidates who have profiles from the test that correlate strongly with a high propensity to commit misconduct or display dishonesty in the workplace can be deleted from consideration for a job.[115]

Training and Development

Investing in employees' training and development now saves a company from having to deal with incompetents or workers whose skills are obsolete down the road.

- An effective orientation program communicates to new employees the values important to the organization. It also teaches employees what is expected from them as members of the organization. These insights into the company can help employees manage their own behavior better. FedEx, for instance, has an extensive orientation program to communicate company values to employees.[116]
- Training programs for new employees can reduce skill gaps and improve competencies.
- Retraining programs can be used for continuing employees whose skills have become obsolete. For example, employees may need periodic retraining on word processing software as the technology changes and more powerful programs become available.
- Training supervisors to coach and provide feedback to their subordinates encourages supervisors to intervene early in problem situations with counseling rather than discipline.
- Career ladders can be developed to give employees incentives to develop a long-term commitment to the organization's goals. When employees know that the organization has a long-term use for their contributions, they are more likely to engage in acts of good citizenship with their coworkers and customers.

Human Resource Planning

Jobs, job families, and organizational units can be designed to motivate and challenge employees. Highly motivated workers seldom need to be disciplined for inadequate performance.

- Jobs should be designed to use the best talents of each employee. It may be necessary to build some flexibility into job designs to put an employee's strengths to best use. One way companies are creating greater job flexibility is through *job banding*. Discussed in Chapter 10, this system replaces traditional narrowly defined job descriptions with broader categories, or bands, of related jobs. By putting greater variety into jobs, job banding makes it less likely that employees will feel so underchallenged or bored that they start avoiding work through absences or tardiness. Job banding has been implemented successfully by companies such as Aetna, General Electric, and Harley Davidson.[117]

- Job descriptions and work plans should be developed to communicate effectively to employees the performance standards to which they will be held accountable.

Performance Appraisal

Many performance problems can be avoided by designing effective performance appraisal systems. An effective performance appraisal system lets people know what is expected of them, how well they are meeting those expectations, and what they can do to improve on their weaknesses.

- The performance appraisal criteria should set reasonable standards that employees understand and have some control over.
- Supervisors should be encouraged to provide continuous feedback to subordinates. Many problems can be avoided with early interventions.
- Performance evaluations for supervisors should place strong emphasis on their effectiveness at providing feedback and developing their subordinates.
- Employee appraisals should be documented properly to protect employers against wrongful discharge or discrimination suits.
- The performance appraisal criteria should measure employee behaviors in addition to performance outcomes so that employees receive feedback on the methods they use to achieve their expected performance goals. This behavioral feedback enables managers to correct employees who choose inappropriate and undesirable means to reach their objectives.[118]

Compensation

Employees who believe that rewards are allocated unfairly (perhaps on the basis of favoritism) are likely to lose respect for the organization. Worse, employees who believe that pay policies do not recognize the value of their contributions are more likely to withhold future contributions.

- Pay policies should be perceived as fair by all employees. Employees deserve rewards for their contributions. It is important to explain to them the procedures used to establish their compensation level.
- An appeal mechanism that gives employees the right to challenge a pay decision should be established. Employees who can voice their frustration with a pay decision through a legitimate channel are less likely to engage in angry exchanges with supervisors, coworkers, or customers.

Summary and Conclusions

Employee Rights

In the employment relationship, both employees and employers have rights. Employee rights fall into three categories: statutory rights (protection from discrimination, safe work conditions, the right to form unions), contractual rights (as provided by employment contracts, union contracts, and employment policies), and other rights (the rights to ethical treatment, privacy, and free speech).

Management Rights

Employers have the right to run their business and make a profit. These rights are supported by property laws, common law, and the values of a society that accepts the concepts of private enterprise and the profit motive. Management rights include the right to manage the workforce and to hire, promote, assign, discipline, and discharge employees. Another important management right is employment at will, which allows an employer to dismiss an employee at any time for any cause. There are three key exceptions to the employment-at-will doctrine: public policy exceptions, implied contracts, and lack of good faith and fair dealing.

Employee Rights Challenges: A Balancing Act

Sometimes the rights of the employer and employees are in conflict. For example, a random drug-testing policy can create a conflict between an employer's responsibility to provide a safe workplace and employees' rights to privacy. HR professionals need to balance the rights of the employee with those of the employer when designing policies that address workplace issues such as random drug testing, electronic monitoring of employees, whistle-blowing, moonlighting, and office romance.

Disciplining Employees

Managers rely on discipline procedures to communicate to employees the need to change a behavior. There are two approaches to discipline. The progressive discipline procedure relies on increasing levels of punishment leading to discharge. The positive discipline procedure uses counseling sessions between supervisor and subordinate to encourage the employee to monitor his or her own behavior. Both procedures are designed to deal with forms of misconduct that are correctable.

Administering and Managing Discipline

To avoid conflict and lawsuits, managers must administer discipline properly. This entails ensuring that disciplined employees receive due process. Managers need to be aware of the standards used to determine whether an employee was treated fairly and whether or not the employee has a right to appeal disciplinary action. For a disciplinary system to be effective, an appeal mechanism must be in place.

Managing Difficult Employees

It is often necessary to discipline employees who exhibit poor attendance, poor performance, insubordination, workplace bullying, or substance abuse. Managing the discipline process in these situations requires a balance of good judgment and common sense. Discipline may not be the best solution in all cases.

Preventing the Need for Discipline with Human Resource Management

The need for discipline can often be avoided by a strategic and proactive approach to HRM. A company can avoid discipline by recruiting and selecting the right employees for current positions as well as future opportunities, by training and developing workers, by designing jobs and career paths that best utilize people's talents, by designing effective performance appraisal systems, and by compensating employees for their contributions.

Key Terms

contract, 458
contractual right, 458
due process, 459
employment at will, 462
employment contract, 458
hot-stove rule, 476
insubordination, 480
management rights, 462
moonlighting, 470
personnel file, 460
positive discipline, 474
Privacy Act of 1974, 460
progressive discipline, 473
right, 457
statutory right, 458
whistle-blowing, 468
workplace bullying, 480
wrongful discharge, 459

✪ Watch It!

Patagonia: Ethics and Social Responsibility. If your instructor has assigned this, go to **mymanagementlab.com** to watch a video case and answer questions.

Discussion Questions

14-1. Why have managers needed to place greater emphasis on employee rights in recent years?

14-2. Do employers have rights? If so, what are these rights?

14-3. In 2003, Dinesh Thakur joined the Indian pharmaceutical company Ranbaxy. Thakur, who went on to become the company's director, uncovered fraudulent practices at the company in drug development, manufacturing, and testing. He was forced to resign in 2005 after exposing the unsafe practices and violations. It wasn't until 2013 that Ranbaxy finally pleaded guilty to seven charges and paid a massive fine of $500 million. The case was only possible due to whistle-blower protection legislation in the United States. Thakur was able to work with the U.S. Food and Drug Administration (FDA) and the U.S. Department of Justice to expose widespread malpractices. What are the incentives and protective measures offered to whistleblowers in your country? How might the involvement of an organization like the FDA help?

14-4. When a whistle-blower steps forward and discloses corruption or misconduct performed by a manager, how does a company benefit? What can HR staff working with management do to reduce the fear and risk to employees from being a whistle-blower?

14-5. Can you think of a job-related reason why a company would decide to restrict dating between employees and enforce a no-dating policy? Do you think employers have a right to restrict any or all of the following off-duty conduct of their employees: (1) smoking cigarettes; (2) engaging in high-risk leisure activities such as skiing, motocross racing, rock climbing, or sky diving; (3) actively supporting a radical political candidate in an election; (4) having a romantic affair outside of the marriage relationship; and (5) joining a religious cult that preaches hatred against minorities? Justify your answer.

MyManagementLab®

If your instructor has assigned this, go to **mymanagementlab.com** for the following Assisted-graded writing questions:

14-6. Many U.S. companies outsource activities, such as manufacturing, to factories in Asia and Latin America. For example, Nike manufactures shoes in Indonesia and Hewlett-Packard uses electrical parts made in Chinese factories for its computers. Should the workers in these overseas factories that are part of the global supply chain for an American company have the same rights as U.S. employees? For example, should workers in overseas factories that make shoes for Nike have the right to the same working conditions as Nike employees working in the United States? List at least three of the advantages of maintaining a policy that offers consistent employee rights on a global basis. Next, provide at least three of the disadvantages of such a policy.

14-7. Compare and contrast the progressive and positive discipline procedures. List the ways they are similar and the ways they are different.

14-8. The administration of discipline usually occurs between a manager and a subordinate employee. Suggest three ways HR staff can contribute to the fairness of the administration of discipline? In addition what are three ways that HR staff contribute to the reduction of the need to administer discipline to employees within a company?

You Manage It! 1: Customer-Driven HR

Incivility Is a Growing Problem at the Workplace

Incivility at the workplace is on the rise according to a study by researchers presented at a recent American Psychological Association meeting. The Civility in America 2011 survey found that 43 percent of Americans reported that they experience incivility at work. Incivility is defined by the Society for Human Resource Management (SHRM) as seemingly inconsequential and inconsiderate words and deeds that violate conventional workplace conduct. In other words, incivility consists of rude conduct, insults, and bad manners.

Behavioral scientists who study incivility suggest that it is on the rise due to the higher stress levels that employees are experiencing originating from increasingly greater performance demands placed on them by managers. Factors that contribute to employee workplace stress include requirements that employees work longer hours with more to do and with fewer resources. Layoffs and downsizing have contributed to the high pressure on the remaining employees to deliver more productivity along with concerns for job security. Employees who are stressed are more likely to snap and get angry over minor errors made by a team member, or they may say hurtful things about a coworker who they perceive is not pulling his or her weight.

When incivility is allowed to continue unabated it can add up to significant costs to businesses in terms of lost productivity. Researchers Christine Porath and Christine Pearson took a survey of 800 managers and employees in 17 industries and asked how employees react to incivility when they experience it. They found that workers who experience incivility react in the following ways:

- 48 percent decreased their work effort.
- 47 percent intentionally decreased the time spent at work.
- 38 percent decreased the quality of their work.
- 80 percent lost work time worrying about the incident of incivility.
- 63 percent lost work time avoiding the perpetrator of incivility.

Organizations that develop ways to minimize incivility at the workplace can expect to be rewarded with a more highly productive workforce. The question remains, how will this be done and what role will the HR department play?

Critical Thinking Questions

14-9. Compare and contrast the differences and the similarities between workplace incivility and workplace bullying (the definition of bullying and some examples of it are described in this chapter of the text). Is there a relationship between bullying and incivility? If so, what would it be?

14-10. Nurses have often reported high frequencies of incidents of incivility when they are working with doctors under stressful conditions in emergency rooms and during surgeries on patients. What effect would these incidents of incivility have on patients receiving medical care at the hospital? What should a hospital administrator do to reduce the high levels of incivility at the hospital when made aware of this problem?

Team Exercise

14-11. A British Workplace Behavior Survey used a sample of 4,000 employees from four large organizations, and discovered three broad categories of ill-treatment at work. These included violence and injury (5 percent reported this), unreasonable treatment (50 percent reported this), and incivility and disrespect (40 percent reported this). The survey found that employers, managers, or supervisors were the main perpetrators (40 percent); clients or customers and the general public accounted for another 27 percent, and co-workers 22 percent. The targets of such behavior were younger workers, certain ethnic minorities, and women. With a team of 4 or 5 students representing the human resource management department, develop an approach to mitigate the level of incivility in an organization using your knowledge of effective human resource management practices. Which human resource practices are most likely to remedy the situation so that employees in an organization can expect to be treated in a civil manner by the other employees and the management? Be prepared to justify the human resource practices that the team recommends when called on by your instructor.

Experiential Exercise: Individual

14-12. In a situation that is commonly experienced by many recent college graduates, you have just been hired to work for one of the large public accounting firms. You have been assigned to work on a team of accountants performing a financial audit for a large corporation located in a different city, which requires overnight travel with the audit team and intense interactions between the team members at the site of the client. Because you are the newest member of the audit team, the other team members take it upon themselves to tease you and make you the target of their jokes to let off steam in this high-pressure work environment. For example, one of the team members gave you a funny-sounding nickname that you do not like, and you have made this known to the team—yet the others persist on calling you the nickname anyway. After some time had passed and you returned to the office of the accounting firm, you were informed that some team members have been spreading offensive and untrue rumors about your off-duty behavior, and you want these rumors to stop. Is there anything that you can do to improve the level of civility of team members on the audit team?

Sources: Based on Porath, C., and Pearson, C. (2013, January-February). The price of incivility: Lack of respect hurts morale—and the bottom line. *Harvard Business Review*, 114–121; Vulcan, N. (2013). What causes incivility in the workplace? *GlobalPost*. *www.everydaylife.globalpost.com*; Woodward, M. (2012, July 16). How to stop incivility in the workplace. *Fox Business*. *www.foxbusiness.com*; Jayson, S. (2011, August 8). Incivility a growing problem at work, psychologists say. *USA Today*. *www.usatoday.com*; Pearson, C., and Porath, C. (2005). On the nature, consequences and remedies of workplace incivility: No time for "nice"? Think again. *Academy of Management Executive*, 19(1), 7–18.

You Manage It! 2: Ethics/Social Responsibility

Background Checks Can Misfire, Harming Employees' Career Prospects

Theodore Pendergrass was shocked in November 2006 when the Walgreens pharmacy chain rejected his application for a store supervisor job. The company told him that a background-screening firm called ChoicePoint reported that a past employer had accused him of "cash register fraud and theft of merchandise" totaling $7,313. "I wanted to cry," Pendergrass said.

The $4 billion background-screening business is booming. Companies large and small are sorting mostly mid- and lower-level job applicants based on information compiled by ChoicePoint, its major rivals, and hundreds of smaller competitors. Some employers have grown more vigilant about hiring since the September 11, 2001, terrorist attacks. Others like the efficiency of outsourcing tasks once handled by in-house human resources departments or bosses who simply picked up the phone themselves. Whatever their motives, employers are becoming more dependent on mass-produced background reports that rely on anonymous—and sometimes inaccurate or unfair—sources.

Pendergrass' difficulties stemmed from a previous job at Rite Aid, a pharmacy company. In late 2005, when he was 25 years old, he had reached the first rung of management as a shift supervisor in a Rite Aid store in Philadelphia. His bosses trusted him to oversee cashiers, bank deposits, and merchandise deliveries. Then, in January 2006, a store official accused him of stealing goods and underpaying for DVDs. He denied the accusations, but the official said police were waiting outside to arrest him if he did not confess. Pendergrass wrote a statement but would not admit to theft. He was soon fired anyway.

Later, at a hearing for unemployment compensation, Pendergrass was vindicated. A state labor referee ruled that Rite Aid had not proved its allegations and awarded him nearly $1,000 in benefits. However, Rite Aid had already submitted its theft report to a database used by more than 70 retailers and run by ChoicePoint, the largest screening firm for corporate employers in the United States. ChoicePoint says that it checks applicants for more than half of the country's 100 largest companies, including Bank of America, UnitedHealth Group, and UPS. Because of Pendergrass' tainted ChoicePoint file, retailers CVS Caremark and Target also rejected him for jobs.

Pendergrass, now 27, makes lattes at a Starbucks in Philadelphia. The coffee chain does not use a screening firm for entry-level hires. Pendergrass earns $17,000 a year—30 percent less than he did at Rite Aid—and fears his career has been derailed. "I worked hard in that store, and none of this stuff was true," he says. "I would be locked up somewhere if I stole $7,000."

Rite Aid declined to comment on Pendergrass. A ChoicePoint spokeswoman says the company's background report merely conveyed information provided by a former employer.

Critical Thinking Questions

14-13. In this case, an employer's right to protect its property is at odds with employees' right to privacy concerning the use of personal employment information and the right to be treated ethically with dignity and respect. Why does there seem to be an imbalance between these conflicting rights, with the employer's rights appearing to take precedence over employees' rights? Do you agree that employers' property rights are more important that employees' rights to privacy and to fair and ethical treatment? Justify your reasoning.

14-14. ChoicePoint is the largest company in the $4 billion background-checking industry. Is there anything ChoicePoint can do, as the industry leader, to be more sensitive and respectful to the privacy rights of employees in how it distributes information to employers? What do you recommend? How would your recommendation affect ChoicePoint's cost of doing business?

Team Exercise

14-15. The federal Fair Credit Reporting Act covers background screeners, but it has not been aggressively enforced. The law says that screeners must use "reasonable procedures" to ensure "maximum possible accuracy." It also requires employers to give a copy of background reports to rejected applicants. An applicant can dispute the information in the report, but the Federal Trade Commission has said employers must wait only five business days before hiring someone else, meaning that objections frequently become pointless. Form a team with four or five students and develop an approach to use the federal regulations to protect employees' employment information in a way that more vigorously protects employees' rights. Keep in mind that the background-checking industry may have a financial interest in maintaining lax enforcement standards of the Fair Credit Report Act to allow it to have maximum flexibility to pursue its own interests. Be prepared to share your recommendation with other class members when called upon by the instructor.

Experiential Exercise: Individual

14-16. Pearson's Acclaim runs a system where digital badges are awarded to individuals when they enroll in a training course or project. Most achievement certificates and degrees are paper-based and not digitized even now. Acclaim aims to create a comprehensive system where credentials can be digitized and then shared using the Internet. Research indicates that over 60 percent of reported employment-frauds are related to false claims on CVs. Organizations like Adobe and Microsoft's Sales Academy have already signed up. The scheme was only launched in 2014, and by the end of 2015, Acclaim hopes to have issued 1 million badges. Make a case either for or against this initiative. Be prepared to share your ideas with other members of the class when called upon by the instructor.

Sources: Based on Terhune, C. (2008, June 9). The trouble with background checks. *BusinessWeek*, 54–58; McGregor, J. (2006, March 20). Background checks that never end. *BusinessWeek*, 40; Balle, J. (2010). Problems with a background check. *www.smallbusiness.chron.com*.

You Manage It! 3: Ethics/Social Responsibility

Employees Should Be Aware of the Risks Before They Attempt to Blow the Whistle

The U.S. Department of Labor, which is charged with enforcing the federal law protecting whistle-blowers at publicly traded companies, has been dismissing complaints on the technicality that workers at corporate subsidiaries are not covered by the law. The government has ruled in favor of whistle-blowers only 17 times out of 1,273 complaints filed between 2002 and 2008, according to Department of Labor records. Another 841 cases were dismissed. Many of the dismissals were made on the grounds that employees worked for a corporate subsidiary, according to Robert Moberly,

Sherron Watkins blew the whistle on Enron and its inaccurate financial reporting in 2002. Four years later, Enron president Jeffrey Skilling was sentenced to twenty-four years in prison after being found guilty of securities fraud and making false statements to auditors, among other crimes.
Source: STEPHEN JAFFE/AFP/Newscom.

a University of Nebraska law professor. The 2011 National Business Ethics Survey provided by the Ethics Resource Center reported that 31 percent of respondents who said they experienced reprisals for blowing the whistle on wrongdoing cited that these reprisals consisted of physical threats to themselves or their property.

Besides the lackluster federal enforcement of incidents of whistle-blowing, organizations are likely to retaliate against the employee who decides to blow the whistle and expose an alleged ethics violation. One way companies retaliate is by questioning the whistle-blower's mental health. The goal of the strategy, known as "nuts and sluts," is to cast doubt on the messenger. National Fuel Gas Company, a utility based near Buffalo, New York, fired Curtis Lee, a highly paid company lawyer, after he alleged that the chief executive and president had ordered him to backdate their stock options on forms submitted to the Security and Exchange Commission (SEC) in a way that made the options worth considerably more. Not only did National Fuel then sue Lee successfully for the return of the documents that might have provided proof, but it also persuaded a local court to ban him from ever repeating the accusations. In addition, the court ruled that he undergo psychiatric treatment, a ruling that was subsequently reversed on appeal on the grounds that it was illegal, but not before Lee had been "treated." An official investigation into the matter was frustrated by the untimely death of the chairman of the company's compensation committee.

Under the "employment at will" doctrine, companies in the United States do not have to give employees a reason for discharging them. Advocates for whistle-blowers believe that the greatest single protection for whistle-blowers would be to make it mandatory for firms to say why they are discharging an employee. The Whistleblower Protection Act has been in force since 1989, and in 2002 the Sarbanes-Oxley Act added additional protection to corporate whistle-blowers. However, these laws have loopholes that companies can use to protect their interests and avoid penalties from retaliating against a whistle-blower.

After reviewing hundreds of laws protecting whistle-blowers, Terrance Miethe, a professor of criminal justice at University of Nevada, concluded that "most legal protection for whistleblowers is illusory; few whistleblowers are protected from retaliatory actions because of numerous loopholes and special conditions of these laws, and the major disadvantage that individual plaintiffs have against corporate defendants," due to the superior availability of resources and legal talent that companies have compared to a whistle-blower.

Critical Thinking Questions

14-17. Why might an employee decide to blow the whistle on another person or practice in a company? What does an employee have to gain from blowing the whistle? What are the potential risks an employee could face by blowing the whistle on the employer?

14-18. How could an employer use the "employment at will" doctrine to defend against an allegation of retaliation from an employee who has been discharged after blowing the whistle on the company?

Team Exercise

14-19. With four or five other students, develop a comprehensive list of factors that represent barriers to whistle-blowing within an organization. Barriers to whistle-blowing come from three sources: (1) the organization itself, (2) an employee's supervisor, and (3) personal factors related to the employee. The team should identify barriers to whistle-blowing from each of these sources. Finally, develop ways to lower the barriers to whistle-blowing from these different sources. Be prepared to discuss ways to lower the barriers to whistle-blowing in organizations when called upon by the instructor.

Experiential Exercise: Individual

14-20. In 2014, the UK Home Office suspended the licenses of 57 private colleges. They launched an investigation into the UK subsidiary of the global testing company Educational Testing Service (ETS). They also suspended international recruitment at three universities. A whistle-blower had alerted authorities to widespread examination fraud. The investigation revealed that around 45,000 immigrants may have fraudulently obtained English language test certificates. UK Visas and Immigration (UKVI) and the National Crime Agency found that there were over 29,000 invalid results and 19,000 questionable results over the period 2012–13. A BBC documentary also showed footage of professionals taking examinations for other people, and cases where the answers were read out to the candidates. A researcher was able to pay a fee to "sit" for an exam in a London-based center approved by the government. A fake-sitter would take the examination for the researcher and all the researcher had to do was pose for a photograph to prove that she had attended. How widespread is examination fraud in your country? What steps would you suggest in order to deal with the problem? Be prepared to share your ideas with other members of the class when called upon by your instructor.

Sources: Based on Tugend, A. (2013, September 21). Opting to blow the whistle or choosing to walk away. *New York Times*, B4; Levitz, J. (2008, September 4). Whistleblowers are left dangling. *Wall Street Journal*, A3; *The Economist*. (2006, March 25). Tales from the back office, 67–68; McKinney, H. (2010, November 20). The hazards of whistleblowing. *www.ehow.com*.

You Manage It! 4: Global

Illegal Immigrants in the Workforce: Opportunity or Challenge?

Illegal immigrant labor is a global HRM issue that arises from people from less developed countries (LDCs) illegally entering more affluent countries to seek employment. Illegal immigrants are likely to work for wages lower than those that are paid to citizens within a country. In addition, they are often paid in cash, and therefore avoid paying taxes on their earned income. This raises issues of unfairness for those who "play by the rules" and pay taxes or who wait their turn to enter the country legally.

Most of the income earned by illegal immigrants goes back to family members in their country of origin. This increases their family's living standards and contributes to the economic stability of their country of origin, reducing its need for foreign economic assistance. Illegal immigrants are often exploited by unscrupulous employers who may not provide safe working conditions or who may force them to work excessive hours beyond what is permitted by the host country's labor laws. Illegal immigrants may not have the same legal rights as the host country's citizens or they may be unaware of their rights; thus, they are easily taken advantage of.

Countries as diverse as Spain, Poland, Italy, and the United States have significant numbers of illegal immigrants in the workforce. In Spain, large numbers of Romanians, Moroccans, Ecuadorans, and Columbians work in the tourist and construction industries. Poland has tens of thousands of illegal immigrants, chiefly from Ukraine. Italy has many Albanians working illegally in its underground economy. Finally, the world's largest illegal immigrant workforce is in the United States, with estimates as high as 10 million illegal immigrants working within its borders in mainly low-wage jobs in industries such as farm labor, meat and poultry processing, lawn care, restaurant labor, and drywall and ceiling tile installation.

In the United States, the illegal immigrant population is so large that it has become an important market segment. Millions of illegal immigrants from Mexico have been issued *matricula* cards from the Mexican consulate (with the approval of the U.S. government) that entitle the card bearers to open bank accounts and to hold driving licenses. Wells Fargo Bank has opened bank accounts for *matricula* card holders, and U.S. Sprint Corp. accepts the card for cell phone contracts. Kraft has developed new drink products with the illegal immigrant consumer in mind. In some parts of the country, entire industries depend on the labor of illegal immigrants. The U.S. Department of Labor estimates that in California, the most important fruit and vegetable producer in the nation, 90 percent of farm labor consists of illegal immigrants. In Texas, restaurants depend heavily on illegal immigrants to clear tables and wash dishes.

With the exportation of millions of higher-paying jobs to India and China through outsourcing arrangements and the presence of a large and growing illegal immigrant workforce for low-wage jobs, U.S. citizens are feeling more uncertain than ever about their own job security and the opportunities that will be available for their children. Depending on how it is framed, the illegal immigrant workforce can be viewed as either a new opportunity providing new markets to serve—or as a challenge that needs to be controlled so that citizens who follow the economic rules, pay their taxes, and obey the law do not feel they are being treated unfairly by their government.

Critical Thinking Questions

14-21. What do you consider to be the primary opportunities related to the issue of illegal immigrants in the workforce? State your reasoning.

14-22. What do you consider to be the main challenges related to the issue of illegal immigrants in the workforce? State your reasoning.

14-23. What makes it so difficult to find an acceptable solution for this issue, assuming that the status quo concerning illegal immigration needs to be changed?

Team Exercise

14-24. With a group of four or five students, determine which workplace rights or benefits illegal immigrant employees and regular employees share, and which ones employees who are citizens or legal residents have that are not available to illegal immigrants. Here are some examples of rights or benefits you can examine to answer this question: Social Security, worker's compensation, unemployment insurance, government safety standards, overtime pay, minimum wage, union membership, and job opportunities working for the U.S. government. What type of employer is most likely to hire illegal immigrants? Be prepared to share your group's findings with the class.

Experiential Exercise: Individual

14-25. This exercise asks you to explore your attitudes concerning illegal immigrants in the workplace.

a. Would you work for an employer who makes it a point to hire illegal immigrants? Why or why not?
b. Would you consume the products of a company that you know purposely hires illegal immigrants? Why or why not?
c. If you worked in a restaurant and found out that some of the employees working there were illegal immigrants, would you inform the restaurant manager? Why or why not?
d. If you were the owner of a restaurant and the only way you could fill the dishwashing jobs was to hire people you expected to be illegal immigrants, would you hire these people? Why or why not?
e. If you were a department manager and you discovered a prospective professional employee had an illegal immigrant providing babysitting services for her children, would you still extend a job offer to this person? Why or why not?

Be prepared to share your answers with other members of the class when called on by your instructor.

Sources: Based on Grow, B. (2005, July 18). Embracing illegals. *BusinessWeek*, 42–49; Justich, R., and Ng, B. (2005). *The underground labor force is rising to the surface.* New York: Bear Stearns Asset Management Inc.; *The Economist.* (2005, September 10). The grapes of wrath, again, 50; Colvin, G. (2005, September 5). On immigration policy, we've got it backward. *Fortune,* 44; *The Economist.* (2010, December 18). Field of tears: They came to America illegally, for the best of reasons, 39–41.

Endnotes

Scan for Endnotes or go to http://www.pearsonglobaleditions.com/Gomez-Mejia.

CHAPTER 15 Working with Organized Labor

MyManagementLab®

When you see this icon, visit **www.mymanagementlab.com** for activities that are applied, personalized, and offer immediate feedback.

CHALLENGES

After reading this chapter, you should be able to deal more effectively with the following challenges:

1. **Understand** why employees join unions.
2. **Describe** labor relations and the legal environment.
3. **Understand** labor relations in the United States.
4. **Become** aware of labor relations in other countries.
5. **Gain** familiarity with labor relations strategy.
6. **Learn** practices for managing the labor relations process.
7. **Recognize** the impact of unions on human resource management.

Working with organized labor can be challenging. One of the greatest challenges managers experience is when union representatives and management are unable to come to an agreement on employee wages, hours, and working conditions and the union decides to exercise its right to strike. On the morning of September 24, 2007, 74,000 members of the United Auto Workers (UAW) left their jobs at General Motors (GM) factories and began picketing in public areas near the factories. The union had just launched a nationwide strike for the first time in 37 years. The union's leader, Ron Gettelfinger, expressed sorrow that a deal could not be reached.[1]

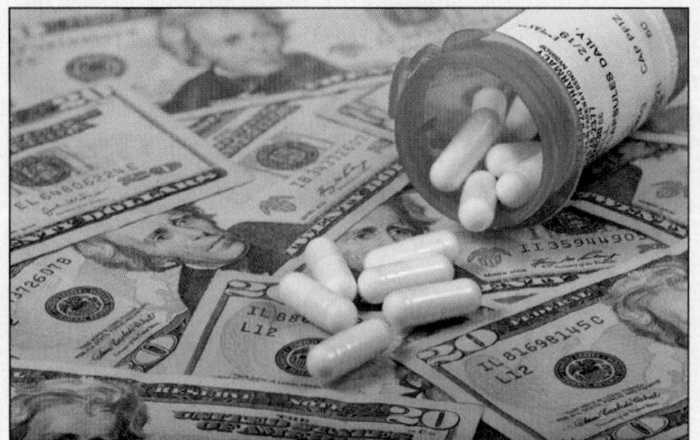

Source: Russell Shively/Shutterstock.

The strike between the UAW and General Motors lasted only two days before a new labor agreement was reached. The big sticking point that led to the breakdown in negotiations was the issue of health care costs. The centerpiece of the agreement that was ratified by the union membership was the creation of an independent trust that took over some $51 billion of health care liabilities for GM's existing employees and over 280,000 of its retired workers. Health care costs added as much as $1,600 to the price of each GM vehicle, and it was critical to management to find a way to reduce these costs. Global competitors in the auto industry in Asia and Europe did not face such expensive health care costs, because governments in other countries often cover the cost of health insurance. Over the years prior to the strike, GM had lost market share in the United States to competitors such as Toyota, Honda, and Hyundai, who had much lower employee health costs than GM.

The trust was set up with about $35 billion and allowed GM to get the liability of providing health care funds for large numbers of retirees off its balance sheet.[2] The union benefited from this deal on health care costs because it protected its members against the possibility that GM would be unable to meet its health coverage obligations for retired union members.[3]

The Managerial Perspective

The relationship between managers and their employees changes in a unionized organization. The law requires managers to meet and confer with elected union representatives when making decisions that affect pay, hours of employment, or working conditions. When unionized employees are dissatisfied with pay or other job factors, the company faces the possibility of a strike or other form of collective action designed to pressure the firm to respond to employees' preferences. Managers, then, need to understand the basics of labor relations and labor law to handle day-to-day labor–management relations effectively.

The presence of a union increases managers' need for HR services. HR specialists in labor relations can help managers develop tactics and strategies to work constructively with the union and its representatives in areas such as negotiating the terms of new labor contracts, interpreting a labor contract, or responding to an employee grievance. Managers that grasp the basics of labor relations will know when to turn to HR specialists and what questions to ask.

In this chapter, we explore the labor–management relationship between companies and unions. We begin by examining why employees join unions and why some employers prefer the workplace not to be unionized. Second, we outline the major U.S. legislation that governs labor issues and describe the current labor-relations climate in the United States and in some other countries. Third, we investigate different labor relations strategies and explore the rules and procedures that govern union activities. Finally, we address the impact of unions on a variety of HR practices.

Learn It!

If your professor has chosen to assign this go to **www.mymanagementlab.com** to see what you should particularly focus on, and take the chapter 15 warmup.

Why Do Employees Join Unions?

A **union** is an organization that represents employees' interests to management on issues such as wages, work hours, and working conditions. Employees participate in administering the union and support its activities with *union dues,* fees they pay for the union's services. The law protects employees' rights to join and participate in unions. The law also requires employers to bargain and confer with the union over certain employment issues that affect unionized employees.

union
An organization that represents employees' interests to management on such issues as wages, work hours, and working conditions.

Employees join unions for different reasons. For example, in Israel, employees join unions because many believe in the social justice the union represents.[4] Employees in the United States seek union representation when they (1) are dissatisfied with certain aspects of their job, (2) feel that they lack influence with management to make the needed changes, (3) believe that their pay and benefits are non-competitive; and (4) see unionization as a solution to their problems.[5] The union's best ally is bad management. If managers listen to employees, give them some say in the policies that affect their jobs, and treat them fairly, employees usually will not feel the need to organize. Managers who ignore their workers' interests and treat them inconsistently often end up having to deal with a union.

Companies usually prefer a nonunion workforce. The primary reason is that wages are typically higher for union employees, which puts unionized companies at a competitive disadvantage if their competitors are not unionized. In addition, unions constrain what managers can and cannot do with a particular employee. For instance, a unionized employee who is doing a particularly good job usually cannot be given a merit raise or promoted over someone who has greater seniority. And many labor agreements spell out the specific work responsibilities of certain employees, which reduces flexibility in work assignments. Of course, many unionized companies flourish, and unions have some very positive social benefits. For example, a study reported that unions boosted productivity at hospitals by 16 percent compared to nonunion hospitals.[6] But given the choice, most managers would prefer a nonunion environment.

The Origins of U.S. Labor Unions

Unions, as we think of them today, were largely unprotected by law in the United States until 1935. The approach of the U.S. government to unions prior to 1935 was simple: In a free market economy, the employment relationship is essentially a private one, and both employee and employer are free to accept or reject this relationship if they find it unsatisfactory. (See the discussion of employment at will in Chapter 14.)

This thinking assumes the employer and the employee to be in similar positions of power: Employees who find their compensation unfair or working conditions unreasonable are free to find another job; employers who are unhappy with an employee's performance can fire that employee. In practice, of course, employers have considerably more power than individual employees. A large steel manufacturer does not miss one employee who quits because there is usually a ready supply of applicants to replace that person. However, a large employer can so dominate a neighborhood, city, or region that there are few or no other employment alternatives. The aircraft assembly plants in Seattle, the auto manufacturers in Detroit, the coal mine operators in Appalachia, and the tire companies in Akron are examples of employers and industries that have dominated their respective regions.

In the Great Depression of the 1930s, millions of workers lost their jobs as employers came under tremendous pressure to cut production costs. These cutbacks put even more pressure on the working class. It was in this environment that union activity as we know it was legalized by the Wagner Act (1935), which attempted to equalize the power of employers and employees. In fact, this goal explains much of the governmental and societal response to union activity during the Depression and in the years following World War II. Unions were widely supported because of the public perception that working people had little power.

Toward the end of the twentieth century, however, public perception had changed. When President Reagan ordered the firing of striking air traffic controllers on August 5, 1981, two days after they began an illegal strike, the terminated employees received little sympathy from society at large, probably because unions were widely perceived to have become too powerful. This action took place in the middle of a period of dramatic decline in strikes in the United States: From a peak of 424 in 1974, strikes decreased to 19 in 2012.[7] However, unions are growing in some fields such as medicine. As unions tackle new issues and represent workers in new professions, public perception of union activities is likely to change.

The Role of the Manager in Labor Relations

labor relations specialist
Someone, often a member of the HR department, who is knowledgeable about labor relations and can represent management's interests to a union.

When a union represents a group of employees in a company, the company needs a staff of specialists who can represent management's interests to the union. These **labor relations specialists**, who are often members of the HR department, help resolve grievances, negotiate with the union over changes in the labor contract, and provide advice to top management on a labor relations strategy.

Still, it is managers who bear the major responsibility for day-to-day labor–management relations. Thus, it is important that they understand the workplace issues associated with unions. First, as we noted earlier, unions generally take hold only in firms where employees are dissatisfied with their jobs, and managers greatly influence how employees perceive their work environment. Second, where there is a union, managers are responsible for the day-to-day implementation of the terms of the labor agreement. The more effectively they carry out this responsibility, the less time the company will spend resolving labor conflicts. Third, managers need to have a basic understanding of labor law so that they do not unintentionally create a legal liability for the company. Finally, individual managers are often asked to serve on committees to hear grievances brought by union members against the company. A manager who understands general labor issues will be better prepared to hear and decide such cases.

Because the nature and function of unions are so dependent on legislation, we look at the specifics of that legislation next.

Labor Relations and the Legal Environment

The key labor relations legislation in the United States consists of three laws enacted between the 1930s and the 1950s: the Wagner Act (1935), the Taft-Hartley Act (1947), and the Landrum-Griffin Act (1959). These laws regulate labor relations in the private sector. Public-sector labor relations are covered by federal or state laws that are patterned after these laws.

In the history of labor relations law in the United States, the government has tried to balance (1) employers' rights to operate their businesses free from unnecessary interference, (2) unions' rights to organize and bargain for their members, and (3) individual employees' right to choose their representatives or to decide that they do not want or need union representation. Before 1935, employer rights were essentially unchecked by federal legislation. After passage of the Wagner Act, however, many felt that union rights were too strongly protected, relative to both employer and individual employee rights. This sentiment led Congress to pass two laws—the Taft-Hartley Act and the Landrum-Griffin Act—in an attempt to achieve balance.

The Wagner Act

The **Wagner Act**, also known as the **National Labor Relations Act**, was passed in 1935 during the Great Depression. It was designed to protect employees' rights to form and join unions and to engage in activities such as strikes, picketing, and collective bargaining. The Wagner Act created the **National Labor Relations Board (NLRB)**, an independent federal agency charged with administering U.S. labor law.

Wagner Act/National Labor Relations Act (1935)
A federal law designed to protect employees' rights to form and join unions and to engage in such activities as strikes, picketing, and collective bargaining.

National Labor Relations Board (NLRB)
The independent federal agency created by the Wagner Act to administer U.S. labor law.

The NLRB's primary functions are (1) to administer *certification elections,* secret ballot elections that determine whether employees want to be represented by a union, and (2) to prevent and remedy unlawful acts called *unfair labor practices.* The NLRB remedies an unfair labor practice by issuing a *cease and desist order,* which requires the guilty party to stop engaging in the unlawful labor practice. The Wagner Act identified five illegal labor practices that can be remedied by the National Labor Relations Board:

1. Interfering with, restraining, or coercing employees to keep them from exercising their rights to form unions, bargain collectively, or engage in concerted activities for mutual protection.
2. Dominating or interfering with the formation or administration of a union or providing financial support for it.
3. Discriminating against an employee to discourage union membership. Discrimination can include not hiring a union supporter, or firing, not promoting, or denying a pay raise to an employee who is a union member or who favors union representation.
4. Discharging or otherwise discriminating against an employee who has filed charges or given testimony under the act's provisions.
5. Refusing to bargain collectively with the union that employees chose to represent them.

The NLRB sometimes has difficulty enforcing its unfair labor practice rules because large corporations often use sophisticated tactics to avoid unions, as described in the Manager's Notebook, "Wal-Mart's Union-Avoidance Tactics."

MANAGER'S NOTEBOOK

Wal-Mart's Union-Avoidance Tactics

Ethics/Social Responsibility

In the summer of 2000, Wal-Mart's Kingman, Arizona, Tire and Lube Express (TLE) employees contacted the United Food and Commercial Workers seeking union representation. The union filed a representation petition on August 28, and two days later a labor relations team from Wal-Mart's corporate headquarters arrived at the store. During the union-organizing campaign, members of the labor relations team did a number of things, including threatening to postpone merit pay increases for the TLE employees during any contract negotiations, engaging in surveillance of employees' union activities, granting benefits and improved working conditions to discourage employees from supporting the union, discriminatorily and disparately applying and enforcing its no-harassment policies to the detriment of employees who supported the union, and discharging and denying COBRA health benefit continuation coverage to employees for supporting the union.

The union filed charges of unfair labor practices with the National Labor Relations Board (NLRB) against Wal-Mart in 2000 due to the unfair way the company treated its employees who favored the union. The NLRB issued its final decision and remedial order nearly 8 years later in June 2008. What took so long? Wal-Mart's legal staff used delay tactics in complying with the law and then appealed the decision to a federal court. By the time Wal-Mart exhausted its appeals on every claim made by the union and eight years had passed, few of the original TLE employees who supported the union remained at the store. In the future, it should not be difficult for Wal-Mart to claim that a majority of employees no longer want a union and to encourage its employees to petition the NLRB to conduct an election to decertify the union.

Sources: Based on Hyman, J. (2008, July 10). A lesson in union avoidance. www.ohioemploymentlaw.blogspot.com/2008/07/lesson-in-union-avoidance.html; Wal-Mart Stores Inc., 352 NLRB No. 103 (2008); Kucera, B. (2008, October 26). Wal-Mart has perfected the art of union-busting, researcher says. *Workday Minnesota. www.truth-out.org*; Brooks, M. (2010, July 1). What else you should know about Walmart. *Chicago Reader. www.chicagoreader.com.* ■■

The Taft-Hartley Act

Taft-Hartley Act (1947)
A federal law designed to limit some of the power acquired by unions under the Wagner Act by adjusting the regulation of labor–management relations to ensure a level playing field for both parties.

The **Taft-Hartley Act**, enacted in 1947 shortly after the end of World War II, was designed to limit some of the power that unions acquired under the Wagner Act and to protect the rights of management and employees. Although the Taft-Hartley Act was basically favorable to management's interests, its goals were to adjust the regulation of labor–management relations to ensure a level playing field for both parties.

Taft-Hartley included remedies from the National Labor Relations Board for six unfair union labor practices:

1. Restraining or coercing employees in the exercise of their rights guaranteed under the act, and/or coercing an employer's choice of a representative in collective bargaining.
2. Causing or attempting to cause an employer to discriminate against an employee who is not a member of a labor union for any reason other than failure to pay the union dues and initiation fees uniformly required as a condition of acquiring or retaining membership in the union.
3. Refusing to bargain in good faith with an employer after a majority of the employees in a unit have elected the union as their representative.
4. Asking or requiring its members to boycott products made by a firm engaged in a labor dispute with another union (*secondary boycott*). However, a union can call a boycott of products produced by its own firm (*primary boycott*).
5. Charging employees excessive or discriminatory union dues as a condition of membership in a union under a union shop clause. (A **union shop clause** requires employees to join the union 30 to 60 days after their date of hire.)
6. Causing an employer to pay for services that are not performed. This practice, often called *featherbedding,* is technically illegal, but the definition of unnecessary or unperformed work is often murky. For example, railroad unions continued to require the presence of firemen on engines long after their main duty (taking care of the fire on a steam engine) was eliminated by the advent of diesel engines.

union shop clause
A union arrangement that requires new employees to join the union 30 to 60 days after their date of hire.

Twelve years later, the Landrum-Griffin Act added a seventh unfair union labor practice: It is illegal for a union to picket an employer for the purpose of union recognition (a practice known as *recognitional picketing*).

Perhaps the most controversial provision of the Taft-Hartley Act is Section 14b, which gives permission to the states to enact right-to-work laws. A **right-to-work law** makes it illegal within a state for a union to include a union shop clause in its contract. Unions negotiate union shop clauses into their contracts to provide greater security to union employees and prevent nonunion employees from receiving union services without paying union dues. A less-restrictive arrangement called the *agency shop clause* requires employees to pay a union service fee (about equal to union dues) but does not require them to join the union. Currently, 24 states have right-to-work

right-to-work law
A state law that makes it illegal within that state for a union to include a union shop clause in its contract.

laws, which make it more difficult to organize and sustain unions in those states.[8] While many of these states are located in the southern or western United States, away from major industrial centers, in 2012 the midwestern industrial states of Indiana and Michigan approved legislation to become right-to-work states.

Several other provisions of Taft-Hartley are noteworthy. First, the act made *closed shops,* which require an employee to be a union member as a condition of being hired, illegal. This provision was modified 12 years later by the Landrum-Griffin Act to allow a closed shop in the construction industry as the only exception. Second, Taft-Hartley allowed employees to get rid of a union they no longer want through a *decertification election* and charged the NLRB with regulating decertification elections. Finally, Taft-Hartley created a new agency, the *Federal Mediation and Conciliation Service,* to help mediate labor disputes so that economic disruptions due to strikes and other labor disturbances would be fewer and shorter.

The Landrum-Griffin Act

The **Landrum-Griffin Act** was enacted in 1959 to protect union members and their participation in union affairs. It allows the government, through the Department of Labor, to regulate union activities. The Landrum-Griffin Act includes the following key provisions:

Landrum-Griffin Act (1959)
A law designed to protect union members and their participation in union affairs.

1. Each union must have a bill of rights for union members to ensure minimum standards of internal union democracy.
2. Each union must adopt a constitution and provide copies of it to the Department of Labor.
3. Each union must report its financial activities and the financial interests of its leaders to the Department of Labor.
4. Union elections are regulated by the government, and union members have the right to participate in secret ballot elections.
5. Union leaders have a fiduciary responsibility to use union money and property for the benefit of the membership and not for their own personal gain. Members can sue and recover damages from union leaders who fail to exercise their fiduciary responsibilities.

Other laws that affect labor relations include the Railway Labor Act (1926, last amended in 1970), the Norris-LaGuardia Act (1932), and the Byrnes Antistrikebreaking Act (1938). Of course, the equal employment opportunity laws discussed in Chapter 3 also apply to unionized workers. Most noteworthy of these other labor laws is the **Railway Labor Act**, which regulates labor relations in the transportation industry. This law covers the railway, airline, and trucking industries that are critical to sustain commerce. It provides dispute settlement procedures if the parties are unable to achieve a labor agreement. The Railway Labor Act has provisions for congressional and presidential intervention in a labor dispute that could be disruptive to interstate commerce. For example, the President intervened in a labor dispute in the airline industry when one of the major airlines forced the union to go on strike because of a breakdown in negotiations.[9]

Railway Labor Act
A law designed to regulate labor relations in the transportation industry.

Although much of U.S. labor relations law is more than five decades old, it would be a mistake to assume that nothing new is happening in this area. More recently, the National Labor Relations Board was considering new rules that would reduce the time required to schedule a union election, which would make it more difficult for management to organize a campaign to defeat the union.[10] In addition, Congress has considered an amendment to the Wagner Act that would eliminate an employer's right to use permanent replacements during an economic strike or work stoppage.[11] In Canada, several provinces have recently enacted laws that restrict employers from using replacement workers during strikes.[12] Clearly, the struggle to find the correct balance of employer, union, and employee rights is ongoing.

We now turn to a description of the current state of labor relations in the United States.

Labor Relations in the United States

Labor relations in the United States evolved from the philosophy of the U.S. labor movement, which accepted the country's capitalist economic structure and wanted to operate within it.[13] U.S. unions have avoided a permanent affiliation with a political party and have focused on improving their members' welfare through dealing directly with the companies that employ their members. The key factors that characterize labor relations in the United States are (1) business unionism,

(2) unions structured by type of job, (3) a focus on collective bargaining, (4) labor contracts, (5) the adversarial nature of labor–management relations and shrinking union membership, and (6) the growth of unions in the public sector.

Business Unionism

business unionism
A form of unionism that focuses on improving workers' economic well-being.

Business unionism is unionism that focuses on "bread-and-butter" issues (such as wages, benefits, and job security) so that workers get a larger slice of the economic pie. U.S. unions, which practice business unionism, have traditionally avoided trying to influence the running of the company, and they provide little input to management on strategic decisions such as how to market a product or what types of new business to enter. It is rare to see U.S. union members on a company's board of directors.[14] U.S. labor laws reinforce this tendency by making wages, hours, and working conditions mandatory topics for bargaining. This means that management is obligated to bargain on these issues in good faith.

Unions Structured by Type of Job

In contrast to unions in some other countries, U.S. unions tend to be organized by type of job. For instance, truck drivers are often members of the Teamsters Union; many public school teachers are members of the National Education Association; and most autoworkers, with the exception of autoworkers in foreign transplant plants, belong to the United Auto Workers, no matter which automaker employs them. Because most unions represent employees from multiple employers, they are typically arranged into *locals* governed by a national body. Each local consists of the union members in a particular geographic location. The local has its own officers and is generally concerned with day-to-day labor practices and disputes. The national organization ties these locals together, governs how locals are organized and operated, and, most importantly, establishes policy for contract negotiations.

The *AFL-CIO,* formed by the merger of the old American Federation of Labor and the Congress of Industrial Organizations, is a confederation of many different unions. Because it represents so many workers (approximately 11.6 million), the AFL-CIO has a tremendous influence on federal labor policies.[15] It also provides support to individual national unions and mobilizes support for laws that are beneficial to working people. Finally, the AFL-CIO resolves disputes between national unions.[16]

In 2005, four large unions representing 4 million employees voted to disaffiliate from the AFL-CIO and become independent. The unions that left the AFL-CIO were the Service Employees International Union, the International Brotherhood of Teamsters, the United Food and Commercial Workers Union, and Unite Here, a union of apparel and hotel workers. These unions wanted the organized labor movement to spend more time and money recruiting new members.[17] Shortly afterward, the Laborers, Carpenters, and United Farm Workers unions joined this group of independent unions and formed Change to Win. Currently, Change to Win is a confederation that represents seven unions with 5.5 million members.[18]

Focus on Collective Bargaining

collective bargaining
A system in which unions and management negotiate with each other to develop the work rules under which union members will work for a stipulated period of time.

work rules
Any terms or conditions of employment, including pay, work breaks and lunch periods, vacation, work assignments, and grievance procedures.

Unions and management are the dominant players in the U.S. labor relations system. Generally, the U.S. government takes a neutral role, allowing the players to make the rules that govern their particular workplace. The mechanism of choice for developing these rules is collective bargaining. Under a **collective bargaining** system, unions and management negotiate with each other to develop the work rules under which union members will work for a stipulated period of time, usually two or three years. **Work rules** include any terms or conditions of employment, including pay, work breaks and lunch periods, vacation, work assignments, and grievance procedures.

Unions that are legally elected by workers in the United States act as the sole representative of those workers' concerns to management. Although unions may compete for recognition, once one is recognized, individual employees cannot choose to be represented by another union.

Labor Contracts

labor contract
A union contract that spells out the conditions of employment and work rules that affect employees in the unit represented by the union.

The product of collective bargaining is a **labor contract** that spells out the conditions of employment and work rules that affect employees in the unit represented by the union. Because both parties enter into the contract voluntarily, one party can use the legal system to enforce the terms of the contract if the other party does not fulfill its responsibilities.

Labor contracts are an important feature of the U.S. labor relations system. In many other countries, such as Germany and Sweden, working conditions and employee benefits are codified into labor laws, but in the United States labor and management have historically established workers' economic benefits without government interference.

The Adversarial Nature of Labor–Management Relations and Shrinking Union Membership

U.S. labor laws view labor and management as natural adversaries who will disagree over the distribution of the firm's profits. For this reason, rules have been put in place so that the pie is distributed peacefully.

In a sense, the U.S. labor relations system is modeled on the U.S. court system. In a court, "justice" may be considered the result of the clash of adversaries, with the district attorney representing the plaintiff's interests and the defense attorney representing the defendant's interests. Similarly, "economic justice" may be considered the result of negotiations between the union (the advocate of the employees) and management (the advocate of the firm's owners). Although this adversarial model worked well for many years in the United States, it has recently become an obstacle to union–management cooperation, which has grown in importance as both labor markets and product markets have become more globally competitive.

As Figure 15.1 shows, 11 percent of the U.S. labor force is unionized.[19] This is down from a peak of about 35 percent in 1945. In addition, only 6.6 percent of the private-sector workforce in the United States is unionized. There are several reasons for this decline: the shrinking base of blue-collar industrial jobs (the traditional area of unionization) due to automation and foreign competition; the increase in employment legislation that provides workers with remedies that address their needs; and the aggressively hostile labor relations strategies of many companies, which have made it difficult for unions to organize workers. Other possible reasons for declining union membership are an increasingly educated workforce, as well as the highly publicized legal problems of some union leaders.

Despite shrinking union membership, unions continue to be an important part of the U.S. labor relations system because they establish wage and benefit patterns that influence nonunion employers. In this way, unions indirectly affect about 40 to 50 percent of the U.S. labor force.

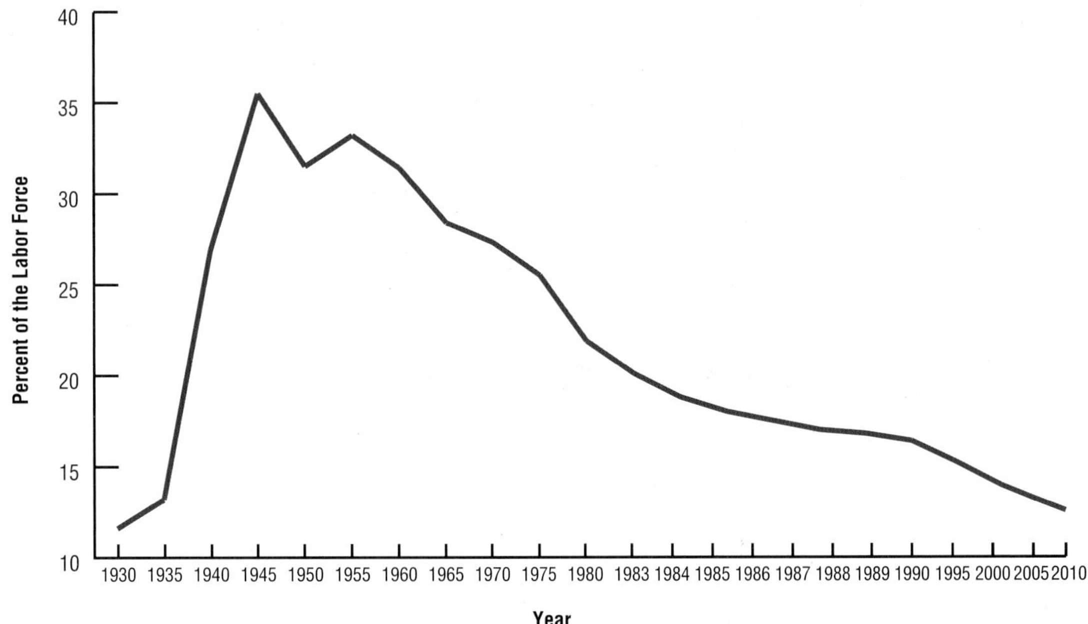

FIGURE 15.1

Union Membership in the United States, 1930–2013

Source: Bureau of Labor Statistics, Department of Labor.

In fact, many employees of nonunion firms benefit from the upward adjustments in their wages and benefits that their employers make to prevent a union from organizing their workers. Unions have also pioneered worker safety measures and antidiscriminatory labor practices. Unless the underlying causes that gave birth to unions are abolished—low wages, unsafe working conditions, health hazards, arbitrary firings, and layoffs—it is a safe bet that unions will not disappear.

The Growth of Unions in the Public Sector

As the percentage of unionized workers in the private sector has declined, the percentage of unionized workers in the public sector has increased substantially. This increase is due in part to the expansion of local government in the 1980s and in part to organizing efforts that have targeted both public-sector and service-sector employees.[20]

Currently, the union membership rate for public-sector workers, which includes those working for federal, state, and local governments, is 36 percent, more than five times higher than the membership rate in the private sector. In addition, since 2010, unionized workers in the public sector represent a majority of all unionized workers in the United States.[21]

Unions in the public sector are in many ways a special case of labor relations, because although public-sector employees are more likely to be organized than private-sector ones, public-sector workers tend to have less bargaining power. There are two main reasons for this difference.

First, governmental power is diffuse. The typical private-sector firm is organized hierarchically so that there is one individual at the top who is in charge. However, governmental bodies in the United States have been intentionally structured so that power is divided among the legislative, executive, and judicial branches. This makes it more difficult for public-sector unions to negotiate and bargain collectively, because the employer's representative often has only limited authority. For instance, a city employees' union may bargain with the mayor's office for higher pay, but the money for the higher salaries has to be appropriated by the city council, which may not concur with the mayor.

The second reason public-sector unions have less power is that many governmental entities severely restrict their employees' right to strike. The reasoning is that the government is a monopoly provider of essential services such as police protection, garbage collection, and highway maintenance. If its employees were to go on strike, there would be no one else to provide these essential services. States differ in restrictiveness on this issue. For instance, Colorado forbids strikes by any state employees, including teachers. In contrast, New York, Michigan, Wisconsin, and some other states give some of their employees the right to strike in certain circumstances.

Because their right to strike is limited, public-sector unions have taken the lead in devising and experimenting with new ways to negotiate, including mandated arbitration and mediation. Their limited economic power has also made public-sector unions less likely than private-sector unions to put pay issues at the top of their agendas. For instance, teachers' unions often focus on such issues as class size, job security, and academic freedom rather than straight salary issues.

Although having government as an employer can present difficulties to unionized workers, it also brings certain advantages. One is that union members, by virtue of the fact that they are also voters, have some political power over their employer. Because voter participation in nonfederal elections is often low in the United States, a well-organized public-sector union can be a powerful force in local politics. In fact, even national candidates court public-sector union support. A second advantage stems from the very diffusion of power we discussed earlier. This makes it possible for the union to play one branch of government against the other in certain circumstances. For instance, a union may be able to achieve a bargaining victory because it has the support of a city council member whose vote the mayor needs on some unrelated issue.

Labor Relations in Other Countries

Labor relations systems vary from country to country because unions mean different things in different countries. In the United States, labor relations involves collective bargaining and labor contracts, but in Sweden and Denmark it involves national wage setting, in Japan it involves enterprise unions that cooperate with company management, in Great Britain it involves union affiliation with the Labour Party, and in Germany it involves union representation on the company's board of directors.[22] Moreover, the shrinking percentage of private-sector employees represented

Percent of Total Civilian Wage and Salary Employees Belonging to Unions													
Year	United States	Canada	Austria	Australia	Japan	Denmark	France	Germany	Italy	Nether-lands	Sweden	Switzer-land	United Kingdom
1965	28	28	46	—	36	63	20	38	33	40	68	32	45
1970	30	31	43	—	35	64	22	37	43	38	75	31	50
1975	29	34	48	—	35	72	23	39	56	42	83	35	53
1980	25	35	47	—	31	86	19	40	62	41	88	35	56
1985	17	36	47	—	29	92	17	40	61	34	95	32	51
1990	16	36	43	34	25	88	—	—	—	28	95	31	46
1995	14	37	39	35	24	78	9	26	32	23	87	23	32
2001	13	30	40	28	20	88	9	30	35	27	79	24	29
2010	11	27	29	19	18	69	8	19	35	19	68	17	27

FIGURE 15.2

Union Membership in Selected Countries, 1965–2010

Sources: Based on *OECD.StatExtracts*. (2013). Trade union density. *www.stats.oecd.org*; Visser, J. (2006, January). Union membership statistics in 24 countries. *Monthly Labor Review,* 45; European Foundation for the Improvement of Living and Working Conditions (2002); *The Economist*. (2003, June 7). Special report: Trade unions, 60; International Labor Organization (1997); and Chang, C., and Sorrentino, C. (1991, December). Union membership statistics in 12 countries. *Monthly Labor Review,* 48.

by unions in the United States is not a world trend. Unions not only represent a large portion of the labor force in most other industrialized countries, but are also important factors in the labor relations systems of many of those countries.

Figure 15.2 compares union membership as a percentage of the labor force in 13 industrialized countries, including the United States. Union membership as a percentage of the labor force is higher in most European countries, with Italy and Sweden having, respectively, 35 percent and 68 percent of their workers represented by unions in 2010. Although unionism declined in Great Britain in the 1980s, British unions still represented 27 percent of the workforce in 2010, more than double the percentage of U.S. workers. Even in Japan, whose firms seek to avoid unions when they locate factories in the United States, 18 percent of workers are unionized. This is significantly higher than the U.S. percentage.[23]

How Unions Differ Internationally

One analysis of unionism around the globe suggests that unions in different countries have different priorities.[24] As we have seen, U.S. unions place a very strong emphasis on economic issues, particularly pay, benefits, and job security. For example, in recent years outsourcing has become a major concern of U.S. unions, because the first jobs to be subcontracted tend to be blue-collar jobs, the union's mainstay.[25] Compared to unions in other countries, U.S. unions place much less emphasis on political issues. Political involvement is just another means to address economic concerns.

At the other end of the spectrum, unions in France tend to be much more politically involved and less concerned with economic issues. The two largest labor confederations in France have clear political orientations, and one is even religiously oriented. Strikes in France tend to focus on political change as the primary means of protecting or improving conditions for union members. In 2010, French unions led a political protest of up to 3 million people, who marched in the streets of France to voice their opposition to a law that would increase the legal minimum retirement age from 60 to 62 years.[26] Unions in Spain also use political tactics to carry out their goals. For example, in 2002 Spanish unions collaborated to organize a one-day general strike to convince the political leaders to reject the government proposal to lower the level of unemployment benefits for Spanish workers. A *general strike* is a work stoppage of all organized labor over a brief, predetermined time period that is designed to influence the government to support a particular political goal representing the interests of workers.[27]

In China, unions are low in both economic and political involvement, because of the pervasive control of the Chinese Communist Party over both political and economic affairs. While the right to strike has been illegal in China, this restriction may be changing after workers in a Chinese Honda plant successfully used the strike in 2010 to achieve higher wages. China is now considering a law that will relax the ban on strikes if the union first attempts to negotiate peacefully with management over the relevant economic issues.[28] Finally, Swedish unions tend to have a high degree of economic and political involvement. Swedish trade unions are often represented on governmental commissions in addition to actively representing their workers in economic affairs.[29] The Manager's Notebook "Chinese Employees Protest Working Conditions at Foxconn and Get Improvements in Workplace Representation" explains how employees gained greater representation in their union at Foxconn as a consequence of negative publicity from poor employee working conditions that attracted a lot of attention in the global media.

MANAGER'S NOTEBOOK

Global

Chinese Employees Protest Working Conditions at Foxconn and Get Improvements in Workplace Representation

Foxconn is the world's largest contract manufacturer and employs over 1.4 million people in China who produce electronic devices for global firms such as Apple, Hewlett-Packard, and Samsung. It received bad publicity in 2010 when a series of 10 employee suicides occurred at the company in protest of harsh working conditions that included long hours of overtime, low wages, and lack of an employee voice to influence managers to make improvements. For example, Foxconn employees routinely worked 16 hours per day, working in silence (talking was forbidden), and with only a few minutes allowed for toilet breaks. In response to the employee suicides, several noisy protest campaigns led by labor activists occurred that created additional bad publicity for Foxconn. These mass protests were followed by a request by Apple Inc., one of Foxconn's largest customers, to have the Fair Labor Association (FLA) audit Foxconn's labor practices.

Although Foxconn employees are supposed to be represented by the official labor union, called the All-China Federation of Trade Unions (ACFTU), the union is under the control of the Communist Party and is dominated by the interests of the employer and the Communist Party. Consequently, few employees are represented at the local ACFTU union at Foxconn.

However, Foxconn decided to make changes in its employment practices and working condition for factory employees in order to improve its reputation as an employer, which was tarnished due to the employee protests that became an international cause. Although employee wages at the company were raised by 25 percent and overtime hours were reduced, the most far-reaching consequence was that the company decided in 2013 to increase the number of employees who would be given a voice within the union committees to represent the interests of Foxconn employees. This greater responsiveness of the union at Foxconn to employee concerns may eventually influence other unions within the ACFTU to give a greater voice to Chinese employees at the workplace.

Sources: Based on Standing, J. (2013, February 4). Foxconn says to boost China worker participation in union. *Reuters. www.reuters.com*; Zhang, L. (2012, March 2). China's marginalized workers are waking up to their rights. *The Guardian. www.theguardian.com*; *The Economist.* (2012, December 15). When workers dream of a life beyond the factory gates, 63–64. ■■

We now turn our attention to two labor relations systems that have achieved high productivity and cooperation between unions and management: those of Germany and Japan.

Labor Relations in Germany

German law requires that all corporations involve workers in decisions at both the plant and the corporate level. This system is sometimes called *industrial democracy.* As practiced in Germany, industrial democracy means workers are represented at the plant level in works councils and at the corporate level through codetermination.

Works councils are committees composed of both worker representatives and managers that have responsibility for governing the workplace. They participate in operational decisions, such as the allocation of overtime, the discipline and discharge of workers, the hiring of new workers, and training.[30] At the plant level, works councils make many decisions on which unions in the United States would bargain with management. In Germany, unions are organized on an industrial basis, with unions representing metal workers, chemical workers, public sector employees, and so on. In recent years some German unions have merged, and the largest unions, such as IG Metall and Verdi, represent a collection of different industries. On issues such as wages, German unions focus on bargaining across industries rather than on bargaining within an industry, as is typical in the United States. However, the unification of Germany's high-wage West and lower-wage East means that unions and employers need more wage flexibility in labor contracts. Currently, more wage agreements are occurring at the company level in Germany.[31] Works councils are also used in several other countries in addition to Germany. Austria, France, Belgium, the Netherlands, and Sweden have enacted laws that require that large companies organize works councils to represent the interests of employees.[32]

works council
A committee composed of both worker representatives and managers who have responsibility for governing the workplace; used in Germany.

Codetermination brings worker representation to a corporation's board of directors. With one-third to one-half of their boards of directors representing workers, German companies are likely to give employees' needs a high priority.[33] (The other board members represent the shareholders.) Not surprisingly, codetermination has fostered a spirit of cooperation between workers and managers. For the German economy, the results have been fewer strikes and higher productivity. For workers, the results have been both greater responsibility and greater security. For example, IG Metall, Germany's largest union, has taken the lead on a number of important issues instead of merely reacting to company proposals. The union's group-work policies, the product of nearly two decades of research and activism, are designed to protect workers from layoff or transfer to lower-paying jobs.

codetermination
The representation of workers on a corporation's board of directors; used in Germany.

Labor Relations in Japan

Japan has developed a successful labor relations system characterized by a high degree of cooperation between unions and management. A key factor in this success has been the Japanese enterprise union. The **enterprise union**, which represents Japanese workers in large corporations such as Toyota, Toshiba, and Hitachi, organizes the workers in only one company. This practice ensures that the union's loyalty will not be divided among different companies. The enterprise union negotiates with management with an eye on the company's long-term prosperity. This labor relations system was long reinforced by large Japanese corporations' offer of lifelong employment, which allowed Japanese workers to feel secure and unthreatened by changes in technology or job characteristics.[34]

enterprise union
A labor union that represents workers in only one large company rather than in a particular industry; used in Japan.

The traditional lifelong employment policy has encouraged cooperation between the enterprise unions and management. Many Japanese executives started their careers as union members right out of school, advanced to a leadership position in the union, and then got promoted into management, all within the same company. Because the enterprise union's legitimacy is unchallenged by management, there is a degree of trust and respect between the union and management in Japan that would be unthinkable in the United States. This fact helps to explain the behavior of Japanese executives who cooperate with a union in Japan but try at all costs to avoid unionization in their U.S. plants.

Unfortunately, there are signs that the labor relations systems in both Germany and Japan are in danger. In Germany, high labor costs for the average factory worker ($47 per hour versus $35 per hour in the United States) and the economic costs of unification with East Germany have forced companies to drive a harder bargain with unions.[35] Competition in global markets has led to downsizings in some of Germany's largest companies and has strained labor relations. For example, Daimler-Benz, Germany's largest industrial company, reduced its workforce by 70,000 jobs and built a new automobile plant in Alabama, where labor costs are much lower than in Germany.[36] And in Japan, a closer look at lifelong employment policies shows that they have always been restricted to the largest companies, applied only to men, and end at age 55. Moreover, downsizing in Japan has made it difficult to sustain lifelong employment policies. NTT, Japan's giant telecommunications company, reduced its workforce by 45,000 jobs, a quarter of its total number of employees. Nissan, the automaker, from 1999 to 2002 laid off 21,000 workers and closed five auto assembly plants.[37]

Labor Relations Strategy

labor relations strategy
A company's overall plan for dealing with labor unions.

A company's **labor relations strategy** is its management's overall plan for dealing with unions. A company's labor relations strategy sets a tone that can range from open conflict with the union to labor–management cooperation. The most important choice affecting a company's labor relations strategy is management's decision to accept or to avoid unions.[38]

Union Acceptance Strategy

union acceptance strategy
A labor relations strategy in which management chooses to view the union as its employees' legitimate representative and accepts collective bargaining as an appropriate mechanism for establishing workplace rules.

Under a **union acceptance strategy**, management chooses to view the union as its employees' legitimate representative and accepts collective bargaining as an appropriate mechanism for establishing workplace rules. Management tries to obtain the best possible labor contract with the union, and then governs employees according to the contract's terms. The labor relations policy shown in Figure 15.3 is an example of a union acceptance strategy.

A union acceptance strategy is likely to result in labor relations characterized by labor–management cooperation or working harmony. The relationship between General Motors and the UAW union at the Saturn auto plant in Tennessee, which operated between 1990 and 2007, was an example of such a strategy. The union negotiated a very flexible contract with management at this plant in exchange for union recognition and job security for its workers. Management could redesign jobs, change technology, and streamline work rules—a degree of flexibility unknown in other unionized General Motors auto plants.[39] In turn, labor was involved in decision making to a degree that was rare in unionized companies. Groups of 5 to 15 workers performed managerial tasks such as hiring. They also elected representatives to higher-level teams that make joint decisions with management on every aspect of the business, from car design to marketing to sticker price.[40] Another tactic used to create a climate of union–management cooperation is the establishment of a joint committee composed of union and management representatives who work to solve long-term problems in the workplace that have a high potential for conflict. At Xerox, management and representatives of the Amalgamated Clothing Workers Union formed joint committees and workplace teams whose collaborative efforts resulted in improved plant

Our objective is to establish a labor policy that is consistent and fair. The purpose is to develop an agreeable working relationship with the union while retaining our full management rights. The rationale behind our labor relations policy is consistency, credibility, and fairness to union representatives and the workers who are in the union. In order to make our policy effective, the Company will:

- Accept union representation of employees in good faith, provided the union represents the majority of our employees;
- Maintain the right of management to manage;
- Adopt procedures by which top management continuously supports the positions of its representatives in implementing the firm's policies and practices in the area of industrial relations;
- Enforce disciplinary policies in a fair, firm, and consistent manner;
- See to it that union representatives follow all Company rules except those from which they are exempted under specific provisions of the labor contract;
- Handle all employee complaints fairly, firmly, and without discrimination;
- See that every representative of management exercises a maximum effort to follow Company policies fairly and consistently; and
- See to it that all decisions and agreements pertaining to the present contract are documented in writing.

FIGURE 15.3
Labor Relations Policy: Union Acceptance Strategy

Source: MANAGEMENT RESOURCES, INC., *The Company Policy Manual,* 1st Edition, © 1992, p. 332. Reprinted by permission of Pearson Education, Inc., Upper Saddle River, NJ.

safety, work flow, and production; reduced grievance rates; and preserved jobs that otherwise would have been eliminated.[41] Southwest Airlines, the most profitable airline in the United States, has had a union acceptance strategy since the time it was founded in 1971. The company founders, Lamar Muse and Herb Kelleher, believed that airline employees needed an effective voice so they could be partners with the organization, and they were convinced that a union should be the mechanism for transmitting the employees' voice to management.[42]

Sometimes teamwork between a union and management happens because of visionary leadership at the top of both organizations. At the Hillsborough County School District, which encompasses the cities of Tampa and St. Petersburg, Florida, the leader of the school board and the president of the local chapter of the American Federation of Teachers (AFT) nurtured collaborative relations between their organizations. They were able to negotiate unique reforms in the schools that included merit pay for top performing teachers, a coaching program for struggling teachers, and a school day that exceeds eight hours.[43]

Unfortunately, the road to union–management cooperation can be rocky. In fact, worker distrust of union–management cooperation threatens to derail teamwork initiatives at an increasing number of companies, especially since the NLRB ruled that management-led employee teams can violate the Wagner Act.[44] For management guidelines in this area, see the Manager's Notebook, "When Is a Team Not a Team?"

Labor relations scholars have found that cooperative labor relations occur more often in industries with patterns of labor contract agreements that foster union–management collaboration, such as the automobile, telecommunications, steel, and construction industries.[45] An example of such a contract provision is one that establishes joint labor–management committees that meet on a regular basis and develop agreements over issues of mutual benefit such as (1) a drug-free workplace, (2) occupational safety rules, (3) gain-sharing plans, (4) equal opportunity for employees with disabilities, and (5) policies that prohibit any type of workplace harassment.[46] Corporate leaders who support a union-acceptance strategy may view unions as an asset rather than as an obstacle to achieving business success. Mark Royse, AT&T's executive vice president of labor relations, says that, "AT&T and its customers benefit from the skills and professionalism of union-represented employees in our business units. Our company has long taken pride in our cooperative and respectful relationship with the unions that represent our employees."[47]

MANAGER'S NOTEBOOK

When Is a Team Not a Team? Guidelines for Employee Involvement Committees

Two conditions determine whether a company's employee involvement (EI) group violates the Wagner Act. A group is illegal if it can be proved to be *both* "employer dominated" and a "labor organization" under the law.

- Determine whether the issues addressed by an EI team clearly constitute "conditions of employment." Until legal developments shed new light on the situation, experts say EI groups should be limited to addressing production, quality, and safety matters.[a]
- Employer domination can be construed if any group of employees is perceived as constituting a "select" group empowered to speak to management on behalf of all employees. Guard against such a charge by periodically rotating employee participants on EI teams.[b]
- Make sure that any such group functions in a way that is strictly independent of management influence. If disputes are settled by means of a negotiation process between employer and employee, employer dominance is often readily established. But if management delegates the authority to resolve grievances to the group and the group resolves such problems on its own, the group is likely to be seen as benign, despite the fact that management played a key role in establishing and encouraging it.[c]
- In a unionized setting, getting union participation in EI committees is virtually a surefire way to avoid litigation.[d] If the company is nonunion, the situation can be trickier. Get visible employee input and make the venture a cooperative and voluntary one.[e] An alternative

would be to let peers nominate employees to participate rather than have management select them.[f]

- *Never* start an EI group during a union organizing campaign. Such activity can readily be seen as union busting.[g]

Sources: [a]Based on *Management Review Forum,* February 1994, © 1994. American Management Association, New York. All rights reserved. [b]*Ibid.;* [c]*Ibid.;* [d]*Ibid.;* [e]*Ibid.;* [f]LeRoy, M. H. (1999). Are employers constrained in the use of employee participation groups by Section 8(a)(2) of the NLRA? *Journal of Labor Research 22*(1), 63–71; [g]*Management Review Forum,* 1994.

Although many small business owners work closely with their workers, they tend to regard such concepts as worker–management teams as a big company's game. According to the NLRB, two-thirds of unfair labor practice complaints are filed against employers with fewer than 100 workers. Because the great majority of small businesses are nonunionized, this record has encouraged unions to target small firms for membership expansion. In recent years, unions won certification at firms with fewer than 50 workers at twice their rate of success at companies employing more than 500 workers.[48] To avoid the loss of management control caused by unionization, many small companies have chosen to pursue a union avoidance strategy.

Union Avoidance Strategy

union avoidance strategy
A labor relations strategy in which management tries to prevent its employees from joining a union, either by removing the incentive to unionize or by using hardball tactics.

Management selects a **union avoidance strategy** when it fears the union will have a disruptive influence on its employees or fears losing control of its workers to a union. Companies that choose a union avoidance strategy are likely to be, at best, in an armed truce with unions and, at worst, in open conflict with them (see Figure 15.3). There are two different approaches to union avoidance: union substitution and union suppression.[49] Which approach a company pursues usually depends on the values of top management.

union substitution/proactive human resource management
A union avoidance strategy in which management becomes so responsive to employees' needs that it removes the incentives for unionization.

UNION SUBSTITUTION In the **union substitution** approach, also known as the **proactive human resource management** approach, management becomes so responsive to employees' needs that it removes the incentive for unionization. Using this approach, IBM, HP, Eli Lilly, and Eastman Kodak avoided unionization and simultaneously developed a reputation as good places to work. Some of the policies that take the union substitution approach are:

- Job security policies that protect the jobs of full-time workers. Among these is a policy that subcontracted, temporary, and part-time workers must be discharged before permanent employees can be laid off.
- Promoting-from-within policies that encourage the training and development of employees.
- Profit-sharing and employee stock ownership plans (see Chapter 11) that share the company's success with its employees.
- High-involvement management practices that solicit employee input into decisions.
- Open-door policies and grievance procedures that try to give workers the same sense of empowerment that they would have under a union contract.[50]

union suppression
A union avoidance strategy in which management uses hardball tactics to prevent a union from organizing its workers or to get rid of a union.

UNION SUPPRESSION Management uses the **union suppression** approach when it wants to avoid unionization at all costs and does not make any pretense of trying "to do the right thing" for its employees. Under this approach, management employs hardball tactics, which may be legal or illegal, to get rid of a union or to prevent the union from organizing its workers.[51]

For example, in the mid-1980s, Continental Airlines' CEO Frank Lorenzo used the U.S. bankruptcy courts to reorganize Continental and escape the company's obligations to employees under its labor contracts with its unions. When the airline emerged from bankruptcy, it had a nonunion workforce with pay levels about 40 percent lower than had prevailed under the union contracts. In another case at about the same time, the *Chicago Tribune* bargained aggressively with its production unions and, when the union workers went out on strike, substituted permanent replacement workers. The result was a completely nonunionized workforce at the newspaper. More recently, in 2000 Wal-Mart used union suppression tactics to reduce its susceptibility to work with a union after the United Food & Commercial Workers union (UCFW) attempted to organize its meat cutters. Wal-Mart's response was to reorganize its supply chain and buy prepackaged meat for its U.S. stores and eliminate most of its meat counter jobs around the country.[52] Caterpillar, the world's largest construction and mining equipment manufacturer, has taken an aggressive stance in its labor negotiations with unions in order to squeeze more profits out of its factories. During contract negotiations in 2012 at its Joliet, Illinois, hydraulic-parts factory, Caterpillar management insisted on making cuts to employee health care and other benefits. This led the International Association of Machinists, representing the employees, to go out on strike. After striking for three months, the union capitulated and accepted the company's settlement terms for a wage freeze and a reduced benefits package. While the union survived the strike and continues to represent the Caterpillar employees in Joliet, its support from employees may have been compromised because it was unable to protect its constituents from a reduction in their compensation.[53]

Sometimes the union suppression approach backfires and management reaps nothing but an angry union, bitter employees, and the worst kind of public relations. In 1990, management at the New York *Daily News,* which was then owned by the Chicago Tribune Company, tried to use replacement workers to intimidate its striking unions, but lost the battle because the media and the public sympathized with the union cause. J. P. Stevens, a textile manufacturer with plants in the southern United States, illegally tried to intimidate its workers by firing union organizers before a union certification election. The NLRB intervened on behalf of the union and ordered J. P. Stevens to recognize and bargain with the union.

In general, the union suppression approach is a higher-risk strategy than the union substitution approach and for this reason is used less frequently. Hardball tactics not only entail legal risks but can also come back to haunt management. Frank Lorenzo's use of the bankruptcy courts to break the company's unions looked like a great success at the time. However, in 1994 Lorenzo's bid to start a new low-fare airline was rejected by the Department of Transportation because of safety and regulatory compliance problems during Lorenzo's stewardship of Eastern Airlines and Continental Airlines. The DOT said that both of these airlines "experienced operational, maintenance, and labor-related problems that were among the most serious in the history of aviation."[54]

A QUESTION OF ETHICS

One strategy for suppressing union activity is to ask certain workers to report to management any union-organizing activities that are taking place at the company. Is this strategy legal? Is it ethical? If you answered "yes" to both questions, do you think it is a good management practice? Why or why not?

Managing the Labor Relations Process

Now that you have some grounding in the history of labor–management relations and relevant law, as well as a sense of the current state of labor relations and corporate strategies in this area, we can examine the specific components of the labor relations process. As Figure 15.4 shows, three phases of labor relations that managers and labor relations specialists must deal with are (1) union organizing, in which employees exercise their right to form a union; (2) collective bargaining, in which union and management representatives negotiate a labor contract; and (3) contract administration, in which the labor contract is applied to specific work situations on a daily basis.

Union Organizing

Union organizing takes place when employees work with a union to form themselves into a cohesive group. The key issues that managers confront in a union organizing campaign are union solicitation, preelection conduct, and the certification election.

UNION SOLICITATION Before it will order a union certification election, the NLRB requires a union to show that there is significant interest in unionization among a company's employees. To meet this requirement, a minimum of 30 percent of the employees in the relevant work unit must sign an authorization card indicating that they want to be represented by a specific union for collective bargaining purposes.

Unions often conduct the early stages of their solicitation effort in private homes or public facilities so that management will not be aware of the organizing drive until the required percentage of workers has signed authorization cards. However, sometimes the union finds it necessary to solicit on company property, which alerts management and gives it the opportunity to respond.

Unions have Web sites where they can communicate with current and potential members.[55] In a drive to organize IBM employees in Colorado, the Communication Workers of America (CWA) alerted employees to a special Web site designed to teach them how to form a union

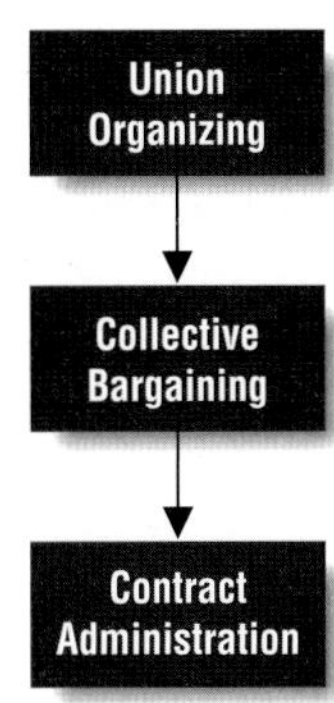

FIGURE 15.4
The Three Phases of the Labor Relations Process

at IBM.[56] The AFL-CIO site (*www.aflcio.org*) discusses union organizing and other issues, such as the pay of the top executives in U.S. public corporations compared to average employee pay and work/family concerns. The Web site gives interested employees a way to turn to unions affiliated with the AFL-CIO to attain social and economic justice.

Management's choice of labor relations strategy guides a company's response to union solicitation. Companies with a union avoidance strategy usually have a "no-solicitation" policy that restricts all solicitations to nonwork areas (for example, solicitation may take place in lunch or break rooms, but not in offices) and nonwork times. A no-solicitation policy makes it more difficult for the union to influence workers' attitudes toward the union and persuade them to sign authorization cards. However, companies that have a no-solicitation policy must be careful to enforce it consistently so that *all* solicitations (including those for charitable causes) are restricted. Singling out union-organizing activities for restriction is an unfair labor practice that can result in an NLRB order to cease and desist the discriminatory policy.

Consistent enforcement of a no-solicitation policy was one of the key factors that led the Supreme Court to rule in favor of Lechmere, Inc., a Newington, Connecticut, store that had banned unions from its premises. The court found that Lechmere did not violate the Wagner Act, largely because it had consistently enforced its no-solicitation policy against all organizations, including the Girl Scouts and the Salvation Army. The court also found that the store's 200 workers were otherwise accessible to the union's nonemployee organizers. The NLRB extended its consistent enforcement of a no-solicitation policy to e-mail communication when it ruled that an organization that allows employees to use e-mail for personal use cannot prohibit employees from corresponding on e-mail about union activities.[57]

PREELECTION CONDUCT If the union can show sufficient employee interest in forming a union, the NLRB will schedule a certification election. During the period before the election, management and union leaders should allow employees to freely exercise their right to vote for or against representation. It is the NLRB's policy to provide an environment in which employees can make an uncoerced choice in their selection of a bargaining agent—or, alternatively, an uncoerced choice not to be represented by any union.

During the preelection period, managers must avoid treating employees in a manner that could be interpreted as using their position to influence the outcome of the election. The NLRB "Notice to Employees" shown in Figure 15.5 indicates some types of conduct that are unacceptable before an election. Managers are prohibited from threatening employees with the loss of their jobs or benefits if they vote for the union. They must also avoid promising employees benefits (such as pay raises or promotions) if they vote against the union. On their side, unions must avoid threatening workers with harm if they do not vote for unionization. The NLRB's rules for permissible conduct during a union election campaign are exceedingly complex and constantly changing; here, however, are some general guidelines for managers:

- ***Threats*** It is unlawful to threaten employees with theoretical dire consequences should the union win the election.
- ***Intimidation*** Employers by law cannot intimidate or coerce employees to vote against the union.
- ***Promises*** Management cannot promise employees benefits or rewards if they vote against the union.
- ***Surveillance*** It is unlawful to secretly or overtly spy on organizing meetings.[58]

It *is* permissible for managers to try to persuade employees before a representation election that they would be better off without a union. Managers can legally do this by:[59]

- Making speeches to groups of employees emphasizing why they do not need a union (legal up to 24 hours before the election).
- Employing a labor relations consultant to assist with the antiunion strategy.
- Sending a personal letter to employees.
- Showing movies that view unions in an unfavorable light.
- Writing memos to employees that summarize all the good things that the employer has provided for them.

NOTICE TO EMPLOYEES

FROM THE

National Labor Relations Board

A PETITION has been filed with this Federal agency seeking an election to determine whether certain employees want to be represented by a union.

The case is being investigated and NO DETERMINATION HAS BEEN MADE AT THIS TIME by the National Labor Relations Board. IF an election is held Notices of Election will be posted giving complete details for voting.

It was suggested that your employer post this notice so the National Labor Relations Board could inform you of your basic rights under the National Labor Relations Act.

YOU HAVE THE RIGHT under Federal Law

- **To self-organization**
- **To form, join, or assist labor organizations**
- **To bargain collectively through representatives of your own choosing**
- **To act together for the purposes of collective bargaining or other mutual aid or protection**
- **To refuse to do any or all of these things unless the union and employer, in a state where such agreements are permitted, enter into a lawful union-security agreement requiring employees to pay periodic dues and initiation fees. Nonmembers who inform the union that they object to the use of their payments for nonrepresentational purposes may be required to pay only their share of the union's costs of representational activities *(such as collective bargaining, contract administration, and grievance adjustments).***

It is possible that some of you will be voting in an employee representation election as a result of the request for an election having been filed. While NO DETERMINATION HAS BEEN MADE AT THIS TIME, in the event an election is held, the NATIONAL LABOR RELATIONS BOARD wants all eligible voters to be familiar with their rights under the law IF it holds an election.

The Board applies rules that are intended to keep its elections fair and honest and that result in a free choice. If agents of either unions or employers act in such a way as to interfere with your right to a free election, the election can be set aside by the Board. Where appropriate the Board provides other remedies, such as reinstatement for employees fired for exercising their rights, including backpay from the party responsible for their discharge.

NOTE:

The following are examples of conduct that interfere with the rights of employees and may result in the setting aside of the election.

- **Threatening loss of jobs or benefits by an employer or a union**
- **Promising or granting promotions, pay raises, or other benefits to influence an employee's vote by a party capable of carrying out such promises**
- **An employer firing employees to discourage or encourage union activity or a union causing them to be fired to encourage union activity**
- **Making campaign speeches to assembled groups of employees on company time within the 24-hour period before the election**
- **Incitement by either an employer or a union of racial or religious prejudice by inflammatory appeals**
- **Threatening physical force or violence to employees by a union or an employer to influence their votes**

Please be assured that IF AN ELECTION IS HELD every effort will be made to protect your right to a free choice under the law. Improper conduct will not be permitted. All parties are expected to cooperate fully with this Agency in maintaining basic principles of a fair election as required by law. The National Labor Relations Board, as an agency of the United States Government, does not endorse any choice in the election.

NATIONAL LABOR RELATIONS BOARD
an agency of the
UNITED STATES GOVERNMENT

THIS IS AN OFFICIAL GOVERNMENT NOTICE AND MUST NOT BE DEFACED BY ANYONE

FORM NLRB-666 (5-90) ★U.S. GOVERNMENT PRINTING OFFICE: 1991-312-471/51356

FIGURE 15.5
NLRB Representation Election Notice to Employees
Source: National Labor Relations Board.

Firms in the United States can also hire consultants who specialize in helping management maintain a nonunion workforce. One study estimated that employers spent an average of $500 per employee on consultants in union election campaigns.[60]

CERTIFICATION ELECTION The NLRB supervises the certification election, determining who is eligible to vote and counting the ballots. The voting is done by secret ballot, and the outcome is determined by the participating voters. If the union receives a majority of the votes, it becomes the certified bargaining agent for all of the unit's employees. This means that it becomes the exclusive agent for both union and nonunion employees in collective bargaining with the employer. The *bargaining unit* consists of all the employees who are represented by a union that engages in collective bargaining with the employer.

If the majority of voters vote against the union, NLRB policy states that no other representation election may be held for a 12-month period. In recent years, unions have won over half of the representation elections held in the United States. In 2011, 1,189 representation elections were

EXHIBIT 15.1 ORGANIZING CAMPAIGNS: A NEW PRIORITY

In recent years, many unions have started to pour significant resources into their organizing campaigns. Here are some examples of recent successful union-organization activities:

- The American Federation of Government Employees won the right to represent 44,000 employees of the Transportation Security Administration (TSA) in a certification election that took place in 2011. This was the largest union election for federal workers in history. The TSA employees represented by the union screen passengers at airport security checkpoints.[a]
- Graduate students work long hours teaching courses, grading papers, and doing laboratory experiments and other important activities at universities for low salaries that average between $11,000 and $15,000 per year. At New York University, graduate students attempted to form a union that was challenged in the courts by the administration. University administration argued that collective bargaining between the students and the university would be an infringement of academic freedom and justified the low wages paid to students by claiming that the graduate assistant work was part of their educational experience. The National Labor Relations Board disagreed with the administration's reasoning and decided to allow the graduate students to form a union organized by the UAW. Consequently, in 2013 New York University became the first private university to have a graduate student union. In addition, several public universities have unions that represent graduate students, including University of Massachusetts, University of California at Berkeley, University of Florida, University of Oregon, and University of Wisconsin at Milwaukee.[b]
- Winning the biggest unionization drive in more than half a century, the Service Employees International Union (SEIU) gained the right to represent 74,000 Los Angeles County home-care workers who feed, bathe, and clean the elderly and disabled. Many said they voted to join a union because they wanted to fight to raise their wages of $5.75 per hour and to obtain two benefits long denied them: health insurance and paid vacations.[c]

Sources: [a]*New York Times*. (2011, June 23). Screeners for T.S.A. select union. *www.nytimes.com*; [b] Brooks, R. (2013, December 12). Graduate students at NYU become the first graduate-student union at a private school (again). *The Village Voice Blogs. blogs.villagevoice.com/runninscared/2013/12/nyu_graduate_students_unionize.php*; Greenhouse, S. (2001, May 15). Graduate students push for union membership. *New York Times*, A-19; [c]Greenhouse, S. (1999, February 26). In biggest drive since 1937, union gains a victory, *New York Times*, A-1, A-15.

held and unions won 69 percent of the certification elections.[61] Exhibit 15.1, "Organizing Campaigns: A New Priority," gives some examples of successful attempts by U.S. unions to organize diverse groups of employees.

Unionized employees who are dissatisfied with a union's representation of their interests have the right to get rid of that union by having a *decertification election.* The NLRB regulates decertification elections with rules similar to those that it uses for certification elections. If a majority of voters vote to decertify, then the union loses its right to represent employees and bargain with the employer over employee pay and working conditions.

The U.S. Congress considered the Employee Free Choice Act (EFCA), which would have allowed workers to form unions without a secret-ballot election. The bill, also known as "Card Check," would allow union organizers to form a union simply by having a majority of employees sign authorization cards expressing their desire to join. It also had provisions to substantially increase the financial penalties for unfair labor practices and would empower an arbitrator to impose a contract if the parties are not able to reach an agreement within 100 days. Unions had pressed for passage of this law because they believe that certification elections with secret ballots make it difficult for unions to overcome management's sophisticated tactics and use of consultants who are adept at convincing employees to vote against union representation, which occurs in nearly half the certification elections. For the most part, management and business owners were against Card Check, because they expected that, if passed, the law would have made it much easier for unions to organize the workforce and gain recognition. The proposed Card Check law was defeated in Congress in 2009.[62] Representatives advocating for management and business owners who were interested in preserving the practice of secret ballot union elections introduced the Secret Ballot Protection Act to Congress in 2013, but it failed to make it to the Senate, which was controlled by Democrats. Thus, it appears that currently the union certification election process will remain unchanged despite the efforts of different parties who would seek to change it.[63]

Collective Bargaining

If union organizing results in certification, the next step in the labor relations process is collective bargaining that results in a labor contract. Most labor contracts last for two to three years, after which they are subject to renegotiation.

Four of the most important issues related to collective bargaining are bargaining behavior, bargaining power, bargaining topics, and impasses in bargaining. In all of these areas, managers must monitor their behavior carefully.

BARGAINING BEHAVIOR Once the NLRB certifies a union as the bargaining agent for a unit of employees, both management and the union have a duty to bargain with each other in "good faith." Refusing to bargain in good faith can result in an NLRB cease-and-desist order that is enforced in the courts. The parties are showing good faith in collective bargaining when:

- Both parties are willing to meet and confer with each other at a reasonable time and place.
- Both parties are willing to negotiate over wages, hours, and conditions of employment (the mandatory bargaining topics).
- The parties sign a written contract that formalizes their agreement and binds them to it.
- Each party gives the other a 60-day notice of termination or modification of the labor agreement before it expires.

In general, *good-faith bargaining* means treating the other party reasonably even when disagreements arise. To show good faith, management should develop different proposals and suggestions for negotiating with the union instead of simply rejecting all union proposals. For example, in the early 1960s a negotiator for General Electric made a single proposal to the union on a take-it-or-leave-it basis, and then refused to negotiate on any of the union's counteroffers. The NLRB interpreted this inflexible approach to bargaining as an unfair labor practice that did not show good faith. For additional insights on how union and management representatives should behave in order to sustain good faith bargaining, see the Manager's Notebook, "Bargaining Etiquette."

A QUESTION OF ETHICS

Suppose at a prebargaining meeting between the company's negotiating team and top management it is decided that the company will give up to a 4-percent raise. When negotiations start, however, the lead management negotiator states that the company cannot afford more than a 2-percent raise, and will go no higher. Is this ethical behavior? What if the situation was reversed, and it was the union negotiator who stated an absolute minimum demand, knowing that the union leadership will accept less? Would that be ethical?

MANAGER'S NOTEBOOK

Bargaining Etiquette

Ethics/Social Responsibility

Here are some guidelines for management and union-bargaining teams to follow so that good faith can be maintained during collective bargaining sessions:

- ***Show courtesy to the other bargaining team*** When the management team takes a caucus break to develop a response to a union proposal, the management team should notify the union team by telephone that they are ready to continue bargaining instead of walking in and interrupting a conversation between the union team members.
- ***Set the tone by being friendly to the other bargaining team*** Team members should shake hands, make eye contact, and show interest in the members of the other bargaining team.
- ***Maintain team solidarity*** Make it a point that all team members will arrive and leave the bargaining sessions at the same time. It is disruptive when team members arrive and leave while bargaining sessions are in progress.
- ***Establish ground rules to deal with difficult bargaining issues*** Rules should cover when caucus breaks occur and for how long they last, the location where the bargaining sessions take place, and whether the bargaining meetings should occur at night. (It is better to avoid bargaining late into the night, because when people are tired their behavior may become less civil.)
- ***Keep negative emotions under control*** If things get heated, take a caucus break, which allows the team members to regroup and calm down. Personal attacks on the opposing bargaining team members should be avoided. Negativity has no place at the bargaining table.

- *Exercise silence* The saying *Silence is golden* is true at the bargaining table. If your bargaining team does not like the offer that the opposing team has put on the table, or your team is waiting for a response, the best course of action may be to sit back and wait instead of criticizing the other side's position. The opposing bargaining team often fills the void of silence by justifying its own position, which may result in a compromise that is closer to your team's bargaining goals.

Sources: Based on Tyler, K. (2005, January). Good-faith bargaining. *HRMagazine,* 49–53; Friedman, S. (2009). Top ten negotiating tactics every meeting manager should know. *www.marketingsource.com*; Dolan, J. (2011). How to overcome the top ten negotiating tactics. *www.myarticlearchive.com.* ■■

BARGAINING POWER In collective bargaining sessions, both parties are likely to take opening positions that favor their goals but leave them some room to negotiate. For example, on the topic of pay raises, the union may initially ask for 8 percent but be willing to go as low as 5 percent. Management may initially offer the union 2 percent but be willing to go as high as 6 percent.

At which point will the parties reach agreement, 5 percent or 6 percent? The party that understands how to use its bargaining power will probably be able to achieve settlement closer to its initial bargaining position. *Bargaining power* is one party's ability to get the other party to agree to its terms. If management has greater bargaining power than the union, it is likely to get the union to agree to a 5 percent pay increase.

An important aspect of a party's bargaining power is how it is perceived by the other party. Each party can engage in behaviors that shape the other party's perceptions. Management that acts in a powerful and intimidating manner may influence the union to make additional concessions. However, aggressive posturing by management may backfire and cause union negotiators to make fewer concessions.

Parties in negotiations have several tactical alternatives. Two bargaining tactics are often used to increase bargaining power: distributive bargaining and integrative bargaining.[64]

distributive bargaining
Bargaining that focuses on convincing the other party that the cost of disagreeing with the proposed terms would be very high.

Distributive Bargaining **Distributive bargaining** focuses on convincing your counterpart in negotiations that the cost of disagreeing with your terms would be very high. In collective bargaining, the cost of disagreement is often a strike. In the United States, strikes usually occur when a labor contract expires without both sides reaching a new agreement. Distributive bargaining tactics tend to be used when the two sides are competing for very limited resources.

Labor uses distributive bargaining when it attempts to convince management that it is willing and able to sustain a long strike that will severely damage the company's profits and weaken the company's position against its competitors. For example, in its 1993 negotiations with UPS, the Teamsters Union presented the company with several key bargaining demands, including substantial pay and benefit increases, improved job security, conversion of part-time jobs to full-time jobs, and less stringent productivity standards. When UPS, after intense contract talks and contract extensions, presented the Teamsters with a contract that did not come close to meeting the union's demands, the Teamsters suspended negotiations and set a strike date. A national strike against UPS could have crippled the company at a time when it was facing stiff competition from nonunion rivals, such as FedEx and Roadway Package Services. Before this happened, however, Ron Carey, the Teamsters' reformist president, hammered out a contract that provided a good economic package and an end to some of the stringent work rules that had long irked union members.[65] As the opening vignette shows, in 2007 General Motors and the UAW were unable to avoid a strike in 2007 when the parties failed to reach a settlement over the issue of health care costs.

Management uses distributive bargaining when it tries to convince the union that it can sustain a long strike much better than union members, who will have to survive without their paychecks. For example, in 1975 management at the *Washington Post* tried to persuade the newspaper's unions that it could sustain a strike and still get the paper out because it had cross-trained managers to do the jobs of union workers. In this instance, management was able to pull it off.

Union leaders may also adopt distributive bargaining tactics when they believe union members are willing to accept the cost of a long strike that is likely to cause a vulnerable company severe economic damage. This situation occurred in 1998 when the UAW struck General Motors over the issue of preventing union jobs from being given to outsourcing firms. GM's motivation for outsourcing was to reduce its labor costs. A two-month strike ensued when there was a strong demand for—but only a short supply of—new General Motors car models. The timing of the strike helped convince management to make concessions to the union after the strike cost GM $2.2 billion in losses.[66]

The United Auto Workers Union and Ford Motor Company conclude their contract negotiations with an agreement.
Source: © Danita Delimont/Alamy.

Integrative Bargaining **Integrative bargaining** focuses on convincing your counterpart in negotiations that the benefits of agreeing with your terms would be very high. Integrative bargaining is similar to a problem-solving session in which both parties are seeking mutually beneficial alternatives. Goodyear Tire & Rubber Co. and the United Steelworkers Union (USW) negotiated an agreement that illustrates the benefits of integrative bargaining. Because of Goodyear's need to become globally competitive, Goodyear placed a high priority on reducing its operating expenses. In exchange for the union's willingness to slash labor costs by $1.15 billion over three years and to eliminate 3,000 jobs, Goodyear agreed to keep, and invest in, all but two of its U.S. factories and to limit imports from its factories in Brazil and Asia. The union accepted the company's terms in a contract in 2003 in the hopes of saving as many of the 19,000 union jobs at Goodyear as possible.[67] The Manager's Notebook, "Guidelines for Integrative Bargaining," shows what both parties need to do to achieve integrative bargaining.

integrative bargaining
Bargaining that focuses on convincing the other party that the benefits of agreeing with the proposed terms would be very high.

MANAGER'S NOTEBOOK

Customer-Driven HR

Guidelines for Integrative Bargaining

Integrative bargaining is the process of identifying a common, shared, or joint goal and developing a process to achieve it. An emphasis on integrative bargaining can lead to cooperation between union and management and the possibility of mutual gains for both. To achieve integrative bargaining, both parties should:

- ***Attempt to understand the other negotiator's real needs and objectives*** The parties should engage in a dialogue in which both sides disclose preferences and priorities, rather than disguise or manipulate them.[a]
- ***Create a free flow of information*** Negotiators must be willing to listen to the other negotiator carefully, and to accept a joint solution that incorporates both parties' needs.[b]
- ***Emphasize the commonalities, and minimize the differences, between the parties*** Specific goals should be reframed to be considered part of a larger, collaborative goal. For example, a safe workplace may be a goal on which both the union and management agree, although they may differ on a specific approach to achieve this goal.[c]
- ***Search for solutions that meet both parties' goals and objectives*** When parties are combative or competitive, they are more likely to focus only on their own objectives and ignore those of the other party. Integrative bargaining is successful only when both parties' needs are met.[d]
- ***Develop flexible responses to the other negotiator's proposals*** Each negotiator should try to accommodate and adapt to the needs of the other party by modifying his or her proposals. Avoid getting stuck in one intractable position that does not provide room to make tactical trade-offs. By behaving flexibly, a negotiator can encourage the other party to reciprocate in a similar fashion and move toward a settlement with mutual gains.[e]

Source: [a]Lewicki, R., Saunders, D., and Barry, B. (2010). *Negotiation* (6th ed.). Burr Ridge, IL: McGraw-Hill Irwin; [b]*Ibid.*; [c]*Ibid.*; [d]*Ibid.*; [e]Das, T. K., and Teng, B. (1998). Between trust and control: Developing confidence in partner cooperation and alliances. *Academy of Management Review, 23,* 491–512. ■■

FIGURE 15.6
Mandatory Bargaining Topics

Wages	Hours	Employment Conditions
Base pay rates	Overtime	Layoffs
Overtime pay rates	Holidays	Promotions
Retirement benefits	Vacation	Seniority provisions
Health benefits	Shifts	Safety rules
Travel pay	Flextime	Work rules
Pay incentives	Parental leave	Grievance procedures
		Union shop
		Job descriptions

It is not unusual in collective bargaining for both sides to use both distributive and integrative bargaining tactics. However, the firm's overall labor relations strategy generally determines what type of bargaining it adopts.[68] Firms with a union acceptance strategy are more likely to mix integrative and distributive bargaining, whereas those with a union avoidance strategy are more likely to focus solely on distributive bargaining. In addition, the strategies selected by the union will influence a firm's bargaining strategies and tactics, because collective bargaining is a dynamic process.

BARGAINING TOPICS The NLRB and courts classify bargaining topics into three categories: mandatory, permissive, and illegal. As mentioned earlier, *mandatory bargaining topics* are wages, hours, and employment conditions. These are the topics that both union and management consider fundamental to the organization's labor relations. Some examples of each of these mandatory topics are shown in Figure 15.6.

The NLRB and courts have interpreted wages, hours, and employment conditions fairly broadly. "Wages" can mean any type of compensation, including base pay rates, pay incentives, health insurance, and retirement benefits. "Hours" can mean anything to do with work scheduling, including the allocation of overtime and the amount of vacation time granted. "Employment conditions" can mean almost any work rule that affects the employees represented by the union. These include grievance procedures, safety rules, job descriptions, and the bases for promotions.

Permissive bargaining topics may be discussed during collective bargaining if both parties agree to do so, but neither party is obligated to bargain on these topics. Some permissive bargaining topics are provisions for union members to serve on the company's board of directors and benefits for retired union members. In the recessionary economy of the early 1990s, some unions swapped wage concessions for equity in the company and a stronger voice in how it is run.

Management–labor agreements in the airline industry have incorporated some novel approaches to rescue faltering airlines and thousands of jobs. For instance, at United Airlines, the unions that represent pilots and machinists traded 15 percent in pay cuts for 55 percent of the company stock and three of 12 board seats in 1994. By 1996, United's stock price had more than doubled and the employee-owned airline was outperforming most of its rivals.[69] However, United Airlines stock plunged in 2001 after the terrorist attack on the United States as United grounded 31 percent of its flights and furloughed 20,000 of its employees. This reversal of company fortunes put a damper on the union's interest in taking additional pay cuts to help the company overcome its latest financial crisis.[70]

Other examples of permissive bargaining topics include allowing management to put the union label on its product, settlement of unfair labor practices, and including supervisors in the labor contract.

Illegal bargaining topics may not be discussed in collective bargaining. Examples of illegal topics are closed shop agreements, featherbedding, and discriminatory employment practices. The NLRB considers the discussion of illegal bargaining topics an unfair labor practice.

IMPASSES IN BARGAINING A labor contract cannot be finalized until the bargaining representatives on both sides go back to their organizations and obtain approval of the contract. Union negotiators typically ask the members to vote on the contract. Most unions require a majority of union members to approve the contract. Management's negotiating team may need approval from the company's top executives. If the parties cannot agree on one or more mandatory issues, they have reached an *impasse* in bargaining. A party that insists on bargaining over a permissive topic to the point of impasse engages in an unfair labor practice.

If the impasse persists because the parties have taken rigid positions, a strike may result. Before a strike is called, either party may ask a mediator to help resolve the impasse. A *mediator* is a neutral third party that attempts to help the parties in a dispute come to a voluntary agreement. Mediators do not have the power to impose their ideas for a settlement on the other parties. Mediators are trained in conflict resolution techniques and are sometimes able to improve communication so that the impasse is resolved. The Federal Mediation and Conciliation Service (FMCS), established by the Taft-Hartley Act, monitors labor disputes and (under certain circumstances) mediates disputes. In addition, the FMCS maintains a list of impartial mediators and arbitrators who are qualified to assist with contract disputes.

If the contract's expiration date approaches and the parties are still at an impasse, the union may ask its members to vote on a strike. If members approve, the strike will start the day after the current labor contract expires. Striking union members withhold their labor from the employer and often publicize their dispute by picketing in front of the employer's buildings. A strike imposes costs on both parties. Striking union members receive no wages or benefits until they return to work, although they may draw some money from the union's strike fund, which is set up to give a small allowance to cover the striking members' basic expenses. However, a long strike may exhaust the strike fund, putting pressure on the union to make concessions in order to get its members back to work.

Workers on strike also face the risk of losing their jobs to permanent replacement workers. Caterpillar, Inc., the world's largest manufacturer of construction equipment, used the threat of hiring permanent replacement workers to win a heated dispute with the UAW. The company set a deadline and told striking workers, "Go back to work or lose your job." The strikers were scared off the picket line and returned to work on management's terms.[71] The use of permanent replacement workers is very controversial, and organized labor is trying to get Congress to pass legislation restricting it.[72] See Exhibit 15.2, "Permanent Replacement Workers: A Strike Against Labor or an Economic Necessity?" for more on this issue.

Sometimes unions are legally bound by their contracts to honor another union's picket line, which makes it more difficult for the company to hire replacement workers. For example, during a strike by the screenwriters at the major U.S. television networks, all the other television production workers left their jobs in a *sympathy strike*. The solidarity of the unions forced the television studios to abandon all production work until they could reach a settlement with the screenwriters.[73]

Management also faces significant strike costs. A strike can force a company to shut down operations and lose customers. In a highly competitive market, such actions may plunge the company into bankruptcy. This is exactly what happened at Eastern Airlines when the International Association of Machinists and Aerospace Workers (IAM) struck the air carrier in a contract dispute in 1989. A strike also poses a threat to a company from a loss of market share to its rivals in highly competitive industries. This is what happened to Boeing in 2000 in the competitive commercial aircraft industry when it sustained a six-week strike of 18,000 engineers and technicians of the Society of Professional Engineering Employees in Aerospace (SPEEA) in the largest white-collar strike occurring in the United States. Eventually the company settled with a contract favorable to the union's demands. The union demanded and obtained in its contract provisions for the company to continue paying for all of the employees' health insurance benefits and to give employees a 5 percent annual pay increase over a three-year period.[74]

Despite the negative outcomes sometimes associated with strikes, they are an important feature of the collective bargaining process. The pressure of an impending strike deadline forces both union and management negotiators to make concessions and resolve their differences. In the United States, less than 0.2 percent of total working time lost is lost because of strikes. Put another way, less working time is lost because of strikes than because of the common cold.[75]

The type of strike we have been discussing thus far, which takes place when an agreement is not reached during collective bargaining, is called an **economic strike**. Another type of strike, called the **wildcat strike**, is a spontaneous work stoppage that happens under a valid contract and is usually not supported by union leadership. Wildcat strikes generally occur when workers are angered by a disciplinary action taken by management against one of their colleagues.

economic strike
A strike that takes place when an agreement is not reached during collective bargaining.

wildcat strike
A spontaneous work stoppage that happens under a valid contract and is usually not supported by union leadership.

EXHIBIT 15.2 PERMANENT REPLACEMENT WORKERS: A STRIKE AGAINST LABOR OR AN ECONOMIC NECESSITY?

When over 6,300 drivers abandoned Greyhound buses during a bitter strike in 1989, the company had 700 new recruits on hand to drive the fleet and 900 more in training. And after the strike ended, most of the new hires remained on the job. Replacement workers also remained on the job after bitter protracted strikes at International Paper and Eastern and Continental Airlines.

Replacing striking workers has been a legal employer option for about 70 years, but it was not until 1981, when President Ronald Reagan fired striking air traffic controllers and kept the air traffic system going with replacements, that employers began using this tactic regularly.

Sometimes when union employees are on strike, management hires replacement workers for temporary jobs that could turn into permanent jobs if the union and management are unable to come to an agreement on a new labor contract. In 2012, 3,300 unionized machinists went on a 10-week strike at Lockheed Martin's fighter jet plant in Fort Worth, Texas, when the union rejected management's proposal of a reduction in employer health insurance coverage and a change in retirement benefits that moved from a generous pension to a more modest 401(k) plan. While the union employees were striking, Lockheed Martin hired 500 replacement workers to keep the fighter jet assembly line moving. When the union and management finally achieved a settlement, the replacement workers were let go.

To organized labor, the hiring of permanent replacement workers undermines the bargaining power granted to unions under the Wagner Act's guaranteed right to strike. Once the unions' trump card, the strike has become a card many unions are afraid to play in an era when strikers fear losing their jobs. Labor advocates argue that permanent replacement is the same as firing striking workers, which is illegal.

The current law on replacement workers derives from a 1938 case, *NLRB v. Mackay Radio & Telegraph Co.*, in which the court declared that, although the company in this case (Mackay) was guilty of firing strikers, in other cases where management has committed no illegal practices, the company is not bound to discharge replacement workers and hire back strikers when they wish to return to work. Labor advocates insist that "not hired back" equals "fired." On their side, employers argue that the ability to hire permanent replacements is necessary to ensure the survival of companies. Jack Schwartz, the labor counsel for National Tea, a New Orleans–based company, echoed the views of many employers when he said that legislation banning permanent replacement workers will encourage companies to relocate to "Mexico or another country where they don't have to worry about that risk."

Sources: Based on Brown, A. (2012, June 28). Lockheed machinists OK new labor deal, end strike. *Bloomberg Businessweek. www.businessweek.com*; Drew, C. (2012, June 16). Lockheed is replacing strikers at fighter plane plant. *New York Times*, B2; Singh, P., and Harish, J. (2001). Striker replacements in the United States and Mexico: A review of the law and empirical research. *Industrial Relations, 40,* 22–53; Budd, J. (1996). Canadian strike replacement legislation and collective bargaining: Lessons for the United States. *Industrial Relations, 3b,* 245–260; *BNA's Employee Relations Weekly.* (1994, January 24). Negotiators for management and labor gauge impact of striker replacements, *12*(4), 87–88; Bernstein, A. (1991, August 5). You can't bargain with a striker whose job is no more. *BusinessWeek, 27;* Kilborn, P. T. (1990, March 13). Replacement workers. Management's big gun. *New York Times.* A24.

Some contracts forbid wildcat strikes and penalize workers who participate in them, sometimes by termination. The preferred method of resolving disputes between unionized workers and management is the grievance procedure. One tool that employers can use against workers is the lockout. A **lockout** occurs when the employer shuts down its operations before or during a labor dispute. Employers may use a lockout during a bargaining impasse to protect themselves from unusual economic hardship when the timing of a strike may ruin critical materials. For example, a brewer must bottle beer by a certain date or the entire batch can be ruined. Because employers have other alternatives to influence the union to make concessions, such as the use of replacement workers, lockouts are rarely used. A 10-month lockout occurred when National Hockey League (NHL) team owners and the Player's Association representing the hockey players failed to come to terms over the owners' demand—citing losses of $273 million the previous year—for a salary cap on each team's wage bill. The lockout resulted in the cancellation of the entire 2004–2005 NHL season. The Player's Association finally caved in and agreed to a deal with the owners that capped each team's total wage bill at $39 million and included a 24-percent reduction in player salaries.[76]

lockout
Occurs when an employer shuts down its operations before or during a labor dispute.

Contract Administration

The last phase of labor relations is contract administration, which involves application and enforcement of the labor contract in the workplace. Disputes occasionally arise between labor and management over such issues as who should be promoted or whether an employee has abused sick leave privileges. The steps taken to resolve such disputes are spelled out in the labor contract.

The mechanism preferred by most unions and managements to settle disputes is the grievance procedure.[77] A **grievance procedure** is a systematic, step-by-step procedure designed to settle disputes regarding the interpretation of the labor contract.

grievance procedure
A systematic, step-by-step process designed to settle disputes regarding the interpretation of a labor contract.

Although employees may attempt to settle their grievances through such alternatives as an open-door policy or a meeting with an employee relations representative in the HR department (see Chapter 13), grievance procedures under union contracts have two significant advantages for employees that no other HRM program can provide:

1. The grievance procedure provides the employee with an advocate dedicated to representing the employee's case to management. This representative is called the **union steward**. Under any other system used to handle grievances, the employee is represented by someone who is either a manager or an agent of management. Such people obviously cannot be entirely dedicated to the employee's position.
2. The last step in the grievance procedure is **arbitration**, a quasi-judicial process that is binding on both parties. The arbitrator is a neutral person selected from outside the firm and compensated by both the union and management (who split the fee). Unlike grievance panels, which are composed of people on the company payroll, the arbitrator has no personal stake in the outcome and can make a tough decision without worrying about how it will affect his or her career.[78]

union steward
An advocate dedicated to representing an employee's case to management in a grievance procedure.

arbitration
The last step in a grievance procedure. The decision of the arbitrator, who is a neutral individual selected from outside the firm, is binding on both parties.

STEPS IN THE GRIEVANCE PROCEDURE Most union grievance procedures have three or four steps leading up to arbitration, the final step. Figure 15.7 illustrates a four-step union grievance procedure. Usually a time limit is set for resolution of the grievance at each step. Later steps in the procedure require more time than earlier steps, and the degree of formality increases with each step. Because the grievance procedure is time consuming and distracts several people from their regular job duties, it is generally advantageous for the company to resolve disputes as early as possible.

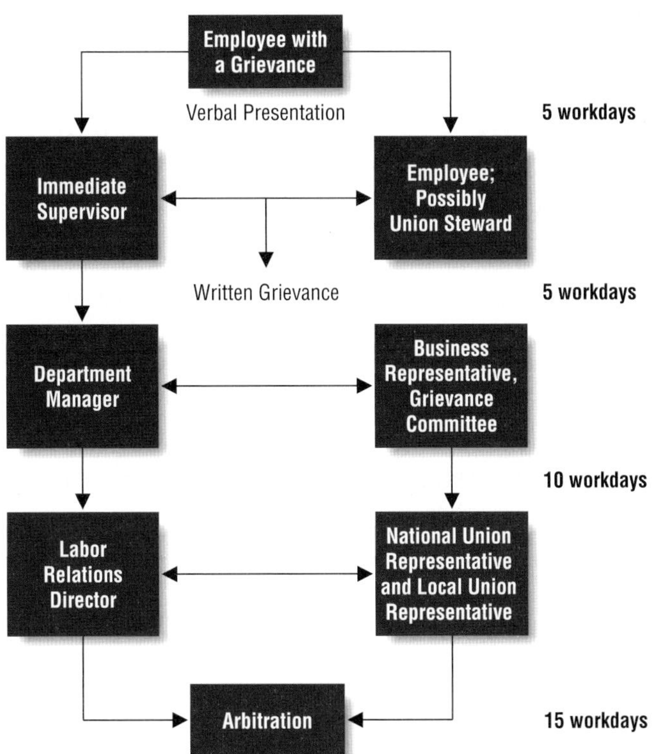

FIGURE 15.7
A Union Grievance Procedure

Source: Adapted from Allen, R., and Keavany, T. (1988). *Contemporary labor relations* (2nd ed.), 530. Reading, MA: Addison-Wesley. Copyright © 1988. Adapted by permission of Pearson Education, Inc., Upper Saddle River, New Jersey.

The key to an effective grievance procedure is training supervisors to understand the labor contract and to work with union stewards to settle grievances at the first step. The labor relations staff in the HR department can make an important contribution here by training and consulting with supervisors.

The first step of the grievance procedure is taken when an employee tells the union steward about his or her grievance. In our example in Figure 15.7, the employee must make the dispute known to the steward and/or the supervisor within five working days of its occurrence. The steward refers to the labor contract to determine whether the grievance is valid and, if it is, tries to work with the employee's supervisor to settle it. The grievance may or may not be put in writing. Most grievances (about 75 percent) are settled at this first step.

If the dispute cannot be resolved at this first step, the grievance is put into writing, and, in our example, the department or plant manager and a union official (such as the union's business representative) have an additional five working days to resolve the issue. At this second step, a formal meeting is usually held to discuss the grievance.

If the second step is unsuccessful at resolving the grievance, the parties move on to the third step. This step usually involves both a corporate manager (for example, the company's director of labor relations) and a local and national union representative. In our example, the labor agreement gives these people 10 days to respond to and resolve the grievance. Grievances that have the potential to set precedents affecting employment policy may get "kicked up" to this level because it is inappropriate for plant supervisors or managers to settle them. For example, a grievance concerning production standards may have widespread implications for all workers if a corporate-wide labor contract is in effect. Because the third step is the last step before arbitration, it is management's final opportunity to negotiate a settlement with the union. It is common for management to try to "cut a deal" with the union at this step.

The final step of the grievance procedure is arbitration. Only about 1 percent of grievances get as far as arbitration; the rest are settled at the earlier steps. Both parties select the arbitrator, before whom the union and management advocates present their case and evidence at a hearing with a quasi-judicial format. The arbitrator then examines the evidence and makes a ruling. Most arbitrators also write an opinion outlining their reasoning and the sections of the labor contract that influenced their decision. This opinion can serve as a guideline for dealing with similar disputes in the future. The arbitrator's decision is final and binding on both parties.

TYPES OF GRIEVANCES Employees initiate two types of grievances. The first is a *contract interpretation grievance* based on union members' rights under the labor contract. If the contract's language is ambiguous, this type of grievance may go to arbitration for clarification. For example, suppose that a labor contract allows workers two 10-minute coffee breaks per day. If management decides it would be more efficient to get rid of coffee breaks, employees may file a contract interpretation grievance to get this privilege restored.

The second type of grievance involves employee discipline. In such cases, the grievance procedure examines whether the employee in question was disciplined for just cause, and management has the burden of proof. An important aspect of these cases is determining whether the disciplined employee received due process. For minor infractions, management is expected to give employees the opportunity to correct their behavior via the progressive discipline procedure (verbal warning, written warning, suspension, discharge). For more serious charges (such as theft), management must provide strong evidence that the discipline was warranted.

BENEFITS OF UNION GRIEVANCE PROCEDURES Union grievance procedures provide benefits to both management and employees. Specifically:

- The grievance procedure protects union employees from arbitrary management decisions; it is the mechanism for organizational justice.
- The grievance procedure helps management quickly and efficiently settle conflicts that could otherwise end up in the courts or result in work stoppages.
- Management can use the grievance procedure as an upward communications channel to monitor and correct the sources of employee dissatisfaction with jobs or company policies.

The Impact of Unions on Human Resource Management

In the absence of a union, management is more likely to develop HRM policies based on the principle of efficiency. For example, a nonunion company is more likely to adopt a meet-the-market pay policy because the market wage is the most efficient way to allocate labor costs (see Chapter 10). But when a union enters the picture, management must develop policies that reflect the preferences of the majority of workers who are represented by the union.[79] In this section, we look at the changes in staffing, employee development, compensation, and employee relations practices that are likely under unionization.

Staffing

Under a labor contract, job opportunities are allocated to people on the basis of seniority. **Seniority** is the length of time a person works for an employer. In a unionized company, promotions, job assignments, and shift preferences are given to the employee with the most seniority in the unit.[80] Layoffs in unionized firms are also governed according to the last in, first out rule (see Chapter 6).[81]

seniority
The length of time a person works for an employer.

Work rules tend to be less flexible in a unionized workplace because they are likely to be formalized in the labor agreement. When labor relations are adversarial, labor contracts are more likely to have inflexible work rules written into them. When labor relations are more cooperative, work rule specifications may purposely be left out of the contract. In certain industries, this gives management the flexibility to adjust to the rapidly changing technological requirements of producing a product or service. For example, unions that have a cooperative relationship with management can play an important role in overcoming barriers to the effective adoption of high-performance work practices that have been linked to organizational competitiveness. Unions can work with management to overcome employees' resistance to change by advocating for change that provides mutually beneficial outcomes for both employees and management.[82]

In the absence of a union, the employer is more likely to allocate job opportunities to employees on the basis of merit.[83] In most cases, merit is determined by a supervisor's judgment of the employee's performance. Supervisors in a nonunion workplace have more power and influence because of their authority to reward employees' efforts with promotions, attractive job assignments, and preferred work schedules. Layoff decisions in nonunion firms are more likely to take both merit and seniority into consideration. Finally, work rules are often more flexible in a nonunion firm because the employer is not tied to a contract and is, therefore, not required to justify to employees any changes made in the way work is done. In nonunion firms it is management alone that determines the most efficient way to produce a product or service and deliver it to the customer.

Employee Development

In unionized companies, the uses of performance appraisal are very limited because the appraisal data usually come from the supervisor, a source that many unions find problematic. Unions tend to balk at using performance appraisal as the basis for making pay and staffing decisions. If performance appraisal is done at all for union employees, it is used simply to provide some feedback on their performance. In a nonunion workplace, however, the performance appraisal is used to determine pay raises, promotions, job assignments, career planning, training needs, and layoff or discharge.[84]

Unionized firms tend to retain their employees longer than nonunion firms do.[85] First, unionized employees are more likely to express their dissatisfaction through the grievance procedure, so this channel may become an alternative to quitting. Second, unionized firms on average pay their employees a higher wage, which may make it more difficult for them to find an equally high-paying job if they leave. Moreover, higher employee retention rates in unionized companies make it more economically feasible for these firms to provide greater investments in training union-represented employees because the firms can expect to retain trained employees long enough to earn positive returns on the investment in training.[86]

Unions themselves have become far more interested in worker training and development. The 1990 contract between General Motors and the UAW, for instance, specified that the company will create Skills Centers (adult educational facilities) for union workers. A total of 36 GM plants in the United States have set up these centers. As unions have stepped up their organizing efforts, many have offered to fund worker training programs. In New York City, for instance, locals of the Amalgamated Labor and Textile Workers Union, the International Ladies Garment

Workers Union, and other major unions work with the Center for Worker Education to provide English as a second language and high school equivalency classes for their members and for worker groups they are trying to organize.[87]

Compensation

A company experiences an increase in total compensation costs when a union organizes its employees. On average, union employees earn 10 to 20 percent higher wages than comparable nonunionized employees.[88]

cost-of-living adjustment (COLA)
A pay raise, usually made across the board, that is tied to such inflation indicators as the consumer price index.

The presence of a union also affects the company's policy on pay raises. Unionized firms avoid using merit pay plans and are likely to give across-the-board pay raises to employees based on market considerations.[89] Across-the-board pay plans are often based on **cost-of-living adjustments (COLAs)** that are tied to inflation indicators such as the consumer price index. About 23 percent of unionized U.S. workers received COLAs in 2002.[90] Unions prefer across-the-board pay raises over merit pay plans because they see the latter as undermining union solidarity by encouraging employees to compete against one another to win higher pay increases. Furthermore, unions are often skeptical of the fairness of merit pay increases because of the potential for favoritism on the part of supervisors (see Chapter 7). Unions apply this same logic to the use of individual pay incentives such as lump-sum bonuses. In contrast, nonunion firms tend to use merit pay and bonuses to encourage competition and recognize their top performers. One notable exception to unions' generally critical predisposition toward merit pay has been the recent adoption of merit pay for teachers in Denver, Colorado. The teachers' union and the school district worked closely to design a plan to reward high-performing teachers that overcame the union's fears that giving rewards on the basis of merit would undermine collaboration between teachers.[91]

Two hundred auto workers picket outside their union's headquarters in Detroit, Michigan, to protest an agreement made by the union and General Motors to reduce newly hired auto workers' wages by half compared to what experienced workers receive at a suburban assembly plant.
Source: w66/ZUMA Press/Newscom.

Unions are less likely to object to group pay incentives because group plans (such as gainsharing or profit sharing) tend to reinforce group cohesion. Each of the Big Three automakers in the United States has negotiated a profit-sharing plan with the UAW. Union employees at Ford Motor Company received profit-sharing bonus checks of $5,000 in 2010, $6,200 in 2011, and $8,300 in 2012 when the company declared profits during those years. However, Ford employees received no profit-sharing bonuses in the three years from 2005 to 2007 when the company reported losses in each of those years.[92] It is not unusual to find gainsharing plans in both union and nonunion companies.[93] However, nonunion firms generally have more flexibility to use both individual and group pay incentives to reward different types of work outcomes.

Unions have generally influenced employers to offer a more valuable benefits package to each employee.[94] Through collective bargaining, they have been able to negotiate packages with a broader array of benefits than nonunion workers receive.

In unionized firms the employer pays for most benefits, whereas in nonunion firms employer and employee share the costs.[95] The result is better health benefits for unionized employees than for their nonunion counterparts. As U.S. health care costs have soared over the last decade, nonunionized companies have begun asking their employees to pay a greater share of these costs through both higher monthly premiums and higher deductibles. Although unionized employers face the same rising health care costs, unions have used collective bargaining to persuade many employers to pursue alternative cost-saving methods, such as managed health care, second opinions, and audits.[96]

In terms of retirement benefits, unions have been able to provide more security for employees by influencing employers to adopt a defined benefit plan, which provides a fixed amount of income to employees upon retirement. Nonunion employers are more likely to adopt a defined contribution plan, which requires only that the employer set aside a fixed portion of the employee's income each month in a plan that meets the ERISA (Employee Retirement Income Security Act) standards for these plans. Under a defined contribution plan, employees do not know how much total income will be available for their retirement until they actually retire (see Chapter 12).

Unions can play an important role in monitoring and enforcing legally required benefits such as workers' compensation and unemployment insurance.[97] In a unionized firm, employees are more likely to receive workers' compensation and unemployment insurance benefits because union representatives give workers information on how to use them. Furthermore, unionized workers are less likely to be discouraged from filing claims for fear of being penalized or challenged by their employer.[98] In contrast, management in a nonunion firm is not as likely to make employees aware of their right to use these government-mandated benefits because a firm's payroll taxes to fund the benefit increase in proportion to the number of employees using the benefit (see Chapter 12).

Employee Relations

The union is an empowerment mechanism that gives employees a voice in the development of work rules that affect their jobs. The labor contract gives employees specific rights. For example, an employee overlooked for promotion may file a grievance and be reconsidered for the promotion if the contract stipulates that the employee has a right to that promotion.

Nonunion employers tend to document their employees' basic rights in an employee handbook (see Chapter 13). However, employee handbooks provide fewer employee rights than labor contracts do. In fact, many of them contain only general guidelines and specifically state that supervisors may need to make exceptions to the written policy from time to time.

The appeals mechanism that a nonunion employer is most likely to use is the open-door policy.[99] Unlike the grievance procedure, which is administered by both the union and management, the open-door policy is controlled by management. It gives management the opportunity to resolve an employee's complaint while balancing both parties' interests. The only recourse open to employees who are unhappy with the resolution of a complaint under the open-door policy is to find legal counsel and go to court to obtain justice—an option more employees are pursuing every year. Under the union grievance procedure, it is much less likely that an employee will take a case to court because judges are usually unwilling to challenge the results of arbitration.

When an employer is investigating a union employee for the purposes of imposing discipline, the employee has a right to have a union representative present during questioning. The right to have a union representative present during a disciplinary investigation is called a *Weingarten right* based on a 1975 Supreme Court case, *NLRB v. Weingarten,* which established this right from an interpretation of the National Labor Relations Act.[100] The union representative in the investigation is likely to be a union steward who is trained in conflict resolution methods and understands employee rights under the labor contract. In 2000, the National Labor Relations Board ruled that nonunion employees are also entitled to *Weingarten rights,* which permits them to have a coworker present when undergoing an investigatory interview that could lead to a disciplinary action. However, the coworker selected as an employee representative in the nonunion setting is likely to have fewer skills at resolving grievances or defusing conflict than a trained union steward.[101]

Summary and Conclusions

Why Do Employees Join Unions?

U.S. employees generally seek representation from a union because they (1) are dissatisfied with certain aspects of their job, (2) lack influence with management to make the needed changes, (3) believe that their pay and benefits are noncompetitive, and (4) see the union as a solution to their problems.

Labor unions were largely unprotected by law in the United States until 1935. Economic conditions during the Great Depression led Congress to try to equalize the power of employers and employees. After several decades of widespread support, unions are today widely perceived as too powerful.

Managers strongly affect how employees perceive the work environment and thus whether they will be susceptible to unionization. Managers must possess enough knowledge of basic labor law to (1) avoid creating a legal liability for the company, (2) implement the terms of labor agreements fairly and impartially, and (3) hear and resolve employee grievances.

Labor Relations and the Legal Environment

The most important laws governing labor relations in the United States are the Wagner Act (1935), the Taft-Hartley Act (1947), and the Landrum-Griffin Act (1959). The Wagner Act created the

National Labor Relations Board, which administers union certification elections and prevents and remedies unfair labor practices.

Labor Relations in the United States

Labor relations in the United States are characterized by (1) business unionism, (2) unions structured by type of job, (3) a focus on collective bargaining, (4) the use of labor contracts, (5) the adversarial nature of labor–management relations and shrinking union membership, and (6) the growth of unions in the public sector.

Labor Relations in Other Countries

The labor relations systems of two key global competitors of the United States, Germany and Japan, have achieved a greater degree of cooperation between unions and management than the U.S. system has. The German system uses works councils and codetermination to involve workers in decisions at all levels of the organization. In Japan, enterprise unions have worked closely with companies for the mutual benefit of both parties. Some believe that economic pressures are straining labor–management relations in these countries today.

Labor Relations Strategy

A labor relations strategy is a company's overall plan for dealing with unions. Companies that choose a union-acceptance strategy view unions as their employees' legitimate representatives and accept collective bargaining as an appropriate mechanism for establishing workplace rules. Companies that choose a union-avoidance strategy use either union substitution or union suppression to keep unions out of the workplace.

Managing the Labor Relations Process

The labor relations process has three phases: (1) union organizing, (2) collective bargaining, and (3) contract administration. In the union organizing phase, management must confront the issues involved with union solicitation, preelection conduct, and the certification election. In the collective bargaining phase, union and management representatives negotiate workplace rules that are formalized in a labor contract. The contract administration phase starts after the labor contract is settled and deals with day-to-day administration of the workplace. A key feature of the contract administration phase is the grievance procedure, a step-by-step process for settling employee disputes about contract interpretations or disciplinary actions.

The Impact of Unions on Human Resource Management

The impact of a union on the way a company manages its human resources is significant. Management can expect that the union will affect virtually every major area of HRM. In a unionized workplace, staffing decisions will be heavily influenced by seniority rather than by merit. Individually focused performance appraisals are severely curtailed, while training programs are emphasized. Unionized employees tend to receive larger compensation and benefit packages. Finally, employee relations processes in a union shop are by definition highly structured.

Key Terms

arbitration, 517
business unionism, 498
codetermination, 503
collective bargaining, 498
cost-of-living adjustment (COLA), 520
distributive bargaining, 512
economic strike, 515
enterprise union, 503
grievance procedure, 517
integrative bargaining, 513
labor contract, 498
labor relations specialist, 494
labor relations strategy, 504
Landrum-Griffin Act (1959), 497
lockout, 516
National Labor Relations Board (NLRB), 495
Railway Labor Act, 497
right-to-work law, 496
seniority, 519
Taft-Hartley Act (1947), 496
union, 493
union acceptance strategy, 504
union avoidance strategy, 506
union shop clause, 496
union steward, 517
union substitution/proactive human resource management, 506
union suppression, 506
Wagner Act/National Labor Relations Act (1935), 495
wildcat strike, 515
works council, 503
work rules, 498

Watch It!

New Haven Federation of Teachers: Collective Bargaining. If your instructor has assigned this, go to **mymanagementlab.com** to watch a video case and answer questions.

Discussion Questions

15-1. Why have labor and management tended to treat each other as adversaries in the U.S. labor relations system?

15-2. How can management's collective bargaining tactics be influenced by the company's labor relations strategy? Provide examples.

15-3. It is often said that "good pay and good management" are the keys to successful union avoidance. Spell out the kind of policies and practices companies should develop if they want to keep their workers from unionizing. Do you think the employee relations practices you've mentioned are less costly or more costly than working with unionized labor?

15-4. Is it necessarily the case that working conditions and rules are less flexible in a unionized organization? Why or why not? If it is the case, then how does this affect management's ability to make what they consider to be quick and important changes? Does unionization mean a lack of cooperation with management?

15-5. Some experts in the field of labor relations believe that when a union can pose a credible threat of a strike to management in the collective bargaining process, both parties—union and management—are motivated to move in the direction of a settlement and reach a labor agreement. They also claim that without a credible strike threat, the two parties are less likely to arrive at a joint agreement. What is the basis for this justification for giving the union the privilege of exercising its right to strike? Do you agree or disagree with this argument? Explain your reasoning.

MyManagementLab®

If your instructor has assigned this, go to **mymanagementlab.com** for the following Assisted-graded writing questions:

15-6. What are two of the advantages and two of the disadvantages of a strike from management's perspective? From the union's perspective?

15-7. Suppose a goal of management is to reduce the number of grievances filed by union employees each year. Provide three ways that the HRM staff can contribute to this goal.

15-8. What, in your opinion, are the three most significant impacts of a union on the management of human resources? Explain, and indicate whether the impact for each one is positive or negative.

You Manage It! 1: Emerging Trends

The Freelancers Union: A New Approach to Unionism?

The Freelancers Union is an organization that represents the interests of self-employed freelance workers. It employs a different approach to unionism than traditional trade unions, most notably because it does not use strikes. In addition, its members do not pay unions dues and the Freelancers Union does not negotiate labor contracts with employers or represent members when they have a grievance. The Freelancers Union offers health insurance through an infrastructure called the Portable Benefits Network (PBN), providing health insurance at costs that are less than half the price of an average HMO premium charged to individuals in the New York City market, where over half of the organization's members are located. The union also offers life and disability insurance, financial services, resources, and discounts to union members. Another benefit that is being considered is to offer 401(k) retirement plans to union members.

The Freelancers Union was started in 2001 by Sara Horowitz, a labor attorney and union organizer. Horowitz believed that unions that had been developed for blue-collar factory workers needed to be brought up-to-date for the twenty-first-century workforce, in which many employees are self-employed yet still need an organization to represent their collective interests.

Horowitz concluded that a union is essentially a means for workers to join together to solve problems. To be effective, it must follow an economic model that makes it independent of government, employers, and other institutions. She rejected the traditional union model of confrontation and of charging membership dues unrelated to the benefits received. Instead, she adopted a customer-centered approach: The Freelancers Union would provide members with a menu of services that they could choose to pay for, thus generating funds to spend on the union's advocacy of labor laws favorable to freelancers. For example, in the United States freelancers are generally not entitled to unemployment insurance, even if a job they have held for as long as 18 months has come to an end.

In 2013, the Freelancers Union had over 200,000 members, and 23,000 received benefits through the PBN. Sara Horowitz expects the Freelancers Union to expand the organization to one million members by 2016. The union serves an unmet need in the market—the growing number of self-employed workers who are ineligible for employer-based benefits. Recently, Horowitz launched a Web site with social networking features for members. It provides a directory that makes it easier for potential employers to find a variety of freelance services offered by the union's members, such as computer programming, event organizing, catering, or any other type of service an employer may be seeking.

Critical Thinking Questions

15-9. How does the Freelancers Union differ from the unions described in this chapter?

15-10. What sources of power does the Freelancers Union use to provide services to its members?

15-11. What can traditional unions, such as those affiliated with the AFL-CIO, learn from the organizing success of the Freelancers Union?

Team Exercise

15-12. With four or five students, assume that you are a team of managers for a corporation that retains the services of freelance computer consultants to provide technical support to company employees. The company has just discovered that all of its freelance computer consultants have recently joined the Freelancers Union. Would the union membership of these freelance consultants affect management's relationship with the consultants for better or for worse? Should the company have a labor relations policy with regard to using consultants who are union members or nonunion members, or should it make no difference? If it is decided that there is a need for a labor relations policy, what should the policy be? Be prepared to share your answers with other members of your class when called upon by the instructor.

Experiential Exercise: Individual

15-13. Assume that you are a self-employed management consultant and a friend tells you about the Freelancers Union. Your friend is a member and asks you to join. You are considering the advantages and disadvantages of joining the Freelancers Union. What would you consider to be the advantages of joining the Freelancers Union? What are the disadvantages of joining the Freelancers Union? As an independent management consultant, does becoming a union member conflict with any of your core personal values? If so, which ones? Ultimately, would you join the Freelancers Union? What was the deciding factor that influenced your decision?

Sources: Based on Greenhouse, S. (2013, March 24). Going it alone, together: The Freelancers Union offers a collective voice—not to mention health insurance—to a growing multitude of independent workers. *New York Times*, Sunday Business 1, 4; Massey, D. (2008, November 21). Freelancers Union forms health insurance company. *www.crainsnewyork.com*; *The Economist*. (2006, November 11). Freelancers of the world, unite! 76; Freelancers Union. (2008). *www.freelancersunion.org*.

You Manage It! 2: Ethics/Social Responsibility

Public Sector Unions in Wisconsin Have been Dealt a Major Setback with a New Law that Weakens Union Bargaining Rights

A controversial new law was enacted in 2011 in Wisconsin that limits the bargaining rights and security of public sector unions within the state. The law, called the Wisconsin Budget Repair Bill, or Act 10, was passed by conservative state lawmakers under the leadership of Republican Governor Scott Walker, who blamed favorable labor contracts negotiated by public sector unions in the past for a state budget deficit of $3.6 billion. The law stipulates that public sector workers need to vote whether to re-unionize every year, prevents unions from automatically collecting union dues from its members, and greatly narrows the scope of collective bargaining topics to only wages. The amount of pay that can be bargained over is limited to the rate of inflation.

During the two years since the law was passed, public sector unions in Wisconsin lost between one-third and two-thirds of their members. For example, the Wisconsin Education Association Council, the state's largest teachers' union, lost about half of its 98,000 members since Act 10 became the law. The law does not affect the bargaining rights of first responder personnel such as local police, firefighters, and state troopers. The law affects all other public sector unions that represent teachers, nurses, municipal employees, social workers, and other job categories that work for city, county, and state government. The success of Wisconsin in limiting public sector union power has influenced legislators in Ohio, Michigan, Tennessee, and Idaho to introduce bills in those state legislatures to limit public sector unions in those states.

Until recently, public sector unions have been considered to be a success story by their increasing union membership growth in the United States. As opposed to the decrease in union membership in private sector firms, public sector unions have accounted for most of the increase in organized labor since the 1960s. However, the shocking setback experienced by public sector unions in Wisconsin—the first state to legalize collective bargaining for government employees back in 1959—has caused labor relations observers to wonder whether the law in Wisconsin is a turning point for public sector unions, making them less relevant for public employees in the years to come.

Critical Thinking Questions

15-14. Are public sector unions in the United States too powerful? What is the source of the power of public sector unions? Do you agree with Governor Walker of Wisconsin, who believes that (1) public sector unions should have their power cut back so the topics for negotiation are limited to only wages, and (2) that unions must hold an election each year to make sure that a majority of employees want the union to continue, or else lose their right to represent public employees?

15-15. Many public sector employees decided to quit being union members in Wisconsin as explained in the case. What alternative ways does a group of public sector employees, such as nurses or teachers, have to improve their employee benefits, working conditions, or salaries without having a union to represent their interests to management in city, county, or state government?

Team Exercise

15-16. With a group of four or five students, assume that you are a group of high school teachers in Wisconsin and that the union that represented the teachers to the board of education in the school district has been disbanded because it did not receive a majority vote in this year's required election. After the union was defeated, the school board announced that the pay for high school teachers would be frozen and no pay raises would be forthcoming. Each teacher in the group believes that he or she deserves a pay raise for the coming year. The group of teachers you are in would like to present a case, in favor of giving teachers pay raises, to the high school principal and the Parent-Teachers Association (PTA) to obtain their support. What kind of data will the teachers need to make a convincing case to the principal and the PTA? For example, will the teachers need data that covers individual teacher performance, school performance, performance of the students, school budget data, school district performance data, or state-wide school district performance data? How will the teachers obtain all of this data to make a rational case for higher pay based on the evidence? Will the school board cooperate and disclose their budget data to the teachers? If the teachers do not have the time or the resources to collect the data they need to make a credible presentation of evidence for higher wages to the principal or PTA, what alternatives do the teachers have to improve their pay? What type of services could a well-functioning union provide the teachers to help them obtain a pay increase from the school board? Be prepared to share your answers to these questions with other members of the class when called on by the instructor.

Experiential Exercise: Individual

15-17. The purpose of this experiential exercise is to reflect on the implications of the Wisconsin law that weakens public sector unions, as explained in this case, by thinking about how you would answer the following questions: Do public sector employees need unions to represent their interests to administrators in government? Is it better to be a member of a weak public sector union or not be a union member at all? Since most employees who work in the public sector have their job security protected by civil service rules that require the application of due process, are public sector unions really necessary to act as an advocate for employees? Do you agree with Governor Walker of Wisconsin that public sector unions are a too powerful a force in local elections that gives support to public officials who cater to their economic interests and works to defeat public officials who oppose union interests, which, unless union power is restrained, lets them obtain an unfair amount of government resources? Be prepared to explain the reasons for your answers when called upon by the instructor.

Sources: Based on Gunn, S. (2013, July 22). Thousands of employees are quitting public sector unions in Wisconsin. *EAGnews. www.eagnews.org*; Frezza, B. (2012, June 5). Governor Walker's victory spells doom for public sector unions. *Forbes. www.forbes.com*; Meiskins, B. (2013, September 13). Convoluted finding in Wisconsin on public sector unions. *Nonprofit Quarterly. www.nonprofitquarterly.org*; Cersonsky, J. (2013, August 2). New labor movement emerges in Scott Walker's Wisconsin. *Salon.* www.salon.org; Greely, B. (2011, February 28). The union, jacked: Why stripping collective bargaining rights from public sector workers is worth debating. *Bloomberg Businessweek*, 8–9; *The Economist.* (2011, February 26). Wisconsin and wider: A dispute in one cold state is having nationwide repercussions, 31–32.

 You Manage It! 3: Customer-Driven HR

When Is a Team a Union?

Amalgamated Tool, a nonunion manufacturer of auto parts in Michigan, suffered such significant financial losses in 2006 that it froze the pay of all its employees to conserve cash. The company also asked its employees to pay a larger share of their health insurance costs. The employees were extremely upset by these actions, and both morale and productivity declined.

To improve morale, Amalgamated's management decided to form several problem-solving employee teams. After meeting to discuss the problems at Amalgamated, the teams presented management with suggestions on how to provide pay raises and health insurance to employees fairly and efficiently. Each problem-solving team had a leader elected by the other team members to present the team's suggestions, but only about 20 percent of Amalgamated's employees were asked to serve on a team. The teams' suggestions were largely adopted by management, and morale and efficiency went up the next year.

On behalf of some dissatisfied Amalgamated employees, a local union filed an unfair labor practice claim stating that management had illegally used the problem-solving teams to form a management-dominated union, in violation of a provision of the Wagner Act that states: "It is an unfair labor practice for an employer to dominate or interfere with the formation of any labor organization or contribute financial support to it."

The National Labor Relations Board sustained the union's position and ordered Amalgamated to cease and desist using its problem-solving teams.

Critical Thinking Questions

15-18. Why did the local union object to the way Amalgamated's management used problem-solving teams?

15-19. What is the difference between a team and a union?

15-20. To avoid the NLRB's cease-and-desist order, what should Amalgamated's management have done differently in using problem-solving teams?

Team Exercise

15-21. Students form into groups of four to six members and role-play National Labor Relations Board members. Each group discusses whether Amalgamated violated the Wagner Act's prohibition of a company "dominating a union or providing financial support to it." Compare conclusions and arguments across groups.

Experiential Exercise: Individual

15-22. It has been estimated that there are around 400 million trade-union members worldwide. A third of the trade-union members live in China, although countries such as Brazil, Russia, and Ukraine are also very highly unionized. Unionization rates differ widely, from 11 percent in the United States, to 25 percent in the United Kingdom, and over 50 percent in Norway. The average for OECD members is around 17 percent. Why do you think that trade union memberships differ so widely across the world? Investigate your country's unionization rates and compare them to those of a neighboring country. What do the rates tell you about the nature of employment? How has it impacted labor relations, pay, and work-conditions? Be prepared to share your answers to these questions with the class.

 You Manage It! 4: Ethics/Social Responsibility

Union Members Protest a 50 Percent Wage Cut at a General Motors Plant

In October 2010, two hundred auto workers picketed outside the locked gates of their union headquarters in Detroit, Michigan, to protest an agreement that let General Motors (GM) pay half the wage rate of current employees to newly hired workers or those called back from layoff at GM's assembly plant in Orion Township, Michigan. The wage cut for the newly hired and returning workers was part of an agreement between the United Auto Workers (UAW) and General Motors that was designed to help GM make money on building the Chevrolet Sonic, a low-price subcompact car, with unionized labor in the United States. In the past, General Motors and other U.S. automakers needed to assemble small cars in Mexico or Korea, where labor costs were lower, which took jobs away from unionized U.S. workers.

The agreement between the company and the union was the first time the union has agreed to a pay cut for workers returning from layoff. The Michigan auto plant builds the Chevrolet Sonic and had previously been closed. U.S. automakers have struggled for years to make money on small cars. Mark Reuss, GM's president for North America, said that the company expected to make money on the Sonic. The UAW deal, he said, was one of the reasons why the small car will be profitable. Others included a highly efficient factory with new equipment and help from state and local governments.

Meanwhile, the auto workers who have been laid off and who were recalled to work in the Orion Township auto plant felt betrayed by their union. Prior to being laid off, the workers earned $28 per hour, and after being recalled were asked to do the same work for $14 per hour. That is why two hundred of these auto workers protested the deal made between the UAW and GM to lower auto worker wages. Gary Bernath, an assistant director of the UAW, said the bankruptcies of GM and Chrysler in 2009 forced the union to make very difficult decisions to safeguard union jobs. In GM's latest contract with the UAW that was settled in 2011, the recalled employees at the Orion Township plant had their wages increased to $16 to $19 an hour, which was still substantially below the $32 per hour wage received by experienced UAW employees who work at other GM assembly plants.

Critical Thinking Questions

15-23. Why did the UAW agree to a 50-percent pay cut for its unionized workers who were being recalled to work in the Orion Township assembly plant? Do you think the local workers who will have their pay reduced by half are justified in protesting the deal made by their union, which is supposed to be representing their interests? Explain the reasons for your position.

15-24. When employees are dissatisfied with the way they are being represented by a union, what are some tactics that employees can use to influence the union leaders to make changes in the union's goals?

Team Exercise

15-25. A big challenge for the GM managers at the auto plant making the Chevrolet Sonic will be maintaining positive employee morale. They will be managing a workforce of 1,550 employees that is composed of 60 percent workers transferred from other GM facilities who will be earning $28 per hour, and 40 percent GM workers recalled from layoffs and new employees doing similar jobs and earning only $14 per hour. With a group of four or five fellow classmates and using your knowledge of HR practice, develop a list of suggestions that managers can use to keep the plant operating efficiently despite the large differences in pay between the two sectors of unionized employees. Be prepared to share your findings with the class when called on by your instructor.

Experiential Exercise: Individual

15-26. Assume you are an employee in a situation similar to the one described in this case, a situation in which you believe your union has not represented your interests fairly and made a deal with management that reduces your pay substantially. You are not free to quit your job because the unemployment rate is high in your community and replacement jobs are scarce. What can you do to cope with being paid a lot less for doing the same job? Will you communicate your dissatisfaction to the union, and if so, how will you do it? Will you communicate your dissatisfaction to management, and if so, how? What do you hope to gain by communicating your feelings to the union and/or management? What are the risks of communicating dissatisfaction to the union and/or management? Is it better to keep quiet and do your job without rocking the boat? What personal values enter into your decision to either be proactive and communicate your dissatisfaction or be silent and avoid controversy?

Sources: Based on Kroh, E. (2014, June 19). A darker future for "tier 2" workers. *Remapping Debate*. www.remappingdebate.org/article/darker-future-tier-2-workers?page=0,1; Breslin, M. (2014, June 17). Two-tiered pay scale for autoworkers raises debate. *Workforce*. www.workforce.com/articles/two-tiered-pay-scale-for-autoworkers-raises-debate; Krisher, T. (2010, October 8) GM, UAW agree on wage deal. *Denver Post*, 7B; Vlasic, B., and Bunkley, N. (2010, October 7). G.M.'s wage-cutting deal clears way for a small car. *New York Times*. *www.nytimes.com*; Slaughter, J. (2011, October 21). UAW members protest 50% wage cut at GM plant, demand a vote. *www.labornotes.org*.

Endnotes

Scan for Endnotes or go to http://www.pearsonglobaleditions.com/Gomez-Mejia.

CHAPTER 16 Managing Workplace Safety and Health

MyManagementLab®

When you see this icon, visit **www.mymanagementlab.com** for activities that are applied, personalized, and offer immediate feedback.

CHALLENGES

After reading this chapter, you should be able to deal more effectively with the following challenges:

1 **Explain** the reasons for safety and health laws, as well as the extent of the employer's responsibility to fund a workers' compensation system and maintain a safe and healthy work environment.

2 **Identify** the basic provisions of the Occupational Safety and Health Act.

3 **Develop** an awareness of contemporary health and safety issues, including AIDS, workplace violence, smoking in the workplace, cumulative trauma disorders, fetal protection, hazardous chemicals, and genetic testing.

4 **Describe** the features of safety programs and understand the reasons for and the effects of programs designed to enhance employee well-being.

Work is engaged in by choice, with employees providing labor for wages. Safety and health regulations help assure that the choice to provide labor does not involve unnecessary risks. Most of us probably share the belief that the majority of employers are mindful of worker safety and take seriously their duty to provide a safe and healthy workplace environment. Although we are probably correct in that belief, there are some examples of unsafe workplace conditions that make it clear that worker safety and health can be an area of real concern. Companies that have received large fines from the Occupational Safety and Health Administration (OSHA) provide some of the most notable and flagrant examples of workplace safety issues. The following are some recent examples of companies that have received fines from OSHA of $100,000 or more.

Source: © Bob Kreisel/Alamy.

- A & B Foundry and Machining in Franklin, Ohio, received a total of over $170,000 in fines from OSHA. Among the safety and health violations that led the fines were a lack of appropriate personal protective equipment and a lack of training for employees. OSHA also cited the company for inoperative safety latches on crane hoists and a lack of guarding on machinery, among other safety regulation violations. Following a previous OSHA inspection, the company also was cited for repeat violations, including failure to provide a fire extinguisher and not providing noise and chemical hazards training.

- Environmental Enterprises, Inc. is headquartered in Cincinnati, Ohio, and has facilities in other states. The company is an environmental management and disposal company that specializes in areas such as hazardous waste management and laboratory chemical packaging. OSHA cited the company with 22 safety and health violations, with fines totaling $325,710. OSHA cited the company for lack of training regarding potentially dangerous interactions among materials and tools. This citation came after a fire and explosion at the company killed one worker and severely burned another worker. OSHA also found that the company willfully disregarded legal requirements by failing to develop and implement hazardous waste handling procedures and by not providing training to employees assigned to handle hazardous waste, among other deficiencies. The OSHA safety citations and health citations regarding Environmental Enterprises can be found at:
  - *www.osha.gov/ooc/citations/EEI_Safety_citations.pdf*
  - *www.osha.gov/ooc/citations/EEI_Health_citations.pdf*
- IVEX Protective Packaging is headquartered in Canada and has facilities in numerous locations. The IVEX operation in Sidney, Ohio, manufactures polyethylene foam and was found to have 21 safety violations, receiving fines from OSHA totaling $128,700. An explosion at the company injured three workers and caused significant damage to the factory. Overall, OSHA concluded that the company has disregarded safety standards and failed to adequately train workers. Citations against the company included lack of detailed operating procedures for its equipment, lack of employee training on equipment operation and maintenance, and not providing flame-retardant clothing for workers exposed to fire hazard, among other safety shortfalls.
- Brillo Motor Transportation received fines totaling $131,000 after terminating one of their truck drivers. The driver had already exceeded the federal limit for allowable driving hours. When the driver refused to violate the law and take on another delivery, he was terminated. OSHA's judgment was that the company's action was to intimidate a worker and could place the worker and public at risk. OSHA's resolution of this case included reinstatement of the driver, paying the driver back wages, and payment of compensatory and punitive damages.

The Managerial Perspective

The examples in the chapter opener dramatically illustrate the devastating consequences of paying insufficient attention to safety concerns and social responsibility. Ensuring a safe working environment is legally mandated. More importantly, it is an obligation for any socially responsible manager. Safety and health must be a priority in all that you do.

An organizational culture that places a greater value on speed or saving money than on safety can result in workplace accidents—some that involve the loss of human life. To disregard safety and health issues can cause more than fines for an organization. It can sever the trust between workers and management, irretrievably damage employee commitment and performance, and ruin an organization's reputation. Managers, then, must understand safety and health issues and take steps to maintain a safe work environment with the help of HR staff.

In this chapter, we consider the contemporary context of the safety and health issue and how managers build and develop safe and healthy working conditions. First, we deal with the legal issues of workplace safety and health by exploring management's legal obligations to fund a workers' compensation system and to provide a safe and healthy workplace. Next we examine a variety of contemporary safety and health issues, including AIDS, violence in the workplace, cumulative trauma disorders, fetal protection, dangerous chemicals, and the use of genetic testing on employees. Finally, we describe and evaluate programs designed to maintain employee safety and health.

Sources: Based on *McClatchy Tribune Business News.* (2013, June 22). Company fined $325,710 for 22 violations after worker dies from burns; Smith, S. (2013). Lack of PPE among 33 OSHA violations at A & B foundry and machining. *EHS Today*, accessed on September 28, 2013 at *http://ehstoday.com/osha/lack-ppe-amond-33-osha-violations-b-foundry-machining*; *McClatchy Tribune Business News.* (2013, July 28). Company fined $128,700 by OSHA; Whistler, D. (2013). Fleet ordered to pay $131,000 to driver terminated for refusing to violate HOS rules. *Fleet Owner*, accessed on September 28, 2013 at *http://fleetowner.com/regulations/fleet-ordred-pay-131000-driver-terminated-refusing-violate-hos-rules*.

Learn It!

If your professor has chosen to assign this go to **www.mymanagementlab.com** to see what you should particularly focus on, and take the chapter 16 warmup.

Workplace Safety and the Law

The most recent data from the Bureau of Labor Statistics indicates that approximately 3 million people were injured on the job in 2011 and in 2012, 4,383 workers died.[1] The number of on-the-job fatalities and injuries has been decreasing in the United States. Part of the reason for the decline in workplace injuries and deaths is hopefully due to improved safety and health conditions in workplaces. However, part of the decline in workplace injuries and fatalities could be due to fewer hours worked in industries that have had a high incidence of worker injuries and fatalities, such as construction.

All levels of government have passed numerous laws to regulate workplace safety. Many of these laws include detailed regulations dealing with work hazards in specific industries such as coal mining and railroads. However, two basic sets of workplace safety laws affect most workers: the various workers' compensation laws at the state level and the Occupational Safety and Health Act of 1970 (OSHA) at the federal level. The objectives, policies, and operations of these two sets of laws are very different.

Each state has its own workers' compensation law, so the provisions for funding and enforcing the law differ by state. As we discussed in Chapter 12, the main goal of the workers' compensation system is to provide compensation to workers who suffer job-related injuries or illnesses. Workers' compensation laws have no safety regulations or mandates, but they do require employers to pay for workers' compensation insurance. Because insurance costs are higher for employers with more workplace accidents and injuries, employers have a financial incentive to create and maintain a safe work environment.

In contrast, OSHA is a federal law designed to make the workplace safer by ensuring that the work environment is free from hazards. The act mandates numerous safety standards and enforces these standards through a system of inspections, citations, and fines. Unlike the workers' compensation laws, however, OSHA does not provide for the compensation of accident victims.[2]

Workers' Compensation

In the early 1800s, people injured on the job went without medical care unless they could afford to pay for it themselves and they rarely received any income until they could return to work. Employees who sued their employers for negligence had little hope of winning, because under U.S. common law the courts habitually ruled that employees assumed the usual risks of a job in return for their pay. In addition, under the *doctrine of contributory negligence*, employers were not liable for an employee's injuries when that employee's own negligence contributed to or caused the injury. And under the *fellow-servant rule*, employers were not responsible for an employee's injury when the negligence of another employee contributed to or caused the injury.

In the early years of the twentieth century—after a host of workplace disasters, including a 1911 fire in a New York City shirt factory that killed more than 100 women—public opinion pressured several state legislatures to enact *workers' compensation* laws. The workers' compensation concept is based on the theory that work-related accidents and illnesses are costs of doing business that the employer should pay for and pass on to the consumer.[3] Since 1948, all states have had workers' compensation programs. These state-administered and employer-funded programs are designed to provide financial and medical assistance to employees injured on the job.

The stated goals of the workers' compensation laws are:[4]

- Providing prompt, sure, and reasonable medical care to victims and income to both victims and their dependents.
- Providing a "no-fault" system in which injured workers can get quick relief without undertaking expensive litigation and suffering court delays.
- Encouraging employers to invest in safety.
- Promoting research on workplace safety.

To be eligible for an award from the workers' compensation system, an employee's injury must have occurred in the course of his or her employment. Sometimes serious accidents, even death, can occur in the workplace, but the accident may not be directly due to the performance of the job. Is the employer still liable for this unfortunate outcome? In many of today's workplaces, job descriptions are more ambiguous and broader than ever before. What is really inside or outside someone's job responsibilities is often not clear. This breadth and ambiguity can encourage flexibility and broad commitment in the workplace, but it may also have the unintended consequence of increasing an employer's exposure to liability for accidents that may occur.

THE BENEFITS OF WORKERS' COMPENSATION Workers' compensation benefits compensate employees for injuries or illnesses occurring on the job. These benefits are:[5]

- ***Total disability benefits*** Partial replacement of income lost as the result of a work-related total disability.
- ***Impairment benefits*** Benefits for temporary or permanent partial disability, based on the degree and duration of the impairment. Injuries are classified as scheduled or nonscheduled. Scheduled injuries are those in which a body part (such as an eye or a finger) is lost; there is a specific schedule of payments for these injuries. Unscheduled injuries are all other injuries (such as back injuries); these are dealt with on a case-by-case basis.
- ***Survivor benefits*** In cases of work-related deaths, the worker's survivors receive a burial allowance and income benefits.
- ***Medical expense benefits*** Workers' compensation provides medical coverage, normally without dollar or time limitations.
- ***Rehabilitation benefits*** All states provide medical rehabilitation for injured workers, and many states provide vocational training for employees who can no longer work at their previous occupation as the result of a job-related injury or illness.

THE COSTS OF WORKERS' COMPENSATION The cost to employers of workers' compensation insurance is directly affected by accidents, with premiums that can increase dramatically and stay high for years as a result of a single injury.[6] Workers' compensation insurance is based on payroll, but premiums paid are modified by an organization's safety record. Workers' compensation insurance premiums average from around 2 percent to more than 4 percent per $100 of wages, but the rate can be much higher in some industries, such as construction.[7]

Unfortunately, the workers' compensation system is subject to fraud by both employers and employees. On the employer side, some companies try to avoid the cost of paying workers' compensation premiums by simply breaking the law and not insuring their employees. An audit in Florida, for example, found that 13 percent of employers did not have workers' compensation insurance. Because premiums are based on payroll, some employers underreport their payroll.[8]

Employee fraud in various forms can also occur. One particularly graphic example of an apparently fraudulent workers' compensation claim involved a worker at a Target store in New Jersey. The worker claimed head and neck injury and was found with boxes around her that had apparently fallen off from a shelf. However, security cameras in the store show that she had arranged the boxes, hit herself in the head with a package of batteries, and ate crackers and a beverage and vomited the material.[9] The claimant now faces criminal charges for fraud and could be sentenced to years of jail time.

Data analytics software is being used by a number of insurance firms to detect possible fraud.[10] However, managers also have a responsibility to confirm workers' compensation claims and reduce fraud. The Manager's Notebook, "Keep 'Em Honest: Preventing Workers' Comp Fraud," further considers fraud possibilities and offers preventative management actions.

Although the occurrence of fraudulent claims should be reduced as much as possible, it is the cause for legitimate workers' compensation claims that should be a central focus of responsible management. If the causes for injuries can be identified and reduced, the costs of the injuries and workers' compensation claims would also be reduced. For example, overexertion is a top cause of workplace injuries.[11] Common examples of overexertion include heavy lifting, pushing, or pulling. Given the prevalence of overexertion injuries, and thus of worker compensation claims, it makes business sense to address those issues, such as correct lifting techniques, that may reduce injury rates and costs. Overexertion is a common cause of injury across companies and industries, but the top causes of injury differ across companies. To effectively manage and control injuries and their costs, managers need to know the causes of injuries at their company and then address them.

Infrequent types of injuries can sometimes be more important than common ones. For example, repetitive motion injuries (such as carpal tunnel syndrome) can result in expensive and lengthy absences from work.[12] Thus, it is important for a manager to consider both frequency as well as costs when determining where to focus attention and resources.

The Occupational Safety and Health Act (OSHA)

Changing political and social values during the 1960s added considerable momentum to the movement to regulate workplace safety. In 1969, the death of 78 coal miners in a mine explosion galvanized public opinion and led to the passage of the Coal Mine Health and Safety Act to regulate mine health and safety.[13] Although no single event is responsible for the passage of the **Occupational Safety and Health Act of 1970 (OSHA)**, the dramatic increase in reported injury rates and workplace deaths during the 1960s (reflecting the inability of workers' compensation laws to give employers adequate incentives to maintain a safe work environment) was probably the major impetus.[14] During the latter part of that decade, the federal government reported that job-related accidents killed more than 14,000 workers and disabled nearly 2.5 million workers annually. In addition, an estimated 300,000 new cases of occupational diseases were being reported every year. OSHA was passed to address the staggering economic and human costs of workplace accidents and health hazards.[15]

Occupational Safety and Health Act of 1970 (OSHA)
A federal law that requires employers to provide a safe and healthy work environment, comply with specific occupational safety and health standards, and keep records of occupational injuries and illnesses.

OSHA's Provisions

OSHA is fairly straightforward. It imposes three major obligations on employers:

- ***To provide a safe and healthy work environment*** Each employer has a general duty to provide a place of employment free from recognized hazards that are likely to cause death or serious physical harm. This *general duty provision* recognizes that not all workplace hazards can be covered by a set of specific standards. The employer is obligated to identify and deal with safety and health hazards not covered by specific regulations.[16]
- ***To comply with specific occupational safety and health standards*** Each employer must become familiar with and comply with specific occupational standards (OSHA's rules deal with specific occupations rather than with industries), and must make certain that employees comply as well.
- ***To keep records of occupational injuries and illnesses*** Under OSHA, employers must record and report work-related accidents and injuries. Organizations with eight or more employees must keep records of any occupational injury or illness resulting in death, lost

work time, or medical treatment and retain these records for five years. The injuries and illnesses must be recorded on OSHA forms and posted annually on an employee bulletin board for all to see. The records must also be made available to OSHA compliance officers, and annual summaries must be prepared.[17] Because record-keeping requirements have been unclear on some points, OSHA issued revised record-keeping standards that are meant to be more flexible and easier to follow.[18] You can view current online materials in English and Spanish by visiting OSHA's Web site at *www.osha.gov*.

MANAGER'S NOTEBOOK

Keep 'Em Honest: Preventing Workers' Comp Fraud

Ethics/Social Responsibility

The number of workers' compensation claims has been going down, but the percentage of claims that are considered questionable has increased. Questionable claims are those that are given closer review and investigation due to the possibility of fraud. A fraudulent workers' compensation claim, if it is accepted as legitimate, can allow the employee to collect compensation while not working. Or, the employee could get another job and collect two incomes. Whatever the motives, fraudulent workers' compensation claims are illegal and unethical. Certainly, valid worker compensation claims need to be supported. However, if fraudulent claims are supported, the increase in claims can increase the premium that the employer is required to pay. There can also be negative effects on the morale and work ethic of the other workers who may suspect or know that a fraudulent claim has occurred and a fellow worker is now being paid for not working.

As a manager, you have a responsibility to take steps to limit fraudulent worker compensation claims and assure that your workers perceive that there is a level playing field in regard to such claims. From a management perspective, it is useful to recognize that workers' compensation fraud can take a number of forms. Probably most obviously, workers' compensation fraud can involve a claim of an injury that is exaggerated or did not occur. Fraudulent workers' compensation claims also occur when a worker is injured when not at work but claims that it happened while on the job. Additionally, fraud can occur through malingering, a situation in which the worker may have suffered a legitimate injury, but continues to display symptoms in order to extend the collection of benefits.

The following are some actions that managers can take to reduce fraudulent claims:

- ***Keep the workplace safe*** A safe work environment lowers the chance of accidents. A safe workplace can also make it more difficult for someone to fake an accident.
- ***Educate employees about the workers' compensation system*** Workers should understand the purpose of the system and how it supports workers with legitimate injury claims. However, they should also understand that there are costs to the employer and that abuse of the system is not a free benefit, but causes real costs for the business. Employees should be made aware of the consequences of fraud and know how to report fraud.
- ***Communicate with the claimant and with others familiar with the incident*** Sharing genuine concern for the employee's well-being is an important management action. However, communication with the injured worker and others can help to confirm that the claim is valid.
- ***Stay in contact with employees on workers' compensation leave*** Let injured employees know that you are looking forward to their return to work. Being proactive in encouraging and helping employees return to work can help to maintain a good relationship with workers who have made a legitimate injury claim. Failed attempts to contact a worker on leave can indicate a possible problem and should be documented. Maintaining communication with employees on leave can also provide some pressure for those who might engage in malingering.

Sources: Based on *Safety Compliance Letter.* (2008, August). Eight tips for managing fraud, 12; Ceniceros, R. (2010). Comp fraudsters working while collecting benefits. *Business Insurance, 44,* 1; Abriola, J. J. (2013, July 1). 4 steps to limiting workers' comp fraud. *Property Casualty 360—National Underwriters*; PR Newswire. (2013, September 24). NICB: Questionable workers' compensation claims increase. ■■

Under the new standard, failure to keep either written or electronic records can result in fines and citations. Falsifying records can result in a fine and a six-month prison sentence. The revised standard also makes it clear that an accident that *could* have caused injury—not just one that *did* cause injury—should be recorded. In other words, close calls count under the OSHA standard.

In addition, the standard clarifies who is an employee under OSHA. For example, a temporary worker from an employment agency doing clerical work for an organization is considered an employee of that organization. However, an independent contractor is an employee only if the business hires and supervises the person. Thus, the Perfect Lawn landscaping crew is not likely to be considered a law firm's employees, but a software specialist the firm hires from an employment agency probably is. This distinction is important because an employer is responsible for keeping records on its employees.

Employees also have responsibilities under OSHA. Although they cannot be cited for violations, they must comply with the relevant safety and health standards. They should also report all hazardous conditions, injuries, or work-related illnesses to their employer. Employee rights under OSHA include the right to file safety or health grievances and complaints to the government, participate in OSHA inspections, and request information on safety and health hazards without fear of discrimination or retaliation by their employer.[19]

Under both OSHA and state *right-to-know regulations*, employers must provide employees with information about hazardous substances in the workplace.[20] OSHA's hazardous substance regulation, known as the **Hazard Communication Standard**, is explained in the Web page reproduced in Figure 16.1.

Hazard Communication Standard
An OSHA standard that gives employees the right to know about hazardous chemicals in the workplace.

The U.S. Supreme Court has upheld an employee's right to refuse to work under conditions where the employee reasonably believes there is an immediate risk of injury or death.[21] If the hazard is of a chemical nature, another federal agency may also be relevant. The Chemical Safety and Hazard Investigation Board, funded by Congress in 1997, is charged with promoting safety and preventing incidents of chemical release.[22] The board works closely with OSHA and the Environmental Protection Agency. A hazard in the form of a chemical spill would result in an accident investigation by the board. The focus of the board is to then make recommendations to companies and government agencies regarding changes in process or equipment that would prevent similar accidents.

Three agencies administer and enforce OSHA: the *Occupational Safety and Health Administration* (the OSH Administration, also known by the acronym *OSHA*), the *Occupational Safety and Health Review Commission (OSHRC)*, and the *National Institute for Occupational Safety and Health (NIOSH)*. States with federally approved safety plans have their own regulatory apparatus.

The Occupational Safety and Health Administration

The Occupational Safety and Health Administration has the primary responsibility for enforcing OSHA. It develops occupational standards, grants variances to employers, conducts workplace inspections, and issues citations and penalties.

- ***Occupational standards*** Occupational standards, which cover hazards ranging from tools and machinery safety to microscopic airborne matter, can be exceedingly complex and detailed. Although many standards are clearly reasonable and appropriate, OSHA has frequently been criticized for adopting infeasible standards or standards whose costs exceed their benefits. The courts, however, generally do not require OSHA to balance the costs and benefits of particular standards, only to demonstrate their feasibility.[23] Some criticize OSHA for not having standards. For example, the agency has been criticized for a lack of specific standards on **combustible dust**.[24] See the Manager's Notebook, "Danger in the Dust," for information about combustible dust and its regulation.

  The development of occupational standards can begin with OSHA, NIOSH, state and local governments, or a variety of other sources, including industry groups and labor organizations. Proposed new standards are published in the *Federal Register*, the official legal news publication of the U.S. government. Comments from interested parties are sought, and hearings regarding the standards may be held. The full text of any adopted standard and the implementation date are then reported in the *Federal Register*.[25]

combustible dust
Dust from sources such as sugar, coal, wood, or flour that can explosively combust.

UNITED STATES DEPARTMENT OF LABOR

All DOL | OSHA | Advanced Search | SEARCH

A to Z Index | En Español | Contact Us | About OSHA

OSHA | QuickTakes Biweekly Newsletter | RSS Feeds | Print This Page | Text Size

Occupational Safety & Health Administration | We Can Help | What's New | Offices

Home | Workers | Regulations | Enforcement | Data & Statistics | Training | Publications | Newsroom | Small Business | OSHA

Hazard Communication

What is Hazard Communication?

Chemicals pose a wide range of health hazards (such as irritation, sensitization, and carcinogenicity) and physical hazards (such as flammability, corrosion, and reactivity). OSHA's Hazard Communication Standard (HCS) is designed to ensure that information about these hazards and associated protective measures is disseminated. This is accomplished by requiring chemical manufacturers and importers to evaluate the hazards of the chemicals they produce or import, and to provide information about them through labels on shipped containers and more detailed information sheets called material safety data sheets (MSDSs). All employers with hazardous chemicals in their workplaces must prepare and implement a written hazard communication program, and must ensure that all containers are labeled, employees are provided access to MSDSs, and an effective training program is conducted for all potentially exposed employees.

The HCS provides people the right-to-know the hazards and identities of the chemicals they are exposed to in the workplace. When employees have this information, they may effectively participate in their employers' protective programs and take steps to protect themselves. In addition, the standard gives employers the information they need to design and implement an effective protective program for employees potentially exposed to hazardous chemicals. Together these actions will result in a reduction of chemical source illnesses and injuries in American workplaces.

- Frequently Asked Questions: Hazard Communication (HAZCOM). OSHA. Provides answers to frequently asked questions, and references applicable interpretation and compliance letters.
- Hazard Communication Standard. OSHA Fact Sheet 93-26, (1993, January). Provides a summary of the HCS standard which applies to all workers exposed to hazardous chemicals in all industrial sectors.
- Hazard Communication Guidelines for Compliance. OSHA Publication 3111, (2000). Also available as a 112 KB PDF, 33 pages. Aids employers in understanding the Hazard Communication Standard and in implementing a hazard communication program.
- Chemical Hazard Communication. OSHA Publication 3084, (1998). Also available as a 248 KB PDF, 31 pages. Answers several basic questions about chemical hazard communication.
- Report of the Hazard Communication Workgroup to the National Advisory Committee on Occupational Safety and Health (NACOSH). OSHA, (1996, September 12). Contains comments and recommendations concerning hazard communication.

Safety and Health Topics

Hazard Communication
- What is Hazard Communication?
- OSHA Standards
- Hazard Determination
- HAZCOM Program
- Globally Harmonized System of Classification
- Additional Information
- Credits

Content Reviewed 12/29/2008

Accessibility Assistance

Contact the OSHA Directorate of Standards and Guidance at 202-693-1950 for assistance accessing PDF materials.

Freedom of Information Act | Privacy & Security Statement | Disclaimers | Customer Survey | Important Web Site Notices | International | Contact Us

U.S. Department of Labor | Occupational Safety & Health Administration | 200 Constitution Ave., NW, Washington, DC 20210
Telephone: 800-321-OSHA (6742) | TTY: 877-889-5627
www.OSHA.gov

FIGURE 16.1

OSHA's Hazard Communication Standard

This excerpt from the OSHA Web site explains that employers must tell their employees how OSHA's hazard communication standard is being put into effect in their workplace.

MANAGER'S NOTEBOOK

Danger in the Dust

Dust may seem innocuous, maybe a housekeeping annoyance, but certainly not a safety hazard. Unfortunately, that is not the case. The reality is that dust from sources such as sugar, coal, wood, and flour production can be combustible if there is an ignition source or sufficient friction. A tragic explosion at a sugar refinery illustrates how deadly dust can be. In February 2008, the Imperial Sugar refinery in Port Wentworth, Georgia, suffered a horrific and fatal explosion. An explosion caused by sugar dust killed 14 workers and injured dozens of others. In 2010, Imperial Sugar announced that it had reached a settlement with OSHA and will pay a penalty totaling $6.05 million.

The dust explosion at Imperial Sugar is not an isolated occurrence. More recently, an explosion of combustible grain dust at a flour mill in North Carolina in April, 2013, collapsed several brick walls and seriously injured a worker. Over the past 25 years, there have been more than 280 dust-related explosions or fires. These incidents have resulted in 119 fatalities and more than 700 injuries. When a combustible dust is airborne and at a sufficient concentration, a flame, spark, or static electricity can result in an explosion.

OSHA is currently working on standards with regard to dust combustion. In the meantime, OSHA has contended that employers have a responsibility to provide a safe workplace and the agency has applied these general standards to regulate the accumulation of combustible dust and ventilation. OSHA has been proactive in regard to addressing the hazard of combustible dust. You can find a poster regarding combustible dust at the following OSHA Web site: *www.osha.gov/Publications/combustibledustposter.pdf.*

Sources: Based on Rubinger, J. (2013). Fight back! Combustible dust. *FeedandGrain.com*, accessed August 2, 2013; *Occupational Hazards.* (2008). Should OSHA adopt a combustible dust standard? *70*, 15–16; O'Rourke, M. (2008). Ashes to ashes, dust to dust. *Risk Management, 55*, 20; *Professional Safety.* (2008). OSHA activity on combustible dust standards. *53*, 22; *Business Wire* (2020, July 7). Imperial Sugar settles OSHA citations. New York; Maxell, M. A. (2010, February). Combustible dust: What you need to know. *Material Handling Management*, 25.

- ***Variances*** Employers may ask OSHA for a temporary (up to one year) variance from a standard when they cannot comply with a new standard by its effective date. OSHA may grant a permanent variance from a particular standard when an employer can demonstrate that it has in place alternatives that protect employees as effectively as compliance with the standard would.[26]
- ***Workplace inspections*** OSHA has the power to conduct workplace inspections to make sure that organizations are complying with OSHA standards. Because it would be impossible to inspect each of the hundreds of thousands of affected workplaces each year, OSHA has established an inspection priority system that calls for inspections to be made in the following order:[27] (1) situations involving "imminent danger" in the workplace; (2) incidents resulting in fatalities or hospitalization of five or more employees; (3) follow-up of employee complaints of unsafe or unhealthful working conditions; and (4) "high-hazard" industries and occupations (for example, mining, farming, construction, and transport).

  OSHA inspectors have the right to enter an establishment without notice to examine work environment, materials, and equipment, and to question both employers and employees. However, this right conflicts with the employer's constitutional protection from warrantless searches. In a 1978 case involving a company's refusal to allow an OSHA inspection until the agency could produce a search warrant, the Supreme Court ruled that the employer does have a right to demand a search warrant before OSHA can make an inspection. Although OSHA can generally obtain a search warrant based on an employee complaint or on the agency's own inspection priority system, some argue that forfeiting the element of surprise makes inspection less effective because it gives employers a means to alter unsafe conditions or practices (for example, erratically using safety equipment) until after the inspection.[28]
- ***Citations and penalties*** OSHA may issue citations and impose penalties for any violations of OSHA standards. The exact penalty varies with the employer's good faith attempts to comply with OSHA regulations, its history of previous violations, the seriousness of the infraction, and the size of the business. These penalties may include criminal penalties as well as substantial fines. In fact, executives of firms that recklessly endanger workers can spend time in jail.[29] For example, five senior executives of Chicago Magnet Wire Company were prosecuted for causing workers' illnesses by allowing them to be exposed to hazardous chemicals, and a supervisor at Jackson Enterprises in Michigan was convicted of involuntary manslaughter in an employee's work-related death.[30]

Fines for violations of OSHA standards may range from no fine for minor violations to mega fines of several million dollars for companies guilty of numerous, repeated, and willful infractions. However, companies can object to OSHA's proposed penalties and may be able to negotiate a lower fine. For example, OSHA fined a BP plant in Augusta, Georgia, when three workers died in an explosion of molten plastic. OSHA accused BP of willfully violating safety rules and fined the company $141,000. BP negotiated a lower classification of violation and paid $119,000 in fines.[31] Critics contend that the negotiation process can yield lowered fines that don't provide companies with enough incentive to improve the safety levels of their operations. OSHA, however, contends that its primary focus is on improving workplaces to protect workers, not on punishing companies.

An important question is whether these fines have any meaningful impact on organizations. One approach to answering this question is to see whether the announcement of fines levied by OSHA has any impact on the value of the firm's stock. If there is no such impact, top executives have little incentive to improve safety and health conditions and avoid future fines. Research suggests that the announcement of OSHA penalties does have a significant negative impact on the firm's stock.[32] However, the downturn in stock prices is a short-term effect that occurs only in the day or two after the announcement of the penalties. Furthermore, it appears that it is simply the announcement of a violation, not the amount of the fine, that impacts the company's stock price.

OSHA offers a free consultation service that works with small businesses to help them identify potential workplace hazards and improve safety management systems. This service is especially useful for small businesses. It provides for a confidential inspection—completely separate from OSHA's inspection program—that does not result in penalties or fines. However, the employer is obligated to correct serious safety and health hazards found in the inspection.

Further information about the consultation service can be found at *www.osha.gov/Publications/3357consultation-sm.pdf*, but the basic procedure works as follows:[33]

1. The employer must contact the OSHA consultant to get things started.
2. An opening conference is scheduled at the work site to discuss the consultant's role and the employer's obligations under the service.
3. Employer and consultant examine workplace conditions together. The consultant may talk to employees, discuss OSHA standards with them, and point out safety problems.
4. In a closing conference, the consultant reviews the findings of the inspection with the employer, detailing both what the employer is doing right and where improvement is needed.
5. After the closing conference, the consultant provides a written report explaining the findings and confirming proposed times within which the employer is to remedy hazards found in the inspection. (These are known as *abatement periods.*)

A QUESTION OF ETHICS

Opponents of "Big Government" claim that excessive regulation of workplace safety hurts productivity and increases costs. They argue that in a free market, employees should be responsible for their own health and safety—that they should be free to choose between taking a wage premium for hazardous work and accepting lower pay for safer work. Would such a policy be ethical? What are its pros and cons?

THE OCCUPATIONAL SAFETY AND HEALTH REVIEW COMMISSION (OSHRC) OSHRC operates independently of OSHA and reviews its citations. An employer can appeal an OSHA citation, an abatement period, or a penalty to OSHRC. Rulings made by this commission can be appealed only through the federal court system.[34]

THE NATIONAL INSTITUTE FOR OCCUPATIONAL SAFETY AND HEALTH (NIOSH) NIOSH exists mainly to research safety and health problems and to assist OSHA in the creation of new health and safety standards. Like OSHA, NIOSH may inspect the workplace and gather information from employers and employees about hazardous materials. In addition, NIOSH trains inspectors and others associated with the enforcement of OSHA.[35]

STATE PROGRAMS OSHA permits states to create their own occupational safety and health programs, and many states have chosen to do so. OSHA will approve a state plan if the state shows that it is able to set and enforce standards, provide and train competent enforcement personnel, and give educational and technical assistance to business. Upon approval of a state program, OSHA funds 50 percent of that program's operating costs and passes primary enforcement responsibility to the state. OSHA continually monitors and evaluates state programs and may withdraw approval if it determines that a state is failing to maintain an effective program.[36]

Logging workers	127.8
Commercial fishing	117
Iron and steelworkers	37
Refuse and recyclable materials collectors	27.1
Farmers and ranchers	21.3
Construction workers	17.4

FIGURE 16.2

Death Rates* for Selected Occupations

*Rates are annual deaths per 100,000 workers.

Source: Based on Bureau of Labor Statistics. (2012). Occupations with high fatal work injury rates, preliminary 2012 data. *www.bls.gov/iif/oshwc/cfoi/cfch0011.pdf.*

THE EFFECTIVENESS OF OSHA Has OSHA been an effective tool for creating a safer and healthier workplace? OSHA's critics suggest that its detailed and expansive regulations produce costs that exceed their benefits. However, many other people feel that while the OSHA-related costs borne by employers are direct and easy to measure, the benefits of an accident-free workplace are not. They point out that it is accident victims—employees—who bear the costs of an absence of health and safety regulations, not the employer.

Indeed, the costs of accidents and illness can be immense. The good news is that there is evidence that the regulations, penalties, and increased awareness brought about by OSHA have significantly improved workplace safety. The Bureau of Labor Statistics' data for 2012 show that workplace fatalities are at their lowest levels since it started collecting workplace fatality data in 1992.[37] Similarly, the rate for injury and illness has declined and is at a historically low level. Nonetheless, some occupations remain dangerous. Figure 16.2 shows the death rate for some of the deadliest occupational areas in the United States.

Managing Contemporary Safety, Health, and Behavioral Issues

Effectively managing workplace safety and health requires far more than reducing the numbers of job-related accidents and injuries. In practice, managers must deal with a variety of practical, legal, and ethical issues, many of which involve a careful balancing of individual rights (particularly the right to privacy) with the needs of the organization (see Chapter 14). Because these issues often give rise to legal questions, HR professionals are frequently called upon to develop and implement policies to deal with them. Among the issues facing employers today are dealing with AIDS in the workplace, workplace violence, cumulative trauma disorders, hearing impairment, fetal protection, hazardous chemicals, and genetic testing.

It is important to recognize that, in addition to these direct challenges, there is also the challenge of employee commitment to safety and health programs. Many organizations face the problem of employees ignoring and even being hostile to safety and health measures. The reason: Employees often view safety and health measures as intrusive and inefficient.

Top managers can generate commitment to safety and health programs by explaining to supervisors and others the rationale for the relevant safety and health practices. For example, it is important that everyone understand the cost of accidents to the organization. Furthermore, the costs (such as fines) for violating safety and health standards should be clearly explained to employees at all levels. Once people understand the link between safety measures and the business's bottom line, resistance to safety programs should largely disappear. Of course, removing human resistance to any kind of program can be a difficult and delicate process that requires time and commitment.

AIDS

Dealing effectively with workplace concerns that arise when an employee contracts acquired immunodeficiency syndrome (AIDS) has become an important workplace health challenge. In the early 1980s, AIDS was scarcely known, but by 1996 the Centers for Disease Control and Prevention reported that two-thirds of organizations with more than 2,500 employees had already experienced an employee with this disease or HIV (the human immunodeficiency virus that leads to AIDS).[38]

Most people in China who have HIV have lost their jobs and cannot find work due to their HIV status.[39] China is now wrestling with the HIV issue, and pressure is mounting to legislate protection against discrimination for Chinese workers with HIV. A sign of a possible shift against HIV discrimination is reflected in a 2012 Chinese court decision regarding an aspiring teacher. The court found the teacher was unlawfully denied employment due to his positive HIV status. The court ordered that damages be paid to the teacher, making him the first person in China to win compensation for HIV employment-related discrimination.[40]

There are federal guidelines regarding AIDS that require organizational compliance. The major sources of these guidelines are OSHA and the Americans with Disabilities Act (ADA).

- ***Create an Exposure Control Plan.*** An exposure control plan must be written and updated annually for all jobs that involve potential exposure to blood and body fluids. The plan should identify risks and preventive techniques.
- ***Provide Training.*** Annual training regarding bloodborne infection needs to be completed by employees who might be exposed to infection while performing their jobs. Unless a medical response can be guaranteed in less than four minutes (a guarantee that would be difficult to make in most situations), training should also include first aid and cardiopulmonary resuscitation (CPR).
- ***Make Available Appropriate Personal Protective Equipment.*** Gloves, masks, and other protective gear need to be available if an accident involving blood or bodily fluid occurs.
- ***Install Bloodborne Pathogen Protection Kits.*** Protection kits typically include protective items such as gloves, shoe covers, and masks. Clean-up items, such as towels, absorbent powder, disinfectant, and biohazard bags should also be in a kit.

FIGURE 16.3

Key Components of OSHA's Bloodborne Pathogens Standards

Sources: Based on *Business Wire.* (2013, March 28). Six essential steps to reducing the impact of a bloodborne pathogen incident; Howe, M. A., Brewer, J. D., and Shane, S. D. (2013). If not you, who? Responding to emergencies in physical education and physical activity settings. *Journal of Physical Education, Recreation, and Dance, 84,* 47–52; McLaughlin, S. B. (2012). Top 10 troubles. *Health Facilities Management, 25,* 39–41; Mitchell, B. (2013). Protecting your people, property and posterior: The top 11 errors in emergency planning. *Security, 50,* 38–39.

OSHA In 1992, OSHA issued the Bloodborne Pathogens Standards, a set of standards meant to lower the accidental occurrence of bloodborne infections, such as HIV and hepatitis. The standards were revised in 2001 and provide steps that must be followed in all workplaces where employees can reasonably be expected to come in contact with blood or other body fluids. For example, people who are in the environmental health, safety, or emergency response professions, among others, fall under this standard. OSHA requires all workers who may come into contact with infectious bodily fluids to be educated about bloodborne pathogens and trained in how to reduce the risks of infection. This preparation should help workers reduce their risks and employers' health care costs. Figure 16.3 summarizes key management steps based on the OSHA standards.

ADA AND THE MANAGER'S ROLE According to ADA guidelines, having HIV infection or AIDS does not necessarily prevent people from performing the essential functions of most jobs.[41] Thus, organizations must make reasonable accommodations for infected employees. Reasonable accommodation might include adjustments to work schedules or workstation modifications. For example, one company gave a manager with AIDS a chair that converted into a sleeping recliner and allowed a 90-minute break in the afternoon.[42] The chair allowed the manager to deal with the drop in his energy level in the afternoon. The manager scheduled all meetings in the morning and came into work extra hours on evenings and weekends, if needed. This arrangement was reasonable and provided an important accommodation for the manager at minimal cost.

ADA guidelines also affect the hiring process. Employers cannot ask job candidates about their HIV or AIDS status or require job candidates to take an HIV test before making a job offer. Testing *can* be done and questions posed after a job offer is made. However, test results must be kept confidential. The job offer cannot be withdrawn on the basis of a positive HIV test unless the employer can demonstrate that the person would pose a direct threat to coworkers or customers and that this threat could not be eliminated through reasonable accommodation. Such demonstration would be all but impossible in most jobs.

In addition to complying with the guidelines issued by federal agencies, some organizations choose to proactively address the AIDS issue by developing an AIDS policy and education programs. Educational programs can provide accurate information about the disease and how it is transmitted. The Manager's Notebook, "Proactive Approaches to AIDS in South Africa," offers examples of companies that go beyond compliance with guidelines in their efforts to deal with AIDS in the workplace.

MANAGER'S NOTEBOOK

Global

Proactive Approaches to AIDS in South Africa

Southern Africa, a beautiful area at the southern tip of the African continent, is in the midst of an HIV/AIDS epidemic. The percentage of adults in this area with HIV exceeds 17 percent, one of the highest rates of infection in the world. While this region accounts for approximately 10 percent of the world's population, it is estimated that over 60% of deaths from AIDs have occurred in Southern Africa. This epidemic has had many negative effects, including reduced life spans and lowered productivity.

Business has been part of the effort to turn around the epidemic and improve the situation in the region. Heineken, Volkswagen, and BMW are examples of companies doing business in the nation of South Africa that have developed notable approaches to HIV/AIDS.

Given the limited public health care available in South Africa, Heineken's operations there provide company health care to the local staff. In the 1990s, Heineken set up a network of in-house clinics that include doctors, nurses, lab technicians, and pharmacists as part of Heineken's staff. The initial internal focus at Heineken broadened to include the local communities. In 2008, Heineken established a foundation that focuses on improving the health of people in the local South African communities where Heineken has operations.

Volkswagen of South Africa has received awards for its efforts to reduce the spread of HIV/AIDS in the region. The company's HIV/AIDS program focuses on prevention, treatment, and care. Their internal program includes an ongoing awareness campaign that emphasizes accurate information and support. A quarterly employee newsletter provides updated information on HIV/AIDS. The program also uses voluntary peer educators to assist in raising awareness and understanding among employees. Volkswagen South Africa provides full medical examinations for employees and has on-site employee assistance practitioners who provide support and counseling. Experts estimate that 11 percent of the country's population, or 5.5 million people, are infected with the HIV virus. The epidemic has cut life expectancy in South Africa to 51 years. Social responsibility requires businesses in South Africa to be proactive about the epidemic and to be part of the larger solution. Volkswagen and BMW are two examples of companies doing business in South Africa that have developed notable approaches to HIV/AIDS.

Volkswagen South Africa employs over 6,000 people in South Africa. The company's HIV program, which has an annual budget of $167,000, provides the following:

- Medical services for employees and their family members
- Antiretroviral therapy for employees and their family members
- Free condoms for employees

BMW South Africa employs approximately 3,000 workers. BMW's HIV/AIDS program features the following components:

- Peer educators
- Training and workshops
- Free condoms
- Voluntary HIV/AIDS counseling and testing
- Antiretroviral therapy

Sources: Based on Anyanwu, J. C., Siliadin, Y. G., and Okonkwo, E. (2013). Role of fiscal policy in tackling the HIV/AIDS epidemic in Southern Africa. *African Development Review*, *25*, 256–275; Chicoine, L. (2012). Aids mortality and its effect on the labor market: Evidence from South Africa. *Journal of Development Economics*, *98*, 256–269; Van Cranenburgh, K. C., and Arenas, D. (2013, June 17). Strategic and moral dilemmas of corporate philanthropy in developing countries: Heineken in sub-Saharan Africa. *Journal of Business Ethics*, published online; Commended: Volkswagen South Africa, case study available at *www.gbchealth.org/commended-company-2012-volkswagen-south-africa*, accessed on October 2, 2013; Bolton, P. L. (2008). Corporate responses to HIV/AIDS: Experience and leadership from South Africa. *Business and Society Review*, *113*, 277–300. ■■

As illustrated in the Manager's Notebook, increasing awareness and educating workers can be positive and proactive steps taken by companies. However, as an upcoming manager, you should be aware that there are boundaries to discussion of AIDS-related issues. Specifically, the ADA includes strict confidentiality provisions in regard to employee medical information. Confidential medical information can be disclosed to supervisory personnel only if they need to know for purposes of providing reasonable accommodation or to safety personnel who might be required to provide emergency medical services to the employee.[43] An employer who discloses an employee's medical condition, such as AIDS, risks violating the employee's right of privacy and the right to work without discrimination as provided by the ADA. Open discussion of the issue of AIDS in the workplace can help create a positive and productive environment, but disclosure of an employee's AIDS status is legally prohibited.

Violence in the Workplace

Media coverage can paint a picture of homicides in the workplace—particularly those carried out by disgruntled current or former employees—to be a fairly common occurrence. Statistics on workplace homicides indicate that it is a relatively infrequent occurrence. According to the Bureau of Labor Statistics, there were 463 homicides that occurred in the workplace in 2012. In addition to the fairly low number, the frequency of workplace homicides has decreased in recent years. The number of workplace homicides in 1994, for example, was 1,080.

Nonlethal violence is a much more common workplace threat than homicide. According to Bureau of Justice statistics, from 1993 to 2000 the average annual number of people who were victims of violent crimes while working was 1.7 million.[44] Violence in the workplace can be lethal or nonlethal and can take a variety of forms, including assaults, threats, and sabotage. Whatever the severity or type, recognizing the threat of violence remains an important workplace issue.[45]

REDUCING ASSAULTS AND THREATS Approximately half of U.S. organizations with 1,000 or more employees report the occurrence of workplace violence. However, approximately 70 percent of U.S. companies do not have policies regarding workplace violence.[46] Proactive management that assesses risks and puts a policy in place should prevent the occurrence of violence in the workplace. Although a criminal trying to rob a business or a disgruntled former employee may seem obvious risks that should be addressed in an organization, another source of risk is domestic violence.

Domestic violence is probably viewed by many people as a private issue, but it can impact the workplace. One study has estimated that one third of domestic violence incidents happen in workplaces, from parking lots to offices.[47] Just how widespread is the problem of domestic violence? Approximately 26 percent of women in the workplace identify themselves as victims or survivors of domestic violence.[48] Domestic violence affects the employee's well-being as well as the company's bottom line. Domestic violence can adversely affect an employee's performance through absenteeism, tardiness, poor performance, and mistakes on the job.

Some states and companies are being proactive about domestic violence. Laws protecting domestic violence victims in the workplace have been put in place in 14 states and in various municipalities. The law in the state of Illinois, for example, offers broad protection for victims of domestic violence. In Illinois, employers with 15 or more employees are prohibited from discriminating or retaliating against domestic violence victims and have a responsibility to make reasonable accommodations for victims, such as transferring the employee and changing phone numbers and work schedules.[49] The clothing retailer Macy's West provides training for managers and sales associates that addresses how to detect warning signs of domestic violence and how to respond to the issue.[50] Liz Claiborne is another company using preventive management to reduce domestic violence. The company trains its managers in how to spot and respond to domestic violence. It also maintains a domestic violence response team that deals with victims. In two years, the company handled more than 40 cases that required more action than simply a referral.

Implementing a workplace violence policy and taking a preventive approach should lower the risk of violence erupting at work. However, the threat can still arise. The Manager's Notebook, "Management Suggestions Regarding Domestic Violence," provides suggestions to help manage a workplace threat due to domestic violence.

REDUCING THREATS FROM SABOTAGE Another form of workplace violence is sabotage. Sabotage is not physical violence, but just the same, it is a violent act. Acts of sabotage can be directed either at a person, such as attempts to damage someone's career, or at an organization, such as attempts to damage equipment or reputation. Most sabotage includes an aspect or motive of revenge. Angry and bitter employees have done everything ranging from putting rodents into food products and needles in baby food to starting company fires and wiping out computer databases.[51]

MANAGER'S NOTEBOOK

Ethics/Social Responsibility

Management Suggestions Regarding Domestic Violence

Domestic violence can spill into the workplace, affecting the abuse victim and others. The following are some management suggestions when there is an identifiable domestic violence threat:

- Request that local law enforcement patrol the workplace, particularly at the beginning and end of an abuse victim's shift.
- Provide closer parking for the abuse victim so that he or she has a shorter walk into the building. Extra parking lot patrols at the beginning and end of each work shift can be an effective use of resources.
- If an escort for the employee to and from the parking lot seems like a good idea, provide someone who is competent in this task. Unless he or she has security training, an escort shouldn't just be the nice person in the office.
- Use monitoring and detection devices, such as surveillance equipment. They can give immediate warning of an on-site problem.
- Temporarily move the employee to another site or work station.
- In an extreme case, provide the employee time off through an administrative leave or sick leave.

For additional information and help with developing policies to prevent workplace tragedies due to domestic violence, go to *www.workplacesrespond.org*.

Sources: Based on Gurchiek, K. (2005). Study: Domestic violence spills over into the workplace. *HRMagazine, 50,* 32, 38; Savard, D., and Kennedy, D. B. (2013). Responding to intimate partner violence in the workplace. *Security Journal, 26,* 249–263; Twigg, T., and Crane, R. (2009). Ending the silence on domestic violence in the workplace. *Dental Economics, 99,* 33–34. ■■

The frequency and prevalence of sabotage is difficult to assess. However, experts suggest that sabotage is increasingly a problem for organizations. Many saboteurs are disgruntled former employees who, as the victims of downsizing or termination, feel underappreciated and unfairly treated by their former employers. Disgruntled employees who retaliate by doing damage to a computer system pose a major concern in organizations.

Whatever form workplace violence may take, managers need to take responsibility for reducing or eliminating violence in the workplace. To this end, they must be sensitive to the causes of workplace violence. Many people feel pressured in their jobs and fear layoffs. Workplace events such as negative performance appraisals, personality conflicts with coworkers or managers, or personal problems such as a divorce add to this existing stress level, and a potentially dangerous person may emerge.

Certainly, managers cannot eliminate all these pressures, which are realities of everyday life in modern organizations. However, they can make sure that employees are treated fairly. Treating employees as though they are expendable will not create commitment to the company and could be enough to trigger a violent reaction. Managers should deal with performance problems by focusing on the behavior and future improvement, rather than condemning the person for past performance problems (see Chapter 7 on performance appraisal). Managers should never discipline employees in front of coworkers; doing so can humiliate the person and incite a violent reaction.[52]

Managers should also take steps to reduce the possibility of hiring workers who might be prone to violence. For example, interviewers might ask job candidates to describe how they reacted to a past management decision they did not agree with and why they did so.[53] The responses to this question and follow-up questions could be quite revealing. Also, interviewers should check for evidence of substance abuse or emotional problems, which might be indicated by careless driving or DWI (driving while intoxicated) entries on driving records. Unexplained gaps in a person's employment history should be carefully examined. Avoiding a **negligent hiring** charge requires thorough background checks.[54]

negligent hiring
Hiring an employee with a history of violent or illegal behavior without conducting background checks or taking proper precautions.

Cumulative Trauma Disorders

Cumulative trauma disorders (CTDs) are also called repetitive stress (or motion or strain) injuries (or illnesses or syndromes). CTDs refer not to one disorder, but rather to a wide array of maladies, from *carpal tunnel syndrome (CTS),* which often affects the wrists of computer keyboard users, to tennis elbow and forearm and shoulder complaints.[55] It has been estimated that CTDs account for more than 16 million lost workdays annually in the United States, with a cost of more than $40 billion.[56]

cumulative trauma disorder (CTD)
An occupational injury that occurs from repetitive physical movements, such as assembly-line work or data entry.

Managers should take steps to reduce CTDs by educating workers and altering the physical arrangement of the workplace if necessary. Figure 16.4 presents suggestions for a production workplace layout that should reduce the likelihood of CTDs. Many of these suggestions can be adapted for nonproduction workers.

Source: © Phorovir/Alamy.

Hearing Impairment

It is widely recognized that loud noise can lead to loss of hearing. However, consistent exposure to loud noise of 95 decibels has also been found to be related to elevated blood pressure and various digestive, respiratory, allergenic, and musculoskeletal disorders. Exposure to loud noise has also been found to lead to disorientation and reduction of eye focus, possibly leading to an increase in the rate of accidents and injuries.[57] Evidence regarding the potential negative health effects of loud noise led OSHA to develop the Occupational Noise Exposure standard. This standard requires organizations to provide hearing protectors free to employees who are exposed to an average of 85 decibels of noise or greater. Regardless of this standard, research findings indicate that, on average, fewer than 50 percent of employees who should wear hearing protectors actually wear them.[58] Furthermore, many employees who wear hearing protectors don't wear them correctly. Part of the problem in dealing with the prevention of hearing loss is getting employees to recognize and take seriously the threat that noise can pose to hearing acuity.

Efforts to prevent hearing loss should not be limited to getting employees to protect their hearing. Reducing the amount of noise in the work environment is a direct and primary way of preventing hearing loss. Although noise reduction isn't always possible, many organizations are finding that new machinery often offers the advantage of quieter operation.[59] Efforts to prevent hearing loss need to be broad-based and include consideration of both system (machinery) and person (employee) factors. The Manager's Notebook,

FIGURE 16.4

Suggestions to Lower the Incidence of CTDs Do

Sources: Based on *Material Handling Management.* (2008). Seven ways to fit the task to the worker, *63*, 34–35.

Do:

- Make certain work surface heights are comfortable and can accommodate chair heights, people sizes, and needed movements.
- Place all supplies and tools within easy reach.
- Keep work below heart level to reduce muscle fatigue.
- Match light intensity to the task so that errors, straining, and fatigue are reduced.
- Adjust work equipment to the worker and the task.

"Say What? Management Steps to the Prevention of Hearing Loss," identifies basic steps for preventing hearing damage in the workplace.

Fetal Protection, Hazardous Chemicals, and Genetic Testing

During the 1970s and 1980s, a handful of large U.S. firms developed workplace policies designed to prevent pregnant employees from exposure to hazardous chemicals that might damage the fetus. These policies were controversial because they tended to restrict women's access to some of industry's better-paying jobs. For example, in 1978 several women working for American Cyanamid underwent sterilization rather than risk losing highly paid jobs.

MANAGER'S NOTEBOOK

Customer-Driven HR

Say What? Management Steps to the Prevention of Hearing Loss

Hearing damage can be invisible and can take years to be recognized. When workers are exposed to excessive workplace noise, hearing loss can get worse over time, but usually only in small increments. It may not be noticed on a day-to-day basis. Given its silent and insidious nature, it is important that management take a proactive approach to limiting hearing loss. Below are some basic steps for developing a hearing loss prevention program.

1. ***How noisy is the environment?*** The first step is to determine the noise level in the workplace. Noise levels that require people to raise their voices to have a conversation could indicate a problem level of noise. However, you can't rely on subjective judgment. You need to use a sound-level meter to determine the levels of noise that workers are exposed to.
2. ***Reduce the noise levels!*** If there is excessive noise, the next logical step is to try to reduce it. Possibilities here include replacement with new machinery that may be significantly quieter or shielding the existing sources of noise.
3. ***Protect the hearing of individual workers*** While reducing overall noise levels helps everyone avoid hearing loss, wearing hearing protection protects only the wearer. To the extent that noise levels can't be sufficiently reduced, the next option is to provide workers with hearing protection.
4. ***Train workers to wear the hearing protection properly*** If workers don't wear hearing protection correctly, it probably won't be doing an adequate job to protect their hearing. Make sure they know how to wear it correctly.
5. ***Motivate workers to wear hearing protection*** Some workers may not want to wear hearing protection. As a manager, you need to make clear that avoiding hearing loss is an important goal to which the organization is committed. You can demonstrate this commitment with the use of brochures, posters, and other sources of information. You can also provide recognition, money, or prizes for work teams whose members are all wearing hearing protection.

Sources: Based on Vallee, L., Ruddy, M., and Bota, K. (2020). Can you hear me now? *Professional Safety, 55,* 26–32. Selwyn, B. (2020). Noise measurement and control. *Professional Safety, 55,* 16–18; Safety Director's Report (2002); Hearing protection strategies for any safety department budget. May newsletter of the Institute of Management and Administration. ■■

The fetal protection controversy came to national attention in 1982 when Johnson Controls, a battery manufacturer, prevented women of childbearing age from working in jobs involving contact with lead. The union sued Johnson Controls for sex discrimination because the company's policy restricted only female employees. The Supreme Court ruled against the company, finding it guilty of illegal sex bias.[60]

This decision caused great concern among companies like General Motors, DuPont, Monsanto, and others with fetal protection policies. These companies argue that their only alternative is to greatly reduce the use of certain substances. But reducing the use of these compounds, they claim, would be both difficult and costly. Critics counter that these companies should do more to protect *all* workers, not simply remove some dangerous substances from the workplace.[61]

Reproductive health concerns are an important workplace issue with the potential to affect thousands of employers and millions of workers. For example, one study of 1,600 pregnant women showed that those who used the old-style video display terminals (VDTs) heavily had a miscarriage rate double that of women who do not use monitors. A study of pregnant women at a Digital Equipment plant in Houston reached a similar conclusion. While old-style VDTs are less common today, the issue still exists in areas that still employ this old technology.[62] The fetal health issue is compounded by the fact that only a handful of companies have comprehensive fetal health policies and research about the effects of many industrial compounds on reproductive health is inconclusive or incomplete. Although some substances (for example, lead) represent clear health threats to fetuses, exposure to many other compounds may not cause problems. However, certain compounds may present significant reproductive hazards to *both* sexes, not just women.

HAZARDOUS CHEMICALS Many thousands of workplace accidents and injuries reported each year have been attributed to exposure to toxic chemicals. In the past, workers were often required to handle chemicals without being fully informed of the hazards involved. In 1983, however, OSHA's hazard communication standard gave employees the right to know about hazardous chemicals in the workplace (see Figure 16.1). The current standard requires manufacturers and users of hazardous chemicals to identify the chemicals, provide employees with information about them, and train employees in understanding the dangers and in how to handle them.[63]

Determining whether a substance might have hazardous effects and the levels at which toxicity is a concern can be a difficult task that requires sorting through a variety of sources. To help streamline this process, the U.S. Department of Labor and health professionals have developed an online decision-support system. The purpose of the system, called **Haz-Map**, is to help users recognize and prevent diseases caused by chemical and biological agents in the workplace.[64] Haz-Map is a useful tool for preventing toxic exposures and for identifying occupational diseases. The site is available to the public at *http://hazmap.nlm.nih.gov/index.html*. An example window from the Web site is presented in Figure 16.5. The site can be searched by hazardous agent as well as by job.

Haz-Map
An online decision support system for recognizing and preventing diseases caused by chemical and biological agents in the workplace.

GENETIC TESTING A new and controversial tool is **genetic testing**, which can be used to identify employees who are genetically susceptible to illness or disability. In 2008, federal legislation was passed that protects employees in regard to genetic testing. The Genetic Information Nondiscrimination Act (GINA) prohibits employers from discriminating against employees on the basis of genetic information. Employers are not allowed to request, require, or buy genetic information. GINA also prohibits health insurers from basing eligibility or premiums on the basis of genetic information.[65]

genetic testing
A form of biological testing that identifies employees who are genetically susceptible to illness or disability.

Safety and Health Programs

We have devoted most of the chapter thus far to discussing physical hazards in the workplace and their impact on both workers and the organization. However, other hazards have major effects on workers, including stress, unsafe behaviors, and poor health habits. To cope with both physical and other types of hazards, companies often design comprehensive safety and health programs.

Safety Programs

A safe working environment does not just happen—it has to be created. The organizations with the best reputations for safety have developed well-planned, thorough safety programs. Concern for safety should begin at the highest level within the organization, and managers and supervisors at all levels should be charged with demonstrating safety awareness, held responsible for safety training, and rewarded for maintaining a safe workplace. Although support for safety has to start at the top, no one knows better than the employees about the job, its risks, and what could be improved. The input and participation of line workers is critical to an effective safety program.[66]

Companies with comprehensive safety programs are likely to be rewarded with fewer accidents, fewer workers' compensation claims and lawsuits, and lower accident-related costs.

Search [ ] as Agent Disease Job Text Search

Haz-Map Search | More Searches | Haz-Map Help | Glossary | References

Browse Haz-Map Search TOXNET

Agent Name	Methyl alcohol
Alternative Name	Methanol
CAS Number	67-56-1
Formula	C-H4-O
Major Category	Solvents
Synonyms	Carbinol; Columbian spirits; Pyroligneous spirit; Wood alcohol; Wood naphtha; Wood spirit; Methanol; [NIOSH] UN1230
Category	Alcohols and Polyols
Description	Colorless liquid with a characteristic pungent odor; [NIOSH]
Sources/Uses	Used as a solvent, alcohol denaturant, antifreeze, and chemical intermediate; [ACGIH] Naturally present in blood and urine and in fruits and vegetables; [CHEMINFO] Used in paint removers, windshield-washing solutions, and duplication fluids; [Olson, p. 260]
Comments	Methanol poisoning can cause blindness and death. The lethal oral dose in humans is 2 to 8 ounces. Most cases have occurred after ingestion. Methanol poisoning after inhalation or skin absorption in the workplace has been reported. [ACGIH] Symptoms of methanol poisoning include initial CNS depression and vomiting followed by metabolic acidosis and severe vision impairment 8-24 hours later. Coma, respiratory failure, and death may ensue. [CHEMINFO] In high-dose reproductive studies in animals, methyl alcohol causes testicular damage and birth defects. [Frazier, p. 179-80] Patients may present with inebriation and gastritis. There is a characteristic latency of 6-30 hours after exposure. Combined osmolar and anion gaps suggest poisoning by methanol or ethylene glycol, but also may occur in severe alcoholic ketoacidosis or diabetic ketoacidosis. [Olson, p. 33]
Exposure Assessment	
BEI	Methanol in urine = 15 mg/L; sample at end of shift;
Skin Designation (ACGIH)	Yes
TLV (ACGIH)	200 ppm
STEL (ACGIH)	250 ppm

FIGURE 16.5
Example Haz-Map Web Page

PEL (OSHA)	200 ppm
MAK	200 ppm
IDLH (NIOSH)	6000 ppm
Excerpts from Documentation for IDLHs	Two human studies showed no effects at vapor concentrations ranging from 160 to 1,000 ppm [McAllister 1954; MDOH 1937]. It has been stated that it probably would be dangerous to be exposed to concentrations of the order of 30,000 to 50,000 ppm for as much as 30 to 60 minutes [Patty 1963].
Vapor Pressure	96 mm Hg
Odor Threshold Low	4.2 ppm
Odor Threshold High	5960 ppm
Lethal Concentration	LC50 (rats) = 64,000 ppm/4 hr
Explanatory Notes	Detection odor threshold from AIHA (mean = 160 ppm); Flash point = 54 deg F; [CAMEO]
Flammability (NFPA)	3: may ignite at ambient temperature
Adverse Effects	
Neurotoxin	Other CNS Neurotoxin
Reproductive Toxin	Yes
Links to Other NLM Databases	
Health Studies	Human Health Effects from Hazardous Substances Data Bank: METHANOL
Toxicity Information	Search TOXNET
Chemical Information	Search ChemIDplus
Biomedical References	Search PubMed
Related Information in Haz-Map	
Processes	Industrial Processes with risk of exposure: • Painting (Solvents) • Semiconductor Manufacturing • Silk-Screen Printing
Activities	Activities with risk of exposure: • Sculpturing plastics • Smoking cigarettes

FIGURE 16.5 (Continued)

Source: http://hazmap.nlm.nih.gob/category-details?id=13&table=copytblagents.

Keep in mind that OSHA considers employee involvement a key feature of a successful safety program. Organizations often involve employees by establishing a safety committee. Although the specific details may vary, the overall purpose of a safety committee is to have employees and managers collaborate to promote workplace safety and health.[67] Safety committees typically evaluate the adequacy of safety procedures; monitor findings and trends; review accidents, illnesses, and safety suggestions; and recommend and evaluate hazard solutions. However, experts recommend that safety committees do not enforce the policies, or they risk being viewed as the "safety police." Instead, the committees should make recommendations that management should implement and enforce.

The creation of safety action teams at Alberto Culver provides an example of the potential that can be realized by including employees in the safety-improvement process.[68] Alberto Culver used safety committees but rarely consulted with employees closest to the work situation—forklift drivers, shipping clerks, and packers. That all changed when the company initiated its first safety action team in 1999. The team collaborated with frontline workers with the purpose of leveraging their knowledge to improve workplace safety. This first team operated in one plant, and within one year the recordable injury rate at the plant dropped by 44 percent and lost time decreased by 70 percent. The results were undeniable, and the safety action team at Alberto Culver (now Unilever) was expanded to 46 global improvement teams involving 425 employees.

Employee Assistance Programs (EAPs)

As we saw in Chapter 13, *employee assistance programs (EAPs)* are programs designed to help employees whose job performance is suffering because of physical, mental, or emotional problems. EAPs address a variety of employee problems ranging from drug abuse to marital problems. Recent surveys indicate that EAPs are offered by most companies, but many workers, approximately 20 percent, do not know their companies offer them.[69] EAPs have the potential to provide effective assistance, but only if employers make their availability known to workers.

Many organizations create EAPs because they recognize their ethical and legal obligations to protect not only their workers' physical health but their mental health as well. The ethical obligation stems from the fact that the causes of organizational stress—climate, change, rules, work pace, management style, work group characteristics, and so forth—are also frequently the causes of behavioral, psychological, and physiological problems for employees.[70] Ethical obligation becomes legal obligation when employees sue the company or file workers' compensation claims for stress-related illnesses. In fact, much of the heightened concern about dealing with the consequences of workplace stress stems from the increasing incidence and severity of stress-related workers' compensation claims and their associated costs.[71]

burnout
A stress syndrome characterized by emotional exhaustion, depersonalization, and reduced personal accomplishment.

Stress often results in **burnout**, a syndrome characterized by emotional exhaustion, depersonalization, and reduced personal accomplishment.[72] People who experience burnout may dread returning to work for another day, treat coworkers and clients callously, withdraw from the organization, and feel less competent in their jobs. Some of the factors that may lead to burnout include ambiguity and conflict when dealing with various job-related issues and problems.[73] A lack of social support can aggravate these effects.

Burnout can lead to serious negative consequences for the individual and for the organization and can have a negative impact on mental and physical health.[74] Mental health problems resulting from burnout can include depression, irritability, lowered self-esteem, and anxiety. Physical problems can include fatigue, headaches, insomnia, gastrointestinal disturbances, and chest pains. Organizational outcomes associated with burnout include turnover, absenteeism, and a decrease in job performance.[75] In addition, sometimes burnout leads to increased drug and alcohol use.[76]

Depression is another topic that merits consideration in any discussion of EAP issues. Clinical depression is a serious mental illness and a bigger problem in the workplace than many people realize. Dr. Ronald Kessler, a health care policy professor at Harvard Medical School, states that depressed workers report "having problems with time and motion, lifting things, and having accidents on the job."[77] Research is consistent with this observation and suggests that depressed workers may be more prone to accidents due to lack of concentration, fatigue, memory difficulties, and slower reaction time. In addition to possible accident-proneness, depression has been linked to decreased productivity. Depression can be treated with counseling and medication, but you should leave this treatment to professionals by referral to your EAP or other source for help.

A manager should refer an employee to an EAP solely on the basis of a performance problem and for no other reason. The case of a manager at a Lucky Stores grocery store illustrates this point.[78] The manager had been a star performer, but employees started complaining about his abusive and hostile manner. Company representatives asked whether he was having "problems" and offered him assistance. He denied having problems, and a transfer to another store did not improve the situation. He was then offered a leave of absence if he contacted the company's EAP. The EAP staff determined he was suffering from stress and diagnosed a mental illness. He was fired after six months of leave.

The store manager brought suit against the company and the court found that although he was not disabled, the company may have perceived him to be disabled. Therefore, the former manager may have had a claim under the ADA. The company and former manager reached an out-of-court settlement. The message of this and some similar cases is that referral to an EAP should be based on work-related performance issues, rather than on inferences or conclusions about the worker's mental or emotional well-being.

Wellness Programs

Whereas EAPs focus on *treating* troubled employees, **wellness programs** focus on *preventing* health problems. Wellness programs have become a popular employee benefit in the United States, with one survey finding that 64 percent of employers offered a wellness program.[79] Wellness programs are also growing in popularity outside of the United States, with approximately 40 percent of employers in Europe, Asia, and Africa now offering this benefit.[80]

wellness program
A company-sponsored program that focuses on preventing health problems in employees.

A complete wellness program has three components:

1. It helps employees identify potential health risks through screening and testing.
2. It educates employees about health risks such as high blood pressure, smoking, poor diet, and stress.
3. It encourages employees to change their lifestyles through exercise, good nutrition, and health monitoring.

Source: © Scott Griessel/Fotolia.

Wellness programs may be as simple and inexpensive as providing information about stop-smoking clinics and weight-loss programs or as comprehensive and expensive as providing professional health screening and multimillion-dollar fitness facilities. Companies are beginning to find that social media is a cost effective means for implementing a wellness program. The Manager's Notebook, "A Social Approach to Wellness," describes recent wellness programs that utilize social media.

MANAGER'S NOTEBOOK

A Social Approach to Wellness

Technology/Social Media

Social media is being integrated into wellness programs, ranging from its use as a marketing tool to a platform for delivering the program.

- ***Social media as a marketing tool*** VCU Medical Center in Richmond, Virginia, used a Facebook campaign to help market its mammography campaign to its female employees. The medical center found the approach to be very cost effective and was very pleased to see a 40% increase in mammograms following its program.
- ***Social media as a delivery platform*** Sprint and Blue Shield of California provide examples of wellness programs that utilized a social networking platform. For its first wellness program on a national scale, Sprint partnered with ShapeUp, a wellness software company, to offer the program. Sprint challenged its U.S. employees to a 12-week "Get Fit" program in which employees could form teams, log their progress online, and challenge each other. Approximately 16,000 of the company's 40,000 employees registered for the program. Only about 45% of those who registered completed the full 12 weeks, but Sprint is positive about the results. During those 12 weeks, Sprint employees lost over 40,000 pounds of weight and logged over 4 billion steps.

Similar to the Sprint approach, Blue Shield of California offered its employees an eight-week fitness challenge via social media. Approximately 1,300 employees walked more than 400 million steps (the equivalent of 200,000 miles).

- ***Other social media–based wellness tools*** There are an increasing number of social media–based wellness tools. In addition to ShapeUp, other companies that offer wellness software include Keas and Limeade. Not all of the social media platforms offer the same features or prices, so it is worth shopping around.

Sources: Based on Davis, A. (2012). Sprint expands wellness through social media. *Employee Benefit News, 26*, 45; Marshall, L. (2011, October). Gain insight into member needs with social media tools. *Managed Healthcare Executive*, 45–46; Rafter, M. V. (2012). Starting a social wellness program. *Workforce Management, 91*, 38. ■■

A QUESTION OF ETHICS

Some feel that wellness and employee assistance programs should be evaluated on a cost–benefit basis and discontinued if these programs' benefits do not exceed their costs. Others feel that because companies create many of the stressful conditions that contribute to employee health problems, they are ethically bound to continue providing these types of programs. What do you think?

THE REWARDS OF GOOD HEALTH HABITS Wellness programs, if implemented effectively, can make a positive contribution to the bottom line in an organization. Although there are costs to starting and maintaining a wellness program, the return in terms of reduced health care costs and absenteeism can greatly offset the investment. A recent study tracked the return on investment for a wellness program at a Midwest utility company.[81] Although the study focused on only one organization, it included over 2,000 employees and looked at the effectiveness of the wellness program over a nine-year period. The findings support wellness programs as a good investment. The overall return on investment was 157 percent, with financial savings from reduced health care costs and less time away from work well exceeding the cost of the wellness program.

These kinds of results indicate that wellness efforts can pay off in tangible ways. In addition, although it may be difficult to measure, people claim that they work better when they feel better and can often better solve problems and be more productive after an exercise break.

Summary and Conclusions

Workplace Safety and the Law

There are two sets of workplace safety laws: (1) workers' compensation, an employer-funded insurance system that operates at the state level, and (2) the Occupational Safety and Health Act (OSHA), a federal law that mandates safety standards in the workplace.

Workers' compensation—which consists of total disability, impairment, survivor, medical expense, and rehabilitation benefits—is intended to ensure prompt and reasonable medical care to employees injured on the job, as well as income for them and their dependents or survivors. It also encourages employers to invest in workplace safety by requiring higher insurance premiums from employers with numerous workplace accidents and injuries.

OSHA compels employers to provide a safe and healthy work environment, to comply with specific occupational safety and health standards, and to keep records of occupational injuries and illnesses. Its safety standards are enforced through a system of inspections, citations, fines, and criminal penalties.

Managing Contemporary Safety, Health, and Behavioral Issues

The most significant safety, health, and behavioral issues for employers are AIDS, violence in the workplace, cumulative trauma disorders, fetal protection, hazardous chemicals, and genetic testing. In all of these areas, line managers must deal with a variety of practical, legal, and ethical questions that often demand a careful balancing of individual rights (especially privacy rights) with the needs of the organization.

Safety and Health Programs

Comprehensive safety programs are well-planned efforts in which management involves employees. Employee assistance programs (EAPs) are designed to help employees cope with physical, mental, or emotional problems (including stress) that are undermining their job performance. Wellness programs are preventive efforts designed to help employees identify potential health risks and deal with them before they become problems.

Key Terms

burnout, 548
combustible dust, 534
cumulative trauma disorder (CTD), 543
genetic testing, 545
Hazard Communication Standard, 534
Haz-Map, 545
negligent hiring, 543
Occupational Safety and Health Act of 1970 (OSHA), 532
wellness program, 549

Watch It!

Herman Miller: Employee Safety. If your instructor has assigned this, go to **mymanagementlab.com** to watch a video case and answer questions.

Discussion Questions

16-1. What is the difference between the objectives of workers' compensation and the objectives of OSHA?
16-2. What kinds of policies do you think would work best to prevent workplace violence?
16-3. Do you think that OSHA standards for combustible dust are needed? Why or why not?
16-4. If a job is potentially hazardous to the fetus of a pregnant employee, should it be legal for the company to restrict the job to men?
16-5. How could genetic testing be used to discriminate?
16-6. How can managers use the organization's reward system to encourage workplace safety?
16-7. Do you think that wellness programs are worth their cost to a company? Explain.
16-8. It was argued in this chapter that an empowerment approach to improving safety could yield positive results. The operation of consultative safety teams including employees was used as an example. However, a participative approach to safety improvement means employee time away from other duties and decreased productivity. Do you think the trade-off may be worth it? Why or why not?
16-9. One of your colleagues argues that domestic violence isn't a concern of the business. Do you agree or disagree? Explain.
16-10. Do you think social media is a useful way for offering a wellness program? Why or why not? What major characteristics do you think a social media–based wellness program should have?

MyManagementLab®

If your instructor has assigned this, go to **mymanagementlab.com** for the following Assisted-graded writing questions::

16-11. Some jobs involve hazards. Some employers pay a higher wage for those jobs, but safety and health regulations suggest that may not be enough. What other basic steps should an employer take to assure worker safety?
16-12. Describe how social media can be used in employee wellness programs.
16-13. Describe why management should address violence in the workplace. Identify a couple of steps that management might take to reduce the threat of workplace violence.

 You Manage It! 1: Ethics/Social Responsibility

Standing Up to Workplace Bullies

As discussed in this chapter, violence in the workplace can take a variety of forms. One form that can be relatively subtle but that can wreak havoc in the workplace is bullying. Just what is bullying? In general, workplace bullying might be described as abrasive or intimidating employee behavior. The Workplace Bullying and Trauma Institute defines *bullying* as repeated, health-harming mistreatment that could include verbal abuse; threatening, humiliating, or offensive behavior; or work interference.

If this type of treatment was directed at a member of a protected class, the bullying could be found to be illegal discrimination. However, if the victim is not a member of a protected class, antidiscrimination law will not offer any protection, at least in the United States. Canada, Australia, and Europe have passed antibullying laws. Workplace antibullying legislation has been introduced in at least 16 states, but none have been passed into law. A federal antibullying law would protect everyone, not just certain subgroups of employees. Critics fear that antibullying legislation could result in liability for employers and a huge number of lawsuits. They also argued that bullying cannot be defined precisely enough, which makes it difficult to outlaw.

Although it may be difficult to define, a recent survey found that 37 percent of employees feel that they have been bullied at work. Research has also found that workers who have been bullied tend to be less satisfied with their jobs, have greater anxiety, and are more likely to quit their jobs. Some accountants have also reported in a recent limited survey that they are more likely to alter numbers in reports when they are pressured by bullies.

Although bullying may not be in violation of federal or state law, organizations that want to be an employer of choice and have effective work teams and a high level of productivity shouldn't tolerate it. Goodwill of Southern California provides an example of what an organization can do to prevent or stop workplace bullying. Goodwill established an interpersonal misconduct policy as a means to operationalize its strategic values of respect, integrity, service, and excellence. Goodwill's policy states that interpersonal misconduct is an individual's behavior that bullies, demeans, intimidates, ridicules, insults, frightens, persecutes, exploits, and/or threatens a targeted individual and would be perceived as such by a reasonable person. Goodwill is targeting patterns of this type of behavior, rather than focusing on isolated incidents. The organization has terminated employees who have violated the policy.

Critical Thinking Questions

16-14. Is workplace bullying different from discrimination? Explain.

16-15. Is workplace bullying different from sexual harassment? Explain.

16-16. Do you think legislation would be an effective tool for managing workplace bullying? Why or why not?

16-17. How could you develop a workplace culture that doesn't tolerate bullying?

16-18. How could you estimate the cost of workplace bullying?

Team Exercise

16-19. A British Workplace Behaviour Survey explored prevalence of a wide range of behaviors that comprise "ill treatment" in the UK workplace. "Ill treatment" included

- 47 percent reported unreasonable treatment
- 40 percent reported denigration and disrespect
- 33 percent experienced both unreasonable treatment and denigration and disrespect
- 6 percent experienced violence

Unreasonable treatment included unmanageable workloads or impossible deadlines, ignoring opinions and views, and withholding information. Denigration referred to being shouted at and treated disrespectfully. The main targets for disrespectful behavior were gay, lesbian, and bisexual employees. Unreasonableness and disrespect are forms of bullying that stop just short of actual violence. It was found that when management ignored behaviors, poor behavior flourished.

As a team, address the issue of measuring bullying in the workplace. How should it be measured? What kind of measurement instrument should be used? How will the criteria be generated? Address these key issues and identify a process that your team would recommend to develop measures of workplace bullying. If possible, generate an example of what a measure might look like. Would it be a rating scale, a checklist, or something else? Also, who would complete the measures? Finally, identify your plan for the resulting data, that is, what would you do with your results? Would you assess individuals with the data? Would you try to identify bullies? What utility would the measurements have?

Share your measurement approach and example with the rest of the class. Describe your management plan with regard to the use of the data. Under the direction of the instructor, the class should select the best measurement approach and the best management plan.

Experiential Exercise: Team

16-20. Workplace bullying can take a variety of forms (see the partial list in the team exercise). With your teammates, identify an episode representing workplace bullying and prepare to role-play this example. Each team presents its role-play example to the class. If needed, the team should explain how the action portrays bullying.

As a class, consider the role-play examples. For each role-play, address what should be done to prevent or eliminate such bullying. (The instructor can lead this class discussion following each role-play.) Also as a class, consider the possible utility of such role-plays. How could the role-play approach be used as part of a program to manage bullying in organizations?

Experiential Exercise: Individual

16-21. Bullying needs to be able to be defined in behavioral terms so that a workplace bullying policy can move from a concept to an operational reality. If bullying could be behaviorally defined, the behaviors could be useful for measuring the occurrence of bullying in a workplace as well as training employees with regard to the kinds of workplace behavior that is not acceptable.

Generate behaviors that illustrate, in your judgment, examples of workplace bullying. In other words, what behavioral incidents would represent examples of workplace bullying? How could these behavioral examples be used in an organization? Share your examples and suggested uses with the rest of the class.

Sources: Adapted from *HR Focus.* (2008). Workplace violence update: What you should know now. *85,* 7–11; Saul, K. (2008). No bullies allowed. *Credit Union Magazine, 74,* 58; Zeidner, R. (2008). Bullying worse than sexual harassment? *HRMagazine, 53,* 28; Greer, O. L., and Schmelzle, G. D. (2009). Are you being bullied? You're not alone. *Strategic Finance, 91,* 41–45.

You Manage It! 2: Emerging Trends

On the Tip of a Beryllium Iceberg?

The Occupational Safety and Health Administration (OSHA) is the agency companies and workers count on, sometimes grudgingly, to make sure that the workplace is a safe as it can be. One of the principal means OSHA uses to ensure workplace safety is by establishing standards for work practices, acceptable levels of chemicals, and so on. Safety isn't just a matter of standards, however; managers and workers must act together to develop a culture of safety so that safety is a guiding value rather than a matter of compliance. What happens, however, if the standards really aren't sufficient to keep people safe? It looks like this may be the case with the standard for exposure to beryllium, and some of the people affected include OSHA's own employees.

Beryllium is an impressive metal: it is lighter than aluminum, yet stiffer than steel. It is an ingredient in atomic bombs and is used in the dental, telecom, and aerospace industries. It shows up in cell phones, computers, cars, and golf clubs. Beryllium is also showing up in recycling operations.

The problem with beryllium is that its dust is toxic. Just a few millionths of a gram can fatally damage lungs and other organs. Exposure to smaller amounts can sensitize the immune system and lead to the development of a disease called *chronic beryllium disease.* Beryllium is increasingly being used in workplaces, but it appears that this use could be placing workers at risk. The National Jewish Medical and Research Center in Denver tests and treats people with chronic beryllium disease. Dr. Lee Newman, a leading expert who works at the Center, considers chronic beryllium disease an unrecognized epidemic whose full extent we have scarcely begun to understand.

A standard for exposure to beryllium exists, but it looks like it may be inadequate to ensure safety. That was the concern of Adam Finkel, an OSHA employee who told a reporter that he thought OSHA was not protecting its own workers from the danger of beryllium. Finkel pushed for tests for all OSHA inspectors. According to Finkel, OSHA's response was to attack and demote him. OSHA denied this charge, and Finkel filed a whistle-blower complaint and settled the case for an undisclosed sum. Perhaps most important, OSHA has since been testing its inspectors for sensitization to beryllium. Of the 271 inspectors tested at the time of this writing, 10 have been found to be sensitized to the metal and are at risk for developing a potentially fatal lung disease. However, as many as 1,000 current and former compliance officers may have been exposed. The largest producer of beryllium, Brush-Wellman Inc. (now Materion Performance Alloys), considers OSHA's current standards to be inadequate. The company has adopted its own exposure standard for airborne beryllium that is one-tenth the level permitted by OSHA.

Critical Thinking Questions

16-22. The beryllium sensitization of OSHA's compliance officers has raised concerns for the thousands of industry workers who are exposed to beryllium. OSHA officers visit the workplaces only sporadically, while industry workers are exposed on a more regular basis. Do you think these workers should be tested for beryllium sensitization? Who should bear the cost of the testing?

16-23. OSHA has been criticized for its inadequate beryllium exposure standards. The agency did try to push through lower exposure limits in the 1970s, but companies stopped passage of the new standards by claiming they couldn't afford to meet the lower standard. Given this history, do you think the companies or OSHA are responsible for today's inadequate exposure standards?

16-24. OSHA could lose credibility with companies over other safety issues due to the beryllium exposure problems. If you were hired as a consultant by OSHA, what would you recommend to reduce the possible damage of the beryllium issue to the agency's reputation and effectiveness?

Team Exercise

16-25. As a team, place yourselves in the position of managers in a company that assesses beryllium. What standard for beryllium exposure would you recommend? Would you defer to OSHA standards, knowing that some of its officers have developed beryllium sensitivity? Or, would you recommend a lower standard? How could this new standard be determined? How should the company go about choosing a safe standard?

Many workers in your company may be concerned, even fearful, regarding their own exposure levels. What are your recommendations for dealing with the concerns of these workers?

As a team, present your recommendations regarding a standard in managing the concerns of the workers. With the guidance of the instructor, the class selects and compiles the best recommendations from the teams.

Experiential Exercise: Team

16-26. It is ironic that OSHA's own officers were exposed to unsafe conditions. More than irony, some people are questioning not only the standards, but the safety culture within OSHA.

Select representatives to serve in the roles of OSHA advisory board members. These representatives are responsible for generating recommendations for OSHA to follow in re-establishing a strong safety culture within the organization. What are the drawbacks if these steps are not taken?

Sources: Adapted from Carey, J. (2005, May). The "unrecognized epidemic": Beryllium can be toxic to the workers who handle it. Where has OSHA been? *BusinessWeek*, 40–42; Minter, S. G. (2005). Erring on the side of disaster. *Occupational Hazards, 67*, 6.

You Manage It! 3: Global

Mental Health: A Global Concern

Hazards in the workplace can pose risks to mental health, just as they can pose risks to physical health. Unfortunately, poor mental health sometimes can have a negative connotation and is often not addressed. Fortunately, the importance of mental health in the workplace is being recognized in multiple countries.

Mental health problems can influence how someone experiences life (including work), how engaged they are, and their effectiveness as an employee. It is estimated that each year one in four people will experience a mental health problem, with depression and anxiety being the most common problems.[a] Further, it is increasingly being recognized that mental health problems can be brought on or exacerbated by workplace conditions. A recent survey found that two-thirds of respondents believe that heavy workloads, unrealistic expectations, and overwork cause or exacerbate mental health problems.

In Europe, stress-related sick leave is estimated to total 91 million working days per year—an enormous loss to European business. Europeans are taking a proactive approach to the problem. In 2005, 52 countries endorsed a "Mental Health Plan for Europe" that highlights the importance of workplace interventions to improve mental health. According to the plan, employers need to recognize and accept mental health as a legitimate concern and take responsibility for minimizing workplace causes of mental health problems. European companies are being advised to conduct an audit or survey to identify workplace characteristics that may be problematic. European companies are also being encouraged to develop mental health policies, take steps to raise awareness and reduce stigma, and introduce preventive and rehabilitative steps. Further description and updates regarding this program can be found online at *www.mhe-sme.org*.

The importance of mental health in the workplace is also being recognized in Canada. A recent Canadian survey of 100 organizations found that over three-quarters of the organizations believe mental health issues are a leading cause of short- and long-term disability claims.[b] Unfortunately, although recognizing the importance of mental health, few Canadian companies seem to be doing much about it. The problem isn't that companies don't want to do anything; they just don't know what actions should be taken to improve employees' mental health. In 2009, the Mental Health Commission of Canada released a report regarding mental health and work titled "Stress at Work, Mental Injury and the Law in Canada: A Discussion Paper for the Mental Health Commission of Canada" (available at *https://www.mentalhealthcommission.ca/English/node/488*). The discussion paper is meant to increase awareness and lead Canadian employers to take on the duty of providing a psychologically safe workplace.

China also recognizes the importance of the mental health of employees. Chinese workers are facing increasing workloads and stress on their jobs, and depression and anxiety are increasing.[c] China announced that it will introduce a program to help employees improve their mental health. The intent of the program is to apply models that have been effective in other countries, such as employee assistance programs, to improve the mental health of Chinese workers. Recently, however, a thirteenth Chinese employee at iPhone-maker Foxconn attempted suicide; ten of the thirteen succeeded in their suicide attempts. Harsh working conditions have been blamed for the rash of suicides.[d]

Critical Thinking Questions

16-27. Mental health problems often have a negative stigma. What, if anything, do you think companies can do to reduce this stigma?

16-28. Recognizing the importance of mental health in the workplace seems like the only moral thing to do. Yet, employers face difficulties in effectively dealing with this area. For example, mental health is less visible and apparent than physical health. How can an employer be protected from feigning and fraud if it takes a liberal approach to dealing with mental health?

16-29. Mental health problems can be caused by many factors outside of the workplace. For example, genetics and family life may predispose or cause mental health difficulties. Nonetheless, these difficulties can show up in the workplace. Does the employer have some responsibility for dealing with these mental health problems? Explain.

Team Exercise

16-30. The European model includes an audit as well as actions to improve mental health. Place yourselves in the position of a mental health task force for a company. As a team, develop steps to address mental health in the workplace. Specifically, what would your team recommend for an audit? What should be measured and how? What actions would you recommend to reduce a negative stigma that can be associated with mental health problems? Finally, identify actions companies can take to improve mental health in the workplace.

Share your team's recommendations with the rest of the class. With the direction of the instructor, the class should put together a combined plan that puts together the best recommendations from the team presentations.

Experiential Exercise: Team

16-31. The increasing importance of mental health in the workplace can be attributed to the characteristics of modern work. Technology has brought about increased efficiency, but also more rapid change and stress. Work must now be accomplished more quickly and often from remote sites. In addition, downsizing and outsourcing have increased pressure and uncertainty for workers. These work characteristics can take their toll on employees' mental health.

However, some experts question whether the workplace has really become more stressful.[e] Work is not meant to be a therapeutic environment. Further, the stress of today's work pales in comparison to working conditions in the past. Previous generations of your family probably worked for little pay, no pension, no health care, and under oppressive conditions. Claiming to be "stressed out" can just be an employee's excuse for time away from work.

Select representatives for two opposing teams reflecting the two positions just described. One team takes the position that mental health in the workplace is an important issue that calls for proactive employer actions. The other team takes the position that mental health is not the employer problem it is made out to be and that special employer actions are not needed. Each team should identify its assumptions and rationale.

As a class, determine whether there was a clear winner to the debate. Is there a consensus in the class on the workplace mental health issue?

Sources: [a]St. John, T. (2005, May). Mental health at work: The hard facts. *Training Journal*, 44–47; [b]Brown, D. (2005). Mental illness a top concern, but only gets band-aid treatment. *Canadian HR Reporter, 18*, 1–3; [c]Xinhua General News Service (2005, June 3). China to introduce special news program for employees' mental health; [d] Foreman, W. (2010, May, 27). Thirteenth employee tries suicide at embattled Chinese factor. *USAToday*. Accessed on December 13, 2010, at *www.usatoday.com/money/world/2010-05-26-foxconnsuicides_N.htm*; [e]Furedi, F. (2005, April 11). Have we become too feeble to cope with life? *The Express* (U.K.), 18.

 You Manage It! 4: Customer-Driven HR

Keeping the Workplace Safe

For every 100 full-time workers, there are, on average, 1.8 assaults reported in the workplace. There are, of course, some industries with higher rates of workplace violence. Social service workers and health service workers experience the highest rates of workplace violence. For example, the average rate of workplace violence in the health care industry is 9 assaults per 100 employees. The elevated rate of incidents of violence in this industry may be less surprising when you consider that front-line health care workers are often working in close proximity with people who may be stressed, under the influence of drugs or alcohol, and often frustrated with wait times. Although rates of violence differ across industries, violent acts can occur in any workplace and cause serious disruption and have lasting effects on employees who had thought that the workplace was a safe environment. As a manager, you have responsibility for the safety of your workers. Possibilities for incidents of violence need to be recognized and reduced as much as possible.

Acts of violence in the workplace can take various forms, such as assaults, robberies, and harassment. Understanding the various types of possible violence can help guide you, as a manager, in effectively taking steps to reduce each type. The Department of Labor classifies workplace violence based on the source of the violence. As summarized in Figure 16.6, the perpetrators of an incident of workplace violence can be an outsider, customer, fellow employee, or someone associated with a fellow employee. Steps you might take, for instance, to reduce threat of violence from an outsider might be quite different from steps to prevent violent acts by coworkers.

Critical Thinking Questions

16-32. What outcomes might be associated with an incident of workplace violence? For example, a worker who experiences abuse and harassment might file a lawsuit against the employer. What other costs might be associated with workplace violence?

16-33. How could you develop a workplace culture that reduces the chances of violence in the workplace?

16-34. Conflict can be a precursor to violence in the workplace. However, supervisors can be reluctant to deal with this warning sign and opt to see whether things work themselves out. Why do you think there is often reluctance to deal with conflict? What would you recommend be done to reduce this reluctance?

Team Exercises

16-35. Consider the four categories of sources of workplace violence. As a team, generate additional examples of each

FIGURE 16.6
Sources of Workplace Violence

Source	Example
Outsider	Criminal
Customer/Client	Abusive Customer
Current/Former Employee	Disgruntled Former Worker
Related to an Employee	Domestic Abuser

source. How likely are each of the possible sources of workplace violence? How severe/important are instances of workplace violence associated with each source? As managers, is there a source that you would focus on first?

a. With your teammates, identify the steps that you would take to manage possible workplace violence associated with each source. Do the actions differ across the sources? From a management perspective, does your team find it useful to categorize workplace violence by source? Why or why not? If not, is there another classification scheme that your team would recommend?
b. Share your assessments regarding frequency and severity of workplace violence for the four sources. With the direction of your instructor, put together the best recommendations from the team presentations. Is there consensus that the source classification scheme is a useful management tool?

Experiential Exercise: Team

16-36. Protecting workers from violence requires proactive management. An initial step in managing workplace violence is often an assessment of risk. For example, have workers experienced incidents of violence on the job? Are there situations in the workplace in which workers might be most vulnerable to an incident of violence?

In addition to an initial assessment, guidelines regarding violence in the workplace should be established. Workers need to know, for example, who to report to regarding an incident of violence as well as know that there are boundaries as to what is acceptable behavior in the workplace.

As a team, what would you include in an assessment of risk of violence? How would you go about collecting the information? Can you find a risk assessment from an actual company? How does this assessment compare to your team's recommended assessment?

Work with your team to develop basic guidelines that you would recommend to an organization to reduce the chances of workplace violence. Recommended steps and content for guidelines can be found in a document prepared for employers and law enforcement agencies at *http://www.theiacp.org/Portals/0/pdfs/Publications/combatingworkplaceviolence.pdf.*

As a team, share your assessment approach and recommended guidelines with the rest of the class. Given the team recommendations, are the recommendations doable and within reasonable cost?

Experiential Exercise: Individual

16-37. Abusive customers appear to be a frequent occurrence. Abuse from customers can take a variety of forms, including verbal abuse, threat of violence, sexual harassment, and physical attack. Such abuse can affect work performance and be a cause for turnover.

Identify a family member or friend who works in retail and ask them for examples of customer abuse that she or he has observed or experienced. Does the person think that customer abuse is a problem in their industry? Why or why not? Does the person's company have any policies or take any action regarding customer abuse?

Based on the information you gather, do you think customer abuse is a problem that management should address? What are your recommendations regarding customer abuse?

Sources: Based on Harris, L. D., and Daunt, K. (2013). Managing customer misbehavior: Challenges and strategies. *The Journal of Services Marketing*, *27*, 281–293; Nierle, B. (2013). What can managers do to mitigate violent employee behaviors? *Public Manager*, *42*, 61–64; *Safety Compliance Letter* (2013, January). Workplace violence: Assessing and responding to risks, Issue 2545; Scott, L. (2012). Workplace violence: A scourge across diverse industries. *Security*, *49*, 22, 26, 28.

Endnotes

Scan for Endnotes or go to http://www.pearsonglobaleditions.com/Gomez-Mejia.

CHAPTER 17 International HRM Challenge

MyManagementLab®

When you see this icon, visit **www.mymanagementlab.com** for activities that are applied, personalized, and offer immediate feedback.

CHALLENGES

After reading this chapter, you should be able to deal more effectively with the following challenges:

1. **Specify** the HRM strategies that are most appropriate for firms at different stages of internationalization.
2. **Identify** the best mix of host-country and expatriate employees given the conditions facing a firm.
3. **Explain** the challenges of expatriate assignments.
4. **Learn** how to effectively manage expatriate assignments and minimize the chances of failure.
5. **Develop** HRM policies and procedures that match the needs and values of different cultures.
6. **Consider** ethical implications of HRM policies and procedures on a global basis.

At the beginning of 2010, Toyota was generally considered to be a winner in the automobile industry, pulling ahead of General Motors, Chrysler, and Ford in the production and sale of cars in the United States and abroad. Toyota's profits were the envy of automobile manufacturers, and there seemed to be no end in sight to Toyota's success. This was an incredible achievement for a company that just a generation ago was relatively unknown and a small industry player. Along the way, the company earned a top-notch reputation for its innovative and sophisticated principles of quality improvement, efficiency, and employee involvement, which came to be known as the Toyota Way.[1]

Source: © Marin Tomas/Alamy.

Then disaster seemed to strike suddenly in the spring of 2010, when Toyota was accused of ignoring problems in the brake system and other vehicle parts. These problems led to several accidents and multimillion-dollar suits. The image of superior vehicles was tarnished dramatically when the company was confronted with a storm of complaints about safety and widespread negative media coverage.

A close look at Toyota's troubles reveals that human resource management practices were partly at fault. Prior to these problems, Toyota's president pressured chief engineers (called *shusas*) to cut cost aggressively. The shusas were evaluated and rewarded for their cost reductions. Many of the customers served by Toyota and the shusas were thousands of miles away in foreign markets, and Toyota had only a skeleton crew of expatriates. Thus, information about vehicle problems did not flow back to corporate headquarters in Japan. "Those engineers [shusas] are placed in Toyota City. They are shielded from market information. . . . [W]hen Toyota customers overseas began to raise questions about the quality of their vehicles, either because they performed unsafely or just looked cheap, Toyota brushed off the complaints and delayed finding solutions."

U.S. operations were overseen by a giant Japanese bureaucracy in Toyota City, with few Toyota representatives keeping a pulse on local conditions in the United States. Lack of delegation to managers of international divisions prevented good communication and quick solutions to problems. In fact, some of the issues "discovered" in 2010 (such as improperly fitting floor mats) were causing problems in the United States as far back as five years earlier. Yet these allegations were ignored in Toyota City; instead, Toyota blamed an overly complaining U.S. culture for the purported problems.

Ignoring these issues when they could have been easily solved has been extremely costly.[2] During 2010–2012, Toyota had to recall approximately 5 million vehicles: for example, 133,469 Priuses, the company's pride car, were recalled to reprogram the antilock braking system when it was found to be too touchy for aggressive use, and 53,281 Sienna minivans were recalled after wire cables that held the spare tires in place were found to be rusting, causing the tires to fall out. *Consumer Reports* uncovered a major flaw in the software of Lexus sport-utility vehicles, leading to the cars rolling over in some situations, thus provoking another 9,411 recalls.[3] Stories about new Toyota vehicle defects seemed to emerge weekly, which seems incredible for a company whose reputation was based on exceptional quality.[4] Currently Toyota is trying to both rebuild its image as a very high-quality car manufacturer and resolve the HR issues that led to these problems.

The Managerial Perspective

As firms such as Toyota become global, many key decisions can no longer be made effectively from corporate headquarters. Thus global companies need to find ways to use certain HR practices (such as appropriate performance evaluation and incentive systems, and recruitment of expatriates) to manage this organizational complexity. Toyota centralized control in corporate headquarters and rewarded cost cutting above everything else, leading to major troubles down the road. There are at least 58,000 multinational companies with 50,000 affiliates worldwide.[5] Managers must select, retain, promote, reward, and train employees to help them meet this global challenge. Even small firms trying to export their products or services via the Internet must cope with the challenges of international business. For the growing number of companies operating in various countries, the HRM system and practices must be successfully adapted to a variety of cultural, socioeconomic, and legal conditions.

Virtually every U.S. company now faces competition from abroad, and the fortunes of most U.S. firms, large and small, are inextricably bound to the global economy.[6] In this chapter, we demonstrate how managers can use HRM practices to enhance their firms' competitiveness in an era of international opportunities and challenges. First, we cover the stages of international involvement, the challenges of expatriate job assignments, and ways to make those assignments more effective. We then discuss the development of HRM policies in a global context and the specific HR concerns of exporting firms.

✪ Learn It!

If your professor has chosen to assign this go to **www.mymanagementlab.com** to see what you should particularly focus on, and take the chapter 17 warmup.

The Stages of International Involvement

As Figure 17.1 shows, firms progress through five stages as they internationalize their operations.[7] The higher the stage, the more the firm's HR practices must be adapted to diverse cultural, economic, political, and legal environments.

- In *stage 1*, the firm's market is exclusively domestic. One firm at this stage today is Boulder Beer, which produces its ales in the Boulder, Colorado, area and seldom sells them

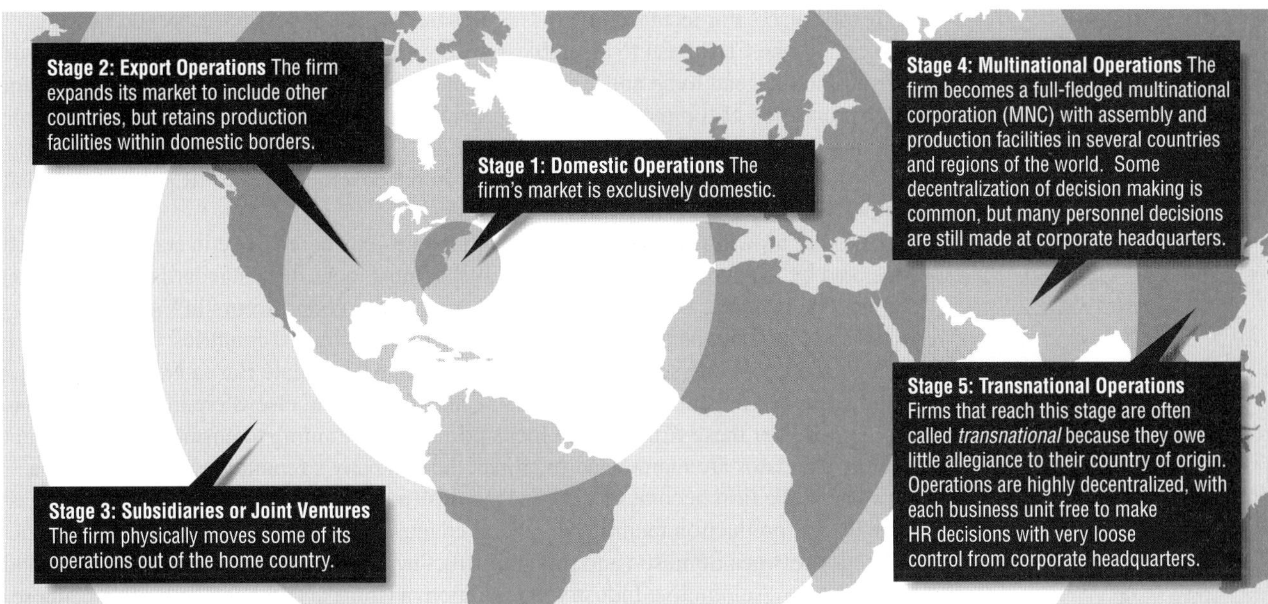

FIGURE 17.1
The Stages of Internationalization

outside the Mountain States region. Another example is Colby Welding, which repairs and rebuilds radiators for sale, primarily in the Phoenix, Arizona, metropolitan area. Many other U.S. firms are still at this stage, but their number is diminishing, particularly in manufacturing. Staffing, training, and compensation for firms at stage I are dictated primarily by local and/or national forces. The only sites considered for plant locations are in the United States, and only the national or regional market is considered in strategic business decisions about production and marketing issues.

- In *stage 2*, the firm expands its market to include foreign countries but retains its production facilities within domestic borders. HRM practices at this stage should facilitate exporting of the firm's products through managerial incentives, appropriate training, and staffing strategies that focus on the demands of international customers.[8]

  An example of a stage 2 firm is Turbo-Tek Enterprises, Inc., located in Los Angeles. It generates $60 million a year in revenues, 38 percent of which comes from overseas sales. The firm's single product is Turbo Wash, a water-spraying attachment for common household hoses. Turbo-Tek's entire manufacturing, packaging, and distribution system is designed with international markets in mind, and the firm's HRM practices play a crucial role in this system. Managerial bonuses are substantially based on foreign sales, and Turbo-Tek rewards its employees for developing innovative ideas to increase exports.

  Falling trade barriers are greatly increasing the number of U.S. firms that fall into stage 2.[9] According to the World Trade Centers Association (WTCA), which has more than 287 licensed world trade affiliates in 88 countries and more than 750,000 companies and individuals, approximately 45 percent of companies with fewer than 500 employees now export products and services—more than three times the number of companies that did so in the 1990s. For instance, after the North American Free Trade Agreement (NAFTA) went into effect in 1993, Treatment Products Ltd. landed contracts with almost every major retail chain in Mexico. Shipments to Mexico tripled to roughly $300,000, about 20 percent of the company's total current exports.[10] The impact of exports on the local community can be huge. For example, during the economic downturn of 2008–2012, Columbus, Indiana, with a population of 40,000, became an export powerhouse with a very low unemployment rate thanks largely to diesel engine–maker Cummins Inc., which added thousands of jobs during this difficult period.[11]

- In *stage 3*, the firm physically moves some of its operations out of the home country. These facilities are primarily used for parts assembly, although some limited manufacturing may take place. For instance, many U.S. apparel manufacturers have opened facilities throughout the Caribbean to assemble a wide variety of garments. The foreign branches or subsidiaries tend to be under close control of corporate headquarters at this stage, and a high proportion of top managers are **expatriates** (employees who are citizens of the corporation's home country). HRM practices at stage 3 need to focus on the selection, training, and compensation of expatriates, as well as on the development of HR policies for local employees where the foreign facilities are located.

expatriate
A citizen of one country living and working in another country.

Another growing segment of firms that may be considered to be in stage 3 are franchises operated by local managers and/or owners that must meet strict standards set by the home office. For example, Starbucks sells its lattes to coffee connoisseurs in Vienna, Austria; KFC and Pizza Hut have more than 12,500 restaurants in 110 countries; Taco Bell has become the number one seller of tacos in Mexico; and Chocolate Bar (a New York eatery and candy store) has opened stores in Dubai, Qatar, Egypt, and elsewhere in the Middle East.[12] HR policies for these firms should focus primarily on training to ensure that consistent quality standards are maintained to protect the company's reputation across the globe.

multinational corporation (MNC)
A firm with assembly and production facilities in several countries and regions of the world.

- In *stage 4*, the firm becomes a full-fledged **multinational corporation (MNC)**, with assembly and production facilities in several countries and regions of the world. Strategic alliances between domestic and foreign firms, such as that between General Motors and the Shanghai Automotive Industry Corporation, a Chinese company, to build a Chinese engine with a Japanese transmission, are very common.[13] Although there is usually some decentralization of decision making for firms at stage 4, many personnel decisions affecting foreign branches are still made at corporate headquarters, typically by an international personnel department. In addition, foreign operations are still managed by expatriates. Amoco (now part of BP), IBM, Rockwell, General Motors, General Electric, and Xerox are all at stage 4. Although China has undoubtedly been the main beneficiary of manufacturing-type jobs during the past 20 years, thanks in large measure to low labor costs, in the next few years Mexico is poised to overtake China as an attractive site for U.S. firms to relocate their manufacturing facilities (see the Manager's Notebook "Will Mexico Overtake China?")

MANAGER'S NOTEBOOK

Global

Will Mexico Overtake China?

For years, low labor costs in China have drained many jobs—particularly in manufacturing—not only from the United States but also from Mexico. For instance, during the past 20 years, hundreds of thousands of low-skilled jobs migrated to China from the *maquilas* (assembly plants, mostly owned by American firms) in Northern Mexico. For Mexico, however, this is likely to change for the better in the near future. According to Bank of America, average wages are now 19.6 percent lower in Mexico than in China, whereas back in 2003 wages were 188 percent higher in Mexico. Combined with the demographic bonus of a young population

Source: © JeffreyIsaacGreenberg / Alamy.

(expected to grow by 20 percent between now and 2020 as compared to 2.9 percent in China) and much lower transportation costs, many manufacturing firms will likely head south rather than go to China.

Source: Based on Reuters (2013). Mexico hourly wages now lower than China. *www.reuters.com*; Miroff, N. (2013). Mexico and China look to trade away old rivalry. *http://washingtonpost.com*; Society for Human Resource Management. (2012). Wage raises in emerging markets outpace developed economies. *www.shrm.org*. ■■

transnational corporation
A firm with operations in many countries and highly decentralized operations. The firm owes little allegiance to its country of origin and has weak ties to any given country.

- In *stage 5,* the most advanced stage of internationalization, firms are often called **transnational corporations** because they owe little allegiance to their country of origin and have weak ties to any given country. Operations are highly decentralized; each business unit is free to make personnel decisions with very loose control from corporate headquarters. The board of directors is often composed of people of different nationalities, and the firm tries hard to develop managers who see themselves as citizens of the world.

  HRM practices at stage 5 companies are designed to blend individuals from diverse backgrounds to create a shared corporate (rather than national) identity and a common vision. For instance, Gillette (which became a business unit of Proctor & Gamble in 2005) conducts an extensive management training program for which local personnel offices in 48 countries search for the best young university graduates who are single and fluent in English. In the words of Gillette's international personnel director, "The person we are looking for is someone who says, 'Today, it's Manila. Tomorrow, it's the U.S. Four years from now, it's Peru or Pakistan.' . . . We really work hard at finding people who aren't parochial and who want international careers."[14]

A QUESTION OF ETHICS
In some areas of the world business practices that are contrary to Western values—such as child labor, payment of bribes to government officials, and sex or race discrimination in hiring and promotion—are common. Should U.S. corporations and their expatriate representatives refuse to engage in such practices even if doing so would put the firm at a competitive disadvantage?

The Rise of Outsourcing

Firms in stages 3 through 5 often outsource their production and services to countries where they find a competitive advantage in lower labor costs. Fewer and fewer firms can grow or even survive unless they engage in some form of outsourcing. Global outsourcing now occurs for all types of jobs and across most industries. For instance, IBM has hired over 100,000 employees in countries such as Brazil, China, and India, where labor costs are low. These employees work in so-called global service delivery centers, which provide a wide array of services for IBM's clients, including software programming, help-desk call centers, financial accounting, and benefits management. Many of those global service employees report both to the local supervisors and to IBM managers thousands of miles away. Another example in a totally different industry is Blue Cross Blue Shield, which has signed alliances with seven overseas hospitals in places such as Turkey, Costa Rica, Singapore, and India and hopes to add more soon. These overseas hospitals will be included in coverage for the insurer's 1.5 million members. As health care costs continue to rise in the United States, "medical travel is going to be part of the solution," says a top Blue Cross executive.

Although some believe that exporting jobs to less-developed countries keeps salaries and benefits at home low, most international business experts believe that it is not realistic to turn the clock back when companies are free to locate wherever they want.[15] Further, consumers benefit from lower prices achieved by outsourcing, and countries that are the recipients of outsourcing use increased earnings to purchase goods and services from the United States. Political leaders are unlikely to push for restrictive legislation to curtail outsourcing in the foreseeable future.

The growth of outsourcing can be attributed to a large extent to the Internet. However, the Internet poses some serious challenges to outsourcing because of problems with online security. Rank-and-file employees are increasingly asked to play a role in fighting Internet-based threats. For instance, in India, which depends heavily on the Internet for much of the outsourcing it receives, there is widespread fear that well-publicized security threats could wreak havoc on the economy. Hence, Indian companies are trying to select workers who can be trusted and are training employees to be on the lookout for any suspicious activity.

As a case in point, two Indian employees who worked for Mphasis BFL LTD, a Citibank subcontractor, logged on to Citi's online system and transferred at least $426,000 from U.S. customers to their own accounts. Because computer systems at Citibank subcontractors in India let local employees see sensitive information about U.S. customers (for example, Social Security number, credit history, and savings account number), the system was open to abuse. This kind of security risk is compounded by hasty selection and training, because attrition in the industry is about 60 percent.[16] But most Indian companies, including Mphasis, are channeling more resources into improving employee screening, reducing attrition, and training employees to spot and report potential security problems. Citibank has no plans to curtail outsourcing to India. "If the industry can keep improving security, it has little to fear in the long-term."[17]

Two additional concerns regarding outsourcing have come to light in the past. One is poor safety. This was recently exemplified, for instance, when drug companies subcontracted with Chinese manufacturers to produce the blood thinner heparin. The contaminated product caused several deaths around the world. Phillips, General Electric, Medtronic, Siemens, and others are setting up the manufacturing of sensitive medical equipment (such as MRIs, CT scanners, and ultrasound and x-ray gear) in China, but many see danger in this trend given recent scandals with unsafe toys, food, and drugs in mainland China.[18] Another concern with global outsourcing is the large number of complaints from clients when they are forced to deal with the firm's customer representatives who are located in foreign countries. Employees in so-called "call centers" often lack sufficient information, may be poorly trained, may have language barriers, and may not be empowered to make decisions to resolve a customer complaint on the spot. These problems mean that firms need to take less-tangible factors into account and not be blinded by the labor-cost savings in subcontracting. It takes years to build a good reputation, and problems of this sort can quickly tarnish a company's image and future profitability. Human resources can help to reduce these problems with outsourcing by having a role in determining how workers are selected, the type of training they receive, the criteria used to reward employees (for instance, quantity versus quality), how new employees are socialized through the orientation program, efficient monitoring systems, and the like.

Falling Barriers

Although the world has always had some degree of economic interdependence, the economic meltdown at the end of the prior decade demonstrates how, for better or for worse, the barriers that separate countries have largely disappeared when it comes to trade, production, services, and finances. For example, most European countries enacted similar economic packages following the initial $700 billion "stimulus" in the United States. China was also forced to announce a similar economic package of $586 billion, a much larger percentage of its gross national product than the United States.[19] As of 2014 most European countries, particularly Spain, Portugal, Italy, Greece and Ireland, are still suffering from the economic malaise that started in the United States back in 2008.

At the firm level, whatever happens to a multinational company in one country will affect many other countries simultaneously. For instance, 70 percent of the components of Boeing's 787 Dreamliner passenger airplane are sourced from foreign suppliers in 40 different countries.[20] So when Boeing faced a recent downturn in the United States, employees in 40 other nations also suffered.

Political rhetoric aside, governments face more limits than ever in enacting and implementing domestic labor legislation (such as social security and minimum wage laws), because firms will simply move their operations elsewhere (see Managers' Notebook "Will Mexico Overtake China?"). Companies now enjoy a great deal of discretion in deciding where they want to set up shop. For individual employees, being a strong contributor is the best job insurance they have, because the protective role of government and labor unions is likely to continue to wane in the future.

Small- and Medium-Size Enterprises Are Also Going Global

Traditionally, only larger and older firms sent production and service off shore, but small and medium-size enterprises (SMEs) are quickly entering this race. These SMEs face some unique human resource challenges. First, many of them are family owned or led by the founder. More often than not, these individuals may have had little international exposure. Second, it may be difficult for these SMEs to delegate control to expatriates or representatives in foreign locations. They may not even know how to start. Third, SMEs that look abroad to gain new customers or partners may be daunted by the complexities involved in navigating complex foreign laws, taxes, and regulations. Fourth, and perhaps most difficult to overcome, most small businesses have had limited experience with people from other cultures. Cultural blunders can get in the way of successful expansion abroad. Consider the following example.

Tom Bonkenburg, director of European operations for St. Onge Company Inc., a small supply-chain consulting firm in York, Pennsylvania, headed to Moscow to develop a partnership with a large firm there. He met the company's Russian branch director. "I gave my best smile, handshake and friendly joke . . . only to be met with a dreary and unhappy look," says Mr. Bonkenburg. Later, however, Mr. Bonkenburg received an e-mail from the Russian branch director, thanking him for a great meeting. Mr. Bonkenburg later learned that Russian culture fosters smiling in private settings and seriousness in business settings. "He was working as hard to impress me as I was to impress him," Mr. Bonkenburg says.[21]

SMEs entering global markets need to put in place recruitment and selection programs to hire employees with the desired international background, appoint the right person to represent the firm overseas, offer sufficient inducements to managers to engage in international activities, and develop the necessary cross-cultural skills to deal with a diverse cultural landscape. According to Kari Herstad, CEO of Culture Coach International Inc., a Newton, Massachusetts, firm that consults with clients on cross-cultural issues: "the important thing to remember is that you don't know what you don't know . . . even subtle cultural insensitivities can have a profound impact."[22]

The Global Manager

Advances in technology and communication and fewer bureaucratic hurdles for short-term, cross-border mobility mean that companies don't need to rely as much on traditional long-term assignments overseas (known as expatriate assignments, discussed next). After at least 100,000 years of human history, it is truly amazing how much things have changed in international connectivity in less than one generation. For instance, a phone call overseas that is almost free today would have cost as much as $100 per minute 25 years ago. That same phone call would have also required the help of an operator on both sides, a process that could have taken eight hours or more for a single call. Fax machines were not widely available until the late 1980s. The ability to send documents overseas in the form of computer attachments was not a viable option in most countries until 15 years ago. Virtual conferences with high-quality connections were not possible until the late 1990s. Traveling to much of Western Europe used to require multiple visas and customs border crossings, and Eastern Europeans were inaccessible behind the so-called Iron Curtain until 1989. English has become the *lingua franca*, or the language of choice, to bridge people whose native language may be French, German, Spanish, or Mandarin. This use of one language (in this case, English) greatly facilitates international communications across over 200 countries. Most leading MBA programs (both in the United States and abroad) are now in English so that language will not be a serious communication roadblock for middle- and upper-level managers interacting across national borders. These changes are truly revolutionary, even though most readers of this book now take them for granted. They have opened a new way of working across the globe, with employees able to choose as the situation demands (for instance, telephone communication, Internet connections, or short-term stays). An employee can be located in a regional office or headquarters yet remain in touch with international operations through short visits or virtually by the touch of a finger. Unlike the traditional expatriate who leaves the home country to take a long-term assignment in another country, these global managers may be expected to interact with people from many different cultures and be able to switch from one culture to another almost instantaneously.

As we will see next, expatriates confront cultural issues, yet they have more time to adapt to local environments. Global managers don't have the opportunity to learn about foreign cultures in a piecemeal fashion. They are supposed to act as integrators and coordinators across national and functional boundaries and to do this under time pressures. According to a recent study, "global managers need to work with people from many cultures simultaneously. They need to form complex cultural understandings, not having the luxury of dealing with each country's issues on a separate and therefore sequential basis. In terms of cross-cultural skills, global managers are expected to tread smoothly and expertly within and between cultures and countries on a daily basis. They need to learn about many foreign cultures' perspectives and approaches to conducting business, be flexible and open-minded toward a multitude of cultures, and have a broad cultural perspective and appreciation for cultural diversity."[23]

From an HR perspective, the scenario described here increases the need to attract, retain, and motivate individuals who are capable of being flexible enough to operate in many cultural environments, sometimes within the space of an 8-hour day or even simultaneously through the use of computer technology. Greater employee diversity at home should help with this process because it sensitizes managers to work with people from very different backgrounds (see Chapter 4). The firm may also need to consider explicitly the person's ability to relate to a diverse audience when it comes to recruitment, selection, appraisals, compensation, and the like. Contrary to some earlier predictions, global managers are not replacing expatriates but are complementing their work. In fact, the number of expatriates has risen sharply in recent years, in tandem with increased globalization. Although expatriates are expensive, many international companies realize that a strong local presence by company loyalists is needed to help manage operations on a continuous basis, to recruit individuals with deep knowledge of the area, to anticipate and deal with political risks, and to protect the company's interest (for instance, ensuring compliance with the firm's quality standards by the subsidiary and its suppliers).We now turn our attention to expatriates.

Determining the Mix of Host-Country and Expatriate Employees

wholly owned subsidiary
In international business, a foreign branch owned fully by the home office.

joint venture
In international business, a foreign branch owned partly by the home office and partly by an entity in the host country (a company, a consortium of firms, an individual, or the government).

ethnocentric approach
An approach to managing international operations in which top management and other key positions are filled by people from the home country.

polycentric approach
An approach to managing international operations in which subsidiaries are managed and staffed by personnel from the host country.

geocentric approach
An approach to managing international operations in which nationality is downplayed and the firm actively searches on a worldwide or regional basis for the best people to fill key positions.

Once a firm passes from the exporting stage (stage 2) to the stage in which it opens a foreign branch (stage 3)—either a **wholly owned subsidiary** (the foreign branch is fully owned by the home office) or a **joint venture** (part of the foreign branch is owned by a host-country entity: another company, a consortium of firms, an individual, or the government)—it must decide who will be responsible for managing the unit. A survey of 151 executives representing 138 large companies identified the choice of management for overseas units as one of their most crucial business decisions.[24]

There are three approaches to managing an international subsidiary: ethnocentric, polycentric, and geocentric.[25]

- In the **ethnocentric approach**, top management and other key positions are filled by people from the home country. For instance, Fluor Daniel, Inc., has 50 engineering and sales offices on five continents and construction projects in as many as 80 countries at any given time. The firm uses a large group of expatriate managers, including 500 international HRM professionals who are involved in recruitment, development, and compensation worldwide and who report directly to a corporate vice president.
- In the **polycentric approach**, international subsidiaries are managed and staffed by personnel from the host country. For instance, General Electric's Tungsram subsidiary in Hungary runs eight factories and employs 8,000 people, almost all of whom are Hungarian nationals.[26]
- In the **geocentric approach**, nationality is deliberately downplayed and the firm actively searches on a worldwide or regional basis for the best people to fill key positions.[27] Transnational firms (those in stage 5) tend to follow this approach. For example, Electrolux has for many years attempted to recruit and develop a group of international managers from diverse countries. Rather than representing a particular country, they represent the organization wherever they are. Most important to Electrolux is the development of a common culture and an international perspective, and the expansion of its international networks.[28]

As Figure 17.2 shows, there are both advantages and disadvantages to using local nationals and expatriates in foreign subsidiaries. Most firms use expatriates only for key positions such as senior managers, high-level professionals, and technical specialists. Because expatriates tend to be very costly (approximately $150,000 to $1,000,000 per person per year depending on location, in 2014 figures), it makes little financial sense to hire expatriates for positions that can be competently filled by foreign nationals. In many locations an expatriate costs 3,000 to 5,000 percent more than a local employee in 2014 figures.[29] In addition, many countries require that a certain percentage of the workforce be local citizens, with exceptions usually made for upper management.

In general, reliance on expatriates increases when:[30]

- ***Sufficient local talent is not available*** This is most likely to occur in firms operating in developing countries. For instance, top managers of Falconbridge and Alcoa (both mining companies operating in Latin America and Africa) are almost always expatriates.

Local

Advantages	Disadvantages
• Lowers labor costs • Demonstrates trust in local citizenry • Increases acceptance of the company by the local community • Maximizes the number of options available in the local environment • Leads to recognition of the company as a legitimate participant in the local economy • Effectively represents local considerations and constraints in the decision-making process • Greater understanding of local conditions	• Makes it difficult to balance local demands and global priorities • Leads to postponement of difficult local decisions (such as layoffs) until they are unavoidable, when they are more difficult, costly, and painful than they would have been if implemented earlier • May make it difficult to recruit qualified personnel • May reduce the amount of control exercised by headquarters

Expatriates

Advantages	Disadvantages
• Cultural similarity with parent company ensures transfer of business/management practices • Permits closer control and coordination of international subsidiaries • Gives employees a multinational orientation through experience at foreign subsidiary • Establishes a pool of internationally experienced executives • Local talent may not yet be able to deliver as much value as expatriates can • Provides broader global perspective	• Creates problems of adaptability to foreign environment and culture • Increases the "foreignness" of the subsidiary • May involve high transfer, salary, and other costs • May result in personal and family problems • Has disincentive effect on local-management morale and motivation • May be subject to local government restrictions

FIGURE 17.2

Advantages and Disadvantages of Using Local and Expatriate Employees to Staff International Subsidiaries

Source: Based on Society for Human Resource Management (2014). Make global assignments a win/win for company, employee, *www.shrm.org*; Amobs, B., and Schlegelamilch, B. (2010). *The New Regional Manager*. New York: Palgrave-McMillan; Deresky, H. (2013). *International Management*. Upper Saddle River, NJ: Prentice Hall; Hamil, J. (1989). Expatriate policies in British MNNs. *Journal of General Management, 14*(4), 20; Sheridan, W. R., and Hansen, P. T. (1996, Spring). Linking international business and expatriate compensation strategies. *ACA Journal,* 66–78; Hill, C. W. (2012). *International Business.* Chicago: Irwin McGraw-Hill; Bozionelos, N. (2009, January/February). Expatriation outside the boundaries of the multinational corporation: A study of expatriate nurses in Saudi Arabia. *Human Resource Management, 48*(1), 11–134.

- ***An important part of the firm's overall business strategy is the creation of a corporate-wide global vision*** For example, Whirlpool Corporation has operations in 40 countries and is deeply committed to the notion of one global company with one global vision. The company has a worldwide leadership program involving extensive use of expatriates, conferences that bring together top executives from different subsidiaries around the world, and global project teams that tackle common problems and facilitate a total international integration process.[31]
- ***International units and domestic operations are highly interdependent*** For example, IBM, HP, and Xerox have specialized manufacturing facilities in different parts of the United States and the world. The outputs of these different facilities (computer chips, software) must be closely monitored and integrated to produce highly sophisticated products such as computers, medical equipment, and photocopying machines. Linking production processes generally calls for greater reliance on expatriate managers and specialists, who can bridge the gaps and tie the units of the organization together.
- ***Technology has dramatically reduced the need for expatriates to link the international units of the firm to the home office*** For instance, a Wal-Mart outpost opens every week

somewhere outside the United States, managed primarily by local employees. Wal-Mart can rely on local employees because it has 1,000 full-time information technology developers in the United States who develop systems that allow close monitoring of the stores from corporate headquarters in Bentonville, Arkansas.

- ***The political situation is unstable*** Corporations tend to rely on expatriates for top management positions when the risk of government intervention in the business is high, when actual or potential turmoil within the country is serious, when the threat of terrorism exists, and when there has been a recent history of social upheaval in the country. Although expatriate top managers may increase tensions between nationalistic groups and a foreign firm, they do provide some assurance to the home office that its interests are well represented locally. Expatriates are also less susceptible to the demands of local political forces. At the same time, as discussed in the You Manage It! feature "Coping with Terrorism," one of the most stressful aspects of an international assignment for many expatriates is precisely the fact that they can become scapegoats when caught in the middle of political and ethnic conflict.
- ***There are significant cultural differences between the host country and the home country*** The more dissimilar the cultures, the more important it is to appoint expatriates who can serve as interpreters or go-betweens. Because this boundary-spanning role demands much cross-cultural sensitivity, the MNC needs to select and carefully train individuals suitable for these positions. This may require considerable career planning.[32]

The Challenges of Expatriate Assignments

Although the number of expatriates as a proportion of the total managerial and professional MNC workforce has declined over the years, their absolute number is on the rise in all regions.[33] A recent survey of 874 MNCs in 24 major industries shows that almost half of firms report an increase in the use of expatriates in the last few years. However, managing expatriates remains a challenge.

The failure rate of U.S. expatriates—that is, the percentage who return prematurely, without completing their assignment—is estimated to be in the 20 to 40 percent range, three to four times higher than the failure rates experienced by European and Asian companies. Perhaps this accounts for the fact that more and more U.S. firms prefer to send Europeans or Asians to foreign assignments, which usually last from one to three years.[34] One reason for the high U.S. failure rate: Two generations of economic dominance and a strong domestic market have contributed to the creation of a colonial mentality in many U.S. companies.[35]

Failures can be very expensive. Premature returnees cost an estimated $250,000 to $700,000 each in 2014 figures, which translates into $6.1 billion per year in direct costs to U.S. firms. The intangible costs of failure include business disruptions, lost opportunities, and negative impact on the firm's reputation and leadership, and are probably many times greater than tangible costs. In addition, the personal hardship on employees and their families, including diminished self-image, marital strife, uprooted children, lost income, and tarnished career reputation, can be substantial.[36]

Why International Assignments End in Failure

Six factors account for most failures, although their relative importance varies by firm.[37] These are career blockage, culture shock, lack of cross-cultural training, an overemphasis on technical qualifications, a tendency to use international assignments as a way to get rid of problem employees, and family problems.

CAREER BLOCKAGE Initially, many employees see the opportunity to work and travel abroad as exciting. But once the initial rush wears off, many feel that the home office has forgotten them and that their career has been sidetracked while their counterparts at home are climbing the corporate ladder. According to a survey by the Society for Human Resources Management (SHRM) conducted in the 1990s, although U.S. companies give themselves high marks for career planning for their expatriate employees, most of their employees do not. Only 14 percent of the 209 expatriate managers who completed the society's questionnaire said their firm's career planning for them was sufficient.[38] Fortunately, this situation may be changing for the better, although there is still a long way to go. A more recent survey this decade in which the SHRM also participated indicates that in comparing the careers of expatriates against employees with no international experience, 41 percent of respondents report that expatriates obtain new positions in the company more easily; 39 percent said that expatriates are promoted faster; and 27 percent say that the expatriate assignment helped them get a better job at another company.[39] A survey of 2,700 managers by Korn Ferry International revealed that more than a third of them view an overseas assignment as positive for their career and that they would consider taking one.[40] However, a survey by consultant giant McKinsey of 450 managers at multinational companies revealed that most managers are reluctant to become expatriates due to fear that relocating will damage their career prospects.[41]

CULTURE SHOCK Many people who take international assignments cannot adjust to a different cultural environment, a phenomenon called **culture shock**. Instead of learning to work within the new culture, the expatriate tries to impose the home office or home country's values on the host country's employees. This practice may trigger cultural clashes and misunderstandings that escalate until the expatriate decides to return home to more familiar surroundings—perhaps leaving a mess behind.

culture shock
The inability to adjust to a different cultural environment.

Lack of "cultural intelligence," or the inability to relate to people from different cultural backgrounds,[42] and being monolingual[43] are often cited as reasons for expatriate failure. Firms can help employees avoid culture shock by using selection tools to choose the employees with the highest degree of cultural sensitivity and who know the local language. Korn Ferry International found that 9 of 10 headhunters worldwide look for prospective expatriates who know at least one foreign language. These headhunters are becoming increasingly sophisticated in the use of a variety of methods (structured interviews, role-playing exercises, assessment centers, and so forth) to identify those who are "prepared to spot cultural differences, some of them startlingly subtle, that can trip the unwary."[44]

LACK OF PREDEPARTURE CROSS-CULTURAL TRAINING Surprisingly, only about one-third of MNCs provide *any* cross-cultural training to expatriates, and those that do tend to offer rather cursory programs.[45] Often the expatriate and his or her family literally pack their bags and travel to their destination with only a U.S. passport and whatever information they could cull from magazines, tourist brochures, and the library. This is a recipe for trouble, as the following example illustrates:

> I once attended a business meeting in Tokyo with a senior U.S. executive. The Japanese go through a very elaborate ritual when exchanging business cards, and the American didn't have a clue. She just tossed some of her business cards across the table at the stunned Japanese executives. One of them turned his back on her and walked out. Needless to say, the deal never went through.[46]

OVEREMPHASIS ON TECHNICAL QUALIFICATIONS The person chosen to go abroad may have impressive credentials and an excellent reputation in the home office for getting things done. Unfortunately, the same traits that led to success at home can be disastrous in another country. Consider the experience of one executive from a large U.S. electronics firm who spent only three months of what was supposed to be a two-year assignment in Mexico:

> I just could not accept the fact that my staff meetings would always start at least a half hour late and that schedules were treated as flexible guidelines with much room to spare. Nobody seemed to care but me! I also could not understand how many of the first-line supervisors would hire their friends and relatives, regardless of competence. What I viewed as nepotism of the worst kind was seen by them as an honorable obligation to their extended families, and this included many adopted relatives or compadres who were not even related by blood.[47]

In a recent survey, 96 percent of respondents rated the technical requirements of a job as the most important selection criteria for international assignments, largely ignoring cultural sensitivity.[48] In more enlightened companies, such as Prudential Relocation (an arm of Prudential Insurance), nearly 35 percent of managers cite "cultural adaptability" as the most important trait for overseas success.[49]

GETTING RID OF A TROUBLESOME EMPLOYEE International assignments may seem to be a convenient way of dealing with managers who are having problems in the home office. By sending these managers abroad, the organization is able to resolve difficult interpersonal situations or political conflicts at the home office, but at a significant cost to its international operations. The following true story was told to one of the authors:

> Joe and Paul were both competing for promotion to divisional manager. The corporate vice president responsible for making the selection decision felt that Joe should get the promotion but also believed that Paul would never be able to accept the decision and would actively try to undermine Joe's authority. Paul also had much support from some of the old-timers, so the only way to avoid the dilemma was to find a different spot for Paul where he could not cause any trouble. The vice president came up with the idea of promoting Joe to divisional manager while appointing Paul as a senior executive at the Venezuelan subsidiary. Paul (who had seldom been out of the country and who had taken introductory Spanish in high school 20 years earlier) took the job. It soon became obvious that the appointment was a mistake. Two months into Paul's tenure, there was a major wildcat strike attributed to his heavy-handed style in dealing with the labor unions, and he had to be replaced.

FAMILY PROBLEMS More than half of all early returns can be attributed to family problems.[50] It is surprising that most firms do not anticipate these problems and develop programs to prevent them. Indeed, few companies consider the feelings of employees' families on international assignments.[51] One expatriate's wife comments:

> A husband who is racked by guilt over dragging his wife halfway around the world, or distracted because she is ill-equipped to handle a foreign assignment, is not a happy or productive employee. . . . Most women actually start out all right. The excitement quickly fades for a traveling wife, though, when her husband abandons her for a regional tour immediately upon arrival and she's left behind with the moving boxes and the responsibility of finding good schools. Or when she is left to hire servants to set up a household without knowing the language . . . [Often] they are asked to jump off their own career paths and abandon healthy salaries . . . just so that they can watch their self-esteem vanish somewhere over the international date line.[52]

The expectations of dual-career couples are another cause of failure in expatriate assignments. MNCs are increasingly confronted with couples who expect to work in the same foreign location—at no sacrifice to either's career. Yet one spouse usually has to sacrifice, and this often leads to dissatisfaction. When 10-year AT&T veteran Eric Phillips was asked to move to Brussels, his wife, Angelinà, had to give up her well-paying job as a market researcher. Although the move represented a terrific career opportunity for Phillips, his wife found it very difficult to adjust.[53]

Difficulties on Return

The expatriates' return home may also be fraught with difficulties. Between 20 and 40 percent of returning expatriates, called *repatriates*, leave the organization shortly after returning home.[54] Some employers report that nearly half of employees leave the company within two years.[55] Four common problems confronting returning expatriates are their company's lack of respect for the skills they acquired while abroad, loss of status, poor planning for the expatriate's return, and reverse culture shock.[56] Figure 17.3 summarizes some of the practices companies can use to counter these problems. We discuss these in greater detail later in this chapter.

LACK OF RESPECT FOR ACQUIRED SKILLS Most U.S. firms are still heavily oriented toward the domestic market, even those that have a long history of operating internationally. The expatriate who has gathered a wealth of information and valuable skills on a foreign assignment may be frustrated by the lack of appreciation shown by peers and supervisors at corporate headquarters. According to a credible survey, only 12 percent of expatriates felt that their overseas assignment had enhanced their career development, and almost two-thirds reported that their firm did not take advantage of what they had learned overseas.[57]

Companies that have relatively low repatriation failure rates attribute their success to intensive interactions with the individual and his or her family before, during, and after the international assignment. Here are some of the practices that increase organizational commitment among expatriate employees:

- ***Advance career planning helps expatriates know what to expect when they return to the United States.*** Management needs to sit down with HR professionals and the employee to lay out a potential career path before the employee goes abroad.
- ***Mentors can make expatriates feel they are vital members of the organization.*** Senior managers and vice presidents should correspond regularly with expatriate employees and meet with them periodically either at the home office or on location.
- ***Opening global communication channels keeps expatriates up-to-date on organizational developments.*** Newsletters, briefings, and, of course, telecommunications technology enable expatriates to stay in constant touch with the home office.
- ***Recognizing the contributions of repatriated employees eases their reentry.*** Repatriated employees whose accomplishments abroad are acknowledged are more likely to stay with the company.

FIGURE 17.3

Communicate to Repatriate

Source: Based on Society for Human Resource Management (2014). Make global assignments a win/win for company, employee, *www.shrm.org*; Deresky, H. (2013). *International management*. Upper Saddle River, NJ: Prentice Hall; Hill, C. W. (2012). *International business*. Chicago: Irwin-McGraw Hill; Shilling, M. (1993, September). How to win at repatriation. *Personnel Journal*, 40. See also Kraimer, M. L., Shaffer, M. A., and Bolino, M. C. (2009, January/February). The influence of expatriate and repatriate experiences on career advancement and repatriate retention. *Human Resource Management, 48*(1), 27–48.

However, given the rapid increase in outsourcing during the past few years, this situation may be changing, particularly among large firms. For instance, only 39 percent of IBM's revenues are now generated within the United States and most of its work is carried out overseas. Other examples of companies in a similar situation include Intel, HP, Oracle, Sun Microsystems, and General Electric.[58] Companies are on the lookout for seasoned managers with international experience to go abroad and run things. According to one analyst, "while an overseas stint used to be a ticket to oblivion, now if you want to rise far in almost any big corporation, you can't afford to ignore the new global order."[59] The financial crash at the end of this century's first decade is propelling this trend as firms try to find strength in growing emergent markets such as China, India, and Brazil to weather weaknesses in the more industrialized countries.

LOSS OF STATUS Returning expatriates often experience a substantial loss of prestige, power, independence, and authority. This *status reversal* affects as many as three-fourths of repatriated employees.[60] One survey shows that disappointment upon return is so profound that 77 percent of returning expatriates would rather accept an international position with another employer than a domestic position with their current company.[61] The following example illustrates:

> When I was in Chile, I had occasions to meet various ministers in the government and other high-ranking industry officials. Basically my word was the final one. I had a lot of latitude because the home office didn't really want to be bothered with what was happening in Chile and therefore was uninformed anyway. I made decisions in Chile that only our CEO would make for the domestic operation. When I returned, I felt as though all the training and experience I had gotten in Chile was totally useless. The position I had seemed about six levels down as far as I was concerned. I had to get approval for hiring. I had to get my boss's signature for purchases worth one-tenth of the values of ones I approved in Chile. To say I felt a letdown would be a significant understatement.[62]

POOR PLANNING FOR RETURN POSITION Uncertainties regarding their new career assignment may provoke much anxiety in returning employees. One survey suggests that more than half of expatriates were unaware of what job awaited them at home.[63] The following story is typical:

> I received a letter from the home office three months prior to the expiration of my assignment in Hungary (where I was responsible for a team of engineers developing a computerized system for handling inventories in four new joint ventures). I was told that I would be assuming the position of Supervisor of Technical Services in corporate headquarters.

> It sounded impressive enough. I was astonished to find out upon return, however, that I was given the honorary title of supervisor with nobody under my command. It smelled like a dead rat to me so I jumped ship as soon as I could.[64]

REVERSE CULTURE SHOCK Living and working in another culture for a long time changes a person, especially if he or she has internalized some of the foreign country's norms and customs. Expatriates are usually unaware of how much psychological change they have undergone until they return home. As many as 80 percent of returning expatriates experience *reverse culture shock*, which sometimes leads to alienation, a sense of uprootedness, and even disciplinary problems.[65] One expatriate who had worked in Spain notes:

> I began to take for granted the intense camaraderie at work and after hours among male friends. Upon returning to the U.S. I realized for the first time in my life how American males are expected to maintain a high psychological distance from each other, and their extremely competitive nature in a work environment. My friendly overtures were often misperceived as underhanded maneuvers for personal gain.[66]

Despite all these difficulties, many managers today are lining up for international assignments as companies gradually realize that employees with international experience can be a valuable asset.[67] Gerber Products has announced that from now on, international assignments will be emphasized as part of normal career development for company executives. As a result, Gerber's country manager in Poland feels he has an edge over many of his colleagues. "My overseas experience sets me apart from the rest of the M.B.A. bunch," he says. "I'm not just one of hundreds of thousands."[68]

Effectively Managing Expatriate Assignments with HRM Policies and Practices

Companies can minimize the chances of failure by creating a sensible set of HRM policies and practices that get to the root of the problems we have discussed. In this section, we look at how selection, training, career development, and compensation policies can help companies avoid these problems.

Selection

The choice of an employee for an international assignment is a critical decision. Because most expatriates work under minimal supervision in a distant location, mistakes in selection are likely to go unnoticed until it is too late. To choose the best employee for the job, management should:

- ***Emphasize cultural sensitivity as a selection criterion*** Assess the candidate's ability to relate to people from different backgrounds. For instance, one large electronics manufacturing firm conducts in-depth interviews with the candidate's supervisors, peers, and subordinates, particularly those whose gender, race, and ethnic origin are different from the candidate's. Personal interviews with the candidate and written tests that measure social adjustment and adaptability should also be part of the selection process.
- ***Establish a selection board of expatriates*** Some HRM specialists strongly recommend that all international assignments be approved by a selection board consisting of managers who have worked as expatriates for a minimum of three to five years.[69] This kind of board should be better able to detect potential problems than managers with no international background.
- ***Require previous international experience*** Although not always feasible, it is highly desirable to choose candidates who have already spent some time in a different country. The major reason the state of Utah is in the forefront of international business is its large Mormon population, whose church requires them to spend a minimum of two years as missionaries in another country. Some schools (such as the American Graduate School of International Management in Phoenix, Arizona) and some MNCs offer overseas internships. A growing number of business schools, including UCLA and the University of Southern California, are broadening their collaboration with universities and businesses abroad. In this way, candidates acquire some knowledge of a country's language and customs before taking on a full-blown expatriate assignment.

- ***Explore the possibility of hiring foreign-born employees who can serve as "expatriates" at a future date*** Japanese companies have been quite successful at hiring young foreign-born (non-Japanese) employees straight out of college to work in the home office in Japan. These recruits enter the firm with little experience and exposure to work in their host country and, thus, are blank slates on which the Japanese MNC can write its own philosophy and values.[70] Some U.S. companies, such as Coca-Cola, have been following a similar practice for years.

- ***Carefully consider the expatriate's ethical values in the selection process*** Of course, ethics is important for all employees, but it is particularly critical for expatriates because they enjoy much discretion and autonomy overseas. One issue that most expatriates will encounter is the temptation to pay bribes to secure local contracts (see the Manager's Notebook, "The Temptation to Pay Bribes"). Even though paying bribes is illegal for U.S. firms, they may justify it by thinking "This is normal here" and "Otherwise, we couldn't get much done." Training can also be helpful in reducing ethical problems, but training most likely will not overcome a person's willingness to commit unethical acts if they don't perceive this as being wrong (for instance, if they believe that the end justifies the means).
- ***Screen candidates' spouses and families*** Because the unhappiness of expatriates' family members plays such a large role in the failure of international assignments, some companies are screening candidates' spouses. For instance, Ford formally assesses spouses on qualities such as flexibility, patience, and adaptability, asking questions such as: "How do you feel about this assignment? Do you feel you can adjust?" Exxon, too, meets with spouses and children during the selection process.[71]
- ***Develop an effective selection program not only for expatriates, but also for those locals who will help the expatriate manager carry out his or her mission*** The international firm should generate a pool of needed human resources at the local level to help accomplish its objectives. The expatriate's job becomes easier if he or she can focus on broader issues while delegating other tasks to expert local staff.

MANAGER'S NOTEBOOK

Ethics/Social Responsibility

The Temptation to Pay Bribes

Despite the fact that paying bribes to foreign officials to secure contracts has been illegal in the United States for over 35 years (since passage of the Foreign Corrupt Practices Act [FCPA] in 1977) and that many European countries also ban this practice, bribes continue to be alive and well when it comes to international management. Consider the following well-publicized cases during the past decade or so:

- Hewlett Packard has been accused of paying several million dollars in bribes for the delivery and installation of an information technology network in Russia.
- Siemens AG paid several million dollars to secure a contract for installing a traffic control system in Moscow. During the past decade, Siemens has paid over $1 billion in fines in the United States and Germany for paying bribes to win contracts in Russia, Argentina, China, and Israel.
- Daimler paid over $100 million in fines after getting caught for improper payments in South America, Africa, Asia, and Eastern Europe.
- Halliburton, a U.S. contractor once headed by former vice president Dick Cheney, paid a fine of nearly $560 million to settle claims by the Securities and Exchange Commission (SEC) and Department of Justice that a former subdivision of the firm paid kickbacks to Nigerian officials.

Cases concerning well-known firms and large sums of money such as the ones listed here most likely represent the tip of the iceberg. Many smaller companies probably pay bribes overseas on a fairly routine basis. In other countries, bribes may be hidden under legitimate business terms such as "commissions," "transaction expenses," and "special fees." ■■

Training

The assumption that people everywhere respond in similar fashion to the same images, symbols, and slogans has hurt U.S. companies offering their products in international markets. See the Manager's Notebook, "The Challenge of Overcoming Cultural Barriers."

MANAGER'S NOTEBOOK

Customer-Driven HR

The Challenge of Overcoming Cultural Barriers

"You think you speak the language, and you discover you don't." That was the reaction of David Rosenberg, a Texan recently assigned to England as a project manager who used trial and error to communicate with British colleagues. For instance, the word *scheme* is interpreted as "service" in England, while in the United States, it has a connotation of deceit.

Cross-cultural communication can present many pitfalls to the unprepared. A U.S. marketing vice president who works overseas says, for instance, that it is sometimes difficult to recognize the word "no" when, as in Japan, it comes couched in terms such as "This is very interesting; we'll certainly give it serious consideration."

Alert Driving, a firm that provides online training courses to companies with vehicle fleets, was surprised to realize that the direct language used in its online training courses was found to be offensive to speakers of many Asian dialects. It was often interpreted by trainees as disrespectful. The company spent about $1 million honing its use of language dialects to avoid cultural blunders in different local markets.

Nonverbal communication is potentially perilous as well. The emphasis of Chinese philosophy on harmony and balance means that it is preferable to give presents in pairs in China. In addition, business gifts should be reciprocated, and the giving of cash is considered to be rude. Pairs of gifts are appreciated in Japan as well and should be presented with both hands, but it's unlucky to give four or nine of anything. In Saudi Arabia, only intimate friends exchange gifts, and always with the right hand.

Training is one of the best ways to ready people to experience cultures around the world. For example, to prepare members of the military at Maxwell-Gunter Air Force Base for combat as well as humanitarian missions, the Air University, which is based there, has adopted a new course on cross-culture competency. Already scheduled to expand over the next five years, the course will focus on kinship, language, religion, sports, and conflict resolution. "This is not a hollow exercise," says the director of the effort. One reason for the emphasis on kinship is because power structures differ in matrilineal and patrilineal societies, a point that could be important in negotiating conflict resolution abroad.

It's equally important to be prepared at home. As more workers from developing nations join the U.S. workforce, working effectively with colleagues from other cultures will grow more important. "You don't have to leave the U.S. to face these issues," said one New York native and owner of a family business who almost made a costly mistake by misconstruing a message from a customer in Louisiana. "We've got plenty big enough differences here." Ninety percent of respondents in a recent survey expect their organizations to grow more culturally diverse over just the next three to five years.

Source: Based on Maltby, E. (2010, January 19). Expanding abroad? Avoid cultural gaffes. *Wall Street Journal*, B-5; Payne, N. Cross-cultural gift giving etiquette. *Business Know-How, www.businessknowhow.com*. Accessed April 12, 2009; Rowell, J. (2009, April 3). Military to lessen culture shock via classroom lessons. *Montgomery Advertiser, www.montgomeryadvertiser.com*; Paton, N. (2009, April 1). How to bestride continents with confidence. *Management Issues, www.management-issues.com*; Sandberg, J. (2008, January 29). Global-market woes are more personality than nationality. *Wall Street Journal*, C-1. For related stories see Kraimer, M. L., Shaffer, M. A., and Bolino, M. C. (2009, January/February). The influence of expatriate and repatriate experiences on career advancement and repatriate retention. *Human Resource Management, 48*(1), 27–48; Benson, G. S., and Pattie, M. (2009, January/February). The comparative role of home and host supervisors in the expatriate experience. *Human Resource Management, 48*(1), 49–68; Herman, J. L., and Tetrick, L. E. (2009, January/February). Problem-focused versus emotion-focused coping strategies and repatriation adjustments. *Human Resource Management, 48*(1), 69–88. ■■

Cross-cultural training sensitizes candidates for international assignment to the local culture, customs, language, tax laws, and government.[72] Ideally, the training process should begin nine to twelve months in advance of the international assignment.[73]

Although training can cost $1,600 and more per manager in 2009 estimates, many companies feel the expense is minor compared to the huge cost of failed expatriate stints. For instance, despite massive cost-cutting moves at General Motors, the auto giant still spends nearly $500,000 a year on cross-cultural training for about 150 Americans and their families headed abroad. GM's general director of international personnel attributes the very low (less than 1 percent) premature return rate of GM expatriates to this training. The experience of a Cortland, Ohio, family transferred to Kenya by GM is typical. The family members underwent three days of cross-cultural training that consisted of a crash course in African political history, business practices, social customs, and nonverbal gestures. The family's two teenagers, who were miserable about moving to Africa, sampled Indian food (popular in Kenya) and learned how to ride Nairobi public buses, speak a little Swahili, and even how to juggle.[74]

One survey found that 57 percent of companies provide one day's worth of cross-cultural preparation; 32 percent provide it for the expatriate employee's entire family; and 22 percent for only the expatriate employee and spouse. Surprisingly, only 41 percent of firms mandated participation in cross-cultural preparation.[75] The least expensive type of cross-cultural training, the *information-giving approach*, lasts less than a week and merely provides indispensable briefings and a little language training. The *affective approach* (one to four weeks) focuses on providing the psychological and managerial skills the expatriate will need to perform effectively during a moderate-length assignment. The most extensive training, the *impression approach* (one to two months), prepares the manager for a long assignment with greater authority and responsibility by providing, for instance, field experiences and extended language training. Ideally, at least a portion of these training programs should be targeted to the expatriate's family. It is also possible (indeed desirable) to use similar "decompression" training programs for returning expatriates to help them cope with reverse culture shock.

Perhaps the most critical part of expatriate training occurs "on the job" and takes place shortly after the expatriate's arrival. Local managers need to be prepared to train incoming expatriates to ensure a smooth transition and to warn them of unexpected cultural pitfalls they may encounter. For instance, Dennis Ross, general manager of offshore operations at Convergys, a call-center company based in Cincinnati, works closely with Convergys' Indian Vice President Jaswinder Ghumman. When Convergys was building its company cafeteria in Gurgaon, a suburb of New Delhi, Ghumman was obliged to point out to Ross that Indian food must be served hot, and the cafeteria had to be able to support hot meal service. In addition, U.S. managers had to be educated on Indian food preferences and learn that cold sandwiches were not considered a meal item. According to Ross, "Who'd have thought tuna on rye could be such a stumbling block? We've succeeded by fostering open communications with our local people by taking nothing for granted."[76]

A key goal of selection and training by multinational firms is to have employees and managers located around the world who understand the norms, values, and expectations of the local community and how these may be blended with the firm's own culture and strategies. For instance, Disney at first faced major problems attracting visitors to the Disneyland Park in Taiwan, which opened in 2005. But by 2012, the situation had changed.

Visitors who do come find themselves in a thoroughly Chinese version of Disneyland. Among the attractions are an employee costumed as Cai Shen Ye, the Chinese god of wealth, and special red New Year's outfits for Mickey and Minnie to celebrate the Year of the Rat, renamed the Year of the Mouse inside the park. The upside-down Chinese character for "luck," a New Year's tradition, even featured a set of mouse ears on top, and the traditional parade down "Main Street USA" includes a dragon dance with traditional Chinese music, bird and flower puppets, and costumed figures representing the gods of longevity and happiness.

Apart from learning how to deal with cultural differences, another major challenge of training programs is to help prospective expatriates navigate risky international environments where politics can interfere with operations. The expatriate should never forget that sovereign governments have the power to facilitate, hinder, or even prevent her or his company from operating in their territories. Often business practices that are normal in the United States are considered illegal or proscribed in other countries (see the Manager's Notebook, "Learning How to Cope with Political Risks").

MANAGER'S NOTEBOOK

Emerging Trends

Learning How to Cope with Political Risks

Two of the most challenging tasks for expatriates and managers dealing with global issues are anticipating and dealing with political risks. Mistakes in these areas can be very costly because the company may miss important business opportunities, may be subject to fines and expensive legal suits, and in the extreme invite undesired government intervention into the business. A few examples within the last five years are listed here:

- IKEA is trying to open retail stores in India, but its business model of having all stores fully owned by the company has made this impossible so far. India's regulations require IKEA to have a local business partner and limit its stake in the joint venture to 51 percent. Unfortunately, according to IKEA's CEO, the company's business model "doesn't lend itself to a joint venture." This means losing out on one of the largest furniture markets in the world, estimated at $380 billion. Ninety-five percent or so of furniture in India is sold through small mom-and-pop shops.
- China has recently threatened retaliation against United Technologies, Boeing, Raytheon, and Lockheed Martin, even though these companies were not responsible for China's anger. Chinese leaders were enraged by U.S. plans to sell helicopters and antimissile systems to Taiwan.
- In a separate case concerning China, the Chinese government is trying to compel foreign automakers that want to produce electric vehicles in China to share critical technologies by requiring the companies to enter joint ventures in which they are limited to a minority stake. The plan is "tantamount to China strong-arming foreign auto makers to give up battery, electric-motor, and control technology in exchange for market access," says a senior executive at one foreign automaker. "We don't like it."
- U.S. firms of all sizes are introducing hotlines so that any employee can anonymously report to company officials what he or she believes is an ethical problem (such as managers falsifying accounting numbers, lying to customers, shortchanging safety requirements, committing or overlooking sexual harassment, overcharging the government, and the like). Many firms are trying to use these hotlines not only in the United States but also in their international operations. But they are encountering some unexpected opposition. For instance, France blocked McDonald's and Exide Technologies from using hotlines, asserting that they violate French privacy law because accusations can be anonymous. Anonymity—a key feature of U.S. hotlines—raises hot-button issues across Europe. In much of the European Union, notes London-based law firm Faegre & Benson LLP, "there is an historical unease over the concept of encouraging individuals to inform against others." The law firm Proskauer Rose LLP says that to Europeans—especially in Germany and France—anonymous reporting can "smack of WWII-era authoritarianism, neighbor spying on neighbor."

Source: Based on Global Political Risks (2013). *www.riskwatchdog.com*; *www.thinkingethics.typepad.com*. (2013). Thinking ethics; *Wall Street Journal* (2010, September 21). IKEA Cozies Up to India, B-10; *BusinessWeek* (2010, February 15), Thunder from China, 8; Gomez-Mejia, L., and Balkin, D. B. (2012). *Management*. Englewood Cliffs, NJ: Prentice Hall; Shirouzu, N. (2010, September 17). China spooks automakers. *Wall Street Journal*, A-1.

Career Development

The expatriate's motivation to perform well on an international assignment, to remain in the post for the duration of the assignment, and to be a high performer upon returning to the home office will depend to a large extent on the career development opportunities offered by the employer. At a minimum, successful career planning for expatriates requires the firm to do three things:

- ***Position the international assignment as a step toward advancement within the firm*** The firm should explicitly define the job; the length of the assignment; and the expatriate's reentry position, level, and career track on return. Some companies are shortening the length of expatriates' assignments. Three-quarters of firms responding to one survey indicate that the typical expatriate assignment is less than 12 months.[77] One reason is to ensure that the expatriate does not become too far removed from the company's mainstream. A second is that in 79 percent of cases, the family remains behind. One obvious drawback of this policy is that it may take a minimum of three to six months for an expatriate to feel comfortable with the local culture, just when it is time to return back home. Successful performance often depends on the establishment of internal and external social networks that take time to develop.
- ***Provide support for expatriates*** Maintaining contact can be accomplished in a number of ways.[78] A popular method is the buddy system, in which a manager or mentor at the home office is appointed to keep in touch with the expatriate and to provide assistance wherever necessary. Another approach has the expatriate employee coming back to the home office occasionally or at specified intervals to foster a sense of belonging to the organization and to reduce reentry shock. Some firms will pay for the expatriate's family to return home with him or her during this time. Although perhaps not a substitute for any of the above, technology now makes it possible for expatriates to be much more connected to the home office on a daily basis. (See the Manager's Notebook "Staying Closer to Home While Far Away.")

MANAGER'S NOTEBOOK

Staying Closer to Home While Far Away

Technology/Social Media

One of the main complaints of expatriates is that they are forgotten in a foreign land. Not long ago an expatriate assignment meant an almost total disconnect from the corporation's mainstream, with survey after survey showing that expatriates often felt "out of sight, out of mind." This translated into a perception that international assignments were not a good way to climb up the corporate ladder. Companies are now finding creative avenues for senior managers in corporate headquarters to remain in close contact with expatriates. For instance, a recent study reports that "one company created web portals that allowed employees to view expat policy statements and also to communicate with bosses, colleagues, and other expats around the world in chat rooms. Another used advanced video conferencing technology." Inexpensive programs requiring minimal investment such as Skype now allow for instant face-to-face communication from almost any country in the world by clicking a few keys—yet this was science fiction in the Star Trek movies of the 1990s.

Source: Based on McEvoy, G.M., and Buller, P.F. (2013). Research for practice: The management of expatriates. *Thunderbird International Business Review*, *55*(2), 213–226; Ananthran, S., and Chan, C. (2013). Challenges and strategies for global human resource executives: Perspectives from Canada and the United States. *European Management Journal*, *31*, 223–233; Zhuang, W. L., Wu, M., and Wen, S. C. (2013). Relationship of mentoring functions to expatriate adjustments: Comparing home country mentorship and host country mentorship. *International Journal of Human Resources*, *24*(5), 905–921; Shaffer, M., Singh, B., and Chen, Y. (2013). Expatriate satisfaction: The role of organizational inequities, assignment stressors and perceived assignment value. *International Journal of Human Resource Management*, *www.tandonline.com*. ■■

Cost-of-Living Index 2015*	
Seoul	155
Tokyo	140
Moscow	125
London	130
Singapore	98
New York	100
Beijing	90
Mexico City	75
Paris	85
Rio de Janeiro	70
Rome	85
Sydney	66
Bombay	65
Toronto	70

Note: *For three-person U.S. family at $100,000 income level

FIGURE 17.4
Living Costs Around the Globe

Source: Estimated by authors from various resources.

- ***Provide career support for spouse*** If the spouse is giving up his or her job to move, it can reduce family income by an average of 28 percent.[79] A recent Merrill Lynch survey indicated that most expatriates now expect the company to provide dual-career support.[80]

Compensation

Firms can use compensation packages to enhance the effectiveness of expatriate assignments. However, compensation policies can create conflict if locals compare their pay packages to the expatriate's and conclude that they are being treated unfairly. Planning compensation for expatriates requires management to follow three important guidelines:

- ***Provide the expatriate with a disposable income that is equivalent to what he or she would receive at home*** This usually requires granting expatriate employees an allowance for price differences in housing, food, and other consumer goods. Allowances for children's schooling and the whole family's medical treatment may also be necessary. The best-known cost-of-living index for world locations is published by Corporate Resources Group, a Geneva-based consulting firm that surveys 97 cities worldwide twice a year.

  The U.S. State Department also maintains a current cost-of-living index for most major cities around the world. Some of the most expensive locations around the world—including Tokyo, Osaka, London, and most Scandinavian cities—cost at least 50 percent more to live in than New York City. For short-term stays, the Runzheimer Guide provides per diem costs for 1,000 cities around the world. This index is used by hundreds of organizations to approve, benchmark, and budget travel expenses.[81]

  Maintaining income equality with the home office is not an exact science (for example, finding housing in Japan comparable to that available in U.S. suburbs is nearly impossible), but as a general rule, it is better to err on the side of generosity. See Figure 17.4 for a comparison of living costs in various cities around the world.
- ***Provide an explicit "add-on" incentive for accepting an international assignment*** The company may provide a sign-on bonus before departure. Or it may offer the employee a percentage increase over his or her home base salary; the standard increase is 15 percent of the base salary.[82] Or it may provide a lump-sum payment upon successful completion of the foreign assignment. Some firms offer a combination of these incentives. Generally, the greatest incentives are reserved for the least desirable locations. For instance, MNCs hoping to lure Western managers to Eastern Europe—where poor air quality, political instability, and a shortage of quality housing make assignments unattractive—often offer packages that include company-paid housing, subsidized shipment of scarce consumer goods, up to four trips home a year, and weekend getaways to Western Europe.[83] Oil companies operating in Colombia amid civil war face a constant threat of terrorism. Expatriates have been kidnapped and murdered. Occidental Petroleum alone has seen its pipeline bombed by rebels about 170 times a year.[84] In this situation, most expatriates receive hardship pay three to five times greater than the pay they would earn at home.
- ***Avoid having expatriates fill the same jobs held by locals or lower-ranking jobs*** Local employees tend to compare their pay and living standards to those of expatriates, and feelings of unfairness are more likely to surface if an expatriate at the same or lower rank than the local is receiving greater pay. Unfortunately, it may be impossible to prevent those feelings of inequity, particularly if a U.S. firm sends one of its top executives overseas. Compared to Western European countries, for instance, U.S. executives may earn as much as 20 times what a similar executive makes locally.

In some local labor markets, such as India, wages are increasing quickly for certain occupations as outsourcing outfits scramble for talent. For instance, controlling for inflation, the salary of a project manager in India in 2014 was more than three times what it was in 2000, and turnover in 2014 is running at 25 to 35 percent annually. As a result, companies in India and other places are starting to hire U.S. talent in order to fill a void at the local level as the cost of native skilled labor rises.[85] Ironically, many skilled Indian workers leave the country each year for the Persian Gulf or Singapore, where wages are higher.[86]

Calculating compensation packages for expatriate employees is one of the most difficult tasks facing MNCs.[87] Compensation used to be a relatively simple issue: Low-level local hires got paid in the local currency, while expatriate managers' pay was pegged to U.S. salaries.

However, in an era of dramatic corporate restructuring to cut costs, expatriate packages based on U.S. salaries are increasingly being considered too expensive. Moreover, as companies move into the later stages of internationalization, they work with a team of international employees operating out of the home office rather than just expatriates.

Still, some companies continue to compensate their expatriates generously. To avoid potential pay inequities when employees are transferred from one international post to another, 3M compares net salaries in both the old and the new country and provides the transferred employee whichever pay package is higher.[88] And Seagram Spirits and Wine Group has come up with an "international cadre policy" for those expatriates who work abroad permanently (as opposed to expatriates who will return to the United States in the future). The package features a standardized cost-of-living adjustment and a global standard employee housing contribution that is the same regardless of location. For temporary U.S. expatriates, Seagram maintains what it terms a "pure expatriate" package that keeps people up to par with U.S. compensation standards.[89]

One thing that makes these pay comparisons easier today is the availability of international pay and benefit surveys on the Web. For instance, Personnel Systems Associates offers a directory of 1,500 such surveys covering hundreds of job titles.[90]

Several other excellent sources that provide comprehensive global pay data include the Radford International Survey (*www.radford.com*), the Culpepper Global Compensation Survey (*www.culpepper.com*), and the ERI Economic Research Institute Survey (*www.erieri.com*).

One issue that continues to complicate compensation design for expatriates is fluctuating exchange rates. For instance, in 2000 each dollar was worth approximately 1.22 euros. By 2005, each dollar was worth .70 euros. By summer 2008, each dollar was worth .54 euros, and by 2014 it was around .66 euros. Pay equity ratios between natives (paid in local currency) and expatriates (paid in dollars) can change very quickly. Firms usually handle this problem by adjusting the pay of employees who are "losing" (those whose currency is being devalued), but this needs to be done carefully because the value of the currency may change again.[91] Paying all employees (locals and expatriates) in U.S. dollars adds even more complexity to the pay equity issue. As recently noted by one analyst, "This has often resulted in distortion of several local pay markets as natives in countries with relatively weak currencies compared with the U.S. dollar (e.g., Africa, Asia-Pacific) who are paid in dollars received compensation of 200 percent to 300 percent more than local norms."[92]

Role of HR Department

A recent survey asked expatriates, "What advice would you have for HR departments about handling expatriates?" According to Professor Joyce Osland, who conducted the study, "What they want most from the HR department is to have unnecessary uncertainty eliminated. There is enough ambiguity overseas—they don't need any more from the HR department. Expatriates want HR to remove obstacles." According to one survey respondent, "The first thing that HR needs to do is to make sure it knows how to handle the logistics such as getting the furniture moved. Because you have all of these little . . . [problems] that take up all of your time when you are trying to deal with other things . . ."[93]

Another survey by Polak International Consultants, an international human resources consulting firm, confirms that most expatriates are unhappy with the services provided by their HR departments; the survey respondents considered the HR department unprepared to meet the requirements of a global workforce. This suggests that a priority in coming years is for multinational corporations' HR departments to be more aware and sensitive to the needs of an international workplace.[94] To achieve this requires not only better service to expatriates but also better tracking of HR trends overseas.

Women and International Assignments

Although in 2014 women represented almost half of all managers in the United States, only 13 percent of U.S. managers sent abroad are women. According to a study by Catalyst, an international consulting firm, there are three misconceptions about women's ability and willingness to handle international assignments: (1) Companies assume that women are not as internationally mobile as men, yet 80 percent of women have never turned down an expatriate assignment offered to them, whereas only 71 percent of men have never turned down expatriate assignments. (2) Companies assume that women encounter more work–life conflict working on a global schedule. However, nearly half of *both* women *and* men report they find work–life balance difficult. (3) Most companies believe clients outside the United States are not as comfortable doing business with women as they are with men. In fact, 76 percent of expatriate women said being a woman had a positive or neutral impact on their effectiveness overseas.[95]

Developing HRM Policies in a Global Context

Firms operating in multiple countries need to worry not just about meeting the special needs of expatriate employees but also about the design and implementation of HRM programs in diverse cross-cultural settings. One company that is widely viewed as exceptional in its achievement of a unified global HRM program—even with two-thirds of its employees working overseas—is Coca-Cola.

In many countries reliance on U.S., or Western, managerial practices is likely to clash with deeply ingrained norms and values.[96] For instance, the open-door style of management, which works well in a culture that readily accepts questioning of authority, will probably not work in countries—such as China—where such behavior is considered unacceptable.[97] Rather than simply transferring abroad HRM practices that are based on the home country's social and cultural standards, managers should mold these practices to the cultural environment in which a particular facility is located.[98]

National Culture, Organizational Characteristics, and HRM Practices

"Culture is important to HRM practices." This statement may seem obvious, but its relevance may be lost in a country such as the United States, where many of the best-known theories of management practice are firmly rooted in Western culture. Geert Hofstede, a Dutch professor, has spent the better part of his professional life studying the similarities and differences among cultures. He has concluded that there are five major dimensions to culture:

1. ***Power distance*** Extent to which individuals expect a hierarchical structure that emphasizes status differences between subordinates and superiors.
2. ***Individualism*** Degree to which a society values personal goals, autonomy, and privacy over group loyalty, commitment to group norms, involvement in collective activities, social cohesiveness, and intense socialization.
3. ***Uncertainty avoidance*** Extent to which a society places a high value on reducing risk and instability.
4. ***Masculinity/femininity*** Degree to which a society views assertive or "masculine" behavior as important to success and encourages rigidly stereotyped gender roles.
5. ***Long-term/short-term orientation*** Extent to which values are oriented toward the future (saving, persistence) as opposed to the past or present (respect for tradition, fulfilling social obligations).[99]

Although Hofstede's research has been criticized for being based largely on the experiences of employees working for only one company (IBM) and for downplaying the importance of cultural differences within countries, other evidence suggests that the five dimensions are a fair summary of cultural differences.[100] They provide clues regarding the general configuration of HRM strategies that are most likely to mesh with a particular culture's values. Figure 17.5 outlines the characteristics of cultures ranking high or low on each of Hofstede's dimensions, lists sample countries falling at each end of the spectrum, and summarizes the organizational features and HRM practices that work best at each end of the scale.

The information in Figure 17.5 has significant implications for international firms. As a general principle, *the more an HRM practice contradicts the prevailing societal norms, the more likely it will fail.*[101] For instance, Hofstede describes management by objectives (MBO) as "perhaps the single most popular management technique 'made in the U.S.A.'"[102] because it assumes (1) negotiation between the boss and employee, or a not-too-large power distance, (2) a willingness on the part of both parties to take risks, or weak uncertainty avoidance, and (3) both supervisors and subordinates seeing performance and its associated rewards as important. Because all three assumptions are prominent features of U.S. culture, MBO "fits" the United States. But in

Power Distance: Organizational Characteristics and Selected HR Practices

Dominant Values	Sample Countries	Organizational Features	Reward Practices	Staffing/Appraisal Practices
		Power Distance		
High				
• Top-down communications • Class divisions seen as natural • Authoritarianism	• Malaysia • Philippines • Mexico	• Centralization and tall organizational structures • Traditional line of command	• Hierarchical compensation system • Difference in pay and benefits reflect job and status differences; large differential between higher- and lower-level jobs • Visible rewards that project power, such as a large office or company car	• Limited search methods in recruitment; emphasis on connections and "whom you know" • Few formal mechanisms of selection • Superior makes selection choice for his or her sphere of influence
Low				
• Egalitarianism • Status based on achievement • Joint decision making	• The Netherlands • Australia • Switzerland	• Flatter organizational structures • Decentralized control • Great degree of worker involvement	• Egalitarian-based compensation systems • Small differences in pay and benefits between higher- and lower-level jobs • Participatory pay strategies (such as gainsharing) more prevalent	• Multiple search methods; extensive advertisement • Formalized selection methods "to give everyone a fair chance" • Superior constrained in making selection choices • Selection based on merit; loyalty to superiors deemphasized

FIGURE 17.5
Cultural Characteristics and Dominant Values

(Continued)

other countries—France, for example—MBO has generally run into problems because of cultural incompatibility:

> The high power distance to which the French are accustomed from childhood ultimately has thwarted the successful utilization of MBO as a truly participative process. . . . The problem is not necessarily with MBO per se but the French managers . . . who are unaware that they are trying to exert control through the implementation of the objectives of MBO almost by fiat.[103]

EEO in the International Context

The globalization of industry raises numerous equal employment opportunity (EEO) issues, only some of which the U.S. courts have addressed. This is not a well-developed area of employment law.[104] However, the following principles seem clear:

- U.S. companies are prohibited from basing employment decisions on employee characteristics such as race, sex, and age. This prohibition applies to international assignments, with

Individualism: Organizational Characteristics and Selected HR Practices

Dominant Values	Sample Countries	Organizational Features	Reward Practices	Staffing/Appraisal Practices
		Individualism		
High				
• Personal accomplishment • Belief in individual control and responsibility • Belief in creating one's own destiny	• United States • Great Britain • Canada	• Organizations not compelled to care for employees' total well-being • Employees look after their own individual interests • Explicit systems of control necessary to ensure compliance and prevent wide deviation from organizational norms	• Performance-based pay • Individual achievement rewarded • External equity emphasized • Extrinsic rewards are important indicators of personal success • Attempts made to isolate individual contributions (i.e., who did what) • Emphasis on short-term objectives	• Emphasis on credentials and visible performance outcomes attributed to individual • High turnover; commitment to organization for career reasons • Performance rather than seniority as criterion for advancement
Low				
• Team accomplishment • Sacrifice for others • Belief in group control and responsibility • Belief in the hand of fate	• Singapore • South Korea • Indonesia	• Organizations committed to high-level involvement in workers' personal lives • Loyalty to the firm is critical • Normative, rather than formal, systems of control to ensure compliance	• Group-based performance is important criterion for rewards • Seniority-based pay utilized • Intrinsic rewards essential • Internal equity guides pay policies • Personal needs (such as number of children) affect pay received	• Value of credentials and visible performance outcomes depends on perceived contributions to team efforts • Low turnover; commitment to organization as "family" • Seniority plays an important role in personnel decisions • "Fitting in" with work group crucial: belief that interpersonal relations are important performance dimension

FIGURE 17.5 ***(Continued)***

the single exception that companies are not required to violate a host nation law. Thus, if a nation prohibits women from working in a specific business context, a U.S. company doing business in that nation is free to offer the particular international assignment covered by this host country law only to men. However, most countries that openly discriminate against their own female citizens are quite flexible in dealing with U.S. companies' female employees. Therefore, companies should not make exclusions automatically.

- Foreign-national employees of U.S. companies working in their own country or in some other foreign country are not covered by U.S. employment law. For instance, the U.S. Supreme Court ruled that a Saudi Arabian citizen working for an American oil company in Saudi Arabia could not sue his employer under Title VII.[105]

Uncertainty Avoidance: Organizational Characteristics and Selected HR Practices

Dominant Values	Sample Countries	Organizational Features	Reward Practices	Staffing/Appraisal Practices
		Uncertainty Avoidance		
High				
• Fear of random events and the unknown • High value placed on stability and routine • Low tolerance for ambiguity	• Greece • Portugal • Italy	• Mechanistic structures • Written rules and policies guide the firm • Organizations strive to be predictable	• Bureaucratic pay policies utilized • Compensation programs tend to be centralized • Fixed pay more important than variable pay	• Bureaucratic rules/procedures to govern hiring and promotion • Seniority an important factor in hiring and promotions • Government/union regulations limit employer discretion in recruitment, promotion, and terminations
Low				
• Unexpected viewed as challenging and exciting • Stability and routine seen as boring • Ambiguity seen as providing opportunities	• Singapore • Denmark • Sweden	• Less-structured activities • Fewer written rules to cope with changing environmental forces • Managers are more adaptable and tend to make riskier decisions	• Variable pay a key component in pay programs • External equity emphasized • Decentralized pay program is the norm	• Fewer rules/procedures to govern hiring and promotions • Seniority deemphasized in personal decisions • Employer provided much latitude in recruitment, promotion, and terminations

FIGURE 17.5 ***(Continued)***

- Under the Immigration Control and Reform Act of 1986, people who are not U.S. citizens but who are living and have legal work status in the United States may not be discriminated against.

Important Caveats

The effectiveness of an HRM practice depends on how well it matches a culture's value system. Even so, managers need to keep several caveats in mind.

- ***"National culture" may be an elusive concept*** For this reason, managers should be careful not to be guided by stereotypes that hold some truth but may not apply to very many people in a culture. Stereotyping is a great danger in large, heterogeneous countries such as the United States, where cultural differences are often huge, but it can also cause problems even in relatively homogeneous nations. For instance, Western German firms hiring Eastern German workers frequently found that the latter reacted negatively to incentive systems that had been used successfully with their Western German counterparts—despite the fact that the two groups shared the same language, ethnicity, and cultural background. The Eastern Germans distrusted such incentive schemes, reported they felt manipulated by management, and shunned those workers who outproduced others.[106] A recent study examining Hofstede's culture dimensions suggests that some cultures are tighter than others, meaning that they exert more pressure on people to conform. Hence, individuals in culturally tighter societies have much less flexibility to diverge from cultural norms.[107]

Masculinity/Femininity: Organizational Characteristics and Selected HR Practices

Dominant Values	Sample Countries	Organizational Features	Reward Practices	Staffing/Appraisal Practices
		Masculinity		
High				
• Material possessions important • Men given higher power and status than women • Rigid gender stereotypes	• Mexico • Germany • United States	• Some occupations labeled as "male," others as "female" • Fewer women in higher-level positions	• Differential pay policies that allow for gender inequities • Tradition an acceptable basis for pay decisions • "Male" traits rewarded in promotions and other personnel decisions	• De facto preferential treatment for men in hiring/promotion decisions into higher-level jobs (even if it is illegal) • "Glass ceiling" for women • Occupational segregation
Low				
• Quality of life valued more than material gain • Men not believed to be inherently superior • Minimal gender stereotyping	• The Netherlands • Norway • Sweden • Finland	• More flexibility in career choice for men and women • More women in higher-level jobs	• Jobs evaluated without regard for gender of job holders • Focus on work content rather than tradition to assess value of different jobs • Well-developed "equity goals" for pay determination	• Gender deemphasized in hiring/promotion decisions for any job • More women in upper-level positions • Occupational integration between the sexes

FIGURE 17.5 ***(Continued)***

- ***Cultures change over time*** Although cultures are generally resistant to change, sometimes the pace of change quickens; hence, employee values and attitudes may differ significantly from one time period to another. This is particularly true when there is rapid economic development and when countries are exposed to foreign influences (see Exhibit 17.1).
- ***Corporate headquarters sometimes blame international personnel problems on cultural factors without careful study*** Often personnel problems have little to do with cultural values and much to do with poor management. For example, a U.S. company introduced individual incentives for R&D employees at its English subsidiary. This policy created intense conflict, lack of cooperation, and declining performance. Top managers blamed the strong role of labor unions in England for these disappointing results. In fact, a large amount of evidence indicates that individual-based incentives are counterproductive when the nature of the task requires extensive teamwork (as is the case in R&D).[108]
- ***Hard data on the success or failure of different HRM practices as a function of national culture are practically nonexistent*** This means that judgment calls, gut feelings, and some trial and error based on a fine-tuned cultural sensitivity and open-mindedness are mandatory in international HRM.
- ***Different cultures often have very different notions of right and wrong*** In many cases, corporate headquarters may have to impose its own value system across multiple nations with conflicting value structures. For example, child labor is common in many Asian and African countries. The corporation may choose to avoid such practices on ethical grounds, but it must recognize that doing so can put it at a competitive disadvantage because local firms that have no qualms about using child labor will have lower labor costs. And, although members of the World Trade Organization and the United Nations have agreed to a set of "core labor standards" prohibiting employment discrimination, exploitive forms of

Long-Term/Short-Term Orientation: Organizational Characteristics and Selected HR Practices

Dominant Values	Sample Countries	Organizational Features	Reward Practices	Staffing/Appraisal Practices
		Long-Term/Short-Term Orientation		
High				
• Future-oriented • Delayed gratification • Long-term goals	• Japan • Hong Kong • China	• Stable organizations • Low employee turnover • Strong company culture	• Long-term rewards • Seniority as basis for pay • Managers rewarded for multiyear accomplishments • No expectation of frequent pay adjustments	• Slow promotions • Promotions from within • High employment security • High emphasis on saving employees' face • High emphasis on coaching versus evaluation • High investment in training and employee development
Low				
• Past- or present-oriented • Immediate gratification • Short-term goals	• United States • Indonesia	• Changing organization • High employee turnover • Weak company culture	• Short-term rewards • Recent performance as a basis for pay • Managers rewarded for annual accomplishments • High expectation of frequent pay adjustments	• Fast promotions • Internal and external hires • Low employment security • Low emphasis on saving employees' face • High emphasis on evaluation versus coaching • Low investment in training and employee development

FIGURE 17.5 (*Continued*)

child labor, and the use of forced labor such as prison labor, violations still occur in many countries, with at least 13 million children working in export industries, such as textiles.[109]

- ***The business laws of other countries often force companies to change their practices*** In some cases, if the firm wants to do business in another country, it must accept local regulations and practices even if these differ significantly from those in the home country.[110]
- ***Multinationals must find the right balance between tailor-made HR policies to fit particular cultures and the need to integrate global consistency with local adaptability*** The current trend in establishing international HR policies appears to be to strive toward integration rather than segmentation of HR policies. The reason for this trend toward integration, according to a recent survey, is that 85 percent of global companies are trying to establish a corporate culture in all locations consistent with the organization's goals and vision. However, 88 percent report that local culture and customs have a "moderate to great" influence on the way they conduct business in particular locations.[111] This requires that organizations try to balance the need for local adaptation with the trend toward global consistency of HR policies.

EXHIBIT 17.1 HRM PRACTICES BECOMING MORE ALIKE AROUND THE GLOBE

Expectations for higher returns from the stock market and investment funds irrespective of national boundaries are forcing firms all over the world to adopt HRM practices that until recently were seen as uniquely American. These include low job security, performance-based pay, flatter organizations, frequent performance appraisals, promotions based on merit, global hiring, "scientific" selection programs, and teaming up with firms across frontiers in part to have access to a broader employee base and expertise. For example:

- When Sony Corp. announced plans to cut 17,000 jobs—10 percent of its workforce—in a sweeping restructuring, long-suffering investors finally had something to feel good about. Sony's American depository receipts (ADRs) promptly soared by more than one-third, to $104.
- Firms such as Toshiba and NEC review employee performance on a regular basis, and employees who do not meet certain objectives are put on probation or terminated. Traditionally, such firms would find makeshift jobs for low performers and keep them on payroll.
- In Mexico, two large firms have instituted HR practices to become more efficient. For instance, Grupo Televisa, the world's largest Spanish-language media company, and Empresas ICA, the country's biggest construction outfit, use batteries of selection devices to hire employees and avoid the traditional "amigismo" practices (i.e., hiring your friends) used by many Latin American firms.
- European conglomerates ranging from Germany's Veba to France's Lagardère Group are bringing in hot new talent from all over the world, a radical practice for European firms.
- Because stock options were expensed in the United States after 2006 (see Chapter 11), making them less attractive from an accounting perspective, the proportion of compensation in the form of stock options is becoming more equal around the world (most countries already required stock options to be included as part of total operating costs).

Although the discussion in this chapter has focused mainly on differences in HRM practices across different countries, global forces are exerting a great deal of influence to make them more similar. Financial investors and the stock market in general appear to favor certain organizational practices (such as pay for performance, promotion based on merit, and restructuring), regardless of nationality, and firms all over the world appear to be responding accordingly, as we see in Exhibit 17.1.

Human Resources Management and Exporting Firms

Our discussion so far has focused on larger firms with international facilities (that is, those in stages 3 to 5 of internationalization). However, the practices we have discussed are also relevant to smaller firms that are interested solely in exporting their products. It is estimated that only about 20 percent of U.S. firms with fewer than 500 employees have ever been active exporters, a percentage that lags way behind that found in most industrialized nations. At least 30,000 small firms in the United States have the potential to export competitively but do not do so.[112]

A number of studies have shown that the key impediments to exporting are (1) lack of knowledge of international markets, business practices, and competition and (2) lack of management commitment to generating international sales.[113] These impediments can be largely attributed to poor utilization of human resources within U.S. firms rather than to external factors. There is some evidence that a company that clearly reinforces international activities in its HRM practices is more likely to fare well in its export attempts.[114] Reinforcing international activities in HRM practices requires a company to:

- Explicitly consider international experience when making promotion and recruitment decisions, particularly to the senior management ranks.
- Provide developmental activities designed to equip employees with the skills and knowledge necessary to carry out their jobs in an international context. Developmental activities that enhance a firm's ability to compete globally include (1) programs designed to provide specific job skills and competencies in international business, (2) opportunities for development and growth in the international field, and (3) the use of appraisal processes that explicitly consider international activities as part of performance reviews.

- Create career ladders that take into account short- and long-term international strategies.
- Design a reward structure that motivates key organizational players to take full advantage of the company's export potential. Reinforcing desired export-related behaviors is likely to increase commitment to foreign sales as managers devote greater attention to skill development, information gathering, and scanning the environment for international opportunities.

The decision to export will require CEOs and senior marketing personnel to spend a significant time away from the office attending trade shows and developing relationships with distributors and companies abroad. Particularly in small companies, this means that the staff back home must be empowered to make decisions regarding the running of the business, with the traveling CEOs and executives keeping in touch via phone, fax, or e-mail.

The process of making the right export connections and establishing relationships used to be slow and painstaking, but the Web is changing all that, opening exports to firms of any size. For instance, net sales of clothing and accessories overseas by U.S. firms through the Internet are projected to soar to $70 billion by 2020. In the first year of its operation, New York-based Girlshop.com, for example, exported $2,000,000 worth of avant-garde merchandise and made $250,000 in operating profit.[115]

To succeed internationally on the Web, however, firms must implement HR practices such as selection and training programs. These services can help firms surmount language barriers, use cutting-edge technology to mix and match products to diverse customer needs, adapt products to different cultural tastes and preferences, engender customer trust, and the like. Although many of these issues also apply to the domestic market, they become more challenging overseas where the market is far more heterogeneous and segmented.[116]

Ethics and Social Responsibility

Globalization increases the possibility that managers, especially those sent to regions very different from their home country, will face ethical dilemmas. For instance, as noted earlier, in many countries what would be considered a bribe in the United States would be considered a commission or an expected gift of reciprocity, part of doing business. Because competition is global, expatriates may feel that if they apply a stricter code of ethics than managers at other firms, the company may be put at a disadvantage, which would reflect poorly on their performance evaluations.

The U.S. Congress passed the Foreign Corruption Practices Act in 1977 as a result of United Brand's $2.5 million bribe to a Honduran government official to reduce the banana tax. The law expressly forbids substantial payments by U.S. firms to foreign officials to influence decisions. The act does not appear to have had an adverse effect on U.S. firms operating overseas. It is even possible that the legislation improved the image of U.S. firms, counterbalancing any losses.[117] Yet despite the act, U.S. expatriates may still be tempted to take the risk of paying foreign bribes to generate more business.

What is ethical and what is legal may differ, and the differences are probably more pronounced when HR practices are considered on a global basis. In many countries, for instance, child labor is not illegal and discrimination against women in employment is viewed as normal. Hence, the multinational firm—and more specifically the expatriates who are often in top management positions overseas—confront tough ethical choices even though legality is not the issue. Consider, for instance, the following story from the late 1990s. Kathie Lee Gifford tearfully confessed on her morning talk show that she had not known that her Wal-Mart outfits were made by Honduran girls paid 31 cents an hour. Made in the U.S.A., a lobbying group, informed consumers that Michael Jordan reportedly earned $20 million a year endorsing Nike sneakers—more than the total annual payroll for the thousands of Indonesians who made them.

The flaying of celebrities like Gifford and Jordan makes it easy to miss the point. As noted by one ethics writer:

> For years, children have been sold as slaves, blinded or maimed for crying or rebelling, or trying to return home, ill-fed, bone-weary, short-lived. They file the scissors blades, mix the gunpowder for the firecrackers, knot the carpets, stitch the soccer balls with needles longer than their fingers. Human-rights groups guess there may be 200 million children around the world, from China to South America, working full time—no play, no school, no chance. All of which raises the question, once the news lands on the front page: How much

are we willing to sacrifice the children of other countries to give our children what they want? Americans search for bargains with enduring passion, but it is hard to find them—such as a handmade rug for only $7,000—without tiny fingerprints on them somewhere. If child-labor and safety laws were truly enforced, trade experts say, whole industries in many countries would collapse, at great cost to both developing and developed economies.[118]

These issues are still with us, although international firms are becoming much more concerned about self-regulation to prevent the worst abuses. Nike, for example, has done much to change the negative image it had a few years back for exploiting young children (often under the age of 10) in Indonesia by paying them a dime per hour (although from time to time similar issues with Nike resurface). It was alleged that many of these children developed permanent disabilities after working in Nike's factories. Many firms and industry groups have developed or are developing their own voluntary code of conduct for foreign operations. For example, the American Apparel Manufacturers Association (AAMA), whose members include Munsingwear, Jockey International, and VF, requires members to pay the existing minimum wage, maintain certain minimum safety standards, and avoid the use of child labor. For a related discussion, see the Manager's Notebook, "Toxic Factories Take Hold of China's Labor Force."

MANAGER'S NOTEBOOK

Ethics/Social Responsibility

Toxic Factories Take Hold of China's Labor Force

Inexpensive, long-lasting, rechargeable, and safe to use, nickel-cadmium batteries quickly became a mainstay in many toys made in China for export to the United States. Yet many U.S. companies have begun phasing these batteries out of their products because their manufacture is so hazardous to Chinese workers. Cadmium, a toxic metal that causes cancer, is banned in Europe and Japan, and cadmium batteries have not been made in the United States for many years.

The United States has seen a wave of recent scares and recalls of products made in China that contain lead and other substances hazardous to consumers. The widespread rejection of nickel-cadmium batteries by U.S. firms such as Hasbro, Mattel, Wal-Mart, and Toys 'R' Us goes further, recognizing a manufacturing component's danger to workers in China, where the vast majority of the world's toys are made.

The response was spurred by a front-page news story that profiled a Chinese engineer. Her blog, written in Chinese and translated by *The Wall Street Journal*, chronicled her experience with the debilitating symptoms of cadmium poisoning acquired at the battery factory where she worked for nine years and against which she has filed a lawsuit. About 400 workers at the company, GP Batteries International Ltd., were also found to have elevated levels of cadmium, making them vulnerable to kidney failure, lung cancer, and bone disease. Hundreds more quit their jobs there.

When the last U.S. cadmium-battery factory closed in 1979, the site required a $130 million clean-up and sparked a multimillion-dollar class action suit by residents of the area. But the unending search for cheaper means of production often sends hazardous manufacturing processes to developing countries, where workers have fewer protections. GP Batteries paid more than $1 million in worker compensation and medical bills, but now outsources production of cadmium batteries to independent factories elsewhere in China.

Source: Based on Stelmach, M. (2013). Sweatshops in China. *www.youtube.com*; *www.waronwant.org*. (2013). Sweatshops in China; *http://toxictort.lawyercentral.com*. Factory toxic gas leak in China. Accessed 2011; Cain Miller, C. (2008, December 18). Green battery start-up begins with drills. *New York Times*, *http://bits.blogs.nytimes.com*; Spencer, J. (2008, February 19). Toys 'R' Us, Mattel phase out cadmium batteries. *Wall Street Journal*, A-1. ■■

Dealing with Political Risks

As noted earlier, the more a firm expands to multiple countries, the more exposed it becomes to political risk. By *political risk,* we mean the possibility that social (and often governmental) pressures in a foreign country may negatively affect the firm's operation. American firms operating in France, for instance, are under a great deal of pressure to avoid layoffs, even if they are overstaffed. Internet providers such as Google and Yahoo! have been widely criticized in the United States for collaborating with the Chinese government, blocking content that the government considers "subversive" and informing authorities on the Internet use of dissidents. In Russia, local companies often pay public officials to raid the offices of business rivals and subject them to criminal investigation, with foreign-owned firms becoming easy targets.[119]

In most of Western Europe, the image of the "ugly American" has resurfaced in recent years, complicating the work of expatriates there. As noted in a 2008 article in *BusinessWeek*, "as credit woes endanger the world economy, they're giving Europeans another reason to resent U.S. influence. Anti-Americanism was already simmering because of the Iraq war, dislike for President George W. Bush, and mistrust of rampaging buyout firms."[120] A U.S. expatriate may feel the heat of Europe's simmering anti-Americanism, even though the subprime mess and the Wall Street crash are not his or her fault.

In short, expatriates are increasingly thrown into the middle of political storms, and they need to be able to respond appropriately to manage potentially damaging situations. This means that besides learning about the foreign culture, expatriates should be prepared to deal with the political forces that they might face. Although this in itself is nothing new, there is little doubt that the political landscape for most companies is far more complex now than it used to be in the not too distant past.

Summary and Conclusions

The Stages of International Involvement

Firms progress through five stages as they internationalize their operations: (1) domestic operations, (2) export operations, (3) subsidiaries or joint ventures, (4) multinational operations, and (5) transnational operations. The higher the stage, the more HR practices need to be adapted to diverse cultural, economic, political, and legal environments.

Determining the Mix of Host-Country and Expatriate Employees

In managing its overseas subsidiaries, a firm can choose an ethnocentric, polycentric, or geocentric approach. Firms tend to rely on expatriates more when sufficient local talent is unavailable, the firm is trying to create a corporatewide global vision, international and domestic units are highly interdependent, the political situation is unstable, and there are significant cultural differences between the host country and the home country.

The Challenges of Expatriate Assignments

An important part of international HRM is managing expatriate employees, both during their international assignments and when they return home. International assignments fail because of career blockage, culture shock, lack of predeparture cross-cultural training, an overemphasis on technical qualifications, the use of such assignments to get rid of troublesome employees, and family problems. Upon returning, expatriates may meet with a lack of respect for their acquired skills, a loss of status, poorly planned jobs, and reverse culture shock.

Enhancing the Effectiveness of Expatriate Assignments

In selecting people for international assignments, employers should emphasize cultural sensitivity, establish a selection board of expatriates, require previous international experience when possible, explore the possibility of hiring the foreign-born who can later serve as "expatriates," and screen candidates' spouses and families. Cross-cultural training programs of various lengths and levels of rigor can be implemented to prepare employees for their assignments. In terms of career development for expatriates, companies should position international assignments as a step toward advancement within the firm and provide support for expatriates. To avoid problems in the compensation area, companies should provide expatriates with enough disposable income and incentive bonuses and avoid having expatriates fill the same or lower-ranking jobs that locals hold in the international operation.

Developing HRM Policies in a Global Context

Managers should not simply transfer abroad HRM practices based on the home country's social and cultural standards. Rather, they should mold these practices to the cultural environments in which the international facilities are located. In general, the more an HRM practice contradicts prevailing societal norms, the more likely it will fail.

Human Resource Management and Exporting Firms

Many firms have the potential to export profitably. A company is more likely to fare better in its export attempts when it clearly reinforces international activities by (1) explicitly considering international experience in hiring decisions, (2) providing developmental activities to equip employees with international skills, (3) creating career ladders for internationally experienced employees, and (4) designing a reward structure that motivates employees to begin export activities.

Key Terms

culture shock, 567
ethnocentric approach, 564
expatriate, 560
geocentric approach, 564
joint venture, 564
multinational corporation (MNC), 560
polycentric approach, 564
transnational corporation, 561
wholly owned subsidiary, 564

Watch It!

Joby: Global HR Management. If your instructor has assigned this, go to **mymanagementlab.com** to watch a video case and answer questions.

Discussion Questions

17-1. As noted in the chapter-opening vignette, Toyota ran into trouble for two reasons. One was that the company centralized most decision making in corporate headquarters. The second was that the CEO pressured top engineers to cut costs to improve profitability. What should an international company do to avoid these pitfalls? What are some potential pitfalls with your recommendations?[121]

17-2. How might an international firm trying to adapt HRM practices to the local culture produce worse results than it would produce by "exporting" HRM practices from the home office?

17-3. What is the likelihood that, in order to protect and to create jobs at home, some developed nations might take steps to curtail the practice of outsourcing to less-developed countries in the future? What are the possible future trends and how might this affect businesses and consumers?

✪ 17-4. U.S. MNCs experience a much higher rate of early returns with their expatriate employees than European and Japanese MNCs do. What explains this difference? What HRM policies and procedures would you develop to reduce this problem?

17-5. Reread the Manager's Notebook, "Toxic Factories Take Hold of China's Labor Force." Do you think it is fair for a company to take advantage of lax environmental standards in other countries? Should a multinational company take special care (even if it is more costly) to invest in equipment to protect workers' health? If employees and their families are aware of the risks they take in working at a particular plant, is the company acting ethically by allowing individuals to work in unsafe conditions? Explain.

✪ 17-6. Some people believe that U.S. MNCs should serve as vehicles for cultural change in developing countries by introducing modern U.S. HRM practices and instilling values (such as punctuality and efficiency) in the workforce that are necessary for industrialization. Do you agree with this assertion? Explain.

17-7. Some people simply cannot adjust to the demands of postings overseas. They find it impossible to adapt to a radically different cultural environment. What is this called and what are the implications to the individual and the organization at home and overseas? Is it just a question of being monolingual or is it more complicated than that?

17-8. Reread the Manager's Notebook, "Learning How to Cope with Political Risks." How do you think firms can better utilize HR practices to avoid the pitfalls illustrated in the Manager's Notebook? Explain.

17-9. What kind of issues might an employee face when they return home after an extended period of service overseas? What are the common problems and how should an organization seek to help the individual to overcome these problems?

MyManagementLab®

If your instructor has assigned this, go to **mymanagementlab.com** for the following Assisted-graded writing questions:

17-10. Outline a set of features that you would put in place if you were asked to design a selection and training program for expatriates. Based on the materials learned in this chapter, explain why you have suggested each of the specific features.

17-11. In recent years many companies sent managers overseas on short-term assignments (for a couple of weeks or less) rather than on a long-term basis. What factors do you think explain this trend? What are the advantages and disadvantages of relying on short-term versus long-term assignments for expatriates? Explain your answer.

17-12. Some experts believe that one way for a multinational firm to avoid political risks in a foreign country is to use local executives for key positions. Why do they reach that conclusion? Do you agree? Explain.

You Manage It! 1: Global

American Universities Moving Overseas

According to a recent report by the *Chronicle of Higher Education,* "[t]oday almost every American university that can afford official letterhead seems to have an international strategy. Although such strategies differ widely, one common element in many is an interest in establishing a branch campus in another part of the world." Hundreds of branch campuses of U.S. universities now operate overseas, and business schools are generally at the forefront. Here are a few current examples:

- Stanford University, the Massachusetts Institute of Technology, and the University of Nevada have opened up campuses in Singapore, a country that has declared its intention to attract 150,000 international students in the near future.
- Johns Hopkins University has a budget of $20 million for its 100,000-square-foot joint venture with Nanyung University in China.
- The president of New York University (NYU), John Sexton, has appeared in television talk shows with Bill Moyers and Richard Heffner to sell his vision of a global university linked by global technology, and taught by global professors. As part of this vision, NYU has already opened branch campuses in Buenos Aires, Shanghai, Singapore, and Tel Aviv, with more coming soon.
- Many traditional U.S. public universities are also entering the race to open foreign branches. For example, Michigan State is setting out for Dubai, while Florida State is heading for Panama.

Apart from the expansion of branch campuses overseas, U.S. universities at home are globalizing rapidly. For instance, 10 percent of the freshmen at the University of Iowa come from foreign high schools. According to the most recent figures by the Institute of International Education, in any single year, more than 200,000 new students come to the United States from China and India alone. At last count, more than half of the PhD's in mathematics, the sciences, and engineering and a growing proportion of PhD's in business are nonresident aliens.

Critical Thinking Questions

17-13. From a human resource perspective, what are the benefits and the pitfalls of a U.S. university pursuing a global strategy as discussed in this case? Explain.

17-14. Do you think the trend discussed in the case will help companies hire more skilled managers and employees to staff foreign operations? Explain.

17-15. Some companies agree that the move toward internationalization by U.S. universities primarily reflect an attempt to get more money because foreign buyers are willing to pay top dollar to obtain a degree from a U.S. institution. Do you agree? Explain.

17-16. Assume that you have two potential candidates for an entry-level expatriate position, one who graduated from a branch campus of a U.S. university overseas and one who graduated from the main campus of the same university in the United States. Also assume that each candidate has equal qualifications. Which candidate would you prefer? Explain.

Team Exercise

17-17. Form teams of five. Each team will come up with a list of five positives and five negatives for the trend discussed in the case. Each team will outline a set of implications of what this trend means for HR practices on a global basis.

Experiential Exercise: Team

17-18. Form an even number of teams of five members each, with one pro team and one con team working for the same university. The pro team is asked to defend the advantage of opening a branch campus, while the con team is asked to take the opposite position. The teams are asked to debate their views in class, with the instructor serving as moderator.

Experiential Exercise: Individual

17-19. Research some recent articles dealing with the recent push by U.S. universities to start training foreign students abroad. Based on what you have read, what would you conclude in terms of the advantages and disadvantages of launching these overseas projects? If you were an HR manager of a multinational firm, would you see this as a positive, negative, or neutral trend? Explain.

Source: Based on Hacker, A., and Dreifus, C. (2010, September 20). The trouble with going global, *Newsweek*, 54–59; U.S. branch campuses abroad: Results of a targeted survey. *http://globalhighered.wordpress.com*. Accessed 2011; McBurnie, G., and Ziguras, C. (2011). The international branch campus, *www.iienetwork.org*; Coclanis, P. A., and Strauss, R.P. (2011). Partnerships: An alternative to branch campuses overseas. *http://chronicle.com*. Accessed 2011.

 You Manage It! 2: Emerging Trends

Coping with Terrorism

One of the concomitants of international assignments is the fear that the expatriate and his or her family may be the target of terrorism. Unfortunately, the expatriate may be seen by some political groups and radical religious extremists as representing a foreign enemy, or by local bandits as a rich foreigner ready for plucking. This fear places a lot of stress on the expatriate, particularly in some parts of the world (such as the Middle East and some South Asia regions). Unfortunately, these regions are precisely the ones where multinationals tend to rely on expatriates most, given the lack of local talent or the suspicion that local personnel cannot be fully trusted.

Although some fears may be exaggerated, the danger is often very real. The Worldwide Incidents Tracking System of the National Counterterrorism Center reports approximately 12,000 terrorist attacks per year, resulting in more than 13,000 deaths. This does not include hijackings, muggings, break-ins, and the like, which obviously add to the anxiety. Many multinationals resort to "compounds" as living quarters for expatriates and their families, but these "increased safety measures do not convey feelings of safety but rather can represent latent danger."

Critical Thinking Questions

17-20. What can a multinational firm do to reduce the level of stress that expatriates may feel as a result of real or perceived terrorist threats? Explain.

17-21. Terrorism-related stress tends to foster negative attitudes towards the local population and this may compound the adjustment problems of the expatriate and family. How can a multinational help deal with this problem? Explain.

17-22. If you were asked to design a set of incentives to induce expatriates to accept an assignment in a risky area, how would you set this up? And once the expatriate accepts the assignment, how would you try to reduce the possibility that the expatriate may return earlier than you would like? Explain.

Team Exercise

17-23. Form groups of five. Each group will analyze recent cases of terrorist attacks where expatriates were the target. Each team will present its findings to the entire class for approximately 10 minutes, to be followed by an open class discussion moderated by the instructor.

Experiential Exercise: Team

17-24. Form teams of five members each. Each team represents a group of HR managers from a large petroleum company operating in a high-risk area. Some students are appointed as CEOs. Teams will role-play with the CEO in front of the entire class, explaining how the company will assess risks and how it plans to reduce fears on the part of expatriates concerning a terrorist attack. The CEO is supposed to ask pointed questions from the team as to the proposed approach to assess the risk and the soundness of the plan to deal with the purported risk.

Experiential Exercise: Individual

17-25. Do some research to learn why many multinationals prefer to send expatriates overseas rather than hire locals in dangerous areas. Based on your research, what are the advantages and disadvantages of using locals versus expatriates in these areas?

Source: Based on Bader, B. and Berg, N. (2013). An empirical investigation of terrorism-induced stress on expatriate attitudes and performance. *Journal of International Management*, *http://dx.doi.gov*; National Counterterrorism Center (2014). Worldwide incidents tracking system. *http://wits.nctc.gov*; Reade, C., and Lee, H.J. (2012). Organizational commitment in time of war. *Journal of International Management*, *18*(1), 85–101; Berger, R. (2011) The golden cage: Western women in the compound in a Muslim country. *Journal of International Women's Studies*, *12*(1), 37–49; Chen, Y., and Bolino, M. C. (2012). Choices, challenges and career consequences of global work experiences: A review and future agenda. *Journal of Management*, *38*(2), 1282–1327.

You Manage It! 3: Global

Two Sides to Every Story

Four years ago, Pressman Company, a U.S.-based firm, entered into a joint venture with a Polish firm to manufacture a variety of plumbing supplies, both for the internal Polish market and for export to neighboring countries. Last week Pressman received the resignation of Jonathan Smith, an expatriate from the home office who nine months ago was appointed general manager of the Polish subsidiary for a four-year term. In the previous 39 months, two other expatriate general managers had also decided to call it quits long before their foreign assignments expired. In addition, 13 of the 28 U.S. technicians sent to work in the Polish facility returned home early. George Stevens, a senior vice president in corporate headquarters, estimates that these expatriates' resignations and early returns have cost the company at least $4 million in direct expenses and probably three times as much in lost production and delayed schedules.

When he heard rumors of widespread discontent in the workforce and a threatened strike, Stevens decided to travel to the Polish facility to find out what was happening. In the course of interviewing five local supervisors and 10 workers with the help of a translator, he repeatedly heard three complaints: first, the American managers and technicians thought they "knew it all" and treated their Polish counterparts with contempt; second, the American employees had unrealistic expectations of what could be accomplished within the stipulated deadlines established at corporate headquarters; and third, American employees were making three times more money than their Polish counterparts and enjoyed looking down their noses at locals by driving fancy cars, living in expensive homes, and hiring an army of maids and helpers.

When he arrived back in the States, Stevens also interviewed Jonathan Smith and five of the technicians who returned early. Some common reasons for their early resignations emerged from these interviews. First, they described their Polish colleagues as "lazy" and "just doing the minimum to get by while keeping a close eye on the clock for breaks, lunches, and go-home time." Pushing them to work harder only provoked anger. Second, they indicated that the Polish workers and managers had a sense of entitlement with little intrinsic motivation and initiative. Third, they complained of loneliness and their inability to communicate in Polish. Finally, most reported that their spouses and children were homesick and longing to return to the States after the first month or so. As he sits in his office, George Stevens is staring blankly out the window, trying to decide what to do.

Critical Thinking Questions

17-26. Based on what you have learned in this chapter, what do you think are the underlying problems in the Polish subsidiary of Pressman Company?

17-27. How would you account for the sharp differences in the perceptions of the Polish locals and U.S. expatriates?

17-28. If you were hired as a consultant by Pressman Company, what steps would you recommend that Stevens take?

Team Exercises

17-29. Students form pairs. One student plays Stevens, the other an HRM consultant. Role-play the initial meeting between these two, with Stevens explaining the problems at the Polish plant and the consultant identifying the additional information that will be needed to get to the root of the difficulties, and how this information might be collected.

Students form into groups of four or five. Each group's task is to make suggestions for the content of a training program for the next group of employees to be sent to Pressman's Polish plant. Besides information from this chapter, use principles you learned from Chapter 4, "Managing Diversity," and Chapter 8, "Training the Workforce," to develop these programs. When the task is finished (approximately 20 minutes), a member from each group should present the group's recommendations to the class. How similar or dissimilar are the groups' recommendations? Why? Which recommendations are likely to be most effective?

Experiential Exercise: Team

17-30. One student will role-play a Polish employee while another role-plays a U.S. expatriate. Each will present his or her perspective to the HR director of Pressman Company (role-played by another student) who will try to understand and bridge the differences between the two. Role-play should last for approximately 10 to 15 minutes, followed by an open class discussion moderated by the instructor.

Experiential Exercise: Individual

17-31. You have been hired as a management consultant located in the United States to offer some suggestions as to how the situation should be handled. First diagnose the causes of the problem based on what you have learned in this chapter. Then develop a set of recommendations to best deal with the situation.

You Manage It! 4: Ethics/Social Responsibility

When in Rome Do as the Romans Do? The Case of Foreign Bribes

According to the anticorruption watchdog Transparency International, senior business executives around the world believe Russia is the country where companies are most likely to pay bribes, followed by China and Mexico. The list of countries with firms *least* likely to pay bribes begins with Belgium, Canada, and the Netherlands. The United States ranks ninth on the list of countries least likely to pay bribes.

Let's take one example. Titan Corporation, based in San Diego, California, has about 12,000 employees dispersed across 60 countries. It was found guilty of bribing the president of Benin. The combined penalties of $28.5 million are the largest imposed on a company in the history of the Foreign Corrupt Practices Act. Titan, with $2 billion in annual sales, mainly from military, intelligence, and homeland security contracts with the U.S. government, pleaded guilty to three felonies before a federal judge in San Diego. According to the Securities and Exchange Commission (SEC), Titan's misconduct was global. Though Titan does business in more than 60 countries, the company has no policy on overseas bribery and failed to monitor its 120 international agents. The SEC said Titan underreported commission payments in its business dealings in France, Japan, Nepal, Bangladesh, and Sri Lanka.

Paul R. Berger, an associate director at the SEC's enforcement division, said that the evidence in the case showed "the virtually complete lack of internal controls" at Titan, along with the company's inability to operate with policies and procedures that would help them detect and deter such problems.

Critical Thinking Questions

17-32. Do you think that Titan is an isolated example or that many companies engage in similar behaviors overseas but are never caught? Do you think it is acceptable for a firm to take the risk and pay a bribe if the firm believes that the chances of getting caught are small and that in the worst-case scenario the fine imposed will be an insignificant fraction of total operating costs? Explain.

17-33. Shortly after Titan pleaded guilty to the bribery charges, it hired Daniel W. Danjczek under a new position title of "vice president for compliance and ethics." Danjczek's job is to "instill ethical behavior at the company." Do you think this is a wise and sincere attempt to redress the company's ethical problems or a public relations gimmick? What would you do to ensure that such an appointment is not perceived by employees as a superficial "quick fix" to improve the firm's ethical reputation? Explain.

17-34. When a company operates in many different countries with widely diverse legal systems and ethical standards, how can it develop and enforce a global set of criteria as to what is right and wrong? Explain.

Team Exercise

17-35. The class is divided into groups of five. Each team will provide Mr. Danjczek with a set of recommendations as to what he should do in his new job to improve the ethical climate at Titan. Depending on class size, each team will present its recommendations to the entire class for approximately 10 minutes, to be followed by open class discussion moderated by the instructor.

Experiential Exercise: Team

17-36. One student will role-play Mr. Danjczek; five other students will role-play international agents of Titan at five different locations (Brazil, Bermuda, Saudi Arabia, Nigeria, and Rumania). Mr. Danjczek is trying to convey the message that the company is serious about its ethical turnabout and that "the old chapter in the company's history of lax ethical standards has come to a close." Local agents believe that this is a wonderful thing to say from a public relations perspective, but that Titan cannot be competitive against other foreign firms that have no qualms about doing whatever they have to do to secure contracts. Role-play should last for about 15 to 20 minutes, after which the instructor will moderate open class discussion of the issues raised.

Experiential Exercise: Individual

17-37. Develop a set of policies to discourage corruption in an organization such as Titan. What are the major challenges in trying to enforce such a policy? What steps would you recommend to increase the probabilities that such a policy will be effectively implemented?

You Manage It! 5: Global

Are Culture-Specific HR Policies a Good Idea?

Over the past 10 years, East Computer Company has grown from a domestic producer of microchips in Boston to a multinational company with assembly plants in four foreign locations. The company's personnel policies were developed five years ago, before East Computer's international expansion, by a task force headed by the vice president for HRM in Boston. The company's CEO has just appointed a new task force to examine the extent to which current domestic personnel policies can be "exported" to East's new international locations. The essential elements of these policies are the following:

1. All job openings are posted to allow any employee to apply for a position.
2. Selection is based on merit. Appropriate selection devices (for example, tests, structured interviews, and the like) are used to ensure proper implementation of this policy.
3. Nepotism is expressly forbidden.
4. Promotion from within is the norm whenever feasible.
5. Equal employment opportunities are available to all, regardless of sex, race, national origin, or religion.
6. Pay for various positions is established through a rational process that includes both job evaluation and market survey data.
7. There is equal pay for equal work, regardless of sex, race, national origin, or religion.
8. Goals are jointly set by supervisor and subordinate, with an annual formal appraisal session at which both parties have the chance to discuss progress toward goal achievement. The appraisal is used both to provide performance feedback to the employee and as a basis for merit pay decisions.

As a first step in evaluating these policies, the vice president for HRM classified the countries where East's facilities are located according to Hofstede's dimensions. She came up with the matrix shown below.

You have been hired by East Computer Company to help management develop personnel policies for each of the four international facilities. Ideally, management would prefer to use the same policies that it uses in the United States to maintain consistency and reduce administrative problems. However, the vice president for HRM has made a strong case for "tailor-made" personnel policies that are suitable to each facility's cultural environment.

Critical Thinking Questions

17-38. Given East Computer Company's present personnel policies, what problems is the company likely to face in each facility if it transports its domestic policies abroad?

17-39. How would you change or adapt each of the company's current personnel policies to better fit the cultural environment of each international facility?

17-40. What set of management recommendations would you provide for keeping, changing, or adapting East Computer Company's HR policies for the United States, Australia, Mexico, England, and Norway? In your recommendations, be sure to mention any risks associated with implementing your recommendations.

Team Exercises

17-41. Students break into groups of five. One student role-plays a consultant who is conducting an exercise to uncover possible problems in uniform application of the company's current policy. Each of the other four students takes the role of advocate for one of the four international locations. Each advocate should make an argument for or against keeping specific parts of East's existing HR policies.

Students form groups of four students, with each group acting as the advocate for one of the four international locations. After deciding which policies to keep and which to change, a representative from each group presents the group's recommendations to the class. After these brief presentations, the class discusses the costs and benefits of culture-specific HR policies.

Experiential Exercise: Team

17-42. Students are divided into groups of five. Using the Internet or any other sources each team will develop an outline of human resource practices that are most likely to succeed in each location based on the materials learned in this chapter.

Experiential Exercise: Individual

17-43. Find some individuals (other students, friends, or relatives) who were either raised in and/or are familiar with a foreign country. Interview them and ask their opinions about how they perceive that country in terms of five of Hofstede's dimensions. On which dimensions is the country high? Low? Based on the interviewee's assessment, is the culture of that country reflected in any human resource practices such as hiring procedures, compensation, performance appraisal, and the like? Several students will be asked to present their finding to entire class (about 5 to 10 minutes each) to be followed by open class discussion moderated by the instructor.

	Cultural Dimensions				
Facility Location	**Power Distance**	**Individualism**	**Uncertainty Avoidance**	**Masculinity**	**Long-Term Orientation**
Australia	Low	High	Medium	Medium	Low
Mexico	High	Low	High	High	Medium
England	Low	High	Low	High	Low
Norway	Low	Medium	Medium	Low	High

Endnotes

Scan for Endnotes or go to http://www.pearsonglobaleditions.com/Gomez-Mejia.

Appendix

HRM and Business Periodicals

The following is an annotated listing of general business publications and specialized HRM publications. Many of these resources may prove helpful to you, not only in your study of HRM but also in your own career development. As we noted in the text, more and more companies are shifting career development responsibilities onto their employees, while providing them with tools for career planning. These resources can be the first in your career-planning toolkit.

General Business Periodicals

Across the Board. Conference Board. 845 Third Avenue, New York, NY 10022. Provides articles that present business topics in nontechnical terms. Articles range from discussions of general business issues to examinations of specific companies and industries.

Black Enterprise. Earl G. Graves Publishing Co. 130 Fifth Avenue, New York, NY 10011. *Black Enterprise* focuses on business, jobs, career potential, and financial opportunities as they relate to African, Caribbean, and African American consciousness. Its annual list of the nation's top black businesses and financial institutions is considered an invaluable accounting of African American business enterprises.

BusinessWeek. McGraw-Hill, Inc. 1221 Avenue of the Americas, New York, NY 10020. The leading general business magazine, *BusinessWeek* offers comprehensive coverage of the news and developments affecting the business world. It includes information on computers, finance, labor, industry, marketing, science, and technology.

Fast Company. P.O. Box 52760, Boulder, CO 80321-2760. Fairly new on the scene, *Fast Company* focuses on a wide variety of business topics and is geared toward giving companies an edge in a very competitive marketplace. The magazine's subtitle is "How smart business works."

Forbes. Forbes, Inc. 60 Fifth Avenue, New York, NY 10011. A general business magazine that celebrates capitalism. Short articles report on company activities, industry developments, economic trends, and investment tips.

Fortune. Time, Inc. Time & Life Building, Rockefeller Center, New York, NY 10020. *Fortune* reports on companies and industries, developments and trends. Its articles tend to be longer than those in other business magazines, and its frequent use of sidebars allows readers to learn more about corollary issues.

Harvard Business Review. Graduate School of Business Administration, Harvard University. Boston, MA 02163. This well-known product of Harvard Business School publishes articles in the areas of business and management. Topics include planning, manufacturing, and innovation. Each issue includes a case study.

Hispanic Business. P.O. Box 469038, Escondido, CA 92046-9038. A general business magazine focusing on a variety of business issues (including career opportunities, entrepreneurial ventures, and legislation) as they relate to Latino workers and Latino-owned businesses in the United States.

Inc.: The Magazine for Growing Companies. Goldhirsch Group, Inc. 38 Commercial Wharf, Boston, MA 02110. Inc. is targeted to the person involved in managing new, small, or growing companies. Articles focus on entrepreneurial ventures, general business topics, and profiles of successful managers.

Journal of Business Ethics. Kluwar Academic Publishers. 101 Philip Dr., Norwell, MA 02061. This journal publishes scholarly articles dealing with the ethical issues confronted in business. It is clearly written, free of technical jargon, and contains articles on such topics as ethics and business schools, competitor intelligence, corporate executives, and disasters.

Management Review. American Management Association. 135 West 50th St., New York, NY 10020. This monthly publication describes management trends, techniques, and issues for middle- and upper-level managers in the corporate and public sector.

Nation's Business: U.S. Chamber of Commerce. 1615 H St. N.W., Washington, DC 20062. *Nation's Business* reports on current business activities and topics such as quality, entrepreneurship, and going public. It is directed mainly to entrepreneurs and small business owners and managers. Each issue contains a feature on issues affecting family businesses.

Small Business Reports. American Management Association. 135 West 50th St., New York, NY 10020. Articles in this monthly magazine tend to offer practical advice for small business owners and managers. However, topics are of interest to all business managers.

The Wall Street Journal. Dow Jones & Co., Inc. 200 Liberty St., New York, NY 10281. With a circulation greater than either the *New York Times* or *USA Today*, this comprehensive national newspaper offers in-depth coverage of national and international finance and business. A must for anyone interested in the business of business.

Working Woman. Working Woman, Inc. 230 Park Avenue, New York, NY 10169. Geared toward the white-collar career woman interested in advancing in her field. Articles focus on career advancement, management, communication skills, money management, and investment information. Features items on new technology, changing demographics, and profiles of successful businesswomen. Of special interest is the annual "Hottest Careers" issue featuring listings of up-and-coming occupations.

HRM Periodicals

Academy of Management Perspectives. Pace University, P.O. Box 3020, Briarcliff Manor, NY 10510. Published quarterly and geared toward executives and students of business, this journal presents straightforward practical articles, many of them written by leading management scholars.

Compensation & Benefits Review. American Management Association. 135 West 50th St., New York, NY 10020. A specialized publication of the American Management Association, this journal contains four to six articles in each issue, covering compensation management and strategy and such diverse topics as job evaluation as a barrier to excellence and compensating overseas executives. One invaluable feature is its condensations of noteworthy articles appearing in other business publications.

CompFlash. WorldatWork Association, 14040 N. Northsight Blvd., Scottsdale, AZ 58260. Published monthly, this newsletter includes short articles and information on the latest trends/statistics useful for compensation management, including the most recent surveys.

Employee Relations Law Journal. Executive Enterprises, Inc. 22 West 21st St., New York, NY 10010. Although geared toward attorneys specializing in employment law, in-house counsel, and HR executives, this journal contains practical advice that is not highly technical. Articles deal with such topics as personnel management techniques, legal compliance, and court cases, and such issues as sex discrimination, privacy in the workplace, and drug testing. Features up-to-date coverage of federal regulatory agency actions.

Employee Relations Weekly. Bureau of National Affairs. 1231 25th Street, N.W. Washington, DC 20037. This government publication covers such workplace issues as EEO developments, health and safety, pay and benefits, and policy and practices. Recent articles have touched on employee committees, domestic partner benefits, and sexual harassment. Useful for discussions of court cases relevant to employee relations.

HRMagazine. Society for Human Resource Management. 606 N. Washington St., Alexandria, VA 22314. Formerly called *Personnel Administrator*, this magazine offers in-depth coverage of all areas of HRM.

Human Resource Management. John Wiley & Sons for the Ross School of Business at University of Michigan in alliance with the Society for Human Resource management. This journal is designed for "bridging research and practice for HR leaders."

International Journal of Human Resource Management. Routledge Journals, 11 New Fetter Lane, London EC4P 4EE. Published monthly, this journal covers research on international HRM issues and trends.

Labor Notes. Labor and Education Research Project. 7435 Michigan Avenue, Detroit, MI 48210. This workers' magazine is as critical of big labor as it is of management. It features nationwide coverage of such issues as contracts, ongoing negotiation, boycotts, working conditions, and problems confronting women and minority workers. Useful for its "shop-floor" view and as counterbalance to the management perspective.

Monthly Labor Review. Bureau of Labor Statistics. U.S. Department of Labor, Washington, DC 20402. The source for U.S. labor statistics. Each issue carries four in-depth articles on labor-related topics.

Organizational Dynamics. American Management Association. 135 West 50th St., New York, NY 10020. Articles deal with appraisal systems and management systems in general, as well as with other relevant aspects of systems administration.

Personnel Journal. 245 Fischer Ave. B-2, Costa Mesa, CA 92626. *Personnel Journal* covers the full range of issues in human resources. Features extensive coverage of current HR policies and practices at actual companies, and each article contains company vital statistics. *Personnel Journal* also sponsors the annual Optimas Awards, which spotlight companies with excellent HR initiatives in a variety of categories.

Public Personnel Management. Personnel Management Association. 1617 Duke St., Alexandria, VA 22314. Research articles useful to personnel administrators in public-sector personnel management. Typical subjects are recruiting, interviewing, training, sick leave, and home-based employment.

Supervisory Management. American Management Association, 135 West 50th St., New York, NY 10020. Within its concise 12-page format, this magazine contains numerous brief articles offering practical advice on such topics as building quality awareness, handling problem employees, and conducting effective meetings.

Training & Development. American Society for Training & Development. 1640 King St., Alexandria, VA 22313. The official magazine of ASTD, *Training & Development* is directed toward HR professionals and other managers. It covers both practical issues and trends in training and development, including such topics as how to make a training video, how to train workers to write more clearly, and the ins and outs of successful diversity training.

Workspan. WorldatWork Association, 14040 N. Northsight Blvd., Scottsdale, AZ 58260. Published monthly, this newsletter includes articles of interest to HR practitioners. It also reports on the resources available to practitioners, as well as positions available in the field.

WorldatWork Journal. WorldatWork Association, 14040 N. Northsight Blvd., Scottsdale, AZ 85260. The *WorldatWork Journal* is a specialized publication of the WorldatWork Association. Issues appear quarterly and feature six to eight articles on such compensation-related topics as pay for performance, compensation strategy, tax considerations, executive pay, and benefits.

Concise Dictionary of HR Terminology

Ability. Competence in performing a job. (47)

Absolute judgment. An appraisal format that asks supervisors to make judgments about an employee's performance based solely on performance standards. (236)

Adverse impact. Discrimination that occurs when the equal application of an employment standard has an unequal effect on one or more protected classes. Also called *disparate impact.* (116)

Affirmative action. A strategy intended to achieve fair employment by urging employers to hire certain groups of people who were discriminated against in the past. (113)

Age Discrimination in Employment Act (ADEA). The law prohibiting discrimination against people who are 40 or older. (123)

Americans with Disabilities Act (ADA). The law forbidding employment discrimination against people with disabilities who are able to perform the essential functions of the job with or without reasonable accommodation. (124)

Appeals procedure. A procedure that allows employees to voice their reactions to management practices and to challenge management decisions. (442)

Apprenticeship. A program in which promising prospective employees are groomed before they are actually hired on a permanent basis. (169)

Arbitration. The last step in a grievance procedure. The decision of the arbitrator, who is a neutral individual selected from outside the firm, is binding on both parties. (517)

Assessment center. A set of simulated tasks or exercises that candidates (usually for managerial positions) are asked to perform. (197)

Attrition. An employment policy designed to reduce the company's workforce by not refilling job vacancies that are created by turnover. (220)

Award. A one-time reward usually given in the form of a tangible prize. (363)

Base compensation. The fixed pay an employee receives on a regular basis, either in the form of a salary or as an hourly wage. (315)

Behavioral appraisal instrument. An appraisal tool that asks managers to assess a worker's behaviors. (238)

Benchmark or key job. A job that is similar or comparable in content across firms. (335)

Benefits mix. The complete package of benefits that a company offers its employees. (394)

Bona fide occupational qualification (BFOQ). A characteristic that must be present in all employees for a particular job. (117)

Bonus program or lump-sum payment. A financial incentive that is given on a one-time basis and does not raise the employee's base pay permanently. (362)

Boundaryless organizational structure. An organizational structure that enables an organization to form relationships with customers, suppliers, and/or competitors, either to pool organizational resources for mutual benefit or to encourage cooperation in an uncertain environment. (76)

Brain drain. The loss of high-talent key personnel to competitors or start-up ventures. (48)

Brainstorming. A creativity training technique in which participants are given the opportunity to generate ideas openly, without fear of judgment. (278)

Bureaucratic organizational structure. A pyramid-shaped organizational structure that consists of hierarchies with many levels of management. (74)

Burnout. A stress syndrome characterized by emotional exhaustion, depersonalization, and reduced personal accomplishment. (548)

Business process reengineering (BPR). A fundamental rethinking and radical redesign of business processes to achieve dramatic improvements in cost, quality, service, and speed. (77)

Business unionism. A form of unionism that focuses on improving workers' economic well-being. (498)

Business unit strategy. The formulation and implementation of strategies by a firm that is relatively autonomous, even if it is part of a larger corporation. (56)

Career development. An ongoing and formalized effort that focuses on developing enriched and more capable workers. (290)

Career path. A chart showing the possible directions and career opportunities available in an organization; it presents the steps in a possible career and a plausible timetable for accomplishing them. (300)

Career resource center. A collection of career development materials such as workbooks, tapes, and texts. (303)

Codetermination. The representation of workers on a corporation's board of directors; used in Germany. (503)

Coinsurance. Payments made to cover health care expenses that are split between the employer's insurance company and the insured employee. (391)

Collective bargaining. A system in which unions and management negotiate with each other to develop the work rules under which union members will work for a stipulated period of time. (498)

Comparability. In performance ratings, the degree to which the performance ratings given by various supervisors in an organization are based on similar standards. (244)

Comparable worth. A pay concept or doctrine that calls for comparable pay for jobs that require comparable skills, effort, and responsibility and have comparable working conditions, even if the job content is different. (342)

Compensable factors. Work-related criteria that an organization considers most important in assessing the relative value of different jobs. (332)

Compensatory damages. Fines awarded to a plaintiff to compensate for the financial or psychological harm the plaintiff has suffered. (122)

Competencies. Characteristics associated with successful performance. (235)

Competency model. Set of competencies associated with a job. (235)

Conciliation. An attempt to reach a negotiated settlement between the employer and an employee or applicant in an EEO case. (127)

Concurrent validity. Extent of correlation between selection and performance scores, when measured at the same time. (192)

Consolidated Omnibus Budget Reconciliation Act (COBRA) of 1985. Legislation that gives employees the right to continue their health insurance coverage for 18 to 36 months after their employment has terminated. (402)

Contingent workers. Workers hired to deal with temporary increases in an organization's workload or to do work that is not part of its core set of capabilities. (95)

Contract. A legally binding promise between two or more competent parties. (458)

Contractual right. A right based on the law of contracts. (496)

Contributions. Payments made for benefits coverage. Contributions for a specific benefit may come from the employer, employee, or both. (391)

Copayment. A small payment made by the employee for each office visit to a physician under a health plan. The health plan pays for additional medical expenses that exceed the copayment at no cost to the employee. (391)

Core time. Time when all employees are expected to be at work. Part of a flexible work hours arrangement. (100)

Core workers. An organization's full-time employees. (95)

Corporate strategy. The mix of businesses a corporation decides to hold and the flow of resources among those businesses. (56)

Cost-of-living adjustment (COLA). A pay raise, usually made across the board, that is tied to such inflation indicators as the consumer price index. (520)

Cross-functional training. Training employees to perform operations in areas other than their assigned job. (277)

Cultural determinism. The idea that one can successfully infer an individual's motivations, interests, values, and behavioral traits based on that individual's group memberships. (170)

Cultural relativity concept of management. The management concept holding that management practices should be molded to the different sets of values, beliefs, attitudes, and behaviors exhibited by a diverse workforce. (153)

Culture shock. The inability to adjust to a different cultural environment. (567)

Cumulative trauma disorder (CTD). An occupational injury that occurs from repetitive physical movements, such as assembly-line work or data entry. (543)

Decentralization. Transferring responsibility and decision-making authority from a central office to people and locations closer to the situation that demands attention. (39)

Deductible. An annual out-of-pocket expenditure that an insurance policyholder must make before the insurance plan makes any reimbursements. (391)

Defined benefit plan or pension. A retirement plan that promises to pay a fixed dollar amount of retirement income based on a formula that takes into account the average of the employee's last three to five years' earnings prior to retirement. (409)

Defined contribution plan. A retirement plan in which the employer promises to contribute a specific amount of funds into the plan for each participant. The final value of each participant's retirement income depends on the success of the plan's investments. (409)

Development. An effort to provide employees with the abilities the organization will need in the future. (265)

Dimension. An aspect of performance that determines effective job performance. (234)

Discrimination. The making of distinctions. In HR context, the making of distinctions among people. (116)

Disparate treatment. Discrimination that occurs when individuals are treated differently because of their membership in a protected class. (116)

Distinctive competencies. The characteristics that give a firm a competitive edge. (60)

Distributive bargaining. Bargaining that focuses on convincing the other party that the cost of disagreeing with the proposed terms would be very high. (512)

Diversity. Human characteristics that make people different from one another. (147)

Diversity audit. A review of the effectiveness of an organization's diversity management program. (197)

Diversity training programs. Programs that provide diversity awareness training and educate employees on specific cultural and sex differences and how to respond to these in the workplace. (194)

Downsizing. (1) A company strategy to reduce the scale (size) and scope of its business in order to improve the company's financial performance. (2) A reduction in a company's workforce to improve its bottom line. (39), (245)

Downward communication. Communication that allows managers to implement their decisions and to influence employees lower in the organizational hierarchy. (459)

Dual-career couple. A couple whose members both have occupational responsibilities and career issues at stake. (321)

Due process. Equal and fair application of a policy or law. (487)

Economic strike. A strike that takes place when an agreement is not reached during collective bargaining. (543)

Egalitarian pay system. A pay plan in which most employees are part of the same compensation system. (352)

Electronic mail (e-mail). A form of electronic communication that allows employees to communicate with each other via electronic messages sent through personal computer terminals linked by a network. (462)

Elitist pay system. A pay plan in which different compensation systems are established for employees or groups at different organizational levels. (352)

Employee assistance program (EAP). A company-sponsored program that helps employees cope with personal problems that are interfering with their job performance. (471)

Employee attitude survey. A formal anonymous survey designed to measure employee likes and dislikes of various aspects of their jobs. (441)

Employee benefits or indirect compensation. Group membership rewards that provide security for employees and their family members. (389)

Employee feedback program. A program designed to improve employee communications by giving employees a voice in policy formulation and making sure that they receive due process on any complaints they lodge against managers. (441)

Employee recognition program. A program that rewards employees for their ideas and contributions. (446)

Employee relations policy. A policy designed to communicate management's thinking and practices concerning employee-related matters and prevent problems in the workplace from becoming serious. (428)

Employee relations representative. A member of the HR department who ensures that company policies are followed and consults with both supervisors and employees on specific employee relations problems. (428)

Employee Retirement Income Security Act (ERISA). A federal law established in 1974 to protect employees' retirement benefits from mismanagement. (408)

Employee separation. The termination of an employee's membership in an organization. (210)

Employee stock ownership plan (ESOP). A corporatewide pay-for-performance plan that rewards employees with company stock either as an outright grant or at a favorable price that may be below market value. (369)

Employment at will. A common-law rule used by employers to assert their right to end an employment relationship with an employee at any time for any cause. (462)

Employment contract. A contract that spells out explicitly the terms of the employment relationship for both employee and employer. (458)

Empowerment. Providing workers with the skills and authority to make decisions that would traditionally be made by managers. (47)

Enterprise union. A labor union that represents workers in only one large company rather than in a particular industry; used in Japan. (503)

Environmental challenges. Forces external to a firm that affect the firm's performance but are beyond the control of management. (30)

Equal Employment Opportunity Commission (EEOC). The federal agency responsible for enforcing EEO laws. (127)

Equal Pay Act (1963). The law that requires the same pay for men and women who do the same job in the same organization. (115)

Essential functions. Job duties that each person in a certain position must do or must be able to do to be an effective employee. (125)

Ethnocentric approach. An approach to managing international operations in which top management and other key positions are filled by people from the home country. (564)

Executive order. A presidential directive that has the force of law. In HR context, a policy with which all federal agencies and organizations doing business with the federal government must comply. (123)

Exempt employee. An employee who is not covered by the provisions of the Fair Labor Standards Act. Most professional, administrative, executive, and outside sales jobs fall into this category. (341)

Exit interview. An employee's final interview following separation. The purpose of the interview is to find out the reasons why the employee is leaving (if the separation is voluntary) or to provide counseling and/or assistance in finding a new job. (213)

Expatriate. A citizen of one country living and working in another country. (560)

Expectancy theory. A theory of behavior holding that people tend to do those things that are rewarded. (363)

Extended leave. A benefit that allows an employee to take a long-term leave from the office, while retaining benefits and the guarantee of a comparable job on return. (168)

External equity. The perceived fairness in pay relative to what other employers are paying for the same type of labor. (317)

Fair employment. The goal of EEO legislation and regulation: a situation in which employment decisions are not affected by illegal discrimination. (113)

Fair Labor Standards Act (FLSA). The fundamental compensation law in the United States. Requires employers to record earnings and hours worked by all covered employees and to report this information to the U.S. Department of Labor. Defines two categories of employees: exempt and nonexempt. (340)

Family and Medical Leave Act (FMLA) of 1993. A federal law that requires employers to provide up to 12 weeks' unpaid leave to eligible employees for the birth or adoption of a child; to care for a sick parent, child, or spouse; or to take care of health problems that interfere with job performance. (400)

Flat organizational structure. An organizational structure that has only a few levels of management and emphasizes decentralization. (74)

Flexible or cafeteria benefits program. A benefits program that allows employees to select the benefits they need most from a menu of choices. (391)

Flexible work hours. A work arrangement that gives employees control over the starting and ending times of their daily work schedules. (100)

Flextime. Time during which employees can choose not to be at work. Part of a flexible work hours arrangement. (100)

Four-fifths rule. An EEOC provision for establishing a prima facie case that an HR practice is discriminatory and has an adverse impact. A practice has an adverse impact if the hiring rate of a protected class is less than four-fifths the hiring rate of a majority group. (117)

Frame-of-reference (FOR) training. A type of training that presents supervisors with fictitious examples of worker performance (either in writing or on video), asks the supervisors to evaluate the workers in the examples, and then tells them what their ratings should have been. (244)

Gainsharing. A plantwide pay-for-performance plan in which a portion of the company's cost savings is returned to workers, usually in the form of a lump-sum bonus. (368)

Genetic testing. A form of biological testing that identifies employees who are genetically susceptible to illness or disability. (545)

Geocentric approach. An approach to managing international operations in which nationality is downplayed and the firm actively searches on a worldwide or regional basis for the best people to fill key positions. (564)

Glass ceiling. The intangible barrier in an organization that prevents female and minority employees from rising to positions above a certain level. (154)

Grievance procedure. A systematic, step-by-step process designed to settle disputes regarding the interpretation of a labor contract. (517)

Health Insurance Portability and Accountability Act (HIPAA). A federal law that protects an employee's ability to transfer between health insurance plans without a gap in coverage due to a preexisting condition. (402)

Health maintenance organization (HMO). A health care plan that provides comprehensive medical services for employees and their families at a flat annual fee. (404)

Health savings account (HSA). A qualified health plan with a high deductible that lets individuals save money for health care expenses with pretax dollars and lets unspent money accumulate as a tax-free stash of money. (406)

High-deductible health plan (HDHP). A way that employers can manage the costs of employee health care plans. The high deductible requires that employees pay for the first few thousand dollars of medical costs each year, which means that the plan pays only when employees have major medical problems. (407)

Hiring freeze. An employment policy designed to reduce the company's workforce by not hiring any new employees into the company. (220)

Hostile work environment sexual harassment. Harassment that occurs when the behavior of anyone in the work setting is sexual in nature and is perceived by an employee as offensive and undesirable. (118)

Hot-stove rule. A model of disciplinary action: Discipline should be immediate, provide ample warning, and be consistently applied to all. (476)

HR audit. A periodic review of the effectiveness with which a company uses its human resources. Frequently includes an evaluation of the HR department itself. (63)

Human resource information system (HRIS). A system used to collect, record, store, analyze, and retrieve data concerning an organization's human resources. (102)

Human resource planning (HRP). The process an organization uses to ensure that it has the right amount and the right kind of people to deliver a particular level of output or services in the future. (178)

Human resources (HR). People who work in an organization. Also called *personnel.* (30)

Human resource strategy. A firm's deliberate use of human resources to help it gain or maintain an edge against its competitors in the marketplace. The grand plan or general approach an organization adopts to ensure that it effectively uses its people to accomplish its mission. (30)

Human resource tactic. A particular HR policy or program that helps to advance a firm's strategic goal. (30)

Individual challenges. Human resource issues that address the decisions most pertinent to individual employees. (45)

Individual equity. The perceived fairness of individual pay decisions. (318)

Individuals with disabilities. Persons who have a physical or mental impairment that substantially affects one or more major life activities. (124)

Informal communications. Also called "the grapevine." Information exchanges without a planned agenda that occur informally among employees. (439)

Information dissemination. The process of making information available to decision makers, wherever they are located. (432)

Insubordination. Either refusal to obey a direct order from a supervisor or verbal abuse of a supervisor. (480)

Integrative bargaining. Bargaining that focuses on convincing the other party that the benefits of agreeing with the proposed terms would be very high. (480)

Internal equity. The perceived fairness of the pay structure within a firm. (317)

Internal Revenue Code (IRC). The code of tax laws that affects how much of their earnings employees can keep and how benefits are treated for tax purposes. (343)

Involuntary separation. A separation that occurs when an employer decides to terminate its relationship with an employee due to (1) economic necessity or (2) a poor fit between the employee and the organization. (215)

Job aids. External sources of information, such as pamphlets and reference guides, that workers can access quickly when they need help in making a decision or performing a specific task. (276)

Job analysis. The systematic process of collecting information used to make decisions about jobs. Job analysis identifies the tasks, duties, and responsibilities of a particular job. (85)

Job banding. The practice of replacing narrowly defined job descriptions with broader categories (bands) of related jobs. (337)

Job description. A written document that identifies, defines, and describes a job in terms of its duties, responsibilities, working conditions, and specifications. (91)

Job design. The process of organizing work into the tasks required to perform a specific job. (83)

Job enlargement. The process of expanding a job's duties. (84)

Job enrichment. The process of putting specialized tasks back together so that one person is responsible for producing a whole product or an entire service. (84)

Job evaluation. The process of evaluating the relative value or contribution of different jobs to an organization. (330)

Job hierarchy. A listing of jobs in order of their importance to the organization, from highest to lowest. (333)

Job-posting system. A system in which an organization announces job openings to all employees on a bulletin board, in a company newsletter, or through a phone recording or computer system. (299)

Job rotation. The process of rotating workers among different narrowly defined tasks without disrupting the flow of work. (84)

Job sharing. A work arrangement in which two or more employees divide a job's responsibilities, hours, and benefits among themselves. (96)

Job specifications. The worker characteristics needed to perform a job successfully. (94)

Joint venture. In international business, a foreign branch owned partly by the home office and partly by an entity in the host country (a company, a consortium of firms, an individual, or the government). (564)

Knowledge worker. A worker who transforms information into a product or service. (431)

Knowledge, skills, and abilities (KSAs). The knowledge, skills, and abilities needed to perform a job successfully. (87)

Knowledge-based pay or skill-based pay. A pay system in which employees are paid on the basis of the jobs they can do or talents they have that can be successfully applied to a variety of tasks and situations. (322)

Labor contract. A union contract that spells out the conditions of employment and work rules that affect employees in the unit represented by the union. (498)

Labor demand. How many workers the organization will need in the future. (178)

Labor relations specialist. Someone, often a member of the HR department, who is knowledgeable about labor relations and can represent management's interests to a union. (494)

Labor relations strategy. A company's overall plan for dealing with labor unions. (504)

Labor supply. The availability of workers with the required skills to meet the firm's labor demand. (178)

Landrum-Griffin Act (1959). A law designed to protect union members and their participation in union affairs. (497)

Line employee. An employee involved directly in producing the company's good(s) or delivering the service(s). (30)

Literacy. The mastery of basic skills (reading, writing, arithmetic, and their uses in problem solving). (279)

Lockout. Occurs when an employer shuts down its operations before or during a labor dispute. (516)

Management by objectives (MBO). A goal-directed approach to performance appraisal in which workers and their supervisors set goals together for the upcoming evaluation period. (240)

Management by walking around (MBWA). A technique in which managers walk around and talk to employees informally to monitor informal communications, listen to employee grievances and suggestions, and build rapport and morale. (440)

Management of diversity. The set of activities involved in integrating nontraditional employees (women and minorities) into the workforce and using their diversity to the firm's competitive advantage. (148)

Management rights. Management's rights to run the business and retain any profits that result. (462)

Manager. A person who is in charge of others and is responsible for the timely and correct execution of actions that promote his or her unit's success. (30)

Medicare. A part of the Social Security program that provides health insurance coverage for people aged 65 and over. (397)

Mentoring. A developmentally oriented relationship between senior and junior colleagues or peers that involves advising, role modeling, sharing contacts, and giving general support. (304)

Merit pay. An increase in base pay, normally given once a year. (362)

Moonlighting. Holding a second job outside normal working hours. (470)

Motivation. (1) A person's desire to do the best possible job or to exert the maximum effort to perform assigned tasks. (2) That which energizes, directs, and sustains human behavior. In HRM, a person's desire to do the best possible job or to exert the maximum effort to perform assigned tasks. (47)

Multimedia technology. A form of electronic communication that integrates voice, video, and text, all of which can be encoded digitally and transported on fiber optic networks. (437)

Multinational corporation (MNC). A firm with assembly and production facilities in several countries and regions of the world. (560)

National Labor Relations Board (NLRB). The independent federal agency created by the Wagner Act to administer U.S. labor law. (495)

Negligent hiring. Hiring an employee with a history of violent or illegal behavior without conducting background checks or taking proper precautions. (543)

Nepotism. The practice of favoring relatives over others in the workplace. (432)

Nonexempt employee. An employee who is covered by the provisions of the Fair Labor Standards Act. (341)

Occupational Safety and Health Act of 1970 (OSHA). A federal law that requires employers to provide a safe and healthy work environment, comply with specific occupational safety and health standards, and keep records of occupational injuries and illnesses. (532)

Office of Federal Contract Compliance Programs (OFCCP). The federal agency responsible for monitoring and enforcing the laws and executive orders that apply to the federal government and its contractors. (128)

Old boys' network. An informal social and business network of high-level male executives that typically excludes women and minorities. Access to the old boys' network is often an important factor in career advancement. (164)

Organizational challenges. Concerns or problems internal to a firm; often a by-product of environmental forces. (38)

Organizational culture. The basic assumptions and beliefs shared by members of an organization. These beliefs operate unconsciously and define in a basic taken-for-granted fashion an organization's view of itself and its environment. (41)

Organizational structure. The formal or informal relationships between people in an organization. (73)

Orientation. The process of informing new employees about what is expected of them in the job and helping them cope with the stresses of transition. (282)

Outcome appraisal instrument. An appraisal tool that asks managers to assess the results achieved by workers. (240)

Outplacement assistance. A program in which companies help their departing employees find jobs more rapidly by providing them with training in job-search skills. (213)

Outsourcing. Subcontracting work to an outside company that specializes in and is more efficient at doing that kind of work. (44)

Patient and Affordable Care Act (PACA). A federal law passed in 2010 that guarantees that affordable health care is available to people in the United States. (403)

Pay grades. Groups of jobs that are paid within the same pay range. (328)

Pay incentive. A program designed to reward employees for good performance. (315)

Pay policy. A firm's decision to pay above, below, or at the market rate for its jobs. (336)

Pay-for-performance system or incentive system. A system that rewards employees on the assumptions that (1) individual employees and work teams differ in how much they contribute to the firm; (2) the firm's overall performance depends to a large degree on the performance of individuals and groups within the firm; and (3) to attract, retain, and motivate high performers and to be fair to all employees, the firm needs to reward employees on the basis of their relative performance. (353)

Peer review. A performance appraisal system in which workers at the same level in the organization rate one another. (243)

Peer trainers. High-performing workers who double as internal on-the-job trainers. (277)

Pension Benefit Guaranty Corporation (PBGC). The government agency that provides plan termination insurance to employers with defined benefit retirement programs. (408)

Performance appraisal. The identification, measurement, and management of human performance in organizations. (233)

Perquisites ("perks"). Noncash incentives given to a firm's executives. (376)

Personnel file. A file maintained for each employee, containing the documentation of critical HR-related information, such as performance appraisals, salary history, disciplinary actions, and career milestones. (460)

Piece-rate system. A compensation system in which employees are paid per unit produced. (359)

Polycentric approach. An approach to managing international operations in which subsidiaries are managed and staffed by personnel from the host country. (564)

Portable benefits. Employee benefits, usually retirement funds, that stay with the employee as he or she moves from one company to another. (408)

Positive discipline. A discipline procedure that encourages employees to monitor their own behaviors and assume responsibility for their actions. (474)

Predictive validity. Extent to which selection scores correlate with performance scores, when performance is measured later in time. (192)

Preexisting condition. A medical condition treated while an employee was covered under a former employer's health plan and requires treatment under a new employer's different health plan. (402)

Preferred provider organization (PPO). A health care plan in which an employer or insurance company establishes a network of doctors and hospitals to provide a broad set of medical services for a flat fee per participant. In return for the lower fee, the doctors and hospitals who join the PPO network expect to receive a larger volume of patients. (405)

Premium. The money paid to an insurance company for coverage. (404)

Privacy Act of 1974. Guarantees the privacy of personnel files for employees of the U.S. federal government. (460)

Problem-solving team. A team consisting of volunteers from a unit or department who meet one or two hours per week to discuss quality improvement, cost reduction, or improvement in the work environment. (79)

Productivity. A measure of how much value individual employees add to the goods or services that the organization produces. (47)

Profit sharing. A corporatewide pay-for-performance plan that uses a formula to allocate a portion of declared profits to employees. Typically, profit distributions under a profit-sharing plan are used to fund employees' retirement plans. (369)

Progressive discipline. A series of management interventions that gives employees opportunities to correct undesirable behaviors before being discharged. (473)

Promotability forecast. A career development activity in which managers make decisions regarding the advancement potential of subordinates. (297)

Protected class. A group of people who suffered discrimination in the past and who are given special protection by the judicial system. (115)

Punitive damages. Fines awarded to a plaintiff in order to punish the defendant. (122)

Quality of work life. A measure of how safe and satisfied employees feel with their jobs. (47)

Quid pro quo sexual harassment. Harassment that occurs when sexual activity is required in return for getting or keeping a job or job-related benefit. (118)

Quotas. Employer adjustments of hiring decisions to ensure that a certain number of people from a certain protected class are hired. (122)

Railway Labor Act. A law designed to regulate labor relations in the transportation industry. (497)

Rater error. An error in performance appraisals that reflects consistent biases on the part of the rater. (244)

Realistic job preview (RJP). Realistic information about the demands of the job, the organization's expectations of the job holder, and the work environment. (283)

Reasonable accommodation. An action taken to accommodate the known disabilities of applicants or employees so that disabled persons enjoy equal employment opportunity. (126)

Recruitment. The process of generating a pool of qualified candidates for a particular job; the first step in the hiring process. (183)

Relative judgment. An appraisal format that asks supervisors to compare an employee's performance to the performance of other employees doing the same job. (236)

Reliability. Consistency of measurement, usually across time but also across judges. (191)

Reverse discrimination. Discrimination against a nonprotected-class member resulting from attempts to recruit and hire members of protected classes. (130)

Right. The ability to engage in conduct that is protected by law or social sanction, free from interference by another party. (457)

Rightsizing. The process of reorganizing a company's employees to improve their efficiency. (217)

Right-to-work law. A state law that makes it illegal within that state for a union to include a union shop clause in its contract. (496)

Selection. The process of making a "hire" or "no hire" decision regarding each applicant for a job; the second step in the hiring process. (183)

Self-managed team (SMT). A team responsible for producing an entire product, a component, or an ongoing service. (87)

Self-review. A performance appraisal system in which workers rate themselves. (243)

Senior mentoring program. A support program in which senior managers identify promising women and minority employees and play an important role in nurturing their career progress. (169)

Seniority. The length of time a person works for an employer. (519)

Simulation. A device or situation that replicates job demands at an off-the-job site. (274)

Situational factors or system factors. A wide array of organizational characteristics that can positively or negatively influence performance. (252)

Skills inventory. A company-maintained record of employees' abilities, skills, knowledge, and education. (300)

Social networking. Interacting over the Internet and sharing text messages, photos, and video clips. (436)

Social Security. A government program that provides income for retirees, the disabled, and survivors of deceased workers, and health care for the aged through the Medicare program. (395)

Socialization. The process of orienting new employees to the organization and the unit in which they will be working; the third step in the hiring process. (183)

Special-purpose team. A team or task force consisting of workers who span functional or organizational boundaries and whose purpose is to examine complex issues. (79)

Staff employee. An employee who supports line employees. (30)

Statutory right. A right protected by specific laws. (458)

Strategic HR choices. The options available to a firm in designing its human resources system. (52)

Strategic human resource (HR) planning. The process of formulating HR strategies and establishing programs or tactics to implement them. (49)

Structured interview. Job interview based on a thorough job analysis, applying job-related questions with predetermined answers consistently across all interviews for a job. (195)

Subordinate review. A performance appraisal system in which workers review their supervisors. (243)

Succession planning. A career development activity that focuses on preparing people to fill executive positions. (297)

Supplemental unemployment benefits (SUB). Benefits given by a company to laid-off employees over and above state unemployment benefits. (399)

Support group. A group established by an employer to provide a nurturing climate for employees who would otherwise feel isolated or alienated. (167)

Taft-Hartley Act (1947). A federal law designed to limit some of the power acquired by unions under the Wagner Act by adjusting the regulation of labor–management relations to ensure a level playing field for both parties. (496)

Team. A small number of people with complementary skills who work toward common goals for which they hold themselves mutually accountable. (78)

Telecommuting. A work arrangement that allows employees to work in their homes full-time, maintaining their connection to the office through phone, fax, and computer. (101)

Teleconferencing. The use of audio and video equipment to allow people to participate in meetings even when they are a great distance away from the conference location or one another. (494)

Title VII (Civil Rights Act of 1964). Section of the Civil Rights Act of 1964 that applies to employment decisions; mandates that employment decisions not be based on race, color, religion, sex, or national origin. (115)

360° feedback. The combination of peer, subordinate, and self-review. (243)

Total compensation. The package of quantifiable rewards an employee receives for his or her labors. Includes three components: base compensation, pay incentives, and indirect compensation/benefits. (315)

Total quality management (TQM). An organization-wide approach to improving the quality of all the processes that lead to a final product or service. (39)

Training. The process of providing employees with specific skills or helping them correct deficiencies in their performance. (265)

Trait appraisal instrument. An appraisal tool that asks a supervisor to make judgments about worker characteristics that tend to be consistent and enduring. (238)

Transnational corporation. A firm with operations in many countries and highly decentralized operations. The firm owes little allegiance to its country of origin and has weak ties to any given country. (561)

Turnover rate. The rate of employee separations in an organization. (210)

Unemployment insurance. A program established by the Social Security Act of 1935 to provide temporary income for people during periods of involuntary unemployment. (398)

Union. An organization that represents employees' interests to management on such issues as wages, work hours, and working conditions. (493)

Union acceptance strategy. A labor relations strategy in which management chooses to view the union as its employees' legitimate representative and accepts collective bargaining as an appropriate mechanism for establishing workplace rules. (504)

Union avoidance strategy. A labor relations strategy in which management tries to prevent its employees from joining a union, either by removing the incentive to unionize or by using hardball tactics. (506)

Union shop clause. A union arrangement that requires new employees to join the union 30 to 60 days after their date of hire. (496)

Union steward. An advocate dedicated to representing an employee's case to management in a grievance procedure. (517)

Union substitution/proactive human resource management. A union avoidance strategy in which management becomes so responsive to employees' needs that it removes the incentives for unionization. (506)

Union suppression. A union avoidance strategy in which management uses hardball tactics to prevent a union from organizing its workers or to get rid of a union. (506)

Universal concept of management. The management concept holding that all management practices should be standardized. (153)

Upward communication. Communication that allows employees at lower levels to communicate their ideas and feelings to higher-level decision makers. (431)

Validity. The extent to which the technique measures the intended knowledge, skill, or ability. In the selection context, it is the extent to which scores on a test or interview correspond to actual job performance. (191)

Vesting. A guarantee that accrued retirement benefits will be given to retirement plan participants when they retire or leave the employer. (408)

Virtual reality (VR). The use of a number of technologies to replicate the entire real-life working environment in real time. (275)

Virtual team. A team that relies on interactive technology to work together when separated by physical distance. (80)

Voice mail. A form of electronic communication that allows the sender to leave a detailed voice message for a receiver. (434)

Voluntary separation. A separation that occurs when an employee decides, for personal or professional reasons, to end the relationship with the employer. (214)

Wagner Act/National Labor Relations Act (1935). A federal law designed to protect employees' rights to form and join unions and to engage in such activities as strikes, picketing, and collective bargaining. (495)

Wellness program. A company-sponsored program that focuses on preventing health problems in employees. (549)

Whistle-blowing. Employee disclosure of an employer's illegal, immoral, or illegitimate practices to persons or organizations that may be able to take corrective action. (468)

Wholly owned subsidiary. In international business, a foreign branch owned fully by the home office. (564)

Wildcat strike. A spontaneous work stoppage that happens under a valid contract and is usually not supported by union leadership. (515)

Work flow. The way work is organized to meet the organization's production or service goals. (73)

Work-flow analysis. The process of examining how work creates or adds value to the ongoing processes in a business. (77)

Work rules. Any terms or conditions of employment, including pay, work breaks and lunch periods, vacation, work assignments, and grievance procedures. (498)

Work–life balance. The balance between an individual's work and personal life. (109)

Worker Adjustment and Retraining Notification Act (WARN). A federal law requiring U.S. employers with 100 or more employees to give 60 days' advance notice to employees who will be laid off as a result of a plant closing or a mass separation of 50 or more workers. (221)

Workers' compensation. A legally required benefit that provides medical care, income continuation, and rehabilitation expenses for people who sustain job-related injuries or sickness. Also provides income to the survivors of an employee whose death is job related. (397)

Workplace bullying. A form of harassment that consists of a persistent pattern of offensive, abusive, intimidating, malicious, or insulting behavior focused at a target employee. (480)

Works council. A committee composed of both worker representatives and managers who have responsibility for governing the workplace; used in Germany. (503)

Wrongful discharge. Termination of an employee for reasons that are either illegal or inappropriate. (459)

Company, Name, and Product Index

H

I

J

K

L

M

N

O

P

Q

R

S

T

U

Subject Index

D

F

Q

R